Rover 3 & 3.5 Litre Workshop Manual Saloon & Coupe (P5)

Rover-British Leyland UK Limited
Solihull, Warwickshire, England

2nd Edition
Issued January, 1966
Technical Publication No. TP367
First Issued January 1965
Plus Supplement
First Issued September 1967

British Leyland Rover

Service Department
Solihull, Warwickshire,
Telephone : 021-743 4242
Telgrams : Rovrepair Solihull
Telex : 33-156

Parts Department
P.O. Box 79
Cardiff
Great Britain
Telephone : Cardiff 33681
Telgrams : Rovparts, Cardiff
Telex : 49-359

Please note that all prices and specifications are subject to alteration without note

Always quote type and number of vehicle when ording

ISBN: 978 185520 1446

By Appointment to Her Majesty Queen Elizabeth II — *Manufacturers of Motor Cars and Land-Rovers*

By Appointment to Her Majesty Queen Elizabeth the Queen Mother — *Suppliers of Motor Cars and Land-Rovers*

Part No. 4661
& Part No. 606358

INTRODUCTION

Layout of the Workshop Manual

This Workshop Manual is designed to assist those responsible for the maintenance and overhaul of the Rover 3 Litre. The subject matter is sectionalised as detailed in the General Index, and the pages are numbered within those sections. A further sub-index and descriptive notes will be found at the beginning of each Section.

Operating instructions and details of routine maintenance will be found in the Owner's Instruction and Maintenance Manuals, a copy of each will be found in the literature pack supplied with the car.

Reference is made throughout the text to the 'left-hand' and 'right-hand' sides of the car, rather than to the 'near-side' and 'off-side'. The 'left-hand' side is that to the left hand when the car is viewed from the rear.

Measurements

All measurements are given in Imperial measure; the Metric equivalent is added where possible, but in certain cases this is not practicable and the Imperial figure must be used.

Workshop Technique

When undertaking any overhaul operation, it is advisable to follow a standard technique, which will ultimately save both time and trouble. Prior to dismantling, the unit should be thoroughly cleaned externally and, as the stripping progresses, components washed in paraffin or petrol before setting out in order on a large drip tray. Small parts, such as nuts and bolts, should be placed in boxes to prevent loss, and shims attached to their respective components to facilitate assembly. All joint washers, lockers, tab washers and split pins must be renewed on assembly.

When the unit is finally rebuilt, use only the recommended lubricants. See Section Y.

Workshop Tools

In order to assist the operator when following details given in this manual, a list of the tools required for the operation has been included.

All sizes quoted refer to the actual spanner size unless otherwise stated. Apart from a very few exceptions, all thread types are either Unified-fine (UNF) or Unified-coarse (UNC).

In addition, details of any special tools which are necessary, are included in the heading of the operation for which they are required. See also Section Z.

NOTE: This publication incorporates all Workshop Manual information appertaining to the Rover 3 litre circulated by means of combined Rover Service News Letters numbered up to 117 and Rover Car Service News Letters Vol. 1 numbered up to 50 and Vol. 2 numbered up to 7.

Rover 3.5 Litre Supplement

The Supplement dealing with the 3.5 Litre Saloon and Coupé models can be found at the back of this manual.

ROVER 3 LITRE Mk I

ROVER 3 LITRE Mk II COUPE

ROVER 3 LITRE Mk IA AND Mk II

ROVER 3 LITRE Mk III, SALOON MODEL

CONTENTS

COMMENCING CAR AND UNIT NUMBERS:

ROVER 3 LITRE Mk I SALOON

1959

Model	Car & Chassis Commencing Numbers	Engine Commencing Number	Gearbox Commencing Number	Rear Axle Commencing Number
4-speed, Home, RHD	625900001	625900001 Basic 8.75:1 626900001-626930000 with Overdrive 8.75:1 626930001-626960000 Basic 7.5:1 626960001 onwards with Overdrive 7.5:1	625900001	625900001 Basic 626900001 Overdrive
4-speed, Export, RHD	626900001			
4-speed, CKD, RHD	627900001			
4-speed, Export, LHD	628900001			
4-speed, CKD, LHD	629900001			
Automatic Transmission, Home, RHD	630900001	630900001 8.75:1 631900001 7.5:1	R5B 1000 Violet plate	625900001
Automatic Transmission, Export, RHD	631900001			
Automatic Transmission, CKD, RHD	632900001			
Automatic Transmission, Export, LHD	633900001			
Automatic Transmission, CKD, LHD	634900001			

1960

Model	Car & Chassis Commencing Numbers	Engine Commencing Number	Gearbox Commencing Number	Rear Axle Commencing Number
4-speed, Home, RHD	625000001	625000001 Basic 8.75:1 626000001-626030000 with Overdrive 8.75:1 626030001-626060000 Basic 7.5:1 626060001 onwards with Overdrive 7.5:1	625000001	625000001 Basic 626000001 Overdrive
4-speed, Export, RHD	626000001			
4-speed, CKD, RHD	627000001			
4-speed, Export, LHD	628000001			
4-speed, CKD, LHD	629000001			
Automatic Transmission, Home, RHD	630000001	630000001 8.75:1 631000001 7.5:1	R5B 1000 Violet plate	625000001
Automatic Transmission, Export, RHD	631000001			
Automatic Transmission, CKD, RHD	632000001			
Automatic Transmission, Export, LHD	633000001			
Automatic Transmission, CKD, LHD	634000001			

1961

Model	Car & Chassis Commencing Numbers	Engine Commencing Number	Gearbox Commencing Number	Rear Axle Commencing Number
4-speed, Home, RHD	625100001	625100001 Basic 8.75:1 626100001 Overdrive 8.75:1 627100001 Basic 7.5:1 628100001 Overdrive 7.5:1	625100001	625100001 Basic 626100001 Overdrive
4-speed, Export, RHD	626100001			
4-speed, CKD, RHD	627100001			
4-speed, Export, LHD	628100001			
4-speed, CKD, LHD	629100001			
Automatic Transmission, Home, RHD	630100001	630100001 8.75:1 631100001 7.5:1	R5B 1000K Violet plate	625100001
Automatic Transmission, Export, RHD	631100001			
Automatic Transmission, CKD, RHD	632100001			
Automatic Transmission, Export, LHD	633100001			
Automatic Transmission, CKD, LHD	634100001			

ROVER 3 LITRE Mk IA SALOON

Model	Car & Chassis Commencing Numbers	Engine Commencing Number	Gearbox Commencing Number	Rear Axle Commencing Number
4-speed, Home, RHD	72500001a	72500001a 8.75:1 without Overdrive 72600001a 8.75:1 with Overdrive 72700001a 7.5:1 without Overdrive 72800001a 7.5:1 with Overdrive	72500001a	72500001a without Overdrive 72600001a with Overdrive
4-speed, Export, RHD	72600001a			
4-speed, CKD, RHD	72700001a			
4-speed, Export, LHD	72800001a			
4-speed, CKD, LHD	72900001a			
Automatic Transmission, Home, RHD	73000001a	73000001a 8.75:1 73100001a 7.5:1	R5B 1000P	72500001a
Automatic Transmission, Export, RHD	73100001a			
Automatic Transmission, CKD, RHD	73200001a			
Automatic Transmission, Export, LHD	73300001a			
Automatic Transmission, CKD, LHD	73400001a			

Note: On 1959-60 3 litre, 4-speed models, the fifth digit in the 6269 and 6260 range of engine numbers is also used to indicate the various types of engines used. See above for details.

COMMENCING CAR AND UNIT NUMBERS—*continued*

Model	Car & Chassis Commencing Numbers	Engine Commencing Number	Gearbox Commencing Number	Rear Axle Commencing Number
ROVER 3 LITRE Mk II SALOON				
4-speed, Home, RHD	77000001A			
4-speed, Export, RHD	77100001A	77000001A 8.75:1		
4-speed, CKD, RHD	77200001A		77000001A	77000001A
4-speed, Export, LHD	77300001A	77100001A 8.0:1		
4-speed, CKD, LHD	77400001A			
Automatic Transmission, Home, RHD	77500001A			
Automatic Transmission, Export, RHD	77600001A			
Automatic Transmission, CKD, RHD	77000001A	77500001A	R5B 1000KP	77500001A
Automatic Transmission, Export, LHD	77800001A			
Automatic Transmission, CKD, LHD	77900001A			
ROVER 3 LITRE Mk II COUPE				
4-speed, Home, RHD	73500001A			
4-speed, Export, RHD	73600001A	77000001A 8.75:1		
4-speed, CKD, RHD	73700001A		77000001A	77000001A
4-speed, Export, LHD	73800001A	77100001A 8.0:1		
4-speed, CKD, LHD	73900001A			
Automatic Transmission, Home, RHD	74000001A			
Automatic Transmission, Export, RHD	74100001A			
Automatic Transmission, CKD, RHD	74200001A	77500001A	R5B 1000KP	77500001A
Automatic Transmission, Export, LHD	74300001A			
Automatic Transmission, CKD, LHD	74400001A			
ROVER 3 LITRE Mk III SALOON				
4-speed, Home, RHD	79500001A			
4-speed, Export, RHD	79600001A	79500001A 8.75:1		
4-speed, CKD, RHD	79700001A		77000001A	79500001A
4-speed, Export, LHD	79800001A	79600001A 8:1		
4-speed, CKD, LHD	79900001A			
Automatic Transmission, Home, RHD	80000001A			
Automatic Transmission, Export, RHD	80100001A	80000001A 8.75:1		
Automatic Transmission, CKD, RHD	80200001A		3EU 1001	80000001A
Automatic Transmission, Export, LHD	80300001A	80100001A 8:1		
Automatic Transmission, CKD, LHD	80400001A			
ROVER 3 LITRE Mk III COUPE				
4-speed, Home, RHD	80500001A			
4-speed, Export, RHD	80600001A	79500001A 8.75:1		
4-speed, CKD, RHD	80700001A		77000001A	79500001A
4-speed, Export, LHD	80800001A	79600001A 8:1		
4-speed, CKD, LHD	80900001A			
Automatic Transmission, Home, RHD	81000001A			
Automatic Transmission, Export, RHD	81100001A	80000001A 8.75:1		
Automatic Transmission, CKD, RHD	81200001A		3EU 1001	80000001A
Automatic Transmission, Export, LHD	81300001A	80100001A 8:1		
Automatic Transmission, CKD, LHD	81400001A			

Location of Car and Unit numbers

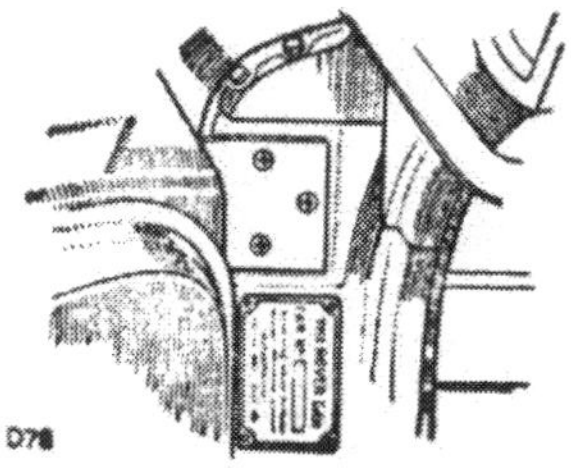

Car and chassis number

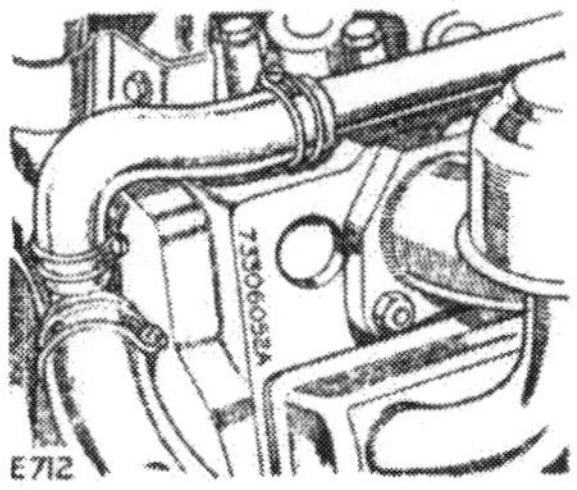

Engine number

Gearbox, number, 4-speed

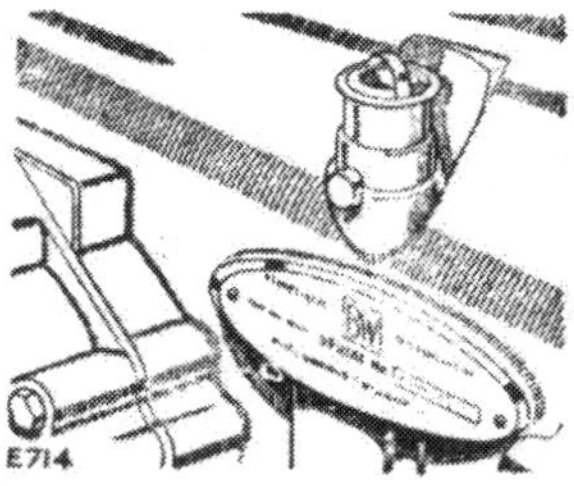

Automatic transmission number, Mk I, IA and II

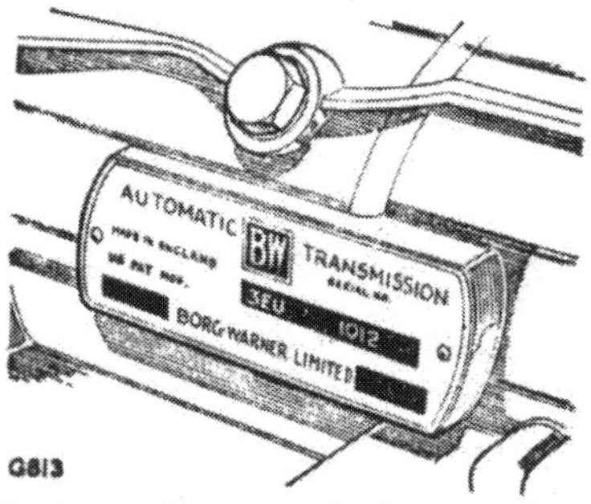

Automatic transmission number, Mk III

Rear axle number

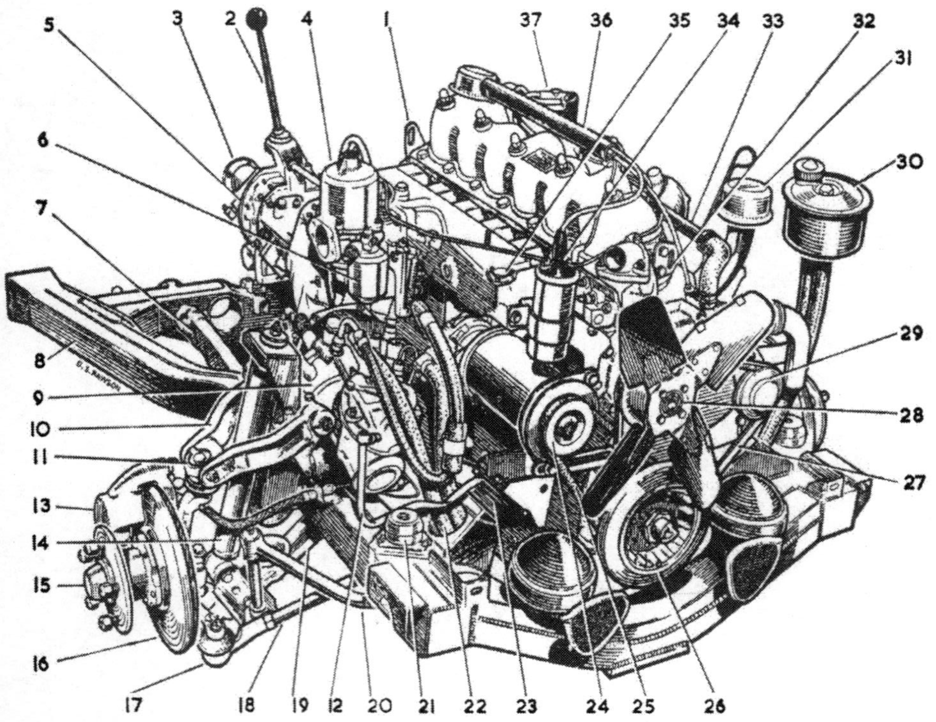

General arrangement of engine, front suspension and sub-frame

1 Rear lifting bracket
2 Change speed lever, remote control
3 Propeller shaft coupling
4 Carburetter suction chamber
5 Overdrive unit
6 Carburetter float chamber
7 Torsion bar, road spring
8 Chassis sub-frame
9 Power steering unit
10 Top link
11 Top ball swivel
12 Earthing strap
13 Brake caliper
14 Shock absorber
15 Front hub
16 Brake disc
17 Steering ball joint
18 Steering link rod
19 Bottom link
20 Torsion rod
21 Body mounting rubber
22 Hydraulic pipes, power steering
23 Engine mounting rubber
24 Dynamo and pulley
25 Dynamo belt
26 Crankshaft damper
27 Fan belt
28 Fan and water pump
29 Jockey pulley
30 Oil reservoir, power steering
31 Engine oil filler and breather
32 Front lifting bracket
33 Heater outlet pipe
34 Ignition coil
35 Thermostat switch
36 Wire carrier, HT leads
37 Distributor

Section A – ENGINE UNIT – Part One

Section A is divided into three parts, namely:

Part I	.. ..	Dismantling and assembling
Part II	.. ..	Components overhaul
Part III	.. ..	Defect location and data

When carrying out a complete engine overhaul, the section can be worked straight through in the order presented.

Alternatively, the individual operations which form the greater percentage of maintenance work undertaken by Distributors and Dealers, are detailed under appropriate headings, and will be found to be complete in themselves.

Some operations are marked with an asterisk * to indicate that they can be carried out with the engine installed. In all other cases it is necessary to remove the engine unit in order to carry out the work detailed.

Brief description of engine

The engine is a six cylinder unit with the block cast integrally with the crankcase, having a bore of 3.063 in. (77,8 mm); a stroke of 4.134 in. (105 mm), and a capacity of 183 cu in. (2,995 cc).

An aluminium alloy cylinder head which is inclined on the cylinder block gives high efficiency combustion chambers. Overhead inlet and inclined side exhaust valves are fitted, and the pistons are of inverted 'V' shape on the crown to conform to the special combustion chamber shape.

The camshaft is driven by a double roller chain and has a hydraulically operated tensioner. The seven bearing crankshaft is fitted with a torsional vibration damper.

Lubrication is by a large capacity oil pump which delivers oil under pressure throughout the engine and a full-flow oil filter is fitted.

Full engine data is to be found in Part Three of Section A.

INDEX—ENGINE UNIT—PARTS ONE, TWO AND THREE

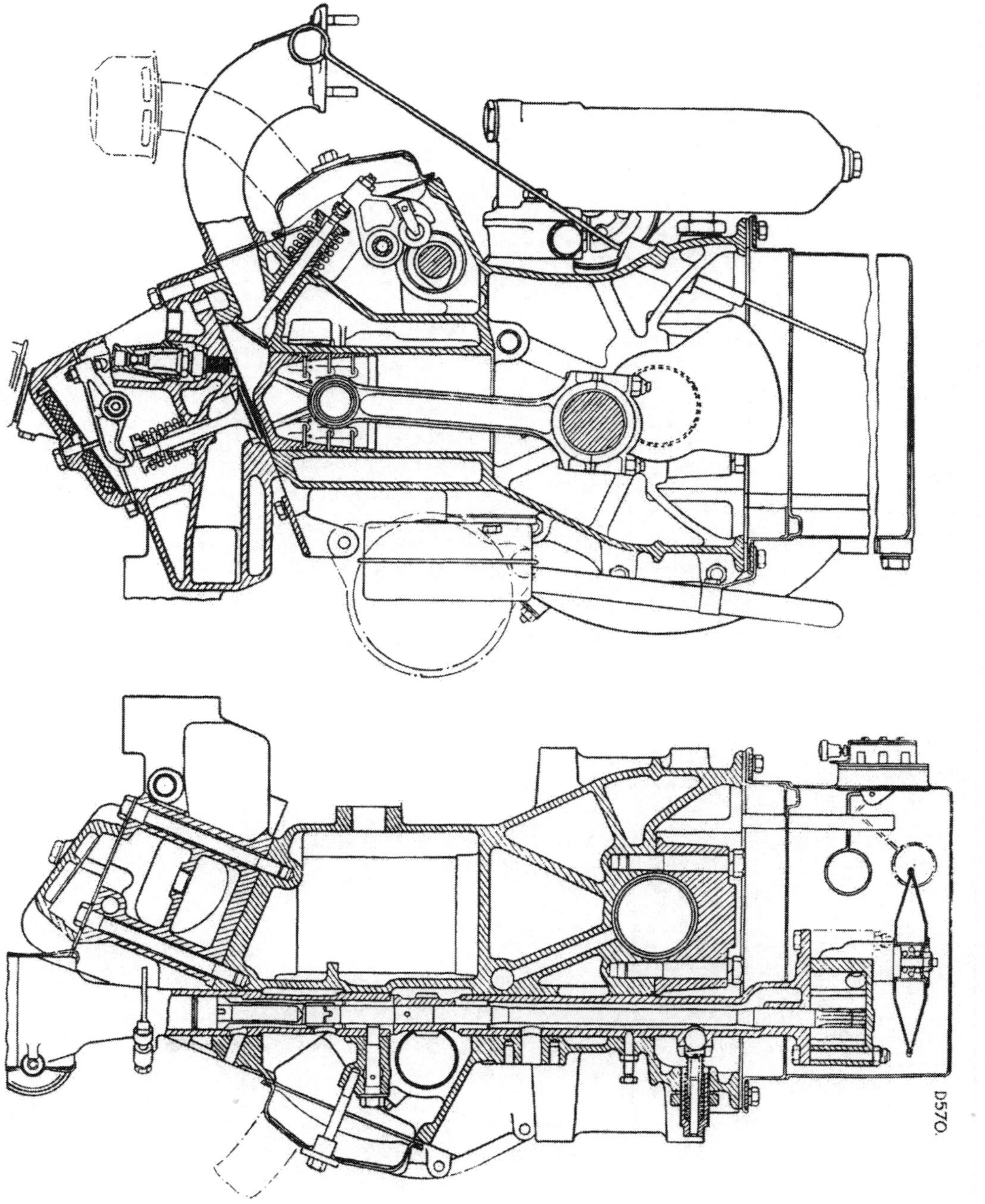

Cross-section of engine, end view. Mk I and Mk IA models illustrated

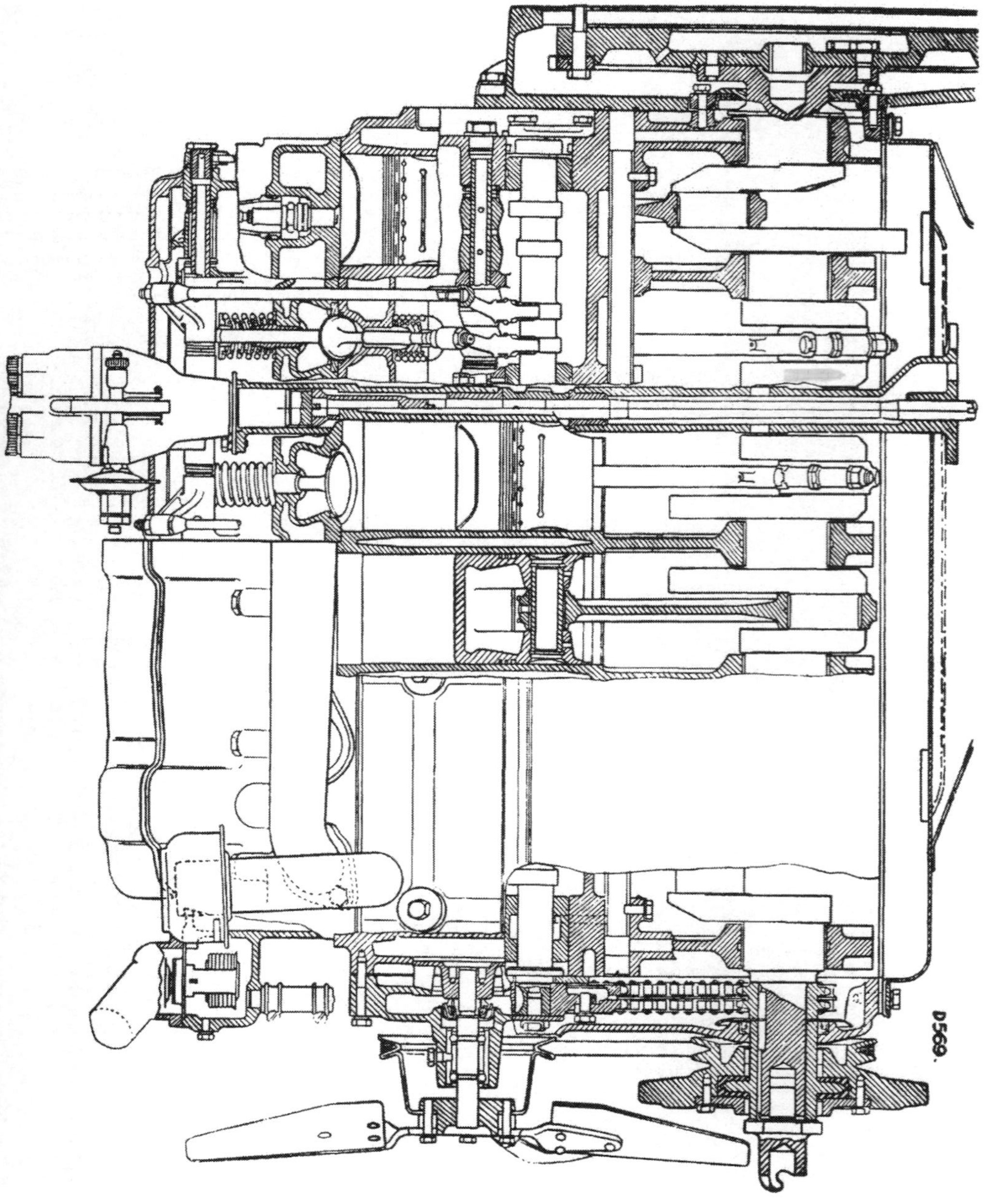

Cross-section of engine, side view. Mk I and Mk IA models illustrated

Section A—Engine Unit, Part One

Bonnet, to remove and refit—Operation A1-1

Workshop hand tools:
Spanner size: ½ in. AF

Bonnet, remove

1. Raise and support the bonnet.
2. **Coupé models only.** Disconnect the wiring to the bonnet lamps by removing one lead from the switch and the other from the fuse box.
3. Remove the springs from the bonnet hinges.
4. Remove the nuts securing the hinge links to the hinge bracket on the bonnet, these face inwards towards the engine. Do not remove the brackets from the bonnet.
5. Lift off bonnet and store in a convenient place.

Bonnet, refit

1. Reverse removal procedure.

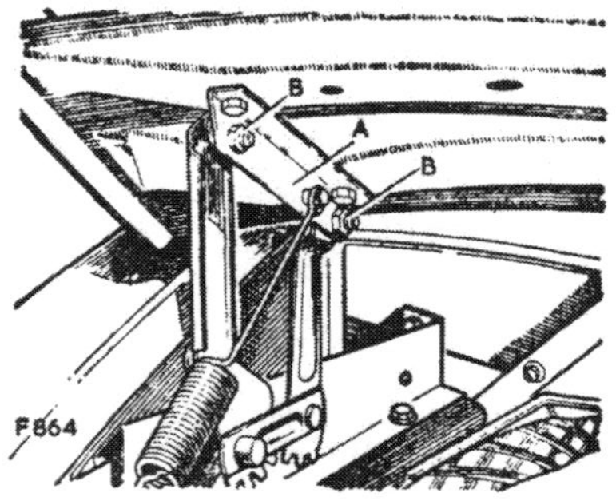

Bonnet hinges
A—Hinge bracket
B—Nuts securing hinge links to hinge bracket

Radiator, to remove and refit—Operation A1-2

Workshop hand tools:
Spanner size: ½ in. AF Screwdriver, medium

Radiator, remove

1. Remove radiator cap and drain off coolant by opening the tap under the radiator and also the tap on the right-hand side of the cylinder block.
2. Disconnect the water hoses, upper and lower.
3. Remove radiator, secured by six set bolts, spring and plain washers.
4. If necessary, remove header tank.

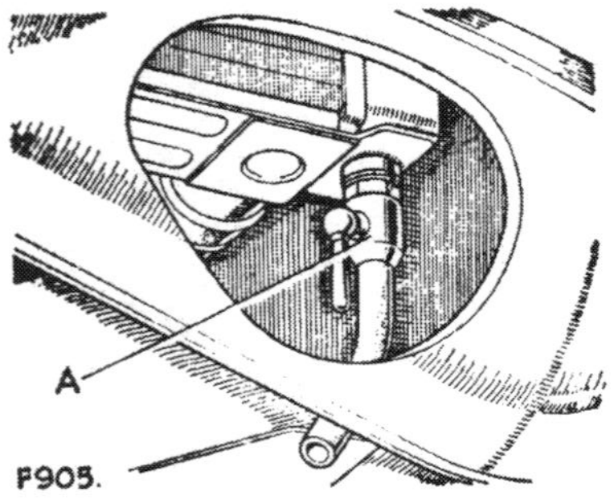

Radiator drain tap
A—Drain tap

Radiator, refit

1. Reverse removal procedure.
2. Refill with coolant, anti-freeze in winter.
   Capacities:
   Mk I, Mk IA and Mk II: 24 Imperial pints; 29 US pints; 13,7 litres.
   Mk III: 26 Imperial pints; 31 US pints; 14,7 litres.
3. When filling the radiator after the cylinder head has been removed, temporarily disconnect the top heater hose. When coolant flows freely from the hose reconnect it; this will avoid an air lock in the heater.
4. Check for leaks after engine has been started.

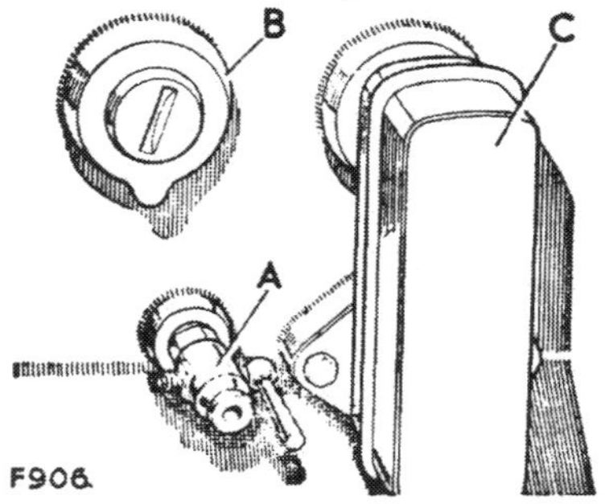

Cylinder block drain tap
A—Drain tap
B—Boss for immersion heater
C—Crankcase breather

Radiator grille, bonnet lock platform and oil cooler, to remove and refit—Operation A1-3

Workshop hand tools:
Spanner sizes: $\frac{7}{16}$ in. AF $\frac{1}{2}$ in. AF $\frac{5}{16}$ in. Whit
Pliers, pointed nose

Grille, remove

1. Remove two top mounting bolts and the mounting bolts situated beneath the lower front body panel.
2. Lift out radiator grille, removing the top first, remove two lower brackets. Where packing pieces are fitted note position to ensure correct refitment.
3. Disconnect the bonnet lock mechanism.
4. Remove the two nuts securing the bonnet lock.
5. Remove the bonnet lock platform secured by four bolts, nuts and washers.

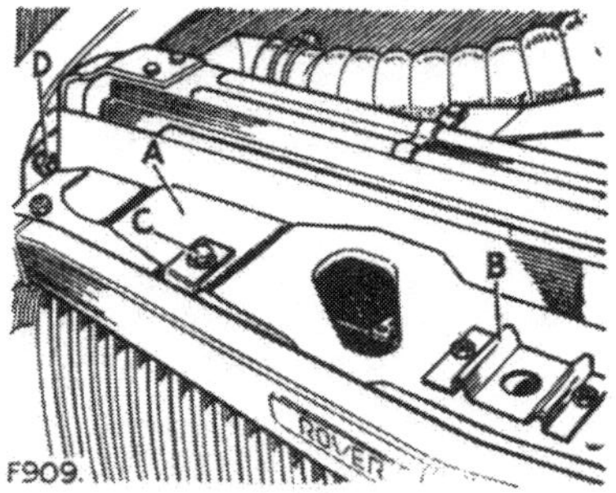

Bonnet lock platform
A—Bonnet lock platform C—Grille fixings
B—Bonnet lock D—Platform fixings

Grille, refit

1. Reverse removal procedure, but do not fully tighten the nuts securing the striker plate.
2. Lower the bonnet and align the striker plate with the lock bolt. The bolt should protrude through the plate approximately ½ in. (12,5 mm).
3. Ensure that the spring retainer on the lock bolt locates at the centre of the striker plate.
4. Check operation of slider catch underneath striker plate, as follows:
   (*a*) Ensure that the catch moves freely to the limit of its travel to the right, thereby allowing full engagement in the groove on the bonnet catch.
   (*b*) Ensure that it completely clears the aperture in the striker plate when the operating rod in the car is pulled.

   Adjust cable operational length as necessary, by repositioning the control rod in the adjustment holes provided.
5. Fit two lower brackets to radiator grille, do not tighten, then pull brackets as far back as possible, and fit radiator grille to body, inserting the bottom in first.
6. Tighten the two lower brackets and secure the remainder with nuts, bolts and spring washers; if removed, refit two packing pieces to mounting brackets and secure with nuts, bolts and flat washers.

Mk III models
Oil cooler, remove

1. Disconnect the two flexible hoses from the oil cooler at the unions beneath the cooler. Use a suitable clean container to collect any fluid from the cooler.
2. Blank off the oil cooler and pipe unions to prevent the ingress of dirt.
3. Remove the two lower oil cooler fixing bolts and lift out the oil cooler.

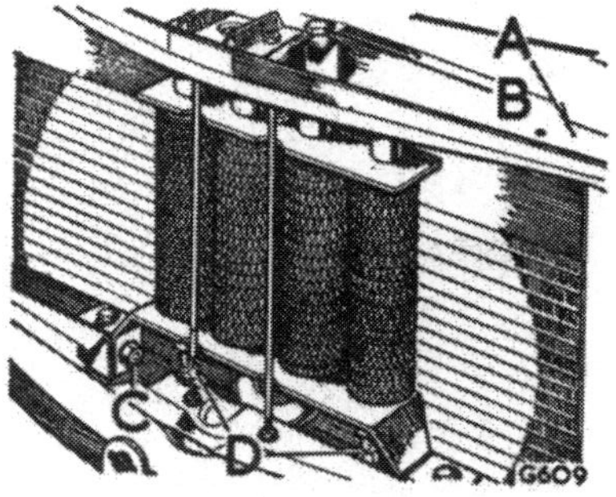

Oil cooler, Mk III models
A—Top grille C—Bolt fixing oil cooler
B—Bolt fixing top grille D—Oil pipe unions

Mk III models
Oil cooler, refit

1. Reverse removal procedure.
2. Check fluid level in automatic transmission; top up if necessary.

*Air cleaner/silencer and elbow, to remove and refit—Operation A1-4

Workshop hand tools:
Spanner size: $\frac{1}{2}$ in. AF
Screwdriver, medium

Air cleaner, remove
Mk I models with oil bath type air cleaner

1. Slacken the hose clips securing the air cleaner top cover to silencer duct.
2. Remove the top cover of the cleaner secured by a wing nut.

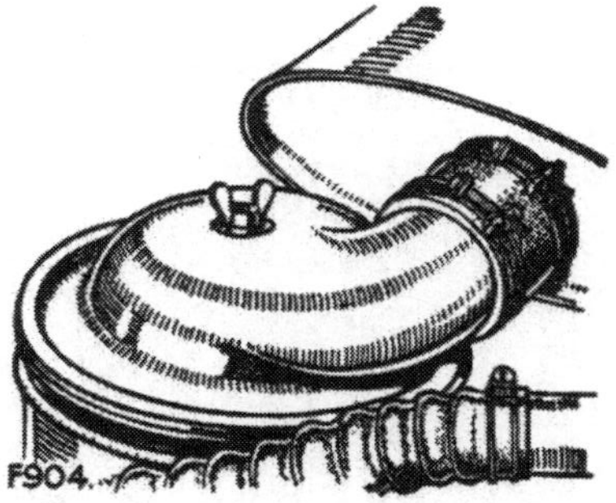

Oil bath type air cleaner

3. Lift out the filter element.
4. Remove the container secured by a horizontal bolt ($\frac{5}{16}$ in. UNF x 3¾ in.), spring washer and nut and by a bolt, nut and washers to a bracket on the dynamo.
5. Clean out all dirty oil and sludge, and wash all the component parts in petrol or paraffin.

Paper element type air cleaner

6. Remove air silencer, secured to elbow by a wing nut and plain washer and by a bolt, bush, washers and nut to a bracket on the cylinder head.

Mk IA, Mk II and Mk III models with paper element type air cleaner

7. Remove air cleaner complete, secured to elbow by a wing nut and plain washer and by a bolt, bush, washers and nut to a bracket on the cylinder head.
8. Unclip the end cover and withdraw the element complete with frame.
9. Remove the end cap and sealing washer secured by a wing nut and plain washer.
10. Discard the old element.

Elbow, remove

11. Disconnect hose from economiser adaptor.
12. Remove elbow from carburetter secured by two nuts and spring washers.

Elbow, refit

13. Reverse removal procedure, using a new joint washer.

Oil bath type air cleaner, refit

14. Replace air silencer.
15. Fit container to support brackets and refill with fresh engine oil to the indicated level, the capacity being approximately 1 pint; 1.2 US pints; 0,5 litres.
16. Ensure that the sealing washers are in good condition and refit top cover.

Paper element type air cleaner, refit

17. Reverse removal procedure.
18. Fit a new paper element and renew sealing washers as necessary.

Operations which are identified by an asterisk (*), can be carried out with the engine installed in the car

Engine, to remove and refit (4-speed models only)—Operation A1-5

Workshop hand tools:

Spanner sizes: $\frac{7}{16}$ in. AF, $\frac{1}{2}$ in. AF, $\frac{9}{16}$ in. AF, $\frac{7}{8}$ in. AF, $\frac{15}{16}$ in. AF, $\frac{3}{8}$ in. Whit, $\frac{3}{8}$ in. BSF, $\frac{1}{2}$ in. BSF

Screwdriver, medium

Special tools:

Engine sling, Part No. 600963

If a service replacement engine is to be fitted, the following parts must be removed from the original engine and fitted to the replacement unit.

Remove and refit: Inlet and exhaust manifolds, starter motor, dynamo, distributor, water pump, jockey pulley and adjusting link for fan belt (late models), carburetter, oil filter, breather filters, breather pipe and bracket. Dipstick (models Mk I and Mk IA only). Vibration damper (models Mk I and Mk IA, also Mk II suffix 'A' and 'B').

If the engine is to be completely overhauled after removal, the work should be carried out in the order presented in this Section, Part One, and in Part Two as necessary. Any components which have been removed to enable the engine to be lifted from the car, should not be refitted until the engine has been re-installed.

Overhaul of the clutch unit will be found in Section C, and for the gearbox see Section D.

Engine unit only, to remove

This operation can be carried out where it is necessary to remove the engine unit only, leaving the gearbox, and, where fitted, the overdrive unit, in position. It does not apply to cars fitted with the automatic transmission unit.

The use of a ramp or inspection pit is not necessary, a suitable mobile hydraulic lifting jack and lifting sling being the equipment required for the operation.

1. Remove bonnet. Operation A1-1.
2. Remove radiator. Operation A1-2
3. Remove radiator grille and bonnet lock platform. Operation A1-3.
4. Remove the two stays from the grille aperture.
5. Remove the air cleaner/silencer and elbow, and the oil bath air cleaner support bracket, where fitted. Operation A1-4.
6. Drain off the coolant.
7. Disconnect the heater water hoses.

Engines suffix 'C' onwards and Mk III Items 8 to 11

8. It is essential to remove the heater unit on suffix 'C' engines and Mk III.
9. Remove the flexible hose, blower to heater, secured by hose clips.
10. Disconnect the control cable from the tap, by removing the circlip and nipple.
11. Remove the heater fixings and lift out the heater.
12. Remove the windscreen washer reservoir.
13. Disconnect the battery, which is situated in the luggage compartment.
14. Drain the engine oil.
15. Disconnect the starter harness, and the leads from the dynamo, ignition coil, oil pressure and mixture control switches, and sump oil level unit.
16. Disconnect the petrol feed pipe and the cold start control from the carburetter.
17. Disconnect the accelerator linkage and on Mk I, Mk IA and Mk II engines up to suffix 'B' remove the countershaft and bracket. On engines suffix 'C' and Mk III models disconnect the control rod between the accelerator lever and the lever on the cross-shaft extension. Disconnect the extension shaft from the cross-shaft by pulling the extension shaft back against the spring.
18. **Overdrive, where fitted.** Disconnect the wiring from the rotary or cam switch (whichever type is fitted) on the accelerator linkage.
19. Unscrew the thermometer bulb from the cylinder head and carefully support the capillary tube out of the way. Late models have electrical temperature gauges, with this type disconnect the wiring at the transmitter on the cylinder head.
20. **Power steering, where fitted.** Disconnect the inlet and outlet pipes from the hydraulic pump attached to the dynamo. Seal the pipe and pump connections to prevent ingress of dirt and loss of fluid.
21. Disconnect the exhaust pipe from the exhaust manifold.
22. Hold the brake pedal down approximately $1\frac{1}{2}$ in. (38 mm), retain in this position to prevent undue loss of fluid, then disconnect and remove the brake vacuum servo unit from the sub-frame. Disconnect the servo pipe, reservoir-to-engine. Seal off the pipes to prevent ingress of dirt, etc.
23. Remove the engine oil filter assembly from the cylinder block.

Operation A1-5—*continued*

24. Disconnect and remove the two horns.
25. Remove the gear change lever assembly. Section D.
26. Remove the speedometer cable from the flywheel housing.
27. Jack up the front end of the car, place suitable stands under the front jacking tubes.
28. **Models with four-point mountings.** Remove the nuts and washers securing the front mountings to engine brackets.

    Fit a suitable sling to the engine brackets, front and rear.

    Remove the nuts and washers securing the bell housing to the engine.

    Remove the clutch return spring (or over-centre spring).

    Carefully lift the engine as high as possible (without damaging the heater unit, where this has been left in position). Draw the engine forward and lift out clear of the gearbox. Ensure gearbox is supported.
29. **Models with five-point mountings.** Remove the nuts and washers securing the front mountings to engine brackets and the mountings between the RH side of cylinder block and the LH side of the flywheel housing.

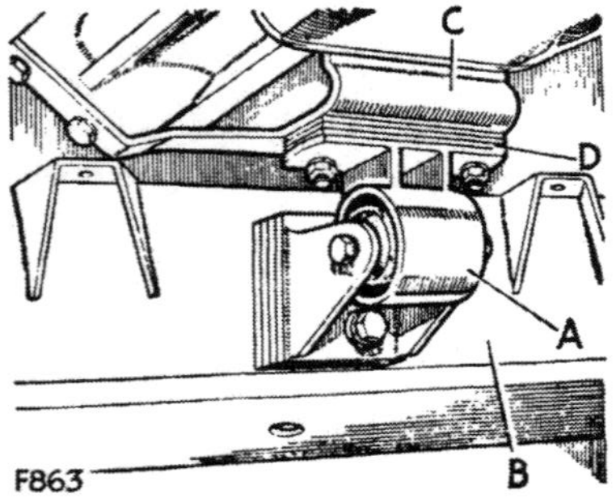

Engine mounting, five-point type

A—Stabiliser bracket to gearbox
B—Sub-frame rear cross-member
C—Reaction bracket
D—Shims

Slacken the $2\frac{3}{4}$ in. long bolt securing stabiliser bracket to sub-frame bracket beneath the speedometer housing (or extension casing on overdrive models).

Remove the nuts and washers securing the stabiliser bracket to reaction bracket.

Using a jack beneath the flywheel housing, raise the engine sufficiently to swing the stabiliser bracket clear. Note the number of shims used under the bracket, and retain for refitting.

Lower the jack and leave in position to support the gearbox.

Remove the nuts and washers securing the bell housing to the engine.

Disconnect clutch return spring (or over-centre spring).

Fit a sling to the engine mounting brackets, front and rear.

Carefully lift the engine as high as possible (without damaging the heater unit, where this has been left in position). Draw the engine forward and lift out. Ensure that the gearbox is supported.

Engine, refit

1. Reverse removal procedure.
2. Fit a suitable sling to the engine lifting brackets.
3. Ensure that the clutch centre plate is correctly aligned.
4. Lift the engine into position on the chassis sub-frame. Ensure correct alignment in relation to the bell-housing.
5. Fit and adjust the accelerator linkage in accordance with the instructions given in Section F.
6. **Engines suffix 'C' onwards and Mk III.** When refitting the heater unit, fit the lower fixing bolts first.
7. Fill engine to correct level with the recommended grade of lubricant. Capacity: 10 Imperial pints; 12 US pints; 5,5 litres; plus 1 Imperial pint; 1.2 US pints; 0,5 litres, after replacing engine oil filter.

   For recommended grades of oil see chart in Section B.
8. Fill radiator with coolant, anti-freeze in winter.
   Capacities:
   Mk I, Mk IA and Mk II: 24 Imperial pints; 29 US pints; 13,7 litres.
   Mk III: 26 Imperial pints; 31 US pints; 14,7 litres.
9. Carry out any adjustments which may be required.

Engine and gearbox (4-speed models), to remove and refit—Operation A1-6

Workshop hand tools:

Spanner sizes: $\frac{7}{16}$ in. AF, $\frac{9}{16}$ in. AF, $\frac{7}{8}$ in. AF, $\frac{15}{16}$ in. AF
$\frac{5}{16}$ in. BSF, $\frac{3}{8}$ in. BSF, $\frac{1}{2}$ in. BSF

Screwdriver, medium

Special tools:

Engine sling, Part No. 600963

If a service replacement engine is to be fitted, the following parts must be removed from the original engine and fitted to the replacement unit.

Remove and refit: Inlet and exhaust manifolds, starter motor, dynamo, distributor, water pump, jockey pulley and adjusting link for fan belt (late models), carburetter, oil filter, breather filters, breather pipe and bracket. Dipstick (models Mk I and Mk IA only). Vibration damper (models Mk I and Mk IA, also Mk II suffix 'A' and 'B').

If the engine is to be completely overhauled after removal, the work should be carried out in the order presented in this Section, Part One, and in Part Two as necessary. Any components which have been removed to enable the engine to be lifted from the car, should not be refitted until the engine has been re-installed.

Overhaul of the clutch unit will be found in Section C, and for the gearbox see Section D.

Engine and gearbox, remove

This operation is carried out with the car on a suitable ramp or over an inspection pit. Where the car is fitted with an overdrive unit, this must be removed before attempting to lift out the engine and gearbox. See Section D. The engine and gearbox (and overdrive where fitted) may also be removed with the sub-frame as an assembly. Section H.

1. Remove bonnet. Operation A1-1.
2. Remove radiator. Operation A1-2.
3. Remove radiator grille and bonnet lock platform. Operation A1-3.
4. Remove the two stays from the grille aperture.
5. Remove the air cleaner/silencer and elbow and the air cleaner support bracket, where fitted. Operation A1-4.
6. Drain off the coolant.
7. Disconnect the water hoses.

Engines suffix 'C' onwards and Mk III
Items 8 to 11

8. It is essential to remove the heater unit on suffix 'C' engines.
9. Remove the flexible hose, blower to heater, secured by hose clips.
10. Disconnect the control cable from the tap, by removing the circlip and nipple.
11. Remove the heater fixings and lift out the heater.
12. Remove the windscreen washer reservoir.
13. Disconnect the battery, which is situated in the luggage compartment.
14. Drain the oil from the engine, gearbox and where fitted, the overdrive unit.
15. Disconnect the starter harness, and the leads from the dynamo, ignition coil, oil pressure and mixture control switches, and sump oil level unit.
16. Disconnect the petrol feed pipe, cold start control and air hose from the carburetter.
17. **Power steering, where fitted.** Disconnect inlet and outlet pipes from the hydraulic pump attached to the dynamo. Seal the pump and pipe connections to prevent ingress of dirt and loss of fluid.
18. **Overdrive, where fitted.** Disconnect the wiring from the rotary or cam switch (whichever type is fitted) on the accelerator linkage.
19. Disconnect the accelerator linkage and on Mk I, Mk IA and Mk II engines up to suffix 'B' remove the countershaft and bracket. On engines suffix 'C' disconnect the control rod between the accelerator lever and the lever on the cross-shaft extension. Disconnect the extension shaft from the cross-shaft by pulling the extension shaft back against the spring.
20. Unscrew the thermometer bulb from the cylinder head and carefully support the capillary tube out of the way. Late models have electrical temperature gauges, with this type disconnect the wiring at the transmitter on the cylinder head.
21. Disconnect the exhaust pipe from the manifold.

Operation A1-6—*continued*

22. Hold the brake pedal down approximately $1\frac{1}{2}$ in. (38 mm), retain in this position to prevent undue loss of fluid, then disconnect and remove the brake vacuum servo unit from the sub-frame. Disconnect the servo pipe, reservoir to engine, and seal the connections to prevent ingress of dirt.
23. Remove the engine oil filter assembly from the cylinder block.
24. Disconnect and remove the two horns.
25. Remove the gear change lever assembly. Section D.
26. Remove the speedometer cable from the flywheel housing.
27. Disconnect the propeller shaft from the gearbox. The flanges are secured by four self-locking nuts. On cars without overdrive, it is necessary to release the centre bearing bracket from the body in order to detach the front propeller shaft flanges, as captive bolts are used.
28. Disconnect the wiring harness from the reverse light switch and where fitted, the overdrive isolation switch. Remove the isolation switch complete with inserts and shims.
29. Disconnect and remove the overdrive solenoid leaving the plunger attached to the solenoid lever.
30. Remove the overdrive, where fitted.
31. Remove the engine and gearbox mounting nuts. Early models have four-point and late models five-point mounting. Models with five-point have a bracket between the speedometer drive housing and the rear cross-member of the chassis sub-frame. When disconnecting this bracket, proceed as follows:

    Slacken the $2\frac{3}{4}$ in. long bolt securing stabiliser bracket to sub-frame bracket beneath the speedometer housing (or extension casing assembly on overdrive models).

    Remove the nuts and washers securing the stabiliser bracket to the reaction bracket.

    Place a jack beneath the flywheel housing. Raise the jack sufficiently to be able to release the stabiliser bracket and swing it clear. Note the number of shims used under the bracket and retain them for refitting. Lower the jack.

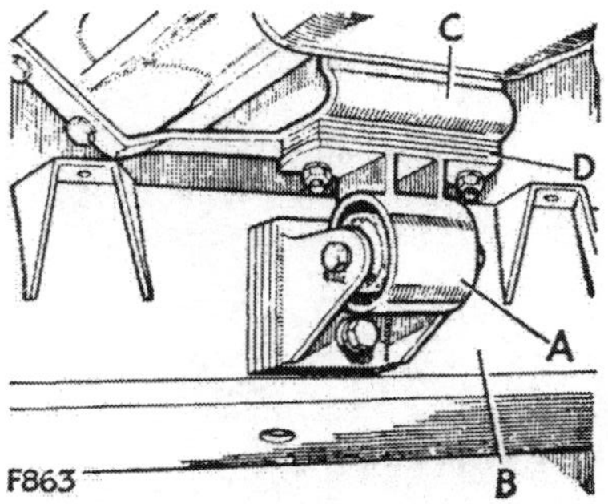

Engine mounting, five-point type

A—Stabiliser bracket to gearbox
B—Sub-frame rear cross-member
C—Reaction bracket
D—Shims

32. Remove the clutch lever return spring (or over-centre spring) and the two clevis pins from the clutch operating lever.
33. Remove the clutch slave cylinder from the bell-housing but do not disconnect the hydraulic pipe, as the cylinder can be supported out of the way.

    Care must be taken to prevent the clutch pedal being depressed, as this will cause the slave cylinder components to be expelled from the cylinder.

34. Fit a suitable sling to the engine lifting brackets front and rear.
35. Ensure the engine is free, start to lift slightly and draw forward. At this stage detach the speedometer cable. Lean the engine sideways in order to give clearance to the clutch slave cylinder mounting when passing the sub-frame cross-member. Take care not to damage the heater unit.
36. Prevent the sump from resting on the steering track rod during the lifting-out operation.
37. Mount the engine and gearbox on to a suitable stand.

Operation A1-6—*continued*

Engine and gearbox, refit

1. Reverse removal procedure.
2. Where the car is fitted with an overdrive unit, this must be fitted separately after the engine and gearbox unit has been fitted into the car.
3. Do not fit the gear change lever assembly until the engine and gearbox are fitted into the car.
4. **Mk II and Mk III models.** The brake vacuum servo unit if completely removed from the car must be replaced (but not secured) before the engine gearbox unit is replaced in the car.
5. **Engines suffix 'C' onwards and Mk III.** When refitting the heater unit, fit the lower fixing bolts first.
6. Fill engine and gearbox to correct levels with the recommended grades of lubricant.

   Capacities:

   Engine: 10 Imperial pints; 12 US pints; 5,5 litres; plus 1 Imperial pint; 1.2 US pints; 0,5 litres, after replacing engine oil filter.

   Gearbox and overdrive, Mk I and Mk IA: 5 Imperial pints; 6 US pints; 2,75 litres.

   Gearbox, Mk II and Mk III: 3 Imperial pints; 3.5 US pints; 1,75 litres.

   Overdrive, Mk II and Mk III: 1.5 Imperial pints; 2 US pints; 0,85 litres.
7. Fill radiator with coolant, anti-freeze in winter.

   Capacities:
   Mk I, Mk IA and Mk II: 24 Imperial pints; 29 US pints; 13,7 litres.
   Mk III: 26 Imperial pints; 31 US pints; 14,7 litres.
8. Check for water and oil leaks. Carry out any adjustments which may be required.

Engine and automatic transmission, to remove and refit—Operation A1-7

Workshop hand tools:

Spanner sizes: $\frac{5}{16}$ in. AF, $\frac{7}{16}$ in. AF, $\frac{1}{2}$ in. AF, $\frac{9}{16}$ in. AF, $\frac{5}{8}$ in. AF, $\frac{7}{8}$ in. AF, $\frac{15}{16}$ in. AF
$\frac{5}{16}$ in. BSF, $\frac{3}{8}$ in. BSF, $\frac{7}{8}$ in. BSF

Small adjustable spanner Screwdriver, medium

Special tools:

Engine sling, Part No. 600963

If a service replacement engine is to be fitted, the following parts must be removed from the original engine and fitted to the replacement unit.

Remove and refit: Inlet and exhaust manifolds, starter motor, dynamo, distributor, water pump, jockey pulley and adjusting link assembly for fan belt (late models). Carburetter, oil filter, breather filters, breather pipe and bracket Dipstick (models Mk I and Mk IA only). Vibration damper (models Mk I and Mk IA, also Mk II suffix 'A' and 'B').

If the engine is to be completely overhauled after removal, the work should be carried out in the order presented in this Section, Part One, and in Part Two as necessary. Any components which have been removed to enable the engine to be lifted from the car, should not be refitted until the engine has been re-installed.

Overhaul of the automatic transmission will be found in Section E or EE.

The automatic transmission unit fitted to Mk I, Mk IA and Mk II models cannot be removed from underneath the car. It must be removed as a unit with the engine. The engine and transmission unit may be removed with the sub-frame as an assembly. Section H.

Engine and automatic transmission, remove

1. Place the car on to a suitable ramp, or over an inspection pit for this operation.
2. Remove the bonnet. Operation A1-1.
3. Remove the radiator. Operation A1-2.
4. Remove radiator grille, bonnet lock platform and oil cooler. Operation A1-3.
5. Remove the two stays from the grille aperture.
6. Remove the air cleaner/silencer and elbow and where fitted the oil bath air cleaner support bracket. Operation A1-4.
7. Disconnect the heater water hoses, heater-to-engine.

Engines suffix 'C' onwards and Mk III
Items 8 to 11

8. It is essential to remove the heater unit on suffix 'C' engines and Mk III.
9. Remove the flexible hose, blower to heater, secured by hose clips.
10. Disconnect the control cable from the tap, by removing the circlip and nipple.
11. Remove the heater fixings and lift out the heater.
12. Remove the windscreen washer reservoir.
13. Disconnect the air hose and petrol feed pipe from the carburetter.
14. Disconnect the exhaust pipe from the manifold.
15. Early models. Unscrew the thermometer bulb from the cylinder head.

    Late models. Disconnect the lead from the water temperature transmitter.
16. Remove the oil filter assembly from the cylinder block.
17. Disconnect and remove the two horns.

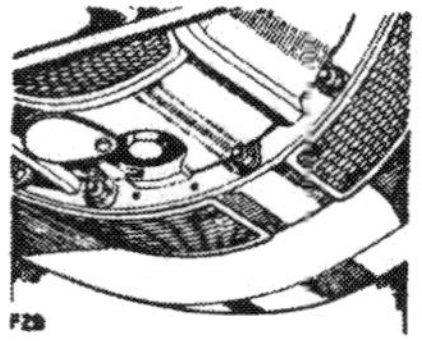

Drain plug for converter, Mk I, IA and II

18. Remove the cover plate from the bottom of the bell-housing and rotate the converter until the drain plug is accessible. Remove the pressure take-off plug (located at the bottom of the reverse servo) to vent the torque converter. Remove drain plug through hole in the bell-housing and drain the fluid from the unit.
19. Drain the fluid sump of the transmission case.

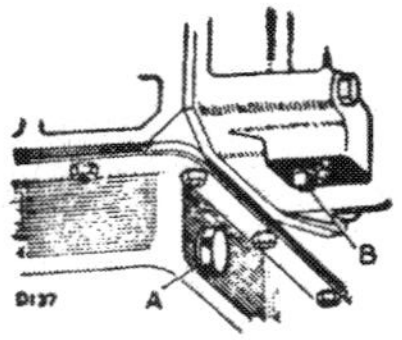

Drain plug and converter pressure take-off plug, Mk I, IA and II
A—Drain plug
B—Converter pressure take-off plug

Operation A1-7—*continued*

20. **Power steering, where fitted.** Disconnect inlet and outlet pipes from hydraulic pump on dynamo, Seal the connections to prevent the ingress of dirt and the loss of fluid.

21. Disconnect the accelerator linkage, and on Mk I, Mk IA and Mk II engines up to suffix 'B' remove the countershaft and bracket. On engines suffix 'C' and Mk III disconnect the control rod between the accelerator lever and the lever on the cross-shaft extension. Disconnect the extension shaft from the cross-shaft by pulling the extension shaft back against the spring.

22. Hold the brake pedal down approximately $1\frac{1}{2}$ in. (38 mm), retain in this position to prevent undue loss of fluid, then disconnect and remove the brake vacuum servo unit from the sub-frame. Seal off the pipes and connections to prevent ingress of dirt.

23. Disconnect the servo pipe engine-to-reservoir where fitted.

24. Detach the speedometer cable from the clip on the flywheel housing.

25. Detach the propeller shaft centre bearing bracket from the body.

26. Disconnect the propeller shaft flange from the output shaft of the transmission.

27. Detach the kickdown operating rod from the transmission case.

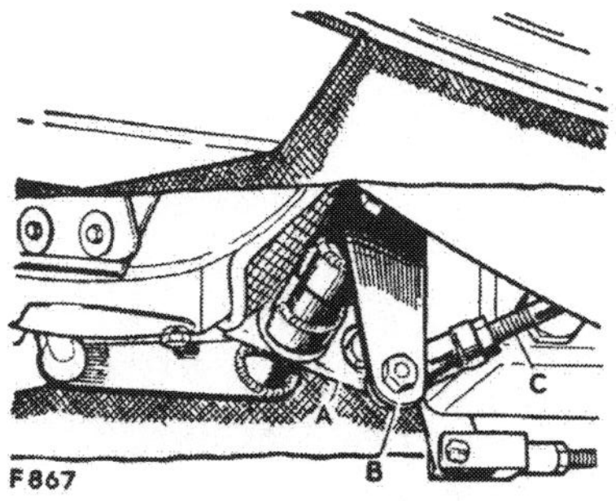

Linkage, automatic transmission. Mk I, IA and II
A—Compensator coupling
B—Cross-shaft lever
C—Control

28. Disconnect the gear selector mechanism at the compensator coupling.

29. Remove the engine mounting nuts. Early models have four-point and late models five-point mounting. Models with five-point mounting have a bracket between the transmission extension casing and the rear sub-frame cross-member. When disconnecting this bracket proceed as follows:

    Slacken the $2\frac{3}{4}$ in. long bolt securing stabiliser bracket to sub-frame bracket beneath extension casing.

    Remove nuts and washers securing stabiliser bracket to reaction bracket.

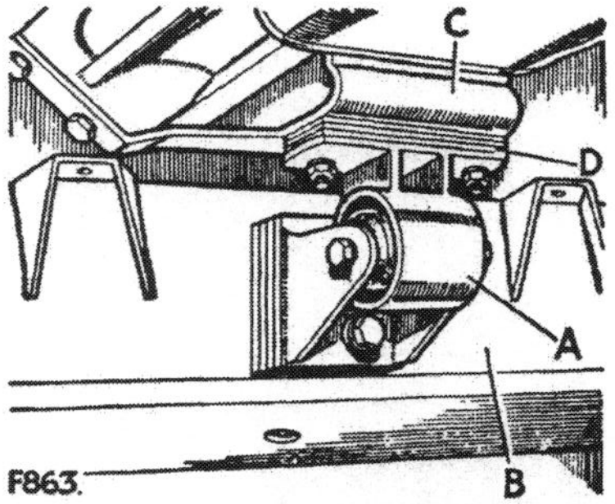

Engine mounting, five-point type
A—Stabiliser bracket to gearbox
B—Sub-frame rear cross-member
C—Reaction bracket
D—Shims

    Place a jack under the automatic transmission main casing. Raise the jack enough to be able to release the stabiliser bracket and swing it clear. Note the number of shims used under the bracket and retain them for refitting. Lower the jack.

30. Fit a suitable sling to the engine lifting brackets front and rear.

31. Ensure the engine is free, start to lift slightly and draw forward. At this stage disconnect the speedometer cable. Continue to pull the unit forwards. Do not let the sump rest on the steering track rod. When lifting the unit away take care not to damage the heater unit.

Operation A1-7—*continued*

32. Mount the unit on a suitable stand. Avoid allowing the transmission case to stand upon its fluid sump either when attached to the engine or not. When the transmission unit is detached from the engine, a special bench cradle is available for this purpose. See Section Z.

Engine and automatic transmission, refit

1. The automatic transmission on Mk I, Mk IA and Mk II models **cannot** be fitted after the engine has been installed; it must be fitted attached to the engine as a unit.
2. Reverse removal procedure.
3. Connect the speedometer cable to the transmission before the unit is finally lowered into position.
4. Adjust the selector mechanism in accordance with the instructions given in Section E for Mk I, Mk IA and Mk II models and Section EE for Mk III models.
5. **Engines suffix 'C' onwards and Mk III.** When refitting the heater unit, fit the lower fixing bolts first.
6. Fill engine and automatic transmission to correct levels with the recommended grades of lubricant.

   Capacities:

   Engine: 10 Imperial pints; 12 US pints; 5,5 litres; plus 1 Imperial pint; 1.2 US pints; 0,5 litres, after replacing engine oil filter.

   Mk I, Mk IA and Mk II automatic transmission units: 15 Imperial pints; 18 US pints; 8,5 litres.

   Mk III automatic transmission unit: 14 Imperial pints; 17 US pints; 8,0 litres.

   For recommended grades of oil see chart in Section B.

7. Fill radiator with coolant, anti-freeze in winter

   Capacities:

   Mk I, Mk IA and Mk II: 24 Imperial pints; 29 US pints; 13,7 litres.

   Mk III: 26 Imperial pints; 31 US pints; 14,7 litres.

8. Check for oil and water leaks. Carry out any adjustments which may be required.

*Distributor and H.T. leads, to remove and refit—Operation A1-8

Workshop hand tools:

Spanner sizes: $\frac{7}{16}$ in. AF, $\frac{3}{8}$ in. AF
Screwdriver, medium Set of feeler gauges

Special tools:

12 volt test lamp

See Section S for distributor overhaul

Distributor and HT leads, remove

1. Disconnect the vacuum advance pipe from the distributor.
2. Detach the sparking plug and HT leads from the distributor cap.
3. Detach the LT lead, coil to distributor.
4. Remove distributor from cylinder block secured by a set bolt and washers.
5. Remove the cork washer from the housing.
6. If necessary, withdraw the short extension shaft

Distributor, refit

1. If the ignition timing has not been disturbed, distributor replacement is straightforward. The engagement of the offset driving shaft will ensure that the original timing setting is maintained.
2. If the timing has been disturbed, or if a replacement distributor has been fitted, proceed as follows:

   Check contact breaker points and set to .014 in. to .016 in. (0,35 mm to 0,40 mm). The octane selector should be set so that the fourth line of the calibrated slide is against the distributor body casing, this setting is for premium grade fuel.

Distributor, adjust

3. (*a*) To set the contact breaker gap slacken off the two large screws securing the contact breaker plate and rotate the small cam screw.

   (*b*) By turning the rotor arm in an anti-clockwise direction, the tension of the automatic advance springs can be felt, giving an indication of whether the mechanism is working correctly.

   (*c*) To replace the automatic advance springs or weights, remove the split pin securing the vacuum control to the contact support plate. Remove the screw securing the cam spindle, disconnect the advance springs and lift out the spindle and weights.

Ignition timing, static full retard

4. Set the ignition timing, using a 12 volt test lamp:

   (*a*) Connect a lead between the distributor low tension terminal and the centre pole of the bulb, and earth the bulb body. Switch on the ignition.

   (*b*) Rotate the distributor; the bulb will glow exactly when the points begin to open, and should coincide with full alignment of the timing mark on the flywheel with the timing pointer. The timing mark indicates a setting of 3° BTDC for engines fitted with 8.75:1 and 8.0:1 compression ratio pistons, using premium grade fuel. For engines fitted with 7.5:1 compression ratio pistons the flywheel should be set to 2° BTDC.

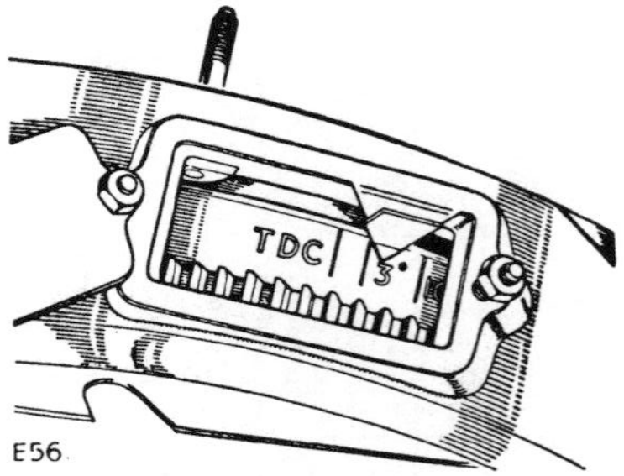

Flywheel timing marks

5. Although no moving parts are visible to indicate the correct operation of the vacuum advance mechanism, this can be checked as follows:

   Fashion a piece of welding wire to clip around a contact plate securing screw, and pass through the gap between distributor body and cap, where the wire must be flattened. Replace the cap, and check when the engine is running slowly. Open the throttle, and the protruding piece of wire should indicate movement of the contact support plate.

Operations which are identified by an asterisk (*), can be carried out with the engine installed in the car

Operation A1-8—*continued*

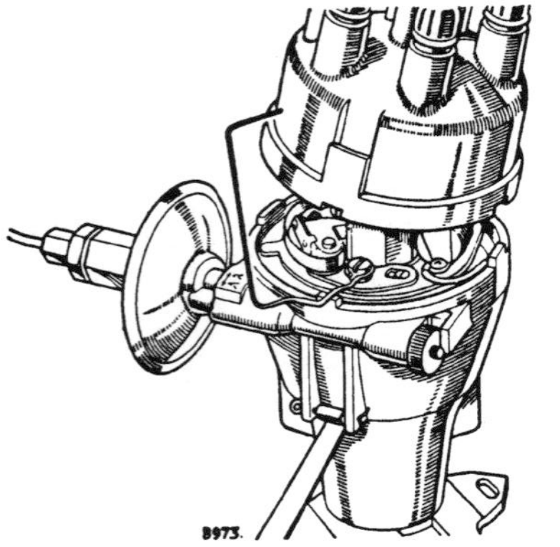

Testing vacuum advance

6. Where the oil pump and drive shaft has been removed from the engine, the replacing of the oil pump will necessitate the re-setting of the distributor short drive shaft as follows:
7. Rotate the flywheel in running direction until the timing mark on the flywheel for Mk I, Mk IA and Mk II models and on the crankshaft damper at the front of the engine for Mk III models is in line with the pointer, with both valves of No. 1 cylinder closed. The timing mark for engines fitted with 8.75:1 or 8.0:1 compression ratio pistons is 3° BTDC, using premium grade fuels. For Mk I, Mk IA and Mk II engines fitted with 7.5:1 compression ratio pistons the timing mark is 2° BTDC.
8. Fit the short extension drive shaft in such a position that the distributor rotor arm is pointing toward number one segment of the distributor cap, and the contact breaker points just about to open. In this position the vacuum advance diaphragm housing of the distributor body should be facing forward.
9. Locate a new cork washer in the recess at the top of the distributor housing.

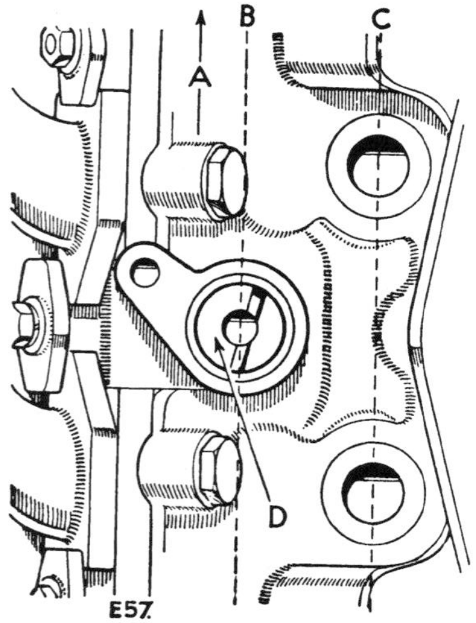

Distributor drive shaft: approximate position of offset slot with flywheel timing marks aligned with pointer

A—Front of engine
B—Centre line through drive shaft
C—Centre line through sparking plug holes
D—Drive shaft

*Sparking plugs, to remove and refit—Operation A1-9

Workshop hand tools:
Set of feeler gauges
Plug spanner

Special tools:
Sparking plug cleaning and testing machine

Sparking plugs, remove

1. Lift the caps and leads from the sparking plugs.
2. Use a plug spanner to remove the plugs and washers.

Sparking plugs, refit

1. Clean the plugs by sand blasting.
2. Reset the gaps to .029 to .032 in. (0,75 to 0,80mm).
3. Test the plugs on a suitable machine.
4. If unsatisfactory, renew as necessary.
5. When fitting new sparking plugs it is essential to fit replacements of the recommended type, that is:

Champion N5 or Lodge HLN	Engines with 8.0:1 compression ratio
Champion N5 or Lodge CLN-H	Engines with 7.5:1 compression ratio
Champion N5 or Lodge HLN	Engines with 8.75:1 compression ratio

Do not over tighten.

6. Replace the 'push-on' lead connectors.

*Water temperature transmitter, to remove and refit—Operation A1-10

Workshop hand tools:
Spanner size: $\frac{5}{8}$ in. AF

Note: Early models are fitted with capillary type temperature gauges, which of course have no electrical connections. When removing this type of instrument care must be taken not to damage the capillary tube between the gauge unit and the thermometer bulb. The tube must have no sharp bends.

Water temperature transmitter, remove

1. Disconnect the battery, situated in the luggage compartment.
2. Disconnect the wiring at the 'Lucar' connector on the transmitter, which is situated in the cylinder head at the front of the engine.
3. Remove the transmitter from the cylinder head.

Water temperature transmitter, refit

1. Reverse removal procedure.
2. Renew joint washer.

*Carburetter, to remove and refit—Operation A1-11

Workshop hand tools:
Spanner sizes: $\frac{7}{16}$ in. AF, $\frac{1}{2}$ in. AF, 2 BA, Small adjustable spanner

See Section Q for carburetter overhaul procedure

Carburetter, remove

1. Remove the air cleaner/silencer. On early models having the oil bath type air cleaner, slacken the hose clips securing the air cleaner top cover to silencer duct. Remove the air cleaner secured by a long horizontal bolt, spring washer and nut and by a nut, bolt and washers to a bracket on the dynamo.

   On late models with paper element type air cleaner, remove the air cleaner/silencer secured by a nut and washer to the elbow, and by nuts and washers to a bracket adjacent to the dynamo.
2. Disconnect the economiser hose adaptor and remove the fixings securing the elbow to the carburetter; withdraw elbow.
3. Disconnect the fuel supply pipe from the carburetter.
4. Disconnect the vacuum pipe for distributor advance mechanism.
5. Remove the hose connection from the economiser union.
6. Disconnect the accelerator linkage, at the throttle lever.
7. Disconnect the cold start control.
8. Remove the carburetter from the cylinder head secured by four nuts and spring washers.

Carburetter, refit

1. Ensure that the fitting faces of the carburetter and cylinder head are clean.
2. Reverse removal procedure, using a new joint washer.
3. Adjust the cold start control. See Section Q.

*Exhaust manifold, to remove and refit—Operation A1-12

Workshop hand tools:
Spanner sizes: $\frac{1}{2}$ in. AF, $\frac{9}{16}$ in. AF

Exhaust manifold, remove

1. Remove the three nuts and spring washers securing front exhaust pipe to manifold.
2. Remove the manifold secured by five nuts and spring washers together with the fixing clamps, also the two nuts and spring washers at the manifold ends.

Exhaust manifold, refit

1. Renew the two joint washers.
2. Reverse removal procedure.
3. Ensure that the manifold nuts are tightened evenly to avoid distortion and damage to the joint washers.

*External oil filter and adaptor, to remove and refit—Operation A1-13

Workshop hand tools:
Spanner sizes: $\frac{5}{8}$ in. AF, $\frac{3}{8}$ in. Whit

Adaptor and oil filter, remove

1. Disconnect the wire from the oil pressure transmitter (coupé models only).
2. Remove the filter and adaptor secured by four bolts and washers to the cylinder block.

Adaptor and oil filter, refit

1. Reverse removal procedure. Use new joint washers.
2. **Coupé models only.** If the oil pressure transmitter has been removed, refit in accordance with instructions given in Section B.

*Water pump, fan blades and fan belt, to remove and refit—Operation A1-14

Workshop hand tools:
Spanner size: $\frac{7}{16}$ in. AF Screwdriver, medium

See Section P for water pump overhaul procedure

Water pump and fan blades, remove

1. Drain coolant and remove radiator. Operation A1-2.
2. Slacken fixing bolts for dynamo or jockey pulley, then remove fan belt. Remove the fan blades, packing piece and fan pulley.
3. Disconnect the heater pipe, thermostat by-pass pipe and water inlet pipe to the water pump. It may be found necessary to detach the ignition coil in order to disconnect the thermostat pipe.
4. Unscrew the nine mounting bolts, noting the fitting sequence.

Layout of single belt system

A—Adjuster bolt
B—Pivot bolt
C—Check at this point, $\frac{5}{16}$ in. to $\frac{7}{16}$ in. (8,0 to 11,0 mm) free movement

Mk I and Mk IA. Remove the water pump which is dowelled to the base of the cylinder block. Remove the joint washer.

Mk II and Mk III. To remove the water pump, tilt upwards off the dowels; this will compress the 'O' ring between pump and cylinder head and will allow the pump to be withdrawn. Remove the joint washer.

Water pump and fan blades, refit

1. Ensure the fitting faces of water pump and cylinder block are clean.
2. Lightly grease a new joint washer and position it on the cylinder block.

   Mk I and Mk IA. Fit the thermostat hose to pump adaptor and fit pump to the dowels on cylinder block, connecting the thermostat hose to the adaptor in the cylinder head. Fit water inlet and heater hose to water pump. Replace ignition coil. Secure with the nine bolts.

   Mk II and Mk III. Lightly smear new 'O' ring with silicone grease MS4, and position it on pump bye-pass outlet. Then fit water pump to cylinder block by tilting it on to the dowels, ensuring that the 'O' ring is not dislocated. Secure pump with the nine bolts. Fit the water inlet and heater hoses to the pump.
3. Refit the packing piece, fan pulley, fan blades and fan belt. With twin belts the fan belt must be fitted to the forward groove of pulley.

Operations which are identified by an asterisk (*), can be carried out with the engine installed in the car

Operation A1-14—*continued*

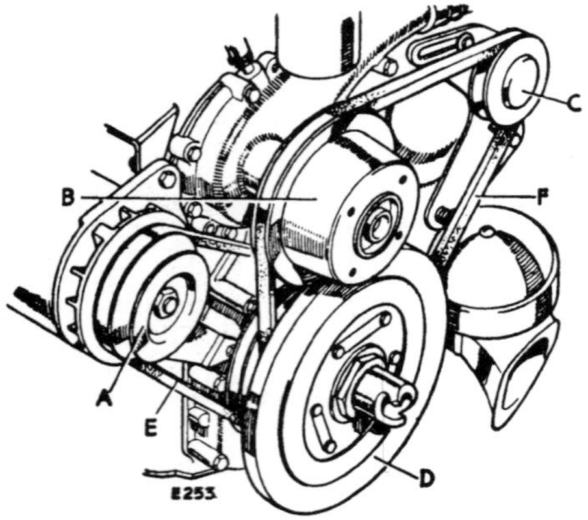

Layout of twin belt system

A—Dynamo pulley
B—Fan/water pump pulley
C—Jockey pulley
D—Vibration damper pulley
E—Dynamo belt
F—Fan belt

4. Adjust the fan belt to the correct tension.
   Single belt system, adjust at dynamo.
   Twin belt system, adjust at jockey pulley.
   Fan belt tension: $\frac{5}{16}$ in. to $\frac{7}{16}$ in. (8,0 to 11,0 mm).
   Dynamo belt: $\frac{5}{16}$ in. to $\frac{7}{16}$ in. (8,0 to 11,0 mm).
   Check by thumb pressure between the pulleys.

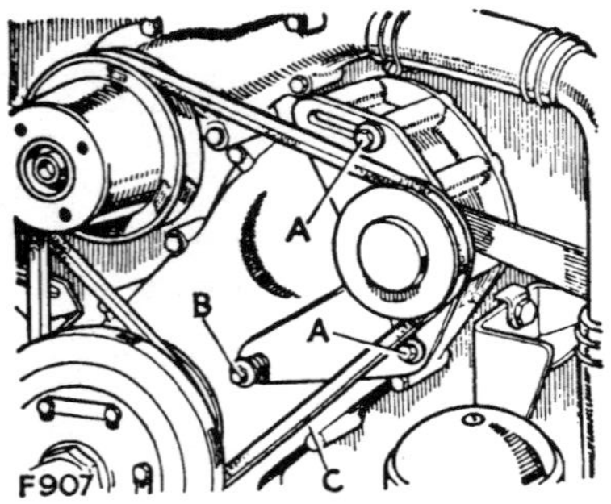

Fan belt adjustment, twin belt system

A—Adjustment bolts
B—Pivot bolts
C—Check at this point, $\frac{5}{16}$ in. to $\frac{7}{16}$ in. (8,0 to 11,0 mm) free movement

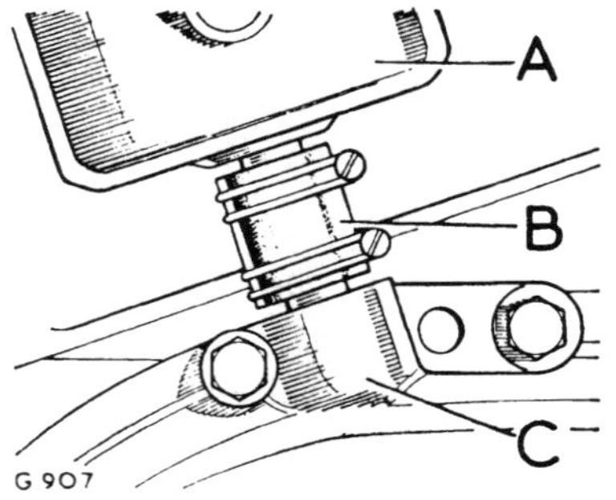

Layout of water pump and cylinder head. Mk I and Mk IA

A—Cylinder head, thermostat housing
B—Rubber hose
C—Water pump

5. Refit the radiator and fill with coolant, anti-freeze in winter. Operation A1-2.

   Capacities:
   Mk I, Mk IA and Mk II: 24 Imperial pints; 29 US pints; 13,7 litres.
   Mk III: 26 Imperial pints; 31 US pints; 14,7 litres.
6. Check for water leaks before starting the engine.

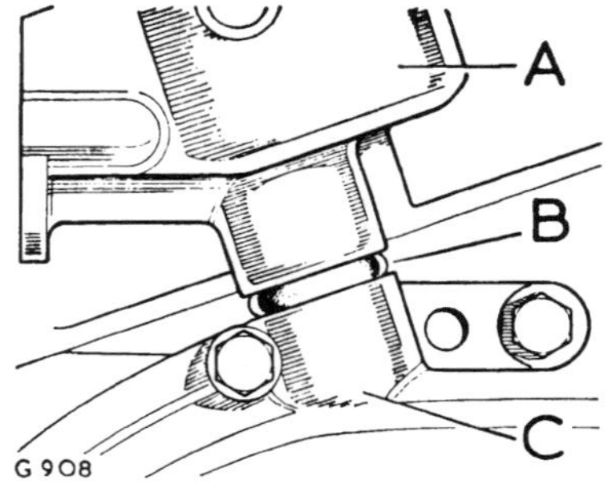

Layout of water pump and cylinder head. Mk II and Mk III

A—Cylinder head, thermostat housing
B—Rubber 'O' ring
C—Water pump

*Dynamo and dynamo belt, to remove and refit—Operation A1-15

Workshop hand tools:
Spanner sizes: $\frac{1}{2}$ in. AF, $\frac{15}{16}$ in. AF $\frac{1}{4}$ in. BSF,

See Section S for dynamo overhaul procedure

Dynamo and dynamo belt, remove

1. Disconnect the battery.
2. **Twin belts. Items 2 and 3.** Remove the radiator. Operation A1-2.
3. Where fitted disconnect the power steering hydraulic pipes from the pump attached to the dynamo and seal the pump ports to prevent the ingress of dirt.
4. Remove the carburetter air cleaner, secured to the elbow by a nut and plain washer, and by a bolt, bush, washers and nut to a bracket on the cylinder head.
5. Disconnect the dynamo wiring and remove the lower securing bolt from the dynamo adjusting link.
6. Push the dynamo towards the engine as far as possible and disengage the driving belt from the dynamo pulley.

Layout of single belt system
A—Adjuster bolt C—Check at this point, $\frac{5}{16}$ in. to $\frac{7}{16}$ in.
B—Pivot bolt (8,0 to 11,0 mm) free movement

7. Remove the two bolts and self-locking nuts from the dynamo mounting bracket and withdraw dynamo.
8. Twin belts. Slacken jockey pulley and remove fan belt.
9. The dynamo belt can now be removed.

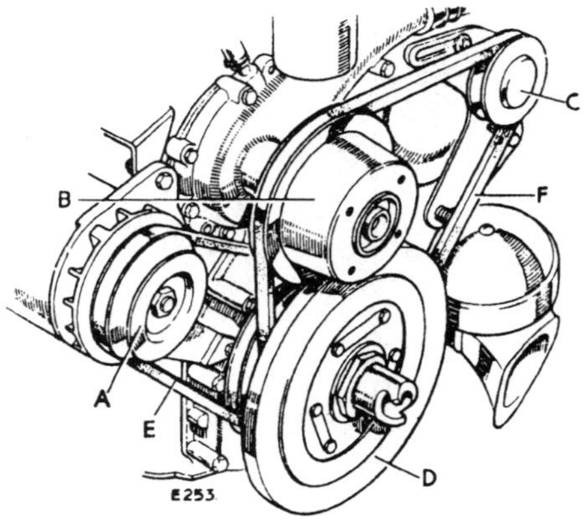

Layout of twin belt system
A—Dynamo pulley D—Vibration damper pulley
B—Fan/water pump pulley E—Dynamo belt
C—Jockey pulley F—Fan belt

Dynamo and dynamo belt, refit

1. Offer the dynamo to mounting bracket and align the bolt holes. Secure with bolts and self-locking nuts.
2. Check the alignment of the dynamo and vibration damper pulleys, correct if necessary by adjusting the dynamo top mounting bracket on the engine. Failure to align pulleys will cause premature belt wear.
3. Pivot the dynamo inwards and fit driving belt between dynamo and crankshaft pulley.
4. Fit the lower securing bolt to the dynamo adjusting link. Do not tighten.
5. Fit the dynamo belt and then the fan belt.
6. Adjust the belts to the correct tension:
   Fan belt $\frac{5}{16}$ in. to $\frac{7}{16}$ in. (8,0 to 11,0 mm).
   Dynamo belt $\frac{5}{16}$ in. to $\frac{7}{16}$ in. (8,0 to 11.0 mm)
   Check by thumb pressure between the pulleys.
7. Connect wiring in accordance with the circuit diagram and reconnect the battery leads.

Operations which are identified by an asterisk (*), can be carried out with the engine installed in the car

Operation A1-15—*continued*

8. **Power steering. Items 7 and 8.** Reconnect the hydraulic pipes to pump.
9. Refit the radiator and fill with coolant, anti-freeze in winter. Operation A1-2.
   Capacities:
   Mk I, Mk IA and Mk II: 24 Imperial pints; 29 US pints; 13,7 litres.
   Mk III: 26 Imperial pints; 31 US pints; 14,7 litres
10. Refit the carburetter air cleaner.
11. Where fitted, bleed the power steering hydraulic system. Section J1.
12. Check dynamo for correct operation.

Fan belt adjustment, twin belt system
A—Adjustment bolts C—Check at this point, $\frac{5}{16}$ in. to $\frac{7}{16}$ in.
B—Pivot bolt (8,0 to 11,0 mm) free movement

*Starter motor, to remove and refit—Operation A1-16

Workshop hand tools:
Spanner sizes: $\frac{9}{16}$ in. AF, $\frac{1}{4}$ in. Whit

See Section S for starter overhaul procedure

Starter, to remove

1. Disconnect the battery leads, and on coupé models disconnect the wiring from the oil pressure transmitter.
2. Remove the external oil filter, adaptor and gasket from the cylinder block, secured by two bolts and washers.
3. Disconnect wiring from starter to solenoid.
4. Remove starter motor, secured by two bolts.

Starter, refit

1. Reverse removal procedure.
2. Fit a new gasket to oil filter and adaptor and secure to cylinder block with four bolts.
3. Check engine oil level, top up if necessary.
4. Connect wiring in accordance with circuit diagram, from starter to solenoid and check operation of starter motor.

Operations which are identified by an asterisk (*), can be carried out with the engine installed in the car

*Rocker oil feed pipe, to remove and refit—Operation A1-17

Workshop hand tools:
Spanner sizes: ⅜ in. AF, $\frac{7}{16}$ in. BSF

Oil pipe, remove

1. Disconnect wiring from oil pressure switch.
2. Remove banjo bolt fixing oil pipe to cylinder block.
3. Remove banjo bolt fixing oil pipe to cylinder head.
4. If necessary, remove oil pressure switch.

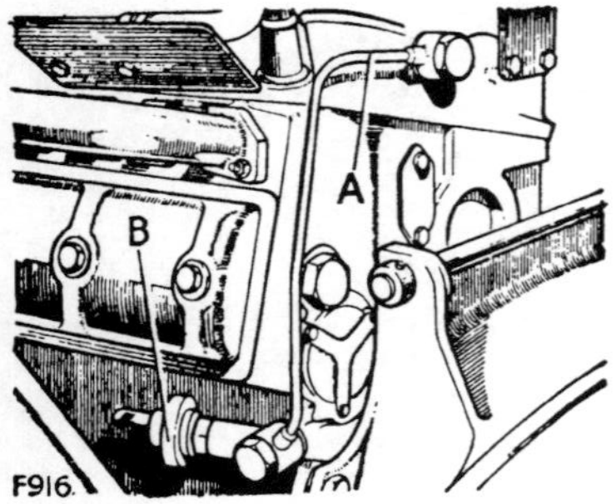

F916

Oil pressure switch and rocker oil feed pipe
A—Rocker oil feed pipe B—Oil pressure switch

Oil pipe, refit

1. Reverse removal procedure.
2. Renew joint washers as required and ensure that a meter plug is fitted to the top banjo union.

Operations which are identified by an asterisk (*), can be carried out with the engine installed in the car

*Cylinder head, to remove and refit—Operation A1-18

Workshop hand tools:
Screwdriver, medium Set of feeler gauges
Spanner sizes: $\frac{7}{16}$ in. AF, ½ in. AF, $\frac{9}{16}$ in. AF
⅝ in. AF, ¾ in. AF, ⅞ in. AF

Special tools:
Torque wrench

See Section A, Part Two, for overhaul and decarbonise instructions

Cylinder head, remove

1. Drain the coolant from the engine and radiator.
2. Remove air cleaner/silencer and elbow. Operation A1-4.
3. Remove distributor. Operation A1-8.
4. Remove carburetter. Operation A1-11.
5. **Mk I, Mk IA and Mk II suffix 'A' and 'B'.** Remove accelerator countershaft and bracket from cylinder head. Where overdrive is fitted disconnect the wiring from the rotary or cam type switch.
   Engines suffix 'C' and Mk III. Disconnect the control rods, throttle lever to bell-crank and bell-crank to cross-shaft.
6. Remove the rocker feed oil pipe.
7. Disconnect the lead from the thermostat switch.
8. Disconnect the radiator top hose from the cylinder head. Where fitted, release the clip on the short by-pass hose between the cylinder head and water pump.
9. Disconnect the heater hose from the cylinder head.
10. Remove the thermometer bulb (or on late models disconnect the wire from the water temperature transmitter).
11. Disconnect the servo brake pipe to manifold.
12. Remove the top rocker cover.
13. Slacken off the cylinder head bolts evenly and remove them, together with the plain washers, then lift off the cylinder head and discard the gasket.

    Mk II and Mk III models. If necessary, remove the inlet manifold secured to the cylinder head by nuts and spring washers; discard gasket.
14. Withdraw the push rods and retain them in their original sequence.

Cylinder head, refit

1. Remove side rocker cover.
2. Replace the push-rods in their original positions.
3. Smear a new cylinder head gasket with oil and place on the face of the cylinder block. The gasket is marked 'This side up'.
4. Use two old cylinder head bolts with their heads sawn off to locate the gasket and head. Cut a screwdriver slot across the diameter of the bolts to facilitate removal when the cylinder head is in position.
5. Position the cylinder head on to the block; as this is being done connect the by-pass hose or sealing washer to the cylinder head. Check that the push-rods are seating correctly.
6. Tighten the cylinder head bolts in order shown and to the following torques:
   (*a*) Bolts 'A' .. 50 lb/ft (7 mkg)
   (*b*) Bolts 'B' .. 30 lb/ft (4 mkg)

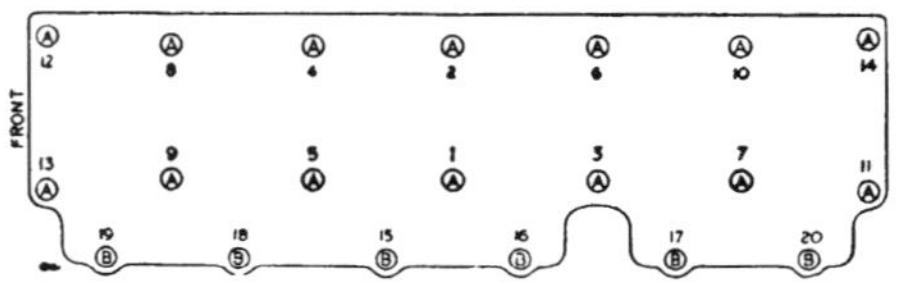

Order of tightening cylinder head bolts

7. Adjust the tappets. Operation A1-26.
8. Replace side rocker cover.
9. Reverse removal procedure for remaining items.
10. Refill cooling system, anti-freeze in winter.
    Capacities:
    Mk I, Mk IA and Mk II: 24 Imperial pints; 29 US pints; 13,7 litres.
    Mk III: 26 Imperial pints; 31 US pints; 14,7 litres.
11. Run engine until hot, recheck cylinder head bolt tightening torques. Check for oil and water leaks Carry out any adjustments necessary.

Operations which are identified by an asterisk (*), can be carried out with the engine installed in the car

*Thermostat, to renew—Operation A1-19

Workshop hand tools:
Spanner size: $\frac{7}{16}$ in. AF Screwdriver, medium

If the thermostat becomes faulty, either overheating or overcooling of the engine may result. To check the operation of the thermostat remove it from its housing, as detailed below. When immersed in hot water the thermostat bellows should commence expansion between 72°C to 77°C (162°F to 171°F) and be complete at 88°C (191°F).

Thermostat, remove

1. Partly drain off the coolant and disconnect the water outlet hose from the outlet pipe.
2. Remove outlet pipe secured to the cylinder head by three $\frac{1}{4}$ in. UNF nuts and spring washers.

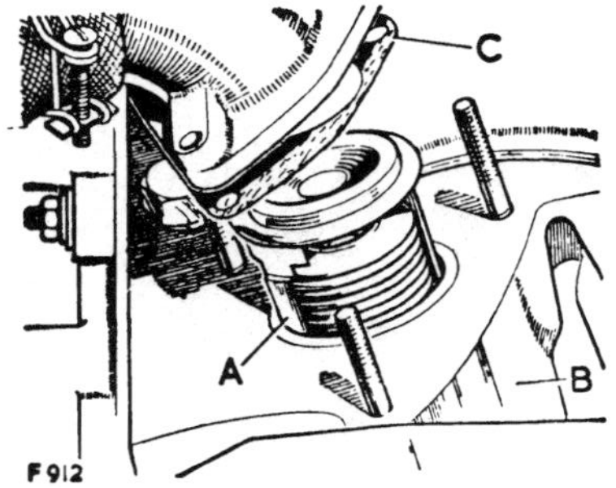

F912

Removing thermostat

A—Thermostat B—Cylinder block C—Joint washer

3. Lift out the thermostat and joint washers.
4. Test thermostat.

Thermostat, refit

1. Reverse removal procedure.
2. If necessary, fit a new thermostat complete with new joint washers.
3. Top up the coolant and check for leaks.

*Engine oil breather pipe, to remove and refit—Operation A1-20

Workshop hand tools:
Spanner sizes: $\frac{7}{16}$ in. AF, $\frac{1}{2}$ in. AF

Oil breather pipe, remove

1. Remove breather pipe, secured to cylinder block by three set bolts and spring washers.

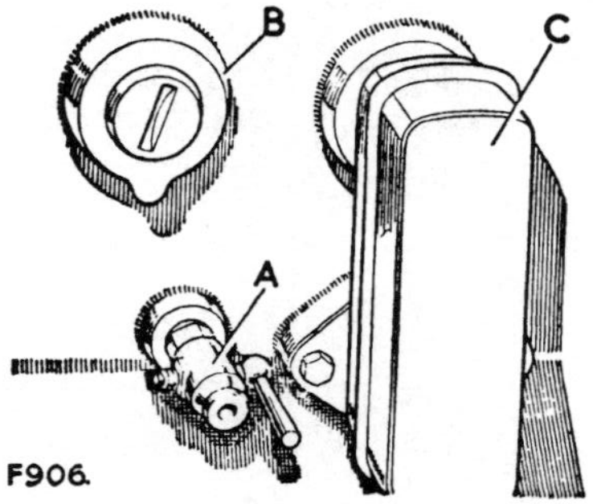

F906

A—Drain tap
B—Immersion heater boss
C—Crankcase breather

Oil breather pipe, refit

1. Reverse removal procedure.
2. Renew joint washer.

*Sump unit for oil level gauge, Mk I, Mk IA and Mk II models, to remove and refit—Operation A1-21

Workshop hand tools:
Spanner size: 3 BA

Sump unit, remove

1. Drain the oil from the sump.
2. Disconnect the wiring from the sump unit.
3. Remove the unit, secured to the RH side of the sump by six set screws and spring washers.

Sump unit, refit

1. Reverse removal procedure.
2. Renew joint washer.
3. Refill the engine to correct level with the recommended grade of lubricant. For recommended grades of oil see chart in Section B.

   Capacity: 10 Imperial pints; 1.2 US pints; 5,5 litres, plus 1 Imperial pint; 1.2 US pints; 0,5 litre, after replacing engine oil filter element.

*Sump and internal oil strainer, to remove and refit—Operation A1-22

Workshop hand tools:
Spanner sizes: $\frac{7}{16}$ in. AF, $\frac{1}{2}$ in. AF, $\frac{5}{8}$ in. AF, Pliers, long nosed

Sump and internal oil strainer, to remove

1. Drain engine oil.
2. Remove dip stick.
3. **Mk I, Mk IA and Mk II models.** Disconnect the lead from sump unit.
4. Disconnect one end of track rod. (Where fitted one end of steering damper).
5. Remove the torsion rod.
6. Where fitted, detach the power steering hydraulic pipes from sub-frame for clearance.
7. Remove the 16 set bolts $\frac{5}{16}$ in. UNF and 2 set bolts $\frac{5}{16}$ in. UNC securing sump to cylinder block.
8. Lower the sump carefully to clear oil filter and remove.
9. Remove joint washer.
10. Remove oil strainer from pump, secured with, a castle nut and split pin.
11. **Mk I, Mk IA and Mk II models.** If necessary, remove sump unit for oil level gauge, secured to right-hand side of sump.

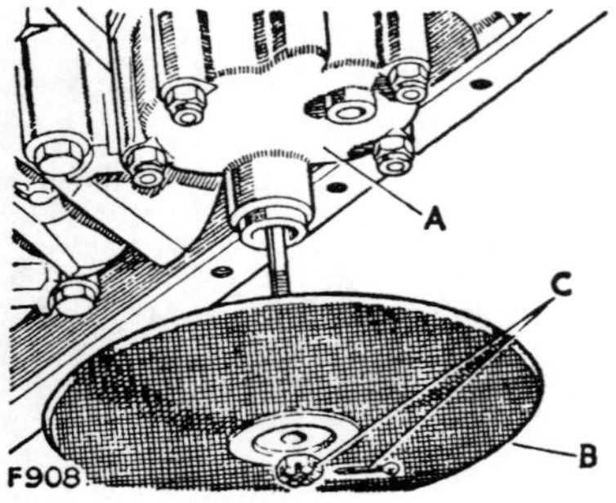

Oil pump strainer

A—Oil pump B—Strainer C—Strainer fixings

Sump and internal oil strainer, refit

1. Reverse removal procedure.
2. Use new sump joint washer.
3. Ensure the two set bolts $\frac{5}{16}$ in. UNC are fitted to the timing cover.
4. **Mk I, Mk IA and Mk II models.** If removed, refit sump oil level unit.
5. Refill the engine to the correct level with the recommended grade of lubricant. For recommended grades of lubricant see chart in Section B.

   Capacity: 10 Imperial pints; 12 US pints; 5,5 litres; plus 1 Imperial pint; 1.2 US pints, 0,5 litres, after replacing filter element.
6. Run the engine and check for oil leaks.

*Oil pump and drive shaft, to remove and refit—Operation A1-23

Workshop hand tools:
Spanner sizes: $\frac{1}{2}$ in. AF, $\frac{5}{8}$ in. AF, $\frac{3}{4}$ in. AF

See Section B for oil pump overhaul

Oil pump and shaft, remove

1. Drain engine oil.
2. Remove the air cleaner and distributor. Operations A1-4; A1-8.
3. Remove the engine sump. Operation A1-18.
4. Remove the non-adjustable oil pressure relief valve.
5. Remove the oil pump locating screw from cylinder block.
6. Withdraw the oil pump.
7. Remove the side rocker cover.
8. Remove the oil feed bolt and lock washer, locating distributor housing inside rocker chamber.
9. Lift out distributor housing.
10. Withdraw drive shaft, upwards.

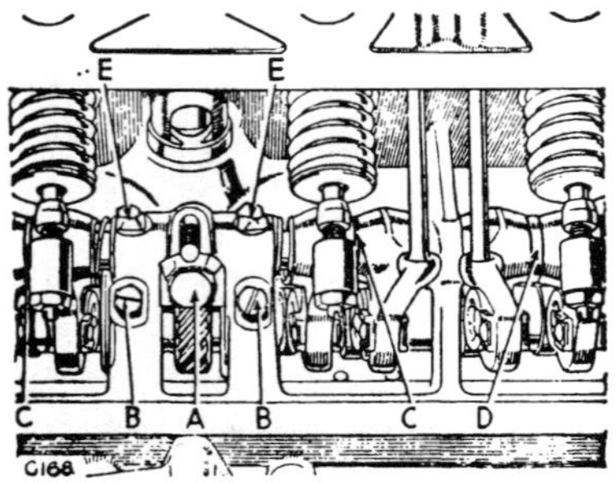

Rocker shaft and oil feed locating screws

A—Oil feed locating bolt
B—Camshaft bearing locating screw:
C—Spacing washer, thin
D—Spacing washer, thick
E—Rocker shaft locating screws

Oil pump and shaft, refit

1. Reverse the removal procedure.
2. It is important that the drive shaft is positioned as detailed in distributor fitting. Operation A1-8.
3. Refill engine to the correct level with the recommended grade of lubricant. Capacity: 10 Imperial pints; 12 US pints; 5,5 litres, plus 1 Imperial pint; 1.2 US pints; 0,5 litres, after replacing engine oil filter element.
4. After final assembly, check the oil pressure which should be: 40 to 50 lb/sq in. at 40 mph (64 kph) in top gear, and with the engine at running temperature.

   To check this, the oil pressure warning light switch may be removed and a suitable external oil pressure gauge temporarily connected in its place. If lower pressures are indicated, the oil pressure relief valve spring should be renewed.

*Vibration damper, to remove and refit—Operation A1-24

Workshop hand tools:

Spanner sizes: $\frac{7}{16}$ in. AF, $\frac{1}{2}$ in. AF, $\frac{1}{4}$ in. BSF
Screwdriver, medium

Special tools:

Spanner for starter dog, Part No. 530102

See Section A, Part Two, for overhaul instructions

(Not applicable to one-piece damper)

Damper, remove

1. Remove radiator. Operation A1-2.
2. Slacken off and remove the driving belt(s).
3. **4-speed models.** Engage top gear and apply hand brake.
4. Prise up the lock on the starting dog lock washer and, using special tool (Part No. 530102), remove the starting dog. Withdraw lock washer and damper from the crankshaft.

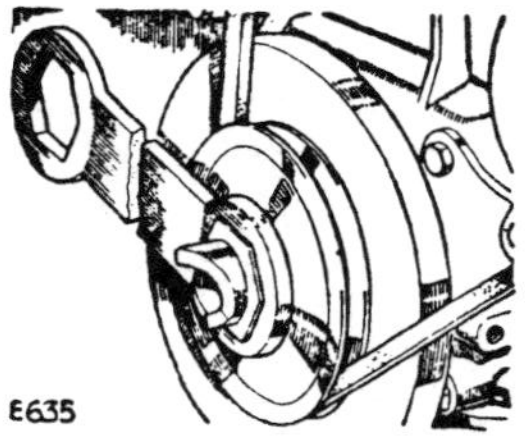
E635

Starter dog spanner

Vibration damper, refit

1. Reverse removal procedure.
2. Use a new lock washer.
3. **Models from suffix letter 'C' onwards and Mk III.** The tightening torque for the starter dog is 200 lb/ft (27,6 mkg).
4. Fill radiator with coolant, anti-freeze in winter.
   Capacities:
   Mk I, Mk IA and Mk II: 24 Imperial pints; 29 US pints; 13,7 litres.
   Mk III: 26 Imperial pints; 31 US pints; 14,7 litres.
5. **Run engine and check for water leaks.**

*Timing chain, tensioner and chainwheels, to remove and refit—Operation A1-25

Workshop hand tools:

Spanner sizes: $\frac{7}{16}$ in. AF, $\frac{1}{2}$ in. AF, $\frac{9}{16}$ in. AF
Screwdriver, medium
Pliers, pointed-nose

Special tools:

Allen key, $\frac{1}{8}$ in. (3 mm)
Spanner for starter dog, Part No. 530102
Extractor, Part No. 507231
Dial test indicator
Bracket for dial test indicator, Part No. 530106

Timing chain, tensioner and chainwheel, remove

1. Remove the radiator. Operation A1-2.
2. Remove the radiator grille and bonnet lock platform. Operation A1-3.
3. **Single belt only.** Ease the tensioner on the fan belt and remove the fan, distance piece and pulley.
4. **Twin belts. Items 4 and 5.** Ease the tensioner on both the fan and dynamo belts and remove.
5. Remove fan, distance piece and pulley.
6. **Mk III models.** Turn the engine over until the exhaust peak ('EP') mark on the crankshaft damper at the front of the engine is corresponding to the timing pointer; this is to ensure the camshaft is in the correct position for assembly.

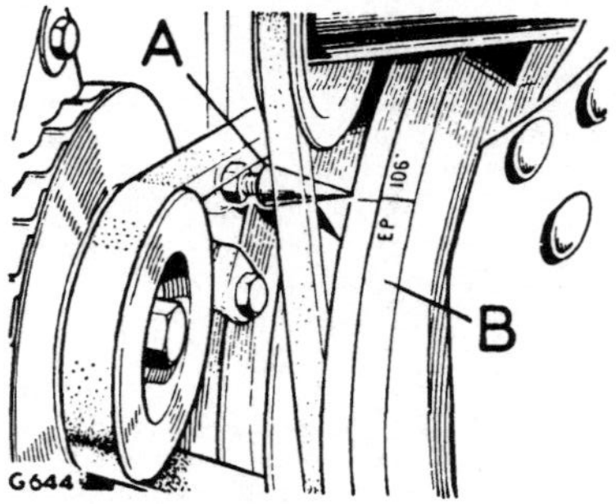

G644

Valve timing marks on crankshaft damper
A—Pointer B—Crankshaft damper

7. Prise up the lock on the starting dog lock washer and, using special tool (Part No. 530102), remove the starting dog. Withdraw the damper from the crankshaft.
8. Remove the dynamo adjusting link.
9. Remove the front cover, secured by eleven set bolts and washers to the cylinder block, and by two UNC bolts to the sump. Take care not to damage sump gasket.
10. Withdraw the oil thrower from the crankshaft.

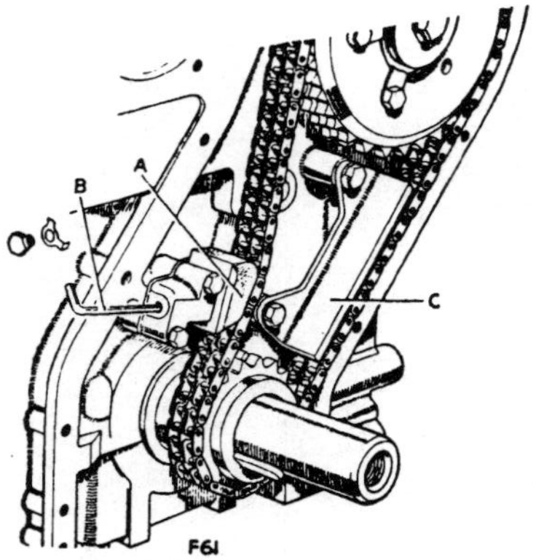

F61

Layout of timing chain adjuster, Allen key in position
A—Chain tensioner
B—Allen key
C—Chain vibration damper plate

11. **Mk I, Mk IA and Mk II models.** Remove the flywheel inspection cover and turn the engine over until the exhaust peak ('EP') mark on the flywheel is corresponding to the timing pointer; this is to ensure the camshaft is in the correct position for assembly.
12. Prise up the lock tab on the timing chain tensioner and remove the plug. With an $\frac{1}{8}$ in. (3 mm) Allen key, relieve the tension of the timing chain tensioner, by turning the key clockwise until the cylinder can be felt to retract into body.
13. Mark the camshaft chainwheel in relation to the camshaft hub in order to ensure correct refitment; prise up the three lock tabs and remove the three bolts, withdraw the camshaft wheel and chain from the camshaft hub, using extractor (Part No. 507231).
14. If necessary, remove the tensioner and backplate assembly, secured by two bolts. Remove the two bolts from the chain vibration damper plate and lift off.

Operation A1-25—*continued*

15. If necessary, remove the camshaft chainwheel hub, using extractor (Part No. 507231).

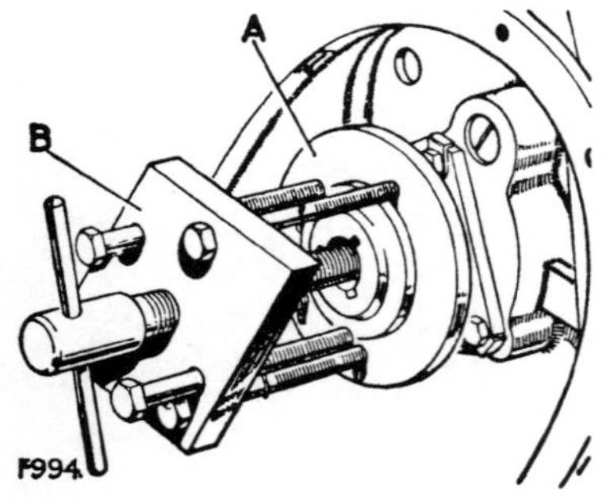

Removing camshaft chainwheel hub

A—Camshaft chainwheel hub
B—Extractor

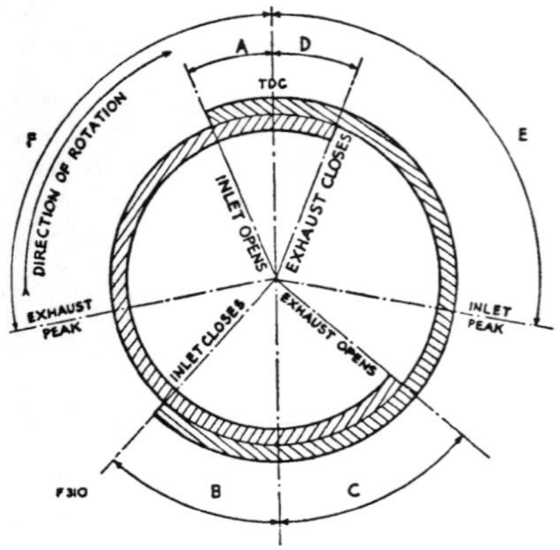

Valve timing diagram

Timing chain, tensioner and chainwheel, refit

1. **Mk I, Mk IA and Mk II models.** The exhaust peak ('EP') mark on the flywheel must be in line with the timing pointer.

	Mk I and Mk IA models		Mk II and Mk III models
	Early camshaft	Late camshaft	
A	17½°	17°	12°
B	40½°	41°	46°
C	52½°	45°	47°
D	27½°	13°	17°
E	101½°	102°	106°
F	102½°	106°	105°

Mk III models. Temporarily fit the crankshaft damper at the front of the engine and ensure that the ('EP') mark on the damper is in line with the pointer. Remove the damper.

2. Temporarily fit the camshaft chainwheel to the camshaft hub.
3. Rotate the camshaft until number one exhaust valve is fully open. The exhaust peak can only be determined by using a dial test indicator mounted on a bracket (Part No. 530106).

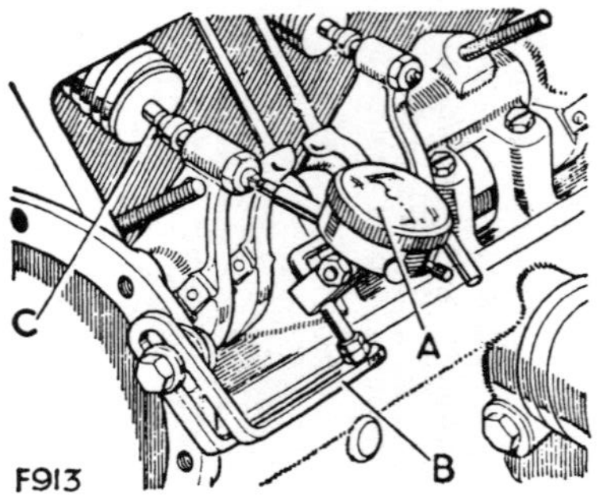

Determining No. 1 exhaust peak

A—Dial test indicator
B—Bracket
C—Exhaust valve

4. Adjustment can be made by alternative use of the three key-ways in chainwheel hub and the three fixing holes in chainwheel.
5. Remove the camshaft chainwheel.

Operation A1-25—*continued*

6. Offer the timing chain and camshaft chainwheel to the camshaft hub and crankshaft chainwheel with no slack on the driving side. Use the marks made during dismantling to assist in the correct realignment.
7. Align the chainwheel with three of the bolt holes in the hub and secure with three lockplates and bolts.
8. Check that the camshaft has not moved during this operation, and re-check the tightness of the chain on the driving side.
9. Prepare the chain tensioner device by inserting an ⅛ in. (3 mm) Allen key into the restraint cylinder and turning clockwise until the restraint cylinder can be felt to be fully retracted into the body. The rubber head of the tensioner should then be free.
10. Mount the tensioner and backplate in position; fit the timing chain vibration damper pad and adjust the position to allow minimum clearance between chain and pad.
11. Turn the Allen key in a clockwise direction until the rubber head of the tensioner moves forward under spring pressure against the timing chain. Do not attempt to force the rubber head on to the chain by external pressure and do not turn the Allen key anti-clockwise.
12. Fit the plug and lock tab to the base of the tensioner.
13. Check the timing by rotating the engine and ensuring that the flywheel 'EP' mark aligns with the pointer at the same time as the dial gauge indicates that No. 1 exhaust valve is fully open.
14. Fit the oil thrower to crankshaft, noting that the oil thrower curves away from the timing chain.
15. Reverse removal procedure for remaining items.
16. Adjust fan and dynamo belt, as applicable. Operation A1-15.

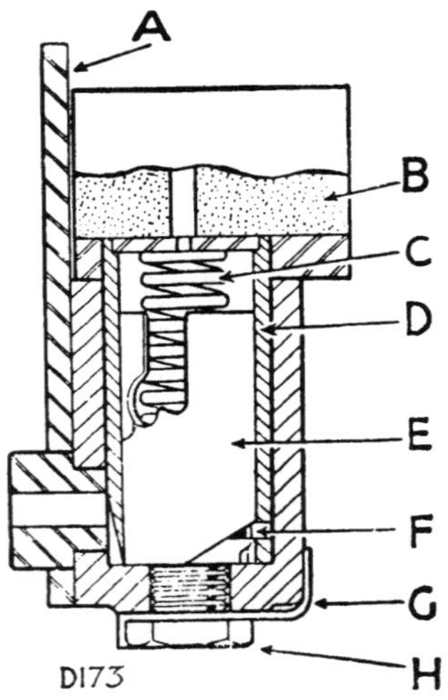

Cross-section of timing chain adjuster

A—Backplate
B—Rubber head
C—Spring
D—Plunger with end piece
E—Cylinder
F—Limit peg
G—Tab washer for plug
H—Plug for Allen key

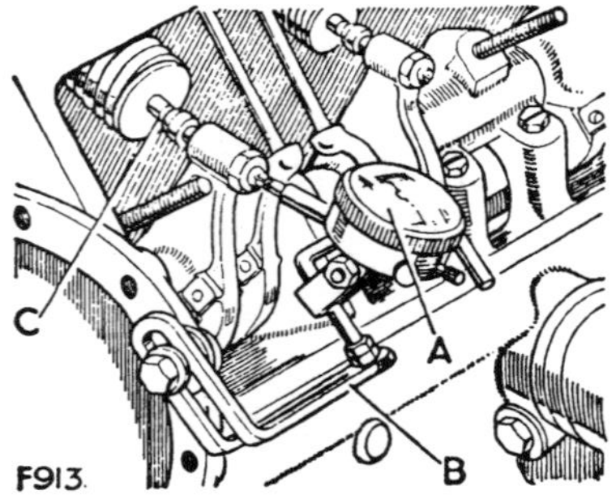

Determining No. 1 exhaust peak

A—Dial test indicator
B—Bracket
C—Exhaust valve

Operation A1-25—*continued*

17. Adjust tappets. Operation A1-26.

18. Fill radiator with coolant, anti-freeze in winter.

    Capacities:

    Mk I, Mk IA and Mk II: 24 Imperial pints; 29 US pints; 13,7 litres.

    Mk III: 26 Imperial pints; 31 US pints; 14,7 litres.

19. Run engine. Check for oil and water leaks. Carry out any adjustments necessary.

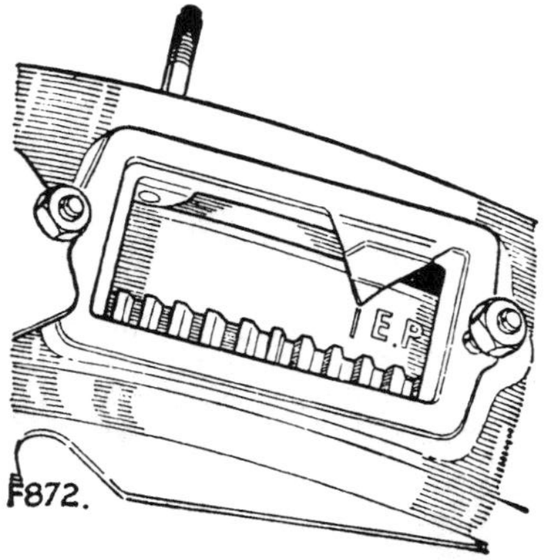

Flywheel valve timing mark. Mk I, IA and II

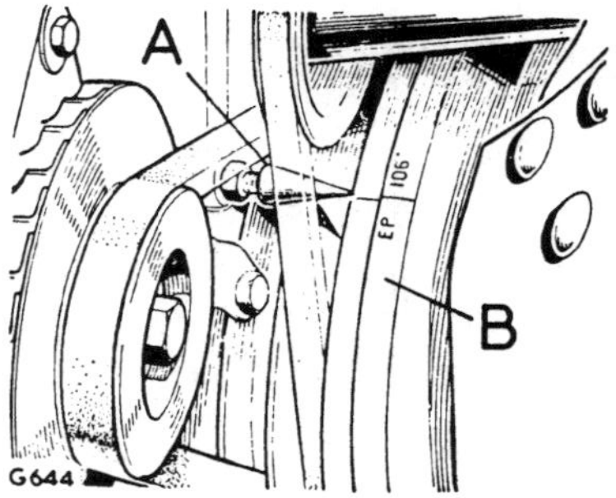

Valve timing mark. Mk III

A—Pointer B—Crankshaft damper

*Tappet adjustment—Operation A1-26

Workshop hand tools:

Spanner size: ½ in. AF Screwdriver, medium Set of feeler gauges

1. Tappet clearance must be checked when the engine is finally assembled and in running order. Reset when the engine is at running temperature.

2. Remove the air cleaner/silencer and elbow. On early models with oil bath type air cleaners, slacken the hose clips between the cleaner top cover and silencer duct. Remove the air cleaner secured by a long horizontal bolt, spring washer and nut, and by a nut, bolt and washers to a bracket adjacent to the dynamo.

   On late models with paper element type air-cleaners, remove the cleaner complete, secured to the elbow by a nut and plain washer, and by a bolt, bush, washers and nut to a bracket on the cylinder head. Disconnect the economiser hose, then remove the carburetter elbow.

3. Remove the side and top rocker covers.

4. Turn the crank in the direction of rotation until number six inlet valve (counting from the front of the engine) is fully open, that is, with the valve spring fully compressed. In this position the tappet for number one inlet valve is on the dwell of the cam.

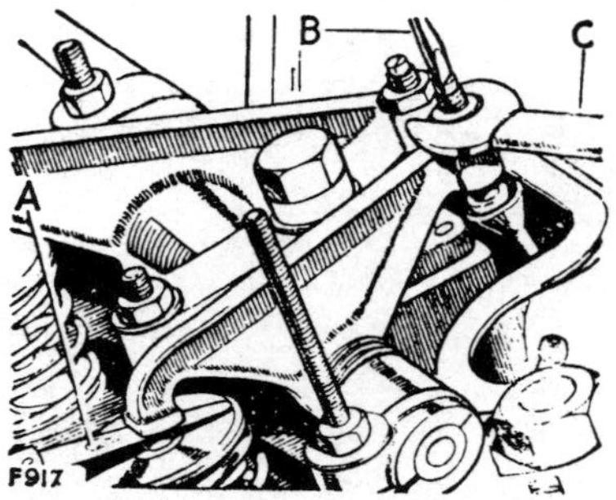

Adjusting tappets, inlet valves

A—Feeler gauge B—Screwdriver C—Tappet spanner

5. Slacken the tappet locknut, then rotate the adjusting screw until there is .006 in. (0,15 mm) clearance between rocker and valve stem when checked with a feeler gauge. Ensure all clearance is taken up at the push-rod ends. Tighten locknut and recheck clearance.

6. Adjust the exhaust valves in a similar manner, using a .010 in. (0,25 mm) feeler gauge.

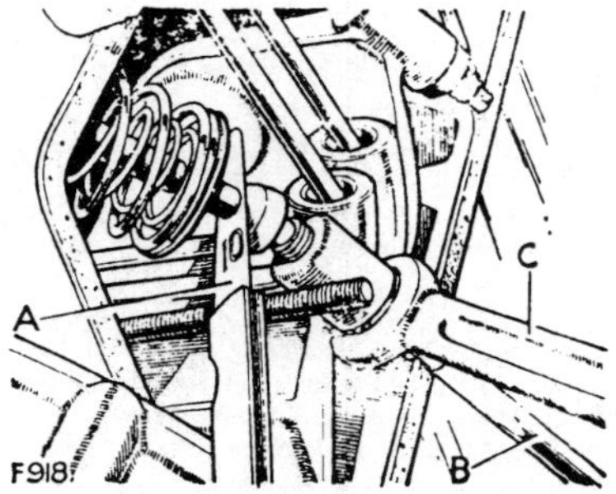

Adjusting tappets, exhaust valves

A—Feeler gauge B—Screwdriver C—Tappet spanner

Tappet clearance:

Inlet valves .006 in. (0,15 mm).

Exhaust valves .010 in. (0,25 mm).

Set No. 1 tappet with No. 6 valve fully open.
Set No. 2 tappet with No. 5 valve fully open.
Set No. 3 tappet with No. 4 valve fully open.
Set No. 4 tappet with No. 3 valve fully open.
Set No. 5 tappet with No. 2 valve fully open.
Set No. 6 tappet with No. 1 valve fully open.

Operations which are identified by an asterisk (*), can be carried out with the engine installed in the car

*Side rockers and shafts, to remove and refit—Operation A1-27

Workshop hand tools:
Spanner sizes: $\frac{7}{16}$ in. AF, $\frac{1}{2}$ in. AF, $\frac{9}{16}$ in. AF, $\frac{3}{4}$ in. AF, 2 BA, Small adjustable, $\frac{1}{8}$ in. Whit
Screwdriver, medium
Pliers, pointed-nose

Special tools:
Extractor, Part No. 262749
Allen key, $\frac{1}{8}$ in. (3 mm)
Spanner for starter dog, Part No. 530102
Dial test indicator
Bracket for dial test indicator, Part No. 530106

Rocker shafts and rockers, remove

1. Remove the radiator. Operation A1-2.
2. Remove the radiator grille and bonnet lock platform. Operation A1-3.
3. Remove the air cleaner/silencer. Operation A1-4.
4. Remove the exhaust manifold. Operation A1-12.
5. Remove the timing chain. Operation A1-25.
6. Remove the top rocker cover and slacken the tappet adjusting screws right back.
7. Remove the side rocker cover and slacken the tappet adjusting screws right back.

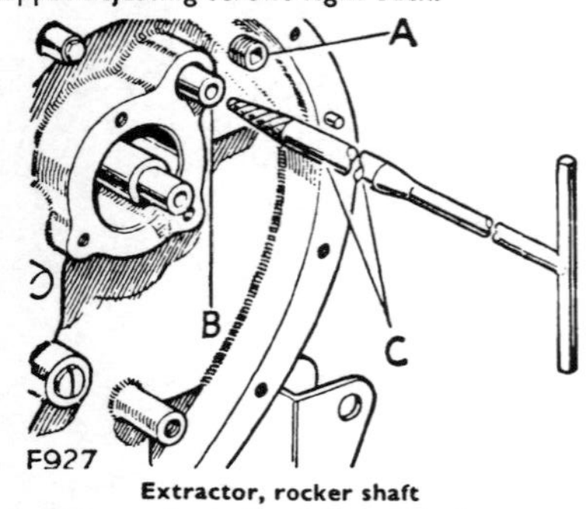

Extractor, rocker shaft
A—Plug B—Rocker shaft C—Extractor

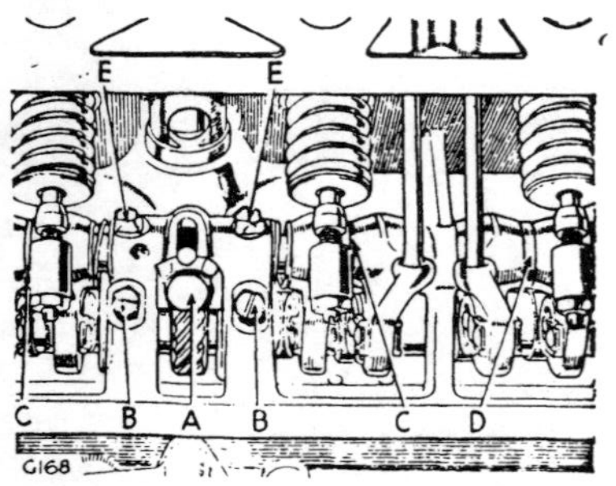

Camshaft and rocker shaft locating screws
A—Oil feed locating bolt
B—Camshaft bearing locating screws
C—Spacing washer, thin
D—Spacing washer, thick
E—Rocker shaft locating screws

8. Remove the end plug from the front end of the rocker shaft.
9. Remove the two locating screws securing front and rear rocker shafts.
10. Remove the oil feed bolt locating the distributor housing.
11. Extract the front and rear rocker shafts using special extractor tool, Part No. 262749.
12. Remove exhaust valve rockers, inlet cam followers, springs and spacers. Note the sequence of assembly. Push-rods should be lifted clear of the rockers as they are removed.
    The rocker shafts can only be removed from the rear when the engine is removed.

Rocker shafts and rockers, refit

1. Replace the rear rockers, cam followers, springs, spacers and shims in the order removed.
2. Feed the rear rocker shaft through the rockers, followers, etc. Ensure the locating screw hole in the shaft is to the front; use the extractor tool to align the hole with the hole in the block.
3. Secure the shaft with the locating screw and lockwasher.
4. Fit the front rocker assembly, in the order removed.
5. Feed the front rocker shaft through the rockers, followers, etc. Ensure the locating screw hole in the shaft is to the rear and in line with the hole in the block. Secure with locating screw and lock or spring washer.
6. Ensure that the inlet push-rods are in position.
7. Replace the end plug.
8. Reverse removal procedure for remaining items.
9. Adjust the tappets. Operation A1-26.
10. Fill radiator with coolant, anti-freeze in winter.
    Capacities:
    Mk I, Mk IA and Mk II: 24 Imperial pints; 29 US pints; 13,7 litres.
    Mk III: 26 Imperial pints; 31 US pints; 14,7 litres.
11. Run engine. Check for oil and water leaks. Carry out any adjustment required.

Operations which are identified by an asterisk (*), can be carried out with the engine installed in the car

*Camshaft, to remove and refit—Operation A1-28

Workshop hand tools:
Spanner sizes: $\frac{7}{16}$ in. AF, $\frac{1}{2}$ in. AF, $\frac{9}{16}$ in. AF, $\frac{5}{8}$ in. AF, Small adjustable, $\frac{3}{16}$ in. Whit
Screwdriver, large Screwdriver, medium
Pliers, pointed-nose
Feeler gauges

Special tools:
Allen key, $\frac{1}{8}$ in. (3 mm)
Spanner for starter dog, Part No. 530102
Extractor, Part No. 507231
Extractor, Part No. 530101
Dial test indicator
Bracket for dial test indicator, Part No. 530106

Camshaft, remove

1. Remove the radiator. Operation A1-2.
2. Remove the radiator grille and bonnet lock platform. Operation A1-3.
3. Remove the air cleaner/silencer. Operation A1-4.
4. Remove the exhaust manifold. Operation A1-11.
5. Remove the timing chain. Operation A1-25.
6. Remove side rockers and shafts. Operation A1-27.
7. Remove the camshaft thrust plate, secured to the cylinder block by three set bolts and lockers.
8. Remove the special set screws locating camshaft bearings.
9. Withdraw the camshaft until the bearings are clear of their housings, using special tool (Part No. 530101).

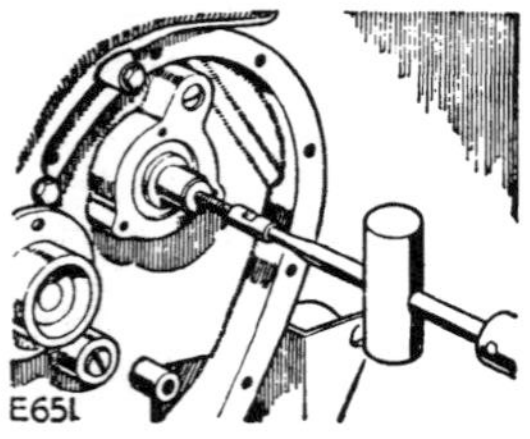

Extractor for camshaft

10. Where two housings are close together it will be advantageous to pass the rearmost bearing through both housings, before removal. The camshaft bearings are easily removed, being of the split type. When all bearings are away from the camshaft, pull the camshaft clear of the engine. Remove the rear cover plate and withdraw the rear camshaft bearing, but note that the cover plate can only be removed when the flywheel housing is removed from the cylinder block. Where bearing removal is necessary the bearing can be drifted out with the aid of a right-angled drift.
11. Keep the bearings in the correct pairs as indicated by the numbers stamped on the end face; these bearings are of soft material and care should be taken to avoid damage should it be necessary to refit the originals.

Camshaft, refit

Important—A camshaft which has been in service in conjunction with a steel gear on the oil pump driving shaft must not be used with a new phosphor bronze oil pump shaft driving gear, otherwise premature failure will result. If it is necessary to change the driving gear the camshaft must also be changed.

1. Before attempting to fit the camshaft bearings to the cylinder block, ensure that the bearing halves fit together correctly on the dowels by checking that no light is visible between the joint faces.
2. The bearings must be fitted dry and should be a hand push fit in the cylinder block; they must always be renewed in paired halves and the numbers stamped on one of the end faces of the bearing halves must be adjacent. Aligning the locating holes in the bearings with the corresponding holes in the housing is important. The rear bearing is provided with four lateral holes for oil relief.
3. Insert the camshaft partly into the cylinder block, allowing the distributor and oil pump drive gear to pass through the first and second intermediate housing webs. Assemble the bearings on to their respective journals on the camshaft. Ensure that the dowelled joint faces are tightly fitted together and the locating holes in the bearings are in line with the holes in the housing webs. Place a suitable distance piece between the first and second intermediate bearings. The width of the distance piece to be approximately the distance between the bearing housings but allowing sufficient clearance for withdrawal.

Operations which are identified by an asterisk (*), can be carried out with the engine installed in the car

Operation A1-28—*continued*

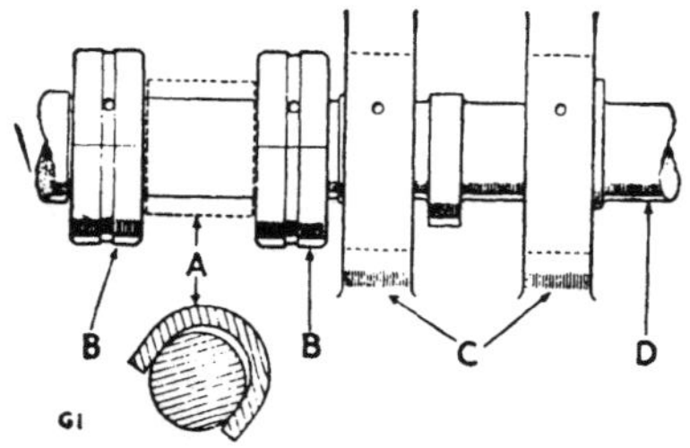

Camshaft fitting with distance piece

A—Distance piece
B—Bearings
C—Bearing housings
D—Camshaft

4. With all the bearings in place and correctly aligned and using a plastic-faced mallet, gently tap the camshaft rearwards until the bearings are fully home in their respective housings and the locating holes are aligned. Remove the distance piece.

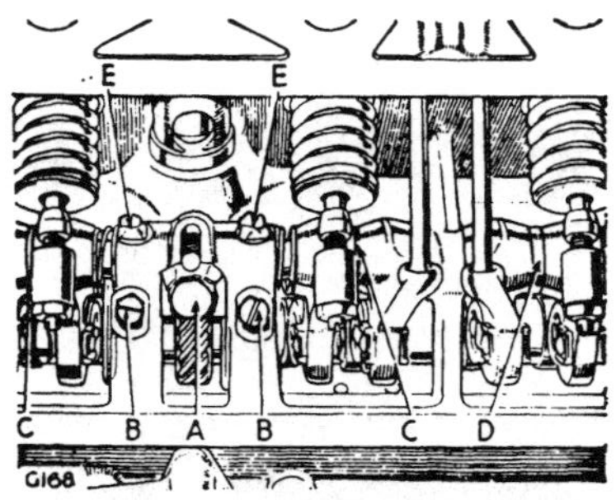

Camshaft bearing set bolts

A—Oil feed locating bolt
B—Camshaft bearing locating screw
C—Spacing washer, thin
D—Spacing washer, thick
E—Rocker shaft locating screws

5. Before fitting the locating set bolts to the bearings and housings, squirt engine oil down the holes to lubricate the bearings. Fit the locating set bolts and spring washers.

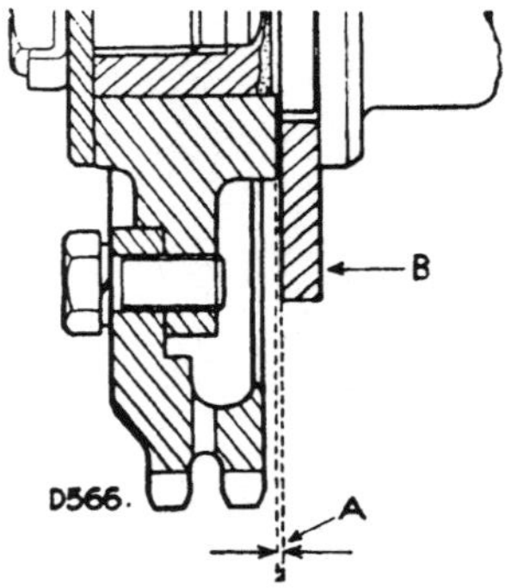

Camshaft end-float

A—.0045 to .0065 in. (0,11 to 0,16 mm) B—Thrust plate

6. Fit the camshaft thrust plate and camshaft hub, noting any alignment marks made previously. The camshaft should have .0045 to .0065 in. (0,11 to 0,16 mm) end-float measured between the hub and the thrust plate. A new thrust plate must be fitted where the end-float is in excess of these tolerances. When a replacement camshaft has been fitted it is important that the correct length of bolt is used for the type of camshaft fitted. Early camshafts had no counterbore at the hub end, later types are counterbored and the thread depth increased.

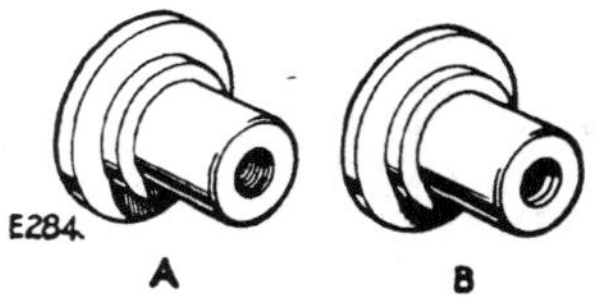

Identification of camshafts

A—Early type, no counterbore
B—Late type, with counterbore

Non-counterbored camshafts use set bolt, Part No. 255245 ($\frac{3}{8}$ in. UNF x $\frac{3}{4}$ in. long) and counterbored camshafts use Part No. 255046 ($\frac{3}{8}$ in. UNF x $\frac{7}{8}$ in. long), to retain the chainwheel hub to the camshaft.

Operation A1-28—*continued*

If the longer bolt is used in a non-counterbored camshaft there is the possibility that the bolt will bottom at the end of the thread before becoming fully tightened. If the shorter bolt is used with a counterbored camshaft there is insufficient thread engagement which may cause premature failure of the thread in service or stripping of the thread during assembly.

7. Reverse removal procedure for remaining items.

8. Fill radiator with coolant, anti-freeze in winter.

   Capacities:

   Mk I, Mk IA and Mk II: 24 Imperial pints; 29 US pints; 13,7 litres.

   Mk III: 26 Imperial pints; 31 US pints; 14,7 litres.

9. Run engine and check for oil and water leaks. Carry out any adjustments required.

*Pistons and connecting rods, to remove and refit—Operation A1-29

Workshop hand tools:
Spanner sizes: $\frac{3}{8}$ in. AF, $\frac{7}{16}$ in. AF, $\frac{1}{2}$ in. AF, $\frac{9}{16}$ in. AF, $\frac{5}{8}$ in. AF, $\frac{3}{4}$ in. AF, $\frac{7}{8}$ in. AF, 2 BA
Small adjustable
Pliers, long-nosed

Special tools:
Torque wrench
Extractor, Part No. 530101
Circlip pliers

See Section A, Part Two, for overhaul instructions

Pistons and connecting rods, remove

1. Remove bonnet. Operation A1-1.
2. Remove the air cleaner/silencer and elbow. Operation A1-4.
3. Remove top rocker cover and distributor cover complete with HT leads.
4. Remove distributor. Operation A1-8.
5. Remove sparking plugs. Operation A1-9.
6. Remove carburetter. Operation A1-11.
7. Disconnect rocker feed oil pipe from cylinder head. Operation A1-14.
8. Remove cylinder head. Operation A1-18.
9. Remove sump. Operations A1-22.
10. Remove oil pump and drive shaft. Operation A1-23.
11. Remove connecting rod caps and bearing shells secured by 'Nyloc' nuts. Ensure that the shells are retained in their respective pairs. It is not necessary to remove the connecting rod bolts.

    When assembling, new locknuts must be used.
12. Draw the pistons and connecting rods up through the cylinder bores.
13. Remove the piston rings.
14. Remove the gudgeon pins located by circlips. Withdraw the gudgeon pins towards the side of the piston which carries the 'X' stamp on the piston crown. Removal of gudgeon pins will be facilitated by the use of extractor (Part No. 530101).

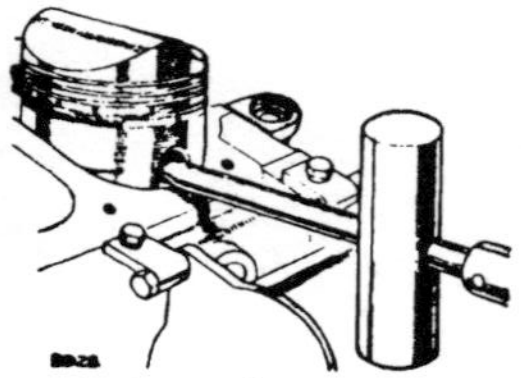

Gudgeon pin extractor

15. If necessary, press out the small end bush from the connecting rod.
16. Mark all components in sets.

Pistons and connecting rods, refit

1. The gudgeon pin should be a good hand push fit into the piston bores at a temperature of 50° to 70°F (10° to 21°C) and should not fall out of the piston under its own weight.
2. Clearance in the connecting rod gudgeon pin bush should be .0002 to .0006 in. (0,005 to 0,015 mm), selective assembly.
3. Fit the pistons to the connecting rods with the oil spray hole in the connecting rods facing the same side as the bore number stamped on the thrust side of the piston crown. New pistons have the machined section of the crown towards the same side as the spray hole in the connecting rods. Use two new circlips to secure each gudgeon pin.
4. Turn the crankshaft until the crankpins relative to numbers 1 and 6 cylinders are at bottom dead-centre. Insert the pistons and connecting rods for these cylinders from the top of the cylinder block, with the oil spray hole in the connecting rod to the RH side of the engine (looking towards No. 1 cylinder) opposite to the camshaft side. Lubricate the piston, crankpins, and bearing shells, before fitment.
5. Secure the big ends to the crankpins, using new self-locking securing nuts, tightened evenly to —bolts with machine-cut threads—30 lb/ft (4 mkg); bolts with rolled threads, identified by a drill point at nut end—25 lb/ft (3,5 mkg).
   New 'Nyloc' nuts must be fitted on every occasion when the connecting rod caps have been disturbed.
6. If the connecting rod bolts have been removed or dislodged, they can be replaced by the use of special tool (Part No. 530101).

Operations which are identified by an asterisk (*), can be carried out with the engine installed in the car

Operation A1-29—*continued*

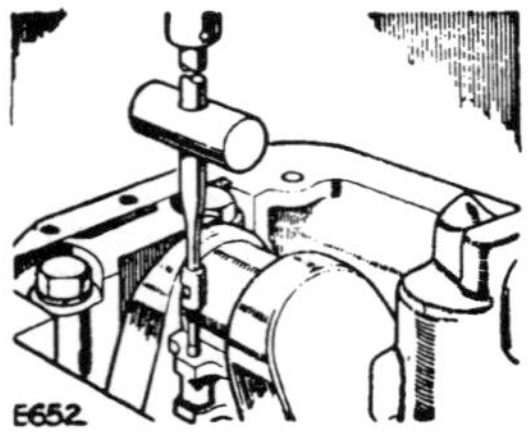

Fitting connecting rod bolts

7. Reverse removal procedure for remaining items.
8. Fill engine to correct level, with correct grade of lubricant. Capacity: 10 Imperial pints; 12 US pints; 5,5 litres, plus 1 Imperial pint; 1.2 US pints; 0,5 litres, if oil filter element has been replaced.

   For recommended grades of oil, see chart in Section B.
9. Fill radiator with coolant, anti-freeze in winter.

   Capacities:
   Mk I, Mk IA and Mk II: 24 Imperial pints; 29 US pints; 13,7 litres.

   Mk III: 26 Imperial pints; 31 US pints; 14,7 litres.
10. Run engine and check for oil and water leaks. Carry out any adjustments required.

*Clutch and flywheel, to remove and refit (4-speed models)—Operation A1-30

Workshop hand tools:

Spanner sizes: 7/16 in. AF, 5/8 in. AF
Screwdriver, medium

Special tools:

Torque wrench
Dial test indicator
Bracket for dial test indicator, Part No. 530106

See Section C for clutch overhaul.

Flywheel, remove

The flywheel can be removed by:

(a) Removal of engine. Operation A1-5.

(b) Removal of gearbox. Section D.

1. Remove the inspection cover from the flywheel housing secured by two (1/4 in. UNF) nuts.
2. Remove the timing pointer.
3. Mark position of pressure plate in relation to flywheel in order to maintain balance condition. Remove self-locking nuts retaining clutch, then lift clutch assembly and clutch plate from flywheel. See Section C for overhaul details.
4. Withdraw the flywheel, secured by eight special set bolts and four lockers to the crankshaft. Use a hide-faced hammer through the starter motor aperture to facilitate removal.
5. If necessary, remove bush for primary pinion.
6. Place the clutch plate, which is marked 'flywheel side' for identification, in position on the flywheel face with the longer end of the central boss away from the flywheel. Handle clutch plate with care.
7. Offer the clutch assembly on to the flywheel, lining up the identification marks made previously. Centralize the clutch plate by means of a 'slave' primary pinion and tighten securing nuts by diagonal selection to prevent distortion of the clutch unit.
8. Remove 'slave' primary pinion.

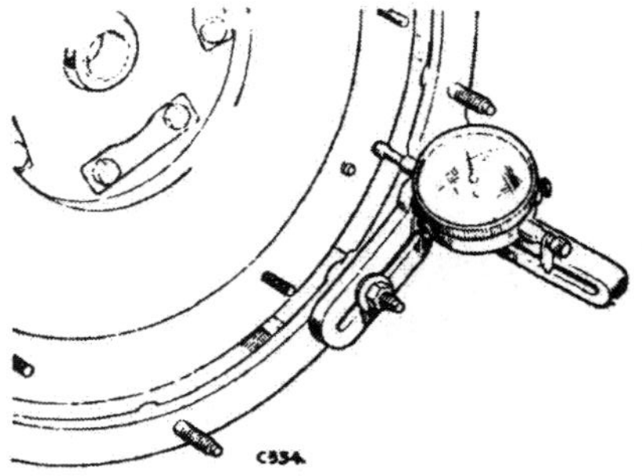

Checking run-out on flywheel face

Flywheel, refit

1. Replace primary pinion bush as necessary.
2. Fit the flywheel to the crankshaft driving flange secured by eight special set bolts and four lockers.
3. Tighten the bolts evenly. Torque loading is 50 lb/ft (7 mkg).
4. Check flywheel run-out on the flywheel face; This should not exceed .005 in. (0,12 mm) at the outer edge of face.
5. When a new or reconditioned clutch unit or starter ring gear is fitted to the original flywheel, any balance weights previously fitted must be removed.

Ring gear, remove

1. Remove securing bolts from ring gear and lift off.

Ring gear, refit

1. Offer ring gear to flywheel, align the bolt holes and tighten fully. The fit of the ring gear to flywheel is .001 in. to .004 in. (0,025 to 0,10 mm) clearance.

Operations which are identified by an asterisk (*), can be carried out with the engine installed in the car

Crankshaft and bearings, to remove and refit—Operation A1-31

This operation to be carried out with the engine removed from the car

Workshop hand tools:

Spanner sizes: 3/8 in. AF, 7/16 in. AF, 1/2 in. AF, 9/16 in. AF, 5/8 in. AF, 3/4 in. AF, 7/8 in. AF, 15/16 in. AF, 1/4 in. BSF, 7/16 in. BSF, 2 BA Small adjustable spanner
Screwdriver, medium
Pliers, long-nosed Plug spanner

Special tools:

Torque wrench
Dial test indicator
Bracket for dial test indicator, Part No. 530106
Allen key, 1/8 in. (3 mm)

Assuming engine removed from car (but not stripped) and mounted on a suitable engine stand

1. Where fitted, remove the automatic transmission and torque converter. Section E or EE.
2. Remove distributor, complete with HT leads. Operation A1-8.
3. Remove sparking plugs. Operation A1-9.
4. Remove carburetter. Operation A1-11.
5. Remove fan and water pump. Operation A1-14.
6. Remove rocker feed oil pipe from cylinder head. Operation A1-17.
7. Remove cylinder head. Operation A1-18.
8. Remove sump. Operation A1-22.
9. Remove oil pump and drive shaft. Operation A1-23.
10. Remove crankshaft vibration damper. Operation A1-24.
11. Remove timing chain tensioner, cam wheel and timing chain. Operation A1-25.
12. Remove pistons and connecting rods. Operation A1-29.
13. Remove clutch assembly (where fitted). Section C.
14. Remove flywheel (where fitted). Operation A1-30.
15. Remove flywheel housing, secured with eight bolts, three nuts and washers.
16. Remove the main bearing cap bolts and lift off the caps. Lift out the crankshaft and place in a suitable stand.
17. Retain the bearing shells in pairs, suitably marked with the number of each respective journal.
18. The rear bearing oil seal halves may be removed from the rear cap and rear face of cylinder block.
19. Remove the crankshaft end-float thrust washers from the upper half of the rear main bearing. Ensure that the thrust washers are retained in the original housings if used again.

Crankshaft, refit

Crankshaft, main bearings and seals

1. Check the main bearing caps by first assembling the caps, without the bearing shells, to the crankcase, ensuring they are correctly located by means of the dowels. Tighten both securing bolts for each cap, to a torque figure of 65 lb/ft (9 mkg), then slacken one bolt of each pair right off. There should be no clearance at the joint face. Bearing caps are numbered in their respective order, from the front of the engine.

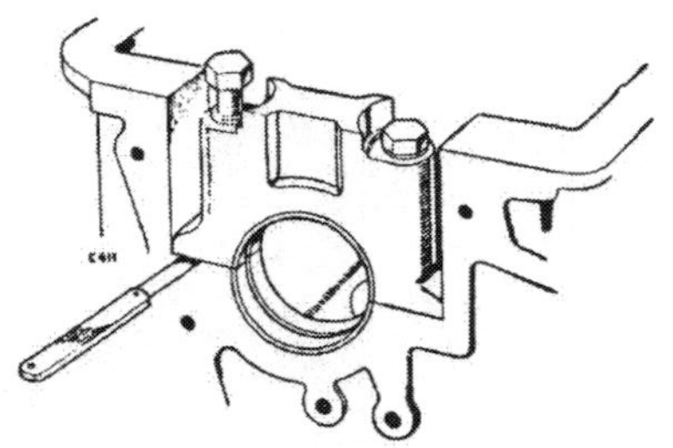

Checking main bearing nip

2. Remove the bearing caps and fit the bearing shells, locating them by means of the tags. Tighten both securing bolts for each cap to a torque figure of 65 lb/ft (9 mkg), then slacken off one bolt of each pair. Check the bearing nip, as illustrated, which should be .004 in. to .006 in. (0,10 to 0,15 mm). The nip can be corrected by selective assembly of bearing shells; these are available in slightly varying thicknesses.
3. When bearing nip has been checked remove the caps and bearing shell bottom halves.
4. Refit the crankshaft and position the thrust bearings at each side of the main bearing shell. Ensure that the white metal faces the crankshaft web.

Operation A1-31—*continued*

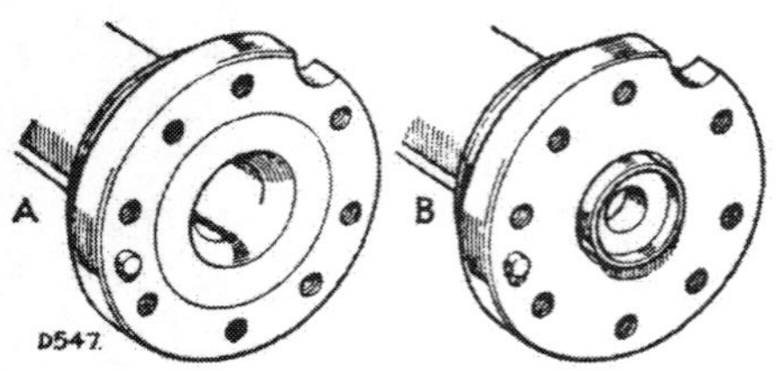

Identification of crankshafts

A—Crankshaft for engine fitted with Borg and Beck clutch
B—Crankshaft for engine fitted with automatic transmission

5. Check the crankshaft end-float which should be .002 to .006 in. (0,05 to 0,15 mm), using a dial test indicator; if the correct reading is not obtained, fit suitable oversize thrust washers, ensuring that any variation of thickness between thrust washers is kept to a minimum of .003 in. (0,07 mm).
6. Refit the bearing caps and bottom half bearing shells, and re-check the crankshaft end-float. The rear bearing cap should be fitted without seals at this stage. Tighten cap bolts to 65 lb/ft (9 mkg).
7. The crankshaft should resist rotation when a .0025 in. (0,06 mm) feeler paper is placed between any one bearing shell and crankshaft journal, and turn freely by hand when the feeler paper is removed. Adjust if necessary by selective assembly of bearing shells. Lubricate the bearing shells before final fitment by lightly smearing with engine oil.

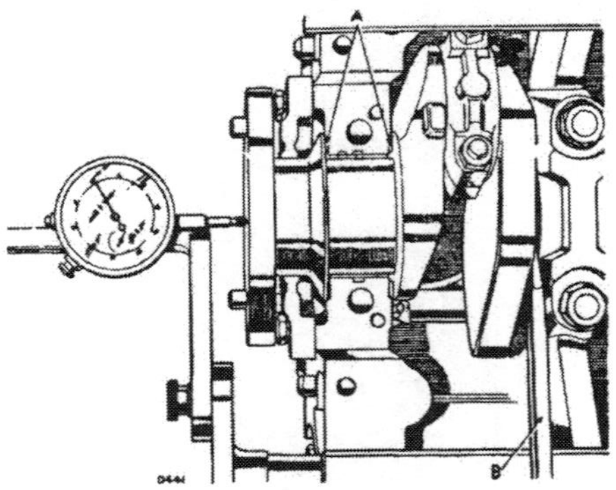

Measuring crankshaft end-float

A—Thrust bearings B—Lever

8. Remove the rear main bearing cap.
9. Fit new rear main bearing oil seals. Operation A1-32.
10. Reverse removal procedure for remaining items.

Crankshaft oil seal, rear, to remove and refit—Operation A1-32

Workshop hand tools:

Spanner sizes:

$\frac{5}{16}$ in. AF, $\frac{7}{16}$ in. AF, $\frac{1}{2}$ in. AF, $\frac{9}{16}$ in. AF, $\frac{5}{8}$ in. AF, $\frac{7}{8}$ in. AF, $\frac{15}{16}$ in. AF, $\frac{5}{16}$ in. BSF, $\frac{3}{8}$ in. BSF, $\frac{7}{8}$ in. BSF

Small adjustable spanner Screwdriver, medium Plug spanner

1. **Mk I, Mk IA and Mk II automatic transmission models.** Remove engine. Operation A1-7.

   Mk III automatic transmission models. Remove automatic transmission unit. See Section EE.
2. **4-speed models.** Remove gearbox. Section D. Engine must be suitably supported on four-point mounting models.
3. **Mk I, Mk IA and Mk II automatic transmission models.** Remove torque converter unit and torque converter from engine. Section E.
4. **Mk I, Mk IA and Mk II automatic transmission models.** Remove flexible drive plate and reinforcing plate from end of crankshaft, secured by eight special bolts and lockers.
5. **4-speed models.** Remove clutch assembly and clutch plate, secured by six self-locking nuts.
6. Remainder of items apply to all models. Remove sump. Operation A1-22.
7. Remove flywheel housing, secured by eight bolts, washers and three nuts.
8. The rear bearing oil seal halves may now be removed from the rear main bearing cap and the rear face of the cylinder block.

   Late models. Lift the split oil seal and garter spring from the crankshaft.
9. Remove the rear main bearing cap and withdraw the 'T' seals.
10. Early type two-piece oil seals should always be replaced by the latest type, as illustrated, and the oil seal must be renewed whenever a crankshaft is removed and replaced for any reason.

    From suffix 'C' onwards and Mk III. These models have a new rear main bearing oil seal to suit larger diameter crankshaft journals.
11. Assemble the garter spring on the oil seal journal of the crankshaft by laying the spring around the journal, this will bring the two ends, the hook and eye, adjacent to one another. Insert the hook into the eye, taking care not to stretch the spring.
12. Move the spring along the journal until it is against the thrower flange.
13. Apply Silicone grease MS4 to the crankshaft oil seal journal and to both sides of the split oil seal sealing lip.
14. Open the split seal sufficiently to allow it to be fitted over the crankshaft oil seal journal. The recess in the oil seal must be towards the thrower flange and garter spring.
15. **Avoid repeatedly fitting and removing the oil seal from the crankshaft as this will damage the sealing lip.**
16. Fit the hook and eye of the garter spring at 90° to the split in the oil seal. Use a small screwdriver or similar tool to gently ease the spring into the recess in the oil seal.

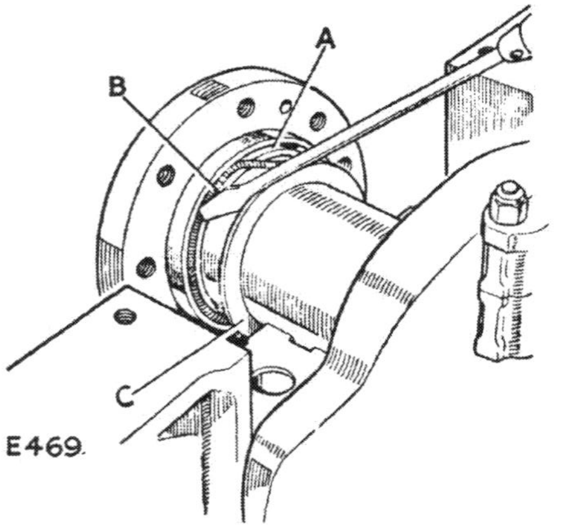

Fitting garter spring to oil seal recess

A—Oil seal recess B—Garter spring C—Thrower flange

17. Rotate the oil seal until the split is vertical and nearest to the cylinder head and in its approximate running position on the journal. This position is important.

Operation A1-31—*continued*

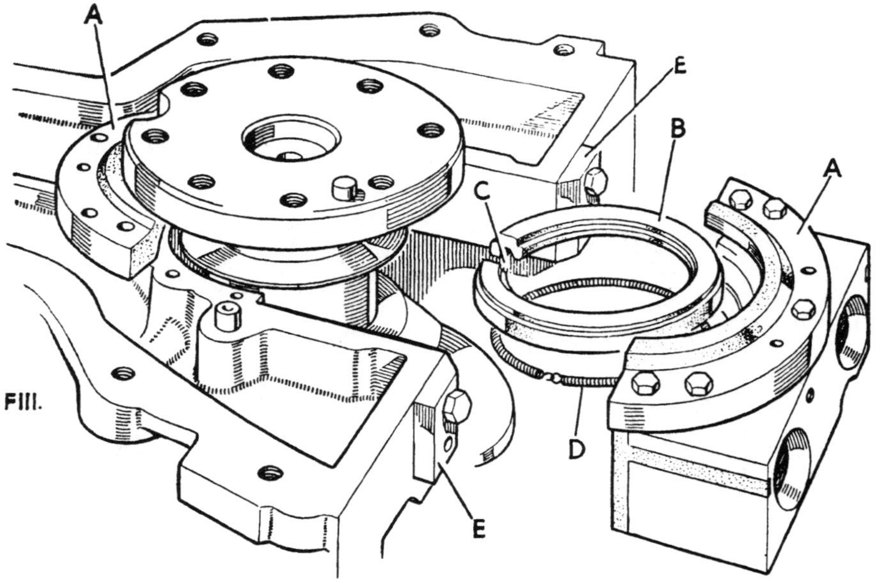

FIII.

Retainer halves, oil seal and garter spring

A—Retainer halves
B—Split oil seal
C—Split line of seal towards top of engine
D—Garter spring, hook and eye midway between split and hinge of oil seal
E—Guides for rear main bearing cap 'T' seals

18. Fit one half of the oil seal retainer on to the crankcase dowels. The oil seal should be compressed to assist assembly; also ensure that it is correctly located in the retainer recess. Bolt the retainer to the crankcase, leaving the two bolts adjacent to the split line finger-tight, fully tighten the remaining three bolts. In order to fit the bolts it will be necessary to rotate the crankshaft, it is essential to hold the seal so that it does not rotate with the crankshaft.

    The latest 'T' seals are coated with molybdenum disulphide and therefore require no lubrication during the fitting operation.

19. Bolt the other half of the oil seal retainer on to the main bearing cap, in the same way. If necessary, Apply Silicone grease MS4 to the 'T' seals and fit them to the main bearing cap. These seals should be left standing proud of the crankcase sump face by $\frac{1}{32}$ in. (0,8 mm). It will be found advantageous to cut a slight lead on to the bottom edges of the side seals as this will prevent them from folding under the cap during fitment, thus causing an oil leak.

20. Fit the main bearing cap with the seal retainer bearing shell and 'T' seals to the crankcase, see illustration, until there is a $\frac{1}{32}$ in. (0,8 mm) gap between the cap and crankcase. Use guides for 'T' seals as illustrated.

21. Ensure that the seal is located in the retainer recess.

22. Pull down the cap slowly, ensuring there is no buckling of the split seal or misalignment of the butt joint.

23. Tighten the cap bolts to 65 lb/ft (9 mkg) torque and re-check that the seal is located correctly in the housing.

24. Finally tighten the four bolts securing the housings adjacent to the split line.

25. Reverse removal procedure for the remaining items.

Section A – ENGINE UNIT – Part Two

Cylinder block, to overhaul—Operation A2-1

Workshop hand tools:
Spanner sizes: $\frac{7}{16}$ in. AF, $\frac{1}{2}$ in. AF, $\frac{9}{16}$ in. AF, $\frac{5}{8}$ in. AF, $\frac{3}{4}$ in. AF
Screwdrivers, medium and large

Special tools:
Reboring jig block, Part No. 261288
Cylinder liner press block, Part No. 246650
Extractor, Part No. 262749

Details of engine removal and stripping are given in Part One of Section A

Cylinder block preparation

1. Clean out the main oil gallery and all oilways, renew all blanking plugs.
2. If necessary, remove the oil gallery pipe from the block by using extractor (Part No. 262749).
3. Clean out the water gallery and water jacket.

Cylinder block, checks

1. Examine the block for cracks and distortion of machined faces.
2. The cylinder block must be checked by first assembling the crankshaft bearing caps (without the bearing shells) to the crankcase. Ensure correct location by means of the dowels. Bearing caps are numbered in their respective order from the front of the engine.
3. Tighten both securing bolts for each cap to 65 lb/ft (9 mkg). Slacken one bolt of each pair right off. There should be no clearance at the joint face. **If there is clearance this indicates that the caps have been filed. The cylinder block is scrap and must be replaced.**
4. Check for stripped threads and general damage to cylinder block.
5. Measure the amount of wear in each cylinder bore.

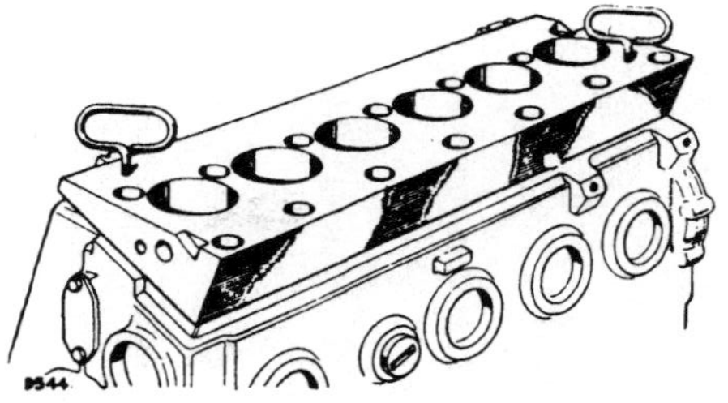

Jig block for reboring

Reboring

1. Although the cylinder head is inclined at an angle of 22°, standard boring equipment can be used in conjunction with a special jig block (Part No. 261288).

Cylinder liners

1. Cylinder liners may be fitted; note the following points:

    (*a*) Machine the cylinder block bores to 3.200 in. plus .001 (81,28 mm plus 0,025).

    This gives an interference fit of .003 to .004 in. (0,07 to 0,10 mm.)

    (*b*) Prior to pressing in the liner, allowance must be made for twist up to $\frac{3}{16}$ in. (5 mm) clockwise. To facilitate realignment should the liner not be positioned correctly at the first attempt, scribe lines down the sides of the liner from the two peaks, and make corresponding marks on the cylinder block.

    (*c*) Press in the liner, using a special press block (Part No. 246650) until the top edge is level with the bottom of the exhaust valve pocket. Blend to the shape of the cylinder block.

Bore to the selected diameter to suit pistons. Liners may only be bored to suit standard or .010 in. (0,25 mm) oversize pistons. For piston selection see Operation A2-4.

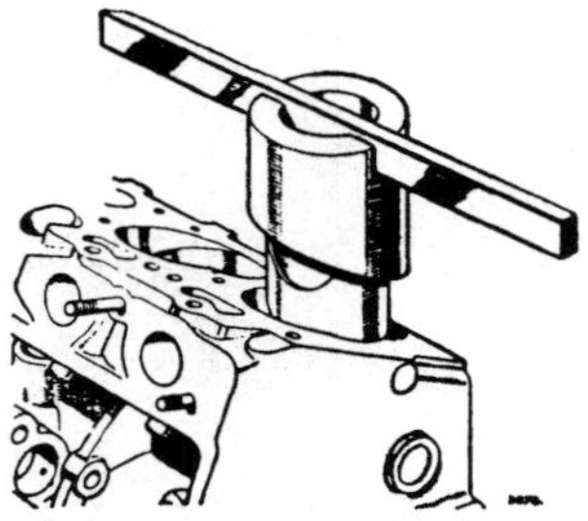

Fitting a cylinder liner

Cylinder head, to overhaul—Operation A2-2

Workshop hand tools:
Spanner sizes: $\frac{7}{16}$ in. AF, $\frac{1}{2}$ in. AF, $\frac{5}{8}$ in. AF, $\frac{3}{4}$ in. AF, 2 BA

Special tools:
Valve spring compressing tool, Part No. 276102
Extractor, Part No. 262749
Drift for inlet valve guide removal, Mk I and 1A, Part No. 274401
Drift for inlet valve guide removal, Mk II and III, Part No. 274400
Drift for inlet valve guide replacement, Mk I and 1A, Part No. 600959
Drift for inlet valve guide replacement, Mk II and III, Part No. 601508

See Section A, Part One, for cylinder head removal instructions

Cylinder head, dismantle

1. Remove the water outlet pipe from the top of the water pump, secured by three nuts and washers. Lift out the thermostat.
2. **Mk I and Mk IA models.** Remove the inlet rocker gear by removing the nuts, spring washers and retaining plates, securing the thrust blocks; remove the shaft locating screws and shaft-end plug. Remove the lifting bracket and using an extractor (Part No. 262749) withdraw the short front shaft, noting that the two oil holes in the shaft face away from the inlet valves, then lift out the rockers, thrust block and springs.
3. Withdraw the rear shaft and rockers in a similar manner. Note that the oil holes in the rocker shaft face away from the valve assemblies. Retain the rocker arms and springs in their correct sequence.

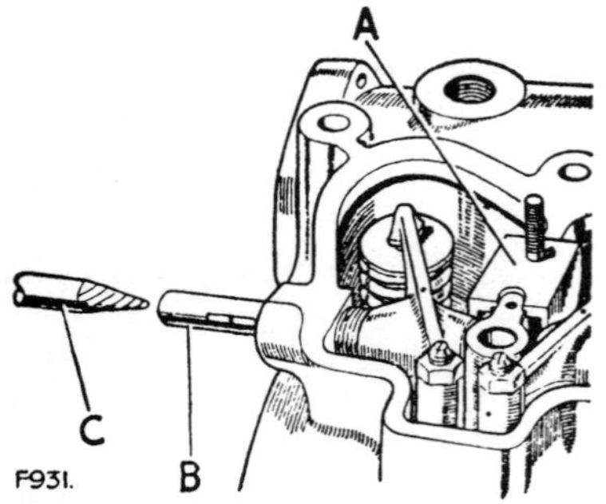

F931.

Extracting inlet rocker shafts, Mk I and Mk IA models

A—Thrust block B—Rocker shaft C—Extractor

4. **Mk II and Mk III models.** Remove the inlet manifold secured with 14 nuts and washers; remove the rocker gear securing nuts and lift off the rocker shaft assembly complete. Take precautions to prevent the rocker shaft assembly from falling apart accidentally.

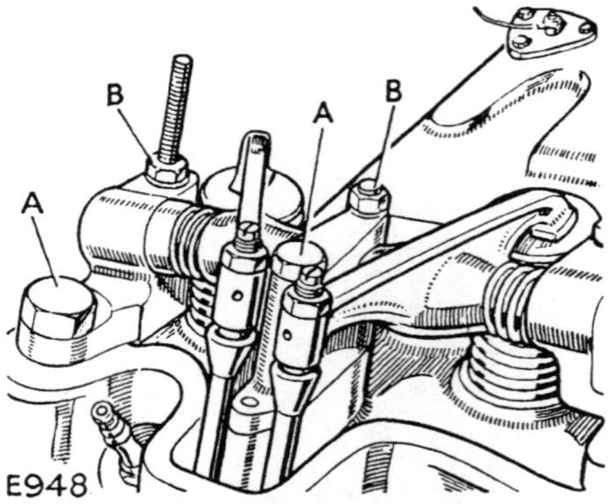

E948

Rocker shaft, Mk II and III models

A—Cylinder head securing bolts B—Rocker gear securing bolts

5. Before removing the inlet valves mark them so that they may be replaced in their original positions. Using a valve spring compressing tool (Part No. 276102), remove the split cones and take out the valves. Retain the springs in pairs; they are selected to ensure an interference fit.

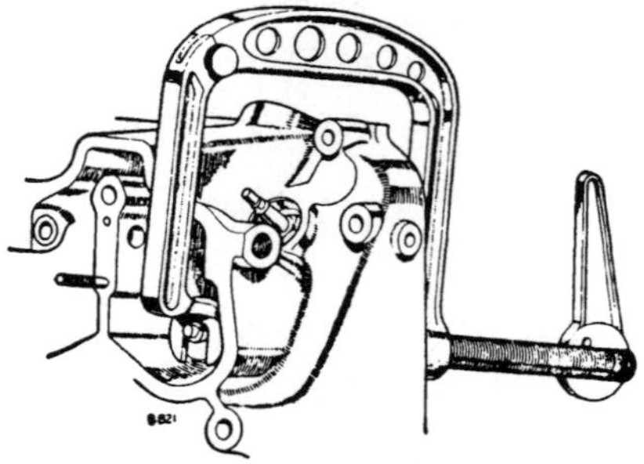

Compressing the inlet valve springs, Mk I and Mk IA cylinder head illustrated

Operation A2-2—*continued*

6. If necessary remove the inlet valve seat insert by carefully grinding the seat insert away; when thin enough, the insert can be prised out.
7. To remove the inlet valve guides, remove the rubber 'O' rings and drift the guide out, using drift (Part No. 274401 for Mk I and Mk IA models and Part No. 274400 for Mk II and Mk III models).

Cylinder head, assemble

1. Where it is necessary to fit new inlet valve seat inserts to the cylinder head, heat the head evenly for a few minutes to approximately 150°F (65°C), the temperature of a normal degreaser, enter the seat squarely into the cylinder head recess, which must be thoroughly clean, and press into position.
2. Valve guides, to refit: replace the steel shim washer on the new valve guides.

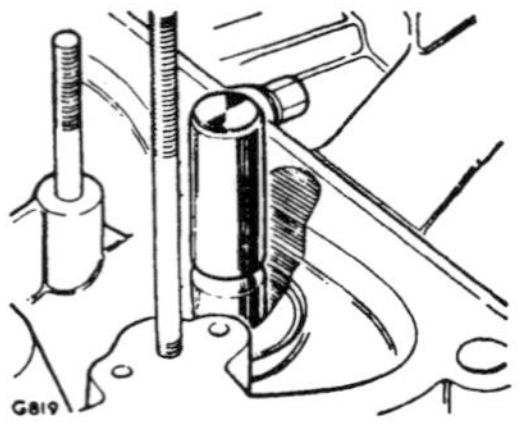

G819

Fitting inlet valve guide

Lubricate the inlet valve guides and carefully drift them into position, using drift (Part No. 600959 for Mk I and Mk IA models and Part No. 601508 for Mk II and Mk III models).

3. Use the valve guide as a pilot and cut the valve seat to 30°.
4. Face the inlet valves to 30° and lap each valve into its respective seat.
5. Wash each valve seat, port and guide with clean paraffin.
6. It is important that new rubber 'O' rings are fitted to each inlet valve guide after all the lapping and preparatory work has been finished. This will ensure that once fitted the valve is not withdrawn through the bore of the seal, thus destroying the seal.
7. Locate each inlet valve into its respective seat and using the compressing tool (Part No. 276102), fit the spring assemblies, caps and split cones.

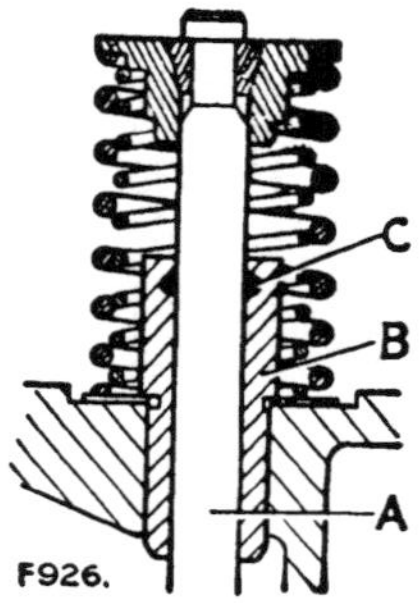

F926.

Inlet valve seal

A—Valve stem B—Valve guide C—Rubber 'O' ring

8. **Mk I and Mk IA models.** Refit the top rocker gear spacers and rocker shafts, with the shaft oil holes facing away from the inlet valve assemblies. Fit the shaft-end plug and the lifting bracket.
9. **Mk II and Mk III models.** Replace the complete top rocker shaft assembly and securing nuts. The shaft is correctly located by the locating set bolts. Refit the inlet manifold with new gasket and secure, using plain washers and nuts.

Pistons and connecting rods, to overhaul—Operation A2-3

Workshop hand tools:

Spanner sizes: $\frac{9}{16}$ in. AF

Special tools:

Set of feeler gauges
Circlip pliers

Details of piston and connecting rod removal are given in Part One of Section A

Note. When dismantling keep all components in sets

Pistons and connecting rods, dismantle

1. Remove piston rings, using a suitable tool.
2. Remove circlips retaining gudgeon pin.
3. Withdraw gudgeon pin towards the side of the piston marked 'X'——— which is stamped on the piston crown.
4. If necessary, press out the gudgeon pin bush from the connecting rod.

Pistons, check

1. New piston assemblies are available for replacement purposes in standard diameter and by .010 in. (0,25 mm) oversizes up to .040 in. (1,00 mm).
2. Standard size pistons are graded in diameter size differences of .0002 in. (0,005 mm). This grading does not apply to oversize pistons.

Grade letter	*Cylinder bore diameter*
'Z' ..	Nominal to minus .0002 in. (0,005 mm)
'A' ..	Nominal to plus .0002 in. (0,005 mm)
'B' ..	.0002 in. (0,005 mm) to .0004 in. (0,01 mm) above nominal
'C' ..	.0004 in. (0,01 mm) to .0006 in. (0,015 mm) above nominal
'D'	.0006 in. (0,015 mm) to .0008 in. (0,02 mm) above nominal

3. When fitting standard pistons in a comparatively new engine, a graded piston, corresponding to the piston removed, should be fitted. However, a check must still be made to ensure that the clearance falls within the limits laid down.
4 For example: If the car has done little mileage and there is no appreciable bore wear, a graded piston of the same size as that taken out should be used; however, if a certain amount of bore wear is apparent, it may be necessary to fit a piston two or three grades larger than the one removed. In the case of a top-limit piston fitted as original equipment, it may be necessary to rebore to the first oversize to obtain the correct piston fit.
5. The grade size of any particular bore is also stamped on the cylinder block exhaust manifold face, using the same letters as stamped on the piston crown.
6. When fitting pistons, standard or oversize, into a new or rebored cylinder block the clearance should be checked as follows:—
   (*a*) Clearance in the bore, measured at the bottom of the piston skirt at right angles to the gudgeon pin—.002 to .0025 in. (0,05 tc 0,06 mm).
   (*b*) Clearance in the bore, measured at the top of the piston skirt at right angles to the gudgeon pin—.003 to .0035 in. (0,08 to 0,09 mm).

In the absence of suitable accurate measuring instruments a long feeler .0035 in. (0,09 mm) thick may be used. Insert the feeler against the thrust side of the bore as illustrated with the piston located crown downward. The piston should become a tight fit when the top of the skirt (immediately below the scraper ring groove) enters the bore. Pistons to be checked without the piston rings fitted.

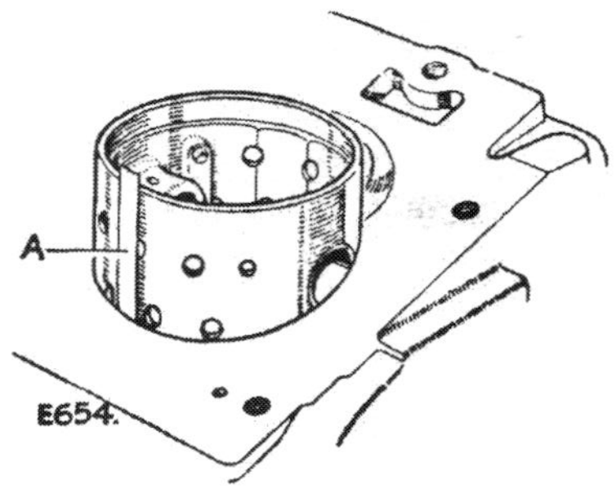

Checking piston clearance with feeler gauge
A—Feeler gauge

Operation A2-3—*continued*

7. To check new piston rings support the ring in the bore with an old piston. Except late models with Duaflex scraper rings.

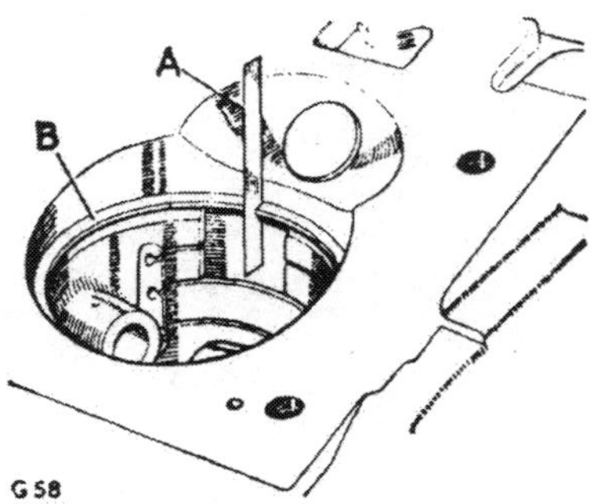

Checking piston ring gap
A—Feeler gauge B—Piston ring

Using a feeler gauge, measure the ring gap, which should be:—

Compression ring ..	.015 to .020 in. (0,4 to 0,5 m m)
Scraper ring, early models	.012 to .017 in. (0,3 to 0,4 mm)

If necessary use a very fine-cut flat file and carefully increase the gap as required.

Compression rings are marked 'TOP' on one face and must be fitted accordingly.

8. Check piston ring side clearance in piston groove, which should be:

Compression ring ..	.0018 to .0038 in. (0,05 to 0,09 mm)
Scraper ring	.002 to .004 in. (0,05 to 0,10 mm)

9. Fit the rings to the piston.
10. Duaflex scraper rings specified for late models are fitted as follows:
   (*a*) Thoroughly clean piston ring grooves and oil drainage holes.
   (*b*) Insert both tangs of expander into the same oil drainage hole. Ensure that they do not cross over.
   (*c*) Fit sidespring into position in groove over expander.
   (*d*) Spiral rails into position in groove, one each side of sidespring, taking care to arrange the gaps all round the piston.
   (*e*) Do not attempt to rotate the complete ring assembly after fitting, but check that it is free in the groove and that back clearance is adequate, by pushing the assembly into the groove at various points.

Connecting rods, check

1. Check connecting rod alignment with a suitable alignment jig.
2. Check that the connecting rods and caps have not been filed.
   (*a*) Select the correct cap for each connecting rod as denoted by the number stamped on the joint faces. This number also indicates the crankpin to which it must be fitted.
   Assemble the connecting rods, less shell bearings, with corresponding numbers together.
   (*b*) Tighten the securing nuts to the correct torque, then slacken one of them right off and check that there is no clearance at the joint face. A clearance indicates that the rods or caps have been filed and the complete connecting rod must be replaced.

Checking ring clearance in groove

Operation A2-3—*continued*

Tightening torque for connecting rod bolts—

Machine-cut thread	30 lb/ft (4 mkg)
*Rolled thread	20 lb/ft (2,8 mkg)

* Identified by a drill point cut into the nut end of the bolt.

New bolts and 'Nyloc' self-locking nuts must be used for final assembly, unless rolled thread bolts and cadmium plated nuts are in use which are known not to have been over-tightened. Use the original bolts and nuts for checking purposes.

Check the bearing nip as follows:

(*a*) Fit the bearing shells and tighten both nuts to correct torque. Slacken one nut right off and check the nip with a feeler gauge, as illustrated. Clearance should be .002 to .004 in. (0,05 to 0,10 mm).

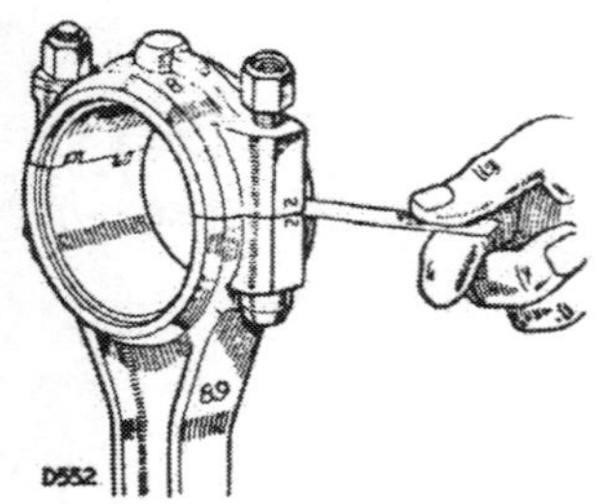

Checking big-end bearing nip

(*b*) Select bearing shells to give correct nip.

3. If it is necessary to replace the gudgeon pin bush, this must be done with the aid of a power press. Ensure that the oil hole in the bearing exactly coincides with the hole in the connecting rod. The bush should be a .001 to .003 in. (0,025 to 0,076 mm) interference fit in the connecting rod. Hone the bush when fitted to the connecting rod to internal diameter .8755 in. — .0005 in. (22,22—0,0127 mm). Ensure correct alignment is maintained whilst honing.

4. To check big-end side clearance assemble connecting rods to respective crankpins. Insert a feeler gauge between the end face of the rod and the crankpin shoulder.

   Side clearance should be .009 to .013 in. (0,23 to 0,33 mm).

5. Remove connecting rods from crankpins. Ensure the bearing shells are kept with respective rods.

Fitting pistons to connecting rods

1. The gudgeon pin should be a good hand push fit into the piston bore at a temperature of 50° to 70°F (10° to 21°C) and should not fall out of the piston under its own weight.

2. Fit a new circlip in the side of the piston opposite the 'X'.

   Place the connecting rod into the piston, ensuring spray hole in connecting rod is to the same side as the bore number stamped on the piston crown, thrust side.

   On new pistons the machined section of the piston crown goes to the same side as the spray hole in the connecting rod. Line up the connecting rod with the gudgeon pin and push pin into position. Fit second new circlip.

Engine, to decarbonise and top overhaul—Operation A2-4

Workshop hand tools:

Spanner sizes: $\frac{7}{16}$ in. AF, $\frac{1}{2}$ in. AF, $\frac{5}{8}$ in. AF, 2 BA

Sparking plug spanner

Screwdrivers, medium and large

Special tools:

Torque wrench

Feeler gauges

Extractor, Part No. 262749

Valve spring compressor, Part No. 276102

A decarbonising gasket set is available

Engine, decarbonise

1. Disconnect the battery.
2. Drain the coolant from the radiator and engine.
3. Remove the air cleaner/silencer and elbow. Operation A1-4.
4. Remove the economiser air hose, and disconnect the petrol feed pipe and cold start control cable.
5. Disconnect the radiator top hose, the thermostat by-pass hose (where fitted) and heater pipes.
6. Disconnect the brake vacuum servo pipe from cylinder head.
7. Remove the accelerator countershaft, return spring and bracket from the engine:

   Disconnect the control rod between countershaft and carburetter spindle lever.

   Disconnect rod from countershaft to accelerator pedal lever.

   Detach the countershaft bracket from the cylinder head and lift out the countershaft complete.
8. **Overdrive, where fitted.** Disconnect the wiring from the rotary (or cam) switch on the bracket. **Do not disturb any other part of the linkage as it is pre-set.**
9. Disconnect the LT lead from coil and distributor.
10. Disconnect the wire from the mixture control switch.
11. Remove the sparking plug leads, distributor cap and the ignition wire carrier from top rocker cover.
12. Remove the top rocker cover and joint washer.
13. Remove the ignition coil from the cylinder head.
14. Disconnect the oil feed pipe between the cylinder block and head.
15. **Mk I and Mk IA models.** Unscrew the thermometer bulb from the cylinder head.
16. **Mk II and Mk III models.** Disconnect the wire from the water temperature transmitter.
17. Disconnect the vacuum pipe between the distributor and carburetter.
18. Remove the distributor, secured by a set bolt and washer.
19. Remove the carburetter.
20. Remove the sparking plugs.

Cylinder head, remove

21. Slacken the cylinder head bolts evenly and remove them, together with the plain washers, then lift off the cylinder head. Remove the gasket from the block face.
22. Withdraw the push rods and retain in original sequence.
23. **Mk I and Mk IA models, items 23 to 26.** Remove the three set screws securing the rocker shafts by first removing the retaining plates secured by nuts and spring washers on the rocker cover studs.
24. Withdraw the rocker shafts, using extractor (Part No. 262749).
25. Remove the rockers, spacers and springs.
26. **Mk II and Mk III models.** Remove the inlet manifold secured by 14 nuts and washers; remove the rocker gear securing nuts and lift off the rocker shaft complete. Do not let the assembly fall apart accidentally.

Operation A2-4—*continued*

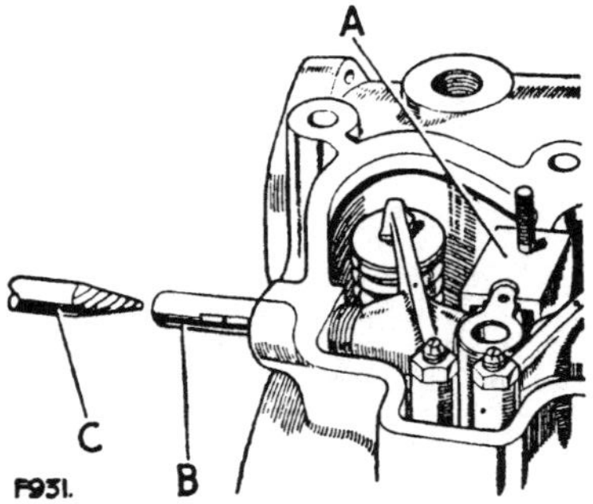

F951.

Extracting inlet rocker shafts, Mk I and Mk IA models

A—Thrust block B—Rocker shaft C—Extractor

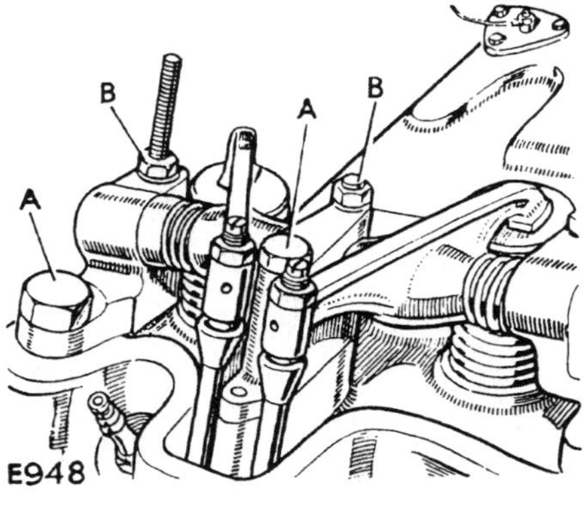

Rocker shaft, Mk II and III models

A—Cylinder head securing bolts
B—Rocker gear securing bolts

27. Mark the inlet valves to ensure they are refitted in their original positions.

28. Compress the valve springs, using valve spring compressor (Part No. 276102). Remove split cones and withdraw valves. Remove compressor and lift off valves. Retain the springs in pairs; they are selected to ensure an interference fit.

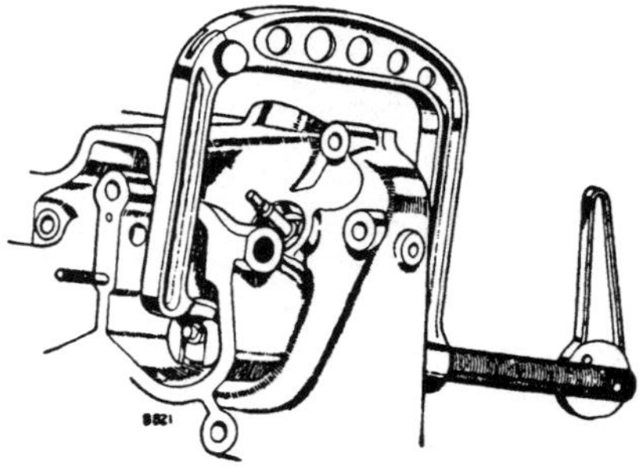

Compressing the inlet valve springs

29. Carefully remove the carbon from the cylinder head and valve ports. The inlet valve seats and valve guides should be replaced only when necessary. See Operation A2-2 for removal instructions.

30. Face the inlet valves to 30° and lap each valve into its respective seat.

31. Wash each valve seat, port and guide with clean paraffin.

    It is important that new rubber "O" rings are fitted to each inlet valve guide after all the lapping and preparatory work has been finished. This will ensure that once fitted the valve is not withdrawn through the bore of the seal, thus destroying the seal.

32. Lightly oil the valve stem and locate each inlet valve into its respective seat. Using the compressing tool (Part No. 276102), fit the spring assemblies, caps and split cones.

Operation A2-4—*continued*

33. **Mk I and Mk IA models.** Refit the top rocker gear spacers and rocker shafts, with the shaft oil holes facing away from the inlet valve assemblies. Fit the shaft-end plug.

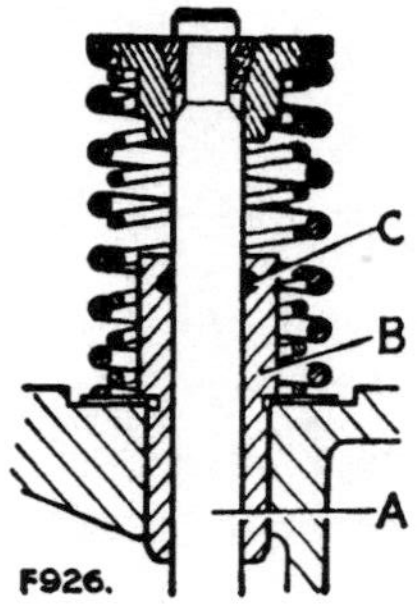

F926.

Inlet valve seal

A—Valve stem B—Valve guide C—Rubber 'O' ring

34. **Mk II and Mk III models.** Replace the complete top rocker shaft assembly and securing nuts. The shaft is correctly located by set bolts.

    Refit and secure the inlet manifold. Use a new gasket.

35. The cylinder head is now ready for reassembly and should be placed to one side until the cylinder block and exhaust valves have received attention.

36. Remove the exhaust manifold and withdraw the gaskets.

37. Remove the side rocker cover and joint washer.

38. Mark the exhaust valves for refitting in correct sequence.

39. Slacken the tappet adjusting screws right off and set each rocker back on its cam.

40. Compress the valve springs, using valve spring compressor (Part No. 276102). Remove split cones and withdraw valves. Remove compressor and lift out valves. Retain the springs in pairs; they are selected to ensure an interference fit.

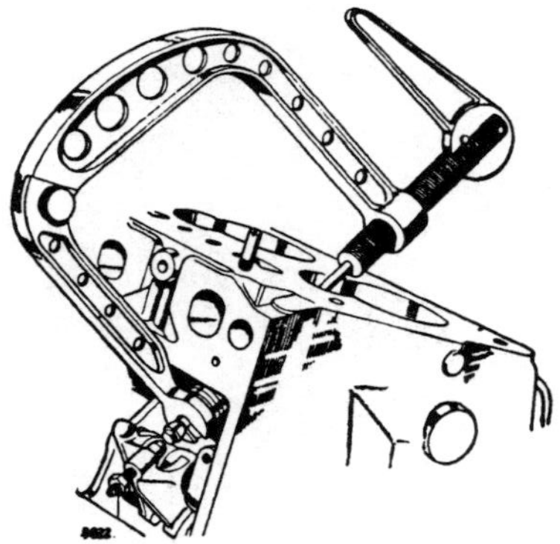

Compressing exhaust valve springs

41. Carefully remove the carbon from the valve ports and piston crowns.

42. The exhaust valves and valve guides should be removed only when necessary. See Operation A2-5 for removal instructions.

43. Face the exhaust valves to 45° then lap each valve to its seat. Wash each valve seat, port and valve guide in clean paraffin.

44. Lightly oil the valve stem and locate each valve into its respective guide. Fit the springs, caps and split cones, using compressor tool (Part No. 276102).

45. Place the push rods into their respective positions.

46. Smear a new cylinder head gasket with oil and place on the face of the cylinder block. The gasket is marked "This side up".

Operation A2-4—*continued*

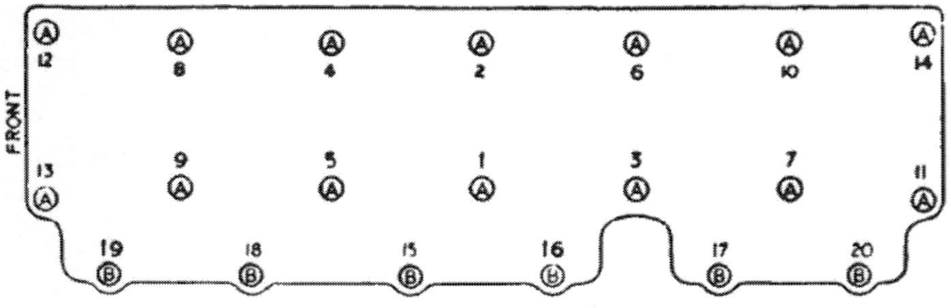

Order of tightening cylinder head bolts

47. Use two old cylinder head bolts with their heads sawn off to locate the gasket and head. Cut a screwdriver slot across the diameter of the bolts to facilitate removal when the cylinder head is in position.

48. Position the cylinder head on to the block; as this is being done connect the by-pass hose or sealing washer to the cylinder head.

    Check that the push rods are seating correctly.

49. Tighten the cylinder head bolts evenly to the following torque in the order illustrated:

    (*a*) Bolts 'A' .. 50 lb/ft (6,9 mkg)

    (*b*) Bolts 'B' .. 30 lb/ft (4 mkg)

50. Adjust the tappets. Operation A1-26.

51. Fit the top and side rocker covers, using Bostik 1776 (Part No. 600193) for the top rocker cover on Mk II models.

52. Fit the sparking plugs, which should have been cleaned and set the gap to .029 to .032 in. (0,75 to 0,80 mm).

53. Connect rocker oil feed pipe.

54. Refit the exhaust manifold, using new gaskets.

55. Refit thermometer bulb or connect water temperature transmitter.

56. Connect the brake vacuum servo pipe to cylinder head.

57. Fit the ignition coil.

58. Refit the accelerator countershaft, bracket and return spring.

59. Connect the operating rods at the ball joints.

60. Fit the carburetter, using a new joint washer.

61. Connect the vacuum advance pipe and petrol feed pipe to the carburetter.

62. Connect the cold start control cable.

63. Connect the radiator and bottom heater hoses, and refill with coolant. When the coolant flows freely from the heater top hose, connect the hose; this will avoid an air lock in the cooling system.

64. Fit the distributor and HT and LT leads. Operation A1-8.

65. Fit the air cleaner/silencer and silencer elbow. Operation A1-4.

66. Connect the battery.

67. The following operations must be carried out with the engine at running temperature:

    (*a*) Readjust the tappets. Operation A1-26.

    (*b*) Adjust the carburetter controls—idling, fast idling and cold start control. Section Q.

*Exhaust valves, seats and guides, to remove and refit—Operation A2-5

Workshop hand tools:
- Spanner sizes:
  - 3/8 in. AF, 7/16 in. AF, 1/2 in. AF, 9/16 in. AF, 5/8 in. AF, 3/4 in. AF, 7/8 in. AF, 2 BA
- Screwdriver, medium
- Pliers, pointed nose

Special tools:
- Valve spring compressing tool, Part No. 276102
- Special protection plate, Part No. 263050
- Valve insert tool, Part No. 262752
- Drift for exhaust valve guide removal, Part No. 274401
- Drift for exhaust valve guide replacement, Part No. 600959
- Spanner for starter dog, Part No. 530102
- Torque wrench
- Allen key, 1/8 in. (3 mm)

Exhaust valves, seats and guides, remove

1. Remove radiator. Operation A1-2
2. Remove radiator grille and bonnet lock platform. Operation A1-3.
3. Remove air cleaner/silencer and elbow. Operation A1-4.
4. Remove distributor. Operation A1-8.
5. Remove exhaust manifold. Operation A1-12.
6. Remove cylinder head. Operation A1-18.
7. Remove fan blades and pulley, secured by four set bolts.
8. Remove the timing chain. Operation A1-25.
9. Remove the side rockers and shafts. Operation A1-27.
10. Remove the valve assemblies, using valve compressor tool (Part No. 276102). Retain the components in their original sets and sequence.

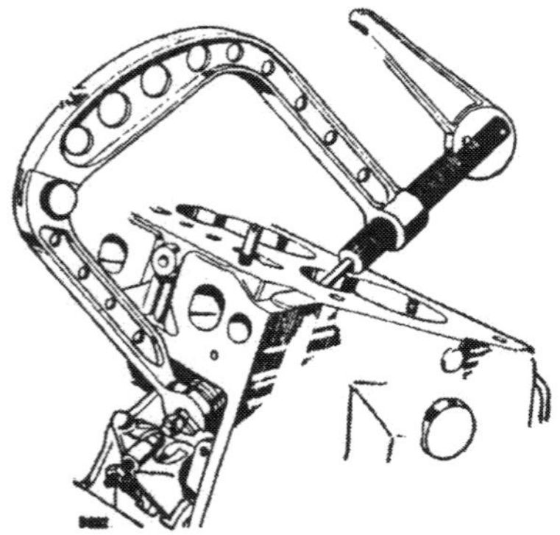

Compressing exhaust valve springs

11. Remove the carbon from the cylinder head, valve ports and piston crowns.

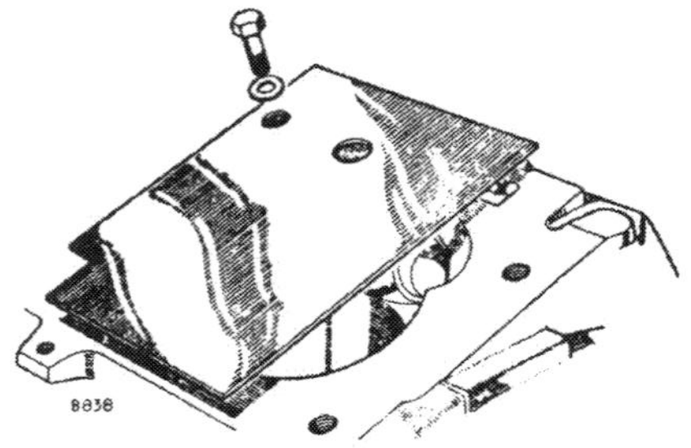

Special protection plate

The exhaust valve guides can be drifted out, using a drift, Part No. 274401, as illustrated.

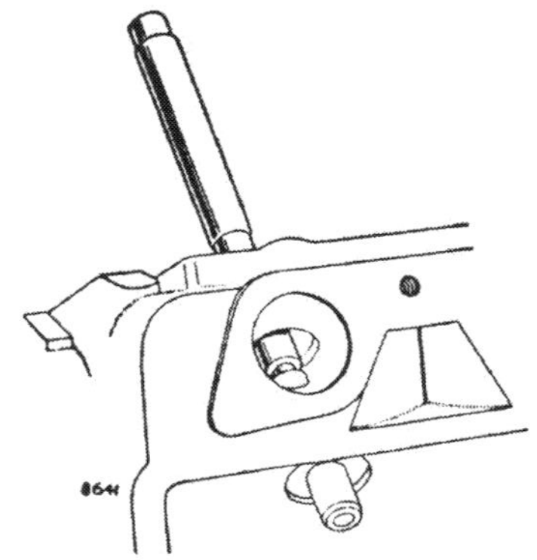

Removing exhaust valve guide with drift

Operations which are identified by an asterisk (*), can be carried out with the engine installed in the car

Operation A2-5—*continued*

12. Owing to the extreme hardness of the seat inserts, great care must be taken during the removal operation to prevent possible injury from flying fragments. A cutting stone should be used, in order to reduce the insert to a minimum thickness, before attempting to break the seat with a chisel. When grinding, take care to avoid damage to the cylinder block.

13. After grinding the seat inserts, secure a protection plate, Part No. 263050 over the cylinder block face and break the seat insert with a suitable chisel applied through the hole in the plate.

Exhaust valves, seats and guides, refit

1. If new exhaust seat inserts are to be fitted, clean the seat recess and pull the new insert into position using a special tool (Part No. 262752). It is not necessary to heat the block or freeze the insert, but light taps on the tool may be required to ensure that the insert enters smoothly. Continue precautions against fragmentation by fitting the protection plate (Part No. 263050) and leaving it in position for a few minutes, as the insert may shatter.

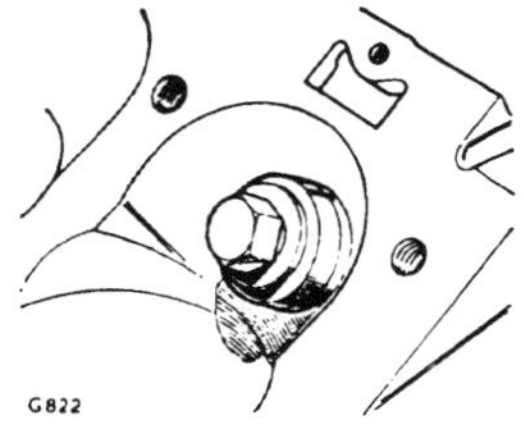

Fitting exhaust valve seat

2. Lubricate the exhaust valve guides and carefully drift them into position, using a drift (Part No. 600959).

3. Face the exhaust valves to 45° and lap each valve into its respective seat.

   The following grinding stones should be used with a power tool:

   First use Black and Decker No. 14198 1½ in. (38.1 mm) 30°–45° stone and then Black and Decker seating stone No. 14370 1½ in. (38.1 mm) 30°–45°.

   Wash each valve, seat, port and guide with clean paraffin.

   Lightly oil valve stem and locate the valves into their respective guides. Using the compressor tool (Part No. 276102), fit the spring assemblies, caps and split cones.

4. Refit the rocker shafts. Operation A1-27, items 1 to 5.

5. Fit the camshaft chain wheel and timing chain and front cover. Operation A1-25, items 1 to 14.

6. Fit the fan blades and pulley.

7. Fit the cylinder head. Operation A1-18, items 1 to 9.

8. Adjust the tappets. Operation A1-26.

9. Fit the exhaust manifold. Operation A1-12.

10. Refit the distributor. Operation A1-8.

11. Refit the air cleaner/silencer and elbow. Operation A1-4.

12. Refit the radiator grille and bonnet lock platform. Operation A1-3.

13. Refit the radiator. Operation A1-2.

Vibration damper (detachable type), to overhaul—Operation A2-6

Workshop hand tools:
Spanner sizes: $\frac{7}{16}$ in. AF

Special tools:
Dial test indicator
Mandrel

For vibration damper removal, see Section A, Part One

Vibration damper, strip

1. Mark the vibration damper flywheel and retaining plate, then remove the six set bolts and locking plates.

2. Press out the driving flange together with retaining plate from the flywheel, and shims, if fitted. Discard shims.

3. Press the driving flange from retaining plate; remove the second rubber disc. If necessary remove bushes from flywheel and retaining plate.

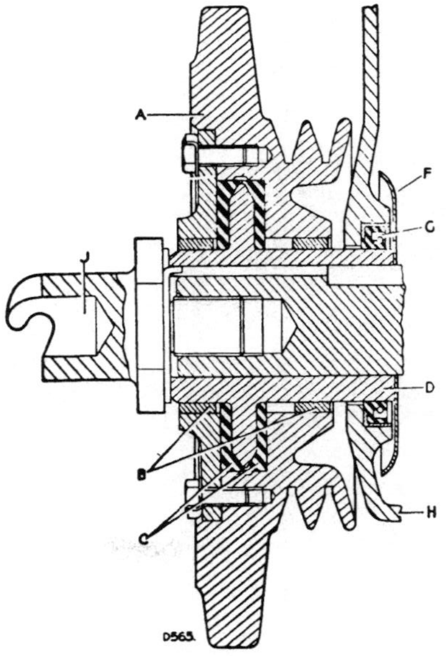

Sectioned view of vibration damper

A—Damper flywheel
B—Bush
C—Rubber disc
D—Driving flange
F—Oil thrower
G—Oil seal
H—Casing
J—Starting handle dog

Vibration damper, rebuild

1. If necessary renew the bushes in the flywheel and retaining plate with an interference fit of .002 in. (0,05 mm) to .004 in. (0,10 mm).

2. Bolt the flywheel and retaining plate together and reamer the bushes to 1.917 in. + .001 (48,6 mm + 0,02), ensuring that the bore is axially concentric, to allow a clearance fit on the driving flange of .001 to .003 in. (0,02 to 0,07 mm).

3. Remove the securing bolts and withdraw the retaining plate from the flywheel.

4. Fit a rubber disc lightly smeared with french chalk to each side of the driving flange, mount the flywheel and retaining plate with the marks on retaining plate and flange aligned, then fit the set bolts and locking tabs.

5. Discard any shims which may have been previously fitted, as these have been found unnecessary.

6. Mount the unit on a suitable mandrel and rotate between centres. Check the run-out with a dial test indicator and adjust to within .005 in. (0,12 mm) by means of the securing bolts. Finally bend up the locking tabs.

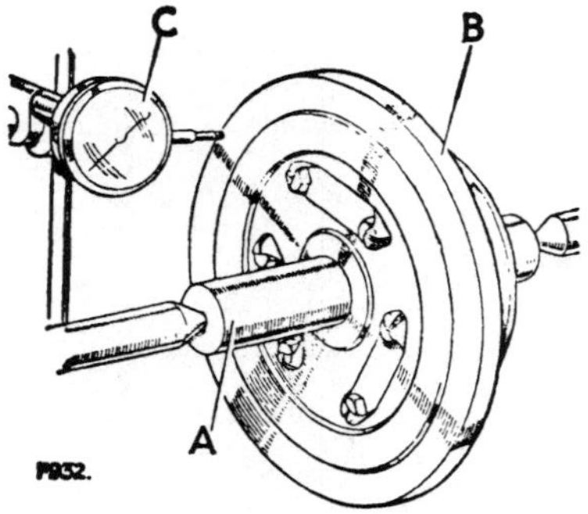

Checking vibration damper run-out

A—Mandrel
B—Vibration damper
C—Dial test indicator

Compression pressure, to check—Operation A2-7

Workshop hand tools:
- Spanner sizes: ½ in. AF
- Plug spanner
- Screwdriver, medium

Special tools:
- Compression gauge

1. Remove the air cleaner/silencer. Operation A1-4.
2. Remove the sparking plugs.
3. Secure the throttle in the fully open position.
4. Insert a suitable compression gauge into the sparking plug hole of each cylinder in turn and crank the engine with the starter motor, for as short a period as possible.
5. Check pressure reading.
6. If the compressor is appreciably less than the correct figure, the piston rings or valves are faulty.

   Low pressure in adjoining cylinders indicates a faulty cylinder head gasket.

Starter motor cranking speed 300 rpm

Compression ratios	7.5:1	8.0:1	8.75:1
Compression pressures	170 lb/in (11,9 kg/cm²)	180 lb/in (12,6 kg/cm²)	190 lb/in (13,4 kg/cm²)

Section A – ENGINE UNIT – Part Three

DEFECT LOCATION

SYMPTOM	*POSSIBLE CAUSE*	*REMEDY*
A—ENGINE FAILS TO START	1. Incorrect starting procedure 2. Starter motor speed too slow 3. Faulty ignition system 4. Water or dirt in fuel system 5. Carburetter flooding 6. Defective fuel pump system 7. Defective starter motor 8. Starter pinion jammed in flywheel 9. Starter pinion not engaging	1. *See Instruction Manual* 2. *Check battery and connections* 3. *See Section S* 4. *See Section Q* 5. *See Section Q* 6. *See Section Q* 7. *See Section S* 8. *Rotate armature shaft with spanner to free pinion* 9. *Clean drive pinion and sleeve with paraffin*
B—ENGINE STALLS	1. Low idling speed 2. Faulty sparking plugs 3. Faulty coil or condenser 4. Faulty distributor points 5. Incorrect tappet clearance 6. Incorrect mixture 7. Foreign matter in fuel system	1. *Adjust carburetter. See Section Q* 2. *Clean and test, renew if necessary* 3. *Renew* 4. *Rectify or renew. See Section Q* 5. *Adjust. See Section A, Part One* 6. *Adjust carburetter. See Section Q* 7. *See Section Q*
C—LACK OF POWER	1. Poor compression 2. Badly seating valves 3. Faulty exhaust silencer 4. Incorrect ignition timing 5. Leaks or restrictions in fuel system 6. Faulty sparking plugs 7. Clutch slip 8. Excessive carbon deposit 9. Brakes binding 10. Faulty coil, condenser or battery	1. *If the compression is appreciably less than the correct figure, the piston rings or valves are faulty. Low pressure in adjoining cylinders indicates a faulty cylinder head gasket* 2. *Rectify or renew* 3. *Renew* 4. *Rectify* 5. *See Section Q* 6. *Rectify* 7. *See Section C* 8. *Decarbonise* 9. *See Section N* 10. *See Section S*
D—ENGINE RUNS ERRATICALLY	1. Faulty electrical connections 2. Defective sparking plugs 3. Low battery charge 4. Defective distributor 5. Foreign matter in fuel system 6. Faulty fuel pump 7. Sticking valves 8. Incorrect tappet clearance 9. Defective valve springs 10. Incorrect ignition timing 11. Worn valve guides or valves 12. Faulty cylinder head gasket 13. Damaged exhaust system	1. *Rectify* 2. *Renew or rectify* 3. *Recharge battery* 4. *Rectify* 5. *See Section Q* 6. *See Section Q* 7. *Rectify or renew* 8. *Adjust* 9. *Renew* 10. *Rectify* 11. *Renew* 12. *Renew* 13. *Rectify or renew*
E—ENGINE STARTS, BUT STOPS IMMEDIATELY	1. Faulty electrical connections 2. Foreign matter in fuel system 3. Faulty fuel pump 4. Low fuel level in tank	1. *Check HT leads for cracked insulation; check low tension circuit* 2. *See Section Q* 3. *See Section Q* 4. *Replenish*
F—ENGINE FAILS TO IDLE	1. Incorrect carburetter setting 2. Faulty fuel pump 3. Sticking valves 4. Faulty cylinder head gasket	1. *See Section Q* 2. *See Section Q* 3. *Rectify or renew* 4. *Renew*
G—ENGINE MISFIRES ON ACCELERATION	1. Distributor points incorrectly set 2. Faulty coil or condenser 3. Faulty sparking plug 4. Faulty carburetter	1. *Rectify. See Section A, Part One* 2. *Renew* 3. *Rectify* 4. *See Section Q*

DEFECT LOCATION—*continued*

SYMPTOM	POSSIBLE CAUSE	REMEDY
H—ENGINE KNOCKS	1. Ignition timing advanced 2. Excessive carbon deposit 3. Incorrect carburetter setting 4. Unsuitable fuel 5. Worn pistons or bearings 6. Distributor advance mechanism faulty 7. Defective sparking plugs 8. Incorrect tappet clearance 9. Incorrect valve timing	1. *Adjust* 2. *Decarbonise* 3. *See Section Q* 4. *Adjust octane selector. See Section S* 5. *Renew* 6. *Rectify. See Section S* 7. *Rectify or renew* 8. *Adjust* 9. *Adjust*
J—ENGINE BACKFIRES	1. Ignition defect 2. Carburetter defect 3. Incorrect valve timing 4. Incorrect tappet clearance 5. Sticking valve 6. Weak valve springs 7. Badly seating valves 8. Excessively worn valve stems and guides 9. Loose timing chain 10. Excessive carbon deposit 11. Incorrect sparking plug gap 12. Air leak in induction or exhaust systems	1. *See Section S* 2. *See Section Q* 3. *Adjust* 4. *Adjust* 5. *Rectify* 6. *Renew* 7. *Rectify or renew* 8. *Renew* 9. *Examine tensioner* 10. *Decarbonise* 11. *Reset* 12. *Renew faulty gaskets or components*
K—BURNED VALVES	1. Insufficient tappet clearance 2. Sticking valves 3. Weak valve springs 4. Excessive deposit on valve seats 5. Distorted valves 6. Excessive mileage between overhauls	1. *Adjust* 2. *Rectify* 3. *Renew* 4. *Re-cut* 5. *Renew* 6. *Decarbonise*
L—NOISY VALVE MECHANISM	1. Excessive tappet clearance 2. Sticking valves 3. Weak valve springs 4. Worn timing chain or chainwheel 5. Worn camshaft bearings 6. Excessive camshaft end-float	1. *Adjust* 2. *Rectify* 3. *Renew* 4. *Renew worn parts* 5. *Renew* 6. *Rectify*
M—MAIN BEARING RATTLE	1. Low oil level 2. Low oil pressure 3. Excessive bearing clearance 4. Burnt-out bearings 5. Loose bearing caps	1. *Replenish as necessary* 2. *See Item N* 3. *Renew bearings; grind crankshaft* 4. *Renew* 5. *Tighten*
N—LOW OIL PRESSURE	1. Thin or diluted oil 2. Low oil level 3. Choked pump strainer 4. Faulty release valve 5. Excessive bearing clearance 6. Excessive camshaft bearing clearance 7. Loose or restricted oil pipe	1. *Drain and refill with correct oil* 2. *Replenish* 3. *Clean* 4. *Rectify* 5. *Rectify* 6. *Renew parts as necessary* 7. *Rectify*
O—RATTLE IN LUBRICATION SYSTEM	1. Hydraulic tensioner inoperative due to low oil pressure 2. Oil pressure relief valve plunger sticking	1. *See Item N* 2. *Remove and clean*
P—ENGINE OVERHEATING	1. Low coolant level 2. Faulty cooling system 3. Faulty thermostat 4. Incorrect timing 5. Defective lubrication system	1. *Check for leaks* 2. *See Section P* 3. *Renew* 4. *Rectify* 5. *See Section B*

GENERAL DATA

Engine type .. .. Water cooled, overhead inlet, side exhaust
Number of cylinders .. .. Six, vertical in line
Capacity .. .. 2,995 cc (183 cu in.)
Bore diameter .. .. 3.063 in. (77,8 mm)
Stroke .. .. 4.134 in. (105 mm)

Basic model

Model	Compression ratio	Brake horse power	Maximum torque	Ignition timing	Compression pressure at cranking speed
Mk I and Mk IA	8.75:1	115 at 4,500 rpm	164 lb ft (22,65 Mkg) at 1,500 rpm	3° BTDC	190 lb sq in. (13,4 kg/cm²)
Mk II and Mk III 4-speed and automatic transmission	8.75:1	134 at 5,000 rpm	169 lb ft (23,37 Mkg) at 1,750 rpm	3° BTDC	190 lb sq in. (13,4 kg/cm²)
Mk II automatic transmission	8.00:1	129 at 4,750 rpm	161 lb ft (22,25 Mkg) at 3,000 rpm	3° BTDC	180 lb sq in. (12,65 kg/cm²)

Models for certain export territories

Model	Compression ratio	Brake horse power	Maximum torque	Ignition timing	Compression pressure at cranking speed
Mk I and Mk IA	7.50:1	109 at 4,500 rpm	155 lb ft (21,4 Mkg) at 1,500 rpm	2° BTDC	170 lb sq in. (11,95 kg/cm²)
Mk II and Mk III 4-speed and automatic transmission	8.00:1	129 at 4,750 rpm	161 lb ft (22,25 Mkg) at 3,000 rpm	3° BTDC	180 lb sq in. (12,65 kg/cm²)

Maximum BMEP, 7.50:1 compression ratio .. .. 131 lb/sq in. at 1,500 rpm
Maximum BMEP, 8.00:1 compression ratio .. .. 133 lb/sq in. at 3,000 rpm
Maximum BMEP, 8.75:1 compression ratio .. .. 140 lb/sq in. at 1,750 rpm
Piston speed at 4,500 rpm .. .. 3,100 ft/minute

Sparking plug type—
7.50:1 .. .. Champion N5 or Lodge CLN-H
8.0:1 and 8.75:1 .. .. Champion N5 or Lodge HLN
Sparking plug gap .. .. .029 to .032 in. (0,75 to 0,80 mm)
Firing point static, full retard .. .. 2° BTDC 7.5:1 compression ratio
3° BTDC {8.00:1 / 8.75:1} compression ratio
Firing order 1-5-3-6-2-4
Contact breaker setting .. .. .014 to .016 in. (0,35 to 0,40 mm)
Valve peak .. .. 106° BTDC. See under Valves

TECHNICAL DETAIL DATA

Air filter

Make	AC Delco
Type	Mk I—oil bath Mk IA, Mk II and Mk III—paper element

Camshaft

Camshafts supplied as replacements are marked '100' between 2 and 3 lobes, and must be timed at 106°. Commencing numbers for Production fitted '100' type camshafts will be found under Valves in this section.

Position	Left-hand side
Material	Steel forging
Drive	Chain
Number of journals	5
Diameter of journal	.999–.9985 in. (25,3–25,2 mm)
Thrust taken	At front
Thrust plate thickness	.216 in.–.2155 in. (5,49–5,46 mm)
End-float	.004 in.–.006 in. (0,10–0,15 mm)

Camshaft bearings

Type	Split Mazak
Number of bearings	6
Bore diameter	1.0 in. (25,4 mm)

Carburetter

Make	SU dust-proofed. Model HD8
Type	Single horizontal, 2 in. (50 mm)
Standard needle	UF or UK models Mk I and Mk IA UR models Mk II and Mk III
Jet	.125 in. diameter (3,17 mm)
Float level	.437 in. (11,2 mm)

Connecting rod

Type	'H' section forging
Length	Centres—7.858 in. (200 mm)
Big-end bearings	Detachable, copper/lead, steel shell, positioned by tab
Clearance on internal diameter	Actual .00075 in.–.0025 in. (0,017–0,063 mm)
End-float of connecting rod on crankpin	.009 in.–.013 in. (0,22–0,33 mm)
Fit of gudgeon pin bush to connecting rod	.001–.003 in. (0,02–0,07 mm) interference fit
Connecting rod bearing nip	.002–.004 in. (0,05–0,10 mm)

Cooling system

Type	Water pump, radiator, fan and thermostat. Pressurised 4.5 to 5.5 lb/sq in. (0,31–0,38 Kg/Cm²)
Capacity	Mk I, Mk IA and Mk II: 24 Imperial pints, 29 US pints, 13,7 litres Mk III: 26 Imperial pints, 31 US pints, 14,7 litres

Crankshaft

Material	Nickel chrome forgings
Balance	Dynamically and statically to within .3 oz/in.
Number of main journals	7

Nominal diameter of main journals	2.250 in. (57,1 mm). Mk I, Mk IA and Mk II suffix 'A' and 'B' 2.625 in. (66,37 mm). Mk II suffix 'C' onwards and Mk III
Width of main journals	1⅛ in. (28,5 mm)
Nominal diameter of crankpin	1⅞ in. (47,6 mm)
Width of crankpin	31/32 in. (24,6 mm)
Thrust taken on the rear main bearing; end-float	.002 in.–.006 in. (0,05–0,15 mm)
Crankshaft damper	Harmonic—Mk I and Mk IA models Torsional—Mk II models
Crankshaft damper	Harmonic—Models Mk I and Mk IA Torsional—Models Mk II and Mk III
Vibration damper run-out	.005 in. (0,12 mm)—Harmonic type only

Cylinder block

Material	Cast iron
Reboring limit	.040 in. (1,0 mm)
Liner reboring limit	.010 in. (0,25 mm)

Cylinder head

	Models Mk I and Mk IA	Models Mk II and Mk III
Material	Aluminium alloy	Aluminium alloy
Type	'F' integral inlet manifold, single carburetter	Separate alloy inlet manifold, single carburetter
Inlet valve seating	Bricromium insert	Bricromium insert
Valve seat angle	30°	30°
Valve seat diameter	1.759 in. (44,6 mm)	1.797 in. (45,2 mm)

Flywheel

Material	Cast iron
Run-out permissible	.005 in. (0,12 mm)
Number of teeth on starter ring	105
Torque converter run-out at impeller hub, maximum permissible	.025 in. (0,63 mm)
EP mark—	
Mk I and Mk IA	102½° engines fitted with early camshaft 106° engines fitted with late camshaft
Mk II	105°
Mk III	105° stamped on crankshaft damper at front of engine

Lubrication system—See Section B

Pistons and gudgeon pins

Pistons—	
Type	Aluminium alloy, inverted 'V' shape crowns to conform to the combustion chamber shape
Piston clearance in bore at top of skirt, at right-angles to gudgeon pin	.003 in.–.0035 in. (0,07–0,09 mm)
Piston clearance in bore at bottom of skirt, at right-angles to gudgeon pin	.002 in.–.0025 in. (0,05–0,06 mm)
Ring groove width—	
Compression	.071 in.–.072 in. (1,80–1,84 mm)
Scraper	.158 in.–.159 in. (4,0–4,03 mm)
Ring groove diameter	2.780 in. (70,6 mm)

Gudgeon pin bore diameter	.874 in. (22,1 mm)
Gudgeon pin—	
Length	2.375 in. (60,3 mm)
Outer diameter	.875 in. (22,2 mm)
Fit in connecting rod bush	.0002 in.–.0006 in. (0,005–0,015 mm) selected clearance
Fit in piston	Good hand push (not to exceed 100 lb (50 kg) at temperature range of 50°F–70°F (10°C–21°C))
Location in piston	By circlips

Piston rings

Number of compression	2
Number of scraper	1
Width of compression	.069 in.–.070 in. (1,75–1,77 mm)
Width of scraper, early models	.155 in.–.156 in. (3,93–3,96 mm)
Clearance in groove—	
Compression	.001 in.–.003 in. (0,02–0,07 mm)
Scraper, early models	.002 in.–.004 in. (0,05–0,10 mm)
Gap when fitted—	
Compression	.015 in.–.020 in. (0,38–0,50 mm)
Scraper, early models	.012 in.–.017 in. (0,30–0,43 mm)
Duaflex scraper rings fitted to late models	See Operation A2-3

Radiator core

Type	Gilled tube, cross-flow
Gill material	Copper

Tappets

Exhaust	Rocker type roller cam follower with adjusting screw and self-aligning pad bearing directly on valve stem
Inlet	Roller type cam follower operating valve rocker through push rod with adjusting screw on rocker
Exhaust tappet clearance	.010 in. (0,25 mm) hot or cold
Inlet tappet clearance	.006 in. (0,15 mm) hot or cold
Rocker clearance on shaft, top and bottom	.0005 in.–.0025 in. (0,0127–0,0635 mm)
Top rocker bushes, press fit in rockers—ream in position to	.500 + .001 in. diameter (12,7 + 0,02 mm)

Tightening torques

Main bearing nuts	65 lb/ft (9 mkg)
Connecting rod nuts with machined thread bolts	30 lb/ft (4 mkg)
Connecting rod nuts with rolled thread bolts (identified by drill point at nut end of bolt)	25 lb ft (3,5 mkg)
Cylinder head bolts, $\frac{3}{8}$ in. (9,5 mm)	30 lb ft (4 mkg)
Cylinder head bolts, $\frac{7}{16}$ in. (11,11 mm)	50 lb ft (6,9 mkg)
Flywheel bolts	50 lb ft (6,9 mkg)
Starter dog, suffix 'C' onwards and Mk III	200 lb ft (27,6 mkg)
Torque converter to drive plate fixing bolts	25–30 lb ft (3,5–4,0 mkg)
Torque converter drive plate to crankshaft fixing bolts	65 lb ft (9 mkg)

Timing chain and wheels

Chain type	'Duplex', pre-stretched, endless
Pitch	.375 in. (9,5 mm)
Number of pitch	76
Diameter of roller	.250 in. (6,3 mm)

Crankshaft timing wheel	Steel, 21 teeth
Camshaft timing wheel	Cast iron, 42 teeth
Chain tensioner	Hydraulic, self-adjusting

Valves

	Inlet	Exhaust
Head diameter	1.797 in. (45,6 mm)	1.265 in. (32 mm)
Valve seat angle	30°	45°
Stem diameter—		
Mk I and Mk IA	.312 in. (7,92 mm)	.343 in. (8,70 mm)
Mk II and Mk III	.343 in. (8,70 mm)	.343 in. (8,70 mm)
Stem clearance in guide	.0002–.0028 in. (0,005–0,07 mm)	.0005–.003 in. (0,012–0,07 mm)
Overall length of valve	3.81 in. (96,8 mm)	4.578 in. (141,5 mm)
Valve material	Silichrome No. 1	XB
Valve opens } Mk I and Mk IA	$17\frac{1}{2}$°; 17°* BTDC	$52\frac{1}{2}$°; 45°* BBDC
Valve closes } Mk I and Mk IA	$40\frac{1}{2}$°; 41°* ABDC	$27\frac{1}{2}$°; 13°* ATDC
Valve opens } Mk II and Mk III	13° BTDC	48° BBDC
Valve closes } Mk II and Mk III	45° ABDC	16° ATDC
Valve peak—		
Mk I and Mk IA	$101\frac{1}{2}$°; 102°* ATDC	$102\frac{1}{2}$°; 106°* BTDC
Mk II and Mk III	106° ATDC	105° BTDC
Inlet valve stem oil seal	'O' ring in valve guide	
Valve lift, inlet	.383 in. (9,73 mm)	.409 in. (10,39 mm)
*Engines numbered: 625100012 onwards 626100076 onwards	627100011 onwards 628100005 onwards	630100139 onwards 631100056 onwards

Valve guides

Length	1.500 in. (38 mm)	2.250 in. (57 mm)
Bore diameter—		
Mk I and Mk IA	.312 in. (7,92 mm)	.343 in. (8,70 mm)
Mk II and Mk III	.343 in. (8,70 mm)	.343 in. (8,70 mm)
Interference fit in head or cylinder block	.0015–.0035 in. (0,03–0,08 mm)	.005–.0025 in. (0,012–0,06 mm)

Valve seats

Interference fit of inlet in head	.003 in.–.004 in. (0,08–0,11 mm)
Interference fit of exhaust in cylinder block	.005 in.–.007 in. (0,12–0,17 mm)

Valve springs

Type	Duplex coil interference fit	
	Inner spring	Outer spring
Free length	1.610 in. (41 mm)	1.768 in. (50 mm)
Number of working coils	6.5	5

Section B – ENGINE LUBRICATION SYSTEM

Brief description of the engine lubrication system

Engine lubrication is by means of a large capacity gear type oil pump located in the sump.

Oil enters the pump through a strainer and having been pressurised, the oil passes through a full-flow paper element type filter which is mounted on the right-hand side of the cylinder block.

From the filter oil under pressure is delivered to the oil gallery and is distributed to the main, big-end and camshaft bearings, also to the timing chain tensioner, distributor drive shaft, cam followers and rocker gear. Each cam is separately fed, and the cylinder bores are lubricated by a jet of oil from each connecting rod.

An oil pressure relief valve, which is not adjustable is located in the side of the pump drive housing. The ball, plunger and spring, are inserted from outside the cylinder block. The valve's function is to allow relief at the pre-determined pressure of 55 to 65 lb/sq in. (3,8 to 4,5 kg/cm^2) at 30 mph (50 kph) in top gear with engine warm.

The oil drains back to the sump from where it is again circulated throughout the system.

INDEX

Oil pump, to overhaul—Operation B-1

Workshop hand tools:
Spanner sizes: $\frac{7}{16}$ in. AF, $\frac{1}{2}$ in. AF Straight edge Feeler gauges

For oil pump removal see Section A

Oil pump, strip

1. Remove the oil pump strainer secured by a castle nut and split pin.
2. Remove the oil pump cover secured by four bolts and self-locking nuts.

   Suffix letter 'C' onwards and Mk III. Four set bolts and spring washers are used.
3. Lift out the gears, if necessary drive out the bush in the idler gear.
4. Remove the idler gear spindle which is screwed into the cover. If necessary drive out the bush at the top of the oil pump body.
5. Clean all parts, examine for wear and renew as necessary.

Oil pump, rebuild

1. If removed, press a new bush into the body and ream in position to .5625 in.+.001 (14,28 mm+0,02). Ensure correct alignment with the bore at the bottom end of the pump body, and the bush should be a light drive fit.
2. If removed, press a new bush in the idler gear. Drill the $\frac{1}{8}$ in. (3,0 mm) oilway and ream in position to .500 in.+.001 (12,7 mm+0,02).
3. If removed, replace the idler gear spindle.
4. Refit the gears and check tolerances as follows:
   (a) Check the radial clearance, which should be .001 to .004 in. (0,02 to 0,10 mm).
   (b) Check the backlash between gears, which should be .008 to .012 in. (0,20 to 0,30 mm).
   (c) Check the end-float of the gears:
   Steel: .002 to .005 in. (0,05 to 0,12 mm)
   Aluminium: .003 to .006 in. (0,07 to 0,15 mm)

   Renew parts as necessary. If the clearances are incorrect, oil flow will be insufficient.
6. When the tolerances are correct, fit the idler gear to the spindle. Mesh the driving gear (steel) with the idler gear, inserting the splined end of the gear first.
7. Fit the housing to the pump cover, renewing the locknuts.
8. Fit the oil strainer.
9. The oil pressure should be 55 to 65 lb/sq in. (3,8 to 4,5 kg/cm²) at 30 mph (50 kph) in top gear with engine warm. To check this the oil pressure warning light switch may be removed and a suitable external oil pressure gauge connected in its place temporarily. If lower pressures are indicated the oil pressure relief valve spring should be renewed.

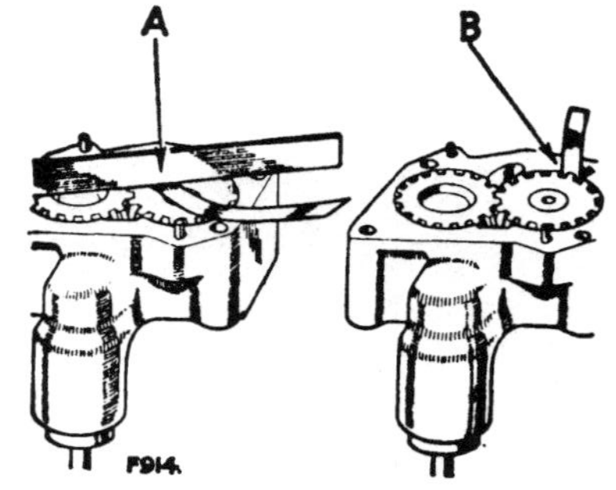

Checking clearance of oil pump gears
A—Checking end-float B—Checking radial clearance

External oil filter, to remove and refit—Operation B-2

Workshop hand tools:
Spanner size: $1\frac{1}{8}$ in. AF

Filter element only, remove and renew

The element of the full-flow oil filter must be renewed every 6,000 miles. This should be done at a routine oil change. To remove the element, proceed as follows:

1. Place a suitable oil tray under the engine.
2. Unscrew the bolt securing the filter container which on early models is at the bottom of the container, and on late models in the top of the filter adaptor, and remove the container complete with the filter element.
3. Remove and discard the used filter element and large rubber washer.
4. Wash the container in clean petrol.
5. Place the new filter element in the container and re-assemble the unit, using the new large rubber washer supplied with the element. Ensure that all the sealing washers are in position and intact, and that the container is correctly located in the top cover assembly.
6. Refill the engine with 11 Imperial pints, 13 US pints (6 litres) of the correct grade of engine oil. Run the engine for five minutes, and check for leaks.
7. Check the oil level after the engine has been switched off and sufficient time has elapsed for the oil around the engine to drain back into the sump. Replenish if necessary.

Oil pressure transmitter, to remove and refit—Operation B-3

Workshop hand tools:
Spanner size: $\frac{5}{8}$ in. A.F.

Oil pressure transmitter, remove

1. The oil pressure transmitter is screwed into the oil filter adaptor on the side of the cylinder block. Its function is to transmit the oil pressure electrically to a gauge which is fitted in addition to the oil pressure warning light.
2. To remove the transmitter, disconnect the electrical connection and use a $\frac{5}{8}$ in. AF spanner to unscrew the complete unit.

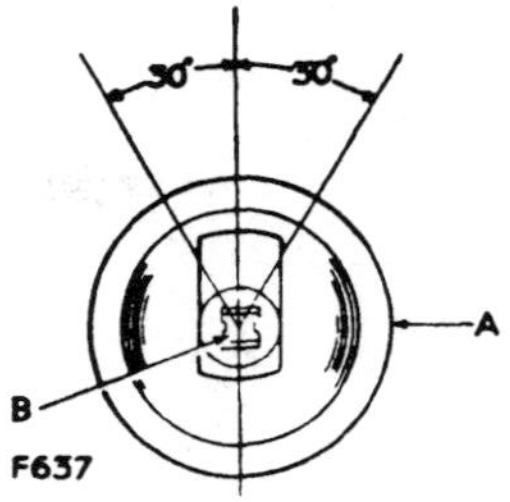

Correct fitting position of oil pressure transmitter
A—Oil pressure transmitter B—Lucar connection

Oil pressure transmitter, refit

1. The oil pressure transmitter must be secured in the vertical position, using a suitable number of shims as necessary.
2. Fit electrical feed lead.

Oil pressure warning light switch, remove and refit—Operation B-4

Workshop hand tools:
Spanner size: $\frac{5}{8}$ in. AF

Oil pressure switch, remove

1. The oil pressure switch is screwed into the oil supply pipe from the cylinder block to the cylinder head.

   Its function is to cause the oil warning light to operate if the oil pressure drops below 8 to 10 lb/sq in. (0,6 to 0,7 kg/cm²).

2. The switch can be removed from the union by disconnecting the electrical connection and using a $\frac{5}{8}$ in. AF spanner to unscrew the complete unit.

3. If a faulty switch is suspected, it can be checked by substitution or by temporarily fitting a pressure gauge in its place.

4. When replacing the switch, fit a new sealing washer.

Rocker oil feed pipe and oil pressure switch

A—Rocker oil feed pipe B—Oil pressure switch

Oil leaks—Operation B-5

1. Whenever any part of the engine lubrication system is dismantled, new gaskets, ring seals or sealing washers should be fitted on assembly.

2. Always tighten flange fixings evenly and securely.

3. Keep the engine clean so that oil leaks can be quickly traced to their source, and never allow a leak to continue without taking remedial action.

DEFECT LOCATION

SYMPTOM	*POSSIBLE CAUSE*	*REMEDY*
A—WARNING LIGHT REMAINS 'ON' ENGINE RUNNING	1. Low oil level 2. Low oil pressure 3. Oil pressure switch unserviceable 4. Electrical fault	1. *Replenish* 2. *See Symptom B* 3. *Renew* 4. *Check circuit*
B—LOW OIL PRESSURE	1. Pump body joints loose 2. Foreign matter on pump ball relief valve seat 3. Relief valve plunger sticking 4. Weak relief valve spring 5. Pump rotors excessively worn 6. Excessively worn bearings; main, connecting rod, big end, camshaft, etc.	1. *Tighten* 2. *Remove and clean* 3. *Remove and ascertain cause* 4. *Renew* 5. *Renew* 6. *Ascertain which bearings and rectify*
C—WARNING LIGHT FAILS TO GLOW When engine is stopped and ignition switch is 'on'	1. Bulb filament is broken 2. Oil pressure switch unserviceable 3. Electrical fault	1. *Renew bulb, see also Section—* 2. *Renew* 3. *Check circuit*

DATA

Engine lubrication system

Lubrication system	
Type	Full pressure, non-adjustable
Nominal pressure	55 to 65 lb/sq. in. (3,8 to 4,5 kg/cm²) at 30 mph (50 kph) in top gear, engine warm
Sump capacity	10 Imperial pints; 12 US pints; 5,5 litres, plus 1 Imperial pint; 1.2 US pints; 0,5 litres, after replacing engine oil filter element
Oil pump position	In engine sump
Type	Spur gear
Drive	Off camshaft
End-float of gears	
Steel	.002 in.–.005 in. (0,05–0,12 mm)
Aluminium	.003 in.–.006 in. (0,07–0,15 mm)
Gear, radial clearance	.001 in.–.004 in. (0,02–0,10 mm)
Backlash between gears	.008 in.–.012 in. (0,20–0,30 mm)
Oil pressure relief spring	
Free length	3.425 in. (87,00 mm)
Load, fitted	17.5 lb at 1.990 in. (7,9 kg at 50,55 mm)
Number of working coils	20
Oil filter	
Full-flow internal	Gauze pump intake strainer
Full-flow external	AC FF 24
Dipstick position	Right-hand side of engine
Oil pressure light	Green light on instrument panel operates when pressure drops below a safe figure
Recommended lubricants	A complete list of recommended lubricants will be found in Section Y of this manual

Section C – CLUTCH

4-SPEED MODELS

Brief description of the clutch assembly

A Borg and Beck 10 in. (254 mm) single dry plate clutch, type BB 45697/35 with hydraulically operated control mechanism is used.

The clutch withdrawal unit utilises a thrust ballrace, which is automatically lubricated by the gearbox oil. The unit housing is bolted to the gearbox.

The hydraulic operating mechanism consists of a ¾ in. (19 mm) bore master cylinder with a combined reservoir, which is mechanically attached directly to the operating pedal and is connected by hydraulic piping to the slave cylinder. A mechanical linkage connects the slave cylinder to the withdrawal unit.

Maintenance attention consists of ensuring that the hydraulic fluid level is maintained to the bottom of the filler neck.

Take precautions to keep all components scrupulously clean when carrying out any work on the hydraulic system.

Should air get into the system, denoted by a spongy operating pedal action, the system must be bled as detailed.

Use only Castrol Girling Crimson Brake Fluid (Specification SAE 70 R3). When replacing the filler cap always ensure that the breather hole is not restricted, and that the sealing washer is in good order.

INDEX

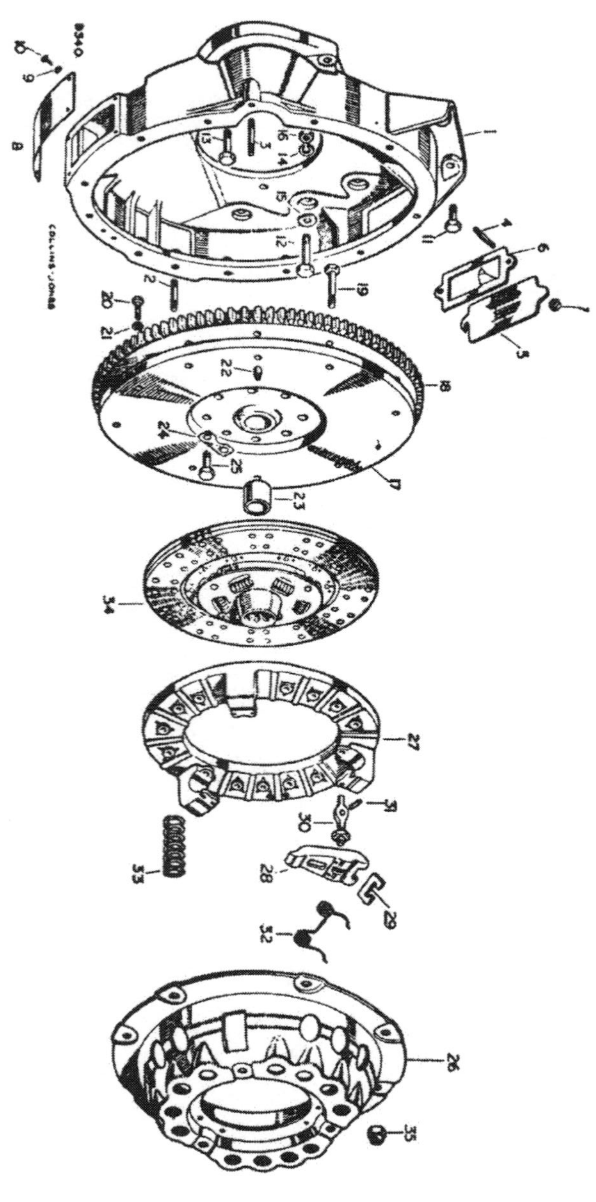

Exploded drawing of clutch

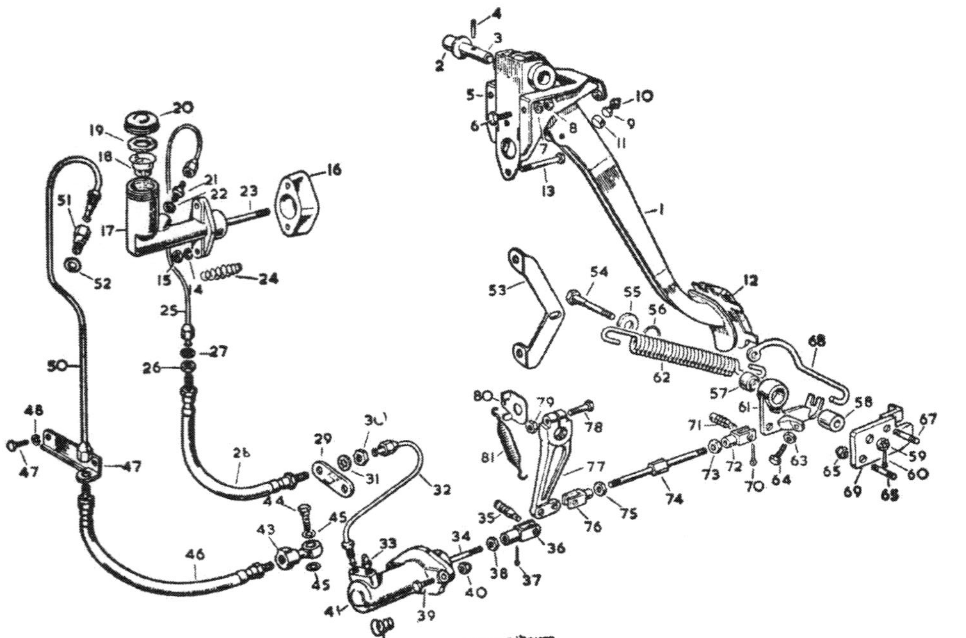

Clutch pedal and cylinders

1 Clutch pedal
2 Bush for bracket
3 Pivot pin for pedal
4 Locating pin
5 Pedal bracket
6 Bolt ($\frac{5}{16}$ in. UNF × $\frac{5}{8}$ in. long)
7 Spring washer
8 Nut ($\frac{5}{16}$ in. UNF) } Fixing pedal bracket to dash (6–8)
9 Bolt ($\frac{1}{4}$ in. UNF × $1\frac{1}{4}$ in. long)
10 Locknut ($\frac{1}{4}$ in. UNF) } For pedal stop (9–10)
11 Rubber pad
12 Rubber pad for clutch pedal
13 Bolt ($\frac{5}{16}$ in. UNF × $2\frac{1}{4}$ in. long)
14 Spring washer
15 Nut ($\frac{5}{16}$ in. UNF) } Fixing clutch master cylinder to dash (13–15)
16 Distance piece for master cylinder
17 Clutch master cylinder
18 Filter
19 Sealing washer for filter
20 Filler cap
21 Adaptor for pipe
22 Joint washer for adaptor
23 Push rod, master cylinder
24 Piston return spring
25 Pipe, master cylinder to hose
26 Special nut
27 Shakeproof washer
28 Hose, early models
29 Bracket for hose, early models
30 Special nut, early models
31 Shakeproof washer, early models
32 Pipe, early models
33 Bleed screw for slave cylinder
34 Push rod, slave cylinder
35 Clevis pin
36 Clevis for push rod
37 Split pin
38 Locknut ($\frac{5}{16}$ in. UNF)
39 Bolt ($\frac{5}{16}$ in. UNF × $1\frac{3}{8}$ in. long)
40 Self-locking nut ($\frac{5}{16}$ in. UNF) } Fixing slave cylinder to bell housing (39–40)
41 Slave cylinder
42 Piston return spring for slave cylinder
43 Banjo for slave cylinder
44 Banjo bolt
45 Gasket for banjo
46 Hose, late models
47 Bolt ($\frac{1}{4}$ in. UNF × $\frac{1}{2}$ in. long)
48 Spring washer
49 Butment bracket, to bulkhead
50 Pipe, late models
51 Adaptor, late models
52 Gasket for adaptor, late models
53 Anchor for clutch return spring
54 Pivot pin
55 Special washer
56 'O' ring
57 Needle bearing
58 Distance piece
59 Castle nut
60 Split pin } Fixing lever to support bracket (54–60)
61 Lever for over-centre mechanism
62 Clutch balance spring
63 Locknut
64 Stop bolt
65 Stud—short
66 Self-locking nut
67 Stud—long } Fixing support bracket (65–67)
68 Hook for balance spring
69 Support bracket
70 Split pin
71 Clevis pin
72 Clevis
73 Locknut
74 Adjusting rod
75 Locknut
76 Clevis
77 Operating lever
78 Pinch bolt for lever
79 Nut
80 Anchor
81 Return spring

*Clutch unit, to remove and refit (4-speed models)—Operation C-1

Workshop hand tools:
Spanner sizes: $\frac{1}{2}$ in. AF, $\frac{9}{16}$ in. AF

Special tools:
Dial test indicator;
Bracket for dial test indicator, Part No. 530106

Clutch unit, remove

The clutch unit may be removed without removing the engine from the car, but if work has to be done on the engine such as renewing rear main bearing oil seals, it is more advantageous to leave the gearbox in situ and remove the engine and clutch from the car.

For details of clutch overhaul see Operation C-5.

1. For engine removal instructions see Section A.

   For gearbox removal instructions see Section D.

2. Remove the clutch unit from the flywheel, secured by (early models) six $\frac{3}{8}$ in. UNF self-locking nuts, and (late models) by six $\frac{5}{16}$ in. UNF bolts and locking washers.

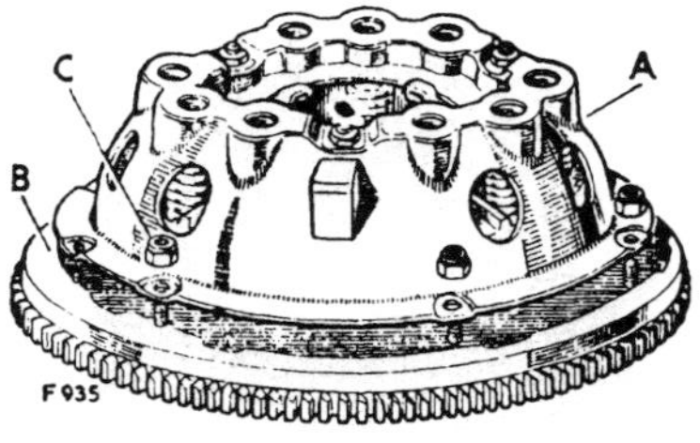

Removing clutch unit from flywheel
A—Clutch unit B—Flywheel
C—Self-locking nut

Clutch unit, refit

1. When a new or reconditioned clutch unit is fitted to the original flywheel, any balance weights previously fitted must be removed. Where only the clutch driven plate is being renewed, the balance weights must be retained in their original positions.

2. These weights can be removed from the flywheel through the starter motor aperture in the flywheel housing.

3. It is most important that clutch plate is checked for run-out within the limits of $\pm$.010 in. (0,25 mm) of the true plane immediately prior to installation. Each side of the plate must be checked and the maximum run-out must not coincide.

   Clutch plates which are outside the acceptable limits must be corrected before installation.

4. Place the clutch driven plate, which is marked 'Flywheel side' for identification, in position on the flywheel face with the longer end of the central boss away from the flywheel. The clutch plate should be handled with care.

5. Offer the clutch unit on to the flywheel, with the identification marking adjacent to that on the flywheel. Centralise the clutch driven plate by means of a slave primary pinion and tighten the securing nuts one turn each at a time, by diagonal selection, to prevent distortion of the clutch unit.

6. Remove the slave primary pinion.

7. Refit the gearbox assembly and refit the clutch slave cylinder.

8. Refit the operating lever and adjust the clutch pedal free movement. Operation C-11.

9. Refit the lever return spring.

10. If necessary bleed the hydraulic system. Operation C-12.

Operations which are identified by an asterisk (*), can be carried out with the engine installed in the car

Clutch master cylinder, to remove and refit—Operation C-2

Workshop hand tools:
Spanner sizes: $\frac{7}{16}$ in. AF, $\frac{9}{16}$ in. AF Circlip pliers

For clutch master cylinder overhaul procedure, see Operation C-6

Clutch master cylinder, remove

1. Remove the air intake elbow. Disconnect the air hose from the elbow, and remove the elbow fixings.

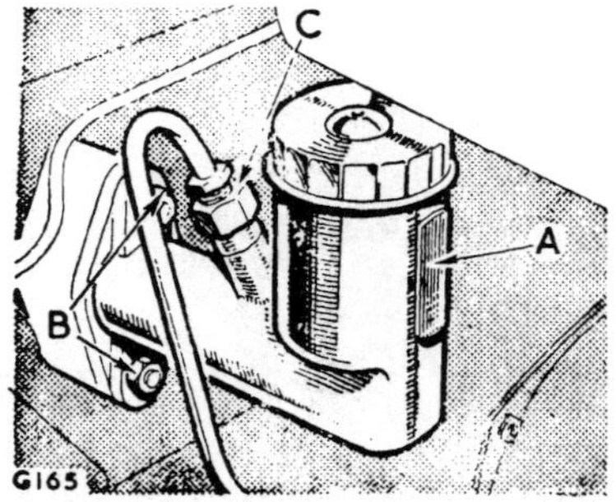

Removing clutch master cylinder
A—Reservoir B—Fixings
C—Hydraulic pipe union

2. Disconnect the hydraulic pipe from the clutch master cylinder.

3. Remove the clevis pin from the clutch operating rod and pedal.

4. Remove the master cylinder and distance piece from the bulkhead, secured by two nuts, bolts and spring washers.

Clutch master cylinder, refit

1. Place the cylinder and distance piece in position and secure by the two bolts, spring washers and nuts.

2. Re-connect the hydraulic pipe line to the master cylinder.

3. Fit the air intake elbow to carburetter.

4. Bleed the hydraulic system at the slave cylinder bleed nipple. Operation C-12.

5. If necessary adjust pedal position. See Operation C-11.

Clutch slave cylinder, to remove and refit—Operation C-3

Workshop hand tools:
Spanner sizes: $\frac{7}{16}$ in. AF, $\frac{1}{2}$ in. AF Pliers

For clutch slave cylinder, to overhaul, see Operation C-7

Slave cylinder, remove

1. Disconnect the hydraulic pipe from the cylinder.
2. Remove the operating rod clevis pin.

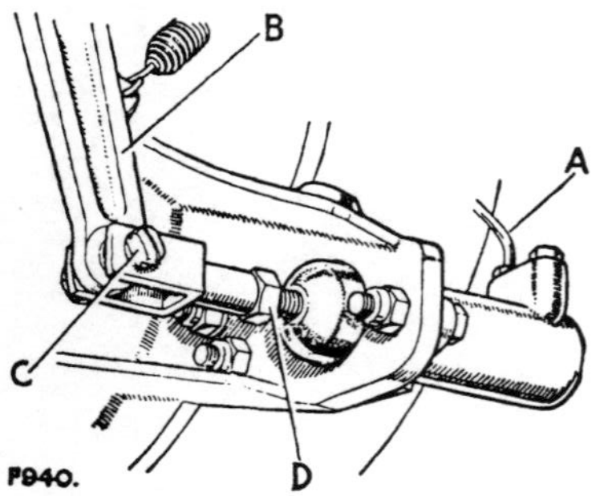

Removing clutch slave cylinder (early models)
A—Hydraulic pipe C—Clevis pin
B—Operating lever D—Adjusting nut

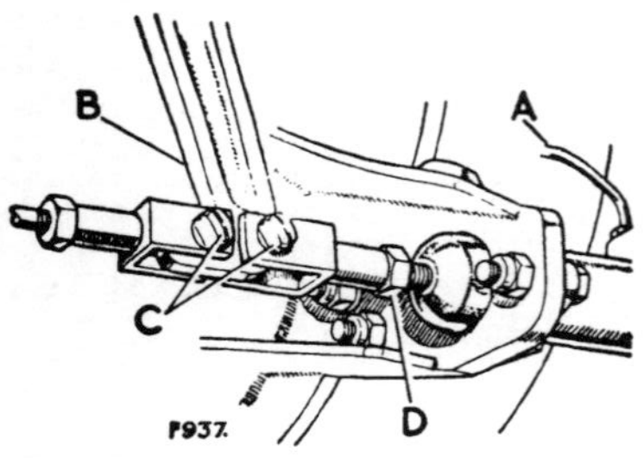

Removing clutch slave cylinder (late models)
A—Hydraulic pipe C—Clevis pins
B—Operating lever D—Adjusting nut

3. Remove the cylinder, secured to the bell housing by two bolts and self-locking nuts.

Slave cylinder, refit

1. Fit the cylinder, secured by two $\frac{5}{16}$ in. UNF x 1$\frac{3}{8}$ in. bolts and self-locking nuts.
2. Connect the hydraulic pipe to the cylinder.
3. Push the slave cylinder push rod and piston fully into its bore until the piston comes to the end of its travel. Adjust the length of the rod so that when it is fitted to the operating lever there is approximately $\frac{1}{16}$ to $\frac{3}{32}$ in. (1,5 to 2,5 mm) free play of piston travel. This adjustment will give approximately $\frac{3}{4}$ in. (20 mm) at the pedal pad. On early models refit the return spring.
4. Bleed the hydraulic system. Operation C-12.

Clutch pedal assembly, to remove and refit—Operation C-4

Workshop hand tools:
Spanner sizes: $\frac{1}{2}$ in. AF, $\frac{7}{16}$ in. AF Pliers, long nosed

For clutch pedal overhaul, see Operation C-9

Clutch pedal assembly, remove

1. Disconnect the pedal return spring and remove the clevis pin connecting the pedal lever to the master cylinder push rod.
2. Place a suitable cover over the front wing to protect the paintwork from spilt brake fluid.
3. Remove the carburetter air intake elbow, Section A.
4. Disconnect the pipe from the clutch master cylinder and insert a suitable plug in the fluid outlet.
5. Remove the clutch master cylinder and distance piece secured to the dash by two bolts, nuts and spring washers.
6. Remove the pedal support bracket secured by four bolts, nuts and spring washers.

Clutch pedal assembly, refit

1. Place the pedal and bracket in position and secure with the fixing bolts, nuts and washers.
2. Fit the distance piece and brake master cylinder to the bulkhead.
3. Adjust the master cylinder operating rod to the correct length, that is until the distance from the bottom of the pedal pad to the floor of the car is 6 in. (152 mm) on RHD cars and 6$\frac{3}{4}$ in. (171 mm) on LHD cars.
4. Fit the pedal return spring anchor plate to the pivot pin and connect the push rod to the pedal. Fit the pedal return spring.
5. Finally adjust the pedal stop 'B' to give a minimum clearance of $\frac{1}{16}$ in. (1,5 mm) free movement at the push rod in the master cylinder.
6. Bleed the hydraulic system. Operation C-12.

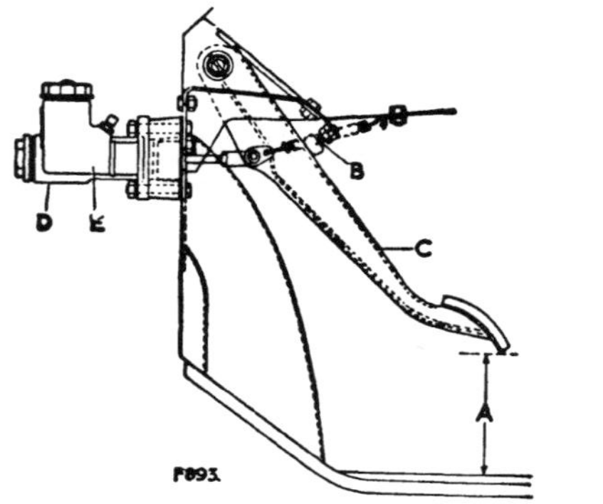

Adjustment of clutch pedal
A—6 in. (152 mm) RHD cars. 6$\frac{3}{4}$ in. (171 mm) LHD cars
B—Pedal stop adjustment
C—Pedal
D—Brake master cylinder
E—Clutch master cylinder

Clutch unit, to overhaul—Operation C-5

Workshop hand tools:

Spanner sizes: $\frac{7}{16}$ in. AF, $\frac{5}{8}$ in. AF, $\frac{11}{16}$ in. AF

Special tools:

Gauge plate, clutch release fingers. Part No. 530103; Surface plate; Scribing block

Clutch unit, strip

1. Mark the cover plate, pressure plate lugs and release levers so that the original balance may be arrived at on assembly.
2. Place the unit under a press with the pressure plate on a wooden block.
3. Press the cover downwards and remove the release lever adjusting nuts.
4. Release the pressure and lift off the cover.
5. With the inner end of the lever and the top of the eyebolt as close as possible, lift the strut over the ridge on the lever and remove the eyebolt, lever and strut from the pressure plate.
6. Clean all the components and lay them out for inspection. Renew damaged or worn parts as necessary.
7. Examine the pressure plate for damage, and regrind if necessary in accordance with the information given in the data section.
8. Check the clutch thrust springs in accordance with the information given in the data section.
9. Examine the flywheel for damage, if necessary remove the engine. Section A.

   See Section X for reconditioning of flywheel.
10. If worn, renew the primary pinion bush in the flywheel, the new bush must be a press fit in the flywheel and the pinion an easy fit in the bush.

Clutch unit, assemble

1. Apply a slight smear of high melting point grease to all moving parts.
2. Assemble the unit by reversing the stripping procedure, ensuring that the marked components are in their correct positions, and using new adjusting nuts.
3. Check the operation of the clutch by operating the levers under a suitable hand press.

Adjusting clutch operating levers

This adjustment must be carried out before the clutch is fitted to the engine, and will be necessary after stripping the unit, or if any new part has been fitted. New adjusting nuts must always be used.

1. Using the original flywheel if removed, or a slave flywheel, surface plate and scribing block; set the scribe to 1.655 in. (42 mm) above the flywheel face by means of the gauge, Part No. 530103.

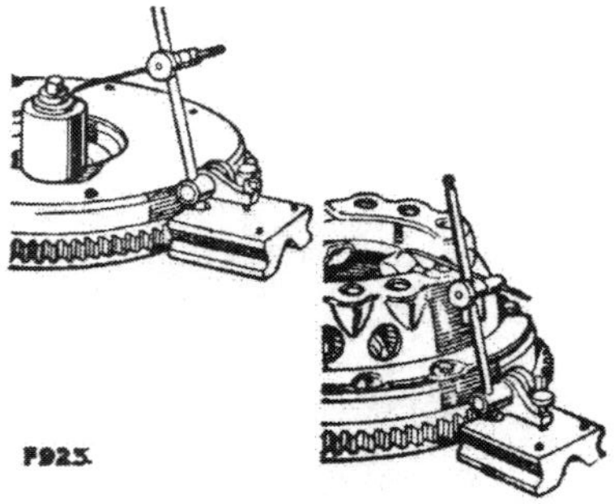
F925

Setting clutch levers

2. Bolt the clutch unit down to the flywheel using three equidistantly spaced $\frac{3}{8}$ in. (9,5 mm) distance pieces in place of the driven plate, which must not be used as it has an allowable run-out of .010 in. (0,25 mm). Gearbox interlocking plungers Part No. 55638 are suitable for this operation.
3. Adjust the operating levers until the top face of each lever is level with the point of the scriber.
4. When the adjusting nuts are finally positioned, lock them to the eyebolts by bending the nut rim into the bolt.
5. Remove the clutch assembly and distance pieces from the flywheel.

Operation C-5—*continued*

Re-lining the clutch plate

6. The clutch plate is balanced and may have small weights attached to the driving member. It is important that only a balanced unit is used.

   (a) Always drill out the old rivets, using a $\frac{5}{32}$ in. (4 mm) diameter drill; never use a punch, which may distort the driven plate.

   (b) Examine the driven plate for cracks and renew as necessary.

   (c) Each facing is secured separately with the rivet heads in the countersunk holes; the plain holes clear the rivet shanks.

   (d) Roll the rivets over securely against the driven plate. If a rolling tool is not available a punch may be used with care.

   (e) Mount the plate on a mandrel between centres; check that the maximum run-out does not exceed .010 in. (0,25 mm).

Clutch master cylinder, to overhaul—Operation C-6

Workshop hand tools:
Spanner sizes: $\frac{7}{16}$ in. AF, $\frac{9}{16}$ in. AF Circlip pliers

See Operation C-2 *for removal procedure*

Master cylinder, overhaul

1. Remove the filler cap and withdraw filter.
2. Remove the retaining circlip and withdraw the push-rod. Apply low air pressure to the intake orifice in order to expel the piston assembly from the cylinder.
3. Clean all components thoroughly in the recommended brake fluid.
4. Carefully examine and renew the internal components as necessary, including all seals.
5. Smear the seals with Wakefield No. 3 rubber grease.
6. Assemble the unit by reversing removal procedure. See illustration for correct order of components.

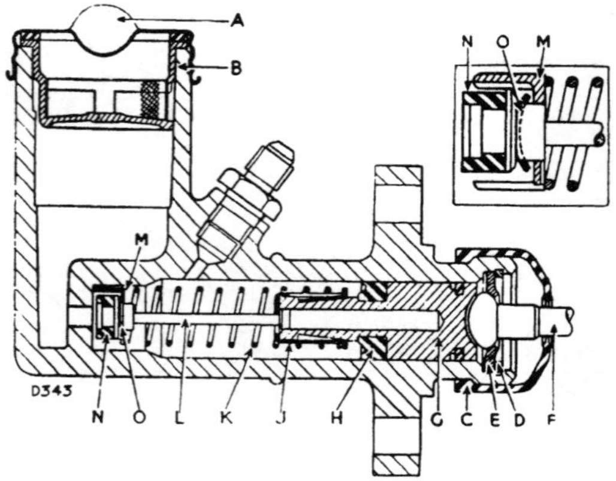

Sectional view of clutch master cylinder

A—Reservoir cap
B—Filter housing
C—Dust cover
D—Circlip
E—Retaining washer
F—Piston push-rod
G—Piston
H—Piston seal
J—Spring retainer
K—Spring
L—Valve stem
M—Valve spacer
N—Valve seal
O—Spring washer

Clutch slave cylinder, to overhaul—Operation C-7

Workshop hand tools:
Spanner size: $\frac{7}{16}$ in. AF

For clutch slave cylinder removal procedure, see Operation C-3

Slave cylinder, overhaul

1. Remove the rubber dust cover and withdraw the push rod.
2. Apply low air pressure to outlet orifice in order to expel the piston and return spring from the cylinder.
3. Clean all the component parts in Castrol Girling Crimson Brake Fluid and inspect the rubber seal and dust cover.
4. Renew worn or defective parts.
5. Smear the seal with Wakefield No. 3 rubber grease.
6. Assemble slave cylinder by reversal of removal procedure.

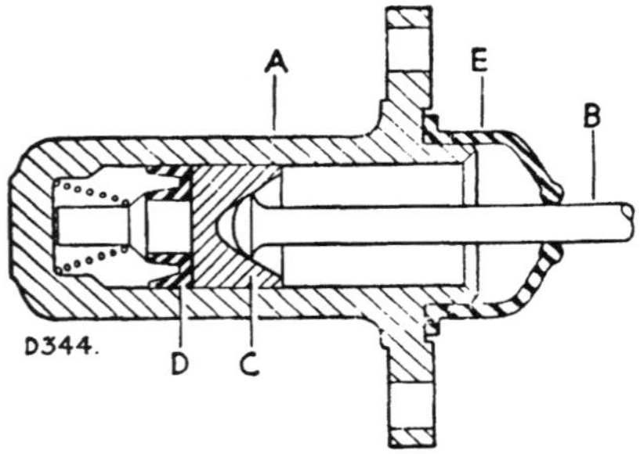

Sectional view of clutch slave cylinder

A—Cylinder housing
B—Piston rod
C—Piston
D—Piston seal
E—Rubber boot

Clutch withdrawal unit, to overhaul—Operation C-8

Workshop hand tools:

Spanner sizes: $\frac{5}{16}$ in. BSF, $\frac{7}{16}$ in. AF Circlip pliers

Clutch withdrawal unit, strip

1. This operation is carried out with the gearbox removed.
2. Remove the pinch bolt and remove the operating lever from the cross-shaft.
3. Withdraw the unit from the bell housing, secured by seven self-locking nuts.
4. Remove the end cover plate from the cross-shaft secured by two set bolts.
5. Remove the circlip and withdraw the shaft from the oil seal side, releasing the operating fork, spring and thrust washer.
6. Remove oil seal.
7. Using a suitable tool, press the withdrawal sleeve from the bearing, an old withdrawal sleeve is suitable for this operation.
8. Press the sleeve bush from the housing.
9. Press out the cross-shaft bushes.
10. Examine all parts for wear, and renew as necessary.

Clutch withdrawal unit, assemble

1. Renew the cross-shaft bushes in the cross-shaft bore, which must be a light drive fit in the bore.
2. Fit the bush for the withdrawal race sleeve which must be a drive fit in the housing.
3. To refit the thrust bearing, press on the sleeve. The bearing must be a light press fit, and should be positioned against the shoulder of the sleeve.
4. Fit a new oil seal in the shaft bore, with the lip of the seal facing inwards.
5. Place the operating fork, spring and thrust washer in position in the housing, with the thrust washer adjacent to the end cover side, and slide in the cross-shaft. Secure the shaft with the distance washer and circlip, and fit the end cover.
6. Using a new joint washer, mount the unit into the bell housing and secure with the seven self-locking nuts.
7. Refit operating lever.

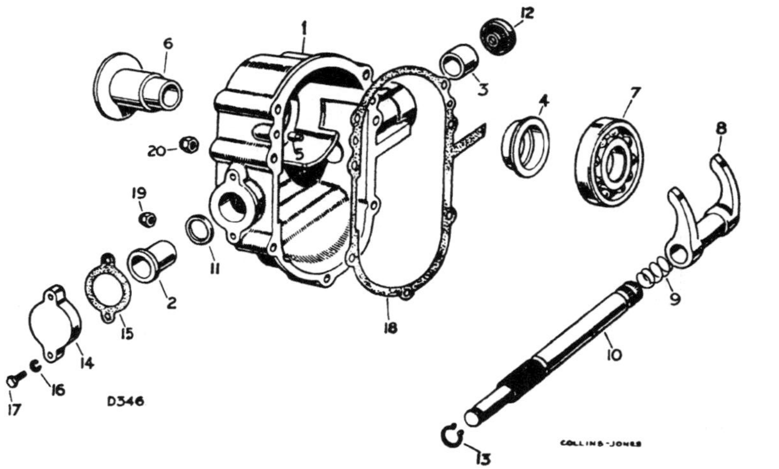

Layout of clutch withdrawal mechanism

1	Clutch withdrawal race housing assembly	10	Cross-shaft for clutch operation
2	Bush for cross-shaft, flanged	11	Thrust washer for cross-shaft
3	Bush for cross-shaft, plain	12	Oil seal for cross-shaft
4	Bush for withdrawal race sleeve	13	Circlip retaining cross-shaft
5	Dowel locating housing	14	End cover for cross-shaft
6	Clutch withdrawal sleeve	15	Joint washer for end cover
7	Withdrawal race thrust bearing	16–17	Fixings, end cover to housing
8	Operating fork for clutch	18	Joint washer for clutch withdrawal housing
9	Spring for fork	19–20	Fixings, housing to bell housing

Clutch pedal, to overhaul—Operation C-9

Workshop hand tools:

Spanner sizes: $\frac{7}{16}$ in. AF, $\frac{1}{2}$ in. AF, $\frac{9}{16}$ in. AF Pliers, long nosed

For clutch pedal removal, see Operation C-4

Clutch pedal, dismantle

1. Remove the small locating pin from the pedal boss and pivot pin and withdraw the pivot pin.
2. Drift out the pivot pin flanged bushes from the bracket.

Clutch pedal, assemble

1. Fit new flanged bushes into the bracket, flanges facing inward.
2. Assemble the pedal lever to support bracket and slide in a new pivot pin. Secure with a new locating pin.

Clutch pedal linkage, to adjust—Operation C-10

Workshop hand tools:

Spanner sizes: $\frac{7}{16}$ in. AF, $\frac{1}{2}$ in. AF, $\frac{9}{16}$ in. AF, $\frac{5}{16}$ in. BSF Pliers, long nosed

If the complete clutch mechanism has been disturbed, re-adjust in the following sequence:

Pedal adjustment—Operation C-11
Adjustment of linkage—Operation C-10
Bleeding the system—Operation C-12

Pedal linkage, adjust. Early models

1. Rotate the clutch cross-shaft clockwise until resistance is felt, that is when the clearance between clutch release fork, release bearing, release sleeve and clutch toggles has been taken up.
2. With the shaft held in this position fit the operating lever to the splines with the lever pointing downwards and approximately 6° forward of the right-angle position measured from the transmission centre-line.
3. Push the slave cylinder push rod and piston into its bore until the piston comes to the end of its travel. Adjust the length of the rod so that when it is fitted to the operating lever, there is approximately $\frac{1}{16}$ to $\frac{3}{32}$ in. (1,5 to 2,5 mm) free play of piston travel. This adjustment will give approximately $\frac{3}{4}$ in. (20 mm) at the pedal pad. Fit the return spring.

Pedal linkage, to adjust

Late models, with over-centre clutch mechanism. Letters in parenthesis refer to illustration on page 15.

Operation C-10—*continued*

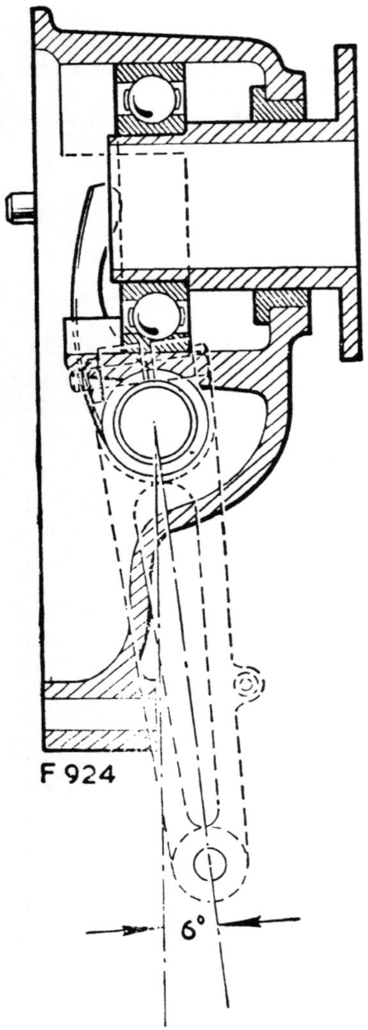

Cross-section of withdrawal unit

4. Disconnect clevis (K) and (Q) from clutch lever (P).

5. Rotate clutch cross-shaft (N) in a clockwise direction, as far as possible, to ensure that all clearance between the clutch withdrawal sleeve and release levers is taken up.

6. If the clutch operating lever has been removed, refit the lever as follows:

   Hold the clutch cross-shaft (N) in the fully clockwise direction.

   Fit the operating lever (P) one spline forward of the vertical position.

7. Push the slave cylinder push rod as far as possible into the bore of the cylinder. Adjust push rod (R) so that with the clevis connected there is approximately $\frac{3}{32}$ in. (2,5 mm) of free play. This adjustment will give the correct pedal free play and the correct clearance between the clutch withdrawal sleeve and release levers.

8. Unscrew adjusting bolt (F) a few turns.

9. Reconnect clevis (K) to lever (P) and adjust length of rod so that the clevis pin (G) is vertically in line with the pivot bolt (C). Then shorten the adjusting rod 'J' by three turns.

10. Whilst the clutch pedal is held fully depressed, adjust bolt (F) so that it abuts on to the stop plate, then tighten the locknut. This adjustment prevents the linkage from going over centre and thus ensures that the clutch does not stick in the disengaged position.

11. Depress the clutch pedal a few times to ensure correct operation of linkage.

12. When routine clutch pedal free play adjustment is carried out, any adjustment of the clutch slave cylinder push rod (R) must be compensated by adjustment of rod (J). For example, if adjustment at rod (R) is shortened by two turns, then the adjustment at rod (J) must be lengthened by one turn to maintain the vertical position of the pivot bolt (C) and clevis (G).

Operation C-10—*continued*

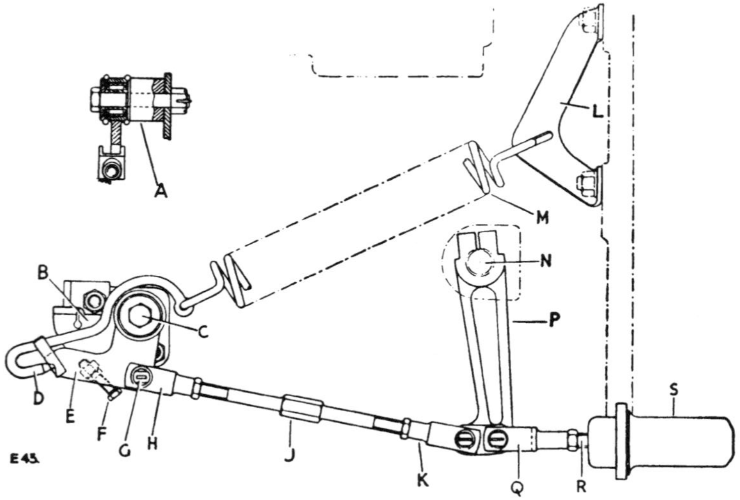

Layout of over-centre clutch linkage

A—Assembly of crank lever
B—Support bracket
C—Pivot bolt
D—Hook for balance spring
E—Crank lever
F—Adjustment bolt
G—Clevis pin
H—Clevis right-hand thread
J—Adjustment rod
K—Clevis left-hand thread
L—Anchor bracket for balance spring
M—Balance spring
N—Clutch cross-shaft
P—Clutch operating lever
Q—Clevis right-hand thread
R—Push rod for clutch slave cylinder
S—Clutch slave cylinder

Clutch pedal adjustment—Operation C-11

Workshop hand tools:

Spanner sizes: $\frac{7}{16}$ in. AF, $\frac{9}{16}$ in. AF   Pliers, long nosed

Pedal position, adjust

1. Adjust the pedal against the pedal stop 'B' to give a distance 'A' of 6 in. (152 mm) for right-hand drive cars and 6¾ in. (171 mm) for left-hand drive cars, from the bottom of pedal pad to floor.
2. Adjust and connect the push rod of master cylinder, so that the pivot pin can be aligned with the hole in pedal and push rod, with the pedal held against the pedal stop 'B'.
3. Fit the pedal return spring with anchor plate to the pivot pin and secure.
4. Finally adjust the pedal stop 'B' to give a minimum clearance of $\frac{1}{16}$ in. (1,5 mm) free movement of the push rod in master cylinder.

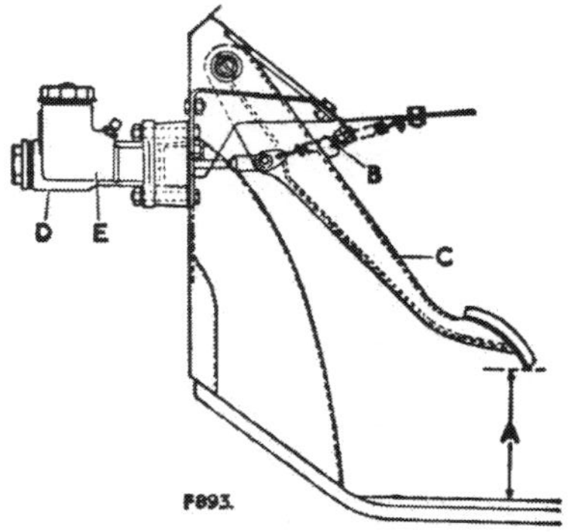

F893

Adjusting clutch pedal

A—6 in. (152 mm) for right-hand drive cars. 6¾ in. (171 mm) for left-hand drive cars
B—Pedal stop screw
C—Clutch pedal
D—Brake master cylinder
E—Clutch master cylinder

Clutch hydraulic system, to bleed—Operation C-12

Workshop hand tools:

Spanner sizes:

$\frac{7}{16}$ in. AF, ½ in. AF

Special tools:

Length of bleed tubing, Transparent container, Castrol Girling Crimson Brake Fluid (Specification SAE 70 R3)

Hydraulic system, bleed

1. Ensure that the pedal travel conforms to the adjustments detailed in Operation C-11.
2. Top up the master cylinder reservoir with Castrol Girling Crimson Brake Fluid (Specification SAE 70 R3) to the bottom of the filler neck.
3. Push one end of a suitable length of tubing over the bleed nipple on the slave cylinder.
4. The other end of the tube should be submerged in clean fluid, held in a suitable transparent container.
5. Slacken the bleed nipple and pump the clutch pedal, pausing at the end of each stroke, until the fluid issuing from the end of the submerged tube is entirely free of air bubbles.
6. Pump the clutch pedal once again and hold fully depressed while the bleed nipple is tightened. Ensure that the end of the tube is still under the fluid surface while tightening the nipple.
7. Replenish the fluid in the master cylinder reservoir as necessary.

NEVER USE FLUID THAT HAS JUST BEEN BLED FROM THE SYSTEM FOR TOPPING UP THE SUPPLY TANK—IT MAY BE AERATED.

DEFECT LOCATION

SYMPTOM	*POSSIBLE CAUSE*	*REMEDY*
A—GRABBING CLUTCH	1. Incorrect release lever adjustment	1. *Adjust*
	2. Oil on clutch lining	2. *Renew. Ensure oil drain holes in housing are not blocked*
	3. Worn clutch plate, lining or flywheel	3. *Renew*
	4. Clutch plate hub sticking on the pinion shaft	4. *Free off the clutch plate and check for wear and distortion. Check the pinion shaft for wear. Renew as necessary*
	5. Worn or binding release levers	5. *Wear on levers usually indicates a binding withdrawal race thrust bearing. Free off bearing and renew levers*
	6. Broken or weak pressure springs	6. *Renew*
	7. Sticking clutch pedal	7. *Free off the pedal and check for damaged or bent parts. Check the return spring*
	8. Damaged or deteriorated engine mountings, or engine loose in sub-frame	8. *Re-tighten or renew*
B—SLIPPING CLUTCH	1. Weak or broken pressure springs	1. *Renew*
	2. Worn clutch linings	2. *Renew and checkpressure plate for scoring*
	3. Incorrect clutch adjustment	3. *Adjust*
	4. Oil on linings	4. *Renew and rectify oil leaks. Ensure oil drain holes in housing are not blocked*
	5. Warped clutch plate	5. *Renew*
	6. Scored or damaged pressure plate	6. *Skim or renew*
	7. Binding release lever	7. *Free off the lever and check for wear. Examine the clutch components for wear or damage and the flywheel for scoring. Renew as necessary*
	8. Binding clutch pedal mechanism	8. *Rectify or renew*
	9. Fractured clutch plate	9. *See item C (5)*
	10. Leaking or faulty hydraulic system	10. *Rectify or renew*
C—DRAGGING OR SPINNING CLUTCH	1. Oil on linings	1. *Renew and rectify oil leak*
	2. Incorrect release lever or pedal adjustment	2. *Adjust*
	3. Incorrect adjustment of operating rod, master or slave cylinder	3. *Adjust*
	4. Dust or other foreign matter in clutch	4. *Clean and renew as necessary*
	5. Bent clutch plate	5. *Ascertain reason for damage, check the remainder of the clutch and renew the plate. A plate may be distorted due to the weight of the gearbox being allowed to hang on the plate during fitting*
	6. Clutch plate hub binding on the pinion shaft	6. *Free off the clutch plate and check for wear and distortion. Check the pinion shaft for wear. Renew as necessary*
	7. Primary pinion bush binding	7. *Renew*
	8. Clutch withdrawal sleeve sticking	8. *Rectify and examine all mating surfaces for wear or scoring*
	9. Warped pressure plate and cover	9. *Renew*
	10. Clutch plate linings too thick	10. *Renew*
	11. Broken linings	11. *Renew. Examine pressure plate for distortion*
	12. Insufficient fluid	12. *Bleed and replenish reservoir. Use only Castrol Girling Crimson Brake Fluid*
	13. Air in hydraulic system	13. *Bleed the system at slave cylinder*
D—RATTLING CLUTCH	1. Weak or broken cross-shaft operating lever return spring	1. *Renew*
	2. Damaged pressure plate	2. *Check reason for damage and renew as necessary*
	3. Weak or broken pedal lever return spring	3. *Renew*
	4. Pinion shaft or clutch plate splines worn	4. *Renew*
	5. Worn or loose primary pinion bush	5. *Renew*
	6. Unequal contact of release levers	6. *Re-adjust*
	7. Incorrect pedal free play	7. *Adjust*
	8. Damaged clutch plate, loose or broken springs, warped clutch plate	8. *Renew*
	9. Withdrawal mechanism worn	9. *Renew*
	10. Excessive transmission backlash	10. *Rectify*
	11. Normal wear in the clutch	11. *Renew as necessary*
E—SQUEAKING CLUTCH	1. Primary pinion bush binding	1. *Rectify and renew*
	2. Primary pinion bush turning in flywheel	2. *Renew*

DEFECT LOCATION—*continued*

SYMPTOM	*POSSIBLE CAUSE*	*REMEDY*
F—VIBRATING CLUTCH OR CLUTCH JUDDER	1. Incorrect clutch balance 2. Loose engine mountings 3. Worn propeller shaft universal joints 4. Loose flywheel 5. Oil or other foreign matter on the clutch lining 6. Contact area of friction surfaces unequal 7. Damaged clutch plate or pinion shaft 8. Pressure plate out of parallel with flywheel face	1. *Rectify and renew as necessary* 2. *Rectify* 3. *Renew* 4. *Tighten, using new locking plates. Check run-out* 5. *Renew and rectify oil leak. Ensure oil drain holes are not blocked* 6. *Rectify or renew* 7. *Renew* 8. *Rectify*
G—STIFF CLUTCH OPERATION	1. Clutch pedal lever pivot pin dry 2. Piston in master or slave cylinder seized	1. *Lubricate* 2. *Renew*
H—CLUTCH NOISY	1. Clutch plate hub splines worn 2. Worn primary pinion bush	1. *Renew* 2. *Renew*
J—FRACTURED CLUTCH PLATE	1. See Item C (5)	1. *Rectify and renew*
K—EXCESSIVE LINING WEAR	1. Produced by overloading or slipping clutch	1. *In the hands of the operator*

DATA

Clutch type	Single, dry plate, Borg and Beck
Plate diameter	10 in. (254,0 mm)
Plate thickness, new	.330 in. (8,4 mm) under load
Operation	Hydraulic
Adjustment	Slave cylinder push rod free travel $\frac{1}{16}$ in. to $\frac{3}{32}$ in. (1,5 mm to 2,5 mm)
Thrust race	Ball bearing
Thrust springs	Quantity: 12 Colour: Cream Poundage: 120 to 130 lb (54 to 59 kg) Free length: 2.680 in. (68,00 mm)
Plate damper springs	Colour: 3 green; 3 black and cream, in overrun slots
Release lever height	From flywheel face, using $\frac{3}{8}$ in. (9,5 mm) diameter distance pieces (gearbox selector plungers): 1.655 in. (42,0 mm)
Pressure plate regrind limit	.010 in. (0,25 mm). Minimum thickness of main body of pressure plate after re-facing .630 in. (16 mm)
Flywheel regrind limit	.030 in. (0,75 mm). Minimum thickness at the outer edge of flywheel after re-facing .742 in. (18 mm)
Master cylinder type	Girling CV
Slave cylinder	Girling
Fluid	Castrol Girling Crimson Brake Fluid (Specification SAE 70 R3)

Section D – GEARBOX AND OVERDRIVE – Part One

Brief description of gearbox assembly

The Rover designed and manufactured gearbox incorporates four forward speeds and reverse with synchromesh engagement for second, third and top gears.

The housing is made of die-cast aluminium.

Gear selection is made by a central floor-mounted lever and the gearbox may be supplied with or without an overdrive unit.

The gear ratios, details of which are given under Data, have been carefully selected to suit the engine output.

Gearbox or gearbox and overdrive removal procedure

Unit to be removed	*Method of removal*	*Operation*
Four-speed gearbox less overdrive	Complete with engine unit or From beneath the car leaving the engine in position	A1-6 D1-3 or D1-4
Four-speed gearbox with overdrive	Remove overdrive and extension casing first, from beneath car then Remove gearbox with engine or Remove gearbox from beneath the car, leaving engine in position	D2-2 A1-6 D2-2 then D1-3 or D1-4
Overdrive and extension casing	Remove from beneath the car	D2-2
Overdrive extension casing only	Must be removed complete with overdrive unit	D2-2

INDEX

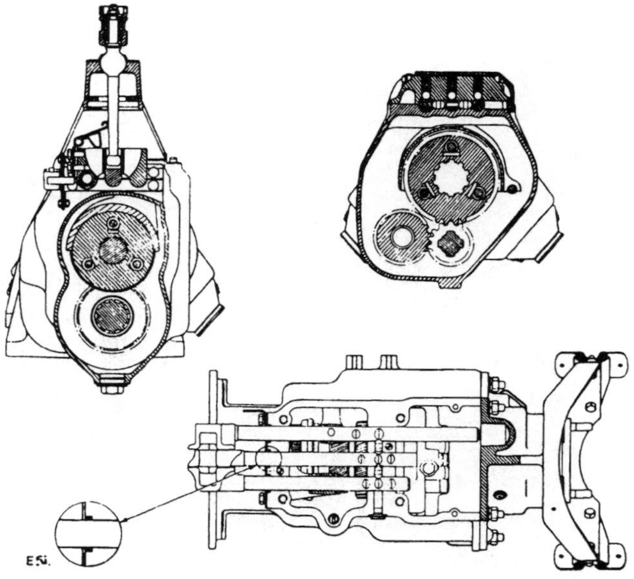

Plan view of gearbox

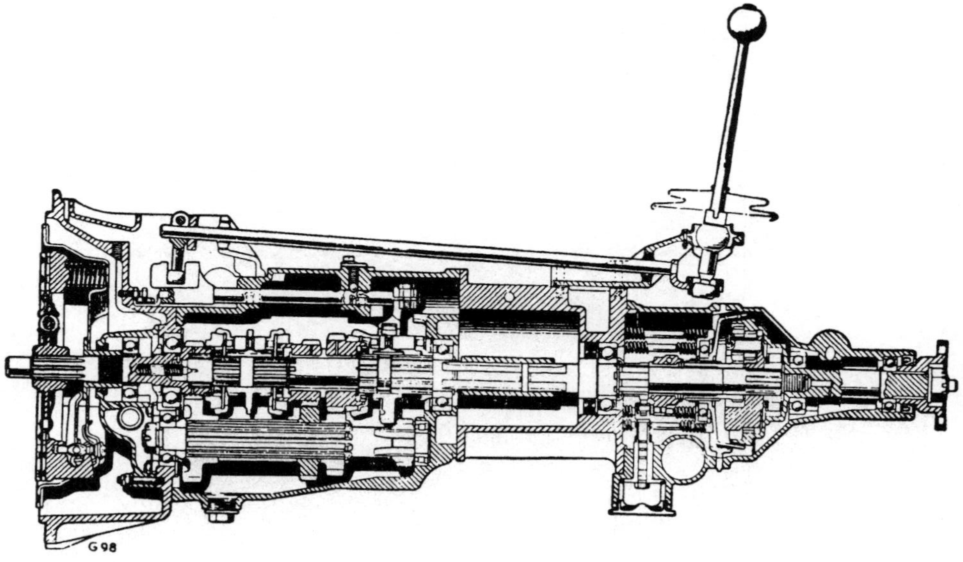

Cross-section of gearbox, side view, late type illustrated

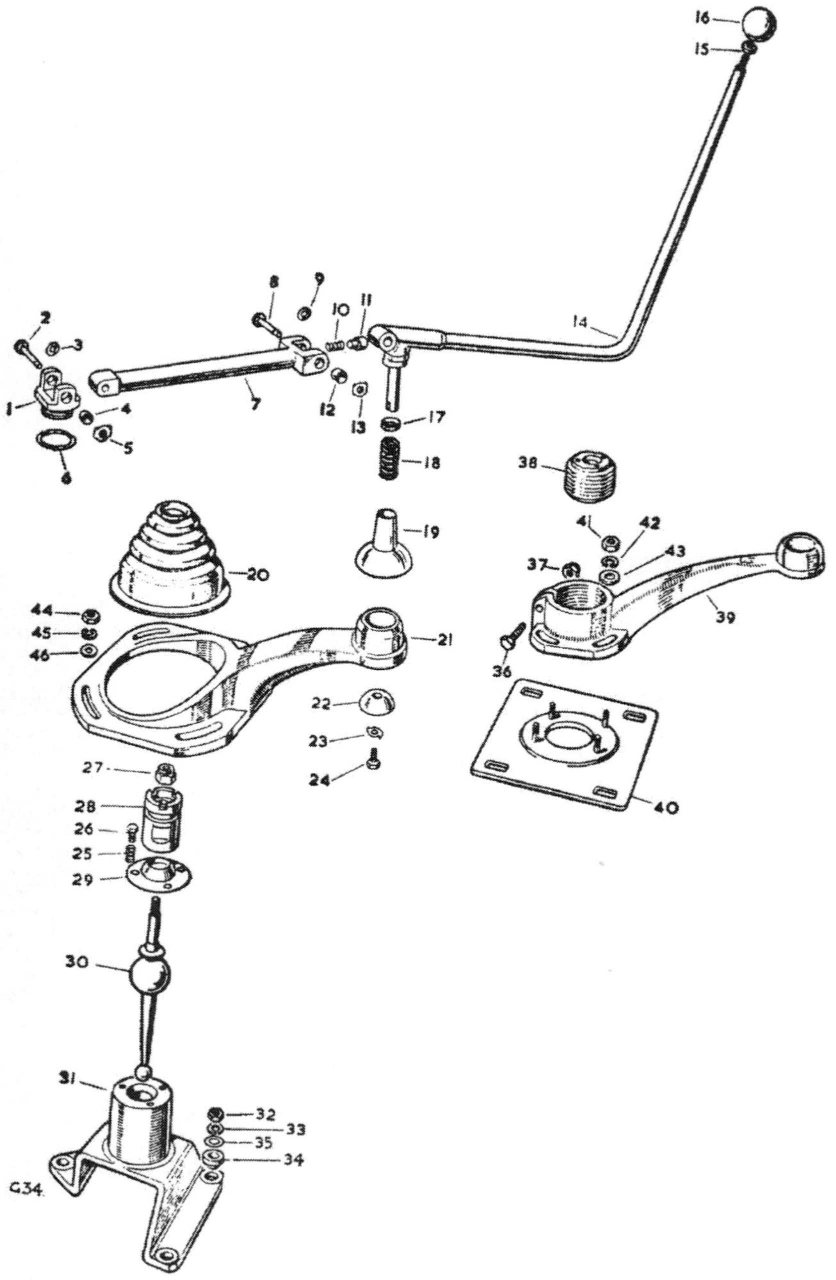

1	Forked end	22	Internal seat
2	Joint pin	23	Lock washer
3	Belleville washer	24	Set bolt (fixing pivot seats)
4	Bush for forked end	25	Spring
5	Special clip	26	Set screw
6	Locker, forked rod to selector lever	27	Self-locking nut
7	Forked rod	28	Insulator housing
8	Joint pin	29	Retainer for selector lever
9	Belleville washer	30	Gear change selector assembly
10	Spring for button	31	Housing assembly
11	Anti-rattle button	32	Nut
12	Bush for rod	33	Spring washer
13	Special clip	34	Rubber bush
14	Gear change lever	35	Plain washer
15	Locknut	36	Bolt
16	Knob	37	Self-locking nut
17	Collar	38	Housing assembly } Threaded
18	Spring	39	Support bracket } Threaded
19	External pivot seat	40	Mounting plate
20	Rubber cover	41–43	Fixings
21	Support bracket	44–46	Fixings

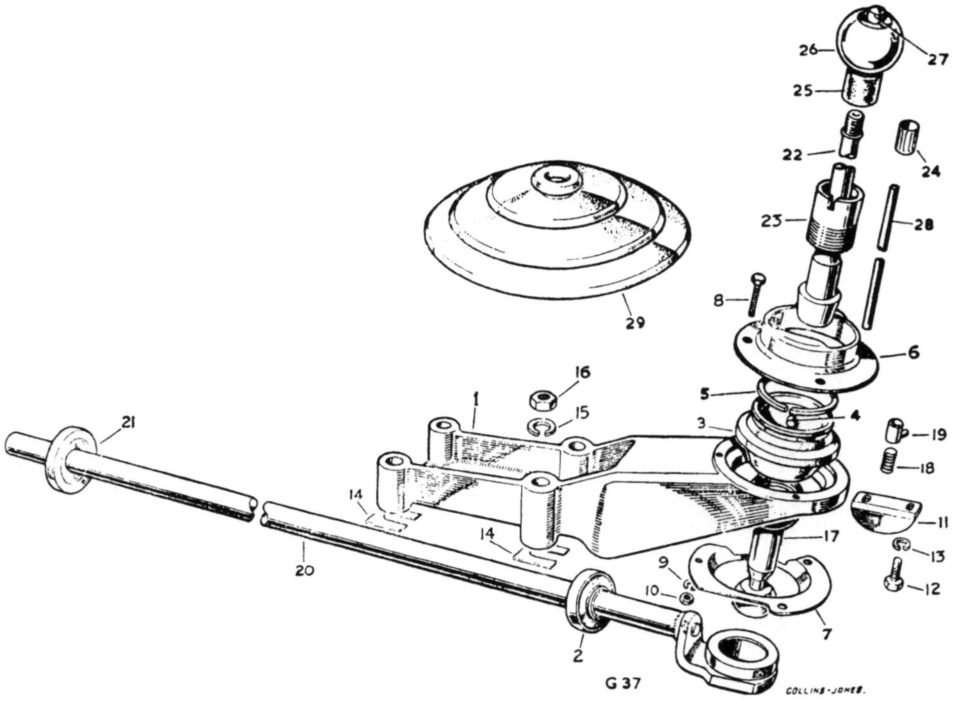

Gear change lever assembly, late type

1	Gear lever support bracket	15–16	Fixings
2	Bush, self-aligning	17	Gear lever lower
3	Spherical seat	18	Reverse stop spring
4	Locating pin	19	Pin for reverse
5	Circlip	20	Gear change shaft assembly
6	Retaining cap, top	21	Reverse stop washer for gear change shaft
7	Retaining cap, bottom	22	Gear change lever
8	Set screw	23	Locknut for base of gear change lever
9	Spring washer	24	Tolerance ring } Fixing gear change lever knob
10	Nut	25	Rubber sleeve } Fixing gear change lever knob
11	Reverse stop plate	26	Knob
12–13	Fixings	27	Button for knob
14	Shim for support bracket to casing	28	Control tube
		29	Grommet

Gear change lever assembly, to remove and refit—Operation D1-1

Workshop hand tools:
Spanner sizes: $\frac{1}{4}$ in. BSF, $\frac{3}{8}$ in. BSF, $\frac{1}{2}$ in. AF, $\frac{9}{16}$ in. AF

Gear change lever assembly, remove—all models

1. Remove the centre section of the front carpet and slide back the front seats as far as possible.

Mk I and Mk IA models, items 2 to 5

2. Remove the four nuts and washers securing the gear change support bracket to the tunnel cover.

3. Raise the large rubber grommet and remove the three small set screws and springs securing the selector lever retaining plate to the gear selector housing.

4. Release the locker securing the selector lever to the fork end and unscrew the lever and insulator housing assembly from the fork end.

5. Lift out the gear change unit.

Mk II and Mk III models, items 6 to 8

6. Remove grommet for gear lever and tunnel cover. Remove four nuts securing gear lever support bracket to gearbox extension.

7. Slacken off pinch bolt securing selector lever.

8. Lift gear lever complete with bracket and withdraw rod from front bush.

   Note position of any shim washers fitted under the bracket, which should be retained and refitted in the original position.

Gear change lever assembly, refit

1. Reverse removal procedure.

Early models (Mk I), item 2

2. Adjust the position of the support bracket on the gearbox cover as necessary.

Late Mk I and Mk IA models, items 3 to 7

3. Adjust gear selector mounting plate so that it is central in the adjustment slots. Leave nuts hand tight at this stage.

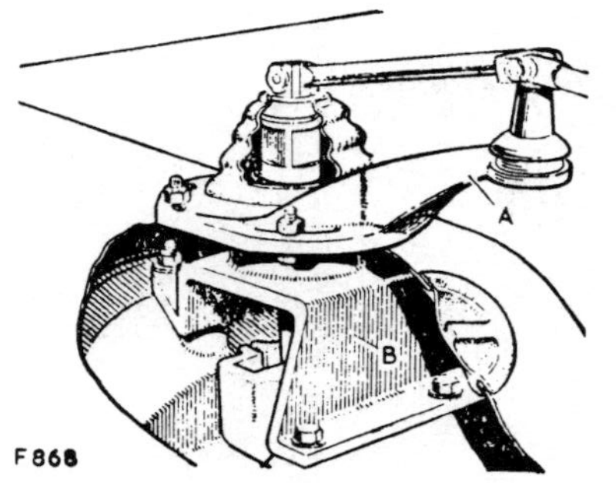

Gear change lever assembly, early Mk I models

A—Support bracket on tunnel cover
B—Housing assembly for gear selector, mounted on gearbox casing

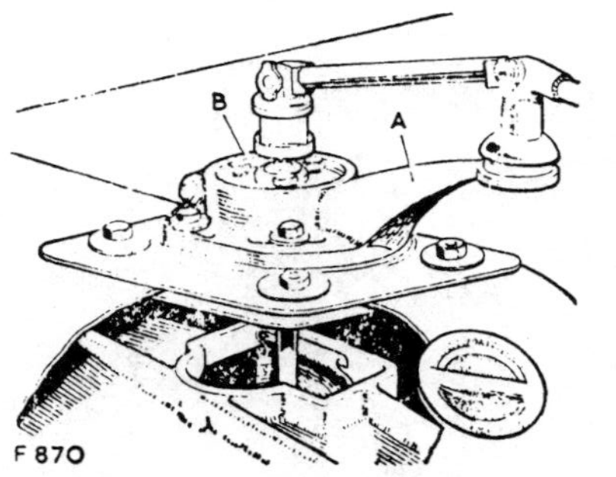

Gear change lever assembly, late Mk I and Mk IA models

A—Support bracket
B—Housing assembly for gear selector, mounted on tunnel cover

4. Set selector lever to approximate height, that is with selector two threads below top of housing, then fit gear selector lever to mounting plate. Ensure selector lever is in neutral and just touching the reverse stop, adjust mounting plate by sliding it fore and aft or from side to side until the selector lever is vertical.

5. When the gear selector lever has been fitted, it is necessary to adjust the position of the 'Vulkollan' pad on the end of the selector in relation to the selector jaws; this is done by slackening off the locking bolt on the support bracket for the gear lever pivot, then with the gear selector lever

Operation D1-1—*continued*

vertical, screw the selector housing clockwise until the 'Vulkollan' pad on the end of the selector lever is fully home in the selector jaw. Turn the housing anti-clockwise three and a half turns, then tighten locking bolt on support bracket for gear lever pivot.

6. After the selector lever height has been set, check that the lever is vertical when in neutral and just touching the reverse stop.

7. Tighten nuts fully and check operation of gear change mechanism.

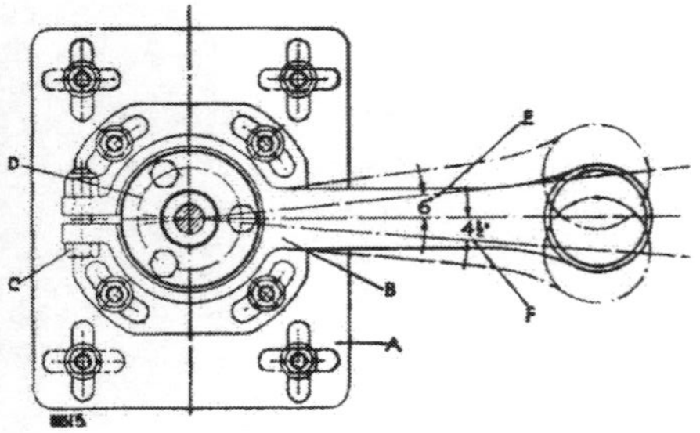

Gear selector mounting plate location

A—Mounting plate for gear selector
B—Support bracket for gear lever pivot
C—Locking bolt on support bracket
D—Housing for selector lever
E—Position of support bracket on right-hand drive models
F—Position of support bracket on left-hand drive models

Remote control gear change lever assembly setting—Mk II and Mk III models, items 8 to 15

8. Ensure that the reverse stop washer, between the selector lever and front bush for gear change shaft, is fitted with the recess towards the rear of the car.

9. Move the gear lever until the bush in the remote control shaft is parallel to the underside of the gear lever support bracket, looking from the rear, and with the gear lever set at an angle of 94° from the remote control shaft.

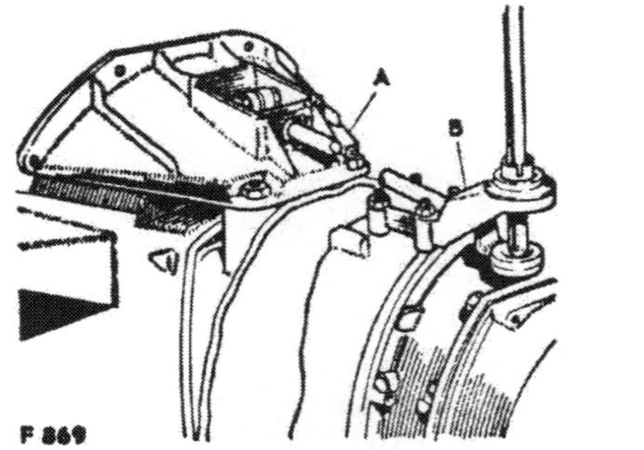

Gear change lever assembly, Mk II and Mk III models
A—Top support stiffener B—Support bracket

10. Measure the gap between the bottom of support bracket and the top of the remote control rod bush; this should be not less than 1.460 in. (37 mm) or more than 1.490 in. (38 mm). Adjust as necessary by fitting shim washers under either front or rear studs of the support bracket as required.

11. Ensure all selector shafts are in neutral, then set gear lever to 94° as detailed above. Move gear lever sideways to the third-fourth position until the bush on the remote control shaft is just clear of the conical part of the gear lever.

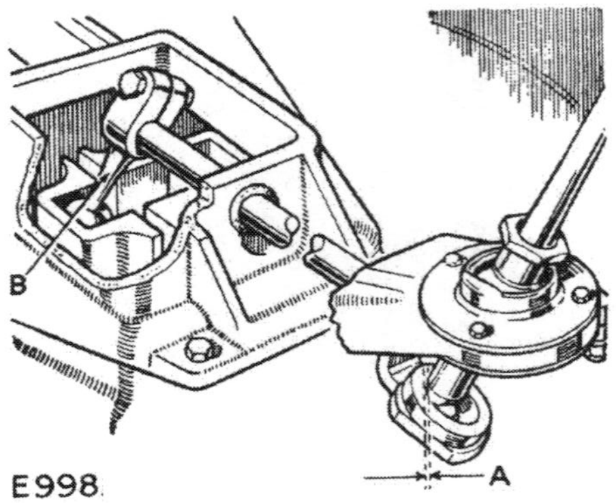

Location of gear lever, when setting selector lever, Mk II and Mk III models
A—Bush just clear of gear lever B—Position of selector lever

Operation D1-1—*continued*

2. With the gear lever held in this position and the selector lever held firmly in the third-fourth gear selector shaft jaw, tighten selector lever clamping bolt.

Select first gear, hold gear lever to the left and check gap between end of reverse stop pin and reverse stop plate, which should be .010–.012 in. (0,25–0,30 mm). Slacken off reverse stop plate bolts to adjust if required.

1 Finally select second gear and check adjustment again.

15 Check that all gears, including reverse, can be engaged.

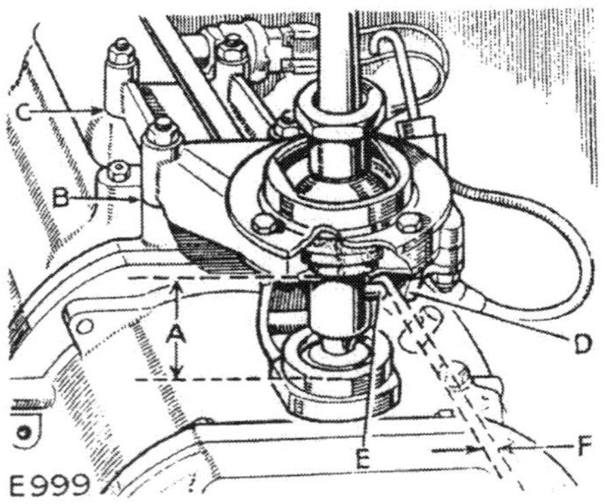

Checking position of gear lever remote control and setting reverse stop plate

A—1.400 in. (37 mm) to 1.490 in. (38 mm)
B—Shim washers under rear studs if required or
C—Shim washers under front studs if required
D—Reverse stop plate
E—Reverse stop pin
F—.010–.012 in. (0,25–0,30 mm)

Gear change lever assemblies, to overhaul—Operation D1–2

Workshop hand tools:

Screwdriver

Spanner sizes: $\frac{1}{4}$ in. BSF, $\frac{5}{16}$ in. BSF, $\frac{3}{8}$ in. BSF, $\frac{1}{4}$ in. AF, $\frac{7}{16}$ in. AF, $\frac{9}{16}$ in. AF

For gear change lever removal instructions, see Operation D1-1

Mk I and Mk IA models

1. Free the lock washer and remove the bolt securing the pivot pin of the lever to the support bracket; remove the internal and external pivot seats and spring.
2. Spring off the two special clips and press out the fork joint pins, taking care not to lose the Belleville washers on each pin.
3. If necessary, press out the bushes from the forked end and rod. Remove the Tufnol anti-rattle button and spring from the rod.
4. Remove the self-locking nut and withdraw the insulator housing from the selector lever.
5. Reassemble the unit: the insulator housing is available only as an assembly, and a new unit should be fitted complete with the top distance washer, which will be found attached to it.
6. Fit new bushes to the forked end and forked rod. Fit the spring and Tufnol button to the forked rod.
7. The joint pins must be an easy fit in the bushes when fitted and must be a press fit in the gear lever and forked rod. The Belleville washers are fitted on the deeper flats of the gear lever and forked rod.
8. When fitted, the heads of the joint pins and the special clips should be clear of the fork end and forked rod.
9. Fit the gear lever to the support bracket at the pivot point, using new components as required; fully tighten the pivot set bolt and lock over the special washer.
10. If necessary, renew the insulator pad in the gear change housing; with the arrow on the pad pointing to the rear along the centre-line of the gearbox, and the word "Top" uppermost.

Mk II and Mk III models, remote control type

11. Remove the three set screws, spring washers and nuts, securing the top and bottom retaining caps to gear lever support brackets.
12. Withdraw the gear lever assembly with the spherical seat from the support bracket and discard.
13. Fit gear lever assembly to the support bracket, less the control tube and push-button fittings, using the original fixings. No lubricant should be used when fitting.
14. Position the rubber grommet over the gear change lever.
15. Insert the control tube into the centre of gear lever and ensure that the tube is pushed firmly down on to the reverse stop pin.
16. Engage reverse gear, then cut off the trim and control tube exactly $\frac{13}{32}$ in. (10 mm) from the top of gear lever.

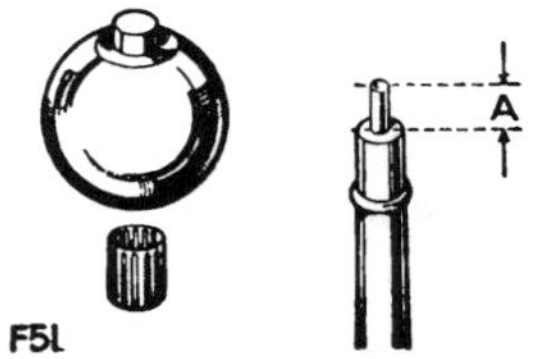

F5L

Cutting control tube for reverse stop

A—$\frac{13}{32}$ in. (10 mm)

17. *Important.* If the tube is cut too long the reverse pin will be below the reverse stop plate when the knob is fitted.

    If the tube is cut too short it will be difficult to engage reverse gear, having to depress the button further down the knob.
18. Fit button in position on control tube and press knob together with rubber sleeve or tolerance ring, on to the gear lever. Check the operation of gear lever in all gears.
19. After fitting, no attempt should be made to loosen the locknut at the base of lever for removal.

4-speed Gearbox, to remove and refit, (early models with 4-point engine mounting) Operation D1–3

Workshop hand tools:

Screwdriver, medium

Spanner sizes: $\frac{1}{2}$ in. AF, $\frac{9}{16}$ in. AF, $\frac{1}{2}$ in. BSF, $\frac{5}{16}$ in. Whit

It is recommended that the car is placed on a suitable ramp or over an inspection pit before commencing this operation

Gearbox, remove

1. Drain the oil from the gearbox, and overdrive unit where fitted.
2. Disconnect the battery, situated in the luggage compartment.
3. Remove the gear change lever assembly. Operation D1-1.
4. Remove the gearbox cover from the floor panel.
5. Remove the front exhaust pipe, secured by there bolts, nuts and spring washers at each flange. Remove securing bracket from bell-housing where fitted.
6. Detach the propeller shaft centre bearing bracket from the propeller shaft tunnel, secured by four bolts, nuts, washers and grommets.
7. Disconnect the front propeller shaft drive flange from the gearbox output flange, secured by four bolts, nuts and washers.
8. Disconnect the wiring from the reverse light switch, and where fitted, from the overdrive solenoid.
9. Support the unit with a jack placed under the flywheel housing. Remove the bolts, nuts and washers fixing the two mountings to chassis sub-frame beneath the speedometer housing (4-speed models) or extension casing assembly on overdrive models.
10. Remove the driving flange from the output shaft of the gearbox, secured by a self-locking nut and washer.
11. Remove the rear mounting bracket, secured to the speedometer drive housing by four nuts and spring washers.
12. Disconnect the clutch pedal return spring, or on late models over-centre spring.
13. Remove the clevis pin from the clutch lever.
14. Remove the clutch slave cylinder secured by two bolts and self-locking nuts to the bell-housing. Do not disconnect the hydraulic pipe as the cylinder can be supported out of the way.

    Prevent the clutch pedal being depressed as this will cause the slave cylinder components to be expelled from the cylinder.
15. Disconnect the speedometer cable.
16. Remove overdrive unit, where fitted. Operation D2-2.
17. Remove the bell-housing fixing nuts and washers.
18. Lower the jack under the flywheel housing as far as possible without straining components.
19. Draw the gearbox and bell-housing assembly rearwards to clear the primary shaft from the clutch unit.
20. Turn the gearbox through 90° to facilitate removal from under the body.

Gearbox, refit

1. Reverse removal procedure.

4-speed Gearbox, to remove and refit, (late models with 5-point engine mounting) Operation D1–4

Workshop hand tools:

Spanner sizes: $\frac{1}{2}$ in. AF, $\frac{9}{16}$ in. AF, $\frac{5}{16}$ in. Whit

It is recommended that the car is placed on a suitable ramp or over an inspection pit before commencing this operation

Gearbox, remove

1. Drain the oil from the gearbox and overdrive unit.
2. Disconnect the battery, situated in the luggage compartment.
3. Remove the gear change lever assembly. Operation D1-1.
4. Remove the gearbox cover from the floor panel.
5. Remove the front exhaust pipe, secured by three bolts, nuts and washers at each flange and by a bracket to the bell-housing.
6. Detach the propeller shaft centre bearing bracket from the propeller shaft tunnel, secured by four bolts, nuts, washers and grommets.
7. Disconnect the wiring from the reverse light switch and the overdrive solenoid.
8. Slacken the $2\frac{1}{4}$ in. long bolt securing stabiliser bracket to sub-frame bracket beneath the speedometer housing on 4-speed models, or extension casing assembly on overdrive models. Remove the nuts and washers securing the stabiliser bracket to the reaction bracket.
9. Place a jack beneath the flywheel housing. Raise the jack sufficiently to support the unit when the two rear mountings are released.
10. Remove fixings from the mounting between the flywheel housing (LH side) and sub-frame.
11. Remove fixings from the mounting between cylinder block (RH side) and sub-frame.
12. Raise the unit with the jack just enough to be able to release the stabiliser bracket and swing it clear. Note the number of shims used under the bracket. Leave the unit jacked up.
13. Remove the driving flange from the output shaft of the gearbox secured by a self-locking nut and washer.
14. Disconnect the clutch pedal return spring, or over-centre spring where fitted.
15. Remove the clevis pin from the clutch lever.
16. Remove the clutch slave cylinder secured by two bolts and self-locking nuts to the bell-housing.

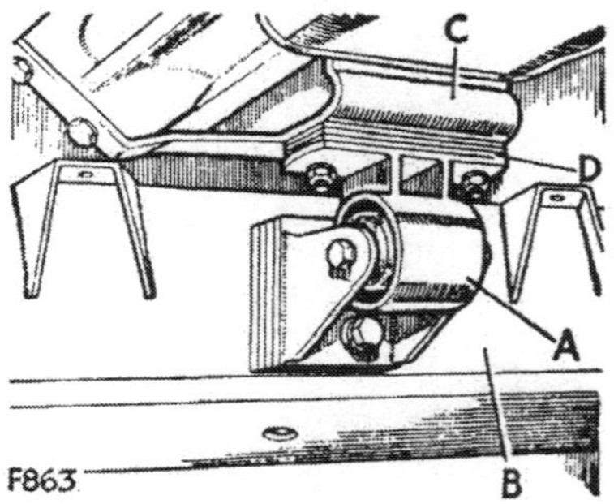

F863

A—Stabiliser bracket to gearbox
B—Sub-frame bracket
C—Reaction bracket
D—Shims

Do not disconnect the hydraulic pipe, as the cylinder can be supported out of the way.

Prevent the clutch pedal being depressed as this will cause the slave cylinder components to be expelled from the cylinder.

17. Disconnect the speedometer cable.
18. Remove overdrive unit, where fitted. Operation D2-2.
19. Remove the bell-housing fixing nuts and washers.
20. Lower the jack under the flywheel housing as much as possible without straining components.
21. Draw the gearbox and bell-housing assembly rearwards to clear the primary shaft from the clutch unit.
22. Turn the gearbox through 90° to facilitate removal from under the body.

Gearbox, refit

1. Reverse removal procedure.
2. Preserve correct engine height and alignment by adding or subtracting shims as necessary, between reaction bracket and stabiliser bracket.

Operation D1–4—*continued*

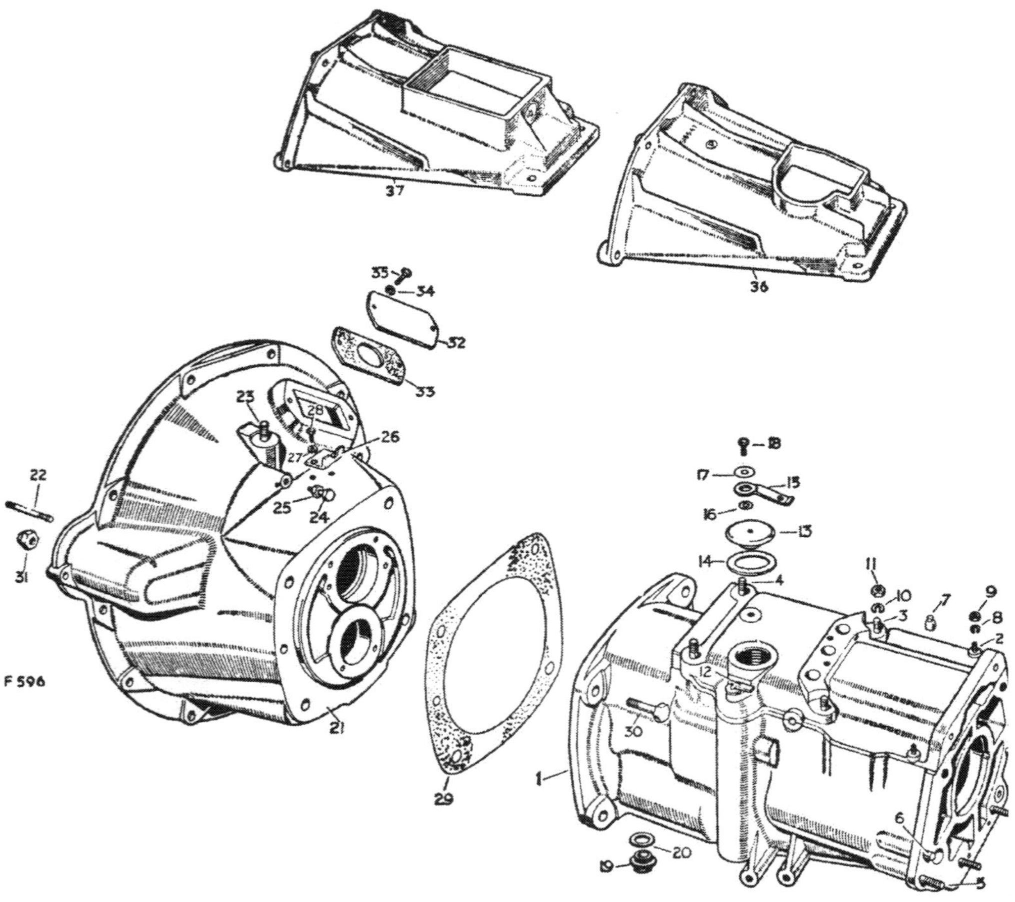

F 596

Gearbox casing and bell-housing

1	Gearbox casing
2–3	Studs for top cover
4	Stud for cover and gear change
5	Stud for speedometer housing
6	Dowel
7	Dowel for cover
8–11	Fixings, top cover
12	Oil level rod
13	Oil filler cap
14	Washer
15	Retaining spring
16–18	Fixings, retaining spring to gearbox cover
19	Drain plug
20	Joint washer
21	Bell-housing
22	Stud for clutch withdrawal housing
23	Stud for gear selector housing
24–25	Second speed stop
26	Bracket for reverse stop
27–28	Fixings, stop bracket
29	Joint washer
30–31	Fixings, bell-housing to gearbox
32	Inspection cover
3–35	Fixings, inspection cover
36	Top support stiffener, Mk IA
37	Top support stiffener, Mk II

Operation D1-4—*continued*

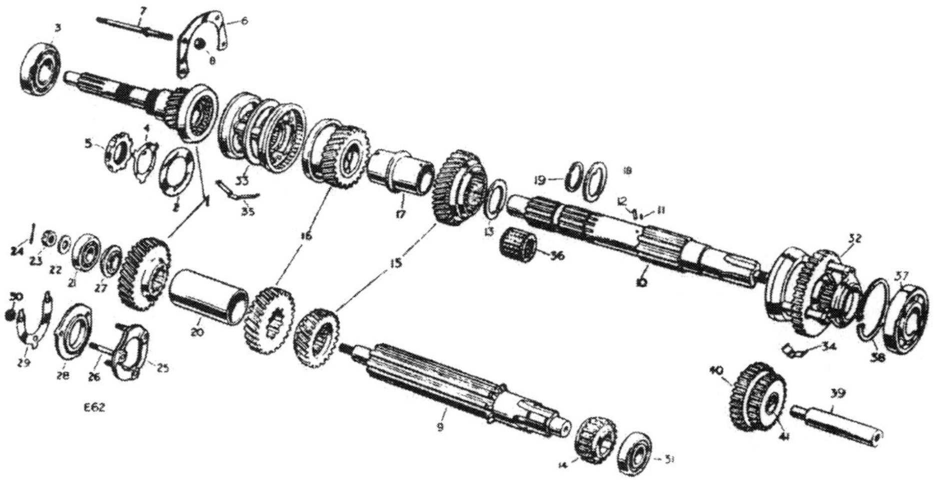

Four-speed gearbox shafts and gears

1	Primary shaft and constant gear	22–24	Fixings, bearing to layshaft
2	Shield for primary shaft	25	Bearing plate
3	Bearing for primary shaft	26	Stud
4–5	Fixings, bearing to shaft	27	Distance piece
6–8	Fixings, bearing to housing	28	Retaining plate
9	Layshaft	29–30	Fixings, plate and bearing
10	Mainshaft	31	Rear layshaft bearing
11	Peg for 2nd gear thrust washer	32	Synchronising clutch, 2nd speed and 1st speed gear
12	Peg for mainshaft bush	33	Synchronising clutch, 3rd and 4th speed
13	Thrust washer, 2nd gear	34	Detent spring for clutch, 2nd speed
14	1st speed layshaft gear	35	Detent spring for clutch, 3rd and 4th speed
15	2nd speed gears	36	Roller bearing for mainshaft
16	3rd speed gears	37	Rear mainshaft bearing
17	Mainshaft bush	38	Circlip for bearing
18	Thrust washer, 3rd speed	39	Shaft for reverse gear
19	Spring ring	40	Reverse gear
20	Sleeve for layshaft	41	Bush for reverse gear
21	Front layshaft bearing		

Gearbox, 4-speed, to overhaul—Operation D1-5

Workshop hand tools:
Feeler gauges
Spanner sizes:
$\frac{1}{4}$ in. BSF, $\frac{5}{16}$ in. BSF, $\frac{3}{8}$ in. BSF

Special tools:
Circlip pliers
Extraction drift, Part No. 266473

For gearbox removal, see Operation D1-3 *or* D1-4

Gearbox, dismantle

1. Support the gearbox on a suitable stand.
2. Remove the speedometer drive housing from the rear of the gearbox casing secured with nuts, bolts and washers.
3. If necessary remove the speedometer drive gear and the rear oil seal from the housing.
4. Remove the operating lever, secured to the cross-shaft by a pinch bolt.
5. Remove the clutch withdrawal unit complete, secured to the bell-housing by seven self-locking nuts.
6. Remove the selector spring retaining plate secured by two bolts and spring washers. Lift out the three small springs.
7. Remove the gearbox oil level rod.
8. Remove the gearbox cover secured by four nuts and washers. Take care that the selector balls and plungers do not fall into the gearbox.
9. Remove the gear selector shafts as follows:

   Engage first gear and remove the reverse selector shaft by lifting and turning.

   Remove the 1st-2nd and 3rd-4th selectors together by pulling the shafts back (away from the bell-housing) and lifting out.
10. Lock the layshaft by engaging two gears and at this stage remove the split pin, castle nut and washer from end of the layshaft (in the bell-housing).

    If the primary shaft or bearing is to be removed from the bell-housing slacken the large special locknut, which has a left-hand thread.
11. Remove the bell-housing securing bolts (two of which are fitted bolts which must not be replaced by standard bolts).
12. Tap off the bell-housing complete with primary shaft and layshaft constant gear, but prevent the layshaft from coming away by tapping it back through the bell-housing bearing.
13. Remove the layshaft constant gear and conical distance piece from the housing.
14. Remove the layshaft front bearing plate, secured by three nuts and a lock plate.
15. Press out the front layshaft bearing and retaining plate. Use extraction drift (Part No. 266473).
16. Remove the four self-locking nuts securing the primary shaft bearing in the bell-housing, and if necessary remove the extension studs.
17. Remove the special locknut (LH thread) and lockwasher. Press the primary shaft together with the bearing and shield from the housing.

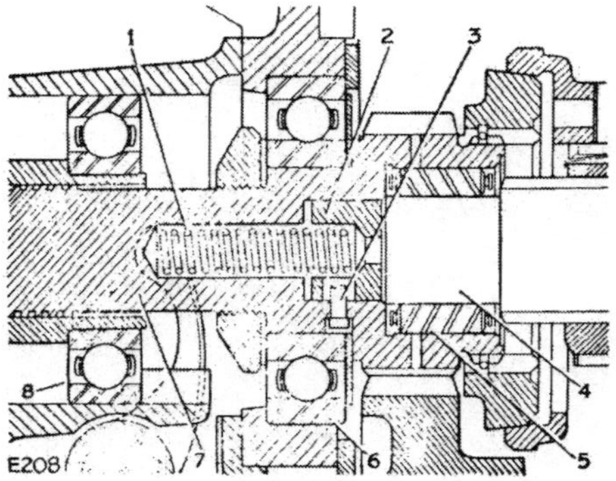

Cross-section of clutch plate decelerator

1. Spring for clutch plate decelerator
2. Button for clutch plate decelerator
3. Pin for clutch plate decelerator
4. Mainshaft
5. Roller bearing for mainshaft
6. Ball bearing for primary pinion
7. Primary pinion
8. Withdrawal race thrust bearing

Operation D1-5—*continued*

18. Press the bearing off the primary shaft and remove the shield. If necessary extract the retaining pin and withdraw the decelerator spring and button.
19. Slide the synchronising clutch off the mainshaft. noting that the annular groove in the inner hub faces the third-speed gear.
20. Withdraw the layshaft complete from the gear-box.
21. Slide off the distance tube, third and second constant gears. If necessary, press off the first layshaft gear and rear bearing.
22. Drive the mainshaft forward out of its bearing in the casing. Use a thimble on the threaded end to protect the thread.
23. Remove the circlip from the bell-housing end of the mainshaft and slide off the first-speed gear and synchronising clutch from the mainshaft.
24. Remove the spring ring, located inside the third-gear recess and slide off the thrust washer, third-speed gear, bush, and second-speed gear.
25. If necessary remove the pegs from mainshaft and remove the rear thrust washer.
26. Remove the internal circlip securing the main-shaft rear bearing inside the casing, heat the casing uniformly to 90–100°F (32,2–37,8°C) which is the temperature of a normal degreaser unit, and press out the bearing.
27. Remove the layshaft rear bearing by using a punch through the two small holes in the casing.
28. Extract the reverse gear shaft and remove the reverse gear.
29. If necessary, press out the second-speed selector fork locating pin.

Gearbox, rebuild

1. Fit the mainshaft and layshaft rear bearings by uniformly heating the casing to 90–100°F (32,2–37,8°C) and pressing the bearing in until it abuts the casing flange. Fit the second-speed selector fork pin, if this was removed.
2. If a new reverse gear bush is fitted it must be a press fit in the gear and both ends should be bell-mouthed to prevent the bush moving in the gear. When fitted, the reverse gear bush should be a sliding fit on the reverse gear shaft.
3. With casing still warm, press in the reverse shaft locating the gear with its smaller wheel to the rear.
4. Secure the mainshaft rear bearing in position with the large internal circlip.
5. If removed, replace the rear thrust washer. Do not fit the large bush locating peg at this stage.

   Slide on the mainshaft bush with the large locating slot to the rear, together with second-speed gear synchromesh cone to the rear.
6. Place the third-speed gear on the bush with the gear wheel against the shoulder, and secure with the second thrust washer and the original spring ring.
7. While pressing the third-speed gear hard against the bush shoulder, the end-float of the second-speed gear, measured between the gear and the bush shoulder, should be between .004 in. to .007 in. (0,10 to 0,18 mm). The third-speed gear end-float should be the same, measured with the second-speed gear pressed hard against the bush shoulder.
8. If the end-float of the gear is insufficient, a new mainshaft bush must be fitted, if excessive it may be reduced by rubbing down the end face of the bush of the gear being checked.

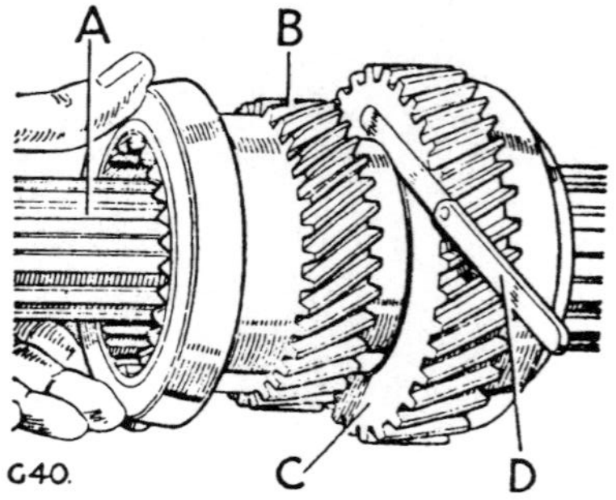

Measuring mainshaft gear end-float

A—Mainshaft C—Second-speed gear
B—Third-speed gear D—Feeler gauge

9. Remove the spring ring, take off the thrust washer, bush and gears, and replace the bush and washer, again securing with the original spring ring.

Operation D1-5—*continued*

10. An end-float of .001 to .008 in. (0,03 to 0,20 mm) for the mainshaft bush is allowed, but this should be kept as low as possible by the use of the thrust washers, which are supplied in four thicknesses—.125 in., .128 in., .130 in. and .135 in. (3,175 mm, 3,25 mm, 3,30 mm and 3,43 mm).

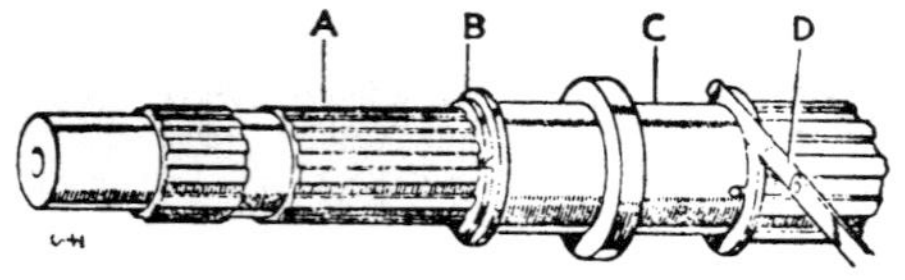

Measuring mainshaft bush end-float

A—Mainshaft C—Bush
B—Spring ring D—Feeler gauge

11. When the tolerances are correct, fit the rear thrust washer and the bush locating peg. Assemble the bush and gears, and slide on the front thrust washer with its groove in line with the small slot in the bush.
12. Secure the assembly with a new spring ring.
13. Slide the first-speed gear and synchronising clutch on to the rear of the shaft, and drive the mainshaft in to the rear bearing of the main casing, securing with the circlip.

Special attention must be paid to the following

(*a*) Layshafts that are fitted with a plain conical distance piece type 'A' should not have any end-float between the gears and distance sleeve when assembled but are to be locked up solid.

(*b*) Layshafts that are fitted with a shouldered conical distance piece type 'B' must have .003 to .005 in. (0,08–0,13 mm) end-float between the gears and distance sleeve when assembled; oversize sleeves are available for end-float adjustments.

(*c*) The layshaft assemblies referred to in (*a*) and (*b*) are interchangeable as assemblies only—component parts are not generally interchangeable.

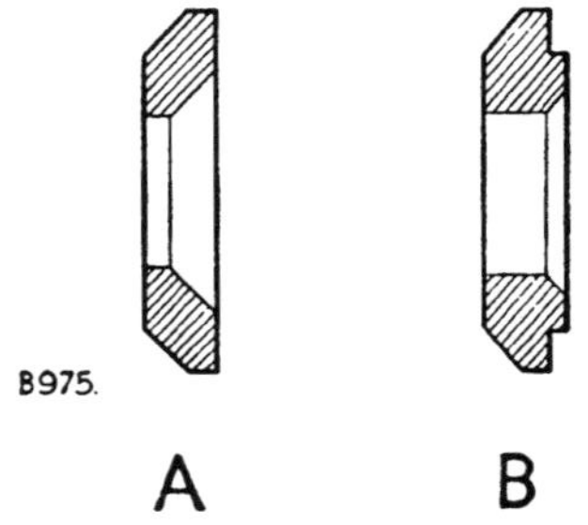

Layshaft distance pieces

14. To check the end-float of gears on the layshaft the component parts should be assembled temporarily as follows:

    Slide the first-speed layshaft gear over the splines on to the rear of the layshaft, with chamfered end of the teeth forward, then fit the rear bearing inner race on to the shaft. The bearing must be a tap fit on shaft.

    Slide the second-speed gear on to the layshaft with flange facing forward and plain side against layshaft shoulder.
15. Slide the third-speed gear on to the layshaft with the larger shoulder facing forward, the distance sleeve, constant gear, distance piece and bearing to follow respectively. Tighten the whole assembly, using the slotted nut and plain washer, then check the end-float, which should be .003 to .005 in. (0,08 to 0,13 mm). The illustration shows a method of checking the layshaft end-float where the bearing has not been removed from the bell-housing.
16. Remove the securing nut, plain washer, bearing, distance washer and constant gear from layshaft and insert shaft complete with distance sleeve, third- and second-speed gears, first-speed gear and rear bearing into gearbox.
17. If removed, refit the decelerator spring to the primary shaft and secure with button and pin. Place the bearing shield on the primary shaft and press the bearing on to the shaft until the shield is held against the shoulder.

Operation D1-5—*continued*

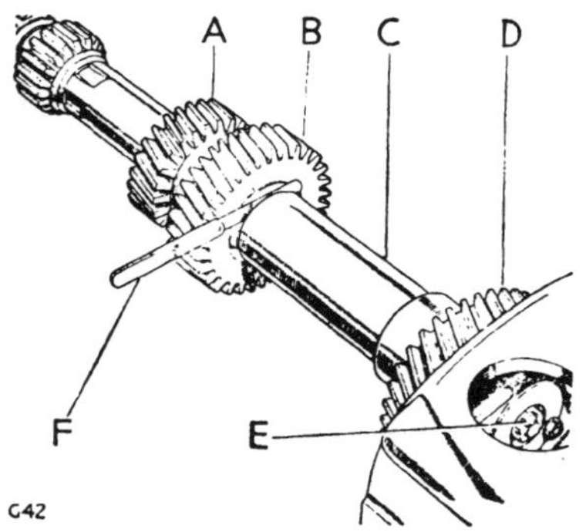

G42

Measuring layshaft end-float

A—Second-speed gear
B—Third-speed gear
C—Distance sleeve
D—Constant gear
E—Slotted nut
F—Feeler gauge

18. Secure the bearing in position with the lock washer and serrated nut, which has a left-hand thread.

19. Warm the bell-housing to 90–100°F, the temperature of a normal degreaser, press in the shaft and bearing, and secure with the short ends of the four clutch withdrawal studs, the retaining plate and self-locking nuts.

20. With the housing still warm, press in the layshaft bearing until it is flush with the rear face of the housing, and secure with the stud plate inserted from the rear, retaining plate, locker plate, and nuts.

21. Place the smaller diameter of the conical distance washer on the layshaft front bearing, and the layshaft constant gear on the washer in mesh with the primary shaft.

22. Slide the third/fourth synchromesh unit, with the cut-away portion of the internal splines to the rear, on to the mainshaft, followed by the mainshaft front bearing.

23. Offer the bell-housing and new joint washer to the gearbox, carefully locating the two shafts and secure with four bolts, two of which are fitted bolts.

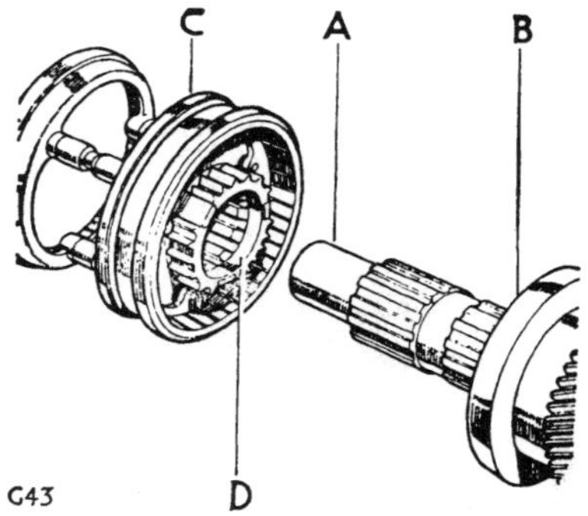

G43

Refitting the third/fourth synchromesh unit

A—Mainshaft
B—Third gear
C—Synchro clutch
D—Recess

24. Engage two gears and secure the layshaft in the bearing with a plain washer, castle nut and split pin.

25. Refit the clutch withdrawal unit and joint washer, and secure with self-locking nuts. For overhaul of clutch withdrawal unit see Operation C-8.

26. The clutch operating lever can be fitted to the operating shaft during refitment of the gearbox unit, see Operation C-10.

27. Slide a new sealing ring on to each selector shaft, followed by the selector forks, securing with pinch bolts.

28. Engage third gear and fit the third/fourth selector, with its sealing ring in the recess outside the gearbox.

29. Partially engage first gear and locate the first/second selector.

30. Engage first gear and enter the reverse selector into the gearbox with the shaft at right-angles to the mainshaft; lower and turn the selector until it can be correctly positioned.

31. With the interlocking plungers in place between the selector shafts, secure the top cover with nuts and spring washers.

Operation D1-5—*continued*

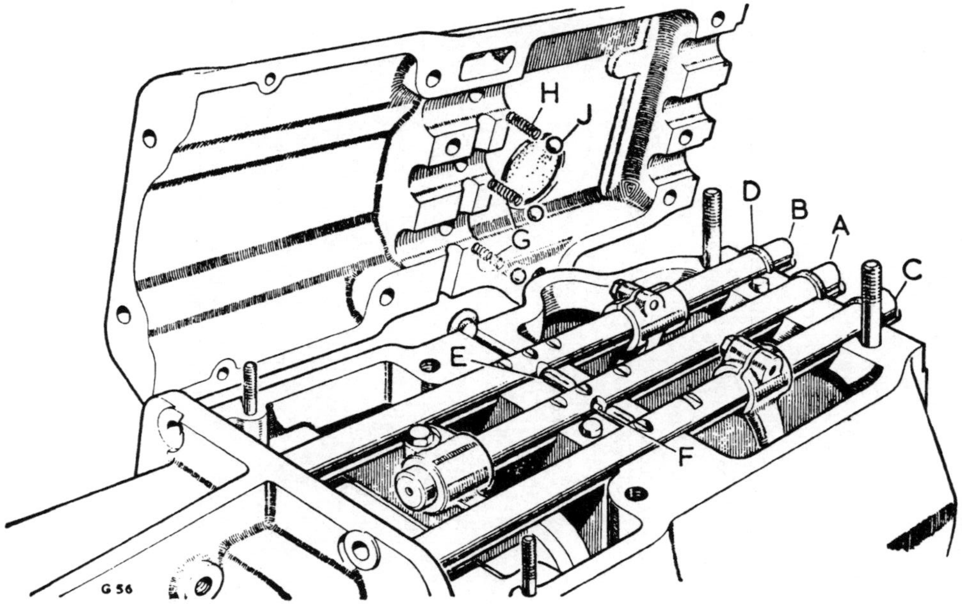

G 56

Gearbox selector shafts in position

A—Selector shaft, 1st and 2nd speeds
B—Selector shaft, 3rd and 4th speeds
C—Selector shaft, reverse speed
D—Sealing ring for shafts
E—Interlocking plungers
F—Interlocking pin
G—Selector spring, forward
H—Selector spring, reverse
J—Steel ball

32. Fit the seal retainers over the selector shaft sealing rings, and secure the retainers and reverse light switch to the gearbox.

33. Drop the selector balls and springs into the bores; insert the rubber plug into interlocking plunger hole, then fit the gasket and retaining plate.

34. Set the first/second selector stop so that when second gear is engaged there is .002 in. (0,05 mm) clearance between stop and jaw.

35. Where applicable, refit the distance piece and speedometer driving gear to the output shaft. Renew the joint washer, and refit the speedometer housing complete with speedometer drive. Fit a new rear oil seal, first smearing it with Molytone 'C'.

Operation D1-5—*continued*

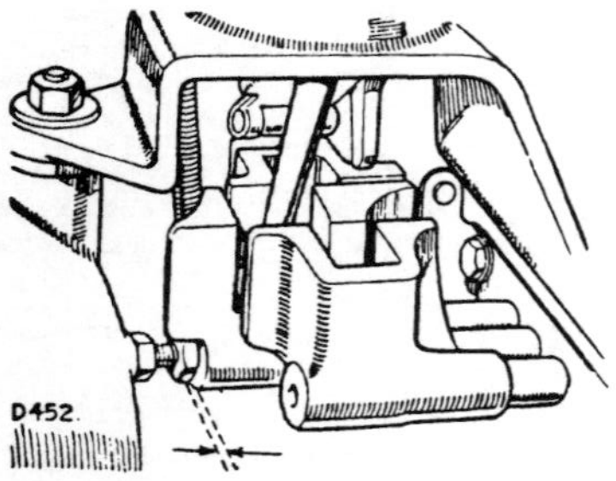

Checking second-speed stop

36. **Early models.** Do not fit the rear mounting bearer plate or driving flange at this stage.

37. **Late models.** Do not fit the driving flange at this stage.

Speedometer drive gear, to remove and refit—Operation D1–6

Workshop hand tools:
Spanner sizes: 2 BA, $\frac{1}{4}$ in. Whit

Spindle, remove

1. **Models without overdrive.** Disconnect the speedometer drive cable at the drive housing, secured by a plate and three set-bolts and spring washers.
2. **Models with overdrive.** Disconnect the speedometer drive cable at the drive housing by unscrewing the knurled nut.
3. Remove the speedometer spindle retaining plate secured by two set screws.
4. Withdraw the spindle bush and spindle.

Spindle, refit

1. Reverse removal procedure.

Section D – GEARBOX AND OVERDRIVE – Part Two

Overdrive unit—General description and working principle

The overdrive unit is attached to the output end of the four-speed gearbox.

The output shaft of the overdrive unit is indirectly driven by an epicyclic train of gears when overdrive ratio is selected, and by direct drive when normal ratio is required; the unit is controlled externally by an electrical circuit and actuated internally by a hydraulic system incorporated in the casing. Use of the overdrive ratio is limited by the electrical control; it can be brought into operation by a switch on the steering column only after top gear has been selected, and reversion to normal drive is possible after the accelerator has been depressed, switches being arranged to operate in conjunction with the gearbox selector mechanism and carburetter controls.

The cross-sectional diagrammatic illustrations show the unit in direct drive and when overdrive is engaged.

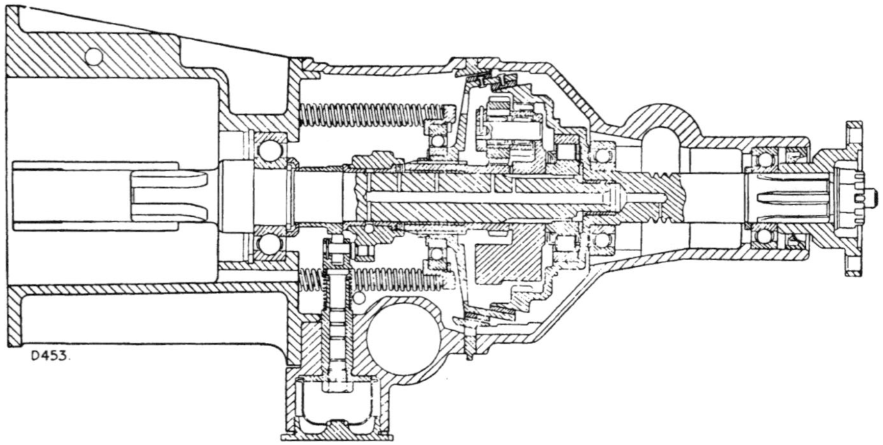

Cross-section of overdrive unit

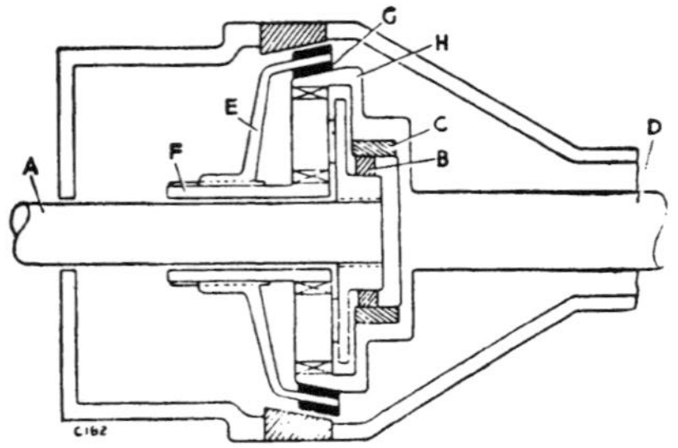

Relative position of component parts, normal ratio

When normal top gear ratio is selected, the drive from gearbox is transmitted to input shaft A, through rollers B, and the outer member C of uni-directional clutch to the output shaft D.

The uni-directional clutch will transmit motion in one direction only, and should the car over-run the engine, the clutch will then function as a free-wheel and thereby deprive the car of the extra braking effect of the engine. To obviate this condition, a cone clutch E, which slides on the sun wheel splined extension F, is pressed by springs so that the inner friction lining G contacts the outer friction cone H of the annulus, thereby locking the gear train and allowing over-run to be transmitted to the engine, and reverse motion, when required, from the gearbox to rear axle.

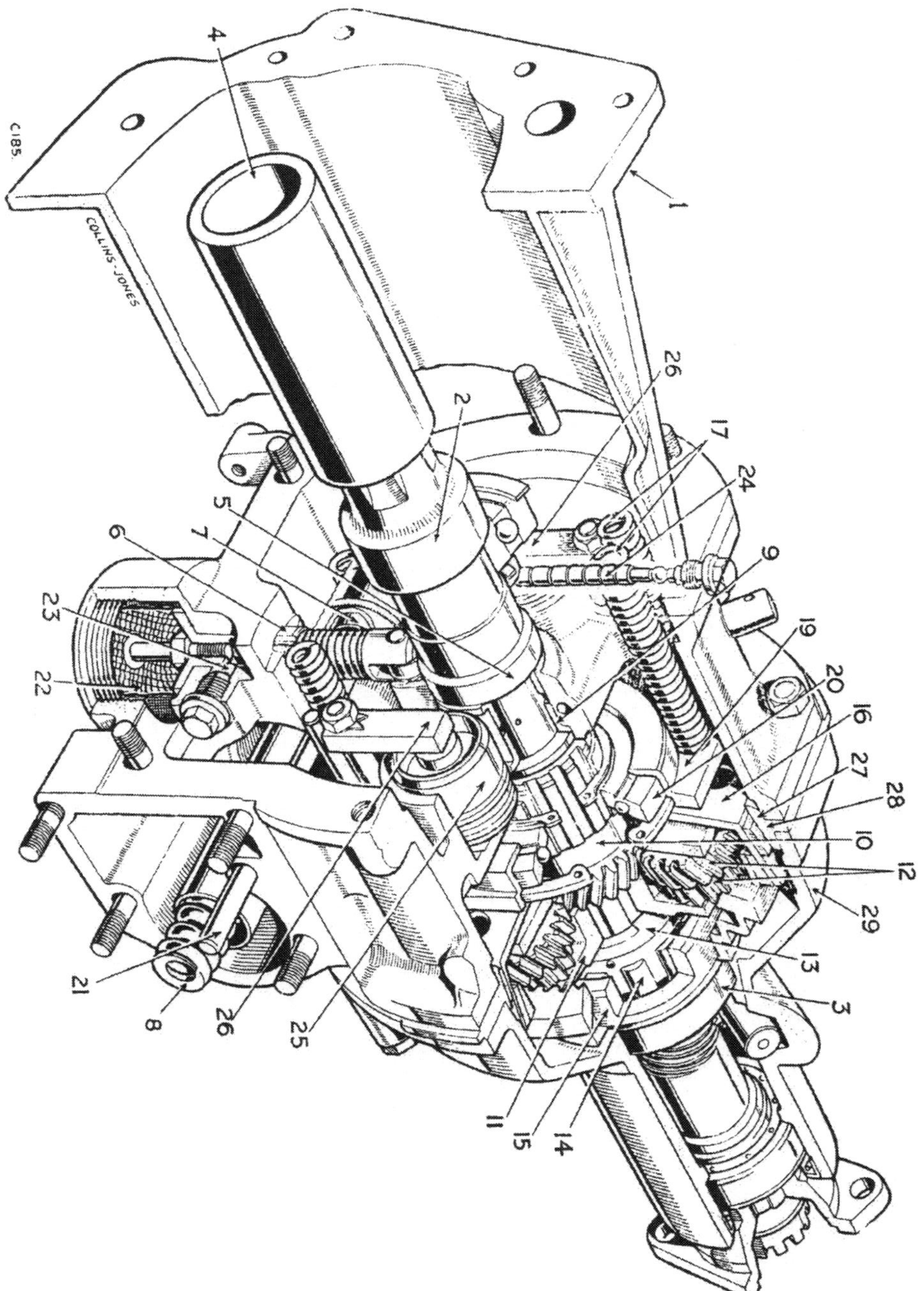

Sectioned view of overdrive unit and extension case

Overdrive unit—General description and working principle—*continued*

1 Extension casing
2 Front end, overdrive input shaft
3 Output shaft and annulus
4 Mainshaft through sleeve
5 Cam
6 Plunger-type pump
7 Pressure piston
8 Accumulator spring
9 Centre case bush
10 Splined extension
11 Sun wheel and planet carrier
12 Planet wheels
13 Uni-directional clutch, inner member
14 Rollers
15 Uni-directional clutch, outer member
16 Cone clutch
17 Springs, 12 off
19 Clutch thrust ring
20 Bearing
21 Operating cross-shaft
22 Filter
23 Non-return valve
24 Operating plunger
25 Operating piston
26 Bridge pieces
27 Cast-iron brake ring
28 Outer friction lining
29 Tail casing

Overdrive unit—General description and working principle—*continued*

Hydraulic pressure developed by a pump in the unit and stored in an accumulator housing is directed to two pistons which thrust forward, overcoming the spring pressure and lock the outer friction lining A of the cone clutch against a cast-iron brake ring B. The cone clutch is splined to the sun wheel extension C which is normally free to rotate on the input shaft D, but it is now stationary and locked indirectly to the outer casing.

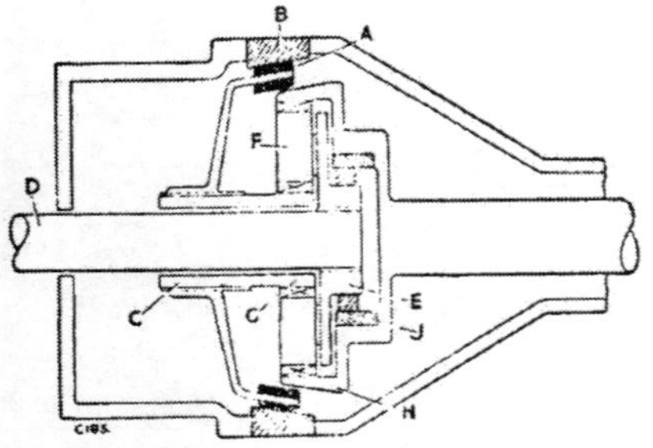

Relative positions of component parts—overdrive ratio

The rotating input shaft D now drives the planet carrier E, which is splined to the shaft, causing the planet wheels F to rotate about the stationary sun wheel G, and drive the internally toothed annulus H at a higher speed than the input shaft. In overdrive, the outer member J of the uni-directional clutch overruns the inner member, thus permitting the input and output shafts to rotate at different speeds.

Over-run is transmitted in the reverse direction when overdrive is engaged.

Arrangement

The extension casing (1) is bolted to rear end of gearbox casing; it supports the overdrive unit and houses the front end of overdrive input shaft (2). An output shaft and annulus (3) of integral construction, supported by two bearings in the tail casing (29), carries the rear end of the input shaft in an oilite bearing fitted to the annulus. Drive to the input shaft is transferred from the gearbox mainshaft through sleeve (4) which is pinned to the input shaft.

A cam (5) splined to the input shaft (2) operates a plunger-type pump (6) which draws lubricating oil from the sump, through a filter (22) and delivers it by way of a non-return valve (23) to an accumulator chamber placed transversely across the bottom of the casing. The pressure is controlled by a piston (7) moving against a spring (8), which is designed to retract to a predetermined point at a given pressure, then the piston uncovers small outlet holes, permitting surplus lubricant to flow at high pressure along a drilling in the input shaft, from where it is forced by centrifugal action through various outlets to the bearings and gears.

Mounted on the input shaft immediately to the rear of the centre case bush (9) and thrust washers is a sun wheel and splined extension (10) of integral construction. This is fitted internally with an oilite bearing and is free to rotate on the shaft. A thrust washer is fitted immediately after the sun wheel, and then a planet carrier (11) which is splined to the shaft, supporting the planet wheels (12). Finally, the inner member (13) of a uni-directional clutch is splined to the shaft.

In direct drive

Motion is transmitted from the shaft (2) to inner member (13) through rollers (14), which are driven up inclined faces and wedge between the inner member (13) and outer member (15) pegged to the annulus (3), thus driving the output shaft.

A cone clutch (16), mounted on the externally splined extension (10), is pressed rearward by twelve springs (17) thrusting from the extension casing (1) on to the clutch thrust ring (19), and exert pressure through the bearing (20). This arrangement causes the inner friction lining of the cone clutch to contact the outer cone of the annulus and rotate with the annulus whilst the springs and thrust rings remain stationary. The effect of pressing the cone clutch on to the annulus is to cause them to rotate at the same speed, lock the gear train and thereby permit car over-run to be transmitted from the annulus (3) and sun wheel (10), through the planet wheels (12) and planet carrier (11) splined to the input shaft. The locked gear train also permits reverse motion.

When overdrive ratio is required

A switch-controlled solenoid partially turns an operating cross-shaft (21), lifting the operating plunger (24) thereby allowing oil stored in the accumulator housing under pressure, to actuate two operating pistons (25) which thrust forward against bridge pieces (26) attached by studs to the cone clutch. The thrusting pistons overcome the spring pressure, then move the cone clutch forward away from the annulus until the outer friction lining (28) is pressed against the cast-iron brake ring (27) and the cone clutch, together with the sun wheels, are stationary, virtually locked to the outer casing.

Overdrive unit—General description and working principle—*continued*

The revolving input shaft (2) now drives the planet carrier (11), splined to the shaft, causing the planet wheels (12) in mesh with the sun wheel (10) and annulus (3) to rotate about the sun wheel and drive the annulus at a higher speed than the input shaft. The outer member (15) of the uni-directional clutch overruns the inner member (13), thus permitting the input and output shafts to revolve at different speeds.

Car overrun is transmitted to the engine from the output shaft and annulus, to the planet wheels (12), planet carrier (11) and input shaft (2).

The speed of the change from high to normal ratio is predetermined by a small metering hole in the operating plunger (24) which restricts the flow of oil from the operating pistons (25) after the operating valve has been closed. Normal change period is approximately a half-second.

Hydraulic control

When the overdrive ratio is selected by the steering column switch, the operating cross-shaft is partially turned, lifting the operating cam A, and operating plunger B, thus moving ball C off its seat. Oil under pressure in the accumulator chamber passes through port D to passage E and to the operating pistons, thereby thrusting them forward against the bridge pieces of the cone clutch, which moves forward compressing the clutch springs.

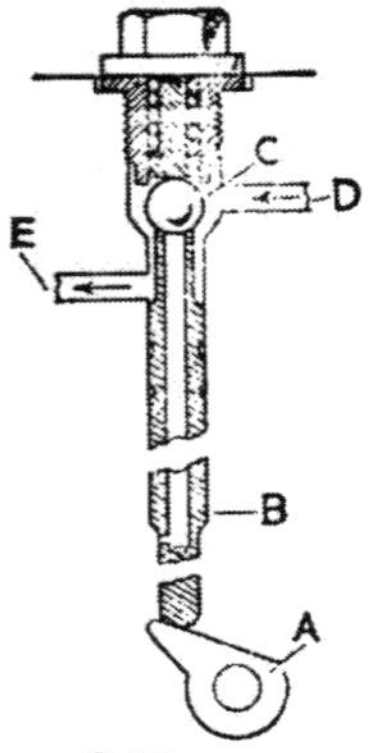

G45

Operating plunger in the overdrive ratio position

Reversion to normal ratio is allowed by the cancelling movement of the steering column switch permitting the operating cam A to return to its former position; the spring F presses the ball C on to the seat, thereby excluding oil from the accumulator chamber The cone clutch springs thrust rearward, forcing the bridge pieces and operating pistons to their former positions. Oil passing from the operating piston chambers enters port E, passes down the centre of the operating plunger B, and out through a small metering hole in the side of the plunger. The speed of the change from overdrive to normal ratio is limited by the size of the metering hole.

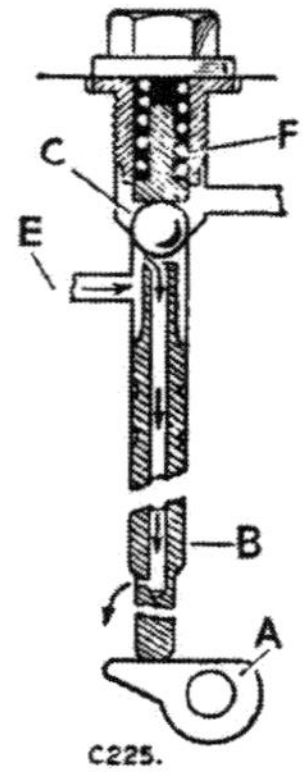

C225.

Operating plunger in normal ratio position

Oil level

The utmost cleanliness must be observed when 'topping-up' with oil or removing any part which could allow dirt or foreign matter to enter the overdrive or gearbox units. Before removing the filler cap, cover plates or plugs, clean carefully round the parts concerned.

Early units had internal oil passages between the gearbox which permitted the use of a common lubricant, the correct oil level being indicated by the gearbox dipstick. Separate drain plugs are provided and both must be removed when draining. Late models have independent lubrication systems, with separate fillers and drain plugs.

Late models are fitted with a magnet in the overdrive drain plug. Any metal particles adhering to it must be removed.

The overdrive unit is fitted with a gauze filter in the sump and the filter should be removed and cleaned in petrol whenever oil is changed.

The exclusion of all foreign matter is essential for trouble-free operation of the overdrive unit.

Hydraulic system checking—Operation D2-1

In the event of the overdrive unit failing in some respect, it will be found expedient to check the electrical side of the system and, in particular, the functioning and setting of the solenoid and operating cross-shaft before carrying out any of the following checks into possible causes of hydraulic failure.

Overdrive cannot be selected

1. Check that the oil level is correct.

   Early models

   These have a common gearbox/overdrive lubrication system, the correct oil level for the overdrive unit being indicated by the gearbox dipstick. The gearbox filler serves for the overdrive unit, but separate drain plugs are provided and both must be removed when draining. Gearbox/overdrive unit capacity 5½ Imperial pints, 6 US pints (3 litres).

   Late models

   The gearbox and overdrive unit have separate lubrication systems. Check level of lubricant with overdrive unit dipstick. Capacity 1½ Imperial pints (0,85 litres).

2. Ensure that anti-friction additives have not been used in the overdrive unit.

3. **Early models**

   Remove the inspection cover (in tunnel cover) giving access to the operating valve.

   Late models

   Remove the tunnel cover.

4. Move the gear lever into top gear position, depress the accelerator pedal, switch the ignition on and operate the control switch on the steering column approximately twelve times to ensure that any pressure in the accumulator chamber is released.

5. Unscrew the operating valve plug and withdraw the spring, plunger and ball. A magnet or forceps will facilitate the removal of these parts.

6. Jack the rear wheels clear of the ground and run the engine with top gear selected, then note if oil is being pumped into the operating valve chamber. If oil appears, a pressure gauge (Part No. 268721) must be fitted to the plug hole, first refitting the operating valve spring, plunger and ball.

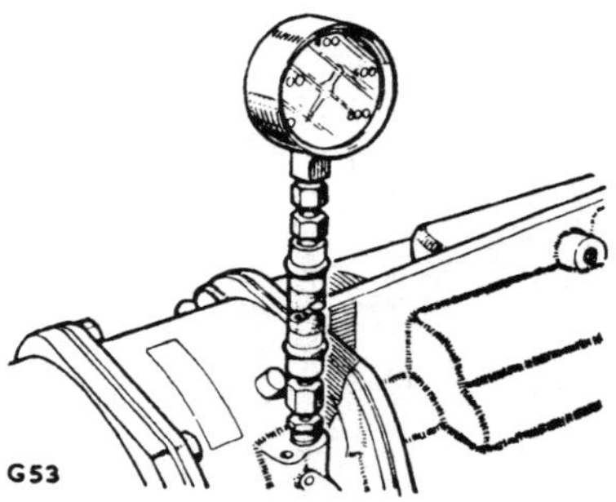

G53

Testing hydraulic pressure

7. Check the developed pressure, which should be 430 lb/sq in. (30,23 kg/cm²). A favourable oil pressure reading will indicate that the cause of failure is mechanical; refer to defect location section.

8. If a low reading is obtained or no oil appears in the operating valve chamber, further checks must be made.

9. Release the oil pressure, as in item 4 above.

10. Remove the drain plug and withdraw the filter for examination and cleaning.

11. Remove the solenoid, solenoid lever and distance piece from the cross-shaft; remove the accumulator chamber cover, taking care to unscrew the two red-painted set bolts lastly and evenly as this cover plate is subject to spring pressure.

12. Withdraw the accumulator spring, noting any packing shims which may adhere to the cover plate around the dowel.

13. Withdraw the spring retaining tube.

14. Test the accumulator spring; compare findings with details in data section.

15. If necessary, remove the red-painted inlet non-return valve plug, which can be seen in the lower left side of the housing.

16. Carefully withdraw the spring, plunger and ball valve. Examine these parts for defects, and check the ball seating for pitting or roughness; if this is the case, the complete overdrive unit must be removed, the pump withdrawn and a new ball valve of the same dimensions as the original must be lapped on to the seat.

Operation D2-1—*continued*

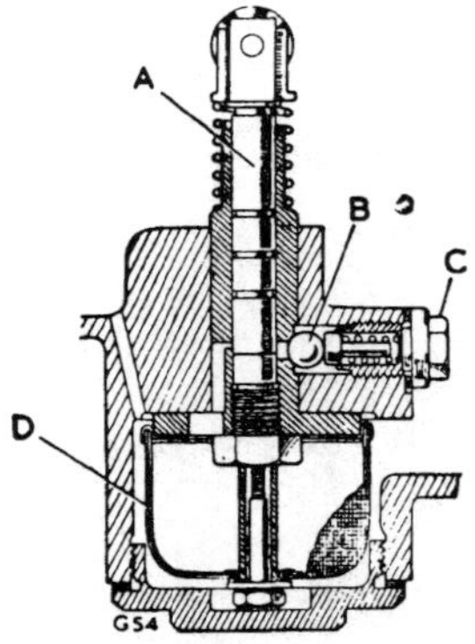

G54

Sectioned view of oil pump and non-return valve

A—Oil pump
B—Non-return valve
C—Red-painted plug
D—Filter

17. Clean all traces of lapping compound before reassembling the unit. Pump withdrawal is dealt with in Operation D2-3.

Unit remains in overdrive, all gear ratios affected.

18 Remove the inspection plate on the right-hand side of the tunnel cover (on early models) above the operating valve plug. On late models, remove the tunnel cover.

19. Switch the ignition 'on', depress the accelerator pedal and, with the gear lever in top gear position, operate the manual control switch on the steering column approximately twelve times to release any hydraulic pressure.

20. Remove the red-painted plug, **but proceed with caution** as the operating plunger valve metering hole may be completely blocked, preventing the relief of oil pressure. Cover the area with rags or clean sacking material, slowly unscrew the plug, allowing for any oil which may be forced upwards past the threads. The operator must ensure that suitable protection is available against any oil soiling the interior of the car.

21. Extract the operating plunger valve, using a magnet or a pair of forceps.

22. Examine the metering hole in the lower side of the plunger for stoppage by foreign matter. Clean and replace the plunger, ensuring that it moves freely in its housing.

23. Refit the components and recheck the overdrive operation.

24. If any of the above checks do not disclose the defect, then reference should be made to the defect location section.

Description of overdrive electrical control and arrangement of components, Mk I and Mk IA

The unit is controlled by switches, a relay unit and a solenoid.

A manual switch on the steering column selects overdrive ratio, but an isolating switch on the gearbox prevents overdrive being engaged unless the car is in top gear. Further restriction by automatic rotary- or cam-type switches, operated by the accelerator linkage, permits engagement when the accelerator has been depressed by more than one-eighth of its full travel

Models Mk I and Mk IA were fitted with an accelerator kick-down switch which disengaged overdrive when rapid acceleration was required. This switch, working through the relay, overrides the steering column selector switch, but unless the column switch was moved to normal position overdrive ratio would be automatically engaged when the accelerator returned beyond half travel.

From Models Mk II onwards the kick-down switch was deleted as a safeguard against over-revving of the engine at high speeds. When rapid acceleration is required, overdrive can be disengaged by means of the switch on the column, but under no circumstances must overdrive be disengaged whilst the car is travelling at speeds in excess of 90 mph (145 kph).

The overdrive circuit described above and the solenoid which operates the overdrive takes its current from the A3 terminal of the normal car circuit. A separate fuse protects the overdrive circuit.

Circuit description and checking procedure, Models Mk I and Mk IA with rotary-type switch

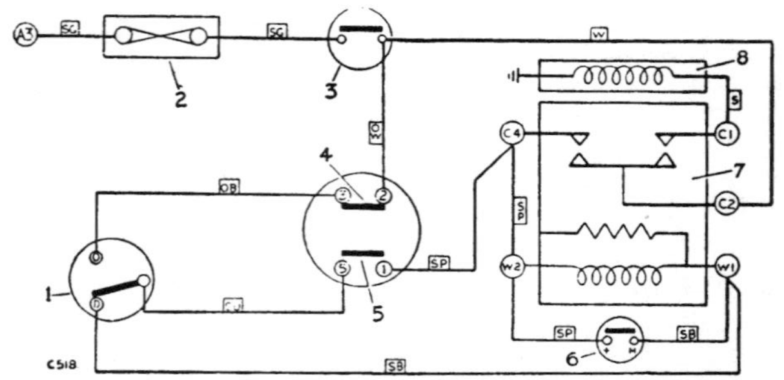

Overdrive electrical circuit, Models Mk I and Mk IA (fitted with rotary switch)

	COMPONENT	*LOCATION OF COMPONENT ON CAR*
1	Overdrive control switch (in 'off' position)	On steering column
2	Fuse—35-amp	Engine side of RH cover panel for dash
3	Isolating switch (closed in top gear only)	On gearbox
4	Rotary switch, shown as two switches — 4 Closed—zero to half throttle	On accelerator linkage
5	Rotary switch, shown as two switches — 5 Open—zero to eighth throttle	On accelerator linkage
6	Kick-down switch	Beneath the accelerator pedal
7	Relay	Adjacent to control box on RH side of dash
8	Solenoid	On side of overdrive unit

Cable colour code

B	Black	O	Orange	G	Green	W	White
U	Blue	P	Purple	S	Slate		

Note: When a cable has two colour code letters, the first denotes the main colour and the second denotes the tracer colour.

Description of overdrive electrical control and arrangement of components, Mk I and Mk IA—*continued*

Arrangement and operation of electrical components

A solenoid (8), mounted on the LH side of the overdrive unit and coupled to the operating cross-shaft, may be energised by current from terminal A3 of the normal car circuit; it is controlled by a series of switches and a relay (7) to select overdrive ratio as required. Fuse (2), fitted to the engine side of the RH cover panel for the dash, protects the circuit from overloading.

Mounted on the gearbox extension casing and operated by the 3rd and 4th speed selector shaft, an isolating switch (3) allows selection of overdrive ratio only after the gear lever has been moved to the top gear position.

A single rotary switch, shown diagrammatically as two switches (4 and 5), is mounted on a support bracket adjacent to the accelerator countershaft, where it is operated by linkage from the countershaft. This switch prevents the selection of overdrive ratio unless the accelerator pedal is depressed between one-eighth and one-half of full travel. Reversion from overdrive to normal top gear ratio is also prevented by the switch unless the accelerator pedal is more than one-eighth depressed.

A kick-down switch (6), fitted immediately beneath the accelerator pedal, is used in conjunction with relay (7), fitted adjacent to the control box on RH side of dash, to permit a full power change from overdrive ratio to normal top gear ratio, by allowing current to flow to both terminals (W1 andW2) of the relay, break the circuit to solenoid and thus override the switch on steering column. Normal top gear ratio will remain engaged after the kick-down switch has been operated until the accelerator pedal is allowed to return beyond half travel, whereon the rotary switch (4 and 5) will complete the relay circuit, re-energise the solenoid and select overdrive ratio again.

Check for electrical or mechanical fault

If the unit is inoperative, check to find out if the fault is electrical or mechanical. Proceed as follows:

(a) Securely jack up the rear wheels of the car.

(b) Start the engine and engage top gear, no overdrive.

(c) Manually move the setting lever on the side of the overdrive unit forward.

(d) If the overdrive unit engages correctly, then it may be presumed that the fault lies in the electrical circuit.

Circuit checking

If an electrical fault is considered to be the reason for the overdrive failing to engage, it will be found expedient to check the following points in the order laid down to localise the trouble.

1. Check the fuse at extreme RH side of dash, adjacent to voltage control box. If the fuse has 'blown', replace, then test the overdrive operation, preferably on the road. If the fuse blows immediately, or after a comparatively short time, the circuit must be tested and checked for earthing or excessive load.

2. If the fuse is intact, select top gear, with ignition 'on', and depress the accelerator pedal to between one-eighth and one-half of full travel and set in this position. Select overdrive at the column switch.

3. Connect one lead of a 12-volt test lamp to a good earth and connect the other lead to terminal W1 on the relay. If the circuit to the relay is in order, the bulb will light.

   (a) If the bulb does not light, the circuit to the relay must be checked as follows:

   Remove the foremost RH inspection plate from the gearbox tunnel cover, and with the test lamp suitably earthed connect the test lead to the isolating switch feed wire (slate with green). If the bulb does not light, the feed from A3 to the switch must be checked.

   (b) If the circuit so far is in order, transfer the test lead to the output terminal on the switch, whereon the bulb should light; if it does not, the fault lies in the isolating switch, which should be reset.

   To do this, screw the switch out of its insert. With the gear lever in top gear position, insert the switch operating plunger and, with finger pressure, ensure that it is in contact with the selector shaft.

   Screw the switch into the insert until approximately $\frac{1}{8}$ in. (3 mm) remains extended.

   Connect the switch in circuit with a test lamp and battery.

   Screw the switch slowly into the insert and stop immediately the bulb lights. Disconnect the test circuit.

   Ascertain the clearance between the switch and insert with a feeler gauge.

Description of overdrive electrical control and arrangement of components, Mk I and Mk IA—*continued*

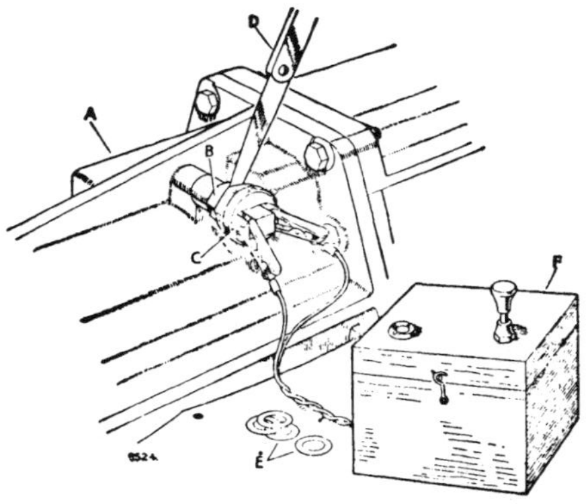

Setting isolating switch

A—Extension casing
B—Insert
C—Isolating switch
D—Feeler gauge
E—Shims
F—Test lamp

Select shims, available in .005 in. (0,12 mm) and .020 in. (0,50 mm) thicknesses, which, when inserted between the switch and insert, will allow the switch to be screwed in a further .010 to .015 in. (0,25 to 0,38 mm) only.

Remove the switch and refit with the selected shims.

Connect the switch to the test circuit again, move the gear lever in and out of top gear; checking that the light is on in top gear position only. Replace the switch if necessary and reset and test as above.

Remove test circuit and connect overdrive wiring to the switch.

(c) If (b) is in order, the rotary and steering column switches must be checked as follows:

With the test lamp suitably earthed, connect the test lead to terminal C4 on the relay, whereon the bulb should light. If it does not, the steering column switch should be checked separately using a battery and test lamp.

Control switch, to replace

With the front wheels in the straight-ahead position, slacken the three Allen screws in the steering wheel hub and remove the horn ring.

Remove the steering wheel securing nut and plain washer, and remove the steering wheel from the splined **shaft**, after noting its correct position.

Remove the four recessed screws in the side of the steering column shroud; remove the four small screws from the top support bracket, thereby releasing the shrouds.

Remove the beading strip from the top and carefully ease both shrouds away from the column.

Remove the overdrive control switch from the shroud and disconnect the wiring harness.

Fit the replacement switch to the shroud and connect the wiring.

Refit the shrouds, ensuring correct location on the dowel. Fit the four recessed screws, but do not fully tighten at this stage.

Fit the top support bracket and top beading strip, then tighten evenly all securing screws, ensuring that both shrouds and beading are firmly in position.

Fit steering wheel on to its original spline, fit the plain washer and tighten the securing nut fully. Fit the horn ring to the steering wheel.

Check that the steering wheel is in the straight-ahead position in relation to the front wheels, and check that the trafficator switch, horn and overdrive switch function correctly.

If the column switch is operating correctly, the rotary switch setting should be checked.

Disconnect and remove the control rod between the rotary switch and the lever on the accelerator countershaft.

Set the lever on the countershaft in the horizontal position and pointing towards the dash.

Slacken the pinch bolt of the lever on the switch and turn the switch spindle in an anti-clockwise direction until the limit of movement is reached; retain this position and set the switch lever so that it is approximately 30° from the vertical and pointing upwards.

Fit the control rod to the lever on the switch and secure in the mid-slot position. Do not connect the rod to the other lever at this stage.

Adjust the control rod as necessary to enable rod to be connected to the lever on the countershaft, without moving the lever, then shorten the control rod by one complete turn clockwise before finally connecting the rod to the lever.

The switch is now correctly set and the circuit should again be tested. If necessary, renew the switch and reset the linkage.

Description of overdrive electrical control and arrangement of components, Mk I and Mk IA—*continued*

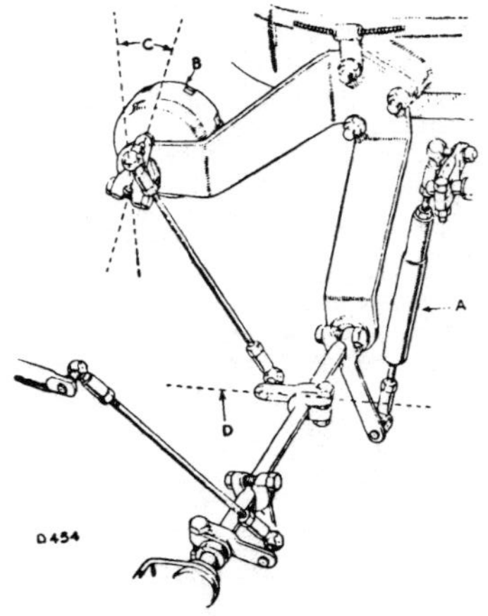

Setting rotary switch and control rods

A—Collapsible rod
B—Rotary switch
C—Switch lever set at 30°
D—Countershaft lever set horizontally

4. To test the relay, suitably earth the test lamp and connect the test lead to terminal C1 on relay. If the bulb fails to light, the relay is faulty and must be replaced.

5. If the bulb lights, proving the relay to be in order, connect the test lead to the snap connector on the solenoid. If the bulb does not light, the feed from the relay to the solenoid must be checked for continuity and, if this is all right, it can usually be taken to mean that the solenoid is at fault and should be replaced.

Solenoid, to replace

Disconnect the wiring to the solenoid at the snap connector. Remove the cover plate.

Remove the solenoid, secured by two screws; leave the plunger attached to the solenoid lever, but slacken the solenoid lever clamp bolt.

Fit the replacement solenoid.

Reverse the removal procedure, leaving the solenoid lever clamping bolt loose, the cover and heat shield unfitted.

Align the setting lever on RH side of the unit with the hole in casing, using a setting bar.

Energise the solenoid by selecting top gear, switching ignition 'on', depressing the accelerator pedal between one-eighth and one-half of full travel and temporarily securing in this position, then operate the switch on steering column.

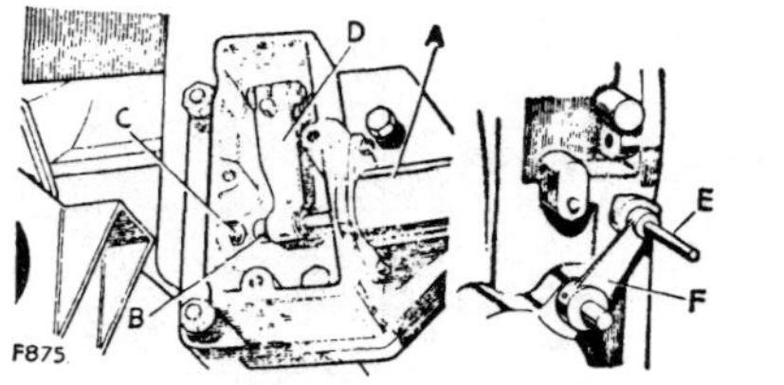

Setting solenoid and lever

A—Solenoid
B—Plunger
C—Rubber buffer
E—Setting bar
F—Cross-shaft lever

Hold the solenoid lever against the foremost part of plunger and tighten the clamping bolt on the solenoid lever.

Remove the setting bar and move the control switch on steering column into 'on' and 'off' positions to check the operation of solenoid.

6. On remote occasions the contacts on the kick-down switch have been known to remain closed after release and should be checked with the test lamp. Connect test lead to switch output lead (slate with black). If the bulb lights, the switch is faulty and must be replaced.

Kick-down switch, to replace

Withdraw the carpet from accelerator pedal area.

Remove the fixings securing switch support to body and lift the switch and bracket clear.

Disconnect the leads from switch.

Remove the set bolts securing the switch to support bracket.

Refit the kick-down switch and connect the leads to switch.

Depress the accelerator pedal to the kick-down switch button.

Ensure that the carburetter butterfly valve is fully open and the collapsible rod is on the point of collapse. If this condition is not achieved, carry out suitable adjustment to the lengths of the collapsible rod and levers.

Description of overdrive electrical control and arrangement of components, Mk I and Mk IA—*continued*

Depress the accelerator pedal to the full kick-down position and ensure that the collapsible rod has telescoped.

Adjustment may be made by altering the length of the control rod between the cross-shaft and accelerator pedal shaft lever.

Overdrive accelerator switch

7. Engage top gear, select overdrive at the steering column switch and switch on ignition.
8. Depress the accelerator pedal very slowly until the solenoid is heard to operate. This signifies engagement of overdrive and this setting should be checked as follows:

   Hold the accelerator pedal stationary at this point, and check the clearance between the carburetter slow running stop and butterfly lever. This clearance should be .050 to .100 in. (1,27 to 2,56 mm).
9. Press the accelerator pedal past full throttle and operate the kick-down switch, whereon the overdrive should disengage. The 'click' from the relay should be audible.
10. Gradually ease the accelerator pedal back to approximately half-throttle position. The overdrive should be heard to re-engage.
11. Allow the accelerator pedal to come right back, switch the overdrive out at the steering column switch, depress the accelerator to approximately ⅛ in. (3,2 mm) throttle opening, at which the overdrive should be heard to disengage.

Circuit description and checking procedure, Models Mk II with cam-type switch

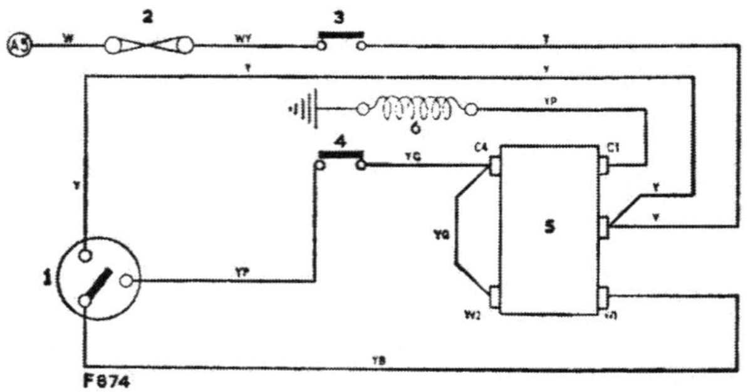

F874

Overdrive electrical circuit, Models Mk II (fitted with cam switch)

	COMPONENT	LOCATION OF COMPONENT ON CAR
1	Overdrive control switch	On steering column
2	Fuse—35-amp	Terminals 7 and 8 in fuse box
3	Isolating switch (closed in top gear only)	Adjacent to fuse box
4	Cam switch	On accelerator linkage
5	Relay	Adjacent to control box on RH side of dash
6	Solenoid	On side of overdrive unit

Cable colour code

W	White	Y	Yellow
G	Green	B	Black
P	Purple		

Note: When a cable has two colour code letters, the first denotes the main colour and the second denotes the tracer colour.

Description of overdrive electrical control and arrangement of components, Mk II and Mk III

Arrangement and operation of electrical components

Current for the overdrive circuit is supplied from the A3 terminal of the car circuit. The unit operating solenoid (6) is controlled by the selector switch on the steering column (1), and by an isolating switch (3) and a cam switch (4), through a relay (5). The overdrive circuit is protected by a 35-amp fuse (2).

Check for electrical or mechanical fault

Proceed as follows:

(a) Securely jack-up the rear wheels of the car.

(b) Start engine, engage top gear and select overdrive.

(c) Manually move the setting lever on the side of the overdrive unit forward.

(d) If the overdrive engages correctly, presume that the fault is in the electrical circuit.

Circuit checking

1. Check the fuse, which if 'blown', replace. Test the overdrive operation, preferably on the road. If the fuse blows immediately, or after a comparatively short time, the circuit must be tested and checked for earthing or excessive load.
2. If the fuse is intact, select top gear, with ignition 'on', and depress the accelerator pedal to between one-eighth and one-half of full travel and set in this position. Select overdrive at the column switch.
3. Connect one lead of a 12-volt test lamp to a good earth and connect the other lead to terminal W1 on the relay. If the circuit to the relay is in order, the bulb will light.

   (a) If the bulb does not light, the circuit to the relay must be checked as follows:

   Remove the gearbox tunnel cover and, with the test lamp suitably earthed, connect the test lead to the isolating switch feed wire. If the bulb does not light, the feed from A3 to the switch must be checked.

   (b) If the circuit so far is in order, transfer the test lead to the output terminal on the switch, whereon the bulb should light; if it does not, the fault lies in the isolating switch, which should be reset, or if still unsatisfactory, replaced.

Disconnect the switch leads.

Slacken the locknut and unscrew switch.

Withdraw plunger using a magnet.

In the remote possibility of the plunger sticking, or if difficulty is experienced in removing the plunger, the sleeve may be unscrewed. Removal of sleeve will either withdraw the plunger also, or allow easier access to it.

Smear the plunger with engine oil and fit into aperture.

With the locknut in position on switch and gear lever in neutral position, screw the switch into gearbox by hand until resistance is felt as the switch extension contacts the plunger, then unscrew one-eighth turn.

Connect the white feed lead to the switch leaving the other lead free. Connect a test lamp between the free terminal of the switch and earth as illustrated, and, with the ignition 'on' check that the contacts are open as indicated by the unlit test lamp bulb.

Move the gear lever into top gear position, then check that the switch contacts are closed as indicated by the lighted test lamp bulb.

If the bulb does not light, unscrew the switch until it does, then move the gear lever into neutral and check that the contacts are open again.

Ensure that the switch remains stationary and tighten locknut.

Recheck switch operation with test lamp, gear lever in top and neutral positions. Reconnect wiring.

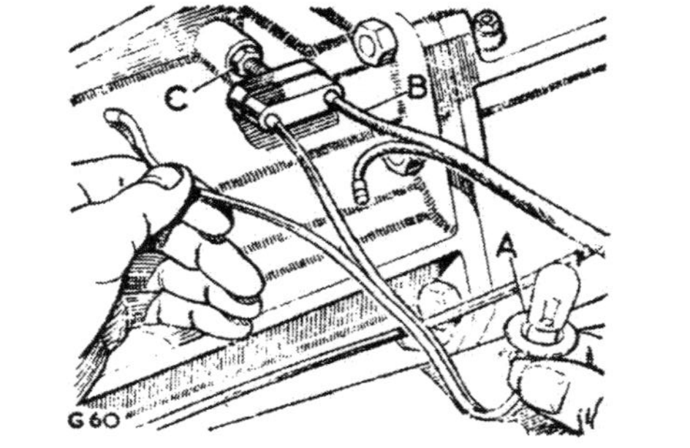

Testing isolating switch

A—Test lamp B—White lead C—Adjusting locknut

Description of overdrive electrical control and arrangement of components, Mk II and Mk III—*continued*

(c) If (b) is in order, the cam and steering column switches must be checked as follows:

With the test lamp suitably earthed, connect the test lead to terminal C4 on the relay, whereon the bulb should light. If it does not, the steering column switch should be checked separately using a test lamp battery. If the column switch is operating correctly, the cam switch setting should be checked and tested again. If it is still faulty, it must be replaced.

Setting overdrive cam switch

(a) Before attempting to set the cam switch, check the full throttle position and adjust as necessary by altering the length of the control rod, accelerator lever to countershaft.

(b) Disconnect the wires from the switch and connect a suitable test lamp.

(c) Rotate the cam by lifting the control rod. The test lamp will go out as soon as the cam depresses the plunger on the switch. This should occur at approximately one-eighth throttle opening.

(d) Unscrew locknut and screw switch in or out until the test lamp goes out at approximately one-eighth throttle opening.

(e) Tighten the locknut. Remove test lamp and reconnect the original wiring.

(f) Road-test the car and, if necessary, carry out final adjustments.

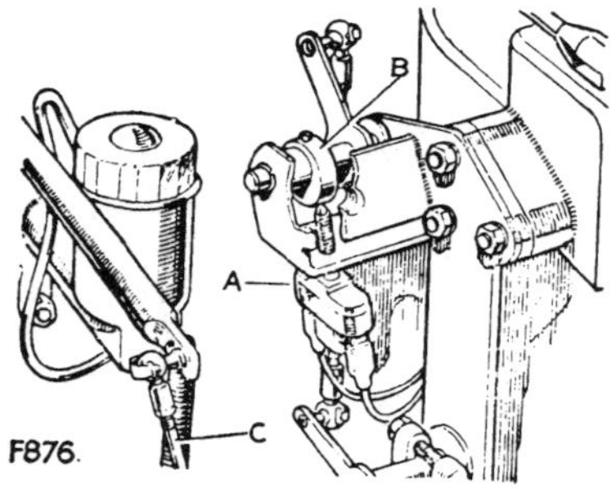

Location of overdrive cam switch and throttle linkage setting

A—Switch B—Cam C—Adjust throttle linkage at this rod

Throttle linkage setting

Check that the carpet does not restrict the accelerator pedal travel. When resetting the accelerator linkage, it is essential to ensure that the full throttle position is reached with the accelerator fractionally above the carpet, otherwise full engine performance will not be available.

Solenoid, to replace

1. Disconnect the wiring to the solenoid at the snap connector. Remove the cover plate.

2. Remove the solenoid, secured by two screws, leave the plunger attached to the solenoid lever; but slacken the solenoid lever clamp bolt.

3. Fit the replacement solenoid.

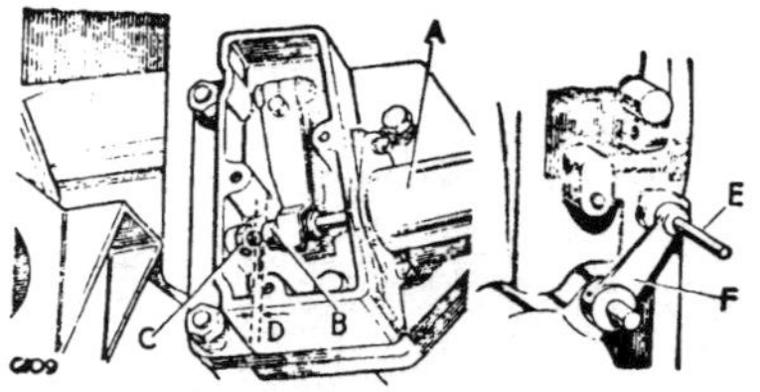

Setting solenoid and lever, late type

A—Solenoid D—.125 in. (3 mm) gap
B—Plunger E—Setting bar
C—Adjustable stop F—Cross-shaft lever

4. Reverse the removal procedure, leaving the solenoid lever clamping bolt loose and the cover unfitted.

5. Align the setting lever on RH side of the unit with the hole in casing, using a setting bar.

6. **Late models.** With the solenoid plunger pressed fully home, the setting screw for the main plunger adjustable stop must be set so that there is a .125 in. (3 mm) gap between the head of the plunger and the end stop. To avoid damage to the contact blade, the main plunger must always be pushed forward by hand before energising the solenoid, whilst the lever clamp bolt is loose. Hold the solenoid lever against the foremost part of plunger and tighten the clamping bolt on the solenoid lever.

Description of overdrive electrical control and arrangement of components, Mk II and Mk III—*continued*

7. Remove the setting bar and move the control switch on the column into 'on' and 'off' positions to check the operation of solenoid.

8. With the front wheels in the straight-ahead position, slacken the three Allen screws in the steering wheel hub and remove the horn ring.

9. Remove the steering wheel securing nut and plain washer, and remove the steering wheel from the splined shaft, after noting its correct position.

10. Remove the four recessed screws in the side of the steering column shroud; remove the four small screws from the top support bracket, thereby releasing the shrouds.

11. Remove the beading strip from the top and carefully ease both shrouds away from the column.

12. Remove the overdrive control switch from the shroud and disconnect the wiring.

13. Fit the replacement switch to the shroud and connect the wiring.

14. Refit the shrouds, ensuring correct location on the dowel. Fit the four recessed screws, but do not fully tighten at this stage.

15. Fit top support bracket and the top beading strip, then tighten evenly all securing screws, ensuring that both shrouds and beading are firmly in position.

16. Fit steering wheel on to its original spline, fit the plain washer and tighten the securing nut fully. Fit the horn ring to the steering wheel.

17. Check that the steering wheel is in the straight-ahead position in relation to the front wheels, and check that the trafficator switch, horn and overdrive switch function correctly.

*Overdrive, to remove and refit—Operation D2-2

Workshop hand tools:
Spanner sizes: $\frac{5}{16}$ in. BSF, $\frac{3}{8}$ in. BSF, $\frac{7}{16}$ in. AF. $\frac{1}{2}$ in. AF, $\frac{9}{16}$ in. AF, 2 BA
Set of feeler gauges

Special tools:
Battery-operated test lamp

See Operations D2-3 and D2-4 for overdrive unit overhaul

Note: The overdrive unit must be removed with the extension casing complete

Overdrive, remove

1. Place the car on a suitable ramp or over an inspection pit before commencing this operation.
2. Disconnect the battery.
3. Drain the gearbox and overdrive units. Late models are fitted with a magnet in the overdrive drain plug. Any metal particles adhering to it must be removed.
4. Disconnect the front driving flange of the propeller shaft from the output shaft flange.
5. Release the handbrake and detach the cross-shaft inner bracket. Remove the detachable cross-member from the underside of the body.
6. Disconnect the wiring harness from the isolating switch and overdrive solenoid. Remove the solenoid wiring from the clip on the overdrive flange.
7. Remove the isolating switch, complete with shims, insert and plunger.
8. Remove the overdrive solenoid fixing screws and remove the solenoid, leaving the plunger attached to the solenoid lever.
9. Disconnect the speedometer cable and remove the speedometer right-angled drive unit.
10. Remove the rear mounting bracket fixings, bracket to sub-frame.
11. Jack up the engine under the flywheel housing high enough to clear the rear mounting brackets from the sub-frame.
12. Remove the eight fixings around the flange, extension case to gearbox.
13. Withdraw the overdrive unit rearwards, then lower the front end down and lift the unit clear.

Overdrive, refit

1. Engage top gear.
2. Offer the overdrive and extension case assembly, complete with a new flange joint washer, up to the gearbox, engage the coupling sleeve on to the gearbox output shaft and secure the unit to the gearbox with the eight fixings.
3. Lower the engine unit to allow the rear mounting brackets to rest on the sub-frame, then secure the mounting brackets to the sub-frame.
4. Connect the front driving flange of the propeller shaft to the output shaft flange.
5. Fit the detachable cross-member to the underside of the body. Refit the inner brake of the hand-brake cross-shaft.
6. Refit the speedometer right-angled drive and connect the speedometer cable.
7. Refit the isolating switch, complete with insert and plunger. If the spacing shims between the switch and insert have been disturbed or removed for any reason, then the following adjustment must be carried out:
   (a) Fit the insert to the extension casing and tighten fully.
   (b) Move the gear lever into the top gear position, insert the plunger and ensure it contacts the selector shaft.
   (c) Screw the switch into the insert until approximately $\frac{1}{8}$ in. (0,3 mm) remains extended, then connect a test lamp and battery to the switch terminals.
   (d) Continue to screw the switch slowly into the insert and stop immediately the bulb lights.
   (e) Check the clearance between the insert and the switch, using a feeler gauge.

Operations which are identified by an asterisk (*) can be carried out with the engine and gearbox installed in the car

Operation D2-2—*continued*

   (f) Select shims, which are available in .005 in. (0,12 mm) and .020 in. (0,50 mm) thicknesses, which, when inserted between the switch and insert, will allow the switch to be screwed in a further .010 in. (0,25 mm) to .015 in. (0,38 mm) only.

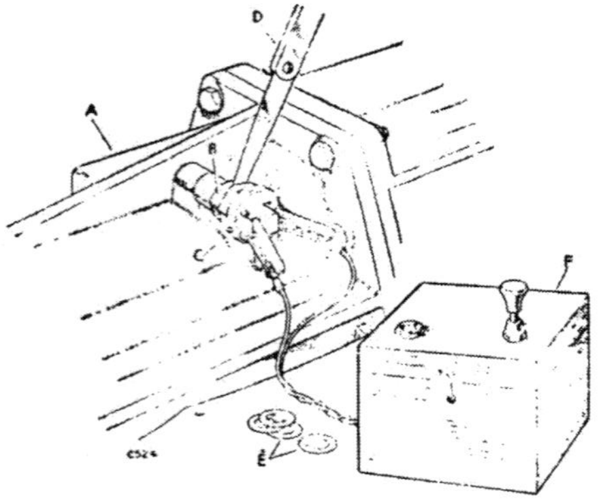

Setting the isolating switch

A—Extension casing
B—Insert
C—Isolating switch
D—Feeler gauge
E—Shims
F—Test lamp

   (g) Remove the switch, fit the selected shims and refit the switch.
   (h) Reconnect the test lamp and battery, move the gear lever in and out of top gear several times and check that the bulb lights only when the gear lever is in the top gear position.
   (i) Remove the test lamp and connect the wiring harness in accordance with the wiring diagram.

Overdrive solenoid, refit and adjust

8. Refit the solenoid to the overdrive unit and adjust the solenoid lever as follows:
   (a) With the solenoid lever clamping bolt loose, align the setting lever on the RH side of the operating cross-shaft with the hole in the casing, using a 12 in. long type setting bar (Part No. 278328). The early short type tool (same part number) must be modified by cutting off approximately $\frac{1}{4}$ in. (6 mm) of its length.
   (b) Connect the battery and solenoid wiring.
   (c) Energise the solenoid by selecting top gear switching the ignition 'on', depressing the accelerator pedal between one-eighth and one-half of full travel, and operating the steering column manual switch.
   (d) Hold the solenoid lever against the foremost part of the plunger and tighten the clamping bolt on the solenoid lever.
   (e) Remove the setting bar and move the steering column manual control to 'off' and 'on' several times to check the operation of the solenoid.
   (f) Refit the solenoid lever cover plate.

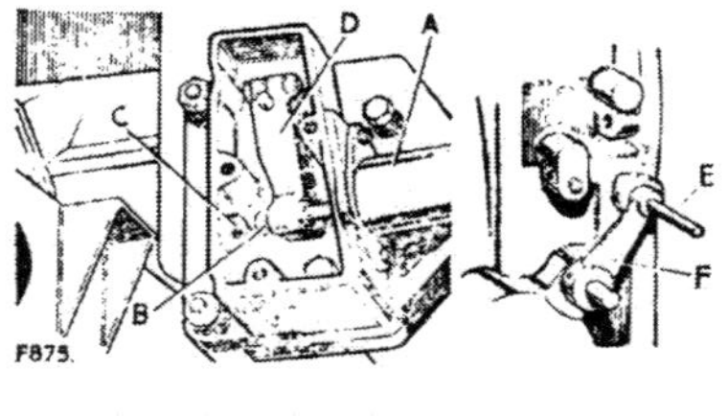

Adjusting solenoid, early type

A—Solenoid
B—Solenoid plunger
C—Rubber buffer
D—Lever
E—Setting bar
F—Cross-shaft lever

9. Refill the gearbox and overdrive units with the correct grade of lubricant. Capacity of complete unit 5 pints (2,75 litres).

Late models—ensure magnet in overdrive drain plug is clean and in position in the plug.

Operation D2–2—*continued*

10. The latest type solenoid, which incorporates a 'delrin' switch actuation push rod, can be used as a replacement on earlier models fitted with an overdrive unit.

    One of the main causes of solenoid burn-out has been due to the incorrect setting of the plunger stop, which on earlier models was in a fixed position and not adjustable. On the later models with the adjustable stop it is important therefore to ensure that it is correctly set. This may be done as follows:

    (a) Remove cover.

    (b) With the solenoid plunger pressed fully home, the setting screw for the main plunger adjustable stop must be set so that there is a .125 in. (3,0 mm) gap between the head of the plunger and the end stop.

    (c) Replace cover.

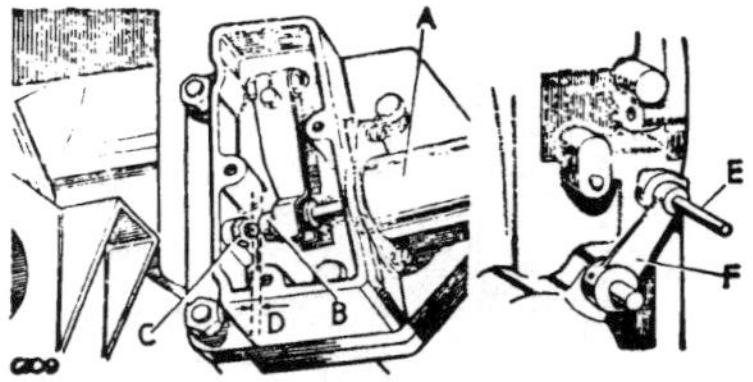

Setting solenoid adjustable stop, late type

A—Solenoid
B—Plunger
C—Adjustable stop
D—.125 in. (3,0 mm) gap
E—Setting bar
F—Cross-shaft lever

Overdrive unit, to dismantle—Operation D2–3

Workshop hand tools:
- Hide-faced hammer
- Screwdrivers, small and medium
- Pin punch Pliers Circlip pliers 'C' spanner
- Spanner sizes: $\frac{5}{16}$ in. AF, $\frac{7}{16}$ in. AF, $\frac{1}{2}$ in. AF, $\frac{9}{16}$ in. AF, $\frac{5}{8}$ in. AF

Special tools:
- Drive shaft oil seal remover, Part No. 268709
- Cone clutch remover, Part No. 268710
- Free-wheel assembly ring, Part No. 268711
- Accumulator piston remover, Part No. 268715
- Pump barrel remover, Part No. 268716
- Tail shaft bearing remover, Part No. 268720

Instructions for removing and refitting the overdrive unit are given in Operation D2-2

Note: From gearboxes numbered 77005682A onwards a new overdrive unit with larger accumulator size and stronger springs has been fitted. Overhaul procedure is basically as the earlier model and is covered in the following operations.

Overdrive unit, dismantle

Caution. Before attempting to dismantle the unit it is necessary to ensure that hydraulic pressure is released from the accumulator chamber.

1. Release hydraulic pressure by operating the setting lever by hand approximately 12 times.
2. Unscrew the large brass drain plug with a 'C' spanner and drain off any excess oil.
3. Remove the solenoid lever compartment cover plate and gasket. Slacken the nut of the pinch bolt retaining the solenoid lever. Remove the two screws retaining the solenoid, disengage the solenoid plunger from the lever and withdraw the solenoid.
4. Withdraw the solenoid lever and spacer.

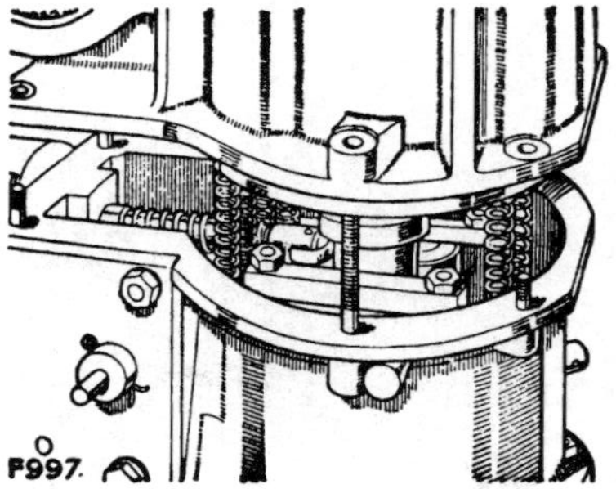

Removing extension casing

Extension casing and input shaft

5. Mount the unit, tail casing downward, in a vice or on a suitable support.
6. Separate the extension casing from the main casing by removing the nuts and washers from the short studs. Remove the two nuts from each of the two long studs last. Failure to release these last may result in injury to the operator.
7. Withdraw the extension case complete with main shaft, oil pump operating cam and collar. Remove and discard the gasket.
8. Remove the circlip securing the bearing to the extension case; then press the shaft and bearing out of the casing.
9. Withdraw the oil pump cam and collar from the input shaft.
10. Prise off the snap ring with a screwdriver and press off the bearing from the shaft. A new snap ring will be required on reassembly.

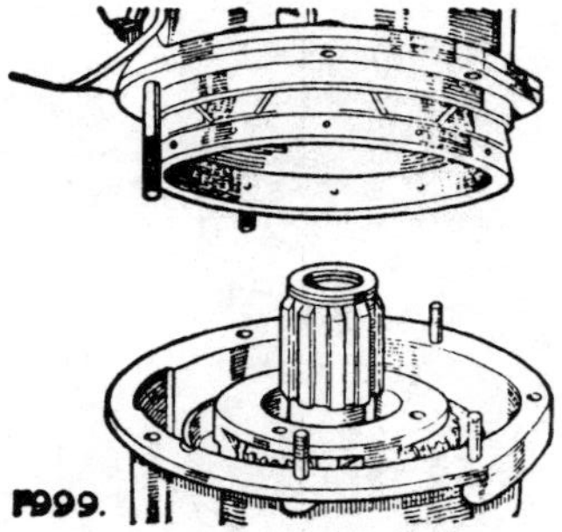

Removing main casing assembly

Main casing

11. Lift the 12 clutch coil springs from the supporting studs.

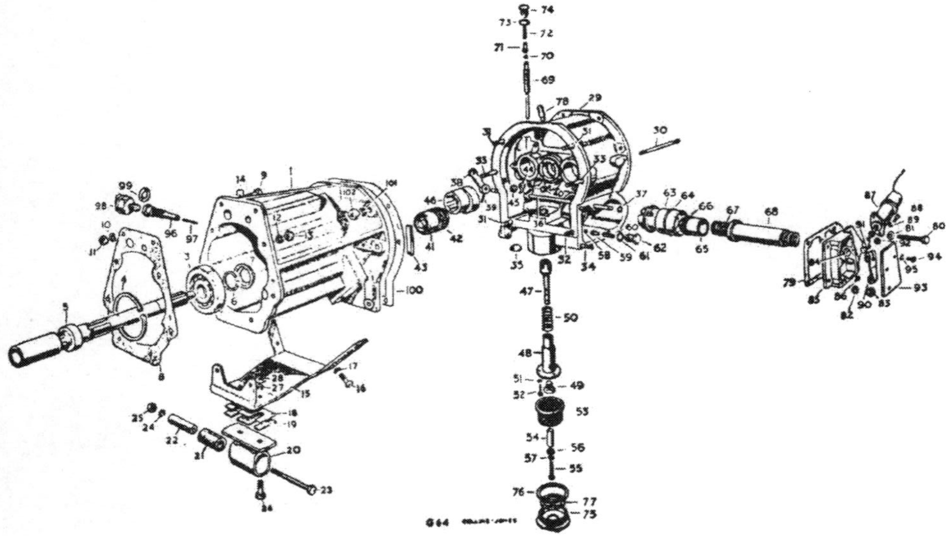

Exploded view of overdrive unit, extension and main casing assemblies

- 1 Extension casing
- 3 Bearing for mainshaft
- 4 Circlip
- 5 Mainshaft
- 6 Split ring
- 7 Spacing collar
- 8 Joint washer, extension casing to gearbox
- 9–14 Fixings, extension casing to gearbox
- 15 Reaction bracket
- 16–17 Fixings, reaction bracket to casing
- 18–19 Shims, reaction bracket to stabiliser bracket
- 20 Stabiliser bracket
- 21 Bush
- 22 Tube, for stabiliser
- 23–25 Fixings, stabiliser bracket to sub-frame bracket
- 26–28 Fixings, stabiliser bracket to reaction bracket
- 29 Main casing assembly
- 30–34 Studs, for main casing
- 35 Core plug
- 36 Valve operating shaft
- 37 Oil seal, for valve operating shaft
- 38 Operating valve setting lever
- 39 Taper pin for lever
- 40 Pump plunger guide peg
- 41 Operating piston
- 42 Operating piston ring
- 43 Bridge piece
- 44–45 Fixings, for bridge piece
- 46 Cam
- 47 Oil pump plunger
- 48 Oil pump body
- 49 Plug
- 50 Plunger spring
- 51–52 Fixings, for oil pump
- 53 Oil filter
- 54 Distance tube
- 55–57 Fixings, for filter
- 58 Steel ball
- 59 Plunger
- 60 Spring
- 61 Copper washer
- 62 Plug
- 63 Accumulator housing
- 64 Oil seal, for housing
- 65 Accumulator piston
- 66 Accumulator piston rings
- 67 Accumulator spring
- 68 Spacing tube
- 69 Operating plunger valve
- 70 Steel ball
- 71 Plunger
- 72 Spring
- 73 Copper washer
- 74 Plug
- 75 Drain plug
- 76 Washer
- 77 Magnet for drain plug
- 78 Breather
- 79 Joint washer
- 80–83 Fixings, for solenoid bracke
- 84 Collar
- 85 Bracket, for solenoid
- 86 Stop, for solenoid
- 87 Solenoid
- 88–89 Fixings, for solenoid
- 90 Operating lever
- 91–92 Fixings, for lever
- 93 Cover plate
- 94–95 Fixings, for cover plate
- 96 Insert
- 97 Plunger
- 98 Isolator switch
- 99 Shim for switch
- 100 Joint washer

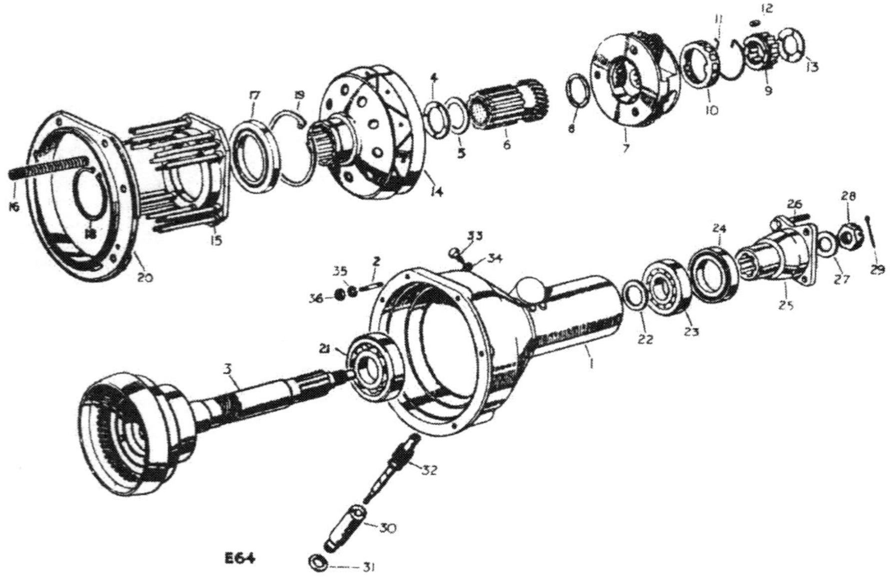
E64

Exploded view of overdrive unit and tail casing assembly

- 1 Overdrive tailshaft casing
- 2 Stud for casing
- 3 Annulus and tailshaft complete
- 4 Spacing washer, bronze, front
- 5 Steel thrust washer (seven thicknesses)
- 6 Sun wheel
- 7 Planet carrier assembly
- 8 Rear thrust washer
- 9 Uni-directional clutch, inner member
- 10 Uni-directional clutch cage
- 11 Spring for uni-directional clutch
- 12 Steel roller
- 13 Thrust washer, between annulus and uni-directional clutch
- 14 Cone clutch
- 15 Cone clutch thrust ring
- 16 Clutch springs
- 17 Thrust bearing
- 18–19 Circlips
- 20 Brake ring
- 21 Front tailshaft bearing
- 22 Spacing washer (five thicknesses)
- 23 Rear tailshaft bearing
- 24 Oil seal
- 25 Flange
- 26 Bolt
- 27–29 Fixings, flange to tailshaft
- 30 Speedometer bearing
- 31 Outer sealing ring
- 32 Speedometer driven gear
- 33 Locking screw
- 34 Copper washer
- 35–36 Fixings, main case to tail-case

Operation D2-3—*continued*

12. Unscrew evenly the nuts securing the main and tail casing, then lift the main case assembly complete with brake ring clear. Note the position of the two thrust washers on top of the sun wheel extension.
13. Prise the locking tabs away from the cone clutch studs and withdraw the cone clutch, use tool (Part No. 268710) if necessary.
14. Withdraw the operating pistons from their housings, using a pair of pliers on the piston pins
15. Remove the piston rings, or on late models the 'O' rings, from the two pistons.
16. Using a hide-faced mallet, tap evenly around the cast-iron brake ring and remove from the main casing.

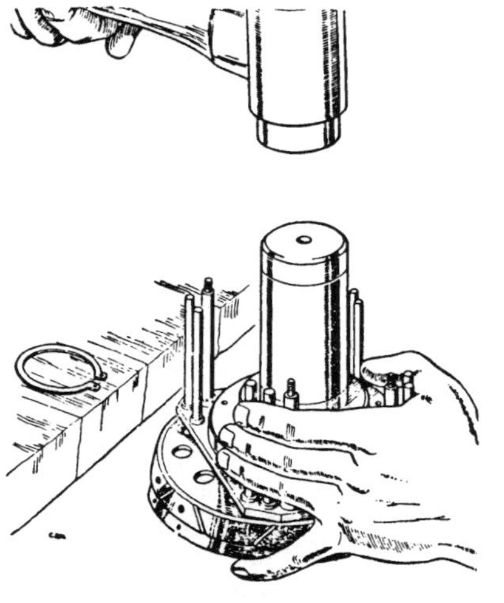

Dismantling cone clutch and thrust ring assembly

17. Unscrew the two nuts securing the side cover and solenoid lever housing. Lastly, remove the red painted set bolts evenly. Withdraw the side cover and housing assembly, then remove the 'O' ring seal from the operating cross-shaft hole in the cover.
18. Withdraw the accumulator spring, tube and packing washer, if fitted. Where packing washers are fitted to the original assembly, these must be retained for refitment.
19. Remove the accumulator housing and piston, using extractor (Part No. 268715), by applying a rotary pull to the wing bolt of the tool.

    Place the assembly into a clean container to avoid soiling or damaging the rubber sealing rings.

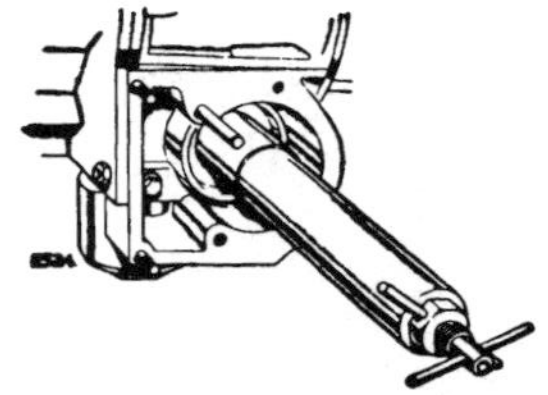

Withdrawing accumulator housing and piston

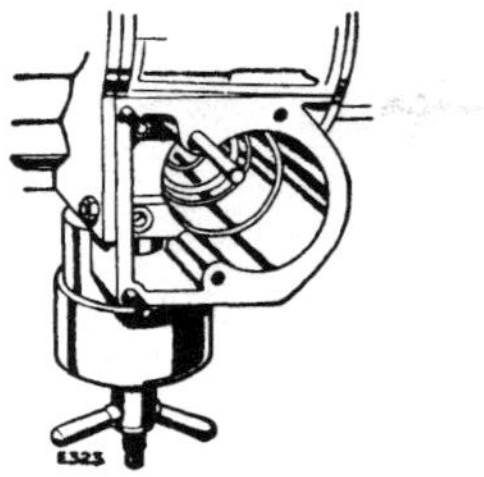

Extracting pump

Operation D2-3—*continued*

20. Before withdrawing the oil pump, the non-return inlet valve, located inside the oil pump housing, must be removed. Failure to remove the valve will result in damage to the casing and pump.

    The non-return inlet valve is retained by a red painted plug, located adjacent to the accumulator assembly aperture. Remove the plug with a socket or tubular box spanner, and withdraw the plug, spring, plunger and ball. Keep the components together in a container.
21. **Early models.** Remove the set bolt, spring washer and distance sleeve securing sump filter and withdraw filter.
22. **Late models.** The filter and magnet assembly are located on and retained by a spigot on the drain plug.
23. Unscrew the two cheese-headed screws in filter aperture and remove the plug in the base of the pump assembly.
24. Withdraw the pump with extractor tool (Part No. 268716).
25. Remove the operating valve plug, which is painted red and is located in the top right-hand side of the casing. Withdraw the spring, plunger, ball and valve.
26. If necessary, drift out the roll pins securing the operating valve setting lever and cam to the operating shaft. Withdraw the shaft from the main case.

Tail casing

27. Remove the two thrust washers from the top of the sun wheel extension.
28. Lift off the sun wheel and remove the rear thrust washer from between the sun wheel and planet carrier. Remove planet carrier, but do not attempt to dismantle this unit.
29. Withdraw the uni-directional clutch, using the assembly ring (Part No. 268711), to retain the rollers. Remove the thrust washer.
30. Unscrew the set bolt securing the speedometer drive bush and withdraw bush and gear.
31. Remove the slotted nut from tailshaft and withdraw the driving flange and plain washer.
32. If necessary, extract the oil seal from end of tail casing, using tool Part No. 268709.
33. Press the annulus and tailshaft from the casing.
34. If necessary, extract the front and rear bearings from the tail casing.

    A special tool (Part No. 268720) is used to remove the front bearing from the shaft. This tool has been designed for use in conjunction with Churchill hand press S4221, RG 4221 or a similar type.
35. Remove packing washer for the small bearing.

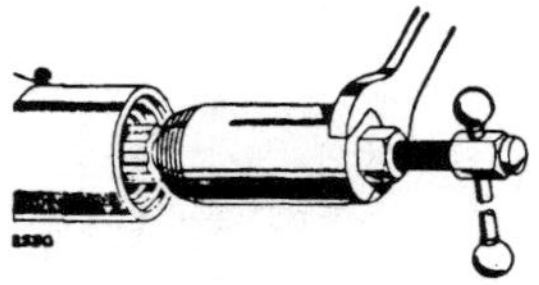

Removing tailshaft oil seal

Overdrive unit and extension case, to assemble—Operation D2-4

Workshop hand tools:
- Hide-faced hammer
- Screwdriver, small and medium
- Pliers, Circlip pliers
- 'C' spanner
- Set of feeler gauges
- Spanner sizes: $\frac{5}{16}$ in. AF, $\frac{7}{16}$ in. AF, $\frac{1}{2}$ in. AF, $\frac{9}{16}$ in. AF, $\frac{5}{8}$ in. AF

Special tools:
- Pump barrel replacer, Part No. 268717
- Accumulator housing 'O' ring replacer, Part No. 268714
- Piston fitting tool, Part No. 268712
- Operating piston fitting tool, Part No. 268713
- Tailshaft bearing replacer, Part No. 268719
- Free-wheel assembly ring, Part No. 268711
- Dummy drive shaft, Part No. 268718

Preparation before rebuild

Extension casing and brake band

1. Clean and inspect the casing for cracks, stripped threads and other damage. Examine the bores of the operating cylinders and accumulator for scores or wear.
2. Check for signs of leaks from the plugged ends of the oil passages. Ensure that the sealing disc beneath the accumulator is tight and not leaking. Inspect the bores of the centre support bushes for wear or damage.
3. Check operating pistons for signs of scores. Renew the sealing rings.
4. Examine pump roller for any undue wear. The roller is secured by a $\frac{1}{16}$ in. diameter Mills pin driven vertically into the curved portion of the pump plunger fork. This pin can be sheared by driving the roller pin through the fork. Later units have floating bronze bush in the pump roller, from which the pin is removed in the same way.
5. Check pump plunger and pump body bore, for wear and scores.
6. Check the valve seat and ball to ensure that they are free from nicks and scratches.
7. Examine the pump spring for distortion
8. Inspect the accumulator piston and sleeve (where fitted) for signs of wear or scores. Examine the piston rings and if necessary renew. Ensure that the 'O' ring on the accumulator sleeve is not damaged.
9. Check accumulator spring for distortion or collapse.
10. Inspect the operating valve for distortion and damage. See that it slides easily in the bore of the casing. Check that the seating at the top is clean and free from scratches. Check that the restrictor jet is clear. Examine the ball and check the spring for distortion.
11. Check the brake ring for signs of wear, scoring or cracks.
12. Clean the filter thoroughly in petrol. Remove all metallic particles from the magnetic ring.

Clutch sliding member

1. Inspect the clutch linings on the clutch sliding member for any signs of excessive wear or charring. If there is any sign of this at all, the sliding member complete must be replaced. It is not possible to fit new linings because the faces have to be fine machined to an accurate angle after riveting.
2. Inspect the pins for the clutch springs and bridge pieces on the thrust ring and see that they are tight and not distorted. The ball race should rotate smoothly. Examine the clutch springs for any sign of distortion or collapse.

Planet carrier and gear train

1. Examine the teeth of the gears and the bearings. If the bush of the sun gear is worn a new gear complete must be fitted as the bore has to be machined concentric with gear teeth after sub-assembly.

Rear casing and annulus

1. Carefully inspect the uni-direction clutch assembly looking for chipped rollers and damaged inner and outer members. Examine the roller cage, the two ears of which should not be damaged and the spring should be checked for distortion or breakage.
2. Examine the speedometer drive worm and the bronze spigot bearing of the annulus under the uni-directional clutch.

Overdrive unit, to assemble

1. Insert the pump plunger and spring into the pump body; to insert this assembly into the maincasing a special tool Part No. 268717 comprising two guide pegs and drift should be used. Screw the pegs into tapped holes in base of pump housing. Position pump assembly with the flattened face of the plunger towards the mainshaft bush and locate by means of the pegs then carefully drift the pump into casing. Remove guide pegs.

Operation D2-4—*continued*

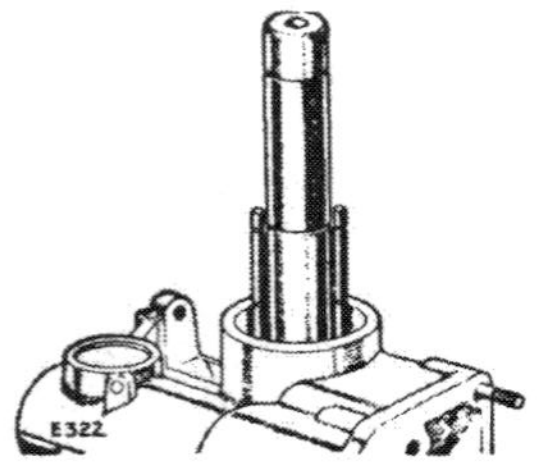

Fitting the oil pump

2. Fit the two cheese-headed screws and spring washers, then fit hexagon-headed plug into pump base.
3. **Early models.** Secure the filter to the pump base with the set bolt, distance piece, plain and spring washer. Fit the drain plug and magnet.

   Late models. Place the magnet into the drain plug recess. Locate the filter on to the peg of the drain plug and fit the plug.
4. Fit the non-return inlet valve ball, which is $\frac{1}{4}$ in. (6,0 mm) diameter, the plunger, spring and plug to transverse bore at side of oil pump. Tap ball lightly with a copper drift to seat it.
5. If removed, fit the valve operating shaft to the maincasing. Locate and secure the setting lever and cam to the shaft and secure with roll pins.
6. Align the hole in valve setting lever with setting hole in casing. Insert the operating plunger valve, narrow solid portion downward, into the bore at top RH side of casing, then fit the valve ball, which is $\frac{5}{16}$ in. (8,0 mm) diameter, then the plunger, spring and plug.
7. Fit new seals to the external diameter of the accumulator housing with the aid of tool Part No. 268714. Note early models have two seals and late models one. Lubricate the parts before fitting, with a little petroleum jelly.

Accumulator housing, seals, pistons and rings to main casing

8. **Early models.** Fit two new rubber seals to external diameter of accumulator piston housing with the aid of tool (Part No. 268714).

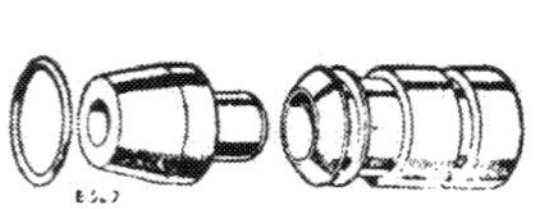

Fitting rubber seals with special tool

9. **Late models.** Fit one new rubber 'O' ring oil seal to the accumulator piston housing.

   (a) Position two wide piston rings in the single groove of the accumulator piston. Ring gap .010 to .015 in. (0,25 to 0,38 mm).

   (b) Position four narrow rings over the two wide rings, spacing the gaps evenly. Ring gap .002 to .006 in. (0,05 to 0,15 mm).
10. Lubricate the internal and external surface of the accumulator housing and, using a special guide tool (Part No. 268712), insert the piston assembly into housing.

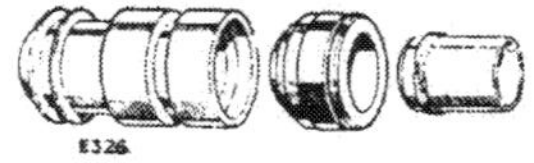

Fitting accumulator piston to housing

11. Press the accumulator housing and piston assembly into the bore, using the spring guide tube, the wide end of which should be located on the housing perimeter. The accumulator spring must not be fitted until the accumulator housing and piston are pressed home.

Operation D2-4—*continued*

12. With the spring guide tube in position, insert the accumulator spring, then position the side cover plate and gasket, complete with oil 'O' ring seal, for operating cross-shaft fitted in recess. If a packing washer was fitted originally, or supplied with a replacement spring, it must be fitted with the spring. The washer is located on the inner side of the cover by a dowel, which also locates the accumulator spring.

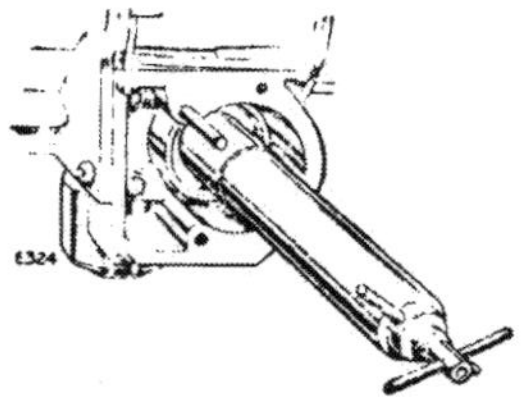

Fitting accumulator housing and piston

13. To compress the spring, tighten evenly the two set bolts, then fit nuts and spring washers. Operate the cross-shaft by hand to ascertain its freedom of movement.

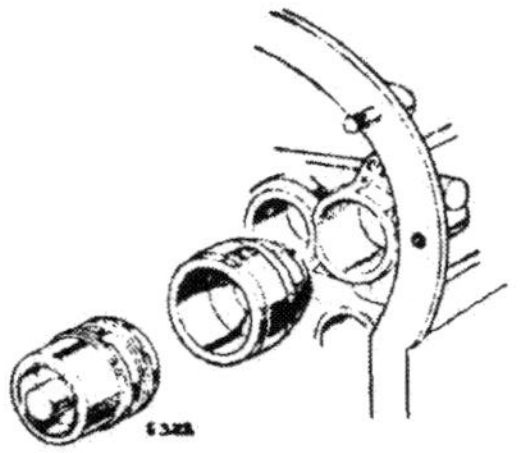

Fitting operating pistons, using special tool; early models illustrated

Operating pistons and rings to main casing

14. **Early models.** Fit a wide piston ring to each groove of the operating pistons and then two narrow rings on top of each wide ring. Space the gaps, which measure:

 Inner ring—.006 to .011 in. (0,15 to 0,27 mm)
 Outer ring—.002 to .006 in. (0,05 to 0,15 mm)

15. **Late models.** Position a new 'O' ring on to each operating piston and lubricate the pistons before inserting them into their bores.

16. Insert the operating pistons into respective bores, crown inwards, actuating knob outwards, using a special guide tool (Part No. 268713).

Brake ring to main casing

17. Position the brake ring by means of the two long studs on main casing rear face and press into position.

18. Ensure that the brake ring is firmly seated with its flange against the casing flange, then ascertain and note the dimension from the face of input shaft bush to joint face of brake ring, as shown at 'A' below. This dimension must be used in conjunction with the dimension obtained at item 40 and used as detailed at item 41.

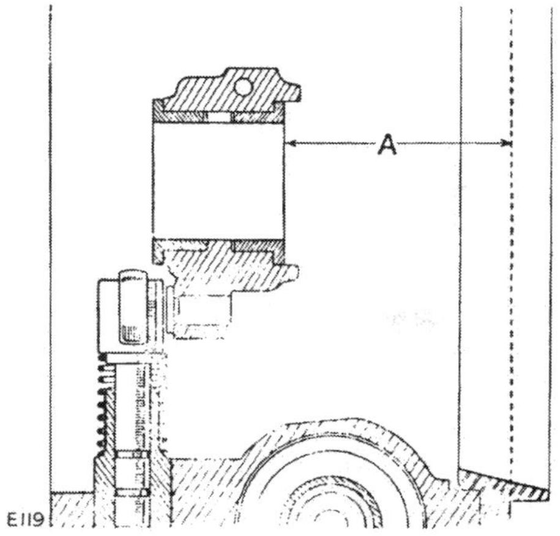

Checking dimension from face of bush to brake ring
For dimension 'A' see script

Operation D2-4—*continued*

Cone clutch, thrust ring and bearing to main casing

19. Press the bearing into housing in thrust ring and secure with a large circlip.

20. Press the bearing and thrust ring on to the cone clutch extension and secure with a small circlip.

21. Fit the cone clutch and thrust ring assembly to the main casing from brake ring side.

22. Turn the unit over and fit the bridge pieces which are secured to the studs protruding through the main casing, using nuts and tab locking washers.

Annulus, bearing, spacing washer, seal, flange, speedometer gear and bush to tail-casing

23. Press the front and larger bearing on to the annulus and tailshaft with the aid of a tool (Part No. 268719).

24. Press the front bearing and tailshaft assembly into the tail casing.

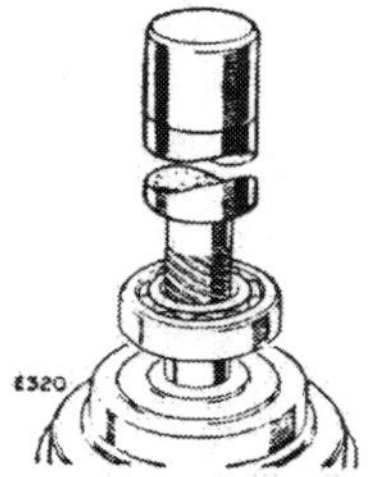

Using special tool to press bearing on to tailshaft

25. Check the dimension between the tailshaft shoulder and the shoulder in tail case for small rear bearing, using a suitable gauge, as shown at 'A' in following illustration.

26. Select a spacing washer, which, when fitted, will allow the annulus and tailshaft to have .005 to .010 in. (0,12 to 0,25 mm) end-float.

27. Fit the chosen washer on to the shaft and press the smaller rear bearing on to tailshaft.

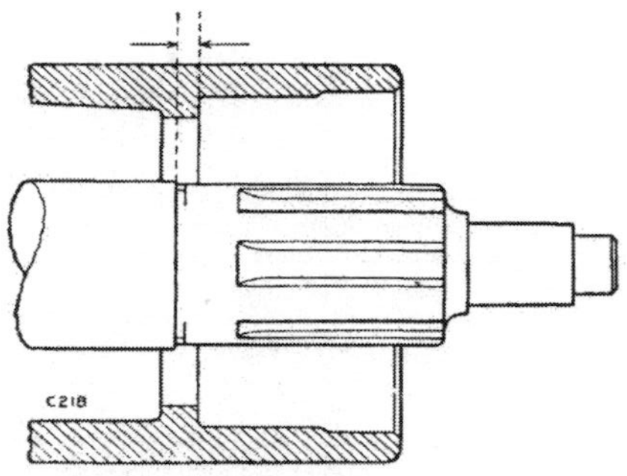

Checking tailshaft for spacing washer dimension
A—Checking position

28. Press the oil seal into position, with the lip facing inwards.

29. Fit the driving flange and plain washer. Secure with a nut and split pin.

30. Locate the speedometer gear and bush, turning the tailshaft to engage gear. Align the holes in casing and bush, then fit the locking screw and copper washer.

Input shaft and bearing to extension casing

31. Press the input shaft bearing on to the shaft and lock in position with a new split ring.

32. Fit the shaft and bearing assembly to the extension casing and press into position. Lock the bearing to casing with a circlip.

Uni-directional clutch assembly

33. Fit the spring and centre member of clutch to cage, locating the spring to cause the rollers (when fitted) to rise up the inclined face of centre member.

34. Position the roller assembly ring (Part No. 268711) to cage and inner member, then feed rollers into position, turning the cage in the free-wheeling direction.

Operation D2-4—*continued*

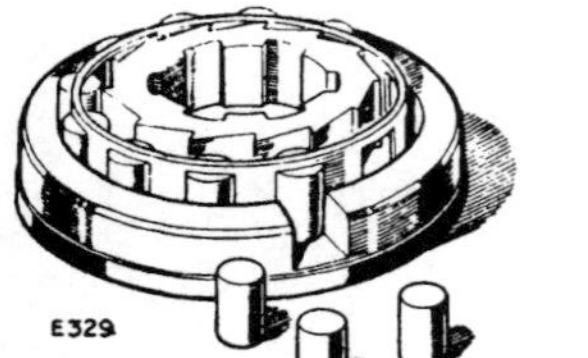

Assembling uni-directional clutch

Main casing assembly to tail casing assembly

35. Mount the tail casing assembly flange downward in a vice or suitable support.
36. Fit the thrust washer, $\frac{31}{32}$ in. (24 mm) internal and $1\frac{5}{8}$ in. (41 mm) external diameter, to the recess annulus.

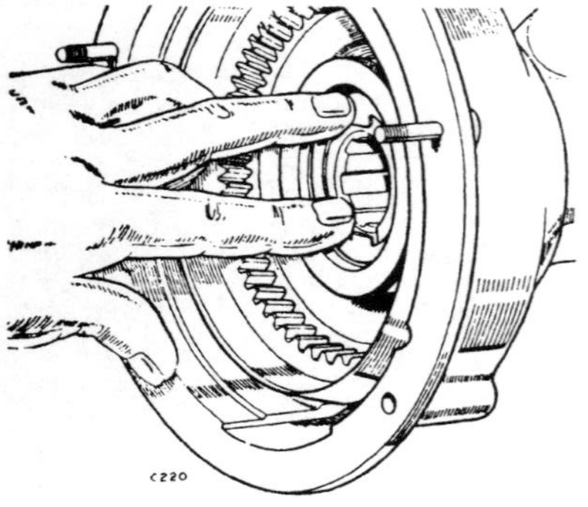

Fitting uni-directional clutch

37. With the assembly ring in position to retain rollers, fit the uni-directional clutch to the annulus with the open side of cage inward, and withdraw the assembly ring.
38. Fit the rear thrust washer, $1\frac{5}{32}$ in. (29 mm) internal and $1\frac{1}{2}$ in. (38 mm) external diameter, to the recess of planet carrier.
39. Turn each planet wheel until the pop marks on teeth align with centre of planet wheel bearings and axle of planet carrier, then fit sun wheel and extension assembly to planet carrier.

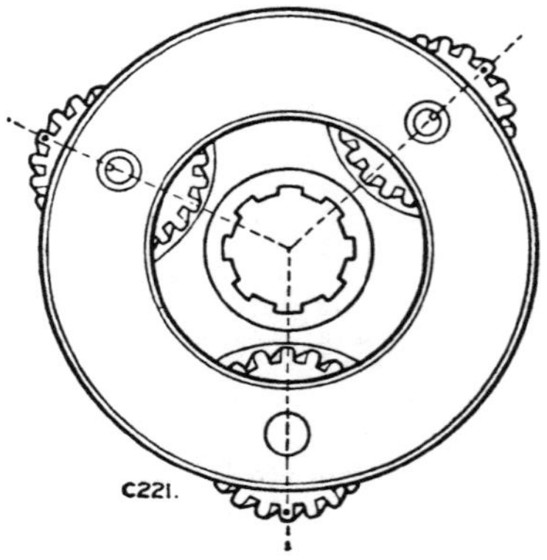

Fitting sun wheel to planet carrier

40. Place the front bronze thrust washer on top of the sun wheel extension. Place a suitable protection on top of thrust washer and tap lightly with a hammer to bed washers, then check the dimension from top of thrust washer to joint face of tail casing, as shown at 'A' in following illustration. This dimension must be used in conjunction with the dimension obtained at item 18 and used as detailed at item 41.
41. Subtract the dimension obtained in item 40 from that determined in item 18, then select a steel washer, $1\frac{5}{32}$ in. (29 mm) internal and 1.60 in. (15,0 mm) external diameter, obtainable in seven thicknesses, to allow an end-float of .008 to .014 in. (0,20 to 0,35 mm) for the sun wheel, planet carrier and uni-directional clutch, when main and tail casing assemblies are bolted together.
42. Place the selected steel washer on top of the thrust washer and insert a dummy drive shaft (Part No. 268718) to facilitate fitment of main casing assembly and retain thrust washers in correct position.
43. Position the main casing assembly and brake ring over tail casing assembly and lower into place. Turn dummy drive shaft and cone clutch to marry sun wheel extension splines with cone clutch splines, then tighten down evenly.

Operation D2-4—*continued*

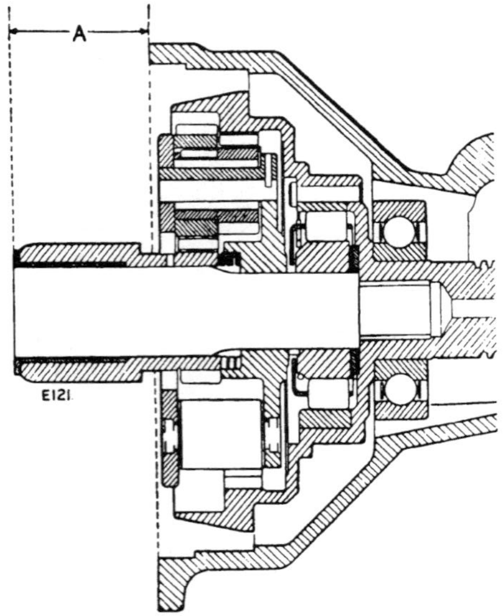

Checking dimension, extension thrust washer to tail casing joint face
For dimension 'A' see script

44. Withdraw the dummy drive shaft and fit a new gasket to joint face of main casing.

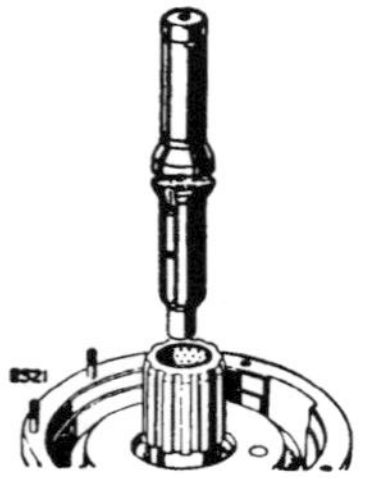

Using dummy drive shaft

Extension casing assembly to main and tail casing assembly

45 Fit the twelve thrust springs to cone clutch extension rods.

46. Fit a spacing collar on to the input shaft of the extension casing assembly and position it over the bearing retaining split ring.
47. Note the relative positions of the splines on input shaft and in planet carrier, then position the oil pump actuating cam, which can be smeared with grease to hold it in position on the input shaft, so that when the extension casing assembly is offered to the main assembly, the lobe of the cam will be farthest from the oil pump plunger. The lobe of the oil pump must be kept away from the pump plunger when assembling. Failure to ensure that these positions are maintained will result in damage to the cam and plunger.
48. Position the extension casing assembly, complete with spacing collar and cam, over the tail casing assembly, then lower into position. The input shaft may be turned a few degrees either way for location purposes, but the amount is limited by the necessity of keeping the lobe of the cam in the correct position. If the shaft does not enter freely, the relative positions of the splines and oil pump cam should be reset. Ensure that the cone clutch springs are correctly located by the raised lobes on the extension casing.
49. Pull the extension casing down into position by tightening evenly on the two longest studs first, then secure finally by means of the remaining fixings.

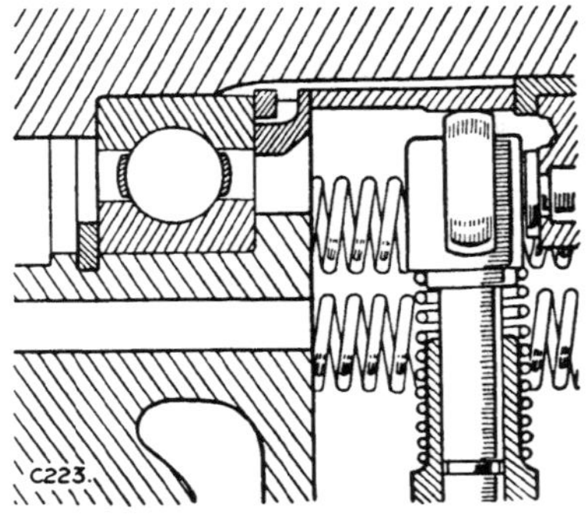

Oil pump cam and plunger in correct relative position for assembly

Overdrive manual switch, to remove and refit—Operation D2-5

Workshop hand tools:
Allen key Screwdriver
Spanner sizes: 2 BA, $\frac{7}{16}$ in. AF, $\frac{1}{2}$ in. AF, $1\frac{5}{16}$ in. AF

Switch, remove

1. Disconnect the battery, situated in the luggage compartment.
2. Remove the horn ring. Do this with the wheels in the straight-ahead position. Slacken the three Allen screws in the steering wheel hub.
3. Remove the steering wheel, secured by a nut and plain washer. **Note the correct position of the steering wheel on its splined shaft.**
4. Remove the shrouds from the steering column, secured by four small screws in the side of the shrouds and four small screws in the top support bracket. Carefully ease both shrouds away from the column after removing the beading strip.
5. Remove the overdrive selector switch from the shroud and disconnect the wiring harness.

Switch, refit

1. Fit the switch to the correct shroud and connect the wiring harness.
2. Refit the shroud assembly, ensuring correct location on the dowel. Fit the four recessed screws, but do not fully tighten at this stage.
3. Fit the top support bracket and the top beading strip, then tighten evenly all securing screws, ensuring that both shrouds and beading are firmly in position.
4. Fit the steering wheel on to its original spline, fit the plain washer and tighten the securing nut fully.
5. Fit the horn ring to the steering wheel.
6. Check that the steering wheel is in the straight-ahead position in relation to the front wheels.
7. Check that the trafficator switch, horn and overdrive switch function correctly.

Rotary switch for overdrive, to remove and refit, Mk I and Mk IA—Operation D2-6

Workshop hand tools:
Spanner sizes: $\frac{7}{16}$ in. AF, $\frac{7}{8}$ in. AF
Screwdriver, small

Rotary switch, remove

1. Disconnect battery, situated in the luggage compartment.
2. Remove the lever from the rotary switch spindle, secured by a clamping bolt and nut.
3. Remove the switch from the bracket secured by a locknut.
4. Disconnect the harness from the switch, noting the wiring sequence.

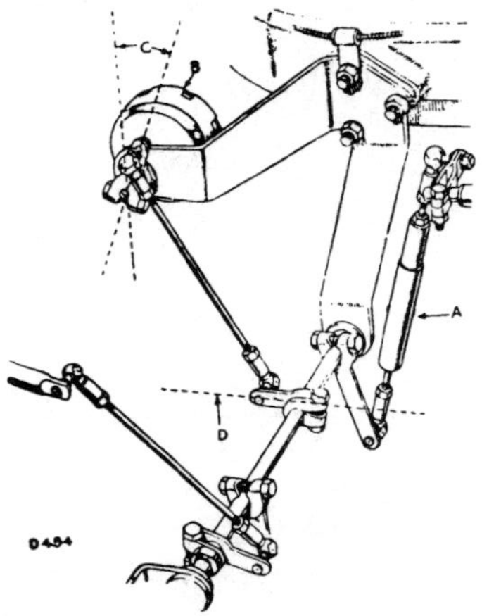

Arrangement of rotary switch and control rods
A—Collapsible rod C—30°
B—Rotary switch D—Horizontal

Rotary switch, refit

1. Connect the harness to the switch in accordance with the circuit diagram.
2. Fit the switch to the bracket, secured by a locknut. The spindle faces away from the engine.
3. Set the control rod ball pin to the mid-slot position in the switch lever.
4. Fit the switch lever to the switch spindle, but do not tighten the clamp bolt.
5. Ensure that the lever on the accelerator countershaft is pointing rearwards in a horizontal position.
6. Turn the switch spindle in an anti-clockwise direction until the limit of movement is reached, using very little pressure; hold the spindle firmly and position the switch lever so that it is approximately 30° from vertical, pointing upwards, then tighten the lever clamping bolt.
7. Adjust the length of the control rod and fit it, but do not tighten. Disconnect one end again and screw the ball joint one complete turn clockwise to shorten the rod slightly. Reconnect the control rod and tighten the locknuts.

Cam switch, to remove, refit and adjust, Mk II and Mk III—Operation D2-7

Workshop hand tools:
Spanner size: $\frac{7}{16}$ in. AF

Cam switch, remove

1. Disconnect the battery, situated in the luggage compartment.
2. Disconnect the two wires from the switch at the Lucar connectors.
3. Slacken the locknut on the switch and screw out the switch from the bracket.

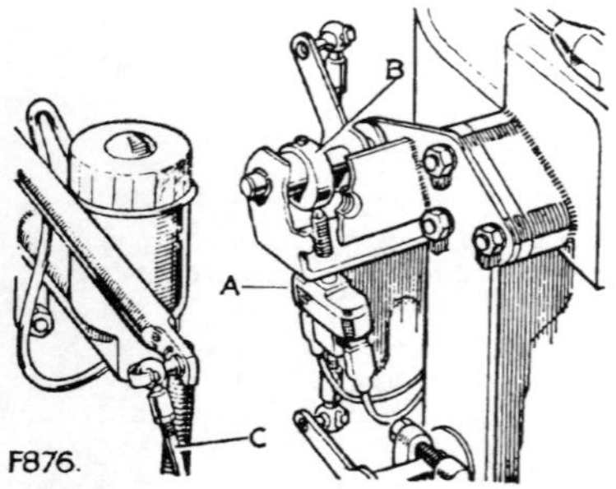

F876.

Overdrive cam switch on accelerator linkage

A—Switch B—Cam
C—Adjust throttle linkage at this rod

Cam switch, refit and adjust, Mk II suffix 'A' and 'B'

1. Reverse removal procedure. Do not tighten the switch locknut at this stage.
2. Before attempting to set the cam switch, check the full throttle position and adjust as necessary by altering the length of the control rod, accelerator lever to countershaft.
3. Adjust the switch, by screwing it in or out on its bracket so that as the cam is rotated (by lifting the control rod) the cam will depress the switch plunger. This should occur at approximately one-eighth throttle opening. Check the operation of the switch by connecting it to a battery-operated test lamp.

Cam switch, refit and adjust, models Mk II suffix 'C' and Mk III

1. Reverse removal procedure.
2. Slacken the clamp bolt of the lever on the carburetter butterfly spindle.
3. Position the lever cam so that the switch plunger is in line with the horizontal groove in the cam.
4. Hold the cam in this position and clamp the carburetter lever to the butterfly spindle with the butterfly in the fully closed position.
5. Screw the switch in or out until the plunger registers in the cam groove by not more than $\frac{1}{64}$ in. (0,4 mm). Tighten the switch locknut.

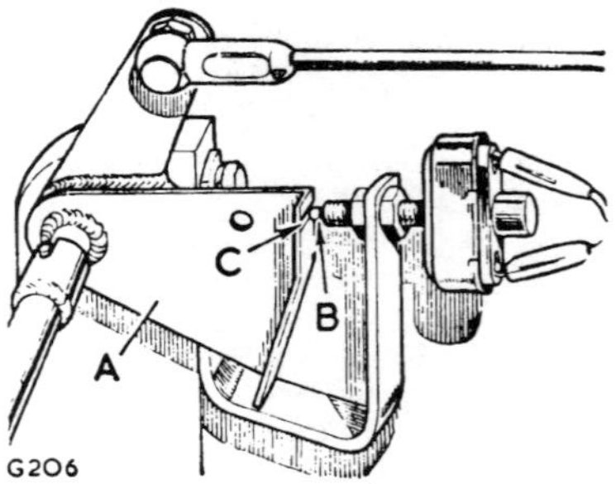

G206

Overdrive cam switch on accelerator linkage Mk II suffix 'C' and Mk III

A—Lever cam B—Switch plunger
C—Groove in cam

Isolating switch, to remove and refit—Operation D2-8

Workshop hand tools:
Screwdriver, small
Feeler gauges
Spanner sizes: 1 in. AF, $1\frac{1}{8}$ in. AF

Special tools:
Test lamp and battery

Isolating switch, remove

Early models, items 1 to 3

1. Disconnect the leads from the isolating switch.
2. Unscrew the switch, then withdraw it complete with spacing shims.
3. If necessary, unscrew the insert and remove the plunger.

Late models, items 4 to 5

4. Disconnect the switch leads.
5. Slacken the locknut and unscrew switch. Withdraw plunger, using a magnet; if plunger is stuck, the sleeve may be unscrewed.

Isolating switch and plunger, refit

Early models

1. Fit the insert to extension casing and tighten fully.
2. Move the gear lever into top gear position, insert the switch operating plunger and, with finger pressure, ensure that it is in contact with the selector shaft.

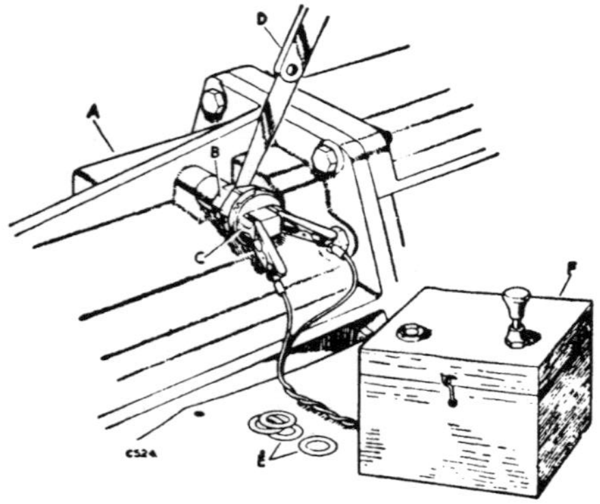

Setting isolating switch

A—Extension casing D—Feeler gauge
B—Insert E—Shims
C—Isolating switch F—Test lamp

3. Screw the switch into the insert until approximately $\frac{1}{8}$ in. (3 mm) remains extended, then connect a test lamp and battery to the switch terminals. Continue to screw the switch slowly into the insert and stop immediately the bulb lights.
4. Ascertain the clearance between the switch and insert, using a feeler gauge.
5. Select shims, available in .005 in. (0,12 mm) and .020 in. (0,50 mm) thicknesses, which, when inserted between the switch and insert, will allow the switch to be screwed in a further .010 to .015 in. (0,25 to 0,38 mm) only.
6. Remove the switch, fit the selected shims and refit.
7. Reconnect the test lamp and battery, move the gear lever in and out of top gear to check that the light appears only when in top gear position.
8. Remove the test lamp and connect the harness leads in accordance with the circuit diagram.

Late models

9. Smear the plunger with engine oil and fit into aperture.
10. With the locknut in position on the switch and the gear lever in the neutral position, screw the switch into gearbox by hand until resistance is felt (as the switch extension contacts the plunger), then unscrew one-eighth turn.
11. Test the switch operation by connecting a test lamp lead to one terminal of switch and the feed lead from the fuse to the other. Earth the second lead of test lamp and, with the ignition switched 'on', check that the contacts are open as indicated by the unlit bulb.
12. Move the gear lever into top gear position, then check that the switch contacts are closed; test bulb should be lit.

Operation D2-8—*continued*

13. If bulb does not light, unscrew the switch until it does, then move gear lever into neutral; light should now be out.

14. Retain switch in position and tighten locknut.

15. Retest as detailed above.

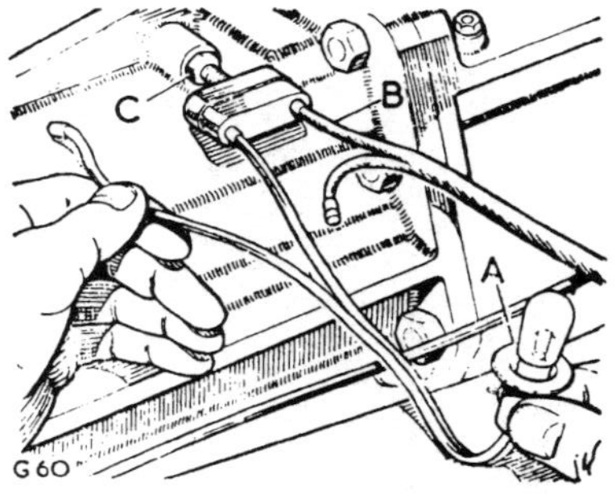

Testing isolating switch

A—Test lamp B—White lead C—Adjusting locknut

Kick-down switch, to remove and refit, Mk I and Mk IA—Operation D2-9

Workshop hand tools:

Spanner sizes: $\frac{5}{16}$ in. AF, $\frac{7}{16}$ in. AF

Kick-down switch, remove

1. Withdraw the carpet from accelerator pedal area.
2. Remove the switch and bracket, secured to body by nuts, bolts and washers.
3. Disconnect the leads from the switch.
4. Remove switch from bracket, secured by two screws.

Kick-down switch, refit

1. Refit the kick-down switch below the accelerator pedal, connecting the leads to switch in accordance with circuit diagram.
2. Depress the accelerator pedal to the kick-down switch button.
3. Ensure that the carburetter butterfly valve is fully open and the collapsible rod is on the point of collapse. If this condition is not achieved, carry out suitable adjustment to the lengths of the collapsible rod and levers.
4. Depress the accelerator pedal to the full kick-down position and ensure that the collapsible rod has telescoped.
5. Adjustment may be made by altering the length of the control rod between the cross-shaft and accelerator pedal shaft lever.

Section D – 4-SPEED GEARBOX AND OVERDRIVE – Part Three

DEFECT LOCATION—Gearbox

SYMPTOM	*POSSIBLE CAUSE*	*REMEDY*
GEARBOX NOISY IN NEUTRAL	1. Primary pinion bearing worn 2. Constant mesh gears incorrectly matched or badly worn 3. Layshaft bearing worn 4. Insufficient oil in gearbox, or incorrect grade of oil	1. *Renew* 2. *Renew* 3. *Renew* 4. *Replenish*
GEARBOX NOISY IN GEAR	1. Worn speedometer gears 2. If the gearbox is noisy in all gears except top, the constant mesh gears may be worn or incorrectly paired or the layshaft bearings may be worn 3. Noise in either the 1st, 2nd or 3rd speed gears only, due to wear 4. Noise in all gears possibly denotes worn primary or mainshaft bearings	1. *Renew* 2. *Renew the constant mesh gears or the layshaft bearings, as necessary* 3. *Renew the pair of gears, as necessary* 4. *Renew bearings and check gear teeth for wear*
OIL LEAKS FROM THE GEARBOX	1. Lubricant level too high 2. Damaged, incorrectly fitted or missing joint washers 3. Damaged or incorrectly fitted oil seals 4. Drain or level plugs loose or threads damaged 5. Cracked or broken gearbox housing	1. *Correct the level* 2. *Renew* 3. *Renew* 4. *Rectify* 5. *Renew*
DIFFICULTY IN ENGAGING GEARS	1. Insulating pad or support bracket incorrectly fitted in gear selector housing 2. Failure to release the clutch completely 3. Clutch spinning or sticking on the primary shaft 4. Second gear stop incorrectly set	1. *Reposition* 2. *In the hands of the operator* 3. *Rectify as necessary* 4. *Adjust to allow .002 in. (0,05 mm) clearance between stop and jaw*
DIFFICULTY IN DISENGAGING GEARS	1. Failure to release the clutch completely 2. Distorted or damaged mainshaft splines	1. *In the hands of the operator* 2. *Renew*
DIFFICULTY IN ENGAGING REVERSE	1. Bush loose in gear 2. Insulating pad or support bracket incorrectly fitted in gear selector housing	1. *Renew* 2. *Reposition*

DEFECT LOCATION—Overdrive

SYMPTOM	POSSIBLE CAUSE	REMEDY
OVERDRIVE DOES NOT ENGAGE	1. Insufficient oil in unit 2. Solenoid not operating, due to faulty solenoid (or electrical circuit) 3. Operational setting incorrect 4. Insufficient hydraulic pressure, due to pump non-return valve not seating 5. Damage to pump roller, plunger or spring	1. *Top up, check for leaks* 2. *Check solenoid, renew as necessary; or check and renew defective wiring* 3. *Reset, check switch on accelerator linkage and solenoid setting* 4. *See Operation D2-1* 5. *Renew*
OVERDRIVE DOES NOT RELEASE	1. Fault in electrical circuit 2. Sticking solenoid plunger or incorrect operational setting 3. Blocked restrictor jet in operating valve	1. *Test wiring, switches and solenoid* 2. *Renew solenoid, or reset solenoid, see Operation D2-2* 3. *See Operation D2-1*
CLUTCH SLIP IN OVERDRIVE	1. Insufficient oil in unit 2. Operational setting incorrect 3. Insufficient hydraulic pressure, due to oil pump non-return valve not seating 4. Pressure correct, but operating valve ball not seating on valve 5. Accumulator assembly worn or scored; anti-friction additives having been used in the oil	1. *Top up, check for leaks* 2. *Reset, check switch on accelerator linkage and solenoid setting* 3. *Remove obstruction or lap seating* 4. *Remove obstruction or lap seating* 5. *Strip unit and clean components, renew cone clutch linings*
CLUTCH SLIP IN REVERSE OR FREE-WHEEL CONDITION ON OVERRUN	1. Operational setting incorrect 2. Operating valve ball not seating in casing 3. Partially blocked restrictor jet in operating valve 4. Anti-friction additives having been used in the oil	1. *Reset, check switch on accelerator linkage and solenoid setting* 2. *Remove obstruction or lap seating* 3. *Remove and clean* 4. *Strip unit and clean components, renew cone clutch linings*
FAULTS—HYDRAULIC Negative or insufficient oil pressure (High ratio cannot be selected)	1. Insufficient oil in sump 2. Dirty filter 3. Inlet non-return valve ball not seating properly 4. Inlet non-return valve spring broken 5. Inlet non-return valve incorrectly assembled 6. Inlet non-return valve plug loose 7. Broken or weak pump plunger spring 8. Excessively worn pump plunger 9. Fatigued or broken accumulator spring 10. Packing washer for accumulator spring not refitted after dismantling (i.e. when a washer was originally fitted or supplied with a replacement spring) 11. Accumulator piston, rings or housing excessively worn 12. Operating piston housings excessively worn	1. *Top up, check for leaks* 2. *Remove and clean* 3. *Remove obstruction—lap seating with spare ball if necessary* 4. *Renew* 5. *Rectify as necessary* 6. *Tighten* 7. *Renew* 8. *Renew* 9. *Renew* 10. *Fit washer* 11. *Renew* 12. *Fit a replacement unit*
Excessive pressure (causing Welch washer in base of main casing to blow)	1. Outlet holes for surplus oil in accumulator chamber obstructed 2. Accumulator piston seized 3. Outlet at centre bearing obstructed	1. *Dismantle unit and clean* 2. *Remove piston and housing, ascertain cause and fit new parts as necessary* 3. *Dismantle and clean*
Normal ratio cannot be selected	1. Operating plunger rod metering hole obstructed 2. Operating plunger stuck 3. Operating valve spring weak or broken 4. Operating valve incorrectly assembled 5. Operating ball valve not seating properly 6. Operating cross-shaft incorrectly set 7. Operating valve plug loose	1. *Remove rod and clear obstruction* 2. *Remove plunger to ascertain cause* 3. *Renew* 4. *Rectify* 5. *Remove obstruction or lap seating* 6. *See Operation D2-2* 7. *Tighten*

DEFECT LOCATION—Overdrive—*continued*

SYMPTOM	POSSIBLE CAUSE	REMEDY
FAULTS—ELECTRICAL **Overdrive ratio cannot be selected**	1. Fuse blown 2. Isolating switch incorrectly set 3. Break in wiring or disconnected lead 4. Faulty switch 5. Relay or solenoid unserviceable 6. Rotary or cam switch on accelerator linkage incorrectly set	1. *Ascertain cause by inspection and testing; rectify fault, renew fuse* 2. *Reset* 3. *Locate and repair* 4. *Test all switches.* 5. *Renew* 6. *Reset*
Overdrive ratio can be selected in any **gear**	1. Isolating switch faulty or incorrectly set 2. Isolating switch plunger sticking	1. *Check setting if still faulty, renew switch* 2. *Remove switch and adaptor; ascertain cause*
Overdrive ratio operates immediately **top gear is selected and cannot be cancelled**	1. Relay plunger sticking in closed position	1. *Renew*
Violent deceleration and possible skidding of rear tyres when steering column switch is used to change from overdrive to normal top gear whilst travelling at high speed	1. Rotary or cam switch on accelerator linkage faulty or incorrectly set	1. *Reset or renew*
Normal top gear ratio cannot be selected	1. Leads disconnected from W1 terminal on relay	1. *Re-connect*
Early models with kick-down switch—normal top gear ratio can be selected by kick-down switch only	1. Control switch on steering column unserviceable, or rotary switch on accelerator linkage faulty	1. *Renew*
Early models with kick-down switch—kick-down switch will not select normal top gear ratio	1. Switch unserviceable 2. Leads broken or disconnected	1. *Renew* 2. *Ascertain cause and rectify*
FAULTS—MECHANICAL **No engine braking effect on car overrun—normal ratio selected**	1. Cone clutch springs fatigued or cone clutch inner lining worn	1. *Strip and replace*
Slipping clutch—overdrive ratio selected	1. Cone clutch outer lining worn 2. Insufficient oil pressure 3. Oil level too low 4. Accumulator spring fatigued 5. Accumulator piston sticking 6. Anti-friction additives in lubricating oil	1. *Strip and renew* 2. *Rectify* 3. *Top up, check for leaks* 4. *Strip and renew* 5. *Strip and investigate cause* 6. *Strip unit and clean components—renew cone clutch linings*
Overdrive ratio cannot be selected	1. Pump plunger return spring fatigued or broken 2. Pump plunger worn excessively 3. Operating cross-shaft and solenoid incorrectly set 4. Operating cross-shaft binding on side cover plate	1. *Strip and renew* 2. *Strip and renew* 3. *Reset* 4. *Check fitment of cover plate and rubber 'O' ring*
Normal top gear ratio cannot be selected	1. Operating cross-shaft binding on side cover plate	1. *Check fitment of cover plate and rubber 'O' ring*

DATA

Gearbox, four-speed

Type	Single helical constant mesh with synchromesh on top, third and second speeds
Gear ratios, four-speed only	
Top	Direct
Third	1.377 : 1
Second	2.043 : 1
First	3.376 : 1
Reverse	2.968 : 1
Gear ratios, four-speed with overdrive	
Overdrive	.778 : 1
Top	Direct
Third	1.377 : 1
Second	2.043 : 1
First	3.376 : 1
Reverse	2.968 : 1
Overall ratios, four-speed only, with 3.9 : 1 rear axle ratio	
Top	3.9 : 1
Third	5.37 : 1
Second	7.968 : 1
First	13.166 : 1
Reverse	11.575 : 1
Overall ratios, four-speed and overdrive, with 4.3 : 1 rear axle ratio	
Overdrive	3.35 : 1
Top	4.3 : 1
Third	5.921 : 1
Second	8.775 : 1
First	14.516 : 1
Reverse	12.762 : 1
Speedometer drive ratios	
Four-speed only	2.142 : 1
Four-speed, with overdrive	2.5 : 1
Oil capacity	
Four-speed gearbox only	$3\frac{1}{2}$ pints (2 litres)
Four-speed gearbox and overdrive unit	5 pints (2,75 litres)
Late models with separate gearbox and overdrive lubrication system Gearbox capacity	3 pints
Overdrive capacity	$1\frac{1}{2}$ pints

DATA—*continued*

Gearbox mainshaft bush end-float	.001 to .008 in. (0,03 to 0,20 mm)
Second and third mainshaft gears end-float	.004 to .007 in. (0,10 to 0,17 mm)
Layshaft end-float	.003 to .005 in. (0,07 to 0,12 mm)
Second and third mainshaft gears, clearance on bush	.002 to .004 in. (0,05 to 0,10 mm)
Reverse gear bush, clearance on shaft	.003 to .005 in. (0,07 to 0,12 mm)
Fit of primary shaft bearing on primary shaft	.0005 in. (0,013 mm) clearance to .0005 in. (0,013 mm) interference
Fit of primary shaft bearing to housing	.0008 to .0033 in. (0,002 to 0,07 mm) interference
Fit of the mainshaft bearing to the case	Zero to .0005 in. (0,013 mm) clearance
Fit of the rear mainshaft bearing to the shaft	Zero to .001 in. (0,02 mm) interference
Synchronising unit, spring loading	
Second	10–15 lbs. (0,45–0,68 kg)
Third–fourth	15–17 lbs. (0,68–0,77 kg)
Second speed selector shaft stop	.002 in. (0,05 mm) clearance when second gear selected
Overdrive unit	
Sun wheel, planet carrier and uni-directional clutch end-float	.008 to .014 in. (0,20 to 0,35 mm)
Annulus and tailshaft end-float	.005 to .010 in. (0,12 to 0,25 mm)
Hydraulic pressure in accumulator chamber	430±10 lb/sq in. (30,23±0,703 kg/cm²)
Accumulator spring, free length	6.428 in. (163 mm)
Identification	Each end coil painted green
Accumulator piston ring gap	
Inner ring	.010 to .015 in. (0,25 to 0,38 mm)
Outer ring	.002 to .006 in. (0,05 to 0,15 mm)
Accumulator piston clearance in housing	.0004 to .0023 in. (0,01 to 0,05 mm)
Accumulator housing clearance in chamber	.0002 to .002 in. (0,005 to 0,05 mm)
Operating piston ring gap	
Inner ring	.006 to .011 in. (0,15 to 0,27 mm)
Outer ring	.002 to .006 in. (0,05 to 0,15 mm)
Operating piston clearance housing	.0004 to .0023 in. (0,01 to 0,05 mm)
Oil pump plunger, clearance in bore	.0002 to .0015 in. (0,005 to 0,04 mm)
Cone clutch springs	
Quantity	12
Free length	Yellow ends $4\frac{9}{16}$ in. (116 mm)
Free length	Red ends $4\frac{13}{32}$ in. (112 mm)

Section E – AUTOMATIC TRANSMISSION
Model 'DG', Rover Mk I, Mk IA and Mk II
Part One

Section E is divided into three parts, namely:

Part I	General description and working principle. Unit removal/refit and adjustment procedure
Part II	Dismantling and overhaul procedure
Part III	Defect location, fault finding chart and data

The main casing of the transmission can only be separated from the engine after the engine and automatic transmission unit has been removed from the car. Certain units, however, can be removed from the main casing whilst the main casing is in the car; these units are:

Valve block
Extension casing
Brake band servos

Instructions for engine and automatic transmission unit removal are given in Section A.

Alternatively, the engine and automatic transmission unit may be removed with the sub-frame as an assembly, see Section H.

Some operations are marked with an asterisk (*) to indicate that they can be carried out with the unit installed in the car.

Driving instructions for the Automatic transmission will be found in the Owner's Instruction Manual.

INDEX

General description

The system consists of a hydraulic torque converter with a direct-drive clutch followed by two planetary gear sets providing two indirect gear ranges and reverse—thus eliminating the clutch pedal and the gear lever.

For low gear the drive is through the torque converter, and reduction of first and second planetary sets to the output shaft. In the intermediate gear a multiple-disc clutch locks up the front planetary set as a unit; drive is then transmitted through the torque converter and reduction of the rear planetary set only.

For direct drive a single-plate hydraulically operated clutch connects the engine output direct to the propeller shaft, thus by-passing both the torque converter and the planetary sets.

There are no internal electrical or vacuum connections throughout the automatic transmission unit, the transmission being hydraulically operated by two oil pumps, one located at the front end of the transmission, driven by the engine through the torque converter. This pump supplies pressure when the engine is idling, during reversing, and low speed operation. Above 25 mph approximately, the rear pump takes over and the front pump exhausts into the transmission sump.

The rear pump, located externally on the extension case, supplies pressure when the car is moving in a forward direction.

A governor valve which is responsive to road speed and torque demand, and the manually operated selector valve described below, controls the system.

The operation of the automatic transmission is controlled by the position of the selector lever, which is indicated by a quadrant pointer.

The lever must be lifted slightly, when engaging P, L or R.

The quadrant is situated in front of the steering wheel and is marked P, N, D, L and R. The selector lever allows selection of the following conditions:

P (park). In this position a pawl is mechanically engaged with a gear on the mainshaft, thus the car cannot be driven, and neither can the car 'roll away' even if the handbrake was not applied; as a further safety measure a hydraulic interlock prevents engagement of the pawl at speeds in excess of 5 mph.

N (neutral). The transmission is completely disengaged and there is no drive.

D (drive). The vehicle can be driven in a forward direction and all changes either "up" or "down" are automatically achieved.

L (low). This locks the transmission in the low range, and no upward changes will take place. It is for use on unusually long and steep gradients or for braking on steep descents and for rocking the car out of mud, sand or snow. A manual change from L (low) to D (normal forward drive) and vice versa, can be readily made at all speeds, though in the interest of engine rpm 35 mph (56 kph) should be taken as the safe maximum for up or down changes.

R (reverse). This provides for reverse driving, without engine braking.

The automatic transmission unit fitted to the Rover 3 Litre can be identified by the violet-coloured serial number plate, which is numbered in the range R5B1000 onwards. Models fitted with 2nd-speed start can be identified by the suffix K after the serial number.

Torque converter assembly

The torque converter consists of a stator, turbine and impeller. The impeller is connected to the engine crankshaft and is therefore the driving member. The turbine is connected to the mainshaft of the transmission and is the driven member. The stator is splined to the front of the transmission through a one-way clutch. The impeller driven by the engine transmits power to the turbine, which in turn transmits power to the transmission. For compactness the direct-drive clutch is enclosed within the torque converter assembly. It consists of three units: a hydraulically operated pressure plate, a driven member and a backing plate. Fluid pressure to the pressure plate locks these three units together, allowing engine torque to be transmitted to the rear axle at 1 : 1 ratio.

As the torque converter can only be serviced as a complete assembly, strip-down procedure has not been included in the following pages.

Gear train

Two planetary sets, each consisting of a ring gear, a carrier with three planet wheels and a sun gear, are carried on the mainshaft and situated one behind the other. Three brake drums and bands named according to their functions and not their location in the case, enable various components of the planetary set to be held stationary. The front drum with band applied is used to engage reverse gear, and is called the reverse drum. In all forward speeds the drum at the rear of the box is held by its brake band, and despite its location is known as the forward drum. The centre drum is held by its band when the selector lever is at 'L' for manual low ratio, and is therefore named the low drum.

The steel brake bands with bonded linings are actuated by hydraulic servos, one on either side of the transmission case and the reaction is taken by adjustable anchors at the opposite side.

A multiple-disc clutch is housed in the low drum and consists of alternate steel, bronze, or paper based clutch plates engaged by hydraulic pressure and retracted by a series of springs. Its function is to lock the front sun gear to the front carrier so that the front planetary set revolves as a unit during intermediate ratio (second gear) operation.

Two one-way clutches, also named according to their functions, are located on the rear sun gear.

The forward one-way clutch in the forward drum prevents the sun gear from rotating opposite to the direction of engine rotation while the reverse one-way clutch in the low drum plate turns the sun gear against engine rotation when reverse is in use.

The extension case bolted to the rear of the transmission carries the rear pump, centrifugal governor and speedometer drive.

The mainshaft, carrying the entire gear train, is supported at the rear by a ball race and at the front by two sets of needle rollers located in the front ring gear and collector ring. It is splined at the front to carry the direct-drive clutch plate and at the rear for the propeller shaft flange. Output from the planetary sets is through the rear carrier splined to the mainshaft.

Hydraulic components

A gear-type pump is mounted on the collector ring at the front of the transmission case and is driven by the converter impeller. The front pump supplies the fluid under pressure to the converter, the hydraulic control valves, and reverse when selected.

A gear-type pump mounted on the extension case takes over from the front pump at about 25 mph (40 kph). It is inoperative in reverse.

The valve block bolted to the bottom of the transmission houses the following: selector valve, converter shuttle valve, accumulator valve, main relief valve, reverse interlock valve, front and rear pump check valves.

The selector valve is operated by the selector lever on the steering column, and directs fluid from either or both pumps, depending on road and engine speeds, to the servos and governor in accordance with the position selected.

The converter shuttle valve regulates the pressure of fluid delivered to the converter. The converter is pressurised but the pressure must be controlled below a maximum to provide a differential between direct clutch and converter pressure to allow clutch engagement, and to avoid distortion of the converter casing. The converter shuttle valve has no spring but is operated solely by fluid pressure.

The accumulator valve increases line pressure after initial application of brake bands at low pressure in the interest of smoothness. The main relief valve regulates the pressure of the front and rear pumps.

The reverse interlock valve prevents application of the reverse band when the car is travelling forward. In addition to the above-mentioned valves, there are three others: the lubrication valve, the parking pawl interlock valve and the governor valve.

The lubrication valve is located in the mainshaft and maintains a head of fluid in the converter when the engine is not running. As the pressure rises the lubrication valve opens and the fluid is returned to the transmission case after bearing and gear train lubrication.

The parking pawl interlock valve is located in the extension case joint face. The piston is retracted by spring pressure so that the parking pawl can only be engaged as long as the piston is not pressurised by the rear pump when the car is moving.

Servos

The reverse servo on the left-hand side of the gearbox case, and low and forward servo on the right-hand side of the gearbox case, apply the bands as required and directed by the selector valve.

Governor

The movement of the governor under the influence of centrifugal force opens or closes the governor valve ports and directs the fluid to the multiple-disc clutch and direct-drive clutch for ratio changes as required by vehicle speed and accelerator positions. One side of the governor is linked to the throttle, thus rendering the governor sensitive to torque demand. A small hydraulic detant works on the governor fork and prevents hunting between intermediate and top ratios. A further detent piston is incorporated on models fitted with 2nd-speed start acting on the governor valve when in intermediate.

1st-speed start models

A spring-loaded pawl engages the governor valve in the intermediate position and prevents engagement of low ratio when kick-down is employed. Before low can be engaged the pawl must be disengaged by releasing the accelerator pedal completely, when the road speed is below 6 mph (9 kph).

2nd-speed start models

The mechanical differences are as follows:

1. The second speed latch control has been discarded and an accelerator detent plunger, to determine the full throttle setting for the box, has been added immediately above and acting on the control shaft detent cam.

2. A stronger booster spring is fitted behind the governor valve.

3. An additional hydraulic detent is fitted, acting on the governor valve when in intermediate.

This affects the car as follows:

Normal starting:

2nd speed or intermediate starts are achieved by the use of a stronger booster spring behind the governor valve, which holds the governor valve in the intermediate position for all normal starts, that is, up to approximately quarter-throttle.

Low starting:

Low or first speed starts, for maximum acceleration, starting on a steep hill or caravan towing, etc., can be made by depressing the accelerator pedal almost to the full throttle position, which is the point when the accelerator pedal touches the top of the spring-loaded plunger located immediately beneath the accelerator pedal. This action rotates the governor control shaft and fork and loads the governor spring, which now overrides the governor valve booster spring, thereby allowing the governor valve to move into the low speed position.

Similarly, depressing the accelerator to full throttle position in intermediate below speeds of approximately 14 to 18 mph (22 to 28 kph) and in top below speeds of approximately 34 to 38 mph (54 to 61 kph) will select low and intermediate respectively.

Above 38 mph (61 kph) and up to 56 mph (90 kph) in top, intermediate is obtained in the same manner, but the accelerator must be depressed past full throttle to the limit of its travel, to move the governor valve into the intermediate position.

Similarly, above 18 mph (28 kph) and up to 25 mph (40 kph) in intermediate, low is obtained by depressing the accelerator to the full kick-down position.

As the intermediate hold cable also positions the governor valve in the intermediate position by loading the governor spring and overriding the booster spring, it will be seen that with the hold control knob pulled out, all starts from rest will be in low speed, the transmission changing up into intermediate as soon as the governor speed is sufficient to pull the control valve into the intermediate setting. This change will be at the normal full throttle speed.

Intermediate gear hold

This is a feature whereby the transmission is held in intermediate gear over an extended speed range. It provides for special driving conditions where constant changes between intermediate and direct drive would be disadvantageous; such as when climbing mountain roads, or when in heavy slow moving traffic streams or towing a caravan.

The intermediate hold does *not* rigidly lock the transmission into intermediate ratio, but it restricts the change-up into direct drive until the speed of the car reaches the speeds given in the following table.

1st-speed start models—These cars normally start in low, but if the car is brought to rest with the intermediate hold in operation the car will then start from rest in intermediate.

2nd-speed start models—These cars normally start in intermediate, except at heavy throttle opening, such as when starting on a gradient. If the car is brought to rest with the intermediate hold in operation the car will then start in low.

Gear change speeds with intermediate gear hold in use

Model	Gear change—up		Gear change—down		Remarks
	1st to 2nd	2nd to 3rd	3rd to 2nd	2nd to 1st	
Mk I 1st-speed start	35 to 38 mph (56 to 61 kph)	57 to 60 mph (91 to 96 kph)	60 mph (96 kph)	If the car is brought to rest, it will re-start in 2nd	
Mk I 2nd-speed start	29 to 31 mph (47 to 50 kph)	60 mph (96 kph)	58 to 56 mph (93 to 90 kph)	28 to 26 mph (45 to 42 kph)	Commencing Engine Nos.: 8.71:1 r 630100001 7.5:1 c r 631100001
Mk IA	30 to 34 mph (48 to 54 kph)	60 to 65 mph (96 to 104 kph)	58 to 56 mph (93 to 90 kph)	28 to 26 mph (45 to 42 kph)	Change speed set at 'Kick-down'
Mk IA	16 to 24 mph (25 to 38 kph)	30 to 34 mph (48 to 54 kph)	31 to 28 mph (49 to 45 kph)	21 to 14 mph (33 to 22 kph)	Change speed set at: 'Full throttle'
Mk II	28 to 32 mph (45 to 51 kph)	55 to 65 mph (88 to 104 kph)	61 to 55 mph (98 to 88 kph)	29 to 26 mph (46 to 41 kph)	Change speed set at: 'Kick-down'
Mk II	20 to 25 mph (32 to 40 kph)	44 to 49 mph (70 to 78 kph)	45 to 40 mph (72 to 64 kph)	23 to 18 mph (37 to 28 kph)	Change speed set at: 'Full throttle'

Mk I models were fitted with a mechanical second speed hold control, which was operated by a knob fitted on the edge of the parcel shelf.

No adjustment can be made to the speed setting.

Mk IA models onwards have electrical control, with a switch mounted on the steering column. The solenoid, which operates the electrical intermediate gear hold, may be adjusted to give gear changes at lower or higher speeds than those quoted above. See Operation E1-7.

It is not practical to convert the early mechanical type mechanism to the electrically operated type.

Mechanical layout

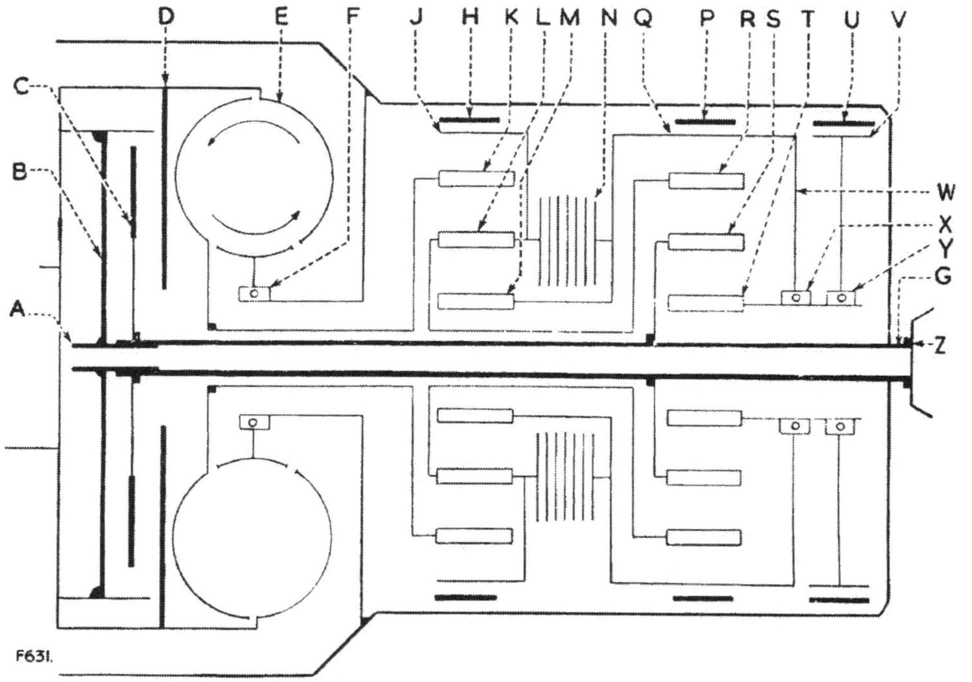

Layout of main components

A—Oil transfer tube
B—Piston
C—Driven plate
D—Backing plate
E—Torque converter
F—Stator one-way clutch
G—Transmission mainshaft
H—Reverse band
J—Reverse drum
K—Ring gear
L—Planet carrier
M—Sun gear
N—Multiple-disc clutch
P—Low band
Q—Low drum
R—Ring gear
S—Planet carrier
T—Sun gear
U—Forward band
V—Forward drum
W—Low drum plate
X—Reverse one-way clutch
Y—Forward one-way clutch
Z—Propeller shaft flange and transmission mainshaft

Front ring gear driven by converter turbine.

Front carrier. Splined to the reverse drum and retained by circlip. Splined to the rear ring gear and locked to the front sun gear when the multiple-disc clutch is engaged.

Front sun gear. Integral with the low drum and therefore can drive the rear sun gear in reverse through the low drum plate and reverse one-way clutch.

Rear ring gear. Splined to the front carrier.

Rear carrier. The output of the gear train splined to the mainshaft.

Rear sun gear. In manual low ratio, held against reverse rotation by the low drum and band and the forward one-way clutch. In automatic low, held by forward band and drum. In reverse, rotated in reverse by the front sun gear through the low drum and plate and reverse one-way clutch.

'P' Park hydraulic layout

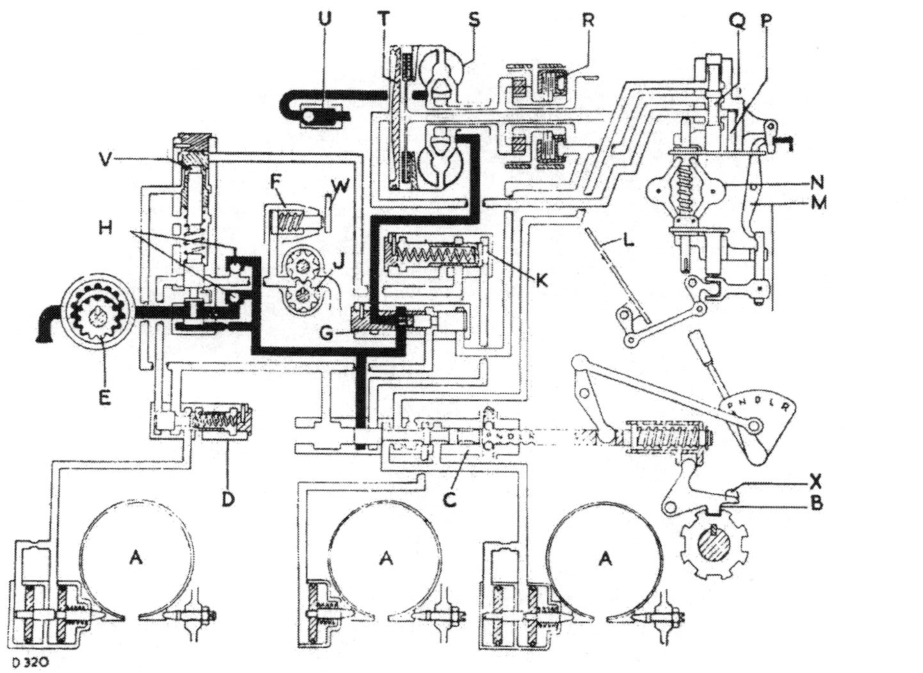

'P' Park hydraulic layout

A—Reverse, low and forward band (free)
B—Parking pawl and interlock engaged
C—Selector valve
D—Reverse interlock valve
E—Front pump
F—Parking pawl interlock piston
G—Converter shuttle valve
H—Front and rear pump ball check valves
J—Rear pump
K—Accumulator valve
L—Accelerator pedal
M—Rocker arm
N—Governor
P—Hydraulic detent
Q—Governor valve
R—Multiple-disc clutch (free)
S—Torque converter
T—Direct drive clutch
U—Lubrication valve
V—Main relief valve
W—Parking pawl interlock
X—Parking interlock

With the engine running, the front pump delivers fluid through the main relief valve and converter shuttle valve to the converter and to the selector valve. The main relief valve regulates the pressure to 20 lb/sq in. (1,41 kg/cm²). The lubrication valve maintains this head of fluid in the converter when the engine is not running, ready for immediate operation. Fluid from the converter returns to the transmission through the lubrication valve.

With the lever at 'P' the selector valve prevents the passage of fluid to the bands, the governor valve and multiple-disc clutch. As the car is stationary the rear pump is not operative and its check valve ball is retained on its seating by fluid pressure from the front pump.

The parking pawl is mechanically engaged.

'N' Neutral hydraulic layout

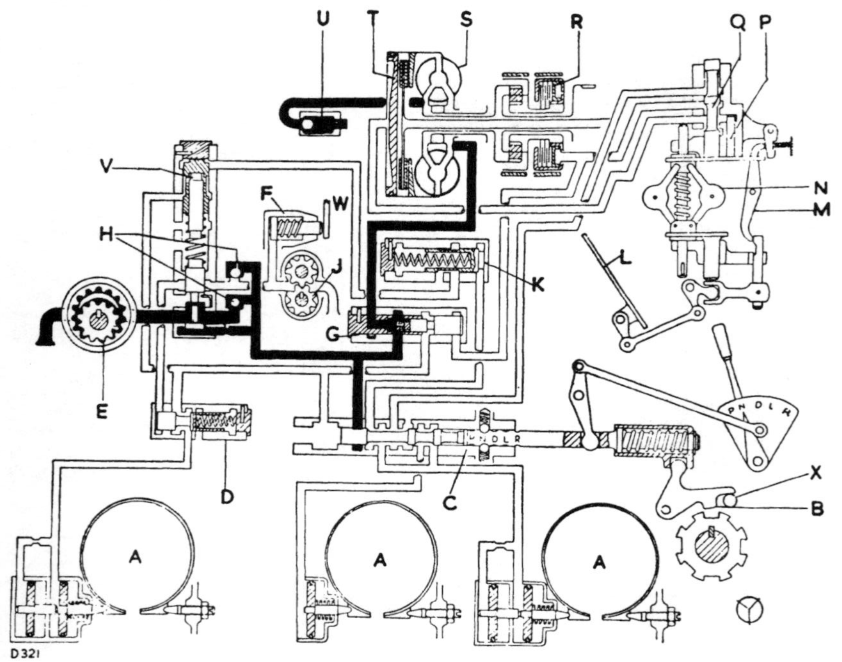

'N' Neutral hydraulic layout

A—Reverse, low and forward band (free)
B—Parking pawl
C—Selector valve
D—Reverse interlock valve
E—Front pump
F—Parking pawl interlock piston
G—Converter shuttle valve
H—Front and rear pump ball check valves
J—Rear pump
K—Accumulator valve
L—Accumulator pedal
M—Rocker arm
N—Governor
P—Hydraulic detent
Q—Governor valve
R—Multiple-disc clutch
S—Torque converter
T—Direct drive clutch
U—Lubrication valve
V—Main relief valves
W—Parking pawl interlock
X—Parking interlock

Hydraulically the conditions are as for 'P' Park. The parking pawl is disengaged mechanically by the movement of the selector lever.

'D' Low ratio automatic powerflow

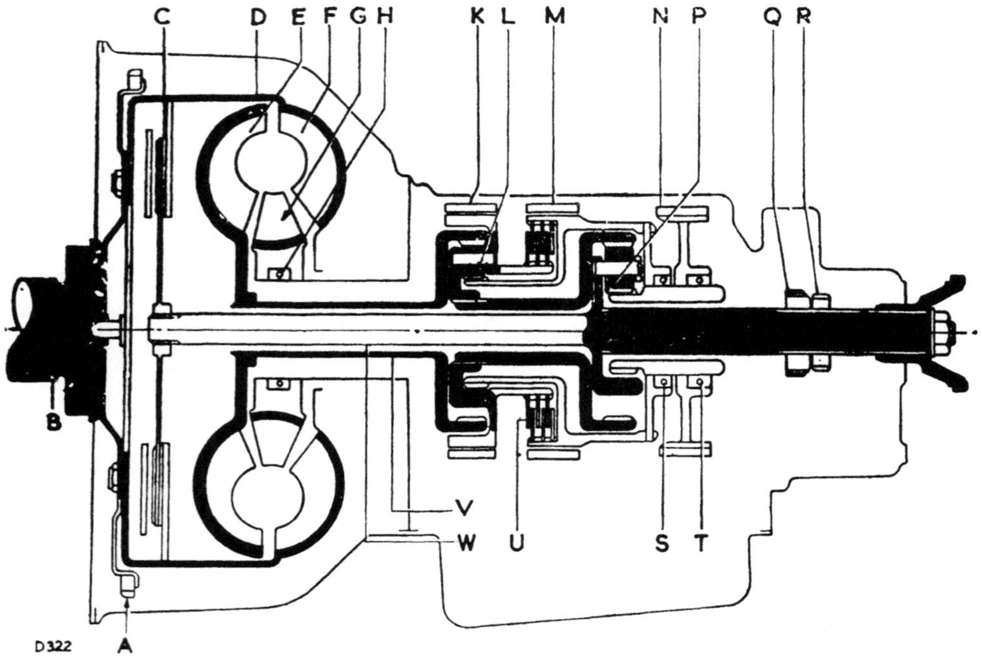

'D' Low ratio automatic powerflow

A—Starting gear
B—Engine crankshaft
C—Direct-drive clutch-driven plate
D—Torque converter
E—Turbine
F—Impeller
G—Stator
H—One-way clutch unit
K—Reverse band
L—Front planetary set
M—Low band
N—Forward band applied
P—Rear planetary set
Q—Parking pawl gear
R—Drive gear for rear pump governor and speedometer
S—Reverse one-way clutch
T—Forward one-way clutch
U—Multiple-disc clutch
V—Front unit ring gear
W—Mainshaft

The forward band only is applied. Low ratio at the output shaft is obtained from the reduction available in each of the planetary sets. Input in each set is through the ring gear, and output through the carrier, both sun gears being held stationary. Drive is from the converter turbine to the front ring gear, and as the ring gear, rotates the planetary wheels of the front set rotate in a clockwise direction and roll round the stationary sun gear; the planet carrier must therefore revolve also in a clockwise or forward direction and at a reduced speed.

The ring gear of the rear planetary set, being splined to the carrier of the front set, must revolve in a clockwise direction, turning the planet wheels clockwise and causing the rear carrier to rotate at a further reduced speed in a forward direction. As the rear carrier is splined to the transmission mainshaft, forward drive low ratio is obtained at the rear axle.

The two sun gears are held in the following manner:

Rear sun gear. Rotation of the rear ring gear and carrier in the forward direction, tends to turn the sun gear in the opposite direction.

An extension of the rear sun wheel carries the forward drum and its one-way clutch, and when the band is applied under these conditions the sun wheel cannot rotate anti-clockwise because the forward one-way clutch allows the sun wheel to turn only in the direction of engine rotation. Reaction in the rear set is therefore taken in the forward band.

Front sun gear. As in the rear planetary set, the reaction of the ring gear, carrier, and planet wheels, tends to turn the sun gear against the direction of engine rotation. The front sun gear is integral with the low drum; the low drum and drum plate must also tend to turn anti-clockwise but are prevented by the reverse one-way clutch in the low drum plate mounted on the rear sun gear, which is locked by the band through the forward one-way clutch.

This prevents anti-clockwise rotation of the drum and plate. The front sun gear is therefore held, and the reaction of both planetary sets is taken by the forward band; when the car overruns the transmission the one-way clutches are unlocked and consequently there is a free-wheel effect operative in automatic low ratio and no engine braking is available.

'D' Low ratio automatic hydraulic layout

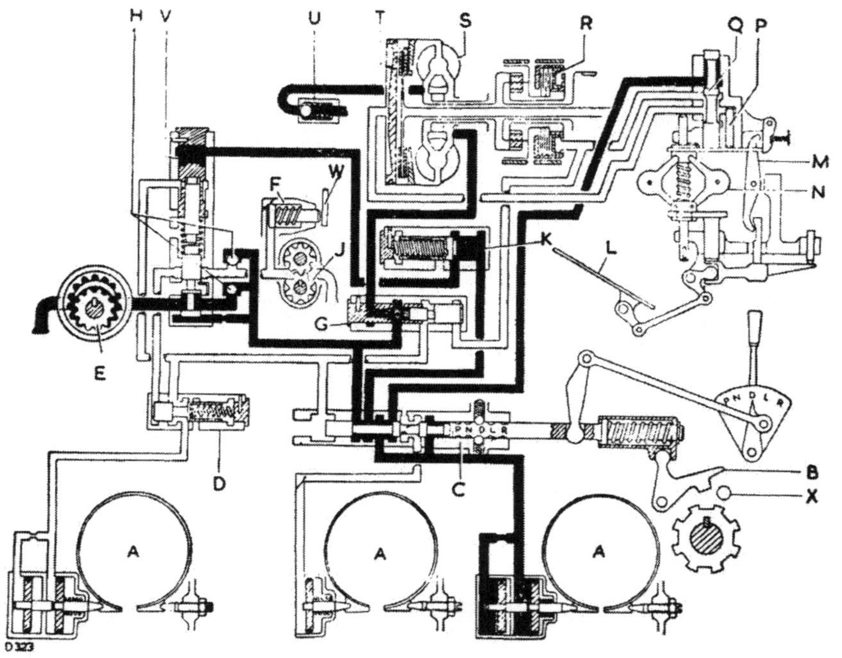

'D' Low ratio automatic hydraulic layout

A—Reverse and low bands (free) Forward band engaged
B—Parking pawl
C—Selector valve
D—Reverse interlock valve
E—Front pump
F—Parking pawl interlock piston
G—Converter shuttle valve
H—Front and rear pump ball check valves
J—Rear pump
K—Accumulator valve
L—Accelerator pedal
M—Rocker arm
N—Governor
P—Hydraulic detent
Q—Governor valve
R—Multiple-disc clutch (free)
S—Torque converter
T—Direct-drive clutch
U—Lubrication valve
V—Main relief valve
W—Parking pawl interlock
X—Parking interlock

Fluid from the front pump at a regulated pressure initially of 20 lb/sq in. (1,41 kg/cm²) is delivered to the converter via the converter shuttle valve and selector valves as in Park, but the movement of the lever to 'D' has moved the selector valve so that the fluid can now pass to the forward band servo and to the accumulator valve and governor. Fluid pressure opens the accumulator valve and a passage to the top of the main relief valve where the fluid pressure moves the piston of the main relief valve on to its stop, thus compressing the main relief valve spring and the line pressure rises to 80 lb/sq in. (5,6 kg/cm²). Pressure in the converter is reduced by the converter shuttle valve nose-piece to a value of 60 lb/sq in. (4,2 kg/cm²). The higher converter pressure reduces cavitation noise and slip.

Fluid is now directed by the selector valve to the governor valve but is blocked until the engine is speeded up and the governor begins to move the valve piston outwards.

The accumulator valve gives a build up in pressure allowing progressive operation of the forward band.

'D' Second gear (intermediate) powerflow

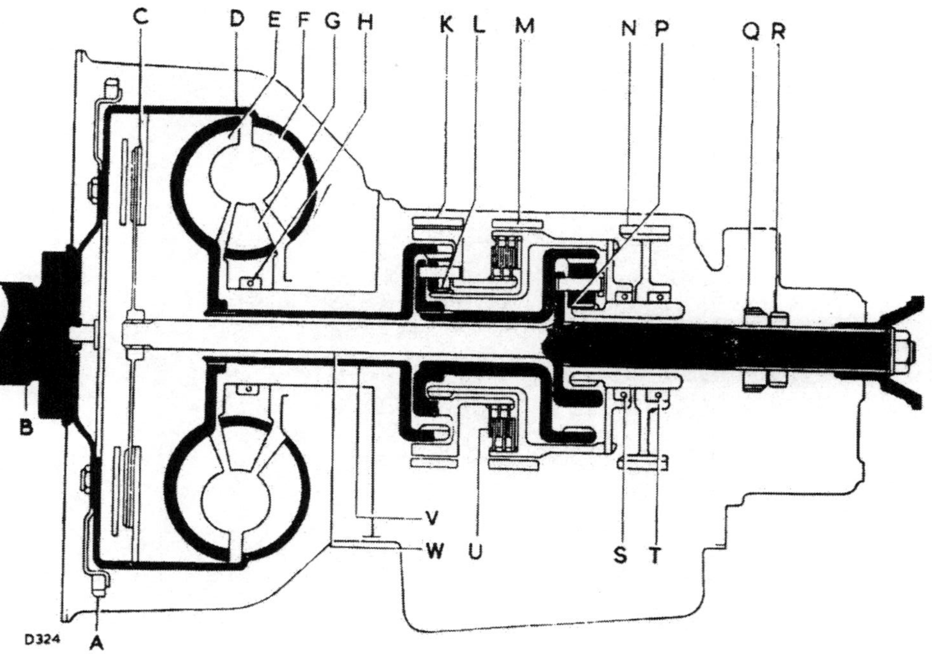

'D' Second gear (intermediate) powerflow

A—Starting gear
B—Engine crankshaft
C—Direct-drive clutch-driven plate
D—Torque converter
E—Turbine
F—Impeller
G—Stator
H—One-way clutch
K—Reverse band
L—Front planetary set
M—Low band
N—Forward band applied
P—Planetary set
Q—Parking pawl gear
R—Drive gear for rear pump governor and speedometer
S—Reverse one-way clutch
T—Forward one-way clutch
U—Multiple-disc clutch (applied)
V—Front unit ring gear
W—Mainshaft

An intermediate ratio is obtained from the reduction available in the rearmost of the two planetary sets while the front set revolves as a unit. The forward band is applied and the multiple-disc clutch engaged. Application of the forward band holds the rear sun gear, and the multiple-disc clutch locks the front sun gear to the front carrier. Drive is from the turbine to the front ring gear. Since the sun gear and carrier are held together the planetary set revolves as a unit without any reductions in speed.

The front carrier turns the rear ring gear at the same speed as the turbine.

The rear ring gear revolves and causes the rear carrier to revolve around the stationary rear sun gear which is held by the forward band, at a reduced speed taking with it the output shaft.

If the car overruns the engine the carrier will drive the sun gear in the direction of engine rotation, unlocking the forward one-way clutch but locking the reverse one-way clutch; the result is that the rear sun gear locks to the rear ring gear through the front planetary set thereby locking up the rear planetary set as a unit. As the front planetary set is locked up by the multiple-disc clutch, both sets are rotating as a unit on the overrun and the engine braking will be in the 1 : 1 ratio.

'D' Second gear (intermediate) hydraulic layout

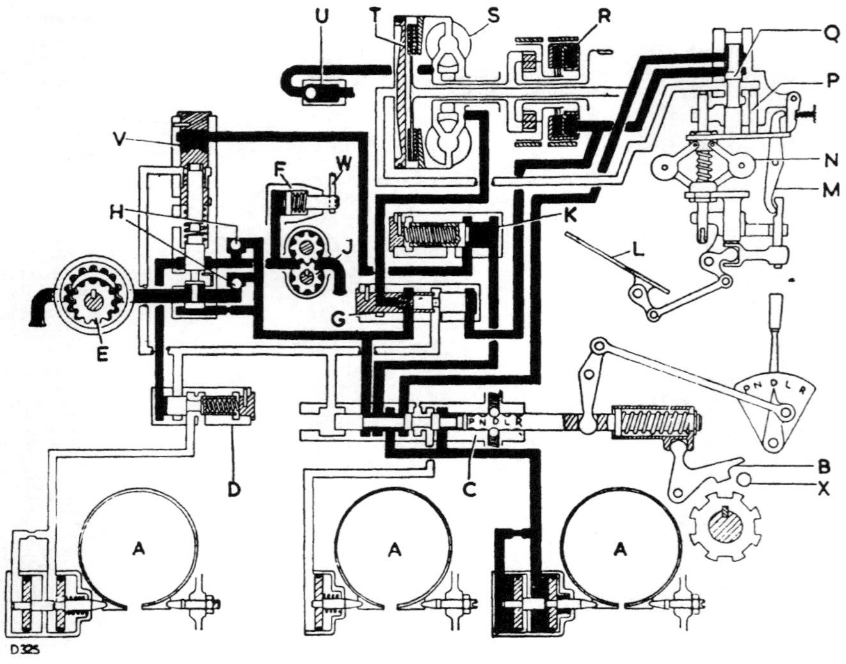

'D' Second gear (intermediate) hydraulic layout

A—Reverse and low bands (free) Forward band engaged
B—Parking pawl
C—Selector valve
D—Reverse interlock valve
E—Front pump
F—Parking pawl interlock piston
G—Converter shuttle valve
H—Front and rear pump ball check valves
J—Rear pump
K—Accumulator valve
L—Accelerator pedal
M—Rocker arm
N—Governor
P—Hydraulic detent
Q—Governor valve
R—Multiple-disc clutch (engaged)
S—Torque converter
T—Direct-drive clutch
U—Lubrication valve
V—Main relief valve
W—Parking pawl interlock
X—Parking interlock

Fluid is pumped through the main relief valve and via the selector valve and accumulator valve to the top of the main relief valve piston giving a line pressure of 80 lb/sq in. (5,6 kg/cm²). As the speed of the car increases, the rear pump closes the front pump check valve and takes over from the front pump completely.

Fluid pressure from the rear pump is directed to the parking pawl and reverse interlock valves, preventing engagement of park or reverse while the car is moving forward at speeds in excess of 5 mph (8 kph).

From the selector valve fluid passes to the forward servo and applies the band, and to the governor valve, from which it is directed to the multi-plate clutch. From the same passage fluid flows to the converter shuttle valve piston, moving it to reduce the orifice through which the fluid passes to the converter; this reduces converter pressure to 30 lb/sq in. (2,1 kg/cm²) for subsequent gear changes.

'D' Direct-drive top powerflow

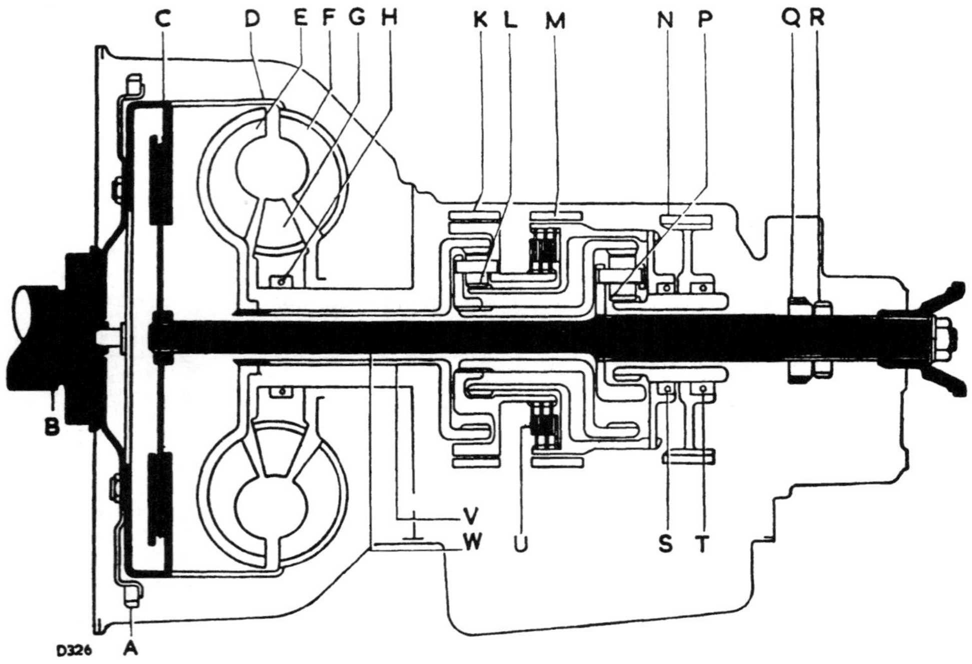

D' Direct-drive top powerflow

A—Starting gear
B—Engine crankshaft
C—Direct-drive clutch (driven)
D—Torque converter
E—Turbine
F—Impeller
G—Stator
H—One-way clutch
K—Reverse band
L—Front planetary set
M—Low band
N—Forward band (applied)
P—Rear planetary set
Q—Parking pawl gear
R—Drive gear for rear pump governor and speedometer
S—Reverse one-way clutch
T—Forward one-way clutch
U—Multiple-disc clutch (applied)
V—Front unit ring gear
W—Mainshaft

In direct-drive top gear a mechanical connection is made between the flywheel and transmission shaft through the engagement of the clutch located in the flywheel part of the converter. The torque converter and planetary sets are by-passed and the ratio is 1 : 1. A spring-centre driven plate is splined to the main transmission shaft and compressed against a backing plate by hydraulic pressure acting behind a pressure plate. Fluid is led behind the pressure plate from the mainshaft through a small removable oil transfer tube, which must not be omitted when assembling. The transmission remains conditioned for the intermediate ratio by continued application of the forward band engagement of the multiple-disc clutch in order to allow an immediate 'kick-down' from top. As soon as the pressure to the direct-drive clutch has been cut off by the governor, the converter and gear train become operative, the forward one-way clutch permits the rotation of the output shaft although the forward band is applied, and the gear train components rotate as dictated by friction.

'D' Direct-drive top hydraulic layout

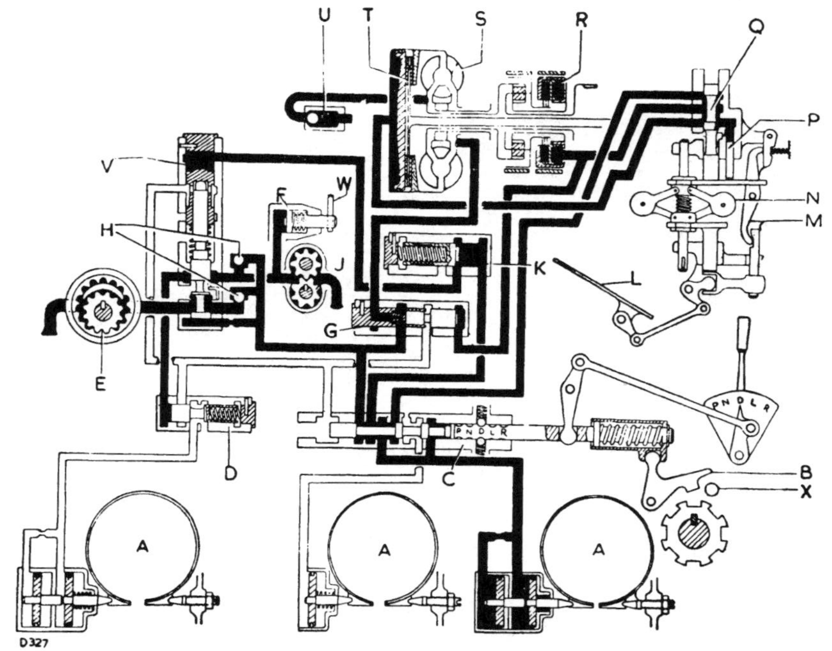

D' Direct-drive top hydraulic layout

A—Reverse and low bands (free) Forward band engaged
B—Parking pawl and interlock
C—Selector valve
D—Reverse interlock valve
E—Front pump
F—Parking pawl interlock piston
G—Converter shuttle valve
H—Front and rear pump ball check valves
J—Rear pump
K—Accumulator valve
L—Accelerator pedal
M—Rocker arm
N—Governor
P—Hydraulic detent
Q—Governor valve
R—Multiple-disc clutch (engaged)
S—Torque converter
T—Direct-drive clutch
U—Lubrication valve
V—Main relief valve
W—Parking pawl interlock
X—Parking interlock

Fluid from the rear pump passes through the check valves and converter shuttle valve to the converter at reduced pressure of 30 lb/sq in. (2,1 kg/cm²), the reduction taking place through the action of the converter shuttle valve. Fluid also passes to the selector valve and is directed to: (*a*) accumulator valve, (*b*) the governor and (*c*) the forward band.

(*a*) From the accumulator valve, when the spring is compressed, fluid is led to the top of the main relief valve piston to maintain the line pressure of 80 lb/sq in.

(*b*) From the governor, line pressure is directed to the piston of the direct-drive clutch, giving a direct drive to the axle and by-passing the planetary sets and multiple-disc clutch.

(*c*) The multiple-disc clutch and forward band are retained in the engaged condition, so that the transmission is conditioned for a rapid change down to intermediate ratio when required.

In the governor valve bushing, fluid is led to a small piston called a hydraulic detent, which butts against a governor valve fork and prevents any tendency for the transmission to hunt between intermediate and top ratios.

'L' Manual low powerflow

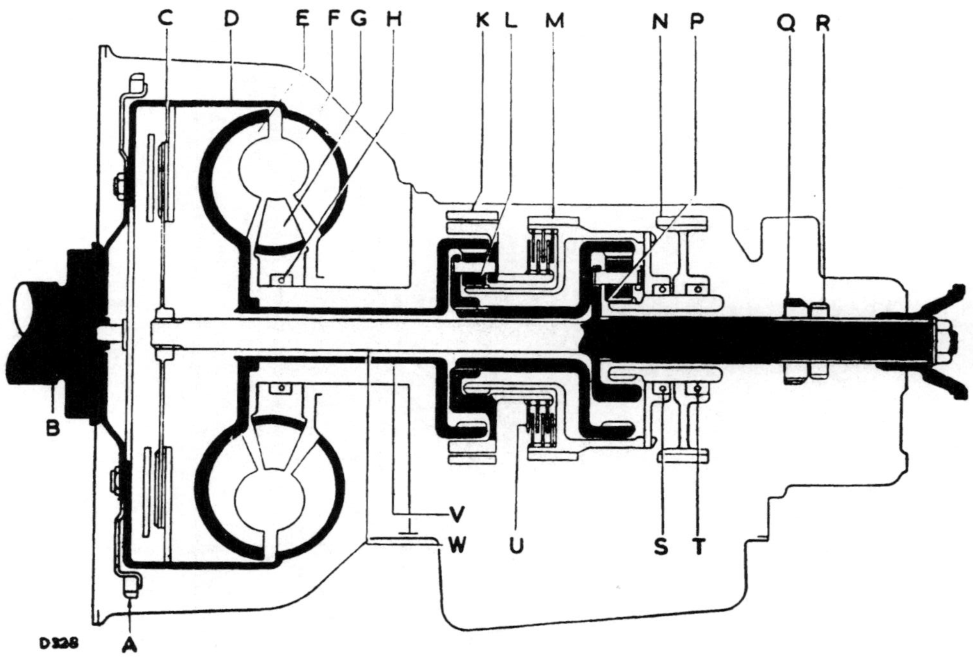

'L' Manual low powerflow

A—Starting gear
B—Engine crankshaft
C—Direct-drive clutch-driven plate
D—Torque converter
E—Turbine
F—Impeller
G—Stator
H—One-way clutch unit
K—Reverse band
L—Front planetary set
M—Low band (applied)
N—Forward band (applied)
P—Rear planetary set
Q—Parking pawl gear
R—Drive gear for rear pump governor and speedometer
S—Reverse one-way clutch
T—Forward one-way clutch
U—Multiple-disc clutch
V—Front unit ring gear
W—Mainshaft

Forward and low bands are applied. Manual low ratio is the same as that obtained automatically in low gear with the control lever at 'D'. In manual low ratio the forward band is applied and the front sun gear is held independently of the rear sun gear. The rear sun gear being held through the forward one-way clutch by the forward band. There is therefore no free-wheel in the transmission, and manual low gives maximum engine braking. The engine should not be used for braking at road speeds greater than 35 mph (56 kph) owing to the risk of causing unnecessary wear and damage to the engine and transmission unit.

'L' Manual low hydraulic layout

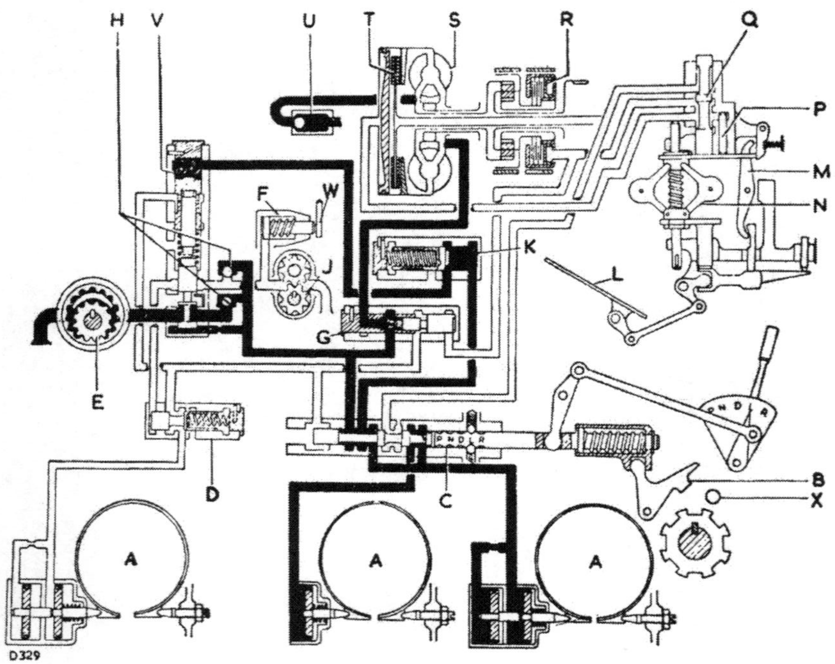

'L' Manual low hydraulic layout

A—Reverse band (free). Low and forward bands (engaged)
B—Parking pawl
C—Selector valve
D—Reverse interlock valve
E—Front pump
F—Parking pawl interlock piston
G—Converter shuttle valve
H—Front and rear pump ball check valves
J—Rear pump
K—Accumulator valve
L—Accelerator pedal
M—Rocker arm
N—Governor
P—Hydraulic detent
Q—Governor valve
R—Multiple-disc clutch (free)
S—Torque converter
T—Direct-drive clutch (free)
U—Lubrication valve
V—Main relief valve
W—Parking pawl interlock
X—Parking interlock

When the car is driven in manual low, conditions of line pressure and forward band application are similar to those described for automatic low, but fluid is now directed to the low band and cut off from the governor valve. Both low and forward bands are now applied and, since the governor is inoperative, the transmission remains in low until the selector valve is once more moved to drive.

If the selector lever is moved from 'D' to 'L', pressure will be at 80 lb/sq in. (5,6 kg/cm²) and application of low band at this pressure gives immediate positive engine braking. The pressure may be supplied by either the front or rear pump, depending on the speed of the car.

'R' Reverse powerflow

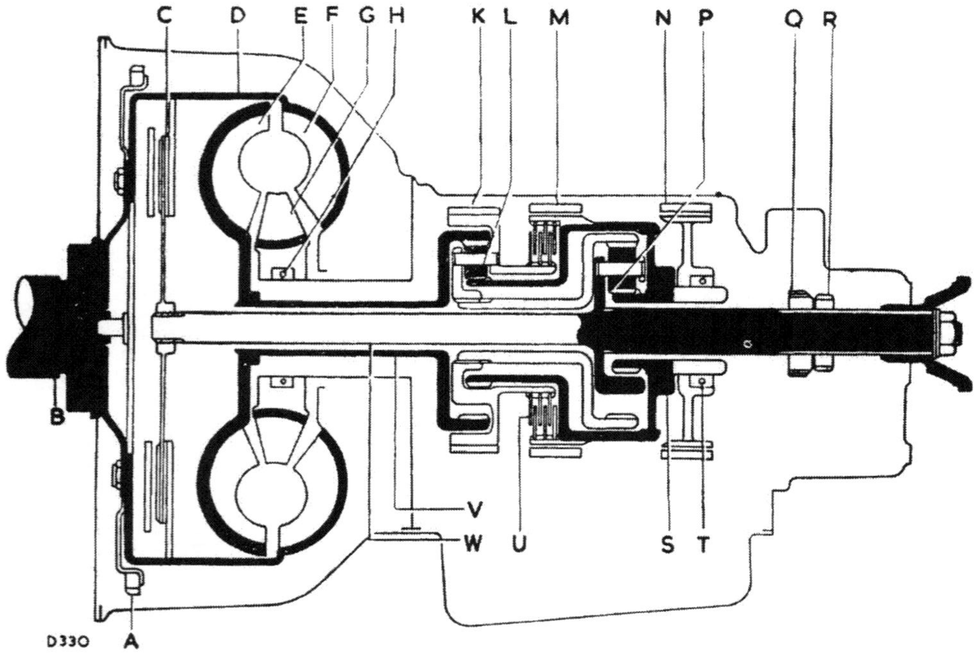

'R' Reverse powerflow

A—Starting gear
B—Engine crankshaft
C—Direct-drive clutch
D—Torque converter
E—Turbine
F—Impeller
G—Stator
H—One-way clutch
K—Reverse band
L—Front planetary set
M—Low band
N—Forward band (applied)
P—Rear planetary set
Q—Parking pawl gear
R—Drive gear for rear pump governor and speedometer
S—Reverse one-way clutch
T—Forward one-way clutch
U—Multiple-disc clutch
V—Front unit ring gear
W—Mainshaft

Reverse is obtained from two planetary sets by holding the carrier in the front set and the ring gear in the rear set. The reverse band is applied.

Drive is from the turbine to the front ring gear, which causes the planet wheels on the carrier to rotate in a clockwise direction. As the carrier is held by the reverse band, rotation of planet wheels causes the front sun gear to rotate in an anti-clockwise direction. The front carrier is held stationary by the reverse band, and as the front carrier is splined to the rear ring gear the rear ring gear is also held. The front sun gear and low drum rotate anti-clockwise and through the locked reverse one-way clutch the rear sun gear also. Rotation of the sun gear in an anti-clockwise direction drives the rear carrier around the stationary ring gear and gives reverse rotation of the output shaft.

Notice that holding the front carrier results in an increase in speed in the front planetary set, while holding the rear ring gear and driving with the sun gear gives the required reduction in the rear planetary set.

A free-wheel action is operative in reverse as the reverse one-way clutch is unlocked when the output shaft overruns the sun gear.

'R' Reverse hydraulic layout

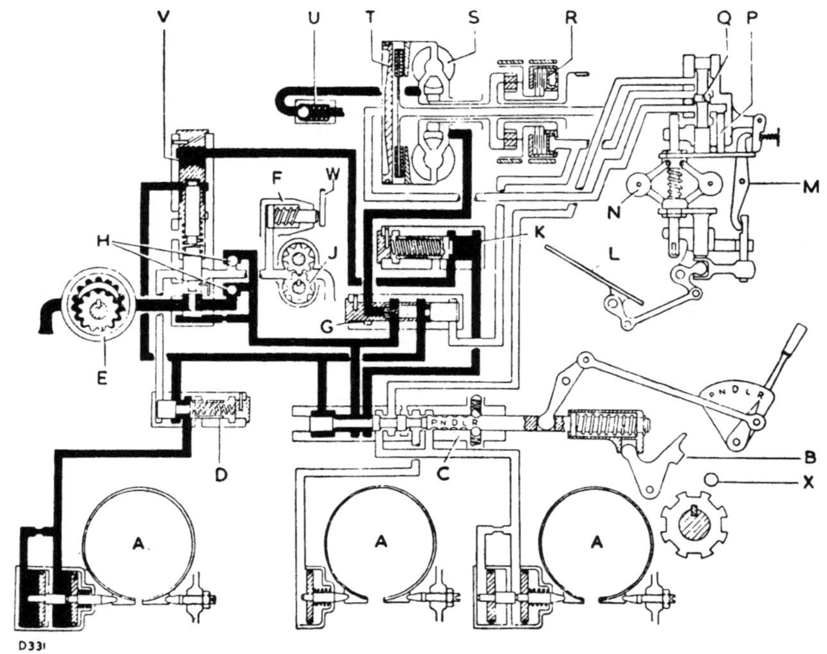

'R' Reverse hydraulic layout

A—Reverse band (engaged)
Forward and low bands (free)
B—Parking pawl
C—Selector valve
D—Reverse interlock valve
E—Front pump
F—Parking pawl interlock piston
G—Converter shuttle valve
H—Front and rear pump ball check valves
J—Rear pump
K—Accumulator valve
L—Accelerator pedal
M—Rocker arm
N—Governor
P—Hydraulic detent
Q—Governor valve
R—Multiple-disc clutch (free)
S—Torque converter
T—Direct-drive clutch
U—Lubrication valve
V—Main relief valve
W—Parking pawl interlock
X—Parking interlock

The rear pump is inoperative in reverse.

Fluid under pressure from the front pump passes to the converter shuttle valve and converter, and to the selector valve. From the selector valve fluid is directed to: (a) the accumulator and main relief valves, (b) reverse servo and the inner piston of the main relief valve.

Fluid pressure opens the accumulator valve and acts on the outer piston of the main relief valve, increasing the line pressure to 80 lb/sq in. (5,6 kg/cm²). Pressure is further increased to 200 lb/sq in. (14 kg/cm²) by leading fluid at line pressure to the inner piston of the main relief valve.

Fluid at 200 lb/sq in. (14 kg/cm²) is directed to the area between the shuttle valve piston and shuttle to move the valve and reduce the orifice through which the fluid must pass to the converter, thus reducing pressure to 60 lb/sq in. (4,2 kg/cm²) in that component.

Fluid at 200 lb/sq in. (14 kg/cm²) is also directed through the reverse interlock valve, opened by spring pressure, and to the reverse servo to apply the reverse band.

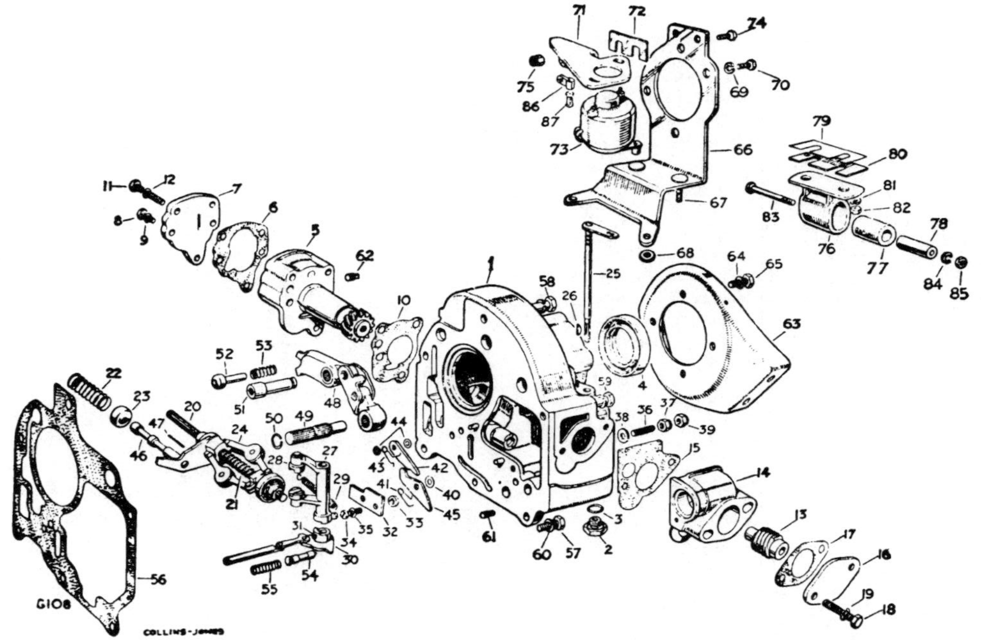

Extension case and components

1	Transmission extension case assembly
2–3	Bush and oil seal for governor control shaft
4	Oil seal, propeller shaft flange
5	Rear oil pump complete
6	Oil pump cover gasket
7	Cover for rear oil pump
8–9	Fixings, cover to pump
10	Joint rear pump to extension case
11–12	Fixings, pump to extension case
13	Gear for speedometer drive
14	Housing for speedometer gear
15	Joint washer, housing to extension case
16	Cover plate for speedometer gear housing
17	Joint washer for cover
18–19	Fixings, cover and housings to extension casing
20	Shaft for governor
21	Spring for governor
22	Spring for governor booster valve
23	Retainer for booster valve spring
24	Governor complete
25	Governor adjusting shaft complete
26	Key for governor shaft
27	Governor adjusting fork
28	Yoke shoes for governor adjusting fork
29	Return spring for governor adjusting fork
30	Detent cam
31	Allen screw, fixing detent cam to governor shaft
32	Stop for governor
33	Spacer for governor stop
34–35	Fixings for governor stop
36–39	Fixings for governor cam stop
40	Washer for rocker arm control (1st-speed start models only)
41	Spring (1st-speed start models only)
42	Pawl (1st-speed start models only)
43	Spring (1st-speed start models only)
44	Plain washer (1st-speed start models only)
45	Rocker arm (1st-speed start models only)
46	Governor control valve
47	Detent piston (two on 2nd-speed start models)
48	Pawl and toggle
49	Shaft for parking brake toggle
50	Circlip fixing pawl and toggle to shaft
51	Pawl pivot pin
52	Parking brake interlock piston
53	Spring for parking brake interlock piston
54	Accelerator detent plunger (2nd-speed start models only)
55	Spring for accelerator detent plunger (2nd-speed start models only)
56	Washer for extension to main casing
57–60	Fixings, extension case to main case
61	Multiple-disc clutch pressure take-off plug
62	Rear pump pressure take-off plug
63	Transmission mounting bracket
64–65	Fixings, bracket to extension case
66	Reaction bracket
67–70	Fixings for bracket
71	Solenoid support bracket (Mk IA and Mk II)
72	Shim (Mk IA and Mk II)
73	Solenoid (Mk IA and Mk II)
74–75	Fixings (Mk IA and Mk II)
76	Stabiliser bracket
77	Bush for stabiliser
78	Tube for stabiliser
79–80	Shim (Fixing stabiliser bracket to reaction bracket)
81–82	Fixings for stabiliser (Fixing stabiliser bracket to reaction bracket)
83–85	Fixings, stabiliser to sub-frame bracket
86	Cable clip
87	Grommet for clip

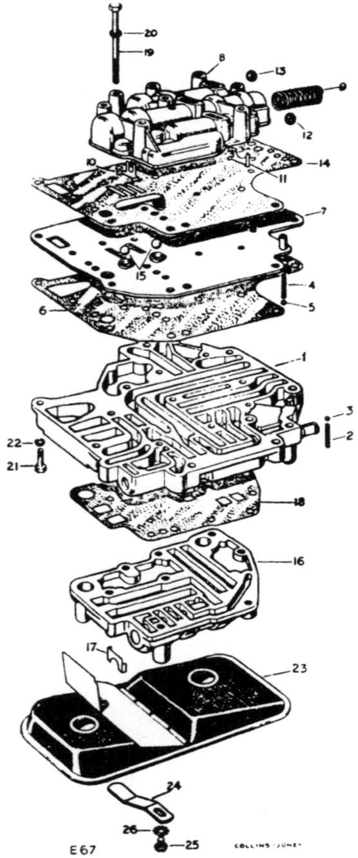

E 67

Valve block and components

1 Manifold
2 Spring } For selector valve detent
3 Ball }
4 Spring } For selector valve detent
5 Ball }
6 Gasket, manifold to base plate
7 Base plate
8 Relief valve body complete
9 Spring } For main relief valve
10 Retainer }
11 Retainer for main relief valve plug
12 Reverse interlock valve spring retainer
13 Accumulator valve spring retainer
14 Gasket base plate to relief valve body
15 Ball check valves
16 Converter valve body
17 Retainer for shuttle valve sleeve
18 Joint washer, manifold to converter valve body
19–20 Fixings, valve block assembly
21–22 Fixings, valve block to unit
23 Oil filter
24 Retainer for oil filter
25–26 Fixings, retainer to converter valve body

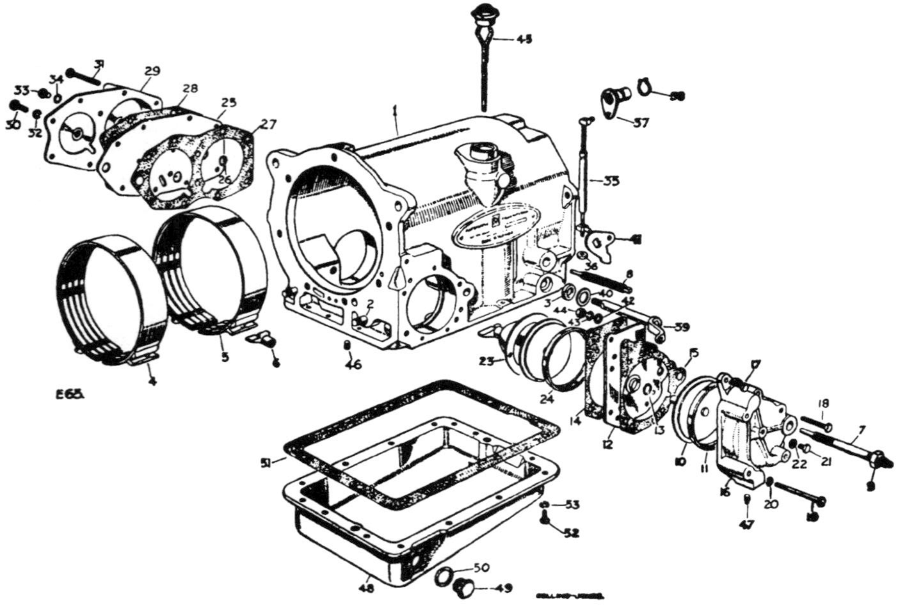

E65

Transmission case and components

1 Transmission casing assembly
2 Stud fixing bell housing to transmission case
3 Oil seal for selector control shaft
4 Reverse brake band
5 Low or forward brake band
6 Side strut for brake band
7 Adjusting screw for low band
8 Adiusting screw for forward band
9 Locknut for adjusting screw
10 Piston complete (reverse servo)
11 Sealing ring for piston
12 Plate, reverse servo cylinder
13 'O' ring seal for plate
14–15 Joint washers for reverse servo cylinder plate
16 Reverse servo
17–20 Fixings, reverse servo to gearbox
21–22 Plug and washer for reverse servo pressure take-off
23 Piston complete (reverse servo)
24 Sealing ring for piston
25 Plate for forward servo
26 'O' ring seal for plate
27–28 Gaskets for forward servo
29 Forward servo
30–32 Fixings, servo to transmission case
33–34 Plug and washer for pressure take-off
35 Parking brake actuating rod
36 Nut fixing bottom swivel to actuating rod
37 Toggle arm lever complete
38 Circlip
39 Selector control shaft
40 Plain washer for control shaft
41 Selector lever for control shaft
42–44 Fixings, lever to control shaft
45 Dipstick for transmission case
46 Allen screw, front pump pressure take-off and direct-drive clutch
47 Converter pressure take-off plug
48 Fluid sump
49 Drain plug
50 Washer for drain plug
51 Joint washer for sump
52–53 Fixings, sump to transmission case

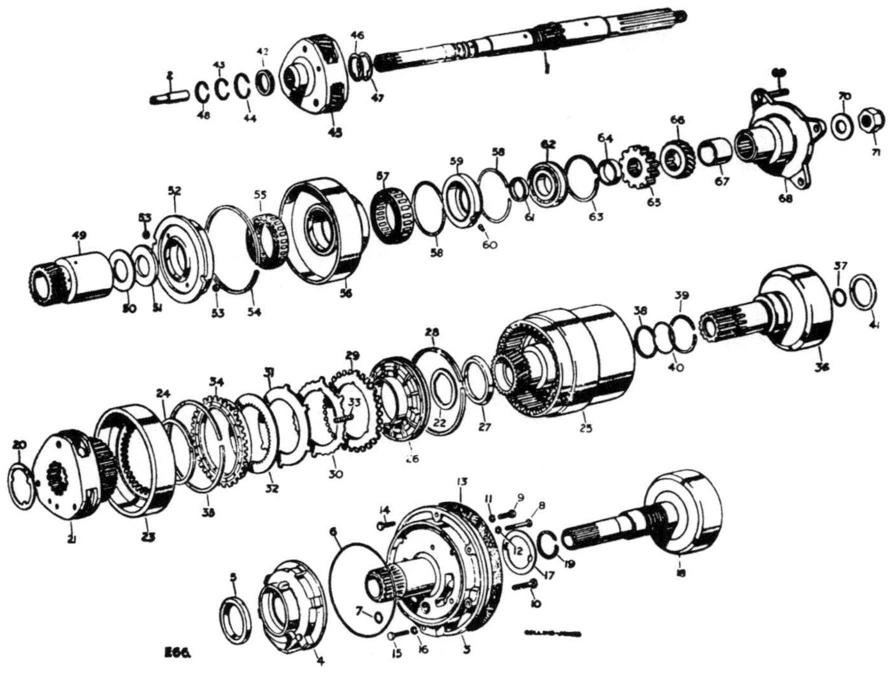

Gear train and components

1 Mainshaft assembly
2 Oil transfer tube
3 Collector ring
4 Front pump body and gears
5 Oil seal
6 'O' ring, large } For collector
7 'O' ring, small } ring
8–12 Fixings, collector ring to oil pump body
13 Joint washer
14–16 Fixings, collector ring to main case
17 Thrust washer
18 Front ring gear
19 Piston ring for front ring gear
20 Thrust washer, front ring gear
21 Front planet carrier
22 Washer for front sun gear
23 Reverse brake drum
24 Snap ring for brake drum
25 Front sun gear and low drum
26 Piston for multiple-disc clutch
27 Sealing ring for piston
28 Piston ring for clutch
29 Retractor plate for clutch
30 Spacer plate for clutch
31 Clutch plate, steel
32 Clutch plate, bronze
33 Spring for clutch
34 Retainer for clutch
35 Circlip fixing clutch
36 Rear ring gear complete
37 'O' ring
38 Circlip for front planet carrier
39 Piston ring, rear ring gear
40 'O' ring
41 Thrust washer, rear planet carrier
42 Oil ring retainer
43 Circlip fixing retainer
44 Piston ring for retainer
45 Rear planet carrier
46 Washer for rear planet carrier
47 Thrust washer, rear planet carrier
48 Piston ring for mainshaft
49 Rear sun gear complete
50 Washer } For rear
51 Spacer } sun gear
52 Reverse one-way clutch lock-up plate
53 Roller for lock-up plate
54 Circlip fixing lock-up plate
55 Reverse one-way clutch
56 Forward brake drum
57 Forward one-way clutch
58 Circlip for forward brake drum
59 Spacer for one-way clutch
60 Pin fixing spacer
61 Spacer for mainshaft rear bearing
62 Rear mainshaft bearing
63 Circlip fixing bearing
64 Small mainshaft spacer
65 Parking brake gear
66 Governor drive gear
67 Large mainshaft spacer
68 Propeller shaft flange
69 Bolt for flange
70 Washer
71 Self-locking nut

Automatic Transmission, to remove and refit—Operation E1-1

Workshop hand tools:
Plastic-faced mallet
Spanner sizes: $\frac{7}{16}$ in. AF, $\frac{5}{8}$ in. AF, $\frac{7}{8}$ in. AF

Special tools:
B-W15A, B-W5, B-W3
Dial gauge Torque wrench

The following units can be removed from the transmission without removing the complete unit from the car; these are:

Valve block. Operation E1-3.
Extension casing. Operation E1-2.
Brake band servos. Operation E1-9.

The main casing of the transmission can only be removed from the engine after the engine has been removed from the car.

Instructions for engine and automatic transmission unit removal are given in Section A.

Alternatively the engine/transmission unit may be removed with the sub-frame as an assembly. Section H.

Warning

Do not flush out the transmission unit with paraffin. Use only type 'A' transmission fluid.

Transmission main casing, remove

1. If the engine/transmission unit has been removed without the sub-frame, mount the engine on a suitable stand.
2. Remove the transmission case and bell housing as an assembly, leave the torque converter attached to the crankshaft.
3. Ensure that the mainshaft oil transfer tube is removed from the converter hub and retained with the transmission assembly.
4. Cover the converter driving hub to prevent the ingress of dirt.
5. Remove the bell housing, secured by two nuts and two bolts.
6. Mount the transmission casing on a bench cradle (Tool B-W 15A).

Transmission main casing, refit

7. Fit the torque and starter ring assembly to the driving plate. The two starter ring securing bolts and back plates fit into the two opposite recesses on the driving plate. Ensure that the dowel locates in its correct position on the driving plate.
8. Fit the securing bolts through the starter motor aperture in the flywheel housing, but do not tighten fully until the torque converter unit has been aligned.
9. Fit the bell housing on to the flywheel housing, with the engine in the vertical position. Secure temporarily with two nuts.
10. Fit the converter aligning flange (Tool B-W3) over the impeller hub of the torque converter and register into the bell housing.
11. Rotate the crankshaft to centralise the torque converter unit.
12. Fully tighten the torque converter securing bolts to a torque loading of 25–30 lb ft (3,5–4 mkg) through the aperture in the flywheel housing.
13. Should difficulty be experienced in engaging the special converter aligning flange, either into bell housing, or on to the impeller hub, check the driving plate for distortion. The two starter ring securing bolt locking plates must be correctly fitted and must not foul the driving plate.
14. If the special aligning tool B-W3 is not available, the run-out of the torque converter can be checked by using a dial test indicator and suitable mounting bracket with the engine in the vertical position.

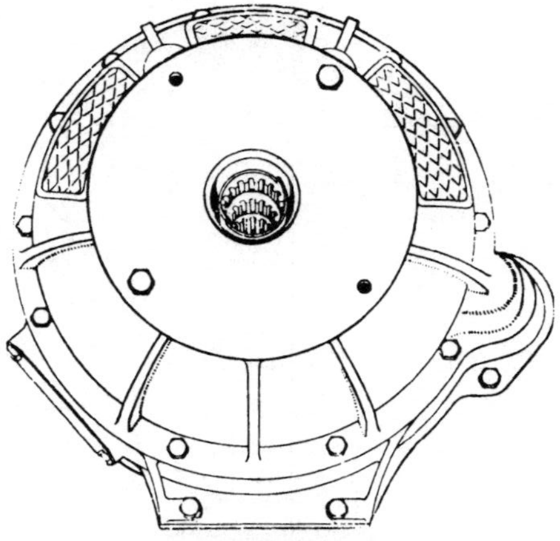

Converter aligning gauge B-W3, engine in vertical position

Operation E1-1—*continued*

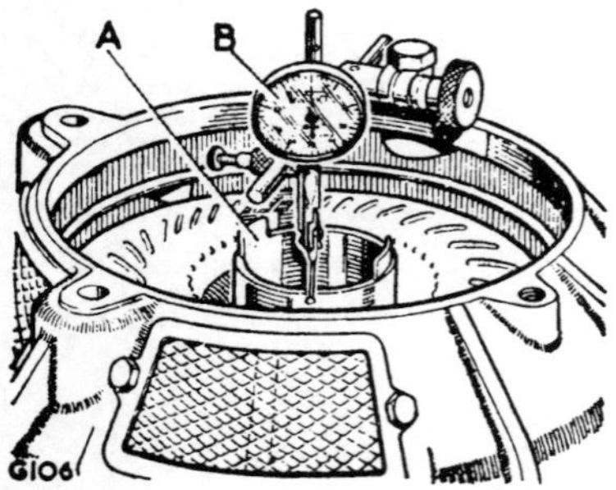

Checking torque converter run-out, with engine in vertical position

A—Torque converter hub B—Dial gauge and bracket

15. Measure the run-out at the impeller hub, which should not exceed .025 in. (0,63 mm). If the reading exceeds this figure the torque converter must be replaced, as excessive hub run-out will scrap the front pump oil seal and bearing.

16. To ensure correct fitting of the transmission to the torque converter, a B-W5 spline aligning fixture should be used. This tool aligns the splines on the transmission unit with the torque converter. Proceed as follows:

(*a*) With bell housing still in position on the flywheel housing, remove retaining clip (Part No. B-W7), from mainshaft spline.

(*b*) Fit the spline aligning tool to the transmission by engaging the sliding pin in the support arm of the tool on to one of the two studs.

(*c*) Slacken off the locking knob.

(*d*) Twist the tool very slightly from side to side to line up the splines, at the same time pushing it right home to the transmission casing; ensure that the two tangs on the tool are fully engaged with the slots in the front pump.

(*e*) Tighten up the locking knob.

Spline aligning fixture B-W5

(*f*) Withdraw the tool from the transmission, taking care not to disturb the relative position of the splines.

(*g*) Insert the tool into the torque converter, again twisting from side to side to align the splines. The sliding pin in the support arm must locate into the stud hole adjacent to the stud used for location purposes on the transmission.

(*h*) Withdraw the tool, ensure that the torque converter is not rotated.

17. Remove bell housing from flywheel housing and fit it to the transmission unit.

18. Ensure that the oil transfer tube is located inside the end of the mainshaft, with the tapered end of the transfer tube facing towards the torque converter.

19. Fit complete transmission unit to the flywheel housing, and secure the bell housing to the flywheel housing, refit starter motor and timing pointer.

*Extension casing, to remove and refit—Operation E1-2

The extension case can be removed for servicing with the transmission *in situ*

Workshop hand tools:
Spanner sizes: $\frac{9}{16}$ in. AF, $1\frac{1}{8}$ in. AF
Plastic-faced mallet

See Operation E2-3 in Part Two of this section, for overhaul procedure.

Extension casing, remove

1. Place the car on a suitable ramp, or over an inspection pit.
2. Remove the centre front carpet and remove the transmission unit cover panel from inside the car.
3. Drain the fluid from the unit.

Late models. Item 4

4. Disconnect the wiring to the 2nd-speed hold solenoid. Remove the solenoid complete with mounting bracket, secured by two bolts and self-locking nuts.
5. Disconnect the speedometer cable at the knurled cap on the speedometer drive housing.
6. Disconnect the control rod or cable from the governor lever on the extension casing.
7. Remove the front propeller shaft. Operation G-1.
8. Move the selector lever fully forward into 'P', park position. The mainshaft is now locked.
9. Remove the transmission unit output flange, secured by a self-locking nut and a washer.

Early models, with four-point mounting

10. Disconnect the rear engine/transmission mountings and support the transmission main casing. Remove the rear mounting bracket secured by four bolts and spring washers to the main casing.

Late models with five-point mounting

11. Slacken the $2\frac{3}{4}$ in. long bolt securing the stabiliser bracket to the sub-frame bracket beneath the extension casing. Remove the stabiliser support bracket from the sub-frame, retaining the shims for reassembly.
12. Remove the extension casing from the main casing, secured by six set set bolts and spring washers.

Extension casing, refit

1. Reverse removal procedure.
2. Fit the governor drive gear spacer, the parking brake gear (with the chamfered face rearwards), the governor drive gear and large spacer on to the mainshaft.
3. Use new joint washers when refitting, and use only petroleum jelly to locate the joint washer.
4. It will be found advantageous to engage 'R', reverse position, when refitting the extension casing to the main casing.
5. Tighten the fixing bolts to a torque of 28 to 33 lb/ft (3,8 to 4,5 mkg).
6. When fitting the universal joint flange, select 'P', park position. Tighten the fixing nut to 60 to 80 lb/ft (8,5 to 11 mkg).

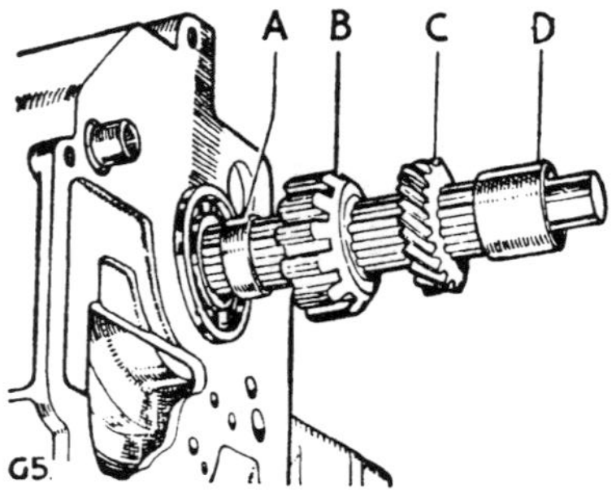

Sequence of mainshaft spacers and components

A—Drive gear spacer C—Governor drive gear
B—Parking brake gear D—Propeller shaft flange spacer

Operations which are identified by an asterisk (*) can be carried out with the transmission unit installed in the car

*Valve block, to remove and refit—Operation E1-3

Workshop hand tools:
Screwdriver, medium
Spanner sizes: $\frac{7}{16}$ in. AF, $\frac{1}{2}$ in. AF, $\frac{9}{16}$ in. AF

Special tools:
Torque wrench

Overhaul procedure is given in Part Two of this Section. Operation E2-1

Valve block, remove

Models fitted with five-point mounting. Item 1

1. Disconnect the front propeller shaft from transmission unit. Support the unit and remove the reaction bracket from transmission case and sump. Retain shims for correct reassembly.
2. Remove the fluid sump, secured by fourteen set bolts and two stiffener strips.
3. Remove the fluid filter, secured by a screw and clip.
4. Remove the valve block, secured by seven set bolts to the main casing.

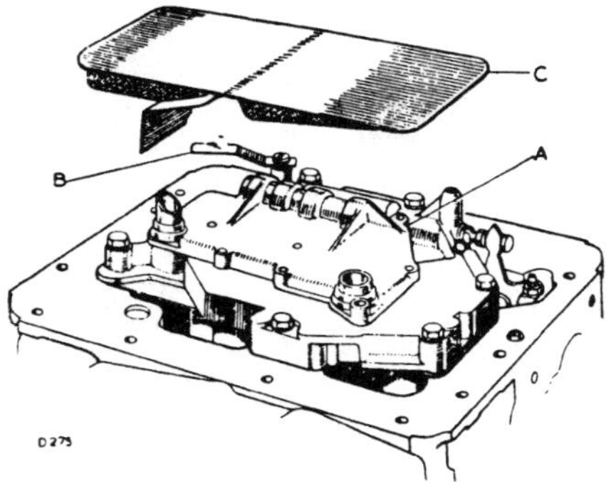

Valve block assembly location
A—Valve block B—Filter clip C—Oil filter

Valve block, refit

1. Place the valve block in position on the transmission case. Turn milled slot in selector valve towards the centre of the valve block, then guide the inner selector control lever into the slot, making sure that the gasket is correctly aligned with the fluid drillings in the casing and valve block.
2. Insert the seven retaining set bolts, check that the selector control lever moves freely through its arc of travel, that is, through the range of five selector positions. Tighten the set bolts to 10–13 lb ft (1,3–1,7 mkg).
3. Fit the filter, using the fluid inlets as guides.
4. Fit the sump, using a new gasket. Tighten the sump bolts to 10–13 lb ft (1,4–1,7 mkg).

Late models with five-point mounting, items 5 and 6

5. Refit the reaction bracket, using the original shims.
6. Fit the propeller shaft.
7. Refill the transmission unit with the recommended grade of fluid to the correct level.

Operations which are identified by an asterisk (*) can be carried out with the transmission unit installed in the car

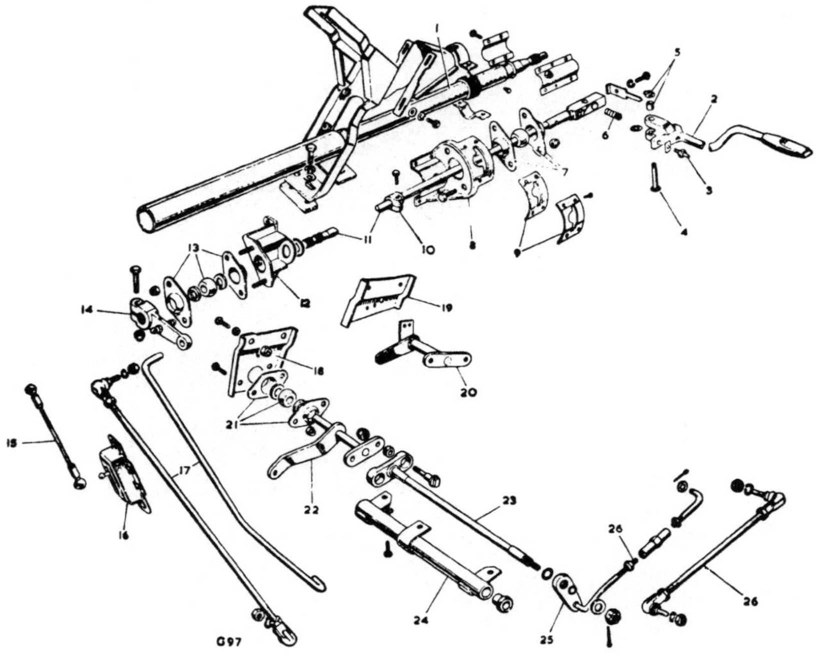

Gear selector shaft assembly

1 Steering column
2 Gear lever assembly
3 Gear selector finger
4 Gear lever joint pin
5 Gear lever joint pin fixings
6 Spring
7 Upper bearing components
8 Upper support bracket and gate
9 Gear selector gate components
10 Clamp
11 Gear selector shaft
12 Lower bearing bracket
13 Lower bearing components
14 Gear selection lever
15 Control rod for starter switch
16 Starter cut-out switch
17 Control rod gear selector lever to compensator—early and late type shown
18 Compensator support bracket—early type
19 Compensator support bracket—late type
20 Compensator—late type
21 Compensator bearing
22 Compensator—early type
23 Cross-shaft
24 Cross-shaft tube
25 Cross-shaft lever
26 Operating rod—early and late type shown

* Gear selector linkage, to remove and refit—Operation E1-4

Workshop hand tools:
Spanner sizes: $\frac{7}{16}$ in. AF, $\frac{1}{2}$ in. AF, $\frac{9}{16}$ in. AF, 2 BA
Pair of long-nosed pliers, Allen key

Linkage, remove

1. Disconnect the battery.
2. Remove the horn ring, secured by three Allen screws situated on the boss of the steering wheel.
3. Withdraw the steering wheel, secured by a nut and washer.
4. Separate the steering column shrouds secured by four screws.
5. Remove the four retaining screws from the shroud support plate.
6. Remove the moulding strip from between the two shrouds and pull both shrouds away from the column as far as possible.
7. Commence to dismantle the gear selector linkage from the engine end. Remove the two control rods from the lever on the selector shaft, these are lever to switch and lever to cross-shaft lever.
8. Remove the selector lever which is splined to the shaft and secured by a pinch bolt.
9. Remove the bearing housing secured to the bracket on the bulkhead by two self-locking nuts. If necessary remove the mounting bracket, secured by nuts and bolts to the bulkhead.
10. From the steering wheel end of the selector shaft remove the six bolts and nuts securing the upper selector bracket to the steering column.
11. The shaft and gear change lever assembly can now be removed from inside the car.

Gear lever assembly, dismantle

12. If necessary remove the gear change lever. Remove the gear selector finger and then the lever which is secured by a joint pin, Belleville washer and a special spring clip.

    Do not loose the small spring between the gear change lever and the end of the selector shaft.
13. Slacken the clamp, secured by a bolt, which is located just below the mounting bracket.
14. Remove the two bolts and self-locking nuts securing the upper bearing housing to the bracket.

Linkage, refit

1. If the gear lever assembly has been dismantled rebuild this first, out of the car.
   (*a*) Fit the selector finger to the gear change lever using a plain and tab washer (item 3).
   (*b*) Fit the upper bearing components to the shaft (item 7).
   (*c*) Fit the clamping collar (item 10).
   (*d*) Fit the upper bracket (item 8).
   (*e*) Loosely bolt the bearing housing (item 7) to the bracket (item 8).
   (*f*) Tighten the clamp pinch bolt (item 10).
   (*g*) Fit the nylon liner and backing plate for the gear selector gate to the bracket located by four small set screws (item 9).
2. Fit assembly to car by reversing removal procedure.
3. Fit the lever on to the lower end of the shaft and adjust the control rods as detailed in Operation

Operations which are identified by an asterisk (*) can be carried out with the transmission unit installed in the car

*Gear selector cross-shaft, to remove and refit—Operation E1-5

Workshop hand tools:
Spanner sizes: $\frac{1}{2}$ in. AF, $\frac{9}{16}$ in. AF, $\frac{7}{16}$ in. AF, $\frac{5}{8}$ in. AF
Pliers, long-nosed

Cross-shaft, remove

1. Remove the control rod between the lever on the end of the selector shaft and the lever on the compensator.
2. Disconnect the operating lever between the lever on the transmission and the lever on the cross-shaft.

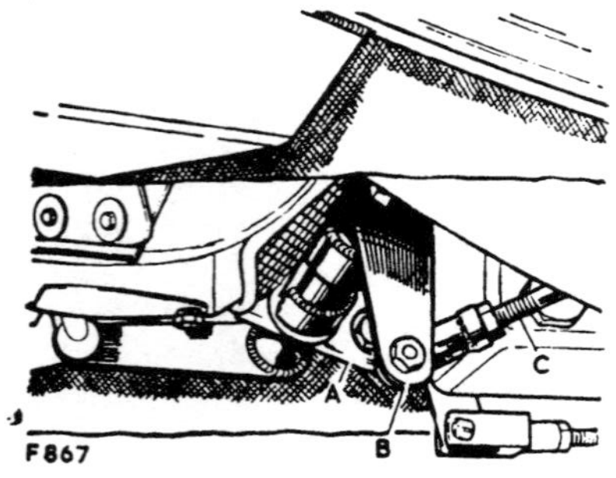

Selector linkage cross-shaft

A—Compensator
B—Lever
C—Control rod, gearbox to cross-shaft lever

3. Remove the compensator, secured by nuts and bolts to a mounting bracket on the body and to the cross-shaft on the underside of the transmission unit.
4. Remove the cross-shaft assembly secured by three bolts to the transmission unit.
5. If necessary, remove the cross-shaft from its mounting tube by removing the splined lever secured by a castle or self-locking nut.

Cross-shaft, refit

1. Reverse removal procedure.
2. For adjustment instructions see Operation E1-6

Operations which are identified by an asterisk (*) can be carried out with the engine and transmission unit installed in the car

Gear selector mechanism and starter cut-out switch setting—Operation E1-6

Workshop hand tools:
Spanner sizes: $\frac{1}{2}$ in. AF, $\frac{9}{16}$ in. AF, $\frac{7}{16}$ in. AF, $\frac{3}{8}$ in. AF
Pliers, long-nosed

Instructions for setting the accelerator linkage will be found in Section F

Selector mechanism setting, RHD models

1. Move selector quadrant to 'N' position.
2. Fit splined selector arm to an appropriate spline to bring it as near horizontal as possible.
3. Tighten pinch bolt.

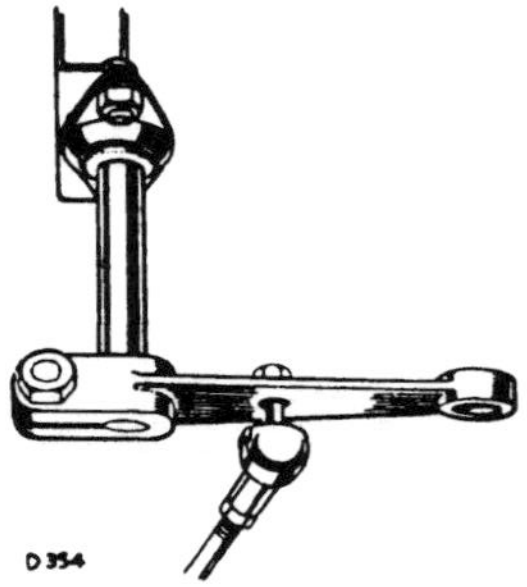

Splined selector lever in position, RHD illustrated

4. Fit control rod (splined selector lever to transmission cross-shaft) and secure at each end with a split pin and washer.
5. Move selector lever to 'P' park position. The splined gearbox cross-shaft arm should now be in a vertical position. If this is not so, remove the split pin, nut and washer and move the arm to an appropriate spline. Replace rubber 'O' ring, washer, nut and split pin.

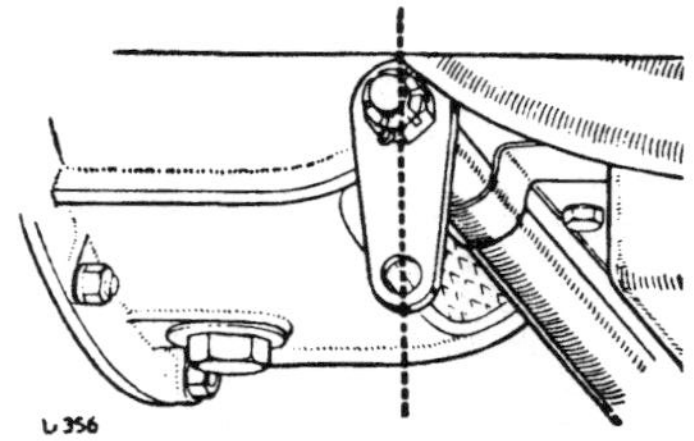

Cross-shaft arm in vertical position, RHD illustrated

6. Move selector lever on transmission to fully forward position, 'P' park.
7. Adjust the adjustable control rod to the necessary length so that it will drop into the cross-shaft splined arm and transmission selector lever. The link fits on the exhaust side of the car with the long end of the link towards the front.

Starter cut-out switch, adjust

8. With the selector lever still at 'P' park, move the starter cut-out switch to the top of its travel.
9. Adjust the control rod for the starter cut-out switch so that it will slide on to the ball joint on the starter cut-out switch and also the ball joint on the splined gear selector lever.
10. Check that the starter will operate in 'P' park or 'N' neutral, but not in 'D' drive, 'L' low or 'R' reverse.
11. Road-test car, trying all positions on selector quadrant.

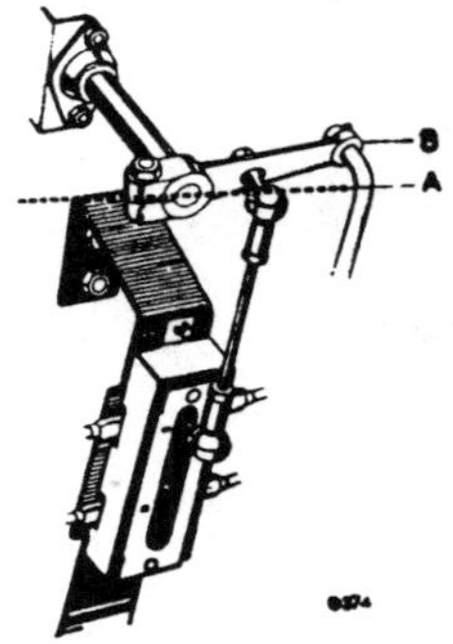

Starter cut-out switch

A—Neutral B—Park

Operation E1-6—*continued*

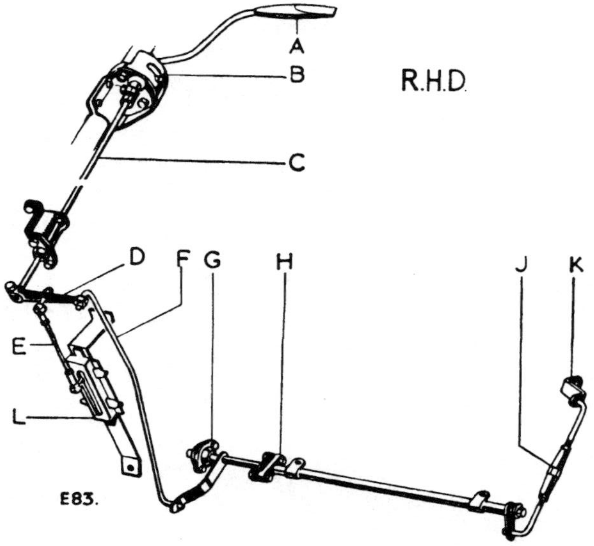

Layout of selector linkage, RHD models

A—Selector lever
B—Selector quadrant
C—Selector shaft
D—Splined selector lever
E—Rod, splined selector lever to cut-out switch
F—Rod, splined selector lever to transmission cross-shaft

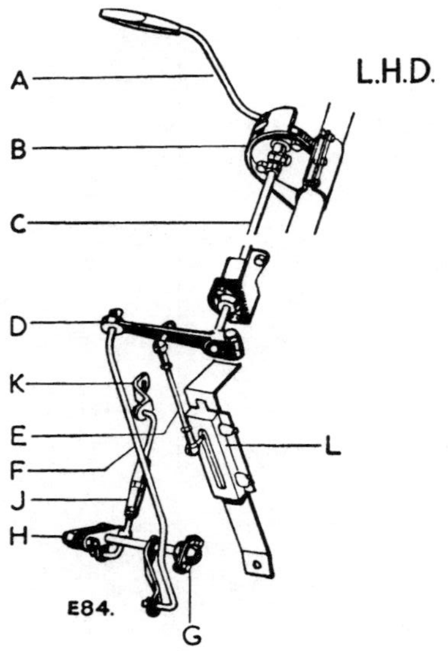

Layout of selector linkage, LHD models

G—Transmission cross-shaft end bearing
H—Transmission cross-shaft compensator
J—Adjustable rod
K—Transmission selector lever
L—Starter cut-out switch

The above illustrations show the early type of control rods. On late models the control rods F and J are of slightly different design and are fitted with nylon ball joints; the general arrangement is, however, unchanged.

Operation E1-6—*continued*

Selector mechanism setting, LHD models

1. Move selector quadrant to 'N' neutral position.
2. Fit splined selector arm to an appropriate spline to bring it as near horizontal as possible. Tighten pinch bolt.
3. Move selector lever to 'P' park position.
4. Adjust the adjustable control rod to the necessary length, so that it will drop into the cross-shaft splined arm and the transmission selector lever. The link fits on the exhaust side of the car with the long end of the link towards the front.
5. Adjust the starter cut-out switch as detailed above

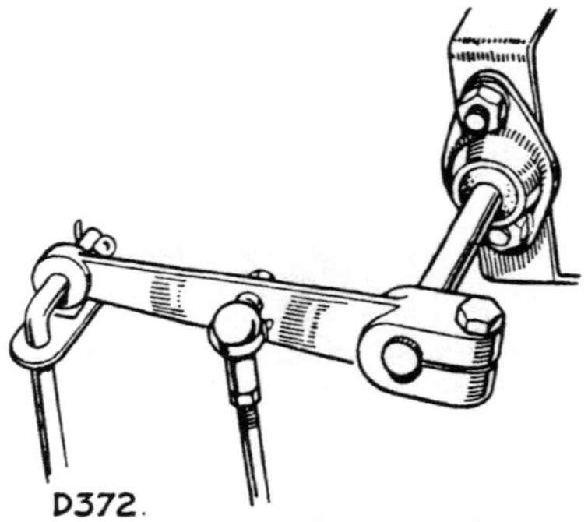
D372.
Splined selector lever in position, LHD models

*Intermediate hold operating speed settings—Operation E1-7

This operation is only applicable to automatic transmission units fitted with electrical intermediate gear hold controls

Workshop hand tools:
Spanner size: $\frac{7}{16}$ in. AF

The intermediate hold is controlled by a solenoid mounted on the transmission unit at the left-hand side. The solenoid is normally set so that the transmission will not change up from low into intermediate until the following speeds have been reached:

Models Mk 1 and Mk IA
30 to 34 mph (48 to 54 kph)

Models Mk II
20 to 25 mph (32 to 40 kph)

Changes from intermediate to direct drive being made at:

Models Mk I and Mk IA
60 to 65 mph (96 to 104 kph)

Models Mk II
44 to 49 mph (71 to 79 kph)

Should it be desirable for the transmission to change up or down at speeds other than those quoted adjust the solenoid as follows:

Solenoid, adjust

1. Place the car on a suitable ramp.
2. From beneath the car slacken the nuts securing the solenoid to mounting bracket.
3. Turn solenoid anti-clockwise (as viewed from below) to the full extent of the slots in the mounting bracket. Tighten the nuts.

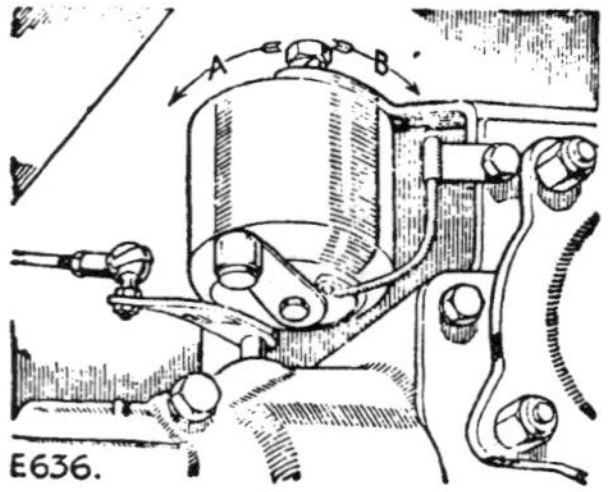

E636.
Adjustment of intermediate hold solenoid

Adjustment of intermediate hold solenoid

Mk IA models

Turn the solenoid in direction of arrow 'B' to give change speeds into direct at 30–34 mph (48–54 kph).

Mk II

Turn solenoid in direction of arrow 'A' to give change speeds into direct at 60–65 mph (96–104 kph).

Turn solenoid in direction of arrow 'B' to give change speeds into direct at 20–25 mph (32–40 kph).

Operations which are identified by an asterisk (*) can be carried out with the transmission unit installed in the car

* Intermediate hold control cable, to remove, refit and adjust—Operation E1-8

This operation is not applicable to models fitted with electrical control

Workshop hand tools:

'C' spanner

Cable, remove

1. Release the cable, secured by a nipple, at the relay on the bulkhead.
2. Remove the overriding spring, where fitted, and disconnect return spring.
3. Release the cable clamping bolt situated between heater and heater motor.
4. Unscrew the chromium bezel, retaining outer cable to control mounting bracket inside the car.

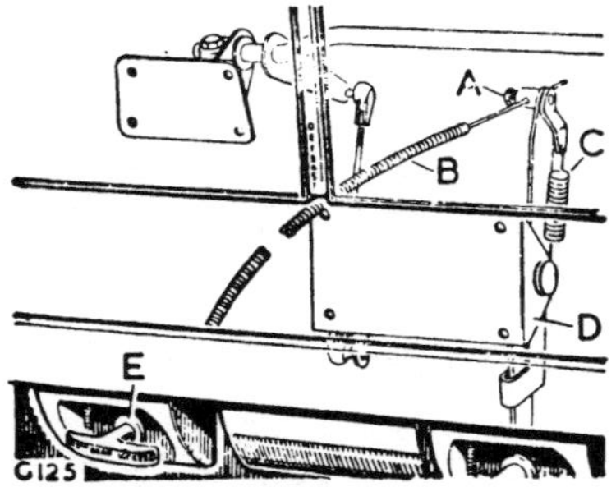

Intermediate hold

A—Nipple
B—Control cable
C—Return spring
D—Accelerator relay box
E—Control knob

5. Completely withdraw the inner cable.
6. Pull the outer cable through the bulkhead and remove from control mounting bracket.

Cable, refit

1. Fit the inner cable to the outer cable.
2. Fit the washer to the outer cable.
3. Secure complete cable to bracket with chromium bezel, pass the bottom of the cable through the bulkhead
4. Pull out the inner cable sufficiently to allow the nipple to be located in the handle.
5. Push both inner cable and handle half-way in.
6. Secure the end of the outer cable in the clamp situated between the heater and the heater motor. The outer cable end should be flush with the clamp. If this is not so, full movement of the lever will not be obtained.
7. Fit a flat washer and spring anchor plate on to clevis pin. Enter clevis pin into lever.
8. Fit a second flat washer on to clevis pin, pass the inner cable through the hole drilled in the end of the clevis pin.
9. Fit the overriding spring (1st speed models) and secure the cable to the lever on the relay with the nipple.
10. Couple up the return spring by hooking on to the relay mounting bracket and hooking on to the anchor plate on the clevis pin.

Control, adjust

11. **1st-speed start models**—Pull out 2nd speed hold handle to the locked position. This should leave no further movement on the control rod relay assembly to governor control shaft.
12. **2nd-speed start models**—Adjust the 2nd-speed (intermediate) hold control, so that when it is pulled out and locked in position, the governor control shaft is against the spring-loaded detent plunger in the extension case. Note that the overriding spring, at the relay end of the cable, is not fitted on models with 2nd-speed start.
13. If there is further movement of the control rod: release the bolt in the ferrule, adjust accordingly and tighten the bolt.
14. Check the action of the 2nd speed hold again.
15. Road-test car, and check performance figures previously laid down.

Operations which are identified by an asterisk (*) can be carried out with the engine and transmission unit installed in the car

*Brake bands, to adjust—Operation E1-9

Workshop hand tools:
Spanner sizes: $\frac{5}{16}$ in. AF, $\frac{3}{4}$ in. AF

Special tools:
B-W2B Brake band adjusting gauge

Brake bands, adjust

1. Remove the plug and copper gasket from the pressure take-off hole in the servo *opposite* the adjustment screw of band to be adjusted. When checking the forward band on early models it may be necessary to remove the transmission mounting rubbers and lower the transmission to provide sufficient clearance to insert the adjusting gauge.
2. Screw the band adjusting gauge B-W2B, carefully into the pressure take-off hole. Correct adjustment is when the plunger is flush with the end of the body of the adjuster, that is with the gauge screwed right in.
3. If the indicator plug becomes flush with the gauge before the gauge is screwed fully home against the transmission case, the band is too tight. **Do not continue screwing the gauge in.** This is a necessary precaution; if the plunger of the gauge is forced beyond the end, by more than $\frac{3}{16}$ in. (4,7 mm) damage will result.

   Loosen the locknut and adjusting screw on the opposite side of the main casing two turns before screwing home the gauge.
4. If with the gauge fully in position the indicator is below the face of the gauge, screw in the adjustment screw and when the indicator becomes flush, tighten the band adjusting screw locknut securely, ensuring that the adjusting screw does not turn.
5. Adjustments completed, remove the gauge and fit the plug using a new copper gasket. **Do not use sealing compound** of any type. Tighten to 28–33 lb ft (3,8–4,5 mkg) torque.

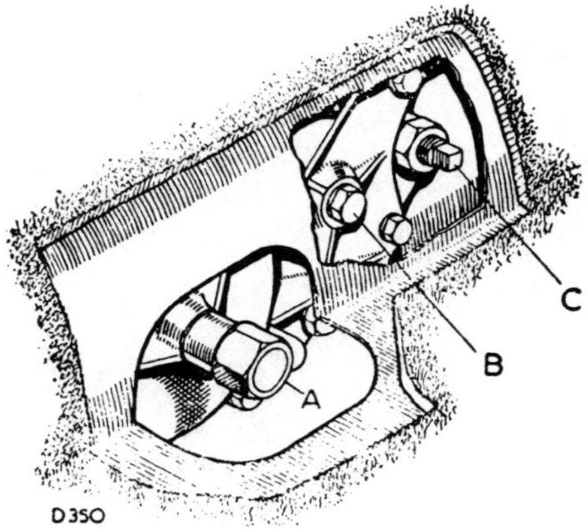

Band adjustment, forward band

A—Band adjusting gauge in low servo
B—Pressure take-off plug for forward servo
C—Reverse band adjusting screw

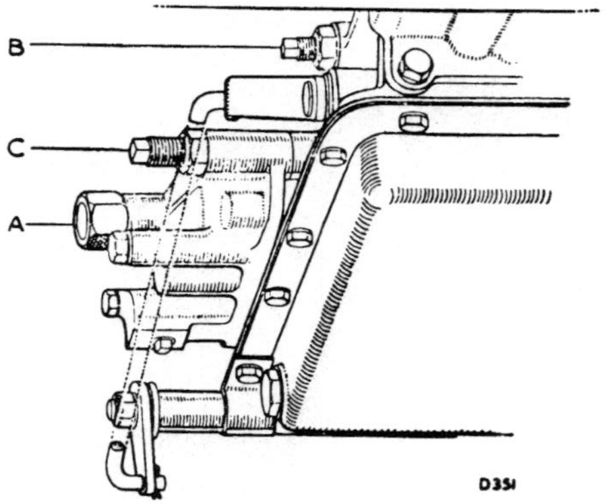

Band adjustment, reverse band

A—Band adjusting gauge in reverse servo
B—Forward band adjusting screw
C—Low band adjusting screw

Operations which are identified by an asterisk (*) can be carried out with the engine and transmission unit installed in the car

Section E – AUTOMATIC TRANSMISSION
Model 'DG', Rover Mk I, Mk IA and Mk II
Part Two

This Section provides the instructions necessary for completely stripping and rebuilding the automatic transmission unit for overhaul and servicing purposes. It should be noted, however, that it is rarely necessary to completely strip the unit, which comprises five basic assemblies, each of which may be stripped without affecting the others. These are:

1. The main case group
2. Gear train
3. Valve block
4. Front pump
5. Extension case

Instructions for the removal of the transmission unit from the car are given in Section A.

Instructions for removing the transmission unit from the engine are given in Part One of this Section.

Before starting to strip any unit, note that absolute cleanliness is essential. Use nylon or non-fluffy material for all cleaning purposes. Use a plastic-headed mallet, as a hide mallet will chip. Do not use paraffin to clean the housings or components—transmission fluid should be used for this purpose.

A bench cradle (Part No. B-W15A) is available, and it is recommended that this should be used.

Valve block, to strip and rebuild—Operation E2-1

Workshop hand tools:
Spanner sizes: $\frac{1}{2}$ in. AF, $\frac{7}{16}$ in. AF
Screwdriver, medium

Special tools:
Spring retainer remover B-W8A
Allen key, small

Valve block, remove

1. Instructions for removing the fluid sump and valve block are given in Part One of this Section. Operation E1-3.

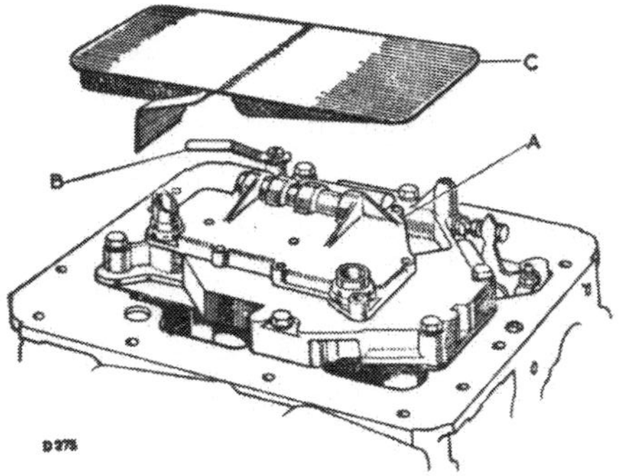

Valve block assembly location

A—Valve block B—Filter clip C—Fluid filter

Valve block, strip

2. Remove the eight bolts from the top of the valve block; remove the main relief valve body by lifting directly upwards.
3. Remove the front and rear oil pump ball check valves from the seats located on the base plate.
4. Remove gasket base plate to transmission casing.
5. Remove the base plate; gasket, base plate to manifold plate, and selector ball and spring.
6. Remove the converter valve body and the gasket from the manifold plate.
7. Turn the selector valve to the position shown.
8. Push the selector valve into the manifold past the detent ball and spring. Failure to take these precautions can result in the selector ball jamming the selector valve.

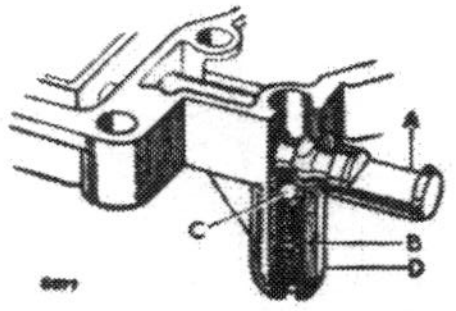

Selector valve position for removal

A—Selector valve C—Selector ball
B—Spring for selector ball D—Housing for selector spring

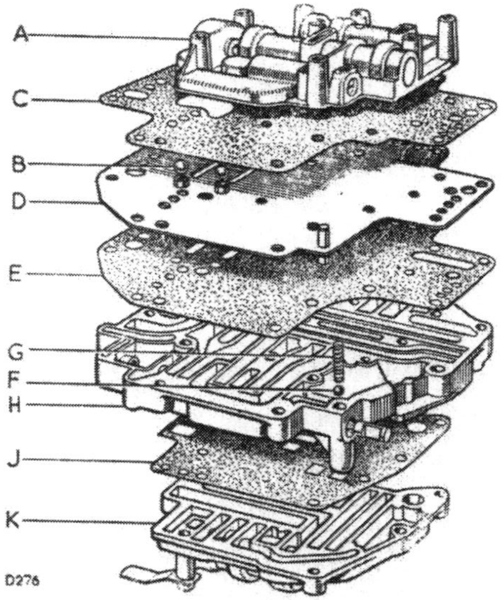

Valve block components

A—Relief valve body
B—Ball check valves
C—Gasket, base plate to transmission casing
D—Base plate
E—Gasket, base plate to manifold plate
F—Selector ball
G—Spring, selector ball
H—Manifold assembly
J—Gasket, converter housing to manifold plate
K—Converter valve body

Operation E2-1—*continued*

9. Should the valve become jammed, it can be released by inserting a piece of bent wire into the selector spring housing, hooking on to the spring and relieving the pressure.
10. On no account should attempts be made to force out the selector valve. The ball is under spring pressure and suitable action should be taken to prevent loss.
11. Remove the selector valve, ball and spring.
12. Remove the reverse interlock valve by compressing the spring and pushing out the retainer, using special tool (Part No. B-W8A). Withdraw spring and reverse interlock piston.

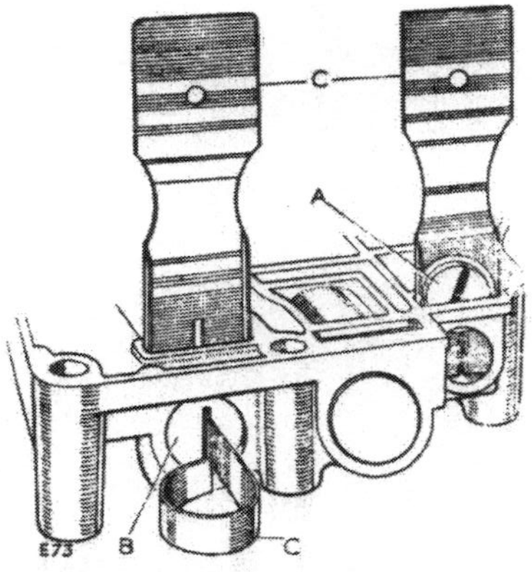

Removing reverse interlock and accumulator valve

A—Reverse interlock valve retainer
B—Accumulator valve retainer
C—Spring retainer remover B-W8A

13. Remove the accumulator valve spring and retainer.
14. Remove retainer for main relief valve plug and withdraw plug.
15. Remove main relief valve outer piston.
16. Remove main relief valve inner piston and spring for main relief valve.
17. Remove retainer for the main relief valve and withdraw main relief valve, taking care to ease the valve through the bore.

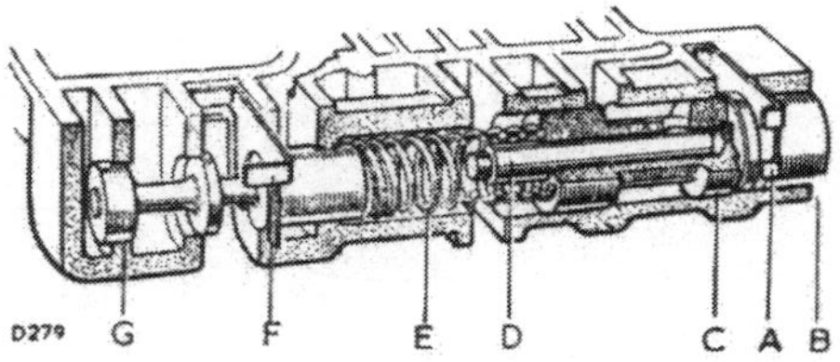

Cross-section main relief valve

A—Plug retainer E—Spring
B—Plug F—Main relief valve retainer
C—Outer piston G—Main relief valve
D—Inner piston

18. From the converter shuttle valve housing remove the shuttle valve sleeve retainer, and withdraw the sleeve, then remove the converter shuttle reverse valve. Withdraw the converter shuttle direct valve from the housing.

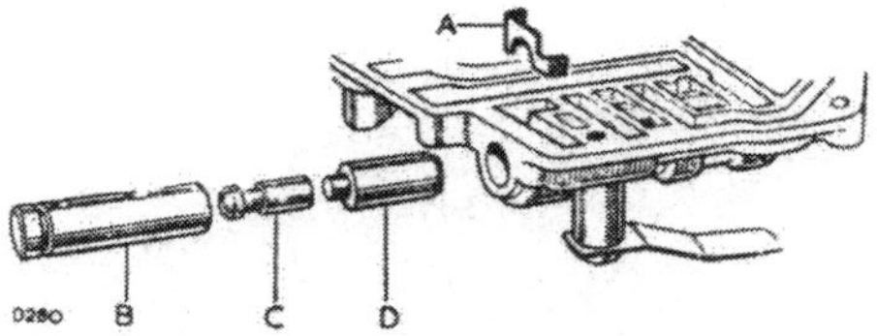

Converter shuttle valve

A—Shuttle valve retainer C—Shuttle valve
B—Shuttle valve sleeve D—Shuttle valve piston

19. Inspect all valves and valve bores for evidence of scratches or scoring and for free operation. All valves have sharp edges for self-cleaning action. In case of burring, careful dressing with an oil stone is permissible, provided valve edges are not rounded.

Valve block, rebuild

1. Place the converter shuttle direct valve into the valve bore so that the top shoulder is towards the end of the bore.

Note: When a new torque converter (Part No. 538212) having paper-based direct-drive clutch linings has been fitted (identified by the letter 'P' painted on a salmon pink panel), a valve block and shuttle valve (Part No. 530099) **must be fitted.**

Operation E2-1—*continued*

2. Insert the converter shuttle valve into the sleeve so that the cone face of the valve can seat inside the sleeve. Insert the sleeve and valve assembly into the valve body with the open end of the sleeve towards the converter shuttle valve piston and secure with retainer.

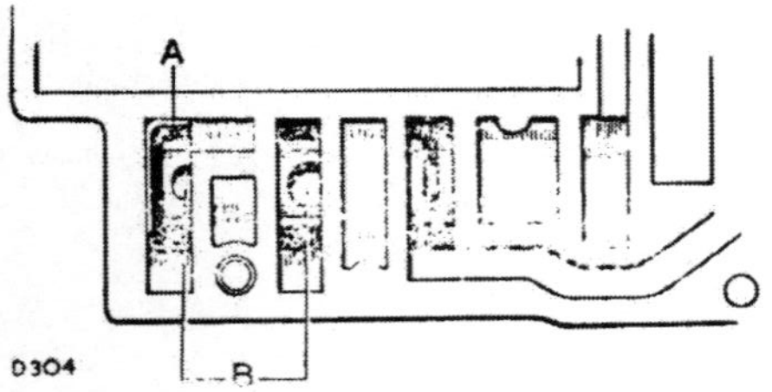

Location of shuttle valve in housing

A—Retainer B—Shuttle valve sleeve

3. Place the accumulator valve spring in the bore of the accumulator valve and insert the valve and spring as an assembly into its housing, with the spring towards the open end of the bore.

   Use tool (Part No. B-W8A) to compress the spring and place the retainer into position. Ensure that the retainer is properly seated.

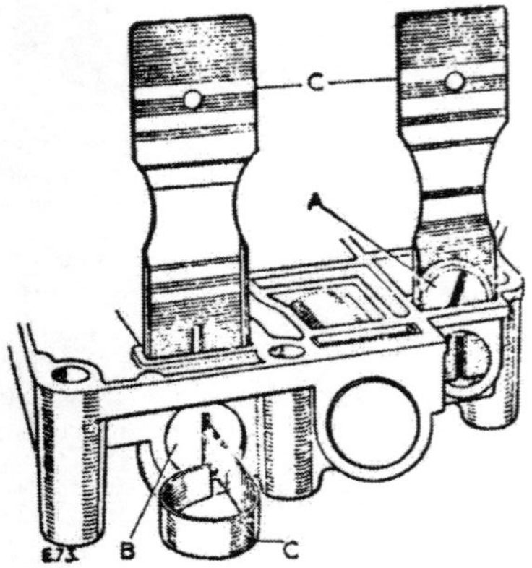

Fitting reverse interlock and accumulator valve

A—Reverse interlock valve retainer
B—Accumulator valve retainer
C—Spring retainer remover B-W8A

4. Place the reverse interlock valve spring into the bore of the valve. Insert the valve and spring as an assembly into the bore of the housing, with the spring towards the open end of the bore. Using tool (Part No. B-W8A), compress the spring and place the retainer into position, ensuring that it is properly seated.

5. Place main relief valve into the bore so that the two waisted lands of the valve are towards the closed end.

6. With the valve right in, place the relief valve retainer into position; ensure that the valve moves freely.

7. Insert the spring into the bore.

8. Place the main relief valve into the bore of the outer piston.

9. Insert the valve as an assembly into the bore of the housing with the main relief valve inner piston towards the spring.

10. Fit the main relief valve plug with the annular groove towards the piston. Insert the retainer as illustrated.

11. Fit detent spring and ball into selector valve housing. Insert the selector valve into the housing, with the milled slot in the selector valve away from the detent housing. Using a small Allen key, press the ball and spring downwards and slide the selector valve into its first detent position.

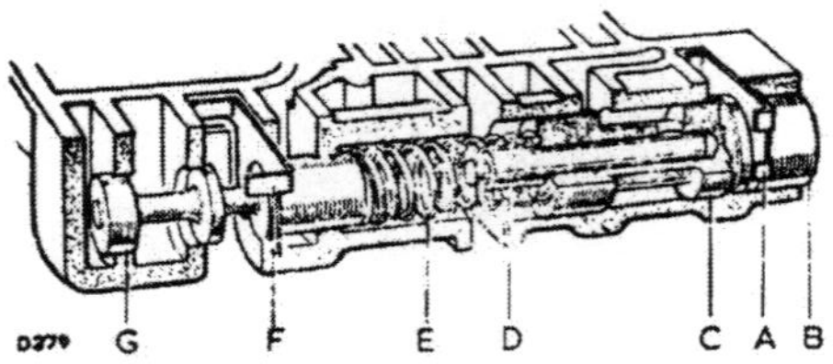

Location of main relief valve retainers

A—Main relief valve retainer
B—Plug retainer
C—Outer piston
D—Inner piston
E—Spring
F—Main relief valve retainer
G—Main relief valve

Operation E2-1—*continued*

12. Place the converter valve body on the bench and fit a new gasket. Fit the manifold to the converter shuttle valve housing. Fit a new gasket to the manifold. Fit the detent ball into the selector valve housing.

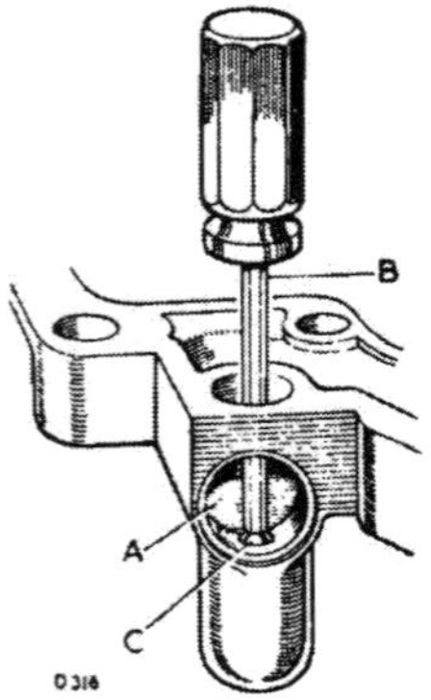

Fitting selector valve detent spring and ball

A—Selector shaft B—Allen key C—Ball

13. Fit the selector valve detent spring into housing in the base plate and fit the base plate to the selector manifold housing, using a new gasket.

14. Fit the two ball check valves to their seatings on the base plate. Fit the main relief valve housing on to the base plate, using a new gasket. Make sure the two ball check valves are not disturbed. Fit the eight securing bolts and tighten to 6 to 8 lb/ft (0,8 to 1,0 mkg).

Valve block, refit to main casing

1. Reverse removal procedure.

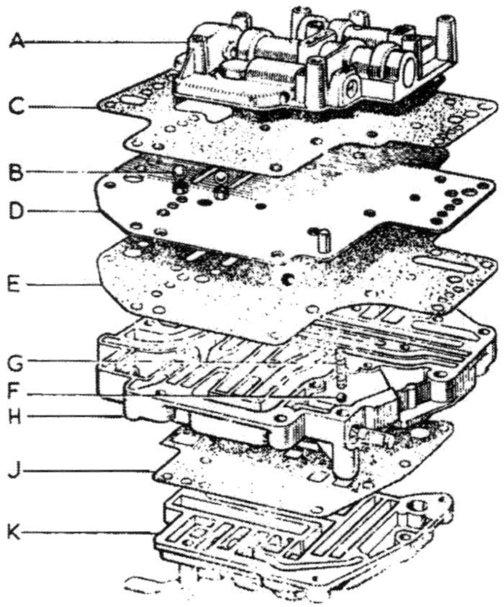

Valve block components

A—Main relief valve block
B—Ball check valves
C—Gasket, base plate to transmission casing
D—Base plate
E—Gasket, base plate to manifold plate
F—Selector ball
G—Spring, selector ball
H—Manifold plate
J—Gasket converter housing to manifold plate
K—Converter shuttle valve housing

Extension casing, to remove from, and refit to, main casing—Operation E2-2

Workshop hand tools:
Spanner sizes: $\frac{9}{16}$ in. AF, $1\frac{1}{8}$ in. AF
Plastic-faced mallet

Special tools:
Bench cradle B-W15A
Torque spanner

Extension casing, remove

1. Absolute cleanliness is essential. Nylon rag or non-fluffy material should be used for cleaning purposes. A plastic-headed mallet should be used, as a hide mallet will chip.

2. Remove bell housing from transmission casing. Fit bench cradle (Part No. B-W15A).

   Move selector valve lever into Park position; that is, fully forward. This locks the mainshaft and facilitates removal of propeller shaft flange nut.

3. Remove the propeller shaft flange, secured by a nut and washer (if necessary using an extractor).

4. Move the selector valve lever out of the Park position.

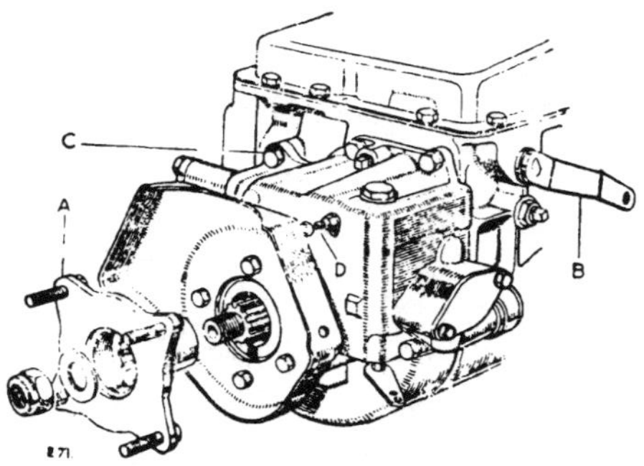

Removal of propeller shaft flange and extension casing (early type illustrated)

A—Propeller shaft flange
B—Selector valve lever in fully forward position
C—Extension casing bolts

5. Remove four bolts securing transmission mounting bracket and remove bracket.

6. Remove six bolts securing extension casing to main casing.

7. Slide the extension casing rearwards, taking care not to drop gears, spacers, piston and springs.

8. Remove the large spacer, governor drive gear, parking pawl gear and small spacer from mainshaft.

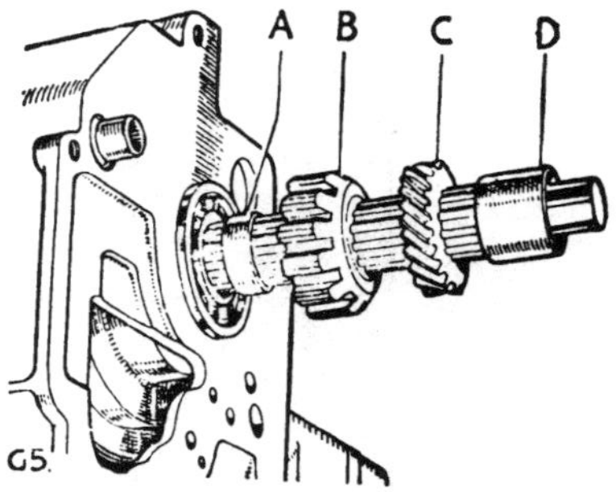

Sequence of mainshaft spacers and components

A—Drive gear spacer
B—Parking brake gear
C—Governor drive gear
D—Propeller shaft flange spacer

Extension casing, refit

1. Place on the mainshaft the governor drive gear spacer, the parking brake gear with the chamfered face towards the rear end, governor drive gear and propeller shaft flange spacer.

2. Place the new gasket into position on the transmission case. Use only petroleum jelly.

3. Move the selector control shaft lever to low position by pulling the lever as far rearward as it will go and then move it one detent forward. This will bring the master spline on the parking brake toggle arm sleeve to approximately a horizontal position.

4. Turn the toggle arm shaft so that the master spline is horizontal and lines up with the master spline on the parking brake toggle arm.

5. Lift the extension casing into position on the shaft. Engage the splines of the toggle arm shaft and sleeve. Push the case forward against the transmission casing and insert the set bolts; tighten to 28 to 33 lb/ft (3,8 to 4,5 mkg).

6. Fit the automatic transmission mounting bracket.

7. Move selector lever into Park position; that is, fully forward, to prevent rotation of the mainshaft.

8. Place the propeller shaft flange on to the mainshaft, ensuring that the propeller shaft bolts are already installed; secure with a plain washer and new self-locking nut; tighten to 60 to 80 lb/ft (8,2 to 11,0 mkg).

Extension casing, to strip and rebuild—Operation E2-3

Transmission unit removed from car

Workshop hand tools:
Spanner sizes: $\frac{7}{16}$ in. AF, $\frac{1}{2}$ in. AF, $\frac{9}{16}$ in. AF, $\frac{1}{2}$ in. BSF
Screwdriver, medium

Special tools:
Allen key
Drive flange oil seal replacer B-W16
Torque spanner

Warning: Do not use paraffin to clean component parts. Use only nylon rag for cleaning purposes.

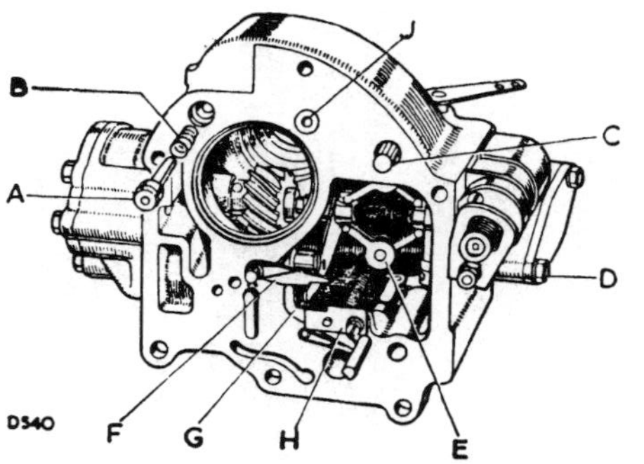

Extension casing components, 1st-speed start models

A—Parking pawl interlock piston
B—Parking pawl interlock spring
C—Shaft for parking brake toggle
D—Speedometer housing securing bolts
E—Governor
F—Second speed latch
G—Rocker arm
H—Stop plate
J—Parking pawl pivot pin

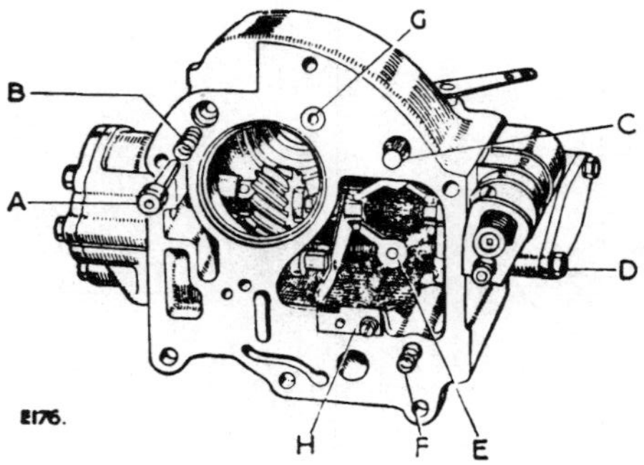

Extension casing components, 2nd-speed start models

A—Parking pawl interlock piston
B—Parking pawl interlock spring
C—Shaft for parking brake toggle
D—Speedometer housing securing bolts
E—Governor
F—Accelerator detent plunger and spring
G—Parking pawl pivot pin
H—Stop plate

Extension casing, to dismantle

1. Remove the parking pawl interlock piston and spring.

2. Remove the parking pawl splined shaft.

3. On 2nd-speed start models remove the accelerator detent spring and plunger.

4. Remove two bolts from end plate and remove speedometer gear housing complete from transmission casing.

5. Remove the nut from the stud securing speedometer shaft retainer. Remove the speedometer shaft retainer.

6. Remove the three screws securing the adaptor for speedometer cable and remove the adaptor.

7. Withdraw the bronze speedometer housing and shaft complete.

8. Withdraw the fibre driven gear from the shaft.

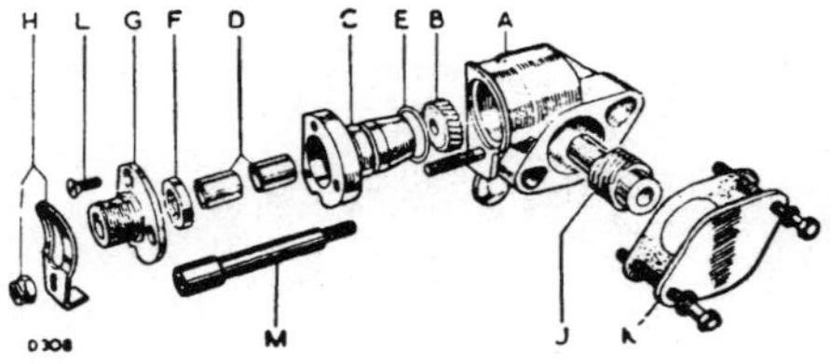

Speedometer drive components

A—Speedometer gear housing
B—Fibre driven gear
C—Bronze speedometer drive housing
D—Bushes
E—Rubber 'O' ring seal
F—Oil seal
G—Speedometer cable adaptor
H—Drive shaft retainer and flange for speedometer spindle
J—Gear for speedometer drive
K—End plate and fixings
L—Screws retaining speedometer drive adaptor
M—Speedometer drive shaft

Operation E2-3—*continued*

9. Withdraw the shaft from the housing.
10. Remove the rubber 'O' ring seal from the housing.
11. Remove oil seal for driven shaft.
12. Using a suitable drift, drive out the bushes from the housing.

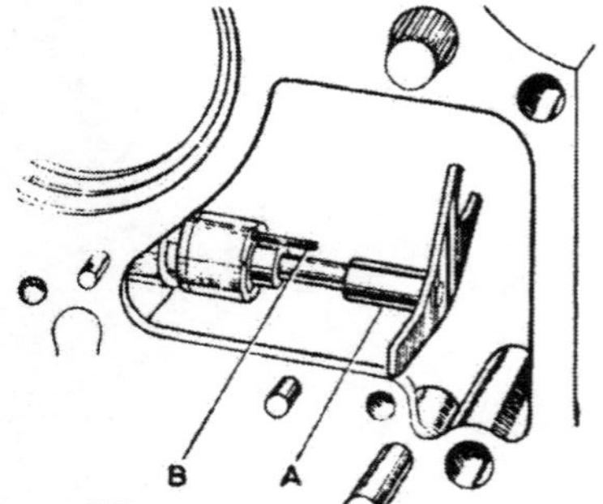

E72

Governor valve and detent piston in bushing, 1st-speed start models

A—Governor valve B—Detent piston

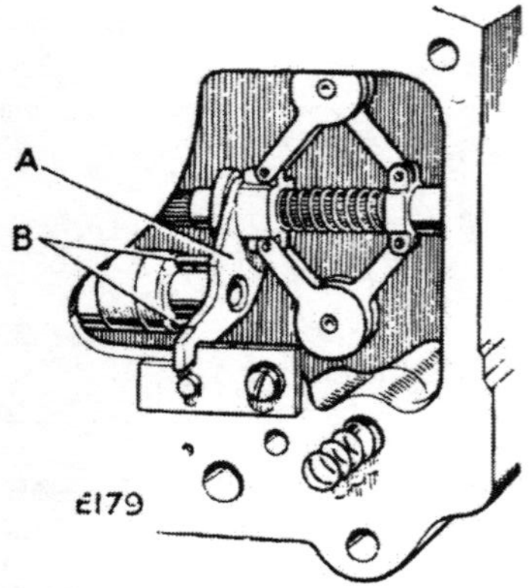

E179

Governor valve and detent pistons in bushing, 2nd-speed start models

A—Governor valve B—Detent pistons

13. Remove the worm drive gear from the speedometer gear housing.
14. Remove the splined shaft from the governor assembly.
15. Remove the governor assembly from the extension casing, and remove governor spring.
16. Remove the governor yoke shoes from the governor fork.

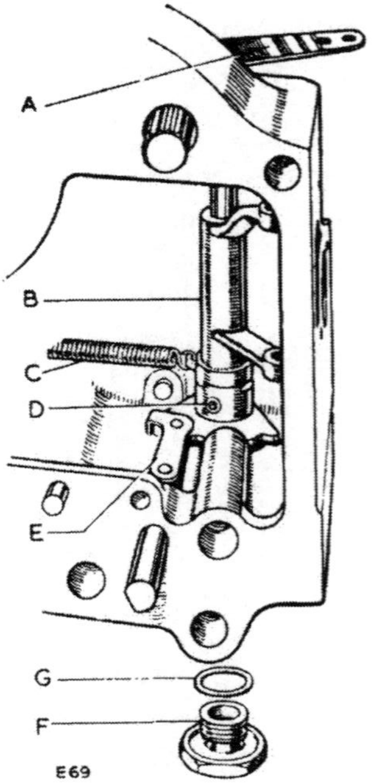

E69

Control shaft and components, 1st-speed start models

A—Control lever
B—Governor fork
C—Spring for governor fork
D—Allen screw
E—Detent cam plunger
F—Bush } For governor
G—Seal } control shaft

Operation E2-3—*continued*

17. Remove the governor valve and top speed detent piston from the sleeve assembly in extension case. On 2nd-speed start models, no attempt should be made to remove the 2nd-speed detent piston, as it is secured on original assembly by a spring ring.
18. 1st-speed start models—remove the split pin, small plain washer, spring for second speed latch and washer from the pivot pin.
19. Unscrew the retaining screw and remove the stop plate and spacer.
20. 1st-speed start models—remove the rocker arm, washer and spring.

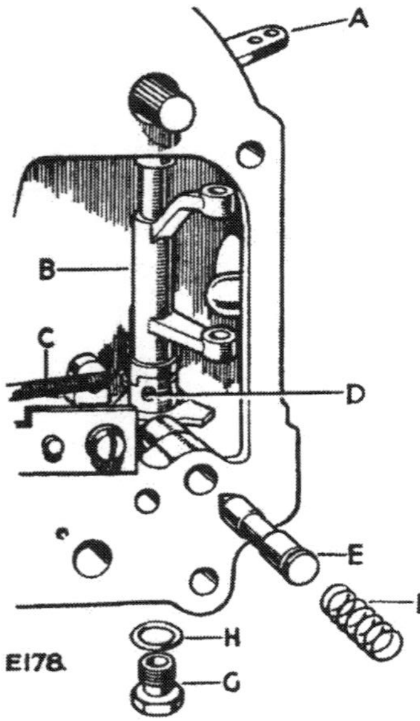

E178

Control shaft and components, 2nd-speed start models

A—C ntrol lever
B—Governor fork
C—Spring for governor fork
D—Allen screw
E—Accelerator plunger
F—Spring
G—Bush } For governor
H—Seal } control shaft

21. To remove the detent cam plunger from the control shaft, hold the adjusting shaft in a suitable position and slacken the Allen screw.
22. 2nd-speed start models—to remove the accelerator detent cam, turn the control shaft to a suitable position and slacken the Allen screw.
23. Remove the control shaft from casing.
24. Remove the governor fork and spring from casing.
25. Remove spring from fork.
26. 1st-speed start models—to remove the detent cam and plunger assembly from casing, swing the detent cam and link towards the governor return spring anchor pin, push the plunger into casing and remove the assembly. Remove the bush and seal from governor adjusting shaft.
27. Remove the parking brake pawl pivot pin, by screwing a bolt ($\frac{5}{16}$ in. UNF x $\frac{3}{4}$ in.) into the end of the pivot pin, and lever the pin out with an open-ended spanner.
28. Remove the toggle assembly from the casing.
29. Remove the rear oil pump, secured by three large retaining set bolts.
30. Remove the booster spring and retainer from the extension case at the rear end of the governor valve.

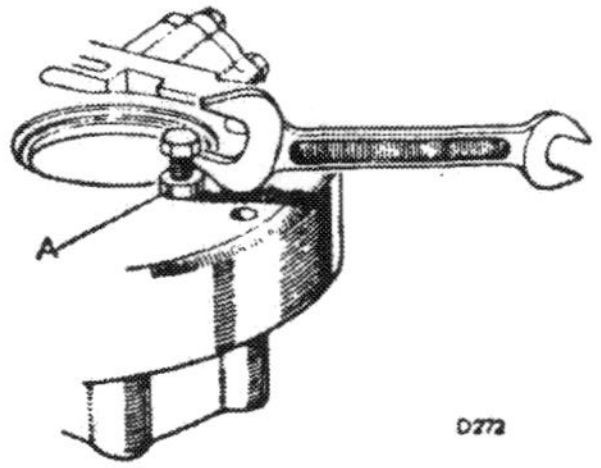

D272

Removal of pivot pin

A—Pivot pin

Operation E2-3—*continued*

31. Remove the extension casing rear oil seal, using a suitable drift or seal extractor. Drive the oil seal rearwards, being careful not to damage the casing.

32. If necessary, remove the protection cap, change speed adjuster bolt, locknut and washer. It is only necessary to remove the adjusting screw when a new governor or governor spring has to be fitted.

Extension casing, assemble

1. Ensure that parts to be assembled are thoroughly clean and serviceable.
2. Examine the splined shaft for distortion or wear.
3. Examine the governor bearing and weight pivots for wear.
4. Examine the governor fork and yoke shoes for wear or damage.
5. 1st-speed start models—examine the detent cam plunger and control shaft for wear.
6. 1st-speed start models—examine the cam and link for wear.
7. 1st-speed start models—examine the second speed latch and rocker arm for wear and check return springs.
8. 2nd speed start models—examine the accelerator plunger and cam for wear.
9. Examine the parking pawl for chipping and check the needle bearings for wear.
10. Check the parking brake pivot and splined shaft for wear.
11. Examine the extension casing for possible damage and stripped threads.
12. Examine the rear pump gears for wear.
13. Examine the propeller shaft flange oil seal for wear.
14. Renew any defective parts.
15. Press a new oil seal into the rear of the extension casing, using oil seal drive flange replacer (Part No. B-W16). The outer surface of the oil seal should be coated with petroleum jelly.
16. Using a new copper washer, refit the change speed adjuster screw, locknut and protection cap.
17. Replace the retainer and booster spring into the governor valve sleeve with the spring to the open end of the sleeve.
18. Fit a new gasket of similar thickness to the one discarded to oil pump end cover and replace end cover, using two small set bolts.

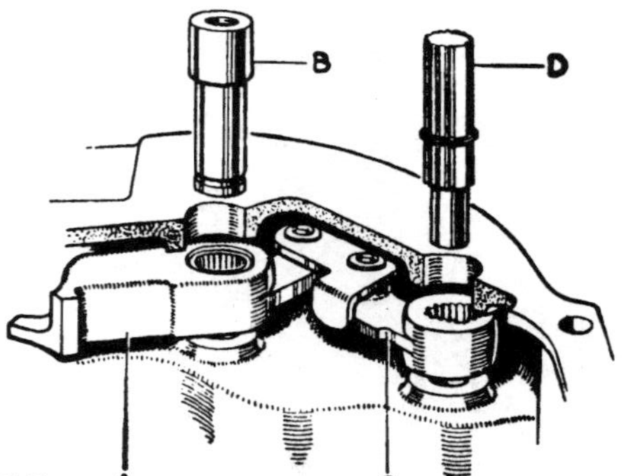

D305

Fitting parking pawl and toggle

A—Parking pawl C—Toggle lever
B—Pivot pin D—Toggle shaft

19. Fit a new gasket to the face of the pump housing and ensure that it does not obstruct the drain hole.
20. Insert the pump into the casing and secure with three set bolts; tighten to 15 to 18 lb/ft (2,07 to 2,48 mkg).

Operation E2-3—*continued*

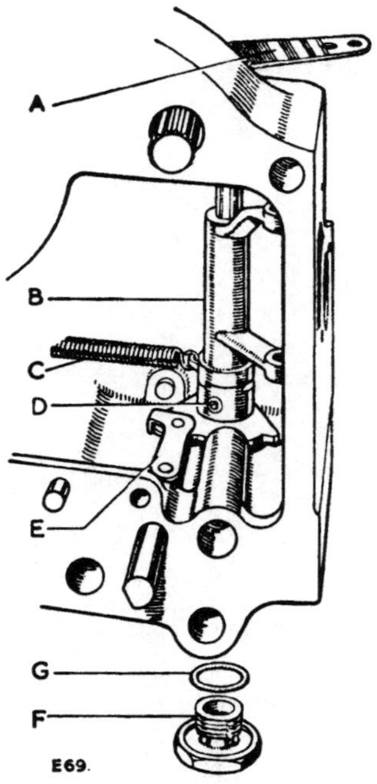

E69.

Control shaft and components, 1st-speed start models

A—Control shaft lever E—Detent cam plunger
B—Governor fork F—Bottom bush
C—Spring for governor fork G—Rubber washer for bottom bush
D—Allen screw

21. Position the parking brake pawl and toggle assembly in the casing with the dog of the pawl pointing downwards.
22. Align the pivot pin hole of the pawl with the hole in the casing and insert the pivot pin.
23. Position the end of the pawl and toggle assembly under the hole in the casing, then align the master splines of the toggle shaft and toggle lever and insert the shaft, plain end first.

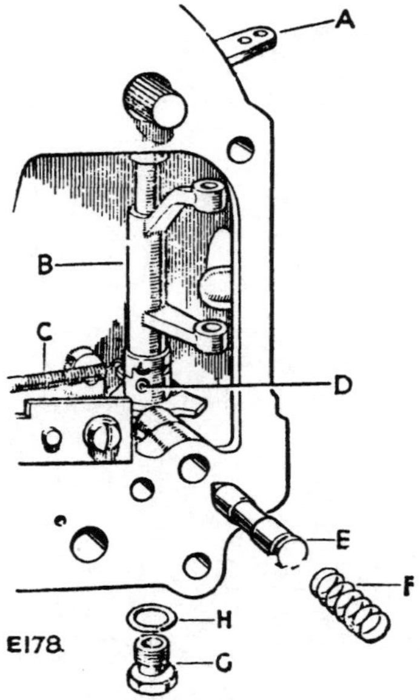

E178

Control shaft and components, 2nd-speed start models

A—Control lever E—Accelerator plunger
B—Governor fork F—Spring
C—Spring for governor fork G—Bush } For governor
D—Allen screw H—Seal } control start

24. Fit a new rubber washer for bottom bush to the governor control shaft bottom bush and replace bush.
25. Place the detent cam into the extension casing, and on 1st-speed start models insert the plunger through the hole in the casing. Turn the detent cam to line up with the governor control shaft bottom bush.
26. Ensure that the Woodruff key is properly installed in the governor control shaft, and insert the shaft into the end of the casing.
27. Fit the return spring to the governor fork.

Operation E2-3—*continued*

28. Position the governor fork in the casing and attach the return spring to the anchor post, loop downwards.

29. Align the Woodruff key in the shaft with the keyway in the detent cam boss, and push the shaft through the governor fork and detent cam into the bottom bush.

30. Ensure that the shaft is fully seated in the bottom bush, then tighten the Allen screw.

31. Insert the top speed detent piston into the governor assembly sleeve.

32. Replace the governor valve into the sleeve assembly.

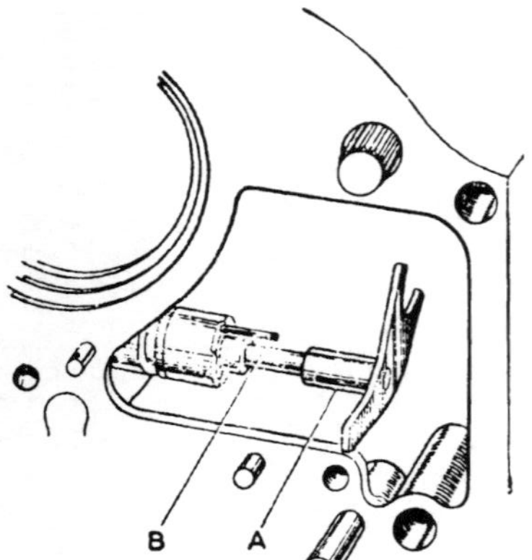

E72

Governor valve and detent piston in sleeve, 1st-speed start models

A—Governor valve B—Detent piston

33. 1st-speed start models—place the large plain washer on to the pin, ensuring that it is correctly placed in relation to the plunger.

34. 1st-speed start models—place the retainer stop plate over the rocker arm as illustrated and slip the distance piece between the plate and case.

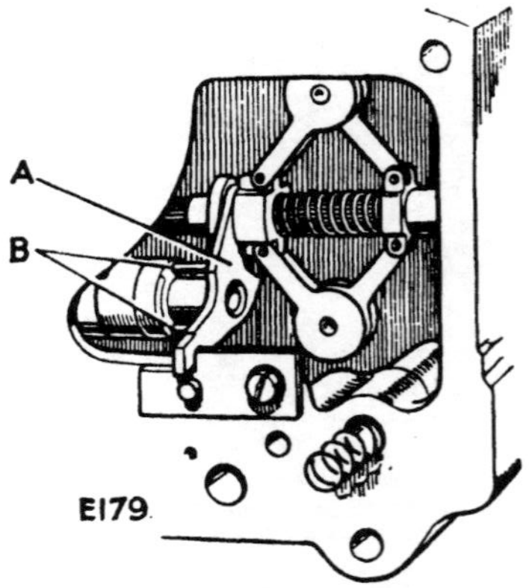

E179

Governor valve and detent pistonsin bushing, 2nd-speed start models

A—Governor valve B—Detent piston

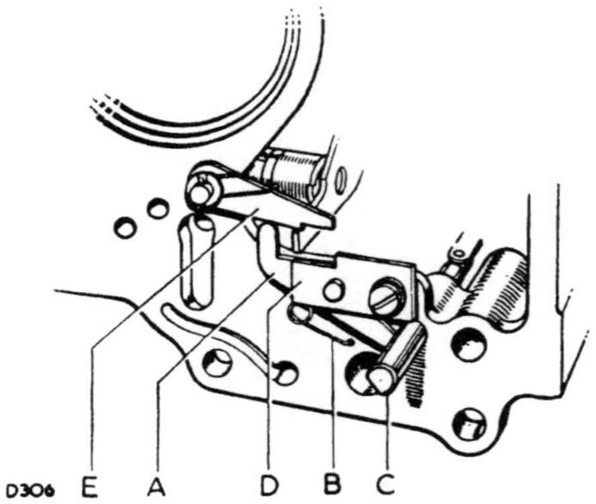

D306

Rocker arm and second speed latch in position, 1st-speed start models

A—Rocker arm
B—Rocker arm spring
C—Accelerator detent plunger
D—Retaining stop plate
E—Second speed latch

Operation E2-3—*continued*

35. Align the distance piece, insert and tighten the retaining screw. Ensure that the rocker arm is still free to move.

36. Place a small plain washer on the pivot pin and replace the second speed latch.

37. Fit spring over extension casing and second speed latch, and fit remaining plain washer and split pin.

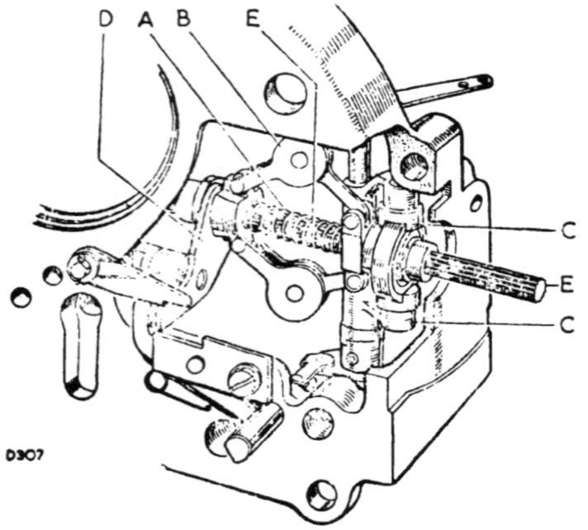

D307

Governor in correct position, 1st-speed start models

A—Governor spring
B—Governor weights
C—Yoke shoes
D—Governor valve fork
E—Governor shaft

38. Insert one end of the governor spring into the governor weights assembly, and by compressing the spring, insert it into the other end.

39. Insert the governor yoke shoes into the governor fork.

40. Align the slots in the shoes and slide the governor bearing into position. Ensure that the fork on the governor valve is correctly positioned between Tufnol washer and governor splined bush.

41. Insert the splined shaft into the governor splined end bush and into the oil pump drive shaft.

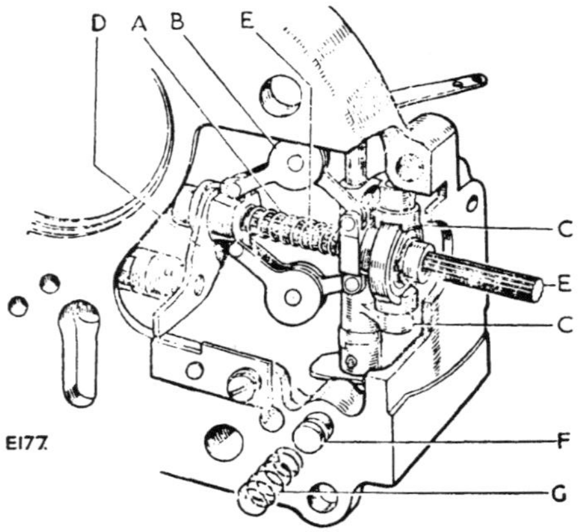

E177

Governor in correct position, 2nd-speed start models

A—Governor spring
B—Governor weights
C—Yoke shoes
D—Governor valve fork
E—Governor shaft
F—Accelerator cam plunger
G—Accelerator plunger spring

When a new governor is installed, or if the governor adjuster screw has been removed from the extension case, check that with the governor fully compressed, that is full kick-down, a .010 in. feeler gauge can be interposed between the two governor end brackets. If the clearance is less than .010 in., remove the cap on the adjuster screw, located on the rear of the extension case, release the locknut and then turn the screw until the necessary gap has been obtained; it may be found necessary to alter this setting to obtain correct kick-down speeds when the car is tested.

42. Using a suitable drift, drive a new bush into the bronze speedometer drive housing.

43. Fit a new oil seal and 'O' ring.

44. Insert the shaft into the housing.

45. Fit the fibre driven gear to the shaft.

46. Fit the worm drive gear to the speedometer gear housing.

Operation E2-3—*continued*

47. Turning the shaft very slightly to engage the gears, fit the speedometer drive housing as an assembly to the speedometer gear housing, aligning the cut-out in the bronze housing with the stud.

48. Fit the adaptor for speedometer cable and secure with three screws.

49. Fit the speedometer shaft retainer and secure with self-locking nut.

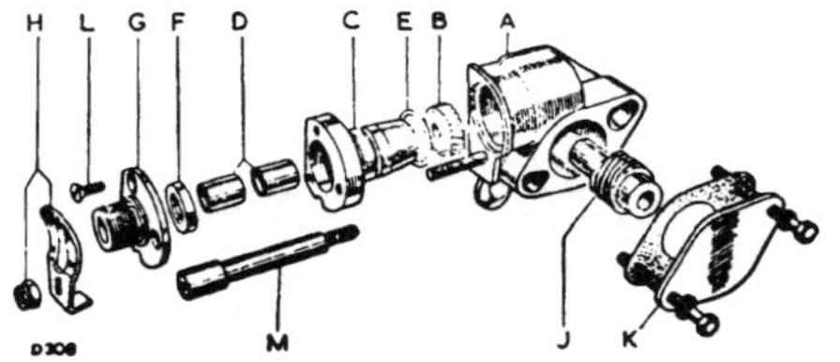

Speedometer housing and components

A—Speedometer gear housing
B—Fibre driven gear
C—Bronze speedometer drive housing
D—Bush
E—'O' ring
F—Oil seal
G—Speedometer cable adaptor
H—Retainer and fixings for speedometer spindle
J—Gear for speedometer drive
K—End plate and fixings
L—Screw retaining speedometer drive adaptor
M—Speedometer drive shaft

50. Fit a new gasket to the face of the speedometer gear housing.

51. Engage the splines of the governor shaft with the worm drive gear.

52. Fit the new gaskets to the end plate and speedometer housing. Ensure that the end plate and gaskets are fitted the correct way round. Secure with two set bolts; tighten to 10 to 13 lb/ft (1,4 to 1,7 mkg).

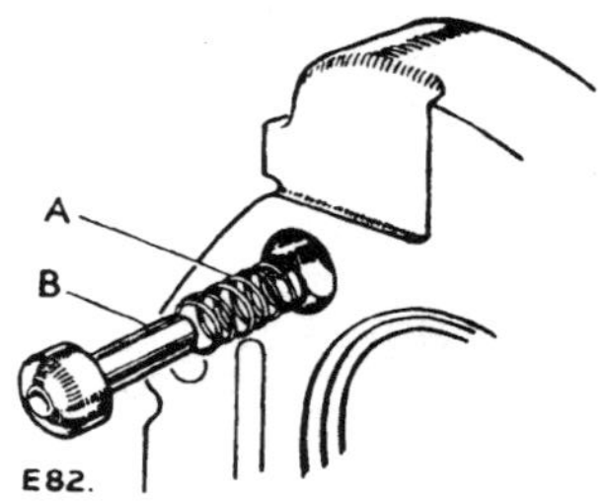

E82.

Parking pawl interlock piston in correct position, 1st-speed start models

A—Spring for interlock piston B—Interlock piston

53. 2nd-speed start models—insert the accelerator plunger and spring; ensure that the plunger is placed in the case with the tapered end downwards.

54. Insert the parking interlock spring and piston.

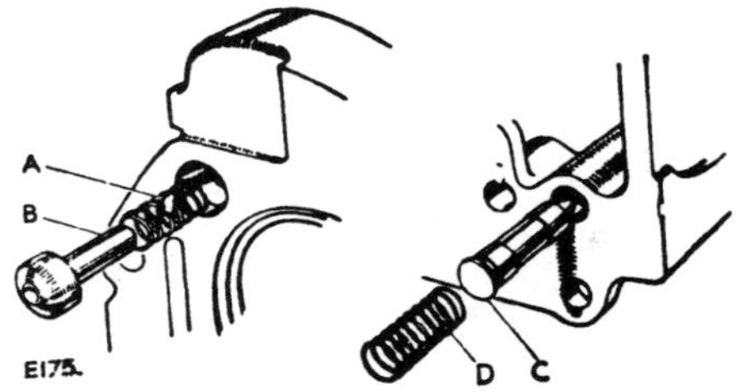

E175.

Parking pawl interlock piston and accelerator plunger in correct position, 2nd-speed start models

A—Spring for interlock piston C—Accelerator plunger
B—Interlock piston D—Spring

Speedometer drive housing, to remove and refit—Operation E2-4

Workshop hand tools:
Screwdriver, medium
Spanner sizes: $\frac{7}{16}$ in. AF, $\frac{1}{2}$ in. AF

Special tools:
Torque spanner

Speedometer drive housing, remove

1. Remove extension casing. Operation E2-2.

2. Remove two bolts from end plate and remove speedometer gear housing complete from extension casing.

3. Remove the nut from the stud securing speedometer shaft retainer. Remove the speedometer shaft retainer.

4. Remove the three screws securing the adaptor for speedometer cable and remove the adaptor.

5. Withdraw the bronze speedometer housing and shaft complete.

6. Withdraw the fibre driven gear from the shaft.

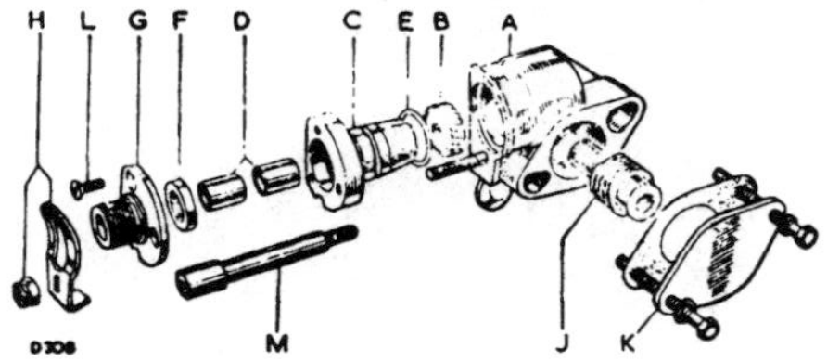

Speedometer drive components

A—Speedometer gear housing
B—Fibre driven gear
C—Bronze speedometer drive housing
D—Bushes
E—Rubber 'O' ring seal
F—Oil seal
G—Speedometer cable adaptor
H—Drive shaft retainer and flange for speedometer spindle
J—Gear for speedometer drive
K—End plate and fixings
L—Screws retaining speedometer drive adaptor
M—Speedometer drive shaft

7. Withdraw the shaft from the housing.

8. Remove the rubber 'O' ring seal from the housing.

9. Remove oil seal for driven shaft.

10. Using a suitable drift, drive out the bushes from the housing.

11. Remove the worm drive gear from the speedometer gear housing.

Speedometer drive housing, refit

1. Using a suitable drift, drive a new bush into the bronze speedometer drive housing.

2. Fit a new oil seal and 'O' ring.

3. Insert the shaft into the housing.

4. Fit the fibre driven gear to the shaft.

5. Fit the worm drive gear to the speedometer gear housing.

6. Turning the shaft very slightly to engage the gears, fit the speedometer drive housing as an assembly to the speedometer gear housing, aligning the cut-out in the bronze housing with the stud.

7. Fit the adaptor for speedometer cable and secure with three screws.

8. Fit the speedometer shaft retainer and secure with self-locking nut.

9. Fit a new gasket to the face of the speedometer gear housing.

10. Engage the splines of the governor shaft with the worm drive gear.

11. Fit a new gasket to the end plate and secure the whole assembly to the extension casing. Ensure that end plate and gasket are fitted the correct way round. Tightening torque for the two bolts is 10 to 13 lb/ft (1,4 to 1,7 mkg).

Rear pump, to remove and refit—Operation E2-5

Workshop hand tools:
Spanner sizes: $\frac{7}{16}$ in. AF, $\frac{1}{2}$ in. AF

Special tools:
Torque spanner

Rear pump, remove

Do not attempt to remove the rear pump from the unit until the extension casing has been removed from the transmission casing. Instructions for the removal of the extension casing from the car are given in Operations E1-2 and E2-2.

1. Remove oil pump, secured by three set bolts and spring washers.
2. Remove the pump cover, secured by two set bolts and spring washers. Shims to be retained for reassembly.
3. Clean and inspect all components for signs of wear.

Rear pump, refit

1. If the pump is worn, replace it with a new one Component parts are not available.
2. If the existing pump is considered to be serviceable refit by reversing removal procedure. Fit new gaskets, using original shims.
3. Tighten securing bolts to 15 to 18 lb/ft (2,0 to 2,4 mkg).

Front pump and collector ring, to remove and refit—Operation E2-6

Workshop hand tools:
Spanner sizes: $\frac{7}{16}$ in. AF, $\frac{1}{2}$ in. AF

Special tools:
Torque spanner Worm drive clip
Mainshaft end-float gauge B-W13

Front pump and collector ring, remove

1. Remove oil transfer tube.
2. Remove the seven set bolts securing the collector ring assembly to main casing.
3. With a plastic hammer, tap the front assembly loose from the casing and slide it forward off the front ring gear.
4. Remove the front ring gear and thrust washer.

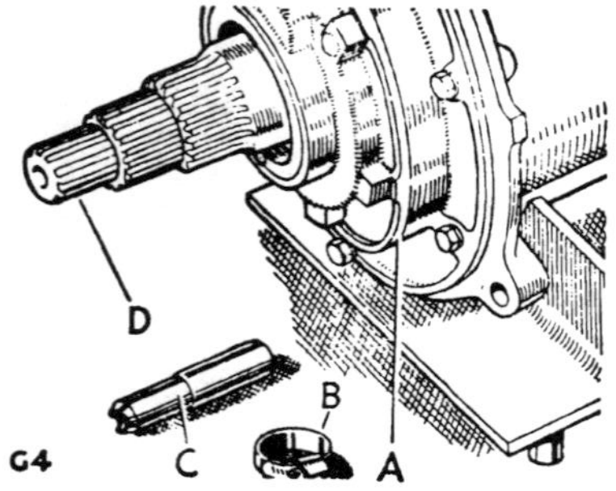

Location of front pump and collector ring

A—Front pump and collector ring
B—Retaining clip
C—Oil transfer tube
D—Mainshaft

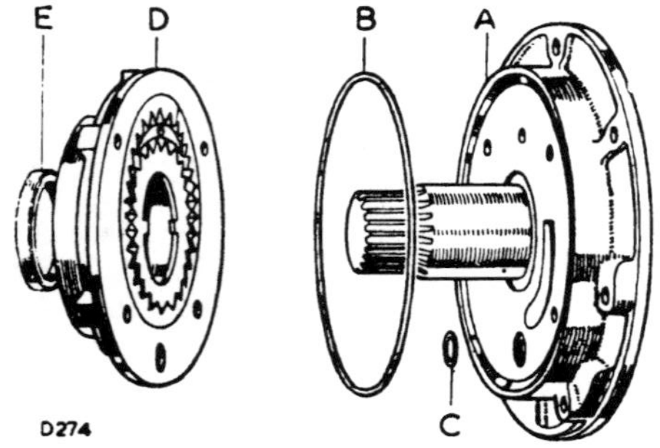

Front pump and collector ring

A—Collector ring
B—Large sealing ring
C—Small sealing ring
D—Pump gears
E—Oil seal

5. Remove the five set bolts securing the front pump assembly to the collector ring and remove pump.
6. Remove large and small rubber sealing rings.
7. Remove pump gear.
8. Drift the oil seal out of the housing. Take care not to damage the pump bush.
9. Clean all parts thoroughly and examine for wear. Renew defective parts.

Front pump and collector ring, refit

1. Replace the pump gears, which must lie flush with the face of the pump body.
2. Position new large and small rubber sealing rings on the collector ring.
3. Align the front pump with the collector ring and secure with five set bolts; tighten to 10 to 12 lb/ft (1,3 to 1,6 mkg).
4. Replace the three oil seal rings on the front ring gear by spreading the ring just enough to permit it to be slipped over the shaft and slipped into the groove. Lock the ends of the ring together. Space the joint in each ring as shown in the illustration.

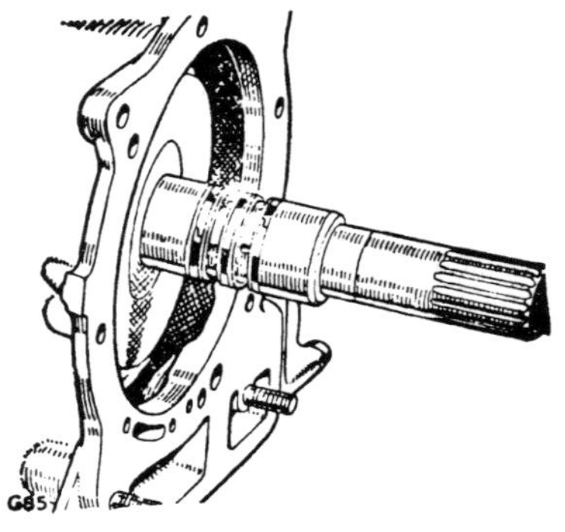

Oil seal rings in position

Operation E2-6—*continued*

5. Check mainshaft end-float with special tool (Part No. B-W13) bolted into the casing.
6. Move the mainshaft rearward as far as possible

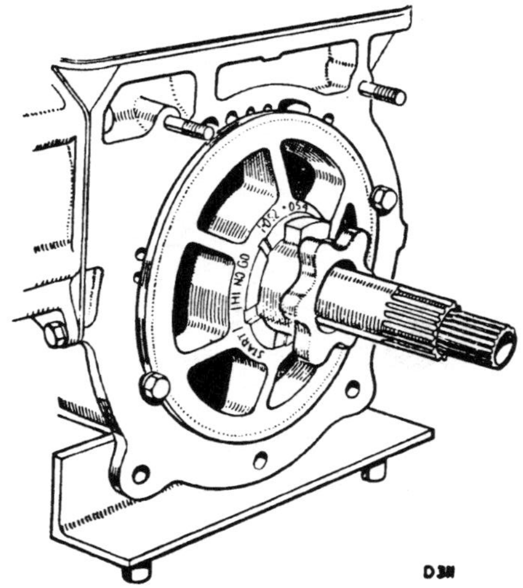

Checking end-float with tool B-W13

7. Turn the hub oi the gauge so that the indicator is over the start step.
8. Rotate the hub anti-clockwise, while pushing the hub inward, maintaining steady pressure.
9. The step over which the indicator is stopped by the next higher step represents the thickness in thousandths of an inch of the thrust washer to be used. For example, if the gauge stops against .061 to .063 a thrust washer with an overall thickness of .061 to .063 in. (1,54 to 1,60 mm) must be fitted.
10. Should the indicator stop over either the high 'No Go' stop or the low 'No Go' stop, the mainshaft assembly cannot be used in that particular transmission case. However, should the indicator stop over the high 'No Go' stop, a check should first be made to see that the front ring gear thrust washer has not become displaced.
11. Remove the gauge, taking great care not to pull out the front ring gear.
12. Having determined the thickness of the thrust washer required, smear the inside bearing face of the collector ring with petroleum jelly and fit the thrust washer with the bronze face towards the transmission casing. Ensure that the tags on the thrust washer are properly located.

Mainshaft, to remove, strip and rebuild—Operation E2-7

Workshop hand tools:

Spanner sizes: $\frac{7}{16}$ in. AF, $\frac{1}{2}$ in. AF, $1\frac{1}{8}$ in. AF
Screwdrivers, medium and small
Two pairs of square-nosed pliers
Set of feeler gauges Plastic-faced mallet
Circlip pliers Worm drive clip
Pump-type oil can filled with transmission fluid
Roll of masking tape

Special tools:

Mainshaft bearing replacer B-W7
Piston installing pins B-W10
Clutch assembly and dismantling tool B-W11A
Lubrication valve test rod B-W12A
Bearing puller B-W55-1

Warning: Do not use paraffin to clean component parts. Use only nylon rag for cleaning purposes.

Mainshaft, remove and strip

1. Remove the transmission main casing. Operation E1-1.
2. Remove the sump and valve block. Operation E1-3.
3. Remove the extension casing. Operation E2-2.
4. Remove the front pump. Operation E2-6.
5. Remove mainshaft bearing circlip.
6. Withdraw mainshaft from transmission casing. This will be facilitated if special tool B-W7 is slipped over the rear end of the mainshaft to give additional support.

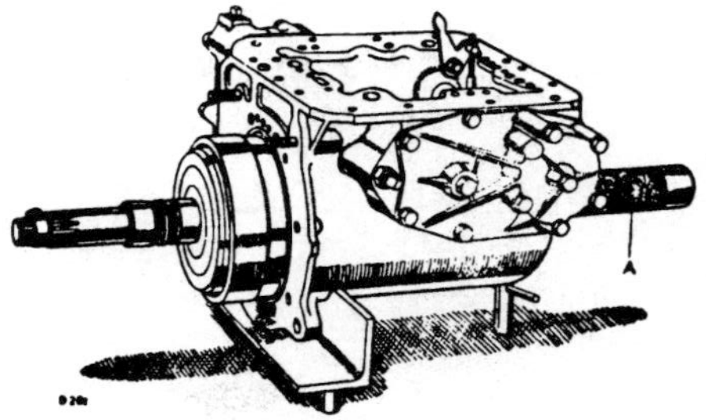

Removing mainshaft assembly

A—Special tool B-W7

7. Place mainshaft assembly in suitable stand with the rear bearing downwards. A simple stand can easily be constructed from a wooden block 8 in. square (203 mm), $8\frac{1}{2}$ in. deep (215 mm) by $8\frac{1}{2}$ in. high (215 mm) and a hole $2\frac{1}{2}$ in. (63 mm) diameter bored through the centre.
8. Slide the front ring gear upward, disengage it from the front planet carrier pinions and remove it from the shaft.
9. Remove front ring gear thrust washer from the front planet carrier.
10. Remove the reverse drum and front planet carrier assembly by sliding it upward off the mainshaft.
11. Remove the front sun gear thrust washer from the hub of the front sun gear.
12. Do not dismantle the front planet carrier and reverse brake drum unless either part is to be renewed. If necessary, remove the snap ring by inserting a small screwdriver into the slot and easing the snap ring out of the groove. Press the planet carrier out of the drum.

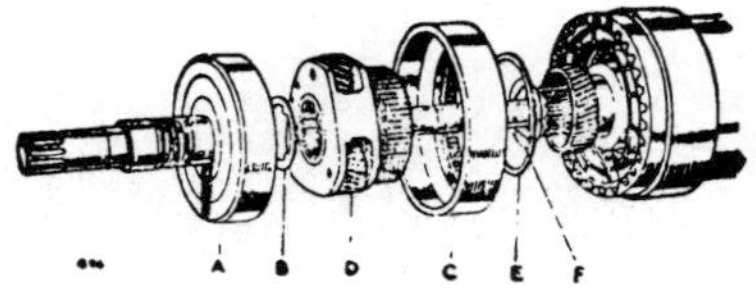

Removing front ring gear and reverse drum

A—Front ring gear
B—Thrust washer for front ring gear
C—Reverse drum
D—Front planet carrier
E—Snap ring
F—Washer for front sun gear

13. Turn the mainshaft over in the stand and, using mainshaft bearing puller (Part No. B-W55-1), remove the bearing and distance piece.
14. Lift off the forward brake drum assembly.
15. Using a small screwdriver, remove the forward one-way clutch unit spacer circlip, and remove the spacer from the drum. Remove the spacer dowel pin.

Operation E2-7—*continued*

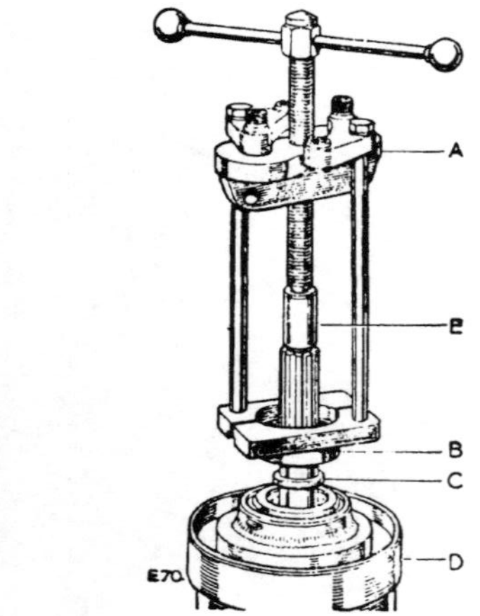

Removal of mainshaft bearings

A—Bearing puller
B—Bearing
C—Distance piece
D—Forward brake drum
E—Protection cap

16. Do not remove one-way clutch unless either brake drum or one-way clutch is to be renewed. If necessary, remove one-way clutch unit from the drum, by removing the retaining circlip with a small screwdriver.

17. Remove the rear sun gear spacer washer, thrust washer and sun gear from the mainshaft.

18. Remove circlip for the reverse one-way clutch lock-up plate; then with a piece of bent wire remove the two plate retaining rollers in the low drum. Remove the lock-up plate.

19. If necessary, the reverse one-way clutch can now be removed from the plate.

20. Pull the mainshaft upward and remove the mainshaft and rear planet carrier as an assembly from the rear ring gear and low brake drum assembly.

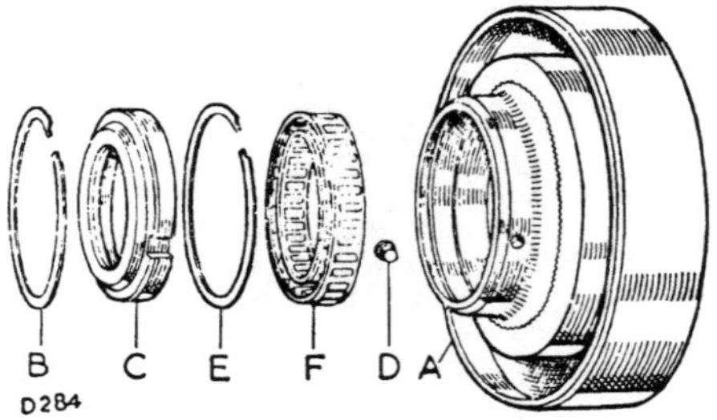

Forward brake drum components

A—Forward brake drum
B—Circlip for clutch unit spacer
C—Clutch unit spacer
D—Dowel pin
E—Circlip for one-way clutch
F—One-way clutch

21. Remove the rear planet carrier front thrust washer.

22. Remove the circlip for rear planet carrier piston ring retainer.

23. Press the shaft out of the seal retainer and planet carrier.

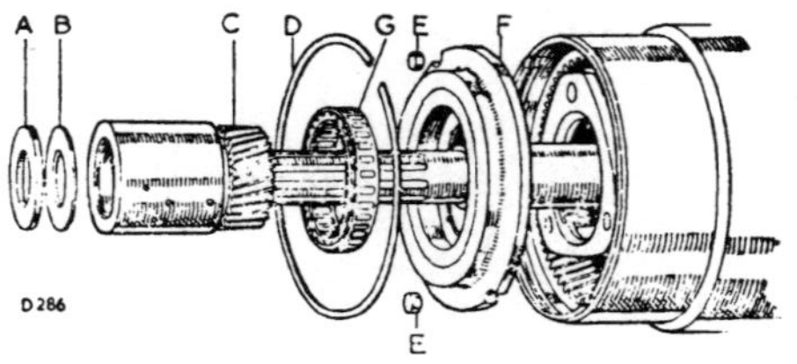

Removing reverse one-way clutch sun gear and components

A—Spacer washer
B—Thrust washer
C—Sun gear
D—Circlip
E—Rollers
F—Lock-up plate
G—One-way clutch

Operation E2-7—*continued*

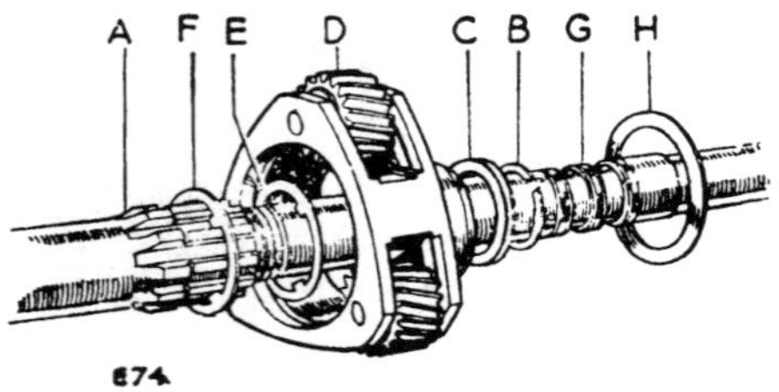

Mainshaft and thrust washers

A—Mainshaft
B—Circlip
C—Piston ring retainer
D—Planet carrier
E—Steel spacing washer
F—Bronze-faced thrust washer
G—Piston rings
H—Rear ring gear thrust washer

24. Remove the seal retainer, rear planet carrier and rear sun gear front thrust washer from the mainshaft.

25. Remove the three piston rings from the mainshaft.

26. Slide the rear ring gear out of the low brake drum.

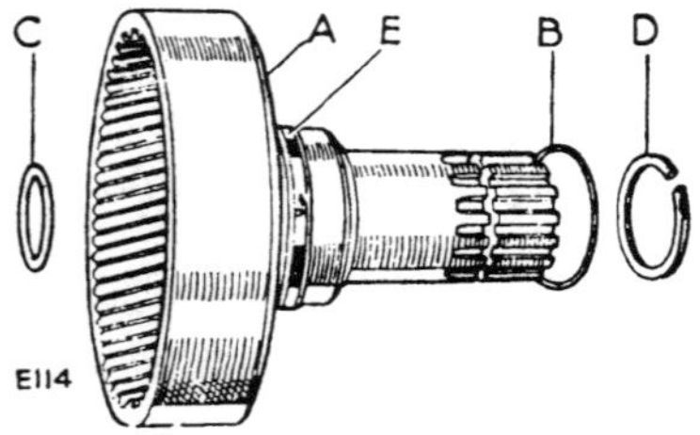

Rear ring gear and seals

A—Rear ring gear
B—Rubber 'O' ring, outer
C—Rubber 'O' ring, inner
D—Spring ring
E—Piston ring

27. With a sharp pointed tool remove the inner and outer rubber 'O' ring seals and remove the piston ring from the rear ring gear.

28. Dismantle the clutch from the sun gear and low brake drum assembly by relieving the clutch spring pressure against the retaining circlip with a suitable clamp or press, in conjunction with tool B-W11A. Remove the circlip and gradually release the spring pressure.

29. Remove the retainer and clutch springs.

30. Mark the lugs and teeth on the top face of clutch plates upon removal for identification on re-assembly.

31. Lift the clutch plates out of the drum.

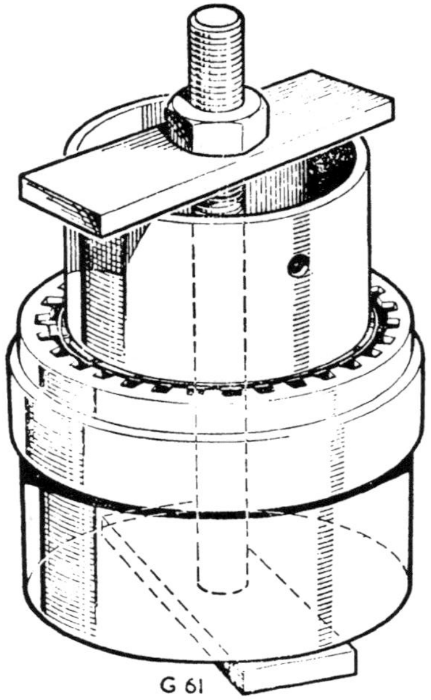

Removing clutch retainer circlip

Operation E2-7—*continued*

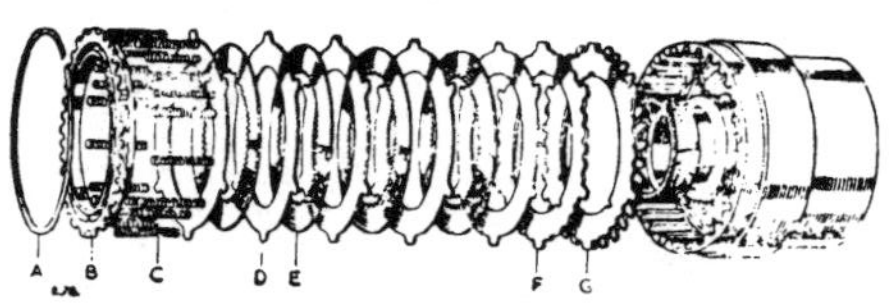

Exploded view of clutch components

A—Circlip
B—Retainer
C—Clutch springs
D—Friction disc, steel
E—Friction disc, bronze
F—Spacer plate
G—Spring plate

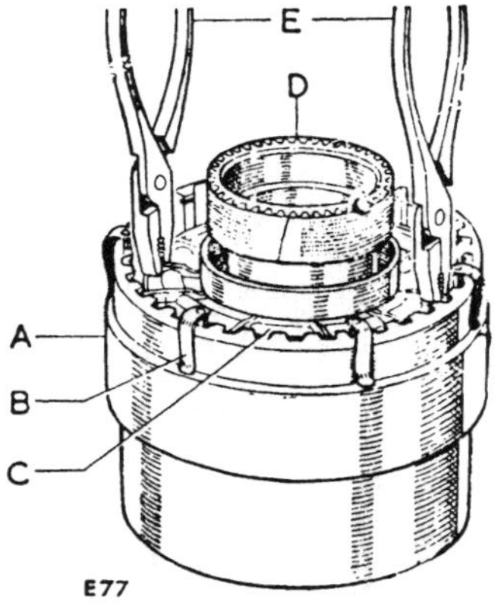

Piston installing pins in use and piston being extracted

A—Low drum
B—Piston installing pins
C—Piston
D—Front sun gear, masked
E—Pliers

32. To prevent damage to the multiple-disc clutch piston inner cylinder bore during removal, wrap two layers of masking tape over the teeth of the front sun gear.

    Using six piston installing pins (Part No. B-W10), remove the clutch piston from the drum.

33. Remove the lipped rubber inner sealing ring and the piston ring from the piston.

34. Clean all component parts thoroughly and examine for wear and damage. Renew any defective parts.

Mainshaft

35. Check the alignment of the mainshaft between centres.

36. Examine the mainshaft carrier splines for wear; the carrier should have no backlash when fitted to the mainshaft.

37. Examine the carrier gears and gear spindles for excessive wear. Carrier and gears are supplied as an assembly only.

38. Examine the driving flange spline for wear; the driving flange should have no backlash when fitted to the mainshaft.

39. Check the parking pawl gear, rear oil pump driving gear and splines for wear.

40. Examine all bearing surfaces on mainshaft for blueing or scoring.

41. Check the tightness of the lubrication valve with special tool (Part No. B-W12A); the tool should be screwed into the valve, then attempt to withdraw; if valve is loose, mainshaft must be replaced.

Checking lubrication valve

42. Place the mainshaft upwards in a hole in the work bench, so that the oil ring lubrication holes are uppermost.

Operation E2-7—*continued*

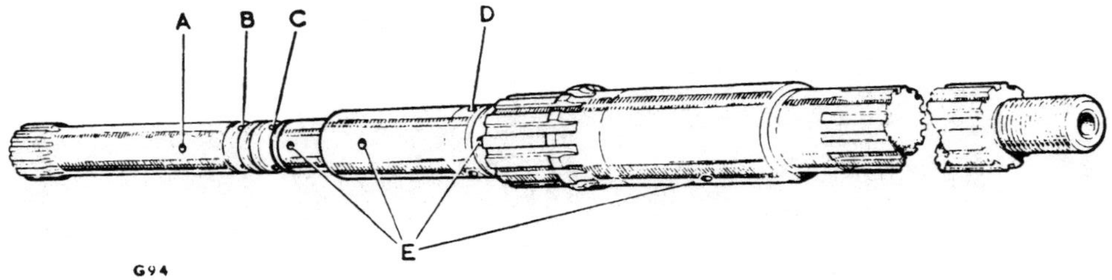

Mainshaft lubrication holes

A—Torque converter to lubrication valve
B—Governor valve to direct-drive clutch
C—Governor valve to multi-disc clutch
D—To multi-disc clutch
E—From lubrication valve to gear train

43. Using a pressure-type oil can (minimum capacity $\frac{1}{2}$ pint; 0,28 litre) with plastic taper nozzle, filled with clean transmission fluid, insert the oil can nozzle into the bottom (rearmost) lubrication hole in the mainshaft. For identification purposes this hole is $\frac{1}{8}$ in. diameter, countersunk, through one wall of the shaft in the centre of the ground diameter.

44. Blank off with the fingers the three holes in the mainshaft, which are located at a right-angle relative to the one in which the oil can nozzle has been inserted, and start pumping.

45. If the valve is tight in the mainshaft and the ball is seating correctly, pressure will build up inside the shaft and no fluid will issue from the top (foremost) $\frac{5}{32}$ in. (3,9 mm) diameter hole nearest to the front end of the shaft.

46. If the valve leaks on its outside diameter, or when there is no non-return action due to incorrect seating of the ball, fluid will emerge from the top (foremost) $\frac{5}{32}$ in. (3,9 mm) diameter hole. A ball which is not seating can often also be diagnosed by an audible rattle when shaking the shaft.

Mainshaft, rebuild and refit

1. Place the front thrust washer for rear sun gear on to the mainshaft splines, with the bronze face towards the rear of the mainshaft.

2. Place the plain steel washer on to the mainshaft, next to the one already fitted.

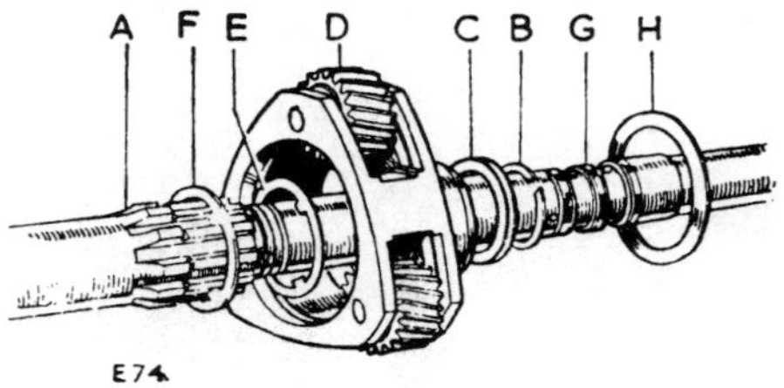

Fitting carrier retainer to mainshaft

A—Mainshaft
B—Circlip
C—Piston ring retainer
D—Planet carrier
E—Steel spacing washer
F—Bronze-faced thrust washer
G—Piston rings
H—Rear ring gear thrust washer

Operation E2-7—*continued*

3. Slide the rear planet carrier on to the front end of the mainshaft, engage the splines and seat the carrier against the thrust washers.

4. Fit a new piston ring to the retainer and make sure it will rotate in its groove.

5. Fit the retainer to the mainshaft from the front end, making sure that the internal bevel on the retainer is towards the carrier. Use a length of metal tubing 12 in. (304 mm) long x $1\frac{1}{4}$ in. (30 mm) inside diameter, to ensure that the retainer is fitted to the shaft squarely.

6. Fit a new retaining circlip to the mainshaft.

7. Fit three new piston rings to the mainshaft.

Multiple-disc clutch, reassemble

8. Make sure that the parts to be assembled are thoroughly clean and serviceable.

9 Examine the inside bushing of the front sun gear and low brake drum, for scoring or excessive wear.

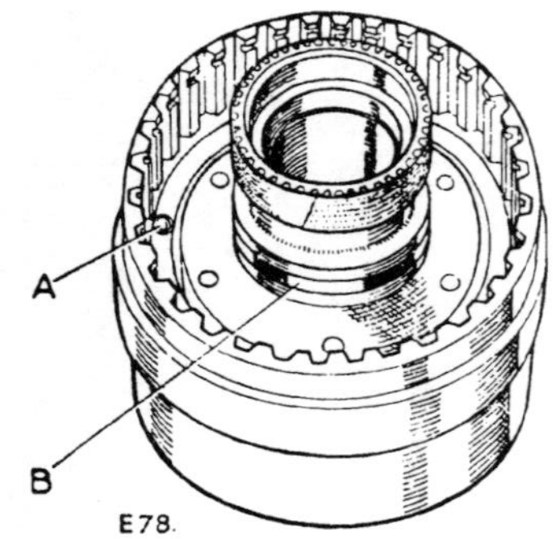

E78.

Multiple-disc clutch ball valve and front sun gear seal

A—Ball valve B—Seal for front sun gear

Item 10 early models only

10. Ensure that the ball valve for the multiple-disc clutch, housed in the low drum, is operating correctly. The ball should be free to move; it is not spring-loaded.

11. Examine the clutch friction plates for wear or blueing.

12. Examine the clutch piston for scoring, with special attention to the inside diameter of the piston.

13. Examine the rear ring gear internal bushing and bearing surfaces for blueing or excessive wear.

14. Place all new seals into a container of clean transmission fluid.

15. Fit a new rubber seal to the front sun gear, with the lip of the seal downwards.

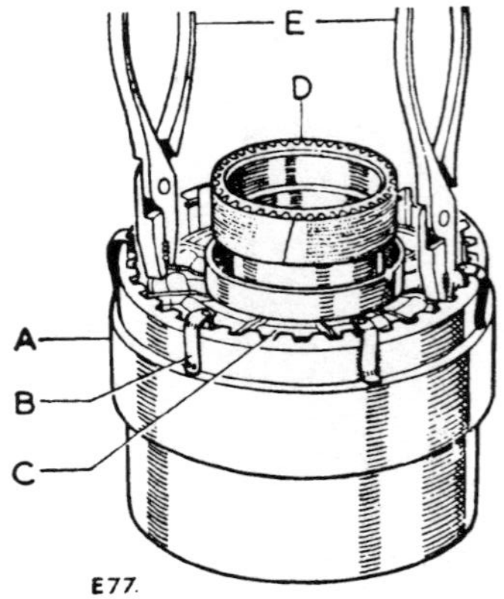

E77.

Piston installing pins in position

A—Low drum
B—Piston installing pins
C—Piston
D—Front ring gear, masked
E—Pliers

Operation E2-7—*continued*

16. Fit a new piston ring to the clutch piston.

17. Place the piston installing pins (Part No. B-W10) into the low drum clutch plate grooves.

18. Wrap two layers of masking tape over the teeth of the front sun gear to prevent possible damage to the multiple-disc clutch inner cylinder bore.

19. Compress the clutch piston ring and slide the piston into the cylinder.

20. Remove the piston installing pins (Part No. B-W10).

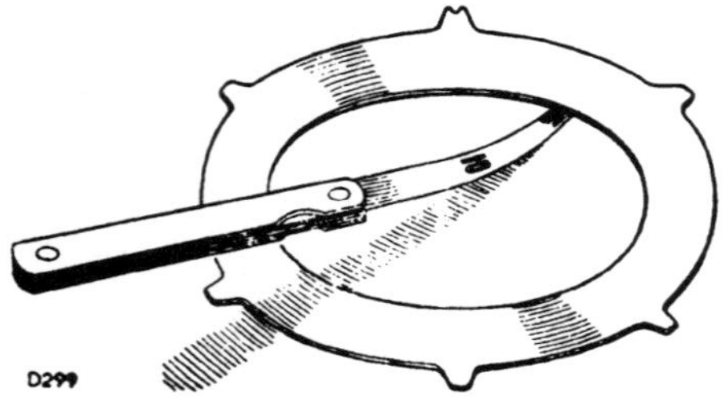

D299

Checking dish on friction plate

21. With a straight edge or face plate and feeler gauge, check the dish on the friction discs; ensure they are all installed with the dish in the same direction. The dishing must be no greater than .010 in. (0,25 mm).

22. If the original clutch plates are to be refitted, ensure that the markings made on dismantling face in the same direction.

23. Assemble the retractor spring plate and the spacer plate into the low drum, so that the offset grooves on the inside diameter of the plates align with each other, and the fully splined half of the spring plate abuts the clutch piston.

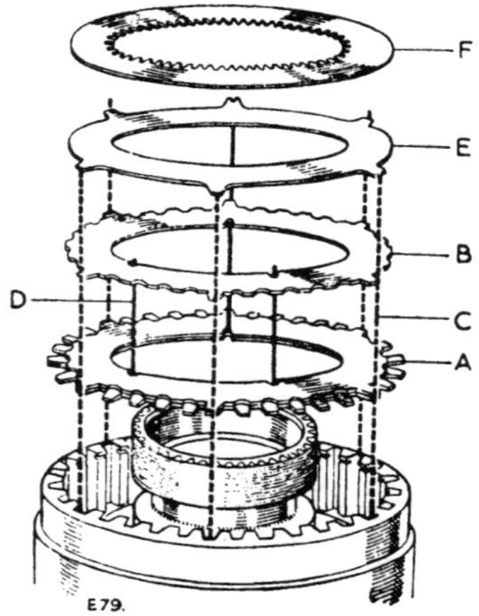

E79.

Alignment of clutch plates and discs

A—Retractor spring plate
B—Spacer plate
C—Master lugs aligned
D—Offset grooves aligned
E—Clutch plate (4 on early models, 5 on late)
F—Clutch disc (3 on early models, 4 on late)

24. Starting with a plate, insert the plates and discs alternately into the drum. Since the lugs are not evenly spaced, make sure that each plate is in the same groove as the master lugs of the retractor spring plate. If a clutch plate is fitted the wrong way round, it will prevent the clutch springs from seating properly. There are seven clutch plates on early models and nine on late models.

25. Centre the friction discs around the sun gear and align the teeth of the friction discs.

Early Mk I models with 12 springs

26. Place the springs into position on the spring plate in the following order: starting from the grooved lug on the top plate, place the spring into No. 1 groove, counting off in a clockwise direction, springs are then placed in the following numbered grooves: 4, 7, 10, 12, 15, 18, 21, 23, 26, 29, 32.

Operation E2-7—*continued*

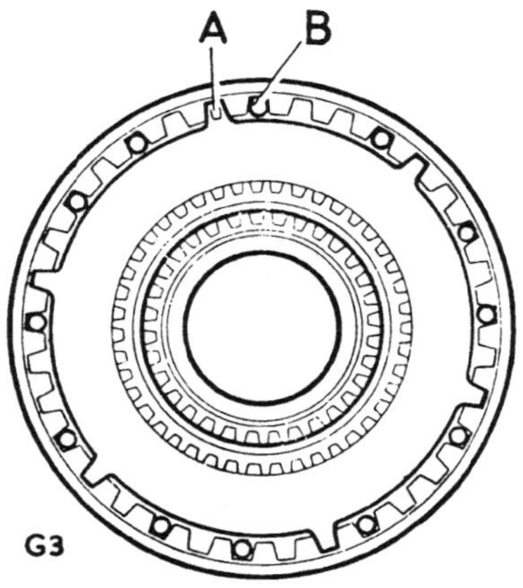

G3

Correct spacing of clutch springs, Mk I models with 12 springs

A—Grooved lug B—Spring

Late Mk I and Mk IA models with 21 springs

27. Place the springs into position on the spring plate as follows:

    (a) Where there are four grooves between lugs, fit four springs.

    (b) Where there are five grooves between lugs, fit three springs.

    An overall total of 21 springs should be fitted.

Mk II models with 27 springs

28. Place the springs into the grooves between the lugs of the top plate. All 27 springs must be fitted.

29. Place the retractor spring retainer over the springs.

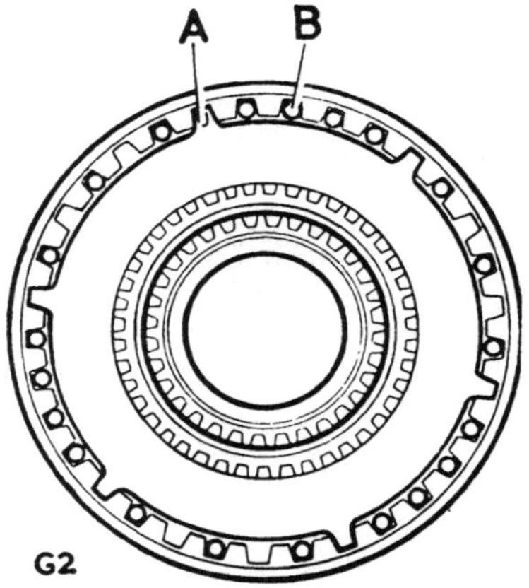

G2

Correct spacing of clutch springs, late Mk I and Mk IA models with 21 springs

A—Grooved lug B—Spring

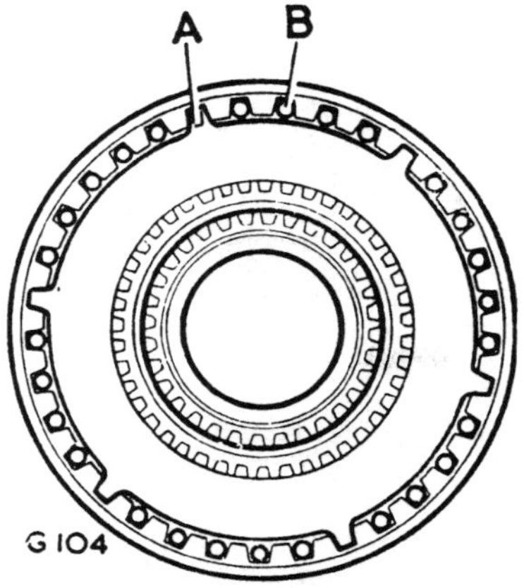

G 104

Correct spacing of clutch springs, Mk II models with 27 springs

A—Grooved lug B—Spring

Operation E2-7—*continued*

30. **Compress the springs with the aid of special tool (Part No. B-W11A) to a position just below the circlip groove in the drum. Place the circlip into position and remove the pressure from the springs.**

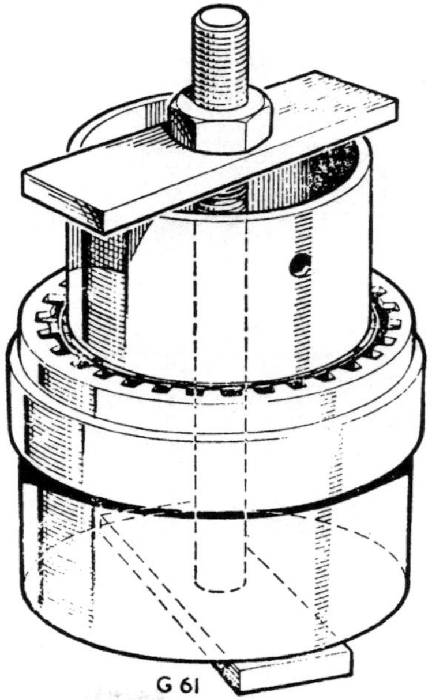
G 61

Refitting clutch retainer circlip

31. **Remove masking tape from teeth of the front sun gear.**

32. **Fit new inner and outer rubber seals for ring gear, also fit new piston ring. Carefully insert the rear ring gear into the low drum without thrust washer.**

33. Place the front thrust washer for the rear planet carrier on to the mainshaft, with the steel face against the face of the planet carrier.

34. Enter the mainshaft and planet carrier assembly into the low brake drum assembly.

One-way clutch and lock-up plate, reassemble

35. Ensure that the parts to be assembled are thoroughly clean and serviceable.

36. Examine the internal bushing in the lock-up plate for slackness, wear or blueing.

37. Examine the reverse one-way clutch for wear or damage to the cage.

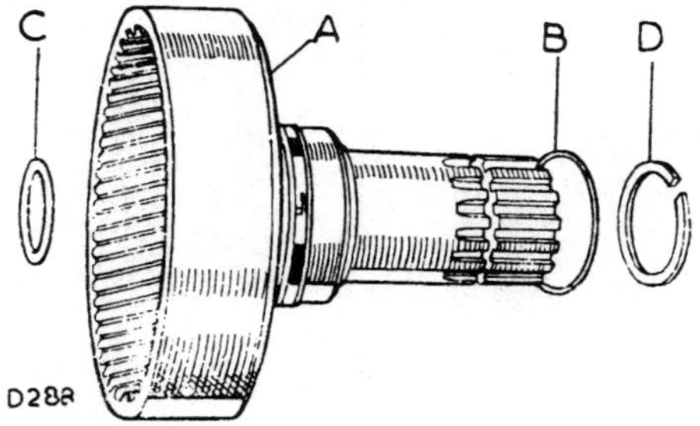

D288

Rear ring gear and components

A—Rear ring gear C—Rubber 'O' ring, inner
B—Rubber 'O' ring, outer D—Piston ring

38. Examine the forward drum, spacer and forward one-way clutch for wear or damage.

39. Examine the rear mainshaft bearing for wear.

40. Renew any defective parts.

41. Place the reverse one-way clutch unit into the low lock-up plate, with the ridge of the one-way clutch outer cage to the top.

Operation E2-7—*continued*

42. Seat the low lock-up plate into the drum, align the cut-outs in the plate and drum and place the rollers into position.

43. Place the circlip into position and make sure it is seated in the groove, and that the circlip is positioned so that the gap is away from the rollers.

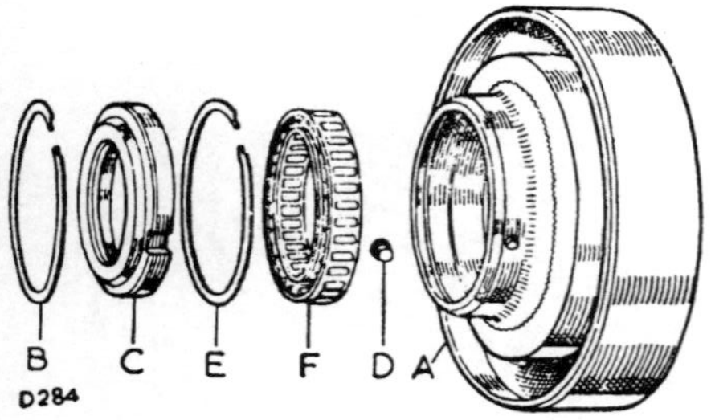

Forward brake drum components

A—Forward brake drum
B—Circlip for clutch unit spacer
C—Clutch unit spacer
D—Dowel pin
E—Circlip for one-way clutch
F—One-way clutch

44. Place the sun gear over the rear end of the mainshaft and enter into the lock-up plate, turning in a clockwise direction.

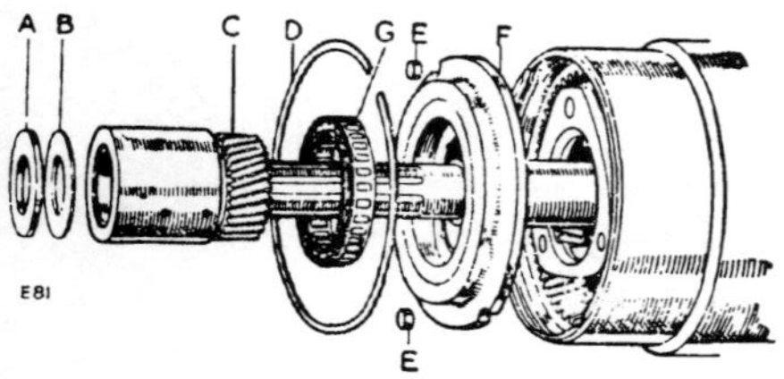

Fitting reverse one-way clutch

A—Spacer washer
B—Thrust washer
C—Sun gear
D—Circlip
E—Rollers
F—Lock-up plate
G—One-way clutch

45. Place the forward one-way clutch unit into the forward brake drum, ensuring that the ridge of the one-way clutch is to the top.

46. Fit circlip retaining one-way clutch.

47. Fit dowel pin and retaining spacer.

48. Fit circlip for retaining spacer into groove.

49. Place the thrust washer for rear sun gear on the shaft, with the bronze face of the thrust washer towards the sun gear.

50. Place spacing washer into position on the thrust washer.

51. Place the forward brake drum assembly over the rear sun gear and ease into position by turning clockwise.

52. Place the distance piece on to the mainshaft.

53. Drift the bearing on to the mainshaft, making sure that the groove on the bearing outer ring is uppermost.

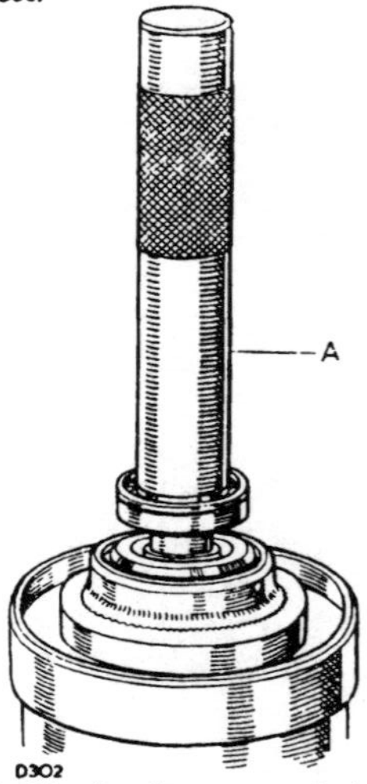

Drifting bearing on to mainshaft

A—Mainshaft bearing replacing tool (Part No. B-W7)

Operation E2-7—*continued*

Reverse drum, reassemble

54. Ensure that the parts to be assembled are thoroughly clean and serviceable.

55. Examine the reverse drum and front carrier assembly for wear or damage.

56. Examine the front ring gear and needle bearings for wear.

57. Turn the mainshaft over in preparation for further operations to be carried out on the front end. If the planet carrier and reverse drum has been stripped, assemble as follows:

58. Align the splines of the front planet carrier and reverse brake drum, press the front planet carrier into position and secure with circlip.

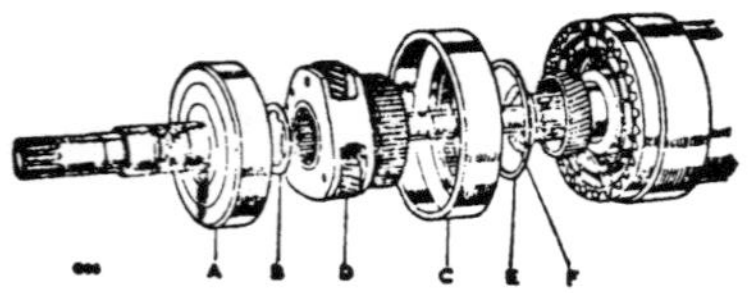

Replacing front ring gear and reverse drum

A—Front ring gear
B—Thrust washer for front ring gear
C—Reverse drum
D—Front planet carrier
E—Snap ring
F—Washer for front sun gear

59. Place the thrust washer for front sun gear into the bore of the front sun gear with the bronze side of the thrust washer towards the threaded end of the mainshaft.

60. Place the reverse drum and front planet carrier assembly into position. It may be necessary to turn the assembly to engage the clutch friction disc teeth. Do not force the assembly into position, as this may cause damage to the teeth.

61. Place the thrust washer for front carrier into position on the rear ring gear shaft splines with the steel face of the washer against the front planet carrier.

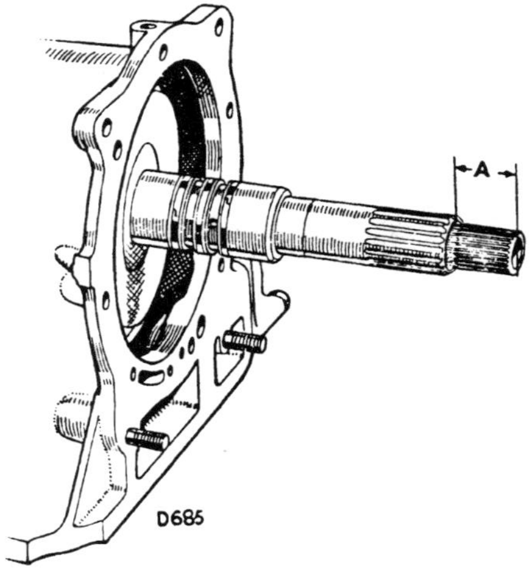

Checking mainshaft dimension

A—$1\frac{3}{16}$ in. (30 mm)

62. Place the front ring gear into position.

63. Check that the mainshaft protrudes $1\frac{3}{16}$ in. (30 mm) from the end of the front ring gear spline. If this measurement is not obtained, it will indicate that either a thrust washer has inadvertently been left out or is not seating properly.

64. Fit worm drive clip on to the front end of the mainshaft to prevent front ring gear from coming forward.

65. Support the mainshaft assembly and insert it into the casing, carefully passing it through the brake bands; again this will be facilitated if special tool B-W7 is slipped over the mainshaft to give additional support.

66. Ensure the brake bands and anchor struts have not been moved out of position.

67. Place the rear mainshaft bearing circlip into position and push circlip back against the rear face of the casing.

Brake bands, to remove and refit—Operation E2-8

Workshop hand tools:
Spanner sizes: $\frac{5}{16}$ in. AF, $\frac{1}{2}$ in. AF, $\frac{3}{4}$ in. AF

Brake bands, remove

1. Slacken off the adjuster for reverse brake band.
2. Remove strut for reverse brake band.
3. Turn brake band through 90° and remove from casing.
4. Repeat the above procedure for the forward and low ratio band brakes.
5. Remove the adjuster screws for brake bands.

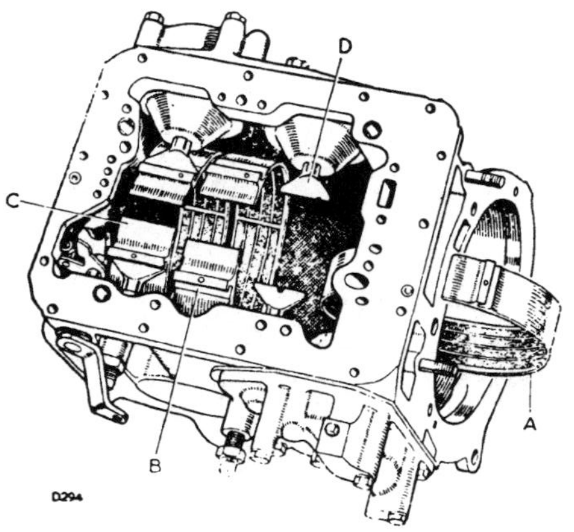

Removal and installation of brake bands

A—Reverse band
B—Low band
C—Forward bands
D—Adjusting shoe

Brake bands, refit

1. Make sure that the parts to be assembled are clean and serviceable.
2. Inspect the brake band linings for wear and the band shoes for damage.
3. Ensure that the offset pin in each band shoe is tight. Renew any defective parts.
4. Low and forward brake bands are lighter in construction than the reverse brake band.
5. Select one of the lighter bands and slip it into the main casing.
6. Turn the band through 90° so that the end with the offset pin is towards the low and forward servo side of the casing. Move the band to the rear of the casing.
7. Place the other light band into the casing in the same manner, and again move band to rear of casing.
8. Place the heavy reverse band into the casing in the same manner as before, but with the offset pin towards the reverse servo side of the casing.
9. All the bands are placed into position in the following manner:
10. Set the band into the guide in the top of the casing, engage each band on to its respective strut, making sure that the pin is in the slot. Pull the shoes of the band together and slip the anchor strut on to the end of the adjusting screw. Release the band and allow the shoe to engage the anchor strut. Make sure that the pins in the brake band shoe are properly engaged in the slots of the struts and that the band is properly positioned in the guide.

Reverse servo, to remove, overhaul and refit—Operation E2-9

Workshop hand tools:
Spanner sizes: $\frac{7}{16}$ in. AF, $\frac{1}{2}$ in. AF, $\frac{3}{4}$ in. AF, $\frac{3}{8}$ in. BSF
Plastic-faced mallet

Special tools:
Torque spanner

Items 1 to 4 are instructions for the removal of the servo unit from the main casing with the transmission unit installed in the car.

Reverse servo, remove

1. Place the car on a suitable ramp, or over an inspection pit.
2. Remove the front exhaust pipe, secured to the exhaust manifold and intermediate exhaust pipe.
3. Remove the exhaust pipe support bracket secured to the bell housing.
4. Disconnect the selector operating rod from transmission unit.

Models fitted with five-point mountings

5. Disconnect the front propeller shaft from transmission unit. Support the unit and remove the reaction bracket from transmission case and sump. Retain shims for correct reassembly.
6. Drain the fluid from the transmission unit.
7. Remove the sump and strainer.
8. Remove the valve block assembly.

Removing the servo from the main casing

9. Remove the reverse outer servo cylinder and plate as an assembly, secured by six bolts.
10. Separate the cylinder plate from the cylinder and remove the gaskets.
11. Remove the reverse outer piston from the cylinder.
12. Push the inner piston assembly outward from the casing by applying pressure to the piston spring retainer.
13. Remove the rubber 'O' ring seal from the cylinder plate with a sharp pointed tool.
14. Remove the rubber piston seals from the pistons.

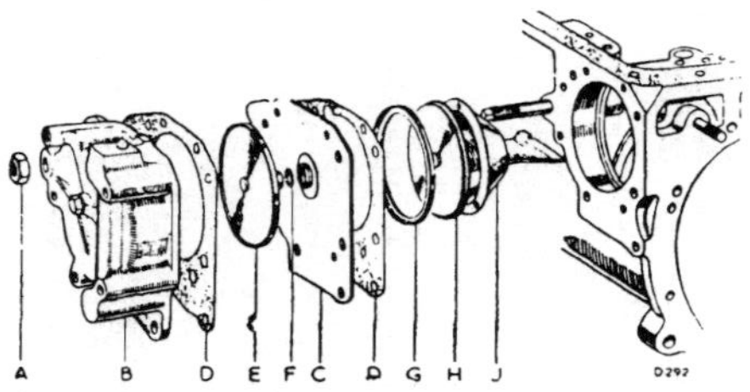

Reverse servo

A—Adjusting screw locknut
B—Reverse outer servo cylinder
C—Cylinder plate
D—Gaskets
E—Outer piston
F—Rubber 'O' ring
G—Rubber piston seals
H—Inner piston
J—Piston spring retainer

15. If necessary remove the pressure take-off plug.
16. Clean all the components, using NYLON RAG only. DO NOT WASH ANY PART IN PARAFFIN.
17. Check the gasket face of the outer servo cylinder for distortion, using a face plate and feeler gauge.
18. Check the cylinder plate for distortion, using a straight edge.
19. Check the servo bore for pitting, scoring or porosity.
20. Check for stripped or damaged threads in the cylinder.
21. Check the inner piston strut for tightness.

Servo, refit

1. Place the new piston seals in a container of clean transmission fluid.
2. Fit new piston seal on to reverse inner piston, being careful not to stretch the seal more than necessary.
3. Lubricate the reverse cylinder with transmission fluid and insert the inner piston, making sure that the offset slot is towards the rear of the casing.
4. Fit the new piston seal on the reverse outer piston, being careful not to stretch the seal more than is necessary.

Operation E2-9—*continued*

5. Lubricate the bore of the reverse outer servo with transmission fluid, and insert the piston at an angle and ease into position.

6. Insert four of the retaining bolts through the reverse outer servo cylinder.

7. Place a new gasket in position on the cylinder face.

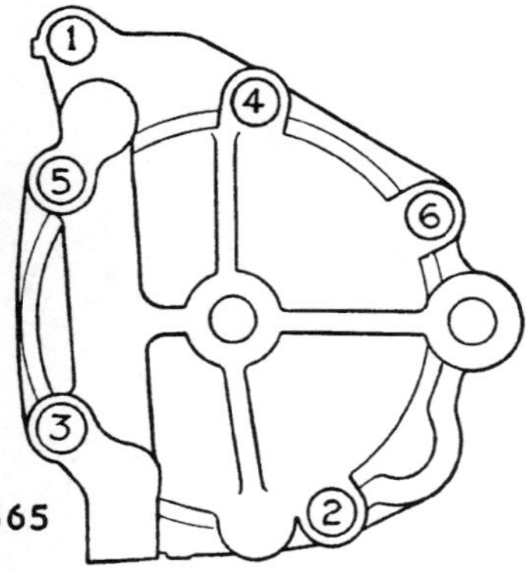

G65

Tighten reverse servo bolts in the order as indicated above

8. Insert a new 'O' ring seal into the cylinder plate.

9. Position the plate over the four bolts on to the servo cylinder, taking care that the outer piston rod is through the plate.

10. Place a new gasket in position over the four bolts on to the plate.

11. Fit the assembly to the main casing, ensuring that the strut engages with brake band. Insert the remaining set bolts and tighten to a torque of 15 to 18 lb/ft (2,0 to 2,4 mkg).

12. Fit the locknut for low adjusting screw loosely in position until adjustment can be made.

13. Adjust the brake band. Operation E1-9.

14. Fit the pressure take-off plug.

15. Refit the valve block.

16. Replace the fluid strainer and sump.

Models with five-point mounting, items 17 and 18

17. Refit the reaction bracket, using the original shims.

18. Refit the propeller shaft, exhaust pipe and operating rod.

19. Refill the transmission unit with recommended grade of fluid to the correct level.

*Forward and low servos, to remove, overhaul and refit—Operation E2-10

Workshop hand tools:
Spanner sizes: $\frac{7}{16}$ in. AF, $\frac{1}{2}$ in. AF, $\frac{9}{16}$ in. AF, $1\frac{1}{8}$ in. AF, $\frac{3}{8}$ in. BSF
Plastic-faced mallet

Special tools:
Torque spanner

Items 1 and 2 are instructions for the removal of the servos from the main casing with the transmission unit installed in the car. If the unit is out of the car, proceed with item 3.

Forward and low servos, remove

1. Place the car on a suitable ramp, or over an inspection pit.

Models fitted with five-point mountings

2. Disconnect the front propeller shaft from transmission unit. Support the unit and remove the reaction bracket from transmission case and sump. Retain shims for correct reassembly.

3. Drain the fluid from the transmission unit.

4. Remove the sump.

5. Remove the locknut for reverse brake band adjusting screw on right-hand side of the main casing.

6. Remove the forward and low outer servo cylinder and plate as an assembly, secured by nine bolts and spring washers.

7. Separate the cylinder plate from the cylinder and remove gaskets.

8. Withdraw the forward servo cylinder outer piston and remove the rubber seal.

9. Remove the rubber 'O' ring seal from the cylinder plate with a sharp pointed tool.

10. Push the forward and low inner pistons outward from the casing by applying pressure to the piston spring retainers.

11. Remove the rubber seals from both pistons.

12. If necessary, remove pressure take-off plugs.

13. Clean all the components, using NYLON RAG only. DO NOT WASH ANY PART IN PARAFFIN.

14. Examine the parts for faults and wear. Renew defective parts as necessary.

15. Check the gasket face of the servo cylinder for distortion, using a face plate and feeler gauge.

16. Check the cylinder plates for distortion.

17. Check the servo bores for pitting, scoring or porosity.

18. Check the servo cylinder tappings for stripped or damaged threads.

19. Check the inner piston struts for tightness.

Servos, refit

1. Use new piston seals, but before fitting them place them in a container of clean transmission fluid.

2. Fit the new piston seals on to the low and forward inner pistons, taking care not to stretch the seals more than necessary.

3. Lubricate the low and forward cylinders with transmission fluid, and insert the inner pistons, making sure that the offset slots in the struts are to the front of the casing.

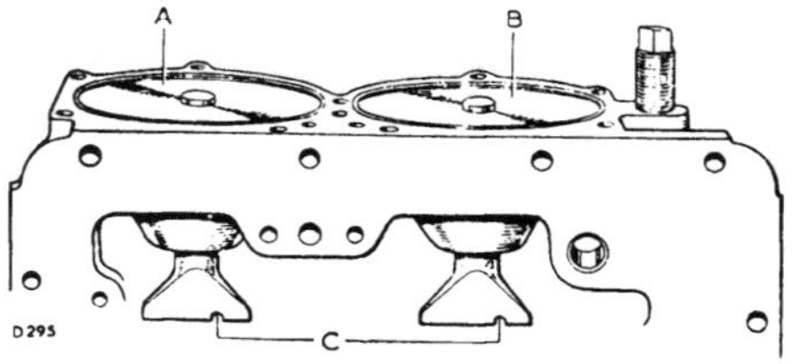

Low and forward inner servo pistons
A—Forward piston B—Low piston
C—Position of slot in strut

4. Fit new piston seals on the low and forward outer pistons, being careful not to stretch the seals more than is necessary.

5. Lubricate the bores of the low and forward outer servo with transmission fluid, and insert the pistons at an angle and ease into position.

6. Insert a new 'O' ring seal into servo cylinder plate.

Operation E2-10—*continued*

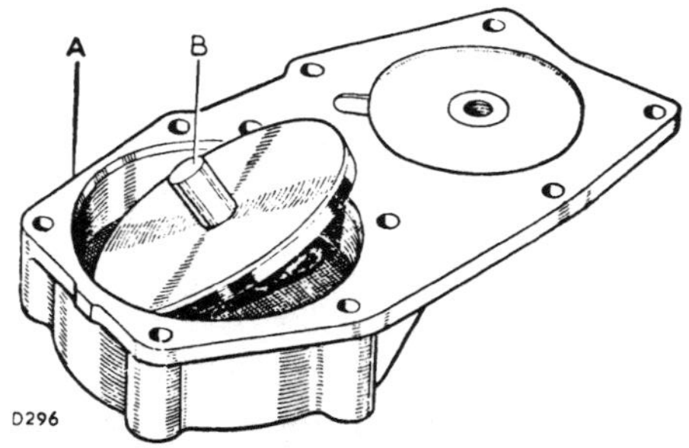

Insertion of forward outer piston

A—Outer servo cylinder B—Outer servo piston

7. Insert four of the retaining set bolts through the outer servo cylinder to retain the gasket and cylinder plate in position.

8. Place a new gasket in position on the servo cylinder face.

9. Position the plate over the four bolts on to the servo cylinder, taking care that the outer piston rod is through the plate.

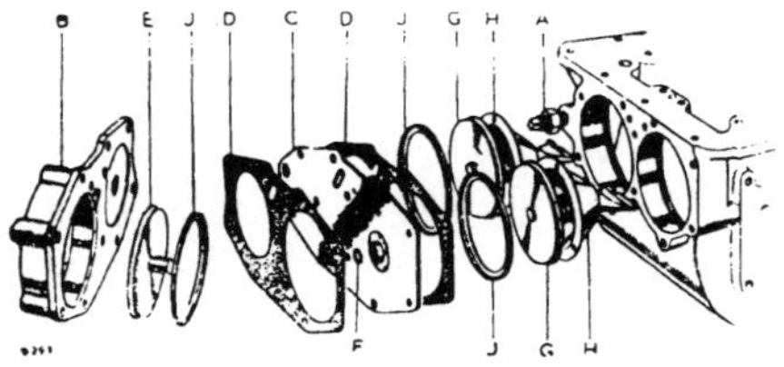

Forward and low servos

A—Adjusting screw locknut
B—Forward and low outer servo cylinders
C—Cylinder plate
D—Gaskets
E—Outer piston
F—Rubber 'O' ring
G—Forward and low inner pistons
H—Piston spring retainer
J—Rubber piston seals

10. Place a new gasket in position over the four bolts on to the plate.

11. Fit the assembly to the main casing, insert the remaining set bolts and tighten to 15 to 18 lb/ft (2,0 to 2,4 mkg).

12. Fit the locknut for reverse adjusting screw loosely in position until adjustment can be made.

13. Fit the pressure take-off plugs, using new washers, but do not tighten at this stage.

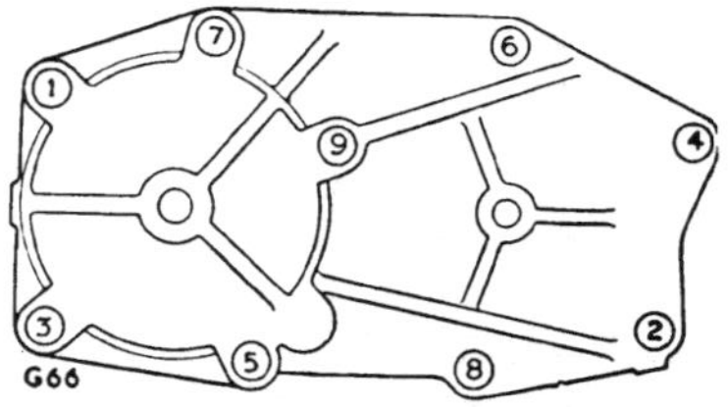

Tighten forward and low servo bolts in the order as indicated above

14. Adjust the brake bands. Operation E1-9.

15. Replace the fluid strainer and sump.

Late models fitted with five-point mounting, items 16 and 17

16. Refit the reaction bracket, using the original shims.

17. Refit the propeller shaft.

18. Refill the transmission unit with recommended grade of fluid to the correct level.

Selector control shaft, to remove, overhaul and refit—Operation E2-11

Workshop hand tools:
Spanner sizes: $\frac{7}{16}$ in. AF, $\frac{1}{2}$ in. AF
Circlip pliers

Selector control shaft, remove

1. Remove the nut, spring washer and plain washer, which secures the selector control shaft inner lever.

2. Pull the shaft assembly outwards and slip the control shaft inner lever off the shaft. Withdraw shaft out of the casing.

3. Remove the oil seal for selector shaft from the casing.

4. Remove the plain washer from the shaft.

5. Remove the circlip from the parking brake toggle shaft sleeve.

6. Remove the rod for toggle shaft sleeve and selector control shaft inner lever from the casing.

7. Unscrew the control shaft inner lever and parking pawl sleeve from each end of the actuating rod. Do not disturb adjusting nut unless replacement is necessary.

8. Remove pressure take-off plugs from main casing.

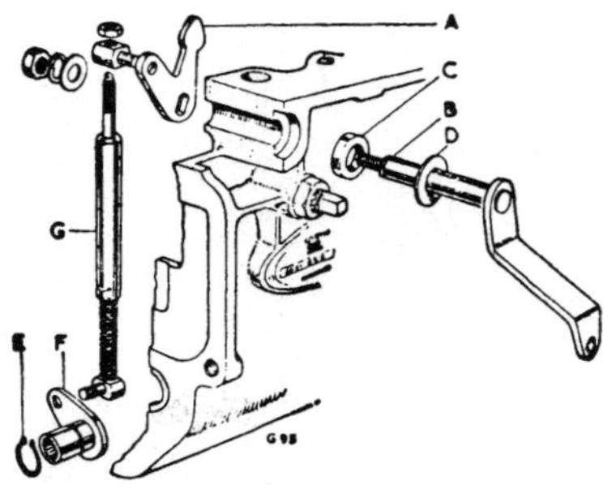

Selector control shaft, main casing

A—Selector inner lever
B—Selector control shaft
C—Oil seal for selector shaft
D—Plain washer for selector shaft
E—Circlip
F—Toggle shaft sleeve
G—Rod for toggle shaft sleeve

Selector control shaft, refit

1. Fit new oil seal for selector control shaft to casing, using the shaft as a guide.

2. Screw the selector control shaft inner lever on to the parking brake actuating rod. Do not fully tighten, but allow approximately one thread free movement.

3. Screw the parking brake sleeve on to the other end of the actuating rod, again do not fully tighten, but leave approximately one thread free movement.

4. Install the assembly into the casing with the parking brake sleeve through the drilling provided.

5. Lubricate the control shaft with one of the recommended transmission fluids, then insert it into the casing with the external lever pointing towards the band adjuster screw.

6. Engage the flats on the selector control shaft into those on the inner lever, with control shaft pointing to the top of casing. Fit plain washer, spring washer and securing nut.

7. Check the operation of the lever.

8. Replace the circlip retaining the parking brake sleeve.

Main casing, to clean and check—Operation E2-12

DO NOT USE PARAFFIN TO CLEAN THE MAIN CASING, USE ONLY TYPE 'A' TRANSMISSION FLUID.

1. Clean the casing, removing all traces of old gaskets.
2. Inspect the casing for stripped threads, cracks and damage to mating surfaces.
3. Make sure the oil drillings and passage ways are free.

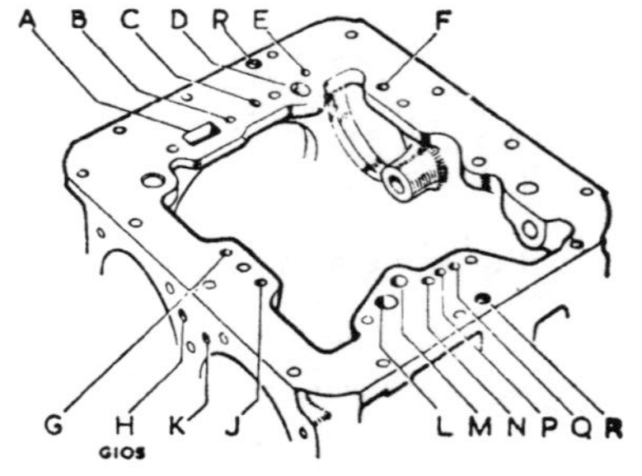

Main casing drillings to be cleaned

A—Front pump inlet
B—Multiple-disc clutch
C—Direct-drive clutch
D—Front pump pressure
E—Converter pressure
F—Reverse pressure
G—Low band servo inlet
H—Low band servo outlet
J—Forward band servo inlet
K—Forward band servo outlet
L—Rear pump inlet
M—Rear pump pressure
N—Governor feed
P—Multiple-disc clutch
Q—Direct-drive clutch
R—Pressure take-off plugs

Section E – AUTOMATIC TRANSMISSION
Model 'DG', Rover Mk I, Mk IA and Mk II
Part Three

Lubrication
Test procedure
Defect location
Data

Lubrication and maintenance

1. Total capacity is approximately 15 pints (8,5 litres).
2. The fluid used in the Automatic Transmission has been specially formulated to meet exacting conditions and no fluids other than those mentioned below must be used.

   This special fluid has to perform four functions:

   (a) To transmit kinetic energy in the torque converter.

   (b) To act as an operating medium for band engagement and clutch.

   (c) To act as a cooling medium.

   (d) To provide efficient lubrication for all transmission components.

It will thus be realised that no ordinary transmission or engine oil will meet these requirements and the only recommended fluids are:

BP	Castrol	Duckham's	Esso	Mobil	Regent Texaco/ Caltex	Shell
Energol ATF Type A	Castrol TQ Automatic Transmission Fluid	Duckham's Nolmatic ATF Type A	Esso Automatic Transmission Fluid	Mobil Fluid 200	Texamatic Fluid 3528	Shell Donax T 6

3. The torque converter and automatic transmission share a common supply of fluid. It is essential, therefore, when checking the level or topping up the automatic transmission, that the engine is run at idling speed to transfer fluid from transmission casing to torque converter, otherwise a false level reading will be obtained.

Check the fluid level

4. The fluid level should be checked every 3,000 miles (5.000 km) and changed every 12,000 miles (20.000 km) as follows:

   (a) Absolute cleanliness is essential, use only nylon rag and clean the filler orifice.

   (b) Apply hand brake and set selector lever at 'L' and raise the transmission fluid temperature by idling the engine to normal engine operating temperature.

   To ensure that the car does not move it is advisable to block the road wheels.

   (c) Remove tunnel carpet and rubber plug to expose dipstick.

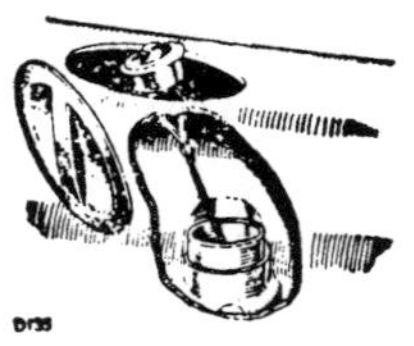

Fluid level dipstick and plug

   (d) Clean area around dipstick hole. Remove dipstick, wipe dry and check fluid level. The difference between full and low mark on dipstick represents approximately 1 pint.

   (e) With the engine still idling and the selector lever still at 'L', add the recommended grade of fluid to bring the level up to the 'full' mark. Do not overfill.

To drain and refill the unit

5. Every 12,000 miles (20.000 km) the transmission fluid must be changed as follows:

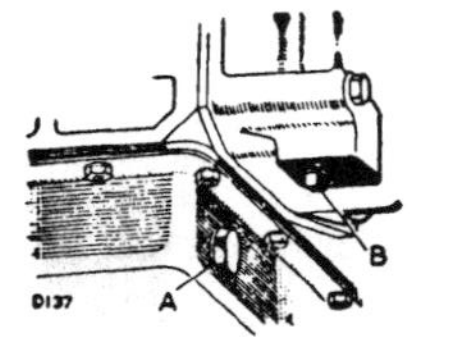

Drain plug and converter pressure take-off plug

A—Drain plug B—Converter pressure take-off plug

(a) Remove the drain plug from the left-hand front of the transmission fluid sump. Take great care if the car has just returned from a run as the fluid may be hot enough to cause serious scalding.

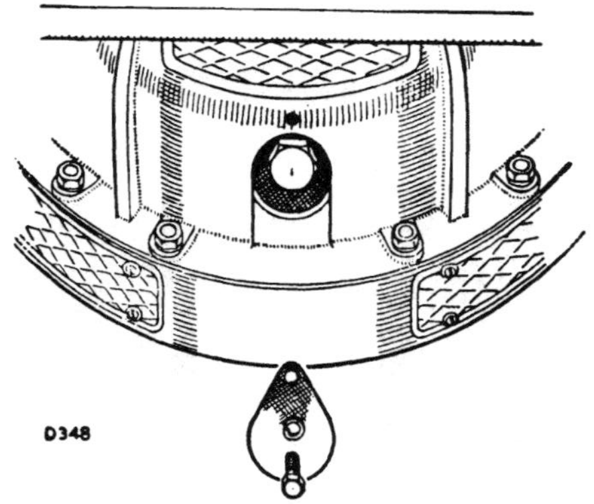

Converter drain plug and cover

(b) The torque converter housing cover plate should be removed and the torque converter rotated until the drain plug is at the bottom. Remove the drain plug and again take care to avoid scalding. Note that early ($\frac{5}{8}$ AF) and late ($\frac{3}{4}$ AF) drain plugs are not interchangeable.

(c) To ensure complete drainage, remove the square-headed converter pressure take-off plug, located at the bottom of the reverse servo housing.

(d) Allow fluid to drain away completely from both transmission casing and torque converter. Replace torque converter drain plug and tighten to 8 to 10 lb/ft (1,10 to 1,38 mkg). Replace pressure take-off plug and tighten to 6 to 7 lb/ft (0,85 to 0,95 mkg). Replace transmission sump drain plug and tighten to 35 to 45 lb/ft (4,85 to 6,25 mkg). Replace torque converter housing cover plate.

(e) Remove the sump and filter.

(f) Clean the sump filter gauze carefully, using only nylon rag to remove any impurities which may have been introduced.

Refilling the unit

6. Place a new gasket on the face of the fluid sump. Fit sump and stiffener plates and tighten to 10 to 13 lb/ft (1,35 to 1,75 mkg).

(a) Clean the area around dipstick hole and remove dipstick. Absolute cleanliness is essential. Use only nylon rag.

(b) Pour in 10 pints (5,8 litres) of the recommended grade of fluid into the transmission through the dipstick hole.

(c) Start the engine and allow to idle for approximately one minute to transfer fluid from transmission case to torque converter. Apply the handbrake and select L (low) on the selector quadrant. As a precaution block the road wheels.

(d) With the engine still idling and the selector lever still at 'L' add additional fluid, up to 5 pints (3 litres), to bring the level up to full mark on dipstick. Do not overfill or underfill and never use anything but the recommended fluid.

(e) Replace dipstick, rubber plug and transmission cover carpet.

Static test procedure—Operation E3-1

Equipment:

Hydraulic pressure test gauge, B-W 1A — Electronic type revolution counter

Test pressure limits for the early and late type transmission units are the same, see chart below.

However, the converter pressures on the latest unit tend towards the higher limits.

TEST PRESSURE LIMITS
Shown in lb/sq. in. Metric equivalents (kg/cm²) in parenthesis

Front pump	N	1,000 rpm	15–30 (1,0–2,1)
	L	1,000 ,,	70–95 (4,9–6,6)
	D	1,000 ,,	70–95 (4,9–6,6)
	R	1,000 ,,	170–250 (11,9–17,5)
Rear pump	D	20 mph	70 min. (4,9 min.)
Low servo	L	1,000 rpm	70–95 (4,9–6,6)
Forward servo	L	1,000 ,,	70–95 (4,9–6,6)
	D	1,000 ,,	70–95 (4,9–6,6)
Reverse servo	R	1,000 ,,	150–250 (10,5–17,5)
Multi-disc clutch	D	15 mph	70–95 (4,9–6,6)
Direct drive clutch	D	25 ,,	70–95 (4,9–6,6)
Torque converter	N	1,000 rpm	10–25 (0,7–1,7)
	L	1,000 ,,	30–60 (2,1–4,2)
	D	30 mph	15–30 (1,0–2,1)
	R	1,000 rpm	25–60 (1,7–4,2)

Rear wheels locked unless road speed quoted — Transmission must be at normal operating temperature

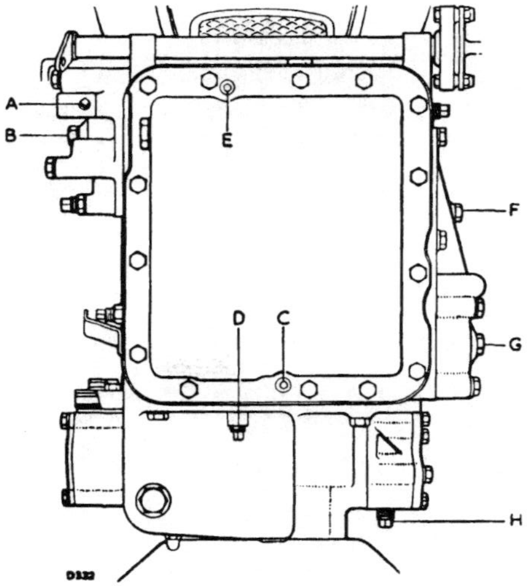

Layout of pressure take-off points from underside of transmission

A—Converter
B—Reverse servo
C—Direct drive clutch
D—Multiple-disc clutch
E—Front pump
F—Low servo
G—Forward servo
H—Rear pump

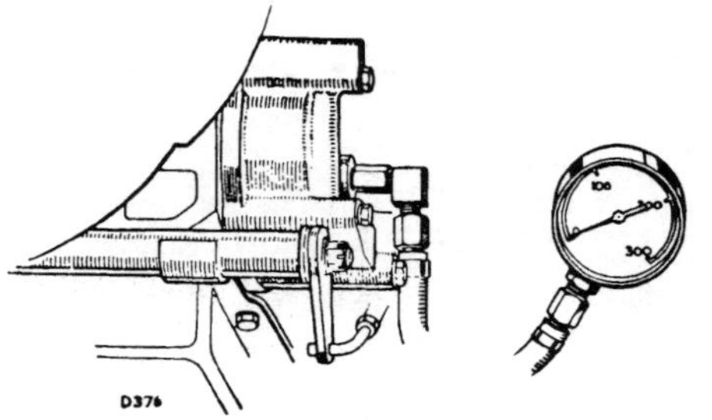

Gauge in position on reverse servo

Test procedure

When locating a fault in the transmission unit, carry out the tests in the following order:

Absolute cleanliness is essential, use transmission fluid type A for cleaning purposes. Only nylon rag or non-fluffy material should be used.

Preliminary checks

Make sure that the engine and transmission is at operating temperature.

Check the fluid level. The fluid level is critical within two pints; the difference between 'full' and 'low' marks on the dipstick represent approximately 1 pint (0,5 litre). If necessary add fluid, through the dipstick hole.

Apply the hand brake firmly, start the engine, select 'L' at the quadrant.

Allow to idle for approximately one minute, to transfer the fluid from the transmission case to the torque converter unit.

Do not race the engine

With the engine still idling and selector lever still at 'L', add extra fluid, to the full mark on the dipstick. Do not overfill.

1. Road-test car, if the fault has not been corrected, check the kickdown and selector linkage; adjust either linkage as necessary and again road-test car.

2. Check the brake band adjustment. Operation E1-9.

Pressure tests

3. If the fault has not been corrected, carry out pressure tests as detailed below, with the engine and transmission at operating temperature.

   Some of the probable reasons which may cause zero or low pressure at the points tested are detailed after each pressure check.

   To avoid overheating of the transmission the engine should not be run at speeds higher than idling for more than 30 seconds when the selector lever is in 'D', 'L' or 'R', and the rear wheels stationary.

Reverse Servo

1. From the centre of the reverse servo, remove the pressure take-off plug and connect gauge.
2. Apply hand and foot brakes firmly, start engine.
3. Move selector lever to 'R' position.
4. Gradually increase engine speed to 1,000 rpm.
5. Check for pressure of 150 to 250 lb/sq. in (10,5 to 17,5 kg/cm²).
6. Remove pressure gauge and, using a new washer, refit pressure take-off plug, tighten to 28 to 33 lb/ft (4 to 4,5 mkg).

   (a) **If the pressure reading is substantially lower than the figure quoted,** remove the fluid sump and valve block; strip the valve block and examine the reverse interlock valve and pump ball check valves. See Operations E1-3 and E2-1.

   (b) **If no pressure reading is obtained,** check the front pump pressure.

   The main relief valve may be stuck in open position; remove sump and strip the valve block and examine for damage or foreign matter.

Low Servo

1. From the centre of low servo remove the pressure take-off plug and connect gauge.
2. Apply hand and foot brakes firmly and start engine.
3. Move selector lever to 'L' position.
4. Increase engine speed gradually to 1,000 rpm.
5. Check for a reading of 70 to 95 lb/sq. in. (4,9 to 6,6 kg/cm²).
6. Remove pressure gauge and using a new washer, refit pressure take-off plug. Tighten to 28 to 33 lb/ft (4 to 4,5 mkg).

   If the reading obtained is substantially below the required pressure, then:

   (a) Remove low servo and examine for damaged seal.

   (b) Remove and strip valve block and examine for foreign matter or damaged gasket. Operations E1-3 and E2-1.

If the pressure reading was correct check low band adjustment, and check for sticking servo piston.

Forward Servo

1. From the centre of the forward servo remove the pressure take-off plug and connect gauge.

2. Apply hand and foot brakes firmly and start engine.
3. Move selector lever to 'L' or 'D' position.
4. Gradually increase engine speed to 1,000 rpm.
5. Check for reading of 70 to 95 lb/sq. in. (4,9 to 6,6 kg/cm²).
6. Remove pressure gauge and using a new washer, refit pressure take-off plug. Tighten to 28 to 33 lb/ft (4 to 4,5 mkg).

   If the reading obtained is substantially below the required pressure, then:

   Remove and strip forward servo, examine piston seal for damage. Operation E2-10.

   If no pressure reading is obtained, check front pump pressure.

   Remove and strip valve block. Examine front and rear pump ball check valves. Ensure they are seating properly. Operations E1-3 and E2-1.

Front pump

1. From the centre of the fluid sump front flange remove the pressure take-off plug with an Allen key, connect gauge. On LHD models it may be necessary to slightly spring the selector cross-shaft forward to enable the pressure gauge adaptor to be fitted.
2. Apply hand and foot brakes firmly and start engine.
3. Move selector lever to 'N' position.
4. Gradually increase engine speed to 1,000 rpm.
5. Check for reading of 15 to 30 lb/sq. in (1,0 to 2,1 kg/cm²).
6. With hand and foot brakes firmly applied and engine running, move selector lever to 'D' or 'L' position, gradually increase engine speed to 1,000 rpm and check for minimum pressure reading of 70 to 95 lb/sq. in. (4,9 to 6,6 kg/cm²). Repeat test in 'R' position and check for reading of 170 to 250 lb/sq. in. (11,9 to 17,5 kg/cm²).
7. Remove pressure gauge and refit plug with Allen key. Tighten fully.

   If either of the readings obtained are substantially below the required pressure, then:

   (a) Remove and strip valve block, examine main relief valve, ensure it is working quite freely in its body. Examine for foreign matter. Operation E2-1.

   (b) Remove and strip front pump and collector ring, examine oil seal rings, gaskets and gasket faces. Examine front pump for wear.

   If no pressure reading is obtained, then:

   (a) Remove and strip valve block, examine for foreign matter or damaged gaskets. Operations E1-3 and E2-1.

   (b) Examine front pump drive fingers on torque converter hub. Operation E1-1.

Converter

1. From the base of the reverse servo remove the converter pressure take-off plug and connect a pressure gauge.
2. Apply hand and foot brakes firmly and start engine.
3. Move selector lever to 'N' position.
4. Gradually increase engine speed to 1,000 rpm approximately.
5. Check for reading of 15 to 20 lb/sq in. (1,0 to 1,4 kg/cm²).

1st-speed start models

6. Move selector lever to 'D' or 'L' position, increase engine speed to 1,000 rpm and check for reading of 30 to 60 lb/sq in (2,1 to 4,2 kg/cm²).

2nd speed start models

7. Move selector lever to 'D' position, increase engine speed to 1,000 rpm and check for reading of 30 to 60 lb/sq in (2,1 to 4,2 kg/cm²).
8. Move selector to 'R' position; on LHD models it will be necessary to remove the selector cross-shaft and to select the 'R' position by hand at the transmission selector lever. Increase engine speed to 1,000 rpm, check for approximate reading of 25 to 60 lb/sq in (1,7 to 4,2 kg/cm²).
9. Remove pressure gauge and refit pressure take-off plug. Tighten to 8 to 10 lb/ft (1,1 to 1,4 mkg). If the reading obtained in the 'N' position is substantially higher than required pressure, then:

   (a) Remove and strip valve block, examine main relief valve, ensure it is working quite freely in its body. Examine for foreign matter. Operations E1-3 and E2-1.

If in the 'D' position the pressure is too high, then:

(a) Strip and examine converter shuttle valve. Ensure that the valve is quite free to move in its sleeve, and no foreign matter is present.

If in the 'R' position the pressure is too low:

(a) Check front pump pressure.

(b) Strip and examine converter shuttle valve, it may be stuck in the closed position.

(c) If the pressure is high in all positions, check the mainshaft lubrication valve.

Rear Pump

1. From the rear pump housing remove the rear pump pressure take-off plug. Connect the pressure gauge.

2. Jack up rear wheels of car and block the front wheels.

3. Start engine and move selector to 'D' position.

4. Increase engine speed gradually until a road speed of 20 mph (32 kph) is attained.

5. Check for pressure reading of 70 lb/sq. in. (4,9 kg/cm^2) minimum.

6. Remove pressure gauge and refit pressure take-off plug. Tighten to 15 to 18 lb/ft (2,0 to 2,5 mkg).

   If the reading obtained is substantially below the required pressure, then check for:

   (a) Faulty rear pump or pump drive.

   (b) Relief valve sticking.

   (c) Front and rear pump ball check valves stuck partially open.

   If no pressure reading is obtained, then check for:

   (a) Front and rear pump ball check valve stuck open.

Multiple-Disc Clutch

1. From the underside of the extension case flange remove the multiple-disc clutch pressure take-off plug, connect gauge.

2. Jack up rear wheels of car, and block the front wheels.

3. Start engine and move selector to 'D' position, gradually increase engine speed to 1,000 rpm, or a road speed of approximately 15 mph (24 kph).

4. Check for a pressure reading of 70 to 95 lb/sq in (4,9 to 6,6 kg/cm^2).

5. Remove pressure gauge and refit pressure take-off plug. Tighten to 8 to 10 lb/ft (1,1 to 1,4 mkg).

   If the reading obtained is substantially below the required pressure:

   (a) Remove and strip multiple-disc clutch and examine clutch piston ring.

   If no pressure reading is obtained, then:

   (a) Examine governor valve, ensure it is quite free in its housing.

   (b) Examine multiple-disc clutch oil passage, ensure it is quite free from obstruction.

   (c) If pressures are correct check multiple disc clutch plates and check piston for free movement.

Direct Drive Clutch

1. From the centre of the fluid sump rear flange remove the pressure take-off plug with an Allen key, connect gauge.

2. Jack up rear wheels of car and block the front wheels.

3. Start the engine and move selector to 'D' position. Check for zero reading.

4. Slowly increase engine speed to 1,500 rpm; at a road speed of 25 mph (40 kph) the transmission should change into direct drive, indicated by a rapid rise in pressure, whilst in direct drive check for minimum reading of 70 to 95 lb/sq. in. (4,9 to 6,6 kg/cm^2).

5. Check direct drive clutch pressure during deceleration, at approximately 650 rpm pressure should fall to zero.

6. Remove pressure gauge and refit plug with Allen key. Tighten to 8 to 10 lb/ft (1,1 to 1,4 mkg).

   If no pressure reading is obtained, then:

   (a) Examine governor valve, ensure it is quite free in its housing.

Stall Speed

The stall speed is the maximum speed at which the impeller can be driven while the turbine is held stationary; it should be noted that this will vary to some extent with the condition of the engine; an engine in poor condition will give a lower stall speed. Engine condition must therefore be considered in interpreting a low stall speed.

The engine must not be run at speed for more than ten seconds during this test.

1. Apply hand and foot brakes firmly; it is also advisable to block the front wheels.

2. Run engine until it reaches working temperature.

3. Ensure that the transmission contains correct quantity of fluid.

4. Connect a revolution counter to the engine.

5. Start engine and move selector lever to 'L' and allow to idle for approximately one minute to ensure circulation of fluid.

6. Depress accelerator to full throttle position and note the revolution counter reading.

1st-speed start models

7. **Mk IA models.** The stall speed of an engine in good condition should be 1,800 to 1,900 rpm.

2nd-speed start models

8. **Mk II models.** The stall speed of an engine in good condition should be 2,100 to 2,300 rpm.

9. Road-test car.

10. Causes for incorrect stall speed may be:

    (a) If the stall speed is below 900 rpm, change torque converter.

    It should be noted that it is not possible to strip the torque converter. Therefore if there is any mechanical fault the torque converter must be changed.

    (b) If the stall speed is higher than the figure given, check the adjustment of low and forward brake bands and condition of forward free-wheel.

Road test procedure—Operation E3-2

Preliminary checks—1st speed start models

Speeds quoted in the following tests are 'true' speeds, allowance for speedometer error may be necessary in practice.

Check that the engine starter will operate in 'P' and 'N' positions—but **not** in 'D', 'L' or 'R'.

Check the freedom of the transmission with the control lever at 'N'. There should be no tendency for the engine to drive the car, nor should there be any engine braking effect. Neutral must not be selected above 70 mph (112,6 kph).

Carry out the tests below with the engine and transmission at working temperature.

1st speed start manual control

(a) With the control in the locked out position, the governor lever should be hard against the stop at the forward limit of its travel.

(b) With the control pushed in, the governor lever should return to the closed throttle position. Adjust the cable as necessary to obtain this condition.

TESTS FOR 1st SPEED START MODELS

PROCEDURE	CHECK
Test One	**ENGINE BRAKING**
Select 'D' and drive car at a road speed of 35 mph (56 kph). Move selector to 'L'	*The car should decelerate immediately and noticeably*
Test Two	**GEAR CHANGE SPEEDS—UPWARDS**
Select 'D' and accelerate gradually from rest	*The transmission should change from:* *1st to 2nd at 4 to 10 mph (6 to 16 kph)* *2nd to 3rd at 17 to 21 mph (27 to 33 kph)*
Test Three	**GEAR CHANGE SPEEDS—DOWNWARDS, ON OVERRUN**
With a closed throttle on the overrun, until the car is just rolling	*The transmission should change smoothly downwards from:* *3rd to 2nd at 20 to 16 mph (32 to 25 kph)* *2nd to 1st at 4 to 2 mph (6 to 3 kph)*
Test Four	**FULL THROTTLE CHANGE-UP SPEEDS**
Select 'D'; release hand brake. Press accelerator pedal to full throttle position, that is just resting on, but not depressing, the kick-down plunger	*That transmission changes from:* *1st to 2nd at 28 to 32 mph (45 to 51 kph)* *2nd to 3rd at 43 to 48 mph (69 to 77 kph)*
Test Five	**FULL THROTTLE CHANGE-UP SPEEDS**
Select 'D'; release hand brake. Press accelerator down to full kick-down position, that is as far down as possible	*That transmission changes from:* *1st to 2nd at 35 to 38 mph (56 to 61 kph)* *2nd to 3rd at 57 to 60 mph (91 to 96 kph)*

TESTS FOR 1st SPEED START MODELS—*continued*

PROCEDURE	CHECK
Test Six	**CHANGING DOWN ON DECELERATION**
Drive normally at 40 mph (64 kph) at part throttle. Apply brakes and bring speed down to approximately 15 mph (24 kph)	*That car should remain in top gear as long as throttle remains open, but should change down to 2nd immediately the throttle is shut*
Test Seven	**2nd SPEED HOLD**
Select 'D'. Engage 2nd speed hold	*That 2nd speed hold control retains 2nd speed until:* *57 to 60 mph (91 to 96 kph)*

Preliminary checks—2nd speed start models

Speeds quoted in the following tests are 'true' speeds, allowance for speedometer error may be necessary in practice.

Check that the engine starter will operate in 'P' and 'N' positions—but **not** in 'D', 'L' or 'R'.

Check the freedom of the transmission with the control lever at 'N'. There should be no tendency for the engine to drive the car, nor should there be any engine braking effect.

Neutral must not be selected above 70 mph (112,6 kph).

Carry out the tests below with the engine and transmission at working temperature.

2nd speed start manual control

(a) With the control in the locked out position, the governor lever should be against the detent plunger in the transmission (full throttle position).

(b) With the control pushed in, the governor lever should return to the closed throttle position. Adjust cable as necessary to obtain this condition.

2nd speed start electric control. Models Mk. IA

(a) With the control switched 'ON' the governor lever should be hard against the stop at the forward limit of its travel.

(b) With the control switched 'OFF' the governor lever should return to the closed throttle position. To adjust, slacken the two bolts securing the solenoid and rotate as necessary to obtain this condition.

The 2nd speed hold, when in operation, maintains the same condition as 'kick-down' with change speeds at:

1st to 2nd at 30 to 34 mph (48 to 54 kph).

2nd to 3rd at 60 to 65 mph (96 to 104 kph).

2nd speed start. Mk II models after March, 1963

(a) With the control switched 'ON' the governor lever should be against the detent plunger in the transmission (full throttle position).

(b) With the control switched 'OFF' the governor lever should return to the closed throttle position. To adjust, slacken the two bolts securing the solenoid and rotate as necessary to obtain the above condition. See Operation E1-7.

TEST FOR 2nd SPEED START MODELS

PROCEDURE	CHECK
Test Eight	**ENGINE BRAKING**
Select 'D' and drive car at a road speed of 25 mph (40 kph). Move selector to 'L'	*The car should decelerate immediately and noticeably*
Test Nine	**GEAR CHANGE SPEEDS—UPWARDS**
Select 'D' and accelerate gradually from rest	*The transmission should change from:* *2nd to 3rd at 17 to 21 mph (27 to 33 kph)*
Test Ten	**FULL THROTTLE CHANGE SPEEDS**
Select 'D'; release hand brake. Press accelerator pedal to full throttle position, that is just resting on, but not depressing, the kick-down plunger	*That transmission changes from:* *1st to 2nd at 20 to 25 mph (32 to 40 kph)* *2nd to 3rd at 44 to 49 mph (72 to 78 kph)* *3rd to 2nd at 40 to 45 mph (64 to 72 kph)* *2nd to 1st at 18 to 23 mph (28 to 37 kph)*
Test Eleven	**FULL THROTTLE CHANGE SPEEDS**
Select 'D'; release hand brake. Press accelerator down to full kick-down position, that is as far down as possible	*That the transmission changes from:* *1st to 2nd at 28 to 32 mph (45 to 51 kph)* *2nd to 3rd at 55 to 65 mph (88 to 104 kph)* *3rd to 2nd at 55 to 61 mph (88 to 98 kph)* *2nd to 1st at 26 to 29 mph (41 to 46 kph)*
Test Twelve	**2nd SPEED HOLD**
Select 'D'. Engage 2nd speed hold	*That 2nd speed hold control retains 2nd speed until: 42 mph (67 kph)*
Test Thirteen	**CHECKING REVERSE AND PARKING SELECTION**
Select 'D'; drive at 5 mph (8 kph). Move selector to 'P'; then into 'R' position	*There should be no effect, that is the car should behave as if it were in 'N'—neutral. If the car comes to rest in 'P' the parking sprag will ratchet, which although not harmful, is not a practice to be encouraged*
Test Fourteen	**CHECKING REVERSE AND PARKING SELECTION**
Select 'D'; drive at 5 mph (8 kph). Move selector to 'R'. Let the car come to a standstill, when reverse should engage.	*That there is no engine braking effect in reverse—a free-wheel action takes place*

TEST FOR 2nd SPEED START MODELS—*continued*

PROCEDURE	CHECK
Test Fifteen	**PARKING POSITION**
With the car stationary, and selector at 'P', release hand brake	*That car cannot be moved*

If this test is carried out on a hill, some difficulty may be experienced when attempting to drive off, owing to the parking pawl not being able to be released.

To release pawl, select lever position *opposite* to the direction of gradient, i.e. if car is facing downhill select 'R'.

Lightly apply pressure to accelerator; this will cause engine to release the load on the pawl allowing it to disengage. Selector can then be used as required.

The rather high change speeds, 1st to 2nd and 2nd to 1st, when intermediate hold is operated on cars prior to March, 1963, solenoid set at 'kick-down' position, can be modified for driving in town traffic by removing the existing valve booster spring and replacing with valve booster spring (Part No. 542295). See Operation E2-3.

This gives the following 1st to 2nd, and 2nd to 1st change speeds. The 2nd to 3rd speeds are unchanged.

With accelerator pedal at full throttle position	Rover Mk II as produced prior to the first week in March, 1963, that is, set at kick-down position	After modification
Change up from 1 to 2 at .... Change down from 2 to 1 at	19 to 25 mph (30 to 40 kph) 24 to 18 mph (38 to 28 kph)	16 to 20 mph (25 to 32 kph) 5 to 0 mph (8 to 0 kph)
With accelerator pedal at kick-down position or intermediate hold in operation	Rover Mk II after March, 1963, solenoid set at full throttle position	
Change up from 1 to 2 at .... Change down from 2 to 1 at	28 to 33 mph (45 to 53 kph) 30 to 25 mph (48 to 40 kph)	23 to 27 mph (37 to 43 kph) 17 to 14 mph (27 to 22 kph)

Note: The new 2 to 1 full throttle down change is virtually at zero road speed, and the transmission does not engage low when stationary until at least full throttle is reached. Performance checks show that there is no measurable increase in the 0 to 40 mph (0 to 64 kph) acceleration time.

SPECIAL TESTS

In cases of direct drive clutch trouble where the symptoms are that the transmission operates normally in indirect ranges but difficulty is experienced in obtaining direct drive, or direct drive is unobtainable, or where it is obtainable only when the foot is momentarily eased off the accelerator, make the following checks and tests:

1. Check fluid level for overfilling.
2. Make sure that the intermediate hold control mechanism disengages correctly.
3. Make the following pressure tests and compare the figures obtained with the ones set out in the table:
   (a) Direct drive clutch pressure at 30 mph (48 kph)
   (b) Torque converter pressure at 30 mph (48 kph)

		Direct drive clutch	Torque converter				Action
		at 30 mph (48 kph)	Low	Inter-mediate	Direct at 30 mph (48 kph)	Reverse	
Normal pressures Normal nominal pressures	lb/sq. in. kg/cm²	80 5,5	60 4,2	30 2,1	30 2,1	60 4,2	If normal pressure readings are obtained and direct drive does not engage correctly, replace torque converter assembly for suspected fault in direct drive clutch
Incorrect pressures Faulty governor, governor valve or bushing	lb/sq. in. kg/cm²	0 0	60 4,2	30 2,1	30 2,1	60 4,2	Service extension case
Lubrication valve blocked or twisted in mainshaft	lb/sq. in. kg/cm²	80 5,6	*80 5,6	*80 5,6	*80 5,6	200 14,0	Replace mainshaft assembly
Converter shuttle valve seized in open position	lb/sq. in. kg/cm²	80 5,6	60 4,2	60 4,2	60 4,2	140 9,8	Service valve block
Faulty direct drive clutch oil seals	lb/sq. in. kg/cm²	80 5,6	60 4,2	30 2,1	60 to 80 4,2 to 5,6 rises slowly	60 4,2	Replace torque converter assembly
Transfer tube missing	lb/sq. in. kg/cm²	65 4,5	80 5,6	30 2,1	45 3,1	60 4,2	Install transfer tube

*If the pressure is found to be 80 lb/sq. in. (5,6 kg/cm²) instead of 30 lb/sq. in. (2,1 kg/cm²) nominal, the lubrication valve should be suspected of leakage, which would cause a build up of pressure in the torque converter and alter the 50 lb/sq. in. (5,6 kg/cm²) differential necessary for correct direct drive clutch operation. A leaking or blocked valve would also affect transmission unit lubrication.

Further checks can only be carried out after removing and dismantling the unit.

To dismantle the unit see Operation E2-7.

Check the lubrication valve for leakage. Use special tool, B-W 12A, to check whether the valve is a tight fit in the mainshaft bore.

Check for a blocked valve or failure of the ball to return on to its seating thus preventing non-return action of the valve. This would cause the torque converter to drain when stationary.

Proceed as follows:

1. Dismantle the transmission unit mainshaft and place shaft upwards in a hole in the work bench, so that the three mainshaft oil rings are uppermost.

2. Use a pressure type oil can (minimum capacity ½ pint (0,28 litre)) with plastic taper nozzle, filled with clean transmission fluid. Insert the oil can nozzle into the bottom (rearmost) lubrication hole in the mainshaft, (for identification purposes this hole is ⅛ in. diameter, countersunk, through one wall of the shaft in the centre of the ground diameter). See Operation E2-7.

3. With your fingers, blank off the three holes in the mainshaft which are located at a right-angle (90°) relative to the one in which the oil can nozzle has been inserted. Start pumping the oil can.

4. If the valve is tight in the mainshaft and the ball is seating correctly, pressure will build up inside the shaft and no fluid will issue from the top foremost $\frac{5}{32}$ in. (3,9 mm) diameter hole nearest to the front end of the shaft.

5. If the valve leaks on its outside diameter, or when there is no non-return action due to incorrect seating of the ball, fluid will emerge from the top foremost $\frac{5}{32}$ in. (3,9 mm) diameter hole. A ball which is not seating can often also be diagnosed by an audible rattle when shaking the shaft.

Mainshaft in position in transmission unit

6. Remove front pump and collector ring assembly, and front ring gear. Insert nozzle of oil can in the $\frac{3}{32}$ in. (2,3 mm) diameter countersunk hole in the mainshaft, adjacent to the lower rearmost oil ring and start pumping. Check for issue of fluid from the $\frac{5}{32}$ in. (3,9 mm) diameter hole nearest to the front end of the mainshaft as described in item 5.

Valve blockage test

To check for lubrication valve blockage, a pressure test must first be carried out as follows:

1. Connect a pressure gauge to the reverse servo pressure take-off and with the hand and foot brakes firmly applied, start the engine.

2. Check the reading and if the pressure in Drive and Low is up to 80 lb/sq in. (5,6 kg/cm²), and in reverse, up to 200 lb sq in. (14,0 kg/cm²) instead of 60 lb/sq in. (4,2 kg/cm²) in all speeds, the following possible causes must be checked:

Cause 1. Valve twisted or displaced in shaft, causing the body of the valve to block the foremost hole in the mainshaft and thus prevent fluid from returning from the torque converter to the transmission unit.

Cause 2. Valve blocked by direct drive clutch lining or metal deposits, foreign matter or collapse of the mainshaft valve spring, preventing fluid from returning from the converter to the transmission unit. The result is that the converter pressure becomes equal to line pressure so that again no pressure differential will be available for operation of the direct drive clutch. Insufficient lubrication of the gear train components may also occur.

To check for correct location of the valve, a special tool—lubrication valve test rod B-W 12A, must be used. With the tool fully screwed home on the valve body, a length of $\frac{9}{16}$ in. (18,2 mm) should protrude from the mainshaft bore.

Late versions of the tool have a ring engraved at this length.

To check valve for blockage, use a pressure type oil can, preferably with a plastic taper nozzle, filled with clean transmission fluid. Insert the oil can nozzle in the top foremost $\frac{5}{32}$ in. (3,9 mm) diameter hole in the mainshaft and start pumping the oil can. See Operation E2-7.

If fluid emerges from the $\frac{3}{32}$ in. (2,3 mm) diameter countersunk hole in the mainshaft adjacent to the lower (rearmost) oil ring, the action of the valve is correct. If pressure builds up and no fluid emerges, the valve is blocked.

In all cases of trouble with the lubrication valve, renew the mainshaft assembly. The valve body is chilled prior to insertion into the shaft and factory installation equipment is essential.

In cases where the transmission operates normally in the direct ranges but 'Direct Drive' or 'Top' is difficult or impossible to obtain, the following checks and tests should be carried out:

(a) Intermediate hold engaged—disengage.

(b) Transmission overfilled—check level.

(c) Oil transfer tube missing—install transfer tube

(d) If (a), (b) and (c) are in order, check the direct drive clutch pressure and the torque converter pressure, in the manner described under Operation E3-1. Compare the pressures obtained with the normal nominal figures shown in the table in Operation E3-1.

If replacement of the torque converter assembly is necessary due to mechanical failure of the direct drive clutch, it is possible that the fluid in the transmission is contaminated with metal dust.

In this event, the transmission unit must be completely dismantled for thorough cleaning of all components, bearings and fluid passages.

Fluid leakage

Cases of fluid leakage from the transmission are in most instances caused by incorrect servicing such as neglect in observing torque specifications or instructions regarding the use of **new** gaskets and washers.

As even slight leakage is likely to be accentuated by the high pressures under operational conditions, a considerable amount of fluid will be lost in a very short time. It is emphasised that any loss of fluid in excess of two pints (1 litre) will cause slip of the friction bands and clutches with risk of **serious damage** to the transmission. It is imperative, therefore, that any cases of fluid loss reported are rectified **with priority,** thus avoiding costly consequential repairs.

DEFECT LOCATION

Classification of faults

Group One	All conditions of slip, that is engine racing	Group Five	All conditions of abnormal external oil leakage
Group Two	All conditions of drag or sticking, that is engine labouring	Group Six	Conditions caused by incorrect functioning of auxiliaries—starter cut-out
Group Three	Irregular gear changes or no drive	Group Seven	Incorrect change-up speeds and inability to attain certain gears
Group Four	All conditions of excessive noise		

Before any attempt is made to carry out the following checks, the transmission and engine should be at operating temperature the transmission fluid level correct and the engine performance satisfactory.

Group One — **TRANSMISSION INOPERATIVE OR EXCESSIVE SLIP IN FORWARD RANGES**

Low or no servo pressure	*Check hydraulic circuit and repair as necessary*
Main relief valve stuck open or partly open	*Check valve block*
Incorrect band adjustment or adjuster broken	*Adjust or renew*
Broken band, or excessively worn lining	*Repair or replace as necessary*
Stuck forward or reverse servo	*Free or replace*
Faulty torque converter	*Check stall speed and renew if necessary*

TRANSMISSION INOPERATIVE OR EXCESSIVE SLIP IN REVERSE

Low or no servo pressure	*Check hydraulic circuit and repair as necessary*
Main relief valve stuck open or partly open	*Check valve block*
Reverse unobtainable	*Check reverse interlocker valve*
Incorrect band adjustment or adjuster broken	*Adjust*
Broken band, or excessively worn lining	*Repair or replace as necessary*
Stuck reverse servo	*Free or replace*
Faulty reverse free-wheel	*Remove unit and replace*

INEFFECTIVE ENGINE BRAKING ON DECELERATION IN MANUAL LOW

Low band slipping	*Adjust or replace as necessary*
Reverse one-way clutch slipping	*Check in second speed hold. Transmission should lock and not allow vehicle to roll back when climbing a gradient, replace parts as necessary*
Check servo pressure	*Rectify as necessary*

SLIP ON ONE TO TWO UP-CHANGE

Low multiple-disc clutch pressure	*Low fluid level, check gaskets and sealing rings*
If pressure is correct, multiple-disc clutch plates damaged or buckled	*Replace necessary parts*
Sticking multiple-disc clutch piston	*Remove unit and rectify*

DEFECT LOCATION—*continued*

Group One—*continued* — **SLIP ON TWO TO THREE UP-CHANGE**

Sticking torque converter shuttle valve	*Free, or replace as necessary*
Check torque converter pressure	*See Operation E3-1*
Check direct-drive clutch pressure	*See Operation E3-1*
Check governor action and governor valve	*See Operation E2-3*
Ensure oil transfer tube is correctly fitted	*See Operation E1-1*
Possible damage to direct-drive clutch	*Change torque converter*

POOR ACCELERATION FROM REST, CAR WILL NOT MOVE AWAY ON STEEP HILLS, PARTICULARLY IN REVERSE. STALL SPEED TEST BELOW 1,000 RPM

Stator free-wheel slipping	*Change torque converter*

TRANSMISSION OPERATES NORMALLY IN INDIRECT RANGES BUT DIFFICULTY IS EXPERIENCED IN OBTAINING DIRECT DRIVE. SOMETIMES DIRECT DRIVE COMPLETELY UNOBTAINABLE, OR DIRECT DRIVE ONLY OBTAINABLE WHEN FOOT IS MOMENTARILY EASED OFF ACCELERATOR

Intermediate hold engaged	*Check that intermediate hold control mechanism disengages correctly*
Faulty operation of direct drive clutch	*Check fluid level for overfilling; correct as necessary*
Check direct drive clutch pressure at 30 mph (48 kph) Check torque converter pressure at 30 mph (48 kph)	*Compare pressures obtained with normal nominal figures shown in the table under special tests at the end of the road test procedure chart*
If normal pressures are obtained and direct drive does not engage correctly	*Replace torque converter assembly for suspected fault in direct drive clutch*
Incorrect pressures:	
Faulty governor, governor valve or bushing	*Remove extension case and service*
Lubrication valve blocked or twisted in mainshaft	*Replace mainshaft assembly*
Converter shuttle valve seized in open position	*Remove and service valve block*
Faulty direct drive clutch oil seals	*Replace torque converter assembly*
Oil transfer tube missing	*Remove transmission unit and fit transfer tube*

Group Two — **POOR PERFORMANCE IN FORWARD RANGES, NORMAL IN REVERSE, AND DELAY IN TAKING UP DRIVE**

Reverse band dragging	*Adjust or replace as necessary*
Check valve block	*See Operation E2-1*
Examine and check forward one-way clutch	*See Operation E2-7*

DEFECT LOCATION—*continued*

Group Two—*continued*	**TRANSMISSION WILL NOT CHANGE AT KICK-DOWN, OR KICK-DOWN SPEED IS INCORRECT**
Accelerator pedal linkage maladjusted—too long	*Adjust*
High oil level interfering with governor action	*Check, drain and refill*
Incorrect operation of governor or valve binding	*Inspect, repair or replace as necessary*
Governor drive shaft worn or splines binding	*Free, or replace as necessary*
	SEVERE OVERHEATING (CAUSING HOT SMELL). TRANSMISSION DRAG AT CONVERTER COUPLING POINT, MAXIMUM SPEED POOR IN DIRECT DRIVE
Stator free-wheel seized	*Change torque converter immediately; otherwise transmission unit will be damaged by overheating*
	CAR DRIVES FORWARD IN NEUTRAL, TRANSMISSION DRAGS IN REVERSE, NORMAL OPERATION IN DRIVE AND LOW
Sticking forward servo	*Remove and strip servo, ensure that outside diameter of piston is free from burrs or ragged edges. Polish servo bore with fine emery cloth. Ensure that the piston rod moves freely in the hole in the steel servo plate. Refit servo—Operation E2-10. Check forward and low band adjustments*
Group Three	**JUDDER ON DECELERATION IN DIRECT DRIVE, NORMAL OPERATION IN LOW, INTERMEDIATE AND REVERSE**
Seized bushing on rear sun gear	*Examine rear sun gear, free wheels and bushings for overheating or seizure. Check that the narrow bush in the low drum plate and forward drum is secure. Replace parts where necessary*
	IRREGULAR GEAR CHANGES
Fluid level too high, irregular governor operation	*Check, drain and refill to correct level*
Sticking governor valve	*Free or replace as necessary*
Binding governor assembly on splined drive shaft	*Free or replace as necessary*
	HARSH GEAR CHANGES
Second to direct drive up-change	*Direct-drive clutch linings loose, change torque converter*
Check fluid level	*Too low, top-up*
	HARSH SELECTION
Sticking accumulator valve	*Free or replace as necessary*

DEFECT LOCATION—*continued*

Group Four	**EXCESSIVELY NOISY OPERATION WITH CAR STATIONARY, SELECTOR LEVER IN DRIVE RANGES**
Low oil level	*Check and fill to correct level*
Filter screen to front pump clogged	*Remove sump and clean filter*
High oil level	*Check and correct level*
Damaged front pump drive fingers on converter hub	*Replace converter*
Converter fouling on bell housing or transmission unit	*Check drive plate and run-out*
Fractured converter vanes	*Replace converter*
Loose direct drive clutch backing plate	*Replace converter*
Faulty stator one-way clutch	*Replace torque converter*
	NOISY AUTOMATIC DRIVE WHEN CAR IS MOVING FORWARD
Damaged or worn rear pump	*Check with car coasting, selector lever in 'N', replace parts as necessary*
Damaged or worn speedometer drive gear or pinion	*Replace worn parts*
Damaged gear train assembly or excessively worn gears or bearings	*Inspect and replace parts as necessary*
Group Five	**LEAKAGE BETWEEN TRANSMISSION AND CONVERTER**
Converter mis-aligned	*Fit in correct alignment, and fit new front pump oil seal and bush*
Damaged front pump oil seal or bush	*Replace oil seal and bush*
Leaking collector ring gasket	*Replace gasket and check gasket surface*
Front pump and collector ring assembly	*Leaking blanking plugs, replace plugs*
Converter leaking on welding seam, leakage from drain plug washer	*Replace converter*
	LEAKAGE AT EXTENSION CASE
Propeller shaft flange oil seal damaged	*Replace oil seal*
Gasket between extension case and transmission case damaged	*Replace gasket*
Leakage at governor control shaft bushing	*Replace bushing*
Leakage at governor control cam stop screw	*Replace stop screw washer*
Oil pump body gasket leakage	*Replace gasket*
Group Six	**STARTER SOLENOID OPERATES WITH SELECTOR LEVER IN 'D', 'L' OR 'R'**
Sliding isolating switch maladjusted	*Adjust correctly*
Sliding isolating switch damaged	*Renew*
Group Seven	**INCORRECT CHANGE-UP SPEEDS**
Check governor linkage adjustment	*Correct as necessary*
Check governor adjustment	*Warning—Do not screw out adjuster more than two to three turns*

DATA

Automatic Transmission

Type		Hydraulic torque converter with direct-drive clutch, followed by two planetary gear sets providing two indirect gear ranges and reverse
Gear ratios:		Torque Converter stalled ratio
Direct (top)	1:1	—
Intermediate (2nd)	1.435:1	2.16
Low (1st)	2.308:1	2.16
Reverse	2.009:1	2.16
Rear axle gear ratio	3.9:1	
Transmission fluid capacity including torque converter		15 Imperial pints (8,5 litres)

Tightening torques

Component	Torque lb/ft	Mkg.
Valve block screw	6 to 8	0,83 to 0,10
Valve block assembly to case screw	10 to 13	1,38 to 3,18
Front pump to collector ring screw (small)	10 to 12	1,38 to 1,65
Front pump to collector ring screw (large)	15 to 18	2,07 to 2,48
Front pump and collector ring to case screw	15 to 18	2,07 to 2,48
Extension case to transmission case screw	28 to 33	3,87 to 4,56
Detent cam adjustment screw locknut	14 to 17	1,93 to 2,35
Detent cam adjustment cap nut	3 to 4	0,41 to 0,55
Rear pump body to extension case screw	15 to 18	2,07 to 2,48
Pump cover to rear pump body set screw	6 to 8	0,83 to 0,10
Speedometer housing and cover to extension case screw	10 to 13	1,38 to 3,18
Reverse cylinder to case screw	15 to 18	2,07 to 2,48
Low cylinder to case screw	15 to 18	2,07 to 2,48
Fluid sump to transmission case screw	10 to 13	1,38 to 1,65
Fluid sump drain plug	35 to 45	4,83 to 6,22
Universal joint flange nut	60 to 80	8,29 to 11,06
Band adjusting screw nut	40 to 50	5,53 to 6,91
Lever to selector control shaft nut	6 to 8	0,83 to 0,10
Parking brake actuating rod nut	3 to 4	0,41 to 0,55
Brake cylinder pressure take-off screw	28 to 33	3,87 to 4,56
Converter drain plug	15 to 20	2,07 to 2,76
Rear pump pressure take-off plug	6 to 7	0,83 to 0,96
Torque converter pressure take-off plug	8 to 10	1,10 to 1,38
Front pump and direct-drive clutch pressure take-off plug	8 to 10	1,10 to 1,38
Multiple-disc clutch pressure take-off plug	8 to 10	1,10 to 1,38
Converter drive plate to crankshaft screw	66	9,12
Transmission to converter housing stud nut	23 to 28	3,18 to 3,87
Transmission to converter housing screw	30	4,14
Converter to drive plate screw	25 to 30	3,5 to 4

Service Tools for Automatic Transmission

The special tools in this section are obtainable only from:

V. L. CHURCHILL & Co. Ltd., P.O. Box No. 3, London Road, Daventry, Northants

Part No.	Tool	Part No.	Tool
B-W 1A	Hydraulic pressure test gauge	B-W 11A	Clutch assembly and dismantling tool
B-W 2B	Brake band adjuster	B-W 12A	Lubrication valve test rod
B-W 3	Converter aligning gauge	B-W 13	Mainshaft end-float gauge
B-W 5	Spline aligning fixture	B-W 15A	Bench cradle
B-W 7	Mainshaft bearing replacer	B-W 16	Drive flange oil seal replacer
B-W 8A	Spring retainer remover	B-W 6312A/1	Mainshaft bearing remover
B-W 10	Piston installing pins	7065	Circlip pliers

Section EE–AUTOMATIC TRANSMISSION, MODEL 35, Rover Mk III
Part One

Section EE is divided into four parts, namely:

Part I ..	..	General description and working principles Test procedure
Part II ..	..	Adjustments Automatic transmission unit, removal and refit Sub-assemblies removal and refit
Part III ..	..	Unit dismantling and overhaul procedure
Part IV ..	..	Defect location Data Recommended lubricants

Model 35 Automatic Transmission units applicable to Rover 3 Litre Mark III models can be identified by the serial number commencing 3EU1001 on a white plate.

The model 35 transmission unit can be separated from the engine and removed from the car leaving the engine in position.

When carrying out a complete unit overhaul, the section can be worked straight through in the order presented.

Alternatively, the individual operations which form the greater percentage of maintenance work undertaken by Distributors and Dealers, are detailed under appropriate headings and will be found to be complete in themselves.

Certain units and operations can be carried out without removing the transmission from the car, these operations are marked with an asterisk (*).

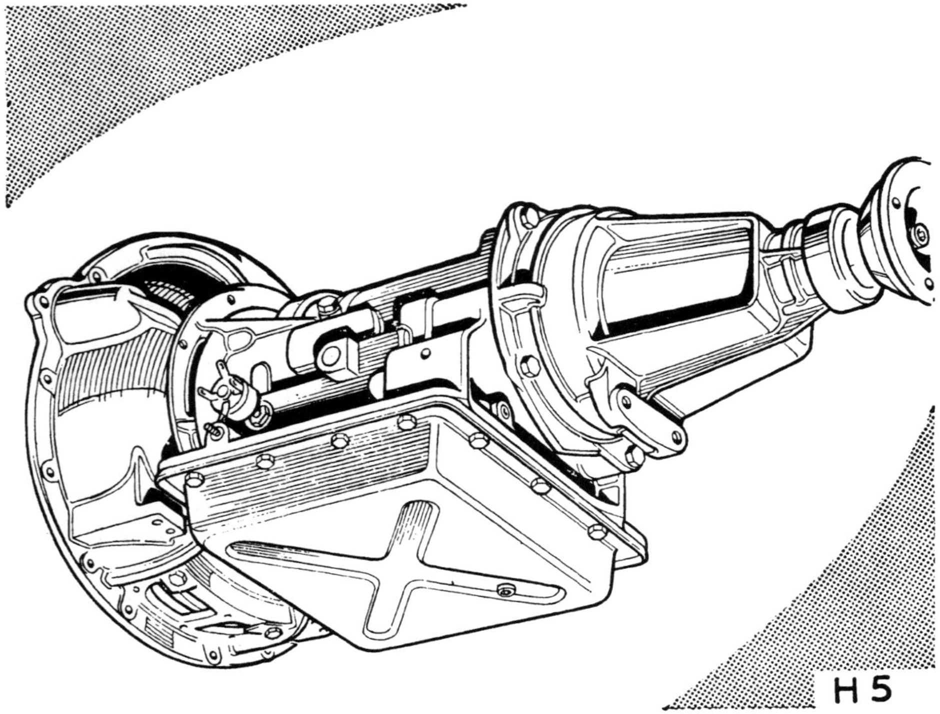

H 5

INDEX—PARTS ONE, TWO, THREE AND FOUR

Automatic transmission, model 35

Description and operation

The model 35, 3-speed automatic transmission is coupled to the engine by a three-element torque converter. Engine power is converted into hydro-kinetic energy and this provides smooth application of driving torque.

Torque multiplication in all gears ratios is provided by the converter, which is infinitely variable between the ratio of 2:1 and 1:1. Extreme low-speed flexibility in 3rd gear is the result. The speed range during which torque multiplication can be achieved is also variable, depending upon the position of the accelerator.

The torque converter

The torque converter consists of an impeller, connected to the engine crankshaft; a turbine connected to the transmission input shaft and a stator incorporating a sprag-type one-way clutch. This assembly is supported by a tube attached to the gearbox; it is co-axial with the input shaft.

The impeller, driven by the engine, causes fluid to flow from its vanes to the turbine vanes and to return to the impeller through the stator vanes.

The vanes of the components are designed and curved to affect the angle of fluid flow when a speed differential exists between impeller and turbine. The angle of the fluid flow from the turbine is changed by the stator vanes in such a way that the fluid from the stator assists in driving the impeller; torque multiplication taking place.

This varies from 2:1 when the turbine is stalled* to 1:1 when the turbine speed reaches approximately 90 per cent of the impeller.

With the speed differential between impeller and turbine achieved the angle of fluid flow from the turbine drives the stator in the same direction as the turbine and impeller. In this state the converter acts as a fluid coupling and no torque multiplication takes place.

The mechanical system

A planetary gear set, having helical involute tooth form throughout, provides three forward speeds and reverse. The planetary gear set comprises of two sun gears (forward and rear); two sets of pinions located in a pinion carrier, and ring gear which is attached to the output shaft.

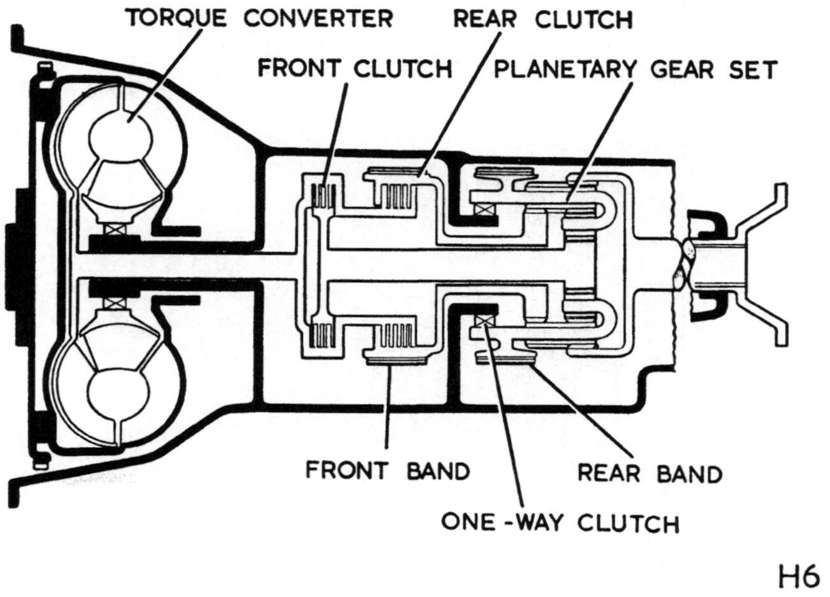

Mechanical layout

* *When the car is held stationary with the engine operating at maximum throttle opening and any one of the driving ranges selected.*

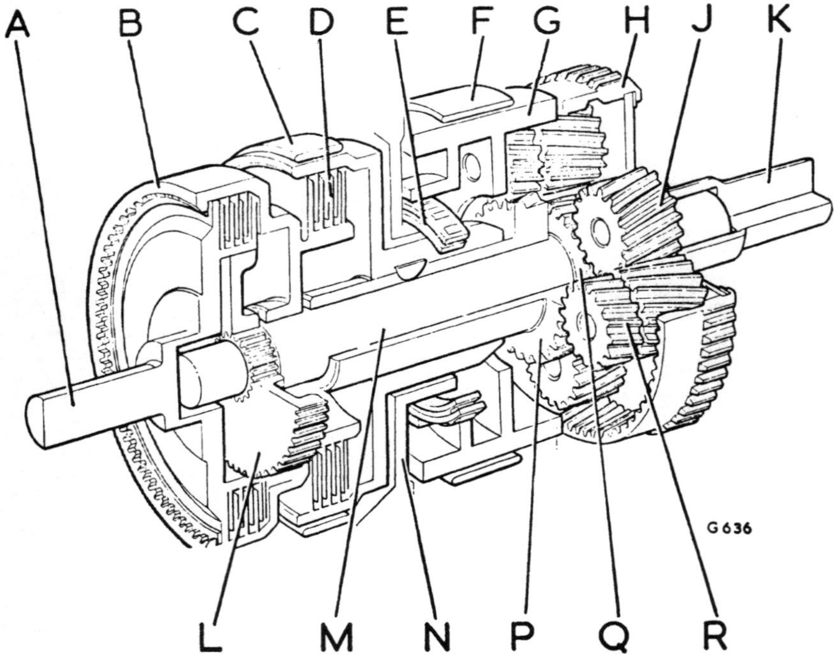

Identification of mechanical parts

A—Input shaft
B—Front clutch
C—Front brake band
D—Rear clutch
E—One-way clutch
F—Rear brake band
G—Planetary gear carrier
H—Ring gear
J—Pinion, short
K—Output shaft
L—Hub for front clutch
M—Shaft for forward sun gear
N—Centre support
P—Reverse sun gear
Q—Forward sun gear
R—Pinion, long

Power enters through one of the sun gears and leaves the gear set through the ring gear. In all forward gears, power enters through the forward sun gear and in reverse through the rear sun gear.

A single set of pinions is engaged when reverse is selected, causing the ring gear to rotate in the opposite direction to the sun gear. A double set of pinions, engaged when forward gears are selected, cause the ring gear to rotate in the same direction as the sun gear.

The pinions are housed in a carrier which locates them in their respective position relative to the two sun gears and the ring gear. The carrier is in the form of a drum which may rotate or be held stationary by a brake band or the one-way clutch.

Gear ratios are engaged by hydraulically operated clutches and brake bands, of which there are two of each.

The clutches

These are operated by hydraulic pistons and connect the torque converter to the gear set.

In forward gears the front clutch connects the converter to the forward sun gear and in reverse the rear clutch connects the torque converter to the reverse sun gear.

Both clutches are of the multi-disc type.

The one-way clutch

This functions in place of the rear brake band when the selector is at the D—Drive position. It prevents anti-clockwise rotation of the planetary gear carrier.

In first gear the gear set therefore freewheels, providing smooth changes 1st to 2nd and vice versa.

The brake bands

There are two bands which hold elements of the gearing stationary to effect lower ratio output and increased torque. Both bands are hydraulically operated by servos.

The front band holds the reverse sun gear stationary; the rear band holds the planetary gear carrier stationary.

In lock-up the pinion or planetary gear carrier is held stationary by the rear band and provides the first gear ratio of 2.39:1.

A double set of pinions are engaged so that the output shaft rotates in the same direction as the input shaft.

In reverse gear the planetary gear carrier is again held stationary, but a single set of pinions causes the driven shaft to rotate in the opposite direction.

For second gear ratio the front band holds the reverse sun gear stationary and the gearing produces a ratio of 1.45:1.

Mechanical power flow—First gear. Lock-up selected

POWER FLOW IN 'L1'

H8

Application of bands and clutches—Front clutch and rear band

Power from the turbine of the torque converter is transmitted through the front clutch to the forward sun gear, which is in mesh with a double set of pinions in the planetary gear carrier.

Power leaves the planetary gear set by the ring gear, which is attached to the driven shaft. The carrier itself is held stationary by the rear brake band.

The reverse sun gear, which is also in mesh with a single set of pinions in the planetary set, rotates freely in the opposite direction to the forward sun gear.

Mechanical power flow—First gear. Drive selected

POWER FLOW IN 'D1'

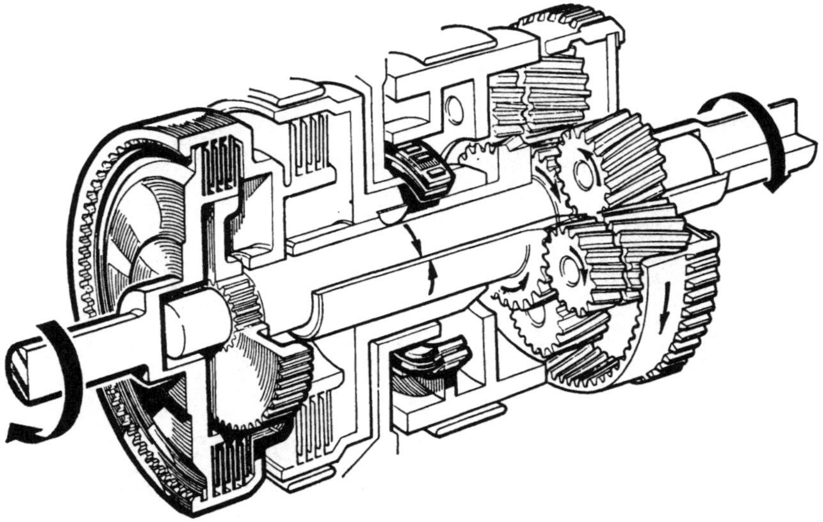

H9

Application of bands and clutches—front clutch and one-way clutch

Power is again transmitted from the turbine of the torque converter to the forward sun gear, through the front clutch. The forward sun gear is in mesh with a double set of pinions in the planetary gear set.

A one-way clutch, incorporated in the carrier of the planetary gears, prevents anti-clockwise rotation of the carrier and allows the gearbox to freewheel when on the over-run.

Power leaves the planet gear set by the ring gear and driven shaft.

Mechanical power flow—Second gear. Lock-up or Drive selected

POWER FLOW IN 'D2' OR 'L2'

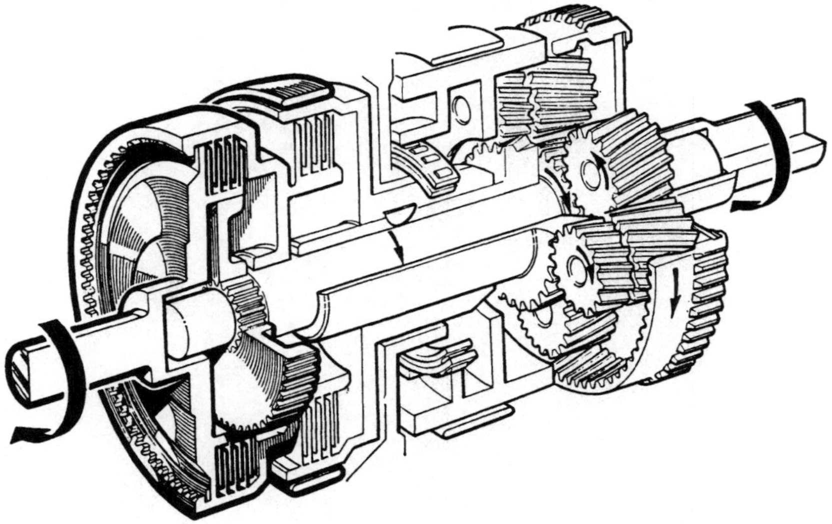

H10

Application of bands and clutches—front clutch and front brake band

The front clutch is applied, connecting the power from the converter to the forward sun gear and the planetary gear set. The front band is applied holding the reserve sun gear stationary, this allows the planetary gear carrier to be driven around the stationary reverse sun gear and provides the reduction of 1.45:1.

Power again leaves the gearbox by the ring gear and driven shaft.

Mechanical power flow—Third gear. Drive selected

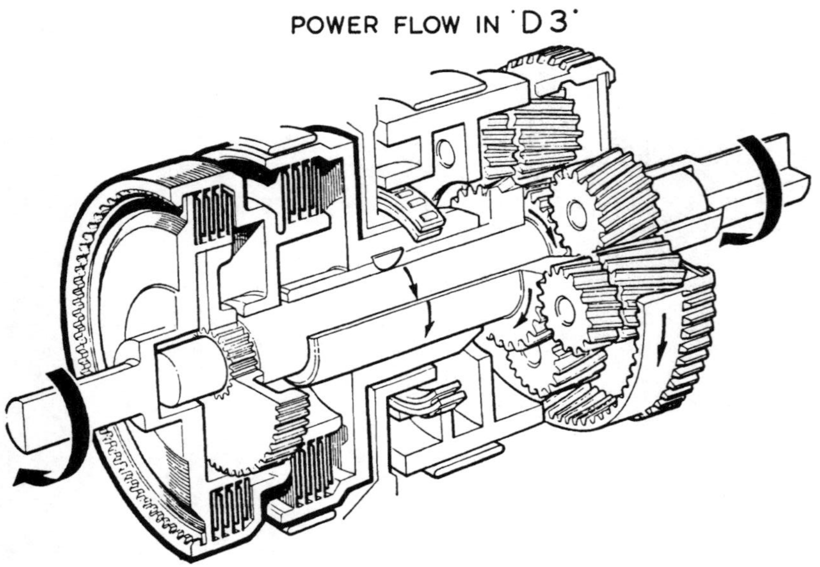

H11

Application of bands and clutches—front clutch and rear clutch

Power enters the gearbox from the torque converter through the front clutch, to the forward sun gear.

The rear clutch is applied which connects the power from the converter to the reverse sun gear; both sun gears being locked together, the gear set rotates as a unit providing a 1:1 ratio.

Mechanical power flow—Reverse selected

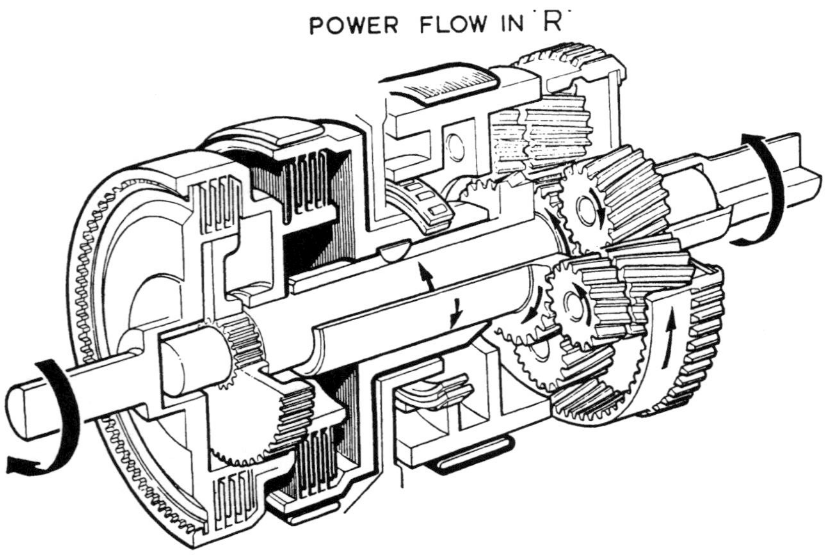

H12

Application of bands and clutches—rear clutch and rear band

Power enters the gearbox from the converter and through the rear clutch to the reverse sun gear.

The rear band is applied which holds the planetary gear carrier stationary. A single set of pinions in the planetary set between the reverse sun gear and the ring gear of the driven shaft provides a reduction of 2.09:1 in the reverse direction to the input shaft.

Neutral and Park

The front and rear clutches are off and no power is transmitted from the converter to the gear set. The front and rear bands are also released, except in 'P' where for constructional reasons the rear band is applied as long as the engine is running.

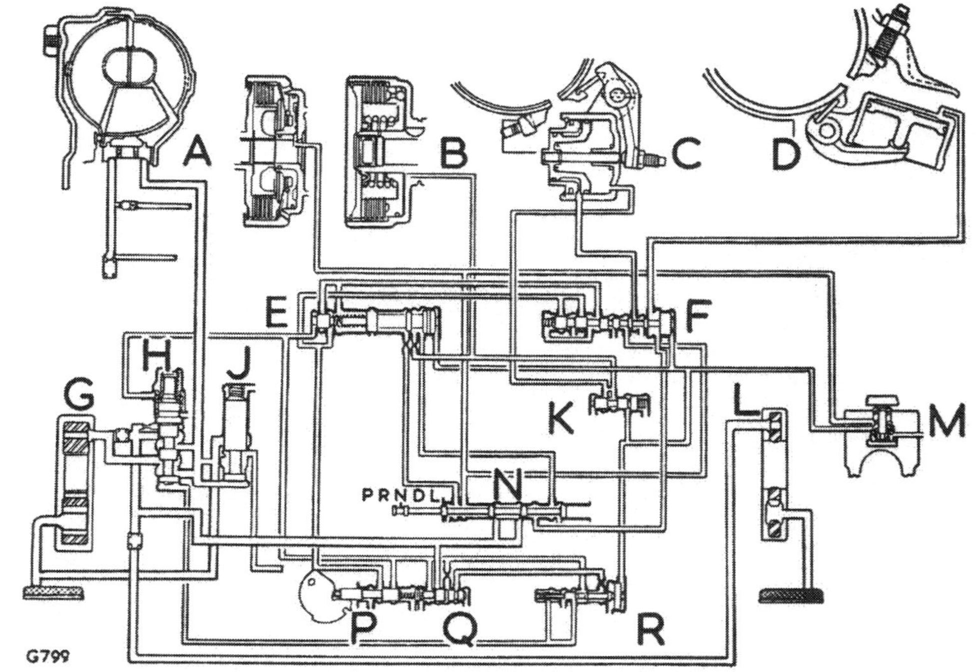

Identification of hydraulic parts

A—Front clutch
B—Rear clutch
C—Front servo
D—Rear servo
E—2 to 3 shift valve
F—1 to 2 shift valve
G—Front pump
H—Primary regulator valve

J—Secondary regulator valve
K—Servo orifice control valve
L—Rear pump
M—Governor valve
N—Manual control valve
P—Downshift valve
Q—Throttle valve
R—Modulator valve

The hydraulic system consists of a front and a rear pump and a centrifugally operated hydraulic governor. Pressure and direction of flow of fluid to the various mechanical components is regulated by a series of valves.

Front pump (G)

The front pump is driven by the converter impeller and is in operation when ever the engine is running. This pump supplies fluid to the hydraulic control system and to the torque converter, and also controls lubrication.

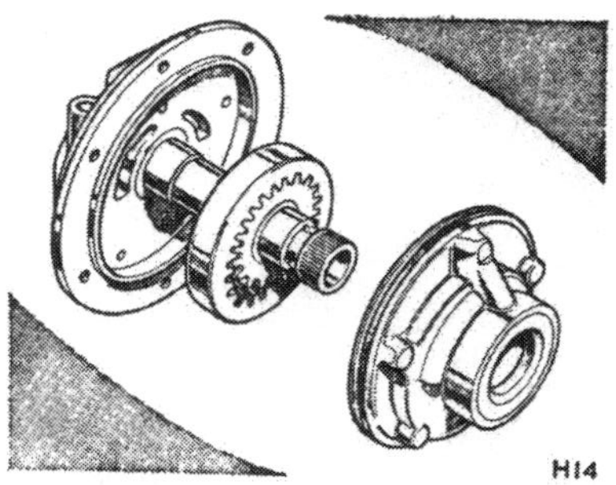

Front pump

Rear pump (L)

The rear pump is driven by the transmission driven shaft and supplements the front pump at road speeds above 25 mph (40 kph) (fluid supply to the hydraulic control system only). This pump enables the engine to be started through the transmission.

Rear pump

Primary regulator valve (H)

The primary regulator valve controls line pressure in the transmission.

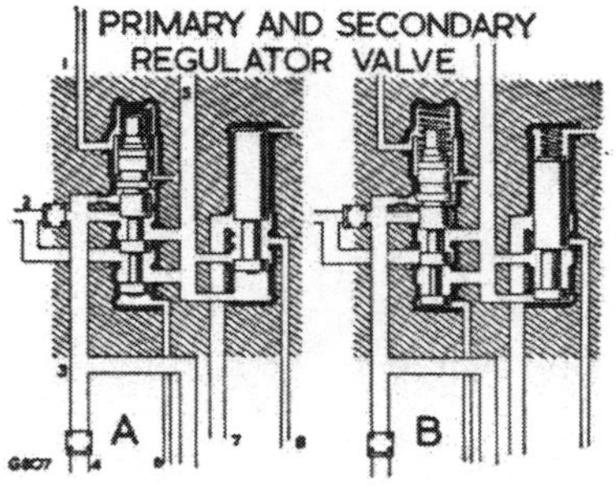

Primary and secondary valve

A—Regulating position
B—Closed position
1—Throttle pressure
2—Front pump pressure
3—Line pressure
4—Rear pump pressure
5—Converter pressure
6—Modulator pressure
7—Return to front pump
8—Lubrication

Secondary regulator valve (J)

The secondary regulator valve controls pressure in the torque converter and also provides lubrication.

Manual control valve (N)

The manual valve is operated by the selector and directs fluid to the shift valves, clutches, servos and governor.

Governor valve (M)

The governor, driven by the output shaft, regulates the fluid pressure applied to the ends of the shift valves, according to the vehicle road speed.

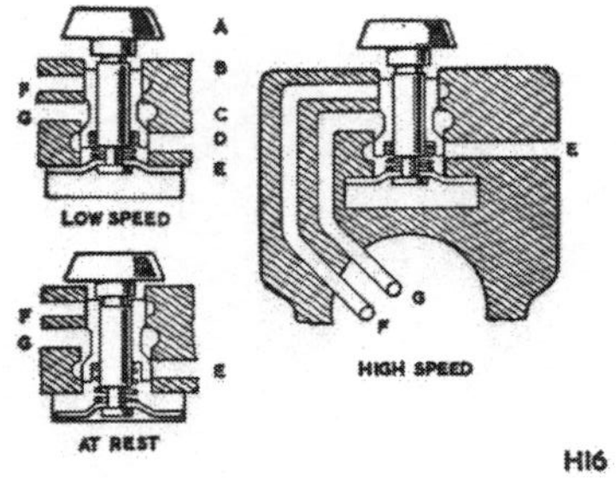

Governor valve

A—Weight for governor
B—Body for governor
C—Valve for governor
D—Spring for governor
E—Exhaust port
F—Main line pressure
G—Governor pressure

Throttle valve (Q)

The throttle valve is operated by the downshift valve via a compression spring and directs fluid to the shift valves to delay upshifts and effect downshifts.

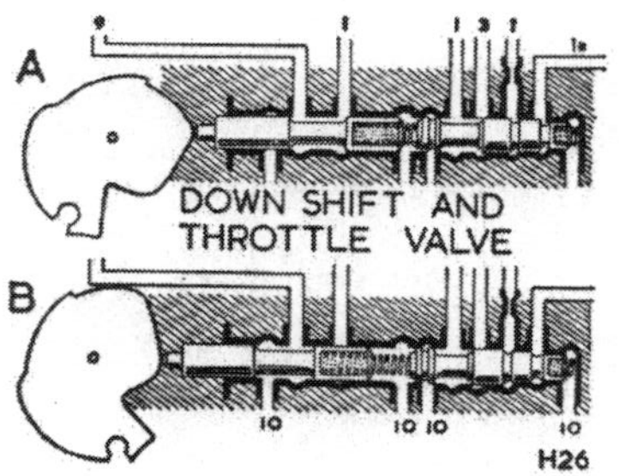

Downshift and throttle valve

A—Kickdown position
B—Part throttle position
1—Throttle pressure
1a—Throttle pressure, modulated
3—Line pressure
9—Kickdown throttle pressure
10—Exhaust ports

Downshift valve (P)

The downshift valve is operated by the downshift cable and cam and directs fluid to the shift valves, further delaying upshifts and effecting downshifts.

Modulator valve (R)

The modulator valve provides high line pressure during stall or part throttle conditions. This valve varies the line pressure relative to throttle and governor pressure.

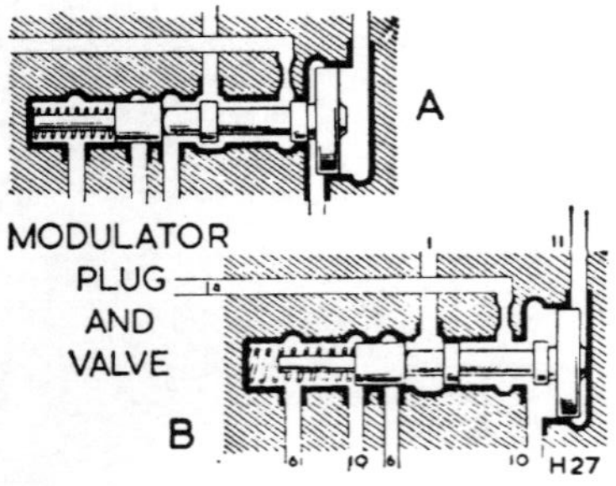

Modulator valve

A—Governor pressure applied
B—Closed position
1—Throttle pressure
1a—Throttle pressure, modulated
6—Modulator pressure
10—Exhaust ports
11—Governor pressure

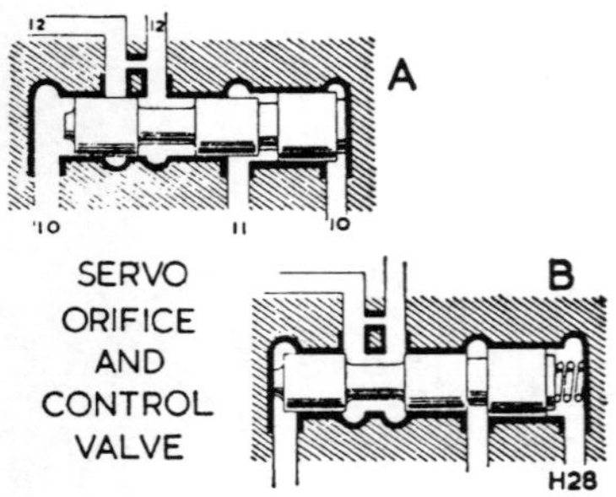

Servo orifice control valve

A—Operation at high speed, orifice in circuit
B—Operation at low speed, orifice by-passed
10—Exhaust ports
11—Governor pressure
12—Line pressure to front servo release

Servo orifice control valve (K)

The servo orifice control valve is operated by governor pressure, and opposed by spring pressure. This valve controls the quality of 2 to 3 and 3 to 2 shifts.

1 to 2 shift valve (F)

The 1 to 2 shift valve is operated by governor pressure and opposed by spring and throttle pressure. This valve effects upshifts or downshifts between 1st and 2nd gears.

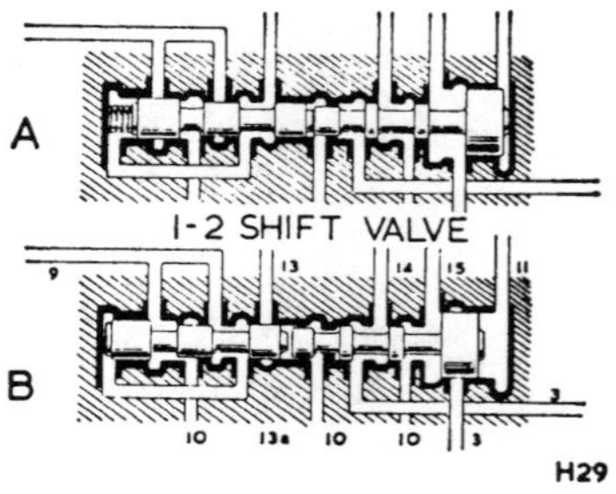

1 to 2 shift valve

A—First gear position
B—Second gear position
3—Line pressure
9—Kickdown throttle pressure
10—Exhaust ports
11—Governor pressure
13—Reduced throttle pressure
13a—Reduced throttle pressure
14—Line pressure to front servo apply
15—Line pressure to rear servo

2 to 3 shift valve (E)

The 2 to 3 shift valve is operated by governor pressure and opposed by spring and throttle pressure. This valve effects upshifts or downshifts between 2nd and 3rd gears.

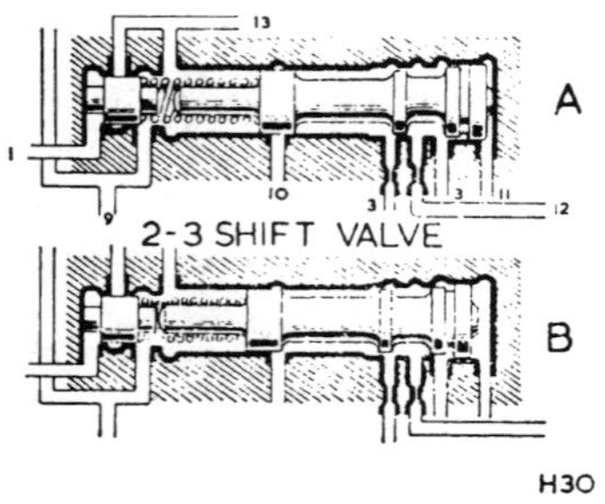

2 to 3 shift valve

A—2nd gear position
B—3rd gear position
1—Throttle pressure
3—Line pressure
9—Kickdown throttle pressure
10—Exhaust port
11—Governor pressure
12—Line pressure to front servo release
13—Reduced throttle pressure

Front servo (C)

The front servo is a double-acting unit, hydraulically operated by line pressure to engage or release the front band (2nd gear).

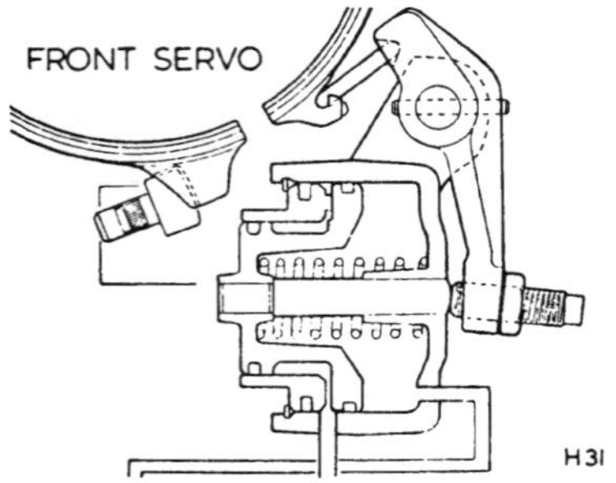

Front servo

Rear servo (D)

The rear servo is a single-acting unit, hydraulically operated by line pressure to apply the rear band (lock-up and reverse gear).

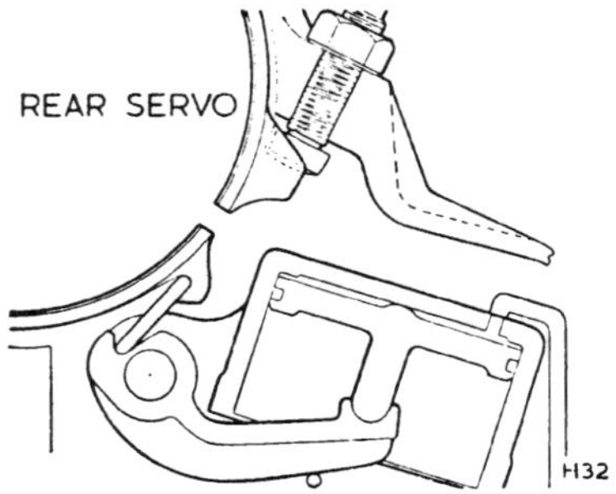

Rear servo

Front and rear clutches (A and B)

Both front and rear clutches are of the wet multi-plate type operated by line pressure.

Hydraulic circuit—Neutral selected, light throttle

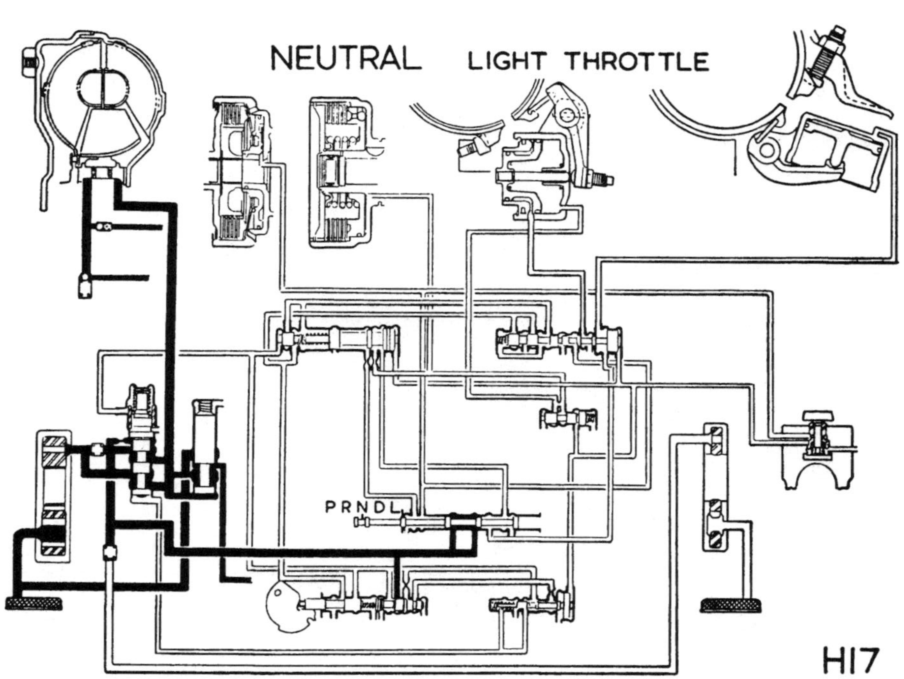

Hydraulic circuit—neutral selected, light throttle

Operation in 'N'

With the engine running, the front pump check valve is open and the rear pump check valve closes due to absence of rear pump pressure.

The primary regulator valve regulates line pressure which is directed to the manual valve and throttle valve. It also permits fluid to reach the secondary regulator valve.

The secondary regulator valve regulates pressure to the converter and lubrication of the front and rear of the gear train.

Excess pressure is exhausted from the primary regulator valve through the secondary regulator valve to the input side of the front pump and also to the oil pan.

Hydraulic circuit—Park selected, light throttle

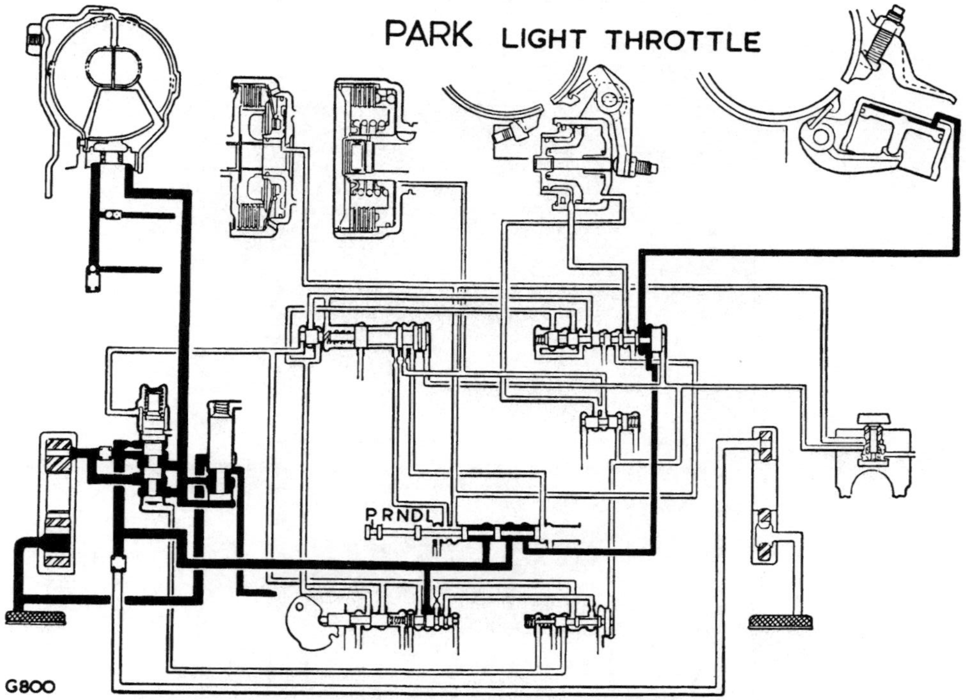

Hydraulic circuit—park selected, light throttle

Operation in 'P'

An internal linkage from the manual valve detent lever engages the parking pawl with teeth formed on the driven shaft ring gear.

With the engine running, the operation of the hydraulic system is identical to 'N' except that the manual valve directs line pressure through the 1–2 shift valve to the rear servo.

This arrangement is based upon the design of the hydraulic system without the rear servo or band performing any function in this selector position.

Hydraulic circuit—Reverse selected, medium throttle

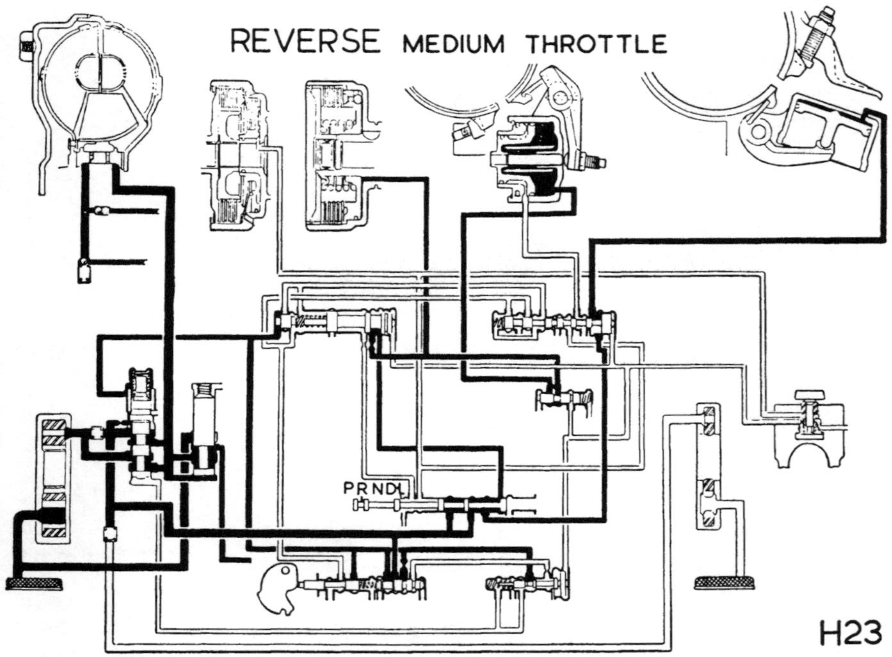

H23

Hydraulic circuit—reverse selected, medium throttle

Operation in 'R'

Pressure control of the front pump is as in 'P' or 'N' but depending upon accelerator pedal depression; throttle pressure is directed to the spring end of the primary regulator valve, thus increasing line pressure in accordance with torque capacity requirements.

The manual valve directs line pressure through the 1–2 shift valve to the rear servo and line pressure through the 2–3 shift valve to the rear clutch and front servo release. Due to absence of governor pressure, the shift valves and servo orifice control valve perform no function in this selector position.

Hydraulic circuit—First gear, drive selected, full throttle

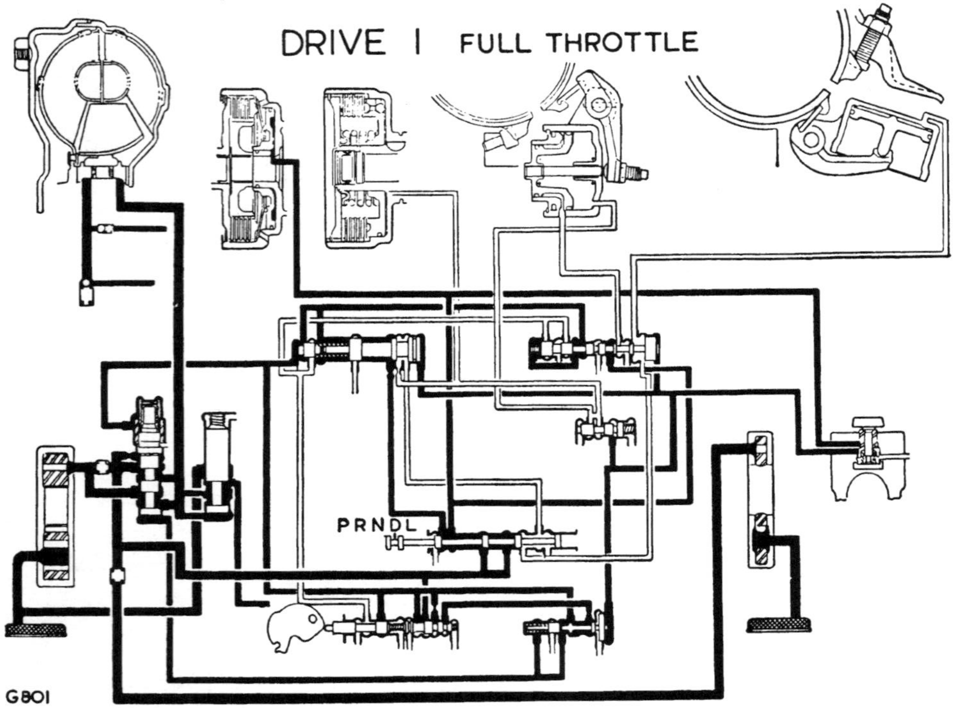

G801

Hydraulic circuit—first gear, drive selected, full throttle

Operation in D 1

Pressure control of the front and/or rear pump will be as in 'R' but with the throttle valve in the full throttle position as illustrated, throttle pressure regulated by the modulator valve plunger acts upon the primary regulator valve opposing throttle pressure and spring force, thus modulating line pressure in the interest of shift quality.

The manual valve directs line pressure to the front clutch, governor feed and 1–2 shift valve for the subsequent 1–2 shift. Line pressure also reaches the 2–3 shift valve for the subsequent 2–3 shift.

The front clutch applied in conjunction with the one-way clutch, permits the car to move off from rest, in first gear.

Hydraulic circuit—Second gear, drive selected, kickdown

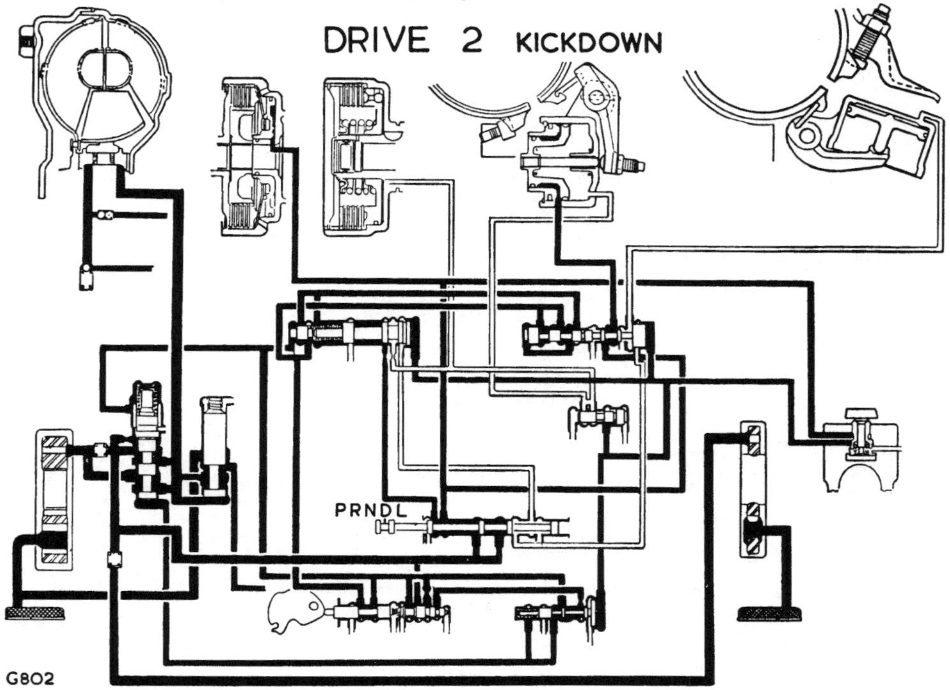

G802

Hydraulic circuit—second gear, drive selected, kickdown

Operation in D 2

Pressure control by the primary regulator valve will be of the rear pump output, the front pump providing torque converter and lubrication requirements. Throttle pressure acts upon the primary regulator valve as in D 1.

Shift control is provided by the 1–2 shift valve moving under influence of governor pressure opposed by spring force and throttle pressure.

With the downshift valve in the forced throttle position, as illustrated, forced throttle pressure acts only upon the 2–3 shift valve, thus further delaying the upshift (or providing a 3–2 downshift at speeds when there is little governor pressure).

This permits line pressure to reach the apply side of the front servo. The front band thus applied, in conjunction with the front clutch, provides 2nd gear.

Hydraulic circuit—Third gear, drive selected, light throttle

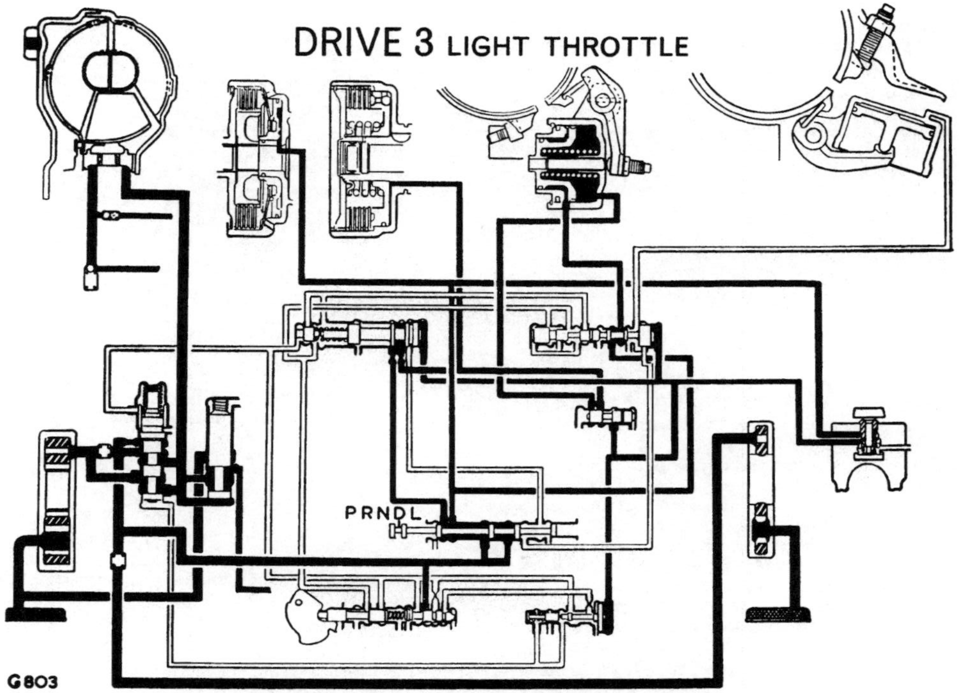

G803

Hydraulic circuit—third gear, drive selected, light throttle

Operation in D 3

Pressure control is as in D 2 except that in the throttle valve position shown (light throttle) no throttle pressure or modulated throttle pressure acts upon the two ends of the primary regulator valve.

Shift control is provided by the 2–3 shift valve moving against spring force under influence of governor pressure. This permits line pressure to reach the rear clutch and the release side of the front servo through the servo orifice control valve. When governor pressure is apparent, the servo orifice control valve closes, forcing line pressure through a .052 in. (1,32 mm) orifice which thus affects the relationship between rear clutch apply and front servo release in accordance with road speed.

Because the release side of the front servo has a larger area than the apply side, the front servo will disengage the band. The rear clutch now engaged in conjunction with the front clutch provides 3rd gear.

The absence of throttle pressure, as mentioned above, will cause the 2–3 shift valve to move early, under influence of governor pressure, thus providing a low-speed 2–3 shift.

Hydraulic circuit—First gear, lock-up selected, medium throttle

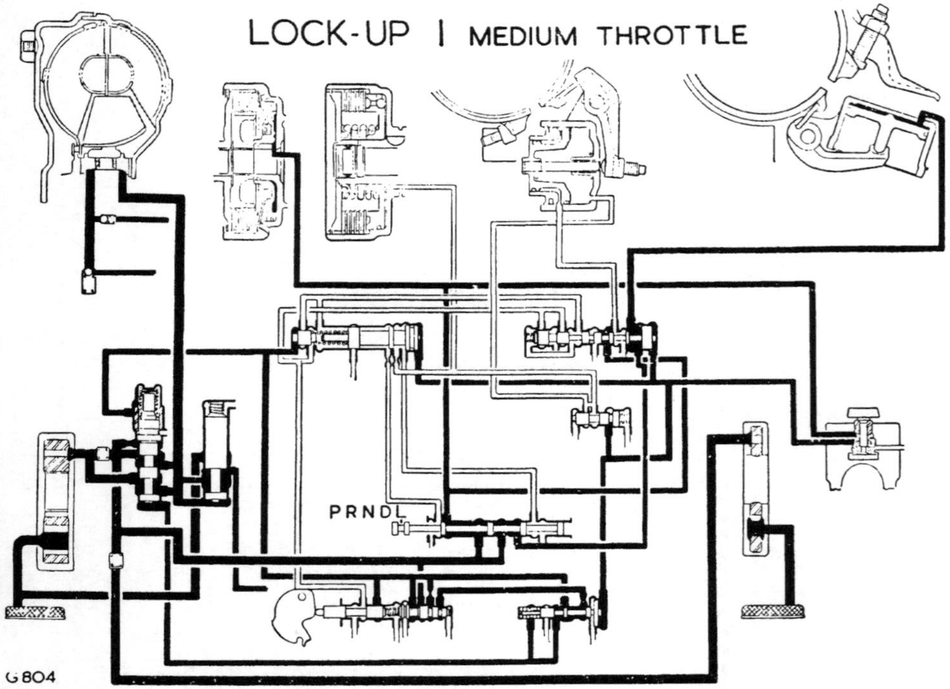

G804

Hydraulic circuit—first gear, lock-up selected, medium throttle

Operation in L 1

Pressure control of the front and/or rear pump will be as in D 1.

The manual valve directs line pressure to the front clutch, governor feed and 1–2 shift valve. In the position illustrated, the 1–2 shift valve is subjected to insufficient governor pressure to overcome spring pressure. The result is that the valve prevents line pressure from reaching the apply side of the front servo but line pressure is open to the rear servo.

At the same time, the manual valve opens to exhaust the rear clutch and front servo release circuit from the 2–3 shift valve. This causes a downshift from 3rd gear whenever 'L' is selected at speed. In this condition governor pressure will move the 1–2 shift valve; the result is that line pressure will then be blocked from the rear servo but open to the apply side of the front servo as in D 2.

Driving procedure

The automatic transmission fitted to the models to which this supplement refers has certain important fundamental differences in its operation by comparison with the automatic transmissions fitted to earlier models. It is important that drivers should familiarise themselves with these features.

The notes which follow have been divided into two sections, the first giving a brief general description of the transmission and its method of handling, and the second, for those who wish to obtain more detailed information and more particularly for using the manual control aspects of the transmission, a supplementary instruction is provided.

General description of controls

In addition to the accelerator pedal there are two controls:

(i) The selector lever

(ii) A kickdown mechanism under the accelerator pedal.

Selector lever

The selector lever moves through a quadrant and by means of a pointer indicates the various positions which are marked 'P', 'R', 'N', 'D' and 'L'. The selector lever falls naturally to the position 'N', 'D', or 'L'; to engage 'P' or 'R', the lever must be lifted towards the steering wheel and then moved to the position required.

Selector lever

P — Park; use this position whenever the car is parked } Never select these positions when car is moving
R — Reverse
N — Neutral
D — Drive; select and leave in this position for all normal forward driving.
L — Lock-up; not normally required. See following detailed description for the use of this selector position. Never select 'L' when road speed is above 75 mph (120 kph) as there is a risk of over-speeding the engine.

Accelerator kickdown mechanism

The accelerator pedal should be depressed to its full extent to operate the kickdown mechanism when:

(i) A lower gear is required for rapid overtaking or hill climbing. The maximum 'kickdown' speeds are pre-set to give optimum performance without over-speeding the engine.

(ii) Maximum acceleration is required, and can safely be used, on starting from rest.

If the accelerator pedal is eased back from the kickdown position during acceleration, upchanges will be made at lower road speeds.

Driving the car

Ensure that the handbrake is firmly applied and that the selector is in either the 'P' or 'N' position. Then operate the combined ignition and starter switch.

As a safety measure an isolation switch prevents the starter being operated in any other position.

With the engine started and idling easily, move the selector lever to either the 'D' or 'R' position as required, release handbrake and gently depress the accelerator pedal. Use foot brake to control car when manoeuvring in confined spaces.

With the selector at 'D', the car will move forward controlled by the accelerator and gear changes will be made automatically depending on road speed and accelerator position; minimum accelerator pedal pressure will result in low upchange speeds. The further the accelerator pedal is depressed the faster the car will go before changing into a higher gear. The kickdown position referred to previously can be used for changing down into a lower gear or to obtain maximum acceleration as required.

Detailed description

The following paragraphs provide a more detailed description including particularly the use of 'L' lock-up.

The drive position ('D') covers a fully automatic range of three ratios operating in conjunction with a torque converter, the ratios being engaged progressively according to car speed and accelerator position.

Top gear will be retained, unless using the kickdown, until the car speed has fallen to about 10 mph (16 kph) when second gear will be automatically engaged.

When the road speed has fallen to about 3 mph (5 kph), first gear will be engaged. Provided road speed is below 55 mph (88 kph), second gear can be obtained by use of the kickdown mechanism and can be held up to a speed of approximately 70 mph (112 kph), at which it will automatically change into top gear.

Similarly, first gear can be engaged below 20 mph (32 kph) and can be held up to approximately 40 mph (64 kph), at which speed it will automatically change into second.

The 'L' position (Lock-up) provides the ability to hold the car in either first gear or second gear and therefore in effect to drive the car in manual control, the torque converter, however, replacing the conventional clutch and multiplying the gearbox ratios.

At any time when first or second gear is in operation in Lock-up, over-run braking is obtained from the gear in question. The Lock-up should never be engaged at speeds above 75 mph (120 kph).

If the selector lever is placed in 'L' when starting from rest, the transmission starts and will remain locked in first gear regardless of road speed or throttle position. This gear gives maximum engine braking but a speed of 45 mph (72 kph) must not be exceeded in first gear.

To move from first gear Lock-up to second gear Lock-up, the lever must be moved to 'D' and then returned to 'L', which will put the transmission into second gear where it will remain locked. Maximum speed in this gear should not exceed 75 mph (120 kph).

The change to top gear is made simply by moving the lever to 'D' and leaving it there.

The maximum recommended speeds in first and second gear, referred to previously, are indicated by yellow figures on the speedometer dial.

When the transmission is in top gear, movement of the lever to 'L' will immediately give second gear but first gear will be automatically selected if the road speed drops below 3 mph (5 kph).

With second gear in operation, first gear can be engaged at speeds below 25 mph (40 kph) by operating the kickdown mechanism, but to change up into second the lever must be moved to 'D' and returned to 'L' as referred to above.

The 'L' position is particularly useful in the following conditions:

(i) For unusually long and steep gradients and descents where a low gear and engine braking are desirable.

(ii) Where hard pulling may be encountered, as in deep snow or heavy mud.

(iii) Where the car is being driven slowly but it is desirable to maintain reasonable engine speed so that the dynamo can balance the heavy electrical load placed upon it by lights, windscreen wiper, heater, etc., e.g. in foggy conditions at night.

(iv) To select and hold a lower gear when overtaking within the permissible maximum speed limits stated previously.

Emergency and manual starting

Emergency starting: The car may be pushed or towed to start the engine. Select 'D', switch on the ignition, set the mixture control and release the handbrake. Tow car until engine fires and starts, this should occur at under 25 mph (40 kph).

For towing, use a rope of sufficient length and exercise the usual care to avoid colliding with the leading vehicle.

Manual starting: Before attempting to start the engine with the starting handle, switch on the ignition, ensure that the selector lever is set to 'P' and the handbrake is hard on.

When manual starting, the starter isolation switch is ineffective and unless the selector lever is set at 'P' there is a danger, once the engine has started, that the car might creep forward, thereby causing personal injury.

Static test procedure

1. Check and if necessary correct the fluid level.
   (a) Apply handbrake firmly and chock the wheels.
   (b) Select 'P'-Park, start engine and allow engine to idle for two minutes.
   (c) Take several dipstick readings.
   (d) Top up as necessary with recommended grade of transmission fluid.
2. When testing or making a diagnosis, it is important that the transmission fluid is at operating temperature but the fluid temperature must **not** exceed 110°C at any time.
3. Check that starter will operate only with the selector in 'P' and 'N' positions—but **not** in 'D', 'L' or 'R'.
4. Check the freedom of the transmission with the selector lever at 'N'. There should be no tendency for the engine to drive the car, nor should there be any engine braking effect.
5. Apply the hand and foot brakes firmly and chock the wheels.

   With the engine at normal idling speed, select 'N–D', 'N–L', and N–R'.

   Transmission engagement should be felt in each position selected.

   Check for slip or clutch squawk.

Stall speeds

'Stall speed' is the maximum speed at which the engine can drive the torque converter impeller whilst the turbine is held stationary. It is dependent on both engine and torque converter characteristics and will vary according to the condition of the engine.

An engine in poor condition will give a lower stall speed.

1. Connect a revolution counter, Rover Part No. 601284, to the engine. See Operation EE2-3.
2. Apply the handbrake firmly and chock the wheels; whilst testing apply the footbrake.
3. Start engine and move selector lever to 'L' and allow to idle for approximately one minute to ensure circulation of fluid.
4. Depress accelerator to full throttle position and note the revolution counter reading.
   DO NOT STALL FOR LONGER THAN TEN SECONDS OR TRANSMISSION WILL OVERHEAT.
5. The stall speed of an engine in good condition should be 2,100 to 2,300 rpm.
6. If the stall speed is below 1,500 rpm change the torque converter.

Road test procedure

1. Check and if necessary correct the fluid level.
   (a) Apply handbrake firmly.
   (b) Select 'P'-Park, start engine and allow engine to idle for two minutes.
   (c) Take several dipstick readings.
   (d) Top up as necessary with recommended grade of transmission fluid.
2. (a) All normal forward running is done in 'D'-Drive. The following table of change speeds apply with the selector linkage correctly adjusted.

Light throttle	mph	kph
1 to 2 2 to 3	8 to 11 12 to 16	13 to 18 19 to 26
Full throttle		
1 to 2 2 to 3	23 to 30 53 to 63	37 to 48 85 to 102
Kickdown		
1 to 2 2 to 3	35 to 43 67 to 79	56 to 69 108 to 127

The speeds in the above table are 'indicated'. Maximum permissible tolerances in both speedometer and transmission have been taken into account, together with tyre make and expansion due to speed.

(b) At 25 mph (40 kph).
'Drive' selected, depress accelerator to full throttle position. Transmission should not change down.

(c) At 40 mph (64 kph).

'Drive' selected, depress accelerator to kick-down position. Transmission should change down into intermediate.

Release the accelerator pedal immediately, when transmission should revert to direct gear.

(d) At 20 mph (32 kph).

'Drive' selected, depress accelerator to kick-down position. Transmission should change down into first gear.

Release the accelerator pedal immediately, when transmission should revert to top gear.

(e) Driving at 30 mph (48 kph) in top gear, select lock-up.

The transmission should change into intermediate, giving engine braking. Slow vehicle to rest. At under 3 mph (5 kph) the transmission should engage first, thus increasing the engine braking.
Accelerate to 30 mph (48 kph) and close throttle. Transmission must not change up.

(f) Stop on a hill and select 'P'-Park.

Note: THIS TRANSMISSION DOES **NOT** INCORPORATE ANY SAFETY INTERLOCKS ON 'PARK' OR 'REVERSE'. 'P' or 'R' must never be selected unless the vehicle is stationary.

Release the brakes when facing up or down hill, the car should remain stationary. On steep slopes some force may be needed to disengage the 'Park' position.

3. At just over 30 mph (48 kph) select 'N', switch off ignition and let car coast. At 30 mph (48 kph) switch on ignition and select 'D'. Engine should start through the rear wheels, indicating that the rear oil pump of the transmission is working.
4. Stop and select 'R'. Release brakes and reverse using full throttle if possible. Check for slip or clutch squawk.

Section EE—AUTOMATIC TRANSMISSION, MODEL 35, Rover Mk III

Part Two

This section provides the instructions necessary for the adjustment and for the removal and refitting of various units of the automatic transmission.

It is rarely necessary to completely dismantle the unit, which has basic assemblies, each of which may be renewed and dismantled without affecting the others.

With the unit removed from the vehicle it should be supported on gearbox cradle, Rover Part No. 601280 when carrying out any of the operations in this section, it will be necessary to remove the torque converter and bell housing. Operation EE2-6 to enable this to be done.

High standards of cleanliness are required when working on the automatic transmission. Petrol, paraffin or an industrial cleaning solvent may be used to clean components. Use nylon rag—never material that is fluffy or that leaves lint—when drying any components.

IMPORTANT

Before any dismantling of the transmission unit is commenced it is essential that the following checks are made in accordance with the procedure as detailed.

1. Fluid level in transmission unit. Operation EE2-4.
2. Gear selector linkage adjustment. Operation EE2-1.
3. Downshift cable adjustment. Operation EE2-3.

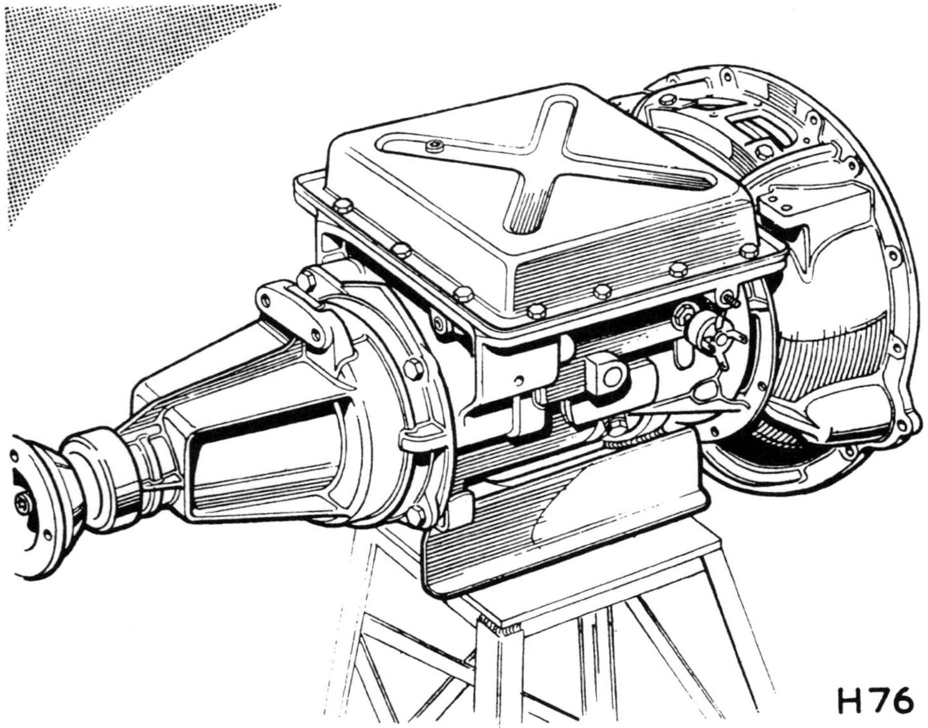

H76

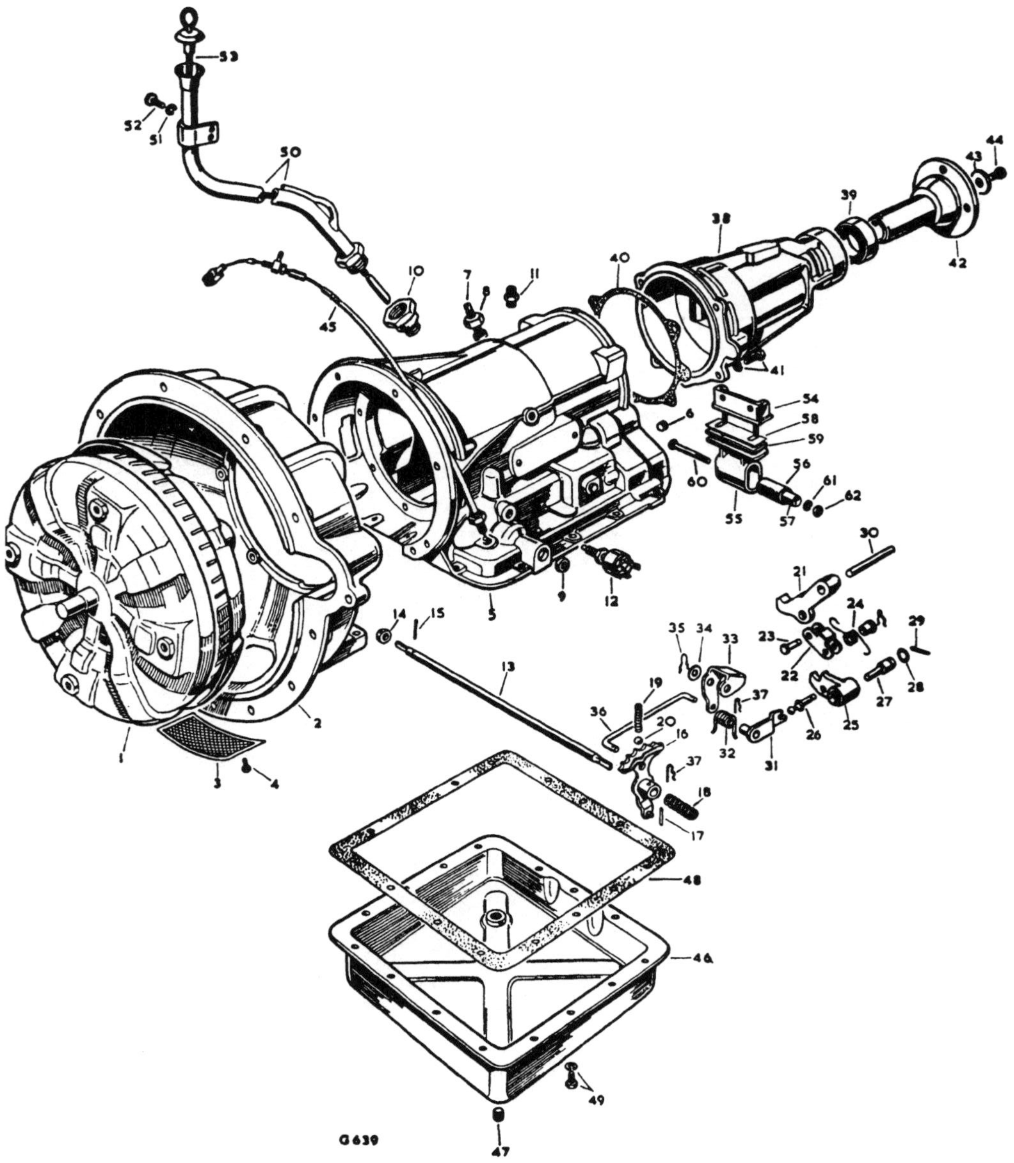

G 639

Transmission case

Transmission case

1 Torque converter assembly
2 Housing for torque converter
3 Stone guard
4 Special bolt fixing stone guard
5 Main case assembly
6 Pipe plug
7 Screw, rear servo adjusting
8 Nut, locking adjusting screw
9 Oil seal, manual control shaft
10 Adaptor for tube connector
11 Connector tube outlet, oil cooler
12 Inhibitor switch
13 Shaft, manual valve lever
14 Collar for shaft
15 Roll pin for collar
16 Lever, manual valve detent
17 Roll pin for lever
18 Spring for lever
19 Spring, manual valve detent
20 Ball ($\frac{3}{8}$ in. dia.), manual valve detent
21 Pawl, parking brake
22 Link for parking brake
23 Pin for toggle link, pawl end
24 Spring, parking brake release
25 Toggle lever
26 Pin for toggle lever, ball ended
27 Pin for toggle lever, shouldered
28 'O' ring for toggle lever
29 Roll pin fixing toggle lever pin
30 Anchor pin for pawl
31 Toggle lift lever, forked
32 Spring for lift lever
33 Torsion lever for parking brake
34 Plain washer for torsion lever
35 Retaining spring for torsion lever
36 Link for parking brake
37 Clip for linkage rod
38 Extension housing assembly
39 Oil seal for housing
40 Gasket for extension housing
41 Special bolt and washer fixing extension housing
42 Coupling flange
43 Plain washer for flange
44 Special screw fixing flange
45 Cable complete
46 Oil pan
47 Drain plug
48 Gasket for oil pan
49 Special bolt and washer fixing oil pan
50 Oil filler tube
51 Spring washer } Fixing oil filler tube
52 Set bolt, $\frac{1}{4}$ UNC x $\frac{1}{2}$ in. } Fixing oil filler tube
53 Dipstick
54 Mounting bracket
55 Stabiliser bracket
56 Bush for stabiliser bracket
57 Tube for stabiliser bracket
58 Shim, 12 SWG
59 Shim, 16 SWG
60 Bolt, $\frac{5}{16}$ UNF x $2\frac{3}{4}$ in. } Fixing stabiliser to sub-frame
61 Spring washer } Fixing stabiliser to sub-frame
62 Nut, $\frac{5}{16}$ UNF } Fixing stabiliser to sub-frame

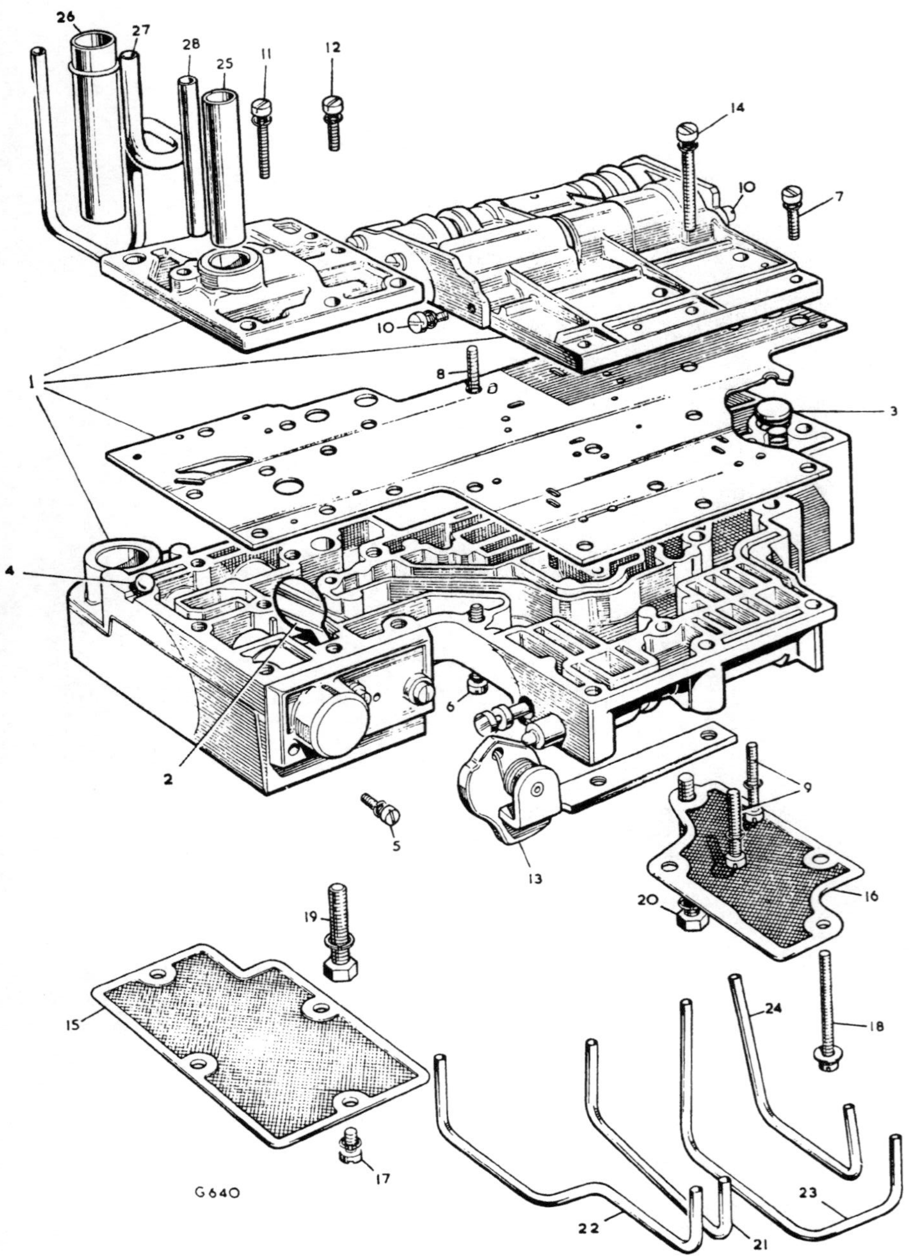

Valve bodies

Valve bodies

1 Valve bodies assembly
2 Check valve, front pump
3 Check valve, rear pump
4 Ball ($\frac{1}{4}$ in. dia.), converter check valve
5 Screw fixing end plate
6 Screw fixing valve body, upper
7 Screw fixing valve body, upper
8 Screw fixing valve body, upper
9 Screw fixing plate
10 Screw fixing end plates to upper valve body
11 Screw fixing plate
12 Screw fixing plate
13 Cam for downshift valve
14 Screw fixing cam
15 Oil strainer, front pump
16 Oil strainer, rear pump
17 Screw fixing strainer, front
18 Screw fixing strainer, rear
19 Bolt fixing valve body
20 Bolt fixing valve body
21 Tube, front servo apply
22 Tube, front servo release
23 Tube, rear clutch
24 Tube, rear servo
25 Tube, front pump outlet
26 Tube, front pump inlet
27 Tube, converter out and oil cooler inlet
28 Tube, converter, in

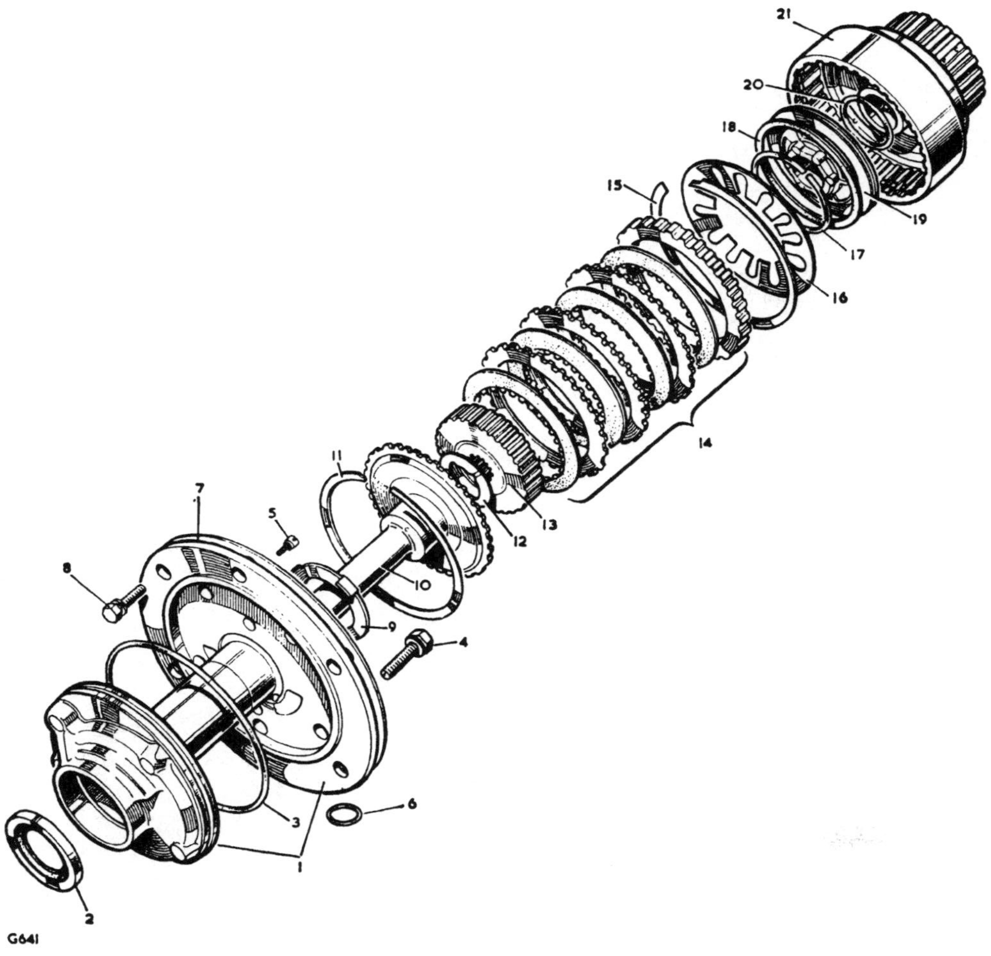

Front pump and front clutch

Front pump and front clutch

1 Front pump assembly
2 Seal for pump
3 'O' ring for pump
4 Bolt ($\frac{7}{8}$ in. long)
5 Screw ($\frac{5}{8}$ in. long)
6 'O' ring for pump tube
7 Gasket, pump adapter
8 Bolt fixing pump
9 Thrust washer
10 Input shaft
11 Snap-ring for input shaft
12 Thrust washer
13 Hub for front clutch
14 Clutch plates
15 Snap-ring for front clutch spring
16 Spring for front clutch
17 Bearing ring for front clutch spring
18 Sealing ring, large, piston front clutch
19 Piston, front clutch
20 'O' ring, small, piston front clutch
21 Cylinder, front clutch

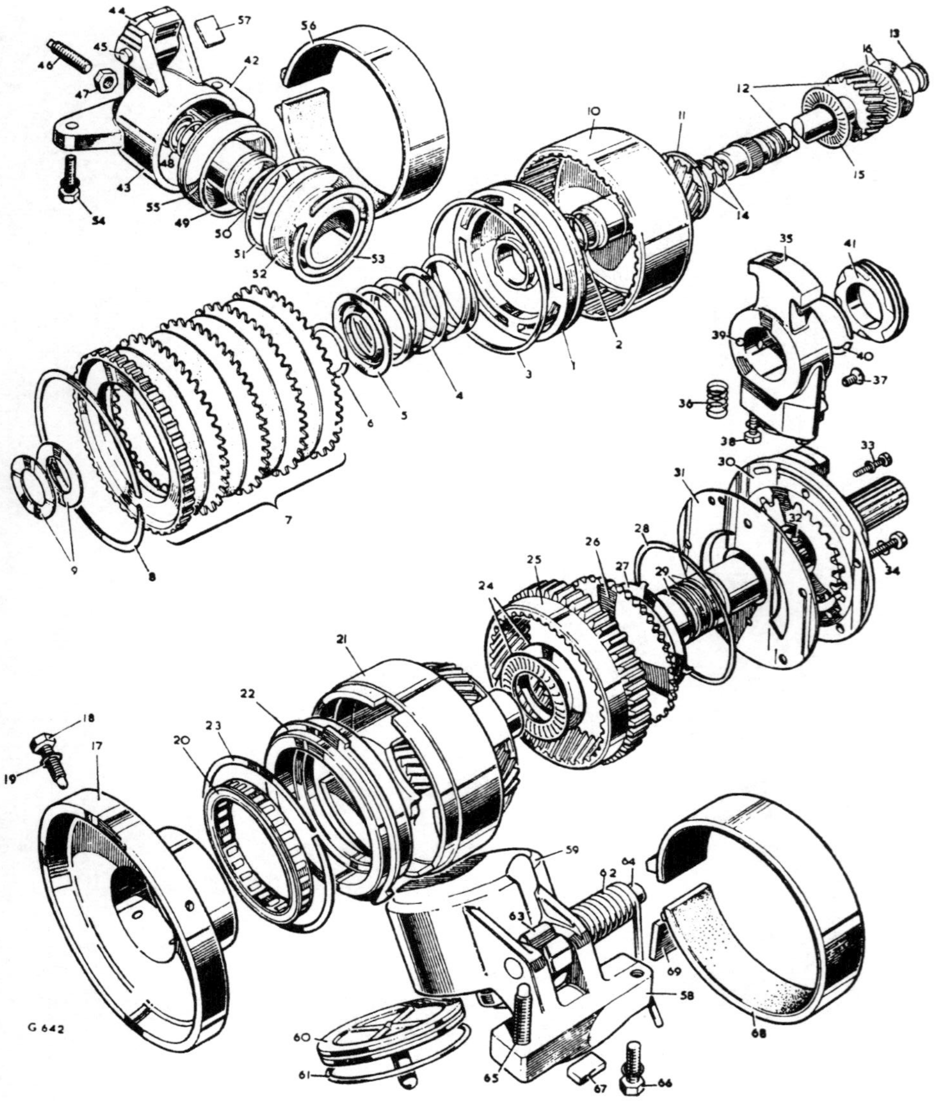

G 642

Rear clutch, rear pump, servo and governor

Rear clutch, rear pump servos and governor

1 Piston assembly, rear clutch
2 'O' ring, small, rear clutch piston
3 Sealing ring, large, rear clutch piston
4 Spring, rear clutch
5 Seat, rear clutch spring
6 Snap-ring for spring
7 Clutch plates
8 Snap-ring
9 Thrust washer
10 Front drum assembly
11 Oil seal ring
12 Forward sun gear
13 Oil seal ring, nylon
14 Oil seal ring
15 Thrust needle bearing
16 Thrust needle bearing and plate
17 Centre support
18 Bolt, centre support
19 Lockwasher, centre support
20 One-way clutch
21 Planet gears and rear drum assembly
22 Outer race, one-way clutch
23 Snap-ring, one-way clutch race
24 Thrust needle bearing and plate
25 Ring gear
26 Driven shaft
27 Thrust washer
28 Snap-ring for ring gear
29 Oil sealing ring, driven shaft
30 Rear pump assembly
31 Plate, rear pump
32 Key, rear pump drive
33 Screw } Fixing
34 Screw } rear pump
35 Governor assembly
36 Spring, governor
37 Lockscrew, governor cover plate
38 Screw, governor
39 Steel ball ($\frac{1}{4}$ in. dia.)
40 Snap-ring, governor
41 Gear, speedometer drive
42 Servo assembly, front
43 Body, front servo
44 Lever, front servo
45 Pivot pin, front servo
46 Adjusting screw, front servo
47 Locknut, adjusting screw
48 Spring, front servo
49 'O' ring, large, front servo piston
50 'O' ring, small, front servo piston
51 Oil sealing ring
52 Sleeve, front servo piston
53 Snap-ring, front servo piston
54 Bolt ($1\frac{3}{8}$ in. long) fixing front servo
55 Piston, front servo
56 Brake band, front servo
57 Strut for brake band
58 Servo assembly, rear
59 Body, rear servo
60 Piston, rear servo
61 'O' ring, piston
62 Spring, rear servo
63 Lever, rear servo
64 Pivot pin, rear servo
65 Bolt, rear servo
66 Bolt fixing rear servo
67 Magnet
68 Brake band, rear servo
69 Strut, brake band

Gear selector linkage, to adjust—Operation EE2-1

Workshop hand tools:
Spanner sizes: Open ended ½ in. AF, 7/16 in. AF

IMPORTANT

The gear selector linkage must be correctly adjusted to give satisfactory operation of the transmission unit. Ensure that the linkage is never allowed to over-ride the transmission detent; a definite 'click' must be felt in each selector position.

Selector lever on steering column at 'N' position

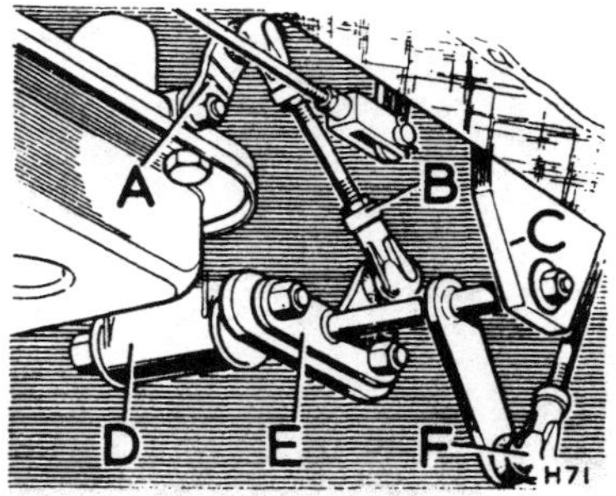

Disconnecting selector linkage, RHD model illustrated

A—Control lever on transmission unit
B—Adjustable rod, cross-shaft to unit
C—Support strap
D—Cross-shaft bracket
E—Cross-shaft
F—Control rod, cross-shaft to selector lever

Manual linkage, to adjust

1. Disconnect the linkage from the transmission lever and select 'N' on the quadrant.
2. Place the selector lever on the transmission in the central ('N') position.
3. Adjust the linkage as necessary at control rod 'B', illustrated, and reconnect linkage. Check quadrant gating in all selector positions, ensuring that linkage is not over-riding the transmission detent.

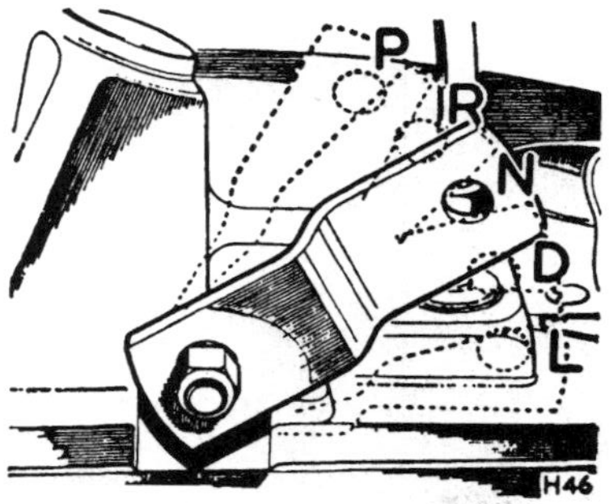

Selector lever on the transmission unit at the 'N'—neutral position

Starter inhibiter switch, to adjust—Operation EE2-2

Workshop hand tools:
Spanner sizes: Open ended 11/16 in. AF

Starter inhibiter switch, to adjust

1. If the unit is in the car, slide back both front seats as far as possible; lift out the carpet from the tunnel cover and remove the tunnel cover.
2. Ensure that the selector linkage is set correctly. Operation EE2-1.

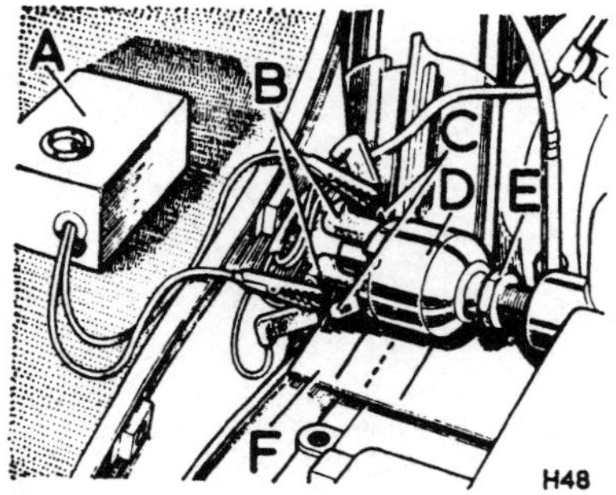

Adjusting inhibitor switch

A—Test lamp
B—Engine isolation terminals
C—Reverse light terminals
D—Starter inhibiter switch
E—Locknut
F—Card

3. Select 'D' (or 'L') position.

Special tools:
Test lamp

4. Disconnect the wiring from the switch at the 'Lucar' connectors.
5. Slacken the locknut and unscrew the switch to its fullest extent.
6. Connect a test lamp (consisting of a small dry battery and bulb) to the pair of terminals which are set at about 45°; these being the reversing light terminals.
7. Screw the switch into the maincase until the test lamp goes out. Note the position of the switch at this point by marking a piece of stiff card held against the transmission case.
8. Now connect the test lamp leads to the other pair of terminals on the switch.
9. Screw the switch in further until the light comes on. Note the position of the switch at this point by marking the card.
10. Turn the switch back until it is midway between the positions marked and tighten the locknut, taking care not to strip the thread of the light alloy switch body.
11. Disconnect the test lamp wiring and reconnect the car wiring.
12. Apply the handbrake firmly and chock the wheels. Apply footbrake during test.
13. Check that the starter operates only when the column selector is at 'P' or 'N'.

*Downshift valve cable, to adjust—Operation EE2-3

Workshop hand tools:
- Spanner size: $\frac{1}{2}$ in. AF
- $\frac{3}{16}$ in. AF, $\frac{1}{4}$ in. AF Allen keys

Special tools:
- Pressure gauge and tachometer, Rover Part No. 601284
- Torque wrench set, Rover Part No. 601285.

IMPORTANT

The downshift valve cable must be correctly adjusted to give satisfactory operation of the transmission unit. For production purposes the adjustment is pre-set at the factory where a stop is crimped on to the inner cable at the engine end.

If, however, the stop has not been crimped, or if it is necessary to check the adjustment of the cable, carry out one of the following two procedures. **Always adjust carburetter first.**

Method A

Adjusting downshift valve cable, using service test gauges

1. Chock front wheels of the car and apply handbrake firmly. Apply footbrake during test.
2. Remove the line pressure take-off plug from the rear of the transmission case, using an Allen key.
3. Connect the line pressure gauge to the pressure take-off point.

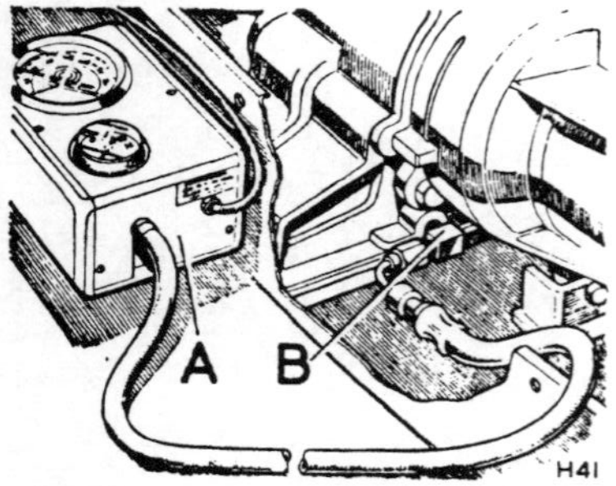

Pressure gauge connected to transmission

A—Pressure gauge
B—Pressure take-off connection

4. Connect the tachometer leads:
   Red lead to battery positive (+).
   The live terminal of the starter solenoid being a convenient take-off point.
   Black lead to battery negative (—).
   Any good earthing point on the engine.
   Green lead to the CB terminal on the side of the distributor.

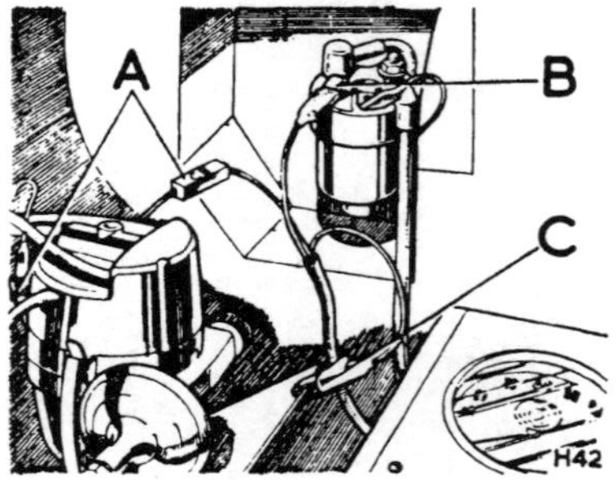

Tachometer connected to engine

A—Contact breaker connection
B—Positive connection
C—Negative connection

5. Start the engine and allow to warm up.
   Take the line pressure reading when engine is running at 500 rpm in 'D'.
   Increase the rpm to 1,000 when the line pressure should increase by 15 to 20 lb sq in. (1,05 to 1,40 kg/cm²).
   If the pressure rise is less than 15 lb sq in. (1,05 kg/cm²), the effective length of the outer cable should be increased by screwing out the cable adjuster.
   If the pressure rise is more than 20 lb sq in. (1,40 kg/cm²), then the effective length of the cable should be decreased by screwing in the cable adjuster.

Operations which are identified by an asterisk (*) can be carried out with the automatic transmission installed in the car.

Operation EE2-3—*continued*

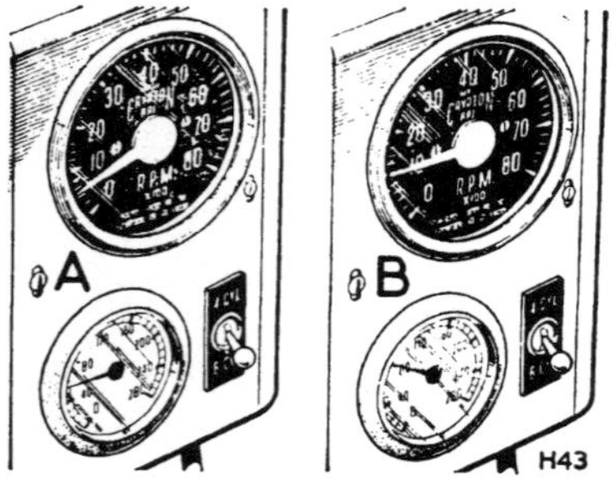

RPM and pressure reading using test gauge

A—500 rpm—Approximate pressure: 60 lb sq in. (4,2 kg/cm²)
B—1000 rpm—Approximate pressure: 80 lb sq in. (5,6 kg/cm²)

Method B

Adjusting downshift valve cable, visual method

1. Drain the fluid from the transmission oil pan and remove the oil pan. Operation EE2-7.
2. Ensure that the accelerator pedal is fully released and that the carburetter butterfly is fully closed.

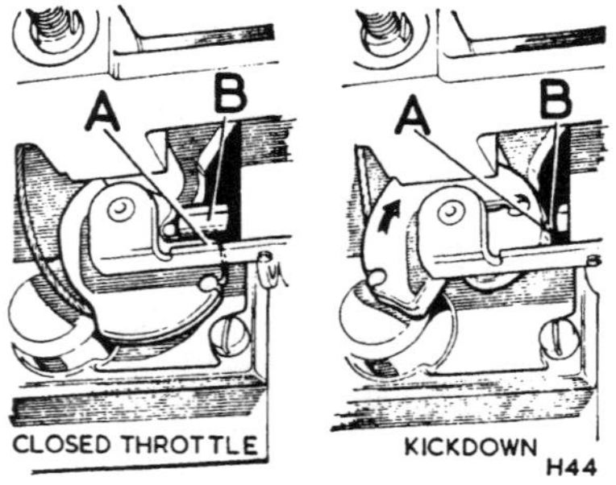

Downshift valve cable adjustment, visual method

Closed throttle { A—Heel of the cam; B—Downshift valve }
Kickdown { A—Constant radius of cam; B—Downshift valve }

3. Check the position of the downshift valve cam; the heel of the cam should contact the full diameter of the downshift valve, with all the slack of the inner cable taken up.
4. With accelerator pedal fully depressed to kick-down position and the carburetter butterfly fully open, the constant radius area of the valve cam should be the point of contact with the downshift valve.

Fluid level, automatic transmission—Every 5,000 miles (8,000 km) Operation EE2-4

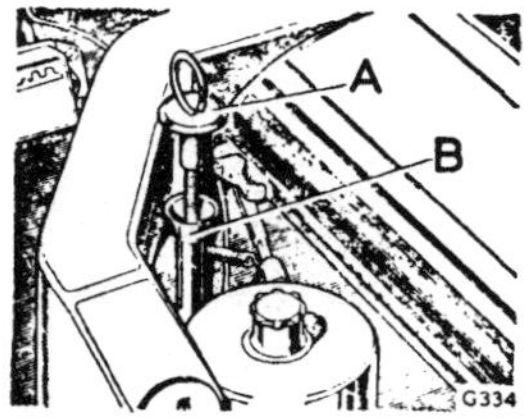

Fluid level dipstick plug in engine compartment

A—Dipstick
B—Tube for dipstick

The torque converter and automatic gearbox are lubricated as one unit. As the fluid for operating the torque converter is fed from the transmission casing it is essential when checking the level or topping-up the automatic gearbox that the engine is run at idling speed for about two minutes to transfer fluid from transmission casing to torque converter, otherwise a false level reading will be obtained. Do not add anti-friction additives to the automatic transmission fluid. Check as follows:

1. Absolute cleanliness is essential. Use only nylon rag for cleaning.
2. Stand car on level ground. Engine idling and selector at the 'P' position.
3. Lift bonnet to expose dipstick, which is adjacent to the air cleaner elbow.
4. Clean area around dipstick hole. Remove dipstick, wipe dry and check fluid level. Take the dipstick reading immediately after the dipstick has been fully inserted to avoid misreadings by splashing. The difference between full and low marks on dipstick represents approximately one pint (0,5 litre). See paragraph 6.
5. With the engine idling and the selector at 'P', add the recommended grade of fluid to bring the level up to the 'full' mark. Do not overfill.
6. When the transmission is hot, top up to the upper mark on the side of the dipstick marked 'HOT'. With transmission cold, top up to the upper mark on the side of the dipstick marked 'COLD'. It is most important to ascertain if the transmission is hot or cold when topping up and to use the appropriate mark, otherwise over-filling or under-filling will result.
7. If significant topping up is required, check for leakage at oil seals and sump joint; rectify immediately.

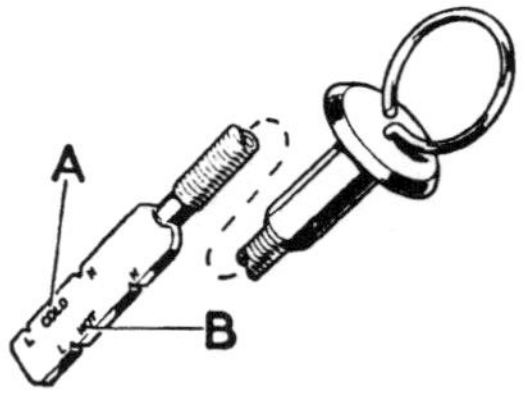

Fluid level dipstick

A—Transmission cold, top up to upper mark on 'COLD' side of dipstick
B—Transmission hot, top up to upper mark on 'HOT' side of dipstick

Automatic transmission, to remove and refit—Operation EE2-5

Important Notes

1. This operation does NOT involve removal of the engine from the car.
2. If necessary, the gearbox can be removed, leaving the torque converter in position. Proceed as detailed in this operation but: Exclude items 4, 11, 20, 22, 23, 24, 27, 28 and 29. Include the following additional items:
   1. Place a suitable container under the centre of the unit, to catch the oil from the torque converter when gearbox is removed.
   2. Remove transmission coupling flange, $\frac{5}{16}$ in. AF Allen key required.
   3. Remove the six bolts securing gearbox to bell housing.
   4. Withdraw unit slightly, then turn anti-clockwise to the inverted position. Allow oil to drain away.
   5. Lift the extension casing up into the car and lower the unit away from beneath the car.

Workshop hand tools:
Pliers: long nosed
Spanner sizes:
Open ended $\frac{7}{16}$ in. AF, $\frac{1}{2}$ in. AF, $\frac{9}{16}$ in. AF, $1\frac{5}{16}$ in. AF
Sockets $\frac{1}{2}$ in. AF, $\frac{9}{16}$ in. AF
Allen key $\frac{1}{4}$ in. AF

Special tools:
Retainer clip for converter, Part No. 601467

High standards of cleanliness are required when working on the automatic transmission. Before attempting to remove or dismantle the unit, clean the outside of the transmission case thoroughly with petrol/paraffin or an industrial cleaning solvent.

Place the car on a suitable floor lifting hoist, but carry out the prior operations before raising the car

Torque converter and gearbox, remove

Prior operations

1. Disconnect the battery.
2. Uncouple the front exhaust pipe at the manifold.
3. Remove the engine oil filter housing.
4. Disconnect the starter motor connections and remove the top fixing bolt.
5. Remove sparking plugs to release engine compression.
6. Withdraw clevis pin from downshift valve cable at bracket on LH side of flywheel housing. Clevis is secured by a split pin.

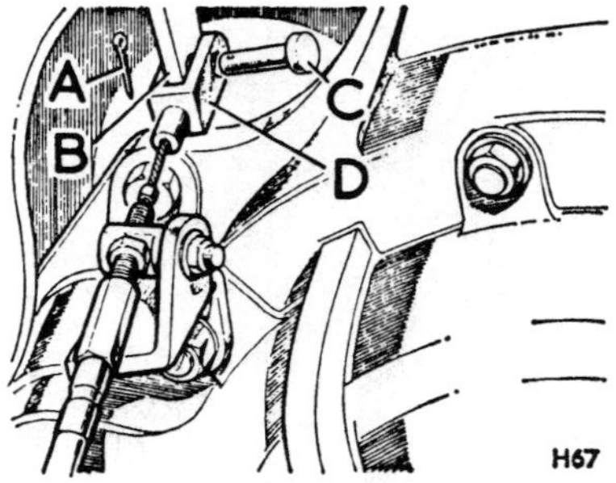

Downshift cable clevis

A—Split pin B—Relay lever C—Clevis pin D—Clevis

From inside the car

7. Push both front seats back as far as possible.
8. Remove the front carpets.
9. Remove the tunnel cover.

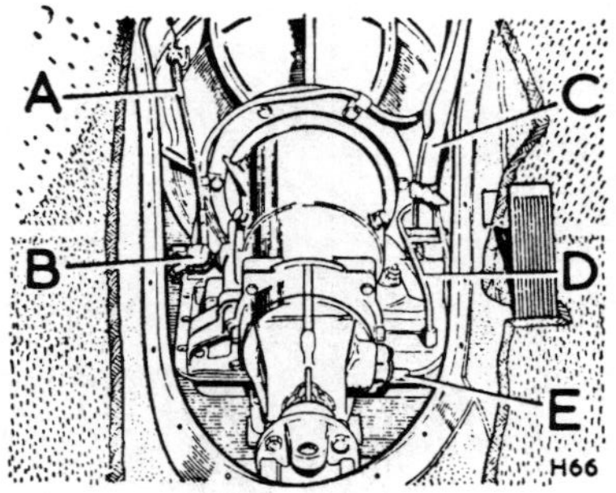

Access to transmission with tunnel cover removed

A—Downshift cable
B—Starter inhibitor switch
C—Dipstick tube
D—Oil cooler pipe
E—Speedometer cable

10. Uncouple the propeller shaft from the driving flange of the transmission unit.
11. Remove the bell housing fixings which are accessible through the tunnel aperture.

Operation EE2-5—*continued*

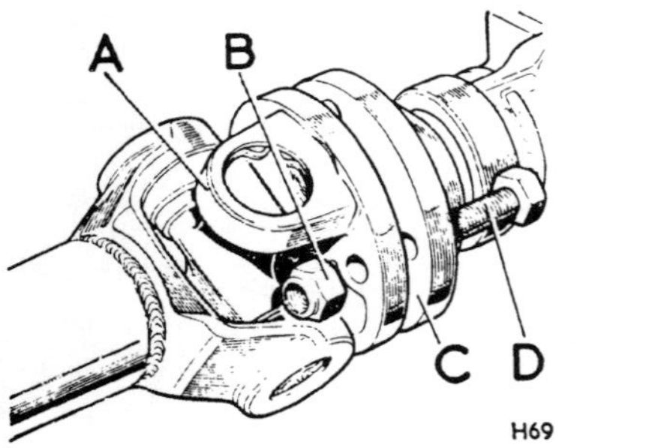

Disconnecting propeller shaft

A—Universal joint
B—Fixing nut
C—Transmission coupling flange
D—Fixing bolt

12. Disconnect the oil cooler pipes at the transmission case end.

13. Unscrew the transmission dipstick tube at the union on the maincasing. Lift out the dipstick and tube through the engine compartment.

14. Detach the wiring from the starter inhibiter switch at the 'Lucar' connectors.

15. Raise the car on the lifting hoist.

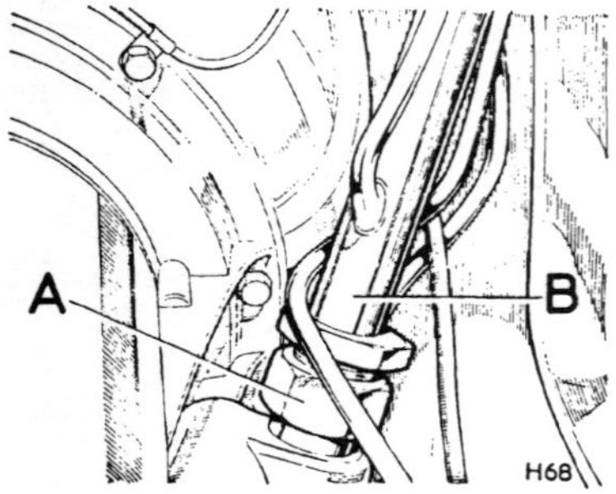

Dipstick tube

A—Union nut
B—Dipstick tube

From below the car

16. Drain the fluid from the oil pan by removing the drain plug with an Allen key. If the car has recently returned from a run take care when draining the fluid as the temperature of the fluid may be hot enough to cause scalding.

17. Disconnect the selector linkage at the lever on the maincasing.

18. Uncouple the front exhaust pipe at the flange adjacent to the rear cross-member of the sub-frame.

19. Disconnect the front exhaust pipe at the bell housing mounting bracket and remove the pipe.

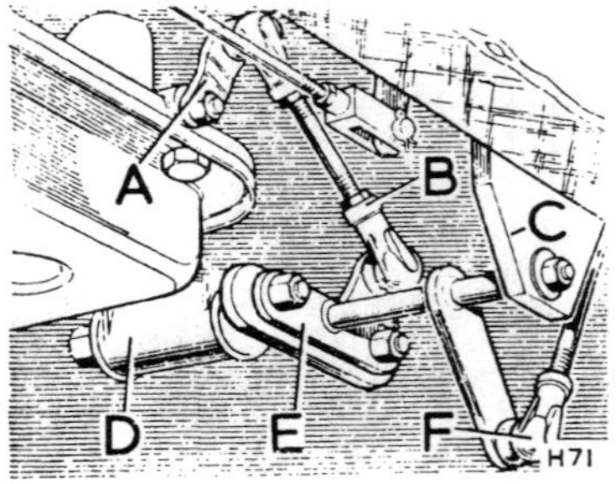

Disconnecting the selector linkage, RHD model illustrated

A—Control lever on transmission unit
B—Adjustable rod, cross-shaft to unit
C—Support strap
D—Cross-shaft bracket
E—Cross-shaft
F—Control rod, cross-shaft to selector lever

20. Remove the stone guards from the torque converter bell housing.

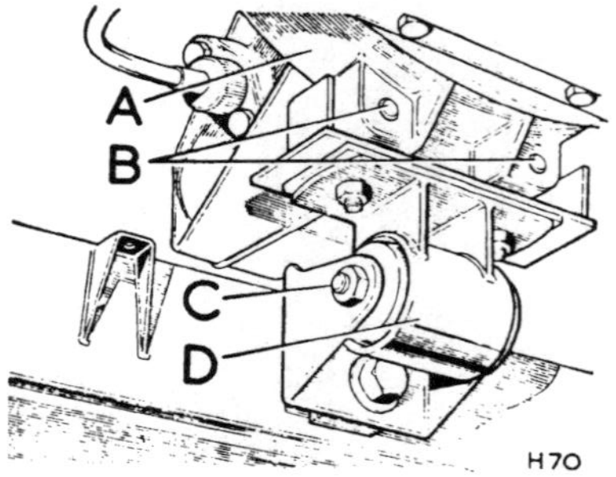

Disconnecting the rear mounting

A—Extension housing
B—Bolts, rear mounting bracket to extension housing
C—Bolt, for stabiliser bracket
D—Stabiliser bracket

Operation EE2-5—*continued*

21. Remove the two bolts securing the mounting bracket to the transmission extension casing and remove the mounting from the cross-member of the sub-frame.

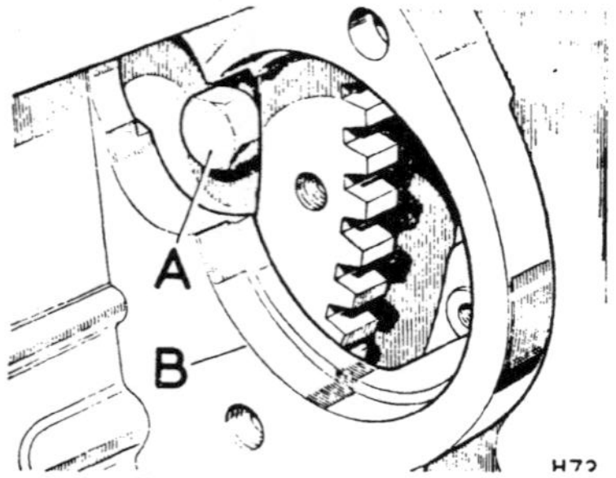

Torque converter removal

A—Bolt, fixing converter
B—Starter motor aperture

22. Remove the starter motor (the upper fixings having been already removed).

23. Rotate the flywheel and remove the four converter mounting bolts through the starter motor aperture.

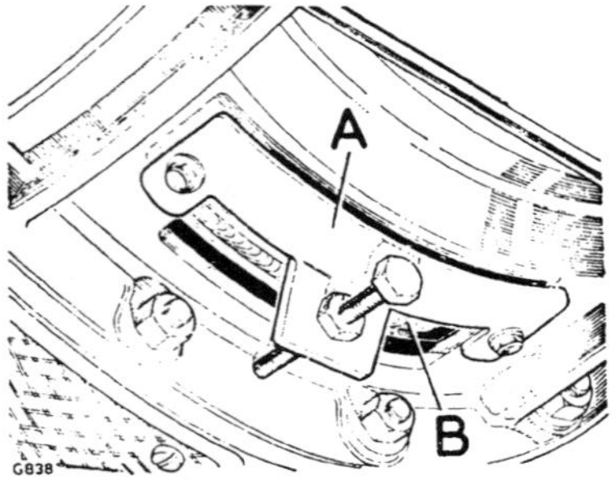

Torque converter clip in position

A—Converter clip
B—Torque converter

24. Secure the retainer clip, Part No. 601467 to the torque converter flange and the bell housing, as illustrated.
25. Detach the propeller shaft centre support bearing from the underside of the body.
26. Place a suitable support beneath the transmission unit.
27. Remove the remaining fixings securing the torque converter bell housing to the flywheel housing.
28. Lift up the transmission unit slightly and pull it back; ease the bell housing off the mounting studs.
29. Lift the extension casing up into the car and lower the unit away from beneath the car.

Torque converter and transmission, refit

1. Reverse removal procedure and ensure that the bolt fixing the bell housing to the flywheel housing are tightened **before** the bolts fixing the torque converter to the engine drive plate.

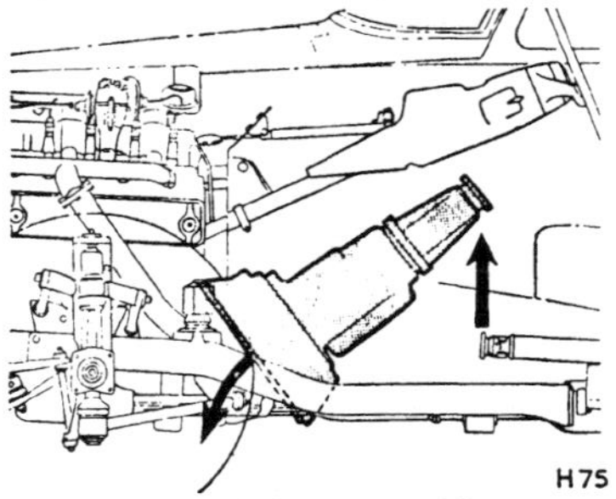

Transmission being removed from car

2. Tightening torques:
   Bell housing to flywheel housing: 30 lb ft (4,0 mkg)
   Torque converter to engine drive plate: 32 lb ft (4,4 mkg)
3. Adjust the selector linkage, starter inhibiter switch and downshift valve cable in accordance with the instructions given in Operations EE2-1, EE2-2 and EE2-3.
4. Fill the transmission with 10 pints (12 US pints, 5,5 litres) transmission fluid of the recommended grade:
   (a) The car should be on a level surface.
   (b) Select 'P' and allow engine to idle for two minutes.
   (c) Add fluid in small quantities. With engine still idling in 'P', wipe dipstick with a non-fluffy rag or clean paper and take frequent readings by inserting the dipstick and withdrawing it immediately.

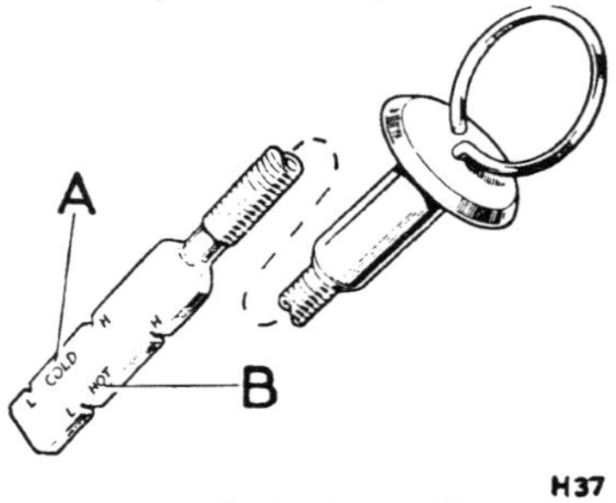

Dipstick, showing markings

A—Use these markings when fluid is cold
B—Use these markings when fluid is hot

   (d) With the transmission cold, fill to the high mark on the side of the dipstick marked 'cold'.

Capacity of transmission unit from dry:
14 Imperial pints; 17 US pints; 8,0 litres.

Torque converter and bell housing, to remove and refit—Operation EE2-6

Workshop hand tools:
Pliers: long nosed

Spanner sizes:
Open ended $\frac{1}{2}$ in. AF, $\frac{7}{16}$ in. AF, $\frac{9}{16}$ in. AF, $1\frac{5}{16}$ in. AF
Sockets $\frac{1}{2}$ in. AF, $\frac{9}{16}$ in. AF
Allen key $\frac{1}{4}$ in. AF

Special tools:
Retainer clip for converter, Part No. 601467

Torque converter and bell housing, to remove

Prior operations:

1. Remove automatic gearbox. Operation EE2-5.
2. Support the transmission unit and remove the retainer clip, Part No. 601467.
3. Withdraw the torque converter taking care during this operation, as the unit will be full of oil.
4. Remove the six bolts and washers securing the bell housing to the main casing and withdraw the bell housing.

Torque converter and bell housing, to refit

1. Reverse removal procedure.
2. Tightening torques:
   Transmission case to bell housing: 8 to 10 lb ft (1,0 to 1,4 mkg)

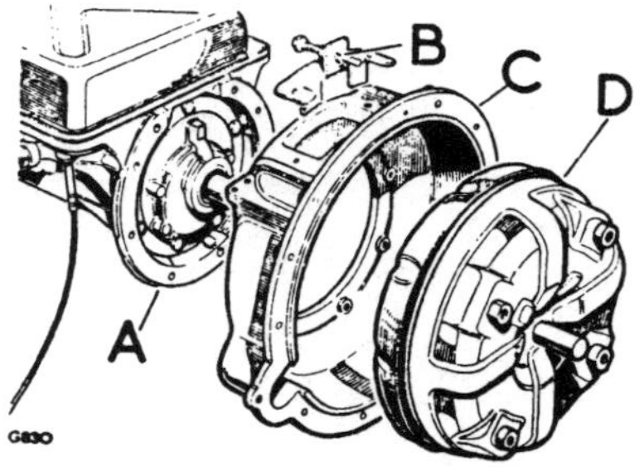

Torque converter and bell housing remove

A—Gearbox unit
B—Retainer clip for converter
C—Bell housing
D—Torque converter

*Oil pan and valve bodies, to remove and refit—Operation EE2-7

Workshop hand tools:

Spanner sizes:
Sockets $\frac{7}{16}$ in. AF, $\frac{1}{2}$ in. AF
Open ended $\frac{7}{16}$ in. AF, $\frac{1}{2}$ in. AF
Screwdriver, large, Allen key $\frac{1}{4}$ in. AF, Pliers, long nosed

Special tools:
Gearbox cradle, Rover Part No. 601280
Torque wrench set, Rover Part No. 601285

Instructions for overhauling the valve bodies is given in Part Three of this Section

Oil pan and valve bodies, to remove

Operations 1 and 2 apply only if the unit is fitted to the car.

1. If necessary, disconnect the selector linkage from the lever on the side of the transmission unit. Remove the cross-shaft bracket secured by two bolts.

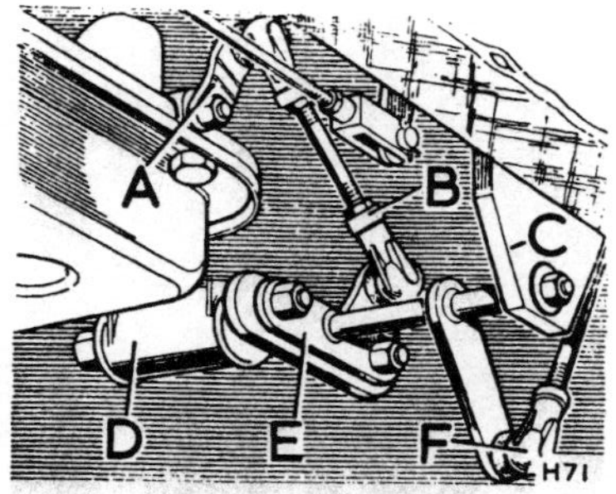

Cross-shaft bracket, RHD model illustrated

A—Control lever on gearbox
B—Adjustable rod (cross-shaft to gearbox)
C—Support strap
D—Cross-shaft bracket
E—Cross-shaft
F—Control rod (cross-shaft to selector lever)

2. Drain the fluid from the oil pan. Take great care if the car has just returned from a run as the fluid will be hot enough to cause scalding.

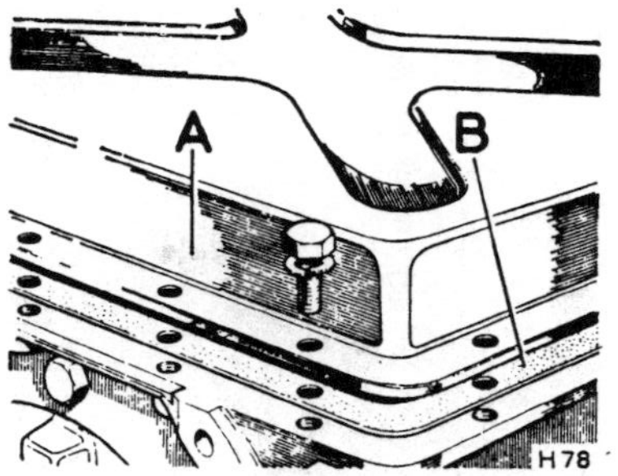

Removing the oil pan

A—Oil pan B—Gasket for oil pan

When the oil has been drained refit the plug. Smear thread of plug with Loctite sealant grade CV, Rover Part No. 601168. It is not possible to completely drain the oil pan.

3. Remove the oil pan and gasket secured by fifteen bolts and spring washers.

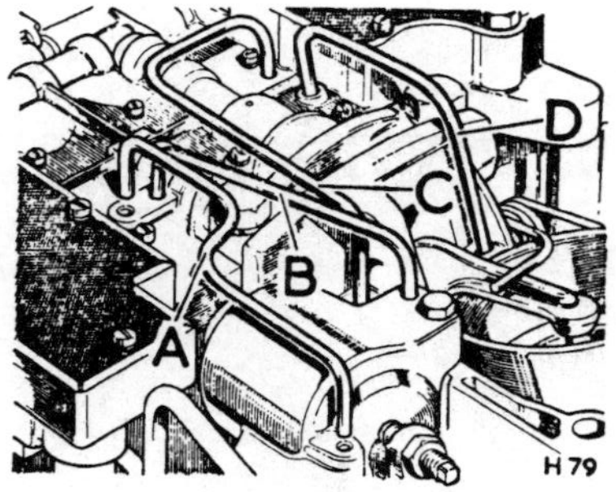

Location of oil tubes in valve body

A—Tube, front servo release
B—Tube, front servo apply
C—Tube, rear clutch
D—Tube, rear servo

4. Withdraw the four oil tubes from the valve bodies assembly. These tubes are a push fit into their respective locations and should be removed by carefully levering out of position with a screwdriver. Take care that no distortion or damage is caused to the tubes.

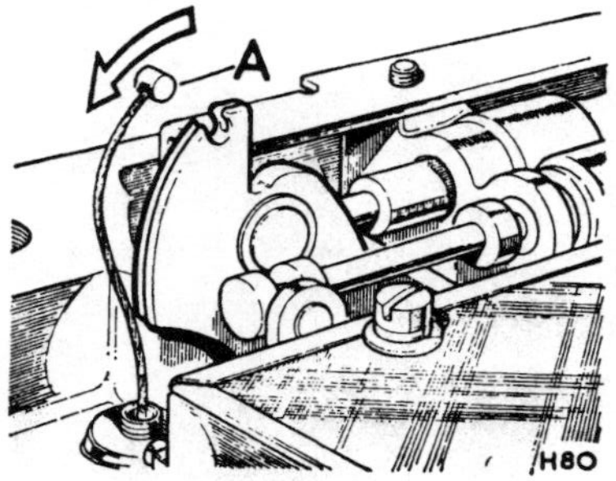

Down-shift valve cam and cable

A—Cable for downshift valve

Operations which are identified by an asterisk (*) can be carried out with the automatic transmission installed in the car.

Operation EE2-7—*continued*

5. If unit is still fitted to the car, disconnect the down-shift cable at the throttle end. Pull the down-shift valve cam forwards, as indicated by the arrow, and release the cable at the valve bodies end.
6. Lift off the valve bodies assembly which is secured by three bolts and spring washers. Take care not to disturb the oil tubes located between the valve body and front pump casing.

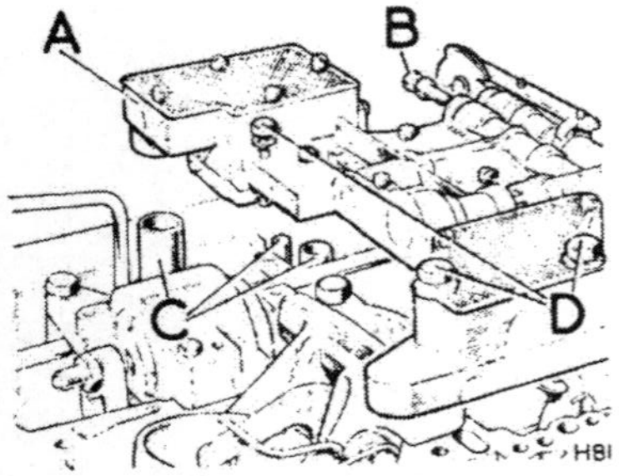

Valve bodies assembly

A—Valve bodies
B—Manual control valve
C—Oil tubes
D—Bolts fixing valve bodies

Oil pan and valve bodies, to refit

1. When placing the valve bodies into position ensure that the oil tubes between valve body and front pump casing are correctly located, flange on front pump inlet tube must be towards front pump, and that the peg on the manual valve detent lever engages in the groove of the manual control valve.

   If the oil tubes have been inadvertently disturbed, it is important that the 'O' ring, which is located at the pump end of the front pump inlet tube, is not omitted or dropped into the transmission casing.

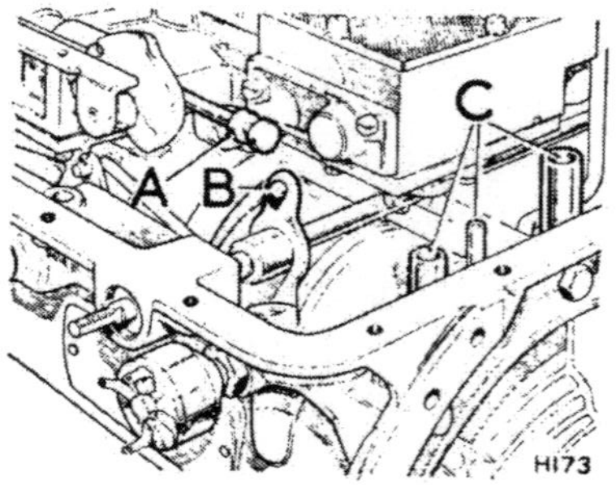

Engaging groove of manual control valve with peg on detent lever

A—Groove in manual control valve
B—Peg on detent lever
C—Oil tubes

2. Tighten the valve bodies securing bolts to a torque of 4 to 5 lb ft (0,55 to 0,7 mkg).
3. Pull down-shift valve cam forward, as indicated by the arrow, and connect the cable. Reconnect cable at accelerator end if unit is still fitted to vehicle.
4. Replace the four oil tubes. Ensure that they are pushed firmly into position.
5. Check adjustment of downshift cable in accordance with method 'B'. Operation EE2-3
6. Use a new oil pan gasket and locate it on transmission casing with petroleum jelly. Fit oil pan and tighten the bolts to a torque figure of 8 to 10 lb ft (1,0 to 1,4 mkg).
7. If unit is in the vehicle, fit and connect the selector linkage. Check adjustment. Operation EE2-1.
8. If the above operation has been carried out with the unit in the vehicle, refill with fluid of the recommended grade. Capacity: 14 Imperial pints, 17 US pints, 8,0 litres.

*Front servo, to remove, refit and adjust—Operation EE2-8

Workshop hand tools:

Spanner sizes:
- Sockets ½ in. AF, $\frac{9}{16}$ in. AF
- Open ended $\frac{7}{16}$ in. AF, ½ in. AF, $\frac{9}{16}$ in. AF
- Screwdriver, large
- Allen key ¼ in. AF

Special tools:
- Gearbox cradle, Rover Part No. 601280
- Torque wrench set, Rover Part No. 601285
- Spintorq screwdriver set, Rover Part No. 601286
- Front servo gauge, Rover Part No. 601287

Instructions for overhauling the front servo are given in Part Three of this Section.

Front servo, to remove

Operations 1 and 2 apply only if the unit is fitted to the car.

1. If necessary, disconnect the selector linkage from the lever on the side of the transmission unit. Remove the cross-shaft bracket secured by two bolts.

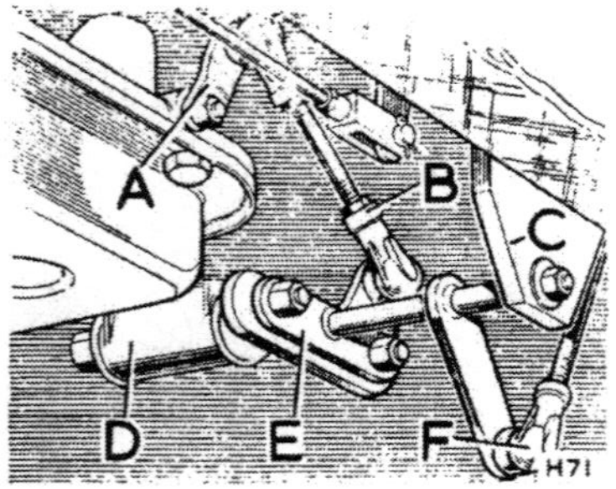

Cross-shaft bracket, RHD model illustrated

A—Control lever on gearbox
B—Adjustable rod (cross-shaft to gearbox)
C—Support strap
D—Cross-shaft bracket
E—Cross-shaft
F—Control rod (cross-shaft to selector lever)

2. Drain the fluid from the oil pan. Take great care if the car has just returned from a run as the fluid will be hot enough to cause scalding. It is not possible to completely drain the oil pan. When the fluid has drained, refit the plug. Smear thread of plug with Loctite sealant grade CV, Rover Part No. 601168.
3. Remove the oil pan and gasket secured by fifteen bolts and spring washers.

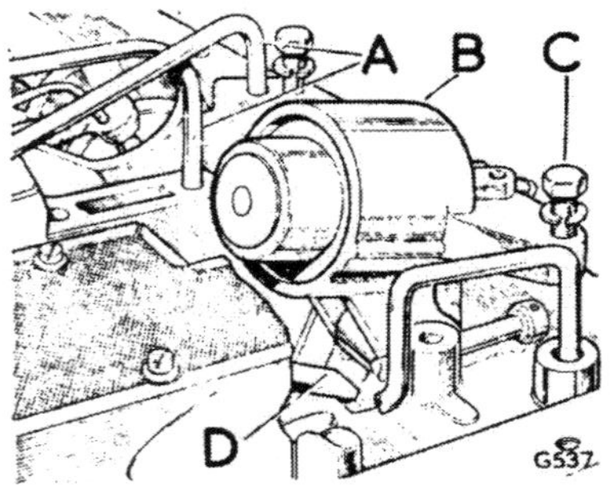

Front servo, removing oil tubes

A—Oil tubes for front servo
B—Front servo
C—Bolt fixing servo
D—Strut for servo

4. Withdraw the two oil tubes fitted between front servo and valve bodies. These tubes are a push fit into their locations. If necessary, very carefully lever them out using a screwdriver. Take care not to cause distortion or damage.
5. Slacken locknut and adjusting screw to relieve tension and remove the front servo, retained by two bolts and spring washers.

   Take care not to lose the servo strut which is a loose item.

Front servo, to refit

1. Install the servo into the main casing. To facilitate location of the servo strut, attach it to the servo lever with petroleum jelly and ensure that it engages with the slot in the brake band. Tighten the two servo fixing bolts to a torque figure of 8 to 10 lb ft (1,0 to 1,4 mkg).
2. Replace the oil tubes. Ensure that they are pushed firmly into position.

Operations which are identified by an asterisk (*) can be carried out with the automatic transmission installed in the car.

Operation EE2-8—*continued*

Front servo, to adjust

The oil pan must be removed to enable the front servo to be adjusted.

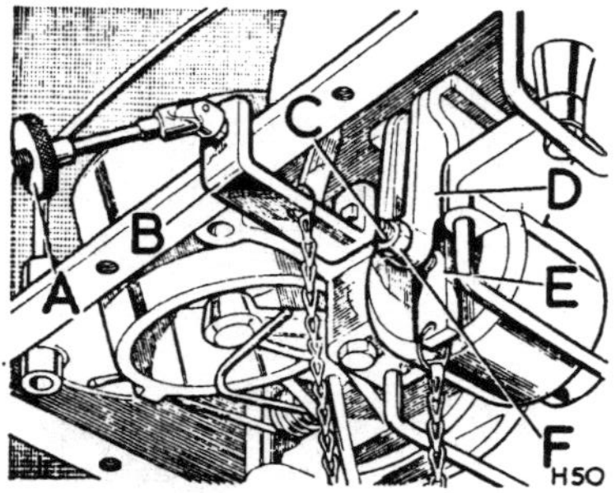

Front brake band, to adjust

A—Spintorq screwdriver
B—Adaptor
C—Adjusting screw for front servo
D—Servo lever
E—Gauge block
F—Locknut for servo adjusting screw

1. Slacken the locknut and unscrew the adjuster Pull the servo lever outwards and place the front servo gauge between the adjusting screw and the servo piston pin.

2. Tighten the servo lever adjusting screw to a torque figure of 10 lb in. (0,11 mkg), using the spintorq screwdriver and the adaptor attached to the gauge block, together with the universal joint.

3. Using a screwdriver between servo body and adjuster lever, release pressure from gauge block and withdraw it.

4. Tighten adjuster lever locknut to a torque figure of 15 to 20 lb ft (2,0 to 2,8 mkg)

5. Use a new oil pan gasket and locate it on transmission casing with petroleum jelly. Fit oil pan and tighten the bolts to a torque figure of 8 to 10 lb ft (1,0 to 1,4 mkg).

6. If the operation has been carried out with the unit in the vehicle, refill with the recommended grade of fluid. Capacity: 14 Imperial pints, 17 US pints, 8,0 litres.

*Rear servo, to remove, refit and adjust—Operation EE2-9

Workshop hand tools:

Spanner sizes:
Sockets, $\frac{1}{2}$ in. AF, $\frac{9}{16}$ in. AF, $\frac{3}{4}$ in. AF
Open ended $\frac{7}{16}$ in. AF, $\frac{1}{2}$ in. AF, $\frac{3}{4}$ in. AF
Screwdriver, large, Allen key, $\frac{1}{4}$ in. AF

Special tools:
Gearbox cradle, Rover Part No. 601280
Torque wrench set, Rover Part No. 601285

Instructions for overhauling the rear servo are given in Part Three of this Section.

Rear servo, to remove

Operations 1 and 2 apply only if the unit is fitted to the car.

1. If necessary, disconnect the selector linkage from the lever on the side of the transmission unit and remove the cross-shaft bracket secured by two bolts.

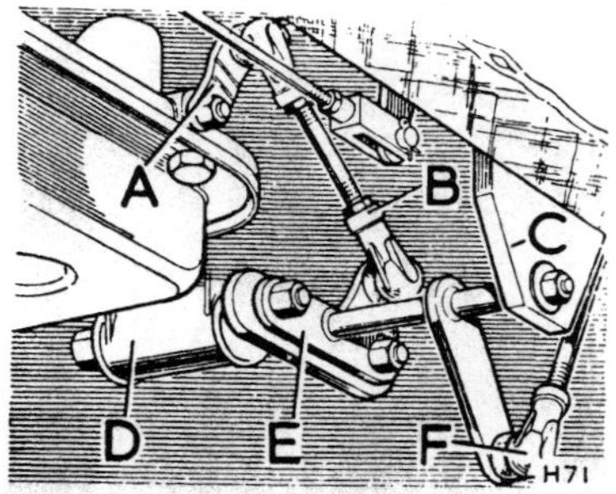

Cross-shaft bracket, RHD model illustrated

A—Control lever on gearbox
B—Adjustable rod (cross-shaft to gearbox)
C—Support strap
D—Cross-shaft bracket
E—Cross-shaft
F—Control rod (cross-shaft to selector lever)

2. Drain the fluid from the oil pan. Take great care if the car has just returned from a run as the fluid will be hot enough to cause scalding. It is not possible to completely drain the oil pan.
When the oil has drained, refit the drain plug. Smear thread of plug with Loctite sealant, grade CV, Rover Part No. 601168.

3. Remove the oil pan secured by fifteen bolts and spring washers.

4. Withdraw the oil tubes between the rear servo and valve body, rear clutch to valve body and front servo to valve body. They are a push fit into their respective locations. If necessary very carefully lever out using a screwdriver. Take care not to cause distortion or damage.

5. Lift off the magnet from the rear bolt then remove the servo retained by two bolts and spring washers. Note that the longer bolt is special as it has a dowel end to locate the centre support. Take care not to lose the servo strut which is a loose item.

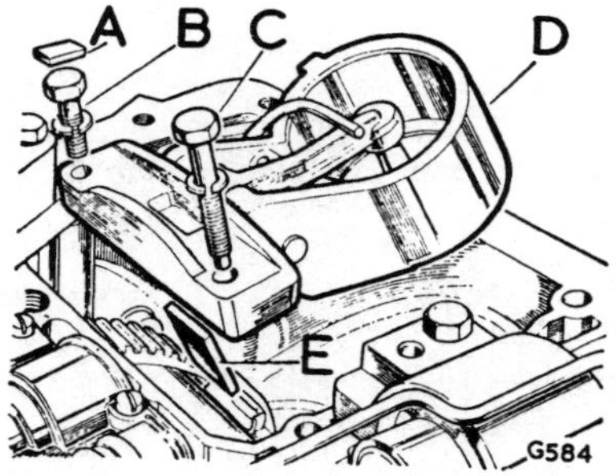

Rear servo, to remove

A—Magnet
B—Bolt fixing servo, short
C—Special bolt fixing servo
D—Rear servo
E—Strut for rear servo

Rear servo, to refit

1. Install the rear servo into the transmission case. Ensure that the brake band is located on the head of the adjustment bolt. To facilitate location of the servo strut, attach it to the servo lever with petroleum jelly, make sure that the strut engages with the slot in the brake band. The special bolt must be fitted into the hole adjacent to the centre cross-support of the transmission case. The magnet should be located on the head of the rear bolt. Tighten the two fixing bolts to a torque figure of 10 to 13 lb ft (1,4 to 1,7 mkg).

2. Replace the oil tubes. Ensure that they are pushed firmly into position.

3. Use a new oil pan gasket and locate it on the transmission casing with petroleum jelly. Fit oil pan and tighten the bolts to a torque figure of 8 to 10 lb ft (1,0 to 1,4 mkg). Connect selector linkage and check adjustment. Operation EE2-1.

Operations which are identified by an asterisk (*) can be carried out with the automatic transmission installed in the car.

Operation EE2-9—*continued*

Rear servo, adjusting the brake band

1. The adjuster for the rear band servo is located on the outside of the transmission case. When the unit is fitted in the car the adjuster is accessible from inside the car by removing the tunnel cover.

2. Slacken the locknut of the adjusting screw.

3. Using the torque wrench adaptor tighten the adjusting screw to a torque figure of 10 lb ft (1,4 mkg), then turn it back one complete turn and tighten the locknut to 25 to 30 lb ft (3,5 to 4,0 mkg).

4. If the operation has been carried out with the unit in vehicle, replace the tunnel cover, then refill unit with recommended grade of fluid. Capacity: 14 Imperial pints (17 US pints, 8,0 litres).

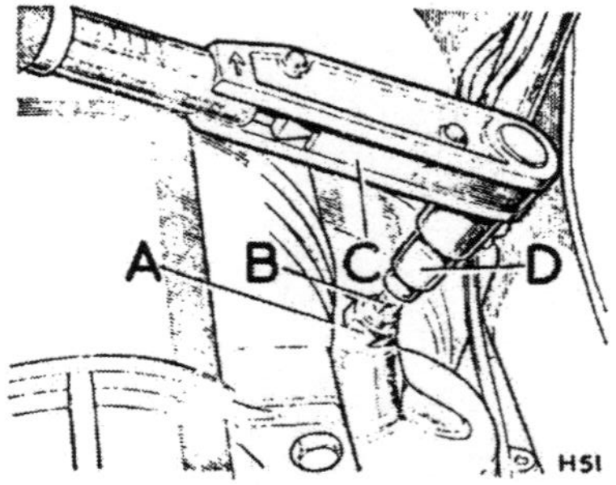

Rear brake band, to adjust

A—Locknut for adjuster
B—External adjusting screw
C—Torque wrench
D—Adaptor for torque wrench

Front pump, to remove and refit—Operation EE2-10

Workshop hand tools:

Spanner sizes:

Sockets $\frac{7}{16}$ in. AF, $\frac{1}{2}$ in. AF
Open ended $\frac{7}{16}$ in. AF, $\frac{1}{2}$ in. AF
Screwdriver, large, Feeler gauges,
Allen key, $\frac{1}{4}$ in. AF

Special tools:

Gearbox cradle, Rover Part No. 601280
Torque wrench set, Rover Part No. 601285
Endplay checking tool, Rover Part No. 601281 or Dial test indicator

Instructions for overhauling the front pump are given in Part Three of this Section

Instructions for the removal of the unit from the car are given in Operation EE2-5

Prior operations

1. Remove the oil pan and valve bodies. Operation EE2-7.

Front pump, to remove

2. Withdraw the oil tubes from the front pump assembly. These tubes are a push fit into their locations.

   Note that the front pump inlet tube has an 'O. ring seal on the end that locates into the front pump assembly, this 'O' ring must be renewed.

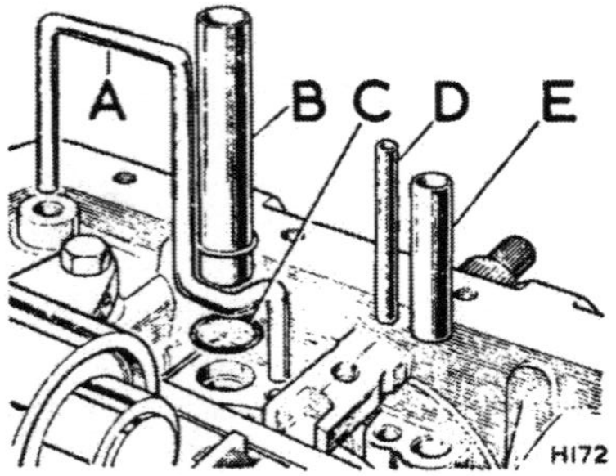

Front pump and converter fluid tubes

A—Tube, converter outlet
B—Tube, front pump inlet
C—'O' ring seal for front pump inlet tube
D—Tube, converter inlet
E—Tube, front pump outlet

3. At this stage measure the gear train end-float This measurement must be made before the removal of the front pump so that compensation for thrust washer wear may be made on re-assembly. Thrust washers are available in two thicknesses .061 in. —.063 in. (1,54 —1,6 mm) and .078 in. —.080 in. (1,97 —2,03 mm).
   Two methods of measuring the end-float are illustrated, depending upon the tools used.

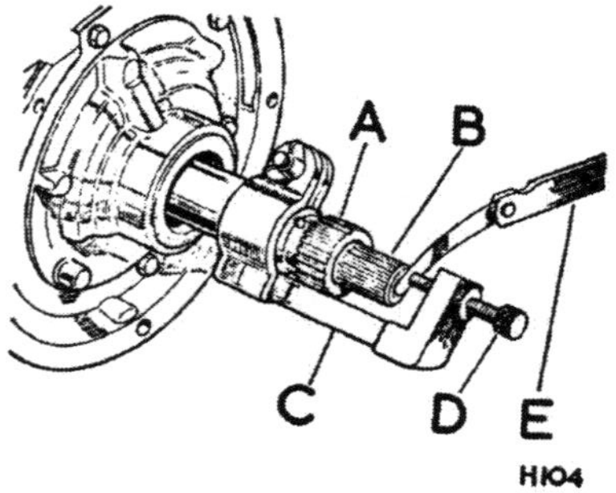

Measuring gear train end-play, using feeler gauges

A—Converter support tube
B—Input shaft
C—End-play checking tool
D—Adjusting screw
E—Feeler gauge

Feeler gauge method, using endplay checking tool, Rover Part No. 601281

(a) Clamp the tool on to the converter support tube.
(b) Pull the input shaft outwards and adjust the abutment screw to just contact the end of the shaft. Tighten knurled locknut.
(c) Push the input shaft inwards and measure the gap between screw and shaft using feeler gauges.
(d) The permissible end-float is .010 in. to .030 in. (0,25 to 0,75 mm). If the reading is outside the permissible limit a new thrust washer must be fitted on reassembly.
(e) Remove endplay checking tool.

Dial test indicator method

(a) Clamp the dial test indicator bracket to one of the holes in the main casing flange.
(b) With the knob of the dial indicator touching the end of the shaft push the shaft inwards.
(c) Zero the indicator then pull the shaft outwards and note the reading, the permissible end-float is .010 in. to .030 in. (0,25 to 0,75 mm). If the reading is outside the permissible limit a new thrust washer must be fitted on reassembly.

Operation EE2-10—*continued*

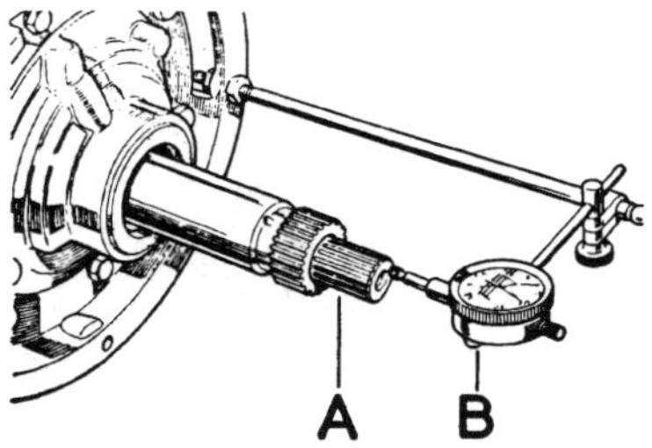

Measuring gear train end-play, using dial test indicator

A—Input shaft B—Dial test indicator

5. Now remove front pump secured by six bolts and spring washers. Hold the input shaft inwards whilst withdrawing the front pump assembly from the main casing, to ensure that the front clutch is not disengaged from the rear clutch assembly.
6. Discard the paper gasket.
7. Retain the tabbed thrust washer, located behind the front pump assembly if the end-float of the gears was within the limits .010 in. to .030 in. (0,25 to 0,75 mm).

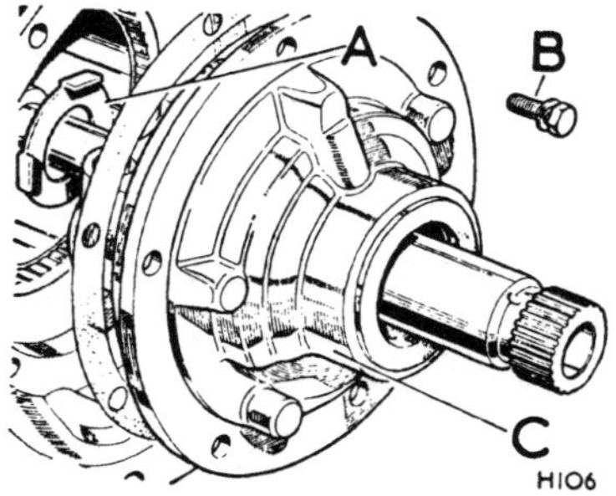

Front pump, removal

A—Tabbed thrust washer B—Bolts for front pump
C—Front pump

Front pump, to refit

1. Fit a new paper gasket between the front pump and the transmission case. Locate the gasket on transmission case with petroleum jelly.
2. If necessary correct the gear train end-float. Thrust washers are selective and available in two sizes, .061 to .063 in. (1,54 to 1,6 mm) and .078 to .080 in. (1,97 to 2,3 mm). Locate the thrust washer on to the pump with petroleum jelly.
3. Check the gear train end-float.
4. Fit the front pump to the transmission case with the oil tube locations facing the valve body. Tighten the six mounting bolts to a torque figure of 8 to 10 lb ft (1,0 to 1,4 mkg).
5. Fit new 'O' ring to the large tube and insert the tube with 'O' ring in the pump. Refit the remaining three tubes.
6. Refit oil pan and valve bodies. Operation EE2–7.

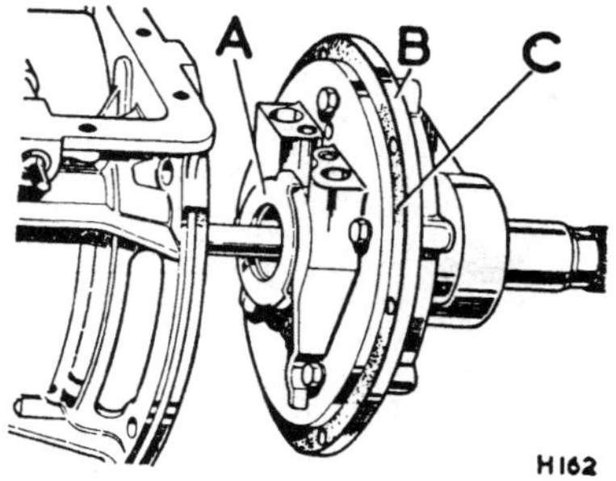

Front pump, to refit

A—Thrust washer for front pump
B—Front pump C—Gasket for front pump

Front brake band, to remove and refit—Operation EE2-11

Workshop hand tools:

Spanner sizes:

Sockets $\frac{7}{16}$ in. AF, $\frac{1}{2}$ in. AF, $\frac{9}{16}$ in. AF
Open ended $\frac{7}{16}$ in. AF, $\frac{1}{2}$ in. AF
Screwdriver, small, Screwdriver, large
Feeler gauges, Allen key, $\frac{1}{4}$ in. AF

Special tools:

Gearbox cradle, Rover Part No. 601280
Torque wrench set, Rover Part No. 601285
Endplay checking tool, Rover Part No. 601281 or Dial test indicator

Prior operations

1. Take off the oil pan and valve bodies assembly. Operation EE2–7.
2. Remove the front servo. Operation EE2–8.
3. Remove the front pump. Operation EE2–10.

Front brake band, to remove

4. Withdraw the brake band through the front of the main casing, take care not to disturb the front clutch and input shaft.

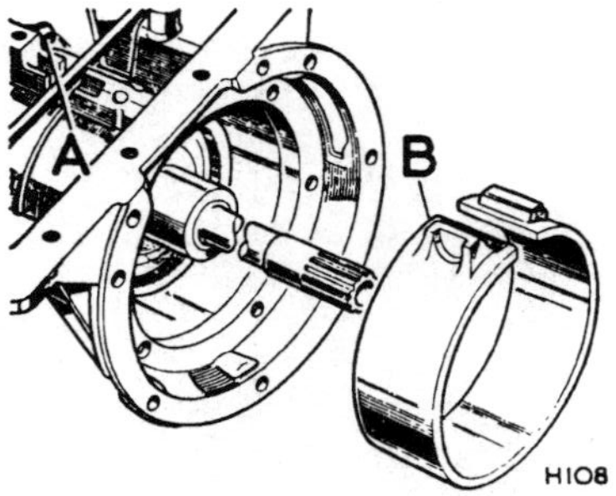

Withdrawing front brake band

A—Support pin in transmission casing
B—Front brake band

Front brake band, to refit

1. Reverse removal procedure, ensuring that the brake band is fitted into the transmission case with the larger external lug located on the support pin in the casing.
2. Tightening torques:
   Bolts, front pump to transmission casing 8 to 10 lbs ft (1,0 to 1,4 mkg).
   Bolts, front servo to transmission casing 8 to 10 lb ft (1,0 to 1,4 mkg).
   Adjusting screw, front servo 10 lb in. (0,11 mkg)
   Locknut, front servo adjuster screw 15 to 20 lb ft (2,0 to 2,8 mkg).
   Bolts, valve bodies 4 to 5 lb ft (0,55 to 0,7 mkg).
   Bolts, oil pan 8 to 10 lb ft (1,0 to 1,4 mkg).

Front clutch, rear clutch and forward sun gear, to remove and refit
Operation EE2-12

Workshop hand tools:

Spanner sizes:

Sockets $\frac{7}{16}$ in. AF, $\frac{1}{2}$ in. AF, $\frac{9}{16}$ in. AF
Open ended $\frac{7}{16}$ in. AF, $\frac{1}{2}$ in. AF
Screwdriver, small, Screwdriver, large
Feeler gauges, Allen key, $\frac{1}{4}$ in. AF

Special tools:

Gearbox cradle, Rover Part No. 601280
Torque wrench set, Rover Part No. 601285
Endplay checking tool, Rover Part No. 601281 or Dial test indicator

Instructions for overhauling the front clutch, rear clutch and forward sun gear are given in Part Three of this Secton.

Prior operations

1. Remove oil pan and valve bodies. Operation EE2-7.
2. Remove front servo. Operation EE2-8.
3. Remove front pump. Operation EE2-10.

Clutch assembly, to remove

4. Withdraw the front brake band.
5. Ease the rear clutch forward with a screwdriver as illustrated and withdraw the assembly of front and rear clutch out through the transmission case. Ensure that the needle thrust bearing and bearing plate, located on the forward sun gear shaft, have not dropped into the planetary gear set.

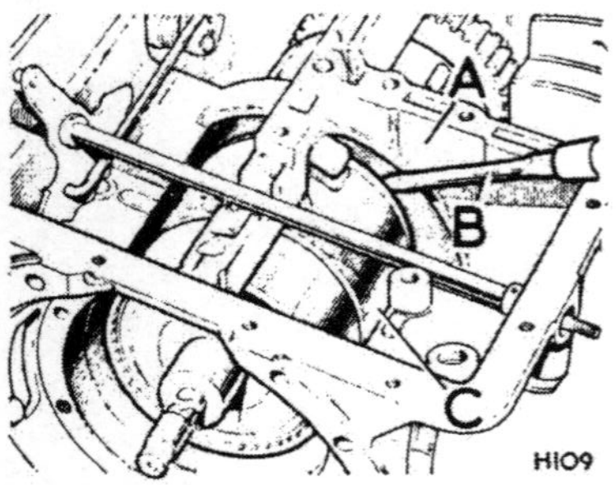

Front and rear clutch withdrawal

A—Centre support
B—Screwdriver, insert in position shown
C—Front and rear clutch assembly

6. Take care not to withdraw front clutch from rear clutch at this stage unless some repair work is to be carried out on these units. If the units are inadvertently disengaged, see Part Three of this Section for assembly procedure.

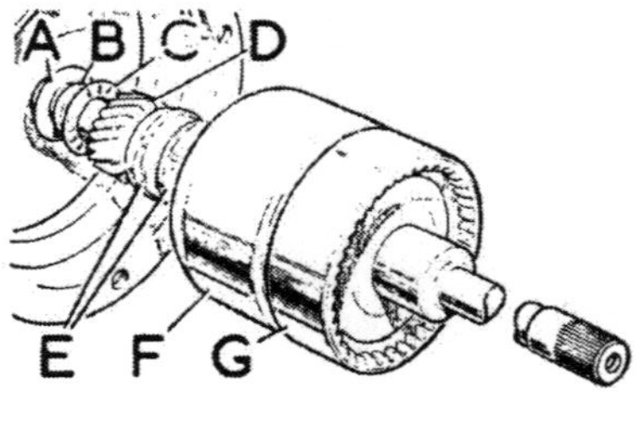

Installing front and rear clutch

A—Bearing plate
B—Nylon seal
C—Needle thrust bearing
D—Forward sun gear
E—Oil sealing rings, rear clutch to centre support
F—Rear clutch
G—Front clutch

Clutch assembly, to refit

1. Fit a new nylon seal on the forward sun gear shaft, then locate the needle thrust bearing followed by the bearing plate, lip towards nylon seal. Ensure oil sealing rings are correctly interlocked.
2. Then install the assembly of front and rear clutch, turn output shaft to engage the gears of the planetary set.
3. Fit the brake band into the transmission case, with the larger external lug towards the support pin in the casing.
4. Then reverse removal procedure.
5. Tightening torques:
   Bolts, front pump to transmission casing 8 to 10 lb ft (1,0 to 1,4 mkg).
   Adjusting screw, front servo 10 lb in. (0,11 mkg).
   Locknut, front servo adjuster screw 15 to 20 lb ft (2,0 to 2,8 mkg).
   Bolts, valve bodies 4 to 5 lb ft (0,55 to 0,7 mkg).
   Bolts, oil pan 8 to 10 lb ft (1,0 to 1,4 mkg).
   Bolts, front servo to transmission casing 8 to 10 lb ft (1,0 to 1,4 mkg).

Centre support and planetary gears, to remove and refit
Operation EE2-13

Workshop hand tools:

Spanner sizes:

Sockets $\frac{7}{16}$ in. AF, $\frac{1}{2}$ in. AF, $\frac{9}{16}$ in. AF
Open ended $\frac{7}{16}$ in. AF, $\frac{1}{2}$ in. AF
Screwdriver, small, Screwdriver, large
Feeler gauges, Allen key, $\frac{1}{4}$ in. AF

Special tools:

Gearbox cradle, Rover Part No. 601280
Torque wrench set, Rover Part No. 601285
Endplay checking tool, Rover Part No. 601281 or Dial test indicator
Spin torque screwdriver set, Rover Part No. 601286

Instructions for overhaul of centre support and planetary gears are given in Part Three of this Section

Prior operations

1. Take off the oil pan and valve bodies assembly. Operation EE2-7.
2. Remove the front servo. Operation EE2-8.
3. Remove the rear servo. Operation EE2-9.
4. Remove the front pump. Operation EE2-10.
5. Withdraw the front brake band. Operation EE2-11.
6. Lift out the front and rear clutch together with the forward sun gear assembly. Operation EE2-12.

Centre support and planetary gears, to remove

7. Remove the two special bolts and lock washers retaining the centre support. These fixings are located on the outside of the transmission case.
8. Withdraw the centre support and planetary gear through the front of the transmission case.
9. Note the needle thrust bearing and plate located on the rear end of the planetary gear assembly.

Centre support and planetary gears, to refit

1. Locate the lipped bearing plate on to the rear of the planet carrier with the lip facing rearward, followed by the needle thrust bearing. Locate in position with petroleum jelly.
2. Position centre support and planetary gears into transmission case.
3. It is most important that the centre support is correctly located. The fluid passages in the support must correspond with those in the main casing, that is, with three drillings towards the valve bodies.
4. The lock washers of the centre support bolts also act as oil retainers and must be fitted with the 'flat rim' facing the bolt head.

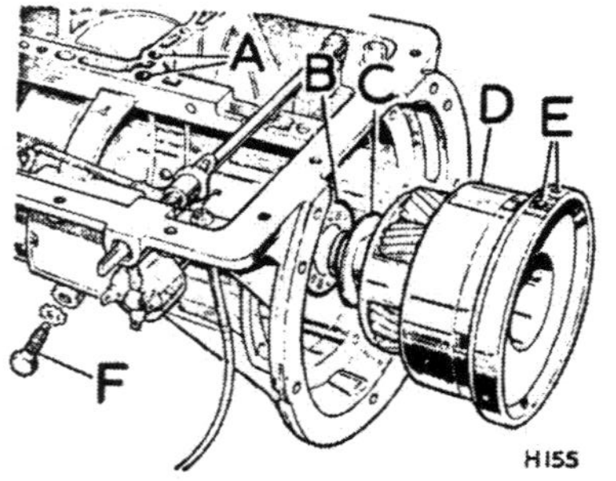

Locating centre support

A—Drillings in transmission casing
B—Needle thrust bearing
C—Thrust plate for needle bearing
D—Planet gear carrier
E—Drillings in centre support
F—Special fixing bolts for centre support

5. Tighten the centre support locating bolts to a torque figure of 10 to 13 lb ft (1,4 to 1,7 mkg).
6. Then reverse removal procedure.
7. Other tightening torques:
   Bolts, front pump to transmission casing 8 to 10 lb ft (1,0 to 1,4 mkg).
   Bolts, front servo to transmission casing 8 to 10 lb ft (1,0 to 1,4 mkg).
   Bolts, rear servo to transmission casing 10 to 13 lb ft (1,4 to 1,7 mkg).
   Adjusting screw, front servo 10 lb in. (0,11 mkg).
   Adjusting screw, rear servo 10 lb ft (1,4 mkg).
   Locknut, front servo adjusting screw 15 to 20 lb ft (2,0 to 2,8 mkg).
   Locknut, rear servo adjusting screw 25 to 30 lb ft (3,5 to 4,0 mkg).
   Bolts, valve bodies 4 to 5 lb ft (0,55 to 0,7 mkg)
   Bolts, oil pan 8 to 10 lb ft (1,0 to 1,4 mkg).

Rear brake band, to remove and refit—Operation EE2-14

Workshop hand tools:

Spanner sizes:
Sockets $\frac{7}{16}$ in. AF, $\frac{1}{2}$ in. AF, $\frac{9}{16}$ in. AF, $\frac{3}{4}$ in. AF
Open ended $\frac{7}{16}$ in. AF, $\frac{1}{2}$ in. AF
Screwdriver, small, Screwdriver, large
Feeler gauges
Allen key, $\frac{1}{4}$ in. AF

Special tools:
Gearbox cradle, Rover Part No. 601280
Torque wrench set, Rover Part No. 601285
Endplay checking tool, Rover Part No. 601281 or Dial test indicator
Spin torque screwdriver set, Rover Part No. 601286

Prior operations

1. Take off the oil pan and valve bodies assembly. Operation EE2–7.
2. Remove front servo. Operation EE2–8.
3. Remove rear servo. Operation EE2–9.
4. Remove front pump. Operation EE2–10.
5. Withdraw front brake band. Operation EE2–11.
6. Remove front and rear clutch. Operation EE2–12.
7. Remove centre support and planetary gears. Operation EE2–13.

Rear band, to remove

8. Withdraw the brake band by tilting the band through 45° to clear the main casing.

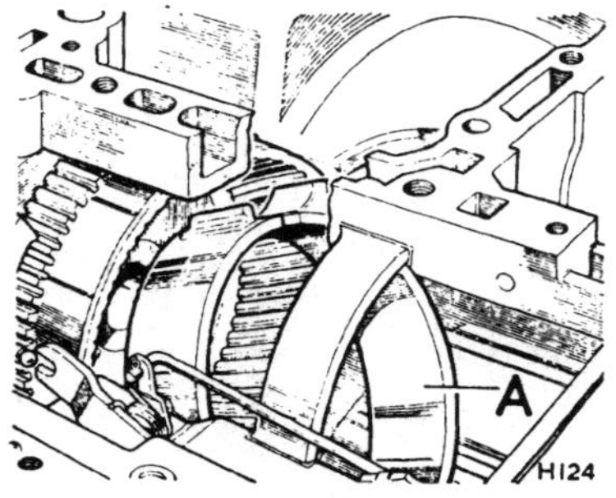

Removing rear brake band

A—Rear brake band

Rear brake band, to refit

1. Reverse removal procedure, ensuring that the band is put in the correct way round, that is, with the slotted lug for the servo strut towards the valve bodies and the larger lug located on the head of the adjuster bolt.
2. Tightening torques:
   Bolts, centre support 10 to 13 lb ft (1,4 to 1,7 mkg).
   Bolts, front pump to main casing 8 to 10 lb ft (1,0 to 1,4 mkg).
   Bolts, front servo to main casing 8 to 10 lb ft (1,0 to 1,4 mkg).
   Bolts, rear servo to main casing 10 to 13 lb ft (1,4 to 1,7 mkg).
   Adjusting screw, rear servo 10 lb ft (1,4 mkg).
   Adjusting screw, front servo 10 lb in. (0,11 mkg).
   Locknut, front servo adjuster screw 15 to 20 lb ft (2,0 to 2,8 mkg).
   Bolts, valve bodies 4 to 5 lb ft (0,55 to 0,7 mkg).
   Bolts, oil pan 8 to 10 lb ft (1,0 to 1,4 mkg).

*Speedometer drive housing, to remove and refit—Operation EE2-15

Workshop hand tools:
Spanner size: $\frac{7}{16}$ in. AF

Speedometer drive housing, remove

1. Withdraw the end of the speedometer cable from the housing, retained by a knurled nut.
2. Remove the speedometer drive housing from its location in the transmission extension case, retained by two set bolts.
3. Withdraw the 'O' ring oil seal from the housing.
4. If necessary renew the driven gear and spindle which may be pulled out of the housing. If the spindle and gear is being withdrawn it will be necessary to unscrew the adaptor from the housing and remove and discard the oil seal.

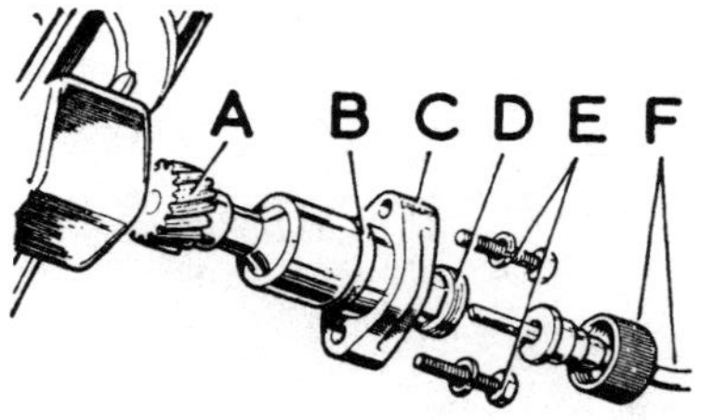

H125

Speedometer cable and housing for driven gear

A—Driven gear
B—Oil seal for housing
C—Housing for driven gear
D—Adaptor for spindle
E—Bolts fixing housing
F—Speedometer cable

Speedometer drive housing, refit

1. Reverse removal procedure.
2. Renew the 'O' ring oil seal on the outside of the housing.
3. If the driven gear and spindle has been withdrawn, renew the oil seal located beneath the adaptor. When replacing the adaptor the threads should be smeared with a little 'Loctite' sealant grade 'AVV', Rover Part No. 600303.

Operations which are identified by an asterisk (*) can be carried out with the automatic transmission installed in the car

*Coupling flange and extension housing, to remove and refit
Operation EE2-16

Workshop hand tools:

Spanner sizes:
Sockets $\frac{7}{16}$ in. AF, $\frac{1}{2}$ in. AF
Open ended $\frac{7}{16}$ in. AF, $\frac{1}{2}$ in. AF
Screwdriver, large, Allen key, $\frac{1}{4}$ in. AF, $\frac{5}{16}$ in. AF

Special tools:
Gearbox cradle, Rover Part No. 601280
Torque wrench set, Rover Part No. 601285

Coupling flange and extension housing, to remove
Items 1, 2, 3 and 4 only apply if unit is fitted to the car.

1. Drain the fluid from the oil pan. Take great care if the car has just returned from a run as the fluid will be hot enough to cause scalding.
2. Disconnect the front propeller shaft at each end and remove.
3. Disconnect rear mounting at gearbox and sub-frame and remove.
4. Disconnect speedometer cable.
5. Lock the box in the park position. If unit is out of vehicle, turn lever clockwise.
6. Withdraw the driving flange secured by 'Wedglok' screw and washer.
7. Remove the extension case secured by four bolts and spring washers. Discard the paper gasket.
8. The speedometer drive pinion can be withdrawn from the shaft if necessary.
9. The oil seal in the extension housing should be levered out with a screwdriver. Press or drift a new seal into position.
10. If necessary remove speedometer driven gear from extension housing.

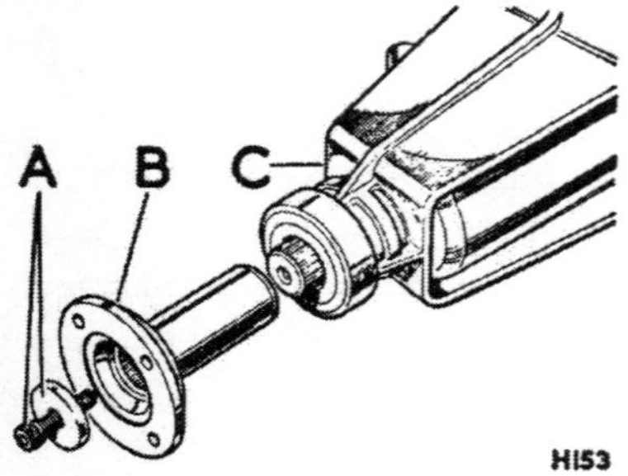

H153

Coupling flange

A—'Wedglok' screw and special plain washer
B—Coupling flange
C—Extension casing

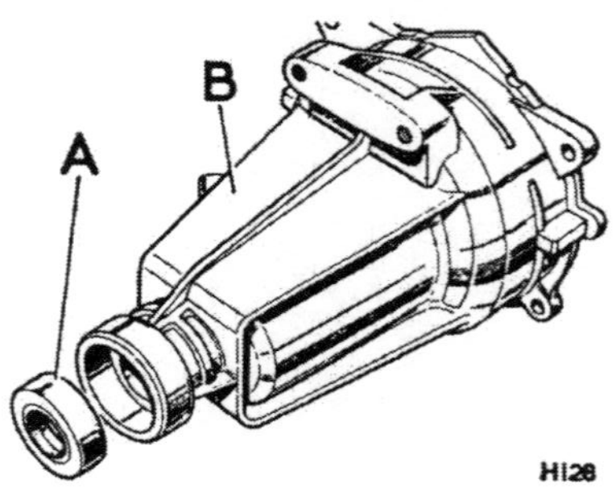

H128

Extension housing oil seal

A—Oil seal B—Extension housing

Operations which are identified by an asterisk (*) can be carried out with the automatic transmission installed in the car

Operation EE2-16—*continued*

Coupling flange and extension housing, to refit

1. Reverse removal procedure, using a new paper gasket for the extension housing.
2. Tighten the bolts securing the extension housing to the transmission case to a torque figure of 8 to 10 lb ft (1,0 to 1,4 mkg).

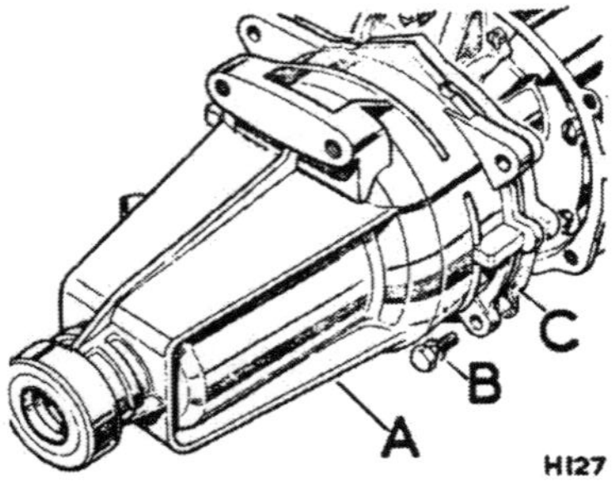

H127

Extension housing, to refit

A—Extension housing
B—Bolts for extension housing
C—Gasket for extension housing

3. Smear the threads of the 'Wedglok' screw retaining the coupling flange to the driven shaft with Loctite sealant grade CV, Rover Part No. 601168. Fully tighten this screw so that flange nips speedometer pinion. Looseness at this point can cause speedometer fluctuation.
4. Release the parking pawl engagement.
5. If the gearbox is completely dismantled, hold the ring gear and driven shaft firmly whilst fitting the extension housing and the coupling flange.
6. If the above operation has been carried out with the unit in the vehicle, refill with fluid of the recommended grade. Capacity: 14 Imperial pints, 17 US pints, 8,0 litres.

*Governor, to remove and refit—Operation EE2-17

Workshop hand tools:

Spanner sizes:
Sockets $\frac{7}{16}$ in. AF, $\frac{1}{2}$ in. AF
Open ended $\frac{7}{16}$ in. AF, $\frac{1}{2}$ in. AF
Allen key, $\frac{1}{4}$ in. AF, $\frac{5}{16}$ in. AF, Screwdriver, large

Special tools:
Gearbox cradle, Rover Part No. 601280
Torque wrench set, Rover Part No. 601285
Snap ring pliers, Rover Part No. 601282

Instructions for dismantling the governor valve are given in Part Three of this Section.

Prior operations

1. Remove the coupling flange and extension housing. Operation EE2-16.

Governor, to remove

2. Release park position, then rotate the driven shaft so that the governor centrifugal weight is at the 6 o'clock position, that is, downwards as illustrated. This is a precaution to prevent the steel retaining ball from being lost when the governor is withdrawn from the shaft.

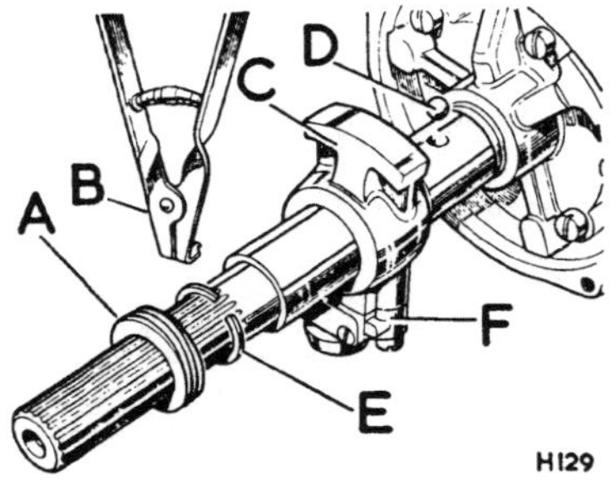

H129

Governor, to remove

A—Speedometer drive gear D—Governor retaining ball
B—Snap ring pliers E—Snap ring
C—Governor sleeve F—Governor body

3. Remove the snap ring locating the governor on to the driven shaft using the special snap ring pliers.
4. Slide the governor off the shaft, taking care not to lose the steel ball which keys the governor to to the shaft.

Governor, to refit

1. Reverse removal procedure.
2. Ensure that the governor is the correct way round, that is, with the governor valve cover plate facing rearwards.

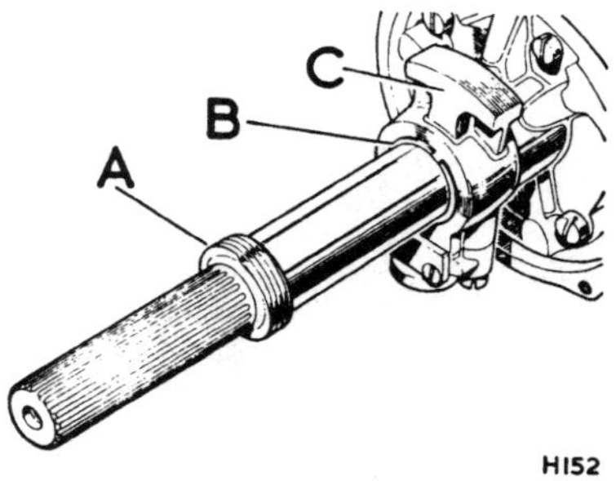

H152

Governor in position on shaft

A—Speedometer drive gear B—Snap ring for governor
C—Governor assembly

3. If the transmission case has been completely dismantled, hold the ring gear and drive shaft firmly in position whilst fitting the governor and the snap-ring.
4. Tightening torques:
   Bolts, securing extension housing, 8 to 10 lb ft (1,0 to 1,4 mkg).

Operations which are identified by an asterisk (*) can be carried out with the automatic transmission installed in the car.

*Rear pump, to remove and refit—Operation EE2-18

Workshop hand tools:

Spanner sizes:
Sockets $\frac{7}{16}$ in. AF, $\frac{1}{2}$ in. AF
Open ended $\frac{7}{16}$ in. AF, $\frac{1}{2}$ in. AF
Allen key, $\frac{1}{4}$ in. AF, $\frac{5}{16}$ in. AF
Screwdriver, large

Special tools:
Gearbox cradle, Rover Part No. 601280
Snap ring pliers, Rover Part No. 601282
Torque wrench set, Rover Part No. 601285
Spintorq screwdriver set, Rover Part No. 601286

Instructions for overhauling the rear pump are given in Part Three of this Section.

Prior operations

1. Remove the coupling flange and extension housing. Operation EE2-16.
2. Remove the governor. Operation EE2-17.

Rear pump, to remove

3. Take out the five screws and spring washers, and one screw with shake-proof washer securing the rear pump to the transmission case.
4. Withdraw the rear pump housing together with the external gear.
5. If necessary lift out the external gear from the housing.
6. Ease the driven gear gently over the three oil seal rings and withdraw from the shaft.
7. Mark the outside face of each gear to ensure that they are refitted the same way round.
8. Withdraw the pump plate from the transmission case.
9. Remove the small key from the driven shaft.
10. Examine all parts for wear and renew as necessary.

Rear pump, to refit

1. Locate the pump plate on to the transmission case with petroleum jelly.
2. If necessary renew the oil sealing rings. Line up rings with gaps uppermost as viewed with the box inverted and centralise them, using a little petroleum jelly to retain the rings in position.
3. Insert the pump drive key into the driven shaft and locate with petroleum jelly.

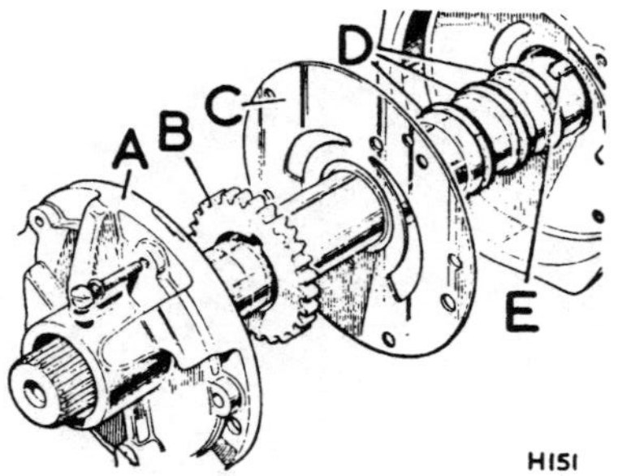

H151

Rear pump components

A—Housing for rear pump C—Backing plate for pump
B—Driven gear for pump D—Oil sealing rings
E—Key for driven gear

4. Ease the pump driving gear over the sealing rings on the shaft and on to the drive key.
5. Slide the pump housing complete with external gear on to the driven shaft. If the unit has been completely dismantled, hold the shaft to prevent it being pushed into the casing.
6. Then reverse removal procedure.
7. Tightening torques:
   Screw, pump securing, five large 4 to 5 lb ft (0,55 to 0,7 mkg).
   Screw, pump locating, one small 20 to 30 lb in. (0,23 to 0,35 mkg).
   Bolts, extension housing, 8 to 10 lb ft (1,0 to 1,4 mkg).

Operations which are identified by an asterisk (*) can be carried out with the automatic transmission installed in the car.

Driven shaft and ring gear assembly, to remove and refit—Operation EE2-19

Workshop hand tools:

Spanner sizes:
- Sockets $\frac{7}{16}$ in. AF, $\frac{1}{2}$ in. AF, $\frac{9}{16}$ in. AF, $\frac{3}{4}$ in. AF
- Open ended $\frac{7}{16}$ in. AF, $\frac{1}{2}$ in. AF, $\frac{9}{16}$ in. AF, $\frac{3}{4}$ in. AF, $1\frac{5}{16}$ in. AF
- Screwdriver, small, Screwdriver, large
- Allen key, $\frac{3}{16}$ in. AF, $\frac{1}{4}$ in. AF, $\frac{5}{16}$ in. AF
- Feeler gauges

Special tools:
- Gearbox cradle, Rover Part No. 601280
- Torque wrench set, Rover Part No. 601285
- Spintorq screwdriver set, Rover Part No. 601286
- Front servo gauge, Rover Part No. 601287
- Endplay checking tool, Rover Part No. 601281 or Dial test indicator
- Snap ring pliers, Rover Part No. 601282

The driven shaft is a service exchange item.

Prior operations

1. All the previous operations detailed in Part Two of this Section.

Driven shaft and ring gear, to remove

2 Withdraw the shaft and ring gear forwards from the transmission case, taking care that the white metal bush in the rear of the transmission case is not damaged. This bush is not serviced separately.

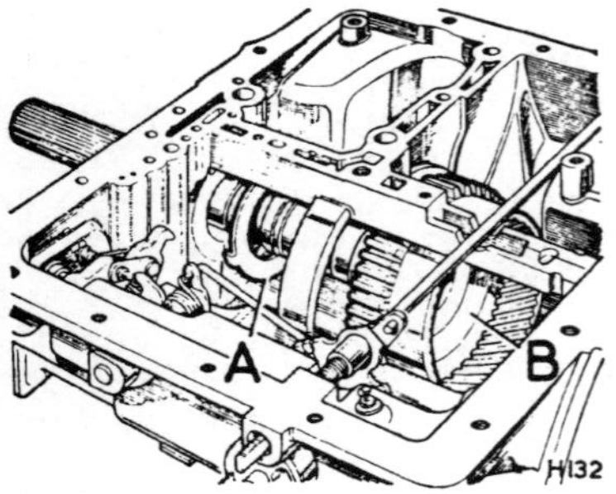

Driven shaft and ring gear assembly, to remove

A—Tabbed thrust washer
B—Driven shaft and ring gear assembly

3. Lift off the tabbed thrust washer located between the driven shaft and the rear bearing of the transmission case.

4. If necessary remove the snap ring and separate the driven shaft from the ring gear. Examine and pressure test the plug in the front of the driven shaft to ensure that it is not loose. A loose plug necessitates a replacement shaft.

5 If necessary remove the three oil sealing rings from the driven shaft.

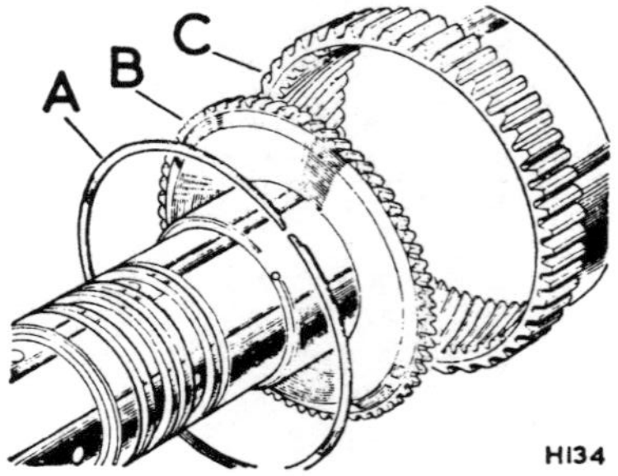

Separating ring gear from driven shaft

A—Snap ring B—Driven shaft C—Ring gear

6. Check components for wear and ensure all oil ways are clear.

7. At this stage check the transmission case for signs of damage or stripped threads. Clear all oil passages with an air line.

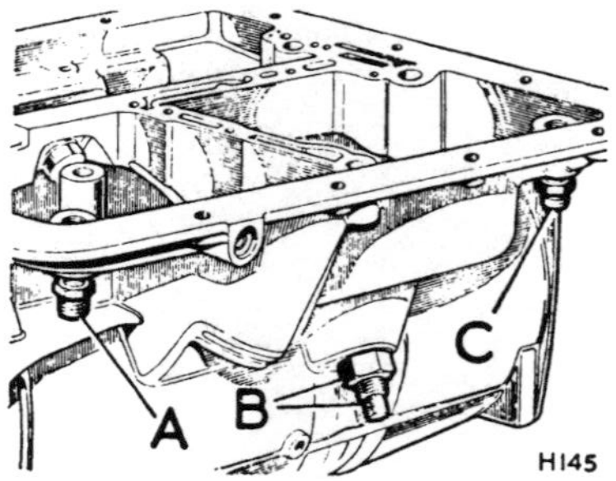

Transmission case details

A—Oil cooler pipe union, inlet
B—Rear brake band adjuster and locknut
C—Oil cooler pipe union, return

Operation EE2-19—*continued*

8. If necessary check or remove the following:
   (a) Rear brake band adjusting screw and locknut.
   (b) Oil cooler pipe unions. If replaced use Loctite Sealant grade AVV, Rover Part No. 600303, on the threads.
   (c) Do not remove the driven shaft bush. This is not a service item.
   (d) Pressure take-off plug at rear face of transmission case.
   (e) Oil dipstick tube adaptor.
   (f) Check that parking brake torsion lever pin is a tight fit.
   (g) Ensure that the front brake band anchor pin is tight.

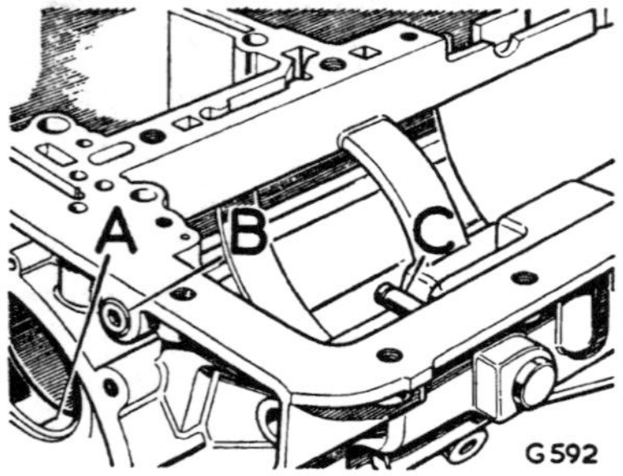

Transmission case details

A—Bush for driven shaft B—Pressure take-off plug
C—Pin for parking brake torsion lever

Driven shaft and ring gear assembly, to refit

1. Fit the driven shaft to the ring gear and secure with snap ring. Check and ensure there is no end-float between driven shaft and ring gear.

2. The snap ring retaining the driven shaft to the ring gear is available in the following thicknesses to enable end-float to be eliminated: .055 in., .057 in. and .059 in. (1,39, 1,44 and 1,49 mm).

3. Fit the three oil sealing rings and line up with gaps uppermost as viewed with the box inverted, centralise the rings in their grooves, retaining them in position with a little petroleum jelly.

4. Locate the tabbed thrust washer on to the boss of the transmission case with petroleum jelly. The tabs of the washer locate on the boss in such a manner that one tab will be pointing upwards, as seen with the box on the gearbox cradle.

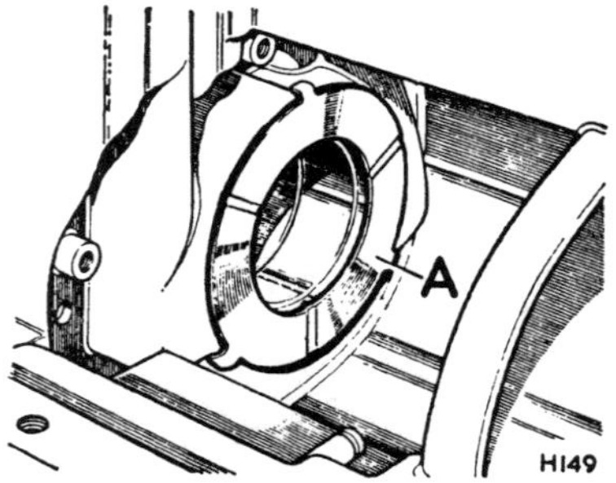

Driven shaft thrust washer

A—Thrust washer

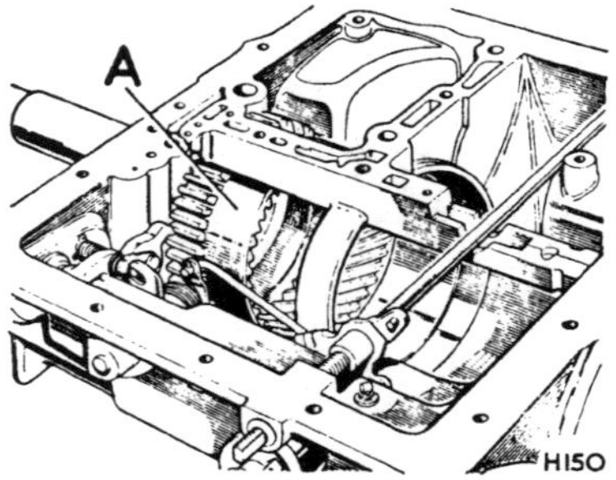

Driven shaft and ring gear, to refit

A—Driven shaft and ring gear assembly

Operation EE2-19—*continued*

5. Insert the driven shaft and ring gear assembly. Great care must be taken when installing it into the transmission case to prevent damage to the bush in the rear of the case.

6. Rotate the driven shaft to bring location hole for governor retaining ball uppermost with the gearbox inverted.

7. Refit rear pump. Operation EE2–18.

8. Refit governor. Operation EE2–17.

9. Refit extension housing and coupling flange. Operation EE2–16.

10. Refit rear brake band. Operation EE2–14.

11. Refit centre support and planetary gears. Operation EE2–13.

12. Refit front and rear clutch. Operation EE2–12.

13. Refit front brake band. Operation EE2–11.

14. Fit a new paper gasket for front pump to the transmission case. Locate with petroleum jelly.

15. If necessary check and correct gear train end-float. See Operation EE2–10.

16. Fit the front pump to the transmission case with the oil tube locations facing the valve bodies. Fit oil tubes to front pump.

17. Install the rear servo into the transmission case. To facilitate the location of the servo strut, attach it to the servo lever with petroleum jelly and ensure that the strut engages with the slot in the brake band. The long special bolt must be fitted into the hole adjacent to centre cross support of the transmission case. The short bolt also locates the magnet.

18. The adjuster for the rear band servo is located on the outside of the transmission case.

19. Slacken the locknut of the adjusting screw.

20. Tighten the adjusting screw to a torque of 10 lb ft (1,4 mkg), then turn the adjusting screw back one complete turn and tighten the locknut to a torque figure of 25 to 30 lb ft (3,5 to 4,0 mkg).

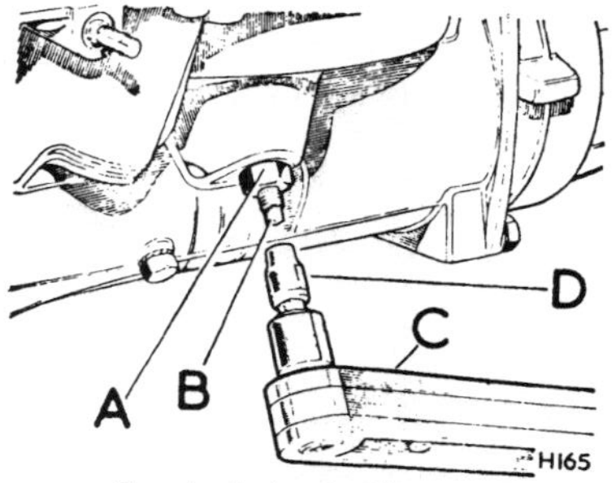

Rear brake band, adjustment

A—Locknut for adjuster
B—Adjusting screw for brake band
C—Torque wrench
D—Adaptor

21. Install the front servo into the transmission case. To facilitate location of the servo strut, attach it to the servo lever with petroleum jelly and ensure that the strut engages with the slot in the brake band.

22. To adjust the front servo, slacken locknut and unscrew the adjuster. Pull the servo lever outwards and place the gauge block between the adjusting screw and the servo piston pin.

23. Tighten the servo lever adjusting screw to a torque figure of 10 lb in. (0,11 mkg), using a torque screwdriver and the adaptor attached to the gauge block.

24. Use a screwdriver between servo body and adjuster lever to release pressure from gauge block and withdraw.

25. Tighten the adjuster lever locknut to a torque figure of 15 to 20 lb ft (2,0 to 2,8 mkg).

Operation EE2-19—*continued*

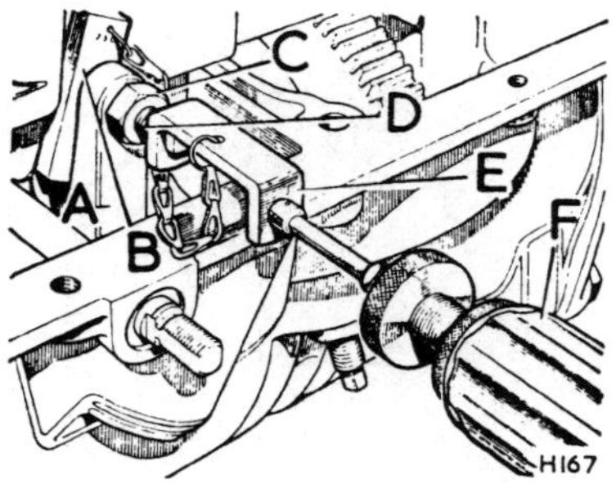

Front brake band, adjustment

A—Servo lever
B—Gauge block
C—Locknut for adjuster
D—Adjuster screw for servo
E—Adaptor
F—Spintoq screwdriver

26. Refit valve bodies and oil pan. Operation EE2–7.

27. Tightening torques for all the previous operations as applicable are:

Bolts, extension housing 8 to 10 lb ft (1,0 to 1,4 mkg).
Bolts, centre support 10 to 13 lb ft (1,4 to 1,7 mkg).
Bolts, front pump to transmission casing 8 to 10 lb ft (1,0 to 1,4 mkg).
Bolts, rear pump to transmission casing 4 to 5 lb ft (0,55 to 0,7 mkg).
Bolts, front servo to transmission casing 8 to 10 lb ft (1,0 to 1,4 mkg).
Bolts, rear servo to transmission casing 10 to 13 lb ft (1,4 to 1,7 mkg).
Adjusting screw, rear servo 10 lb ft (1,4 mkg).
Adjusting screw, front servo 10 lb in. (0,11 mkg).
Locknut, front servo adjusting screw 15 to 20 lb ft (2,0 to 2,8 mkg).
Locknut, rear servo adjusting screw 25 to 30 lb ft (3,5 to 4,0 mkg).
Bolts, valve bodies 4 to 5 lb ft (0,55 to 0,7 mkg).
Bolts, oil pan 8 to 10 lb ft (1,0 to 1,4 mkg).

Manual valve lever control shaft, to remove and refit—Operation EE2-20

Workshop hand tools:

Spanner sizes:

Sockets $\frac{7}{16}$ in. AF, $\frac{1}{2}$ in. AF
Open ended $\frac{7}{16}$ in. AF, $\frac{1}{2}$ in. AF
Screwdriver, large, Pin punch $\frac{1}{8}$ in. diameter (3 mm), Pointed nose pliers, Brass drift, Allen key, $\frac{1}{4}$ in. AF, Hammer, light

Special tools:

Torque wrench set, Rover Part No. 601285

Prior operations

1. Remove oil pan and valve bodies. Operation EE2-7.

Manual valve lever control shaft, to remove

2. Remove the spring clip retaining the parking brake link at the torsion lever end.
3. Drive out the $\frac{11}{16}$ in. (17 mm) long roll pin from the manual valve detent lever on the manual control shaft with a suitable drift. Take care not to drop the pin. Remove the detent ball and spring.
4. Remove the operating lever from the end of the shaft outside the box.

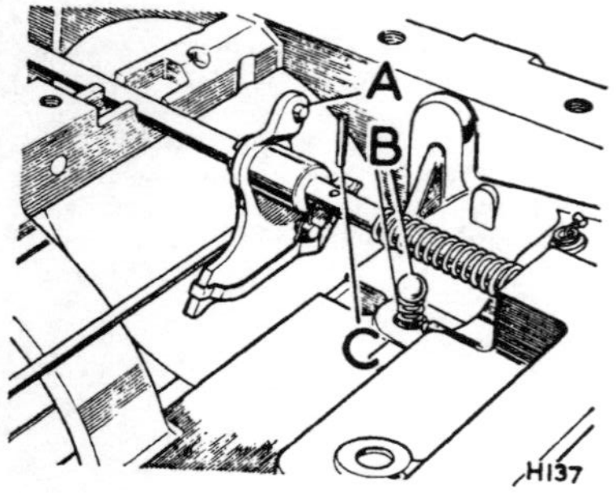

Roll pin being drifted out

A—Manual detent lever B—Detent ball and spring C—Roll pin for lever

5. Turn the shaft to enable the $\frac{5}{8}$ in. (15 mm) long roll pin to be driven out from the opposite end of the shaft, taking care not to drop the pin.
6. Withdraw the shaft, taking off the collar, lever assembly and bias spring.
7. Clean and examine all the components. Renew defective parts.

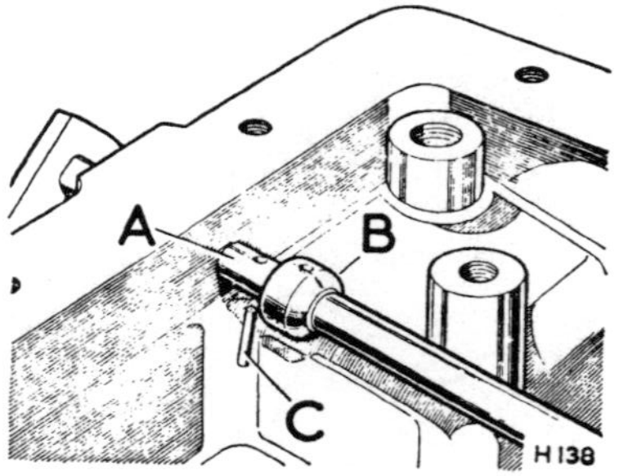

Roll pin for collar, to remove

A—Manual control shaft B—Collar C—Roll pin

Manual valve lever shaft, to refit

1. Renew the oil seals in the transmission case.
2. Insert the end of the shaft into the case and slide on the collar, chamfer facing inwards, then slide on the detent lever and bias spring.
3. Secure the lever to the shaft with an $\frac{11}{16}$ in. (17 mm) long pin.

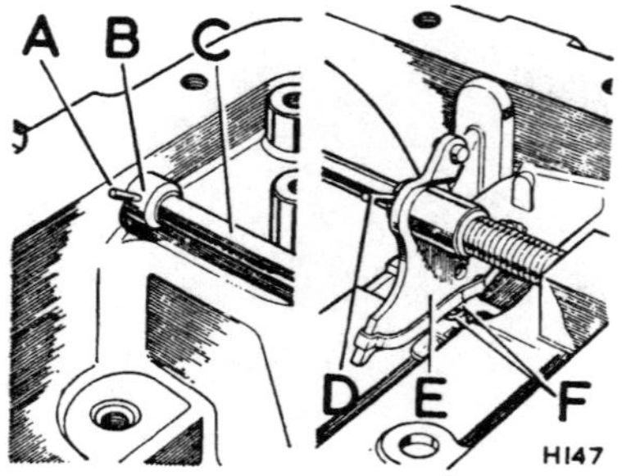

Manual control shaft, fitting roll pins

A—Roll pin for collar—$\frac{5}{8}$ in. long (15 mm)
B—Collar for manual control shaft
C—Manual control shaft
D—Roll pin for detent lever—$\frac{11}{16}$ in. long (17 mm)
E—Detent lever
F—Ball and spring for detent lever

Operation EE2-20—*continued*

4. Locate the lever detent ball and spring and compress the spring with a suitable tool. Slide the detent lever into position. Then secure the collar to the shaft with a $\frac{5}{8}$ in. (15 mm) long roll pin.
5. Connect the link rod to the detent lever and fit retainer.

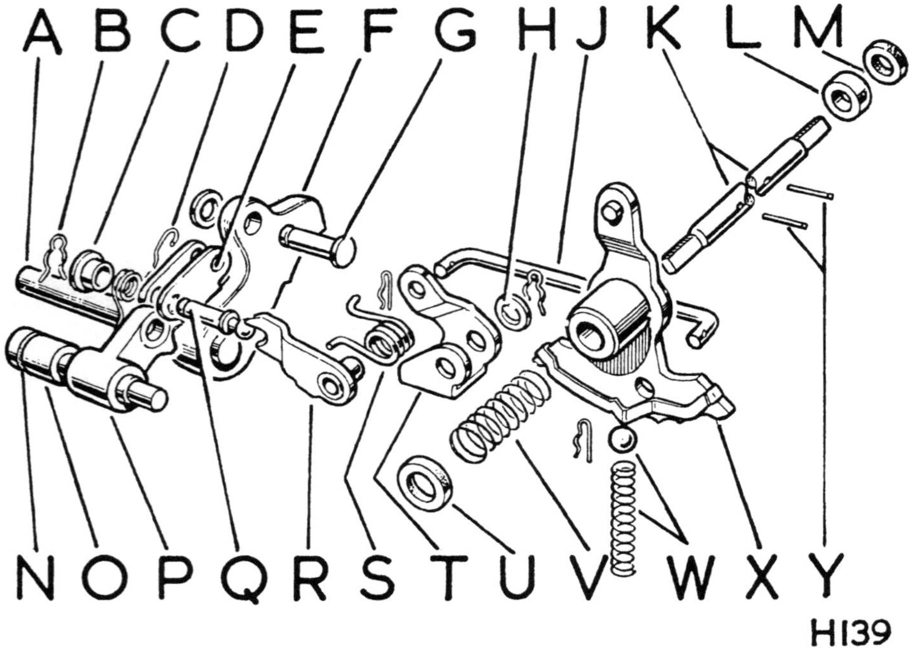

Manual valve shaft, link and parking pawl and torsion lever assembly

A—Anchor pin
B—Circlip for toggle lever pin
C—Retainer for spring
D—Parking brake release spring
E—Toggle link
F—Parking brake pawl
G—Pin for toggle link
H—Plain washer for torsion lever
J—Linkage rod, detent lever to torsion lever
K—Manual valve lever shaft
L—Collar for shaft
M—Oil seal for manual lever shaft, collar end

N—'O' ring for toggle pin
O—Toggle pin
P—Toggle lever
Q—Pin for toggle lever
R—Toggle lift lever
S—Toggle lever spring
T—Torsion lever
U—Oil seal for manual lever shaft, detent lever end
V—Bias spring
W—Detent ball and spring
X—Detent lever
Y—Roll pins fixing collar and lever

*Parking pawl and torsion lever assembly, to remove and refit—Operation EE2-21

Workshop hand tools:

Spanner sizes:
Sockets $\frac{7}{16}$ in. AF, $\frac{1}{2}$ in. AF
Open ended $\frac{7}{16}$ in. AF, $\frac{1}{2}$ in. AF
Screwdriver, large, Hammer, Pin punch $\frac{1}{8}$ in. diameter (3 mm), Pointed nose pliers, Magnet, Allen key, $\frac{1}{4}$ in. AF, $\frac{5}{16}$ in. AF

Special tools:
Torque wrench set, Rover Part No. 601285

Prior operations

1. Remove oil pan and valve bodies. Operation EE2–7.
2. Remove extension housing and coupling flange. Operation EE2–16.

Parking pawl and torsion lever assembly, to remove

3. Tap out the roll pin locating the parking pawl toggle pin in the transmission case.

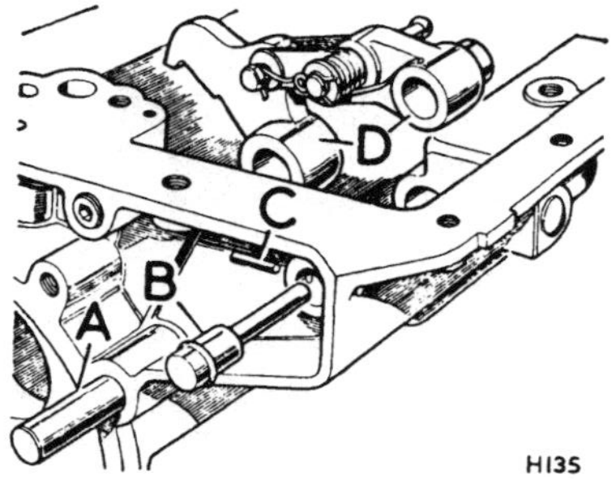

Parking pawl and torsion lever assembly

A—Parking pawl anchor pin C—Retaining roll pin
B—Parking brake toggle pin D—Parking pawl assembly

4. Use a suitable magnet to withdraw the toggle pin complete with 'O' ring, also the anchor pin.
5. Lift out the parking pawl assembly.
   If necessary the parking pawl assembly can be dismantled as follows:
6. Remove spring clip from the toggle lever pin, withdraw spring retainer and disconnect release spring.
7. Separate the components by withdrawing the toggle lever pin and toggle link pin, note plain washer on link pin.

Item 8 can only be carried out after the removal of the rear servo and sliding the brake band fully to the rear.

8. Remove the spring clip retaining the link rod, also the spring clip retaining the torsion lever assembly to the pin in the casing and withdraw the assembly.

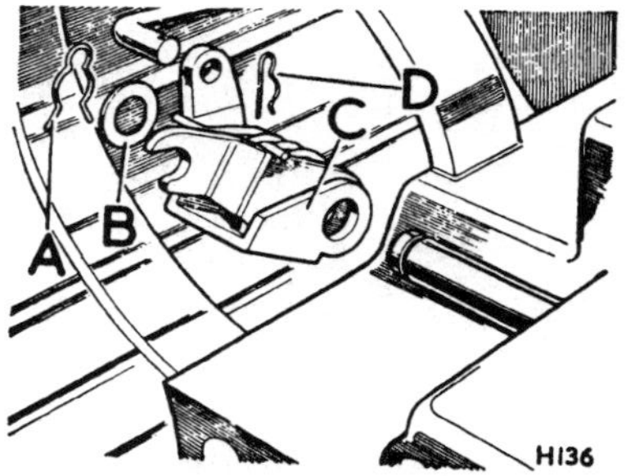

Torsion lever assembly

A—Spring clip for torsion lever
B—Plain washer for torsion lever
C—Parking brake lever and toggle assembly
D—Spring clip for link

Parking pawl and torsion lever, to refit

1. Examine components for wear, renew as necessary and assemble by reversing dismantling procedure.
2. Use a new 'O' ring on the toggle pin.

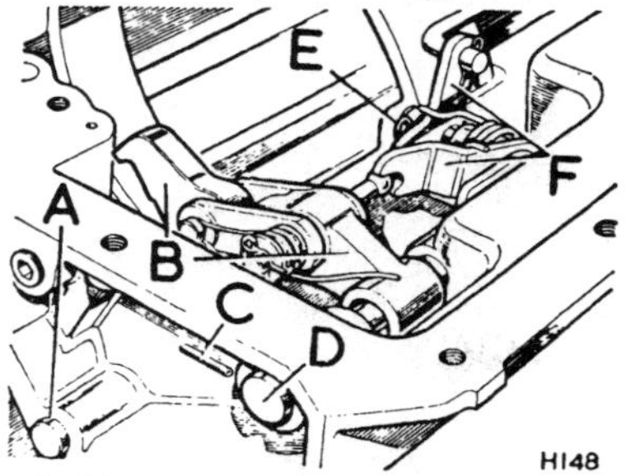

Parking pawl and torsion lever assembled

A—Anchor pin for parking pawl
B—Parking pawl assembly
C—Roll pin for toggle pin
D—Toggle pin
E—Spring clip for torsion lever
F—Torsion lever assembly

Operations which are identified by an asterisk (*) can be carried out with the automatic transmission installed in the car.

*Starter inhibiter switch, to remove and refit—Operation EE2-22

Workshop hand tools:

Spanner sizes:
Open ended $\frac{11}{16}$ in. AF

Inhibiter switch, to remove

1. Disconnect the battery, situated in the luggage compartment.
2. Remove gearbox tunnel cover.
3. Disconnect the wiring at the switch connections.

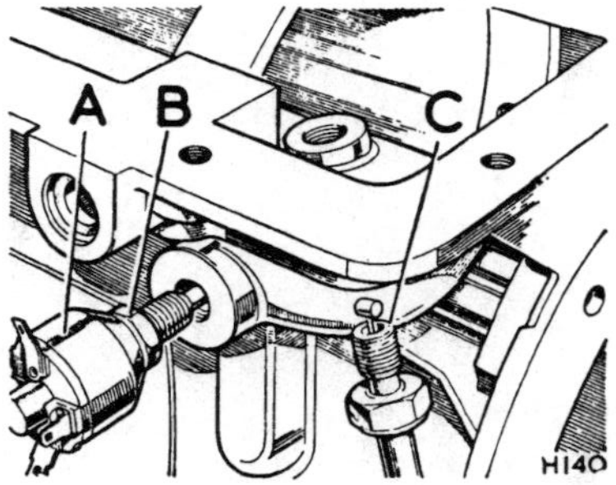

Starter inhibiter switch, to remove

A—Inhibiter switch B—Switch locknut
C—Downshift valve cable

The illustration shows the switch being removed after the gearbox has been dismantled, but this operation can be carried out without dismantling the gearbox.

4. Slacken the switch locknut.
5. Screw the switch from the transmission case by hand.

Inhibiter switch, to refit

1. Reverse removal procedure.
2. For adjustment, see Operation EE2–2.

Operations which are identified by an asterisk (*) can be carried out with the automatic transmission installed in the car.

*Downshift valve cable, to remove and refit—Operation EE2-23

Workshop hand tools:

Spanner sizes: Sockets $\frac{7}{16}$ in. AF, $\frac{1}{2}$ in. AF Open ended $\frac{7}{16}$ in. AF, $\frac{1}{2}$ in. AF, $\frac{3}{4}$ in. AF
Allen key, $\frac{1}{4}$ in. AF

Cable, remove

1. Drain the fluid from the oil pan. Take great care if the car has just returned from a run as the fluid will be hot enough to cause scalding. When the oil is completely drained refit the drain plug.

   Smear threads of plug with Loctite sealant grade CV, Rover Part No. 601168. It is not possible to completely drain the oil pan.

   Disconnect the selector linkage from the lever on the side of the tıansmission unit. Remove the cross-shaft bracket secured by two bolts. Remove the oil pan.

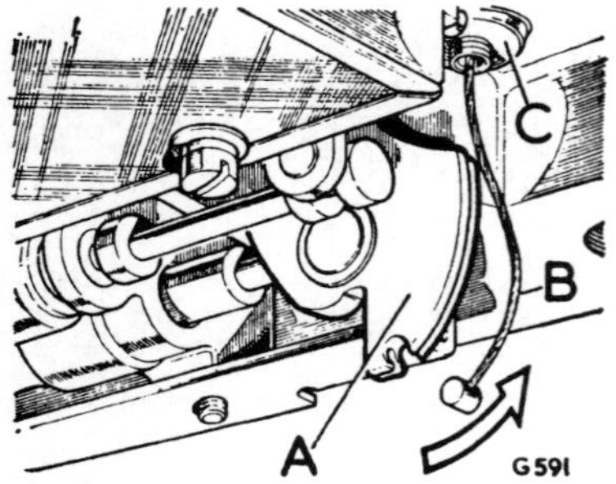

Downshift valve cable, to remove at transmission unit

A—Downshift valve cam B—Cable C—Ferrule for cable

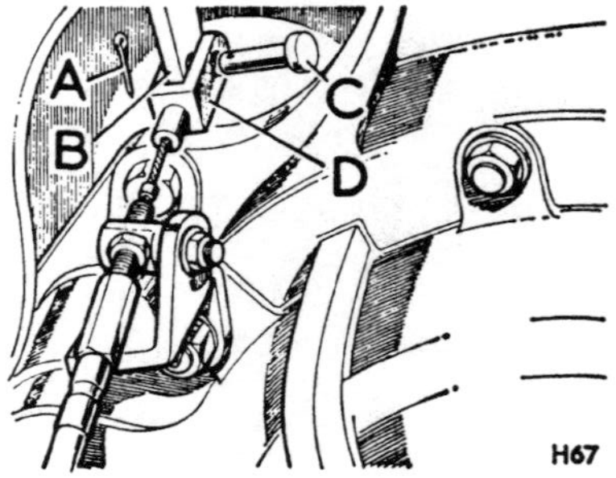

Downshift valve cable, to remove at engine

A—Split pin C—Clevis pin
B—Relay lever D—Cable end

2. Pull the downshift valve cam forward in direction of arrow and disconnect the cable from the valve bodies end.
3. Disconnect the cable at the engine end.
4. Unscrew the ferrule of the cable from the transmission case.

Cable, refit

1. Reverse removal procedure.
2. Tightening torque:
   Bolts, oil pan 8 to 10 lb ft (1,0 to 1,4 mkg).
3. If the above operation has been carried out with the unit in the vehicle, refill with fluid of the recommended grade. Capacity: 14 Imperial pints, 17 US pints, 8,0 litres.
4. To adjust cable, see Operation EE2–3.

*Air pressure checks—Operation EE2-24

Workshop hand tools:

Spanner sizes:
Open ended $\frac{7}{16}$ in. AF, $\frac{1}{2}$ in. AF
Sockets $\frac{7}{16}$ in. AF, $\frac{1}{2}$ in. AF

Special tools:
Torque wrench set, Rover Part No. 601285

Air pressure checks to determine whether the clutch and brake bands are operating, can be made with the transmission unit in the car, or on the bench.

If the clutch and bands operate satisfactorily with air pressure, faulty operation of the transmission must be due to malfunction of the hydraulic control system.

The valve bodies assembly must then be dismantled, cleaned, inspected and reassembled.

Instructions for dismantling the valve bodies assembly is given in Part Three of this Section.

Prior operations, necessary if the unit being tested is fitted in the car.

1. Remove the oil pan and valve bodies assembly. Operation EE2–7.
2. Remove the extension housing and coupling flange. Operation EE2–16.

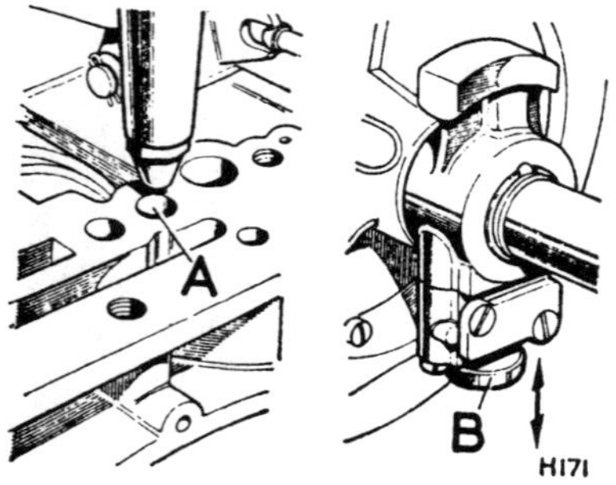

Front clutch and governor feed pressure check

A—Drilling in transmission case
B—Governor weight

Front clutch and governor feed

3. Apply air pressure to the drilling A in the transmission case.
   (a) Listen for thump indicating that the clutch is functioning.
   (b) Rotate driven shaft so that the governor weight is in the six o'clock position. Apply and release air pressure and observe whether governor weight rises and falls. If the unit is on the bench, apply air pressure and rotate the driven shaft by hand and observe that the input shaft rotates.

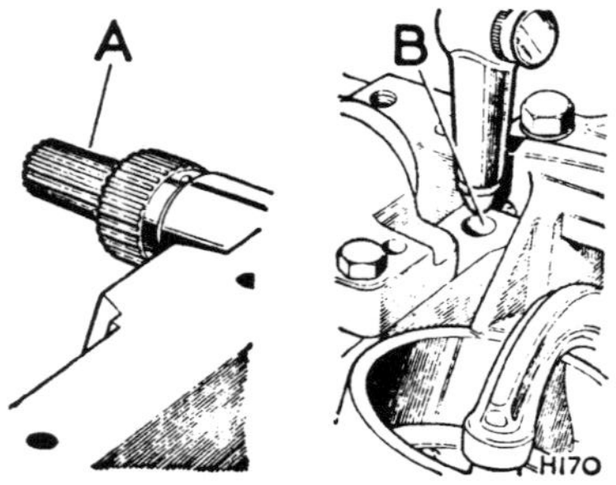

Rear clutch pressure check

A—Input shaft B—Drilling in transmission case

Rear clutch

4. Apply air pressure to the drilling A in the transmission case.
   (a) If the unit is on the bench, apply air pressure and try to turn the input shaft by hand; note resistance as long as air pressure is applied. Keep air pressure applied for several seconds to check for leaks.
   (b) Listen for thump as air pressure is released indicating that clutch is releasing and not sticking.

Front servo

5. Apply air pressure to the servo apply tube location on servo body, adjacent to the rear retaining bolt. Observe the movement of the piston pin indicating that the servo is working.

Operations which are identified by an asterisk (*) can be carried out with the automatic transmission installed in the car

Operation EE2-24—*continued*

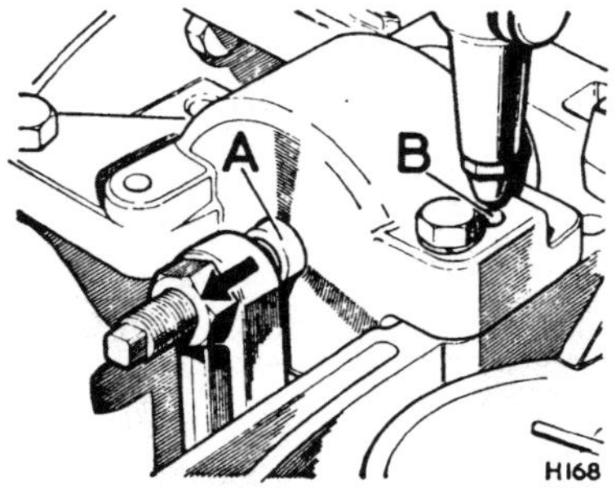

Front servo pressure check

A—Piston pin B—Servo apply tube location

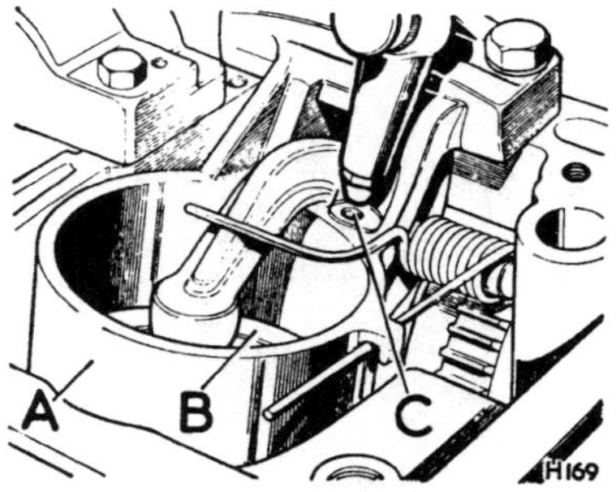

Rear servo pressure check

A—Cylinder B—Piston C—Oil tube location

Rear servo

6. Apply air pressure to tube location on the servo body.

   Observe movement of servo lever indicating servo is working.

On completion of tests continue assembly of the unit or if the unit tested, is fitted in the car, fit the following:

Extension casing and coupling flange. Operation EE2-16.

Oil pan and valve bodies assembly. Operation EE2-7.

Tightening torques:

Bolts, securing valve bodies assembly to transmission casing 4 to 5 lb ft (0,55 to 0,7 mkg).

Bolts, securing extension housing to transmission casing 8 to 10 lb ft (1,0 to 1,4 mkg).

Bolts, securing oil pan to transmission casing 8 to 10 lb ft (1,0 to 1,4 mkg).

*Oil cooler, to remove and refit—Operation EE2-25

Workshop hand tools:
Spanner sizes: $\frac{7}{16}$ in. AF, $\frac{1}{2}$ in. AF, $\frac{5}{16}$ in. Whit
Pliers, pointed nose

Oil cooler, remove

1. Remove the radiator grille by raising the bonnet and taking out the two top mounting bolts and the mounting bolts situated beneath the lower front body panel. Lift the top of the grille out first and remove two lower brackets. Where packing pieces are fitted note position to ensure correct refitment.

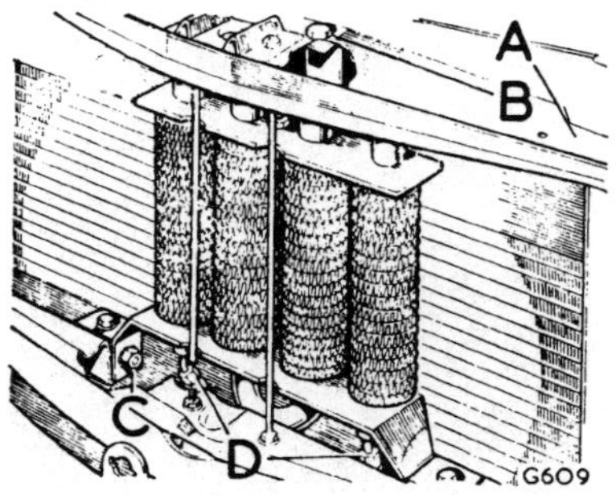

Oil cooler

A—Top grille C—Bolt fixing oil cooler
B—Bolt fixing top grille D—Oil pipe unions

2. Disconnect the bonnet lock mechanism.
3. Remove the two nuts securing the bonnet lock.
4. Remove the fixings securing the bonnet lock platform and oil cooler hanger bracket. Lift out the bonnet lock platform.
5. Disconnect the two flexible hoses from the oil cooler at the unions beneath the cooler. Use a suitable clean container to collect any fluid from the cooler.
6. Blank off the oil cooler and pipe unions to prevent the ingress of dirt.
7. Remove the two lower oil cooler fixing bolts and lift out the oil cooler.

Oil cooler, refit

1. Reverse removal procedure.
2. Check fluid level in automatic transmission topping up if necessary.

*Oil cooler pipes, to remove and refit—Operation EE2-26

Workshop hand tools:
Spanner sizes: $\frac{7}{16}$ in. AF, $\frac{1}{2}$ in. AF, $\frac{5}{16}$ in. Whit

Oil cooler pipes, remove

1. Disconnect the two flexible hoses from the oil cooler at the unions beneath the oil cooler. Also disconnect the two pipes at the automatic transmission end. Use a suitable clean container to collect any fluid from the pipes.
2. Remove clips retaining pipes.
3. If necessary, disconnect flexible pipes from the bundy pipes.

Oil cooler pipes, refit

1. Reverse removal procedure.
2. Check fluid level in automatic transmission, top up as required.

Operations which are identified by an asterisk (*) can be carried out with the automatic transmission installed in the car.

Operation EE2-26—*continued*

1 Oil cooler
2 Union nut } Oil cooler connections
3 Olive for union nut } Oil cooler connections
4 Hanger bracket for oil cooler
5 Bolt (¼ in. UNF x ⅝ in. long) } Fixing hanger bracket to body at bonnet locking platform
6 Plain washer
7 Spring washer
8 Locknut
9 Mounting bracket for oil cooler and radiator grille
10 Bolt (¼ in. UNF x ⅝ in. long) } Fixing oil cooler to mounting brackets
11 Plain washer
12 Spring washer
13 Bolt (¼ in. UNF x ⅜ in. long) } Fixing oil cooler to hanger bracket
14 Spring washer
15 Feed pipe complete
16 Return pipe complete
17 Union nut } For feed and return pipes
18 Olive } For feed and return pipes
19 Flexible pipe, oil connection
20 Support bracket for pipe clip
21 Pipe clip (double)
22 Pipe clip (single)
23 Bolt (2 BA x ⅜ in. long) } Fixing clips to support brackets at sump fixings
24 Bolt (2 BA x ¾ in. long)
25 Spring washer
26 Nut (2 BA)
27 Drive screw fixing clip to flywheel housing

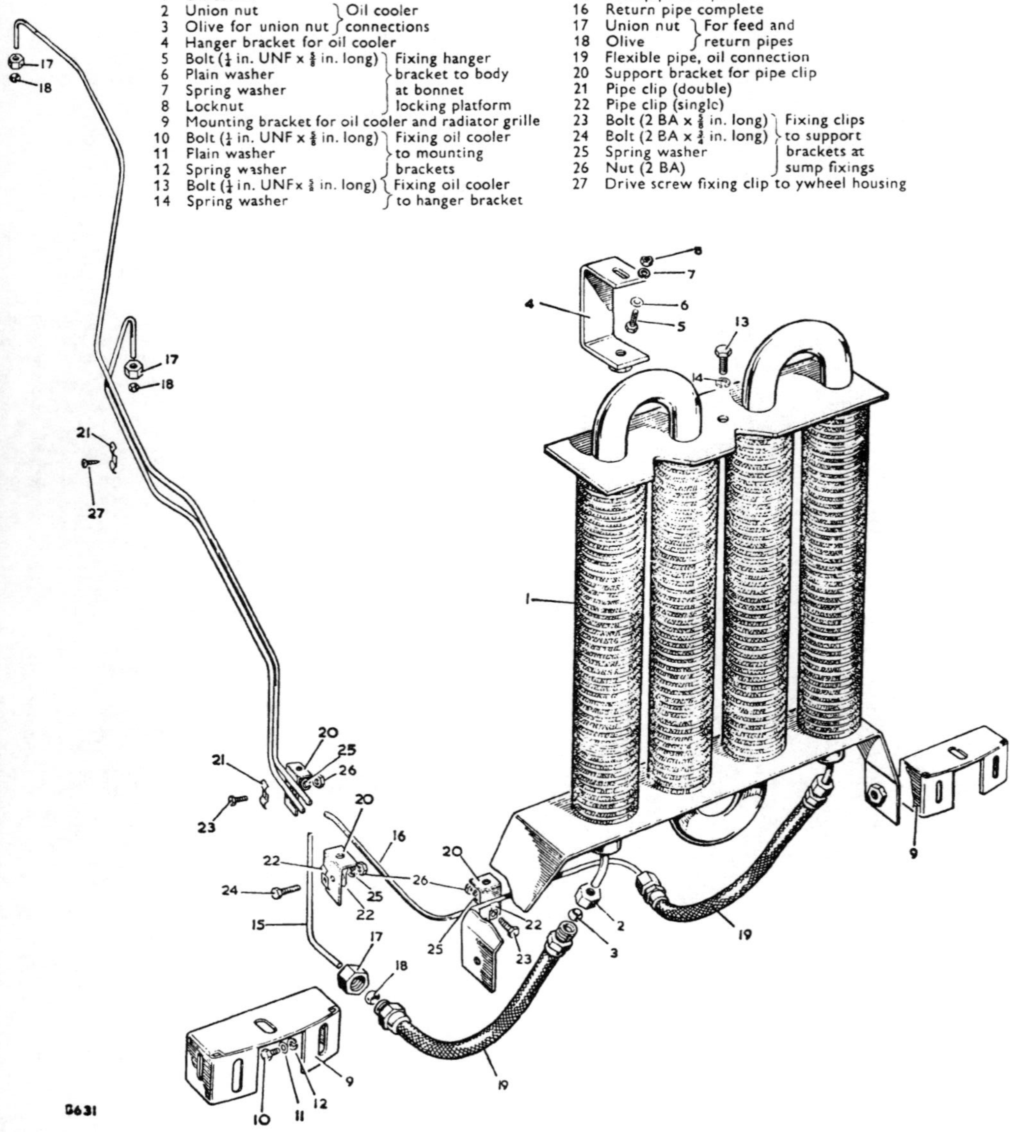

Oil cooler and pipes

Section EE—AUTOMATIC TRANSMISSION, MODEL 35, Rover Mk III

Part Three

This section provides the instructions necessary for overhauling the various units of the automatic transmission.

High standards of cleanliness are required when working on the automatic transmission. Petrol, paraffin or an industrial cleaning solvent may be used to clean components. Use nylon rag—never material that is fluffy or that leaves lint when drying any components.

Valve bodies, to overhaul—Operation EE3-1

Workshop hand tools:
Screwdriver, medium

Special tools:
'Spintorq' screwdriver set, Rover Part No. 601286

Instruction for the removal of the valve bodies assembly is given in Part Two of this Section.

Valve bodies, to dismantle

1. Withdraw the manual control valve.
2. Remove the front and rear pump oil strainers, secured by screws, plain and spring washers.

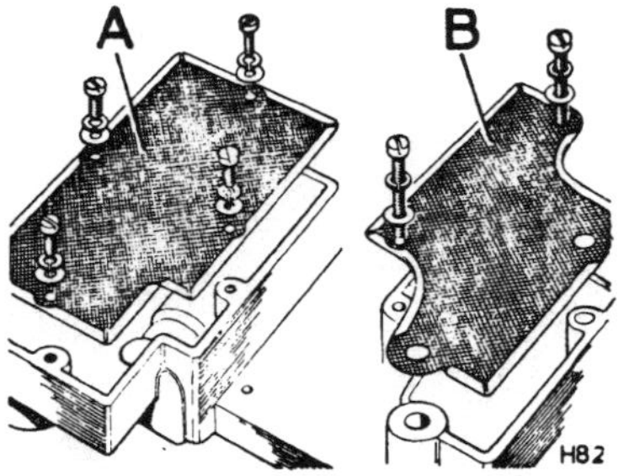

Oil strainers, front and rear pump

A—Oil strainer, front pump
B—Oil strainer, rear pump

3. Remove eight screws and spring washers securing the lower valve body to the upper valve body, two screws and washers are located in the oil strainer housing, these retain the governor line plate.

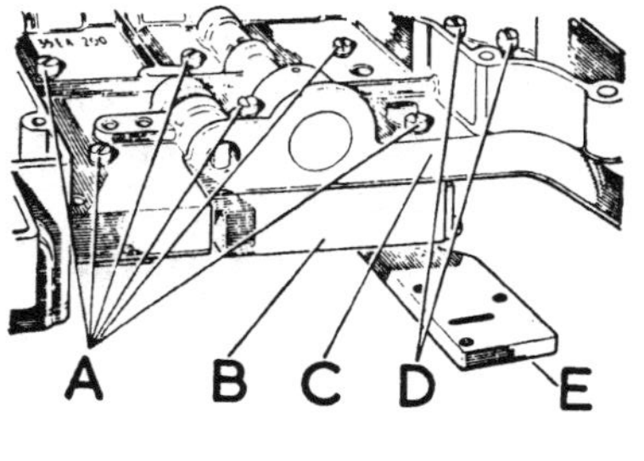

Valve bodies

A—Screws for valve bodies
B—Upper valve body
C—Lower valve body
D—Screws for governor line plate
E—Governor line plate

4. Turn the unit over and remove the oil tube collector plate, secured by six short and two long screws and spring washers, to the lower valve body.

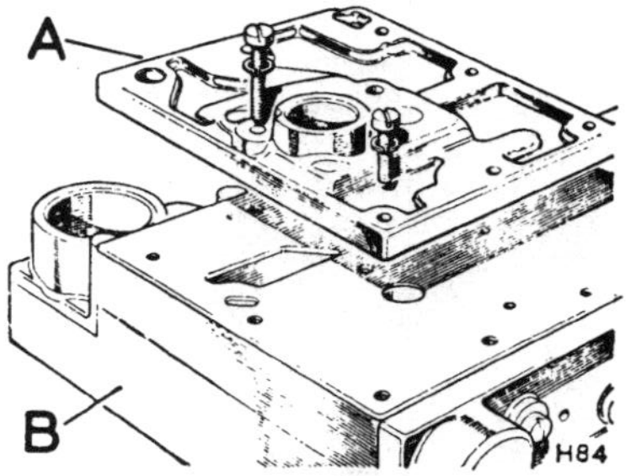

Oil tube collector plate

A—Oil tube collector plate
B—Lower valve body

5. Remove the down-shift valve cam, which is secured by two screws and spring washers.
6. Remove the two remaining screws securing the upper valve body to the lower valve body and separate the two bodies.

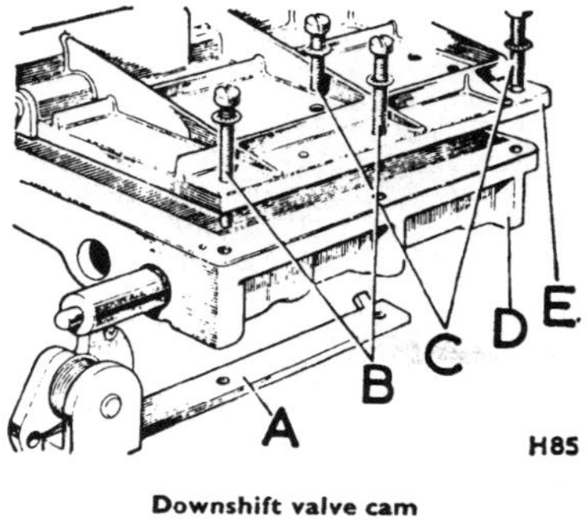

Downshift valve cam

A—Downshift valve cam
B—Screws fixing valve cam
C—Screws fixing upper to lower valve body
D—Lower valve body
E—Upper valve body

Operation EE3-1—*continued*

7. Lift off the separating plate.
8. Take all the loose valves and components from the lower valve body, these are:

   Front pump check valve, spring steel reed valve.

   Rear pump check valve and spring, disc and coil spring.

   Converter check valve and spring, ball and coil spring.

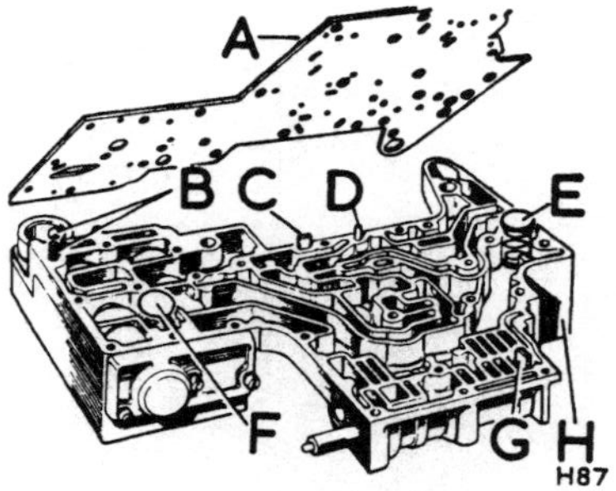

Separating plate, to remove

A—Separating plate
B—Converter 'out' check valve spring, 11/16 in. (18 mm) long, 7/32 in. (5,5 mm) diameter
C—Servo orifice valve stop
D—Dowel pin for modulator valve
E—Rear pump check valve spring, 5/8 in. (16 mm) long, 13/32 in. (10 mm) diameter
F—Front pump check valve
G—Stop for throttle valve spring
H—Lower valve body

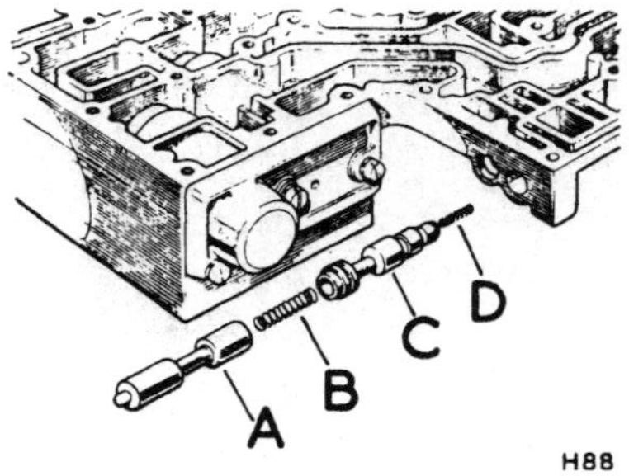

Downshift and throttle valve

A—Downshift valve
B—Throttle valve spring, 1 3/16 in. (30 mm) long, 15/64 in. (6 mm) diameter
C—Throttle valve
D—Throttle return spring, 25/32 in. (20 mm) long, 9/64 in. (3.5 mm) diameter

9. Withdraw the down-shift valve, then tilt valve body to allow throttle valve and spring to slide out, finally remove spring retainer.

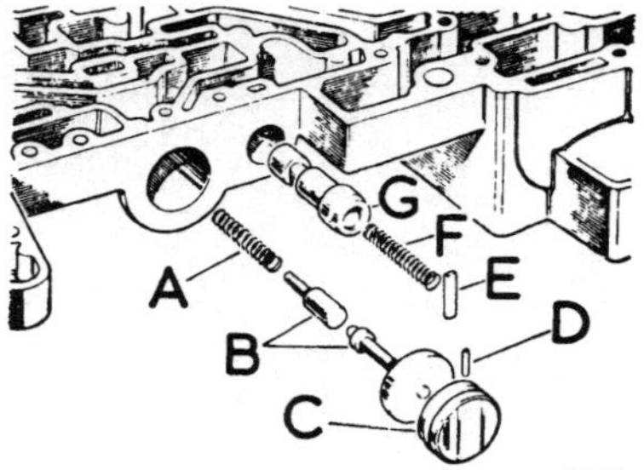

Modulator and servo orifice valve components

A—Spring, modulator valve, 1 in. (25 mm) long, 3/16 in. (4,5 mm) diameter
B—Modulator valve
C—Plug, modulator valve
D—Dowel pin for modulator valve
E—Stop for servo orifice valve
F—Spring, servo orifice control valve, 1 7/32 in. (30 mm) long, 13/64 in. (5 mm) diameter
G—Servo orifice control valve

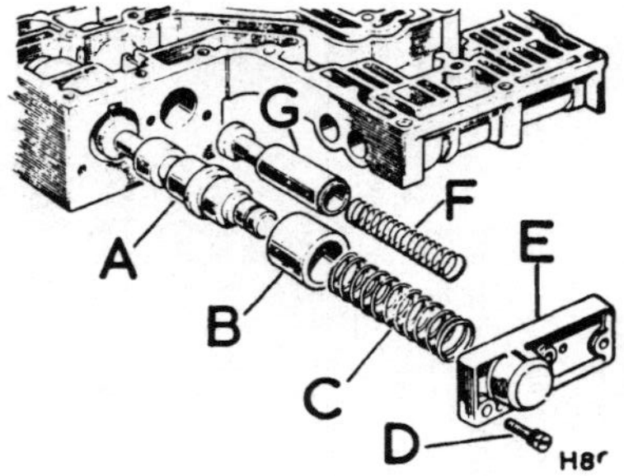

Primary and secondary regulator valves

A—Primary regulator valve
B—Sleeve, primary regulator valve
C—Spring, primary regulator valve, 2 27/32 in. (72 mm) long, 5/8 in. (16 mm) diameter
D—Screw fixing cover plate
E—Cover plate
F—Spring, secondary regulator valve, 2 19/32 in. (66 mm) long, 15/32 in. (12 mm) diameter
G—Secondary regulator valve

Operation EE3-1—*continued*

10. Turn the valve body over to remove:
    Orifice control valve stop.
    Modulator valve dowel.
    It may be necessary to depress the valve plug to release the dowel pin. Withdraw the plug, valve, spacer and spring of the modulator valve and the servo orifice control valve spring and valve.

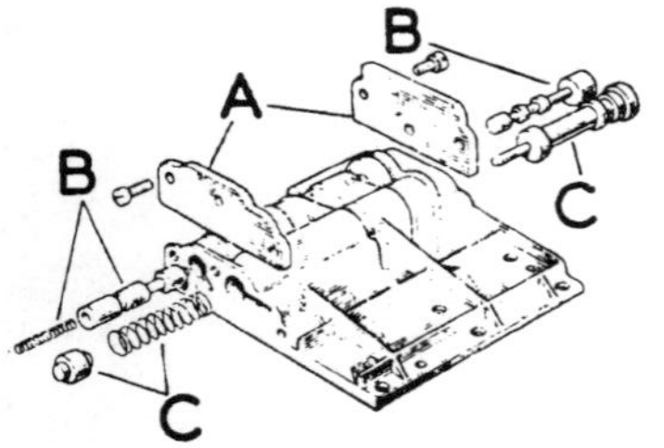

H86

Upper valve body components

A—End cover plates
B—1st, 2nd shift valve, plunger and spring, 1 $\frac{3}{32}$ in.(28 mm) long, $\frac{15}{64}$ in. (6 mm) diameter
C—2nd, 3rd shift valve, plunger and spring, 1 $\frac{19}{32}$ in. (40 mm) long, $\frac{23}{64}$ in. (9 mm) diameter

11. Remove the lower body end-plate, secured by three screws and spring washers. Withdraw the primary and secondary regulator valve components. Note there is considerable spring pressure behind the cover plate.
12. Dismantle the upper valve body, which has already been removed from the lower valve body. The upper body end-plates are each retained by three screws and spring washers. Remove the plates and withdraw the valve components.

Preparation before rebuild

1. Carefully clean all the components, using petrol as the cleaning medium. Use only nylon or non-fluffy rag. Clear fluid passages with the aid of an air line. Assemble parts dry to check fit in bores.
2. Examine all components for wear and verify the free movement of all the valves in their bores.

Valve bodies, rebuild

1. Note that no gaskets are used throughout the valve bodies assembly. It is essential that a torque screwdriver is used exclusively on reassembly.
2. Assemble the upper valve body in the order as illustrated. Tighten the six end-plate fixing screws to 20 to 30 lb in. (0,23 to 0,35 mkg).
3. Place on one side until required for final assembly.
4. Assemble in accordance with the illustration the servo orifice control valve and secure with the stop.

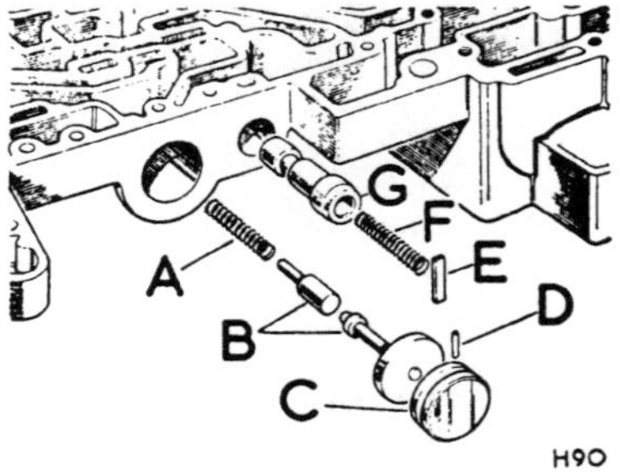

H90

Modulator and servo orifice valve components, to assemble

A—Spring, modulator valve, 1 in. (25 mm) long, $\frac{3}{16}$ in. (4,5 mm) diameter
B—Modulator valve and plug
C—Retaining plug
D—Dowel pin, modulator valve
E—Stop, servo orifice valve
F—Spring, servo orifice control valve, 1 $\frac{7}{32}$ in. (30 mm) long, $\frac{13}{64}$ in. (5 mm) diameter
G—Servo orifice control valve

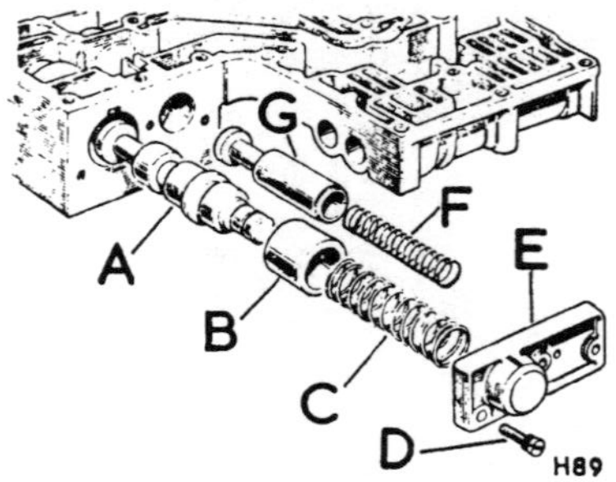

H89

Primary and secondary regulator valves, to reassemble

A—Primary regulator valve
B—Sleeve, primary regulator valve
C—Spring, primary regulator valve, 2 $\frac{27}{32}$ in. (72 mm) long, $\frac{5}{8}$ in. (16 mm) diameter
D—Screw fixing cover plate
E—Cover plate
F—Spring, secondary regulator valve, 2 $\frac{19}{32}$ in. (66 mm) long, $\frac{31}{64}$ in. (12 mm) diameter
G—Secondary regulator valve

Operation EE3-1—*continued*

5. Fit the modulator valve to the lower valve body, and secure the assembly with the dowel pin.
6. Insert the primary and secondary regulator valves into the lower valve body and fit the cover plate. Tighten the three screws securing the cover plate to the body to a torque figure of 20 to 30 lb in. (0,23 to 0,35 mkg).
7. Place the three check valves, front pump, rear pump and converter 'out', into position on the lower valve body. Place the stop for throttle valve spring into position.

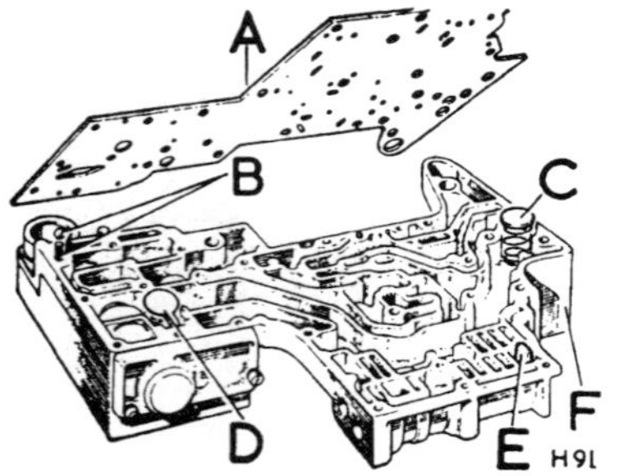

H9l

Lower valve body components, to assemble

A—Separating plate
B—Converter 'out' check valve spring, $\frac{45}{64}$ in. (18 mm) long, $\frac{7}{32}$ in. (5,5 mm) diameter
C—Rear pump check valve spring, $\frac{5}{8}$ in. (16 mm) long, $\frac{13}{32}$ in. (10 mm) diameter
D—Front pump check valve
E—Stop for throttle valve spring
F—Lower valve body

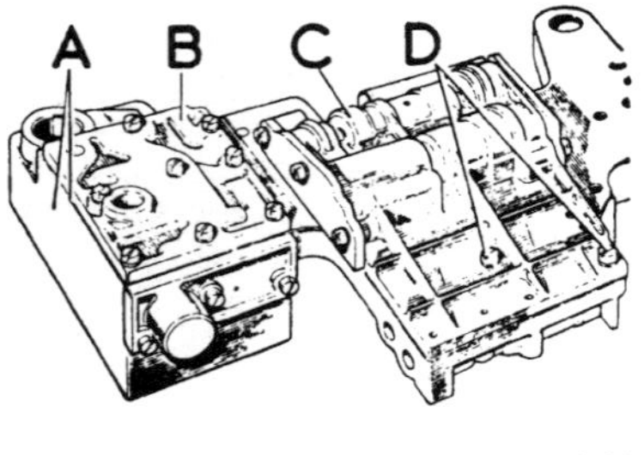

H92

Valve bodies, to reassemble

A—Separating plate and lower valve body
B—Oil tube collector plate
C—Upper valve body
D—Screws fixing valve bodies

8. Carefully place the separating plate into position, ensuring that the valves beneath it are locating correctly.
9. Position the upper valve body assembly on to the separating plate and locate with the two screws as shown, but do not fully tighten the screws at this stage.
10. Fit the oil tube collector plate to the valve body. Tighten the eight fixing screws (six short and two long) to 20 to 30 lb in. (0,23 to 0,35 mkg).
11. Place the governor line plate into position on the valve bodies. Turn the unit over and secure the plate loosely with the two screws located inside the oil intake chamber of the valve body. Before finally tightening these two screws to 20 to 30 lb in. (0,23 to 0,35 mkg) insert the other two long screws loosely (these also locate the oil strainer) to ensure correct alignment. After tightening, remove the long screws.
12. Fit the six remaining screws securing the upper valve body to the lower valve body. Tighten to a torque figure of 20 to 30 lb in. (0,23 to 0,35 mkg).

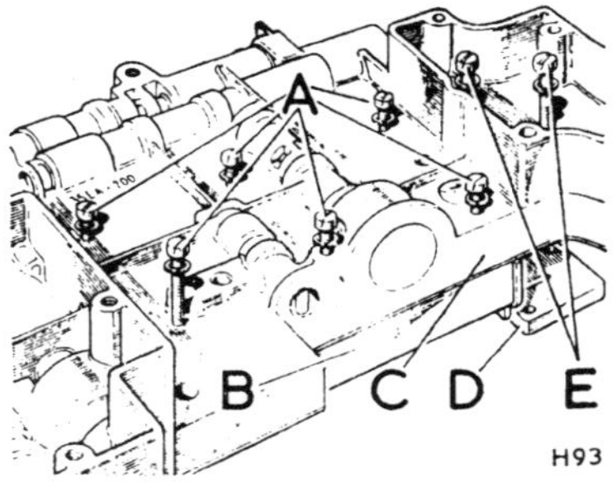

H93

Valve bodies and line plate, to reassemble

A—Screws fixing valve bodies
B—Upper valve body
C—Lower valve body
D—Line plate
E—Screws fixing line plate

13. Fit the down-shift valve and throttle valve in the order illustrated overleaf.

Operation EE3-1—*continued*

14. Fit the down-shift valve cam. To ensure that the return spring is correctly tensioned, the cam should be turned in the direction of the arrow and held in this position whilst the assembly is secured to the valve body with two screws and spring washers.

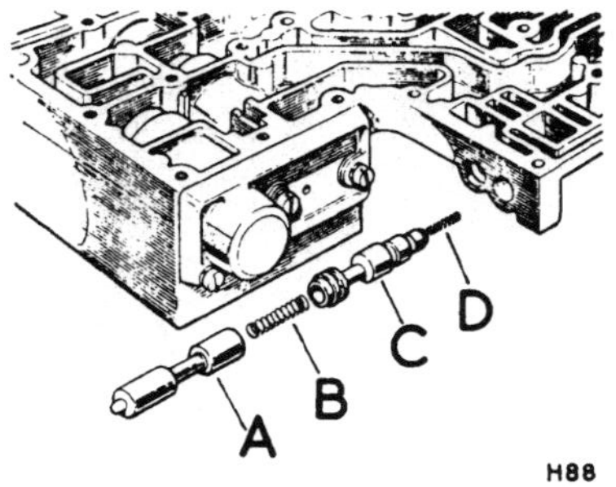

Downshift and throttle valve, to reassemble

A—Downshift valve
B—Throttle valve spring, $1\frac{3}{16}$ in. (30 mm) long, $\frac{15}{64}$ in. (6 mm) diameter
C—Throttle valve
D—Throttle return spring, $\frac{13}{16}$ in. (20 mm) long, $\frac{9}{64}$ in. (3,5 mm) diameter

15. Replace the two pump strainers, tightening the screws to 20 to 30 lb in. (0,23 to 0,35 mkg).

16. Insert the manual control valve.
The valve body assembly is now completely assembled.

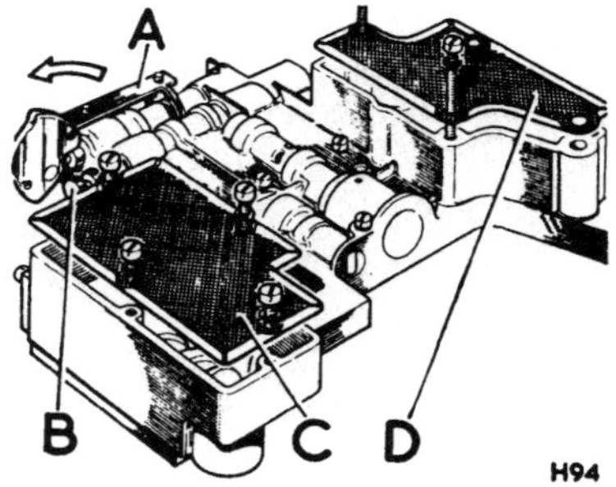

Downshift valve cam and oil strainers, to reassemble

A—Downshift valve cam assembly
B—Manual control valve
C—Oil strainer, front pump
D—Oil strainer, rear pump

Front servo, to overhaul—Operation EE3-2

Workshop hand tools:
Spanner sizes: Open ended $\frac{1}{2}$ in. AF $\frac{9}{16}$ in. AF, Screwdriver, small, Drift, Light hammer
Instruction for the removal and refitting of the front servo is given in Part Two of this Section

Front servo, dismantle

1. Use a screwdriver to prise out the snap ring.
2. Withdraw the sleeve and piston from the body of the servo and separate the components.

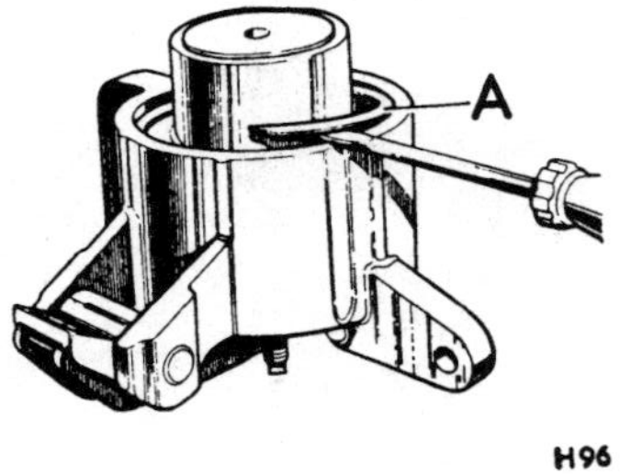

Front servo, dismantle

A—Snap ring

3. Remove the large and small 'O' ring from the piston and the seal from the piston sleeve.
4. Remove the adjusting screw, operating lever and pivot pin.

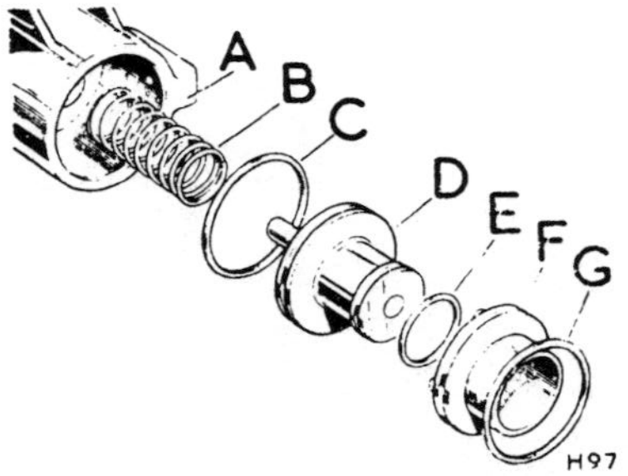

Front servo components

A—Servo body
B—Piston retracting spring
C—'O' ring for piston, large
D—Piston assembly
E—'O' ring for piston, small
F—Piston sleeve
G—Sealing ring for piston sleeve

Preparation before rebuild

1. Clean all components, using petrol and nylon rag. Examine all components for defects.
The nominal free length of the spring is $\frac{31}{32}$ in. (24,5 mm).

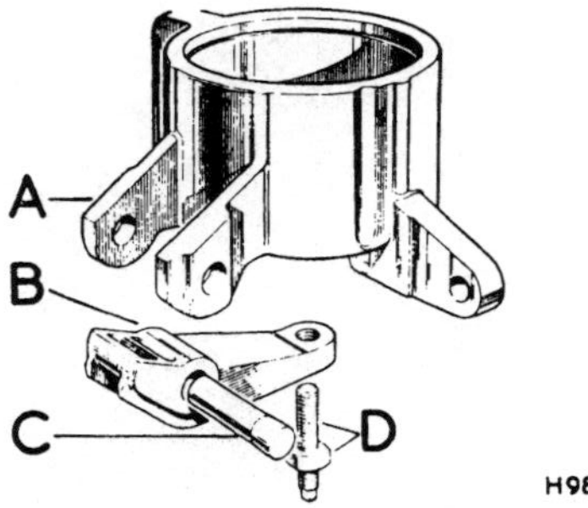

Front servo body

A—Servo body
B—Operating lever
C—Pivot pin
D—Adjusting screw and locknut

Front servo, rebuild

1. Renew the 'O' ring and the square section oil sealing ring.
2. Prior to assembly lubricate the components with clean transmission fluid.
3. Assemble the components and secure with the snap ring. Note that the collar of the sleeve fits inwards.

Rear servo, to overhaul—Operation EE3-3

Workshop hand tools:
Drift, Light hammer

Instruction for removal and refitting of the rear servo is given in Part Two of this Section

Rear servo, to dismantle

1. Release return spring from lug on servo body.

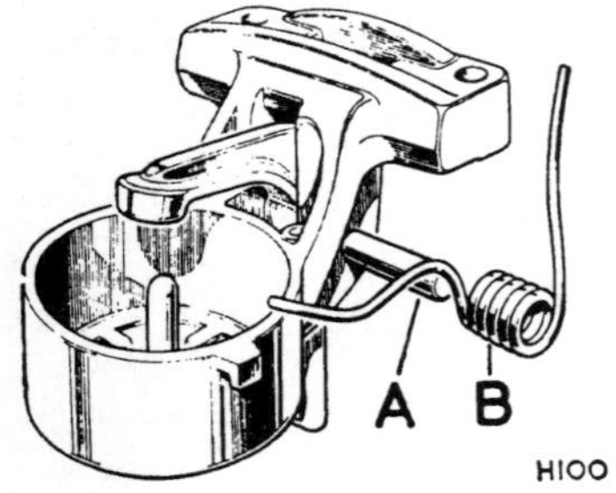

Rear servo, to dismantle

A—Pivot pin for spring and lever
B—Return spring for servo

2. Withdraw piston by manoeuvring it out between body and lever as shown in the illustration.

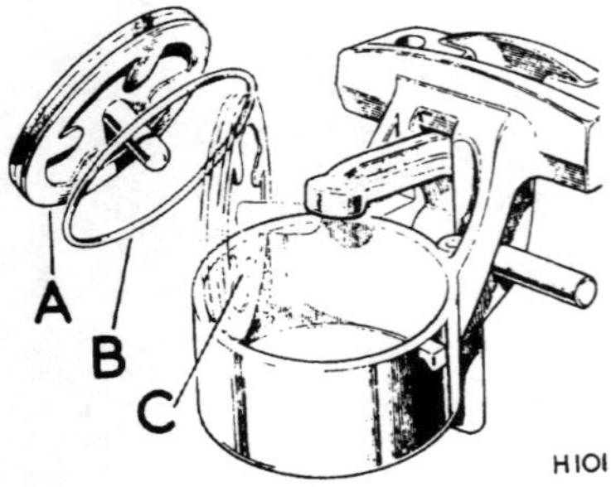

Rear servo piston

A—Servo piston
B—Sealing ring for piston
C—To withdraw, turn as shown

3. Remove the 'O' ring from the piston.
4. Drift out the pivot pin, then withdraw the operating arm.

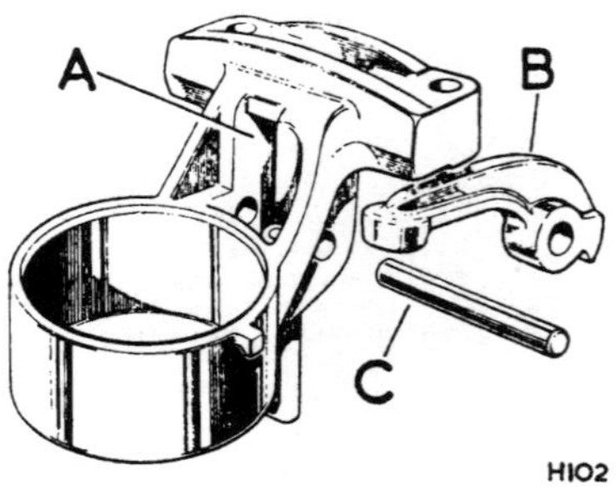

Servo operating lever, removal

A—Servo body
B—Operating lever for servo
C—Pivot pin for spring and lever

Preparation before rebuild

1. Clean and examine all the components for defects. Use petrol and nylon rag for cleaning purposes.

Rear servo, rebuild

1. Renew the piston 'O' ring.
2. Prior to assembly of the piston into the body, lubricate all components with transmission fluid.
3. Reverse dismantling procedure.

Front pump assembly, to overhaul—Operation EE3-4

Workshop hand tools:

Spanner sizes:
Socket ½ in. AF
Screwdriver, medium, Plastic-faced hammer

Special tools:
'Spintorq' screwdriver set, Rover Part No. 601286
Torque wrench set, Rover Part No. 601285

Instruction for the removal and refitting of the front pump is given in Part Two of this Section

Front pump, dismantle

1. Separate the pump housing from the adaptor and converter support by removing the five bolts and spring washers and the small locating screw and spring washer.

   If necessary tap the assembly lightly with a plastic-faced hammer to separate the housing and adaptor.

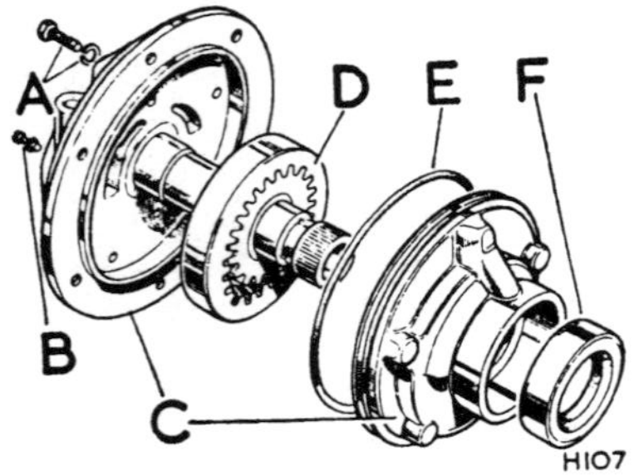

Front pump assembly

A—Bolts for front pump
B—Locating screw and washer
C—Two halves of pump assembly
D—Pump gears
E—'O' ring, large
F—Outer oil seal

2. Mark the outside face of each pump gear to ensure they are fitted the same way round on assembly. Lift out the gears.
3. Remove the large 'O' ring from the outside diameter of the pump housing and discard.
4. Prise out the lipped oil seal from the pump housing and discard.

Preparation before rebuild

1. Clean all parts thoroughly and examine for wear and defects. Renew the seal and 'O' ring and if necessary the fixing bolts and washers.
2. The bushes in the converter support tube are not service items.

Front pump assembly, rebuild

1. Position the new large 'O' ring on to the pump housing and fit a new lipped oil seal.
2. Assemble the pump gears; locate in position with petroleum jelly the correct way round, as marked, position the pump housing to the adaptor and converter support. Loosely locate with the five bolts and spring washers and small screw and washer. Then push the pump housing into the adaptor. Tighten the five bolts to a torque figure of 17 to 22 lb ft (2,3 to 3,0 mkg) and the screw to a torque figure of 25 to 35 lb in (0,3 to 0,4 mkg).

Front clutch assembly, to overhaul—Operation EE3-5

Workshop hand tools:
Screwdriver, small

Instruction for the removal and refitting of the front clutch is given in Part Two of this Section.

Front clutch, to dismantle

1. Separate front clutch from rear clutch.
2. Use a screwdriver to remove the snap ring retaining the input shaft. Lift off the input shaft.

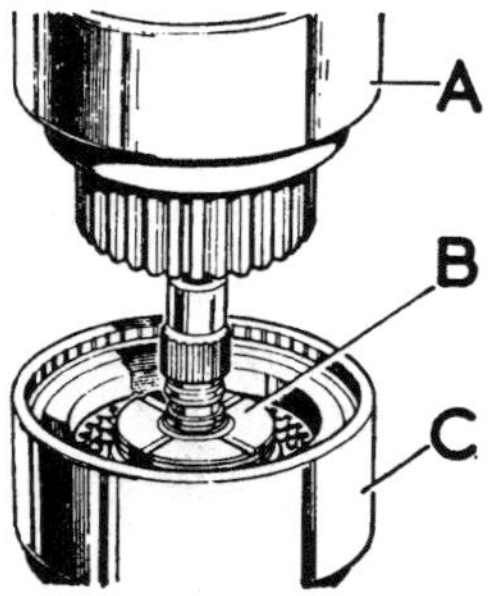

Front and rear clutch

A—Front clutch B—Thrust washers
C—Rear clutch

3. Remove the bronze thrust washer, located in the recess of the clutch hub, and lift out the clutch hub.

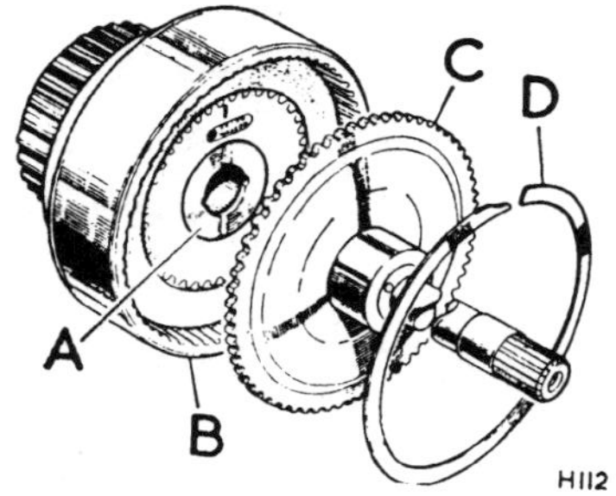

Input shaft and front clutch assembly

A—Bronze thrust washer C—Input shaft
B—Front clutch cylinder D—Snap ring

4. Withdraw the clutch plates, four inner and three outer. The outer 'drive' plates are steel and the inner friction plates are paper-faced.
5. Lift out the pressure plate.

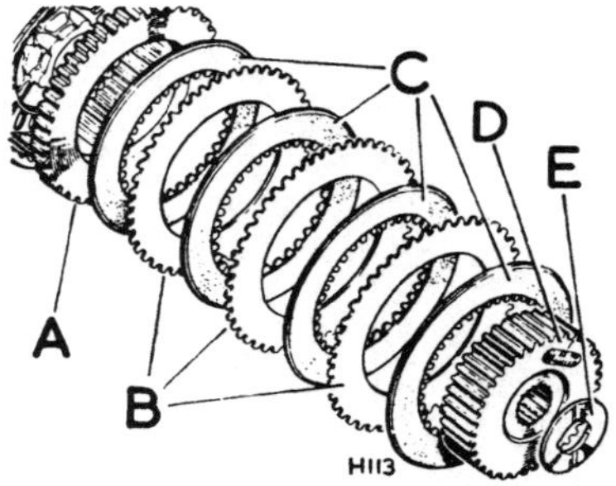

Hub and clutch plates, to remove

A—Pressure plate C—Inner clutch plates
B—Outer clutch plates D—Clutch hub
E—Bronze thrust washer

6. Prise out the inner snap ring with a screwdriver and remove the diaphragm type spring. Note that the inner edge of the diaphragm spring is dished inwards.

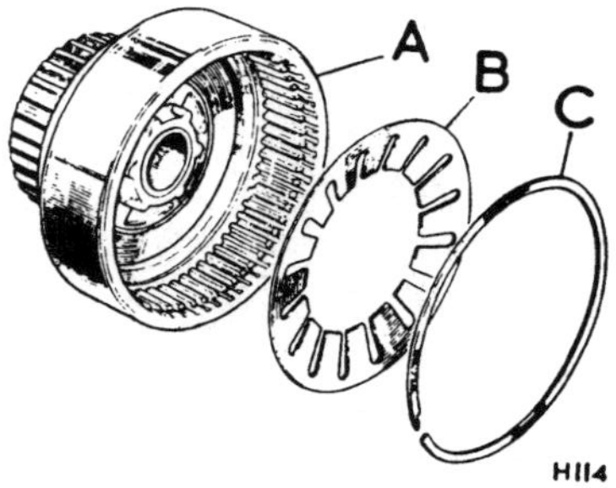

Clutch spring, to remove

A—Clutch cylinder B—Diaphragm spring
C—Snap ring

7. Remove the clutch piston. This may be facilitated by applying an air line through the hole in the internal bore whilst the second hole is blanked off.
8. Withdraw the bearing ring from the top of the piston.
9. Remove the large sealing ring from the piston.
10. Remove the small 'O' ring from the cylinder spigot.
11. Check that the reed valve on the piston is not bent and that it can be closed with light finger pressure.

Operation EE3-5—*continued*

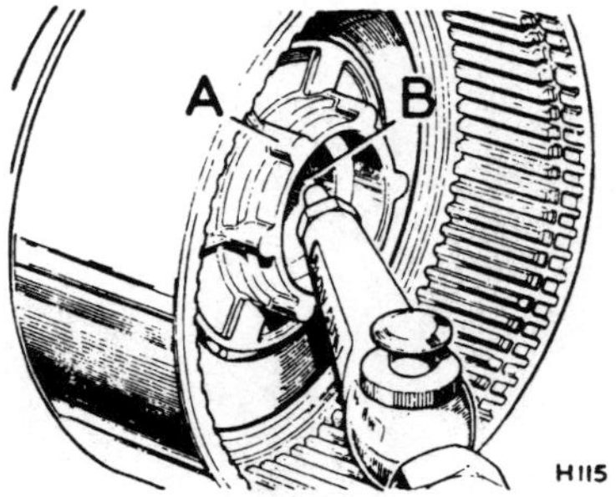

Clutch piston, to remove

A—Piston
B—Drilling to which air pressure is applied

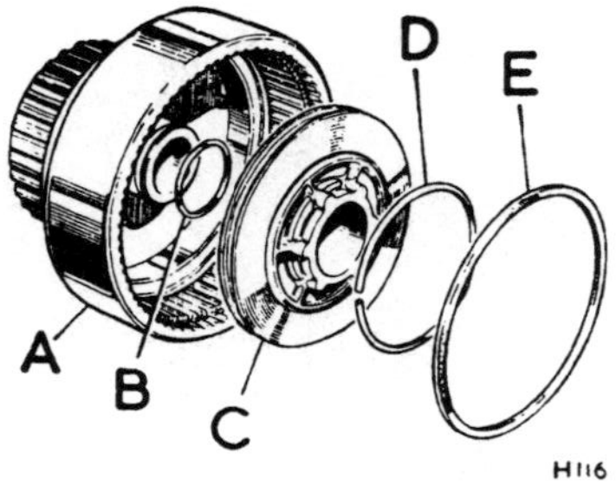

Front clutch piston components

A—Clutch cylinder C—Piston
B—Inner 'O' ring seal D—Spring bearing ring
E—Seal for piston

Preparation before rebuild

1. Clean the component parts thoroughly and inspect for defects. Use nylon rag and petrol for cleaning purposes.

Front clutch, rebuild

1. Lubricate the cylinder with clean transmission fluid. Smear a new small 'O' ring with clean fluid and fit the ring into the cylinder.
2. Fit new sealing ring on to the clutch piston, after lubricating both parts with clean transmission fluid. Place the bearing ring into position in its groove on top of the piston.
3. Replace the diaphragm spring, dished edge inwards, and secure in position with the snap ring.
4. Install the clutch pressure plate with the plain side uppermost.
5. Replace the clutch plates; an inner splined plate first, followed by an outer splined plate, alternately.
6. Line up the internal teeth of the inner plates then fit the clutch hub, with the flat face uppermost. If necessary, turn the hub slightly to pick up the splines of the clutch plates.
7. Place the bronze thrust washer into the recess of the hub.
8. Fit the input shaft to the cylinder and secure with the large snap ring.

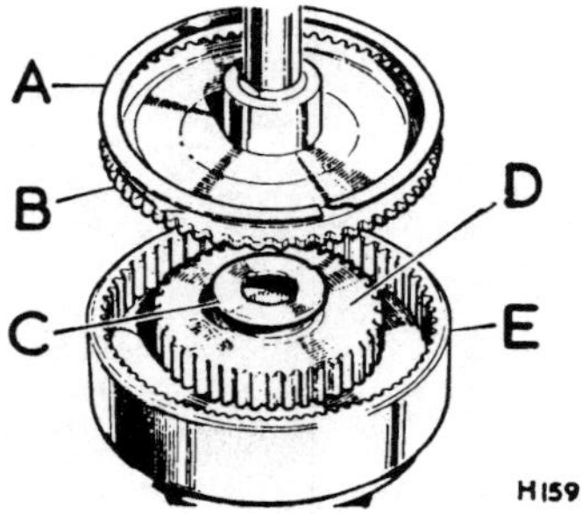

Clutch plates and hub

A—Snap ring for input shaft C—Bronze thrust washer
B—Input shaft flange D—Clutch hub
E—Clutch cylinder

9. Support the rear clutch and forward sun gear assembly in a vertical position, centralise the two sealing rings on the shaft of the forward sun gear assembly. Lubricate freely with petroleum jelly and gently lower the front clutch cylinder into position.
10. Take care not to disengage the front clutch from rear clutch during handling.

Rear clutch, to overhaul—Operation EE3-6

Workshop hand tools:
Screwdriver, small

Special tools:
Clutch spring compressor, Rover Part No. 601283
Snap ring pliers, Rover Part No. 601282
Rear clutch piston and seal inserter, Rover Part No. 601290

Instruction for the removal and refitting of the rear clutch is given in Part Two of this Section.

Rear clutch, to dismantle

1. With the front and rear clutch assembly in a vertical position, carefully lift off the front clutch and place on one side.
2. Remove needle thrust bearing and lipped thrust plate from rear end of shaft, also the steel and bronze thrust washers from the rear clutch housing.

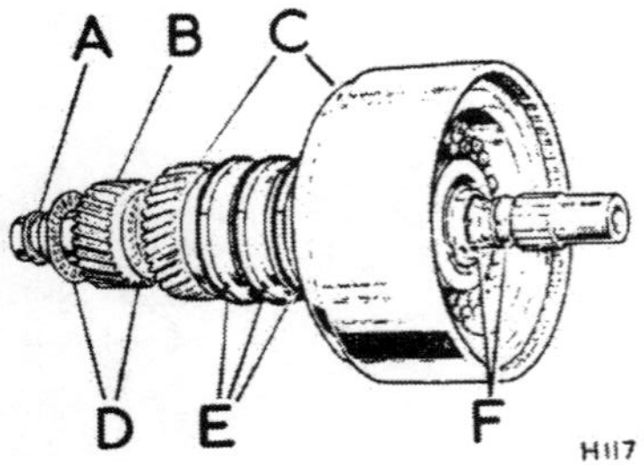

Rear clutch, to dismantle

A—Rear end sealing ring, nylon
B—Forward sun gear and shaft
C—Rear clutch assembly
D—Needle thrust bearing
E—Large sealing rings
F—Front end oil sealing rings

3. Remove the oil sealing rings from the front end of the forward sun gear shaft before attempting to remove the forward sun gear assembly.
4. Withdraw the forward sun gear assembly from the clutch, noting the position of the needle thrust bearing between the two gears. The sun gear cannot be removed from its shaft.
5. Use a screwdriver to remove the outer snap ring retaining the clutch components.
6. Invert drum and remove plates. Mark plate serrations to ensure correct assembly if original plates are being replaced.

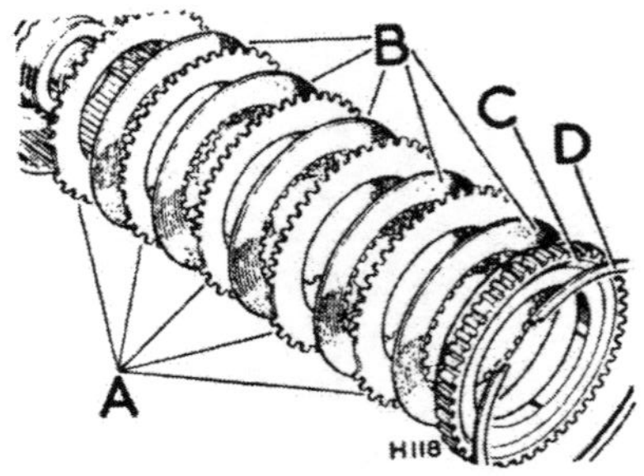

Rear clutch components

A—Outer clutch plates C—Pressure plate
B—Inner clutch plates D—Snap ring for pressure plate

7. Lift out the pressure plate and clutch plates. Note that the outer plates are dished and the inner plates are paper-faced.

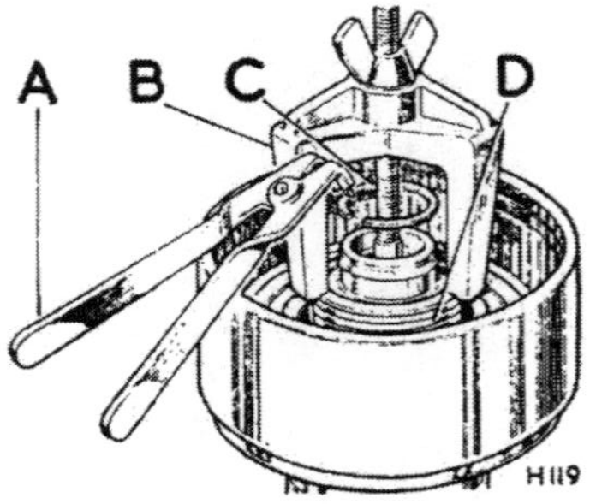

Clutch piston spring, to remove

A—Snap ring pliers
B—Clutch spring compressor
C—Snap ring for piston spring
D—Piston spring

8. Insert threaded rod of service tool, Rover Part No. 601283, through clutch and use legs of tool together with the wing nut to compress the

Operation EE3-6—*continued*

clutch spring. Use snap ring pliers, Rover Part No. 601282, to remove the circlip. Rotate the snap ring gap to the milled flat on the boss of the drum to facilitate removal.

Remove spring compression tool.

9. Withdraw spring seat and spring.
10. To facilitate removal of the piston use an air line through the hole adjacent to the drum, as illustrated.

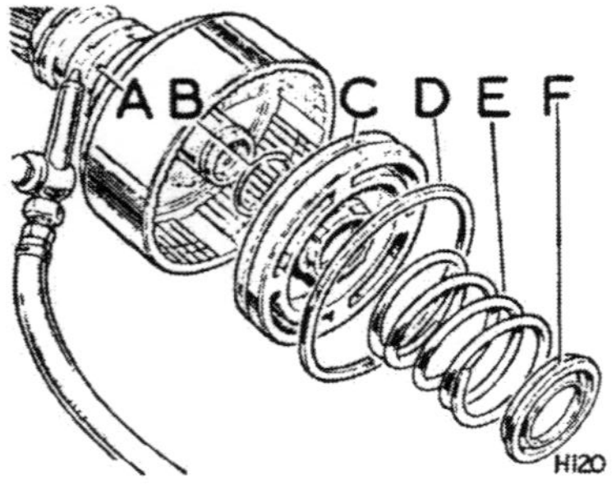

Clutch piston removal

A—Orifice for air line D—Seal for piston
B—Inner 'O' ring, small E—Clutch spring
C—Piston F—Clutch spring seat

11. Remove the 'O' ring from the inner boss of the drum and the oil seal from the piston.

Preparation before rebuild

1. Use petrol and nylon rag to clean all the components.
2. Examine all the parts for wear or defects.
3. Check that the reed valve on the piston is not bent or stuck open and that it can be closed with light finger pressure.

Rear clutch, rebuild

1. Fit new 'O' ring to boss in clutch cylinder.
2. Fit new sealing ring to piston.
3. Locate the rear clutch piston and seal inserter in clutch cylinder then install piston flat side downwards, ensure that it is correctly aligned with the bore during fitting. Remove the rear clutch piston and seal inserter.

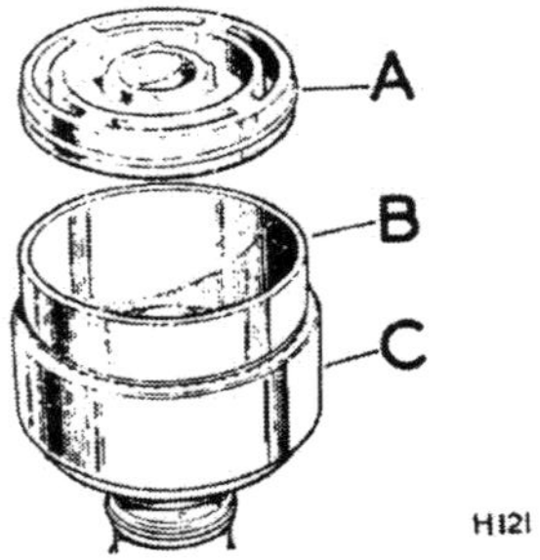

Clutch piston, to refit

A—Piston
B—Rear clutch piston and seal inserter
C—Clutch cylinder

4. Locate the piston spring and spring seat on to the piston. Position circlip on spring seat then use the special tool to compress the spring. Fit the circlip, using circlip pliers.
5. Fit the clutch plates, noting that an outer plate is fitted first. The dishing of the outer plates must all face in one direction, but it does not matter which way the dishing of the plates face in the drum. If necessary check for dishing on a flat surface.

   Replace the pressure plate with the flat face inwards and secure the plates with the snap ring.
6. Fit new oil sealing rings to the rear outer boss of the drum.
7. Place a needle thrust washer over the shaft against the front face of the forward sun gear, then insert shaft into the clutch.

Operation EE3-6—*continued*

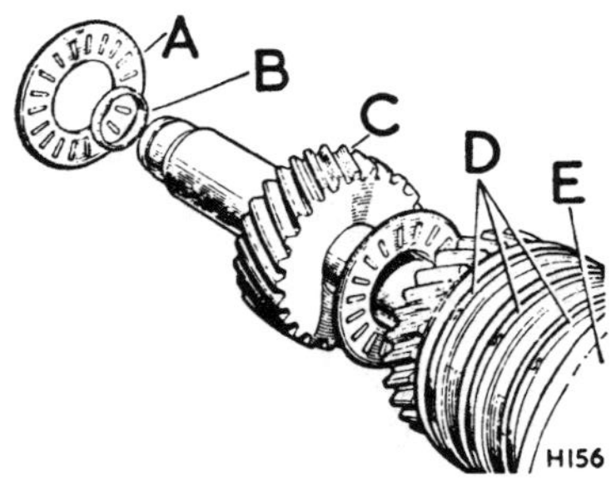

Forward sun gear and rear clutch

A—Needle thrust bearing
B—Nylon ring
C—Forward sun gear
D—Oil sealing ring, clutch to centre support
E—Rear clutch

8. Fit two new oil sealing rings to the front end of the forward sun gear shaft.

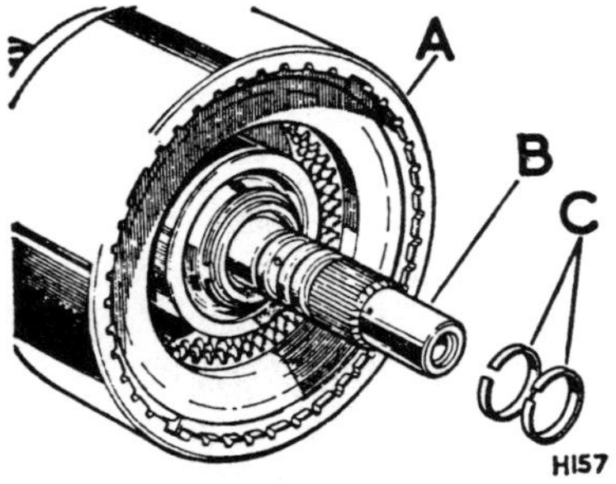

Oil sealing rings, to fit

A—Rear clutch
B—Forward sun gear shaft
C—Oil sealing rings

9. Locate the steel and bronze thrust washer over the centre hub of the drum and retain with petroleum jelly.

10. With the assembly in a vertical position, first line up the internal teeth of the clutch plates then centralise the small oil sealing rings on the shaft, lubricating with petroleum jelly and gently lower the front clutch over the shaft.

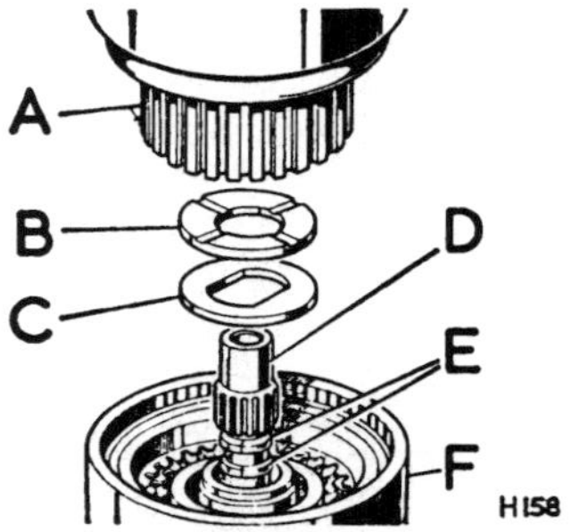

Front and rear clutch

A—Front clutch
B—Bronze thrust washer
C—Steel thrust washer
D—Forward sun gear shaft
E—Oil sealing rings
F—Rear clutch

11. If difficulty is experienced when carrying out this operation the front clutch should be checked to ensure that the internal thrust washer has not been displaced.

12. Fit new nylon sealing ring to rear end of forward sun gear shaft and place needle thrust washer in position and retain with petroleum jelly.

Planet gears and rear drum, to overhaul—Operation EE3-7

Workshop hand tools:
Screwdriver, small, Screwdriver, large, Mallet, plastic faced

Instruction for the removal and refitting of the planet gear and rear drum assembly is given in Part Two of this Section.

Rear drum, to dismantle

1. Remove needle thrust bearing and plate from the rear end of the drum.
2. Separate the centre support from the planet gear assembly.
3. Withdraw the one-way clutch from its outer race.
4. Support the drum in a soft-jawed vice. Prise out the snap ring with a screwdriver. Remove the one-way clutch outer race by levering with a large screwdriver alternately in the three slots. This race is a tight fit. Take care not to damage outer surface of drum.

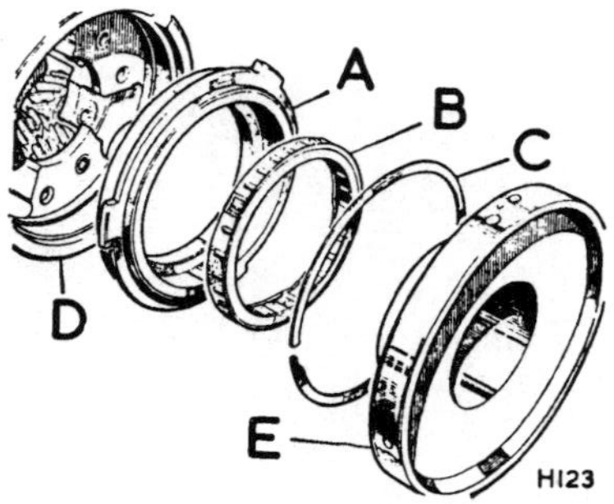

Planet gears and rear drum assembly

A—Outer race for one-way clutch
B—One-way clutch
C—Snap ring for outer race
D—Planet carrier
E—Centre support

Preparation before rebuild

1. Clean all the components using transmission fluid and nylon rag. Examine all components for defects.

Rear drum, rebuild

1. Lubricate all the components with clean transmission fluid.
2. Lightly tap the one-way clutch outer race into position using a soft-faced mallet and ensure correct alignment. Secure with the snap ring.
3. Position the one-way clutch in the outer race with the lip of the one-way clutch outwards.
4. Place the centre support into position on the drum.
5. First place the bearing plate lip outwards, followed by the needle thrust washer in position at the rear of the assembly and retain using petroleum jelly.

Governor, to overhaul—Operation EE3-8

Workshop hand tools:
Screwdrivers, medium and large

Special tools:
'Spintorq' screwdriver, Rover Part No. 601286

Instruction for the removal and refitting of the governor is given in Part Two of this Section.

Governor, dismantle

1. Remove the two screws and spring washers retaining the body to the governor sleeve.
2. Compress and withdraw the retainer and remove the governor weight, valve and spring.
3. If necessary remove the governor cover plate retained by two countersunk-head lock screws.

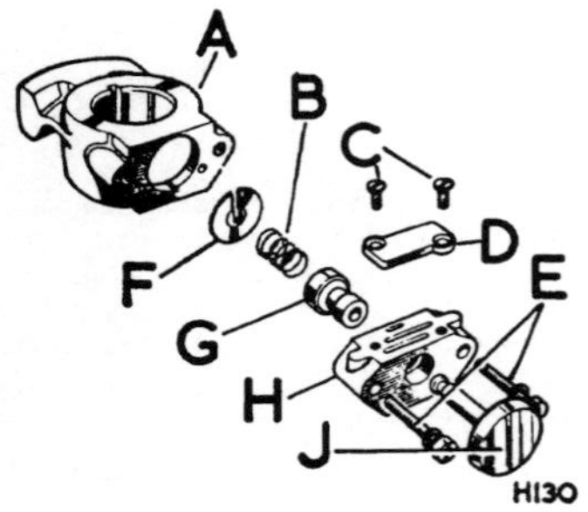

Governor assembly

A—Sleeve for governor
B—Spring for governor
C—Countersunk head lock screws
D—Cover plate
E—Screws fixing governor body
F—Retainer for spring
G—Valve for governor
H—Body for governor
J—Weight for governor

Preparation before rebuild

1. Clean and examine all components. Use nylon rag and transmission fluid for cleaning.

Governor, rebuild

1. Reverse removal procedure.
2. Align oil holes between body and sleeve.
3. Tighten the screws retaining the cover plate to the valve body to a torque figure of 20 to 30 lb in. (0,23 to 0,35 mkg).
   The screws retaining the valve body to the sleeve should be fully tightened using a large screwdriver.

Section EE—AUTOMATIC TRANSMISSION, MODEL 35, Rover Mk III

Part Four

This section covers a quick reference defect location chart, general data, recommended lubricants, a list of tightening torques and special tools.

MODEL 35—QUICK REFERENCE DEFECT LOCATION CHART

Note: The numbers indicate the recommended sequence of fault investigation.
See opposite page for Action Key

	1	2	3	4	5	6	7	8	9	10	11	12	13
ENGAGEMENT OF R, D or L													
Bumpy	D	B	d	f	c	O	Q	—	—	—	—	—	—
Delayed	A	C	D	a	d	c	b	s	N	P	S	X	q
None	A	C	a	b	c	d	V	W	X	Z	—	—	—
TAKE-OFF													
None forward	C	c	b	N	T	—	—	—	—	—	—	—	—
None reverse	C	F	m	n	c	b	a	S	P	—	—	—	—
Seizure reverse	E	O	—	—	—	—	—	—	—	—	—	—	—
No neutral	C	O	c	—	—	—	—	—	—	—	—	—	—
UPSHIFTS													
No. 1 to 2	C	E	h	m	R	f	g	a	b	c	—	—	—
No. 2 to 3	C	h	n	p	P	f	g	a	b	c	—	—	—
Above normal speeds	B	f	h	m	n	p	g	b	c	d	—	—	—
Below normal speeds	B	f	h	p	b	c	—	—	—	—	—	—	—
UPSHIFT QUALITY													
Slip 1 to 2	A	B	C	E	R	d	f	a	b	c	—	—	—
Slip 2 to 3	A	B	C	E	P	R	d	f	a	b	c	—	—
Rough 1 to 2	B	E	d	f	g	h	T	U	N	c	—	—	—
Rough 2 to 3	B	E	d	f	Q	c	—	—	—	—	—	—	—
Seizure 1 to 2	F	Q	T	U	b	c	—	—	—	—	—	—	—
Seizure 2 to 3	E	a	b	c	—	—	—	—	—	—	—	—	—
DOWNSHIFTS													
No 2 to 1	B	m	h	S	—	—	—	—	—	—	—	—	—
No 3 to 2	B	m	h	Q	R	—	—	—	—	—	—	—	—
Involuntary high speed 3 to 2	A	a	P	—	—	—	—	—	—	—	—	—	—
Above normal shift speeds	B	h	p	f	b	c	—	—	—	—	—	—	—
Below normal shift speeds	B	h	p	f	b	c	m	n	—	—	—	—	—
DOWNSHIFT QUALITY													
Slip 2 to 1	T	—	—	—	—	—	—	—	—	—	—	—	—
Slip 3 to 2	E	R	l	d	f	a	b	c	P	—	—	—	—
Rough 2 to 1	T	N	b	—	—	—	—	—	—	—	—	—	—
Rough 3 to 2	E	l	d	f	c	P	Q	R	—	—	—	—	—
LINE PRESSURE													
Low, idling	A	C	D	d	c	a	s	b	W	—	—	—	—
High, idling	B	D	d	f	e	—	—	—	—	—	—	—	—
Low at stall	A	B	d	g	f	a	c	b	h	X	—	—	—
High at stall	d	f	g	c	—	—	—	—	—	—	—	—	—
STALL SPEED													
Below 1,000	Z	—	—	—	—	—	—	—	—	—	—	—	—
Over 2,000	A	C	F	a	b	c	d	N	P	S	T	V	Z
NO PUSH START	A	C	s	Y	F	E	N	a	b	c	d	V	—
OVER-HEATING	A	E	F	Z	—	—	—	—	—	—	—	—	—

PRELIMINARY ADJUSTMENT FAULTS

A Fluid level incorrect.
B Downshift valve cable incorrectly assembled or adjusted.
C Manual linkage incorrectly assembled or adjusted.
D Incorrect engine idling speed
E Incorrect front band adjustment.
F Incorrect rear band adjustment

MECHANICAL FAULTS

N Front clutch slipping due to worn plates or faulty parts.
O Front clutch seized or plates distorted.
P Rear clutch slipping due to worn plates or faulty check valve in piston.
Q Rear clutch seized or plates distorted.
R Front band slipping due to faulty servo, broken or worn band.
S Rear band slipping due to faulty servo, broken or worn band.
T One-way clutch slipping or incorrectly installed.
U One-way clutch seized.
V Input shaft broken.
W Front pump drive tangs on converter hub broken.
X Front pump worn.
Y Rear pump worn or driven key broken.
Z Converter blading and/or one-way clutch failed.

HYDRAULIC CONTROL FAULTS

a Oil tubes missing or not Installed correctly.
b Sealing rings missing or broken.
c Valve body assembly screws missing or not correctly tightened.
d Primary regulator valve sticking.
e Secondary regulator valve sticking.
f Throttle valve sticking.
g Modulator valve sticking.
h Governor valve sticking, leaking or incorrectly assembled.
l Orifice control valve sticking.
m 1 to 2 shift valve sticking.
n 2 to 3 shift valve sticking.
p 2 to 3 shift valve plunger sticking.
q Converter 'out' check valve missing or sticking.
s Pump check valve missing or sticking.

DATA

Type	Hydraulic torque converter, providing torque multiplication between the ratios 2:1 and 1:1. Planetary gear set, comprising two sun gears, two sets of pinions, a pinion carrier and a ring gear. The various mechanical ratios are obtained by the engagement of hydraulically operated multi-disc clutches and brake bands.
Gear ratios:	Torque converter stall ratio
Direct (top) 1:1 (Torque converter ratio)	2.16
Intermediate (2nd) 1.45:1 (Torque converter ratio)	2.16
Low (1st) 2.39:1 (Torque converter ratio)	2.16
Reverse 2.09:1 (Torque converter ratio)	
Rear axle gear ratio	3.54:1
Engine torque	160 lb ft at 2,650 rpm
Transmission fluid capacity from dry	Torque converter: 9 pints Gearbox: $4\frac{1}{4}$ pints Cooler and pipes: $\frac{3}{4}$ pints TOTAL: 14 pints
Fluid temperature	Normal operating range 80° to 100°C approximately
Identification	The Rover automatic transmission model 35 has a white nameplate attached to the side of the transmission maincasing with the commencing serial number 3EU 1001

Recommended lubricants

BP	Castrol	Duckham's	Esso	Mobil	Regent Texaco/ Caltex	Shell
Energol ATF Type A	Castrol TQ Automatic Transmission Fluid	Nolmatic ATF Type A	Esso Automatic Transmission Fluid	Mobil Fluid 200	Texamatic Fluid 3528	Shell Donax T 6

Tightening torques

Component	Torque lb ft	Torque mkg
Torque converter to drive plate	25 to 30	3,5 to 4,0
Drive plate to crankshaft	50	7,0
Transmission case to bell housing	8 to 10	1,0 to 1,4
Extension housing to transmission case	8 to 10	1,0 to 1,4
Oil pan to transmission case	8 to 10	1,0 to 1,4
Front servo to transmission case	8 to 10	1,0 to 1,4
Rear servo to transmission case	10 to 13	1,4 to 1,7
Pump adaptor to front pump body (locating screw)	2 to 3 (25 to 35 lb in.)	0,3 to 0,4
Pump adaptor to front pump body	17 to 22	2,3 to 3,0
Pump adaptor to transmission case	8 to 10	1,0 to 1,4
Rear pump to transmission case	4 to 5	0,55 to 0,7
Rear pump to transmission case (locating screw)	1.7 to 2.5 (20 to 30 lb in.)	0,23 to 0,35
Centre support to transmission case	10 to 13	1,4 to 1,7
Outer lever to manual valve shaft	10 to 15	1,4 to 2,0
Pressure take-off plug	4 to 5 (50 to 60 lb in.)	0,55 to 0,7
Oil pan drain plug	10 to 14	1,4 to 1,9
Oil tube collector to lower valve body	1.7 to 2.5 (20 to 30 lb in.)	0,23 to 0,35
Governor line plate to lower valve body	1.7 to 2.5 (20 to 30 lb in.)	0,23 to 0,35
Lower body end plate to lower valve body	1.7 to 2.5 (20 to 30 lb in.)	0,23 to 0,35
Upper body end plate, front or rear, to upper valve body	1.7 to 2.5 (20 to 30 lb in.)	0,23 to 0,35
Upper valve body to lower valve body	1.7 to 2.5 (20 to 30 lb in.)	0,23 to 0,35
Valve bodies assembly, to transmission case	4 to 5 (55 to 66 lb in.)	0,55 to 0,7
Pump strainers to lower valve body	1.7 to 2.5 (20 to 30 lb in.)	0,23 to 0,35

Tightening torques (*continued*)

Component	lb ft	mkg
Downshift valve cam bracket to valve body	1.7 to 2.5 (20 to 30 lb in.)	0,22 to 0,35
Body to governor sleeve	Tighten fully with large screwdriver	
Cover plate to governor body	1.7 to 2.5 (20 to 30 lb in.)	0,23 to 0,35
Adjusting screw, front servo	10 lb in.	0,11
Locknut, front servo lever	15 to 20	2,0 to 2,8
Adjusting screw, rear servo	10	1,4
Locknut, rear servo to case	25 to 30	3,5 to 4,0
Starter inhibiter switch lock nut	4 to 6 (48 to 72 lb in.)	0,55 to 0,8
Downshift valve cable adaptor to transmission case	8 to 9 (96 to 108 lb in.)	1,0 to 1,2
Filler tube connector adaptor to transmission case	20 to 30	2,8 to 4,0
Filler tube to connector sleeve nut	17 to 18	2,3 to 2,4
Stone guards to converter housing	1.4 to 1.6 (17 to 19 lb in.)	0,19 to 0,22
Coupling flange to driven shaft	20 to 25	2,8 to 3,5
Oil cooler to transmission case connector	6 to 10 (72 to 120 lb in.)	0,8 to 1,4
Extension housing to mounting bracket on sub-frame	25	3,5
Torque converter housing to flywheel housing	30	4,0

Special tools

Below will be found details of special tools which are recommended to facilitate service work on the model 35 automatic transmission.

All tools are illustrated in the appropriate sections, together with an explanation of their use.

Special service tools for the model 35 automatic transmission

	Rover Part No.
Service tool kit assembly	601279
Comprising the following 11 items:	
Gearbox cradle	601280
End-play checking tool	601281
Snap ring pliers	601282
Clutch spring compressor	601283
Pressure gauge and tachometer	601284
Torque wrench set	601285
'Spintorq' screwdriver set	601286
Front servo gauge	601287
Locknut wrench	601288
Service tool box	601289
Rear clutch and seal inserter	601290
Retainer clip for torque converter	601467

All the tools listed may be ordered from the Rover Parts Department or through any Rover distributor or dealer.

Spring identification

	Free length	*Diameter*
Converter 'out' check valve	$\frac{45}{64}$ in. (18 mm)	$\frac{7}{32}$ in. (5,5 mm)
Rear pump check valve	$\frac{5}{8}$ in. (16 mm)	$\frac{13}{32}$ in. (10 mm)
Throttle valve	$1\frac{3}{16}$ in. (30 mm)	$\frac{15}{64}$ in. (6 mm)
Throttle return	$\frac{13}{16}$ in. (20 mm)	$\frac{9}{64}$ in. (3,5 mm)
Modulator valve	1 in. (25 mm)	$\frac{3}{16}$ in. (4,5 mm)
Servo orifice control	$1\frac{7}{32}$ in. (30 mm)	$\frac{13}{64}$ in. (5 mm)
Primary regulator valve	$2\frac{27}{32}$ in. (72 mm)	$\frac{5}{8}$ in. (16 mm)
Secondary regulator valve	$2\frac{9}{32}$ in. (66 mm)	$\frac{31}{64}$ in. (12 mm)
1st, 2nd speed shift valve	$1\frac{3}{32}$ in. (28 mm)	$\frac{15}{64}$ in. (6 mm)
2nd, 3rd speed shift valve	$1\frac{19}{32}$ in. (40 mm)	$\frac{23}{64}$ in. (9 mm)

Section F – ACCELERATOR LINKAGE

Brief description of accelerator linkage

(*Right hand drive models illustrated*)

Various types of accelerator linkage have been used on 3 litre models. As it is very important that the linkage is correctly assembled and adjusted, each type of linkage layout has been illustrated and complete instructions for dismantling, rebuilding and adjusting, have been given. It is only necessary to remove the accelerator shafts from the body for complete overhaul.

During engine overhaul or engine removal the linkage need only be disconnected between the engine and the body.

INDEX

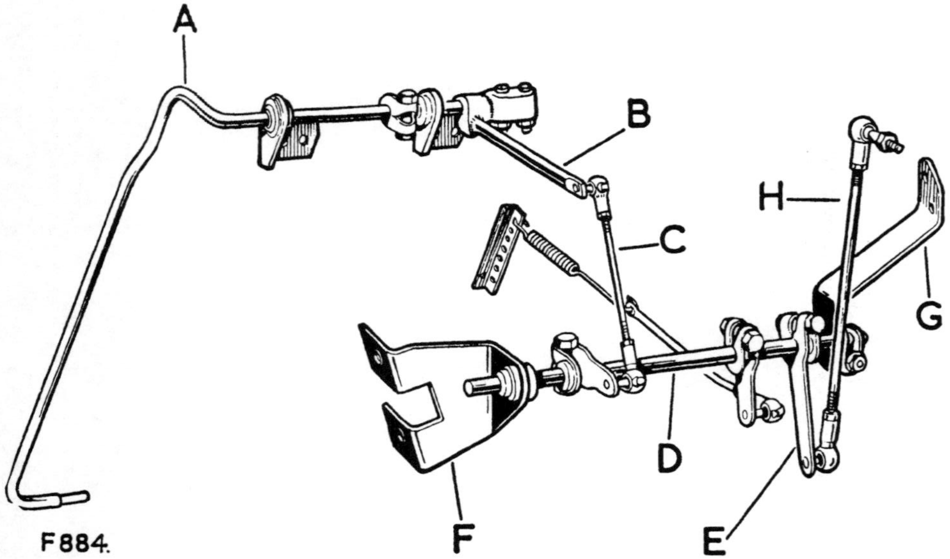

F884.

Layout of accelerator linkage, early 4-speed models without overdrive

A—Accelerator shaft
B—Accelerator lever
C—Control rod
D—Countershaft
E—Countershaft lever, carburetter end
F—Countershaft bracket on wing valance
G—Countershaft bracket on engine
H—Control rod

Linkage, to remove, refit and adjust, Models Mk I and Mk IA 4-speed without overdrive—Operation F-1

Workshop hand tools:

Spanner size: $\frac{7}{16}$ in. AF Screwdriver, medium

Linkage, remove

1. Disconnect the control rod C from the lever assembly B.
2. Disconnect the control rod H, countershaft to carburetter from the lever E.
3. Disconnect the return spring between the countershaft and bulkhead.
4. Remove the countershaft brackets F and G from the engine and wing valance, secured by nuts, bolts and washers. Lift out the countershaft assembly D.
5. Disconnect the accelerator pedal from the accelerator lever, secured by a washer and split pin.
6. Remove the accelerator pedal from the floor, secured by screws and countersunk washers.
7. Remove the accelerator shaft and lever assembly, secured by nuts, bolts and washers to the dash.

Linkage, refit

1. Reverse removal procedure.

Linkage, to adjust

2 Adjust the carburetter throttle lever so that it moves through $51\frac{1}{2}°$ above and $23\frac{1}{2}°$ below horizontal to open and close the butterfly valve fully.

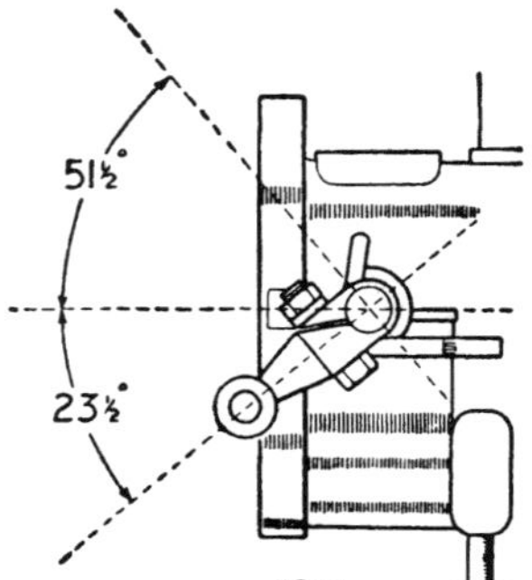

C543.

Setting throttle lever

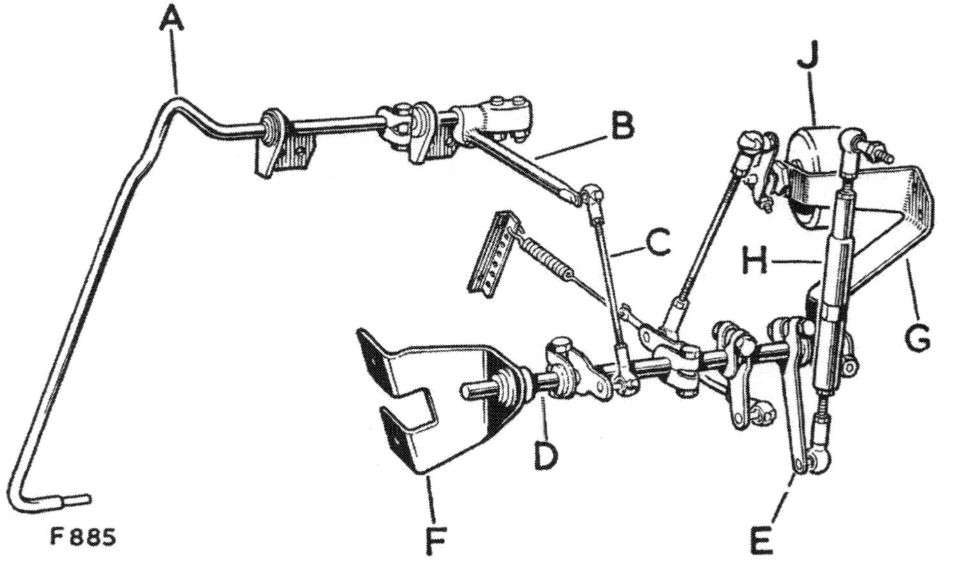

Layout of accelerator linkage, 4-speed models, with overdrive (rotary switch)

A—Accelerator shaft
B—Accelerator lever
C—Control rod
D—Countershaft
E—Countershaft lever
F—Countershaft bracket on wing valance
G—Countershaft bracket on engine
H—Collapsible control rod
J—Rotary switch

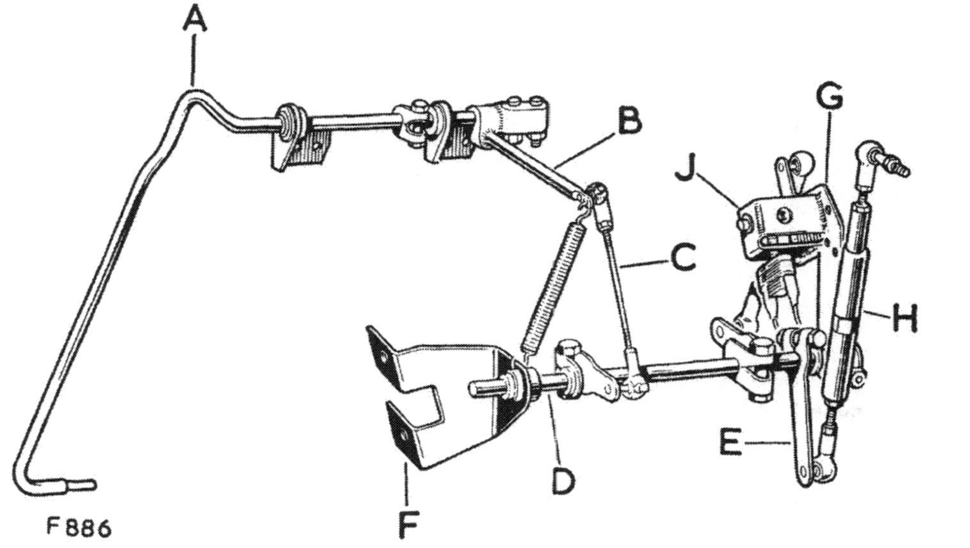

Layout of accelerator linkage, 4-speed models, with overdrive (cam switch)

A—Accelerator shaft
B—Accelerator lever
C—Control rod
D—Countershaft
E—Countershaft lever
F—Countershaft bracket on wing valance
G—Countershaft bracket on engine
H—Collapsible control rod
J—Cam switch

Linkage, to remove, refit and adjust, Models Mk I, Mk IA and Mk II, suffix letters 'A' and 'B' 4-speed with overdrive—Operation F-2

Workshop hand tools:

Spanner size: $\frac{7}{16}$ in. AF Screwdriver, medium

Linkage, remove. Models fitted with rotary or cam type switches

1. Disconnect the control rod C from the lever assembly B.
2. Disconnect the collapsible control rod H, countershaft to carburetter, from the lever E.
3. Disconnect the throttle return spring.
4. Disconnect the wiring from the rotary (or cam) type switch.
5. Remove the countershaft bracket F from the wing valance, secured by nuts, bolts and washers.
6. Remove the bracket G countershaft to engine. Lift out the countershaft assembly complete.
7. Disconnect the accelerator pedal from its lever by removing the split pin and washer.
8. Remove the accelerator pedal secured by screws and countersunk washers to the floor.
9. Remove the accelerator shaft and lever assembly A, secured by bolts, nuts and washers to the dash.

Linkage, refit

1. Refit the linkage by reversing removal procedure and adjusting as follows:

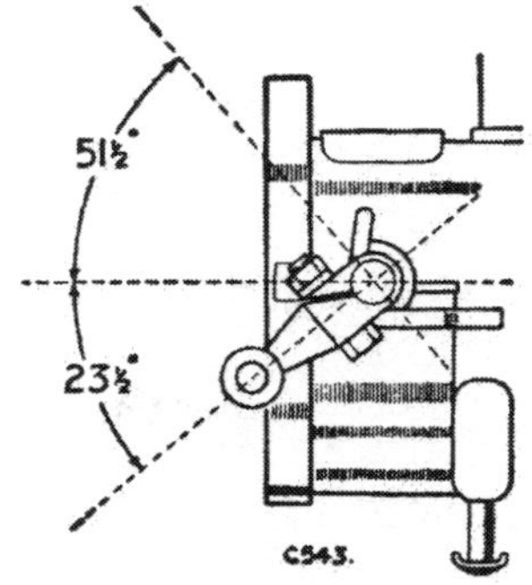

Setting throttle lever

2. If necessary adjust the carburetter throttle lever so that it moves through 51½° above and 23½° below horizontal to open and close the butterfly fully.

Linkage with rotary type switches

3. With the accelerator pedal depressed to kick-down button, ensure that the carburetter butterfly is fully open and the collapsible rod is on the point of collapse; if this state is not achieved, carry out suitable adjustments to the collapsible rod and levers.
4. Depress the accelerator pedal to full kick-down position and ensure that the collapsible rod collapses.
5. The switch control lever fitted on the accelerator countershaft must be pointing rearwards in a horizontal position.
6. Ensure that the control rod ball pin attached to the switch lever is in the mid-slot position, then fit the lever to the switch spindle loosely.
7. Turn the switch spindle in an anti-clockwise direction until the limit of movement is reached, using very little pressure; hold the spindle firmly, position the switch lever until it is 30° from vertical and pointing upwards. Then tighten the clamping bolt.

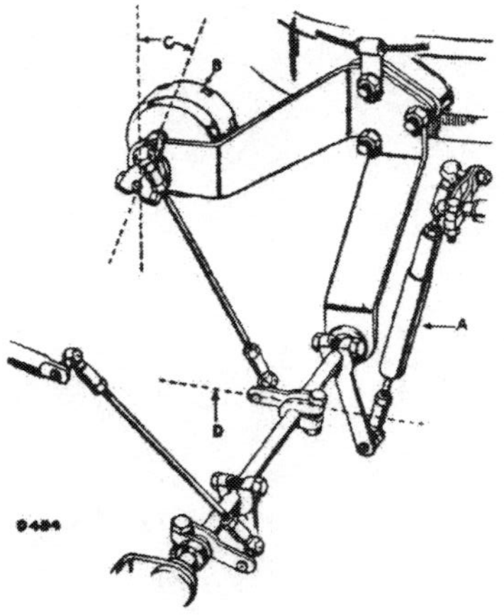

Arrangement of overdrive rotary switch and control rods, 4-speed models

A—Collapsible rod
B—Rotary switch
C—30°
D—Control lever horizontal

Operation F-2—*continued*

8. Adjust the length and fit the control rod between the countershaft and rotary switch, then disconnect one end of the rod and screw the ball joint in, one complete turn.

Linkages with cam type switches

1. Check the full throttle position and adjust as necessary by altering the length of the control rod, accelerator lever to countershaft.
2. Disconnect the wires from the switch and connect a suitable test lamp.
3. Engage top gear, select overdrive on the steering column switch; switch on ignition.
4. Rotate the cam by lifting the control rod. The test lamp will go out as soon as the cam depresses the plunger on the switch. This should occur at approximately one-eighth throttle opening.
5. To adjust, unscrew the locknut and screw the switch in or out until the lamp goes out at approximately one-eighth throttle opening.

   Tighten the locknut. Remove the test lamp and connect the original wiring.

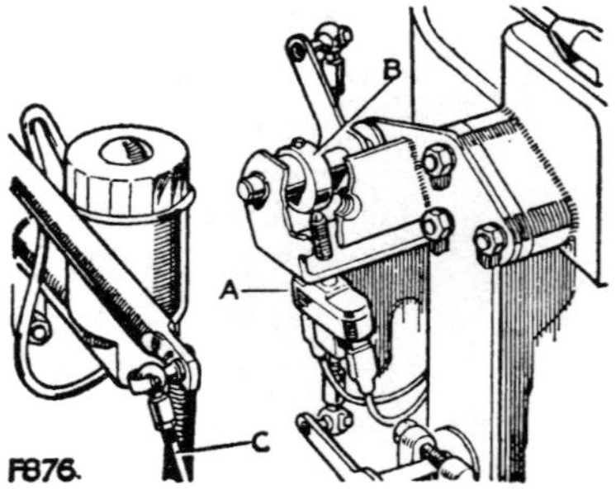

F876

Arrangement of overdrive cam switch and control rods, 4-speed models

A—Switch B—Cam

C—Adjust throttle linkage at this rod

6. Check that the carpet does not restrict the accelerator pedal travel. Full throttle position should be reached with the pedal fractionally above the carpet.
7. Road test the car. If necessary re-adjust.

Linkage, to remove, refit and adjust. Automatic transmission with manual second speed hold—Operation F-3

Workshop hand tools:

Spanner size: $\frac{7}{16}$ in. AF Screwdriver, medium

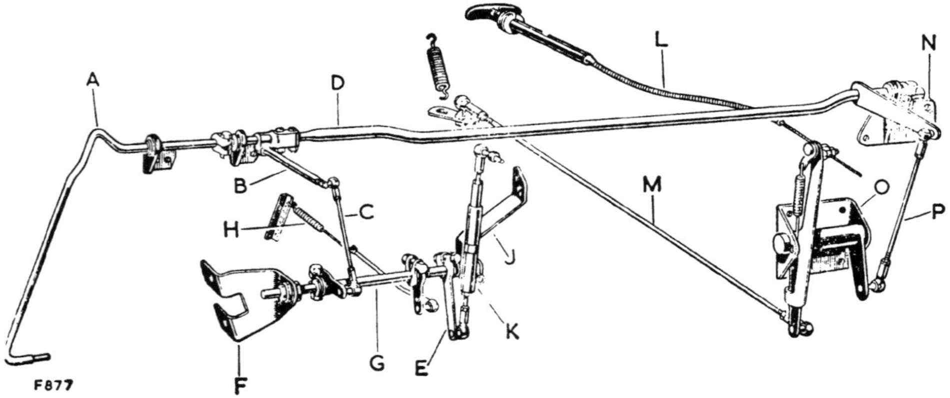

F877

Layout of accelerator linkage, automatic transmission models with manual second speed hold

A—Accelerator shaft
B—Accelerator lever
C—Control rod
D—Accelerator shaft extension
E—Countershaft lever
F—Countershaft bracket on wing valance
G—Countershaft
H—Return spring
J—Countershaft bracket on engine
K—Collapsible control rod
L—Second speed hold control cable
M—Control rod relay to gearbox
N—Extension shaft bearing bracket
O—Relay box
P—Control rod

Linkage, remove

1. Disconnect the second speed hold control cable L, at the relay box, by unscrewing the special nut and bolt on the cable end. Withdraw the overriding spring from the cable.
2. Remove the lever return spring from the relay.
3. Remove the control rod P, between the cross-shaft and relay.
4. Remove the control rod M, between the relay and the gearbox.
5. Remove the collapsible rod K.
6. Disconnect the countershaft lever return spring H.
7. Remove the control rod C, between the accelerator shaft and countershaft.
8. Remove the countershaft brackets F and J from from the wing valance and engine, and lift out the countershaft G, complete.

Operation F-3—*continued*

9. Remove the relay O, secured by nuts, bolts and washers.
10. Disconnect the accelerator extension shaft D, from the accelerator shaft A, by removing the cotter retaining nuts and driving out the cotters.
11. Remove the three bolts, nuts and washers securing the extension shaft bearing bracket N, and remove the extension shaft.
12. Remove the two handbrake pulleys.
13. Disconnect the accelerator pedal secured by a split pin and washer.
14. Remove the accelerator shaft A, secured by nuts, bolts and washers to the dash.
15. Remove the accelerator pedal, secured by screws and washers.
16. Remove the accelerator pedal spring-loaded stop, secured by bolts, nuts and washers.

Linkage refit

1. Reverse removal procedure.
2. Check and if necessary adjust the carburetter throttle lever so that it moves through $51\frac{1}{2}°$ above and $23\frac{1}{2}°$ below horizontal to open and close the butterfly valve fully.

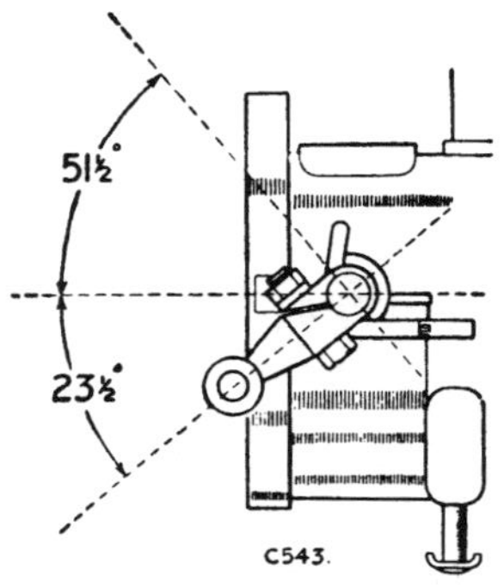

Setting throttle lever

3. Fit the countershaft return spring in approximately the fourth hole down. The correct hole may be ascertained by the feel of the accelerator pedal when the kickdown adjustment has been made.
4. Check the linkage setting. Depress the accelerator to full throttle, that is just resting on the spring-loaded pedal stop; then check that the butterfly is fully open and that the collapsible rod is on the point of collapse. If necessary adjust the collapsible rod and levers.
5. Depress the accelerator fully, compressing the spring-loaded pedal stop. The collapsible rod should now have collapsed.

Adjustment for cars fitted with short travel dipper switch type pedal stop

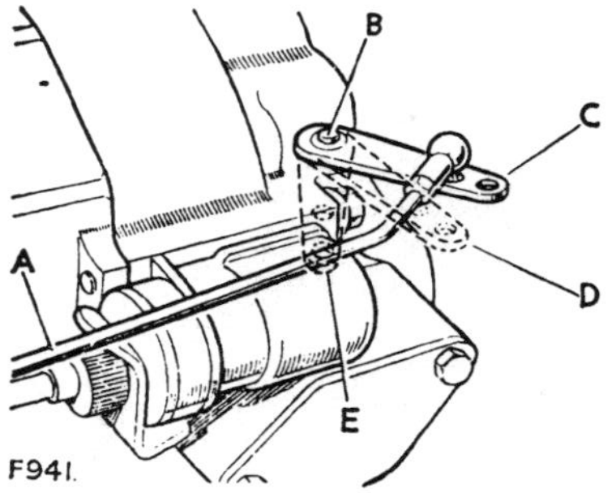

Setting governor control shaft lever

A—Control rod C—Fully rearward
B—Control shaft D—End of free movement
E—Fully forward

6. Fit the control rod A, to the inner hole of the lever on the governor control shaft B, and push the lever to the fully rearward position C. Move the lever forward until the loading of the governor spring can be felt, that is at the end of the free movement D.

   Move the lever back from this position approximately $\frac{1}{8}$ in. (3 mm) and hold this position.

Operation F-3—*continued*

Adjust and couple up the control rod A to the lever on the relay, which should be clear of the bulkhead.

7. With the accelerator depressed in the full kickdown position and the governor control shaft rod in the fully forward position, adjust and connect the control rod between the accelerator cross-shaft lever and relay assembly.
8. Ensure that all links are tight.

Adjustment for cars fitted with long travel plunger type stop

9. Fit the control rod A, to the inner hole on the lever of the governor control shaft B, and push the control shaft to the fully rearward position. With the shaft held in this position connect the other end of the control rod A, to the lever on the relay. The relay lever must be clear of the bulkhead.
10. With the accelerator depressed in the full kickdown position and the governor control shaft lever in the fully forward position, adjust and connect the control rod between the accelerator shaft extension, and the relay.
11. With the accelerator depressed in the full kickdown position and the governor control shaft rod in the fully forward position, adjust and connect the control rod between the accelerator cross-shaft lever and the relay assembly.
12. Ensure that all links are tight.
13. Fit a flat washer and spring anchor plate on to the clevis pin for second speed hold cable. Enter clevis pin into lever, and fit a second flat washer on to the clevis pin and pass the cable through the hole drilled in the clevis pin. Secure the inner cable with a spring (first speed start only), ferrule and clamping bolt.
14. Couple up the return spring by hooking on to the relay mounting bracket and the anchor plate on the clevis pin.

1st speed start models, items 15 and 16

15. Pull out the second speed hold cable to the locked position, this should leave no further movement on the control rod relay assembly to governor control shaft.
16. If there is further movement of the control shaft, release the bolt in the ferrule, adjust accordingly and tighten the bolt. Re-check the action of second speed hold.

2nd speed start models, items 17 and 18

17. Adjust the second speed hold control, so that when it is pulled out and locked in position, the governor control shaft is against the spring-loaded detent plunger in the extension case. Note that the over-riding spring, at the relay end of the cable, is not fitted.
18. Ensure that all links are tight.
19. Road test car and check performance figures. See Automatic Transmission. Road Test Procedure.
20. If, when the car is driven, the kickdown is not instantaneous but lags, shorten the accelerator extension to relay assembly control rod, approximately two turns.
21. If the kickdown is operating before full kickdown is reached, check the collapsible rod. It will probably be found it is collapsing too early. Adjust as necessary.
22. When the car is road tested and it moves off from a standstill in intermediate and not low, re-check the setting of the governor control lever.

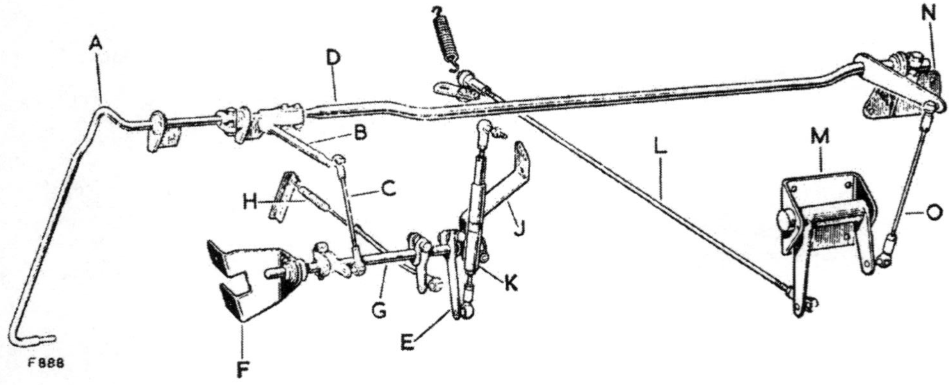

Layout of accelerator linkage, automatic transmission models with electrical second speed hold

A—Accelerator shaft
B—Accelerator shaft lever
C—Control rod
D—Accelerator extension shaft
E—Countershaft lever
F—Countershaft bracket on wing valance
G—Countershaft
H—Return spring
J—Countershaft bracket on engine
K—Collapsible rod
L—Control rod relay to gearbox
M—Relay box
N—Extension shaft bearing bracket
O—Control rod

Linkage, to remove, refit and adjust. Mk I and Mk II suffix 'A' and 'B' automatic transmission with electrical second speed hold—Operation F-4

Workshop hand tools:

Spanner size: $\frac{7}{16}$ in. AF Screwdriver, medium

Linkage, remove

1. Remove the control rod L, accelerator relay to gearbox.
2. Remove the control rod O, accelerator extension shaft to relay.
3. Disconnect the collapsible rod K, between countershaft and carburetter.
4. Disconnect the control rod and return spring H, between countershaft and bulkhead.
5. Disconnect the control rod C, between accelerator shaft and countershaft.
6. Remove countershaft brackets F and J, countershaft to engine, and countershaft to wing valance. Lift out the countershaft.
7. Remove relay N, secured to bulkhead by bolts, nuts and washers.
8. Remove the split pin and washer securing accelerator lever to pedal.
9. Disconnect the accelerator shaft A, from the accelerator extension shaft D, by drifting out the cotter pins secured by nuts and washers.
10. Remove the extension shaft bearing bracket N, secured to the bulkhead by bolts, nuts and washers. Lift out the shaft.
11. Remove the accelerator lever and shaft secured to the bulkhead by two brackets and bolts, nuts and washers. Withdraw the accelerator lever through the aperture in the bulkhead.
12. Remove the accelerator pedal secured by screws and countersunk washers to the floor.
13. Remove the accelerator pedal spring-loaded stop, secured by bolts, nuts and washers to the floor.

Linkage, refit

1. Reverse removal procedure.

Linkage, adjust

2. With the governor control shaft held in the fully rearward position, fit the control rod relay lever to governor control shaft so that the relay lever does not foul the bulkhead.
3. With the accelerator depressed in the full kick-down position and the governor control shaft rod in the fully forward position adjust and connect the control rod between the accelerator extension lever and the relay assembly.
4. Ensure that all links are tight.
5. Road test car and check performance figures previously laid down.
6. If when the car is driven, the kickdown is not instantaneous but lags, shorten the accelerator cross-shaft relay assembly control rod, approximately two turns.
7. If the kickdown is operating before full kickdown is reached, check the collapsible rod. It will probably be found it is collapsing too early. Adjust as necessary.
8. When the car is road tested it moves off from a standstill in intermediate and not low, re-check the setting of the governor control shaft lever.

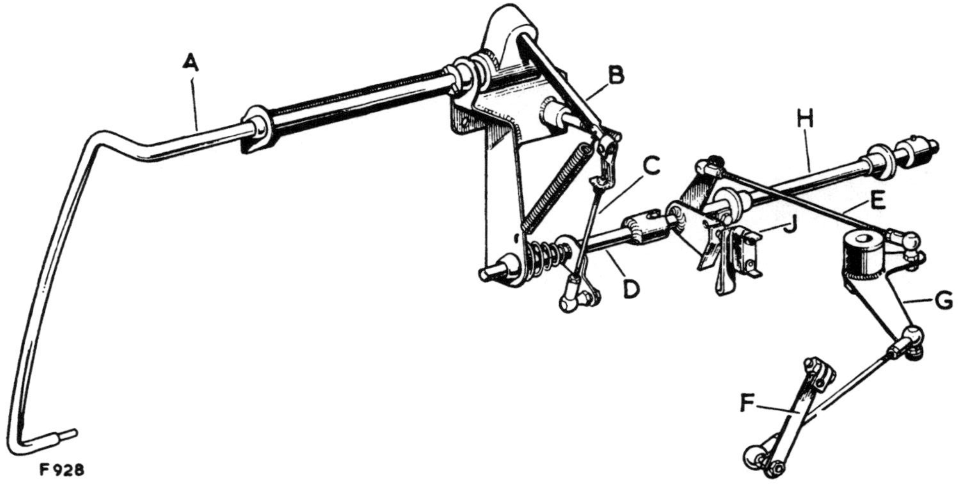

Accelerator linkage, Mk II, suffix 'C' and Mk III, 4-speed models

A—Accelerator shaft
B—Accelerator lever assembly
C—Adjustable control rod
D—Extension shaft
E—Control rod
F—Throttle lever
G—Bell-crank lever
H—Cross-shaft
J—Cam switch

Linkage, to remove, refit and adjust. Mk II 4-speed models, suffix 'C' and Mk III 4-speed models—Operation F-5

Workshop hand tools:
Spanner sizes: $\frac{5}{16}$ in. AF, $\frac{1}{2}$ in. AF, $\frac{3}{4}$ in. AF
Screwdriver, medium, Hammer, medium, Pinpunch, Pliers

Linkage, disconnect

1. Disconnect the control rod from the lever assembly B. Disconnect the return spring.
2. Pull the extension shaft D, back against the conical spring and disconnect the shaft from the cross-shaft H.

Linkage, remove

3. Disconnect the accelerator pedal from the lever A, secured by a split pin and washer.
4. Remove the hand brake cable pulley from the pedal lever mounting bracket.
5. Remove the pedal lever assembly complete with mounting bracket, secured to the dash by nuts, bolts and spring washers.
6. If necessary remove the pedal lever A, from its mounting bracket by driving out the pin securing the accelerator lever to the shaft.
7. Disconnect the control rod E, from the lever on the cross-shaft H, and from the bell-crank lever beneath the inlet manifold.
8. Disconnect the control rod from the bell-crank lever G, to the carburetter throttle lever F.
9. Remove the bell-crank lever G, which is secured by a hexagon-headed pin to the inlet manifold.
10. Remove the cross-shaft assembly, which is located through two brackets on the flywheel housing, by driving out the pin securing the collar to the end of the shaft.
11. Remove the accelerator pedal, secured to the floorboards by screws and washers.

Linkage, refit

1. Reverse removal procedure.
2. Before the engine is tested, adjust the linkage.
3. Adjust the control rod C and the throttle lever F to obtain maximum throttle opening. Check that the carpet does not restrict the accelerator pedal travel. Full throttle position should be reached with the pedal fractionally above the carpet.

Adjusting the linkage on the engine

4. Position the lever cam so that the switch plunger is in line with the cam groove.
5. Adjust the switch by unscrewing the locknut and screwing the switch in or out until the plunger registers in the cam groove by not more than $\frac{1}{64}$ in. (0.4 mm).
6. Hold the cam in this position and clamp the carburetter lever to the butterfly spindle with the butterfly in the closed position.

Adjusting linkage, engine to body

7. Press down the accelerator pedal until it is just resting on the spring-loaded pedal stop, without depressing the stop. Maintain the pedal in this position.
8. Adjust the control rod until the carburetter butterfly is fully open.
9. Release the accelerator pedal and check that full throttle at the pedal gives full butterfly opening.

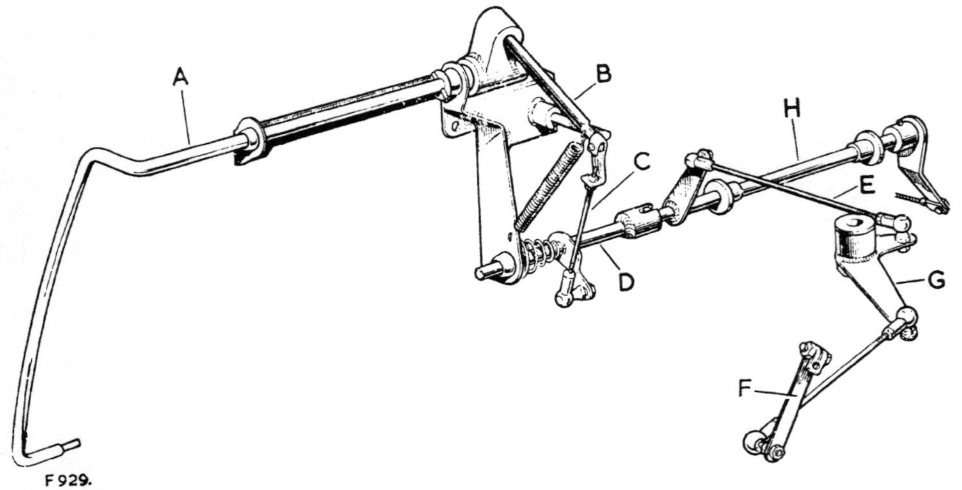

Accelerator linkage, Mk II, suffix 'C', automatic transmission models

A—Accelerator shaft
B—Accelerator lever assembly
C—Adjustable control rod
D—Extension shaft
E—Control rod
F—Throttle lever
G—Bell-crank lever
H—Cross-shaft

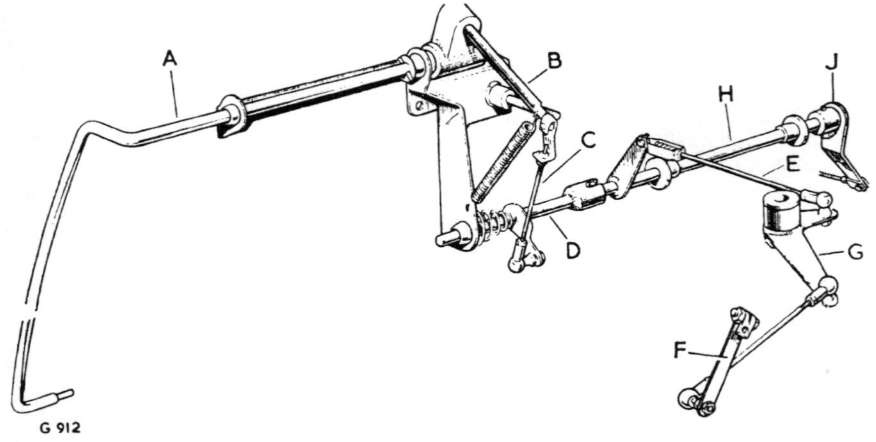

Accelerator linkage, Mk III cars with model 35 automatic transmission

A—Accelerator shaft
B—Accelerator shaft lever
C—Adjustable control rod
D—Extension shaft
E—Control rod, spring-loaded
F—Throttle lever
G—Bell-crank lever
H—Cross-shaft
J—Lever down shift cable

Linkage, to remove, refit and adjust. Mk II suffix 'C' and Mk III automatic transmission models—Operation F-6

Workshop hand tools:
Spanner sizes: $\frac{5}{16}$ in. AF, $\frac{1}{2}$ in. AF, $\frac{3}{4}$ in. AF
Screwdriver, medium, Hammer, medium, Pinpunch, Pliers

It is not normally necessary to carry out adjustments to the accelerator linkage, except when the lengths of the control rods or the setting of the throttle lever has been disturbed.

Linkage, disconnect

1. Disconnect the control rod from the lever assembly B.
   Disconnect the return spring.
2. Pull the extension shaft D, back against the conical spring and disconnect the shaft from the cross-shaft H.

Linkage, remove

3. Disconnect the accelerator pedal from the lever A, secured by a split pin and washer.
4. Remove the pedal lever assembly, secured to the dash by nuts, bolts and spring washers.
5. If necessary remove the pedal lever A, from its mounting bracket by driving out the pin securing the accelerator lever to the shaft.
6. Disconnect the control rod E, from the lever on the cross-shaft H, and from the bell-crank lever G, beneath the inlet manifold.
7. Disconnect the control rod from the bell-crank lever G, to the throttle lever F.
8. Remove the bell-crank lever G, which is secured by a hexagon headed pin to the inlet manifold.
9. Remove the cross-shaft, which is located through two brackets on the flywheel housing, by driving out the pin securing the lever J, to the end of the shaft.
10. Remove the accelerator pedal, secured to the floor by two screws and washers.

Linkage, refit

1. Reverse removal procedure.
2. Before the engine is tested, adjust the linkage.

Adjusting the linkage on the engine, Mk II

3. Rotate the accelerator cross-shaft until the governor lever is in the full kickdown position. Retain this position.
4. Open the carburetter butterfly to full throttle position. Retain this position.
5. Clamp the carburetter lever to the butterfly spindle.

Adjusting linkage, engine to body, Mk II

6. Press the accelerator pedal down to the full throttle position, that is with the pedal just resting on, but not depressing the spring-loaded stop. Maintain this position.
7. Rotate the extension cross-shaft until the full throttle detent in the gearbox can be felt.
8. Adjust the control rod to maintain this condition.
9. Release the accelerator pedal and check for freedom of movement.
10. Check that full kickdown at the pedal gives full butterfly opening.

Adjusting linkage on the engine and transmission, Mk III

11. Adjust down shift cable abutment screw until the thread is centralised on the bracket as shown below.

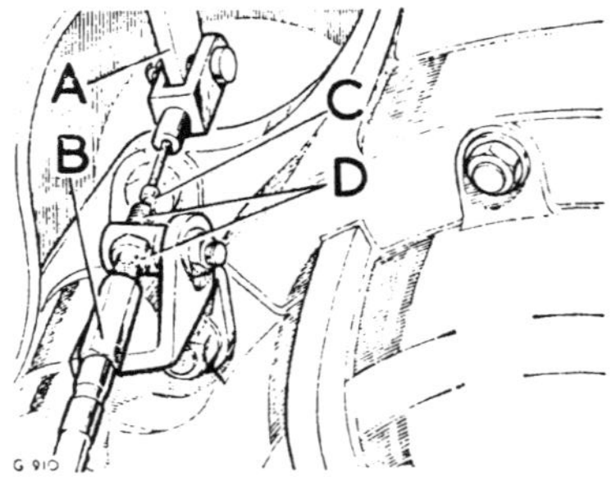

Adjustment of down shift cable

A—Lever for cross-shaft
B—Abutment screw for down shift cable
C—Gap between end of abutment screw and crimp on cable .015 in. (0,38 mm)
D—Thread centralised in bracket

12. Slacken the pinch bolt of the carburetter throttle lever (F) and with the throttle butterfly in the idling position, move the carburetter throttle

Operation F-6—*continued*

lever until there is a gap of .015 in. (0,38 mm) between end of abutment screw and the crimped stop on the inner cable.

Hold lever in this position and then tighten pinch bolt.

13. Check that the down shift cable extends 1.468 in. (37 mm), measured between the end of the abutment screw and the crimped stop of the inner cable when the throttle is fully open.

 At this position the accelerator pedal is just resting on the kickdown plunger.

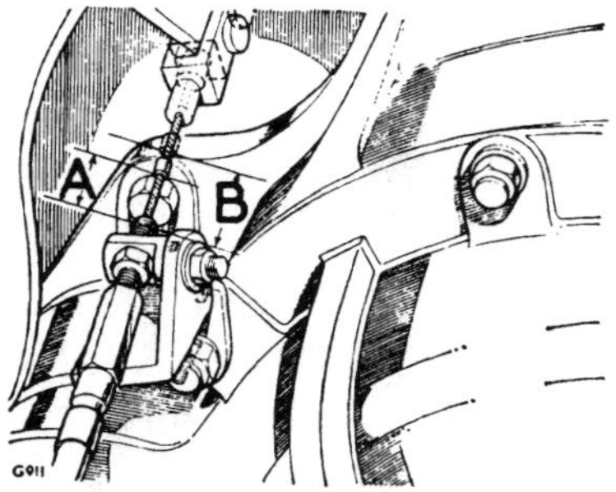

Position of crimped stop on inner cable at full throttle and kickdown position

A—Full throttle position, $1\frac{15}{32}$ in. (37 mm)
B—Kickdown position, $1\frac{3}{4}$ to $1\frac{13}{16}$ in. (44 to 46 mm)

14. Check that down shift cable extends $1\frac{3}{4}$ in. to $1\frac{13}{16}$ in. (44 mm to 46 mm), measured between the end of the abutment screw and the crimped stop on the inner cable when the throttle is at the kickdown position, that is the spring-loaded control rod fully extended.

Adjusting linkage, engine and transmission to body, Mk III models

15. Depress the throttle pedal so that it is just resting on the kickdown plunger, and retain in this position.
16. Adjust control rod C so that a clearance of .001 in. to .005 in. (0,02 mm to 0,12 mm) exists between the carburetter butterfly stop and stop on carburetter body.
17. Check that the throttle closes fully and that crimped stop on the inner cable is .015 in. (0,38 mm) from the end of the abutment screw for the down shift cable.

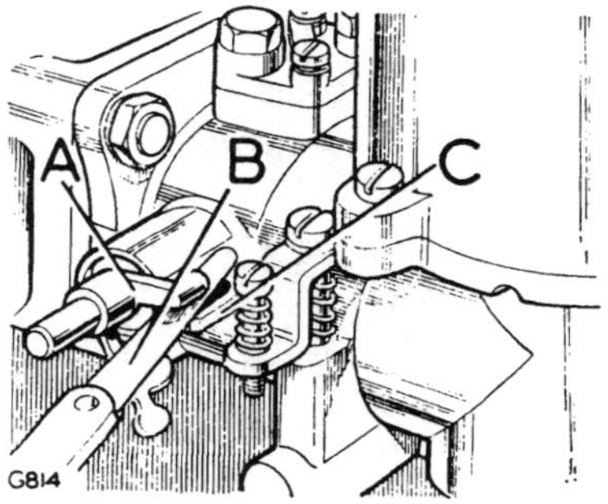

Clearance at carburetter butterfly stop

A—Carburetter butterfly stop
B—Feeler gauge
C—Stop on carburetter body

Section G – PROPELLER SHAFTS

Brief description of propeller shafts

An open type, two-piece Hardy Spicer propeller shaft having a flexible mounted ball-race type centre bearing transmits the drive from the gearbox to the rear axle.

The needle roller bearings of the universal joints are pre-packed with lubricant on assembly, and require no further attention.

A grease nipple, for the lubrication of the sliding joint splines, is fitted and should receive attention every 3,000 miles (5.000 km).

INDEX

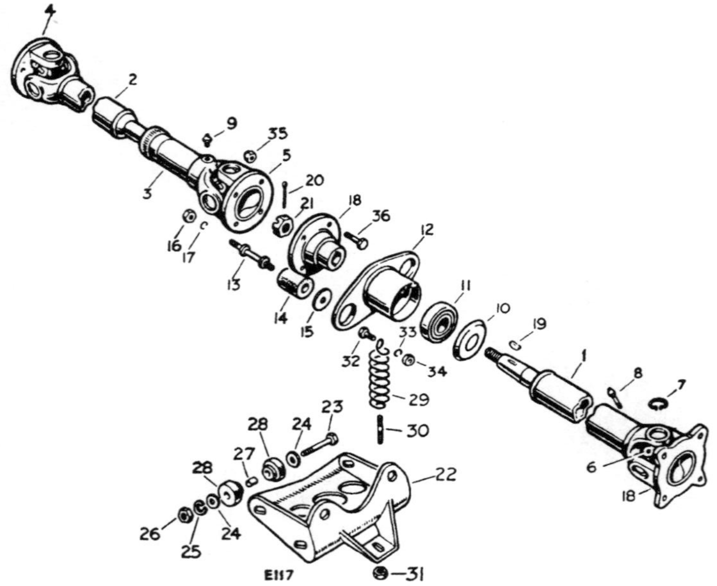

Propeller shaft components (4-speed gearbox)

1	Propeller shaft, front
2	Propeller shaft, rear
3	Splined end, rear shaft
4	Flange, rear shaft
5	Flange, front, rear shaft
6	Journal
7	Circlip
8	Grease nipple for journal, where fitted
9	Grease nipple for shaft
10	Dust shield
11	Bearing for shaft
12	Bearing support and plate
13	Special support stud
14	Rubber bush
15	Plain washer
16–17	Fixings, special stud
18	Flange, front shaft
19	Woodruff key
20–21	Fixings, for flange
22	Bracket for centre bearing
23–26	Fixings, bracket centre bearing
27	Support spring
28–32	Fixings, support spring
33–34	Fixings, for coupling propeller shafts

Propeller shafts, to remove, separate and refit—Operation G-1

Workshop hand tools:

Spanner sizes: $\frac{7}{16}$ in. AF, $\frac{1}{2}$ in. AF, $\frac{9}{16}$ in. AF, $\frac{3}{8}$ in. BSF, $\frac{3}{4}$ in. BSF

Propeller shafts, remove

1. Disconnect the front flange of the front propeller shaft, and the rear flange of the rear shaft.
2. Remove the centre bearing support bracket secured by four bolts, nuts and washers, to the underside of the body. Remove the propeller shafts front and rear as an assembly.
3. Disconnect the centre bearing support spring from the bearing housing and support bracket.
4. Detach the support bracket from the centre bearing housing secured by nuts, flat washers and rubber bushes.
5. Disconnect the front and rear shafts at the flange coupling.

Shafts and support bracket, refit

1. Fit the flanges of the front and rear shafts together and fit new self-locking nuts on to the coupling bolts.
2. Fit the support spring to the centre bearing housing.
3. Fit the rubber bushes into the centre bearing housing, fitting at the same time the centre bearing support bracket. Secure with plain washers and nuts, but do not tighten at this stage.
4. Connect the support spring to the support bracket but do not tighten at this stage.
5. Offer up and secure the front propeller shaft flange to front coupling flange and the rear propeller shaft flange to the differential coupling flange.
6. Secure the support bracket to the body with the four fixings so that the centre bearing housing plate is central on the rubber bushes and situated at an equal distance from each end of the rubber bush. Tighten the nuts securing the rubbers and the support bracket fixings.
7. Adjust the support springs to a vertical position and tighten securing nuts.
8. Lubricate the sliding joint of the rear propeller shaft. See recommended lubricants. Note very early models were fitted with grease nipples on the journals, lubricate sparingly with the recommended lubricant.

   Later models have pre-packed universal joint bearings, and require no attention.

Front propeller shaft, to strip and rebuild—Operation G-2

Workshop hand tools:
Spanner sizes: $\frac{7}{16}$ in. AF, $\frac{1}{2}$ in. AF, $\frac{9}{16}$ in. AF, $\frac{3}{8}$ in. BSF, $\frac{3}{4}$ in. BSF

For propeller shaft removal, see Operation G-1

Propeller shaft, strip

1. Remove the split pin and special castle nut securing the drive flange to the shaft.
2. Drift off the flange from the tapered shaft.
3. Press the shaft, complete with bearing and dust shield, from the bearing support tube.
4. Remove the two Woodruff keys from the shaft.
5. Press the centre bearing and dust shield off the shaft.
6. Dismantle the universal joints. Operation G-4.

Propeller shaft, rebuild

1. Fit the dust shield and bearing to the shaft, ensuring that the bearing is a light drive fit on the shaft.
2. Press the bearing housing on to the bearing, ensuring that this also is a light drive fit.
3. Fit the two Woodruff keys to the shaft and with the four flange bolts in position in the flange, fit the flange to the shaft. Secure with a castle nut and split pin.

Rear propeller shaft, to strip and rebuild—Operation G-3

For propeller shaft removal, see Operation G-1

Rear propeller shaft, strip

1. Unscrew the dust cap and withdraw the sliding joint from the splined shaft.
2. Remove the felt seal and retainer.
3. Dismantle the universal joint. Operation G-4.

Rear propeller shaft, rebuild

1. With the universal joints fitted, smear the splines of the sliding joint and splined shaft with oil and replace the joint on the shaft, making sure that the arrows marked on the splined sleeve yoke and shaft are in line.
2. Refit the felt seal and retainer and screw up the dust cap as far as possible by hand.

Universal joints, to overhaul—Operation G-4

Workshop hand tools:
Circlip pliers, Hammer, soft-faced, Small brass drift

For propeller shaft removal, see Operation G-1

1. Remove the bearing circlips from the front universal joint; if necessary tap the end of the bearing to relieve the pressure against the circlip.
2. With one of the splined sleeve (or shaft) yoke lugs uppermost, tap the radius of the yoke with a soft-faced hammer. The top bearing should then emerge.

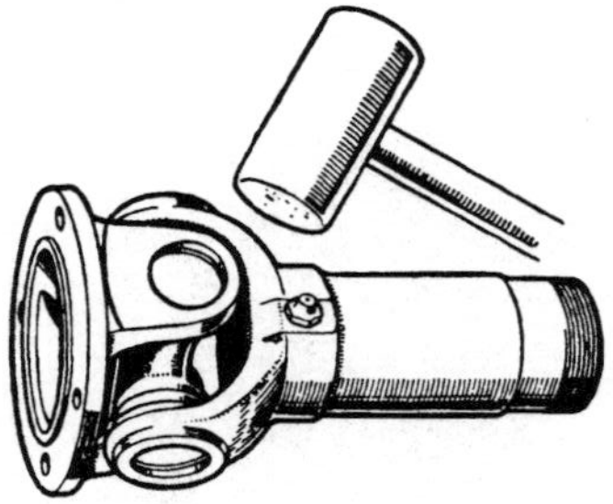

Removing a yoke bearing, stage 1

3. Turn the joint over and withdraw the bearing downwards, to avoid dropping the needle rollers. It may be necessary to tap the bearing race from the inside with a small drift.

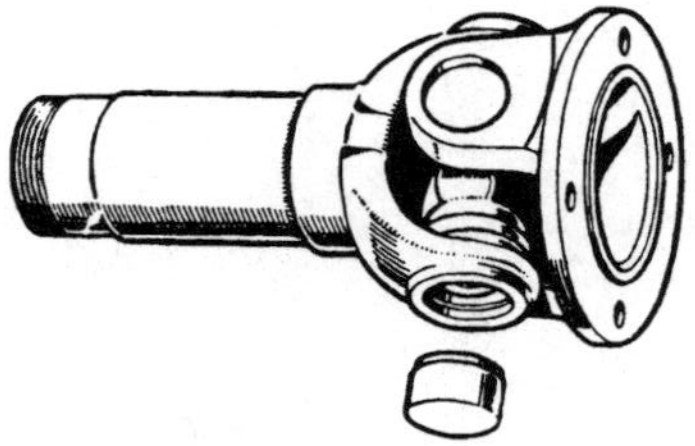

Removing a yoke bearing, stage 2

4. Repeat operations 2 and 3 for the opposite bearing.
5. The splined sleeve (or shaft) yoke can now be removed from the spider.
6. Rest the flange yoke on a piece of tubing and drive out the two remaining bearings, using a brass drift.

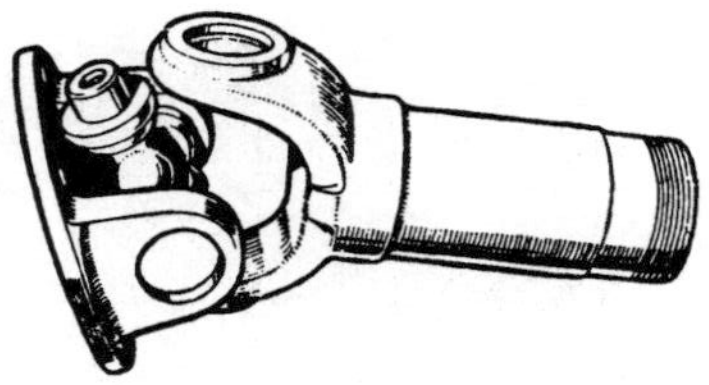

Removing the splined sleeve

7. The rear universal joint may be dismantled in a similar manner.
8. Clean all parts, inspect and renew as necessary.

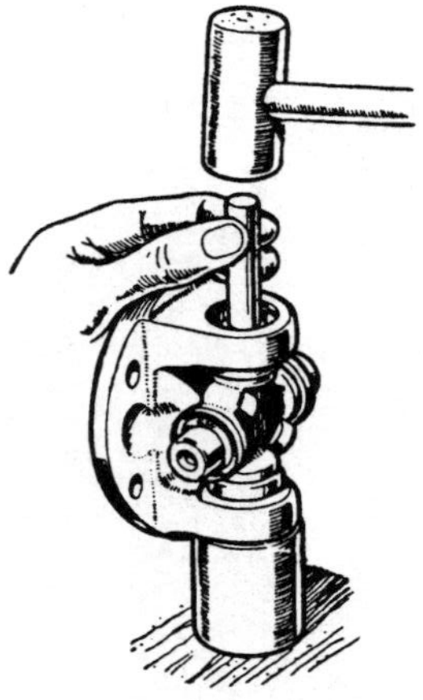

Removing the flange yoke

9. The parts most likely to show signs of wear after long usage are the bearing races and the spider journals. Should looseness in the fit of these parts, load markings or distortion be observed, they must be renewed complete.
   Replacement journal assemblies comprise a spider complete with cork oil seals and four bearings which will be found to be pre-packed with the correct amount of lubricant.

Operation G-4—*continued*

10. The other parts likely to show signs of wear are the splined sleeve yoke and splined shaft. A total of .004 in. (0,1 mm) circumferential movement, measured on the outside diameter of the splines, should not be exceeded. If wear beyond this limit has taken place, a new propeller shaft complete must be fitted.

11. The journals fitted to the propeller shaft of the 3 litre are of a larger overall size than the journals used on other Rover models.

    Identification:

    3 litre: 3.355 in. (85 mm) overall diameter, depth of ground portion of cup .555 in. (14 mm). Other Rover models: 2.940 in. (75 mm) overall diameter, depth of ground portion of cup .445 in. (11 mm).

12. Assemble the needle rollers in the bearing races using a smear of vaseline to retain them in place.

13. Insert the spider into the flange yoke holes and tap the first bearing and oil seal into position. The bearing races should be a **light drive** fit in the yoke trunnions. If any of the yoke holes are oval, a new propeller shaft or flange must be fitted.

14. Repeat the operation for the remaining bearings of the two shafts, front and rear.

15. Replace the circlips in their grooves. If the joint is stiff, tap with a soft-faced hammer to relieve any pressure on the ends of the journals.

16. Clean off any excess grease.

DEFECT LOCATION

SYMPTOM	*POSSIBLE CAUSE*	*REMEDY*
A—VIBRATING PROPELLER SHAFT	1. Misalignment	1. *Ensure that the universal joint yokes on the shaft are in line with each other. Check that the arrows on splined sleeve and the outer tube are in line with each other*
	2. Worn splines	2. *Renew as necessary*
	3. Worn coupling flange bolt holes	3. *Ensure that flange bolt holes are not oval, due to loose nuts. This could cause slight misalignment of the flanges. Renew as necessary*
	4. Securing bolts on flanges and support bracket loose	4. *Rectify*
	5. Centre bearing rubber mounting fatigued and weak support spring	5. *Renew as necessary*
B—PROPELLER SHAFT NOISY	1. Worn universal joints	1. *Renew*
	2. Lack of lubrication	2. *Lubricate, or renew bearings if cork seals are defective*
	3. Securing nuts loose	3. *Rectify*
	4. Worn splines	4. *Renew*
	5. Worn centre bearing	5. *Renew*

DATA

Type .. .. Open shaft

Universal joint .. .. Hardy Spicer needle bearing. Late type are pre-packed with grease

Shaft length, flange to flange .. ..

Model	*Position*	*Length*
4-speed	Front	41 25/32 in. (1,6 m)
4-speed with overdrive	Front	25 5/32 in. (639 mm)
Automatic transmission, Mk I, Mk IA and Mk II	Front	41 25/32 in. (1,6 m)
Automatic transmission, Mk III	Front	39 15/16 in. (1,0 m)
All	Rear	24 3/4 in. (628 mm)

Centre bearing type .. .. .. Ball bearing, pre-packed with grease

Section H – SUB-FRAME

Brief description of the sub-frame

The front end chassis unit or sub-frame is of strong box section construction. This unit, which carries the engine, transmission, suspension, steering and brakes, is bolted on to the welded steel body.

The sub-frame, complete with the engine and transmission units in situ and with the front wheels on, can be removed from the body for servicing purposes.

INDEX

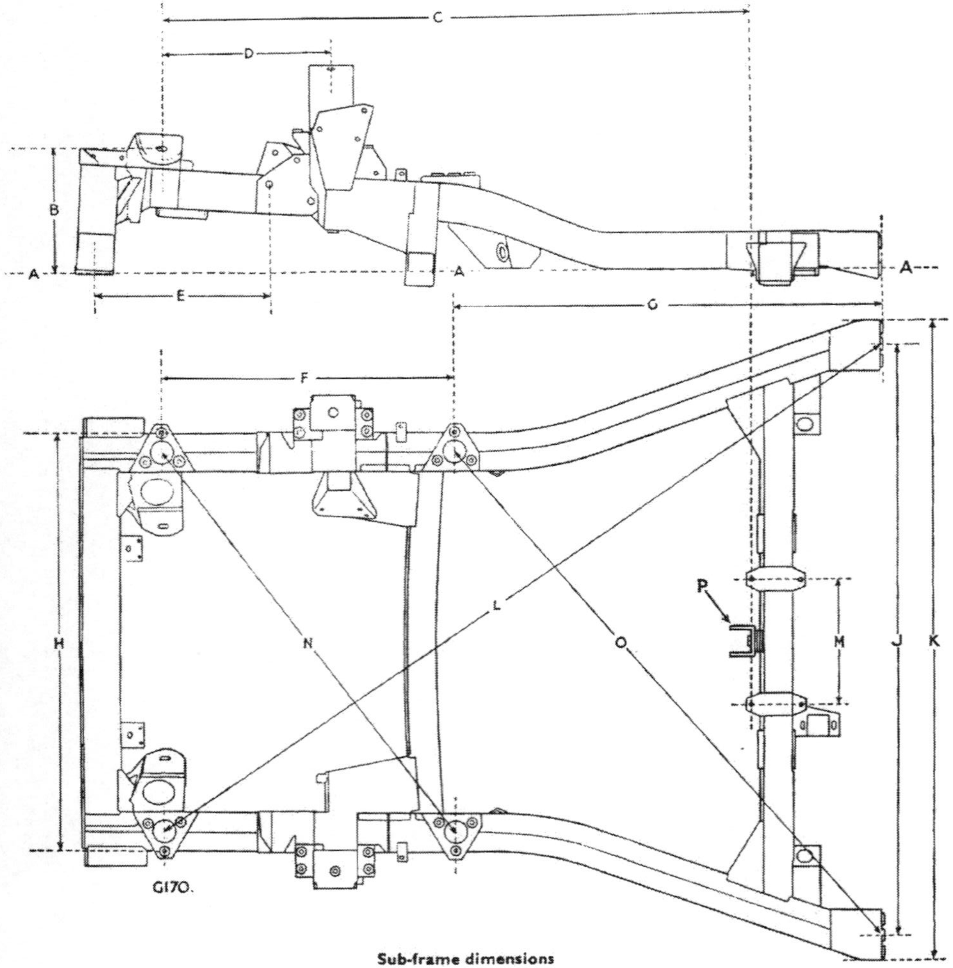

Sub-frame dimensions

A—Chassis datum line
B—$9\frac{11}{16}$ in. $\pm\frac{1}{16}$ in. (246,0±1,5 mm)
C—$45\frac{5}{16}$ in. $\pm\frac{1}{32}$ in. (1151,0±0,8 mm)
D—$13\frac{3}{16}$ in. (335,0 mm)
E—$13\frac{19}{32}\pm\frac{1}{32}$ in. (345,5±0,8 mm)
F—$22\frac{1}{2}$ in. (571,5 mm)
G—$32\frac{19}{32}$ in. (828,0 mm)
H—33 in. (838,0 mm)
J—$46\frac{3}{8}$ in. (1178,0 mm)
K—$50\frac{1}{2}$ in. (1283,0 mm)
L—$70\frac{13}{64}$ in. (1783,0 mm)
M—$9\frac{3}{4}\pm\frac{1}{32}$ in. (247,5±0,8 mm)
N—$37\frac{1}{2}$ in. (925,5 mm)
O—$50\frac{1}{4}$ in. (1276,0 mm)
P—Position, five-point mounting bracket

Sub-frame checking procedure—Operation H-1

1. Remove the sub-frame complete with engine, transmission and steering from the car.
2. All units must be removed from the sub-frame.
3. Measure the sub-frame and check the dimensions against the ones given in the diagram.
4. Repair the sub-frame where possible.
5. Check the body for distortion; repair if necessary. See Section U.
6. Fit the sub-frame to the body and check that the pick-up points coincide. If a new sub-frame is available, preferably use this to check the body pick-up points.
7. If a new sub-frame has to be fitted to car having four-point mountings, the latest type sub-frame (five-point mountings) will be supplied and a conversion kit, Part No. 530149 will be required.

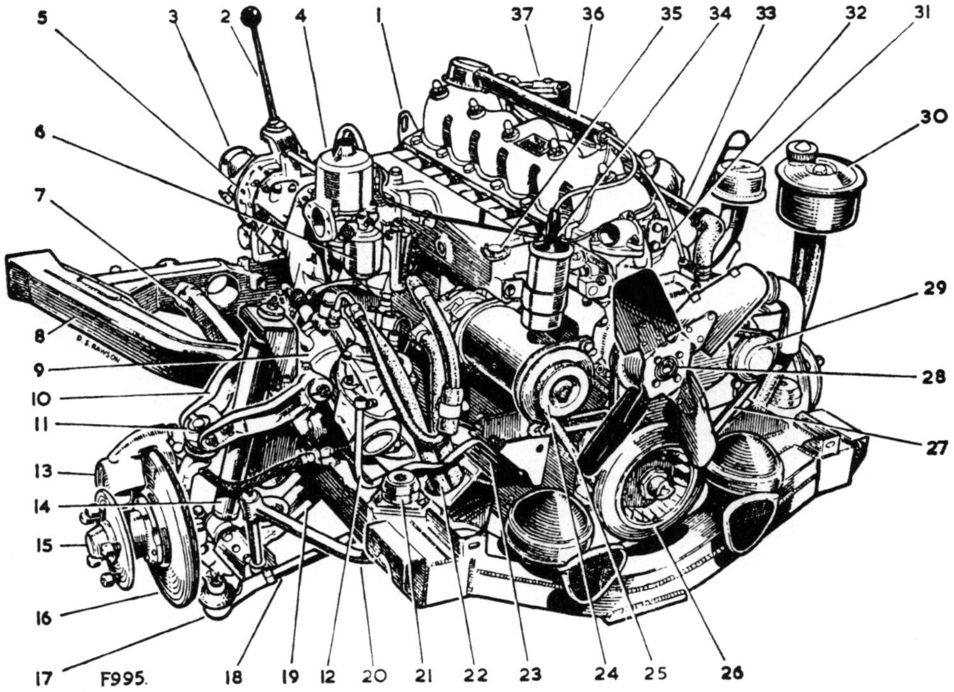

F995.

Engine, transmission and sub-frame assembly

1 Rear lifting bracket
2 Change speed lever, remote control
3 Propeller shaft coupling
4 Carburetter suction chamber
5 Overdrive unit
6 Carburetter float chamber
7 Torsion bar, road spring
8 Chassis sub-frame
9 Power steering unit
10 Top link
11 Top ball swivel
12 Earthing strap
13 Brake caliper
14 Shock absorber
15 Front hub
16 Brake disc
17 Steering ball joint
18 Steering link rod
19 Bottom link
20 Torsion rod
21 Body mounting
22 Hydraulic pipes, power steering
23 Engine mounting
24 Dynamo and pulley
25 Dynamo drive belt
26 Crank damper
27 Fan belt
28 Fan and water pump
29 Jockey pulley
30 Oil reservoir, power steering
31 Engine, oil filler and breather
32 Front lifting bracket
33 Heater outlet pipe
34 Coil
35 Thermostat switch
36 Wire carrier, HT leads
37 Distributor

Sub-frame, with engine and transmission unit, to remove—Operation H-2

Workshop hand tools:

Spanner sizes:
$\frac{5}{16}$ in. AF, $\frac{1}{2}$ in. AF, $\frac{9}{16}$ in. AF, $\frac{3}{4}$ in. AF, $\frac{7}{8}$ in. AF, $\frac{15}{16}$ in. AF
Screwdrivers, small and medium Pliers

The sub-frame can be removed from the car with the engine and transmission unit mounted upon it. This operation is carried out with the aid of suitable lifting equipment. The following information is basically applicable to both automatic and 4-speed transmission cars, and any detail which differs between the two models is clearly defined for guidance.

Sub-frame, remove

1. Remove the radiator cap and drain the cooling system by opening the tap under the radiator, and the tap on the right-hand side of the cylinder block.

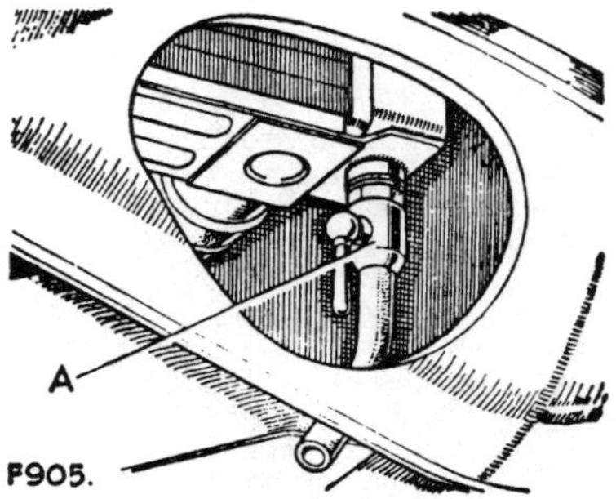

F905.

Radiator drain tap
A—Drain tap

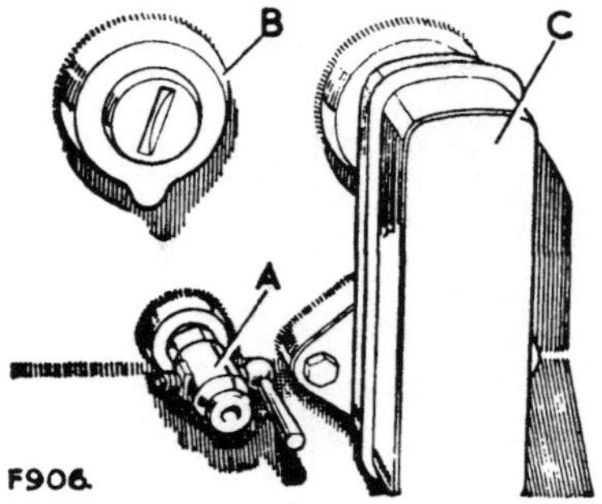

F906.

Cylinder block drain tap
A—Drain tap B—Boss for immersion heater
C—Crankcase breather

2. Disconnect the battery, situated in the boot.
3. Remove the bonnet, leaving the brackets attached to the bonnet—this ensures correct alignment when refitting. Where necessary disconnect the windscreen washer pipes; on coupé models, disconnect the bonnet light wiring.

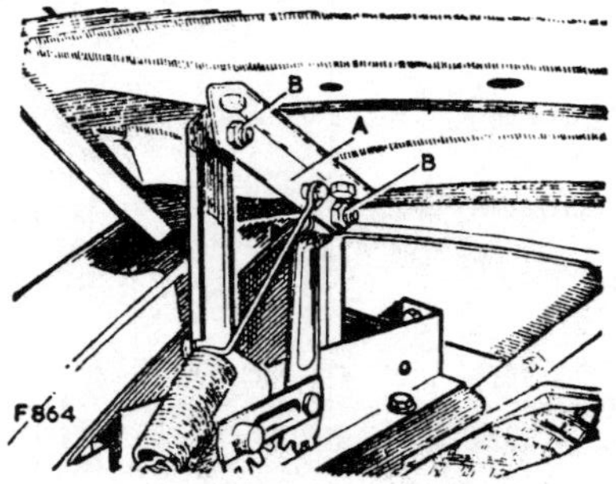

F864

Bonnet hinges
A—Hinge bracket
B—Nuts securing hinge links to hinge bracket

4. Remove the air cleaner, silencer and elbow:

Mk I models

(a) Slacken the hose clips securing the air cleaner top cover to silencer duct.

(b) Remove air silencer, secured to elbow by a wing nut and plain washer and by a bolt, bush washers and nut to a bracket on the cylinder head.

(c) Remove air cleaner secured by a horizontal bolt ($\frac{5}{16}$ in. UNF × $3\frac{3}{4}$ in.), spring washer and nut and by a bolt, nut and washer to a bracket on the dynamo.

Operation H-2—*continued*

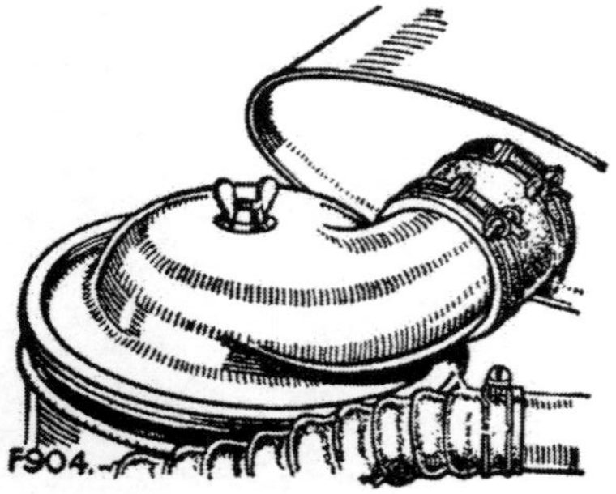

Oil bath type air cleaner

G152

Paper element type air cleaner

Mk IA, Mk II and Mk III models

Remove air cleaner complete, secured to elbow by a wing nut and plain washer and by a bolt, bush washers and nut to a bracket on the cylinder head.

All models

Disconnect the hose from the economiser adaptor. Remove the elbow from the carburetter secured by two nuts and spring washers.

5. Disconnect the fuel feed pipe from the carburetter and disconnect the cold-start control cable.
6. Disconnect the thermometer bulb from the cylinder head. On early models having a capillary tube, unscrew the bulb from the cylinder head.
7. Remove the screen washer reservoir.
8. Disconnect the water hoses, upper and lower, and heater hoses.
9. Remove radiator, secured by six set bolts, spring and plain washers.
10. Disconnect the starter harness, and the leads from the dynamo, ignition coil, oil pressure and mixture control switches, sump oil level unit, horns and starter inhibiter switch as applicable.

Models Mk I and Mk IA. Item 11

11. Disconnect the brake servo vacuum pipes, servo-to-reservoir and reservoir-to-manifold.
12. Disconnect the hydraulic brake pipe between the servo unit and the junction on the bulkhead. Depress the brake pedal and lock in position to prevent loss of fluid. Seal off all pipes to prevent ingress of dirt.

Power steering. Item 13

13. Remove reservoir from bracket on left-hand wing valance and secure reservoir to engine.

Overdrive. Item 14

14. Disconnect the wiring from the switch actuated by the throttle linkage.
15. Disconnect the throttle linkage.

(a) **Mk I, Mk IA and Mk II suffix 'A' and 'B' models**

Disconnect the collapsible control rod from the lever on the carburetter butterfly spindle. Remove the countershaft and bracket (engine to wing valance). Do not disturb any other part of the linkage as it is pre-set.

(b) **Mk II suffix 'C' and Mk III models**

Disconnect the control rod between the accelerator shaft and the cross-shaft extension. Pull the extension shaft back against its conical spring to disconnect it from the cross-shaft.

All models. Items 16 to 18

16. Disconnect the front exhaust pipe from the exhaust system fitted to the body.
17. Disconnect the speedometer drive, at the gear-box.
18. Disconnect and remove the forward longitudinal handbrake rod and return spring.

Operation H-2—*continued*

4-speed models

19. Remove the gear change lever assembly.

(a) Remove the centre section of the front carpet and slide back the front seats as far as possible.

(b) **MkI and Mk IA models**

Remove the four nuts and washers securing the gear change support bracket to the tunnel cover. Raise the large rubber grommet and remove the three small set screws and springs securing the selector lever retaining plate to the gear selector housing.

Release the locker securing the selector lever to the fork end and unscrew the lever and insulator housing assembly from the fork end. Lift out the gear change unit.

(c) **Mk II and Mk III models**

Remove grommet for gear lever and tunnel cover. Remove four nuts securing gear lever support bracket to gearbox extension. Slacken off the pinch bolt securing selector lever. Lift gear lever complete with bracket and with-draw rod from front bush. Note position of any shim washers fitted under the bracket, which should be retained and refitted in the original position.

20. Disconnect the wiring from the reverse light switch on the gearbox and where overdrive is fitted disconnect the feed wire from the overdrive isolation switch and operating solenoid.
21. Disconnect the return spring and remove the clevis pin from the clutch lever.
22. Remove the clutch slave cylinder from the bell-housing, but do not disconnect the hydraulic pipe as the cylinder can be supported out of the way. Fit a suitable metal clip over the cylinder to prevent cylinder components from being expelled by depression of the clutch pedal.

Overdrive models. Item 23

23. Remove the detachable cross-member from body floor, situated below the overdrive casing.

Automatic transmission. Items 24 to 29
Mk I and Mk IA. Items 24 and 25
Mk II. Items 26 and 27

24. Disconnect the gear selector-to-cross-shaft com-pensator coupling.
25. Remove the control rod, relay to governor control shaft.
26. Disconnect the gear selector-to-cross-shaft com-pensator coupling.
27. Pull the extension shaft, at engine side of bulkhead, back against the conical spring and disconnect from the cross-shaft.

Mk III. Items 28 and 29

28. Disconnect cross-shaft bracket at sump and also the adjustable rod, cross-shaft to transmission unit.
29. Pull the extension shaft, at engine side of bulkhead, back against the conical spring and disconnect from the cross-shaft.

All models. Items 30 to 38

30. Disconnect the propeller shaft at gearbox output shaft.

F867

Linkage, automatic transmission, Mk I, Mk IA and Mk II models

A—Compensator coupling
B—Cross-shaft lever
C—Control rod

31. Mark the steering shaft and coupling on the steering box in relation to each other and remove the steering wheel and shaft.
32. **Models fitted with single inner column bearing:** Remove the steering wheel and with-draw the steering shaft from the coupling. See Section J.

Operation H-2—*continued*

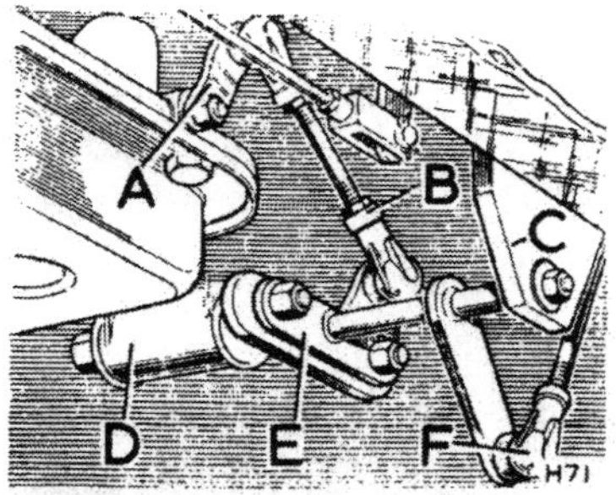

Linkage, automatic transmission, Mk III RHD model illustrated

33. **Models fitted with double inner column bearing:** Remove the steering wheel and the steering shaft complete with outer column from the coupling. See Section J.

34. Disconnect the earth strap, wing valance to sub-frame, at the right-hand side of engine compartment.

35. Remove the front bumper bar complete with mounting brackets.

36. Disconnect the hydraulic brake pipe between the servo unit and the junction on the bulkhead. Depress the brake pedal and lock in position to prevent loss of fluid. Seal off all pipes to prevent ingress of dirt.

37. Position a trolley jack under the rear sub-frame cross-member. Remove the six sub-frame mounting bolts, four being situated in the engine compartment and two at the rear of the sub-frame. Using a suitable sling attached to the front of the body, carefully lift the front end clear of the sub-frame and engine assembly.

38. Wheel the sub-frame assembly clear and lower the body on to suitable stands placed under the front jacking tubes.

Sub-frame, with engine and transmission unit to refit—Operation H-3

Workshop hand tools:

Spanner sizes: $\frac{5}{16}$ in. AF, $\frac{1}{2}$ in. AF, $\frac{9}{16}$ in. AF, $\frac{3}{4}$ in. AF, $\frac{7}{8}$ in. AF, $\frac{15}{16}$ in. AF

Pliers

Special tools:

Torque spanner

Sub-frame, refit

1. Using a suitable sling, firmly attached to the front end of the car, carefully lift the front end high enough to allow the sub-frame assembly to be wheeled into position beneath it.

2. Align the sub-frame assembly, which must be supported at the rear, to the car, and carefully lower the front end of the car on to the sub-frame, ensuring that all fittings are clear. To assist in aligning the mounting bolts, two $\frac{1}{2}$ in. UNF × 4 in. bolts which have had the head removed and the shank tapered, can be screwed into the front mountings on the sub-frame to serve as a guide tool as the body is lowered.

3. After checking the alignment of the mounting bolt holes, smear the mounting bolts with Lithium grease, fit the six mounting bolts; it is advisable to fit the two rear mounting bolts first. Do not tighten fully until all bolts are in position, then tighten to 50 to 55 lb/ft (6,9 to 7,6 mkg).

4. Connect the front universal joint flange of the front propeller shaft to the output shaft driving flange, and refit the centre bearing mounting bracket. Check that the centre bearing housing plate is central on the rubber bushes and situated at an equal distance from each end of the rubber bush; if necessary adjust the support spring to a vertical position.

Models with overdrive

5. Refit the detachable body cross-member to the underside of the car body.

6. Refit the steering column and steering wheel. See Section J.

7. With the road wheels and steering wheel in the straight-ahead position and the marks on the couplings aligned, fit the flexible coupling and locating plates to the steering box and steering column shafts.

8. Connect the hydraulic brake pipes, front-to-rear.

9. Fit the earth strap, right-hand wing valance to sub-frame, ensuring that a good metal-to-metal connection is made.

10. Connect the reverse light switch and where necessary the overdrive isolation switch and solenoid harness.

Four-speed models. Items 11 and 12

11. Refit the clutch slave cylinder and where fitted the over-centre clutch mechanism. See Section C.

12. Fit the gear change lever assembly. See Section D.

All models. Item 13

13. Connect the accelerator linkage. See Section F.

Automatic transmission. Item 14

14. Connect the gear selector linkage and starter inhibiter switch.

All models

15. Connect the speedometer drive cable to the transmission.

16. Re-connect the exhaust system. See Section R.

17. Re-connect the handbrake mechanism. See Section N.

18. Connect the wiring to the following:

    Coil and ignition system.

    Thermometer. (On early models having a capillary tube, fit the thermometer bulb to the cylinder head.)

    Choke warning light.

    Dynamo.

    Horns.

    Oil pressure switch.

    Windscreen washer.

    Sump gauge unit.

    Starter motor.

19. Fit the cold-start control cable to the carburetter and connect the fuel feed pipe.

20. Fit the radiator and connect the hoses and heater hoses. Fill the system with coolant. For capacities see Section P.

Power steering. Item 21

21. Connect the power steering hoses. See Section J-1.

22. Fit the front bumper. See Section U.

23. Fit the bonnet. See Section U.

24. Bleed the brakes. See Section N.

25. Bleed the clutch system. See Section C.

26. Fit the carburetter elbow and the air cleaner and silencer.

Operation H-3—*continued*

27. Items 27, 28 and 29 are only necessary if the engine, transmission and, where applicable, power steering oils have been drained off or if any overhaul work to these units has been carried out.

28. Fill the engine (and oil bath air cleaner where fitted) to the correct levels, with recommended grade of engine oil. See Sections A and Y.

29. **Four-speed transmission**—fill the gearbox and overdrive, where fitted, with the recommended grade of oil. See Section D.

30. **Automatic transmission and power steering units**—the transmission and power steering units must be filled with the correct grade of fluid.

    See Section E for automatic transmission.

    See Section J-1 for power steering.

31. Connect the battery terminals.

    Caution: Do not attempt to start the engine unless there is fluid in both automatic transmission and power steering units where fitted.

32. Adjust the carburetter controls—idling speed, fast idling and cold-start control. See Section Q.

Power steering. Item 33

33. Bleed the system. See Section J-1.

34. Check that all the fixing bolts are tight and that split pins have been fitted where applicable.

Manual steering. Item 35

35. Adjust the steering lock stops, check the length of the track rod and the adjustment of the steering links. See Section J.

Power steering. Item 36

36. Check the length of the track rod and the adjustment of the steering links. See Section J-1.

Manual and power steering

37. Check the steering alignment, $\frac{1}{16}$ in. (1,5 mm) toe-in to $\frac{1}{16}$ in. (1,5 mm) toe-out.

38. Adjust the torsion bar height. See Section K.

Sub-frame, to strip and rebuild—Operation H-4

Workshop hand tools:

Spanner sizes: $\frac{1}{2}$ in. AF, $\frac{9}{16}$ in. AF, $\frac{5}{8}$ in. AF, $1\frac{1}{4}$ in. AF, $\frac{3}{8}$ in. BSF

Screwdriver, medium Pliers

Special tools:

Torque spanner

Sub-frame, to strip

1. Remove the engine and transmission unit from the sub-frame.

2. Support the sub-frame on suitable stands and remove the road wheels.

3. Remove the steering track rod, steering links and where fitted the steering damper. Remove the steering box and relay. See Section J and J-1.

4. Remove the brake servo unit from the sub-frame.

Mk I models with drum brakes. Item 5

5. Disconnect the brake hoses and remove the brake drums and hubs. See Section N and K.

Mk II and Mk III models with disc brakes. Item 6

6. Disconnect the brake hoses and remove the disc brake assemblies and hubs. See Sections N and K.

7. Remove the stabilising torsion rod and link pins. See Section K.

8. Remove the front shock absorbers. See Section K.

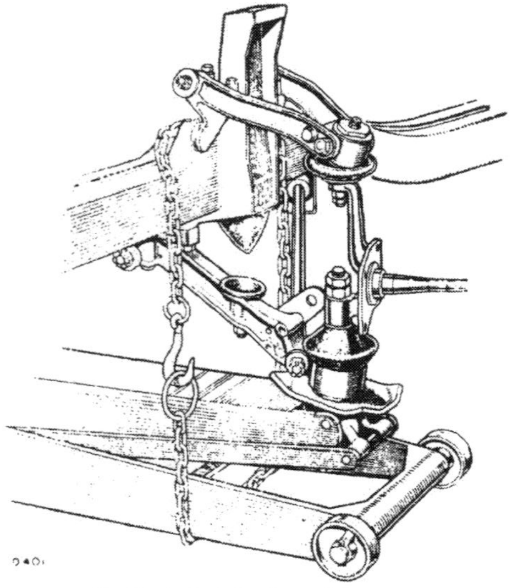

Trolley jack chained to sub-frame

9. Place a trolley jack under the extreme outer end of the bottom link, with the jack at right-angles to the centre-line of the sub-frame. Secure the jack with a suitable chain to the sub-frame, ensuring that the chain passes under the jack and is kept taut and in a near-vertical position to allow for jack movement when lowering the bottom link, and also to prevent the sub-frame from lifting during the torsion bar removal operation.

10. Jack up the bottom link and place two suitable hard wooden blocks between the top links and their respective rebound rubbers.

11. Remove the locking nut from the lower ball swivel pin, and slacken the securing nut on both upper and lower ball swivel pins by approximately $\frac{1}{64}$ in. (0,4 mm).

12. With the wooden blocks in position, carefully lower the jack sufficiently to subject the ball swivel pins to torsion bar tension. Do not remove the jack.

13. Smartly tap the stub axle eye around both upper and lower swivels, to release the swivel pins from their tapers. The securing nuts will prevent damage to the threads of the pins. Ensure that the stub axle is free on both tapers before raising the bottom link again.

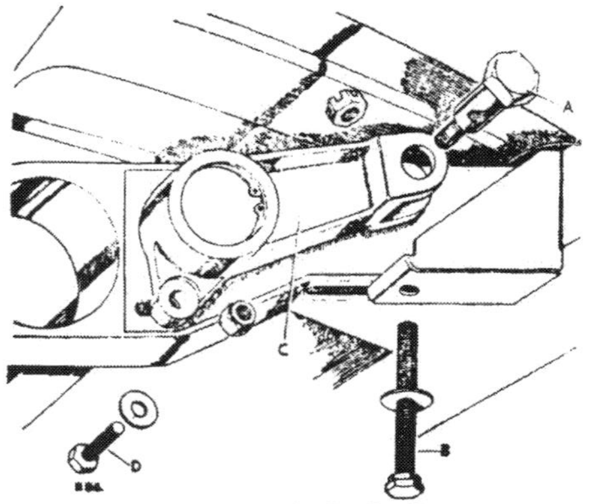

Arrangement of adjusting lever

A—Trunnion for adjusting lever
B—Adjusting bolt
C—Adjusting lever
D—Clamping bolt for adjusting lever

Operation H-4—*continued*

14. Jack up the bottom link again, to relieve the load on the nuts securing the swivel pins, remove the lower nut and gradually lower the bottom link to its fullest extent, allowing the torsion bar tension to be relieved.
15. Remove the split pin and castle nut from the top of the adjusting bolt. Remove the locknut and clamping bolt from the adjusting lever and the locknut from the adjusting trunnion bolt, which is situated inside the rear cross-member
16. Unscrew the adjusting bolt from the adjusting lever trunnion and remove the bolt complete with the seat washer.
17. Slight downward pressure may be required on the bottom link in order to withdraw the trunnion bolt, at the same time care must be taken to ensure that the radius rod is not subjected to undue strain.
18. Withdraw the adjusting lever from the end of the torsion bar. Pull the torsion bar rearwards, out of the bottom link housing. Do not disturb the order of the torsion bar leaves—any re-arrangement will affect the characteristics of the bar.
19. Detach the top ball swivel joint and stub axle from the top links. Remove the securing nut and withdraw the stub axle from the swivel pin taper.
20. Loosen the lock plates and remove the bolts fixing the bottom link pin housing to the sub-frame. Detach the bottom link from the front end of the radius rod.
21. Remove the top links, noting the fitting sequence of the plain washers. It is recommended that the top links are identified in some way to assist in the rebuild.
22. Remove the top link mounting arms, which should be marked to assist identification when assembling.
23. Remove the radius rod from the sub-frame mounting bracket, noting the sequence of the plain washers.
24. Remove the top link and bottom link rebound rubbers.
25. Remove the front engine mountings, radiator supports and horns and if necessary remove the six sub-frame mountings, all brake pipes and clips. Unscrew the steering lock adjuster screws, (where fitted).

Sub-frame, to rebuild

1. Ensure that the sub-frame is safely supported on suitable stands. Fit the front engine mountings, radiator supports, and horns; fit the top link and bottom link rebound rubbers.
2. Fit the six sub-frame mountings, all the brake pipes and clips. Screw in the steering lock adjusters (where fitted).
3. Fit the short shouldered end of the radius rod to the sub-frame mounting bracket, turning the rod to a position to facilitate fitting of the split pin. Ensure that the thick washer is fitted with the chamfer on the internal diameter towards the radius of the rod shoulder. After fitting the rubbers, cup washers and plain washer, the castle nut can be fully tightened and split pinned.
4. Fit the bottom link and ball swivel assembly to the sub-frame and radius rod. The radius rod mounting sequence is:
   (a) Thick washer with the chamfered internal diameter fitted to the rod shoulder.
   (b) Rubber bush (fitted in bottom link).
   (c) Plain washer.
   (d) Castle nut and split pin.

   The castle nut can be tightened and split pinned. Use new lock plates when securing the bottom link pin housing to the sub-frame.
5. Ensure that the grease sleeves are fitted to the torsion bars and are filled with the correct grade of lubricant.
6. It is important that the torsion bars are fitted to their respective sides, because of the 'set' of the spring leaves. When fitting new torsion bars, the right-hand side bar is identified with red paint, the left-hand bar has no identification mark; ensure that each is fitted to the correct side.

   Torsion bars must be replaced as a complete assembly and the arrangement of the leaves must not be disturbed.
7. With the edges of the leaves pointing inwards and down to the sub-frame centre-line, and the chamfered end of the bar to the rear, slide the bar forward into its respective bottom link housing.
8. Locate the adjusting lever on to the end of the torsion bar and register into the sub-frame aperture.

Operation H-4—*continued*

9. To fit the trunnion bolt to the adjusting lever, it may be necessary to apply a slight downward pressure on the bottom link, at the same time care must be taken to ensure that the radius rod is not subjected to undue strain.
10. Slide the seat on to the adjusting bolt and thread the bolt into the trunnion.
11. Jack up the bottom link slightly to relieve any stress imposed on the radius rod.
12. Fit the trunnion plain washer and locknut, and the adjusting lever clamping bolt, plain washer and locknut. Do not tighten at this stage.
13. Fit the castle nut and split pin to the adjusting lever bolt. Do not run the castle nut right down the threaded bolt—only far enough to allow the split pin to be fitted.

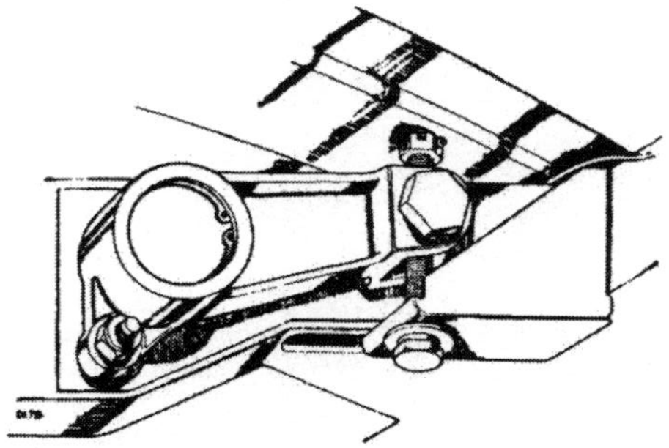

Position of castle nut and split pin

14. Fit the top link mounting arms, one right-hand and one left-hand respectively, to the sub-frame.
15. Fit the respective top links to the mounting arms and secure with castle nuts and split pins.
16. Fit the top ball swivel, complete with rubber boot, to the top arm of the stub axle, securing with a new self-locking nut and tighten to 45 lb/ft (6,0 mkg).
17. Fit the top ball swivel joint and stub axle assembly to the top links; the left-hand side stub axle has a right-hand thread for the bearing nuts, and the right-hand side stub axle has a left-hand thread.

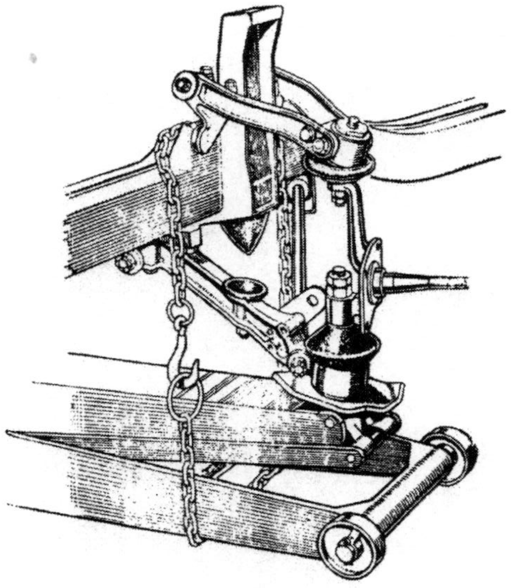

Trolley jack chained to sub-frame

18. Position a trolley jack under the extreme outer end of the bottom link, with the jack at right-angles to the sub-frame centre line. Secure the jack with a suitable chain to the sub-frame, ensuring that the chain passes under the jack. The chain should be taut and in a near-vertical position, to prevent the sub-frame from lifting when jacking up the bottom link.
19. Raise the bottom link, at the same time carefully guiding the lower arm of the stub axle on to the lower ball joint swivel pin, taking care to prevent damaging the threads. Fit a new steel nut and self-locking nut and tighten both nuts to 75 to 80 lb/ft (10 to 11,0 mkg). Ensure that the swivel pin rubber boot fits snugly under the shield on the stub axle. Lower the jack and remove the chain.

On early models two identical plain steel nuts were used on the lower ball swivel pin, on later models a steel nut and self-locking nut were used; this modification may be carried out to earlier models.

Operation H-4—*continued*

20. Fit the front shock absorbers, using new mounting rubbers. Fit the lower mounting bracket and mounting plate to the bottom link and fit the shock absorber lower mounting bolt.

21. The stabilising torsion rod, with its rubber bushes and support brackets, can be fitted to the sub-frame; fit the link pins, distance tubes, cup washers, new rubbers and nuts, and secure to the shock absorber lower mounting bracket.

22. Refit the hub assemblies. See Section K.

23. Fit the brake assemblies. See Section N.

24. Fit the brake hose to the brake assemblies.

25. Secure the brake servo unit to its mounting on the sub-frame.

26. Fit the steering and relay boxes. See Sections J and J-1.

27. The length of the steering links must be adjusted so that when fitted with the front wheels in the straight-ahead position and the toe-in correctly set the turning circle on right- and left-hand lock is the same.

28. Ensure that the ball joint body is parallel with the respective steering and drop arms, in order to allow full movement.

29. Fit the track rod to the outer hole of the drop arms. The track rod length should be—manual steering $24\frac{1}{4}$ in. (616,0 mm), power steering—$23\frac{15}{16}$ in. (608 mm) between ball joint centres. Ensure that the ball joints are aligned to allow full unrestricted movement of the steering linkage.

30. Refit the road wheels.

DATA

Steering arm nuts, tightening torque	45 lb/ft (6,22 mkg)
Hub end-float	.004 to .006 in. (0,10 to 0,15 mm)
Length of track rod between ball joint centres:	
Manual steering..	$24\frac{1}{4}$ in. (616 mm)
Power steering	$23\frac{15}{16}$ in. (608 mm)
Torsion bar height	See Section K
Tyre pressures	See Section V

Section J — MANUAL STEERING

Brief description of steering system

The Burman re-circulating ball, worm and nut unit with variable ratio is used to give high overall efficiency. The ratios of the earlier unit are 17.6:1 straight ahead and 28.5:1 on full lock. The latest steering ratios are 20.3:1 straight ahead and 24.5:1 on full lock.

The 17 in. steering wheel gives 4½ turns from lock to lock providing the car with a turning circle of 38 ft 6 ins. An hydraulic telescopic shock absorber is incorporated for steering damping on saloon models from suffix letter 'B' onwards.

INDEX

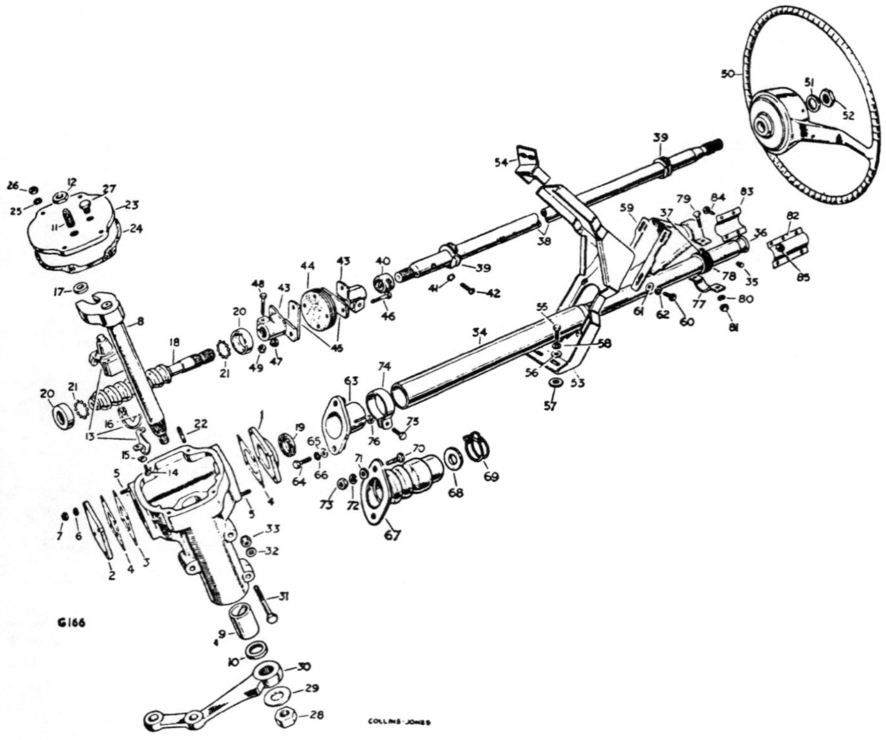

G166

Layout of steering unit assembly

1	End cover plate, upper
2	End cover plate, lower
3	Joint washers, steel
4	Joint washers, paper
5	Stud
6–7	Fixings, end cover plate
8	Rocker shaft
9	Bush for rocker shaft
10	Oil seal
11	Adjusting screw
12	Nut for adjusting screw
13	Main nut assembly
14	Set bolt
15	Lock washer
16	Steel balls ($\frac{3}{8}$ in.)
17	Roller for main nut
18	Inner column
19	Oil seal for inner column
20	Adjustable ball race
21	Steel balls
22	Stud
23	Top cover plate
24	Joint washer
25–26	Fixings, top cover plate
27	Oil filler plug
28–29	Fixings, drop arm
30	Drop arm
31–33	Fixings, steering box to sub-frame
34	Outer column assembly
35	Dowel for shrouds
36	Bearing for outer column
37	Dowel for steering column support bracket
38	Steering column shaft
39	Spring washer
40	Clamping ring for shaft
41	Shakeproof washer } Fixing clamping ring to shaft
42	Set screw } Fixing clamping ring to shaft
43	Coupling flange
44	Flexible coupling disc
45	Locating plate
46–47	Fixings, flanges, disc and locating plates
48–49	Fixings, coupling to steering box and steering shaft
50	Steering wheel
51–52	Fixings, steering wheel
53	Mounting bracket
54	Steering column tie bracket
55–58	Bracket fixings
59	Support bracket
60–62	Fixings, support bracket
63	Anchor bracket
64–66	Fixings, anchor bracket
67	Grommet for steering column
68	Felt washer for grommet
69	Hose clip
70–73	Fixings for grommet
74	Clamp
75–76	Fixings, for clamp
77	Clip for steering column
78	Tape for clip
79–81	Fixings, clip
82	Clamp plate
83	Strengthening plate
84–85	Fixings, plates to outer column

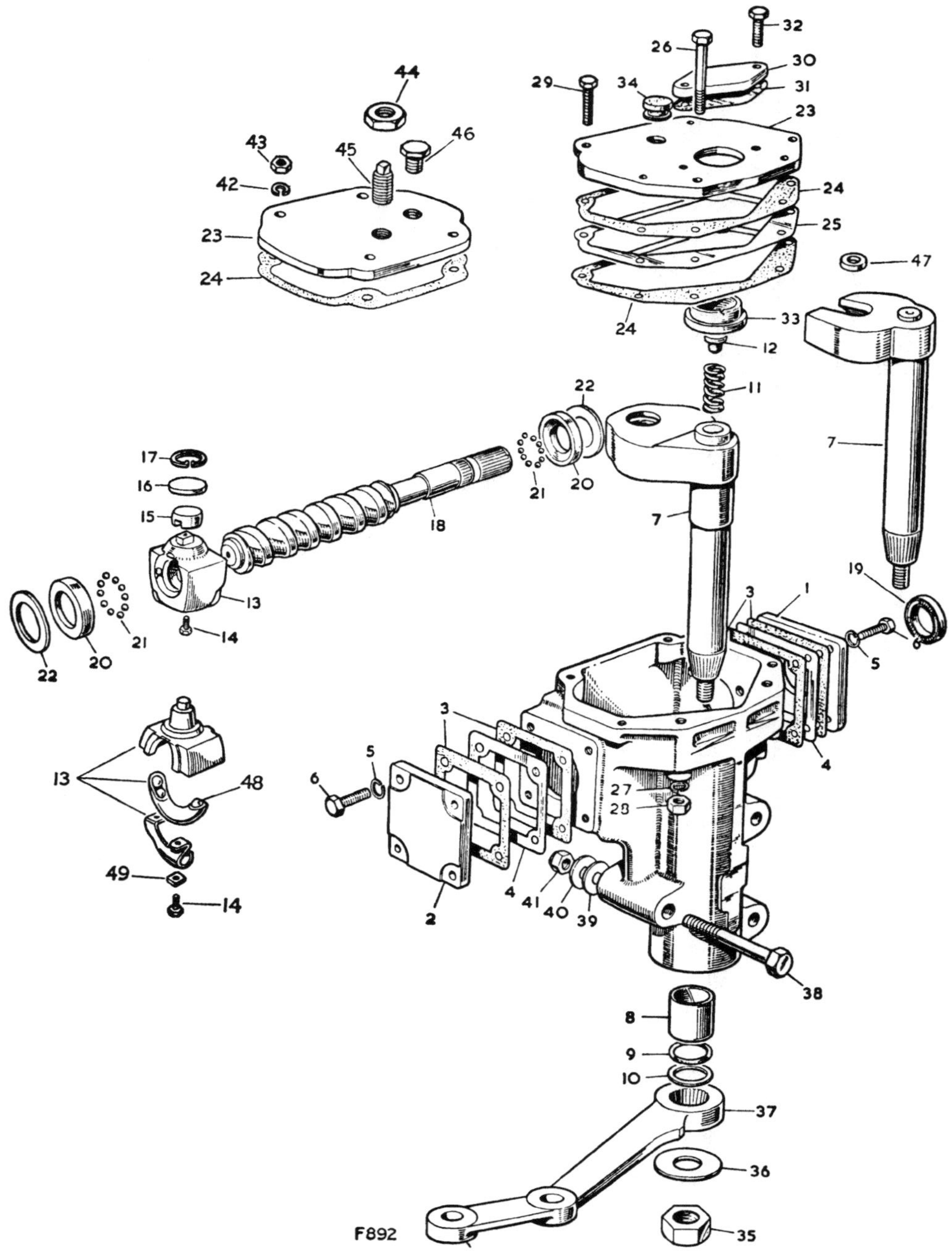

F892

Layout of steering box

1	End cover plate, upper	17	Circlip	34	Oil filler plug
2	End cover plate, lower	18	Inner column	35	Nut
3	Joint washer, paper	19	Oil seal	36	Lock washer
4	Joint washer, steel	20	Adjustable ball race	37	Drop arm
5	Spring washer	21	Steel balls	38	Bolt
6	Set bolt	22	Spacer washer	39	Packing washer
7	Rocker shaft	23	Top cover plate	40	Plain washer
8	Bush for rocker shaft	24	Joint washer, paper	41	Self-locking nut
9	Oil seal for rocker shaft	25	Joint washer, steel	42	Spring washer
10	Washer for oil seal	26	Dowel bolt	43	Nut
11	Spring for rocker shaft	27	Spring washer	44	Nut for adjusting screw
12	Button for rocker shaft	28	Nut	45	Adjusting screw
13	Main nut assembly	29	Set bolt	46	Oil filler plug
14	Bolt	30	Cover plate	47	Roller for main nut
15	Roller for main nut	31	Joint washer	48	Steel balls
16	Thrust washer	32	Bolt	49	Lock washer
		33	Bush		

Steering box, remove and refit—Operation J-1

Workshop hand tools:

Spirit level Rule Screwdriver Hammer

Spanner sizes: $\frac{5}{16}$ in. AF, $\frac{7}{16}$ in. AF, $\frac{1}{2}$ in. AF, $\frac{11}{16}$ in. AF, $\frac{3}{4}$ in. AF, $\frac{7}{8}$ in. AF, 3 BA

Special tools:

Alignment equipment

Steering box, remove

1. Place the car with the front road wheels in the straight-ahead position.
2. Remove the carburetter air intake elbow—Section A.
3. Disconnect the choke cable at the carburetter.
4. Remove the ball joints from the steering box drop arm; this will be facilitated by tapping smartly around the drop arm eye.
5. Mark the steering shaft flange and flexible rubber coupling to ensure correct refitment. Remove the two nuts and bolts securing the steering shaft flange to the rubber coupling, taking care to prevent pushing the steering shaft upwards. Should this occur, the horn contact will be disturbed. A suitable clip can be secured to the shaft adjacent to the bulkhead to prevent the shaft from moving upwards.
6. Remove the three steering box mounting bolts and detach the steering box from the sub-frame, complete with drop arm and flexible rubber coupling.

Steering box, refit

1. Reverse removal procedure.
2. Tighten the steering box securing bolts to a torque of 50 lb/ft (7,0 mkg).
3. Refill the steering box with the correct grade of lubricant—Section Y.
4. Ensure that the ball joints are aligned with their companion joint at the opposite end of the rod and link to allow full free movement of these parts.
5. If necessary, adjust the wheel alignment and toe-in—Operation J-9.

Steering box, overhaul—Operation J-2

Workshop hand tools:

Spirit level, Rule, Screwdriver, Hammer

Spanner sizes: $\frac{5}{16}$ in. Whit, $\frac{5}{16}$ in. AF, $\frac{7}{16}$ in. AF, $\frac{1}{2}$ in. AF, $\frac{9}{16}$ in. AF, $\frac{11}{16}$ in. AF, $\frac{3}{4}$ in. AF, $\frac{7}{8}$ in. AF, $\frac{15}{16}$ in. AF, $1\frac{1}{8}$ in. AF, 3 BA

Special tools:

Alignment equipment

Drop arm removal tool, Part No. 600446

See *Operation J-1 for steering box removal*

Steering box, strip

1. Withdraw the retaining nut and washer and mark the drop arm in relation to the rocker shaft to ensure correct refitment and remove the drop arm, using special tool Part No. 600446.

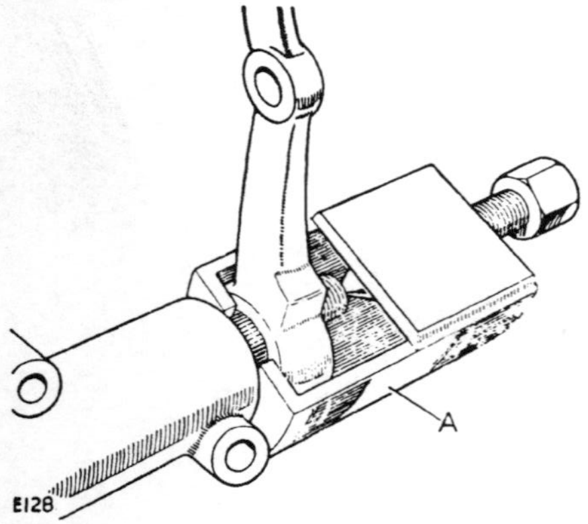

Drop arm removal tool
A—Withdrawal tool

2. Mark the coupling flange in relation to the worm shaft, then withdraw the clamping bolt and remove the flange.
3. On the latest type of box fitted to Mk II models suffix letter 'B' onwards, remove the cover plate and distance piece for rocker shaft spring, undoing the bolts evenly to prevent distortion of the cup.
4. Withdraw the spring and the adjuster cup.
5. On all models remove the top cover and drain off the oil.
6. Lift off the main nut roller and remove the rocker shaft.
7. Holding the steering box in a vice, remove the bottom end cover, together with shims and joint washers.
8. Remove the top end cover, complete with oil seal, joint washer and shims (if fitted).
9. Remove the top and bottom outer races and ball bearings.
10. Rotate the worm shaft until the main nut, complete with 12 ball bearings, and the worm shaft can be removed from the box.
11. If necessary press out the rocker shaft bush and oil seal from the box.
12. If necessary remove the transfer tube from the main nut.

Steering box, rebuild

On cars from suffix letter 'B' onwards a redesigned steering drop arm of thicker section and with a raised ball centre was fitted to improve the steering geometry.

If it is found necessary to change a drop arm on the steering box, it must be established that the replacement is of the same design as that fitted to the steering relay.

Examine the steering box components for signs of wear or damage and renew as necessary.

1. If removed, refit the rocker shaft bush, which should be a light drive fit in the housing. Renew the oil seal.
2. Fit a new oil seal to the top end cover. Fit the top end outer race, without bearings, to the steering box and fit the top end cover, with new joint washer, and any shims which may have been fitted originally.
3. Hold the steering box in the vice so that the top end cover faces downwards.
4. Retain the 12 large ball bearings in the main nut with grease.
5. Position the main nut inside the worm housing and insert the worm shaft, splined end first, into the main nut. Rotate the worm shaft in through the main nut.

Operation J-2—*continued*

6. Lower the worm shaft into the outer race of the top bearing, splined end first, far enough to allow the 10 small ball bearings to be inserted between the shaft and outer race.
7. Assemble 10 ball bearings into the bottom outer race, retaining with grease, and carefully fit to the end of the shaft and steering box.
8. Fit the bottom end cover, shims and joint washers. With the steering box and worm shaft still in the vertical position, adjust the worm shaft so that it can be turned by hand but has no end-float. Add alternative shims and joint washers under the bottom end cover to achieve this condition.
9. Insert the rocker shaft into the steering box and locate the main nut. Rotate the worm shaft until the main nut is centrally positioned.
10. At this stage the box can be turned to a horizontal position and be filled with the correct grade of oil (Section Y).
11. On earlier steering boxes fitted with an adjusting screw, refit the main nut roller and cover plate, ensuring that the roller locates in the slot in the cover.
12. Ensure that the main nut is central on the worm shaft, tighten the cover fixings and adjust the rocker shaft end float by screwing down the adjuster by hand until it contacts the rocker shaft; tighten a further tenth of a turn and then tighten the locknut.

Steering box lubrication
A—Oil filler plug B—Adjusting screw

13. On later steering boxes fitted with a spring cap bolted to the top rocker cover. Fit the top rocker cover, using all shims and joint washers removed, and tighten.
14. Add or remove shims so there is the minimum of end-float in the rocker shaft, but ensure there is no pre-load; when end-float adjustment is correct replace adjuster cup and the spring. Refit the distance piece and cover plate for spring, using a new joint washer. Top cover joint washers and shims are available in .003 in. (0,07 mm) and .010 in. (0,25 mm) thicknesses.

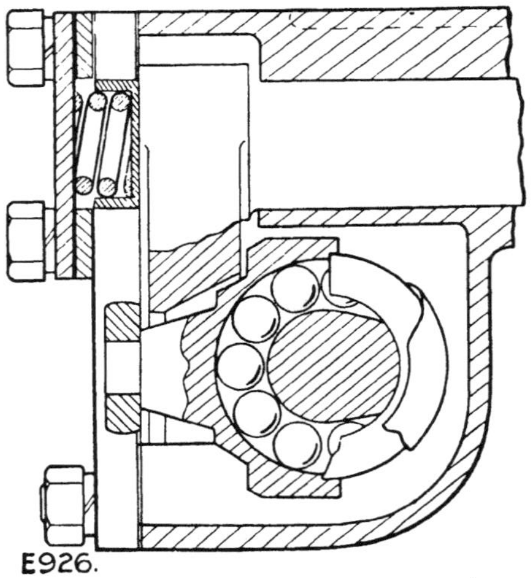

Cross-section of steering box with adjuster spring

15. Refit the steering drop arm, taking care to align the markings on arm and shaft, fit a new locking plate and tighten the nut fully.
16. The coupling flange should be fitted to the steering worm shaft on the original splines, as marked before removal.

Steering box, adjust—Operation J-3

Workshop hand tools:
Spanner size: $\frac{15}{16}$ in. AF

Steering box, adjust, early models

1. With the road wheels in the straight-ahead position, slacken the adjuster locknut. Turn the square-headed adjuster by hand until contact is made with the top of the rocker shaft. Tighten a further tenth of a turn and lock the adjuster with the locknut.

   If this adjustment is carried out with the wheels not in the **straight-ahead position,** serious damage to the steering box may result.

2. Later type steering box with spring cap, is non-adjustable. Overhaul procedure detailed in Operation J-2.

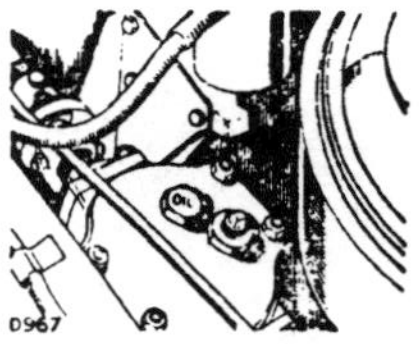

Early type steering box with rocker shaft adjuster screw

Hydraulic steering damper, remove and refit—Operation J-4
Mk II cars suffix 'B' onwards

Workshop hand tools: Scriber
Spanner sizes: $\frac{1}{2}$ in. AF, $\frac{9}{16}$ in. AF

Hydraulic steering damper, remove

1. Remove nut securing lower damper mounting to support bracket.
2. Remove nut securing upper damper mounting to track rod bracket.
3. Remove damper from car.

Hydraulic steering damper, replace

1. Refit the damper to the car by reversing removal procedure.
2. Raise the car to allow the steering to be turned freely from lock to lock.
3. Turn the steering to full RH lock and extend the damper to the fullest extent, by moving the clamp bracket along the track rod. Mark the position of the clamp bracket on the track rod.
4. Turn the steering to full LH lock and fully compress the damper, by moving the clamp bracket along the track rod. Mark the position of the clamp bracket on the track rod.
5. Move the clamp bracket so that it is midway between the scribe marks on the track rod and square to the damper. In this position tighten the clamping bracket fixing bolts.

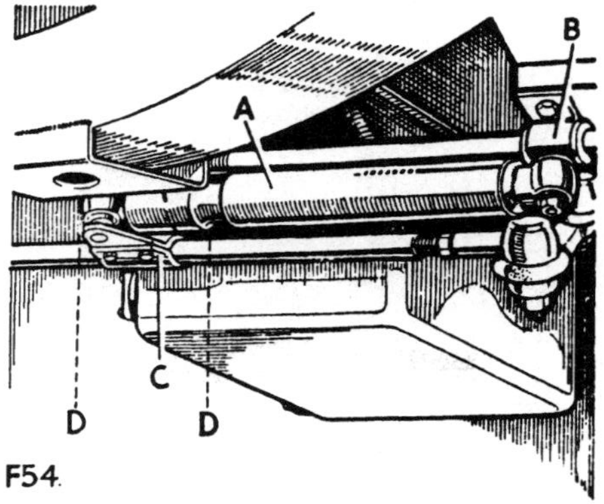

F54

Steering damper in position

A—Steering damper, telescopic
B—Torsion rod bracket assembly
C—Track rod clamp bracket
D—Position of clamp bracket midway between scribe marks previously made

Steering relay, remove and refit—Operation J-5

Workshop hand tools: Hammer
Spanner size: $\frac{11}{16}$ in. AF

Steering relay, remove

1. Remove the ball joints from the steering relay drop arm by smartly tapping the eye of the drop arm around each ball joint pin.
2. Remove the three mounting bolts and detach the relay unit from the sub-frame, noting that in the case of the latest unit there is a spacing washer between relay and frame at each fixing bolt.

Steering relay, refit

1. Reverse removal procedure

Steering relay, overhaul—Operation J-6

Workshop hand tools:

Hammer, Screwdriver, Feeler gauges
Spanner sizes: $\frac{7}{16}$ in. AF, $\frac{11}{16}$ in. AF, $\frac{15}{16}$ in. AF, $1\frac{1}{8}$ in. AF

Special tools:

Drop arm removal tool, Part No. 600446
Spring balance

See Operation J-5 for steering relay removal

Operation J-6 applicable to Mk I, Mk IA and Mk II models with suffix letter 'A'. For steering relay overhaul on Mk II models suffix 'B' onwards see Section J-1

Steering relay, strip

Cars up to suffix 'B' had a friction damper incorporated in the steering relay, cars suffix 'B' onwards have no damper incorporated with the relay but utilise an hydraulic telescopic steering damper at the track rod.

1. Withdraw the retaining nut and washer and mark the drop arm lever in relation to the relay shaft and remove drop arm. The removal of the drop arm will be facilitated by the use of the special drop arm removal tool, Part No. 600446.
2. Remove the rubber cover, adjusting screw and locknut from the top of the unit.
3. Remove top cover from relay.
4. Carefully note the position of the top steel adjusting plate, which is aligned to the cover by dowels. The second, or pressure, plate has two

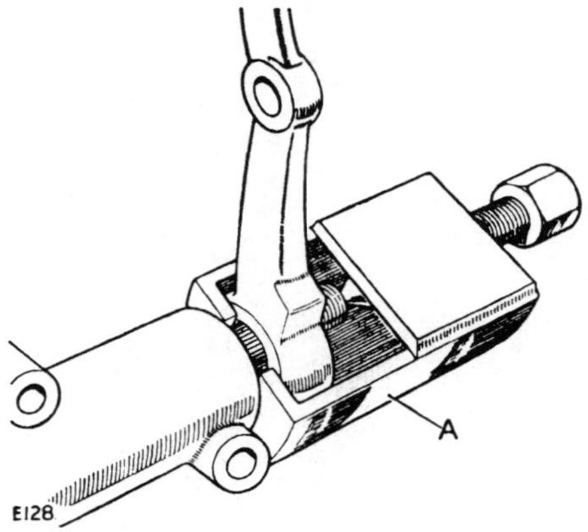

Drop arm removal tool
A—Withdrawal tool

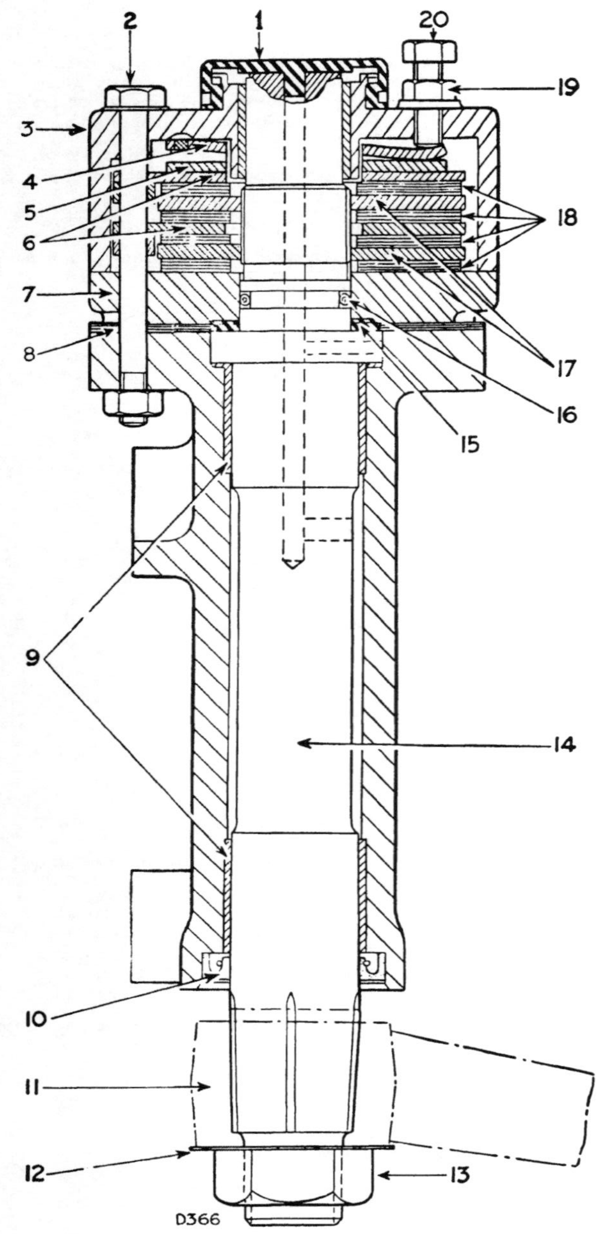

1 Rubber cover
2 Fixing bolt
3 Damper housing
4 Adjuster plate
5 Pressure plate
6 Fixed plate
7 Mounting plate
8 Shims
9 Bushes
10 Oil seal
11 Drop arm
12 Lock washer
13 Fixing nut
14 Relay shaft
15 Thrust washer
16 Rubber sealing ring
17 Splined steel rotor plates
18 Wooden friction discs
19 Locknut
20 Adjusting bolt

Cross-section of steering relay, Mk I, Mk IA and Mk II models with suffix letter 'B'

Operation J-6—*continued*

'dents' formed on it, these being uppermost; this plate is dowelled to the third fixed upper plate. Below this plate are more discs, in this order:

One wooden disc.
One steel splined rotor plate
One wooden disc
One fixed steel plate, intermediate
One wooden disc
One steel splined rotor plate
One wooden disc
One alloy mounting plate.

The wooden friction discs apply only to Mk I and early Mk IA cars, later cars were fitted with Ferodo friction discs.

5. On early 3 litre cars the alloy mounting plate is fixed to the relay housing by three Unbrako type screws. Before removing the mounting plate, mark the plate and housing to ensure correct assembly.

6. Later models have a relay housing with a flange dimensionally the same as the mounting plate, the four fixing bolts passing through the flange. Detach the mounting plate, noting the thickness of the steel shims which are situated below it.

7. The shaft can now be withdrawn complete with oil seal ring and thrust washer.

8. If necessary, remove the oil seal and two bushes from the relay housing.

Steering relay, reassemble

1. Renew the bushes in the relay.

2. Fit the thrust washer to the relay shaft, and place the shaft in the housing. Place the alloy mounting plate on the housing flange, without any shims. Using a feeler gauge, measure the gap between the flange and mounting plate, which must be firmly held in position.

3. Prepare shims to this dimension plus .001 to .006 in. (0,02 - 0,15 mm). This measurement will allow relay shaft end-float, which should be kept to a minimum.

4. Remove the mounting plate and relay shaft from the housing.

5. Fit the new oil seal with its open end inwards and refit the shaft.

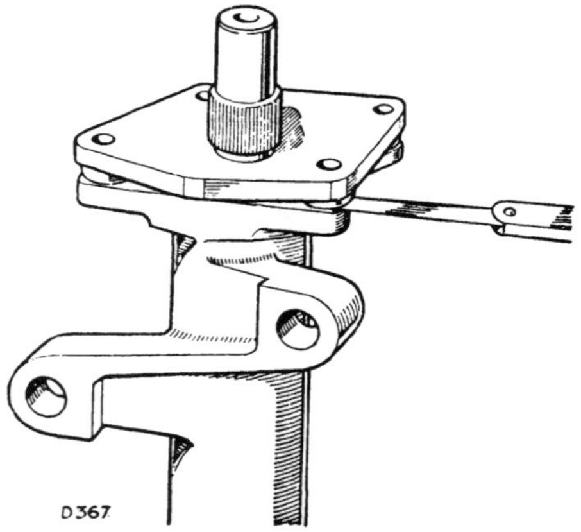

Measuring for shim dimension

6. Place the required amount of steel shims on the housing flange and fit the alloy mounting plate. Early type housing has the mounting plate fixed by three screws. Remove all traces of oil.

7. Replace the wooden or friction discs and steel plates, ensuring correct alignment and fitting sequence. The discs should be smeared with the appropriate lubricant (Section Y) on both sides before fitting. These discs are available in two sizes, .080 in. (2,0 mm) and .093 in. (2,4 mm) thick. When fitting new discs, check that the total thickness of all discs and steel plates will allow maximum adjusting bolt movement, with the cover fitted; ensure that the cover fits correctly on to the mounting plate and if necessary replace thick discs with thinner ones to obtain this condition. Ensure that the fixed steel plates are aligned with the cover fixing bolt and that the adjusting plate is fitted so that the two dowels locate in the cover, opposite the adjusting bolt hole.

8. Refit the top cover with washers and shims.

9. Check the shaft end-float, which should be .001 in. to .006 in. (0,02 to 0,15 mm). Correct as necessary by the addition or removal of shims.

10. Fit the drop arm to the relay shaft, aligning the splines to the correct position. Fit a new lock plate and tighten the nut fully.

Operation J-6—*continued*

11. Fit the rubber cover and adjusting screw. With the unit still held firmly in the vice adjust the screw to give a friction loading of 24-26 lb (11-12 kgs) measured at the end of the drop arm lever. When this reading is obtained tighten the adjusting screw locknut. Re-check friction loading.

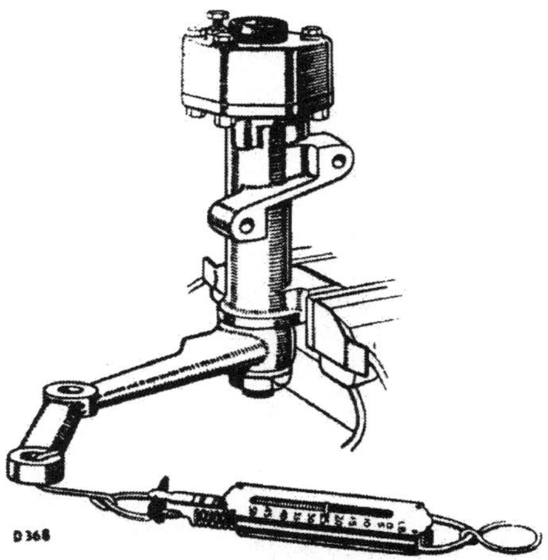

Checking relay friction loading

Steering relay, adjustment—Operation J-7

Workshop hand tools:

Hammer, Screwdriver, Spirit level, Rule

Spanner sizes: $\frac{5}{16}$ in. AF, $\frac{7}{16}$ in. AF, $\frac{11}{16}$ in. AF, $\frac{3}{4}$ in. AF, $\frac{7}{8}$ in. AF, $\frac{15}{16}$ in. AF

Special tools:

Alignment equipment

Steering relay, adjust

The friction loading adjustment refers only to relays incorporating friction dampers, on cars prior to suffix 'B'.

1. Disconnect the steering link and track rod ball joints from the relay drop arm.
2. Using a suitable spring balance, measure the loading of the relay at the end of the drop arm. This should be 24-26 lb (11-12 kgs). If necessary adjust the screw on the top of the unit to give this friction loading.
3. Check the relay shaft end-float, which should be .001 to .006 in. (0,25 to 0,15 mm). Should a reading in excess of .006 in. (0,15 mm) be obtained, the unit should be removed and the end-float adjusted by suitable shims, inserted between the flange and mounting plate.
4. After checking the unit, refit the steering link and track rod ball joints to the relay drop arm.
5. Check wheel alignment, Operation J-9.

Steering column and bearings, remove and refit—Operation J-8

Workshop hand tools: Allen key, Screwdriver

Spanner sizes: 2 BA, $\frac{7}{16}$ in. AF, $\frac{1}{2}$ in. AF, $\frac{15}{16}$ in. AF

Steering column and bearings, remove

1. With the front road wheels in the straight-ahead position, slacken the three Allen screws in the steering wheel hub and remove the horn ring.
2. Unscrew the steering wheel securing nut and remove the steering wheel from the splined steering shaft, after noting its correct position.
3. Remove the four recessed screws in the side of the steering column shroud; remove the four small screws from the top support bracket, thereby releasing the shrouds.
4. Remove the beading strip from the top and carefully ease both shrouds away from the column.
5. When fitted, remove the Borg-Warner control, or the overdrive switch control from the steering column. Where-ever possible avoid disturbing the mechanism of these controls.
6. The shroud fitted to the same side as the headlight and trafficator switch can be detached by removing the two trafficator switch securing screws.
7. Mark one of the trafficator cancelling fingers in relation to the outer column, to ensure correct refitment.
8. Remove the pinch bolt securing steering shaft to the coupling on steering box.
9. On models with the single bearing shaft clean off any surplus paint on the shaft and carefully withdraw the shaft into the car interior, out of the outer column. Retain the special double coil spring washer.
10. Lever the bearing out of the outer column.
11. On models with the double bearing shaft, remove the clamp bracket securing outer column to support bracket fitted to dash, then remove the support bracket from dash.
12. Loosen the clip securing rubber grommet to the bottom of outer column.
13. Temporarily replace the steering wheel and remove the outer column complete with shaft from the car.
14. With the outer column held securely in a suitable vice, remove the horn ring and horn button, flasher trip ring and the bottom adjustable clamp ring

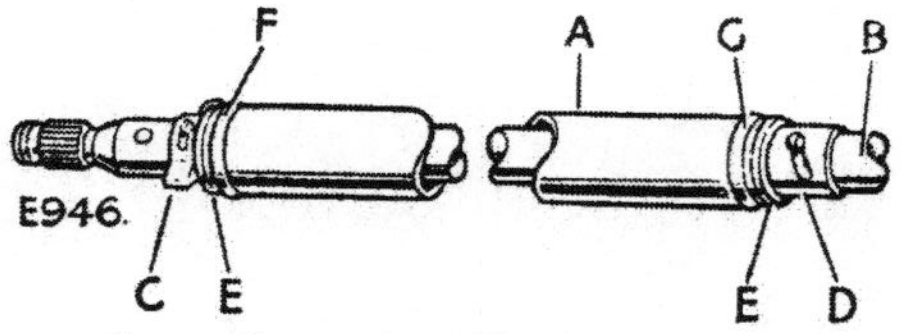

Outer column and steering shaft assembled

A—Outer column
B—Shaft
C—Flasher trip ring
D—Adjusting ring
E—Spring
F—Bearing, top
G—Bearing, bottom

15. Remove the shaft from the outer column, retaining the coil springs.
16. Tap out top and bottom bearings.

Steering column and bearings, refit

1. Carefully press in the new bearings first lightly lubricating them with grease.
2. On models with the double bearing shaft, refit by reversing the removal procedure ensuring that the coil springs are compressed so as to give a minimum amount of shaft up and down movement, but ensure that the shaft rotates freely.
3. On models with the single bearing shaft, slide the double coil spring washer on to the shaft and carefully insert the shaft into the top bearing and outer column. Align the marks made previously on the trafficator ring and outer column, and engage the lower end into the splines of the coupling flange.
4. Push the steering shaft downwards to load the double coil spring and fit and tighten the pinch bolt.
5. On all models complete the reassembly by reversing the removal procedure.

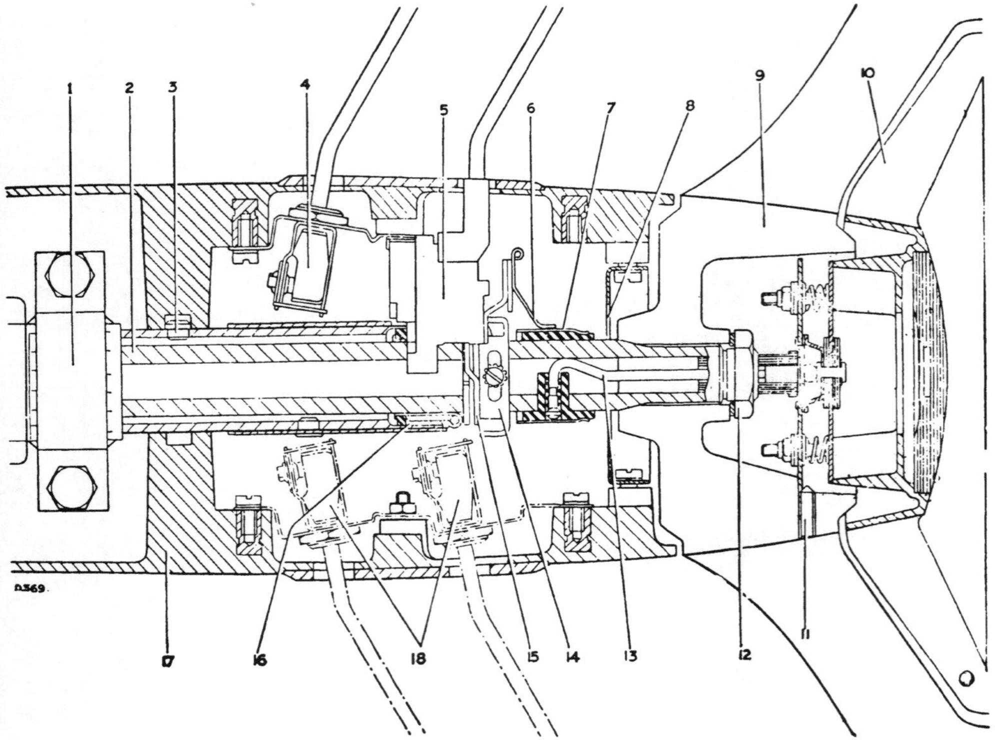

Cross-section of upper column

1 Clip for column
2 Steering column shaft
3 Dowel for shroud
4 Headlamp switch assembly
5 Trafficator switch
6 Horn contact arm
7 Horn slip ring assembly
8 Support bracket
9 Steering wheel
10 Horn ring assembly
11 Allen screw
12 Locknut for steering wheel
13 Horn contact cable
14 Flasher trip ring
15 Double coil spring washer
16 Bearing assembly
17 Shroud
18 Auxiliary switches

Wheel alignment, to set—Operation J-9

Workshop hand tools:

Spirit level, Rule

Spanner sizes: $\frac{5}{16}$ in. AF, $\frac{3}{4}$ in. AF, $\frac{7}{8}$ in. AF

Special tools:

Alignment equipment

Wheel alignment, to set

1. All checking must be carried out on a flat floor with the wheels in the straight-ahead position.
2. The front suspension height must be set correctly as detailed in Section K.
3. Adjust the height of the body at the rear with a suitable jack until the body is exactly horizontal, which can be checked by using a spirit level placed on the flat surface of the door sill.
4. It is important only to check when the static height is correct, because a variation of 1 in. (25 mm) in the height at the front alters the camber and castor angles by approximately 1°.
5. The length of the track rod should be $24\frac{1}{4} \pm \frac{1}{4}$ in. (616,0±6,5 mm) which allows for adjustment of the front wheel toe-in. The track rod locknuts are left-hand and right-hand threaded. The wheel alignment is $\frac{1}{16}$ in. (1,5 mm) toe-in to $\frac{1}{16}$ in. (1,5 mm) toe-out.
6. The length of the steering links must be so adjusted that, when fitted with the front wheels in the straight-ahead position, and the toe-in correctly set, the turning circle on right- and left-hand lock is the same.
7. If the swivel pin inclination angle is suspected of being incorrect, the stub axle assembly should be dismantled and checked as follows:
8. Set up the stub axle with the swivel axis vertical.
9. This is found by placing alignment bars through the swivel eyelets.
10. Measure the angle to the vertical, from the flat face at the rear of the hub bearing track. This angle should read 6°.

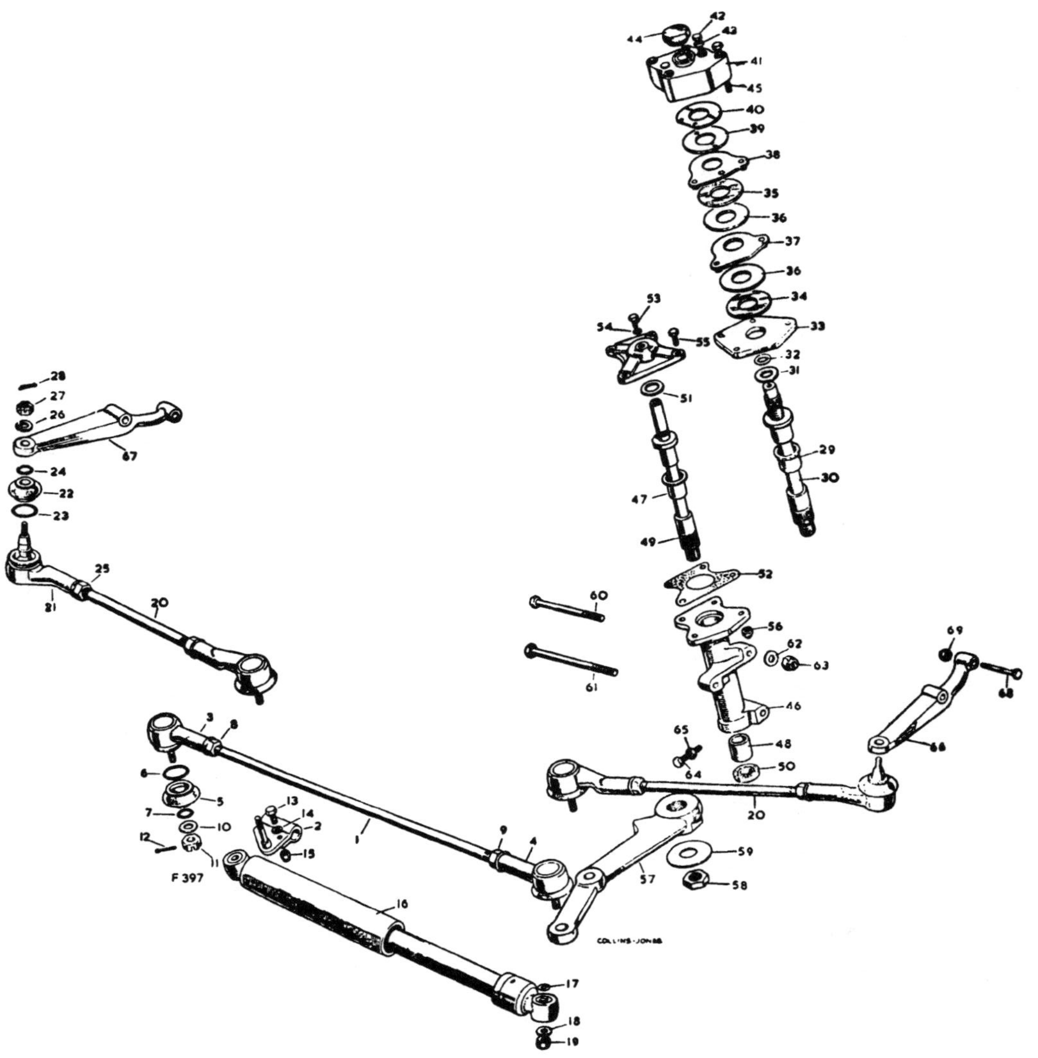

Layout of steering linkage

1	Track rod	
2	Clamp bracket for damper	
3	Ball joint assembly, RH	
4	Ball joint assembly, LH	
5	Rubber boot	
6	Spring ring	
7	Spring ring	
8	Locknut	
9	Locknut	
10	Plain washer	
11	Castle nut	
12	Split pin	
13	Bolt	Mk II models suffix letter 'B' onwards
14	Plain washer	Mk II models suffix letter 'B' onwards
15	Self-locking nut	Mk II models suffix letter 'B' onwards
16	Steering damper	Mk II models suffix letter 'B' onwards
17	Plain washer, small	Mk II models suffix letter 'B' onwards
18	Plain washer, large	Mk II models suffix letter 'B' onwards
19	Self-locking nut	Mk II models suffix letter 'B' onwards
20	Steering link	
21	Ball joint assembly, cranked	
22	Rubber boot	
23	Spring ring	
24	Spring ring	
25	Locknut	
26	Plain washer	
27	Castle nut	
28	Split pin	
29	Bush	Mk I, Mk IA and Mk II models with suffix letter 'A'
30	Shaft	Mk I, Mk IA and Mk II models with suffix letter 'A'
31	Thrust washer	Mk I, Mk IA and Mk II models with suffix letter 'A'
32	Rubber sealing ring	Mk I, Mk IA and Mk II models with suffix letter 'A'
33	Mounting plate	Mk I, Mk IA and Mk II models with suffix letter 'A'
34	Friction disc	Mk I, Mk IA and Mk II models with suffix letter 'A'
35	Friction disc	Mk I, Mk IA and Mk II models with suffix letter 'A'
36	Rotor plate	Mk I, Mk IA and Mk II models with suffix letter 'A'
37	Fixed plate, intermediate	Mk I, Mk IA and Mk II models with suffix letter 'A'
38	Fixed plate, upper	Mk I, Mk IA and Mk II models with suffix letter 'A'
39	Pressure plate	Mk I, Mk IA and Mk II models with suffix letter 'A'
40	Adjuster plate	Mk I, Mk IA and Mk II models with suffix letter 'A'
41	Damper housing	Mk I, Mk IA and Mk II models with suffix letter 'A'
42	Bolt	Mk I, Mk IA and Mk II models with suffix letter 'A'
43	Nut	Mk I, Mk IA and Mk II models with suffix letter 'A'
44	Rubber plug	Mk I, Mk IA and Mk II models with suffix letter 'A'
45	Bolt	Mk I, Mk IA and Mk II models with suffix letter 'A'
46	Housing assembly	
47	Bush, top	
48	Bush, bottom	
49	Shaft	Mk II models suffix letter 'B' onwards
50	Oil seal	Mk II models suffix letter 'B' onwards
51	Thrust washer	Mk II models suffix letter 'B' onwards
52	Shim	Mk II models suffix letter 'B' onwards
53	Set bolt	Mk II models suffix letter 'B' onwards
54	Washer	Mk II models suffix letter 'B' onwards
55	Bolt	Mk II models suffix letter 'B' onwards
56	Self-locking nut	Mk II models suffix letter 'B' onwards
57	Drop arm	
58	Nut	
59	Lockwasher	
60	Bolt	
61	Bolt	
62	Plain washer	
63	Self-locking nut	
64	Special bolt	Steering lock stop
65	Locknut	Steering lock stop
66	Track rod lever, LH	
67	Track rod lever, RH	
68	Bolt	
69	Self-locking nut	

Steering linkage, remove and refit—Operation J-10

Workshop hand tools:

Hammer, Spirit level, Rule

Spanner sizes: $\frac{5}{16}$ in. AF, $\frac{11}{16}$ in. AF, $\frac{3}{4}$ in. AF, $\frac{7}{8}$ in. AF

Special tools:

Alignment equipment

Steering linkage, remove

1. The steering ball joints have been designed in such a way as to retain the initial filling of grease for the normal life of the ball joint; however this applies only if the rubber boot remains in position on the joint. The rubber boots should be checked every 3,000 miles (5.000 km) to ensure that they have not become dislodged or the joint damaged.
2. To replace the rubber boots or the ball joints complete, remove the ball end from the lever by tapping smartly around the eye of the pin.
3. Remove the rubber boot.
4. Thoroughly clean all parts.
5. Apply grease around the taper, and fill the rubber boot.
6. Place the castle nut upside down on the pin and screw on a few threads, then place the ball joint uder a press or between the jaws of a vice and carefully force the pin and ball down against the spring. In this position the interior of the ball joint can be cleaned and lubricated.

Steering linkage, refit

1. Reassemble, using new rubber boots and spring rings.
2. When refitting track rod and ball joints to the drop arms, ensure that the ball joints are aligned with each other, in order to allow full unrestricted movement of steering linkage.
3. When refitting steering links, ensure that the ball joint body is parallel with respective steering arms, in order to allow full movement.
4. Adjust the alignment as detailed in Operation J-9.

Steering lock stops, adjust—Operation J-11

Workshop hand tools:

Spanner size: $\frac{1}{2}$ in. AF

Steering lock stops, adjust

1. Slacken the locknuts and screw in both adjusting bolts.
2. Turn the steering wheel so that the front wheels are on full right-hand lock as far as the steering box permits, without straining.
3. Turn the wheels back off full lock slightly, to relieve any strain imposed on the steering mechanism and screw out the left-hand side adjusting bolt until the head just touches the drop arm lug; unscrew the bolt a further half-turn, then tighten the locknut.
4. Repeat for the left-hand lock, then check the turning circle of the car, which should be approximately 38 ft 6 in. (11,7 m).

DEFECT LOCATION

SYMPTOM	*POSSIBLE CAUSE*	*REMEDY*
A—EXCESSIVE LOOSENESS OR BACKLASH IN THE STEERING	1. Steering rocker shaft incorrectly adjusted or worn 2. Steering linkage loose or worn 3. Suspension ball swivel joints worn 4. Loose or worn front wheel bearing 5. Steering box mounting bolts loose 6. Steering shaft flexible coupling loose	1. *Adjust or renew* 2. *Check all ball joints for wear. Renew as necessary* 3. *Renew* 4. *Rectify* 5. *Rectify* 6. *Rectify*
B—TIGHT STEERING	1. Low or unequal tyre pressures 2. Steering box oil level low 3. Steering rocker shaft adjusted too tightly	1. *Rectify* 2. *Rectify* 3. *Adjust in accordance with Operation J-3*
C—CAR PULLS TO ONE SIDE	1. Incorrect camber, castor or swivel pin inclination 2. Uneven or worn tyres and low pressures 3. Brakes binding 4. Top and bottom suspension ball swivels dry or tight 5. Tight or dry wheel bearings 6. Incorrect wheel alignment	1. *Check suspension, wheel alignment and torsion bar height* 2. *Rectify* 3. *Rectify* 4. *Renew as necessary* 5. *Inspect for damage, renew or lubricate as necessary* 6. *Adjust to $\frac{1}{16}$ in. (1,5 mm) toe-in to $\frac{1}{16}$ in. (1,5 mm) toe-out*
D—CAR WANDERS	1. Incorrect castor 2. Incorrect wheel alignment 3. Worn suspension ball swivels 4. Worn front wheel bearings 5. Tight steering 6. Unequal tyre pressures or worn tyres 7. Loose rear axle 'U' bolts 8. Damaged sub-frame	1. *Check for wear or damage to suspension* 2. *Reset to $\frac{1}{16}$ in. (1,5 mm) toe-in to $\frac{1}{16}$ in. (1,5 mm) toe-out* 3. *Renew as necessary* 4. *Renew as necessary* 5. *Check steering box and relay adjustment. Check ball joints* 6. *Rectify* 7. *Rectify* 8. *Examine for alignment and rectify as necessary*
E—LOW OR HIGH SPEED SHIMMY	1. Excessive castor 2. Worn steering ball joints 3. Loose wheel bearings 4. Wheels out of balance 5. Under-inflation or unequal inflation of front tyres 6. Loose engine or sub-frame mountings 7. Faulty front shock absorbers 8. Worn steering box or linkage 9. Loose or damaged flexible steering shaft coupling	1. *Check for wear or damage to suspension* 2. *Renew* 3. *Rectify* 4. *Rectify* 5. *Rectify* 6. *Rectify* 7. *Renew* 8. *Rectify* 9. *Renew*

DATA

Steering unit type	Re-circulating ball, variable ratio
Ratio (cars prior to suffix 'B')	17.6:1 straight ahead 26.9:1 full lock
Ratio (suffix 'B' onwards)	20.3:1 straight ahead 24.5:1 full lock
Steering rocker shaft end-float	Nil
Relay shaft end-float	.001 - .006 in. (0,025 - 0,15 mm)
Steering worm shaft end-float	Nil
Relay shaft, clearance in bushes	.003 - .0045 in. (0,08 - 0,12 mm)
Relay loading	24 - 26 lb (11 - 12 kg) at end of drop arm
Fit of steering top bearing assembly to outer column	.0025 - .0065 in. (0,06 - 0,17 mm) interference fit
Thickness of wooden friction discs	.080 in. and .093 in. (2,0 mm and 2,4 mm)
Wheel alignment	$\frac{1}{16}$ in. (1,5 mm) toe-in to $\frac{1}{16}$ in. (1,5 mm) toe-out
Track, front	55 in. (1,4 m)
Static unladen and steering geometry	See Section K
Turning circle	38 ft. 6 in. (11,7 m)
Steering wheel turns, lock to lock	$4\frac{1}{4}$
Steering box lubrication	SAE 90
Tightening torque; steering box mounting bolts	50 lb ft (7,0 mkg)

Section J1 – POWER STEERING

Brief description of the power steering system

The outward appearance of the power steering unit differs little from that of the conventional steering box.

If the power assistance should fail, the driver still has full mechanical control over the steering, the movements of which are transmitted to a standard type linkage.

A reservoir, mounted on the wing valance, supplies fluid to a mechanical pump driven by the dynamo.

The pump supplies fluid at pressure to the steering box. An element type filter incorporated in the reservoir and a pressure relief valve located in the pump have been designed to eliminate the possibility of the control valve jamming, due to either excessive load or foreign matter in the fluid.

The ratios of the power steering unit are:

Early models—15.6:1 straight ahead, 10.2:1 full lock.
Late models: 16:1 straight ahead, 11.3:1 full lock.

Operating principle

With the steering in the straight-ahead position and the engine running, the valve spool occupies a central position relative to the valve side plates. In this condition fluid entering from the pump is free to circulate round the spool and through drillings to each side of the piston. The fluid can also pass from the unit and return to the reservoir.

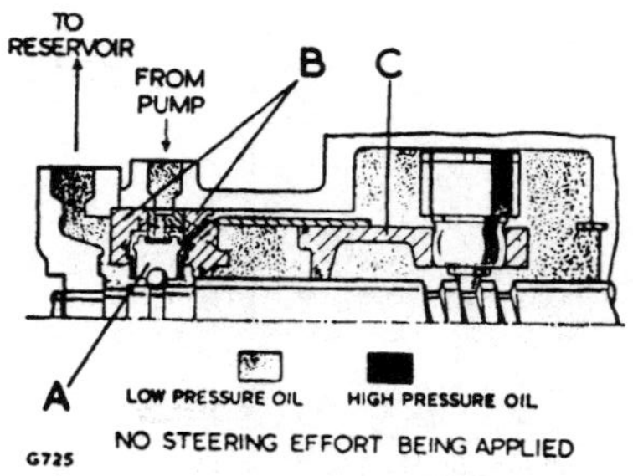

Steering wheel in straight-ahead position and no steering effort being applied

A—Valve spool B—Valve side plates C—Piston

Without restriction in the unit, the fluid can circulate freely throughout the entire system and the relief valve in the pump will restrict the pressure output to between 50 to 100 lb sq in. (3,5 to 7 kg/cm²).

No power assistance is available at this stage.

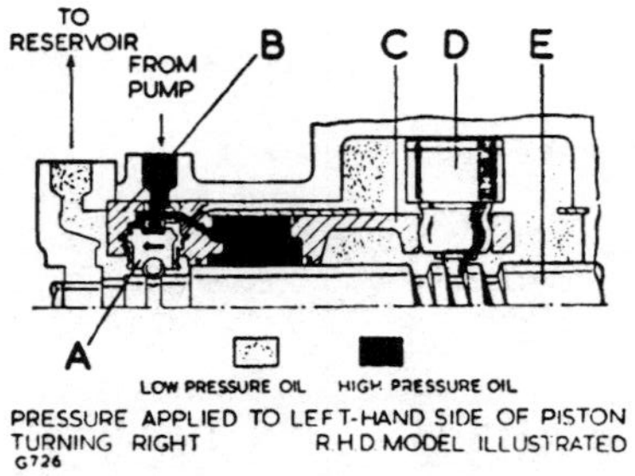

Turning right, RHD model illustrated

A—Valve spool
B—Valve side plate
C—Piston
D—Rocker shaft
E—Camshaft

Turning right

Rotation of the steering wheel to the right causes the valve spool to move to the left towards the valve side plate against spring plate tension. This action causes a restriction of flow to one side of the piston and at the same time allows the opposite side of the piston to become influenced by pump pressure. The piston then pushes the rocker shaft thereby creating power assistance to turn the camshaft.

Fluid on the low pressure side of the piston can return to the reservoir as displacement takes place.

If the swivelling resistance of the front wheels is high, this produces high restrictive effort in the steering box and accordingly, if the steering wheel is held in the 'full lock' position, pump pressure increases and forces the piston along inside the sleeve causing the front wheels to turn. Under these conditions the pump pressure can be as high as 750 lb sq in. (52 kg/cm²).

Turning left

The valve spool has moved against the opposite side of the valve plate due to rotation of the steering wheel to the left. The action of the spool has now cut off the return of the fluid to the opposite side of the piston and allowed the pump-pressure to build up. This in turn acts against the piston and forces the rocker shaft to assist in turning the camshaft.

Brief description of the power steering system—*continued*

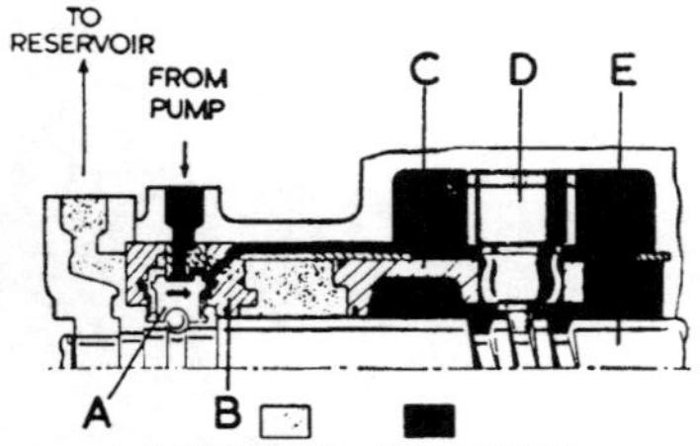

Turning left, RHD model illustrated

A—Valve spool
B—Valve side plate
C—Piston
D—Rocker shaft
E—Camshaft

Fluid on the low pressure side of the piston is displaced by piston movement through the drillings and out to the reservoir.

In both diagrams the pressure differential to the piston on the side appropriate to the direction of travel will increase progressively up to the maximum available, depending upon engine rpm and the swivelling resistance of the front wheels.

INDEX

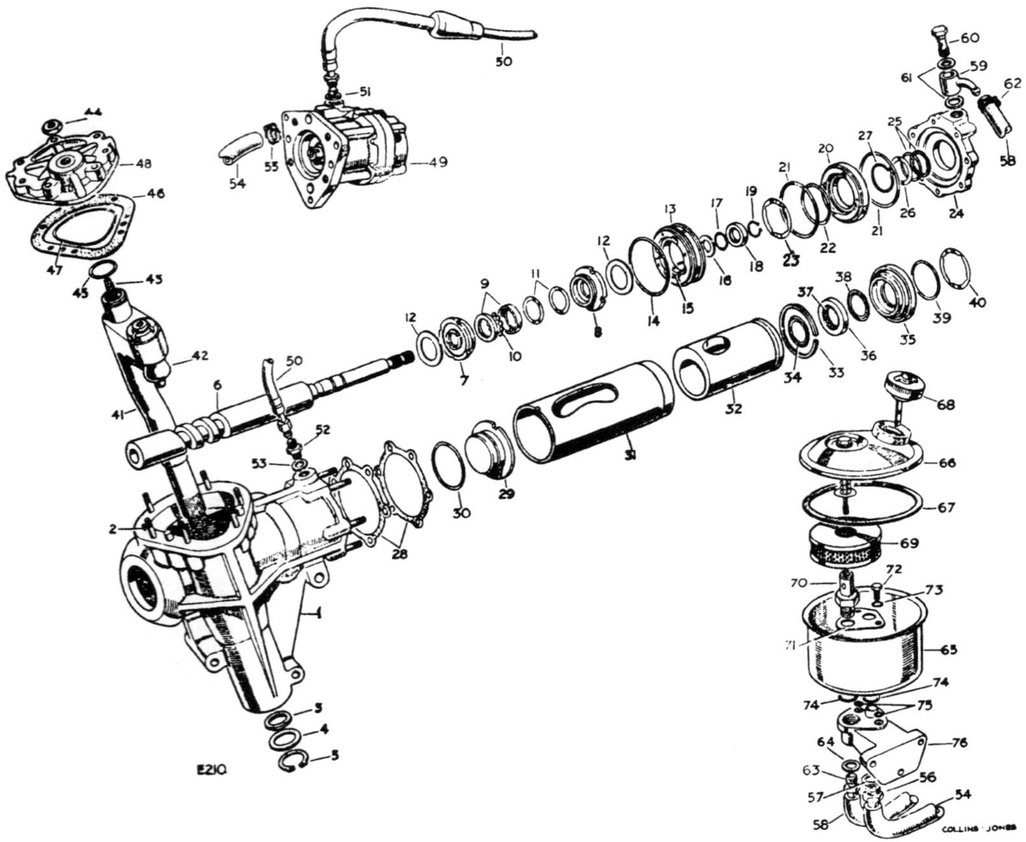

Layout of power steering, dismantled

1 Steering box (RHD illustrated)
2 Tube locating pin
3 Rocker shaft oil seal
4 Retaining washer for oil seal
5 Circlip for oil seal
6 Camshaft (RHD illustrated)
7 Inner half spool
8 Outer half spool
9 Ball cup
10 Ball bearing
11 Ball bearing shims
12 Valve plate spring
13 Valve centre
14 Seal for valve centre
15 Spool locking pin
16 Washer for end seal bush
17 'O' ring for end seal bush
18 Bush, camshaft end seal
19 Circlip for end seal bush
20 Valve side plate, outer
21 Seals for outer valve side plate
22 'O' ring valve seal
23 Seal plate for valve spring
24 End cover
25 End cover sealing ring
26 Washer for sealing ring
27 Circlip for oil seal
28 Shims
29 Bearing housing complete
30 Bearing housing outer sealing ring
31 Piston sleeve (RHD illustrated)
32 Piston
33 Piston ring
34 Piston tube sealing ring
35 Valve side plate, inner
36 Bearing
37 Ball bearings
38 Inner valve side plate sealing ring
39 'O' ring valve seal
40 Seal plate for valve spring
41 Rocker shaft
42 Peg assembly
43 Adjusting screw
44 Adjusting screw locknut
45 Rocker shaft sealing ring
46 Aluminium gasket for top cover
47 Top cover sealing ring
48 Top cover (RHD illustrated)
49 Pump
50 Flexible pipe, pump to steering box
51 Washer, pipe, pump to steering box pump end
52 Adaptor pipe, pump to steering box
53 Washer for adaptor
54 Pipe, pump to reservoir
55 Hose clip
56 Adaptor } For pipe at
57 Sealing ring } reservoir
58 Flexible pipe, steering box to reservoir
59 Banjo
60 Banjo bolt
61 Washer for banjo bolt
62 Hose clip
63 Adaptor } At
64 Washer } reservoir
65 Reservoir
66 Reservoir cover
67 Cover sealing ring
68 Filler cap and dipstick
69 Filter element
70 Adaptor
71 Reinforcement plate
72–73 Fixings for reinforcement plate
74 Large sealing rings
75 Small sealing rings
76 Bracket

Power steering, test—Operation J1-1

Workshop hand tools:
Spanner sizes: $\frac{7}{16}$ in. AF, $\frac{11}{16}$ in. AF
Bleed tube, container

Special tools:
Pressure test gauge, Part No. 268721
Special adaptor, Part No. 601304

Power steering test

If there is a lack of power assistance evident, it is important that the pressure of the hydraulic pump, which is bolted to the rear of the dynamo, is checked and if necessary corrected or a replacement unit fitted before any action is taken to replace the complete steering unit.

This operation together with the fault finding chart at the end of the operation gives information on how to check this point and also covers other faults on the power steering system which are best diagnosed before attempting removal and overhaul of the system.

1. The hydraulic pressure test gauge, Part No. 268721, may be used in conjunction with the special adaptor (as illustrated) for testing the power steering system. This gauge is calibrated to read up to 800 lb psi (56 kg/cm²) and the normal maximum pressure which may be expected in the power steering system is 750 lb psi (53 kg/cm²).
2. Under certain fault conditions of the hydraulic pump, it is possible to obtain pressures up to 1,500 lbs psi (105 kg/cm²). Therefore it is important to realise that the pressure upon the gauge is in direct proportion to the pressure being exerted upon the steering wheel. When testing, apply pressure to the steering wheel very gradually while carefully observing the pressure gauge. Should it be obvious that the test gauge is going to be overloaded, then a fault exists in the pressure relief valve and the steering wheel must be released immediately, otherwise the gauge will be damaged.

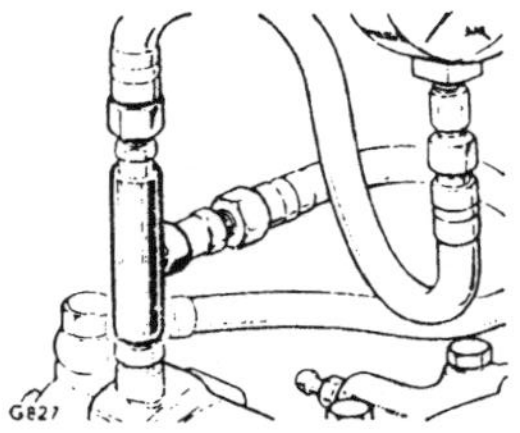

Adaptor for testing power steering system

3. Fit the adaptor in the high pressure pipe line, which runs from the hydraulic pump to the top of the steering box, at the steering box end, as illustrated.
4. Remove the high pressure pipe at the steering box end and fit the adaptor in its place, using sealing washer, Part No. 518953. Refit high pressure hose to the union in the adaptor. Attach the pressure gauge to the adaptor, using sealing washer, Part No. 518953.
5. Bleed the system as detailed in Operation J1-9, taking care while doing so not to overload the pressure gauge.
6. With the system in good condition the pressures should be as follows:
   (a) Steering wheel held hard on full lock and engine running at a 1,000 rpm, the pressure should be 650 to 750 lb psi (45 to 52 kg/cm²).
   (b) With engine idling and steering wheel held hard on full lock the pressure should be 400 lb psi (28 kg/cm²) minimum.

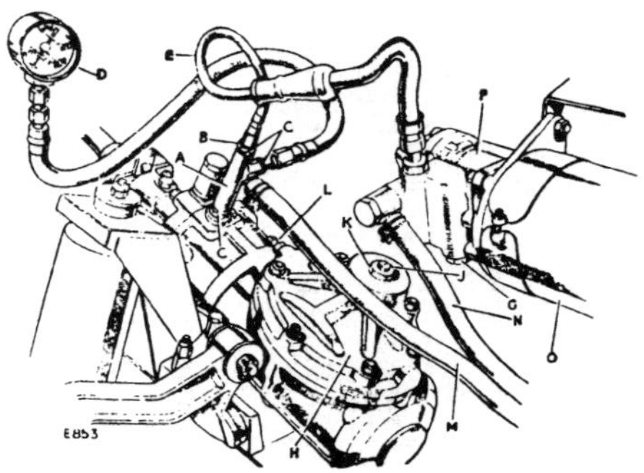

Testing power steering pump, showing special adaptor in position

A—Special adaptor
B—Union
C—Sealing washers
D—Pressure gauge
E—Pipe, high pressure, pump to steering box
F—Hydraulic pump
G—Plug for relief valve
H—Power steering box
J—Rocker shaft adjuster bolt
K—Locknut for rocker shaft adjuster bolt
L—Bleed screw
M—Pipe, low pressure, steering box to reservoir
N—Pipe, low pressure, reservoir to hydraulic pump
O—Dynamo

Operation J1-1—*continued*

These checks should be carried out first on one lock, then on the other.

(c) Release steering wheel and allow engine to idle; pressure should be 100 lb psi (7 kg/cm²) maximum.

Never hold steering wheel on full lock for more than 30 seconds in any one minute to avoid causing the oil to overheat and possible damage to the seals.

7. Failure to build up pressure when items 1 and 2 of the fault finding chart have been eliminated is usually due to a fault in the hydraulic pump relief valve.
8. Should a lack of pressure occur only on one lock, then the cause is undoubtedly a fault in the steering box valve and spool.
9. As it is not possible to distinguish between lack of pressure in the hydraulic pump and a leaking steering box piston seal or worn components in the steering box, it will always be necessary to recheck the pressure after any rectification to the hydraulic pump or after hydraulic pump replacement. If pressure is still low, transfer attention to the steering box and rectify or replace as necessary.

FAULT-FINDING CHART
POWER STEERING

FAULT	CAUSE	TEST ACTION	REMEDY
Insufficient power assistance when parking	(1) Lack of oil	Check hydraulic fluid tank level	If low, fill and bleed the system. Operation J1-9.
	(2) Engine idling speed too low	Try assistance at fast idle	If necessary, reset idle speed.
	(3) Driving belt slipping	Run engine at fast idle and operate steering.	If red light comes on, adjust the driving belt. Operation J1-10.
	(4) Defective hydraulic pump and/or pressure relief valve	(a) Fit pressure gauge between high pressure hose and steering box, with steering held hard on full lock, see Note 1, and engine running at 1000 rpm the pressure should be 650-750 lb/sq in. (45/52 kg/cm²) with engine idling the pressure should be 400 lb/sq in. (28 kg/cm²) minimum (b) Release steering wheel and allow engine to idle, pressure should be 100 lb/sq in. (7 kg/cm²) maximum	If pressure is outside limits (high or low) after checking items 1 and 3, see Note 2. If pressure is greater, check steering box for freedom and self-centring action.
Poor handling when car is in motion	Lack of castor action	This is caused by over-tightening the rocker shaft backlash adjusting screw on top of steering box	It is most important that this screw is correctly adjusted. Instructions governing adjustment are given in Operation J1-5 and must be strictly adhered to.
Hydraulic fluid leaks	Damaged pipework, loose connecting unions, etc.	Check by visual inspection; leaks from the high pressure pipe lines are best found while holding the steering on full lock with engine running at fast idle speed (see Note 1). Leaks from the steering box tend to show up under low pressure conditions, that is, engine idling and no pressure on steering wheel	Tighten or renew as necessary.
Excessive noise	(1) If the high pressure hose is allowed to come into contact with the body shell, or any component not insulated by the body mounting, noise will be transmitted to the car interior	Check the loose runs of the hoses	Alter hose route or insulate as necessary.
	(2) Noise from hydraulic pump	Check oil level and bleed system. (Operation J1-9)	If no cure, change hydraulic pump.
	(3) Whine from jockey pulley	—	Replace complete unit. This will ensure that all the latest modifications are incorporated and that the bearings have been packed with Shell Nerita 3 grease.
Cracked steering box	Excessive pressure due to faulty relief valve in hydraulic pump	Check by visual inspection	Fit new steering box and rectify hydraulic pump or replace as necessary.

Note 1. Never hold the steering wheel on full lock for more than 30 seconds in any one minute, to avoid causing the oil to overheat and possible damage to the seals.

Note 2. High pressure—In general it may be assumed that excessive pressure is due to a faulty relief valve in the hydraulic pump.
Low pressure—Insufficient pressure may be caused by one of the following:

1. Low fluid level in reservoir } Most usual cause of
2. Fan belt slip } insufficient pressure
3. Leaks in the power steering system
4. Faulty relief valve in the hydraulic pump
5. Fault in steering box valve and spool
6. Leak at piston sealing in steering box
7. Worn components in either steering box or hydraulic pump

Steering box oil seals, remove and refit—Operation J1-2

Workshop hand tools:
Spanner sizes: ½ in. AF, ¾ in. AF, 1⅛ in. AF
Screwdriver, Allen key, Hammer, Circlip pliers,
Feeler gauges

Special tools:
Drop arm removal tool, Part No. 521588

Various oil leaks which may occur on the power steering box are usually caused through faulty oil seals. These can often be rectified without completely stripping the box.

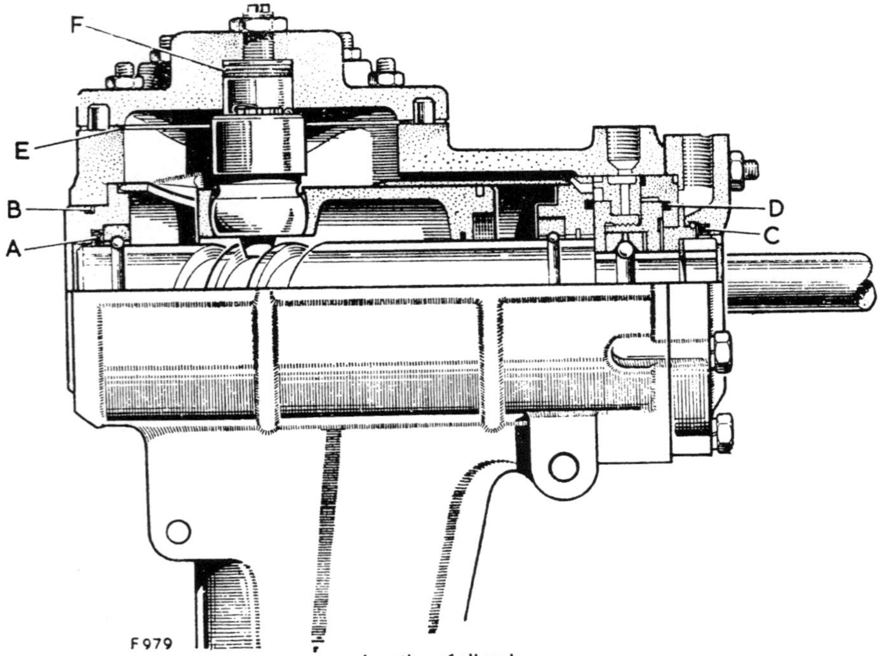

F979

Location of oil seals

A—Bearing housing internal seal
B—Bearing housing external seal
C—End cover oil seal
D—Square sectioned outer seal
E—Top cover sealing ring
F—Rocker shaft oil seal

Oil leaks from bearing housing

To rectify oil leaks from the bearing housing replace the internal two-piece and the external oil seals of the bearing housing.

1. Lever away the locking tab and remove the drop arm securing nut.
2. Withdraw the drop arm, using special tool, Part No. 521588.
3. Remove the Allen screw, locknut for adjusting screw and the nuts securing the top cover from the body.
4. To remove top cover, screw in the adjuster until the thread is clear of the threaded insert in the cover; if necessary, ease up the top cover as the adjuster is rotated. The cover, aluminium washer and sealing ring can now be lifted off.

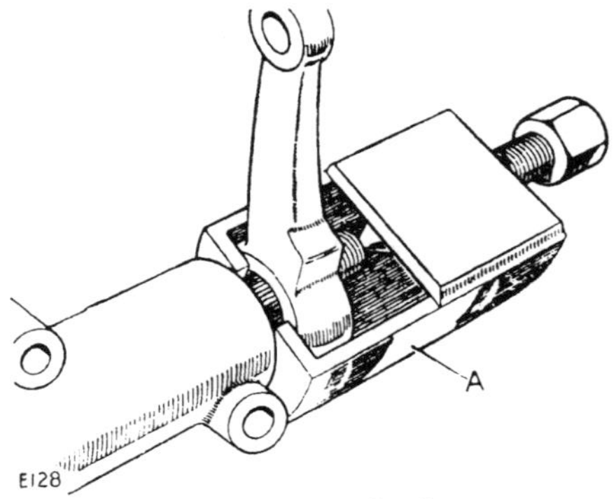

E128

Drop arm removal tool
A—Special tool

Operation J1-2—*continued*

5. Rotate camshaft until rocker shaft peg is in the central position, tap the rocker shaft up until the peg is clear of the piston and piston sleeve and support on edge of housing and secure in this position. Care must be taken that when tapping the rocker shaft up it is not allowed to foul and so damage the piston sleeve.

6. Using masking tape, cover the splines on the end of the camshaft to prevent accidental damage to seals, etc.

7. Remove the nuts and spring washers securing the end cover to the steering box and withdraw the end cover, shims and outer valve side plate 'O' ring. Discard the shims.

8. From the end cover, remove the circlip, seal retaining washer and the two-piece seal.

9. Remove the circlip and withdraw the shaft bush, seal and plain washer. A suitable collar, $1\frac{1}{4}$ in. (31 mm) long by $\frac{15}{32}$ in. (12 mm) diameter, should be positioned over the shaft and retained with the original circlip as illustrated. This will ensure that the valve components are locked together and will facilitate removal.

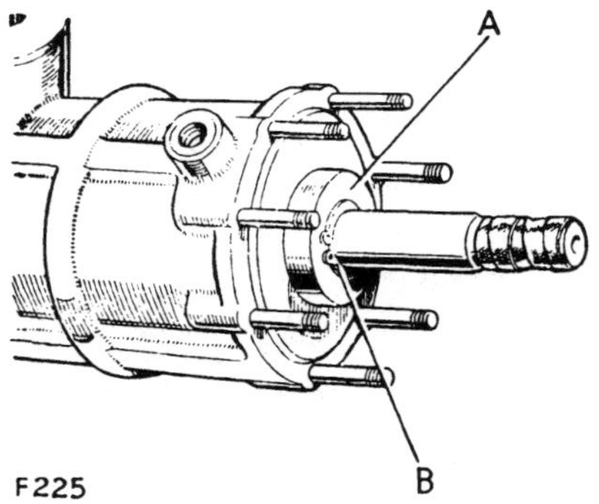

F225

Slave collar in position on shaft
A—Collar B—Circlip

10. Gently tap the camshaft end bearing housing assembly inwards until clear of its location with the bearing housing held in position on the piston sleeve, press the camshaft assembly clear of the steering box. Do not attempt to withdraw assembly by pulling the camshaft.

11. From the end bearing housing, remove the thirty $\frac{5}{32}$ in. dia. ball bearings, the two-piece oil seal located below the ball cup and the oil seal from the outer diameter.

12. From the steering box remove the circlip, retaining washer and rocker shaft oil seal.

13. Care must be taken that the camshaft assembly is not moved or lifted by the camshaft, as this may cause the valve components to become displaced making it necessary to dismantle and reassemble the unit.

14. Remove the bearing housing from the camshaft assembly.

15. Fit a new seal to the outer diameter and a new two-piece oil seal to the inner diameter of the bearing housing. Locate the thirty $\frac{5}{32}$ in. dia. ball bearings in the bearing housing race and retain with a smear of Silicone MS4 grease. Fit the bearing housing to the camshaft and allow the shoulder to enter and locate in the sleeve.

16. Fit new round sectioned sealing rings to the inner valve side plate and valve centre.

17. Fit new rocker shaft oil seal into the casing and retain with washer and circlip.

18. Check that the dowel marks are in line, then offer the complete camshaft assembly to the steering box and push in until the piston sleeve is parallel with the rocker shaft cut-away in the box. Ensure that the grooves in the bearing housing and piston sleeves are in line with the locating pin in the body.

19. Fit the rocker shaft into the casing so that the peg assembly is clear of the sleeve, support on edge at housing and secure in this position.

Operation J1-2—*continued*

20. Using a suitable tube located over the camshaft and on to the valve side plate, press the camshaft assembly into position, ensuring that the slot in the bearing housing and sleeve locate with the dowel in the casing.

21. Allow the rocker shaft peg assembly to enter and locate in the piston and cam track.

22. Remove the circlip and slave collar; slide on the plain washer, a new seal and the camshaft end bush. Secure the assembly with the circlip.

23. Fit a new two-piece seal to the end cover, replace retaining washer and spring clip. Fit cover and tighten bolts to a torque figure of 180 to 200 lb ft (24 to 27 mkg).

24. Measure the clearance between the cover and the body. This should be .002 in. (0,07 mm) minimum after torque loading, thus ensuring that the piston sleeve is positively locked in position.

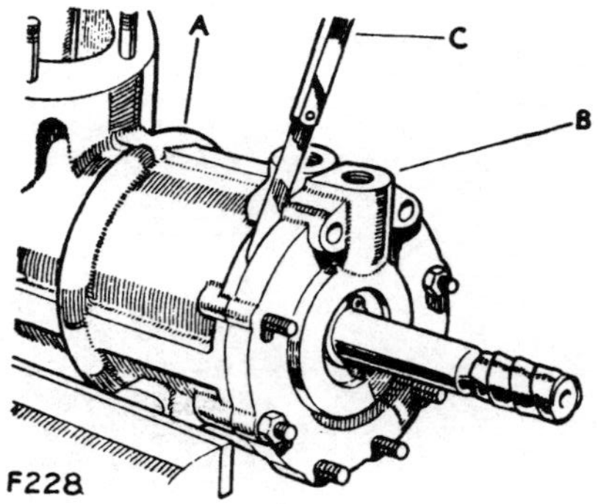

F228

Measuring clearances between housing and cover
A—Housing B—Cover C—Feeler gauge

25. Fit a new rocker shaft sealing ring. Position the aluminium washer and rubber sealing ring on the steering box top surface.

26. Allow the adjusting screw to enter the threads in the top cover and rotate in an anti-clockwise direction to pull the cover down. Secure the cover with special screw, nuts and spring washers.

27. Fit sealing rubber to drop arm and secure with nut and lock washer. Remove masking tape from camshaft splines.

28. Adjust rocker shaft end-float as detailed in Operation J1-5.

Oil leaks from end cover

To rectify oil leaks from the end cover replace the end cover internal two-piece oil seal, end bush 'O' ring and the square sectioned outer side plate seal.

1. Using masking tape, cover the splines on the end of the camshaft to prevent accidental damage to seals, etc.

2. Remove the nuts and spring washers securing the end cover to the steering box and withdraw the end cover, shims and outer valve side plate 'O' ring.

3. From the end cover, remove the circlip, seal retaining washer and the two-piece seal

4. Remove end seal bush circlip and withdraw shaft bush and seal.

5. Fit new end seal bush 'O' ring and replace the bush and circlip.

6. Fit a new square sectioned outer side plate seal and replace the end cover shims.

7. Fit a new two-piece oil seal to the end cover and replace the sealing ring washer and circlip.

8. Replace end cover springs, washers and nuts.

9. Adjust rocker shaft end-float as detailed in Operation J1-5.

Operation J1-2—*continued*

Oil leaks from top cover

To rectify oil leaks from the top cover, replace the top cover sealing ring together with the rocker shaft sealing ring.

1. Remove the Allen screws, locknut for adjusting screw and the nuts securing the top cover from the body.
2. To remove top cover, screw in the adjuster until the thread is clear of the threaded insert in the cover; if necessary, ease up the top cover as the adjuster is rotated. The cover, aluminium washer and sealing ring can now be lifted off.
3. Fit a new rocker shaft sealing ring. Position the aluminium washer and rubber sealing ring on the steering box top surface.
4. Allow the adjusting screw to enter the threads in the top cover and rotate in an anti-clockwise direction to pull the cover down. Secure the cover with special screw, nuts and spring washers.
5. Fit sealing rubber to drop arm and secure with nut and lock washer. Remove masking tape from camshaft splines.
6. Adjust rocker shaft end-float as detailed in Operation J1-5.

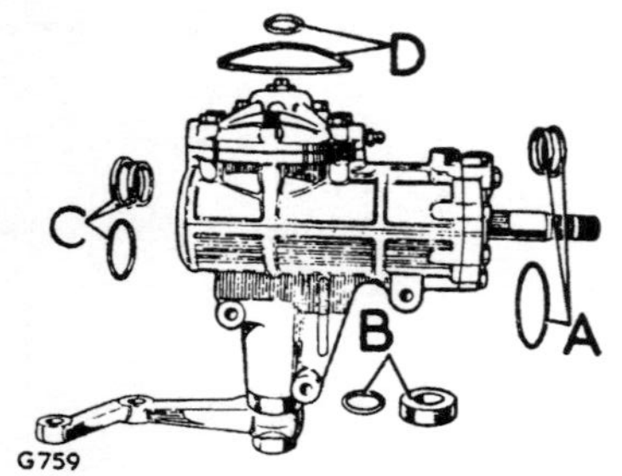

G759

Oil seals

A—End cover, large 'O' ring, two-piece seal
B—Rocker shaft, small rubber seal, foam rubber
C—End bearing housing, square section seal, two-piece
D—Top cover, small seal on peg, square section shaped

Oil leak from rocker shaft

To rectify oil leaks from the rocker shaft, replace rocker shaft oil seal.

1. Lever away the locking tab and remove drop arm securing nut.
2. Withdraw drop arm, using special tool, Part No. 521588.
3. Remove the Allen screw, locknut for adjusting screw and the nuts securing the top cover from the body.
4. To remove top cover, screw in the adjuster until the thread is clear of the threaded insert in the cover; if necessary, ease up the top cover as the adjuster is rotated. The cover, aluminium washer and sealing ring can now be lifted off.
5. Rotate camshaft until rocker shaft peg is in the central position, tap the rocker shaft up until the peg is clear of the piston and piston sleeve and support on edge of housing and secure in this position. Care must be taken that when tapping the rocker shaft up it is not allowed to foul and so damage the piston sleeve.
6. From the steering box remove the circlip, retaining washer and rocker shaft oil seal.
7. Fit new rocker shaft oil seal into the casing and retain with washer and circlip.
8. Allow the rocker shaft peg assembly to enter and locate in the piston and cam track.
9. Fit a new rocker shaft sealing ring. Position the aluminium washer and rubber sealing ring on the steering box top surface.
10. Allow the adjusting screw to enter the threads in the top cover and rotate in an anti-clockwise direction to pull the cover down. Secure the cover with special screw, nuts and spring washers.
11. Fit sealing rubber to drop arm and secure with nut and lock washer. Remove masking tape from camshaft splines.
12. Adjust rocker shaft end-float as detailed in Operation J1-5.

Steering box, remove and refit—Operation J1-3

Workshop hand tools:
Spanner sizes: 2 BA, 3 BA, $\frac{7}{16}$ in. AF, $\frac{1}{2}$ in. AF, $\frac{11}{16}$ in. AF, $\frac{13}{16}$ in. AF, 1 in. AF
Allen key; Hammer; Screwdriver; Pliers; Bleed tube and container

Special tools:

Steering box, remove

It is important that whenever any part of the system, including the flexible piping, is removed or disconnected, that the utmost cleanliness is observed.

All ports and hose unions should be suitably sealed off to prevent ingress of dirt, etc.

If metallic sediment is found in any part of the system, the system should be systematically checked throughout, the cause rectified and the entire system thoroughly cleaned.

The engine must never be started until the reservoir has been filled. Failure to observe this rule will result in damage to the pump.

1. Remove the reservoir filler cap. Disconnect the return pipe from the steering box, drain and discard the oil.
2. Remove the air silencer elbow and cleaner, Section A.
3. Disconnect choke cable at carburetter.
4. Disconnect the flexible hoses from the steering box.
5. Disconnect and remove horn, Section S.
6. Set road wheels in the straight-ahead position and remove the steering wheel.
7. Remove the four recessed screws in the side of the steering column shroud; remove the four small screws from the top support bracket, thereby releasing the shrouds.
8. Remove the beading strip from the top and carefully ease both shrouds away from the column.
9. When fitted, remove the Borg-Warner control, or the overdrive switch control from the steering column. Wherever possible avoid disturbing the mechanism of these controls.
10. On earlier models with a single bearing steering column, remove the pinch bolt locking the steering shaft to the coupling flange and carefully withdraw the shaft approximately 3 in. (76 mm) into the car interior.
11. Retain the special double coil spring washer.
12. On latest models with a double bearing steering column, remove the clamp bracket securing outer column to support bracket fitted to dash—then remove the support bracket from dash.
13. Loosen the clip securing rubber grommet to the bottom of outer column.
14. Remove the pinch bolt securing steering shaft to the coupling on the steering box.
15. Temporarily replace the steering wheel and remove the outer column complete with shaft from the car.
16. On all models disconnect the steering links at the steering box drop arm.
17. Remove the steering box from the sub frame.

Steering box, refit

1. Reverse removal procedure, ensuring that the horn pick-up arm fits correctly on to the horn contact ring.
2. Tighten the steering box securing bolts to a torque of 50 lb/ft (70 mkg).
3. Fill reservoir with recommended lubricant (Section Y) and bleed the system as detailed in Operation J1-9.
4. Test the steering system for leaks, with the engine running, by holding the steering hard on full lock in both directions. Do not maintain this pressure for more than 30 seconds in any one minute, to avoid causing the oil to overheat and possible damage to the seals.
5. Road test the car.

Steering box, overhaul—Operation J1-4

Workshop hand tools:

Spanner sizes: 2 BA, 3 BA, $\frac{7}{16}$ in. AF, $\frac{1}{2}$ in. AF, $\frac{11}{16}$ in. AF, $\frac{3}{4}$ in. AF, $\frac{15}{16}$ in. AF, 1 in. AF, $1\frac{1}{8}$ in. AF
Allen key; Hammer, soft faced; Screwdriver; Pliers; Bleed tube; Container; Circlip pliers; Wooden drift; Feeler gauge

Special tools:

Drop arm removal tool, Part No. 521588;
Special 'C' spanner, Part No. 525375;
Special collar, Part No. 601303;
Piston ring clamp

For steering box removal see Operation J1-3

Steering box, strip

1. Lever away the locking tab, and remove the drop arm securing nut.
2. Tear away the foam seal, which is situated between the housing and the drop arm. Then withdraw the drop arm, using special tool (Part No. 521588).

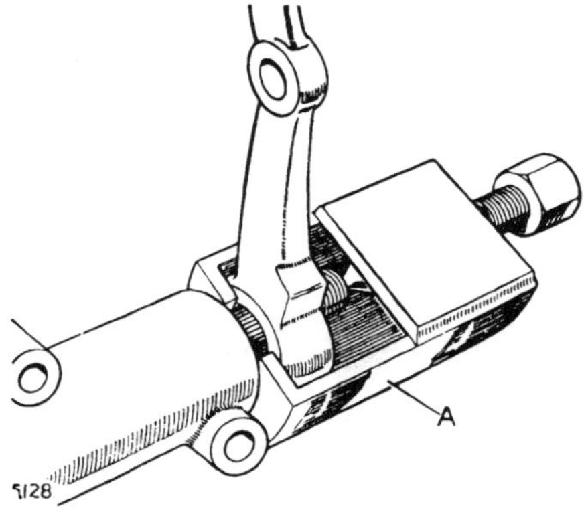

Drop arm removal

A—Special tool

3. Remove the Allen screw, locknut for adjusting screw and the nuts securing top cover to body.
4. Screw the adjuster through the cover, to ease up the cover, and remove cover, aluminium washer and square-section seal.
5. Rotate the camshaft until rocker shaft peg is in the central position.
6. Cover the splines on the end of camshaft with masking tape to prevent accidental damage to seals and components in the course of dismantling.
7. Remove the fixings securing end cover to the steering box and withdraw the end cover, shims and outer valve side plate 'O' ring. Discard the shims.

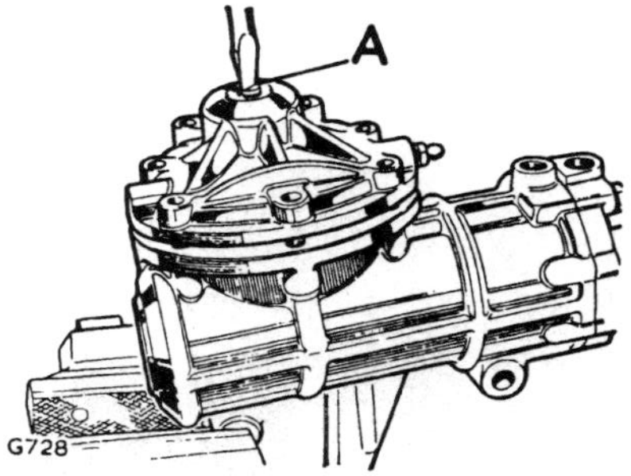

Top cover removal

A—Adjusting screw

8. From the end cover, remove the spring ring, seal retaining washer and the two-piece seal. Observe the circlip and oil seal bush behind which are located a rubber 'O' ring and plain washer.

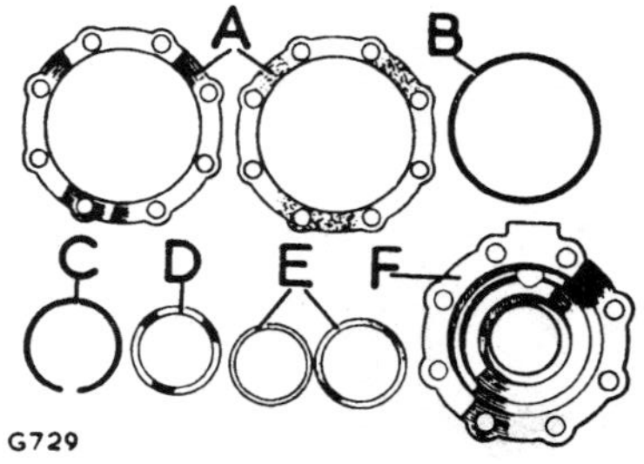

Component parts of end cover

A—Plastic shims, early models
B—'O' ring
C—Spring ring
D—Retaining washer
E—Two-piece seal
F—End cover

9. Remove the circlip and withdraw the shaft bush, 'O' ring seal and plain washer. Care should be taken not to disturb the valve outer side plate.

Operation J1-4—*continued*

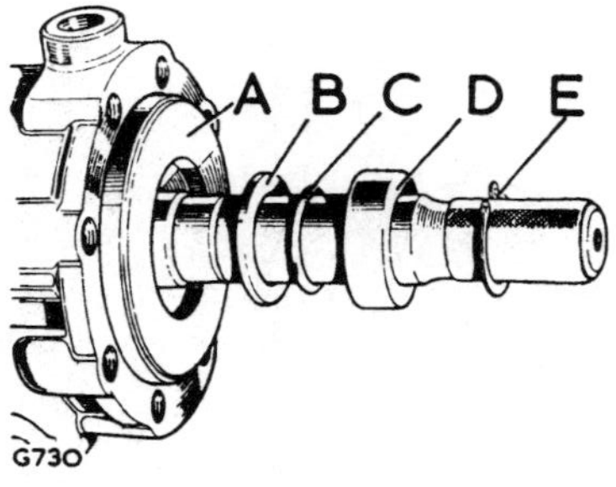

Removing oil seal bush and plain washer

A—Valve outer side plate
B—Plain washer
C—'O' ring
D—Bush
E—Circlip

10. A collar, suitable for the next sequence of operations is required. This collar can be manufactured to the dimensions given, or obtained under Part No. 601303.

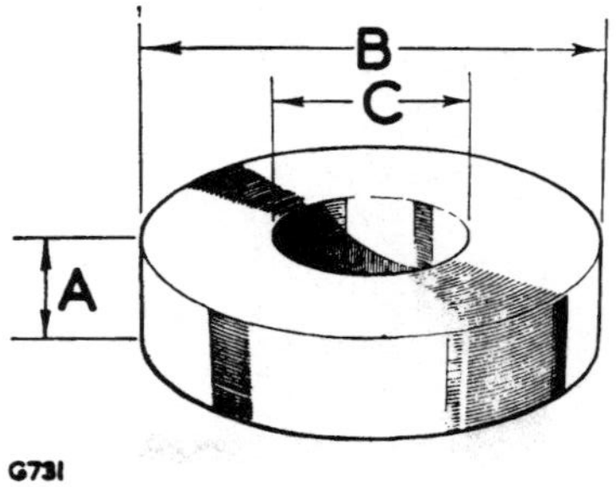

Special collar retaining valve spool

A—$\frac{1}{2}$ in. (12,5 mm) B—2 in. (50,5 mm) C—$\frac{7}{8}$ in. (22 mm

11. Position the collar over the shaft and retain in position with the original circlip as illustrated. This will ensure that the valve components are locked together to facilitate removal from the housing.

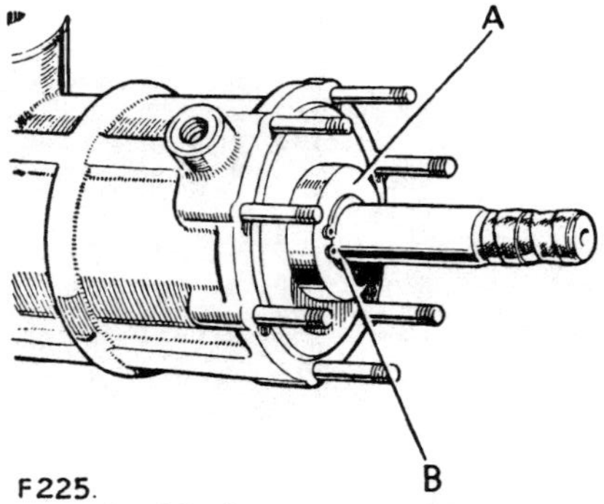

Special collar in position on shaft

A—Collar B—Circlip

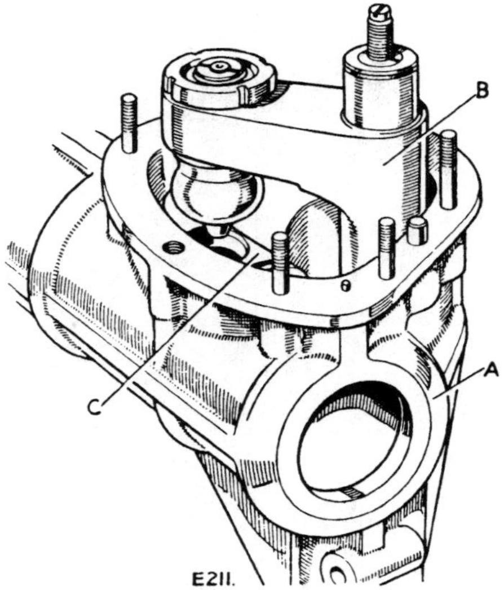

Rocker shaft on edge of housing

A—Steering box housing
B—Rocker shaft on edge of housing
C—Camshaft and piston sleeve

Operation J1-4—*continued*

12. Tap the rocker shaft up until the peg is clear of the piston and piston sleeve, taking care that the peg does not foul the piston sleeve, causing damage to the sleeve. Support the arm of the rocker shaft on the edge of the housing and secure in this position.
13. Exert pressure on the camshaft end bearing housing and push the camshaft assembly in the direction indicated, clear of the steering box. Do not attempt to withdraw the assembly by pulling the camshaft, otherwise the end cover ball bearings may be dislodged.

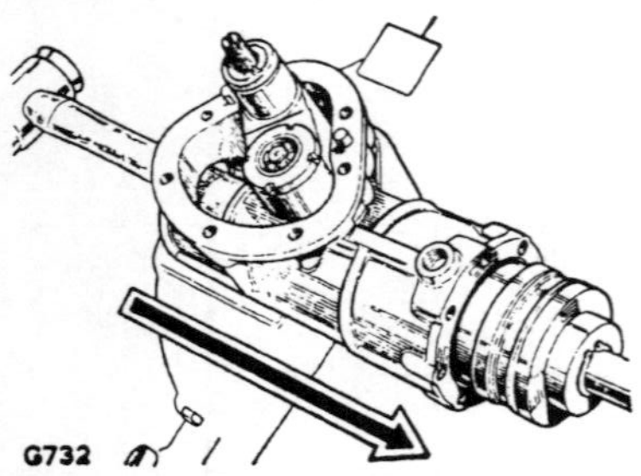

G732

Camshaft assembly, removal from housing

14. Place the camshaft assembly with the bearing housing downwards on a suitable clean working surface. Remove the circlip and special collar.

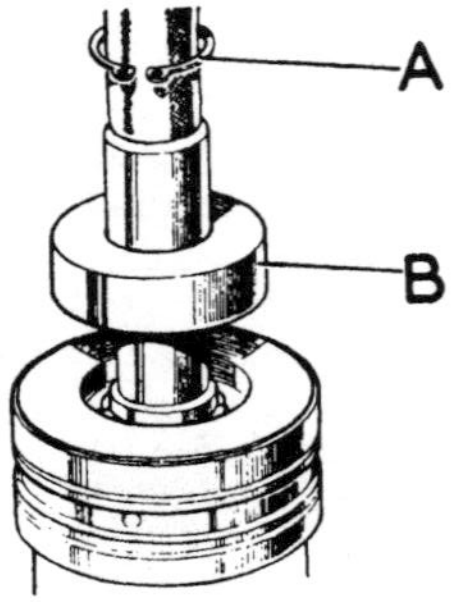

G733

Removal of collar and circlip

A—Circlip B—Special collar

15. Lift off the valve outer side plate together with the large diameter 'O' ring.
16. Remove the seal plate and 'O' ring from the valve outer side plate.

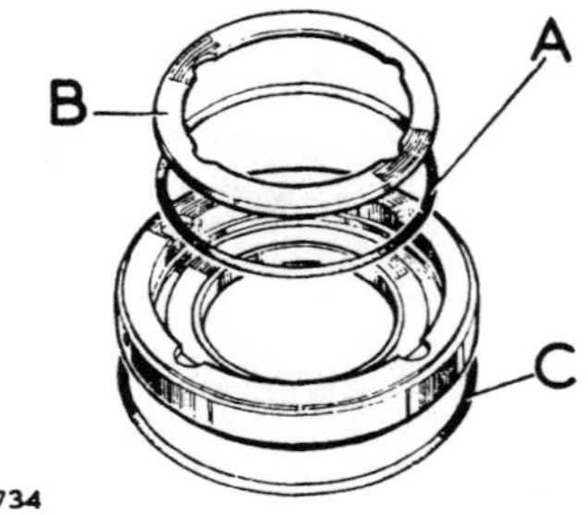

G734

View of outer side plate, showing seal and seal plate

A—'O' ring B—Seal plate C—Large 'O' ring

17. Lift off the valve plate spring.

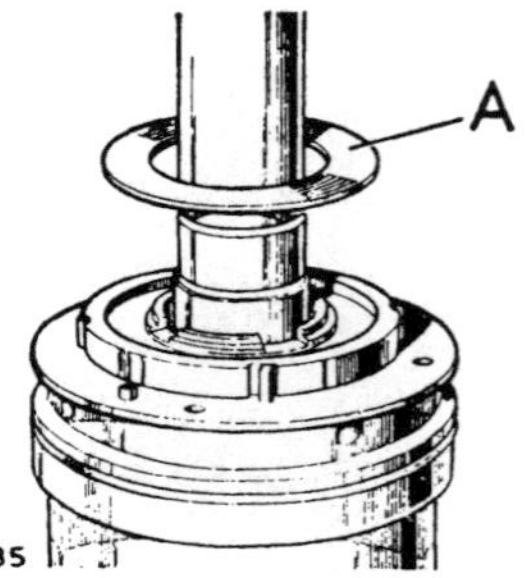

G735

Removal of valve plate spring

A—Valve spring plate

18. Withdraw the four spool locking pins.
19. Unscrew the two spool halves, using special tool (Part No. 525375).

Operation J1-4—*continued*

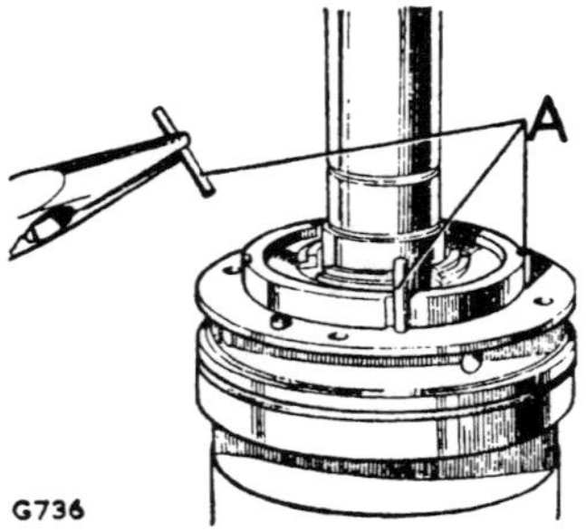

G736

Removal of spool locking pins

A—Locking pins

20. Locate the 'C' spanner part of special tool over the valve centre and screw the threaded pins through two holes in the centre and into the aligning holes of the female half of the spool.

The other part of the tool locates, as shown, over the male spool half. After unscrewing the male half, lift it off.

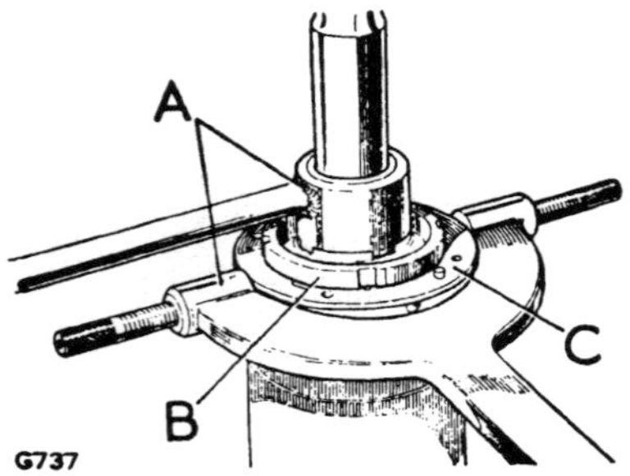

G737

Separating spool halves, using special tool

A—Special tool (Part No. 525375)
B—Male spool half
C—Valve centre

21. Lift off the valve centre together with the large diameter 'O' ring and the female half of the valve spool.

Lift the camshaft slightly and tip the whole assembly to allow the steel balls to drop out. Then lift off the spool female half.

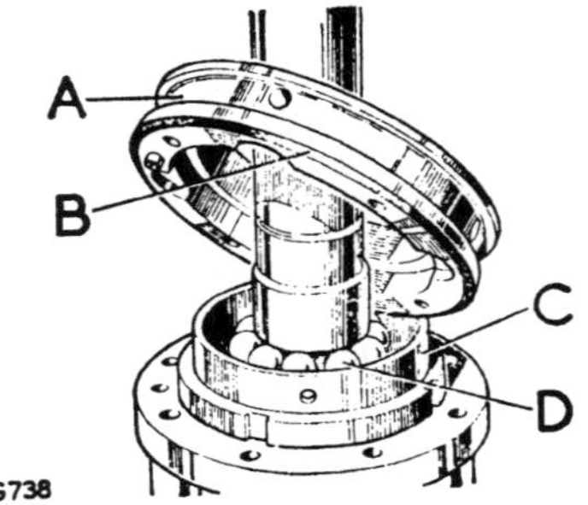

G738

Removal of valve centre and spool

A—Valve centre C—Valve spool, female half
B—'O' ring D—Steel balls

Where it is necessary to renew spool parts proceed as follows:

22. Lift out the bearing housings from within each spool half. Underneath the housing in the male half, shims may be found and a rubber 'O' ring inside the female half.

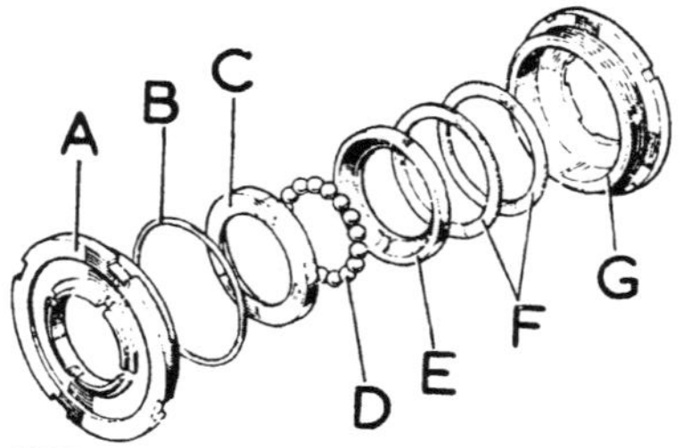

G739

Components of the valve spool

A—Female, lower, spool half
B—'O' ring
C—Bearing housing
D—Ten steel balls
E—Bearing housing
F—Shims
G—Male, upper, spool half

Operation J1-4—*continued*

23. Remove the inner valve plate spring, seal plate and 'O' ring from the valve inner side plate.

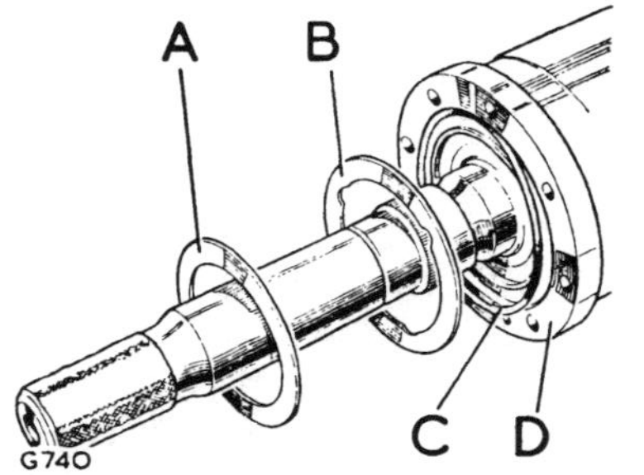

Inner valve side plate components

A—Valve plate spring
B—Seal plate
C—'O' ring
D—Valve inner side plate

24. Lift the piston and camshaft assembly out of the end bearing housing. Carefully withdraw the camshaft from the piston and sleeve in the direction indicated in the illustration. At the opposite end of the piston sleeve the camshaft is supported by another ball race. Care must be taken, when removing the camshaft, not to displace and lose the steel balls of the bearing.

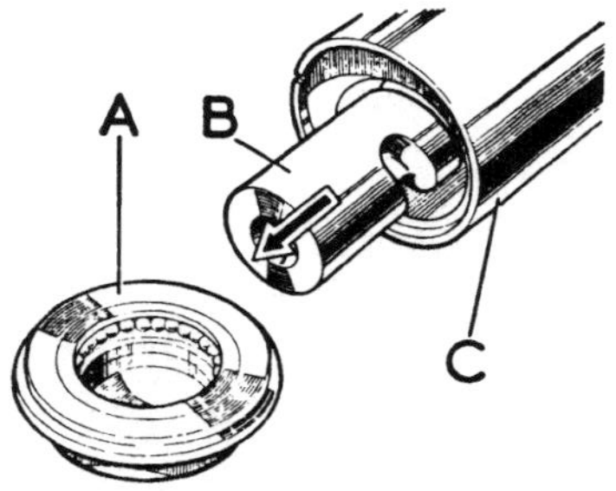

G741

Camshaft removal

A—End bearing housing B—Camshaft C—Piston sleeve

25. Withdraw the piston from the sleeve, and if necessary remove cast iron piston ring. Remove the two-part seal from the piston. This seal consists of a black square-section seal which fits in the bottom of the groove; a smaller diameter white plastic seal fits into the same groove on top of the black seal.

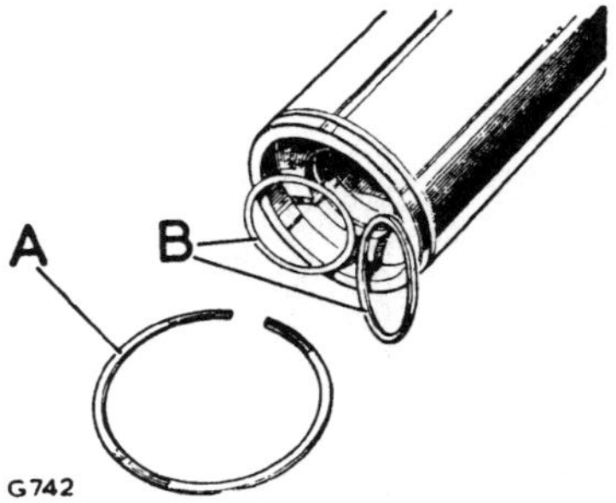

G742

Piston ring and seals

A—Cast iron ring B—Two-piece seal

26. Should it be necessary, the inner valve side plate can be removed from the piston sleeve; first remove the thirty steel balls from their groove, inside the plate, then gently tap the plate from the inside of sleeve, using a wooden drift.

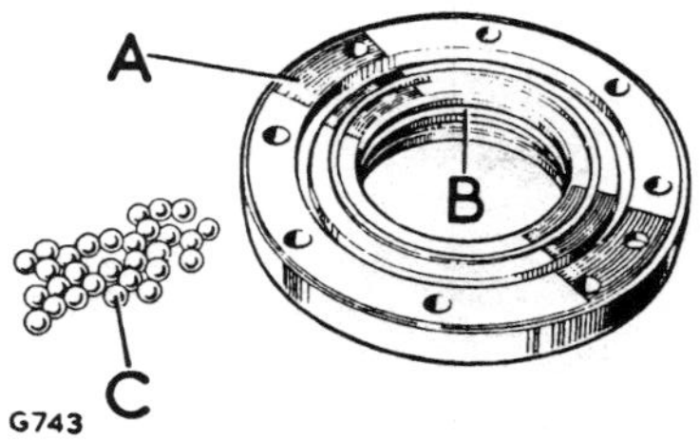

G743

Inner valve side plate seal and steel balls

A—Valve side plate B—Two-piece seal C—Steel balls

Operation J1-4—*continued*

27. With the inner valve side plate removed from piston sleeve, remove the white plastic and black seal from the groove.

28. From the end bearing housing, remove the square section seal from the shoulder part of housing and the two-piece seal from the internal groove.

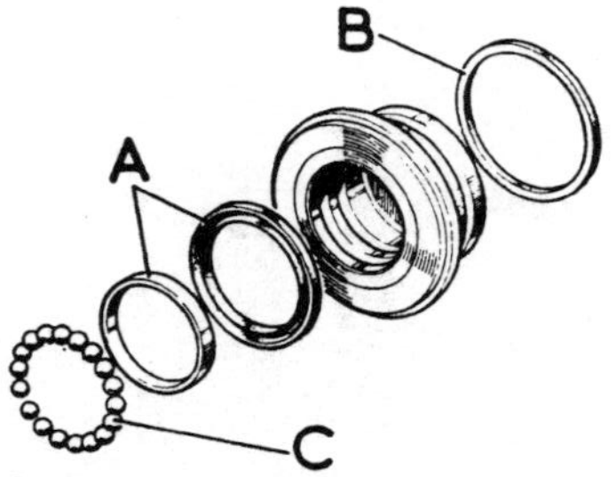

G744

End bearing housing components

A—Two-piece seal B—Square section seal C—Steel balls

29. Withdraw the rocker shaft from the steering box and remove the circlip, retaining washer and oil seal.

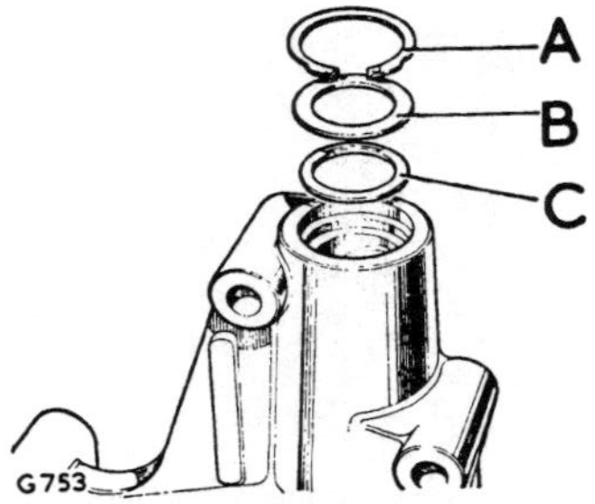

Steering box rocker shaft seals

A—Circlip B—Retaining washer C—Seal

Operation J1-4—*continued*

Inspection before steering box rebuild

Examine all component parts for wear or damage and renew as necessary.

Check valve spring plates for flatness. Any dishing beyond .0025 in. (0,06 mm) means renewal of the plates, in pairs.

All seals must be renewed. All plastic seals, with the exception of the end cover seal, should be warmed in hot water to make them more pliable before fitting.

Examine the inner side plate and the end bearing housing. The ball race housing is a part of the end bearing; this applies also to the inner valve plate.

If a ball bearing has been lost, replace with a complete set of thirty new ball bearings of $\frac{5}{32}$ in. (4,0 mm) diameter.

Ensure that the spool halves are in a good condition, and that the threads are not damaged.

Check that the spring plate locations are free from burns or scores.

If the spool halves or bearing halves are damaged in any way they are only replaceable as assemblies.

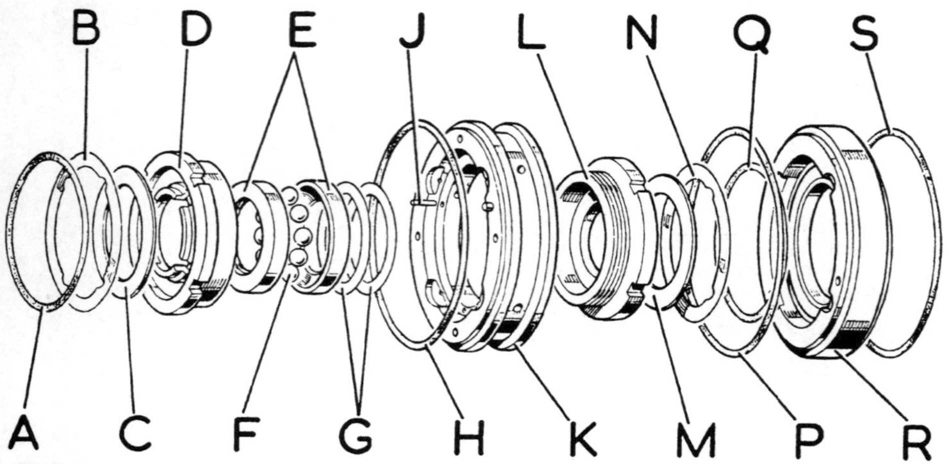

G794

Layout of valve spool

A—'O' ring for valve seal
B—Seal plate
C—Valve plate spring
D—Female spool half
E—Bearing cups
F—Ball bearings
G—Shims for ball bearings
H—Seal ring for valve centre
J—Spool locking pin
K—Valve centre
L—Male spool half
M—Valve plate spring
N—Seal plate
P—Sealing ring for outer valve side plate
Q—'O' ring for valve seal
R—Outer valve side plate
S—Sealing ring for outer valve side plate

Operation J1-4—*continued*

Steering box, rebuild

1. Fit the black rubber seal to the inner bore of the piston. Warm the white seal in hot water and fit to the piston over the top of black seal.
2. Locate a new cast-iron piston ring into the piston sleeve bore, and check ring gap, which should be .004 in. to .008 in. (0,10 to 0,20 mm). Fit the piston ring into the groove around piston.
3. Make a pencil mark adjacent to the single blind hole on the inner valve plate outer diameter. This is for the purpose of alignment at a later stage of assembly.

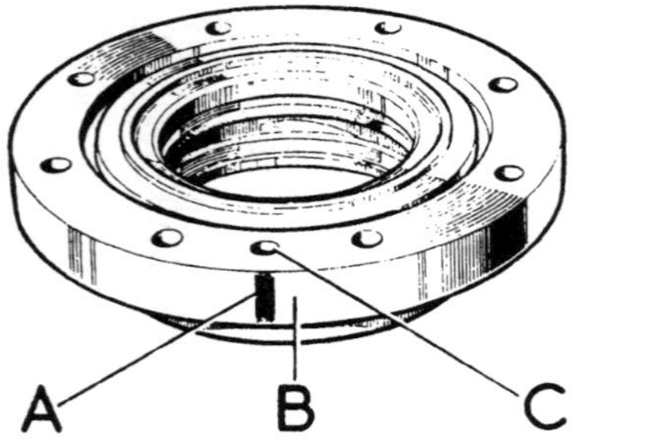

G783

Marking inner valve side plate

A—Pencil mark B—Inner valve side plate C—Blind hole

4. Using a suitable press, fit the piston sleeve into its location in the inner valve side plate.
5. Using a piston ring clamp over the piston ring, insert the piston into the sleeve. Ensure that the piston gap is located on the opposite side of the cutaway in the sleeve and that the hole in the piston registers with the cutaway.
6. Fit a new two-piece oil seal to the valve inner side plate. The white plastic seal is fitted last on top of the black rubber seal.
7. Locate the thirty $\frac{5}{32}$ in. (4,0 mm) diameter ball bearings into the inner side plate ball race, and retain with a smear of silicone compound MS4.

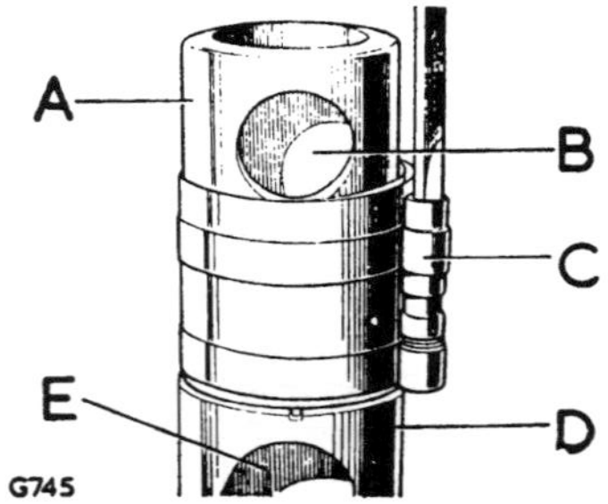

G745

Assembly of piston and sleeve

A—Piston
B—Hole in piston
C—Piston ring clamp
D—Piston sleeve
E—Cutaway in sleeve

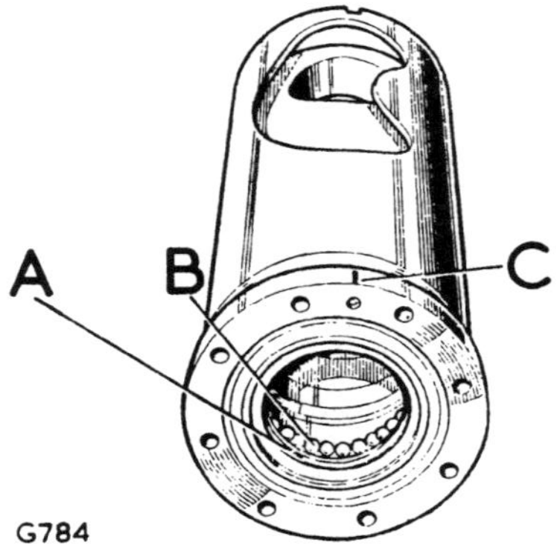

G784

Assembly of piston, sleeve, seals and bearing

A—Two-piece seal
B—Ball bearings
C—Pencil alignment mark

8. Fit a new square-section outer seal into the groove of end bearing housing.

Operation J1-4—*continued*

9. Fit a new two-piece inner seal to the end bearing housing as described in item 1. Locate the thirty $\frac{5}{32}$ in. (4,0 mm) ball bearings into the bearing housing groove and retain with a smear of Silicone compound MS4.

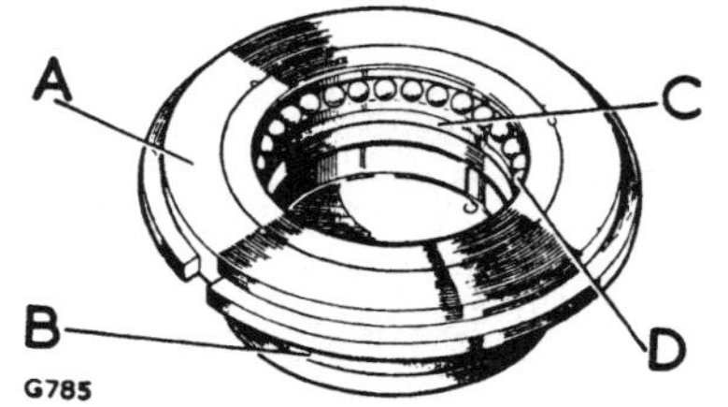

G785

Assembly of end housing, seals and bearing

A—Bearing housing C—Two-piece seal
B—Square seal D—Bearing

10. Fit to the camshaft the male and female spool halves, together with the bearings, 'O' ring and the original internal shims. With the spool halves tight and the master locking pin grooves accurately aligned, check that the spool assembly is free to rotate on the camshaft without end-float. This operation must be carried out with extreme care to ensure correct operation of the power steering.

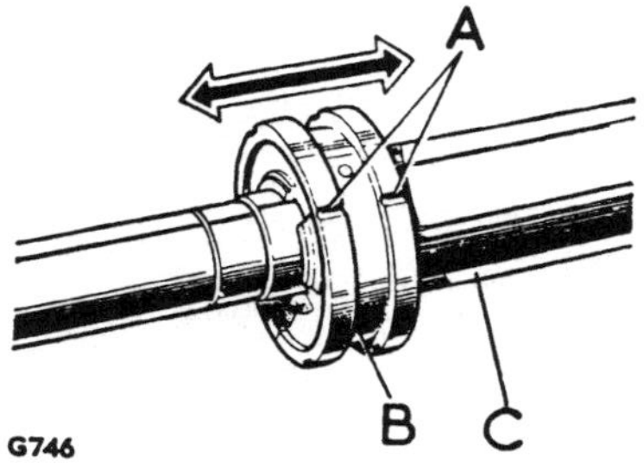

G746

Checking valve spool end-float

A—Locking pin grooves B—Spool assembly C—Camshaft

11. If there is tightness of the bearing, or end-float of the spool, adjust by means of the shims, which fit behind the bearing housing male spool half. These shims are available in the following sizes:
    .002 in. (0,05 mm)
    .003 in. (0,07 mm)
    .005 in. (0,12 mm)
    .010 in. (0,25 mm)
    .015 in. (0,38 mm)
12. Where a new spool assembly is to be fitted, it must be checked in the manner described, and shims added or removed to obtain the condition described in item 10.
13. Remove the spool halves and retain, together with the correct shimming, before fitting the camshaft into the piston sleeve and end housing.
14. Carefully fit the camshaft, from the forward end of the piston and sleeve assembly, into the end bearing housing, so that the camshaft stands vertical.

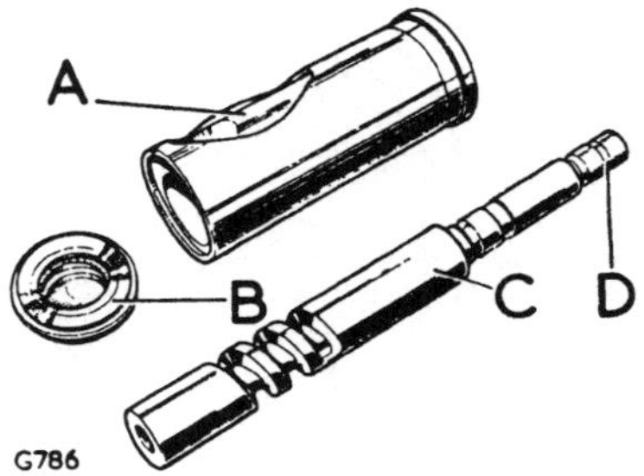

G786

Camshaft, piston sleeve and end bearing assemblies

A—Piston sleeve assembly C—Camshaft
B—End bearing housing assembly D—Masking tape

15. Taking care not to dislodge the bearings in the piston, lower the piston and sleeve assembly over the camshaft. Align the small cutaway with the slot in the end bearing housing, then ensure that the sleeve is fully engaged on the housing.
16. Fit the 'O' ring-seal to the inner valve side plate. Place a seal plate in position over the seal.

Operation J1-4—*continued*

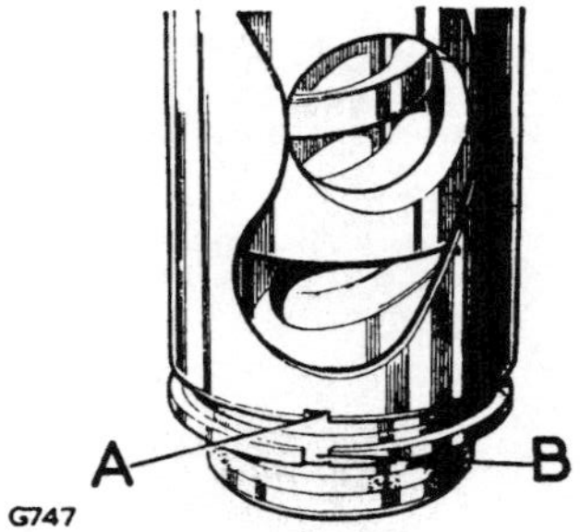

G747

Assembly of piston and sleeve to camshaft

A—Small cutaway in piston sleeve
B—Slot in end bearing housing

17. Fit the 'O' ring seal into the female spool half. Turn spool half over, and fit valve spring plate on to the outer face of spool half. Retain in position with a smear of Silicone Compound MS4.

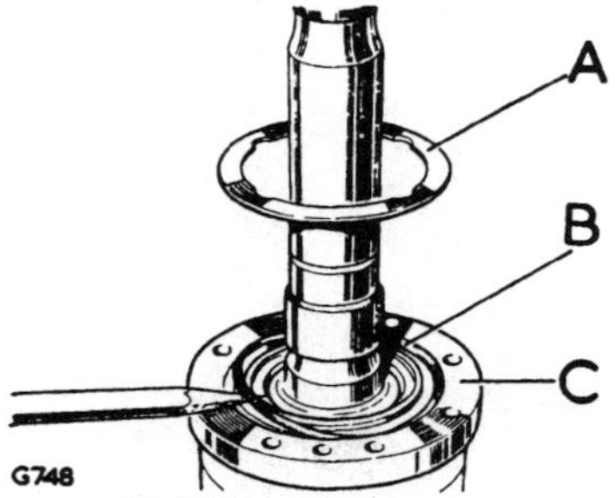

G748

Assembly of 'O' ring seal and seal plate

A—Seal plate B—'O' ring seal C—Valve side plate

18. Position the female spool half on to the inner valve side plate, taking care not to dislodge the valve spring plate.
19. Fit the bearing half, together with the ten ball bearings, into the female spool half. To insert the balls it will be necessary to raise the camshaft very slightly.

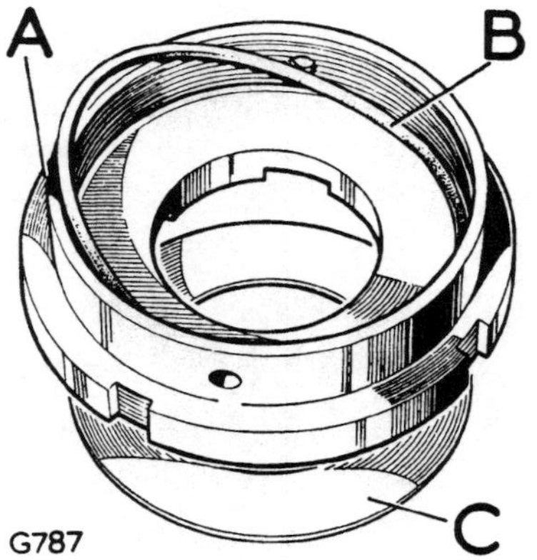

G787

Assembly of 'O' ring, valve spring plate to spool half

A—Female spool half B—'O' ring seal C—Valve spring plate

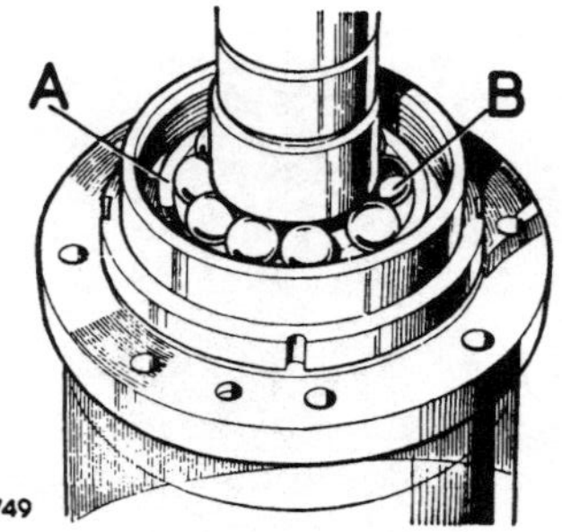

G749

Assembly of bearing half and bearings

A—Bearing half B—Bearings

20. Mark the outer diameter of the valve centre in line with the hollow dowel, and locate the valve centre on to the inner valve side plate, ensuring correct positioning of the dowel and alignment of pencil marks.

Operation J1-4—*continued*

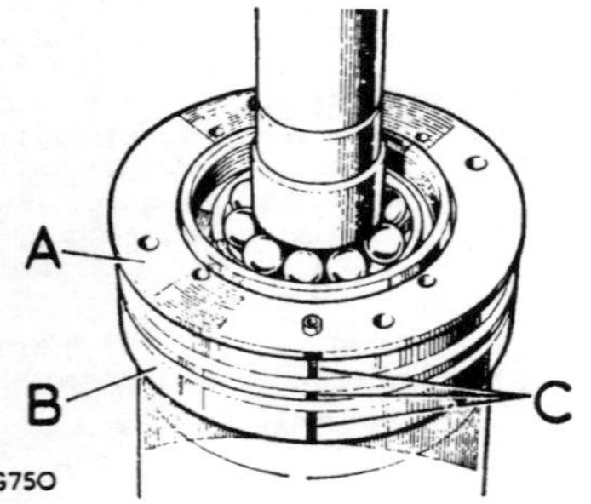

G750

Assembly of valve centre

A—Valve centre B—Inner valve side plate C—Pencil marks

21. Fit the shims previously selected, as detailed in items 10, 11, 12 and the remaining bearing half into the male spool half, retaining the shims in position with Silicone Compound MS4.

22. Fit the two spool halves together and fully tighten with the special 'C' spanner (Part No. 525375).

23. With the spool assembly fully tightened, insert the four locking pins, ensuring that the reduced diameter groove in the spool half corresponds with the holes in valve centre, to give an exact fit of the locking pins.

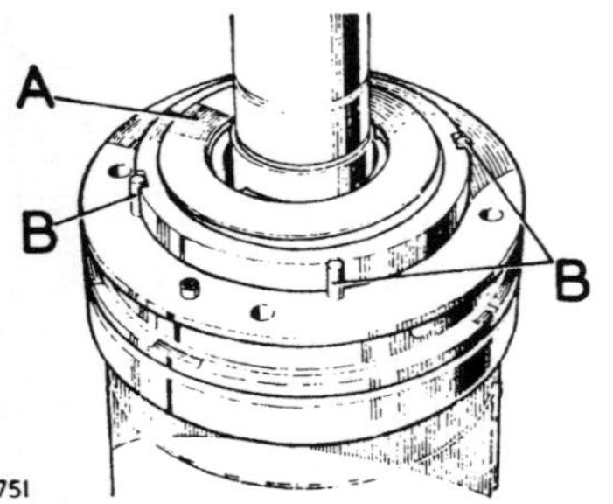

G751

Assembly, locking pins and valve plate

A—Valve spring plate B—Locking pins

24. Locate the valve spring plate in the recess of the spool outer face, retaining in position with a smear of Silicone Compound MS4.

25. Fit a new inner sealing ring to the outer valve side plate, and position the seal plate on top, retain with a smear of Silicone Compound MS4. Mark the position of dowel hole on to the side plate.

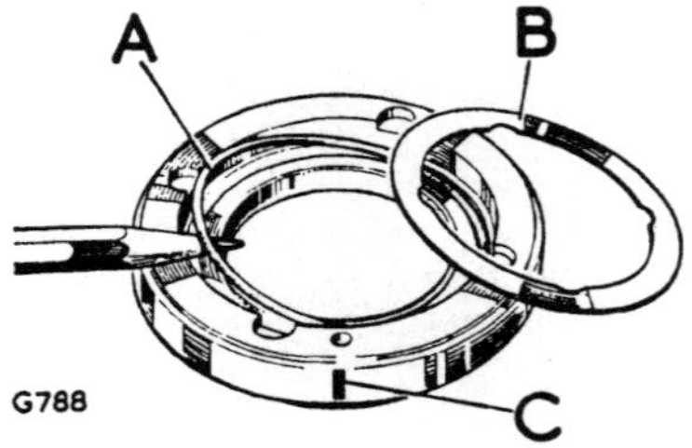

G788

Assembly, outer valve side plate

A—Inner sealing ring B—Seal plate C—Dowel position mark

26. Fit the outer valve side plate assembly to the valve centre and ensure that the dowel fits exactly in the locating hole in outer side plate, using the marks to align the dowels.

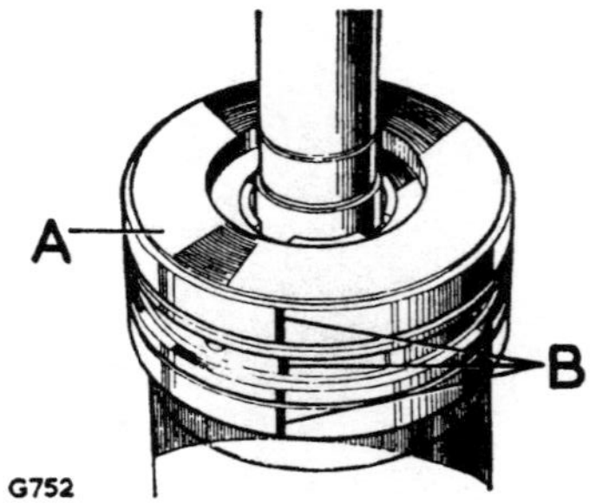

G752

Assembly, outer and inner valve side plates

A—Outer valve side plate B—Pencil marks

Operation J1-4—*continued*

27. Fit the slave collar previously used for dismantling and secure to the camshaft with the circlip.

28. Fit new 'O' ring seals to the inner valve side plate and to the valve centre.

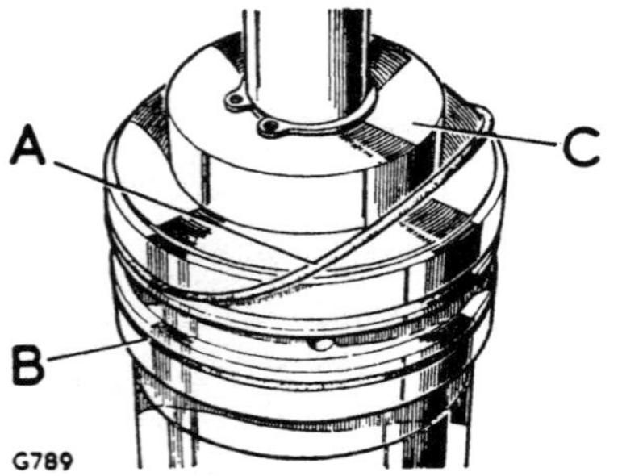

G789

Assembly, special collar and 'O' ring seals

A—'O' ring seal, valve centre
B—'O' ring seal, valve side plate
C—Special collar retained with circlip

29. The camshaft and piston sleeve assembly is now prepared for refitting to the housing.

30. Fit a new rocker shaft oil seal into the casing and retain in position with washer and circlip.

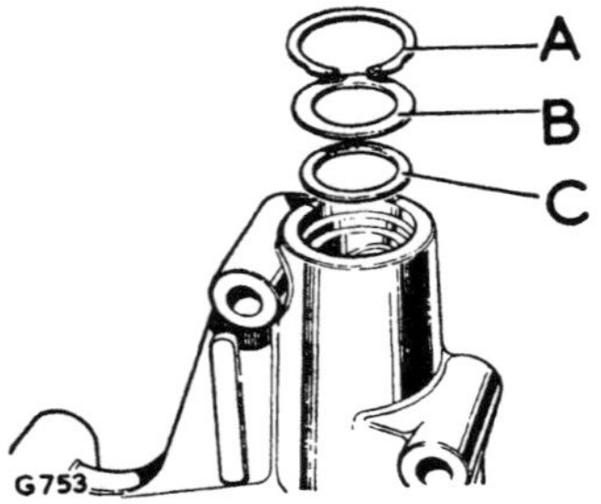

G753

Steering box rocker shaft seals

A—Circlip B—Retaining washer C—Seal

31. Check that the dowel marks are in line—then offer the complete camshaft and sleeve assembly to the steering box, and push in until the piston sleeve is parallel with the rocker shaft cutaway in the casing. Ensure that the grooves in the bearing housing and piston sleeve are in line with the locating pin in the casing. Once the camshaft assembly has entered the steering box, any attempt to withdraw the camshaft assembly will result in the end bearing housing becoming dislodged from both sleeve and camshaft.

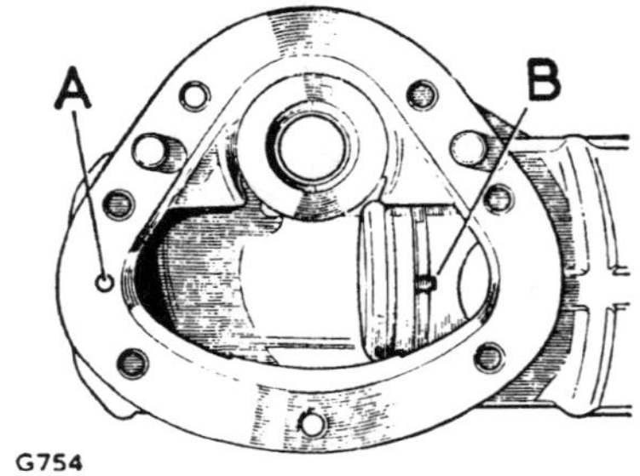

G754

Assembly, camshaft to casing

A—Casing locating pin B—Piston sleeve

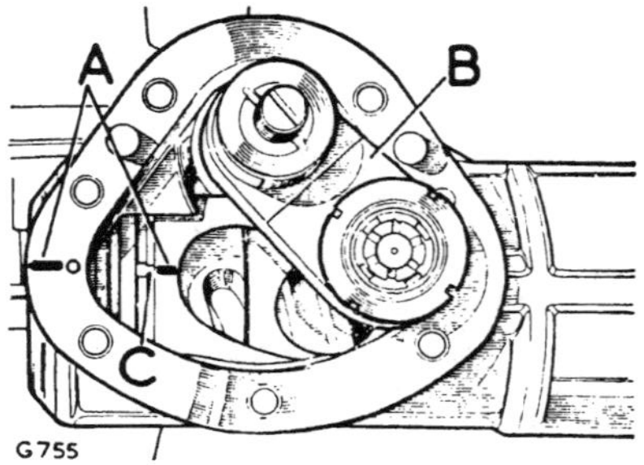

G755

Rocker shaft in temporary position

A—Pencil marks, sleeve and casing
B—Rocker shaft supported
C—Piston groove

Operation J1-4—*continued*

32. Fit the rocker shaft into the casing, and support the shaft on the edge of the casing cover face, and secure in this position.

33. Use a suitable tube, located over the camshaft on to the valve side plate, and press the camshaft assembly into position. Ensure that the slot in the bearing housing and sleeve locate with the dowel in the casing. Care should be taken during this operation not to dislodge the 'O' ring seals fitted to the valve centre, and to facilitate entry of the seals, lightly smear with Silicone Compound MS4.

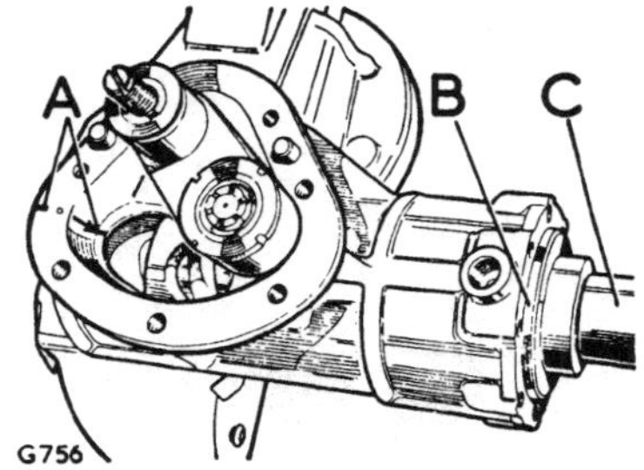

G756

Assembly, camshaft to casing

A—Pencil marks B—'O' ring valve centre C—Tube

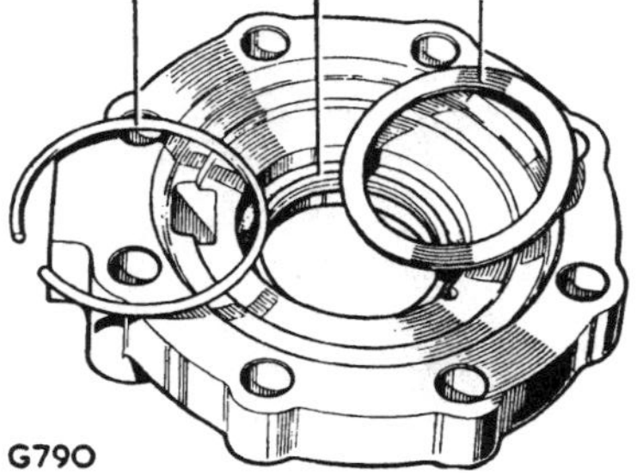

G790

Assembly, end cover

A—Spring ring B—Two-piece seal C—Retaining washer

34. Allow the rocker shaft peg assembly to enter and locate in the piston sleeve and cam track.

35. Fit a new two-piece seal to the end cover, and fit retaining washer and circlip.

36. Remove the special distance collar, used for assembly, taking care not to displace the valve outer side plate.

37. Fit a new 'O' ring seal into the end bush. Cover the camshaft spline with masking tape to protect the 'O' ring in bush. Fit the flat washer and end bush to camshaft and retain with circlip.

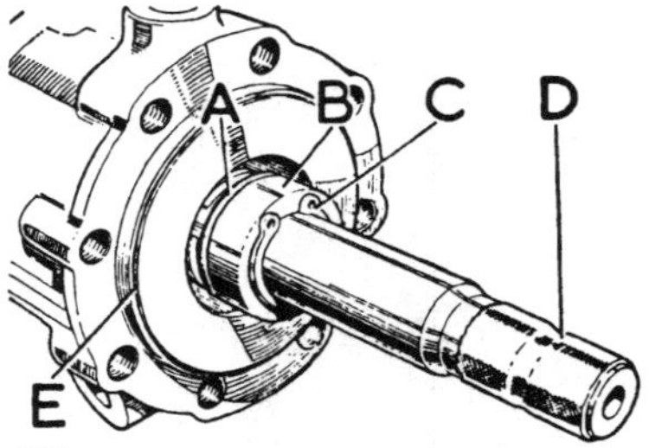

G791

Assembly, camshaft end bush

A—Flat washer
B—End bush
C—Circlip
D—Masking tape
E—'O' ring seal groove

38. Discard any plastic shims which may have been previously fitted between cover and steering box.

39. Fit the large 'O' ring seal to the outer valve side-plate and lightly smear with Silicone Compound MS4 prior to fitting of end cover.

40. Fit the end cover and retain in position with four set bolts; tighten to 180 to 200 lb ft (24 to 27 mkg). Ascertain the clearance between the casing and end cover with a feeler gauge. This should be .002 in. (0,07 mm) minimum after torque loading, thus ensuring that the piston sleeve is positively locked in position.

Operation J1-4—*continued*

Shims are available in the following sizes:
.0025 in. (0,06 mm)
.005 in. (0,12 mm)
.010 in. (0,25 mm)

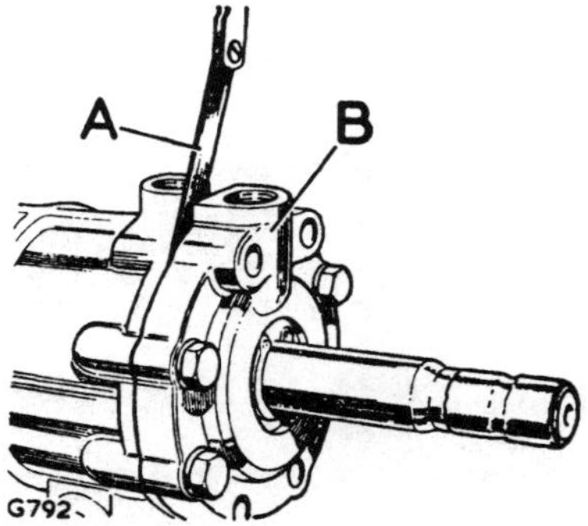

G792

Checking end cover clearance

A—Feeler gauge B—End cover

41. Smear a new top sealing ring with Silicone Compound MS4 and fit to the end of rocker shaft.

42. Place the aluminium washer and a new square-section rubber seal in position on the top surface of the steering box casing. Turn the camshaft so that the rocker shaft is in mid-position.

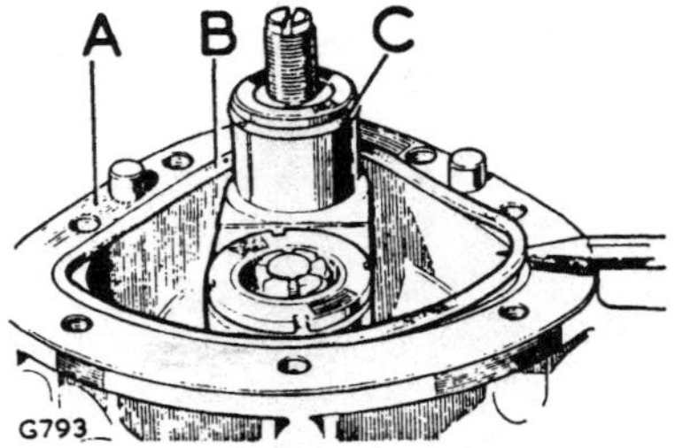

G793

Positions of aluminium washer and seals

A—Aluminium washer B—Rubber seal C—Sealing ring

43. Locate the top cover on to the boss of rocker shaft, and ensure the seal remains in position. Enter the thread of adjusting screw into the cover by rotating the screw in an anti-clockwise direction to pull the cover down. Check that the dowels engage correctly, and secure the top cover with the fixings.

44. With the rocker shaft set in mid-position, fit a new foam rubber seal over the rocker shaft up against the casing. Fit the drop arm pointing forward to the front of the car. Tighten the securing nut fully and lock over the lock washer.

Rocker shaft end-float, to adjust

45. Secure the steering box firmly in a vice by the mounting bosses.

46. Rotate the camshaft and ensure the drop arm is in the straight-ahead position.

47. Screw the adjusting screw in or out to obtain a condition whereby there is no perceptible back-lash at drop arm when in the straight-ahead position.

48. Move the drop arm throughout its full travel from lock to lock, by rotating the camshaft, and ensure there is no stickiness or hesitation in the straight-ahead position. If necessary rotate the adjusting screw clockwise in small amounts until the drop arm can be moved freely from lock to lock. This adjustment is very sensitive, movements of the adjusting screw of 10° will often have a significant effect.

49. When adjustment has been completed, fully tighten the adjusting screw locknut.

50. When the steering unit has been fitted to the car, it must be road tested and any final adjustment made as required. See Operation J1-5.

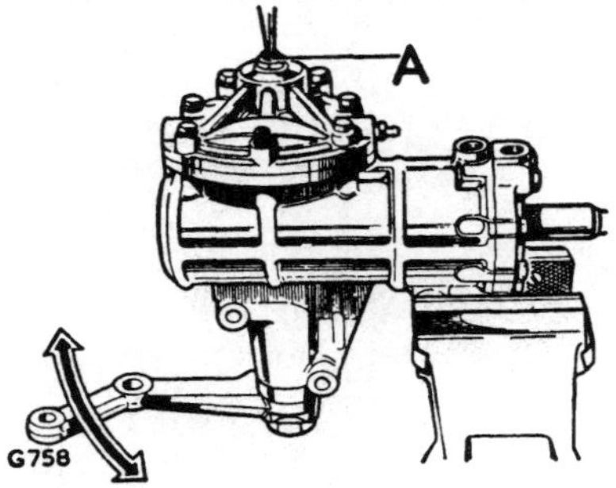

G758

Adjusting rocker shaft end-float

A—Adjusting screw

Rocker shaft end-float, adjust—Operation J1-5

Workshop hand tools:
Spanner size: $\frac{3}{4}$ in. AF
Screwdriver

Special tools:

Rocker shaft end-float, adjust, unit on bench

1. Rotate the camshaft until the steering box is in the straight ahead position.
2. With the steering unit securely fixed in a vice, rotate the adjusting screw until there is no perceptible backlash at the drop arm, when in the straight ahead position.
3. Then move the drop arm throughout its full travel from lock to lock and ensure there is no stickiness or hesitation in the straight ahead position. If necessary rotate the adjusting screw clockwise in small amounts until the drop arm can be moved freely from lock to lock. The rocker shaft adjustment is very sensitive, movements of the screw of 10° will often have a significant effect.
4. When the steering unit has been refitted to the car it must be road tested and any final adjustment made as required as detailed below.

Rocker shaft end-float, adjust, unit installed

1. Check tyre pressures. (Section V).
2. Run car for at least 5 miles (8 km) to thoroughly warm steering system, tyres, etc.
3. At speeds of 2 to 6 mph (3 to 10 kph) when running in a straight line over a bumpy surface check for 'peg rattle'. This is a low frequency knock occurring in phase with road wheel disturbance by bumps, which can both be felt on the steering wheel and sometimes heard.

   If it is present the rocker shaft adjusting screw should be turned clockwise in small amounts while the steering is gently oscillated through the free play area, the car being stationary with the wheels straight ahead.

   As soon as a trace of stickiness is felt the adjusting screw should be locked.

   This adjustment is very sensitive, movements of the screw of 10° often having a significant effect.

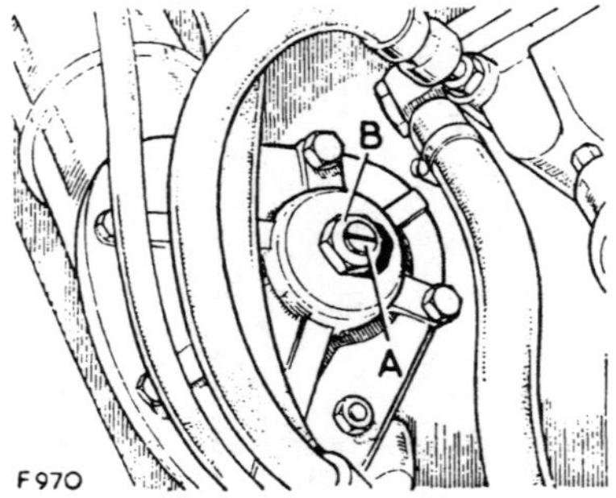

F970

Rocker shaft adjustment

A—Rocker shaft adjustment screw
B—Locknut

4. Next drive the car at speeds between 35 mph (56 kph) and 55 mph (88 kph) and check that the steering wheel self-return action from small angles is adequate.

   If more than very slight stickiness is observed, the steering box adjusting screw should be screwed outwards just enough to remove the stickiness, probably only 5 to 15°, and then re-locked.
5. If re-adjustment was necessary, repeat check 3 to assess effect on 'peg rattle'.
6. If it is not possible by adjustment to reach a satisfactory compromise between 'peg rattle' and steering wheel return, this will probably be due to the position of the 'high spot' in the steering box being just away from the straight-running position. In this case it will be necessary to centralise the steering box drop arm by adjustment of the side steering rods. The car should then be re-tested and re-adjusted as previously described.

Hydraulic pump, remove and refit—Operation J1-6

Workshop hand tools:
Spanner sizes: $\frac{7}{16}$ in. AF, $\frac{1}{2}$ in. AF, $\frac{5}{8}$ in. AF, 1 in. AF
Screwdriver; Bleed tube; Container

Special tools:

Hydraulic pump, remove

1. Remove the reservoir filler cap. Disconnect the return pipe from the steering box and allow the oil to drain into a suitable receptacle. This oil must not be used again. Refit pipe to steering box.
2. Remove the air silencer, aluminium elbow and oil bath cleaner, Section A.
3. Disconnect the suction hose from the pump end cover by removing the banjo bolt.
4. RHD models. Disconnect the high pressure hose from the steering box, slacken the union at the pump and rotate the hose to remove.
5. Remove the crankcase breather and gasket.
6. LHD models. Slacken the high pressure hose connection at the pump.
7. Remove the nuts securing the pump to the dynamo, taking care not to lose the composite coupling, and withdraw.
8. LHD models. Rotate the pump bodily to disconnect the high pressure hose.

Hydraulic pump, refit

1. RHD models. Fit the pump to the dynamo and tighten the fixings.
2. LHD models. Fit the pump to the high pressure hose and rotate bodily until the hose is practically tight. Fit the pump to the dynamo, tighten the fixings and tighten the high pressure hose connection.
3. Connect the suction hose to the pump and tighten the banjo bolt.
4. Fit the crankcase breather to the crankcase, using a new gasket.
5. Refill the system with the correct grade of oil (Section Y). Total capacity 4 pints (2 litres). Bleed the system as laid down in Operation J1-9.
6. Test the steering system, with the engine running, by holding the steering hard on full lock in both directions. Do not maintain this pressure for more than 30 seconds in any one minute to avoid causing the oil to overheat and possible damage to the seals.
7. Replace the air cleaner assembly, Section A.
8. Road test the car.

Operation J1-6—*continued*

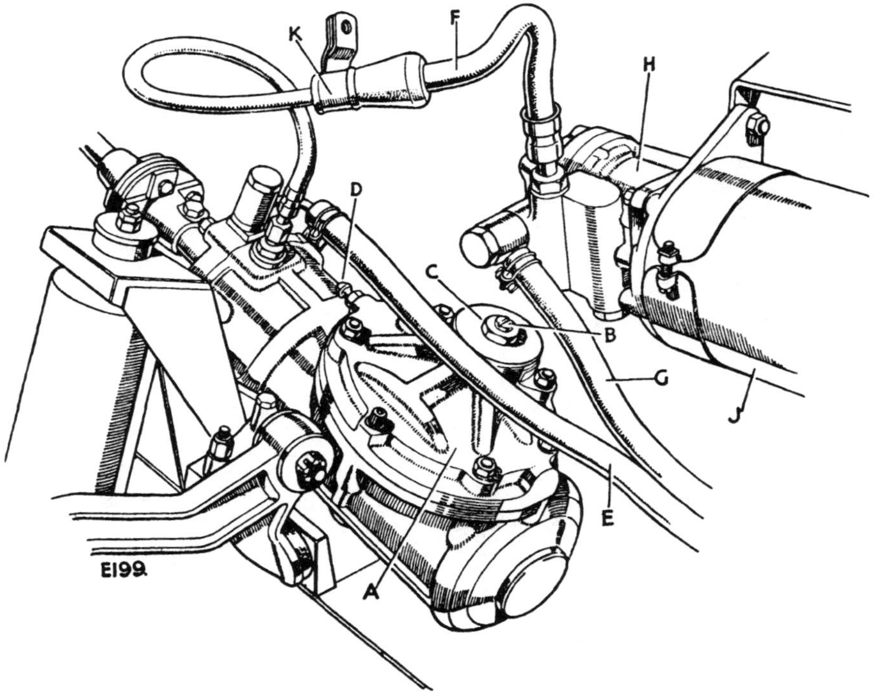

Power steering arrangement

A—Steering box
B—Rocker shaft adjusting screw
C—Adjusting screw locknut
D—Bleed screw
E—Pipe, steering box to reservoir
F—Pipe, pump to steering box
G—Pipe, reservoir to steering box
H—Pump
J—Dynamo
K—Clip, fixing pipe to air cleaner

Hydraulic pump, overhaul—Operation J1-7

Workshop hand tools:

Spanner sizes: $\frac{7}{16}$ in. AF, $\frac{1}{2}$ in. AF, $\frac{5}{8}$ in. AF, 1 in. AF
Screwdriver; Bleed tube; Container; Feeler gauge;
Straight-edge

Special tools:

Torque spanner

Hydraulic pump, strip

Thoroughly clean the exterior of the pump assembly, using care so that dirt does not enter the inlet or outlet holes.

During assembly operations, extreme caution should be used to prevent any dirt from entering the pump.

All parts should be lightly oiled before assembly.

1. Clamp body in vice.
2. Unscrew adaptor screw and remove adaptor, fibre washer and gasket. The venturi flow director is pressed into cover, and should not be removed.
3. Remove screws securing pump body to cover and remove pump from vice. Separate cover from body vertically to prevent parts from falling out.
4. Remove 'O' ring seals from grooves in pump body. Remove thrust washer from pump cover.
5. Remove snap ring from shaft, and remove rollers and carrier.
6. Remove shaft from body.
7. Lift out cam lock peg.
8. Remove shaft seal from body, ensuring that no damage is caused to shaft bushing.

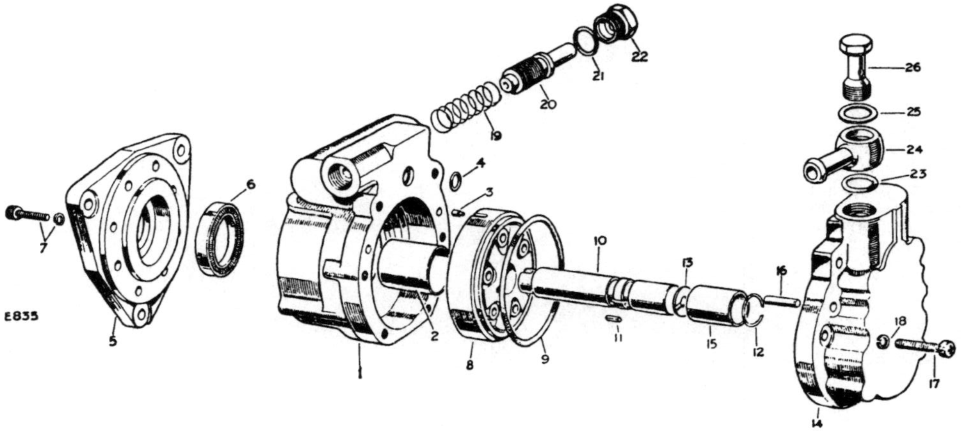

Exploded view of pump

1 Body for pump
2 Bush for shaft in body
3 Cam lock peg in pump body
4 'O' ring for by-pass in pump body
5 End plate
6 Oil seal end plate to body
7 Special screw and washer fixing end plate to body
8 Vane carrier and roller vanes
9 'O' ring for vane carrier to body
10 Shaft } For vane
11 Drive pin } carrier
12 Retaining clip
13 Thrust washer, shaft to end cover
14 Cover for pump
15 Bush for shaft in end cover
16 Dowel for fixing end cover to body
17 Special screw } Fixing end cover
18 Lock washer } to body
19 Control spring for valve assembly
20 Valve assembly in pump body
21 Valve cap 'O' ring
22 Valve cap in pump body
23 Seal for adaptor in cover
24 Adaptor for end cover
25 Fibre washer for adaptor
26 Adaptor screw fixing adaptor to end cover

Operation J1-7—*continued*

9. Remove valve cap, valve and valve spring from body. Place all parts where they will not be damaged, or subject to contamination.

10. Wash all parts in a suitable solvent, air dry, or wipe clean with a lint-free cloth if air is not available.

11. Check pump body and cover for wear. Replace either part if faces or bushes are worn.

Hydraulic pump, rebuild

1. Install new shaft seal in pump body with lip towards carrier pocket. Care should be taken to ensure that damage is not caused to lip of seal. Grease lip of new seal.

2. Replace cam lock peg in hole in pocket. Inspect cam for wear and replace if worn or damaged. Install in pocket with slot over retaining pin. Ensure that cam is seated on pocket face.

3. Insert the shaft from the seal side of the body, ensuring that there are no sharp edges on the shaft to cut the seal lip.

4. Replace carrier key in shaft.

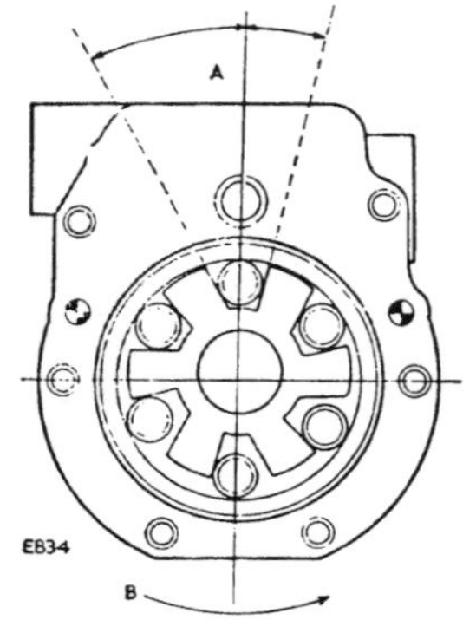

Installation of vane carrier
A—Greater angle in leading position
B—Direction of rotation

5. Inspect carrier and place in pocket, ensuring correct installation, that is correct face of slots driving rollers (see illustration). Replace snap ring.

6. Inspect rollers paying particular attention to the finish on the ends.

   Replace if scored, damaged or out of round.

7. Using a straight-edge across the cam surface, and feeler gauge, check end clearance of carrier and rollers in pump body. If end clearance exceeds .002 in. (0,05 mm) replace carrier and rollers.

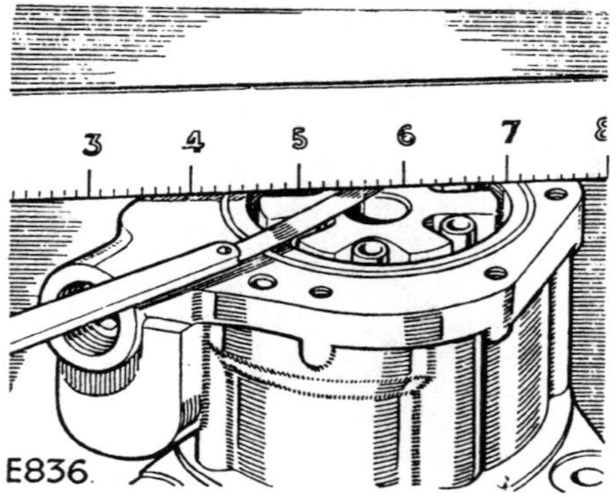

Checking clearance of carrier and roller in pump body

8. Replace flow control valve spring in bore; spring tension should be 8 to 9 lb (3,6 to 4,0 kg) at .820 in. (21 mm) long. If not, replace with new spring.

9. Replace valve in bore inserting valve so that exposed ball end enters last. Ensure that valve is not sticking.

10. Replace 'O' ring on valve cap and assemble in pump. Tighten cap to a torque of 30 to 35 lbs ft (4,0 to 4,9 mkg).

11. Install new 'O' rings in cover joint face.

Operation J1-7—*continued*

12. Insert thrust washer into bearing bore in pump cover.

13. Replace cover on pump body.

14. Secure cover with six cap screws, tighten evenly to a torque of 18 lbs ft (2,5 mkg). Check shaft for free rotation after tightening cap screws. There must be no bind.

15. Install new 'O' ring gasket in groove on to end of cover housing.

16. Replace adaptor and adaptor screw.

17. The plug in the top of cover housing is used purely for sealing purposes and if removed, care should be taken to ensure that an air-tight seal is obtained when plug is replaced.

Reservoir, remove and refit—Operation J1-8

Workshop hand tools:
Spanner sizes: $\frac{7}{16}$ in. AF, $\frac{1}{2}$ in. AF, 1 in. AF
Screwdriver; Bleed tube; Container

Special tools:

Reservoir, remove

1. Remove the reservoir filler cap, disconnect the return pipe from the steering box end cover, drain and discard the oil.

   Refit the return pipe to the steering box end cover.

2. Remove the fixings and withdraw the reservoir complete, then disconnect the flexible hoses. If the reservoir is not going to be replaced immediately, the pipes must be sealed to prevent ingress of dirt.

3. Remove the top cover and oil filter element.

Reservoir, refit

1. Reverse the removal procedure, fitting new oil filter element, ensuring correct fitting of ring seal.

2. Refill the system with the correct grade of lubricant (Section Y). Total capacity 4 pints (2 litres). Bleed the system as detailed in Operation J1-9.

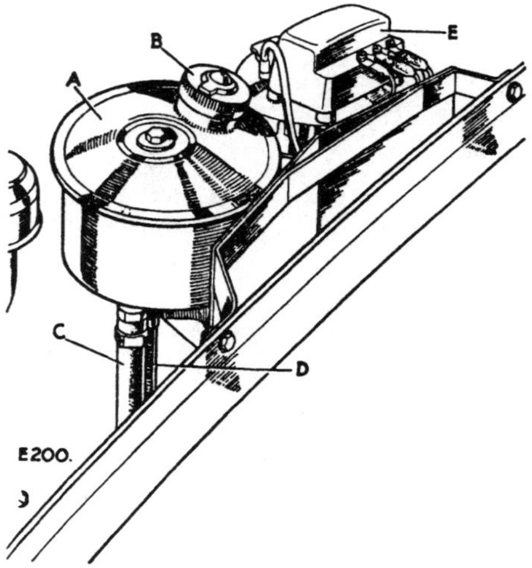

Power steering reservoir

A—Reservoir
B—Filler cap
C—Flexible pipe, reservoir to steering box
D—Flexible pipe, reservoir to pump
E—Screen washer

Refilling and bleeding the system—Operation J1-9

Workshop hand tools:
Spanner sizes: $\frac{7}{16}$ in. AF
Bleed tube; Container

Special tools:

Bleeding the system

1. Refill the steering oil reservoir to the top with the recommended oil. (Section Y) total capacity 4 pints (2 litres).

2. Start the engine and run at fast idle speed for one minute. It is important that the engine is not switched off until the steering box has been bled, as air trapped in the system can force fluid out through the reservoir filler.

3. Fit a rubber tube, which must be a tight fit, to the bleed screw on the steering box top cover. Insert the other end into a suitable container of not less than 4 pints (2 litres) capacity. Slacken the bleed screw, then turn the steering wheel from lock to lock until a steady stream of oil, free of air, is seen. Add more oil as necessary during this operation.

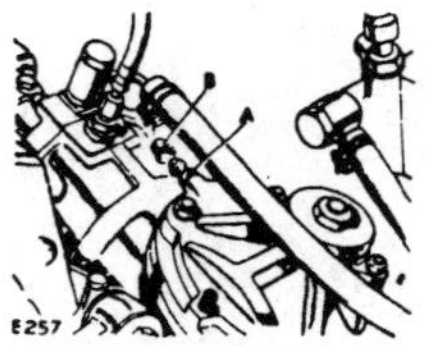

Bleeding the steering box

A—Bleed screw B—Dust cover

4. Tighten the bleed screw, and bring the oil level up to the 'full' mark on the reservoir dipstick, with the engine running. Remove the rubber tube and the container. Refit the dust cover to the bleed screw.

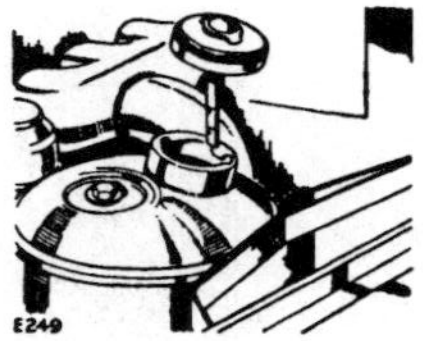

Oil filler and dipstick

5. Check all hose joints, and pump and steering box for oil leaks under pressure by holding the steering hard on full lock in both directions. Do not maintain this pressure for more than 30 seconds in any one minute, to avoid causing the oil to overheat and possible damage to the seals.

Dynamo belt tension, adjust—Operation J1-10

Workshop hand tools:
Spanner sizes: $\frac{7}{16}$ in. AF, $\frac{1}{2}$ in. AF
Screwdriver

Special tools:

Dynamo belt tension, adjust

1. Drain coolant and remove radiator block. Section A.
2. On early models remove air cleaner. Section A.
3. Slacken the pivot bolts securing the dynamo to the mounting bracket and slacken the adjusting bolt.
4. Pivot the dynamo inwards or outwards as necessary and adjust until the correct tension has been obtained, which is $\frac{5}{16}$ in. to $\frac{7}{16}$ in. (8 to 11 mm), by thumb pressure between dynamo and crankshaft pulleys. See point marked 'C' on illustration.
5. Tighten the dynamo adjusting bolt and the securing pivot bolts.

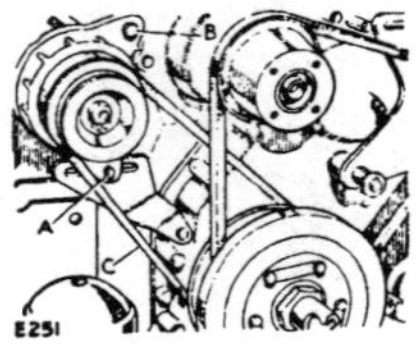

Dynamo belt adjustment
A—Adjusting bolt B—Pivot bolt
C—Check at this point— $\frac{5}{16}$ in. (8 mm) movement

6. On early models refit the air cleaner. Section A.
7. Refit the radiator block, Section A, refill with coolant, capacity 22½ pints (13 litres), run the engine and check for coolant leaks.

Fan belt tension, adjust—Operation J1-11

Workshop hand tools:
Spanner sizes: $\frac{1}{2}$ in. AF
Screwdriver; Circlip pliers

Special tools:

Fan belt tension, adjust

1. Drain off the coolant and remove the radiator block. Section A.
2. Slacken the two bolts securing the jockey pulley to the front cover.
3. Pivot the pulley assembly inwards or outwards as necessary and adjust until the correct tension is obtained, which is $\frac{5}{16}$ in. to $\frac{7}{16}$ in. (8 to 11 mm) by thumb pressure between jockey and fan pulleys.
4. Tighten the jockey pulley fixing bolts.
5. Refit the radiator block, Section A. Refill with coolant, capacity 22½ pints (13 litres), run the engine and check for coolant leaks.

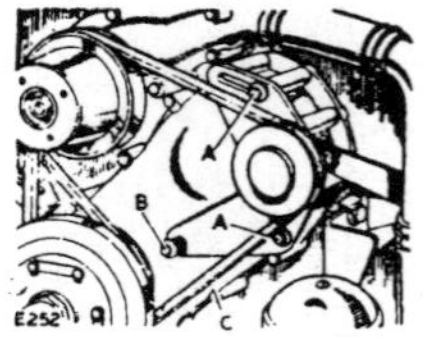

Fan belt adjustment
A—Securing bolt B—Pivot bolt
C—Check at this point— $\frac{5}{16}$ to $\frac{7}{16}$ in. (8 to 11 mm) movement

Jockey pulley, remove and refit—Operation J1-12

Workshop hand tools:
Spanner sizes: $\frac{1}{2}$ in. AF
Screwdriver; Circlip pliers

Special tools:

Jockey pulley, remove

1. Drain off the coolant and remove the radiator block. Section A.
2. Remove the fan belt by slackening the two bolts securing the jockey pulley assembly to the front cover and pivoting the pulley inwards.
3. Remove the two securing bolts, circlip, plain washer and coil spring from the pivot pin.

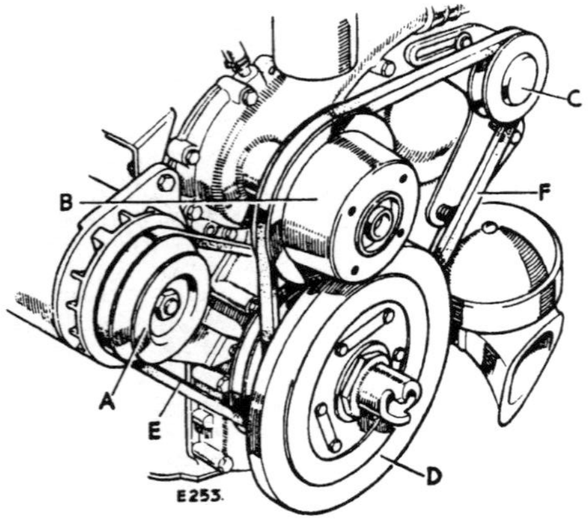

Layout of pulleys and driving belts
A—Dynamo pulley D—Vibration damper
B—Fan pulley E—Dynamo belt
C—Jockey pulley F—Fan belt

Jockey pulley, refit

1. Reverse removal procedure.
2. Adjust fan belt to correct tension. Operation J1-11.
3. Refit radiator block, Section A. Refill with coolant, capacity 22½ pints (13 litres), run the engine and check for coolant leaks.

Steering relay, remove and refit—Operation J1-13

Workshop hand tools:
Spanner sizes: $\frac{11}{16}$ in. AF
Hammer

Special tools:

Steering relay, remove

1. Remove the ball joints from the steering relay drop arm by smartly tapping the eye of the drop arm around each ball joint pin.

2. Remove the three mounting bolts and detach the relay unit from the sub-frame, noting that there is a spacing washer between relay and frame at each fixing bolt.

Steering relay, refit

1. Reverse removal procedure.

Steering relay, overhaul—Operation J1-14

Workshop hand tools:
Spanner sizes: $\frac{7}{16}$ in. AF, $\frac{11}{16}$ in. AF, $1\frac{3}{8}$ in. AF
Screwdriver; Hammer

Special tools:
Drop arm removal tool, Part No. 600446

See Operation J1-13 for steering relay removal

Steering relay, strip

1. Withdraw the retaining nut and washer and mark the drop arm lever in relation to the relay shaft and remove drop arm. The removal of the drop arm will be facilitated by the use of the special drop arm removal tool, Part No. 600446.

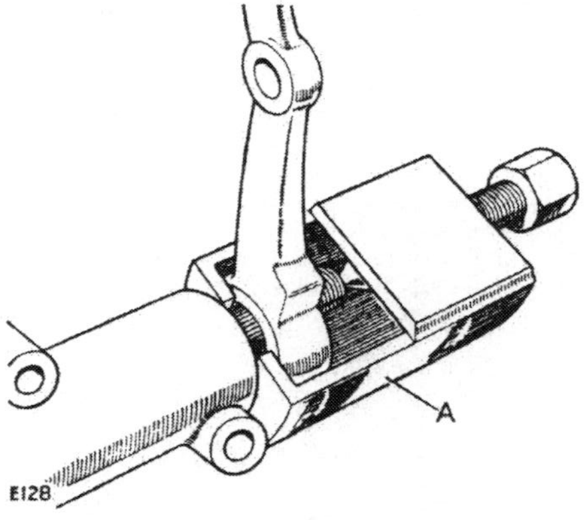

Drop arm removal tool
A—Withdrawal tool

2. Remove the top cover from the relay and preserve the shims and thrust washer.

3. Press the shaft out of the housing.

4. Remove the oil seal from the bore of the housing.

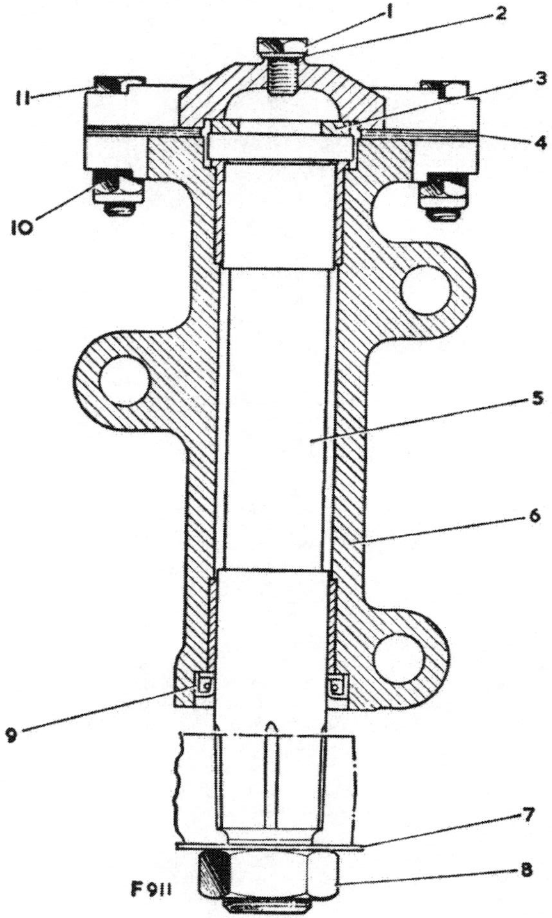

1	Oil filler plug	7	Lockwasher for shaft nut
2	Washer for plug	8	Nut for shaft
3	Thrust washer for shaft	9	Oil seal for shaft
4	Shims for top cover	10	Self-locking nut } Fixing top cover
5	Shaft	11	Bolt } Fixing top cover
6	Housing		

Operation J1-14—*continued*

Steering relay, rebuild

1. If renewed, the bushes should be a drive fit in the housing and the shaft must be a sliding fit in them when fitted.

2. Fit the oil seal with its open end inwards.

3. Reverse removal procedure.

4. Check the shaft end-float, which should be .001 to .006 in. (0,02 to 0,15 mm). Correct as necessary by the addition or removal of shims between the cap and the flange as illustrated.

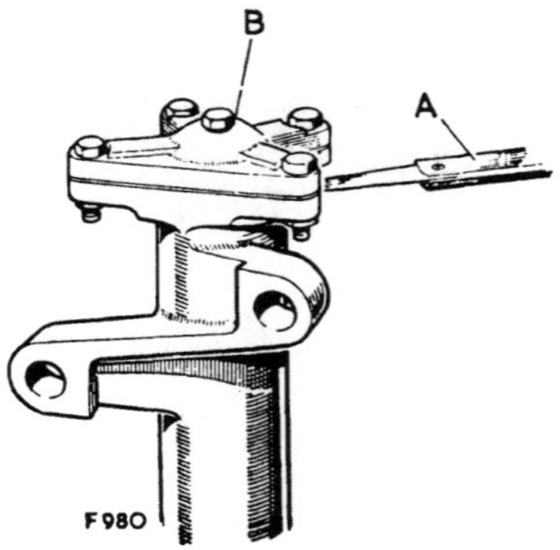

Measuring for shim dimension

A—Feeler gauge B—Cap

Steering relay, adjustment—Operation J1-15

Workshop hand tools:

Spanner sizes: $\frac{5}{16}$ in. AF, $\frac{11}{16}$ in. AF, $\frac{3}{4}$ in. AF, $\frac{7}{8}$ in. AF
Hammer; Pliers; Feeler gauge; Spirit level; Rule

Special tools:

Alignment equipment

Steering relay, adjust

1. Disconnect the steering links and track rod ball joints from the relay drop arm.

2. Check the end-float, which should be .001 to .006 in. (0,02 to 0,15 mm). Should a reading in excess of .006 in. (0,15 mm) be obtained, the unit should be removed and the end-float adjusted by suitable shims, inserted between the flange and cap, as detailed in Operation J1-14.

3. After checking the unit, refit the steering link and track rod ball joints to the relay drop arm. Check wheel alignment as detailed in Operation J1-18.

Steering column and bearings, remove and refit—Operation J1-16

Workshop hand tools:

Spanner sizes: 2 BA, $\frac{7}{16}$ in. AF, $\frac{1}{2}$ in. AF, $\frac{15}{16}$ in. AF
Allen key; Screwdriver

Special tools:

Steering column and bearings, remove

1. With the front road wheels in the straight-ahead position, slacken the three Allen screws in the steering wheel hub and remove the horn ring.

2. Unscrew the steering wheel securing nut and remove the steering wheel from the splined steering shaft, after noting its correct position.

3. Remove the four recessed screws in the side of the steering column shroud; remove the four small screws from the top support bracket, thereby releasing the shrouds.

4. Remove the beading strip from the top and carefully ease both shrouds away from the column.

5. When fitted, remove the Borg-Warner control, or the overdrive switch control from the steering column. Wherever possible avoid disturbing the mechanism of these controls.

6. The shroud fitted to the same side as the headlight and trafficator switch, can be detached by removing the two trafficator switch securing screws.

7. Mark one of the trafficator cancelling fingers in relation to the outer column, to ensure correct refitment.

8. Remove the pinch bolt securing steering shaft to the coupling on steering box.

9. On models with the single bearing shaft, clean off any surplus paint on the shaft and carefully withdraw the shaft into the car interior out of the outer column. Retain the special double coil spring washer.

10. Lever the bearing out of the outer column.

11. On models with the double bearing shaft, remove the clamp bracket securing outer column to support bracket, fitted to dash, then remove the support bracket from dash.

12. Loosen the clip securing rubber grommet to the bottom of outer column.

13. Temporarily replace the steering wheel and remove the outer column complete with shaft from the car.

14. With the outer column held securely in a suitable vice, remove the horn ring and horn button, flasher trip ring and the bottom adjustable clamp ring.

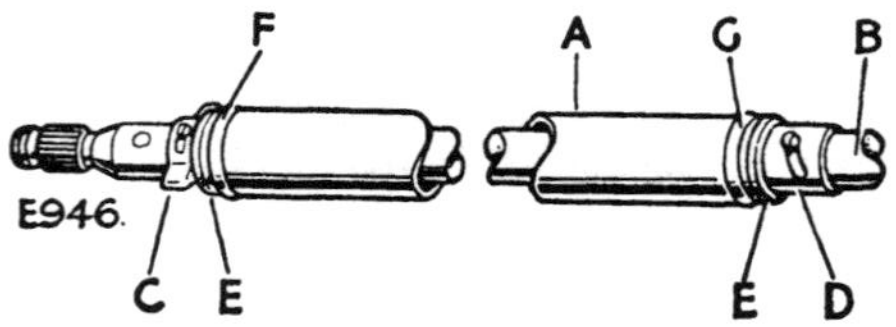

Outer column and steering shaft, assembled

A—Outer column
B—Shaft
C—Flasher trip ring
D—Adjusting ring
E—Spring
F—Bearing, top
G—Bearing, bottom

Steering column and bearings, refit

1. Carefully press in the new bearings first lightly lubricating them with grease.

2. On models with the double bearing shaft, refit by reversing the removal procedure ensuring that the coil springs are compressed so as to give a minimum amount of shaft up and down movement, but ensure that the shaft rotates freely.

3. On models with the single bearing shaft, slide the double coil spring washer on to the shaft and carefully insert the shaft into the top bearing and outer column. Align the marks made previously on the trafficator ring and outer column, and engage the lower end into the splines of the coupling flange.

4. Push the steering shaft downwards to load the double coil spring and fit and tighten the pinch bolt.

5. On all models complete the reassembly by reversing the removal procedure.

Operation J1-16—*continued*

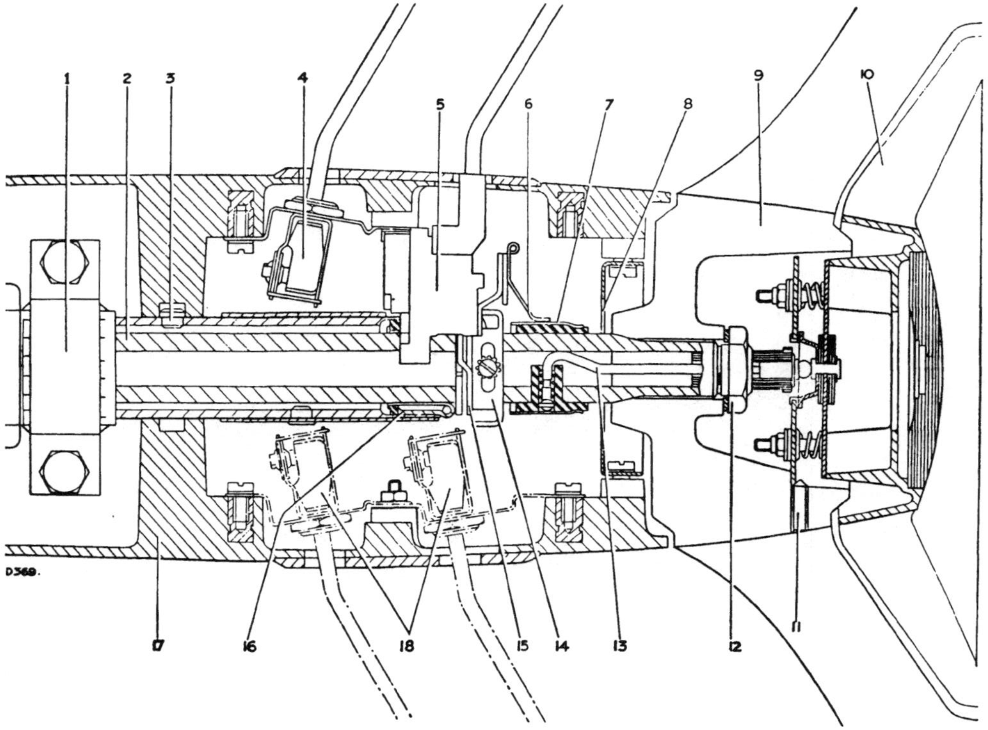

Cross-section of upper column

1 Clip for column
2 Steering column shaft
3 Dowel for shroud
4 Headlamp switch assembly
5 Trafficator switch
6 Horn contact arm
7 Horn slip ring assembly
8 Support bracket
9 Steering wheel
10 Horn ring assembly
11 Allen screw
12 Locknut for steering wheel
13 Horn contact cable
14 Flasher trip ring
15 Double coil spring washer
16 Bearing assembly
17 Shroud
18 Auxiliary switches

Steering linkage, remove and refit—Operation J1-17

Workshop hand tools:
Spanner sizes: $\frac{5}{16}$ in. AF, $\frac{11}{16}$ in. AF, $\frac{3}{4}$ in. AF, $\frac{7}{8}$ in. AF, 1 in. AF
Hammer; Pliers; Spirit level; Rule

Special tools:
Alignment equipment

Steering linkage, remove

1. The steering ball joints have been designed in such a way as to retain the initial filling of grease for the normal life of the ball joint; however this applies only if the rubber boot remains in position on the joint. The rubber boots should be checked every 3,000 miles (5.000 km) to ensure that they have not become dislodged or the joint damaged.

2. To replace the rubber boots or the ball joints complete, remove the ball end from the lever by tapping smartly around the eye of the pin.

3. Remove the rubber boot.

4. Thoroughly clean all parts.

5. Apply grease around the taper, and fill the rubber boot.

6. Place the castle nut upside down on the pin and screw on a few threads, then place the ball joint under a press or between the jaws of a vice and carefully force the pin and ball down against the spring. In this position the interior of the ball joint can be cleaned and lubricated.

Steering linkage, refit

1. Reassemble, using new rubber boots and spring rings.

2. When refitting track rod and ball joints to the drop arms, ensure that the ball joints are aligned with each other, in order to allow full unrestricted movement of steering linkage.

3. When refitting steering links, ensure that the ball joint body is parallel with respective steering arms, in order to allow full movement.

4. Adjust the alignment as detailed in Operation J1-18.

Operation J1-17—*continued*

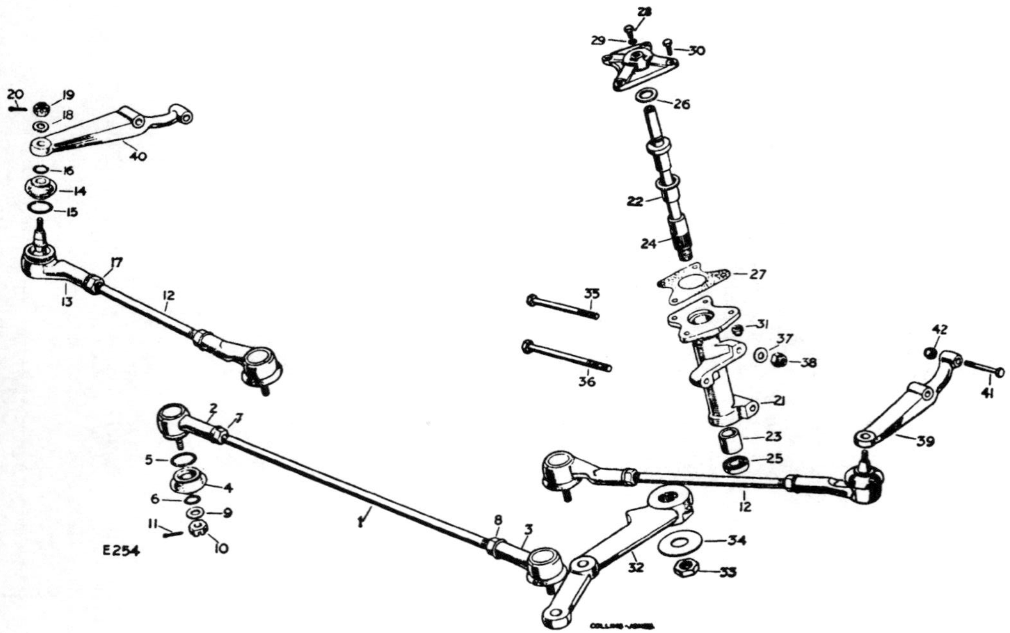

Layout of steering linkage

1	Track rod	21	Housing assembly for relay
2	Ball joint assembly, RH thread	22	Bush for housing, top
3	Ball joint assembly, LH thread	23	Bush for housing, bottom
4	Rubber cover	24	Shaft for relay
5	Spring ring	25	Oil seal
6	Spring ring	26	Thrust washer
7–8	Fixings, ball joints to track rod	27	Shims
9–11	Fixings, ball joints to drop arms	28–31	Fixings, relay top cap to body
12	Steering link	32	Drop arm
13	Ball joint assembly	33–34	Fixings for drop arm
14	Rubber cover for ball	35–38	Fixings, relay to sub-frame
15	Spring ring	39	Track rod lever, LH
16	Spring ring	40	Track rod lever, RH
17	Locknut	41–42	Fixings for track rod lever
18–20	Fixings, ball joints		

Wheel alignment, to set—Operation J1-18

Workshop hand tools:
Spanner sizes: $\frac{5}{16}$ in. AF, $\frac{3}{4}$ in. AF, $\frac{7}{8}$ in. AF
Spirit level; Rule

Special tools:
Alignment equipment

Wheel alignment, to set

1. All checking must be carried out on a flat floor with the wheels in the straight-ahead position.
2. The front suspension height must be set correctly as detailed in Section K.
3. Adjust the height of the body at the rear with a suitable jack until the body is exactly horizontal, which can be checked by using a spirit level placed on the flat surface of the door sill.
4. It is important only to check when the static height is correct, because a variation of 1 in. (25 mm) in the height at the front alters the camber and castor angles by approximately 1°.
5. The length of the track rod should be $24\frac{1}{4}\pm\frac{1}{4}$ in. (616,0$\pm$6,5 mm) which allows for adjustment of the front wheel toe-in. The track rod locknuts are left-hand and right-hand threaded. The wheel alignment is $\frac{1}{16}$ in. (1,5 mm) toe-in to $\frac{1}{16}$ in. (1,5 mm) toe-out.
6. The length of the steering links must be so adjusted that, when fitted with the front wheels in the straight-ahead position, and the toe-in correctly set, the turning circle on right- and left-hand lock is the same.
7. If the swivel pin inclination angle is suspected of being incorrect, the stub axle assembly should be dismantled and checked as follows:
8. Set up the stub axle with the swivel axis vertical.
9. This is found by placing alignment bars through the swivel eyelets.
10. Measure the angle to the vertical, from the flat face at the rear of the hub bearing track. This angle should read 6°.

DEFECT LOCATION

SYMPTOM	POSSIBLE CAUSE	REMEDY
A—LACK OF SELF-CENTRING	1. Insufficient rocker shaft end-float	1. *Adjust end-float*
B—EXCESSIVE LOOSENESS OR BACKLASH IN THE STEERING	1. Steering rocker shaft incorrectly adjusted 2. Steering linkage loose or worn 3. Suspension ball swivel joints worn 4. Loose or worn front wheel bearings 5. Steering box mounting bolts loose 6. Steering shaft flexible coupling loose	1. *Adjust* 2. *Check all ball joints for wear, renew as necessary* 3. *Renew* 4. *Rectify* 5. *Rectify* 6. *Rectify*
C—TIGHT STEERING	1. Low or unequal tyre pressures 2. Steering rocker shaft adjusted too tightly	1. *Rectify* 2. *Adjust end-float*
D—CAR PULLS TO ONE SIDE	1. Incorrect camber, castor or swivel pin inclination 2. Uneven or worn tyres and low pressures 3. Brakes binding 4. Top and bottom suspension ball swivels dry or tight 5. Tight or dry wheel bearings 6. Incorrect steering toe-in	1. *Check suspension, wheel alignment and torsion bar height* 2. *Rectify* 3. *Rectify* 4. *Renew as necessary* 5. *Inspect for damage, renew or lubricate as necessary* 6. *Adjust as detailed in Operation J1-18*
E—CAR WANDERS	1. Incorrect castor 2. Incorrect toe-in 3. Worn suspension ball swivels 4. Worn front wheel bearings 5. Tight steering 6. Unequal tyre pressures or worn tyres 7. Loose rear axle 'U' bolts 8. Damaged sub-frame	1. *Check for wear or damage to suspension* 2. *Adjust as detailed in Operation J1-18* 3. *Renew as necessary* 4. *Renew as necessary* 5. *Check steering box and relay adjustment Check ball joints* 6. *Rectify* 7. *Rectify* 8. *Examine for alignment and rectify as necessary*
F—LOW OR HIGH SPEED SHIMMY	1. Excessive castor 2. Worn steering ball joints 3. Loose wheel bearings 4. Wheels out of balance 5. Under-inflation or unequal inflation of front tyres 6. Loose engine or sub-frame mountings 7. Faulty front shock absorbers 8. Worn linkage 9. Loose or damaged flexible steering shaft coupling	1. *Check for wear or damage to suspension* 2. *Renew* 3. *Rectify* 4. *Rectify* 5. *Rectify* 6. *Rectify* 7. *Renew* 8. *Rectify* 9. *Renew*
G—ROCKER SHAFT PEG RATTLE	1. Excessive rocker shaft end-float	1. *Adjust end-float*

DATA

Steering unit type	Integral, power assisted, variable ratio
Ratios: (early box)	15.6:1 straight ahead. 10.2:1 full lock
(later box)	16:1 straight ahead. 11.3:1 full lock
Relay shaft end-float	.001 to .006 in. (0,02 to 0,15 mm)
Relay shaft, clearance in bushes	.003 to .004 in. (0,08 to 0,12 mm)
Wheel alignment	$\frac{1}{16}$ in. (1,5 mm) toe-in to $\frac{1}{16}$ in (1,4 mm) toe-out
Track, front	55 in. (1,4 m)
Tightening torque; steering box mounting bolts	50 lb/ft (7,0 mkg)
Static unladen geometry: See Section K	
Turning circle	38 ft 6 in. (11,7 m)
Steering wheel turns, lock to lock	3
Capacity of system	4 Imperial pints (2 litres)

Section K – FRONT SUSPENSION

Brief description of the front suspension

The independent front suspension is operated by ball jointed transverse wishbones, laminated torsion bars and anti-roll bars. Control is by hydraulic telescopic shock absorbers.

Early type swivel ball joints require lubrication attention, but on later models the ball joints and bearings are sealed against the ingress of dust and water and do not require attention in this respect.

Rubber bushes requiring no lubrication are also extensively used.

INDEX

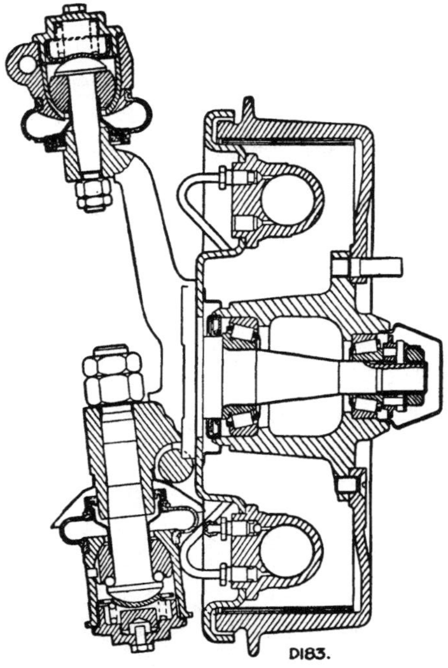

Cross-section of front suspension with drum type brakes

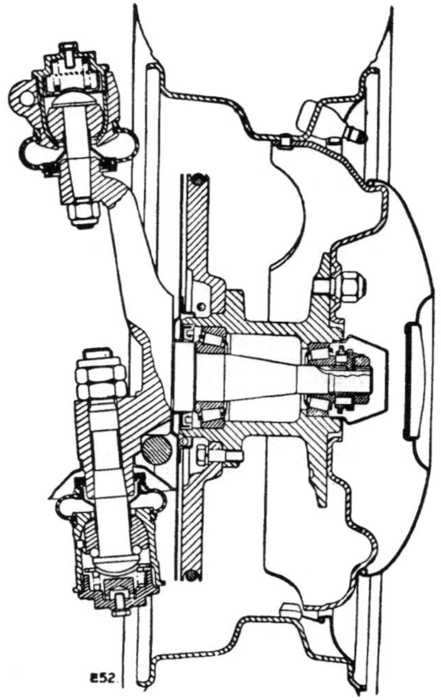

Cross-section of front suspension with disc brakes

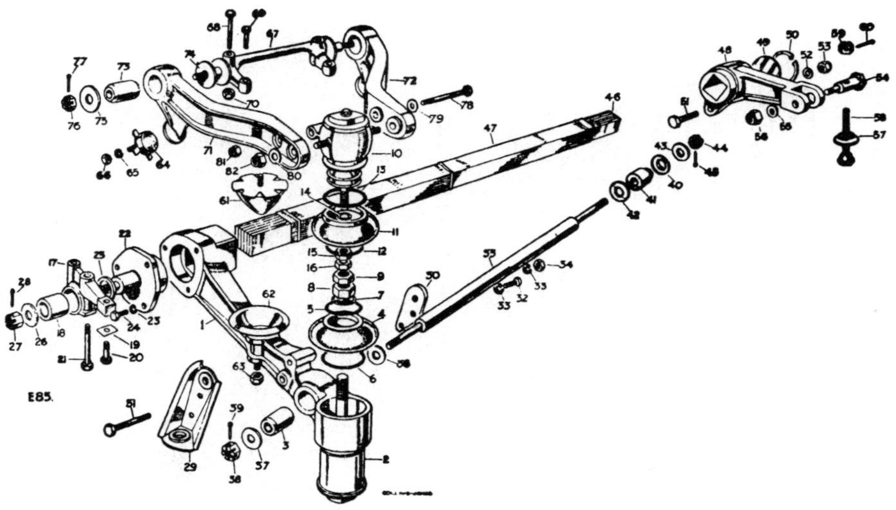

Layout of front suspension

1	Bottom link
2	Bottom ball swivel
3	Flexible bush for radius arm
4	Rubber boot for ball swivel
5	Retaining spring, small, for boot
6	Retaining spring, large, for boot
7	Joint washer
8	Securing nut
9	Special self-locking nut
10	Top ball swivel
11	Rubber boot for ball swivel
12	Retaining spring, small, for boot
13	Retaining spring, large, for boot
14	Joint washer
15	Nut
16	Self-locking nut
17	Link mounting pin housing
18	Flexible bush
19	Tab washer
20–21	Fixings, link mounting to sub-frame
22	Bottom link mounting pin
23–24	Fixings, pin to bottom link
25–28	Fixings, link mounting pin housing to mounting pin
29	Shock absorber and anti-roll bar bracket
30	Shock absorber mounting plate
31-34	Fixings, bracket to bottom link
35	Radius rod
36–39	Fixings, radius rod to bottom link
40–45	Fixings, radius rod to sub-frame
46	Torsion bar assembly
47	Grease sleeve for torsion bar
48	Torsion bar adjusting lever
49	Retaining plate
50	Circlip
51–53	Fixings, adjusting lever
54	Trunnion for adjusting lever
55–56	Fixings, trunnion to sub-frame
57	Adjusting lever bolt seat
58	Adjusting bolt for lever
59	Castle nut retaining adjusting pin
60	Split pin
61	Bump rubber, front
62	Bump stop for front spring
63	Self-locking nut fixing bump stop to bottom link
64	Rebound stop rubber
65–66	Fixings, rubber to sub-frame
67	Top link mounting arm
68–70	Fixings, mounting arm to sub-frame
71	Top link complete, front
72	Top link complete, rear
73	Bush for top link
74–77	Fixings, top link to mounting arm
78–82	Fixings, top link to swivel housing

Front hub, remove and refit—Operation K-1

Workshop hand tools:
Screwdriver
Spanner sizes: ¾ in. AF, 1⅛ in. AF

Special tools:
Front hub adjustment spanner, Part No. 263057
Bracket for dial test indicator, Part No. 530106
Dial test indicator

Front hub, remove

1. Jack up the car and place suitable stands under the forward jacking points. Remove the road wheel and prise off the hub cap.

Drum brake models, items 2 to 5

2. Remove the drum.
3. Release the lock washer and remove the outer nut (left-hand thread on the right-hand side and right-hand thread on the left-hand side).
4. Remove the key washer, inner nut and peg.
5. Remove hub.

Disc brake models, items 6 to 10

6. Remove brake pads, Section N, and prise up tab washers on caliper securing bolts; remove bolts and withdraw caliper.
7. Suspend the caliper with a suitable piece of wire to avoid damaging the brake hose.
8. Insert packing between the caliper pistons to prevent them becoming dislodged.
9. Release the lock washer and remove the outer nut (left-hand thread on the right-hand side and right-hand thread on the left-hand side). Remove the key washer, inner nut and peg.
10. Withdraw hub complete with disc.
11. If necessary remove the oil seal and roller bearings from the hub.

Front hub, refit

1. Replace the hub bearing outer races, which must be a press fit in the hub.
2. Drop the larger bearing into its outer member and press the oil seal into the hub with the lip towards the bearing. Pack the bearing lightly with grease.

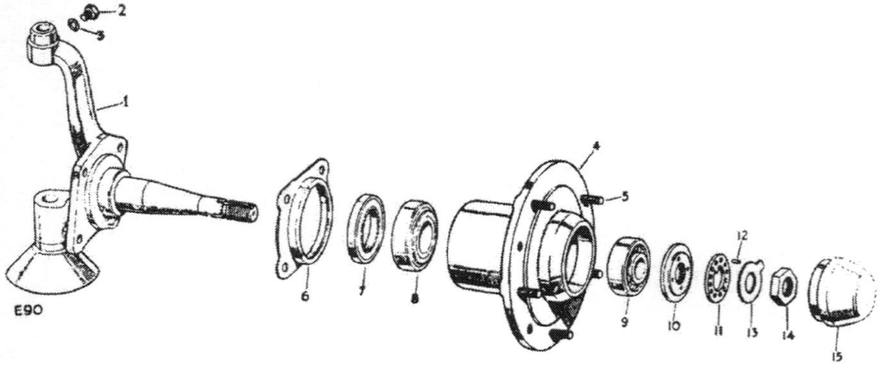

Layout of front hub

1 Stub axle assembly
2 Plug for stub axle oilway
3 Joint washer for plug
4 Front hub assembly
5 Stud for road wheel
6 Oil thrower ring for front hub
7 Oil seal for inner bearing
8 Bearing for hub, inner
9 Bearing for hub, outer
10 Inner nut
11 Key washer
12 Peg for key washer
13 Lock washer
14 Outer nut
15 Hub cap

Operation K-1—*continued*

3. When refitting the hub to a vehicle equipped with disc brakes a concentric ring of Prestik 5686 sealing compound must be applied between the shield and the axle face in order to prevent the possible ingress of water which may cause damage to the front wheel bearings.
4. Offer the hub to the stub axle and fit the smaller inner member of the outer race, also lightly greased.
5. Replace the inner nut and tighten with a special tool (Part Number 263057) to remove all end-float. Slacken off two holes and mount a dial test indicator and bracket (Part No. 530106) on a wheel stud, then check the end-float which should be .004 in. to .006 in. (0,1 to 0,15 mm).

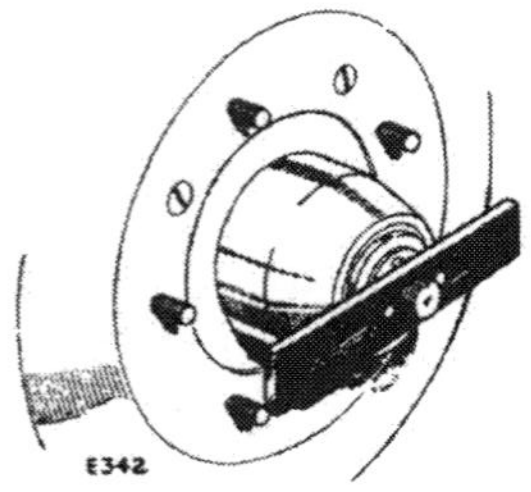

Hub adjustment

6. If necessary adjust the inner nut to allow the correct end-float, then lock the inner nut with the peg and key washer. Fit the locking tab washer and tighten the outer nut.
7. On disc brake models check disc radial run-out. See Section N.
8. Re-check the end-float and lock the outer nut with the tab washer if the reading is satisfactory, but should the reading be incorrect the outer nut must be removed together with the tab washer, peg and key-washer to allow re-adjustment of the inner nut. **The final reading must be taken with the outer nut fully tightened.**
9. Refit drum or caliper whichever appropriate.
10. Repack with grease. Refit hub cap and road wheel.

Measuring hub end-float

Torsion rod, remove and refit—Operation K-2

Workshop hand tools:
Spanner sizes: $\frac{1}{2}$ in. AF, $\frac{9}{16}$ in. AF

Torsion rod, remove

1. Jack up car and place suitable stands under forward jacking points. Remove road wheels.
2. Remove the rod link pins, distance tubes, rubbers, cup washers and nuts.
3. Remove the two support brackets and rubber bushes attached to chassis sub-frame.
4. Remove torsion rod.

Torsion rod, refit

1. Reverse removal procedure.

Shock absorbers, remove and refit—Operation K-3

Workshop hand tools:
Spanner sizes: $\frac{9}{16}$ in. AF, $\frac{5}{8}$ in. AF

Shock absorber, remove

1. Jack up car and remove road wheels.
2. Remove the bottom shock absorber mounting bolt and locknut and loosen the two mounting plate nuts and bolts.
3. Remove the top shock absorber mounting nuts, washers and rubbers.
4. Lift out the shock absorber, pulling clear at the bottom mounting first and then drawing the top of the shock absorber out of the top mounting.
5. The shock absorbers are not adjustable and cannot be dismantled; if trouble is experienced, a replacement shock absorber must be fitted.
Test the action of a shock absorber by holding it vertically in the normal working position; if tested horizontally, the ball valves do not function correctly, giving the effect of a faulty unit.

Shock absorber, refit

1. Fit new rubber bushes and reverse removal procedure.

Torsion bar, adjust—Operation K-4

Workshop hand tools: Rule.
Spanner sizes: $\frac{5}{16}$ in. AF, $\frac{3}{4}$ in. AF

Torsion bar, adjust

1. Place the car, unladen, on level ground.
2. Check the front tyres to see that they are evenly matched regarding tyre wear, and see that they are inflated to their correct pressure. Front and rear 26 lb/sq in. (1,8 kg/cm²).
3. Disconnect the shock absorbers then rock the car up and down at the front to allow the suspension to take up a static position.
4. Then check and note the dimensions at the following points, as illustrated:
   (a) Point 'A' from the base of the bottom suspension ball joint to the ground.
   (b) Point 'B' from centre line of bottom link mounting pin to the ground.

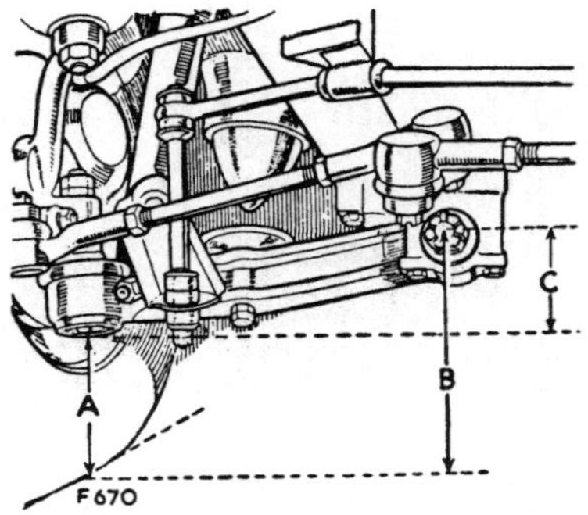

Checking car height

A—Base of ball joint to the ground
B—Centre line of bottom link mounting to the ground
C—Represents the difference between the dimensions obtained at 'A' and that at 'B'

5. Subtract the dimensions obtained at point 'A' from that obtained at point 'B' and the result should read:

Mk I and IA

Non-sealed ball joints $4\frac{5}{8}$ in. (117 mm).

Mk II

High suspension:
Non-sealed ball joints $4\frac{5}{8}$ in. (117 mm).
Sealed ball joints $3\frac{7}{8}$ in. (98 mm).

Low suspension:
Non-sealed ball joints $3\frac{5}{8}$ in. (92 mm).
Sealed ball joints $2\frac{7}{8}$ in. (73 mm).

Mk III

High suspension:
Sealed ball joints $3\frac{7}{8}$ in. (98 mm).
Low suspension:
Sealed ball joints $3\frac{3}{8}$ in. (85 mm).

6. If the correct reading is not obtained, then:
   (a) Slacken the adjuster lever trunnion self-locking nut.
   (b) Slacken adjuster lever clamping bolt.
   (c) By movement of the adjuster lever bolt, the torsion bar height may be altered.
   (d) After the adjustment has been made and the correct reading obtained, tighten fully the adjuster lever clamping bolt and the trunnion self-locking nut.

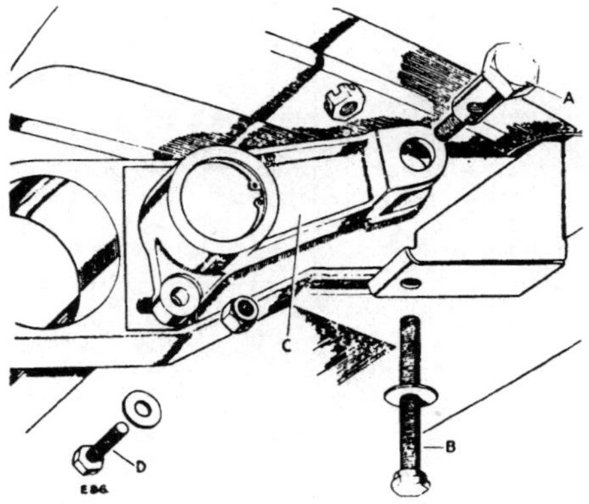

Arrangement of adjusting lever

A—Trunnion for adjusting lever
B—Adjusting bolt
C—Adjusting lever
D—Clamping bolt for adjusting lever

Torsion bar, remove and refit—Operation K-5

Workshop hand tools:

Soft faced hammer, Screwdriver

Spanner sizes: $\frac{1}{2}$ in. AF, $\frac{9}{16}$ in. AF, $\frac{5}{8}$ in. AF, $\frac{11}{16}$ in. AF, $\frac{3}{4}$ in. AF, $1\frac{1}{8}$ in. AF

Special tools:

Torque spanner

Front hub adjustment spanner, Part No. 263057

Dial gauge. Dial gauge bracket

Torsion bar, remove

Caution: It is most important that the torsion bar tension is completely relieved before attempting torsion bar removal. Failure to observe this may result in injury to the operator.

1. Jack up the front of the car and support on suitable stands at the front jacking points.
2. Remove the road wheels. Disconnect the steering arms from the steering links.
3. Disconnect the brake hoses.
4. **Drum brake models.** Remove brake drum.
5. **Disc brake models.** Remove calipers.
6. Remove torsion rod, Operation K-2.
7. Remove shock absorbers, lower mounting.
8. Detach radius rod from bottom link.

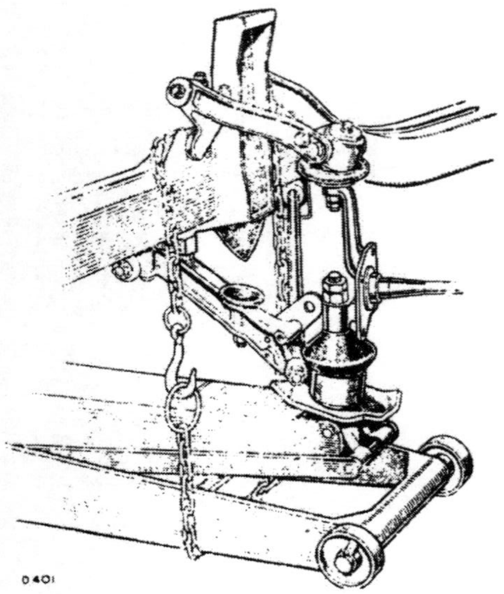

0401

Trolley jack chained to sub-frame

9. Place a trolley jack under the extreme outer end of the bottom link, with the jack at right angles to the car centre-line. If this operation is being carried out on a car with the engine removed or when the sub-frame is removed from the car, the trolley jack should be secured with chains to the sub-frame before attempting torsion bar removal. Raise the suspension until the car is about to lift off the stand under the jacking point.
10. Remove the locking nut from the lower ball swivel pin and slacken the securing nut approximately $\frac{1}{8}$ in. (0,3 mm).
11. Place two suitable hard wooden blocks between the top links and the rebound rubbers, then lower the jack in order to subject the lower ball swivel pin to torsion bar tension. Smartly tap the stub axle eye around the swivel to release the swivel pin from its taper.
12. Jack up slightly to relieve the load on the nut securing the swivel pin, remove the lower nut and carefully lower the suspension to its fullest extent, thereby relieving torsion bar tension.
13. Remove the bottom link mounting from the sub-frame.

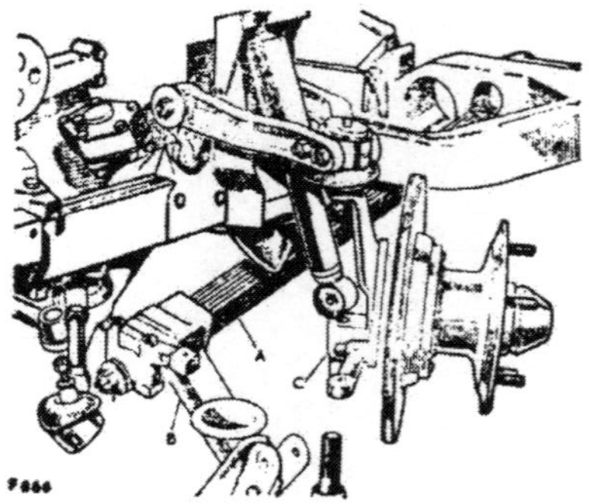

Withdrawing torsion bar, showing bar, bottom link and mounting

A—Torsion bar B—Lower link C—Stub axle

Operation K-5—*continued*

14. Remove the torsion bar from the rear adjustment point and lower bar out complete with bottom link.
15. Do not disturb the order of the torsion bar leaves. Any rearrangement of the leaves will affect the characteristics of the torsion bar.

Torsion bar, refit

It is important that the torsion bars are fitted to their respective sides, because of the 'set' of the spring leaves. When fitting new torsion bars the right-hand side bar is identified with red paint, the left-hand bar has no identification mark; ensure that each is fitted to the correct side.

1. With new torsion bars fit the grease sleeve using the recommended grade of lubricant (Section Y) to fill the sleeves before fastening.
2. Refit radius rod to bottom link.
3. Refit the torsion bar complete with bottom link to rear adjustment point.
4. Secure the bottom link mounting to the sub-frame.
5. Place a trolley jack under the extreme outer end of the bottom link; if the engine has been removed from the car or the sub-frame is removed the trolley jack should be secured to the sub-frame with a suitable chain. Raise the bottom link, at the same time guiding the lower arm of the stub axle on to the lower ball joint swivel pin, taking care to prevent damaging the threads. Fit a new steel nut and self-locking nut and tighten both nuts to 75-80 lb/ft (10,0-11,0 mkg).

   On early models two identical plain steel nuts were used on the lower ball swivel pin. On later models a steel nut and self-locking nut is used.

   This modification may be carried out to earlier cars.
6. Refit shock absorbers, lower mounting.
7. Refit torsion rod. Operation K-2.
8. **Drum brake models.** Refit brake drum.
9. **Disc brake models.** Refit caliper.
10. Connect the brake hoses. Bleed and adjust the brakes. (Section N.)
11. Connect the steering arm to the steering links; check wheel alignment and adjust, if necessary. (Section J.)
12. Check the tightness of all suspension points and adjust the height of the torsion bar in accordance with Operation K-4.

Top and bottom links, remove and refit—Operation K-6

Workshop hand tools:

Soft faced hammer, Pliers, Screwdriver

Spanner sizes: $\frac{1}{2}$ in. AF, $\frac{9}{16}$ in. AF, $\frac{5}{8}$ in. AF, $\frac{11}{16}$ in. AF, $\frac{3}{4}$ in. AF, $\frac{15}{16}$ in. AF, $1\frac{1}{8}$ in. AF

Special tools:

Torque spanner
Front hub adjustment spanner, Part No. 263057
Dial gauge
Dial gauge bracket

Top and bottom links, remove

1. Remove from hub, Operation K-1.
2. Remove torsion rod, Operation K-2.
3. Remove shock absorbers, Operation K-3.
4. Remove torsion bar, Operation K-5.
5. Remove torsion bar from bottom link assembly.
6. Remove split pin, castle nut and washer and withdraw bottom link mounting pin and housing from bottom link.
7. Detach the top ball swivel joint and stub axle from the top links.
8. Remove the top link mounting arm bolts and remove the top links, noting the fitting sequence of the plain washers. It is recommended that the top links are identified in some way, to assist in the rebuild of the suspension.

Top and bottom links, refit

1. Fit new bushes to:
   (a) Top links;
   (b) Bottom links;
   (c) Bottom link pin housings.
2. Reverse the removal procedure.

Top ball swivel rubber boot, remove and refit—Operation K-7

Workshop hand tools:

Soft faced hammer

Spanner sizes: $\frac{7}{16}$ in. AF, $\frac{9}{16}$ in. AF, $\frac{11}{16}$ in. AF

Special tools:

Ball swivel rubber boot replacing tool, Part No. 511041. Torque spanner

Top ball swivel rubber boot, remove

The rubber boots around the ball swivels should be checked every 3,000 miles (5.000 km) to ensure that they have not been damaged or dislodged. If replacement is necessary, proceed as follows:

1. Jack up and support the car on suitable stands at the front jacking points. Remove the road wheels.
2. Place a trolley jack at right angles to the car centre-line, and jack up under the extreme outer end of the bottom link.
3. Remove the bolt fixing the top ball swivel to the top links and slacken the two self-locking nuts of the ball swivel.
4. Remove the locknut and slacken the self-locking nut of the top ball swivel pin approximately $\frac{1}{8}$ in. (4 mm).
5. Place suitable wooden blocks between the top links and the rebound rubbers, to hold the top links up.
6. Lower the jack slightly, to subject the top swivel pin taper to torsion bar tension and tap smartly around the upper eye of the stub axle. This will release the eye from the pin, and the nut will prevent damage to the threads of the swivel pin.
7. Jack up again sufficiently to relieve the pressure on the nut and remove the nut. Lift the top links and ball swivel clear of the stub axle eye.
8. Prevent the hub assembly from straining outwards.
9. Turn the ball swivel through 180° and remove the rubber boot and spring rings.

Top ball swivel rubber boot, refit

1. Fit new spring rings and rubber boots to the ball swivel, using special tool, Part No. 511041.

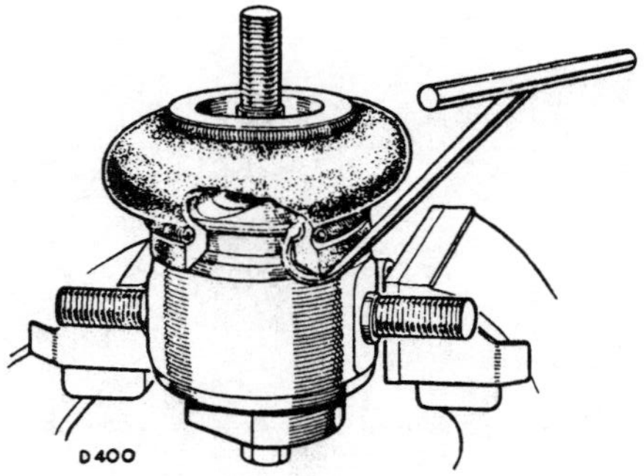

Refitting rubber boot with special tool

2. Jack up bottom link slightly and guide the swivel pin into the upper eye of the stub axle.
3. Fit the swivel pin self-locking nut and tighten to 45 lb/ft (6,2 mkg), fit the bolt and nut fixing the top links to ball swivel, also tighten the two self-locking nuts securing the top links to ball swivel joint.
4. Lower and remove the trolley jack.
5. On models provided with a lubrication point, refill with correct lubricant as detailed in Operation K-9. On the sealed type swivel no lubrication is required.
6 Refit the road wheels and remove the jacking stands from beneath the car.

Bottom ball swivel rubber boot, remove and refit—Operation K-8

Workshop hand tools:

Soft faced hammer

Spanner sizes: $\frac{1}{2}$ in. AF, $\frac{7}{16}$ in. AF, $\frac{9}{16}$ in. AF, $\frac{5}{8}$ in. AF, $\frac{11}{16}$ in. AF, $1\frac{1}{8}$ in. AF

Special tools:

Ball swivel rubber boot replacing tool, Part No 511041

Torque spanner

Bottom ball swivel rubber boot, remove

The rubber boots round the ball swivels should be checked every 3,000 miles (5.000 km) to ensure that they have not been damaged or dislodged. If replacement is necessary, proceed as follows:

1. Jack up and support the car on suitable stands at the front jacking points. Remove the road wheels.
2. Disconnect the steering link from the steering arm and with the jack under the bottom link and suitable blocks between the top links and rebound rubbers, remove the locknut from the lower swivel pin.
3. Slacken the securing nut of the lower swivel pin approximately $\frac{1}{8}$ in. (4 mm), lower the jack slightly and tap smartly around the lower eye of the stub axle. This will release the swivel pin from the eye and the bottom link can be jacked up again slightly to release the securing nut.
4. Remove the shock absorber lower mounting bolt, torsion rod, and shock absorber mounting bracket.
5. Lower the bottom link carefully a short distance and lift the stub, and hub assembly off the lower swivel pin.
6. To hold the hub assembly out of the way in order to remove the joint rubber, place thick wooden blocks between the top links and rebound rubbers, and swivel the hub to the rear.
7. Remove the old spring rings and the rubber boot.

Bottom ball swivel rubber boot, refit

1. Fit new spring rings and rubber boots to the ball swivel, using special tool, Part No. 511041.
2. Lift the hub assembly on to the lower ball swivel pin, fit a new securing nut and self-locking nut, tighten both nuts to 75-80 lb/ft (10,0-11,0 mkg)
3. Refit the shock absorber and torsion rod mounting bracket and secure lower shock absorber mounting.
4. Re-connect the torsion rod to the mounting bracket and connect the steering link to the steering arm.
5. Lower and remove the trolley jack
6. On models provided with a lubrication point refill with correct lubricant as detailed in Operation K-9. On the sealed type swivel no lubrication is required.
7. Refit the road wheels and remove the jacking stands from beneath the car.
8. Check steering alignment and adjust, if necessary. (Section J.)

Ball swivel joints, lubricate—Operation K-9

Workshop hand tools:

Spanner size: $\frac{7}{16}$ in. AF

Ball swivel joints, lubricate

On models suffix 'C' onwards and Mk III the ball swivels are of the pre-packed sealed type and require no lubrication. The earlier type of joint requires the oil level topping up every 12,000 miles (20,000 km) as follows:

1. Jack up the front of the car and remove the road wheels. Unless the ball swivels are filled with the suspension on the rebound, overfilling can result, and the oil will be pumped out from under the rubber boot.

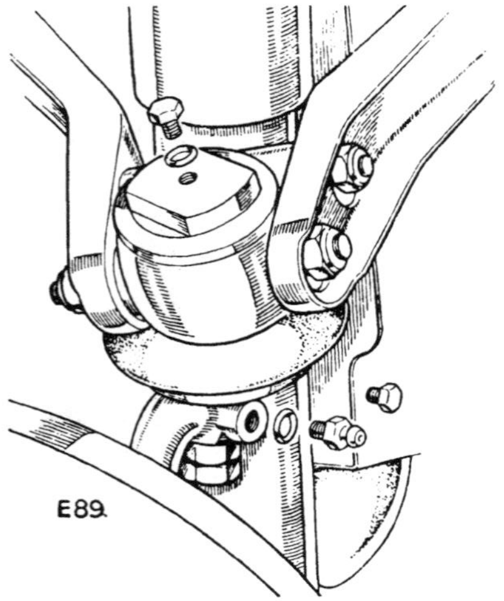

Plugs for upper ball swivel

2. Remove the two plugs in the ball swivel. Screw in a $\frac{1}{4}$ in. UNF straight grease nipple into the lower hole of the top ball swivel, and a $\frac{1}{4}$ in. UNF cranked grease nipple into the lower hole of the bottom ball swivel. The upper plug on the right-hand side of car faces forward and on the left-hand side of car faces to the rear.
3. With a hand oil gun filled with one of the recommended lubricants (Section Y), pump oil in steadily until it is seen to seep from the top hole.
4. Refit the top plugs of each swivel, remove the grease nipples and refit the lower plugs.

Under no circumstances must a pressure gun be used for filling the ball swivels, because of possible damage to the rubber boot.

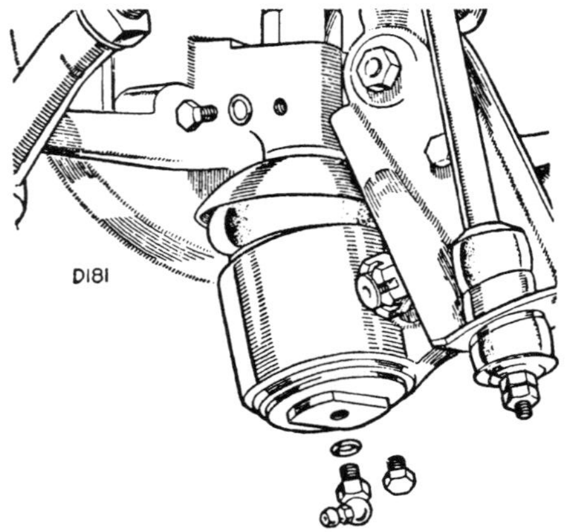

Plugs for lower ball swivel

Ball swivels, remove and refit—Operation K-10

Workshop hand tools:
Soft faced hammer, Screwdriver
Spanner sizes: $\frac{1}{2}$ in. AF, $\frac{7}{16}$ in. AF, $\frac{9}{16}$ in. AF, $\frac{5}{8}$ in. AF, $\frac{11}{16}$ in. AF, $\frac{3}{4}$ in. AF, $1\frac{1}{8}$ in. AF

Special tools:
Torque Spanner, Front hub adjustment spanner, Part No. 263057, Dial gauge, Dial gauge bracket, Ball swivel rubber boot replacing tool, Part No. 511041, Press

Ball swivels, remove

1. Remove front hub, Operation K-1.
2. Remove torsion rod, Operation K-2.
3. Remove shock absorbers, Operation K-3.
4. Remove torsion bar, Operation K-5.
5. Remove torsion bar from bottom link assembly.
6. To remove the lower ball swivel joint from the bottom link for renewal purposes, remove the rubber boot and spring rings.
7. Place the bottom link under a suitable press and carefully remove the housing from the bottom link eye. Care must be taken to prevent damaging the bottom link during this operation.
8. To remove the top ball swivel joint for renewal purposes detach the swivel joint and stub axle together from the top links.
9. Remove the securing nut and withdraw the stub axle from the swivel pin taper.

Ball swivels, refit

1. Fit a new rubber boot and spring rings to the top ball swivel joint; fit the ball swivel joint to the top arm of the stub axle, securing it with a new self-locking nut, and tighten to 75-80 lb/ft 10,0-11,0 mkg).
2. Fit the top ball swivel joint and stub axle assembly to the outer end of the top links.
3. Press the lower ball swivel joint into the large eye of the bottom link from the lower face, ensuring location by aligning the 'flat' on the outer diameter of the ball swivel joint with the shoulder on the lower side of the bottom link eye. Take care to prevent damage to the ball swivel joint oil seal when pressing into the link eye. Fit the new rubber cover and spring rings to the ball swivel joint.
4. To reassemble front suspension reverse the removal procedure.

Radius rod, remove and refit—Operation K-11

Workshop hand tools:
Soft faced hammer. Screwdriver
Spanner sizes: $\frac{1}{2}$ in. AF, $\frac{9}{16}$ in. AF, $\frac{5}{8}$ in. AF, $\frac{11}{16}$ in. AF, $\frac{3}{4}$ in. AF, $1\frac{1}{8}$ in. AF

Special tools:
Torque Spanner. Front hub adjustment spanner, Part No. 263057. Dial gauge.
Dial gauge bracket

Radius rod, remove

1. Remove front hub, Operation K-1.
2. Remove torsion rod, Operation K-2.
3. Remove shock absorbers, Operation K-3.
4. Remove torsion bar, Operation K-5.
5. Remove split pin, castle nut and washer and withdraw radius rod from sub-frame.

Radius rod, refit

1. Re-bush radius rod at both sub-frame and bottom link mounting points.
2. Reverse removal procedure.

DEFECT LOCATION

SYMPTOM	POSSIBLE CAUSE	REMEDY
A—CAR PULLS TO ONE SIDE	1. Incorrect camber 2. Incorrect or unequal castor 3. Uneven tyre pressure or worn tyre 4. Brakes binding 5. Top and bottom suspension ball swivels dry or tight 6. Tight or dry front wheel bearings 7. Incorrect front wheel alignment	1. *Check for worn bushes or damage to front suspension. Check torsion bar height* 2. *Check front wheel alignment and angles* 3. *Rectify as necessary* 4. *Rectify as necessary* 5. *Renew as necessary* 6. *Inspect for damage, renew or lubricate as necessary* 7. *Adjust to 1/16 in. (1,5 mm) toe-in to 1/16 in. (1,5 mm) toe-out*
B—CAR WANDERS	1. Incorrect castor 2. Incorrect front wheel alignment 3. Worn top or bottom suspension ball swivels 4. Worn front wheel bearings 5. Tight steering 6. Damaged sub-frame 7. Loose rear axle 'U' bolts 8. Unequal tyre pressures 9. Worn tyres	1. *Check for wear or damage to suspension* 2. *Reset to 1/16 in. (1,5 mm) toe-in to 1/16 in. (1,5 mm) toe-out* 3. *Renew as necessary* 4. *Renew as necessary* 5. *Rectify* 6. *Examine for alignment, and rectify as necessary* 7. *Rectify* 8. *Rectify* 9. *Renew*
C—LOW SPEED SHIMMY	1. Excessive castor 2. Worn top or bottom suspension ball swivels 3. Loose steering 4. Loose wheel bearings 5. Worn steering ball joints 6. Wheels out of balance 7. Worn front tyres	1. *Check for wear or damage to suspension* 2. *Renew as necessary* 3. *Rectify, with reference to appropriate steering section* 4. *Rectify* 5. *Renew* 6. *Rectify* 7. *Renew*
D—HIGH SPEED SHIMMY	1. Eccentric wheels and tyres 2. Wheels out of balance 3. Under-inflation of front tyres 4. Unequal inflation of front tyres 5. Loose engine mountings 6. Faulty shock absorbers 7. Worn or loose front wheel bearings 8. Loose sub-frame mountings	1. *Check for buckled or bent wheels and damaged outer covers. Rectify as necessary* 2. *Rectify* 3. *Rectify* 4. *Rectify* 5. *Check rubber mountings for damage, renew or tighten as necessary* 6. *Renew as necessary* 7. *Rectify as necessary* 8. *Rectify*
E—WHEEL TRAMP	1. Unequal tyre pressures 2. Unbalanced wheels or tyres 3. Faulty front shock absorber	1. *Rectify* 2. *Rectify* 3. *Renew*
F—EXCESSIVE TYRE WEAR	1. Incorrect camber 2. Incorrect wheel alignment 3. Incorrect tyre inflation 4. Fast cornering 5. Wheel wobble 6. Worn suspension ball swivel joints 7. Harsh or unequal braking 8. Failure to change wheel and tyre positions	1. *Check for worn bushes or damage to front suspension. Check torsion bar height* 2. *Reset to 1/16 in. (1,5 mm) toe-in to 1/16 in. (1,5 mm) toe-out* 3. *Rectify* 4. *Fast cornering will cause a scuffing action on the tyres, resulting in rapid wear* 5. *Check the wheel and outer cover for damage. Rectify as necessary* 6. *Renew as necessary* 7. *Rectify as necessary* 8. *Rectify*
G—FRONT END NOISY	1. Looseness in front suspension 2. Front shock absorbers noisy 3. Worn shock absorber rubber bushes	1. *Check all nuts and bolts, check rubber mountings for wear and renew as necessary. Check wheel alignment* 2. *Renew as necessary* 3. *Renew as necessary*

DATA

Front suspension	Laminated square section torsion bar
Hydraulic dampers	Telescopic anti-aeration non-adjustable
Front wheel alignment	1/16 in. (1,5 mm) toe-in to 1/16 in. (1,5 mm) toe-out

	Mk I and IA Saloon *Mk II Export Saloon*	*Mk II Saloon and Coupé*	*Mk III Saloon and Coupé*
Castor angle	1° negative	¼° positive	¼° negative
Camber angle	2°	1½°	1¾°
Swivel pin inclination	4°	4½°	4½°

Static unladen position as detailed in Operation K-4

For setting wheel alignment and steering angles see Section J

Front suspension height

Mk I and Mk IA
- Non-sealed ball joints .. .. 4⅝ in. (117 mm)

Mk II
- High suspension
  - Non-sealed ball joints .. .. 4⅝ in. (117 mm)
  - Sealed ball joints .. .. 3⅞ in. (98 mm)
- Low suspension
  - Non-sealed ball joints .. .. 3⅝ in. (92 mm)
  - Sealed ball joints .. .. 2⅞ in. (73 mm)

Mk III
- High suspension
  - Sealed ball joints .. .. 3⅞ in. (98 mm)
- Low suspension
  - Sealed ball joints .. .. 3⅜ in. (85 mm)

Hub end-float	.004 to .006 in. (0,10 to 0,15 mm)
Torsion bar identification	Right-hand side marked with red paint
Lubrication, ball swivels	Top up every 12,000 miles (20.000 km)
Tightening torques	
Nut for upper ball swivel	45 lb/ft (6,2 mkg)
Nut for lower ball swivel	75 to 80 lb/ft (10,0 to 11,0 mkg)

Mk II and Mk III Saloon and Coupé models with export suspension are identified by the letter 'H' stamped adjacent to the word 'ROVER' on the car serial number plate attached to the left-hand 'A' post.

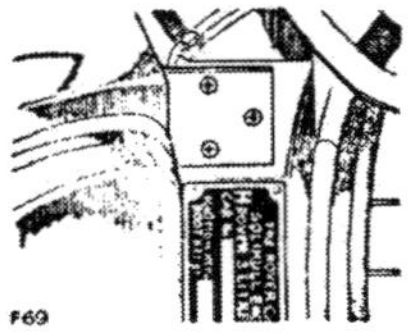

F69

Location of identification letter on cars fitted with high suspension

Section L – REAR SUSPENSION

Brief description of rear suspension

The rear suspension arrangement utilises semi-elliptic leaf springs of progressive rate. Attached at the front by eccentric rubber-bushed bearings and at the rear by rubber cushion shackles requiring no maintenance.

The springs are enclosed by grease gaiters. Control is by hydraulic telescopic shock absorbers.

INDEX

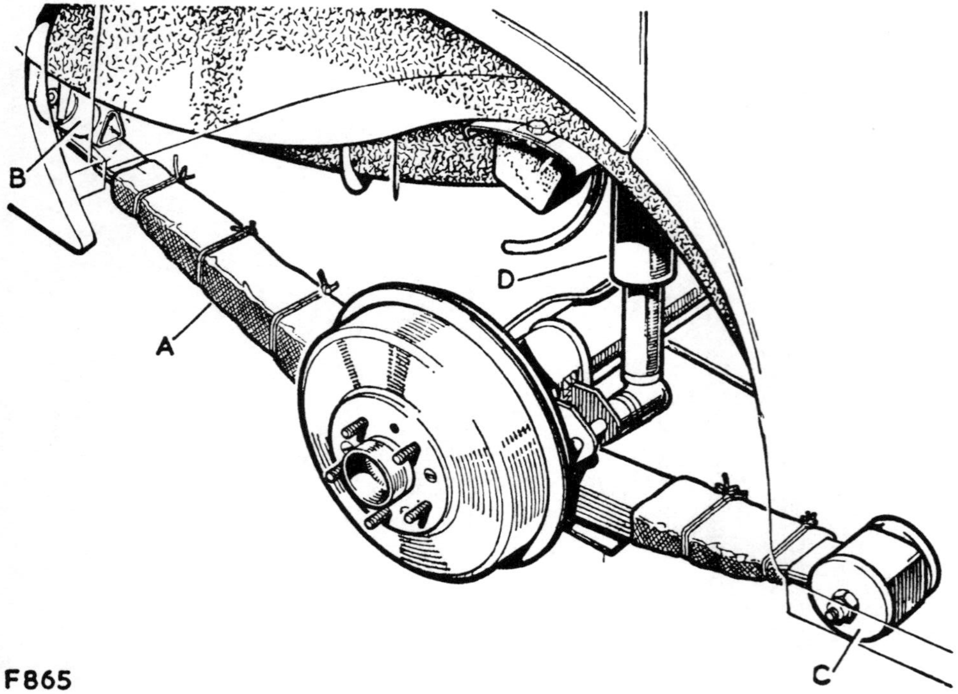

F865

Rear suspension layout

A—Spring
B—Rear spring mounting
C—Front spring mounting
D—Telescopic shock absorber

Rear spring, remove and refit—Operation L-1

Workshop hand tools:
Spanner sizes: $\frac{9}{16}$ in. AF, $\frac{11}{16}$ in. AF, $\frac{7}{8}$ in. AF

Rear spring, remove

1. Jack up the car under the differential housing and place axle stands under the rear jacking points. Lower the car sufficiently to rest on the stands.
2. Remove the road wheels.
3. With the axle assembly supported by the jack in order to keep the spring under tension, remove the self-locking nuts from the front shackle bolt and the rear rubber mountings.

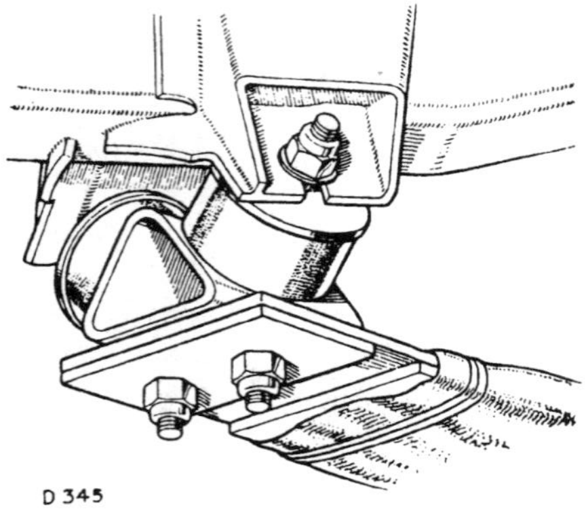

D 345

Rear road spring, rear mounting

4. Detach the shock absorber from the lower mounting.
5. With a suitable bar inserted into the rear rubber mounting spring bracket, lever the mounting studs clear of the body bracket.
6. Lower the jack sufficiently to relax the spring, taking care to prevent stretching the brake flexible hose. Place supports under the axle.
7. Remove the 'U' bolt locknuts, securing nuts and base plate, then lower the rear end of the spring to the ground and remove the wedge, where fitted.
8. Drift out the front shackle bolt and lift the spring away.

Rear spring, refit

1. Offer the rear spring front shackle into position, fit the shackle bolt with one distance washer either side, located inside the front anchor bracket. Fit the self-locking nut but do not tighten at this stage.
2. Lift the spring to the axle and fit the wedge, where used, 'U' bolts, and base plate. Do not tighten at this stage.
3. Jack the axle up slightly, at the same time using a suitable bar, lever the rear rubber mounting studs into the slots of the rear spring hanger bracket.
4. Ensure that the studs are correctly fitted, then replace flat washers and nuts, but do not tighten at this stage.
5. Refit the shock absorber to the lower mounting. Refit the road wheels.
6. Continue to jack up the car and remove the axle stands from the jacking points, then lower the car on to the road wheels.
7. In this position tighten the spring front shackle bolt self-locking nut and the rear mounting securing nuts. Tighten the 'U' bolt securing nuts, and fit the locknuts.

Grease gaiters, remove and refit—Operation L-2

Workshop hand tools:
Spanner sizes: $\frac{9}{16}$ in. AF, $\frac{11}{16}$ in. AF, $\frac{7}{8}$ in. AF

Grease gaiters, remove

1. Remove road spring (Operation L-1).
2. Untie the gaiter and withdraw from spring.

Grease gaiters, refit

1. Re-pack with correct grade of lubricant (Section Y).
2. Refit gaiter to spring and tie in place.
3. Apply a suitable adhesive between the ends of the gaiter and the springs.
4. Refit road spring (Operation L-1).

Rear spring, overhaul—Operation L-3

Workshop hand tools:
Spanner sizes: $\frac{9}{16}$ in. AF, $\frac{11}{16}$ in. AF, $\frac{7}{8}$ in. AF

Rear spring, overhaul

1. Remove rear spring (Operation L-1).
2. The main leaf only is supplied as a replacement, so that the complete spring must be renewed if any other leaf is broken.
3. To remove the main leaf, remove the grease gaiter (Operation L-2), then carefully heat the tags of the spring clips until they can be bent upwards and the link removed. Open the clips, and remove the spring centre bolt. Remove the main leaf.
4. Fit a new main leaf and re-assemble the spring. Refit the spring gaiter (Operation L-2).
5. In the event of a new shackle bush being fitted it must be a drive fit. Ensure it is correctly aligned, as illustrated.
6. If necessary, renew rubber mountings.

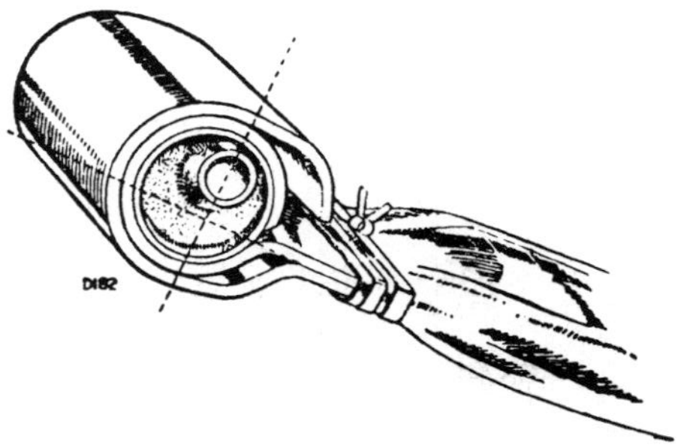

Position of spring shackle bush

Shock absorbers, remove and refit—Operation L-4

Workshop hand tools:
Screwdrivers. Spanner sizes: $\frac{7}{16}$ in. AF, $\frac{9}{16}$ in. AF, $\frac{11}{16}$ in. AF

Shock absorbers, remove

The shock absorbers are of the non-adjustable type and cannot be dismantled. If trouble is experienced, a replacement unit should be fitted.

1. To remove the shock absorbers it is necessary to release the back panel of the boot trim, in order to remove the four rear seat backrest fixings, which are located just above the petrol tank.
2. Remove the rear seat, backrest and felt packing.
3. Remove the drive screws securing the two shock absorber access panels, and remove the shock absorber top fixings.
4. Remove the lower mounting nut and bolt and withdraw the shock absorber unit.

To test the action of the shock absorbers, check the movement in a vertical position. If tested horizontally the valves will not function correctly, giving the effect of a faulty unit.

Shock absorbers, refit

1. Fit new rubbers and washers to top and bottom fixings.
2. Reverse the removal procedure.

DATA

Overall length (fitted)	50 in. (1270,0 mm)
Number of leaves	8 including auxiliary
Width of leaves	3 in. (76,2 mm)
Thickness of leaves:	
Main	.218 in. (7,8 mm);
Remainder	.171 in. (4,3 mm);
Auxiliary Mk I, IA, II high suspension	.468 in. (11,8 mm);
Auxiliary Mk II Saloon and Coupé	.406 in. (10,3 mm).
Bore of spring eye	1.836 in. + .010 (45,7 mm + 0,254)

Section M—REAR AXLE

Brief description of rear axle

The rear axle is of conventional semi-floating design with the final drive taken through spiral bevel gearing.

On models fitted with a four-speed gearbox and overdrive the final drive ratio is 4.3:1, on Mk I, Mk IA and Mk II models with automatic transmission the ratio is 3.9:1, and on Mk III models with automatic transmission it is 3.54:1.

The capacity of the differential is 3 pints, 3.5 US pints or 1.75 litres.

INDEX

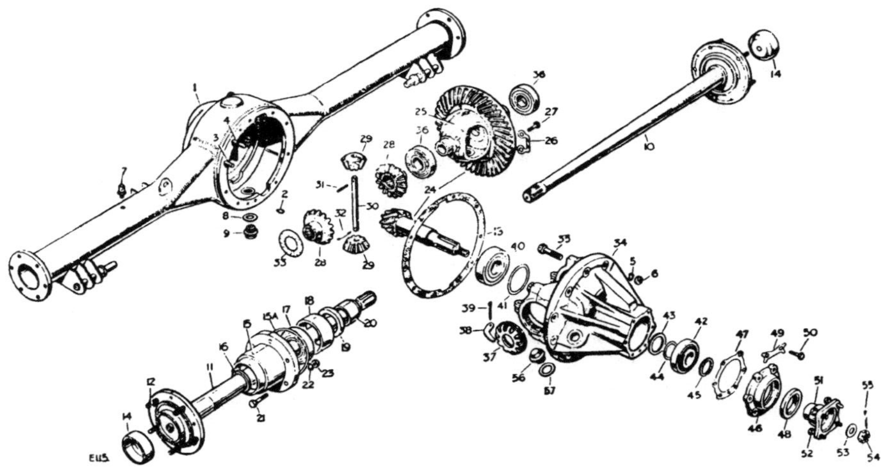

Layout of rear axle

1	Axle casing
2	Dowel locating differential
3–6	Fixings, differential to axle
7	Breather
8–9	Oil drain plug
10–11	Axle shafts
12	Stud for road wheel
13	Joint washer for differential
14	Extension piece for wheel changing
15	Housing for hub bearing
15A	'O' ring for bearing housing
16	Distance washer
17	Bearing for hub
18	Sleeve for oil seal
19	Oil seal for hub
20	Retaining collar
21–23	Fixings, for bearing housing
24	Crownwheel and bevel pinion
25	Differential casing
26–27	Fixings for crownwheel
28	Differential wheel
29	Differential pinion
30	Spindle for pinion
31–32	Fixings for spindle
33	Thrust washer for differential
34	Bevel pinion housing
35	Bolt fixing bearing cap
36	Roller bearings for differential
37	Serrated nut } For bearing adjustment
38	Lock tab } For bearing adjustment
39	Split pin } For bearing adjustment
40	Rear bearing for bevel pinion
41	Shim for pinion position
42	Front bearing for bevel pinion
43	Washer
44	Shim for bearing pre-load
45	Distance washer
46	Retainer for oil seal
47	Joint washer for retainer
48	Oil seal for pinion
49–50	Fixings for retainer
51	Driving flange
52	Driving bolt
53–55	Fixings for driving flange
56–57	Oil level filler plug

Rear axle complete, remove and refit—Operation M-1

Workshop hand tools:

Screwdriver, Pliers, Bleed Tube, Glass Container
Spanner sizes: $\frac{7}{16}$ in. AF, $\frac{1}{2}$ in. AF, $\frac{9}{16}$ in. AF, $\frac{5}{8}$ in. AF, $\frac{11}{16}$ in. AF

Rear axle complete, remove

1. Jack up the car, support at rear jacking points and remove the road wheels. Drain the oil.
2. Disconnect the rear propeller shaft from the differential driving flange.
3. Depress the brake pedal, wedging in position to avoid wastage of brake fluid, and disconnect the flexible brake pipe to the axle.
4. Disconnect the rear hand brake longitudinal rod, relay-to-compensator.
5. Disconnect the shock absorbers at the lower mounting.
6. Remove the spring rear mounting nuts and flat washers securing the rubber mountings to the body brackets. place a jack under the axle and raise slightly. With a suitable lever guide the rubber mounting studs out of the bracket slots, then lower the axle and springs.
7. Support springs and remove 'U' bolt locknuts and securing nuts. Remove wedges and, where fitted, withdraw the axle assembly to the rear.

Rear axle complete, refit

1. To refit rear axle reverse the removal procedure.
2. Bleed the brake system, Section N, and check hand brake adjustment.
3. Refill the axle with the correct grade of lubricant, Section Y, capacity 3 Imperial pints, 3.5 US pints (1,75 litres).

Axle shaft, remove and refit—Operation M-2

Workshop hand tools:

Screwdriver, Pliers, Bleed Tube, Glass Container
Spanner sizes: $\frac{7}{16}$ in. AF, $\frac{1}{2}$ in. AF, $\frac{9}{16}$ in. AF

Axle shaft, remove

1. Jack up the rear of the car and drain off the axle oil.
2. Remove the road wheel and brake drum, depress the brake pedal and wedge in position to prevent wastage of brake fluid.
3. Disconnect the brake pipe from the brake wheel cylinder and the brake cross-rod from the draw link.
4. Remove the six bolts securing the bearing housing to the axle casing and withdraw the axle shaft complete with brake anchor plate. Remove the rubber 'O' ring, fitted to late models.

Axle shaft, refit

1. To refit axle shaft reverse the removal procedure.
2. Bleed the brake system, Section N, and check hand brake adjustment.
3. Refill the axle with the correct grade of lubricant, Section Y, capacity 3 Imperial pints, 3.5 US pints (1,75 litres).

Hub assembly, remove and refit—Operation M-3

Workshop hand tools:

Screwdriver, Pliers, File small, Bleed Tube, Glass Container

Spanner sizes: $\frac{7}{16}$ in. AF, $\frac{1}{2}$ in. AF, $\frac{9}{16}$ in. AF

Special tools:

Axle shaft retaining collar tool, Part No. 275870
Adaptor 514576

Hub assembly, remove

1. Remove axle shaft, Operation M-2.
2. Remove brake components from anchor plate.
3. The hub components are retained by a collar pressed tightly on to the axle shaft, which must be removed by using special tool, Part No. 275870 and adaptor 514576.
4. Place the extractor body of special tool 275870 in a vice, tightening the vice jaws on to the pads provided for this purpose.

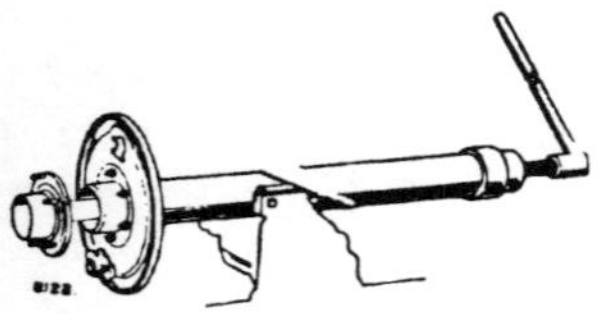

Stripping rear axle shaft

5. Fit the short adaptor over the splined end of the axle shaft and then insert the axle shaft into the tool. Secure the bearing housing to the tool flange by six bolts and nuts. Fit the spanner and turn in a clockwise direction, this will press the axle shaft out of the bearing housing.

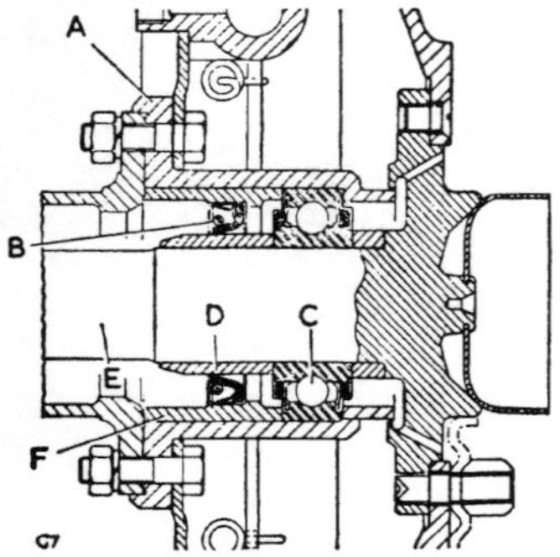

Cross-section of rear hub, early models

A—Bearing housing
B—Oil seal
C—Rearing
D—Retaining collar
E—Axle shaft
F—Sleeve for oil seal

6. Remove the felt seal, if fitted, then press the bearing and sleeve from the housing and press the oil seal from the sleeve.

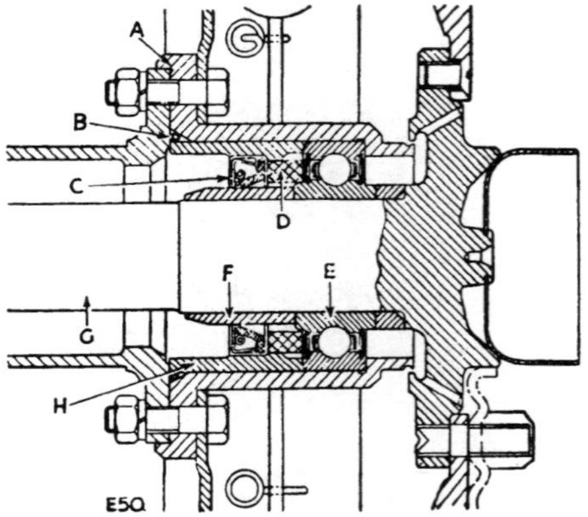

Cross-section of rear hub, late models

A—Bearing housing
B—'O' ring
C—Oil seal
D—Felt seal
E—Bearing
F—Retaining collar
G—Axle shaft
H—Sleeve for oil seal

7. The bearing, which is packed with grease on assembly, must be renewed if it shows signs of a leak.
8. The wheel studs, which are threaded into the axle flange, can be removed after the peened-over end has been filed away. Late models have serrated studs which can be drifted from the axle flange.
9. Ensure that the three drillings in the shaft flange are not blocked, and check axle breather for obstruction.

Hub assembly, refit

1. Press the bearing into the housing until it abuts the shoulder.
2. Place the distance washer on the axle shaft with the chamfered inner diameter toward the shoulder, position the brake anchor plate on to the housing and place them on to the shaft.

Operation M-3—*continued*

3. Position a new retaining collar on the shaft and press it on by use of special tool, Part No. 275870. With the tool acting as a ram use the weight of the extractor to drive the retaining collar home as follows:
4. Support the shaft assembly on a suitable hard wooden block.

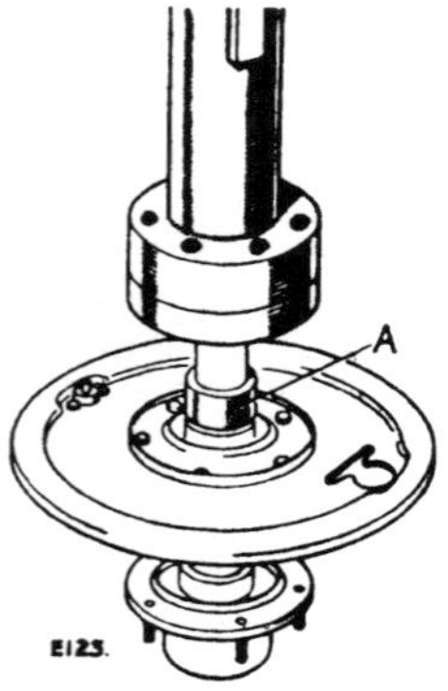

Assembling rear axle shaft

A—Collar

5. Fit the adaptor plate, Part No. 514576 to the extractor body with the boss towards the retaining collar.
6. Lift the extractor tool with adaptor fitted on to the axle shaft, as illustrated, ensuring that the screw is fully clear of the axle shaft. Then, using the weight of the tool, ram the retaining collar fully home. During this operation ensure that the brake anchor plate is not nipped between the hub and axle shaft.
7. Press the oil seal into the sleeve up to the shoulder, so that the lip of the oil seal is towards the axle shaft splines.
8. Late models. Fit a new felt ring to the bearing side of the oil seal fitted to the sleeve.
9. Place a smear of grease on the bearing side of the seal before fitting sleeve, then press the sleeve unit into the housing.
10. Refit the brake components to the brake anchor plate.
11. Refit axle shaft, Operation M-2.
12. Bleed the brake system, Section N, and check hand brake adjustment.
13. Refill the axle with the correct grade of lubricant, Section Y, capacity 3 Imperial pints, 3.5 US pints (1,75 litres).

Hub bearing housing, modify—Operation M-4

Workshop hand tools:

Screwdriver, Pliers, File small, Bleed tube, Glass container

Spanner sizes: $\frac{7}{16}$ in. AF, $\frac{1}{2}$ in. AF, $\frac{9}{16}$ in. AF

Special tools:

Axle shaft retaining collar tool, Part No. 275870
Adaptor 514576

The hub assembly must be removed as detailed in Operation M-3 prior to carrying out this operation

Hub bearing housing, modify

Early type bearing housings may be modified as detailed below, to incorporate a rubber 'O' ring and felt seal, to prevent any tendency towards oil seepage. Proceed as follows:

1. Remove axle shaft, Operation M-2.
2. Remove hub assembly, Operation M-3.
3. If the modification is being carried out to rectify oil seepage, the original bearing should be renewed.
4. Machine the hub bearing housing to the dimensions shown in the illustration. The 30° taper machining should be to a high standard, to ensure a smooth finish.
5. Refit hub assembly, Operation M-3.
6. Refit axle shaft, Operation M-2.
7. Refill the axle with the correct grade of lubricant, Section Y, capacity 3 Imperial pints, 3.5 US pints (1,75 litres).

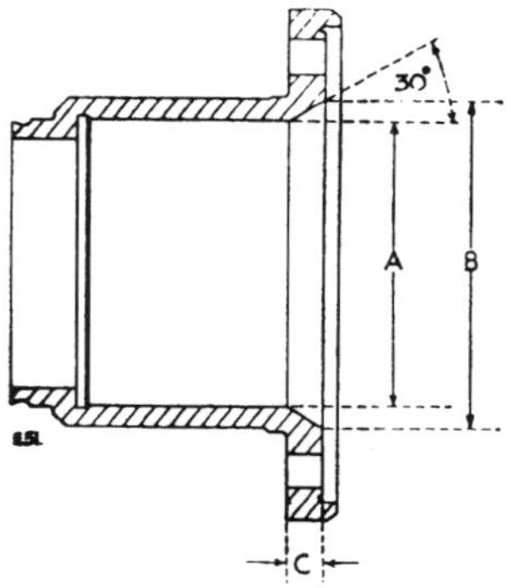

Bearing housing machining details

A—3.1494 in. +.001 (79,98 mm +0,025)
B—3.437 in. +.016 (87,29 mm +0,40)
C—.375 in. +.008 (9,5 mm +0,20)

Differential, remove and refit—Operation M-5

Workshop hand tools:

Screwdriver, Pliers, Bleed tube, Glass container

Spanner sizes: $\frac{7}{16}$ in. AF, $\frac{1}{2}$ in. AF, $\frac{9}{16}$ in. AF, $\frac{5}{8}$ in. AF

Differential, remove

1. Partly withdraw both axle shafts, Operation M-2.
2. Disconnect the rear propeller shaft from the differential driving flange.
3. Remove the nuts and spring washers and lift out the differential assembly.

Differential, refit

1. To refit differential, reverse the removal procedure.
2. Refill the axle with the correct grade of lubricant, Section Y, capacity 3 Imperial pints, 3.5 US pints (1,75 litres).

Differential, overhaul—Operation M-6

Workshop hand tools:

Screwdriver, Pliers, Chisel, Hammer, Drift, Feeler gauge, File small, Bleed tube, Glass container.

Spanner sizes: $\frac{5}{16}$ in. Whit, $\frac{3}{8}$ in. Whit, $\frac{7}{16}$ in. AF, $\frac{1}{2}$ in. AF, $\frac{9}{16}$ in. AF, $\frac{5}{8}$ in. AF, 1 in. AF

Special tools:

Spanner, Part No. 530105;
Extractor, Part No. 262757;
Gauge, Part No. 262761 or 600299;
Press block, Part No. 262758;
Tool for pinion pre-load, Part No. 600968;
Bracket, Part No. 530106;
Torque wrench;
Dial test indicator

The differential unit must be removed as detailed in Operation M-5 prior to carrying out this operation

Differential, strip

1. Withdraw the bolts and remove the differential bearing caps, marking them so that they may be assembled in the same position.
2. Remove the serrated adjusting nuts.
3. Lift out the differential assembly. If the differential bearings are not to be replaced, keep the outer races separate so that they may be assembled to the original inner races.
4. Remove the set bolts and lockers securing the crownwheel and take off the crownwheel. Note the position of the two shouldered fitting bolts which are located diametrically opposite to each other.
5. Extract the split pin and tap out the differential wheel spindle.
6. Take out the differential wheels and pinions, together with the thrust washers.
7. Remove the differential bearings. If a drawing tool is not available, carefully tap off the bearing with a chisel inserted between the casing and bearing.

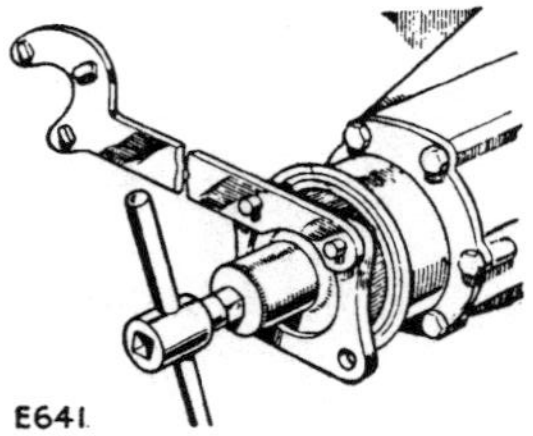

Removing pinion nut using special tool

8. Remove the pinion driving flange, using special tool, Part No. 530105, followed by the pinion oil seal retainer and joint washer. On late models there is also a brass joint washer.

The washer has a flat on its inner diameter which forms an oil reservoir, thus increasing lubrication of bearing; it is located between the pinion housing and the oil seal housing and is assembled using Hylomar sealing compound SQ 32M on both sides.

Differential units fitted with the latest joint washer can be identified by the protruding tags on the washer.

These joint washers may be used on earlier vehicles.

9. Take out the pinion and large inner race from the rear of the casing, and the distance washer and small inner race from the front.

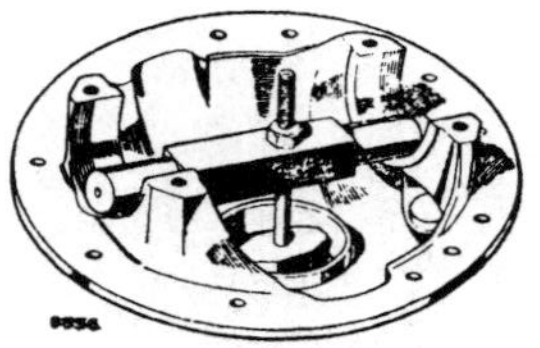

Removing pinion rear bearing outer member using special tool

10. Remove the shims from the pinion and press off the rear inner race. Later type differential units will have two thrust washers, one either side of the shims.
11. Press out the pinion bearing outer members. A special tool, Part No. 262757 will be required for the rear member.
Retain the shims which will be free when the member is removed.

Operation M-6—*continued*

Differential, rebuild

The crownwheel and pinion are lapped together when manufactured and are supplied, and must only be fitted, in pairs.

1. Smear a new oil seal with Molytone 'C' and fit it into the retainer with the seal lip towards the rear. Use a jointing compound between seal and casing. Retainer and seal should now be put to one side until pinion pre-load has been checked.
2. Press the outer members of the pinion bearing into the casing.

   A press block, Part No. 262758 will be required for tne rear member.

   Do not replace the larger shims at this stage.

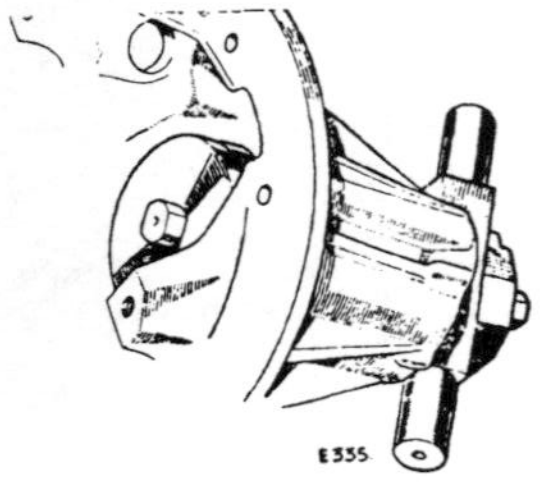

Replacing pinion rear bearing outer member

3. Press the larger pinion bearing on to the pinion until it abuts the shoulder.
4. Place a number of the small shims on the pinion, place the pinion in position and secure temporarily with the front bearing, distance washer, driving flange, plain washer and nut. Later types must have a thrust washer either side of the small shims. Do not fit the oil seal at this stage.
5. When the driving flange nut is tightened to 85 lb/ft (11,75 mkg), using a torque wrench, the effort required to turn the pinion should be 9 to 14 in./lb (0,10 to 0,16 mkg). Check as follows:
6. Hold the casing in a vice and bolt special tool. Part No. 600968, to the driving flange.

   Slide the weight along the bar until the pinion turns; the weight should then be between 9 and 14 in. (23 and 35 cm) from the centre of the pinion.

   Increase the pre-loading, when below 9 in./lb (23 cm), by removing shims, and reduce the pre-loading, when above 14 in./lb (35 cm), by increasing the number of shims.
7. When the loading of the pinion is correct, measure the distance between the axis of the crownwheel and the end face of the pinion.

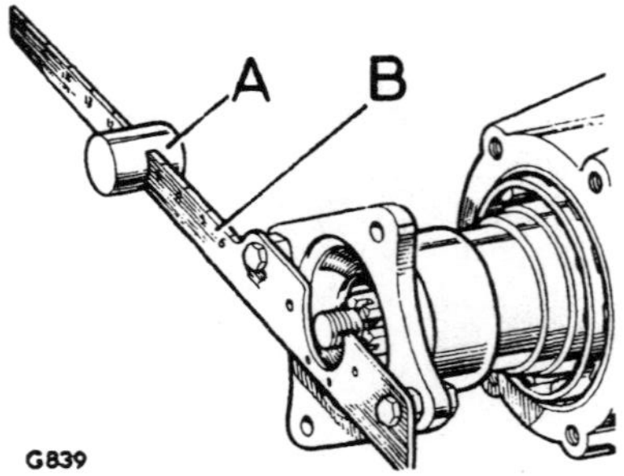

Measuring pinion bearing pre-load

A—Weight B—Bar

This dimension, 3.000 to 3.002 in. (76,2 to 76,25 mm), can only be checked with gauge, Part No. 262761 or 600299, measuring the amount the pinion must be raised.

When gauge, Part No. 262761 is used, that is with a round gauge, it is necessary to use a .002 In. (0,05 mm) feeler gauge.

Operation M-6—*continued*

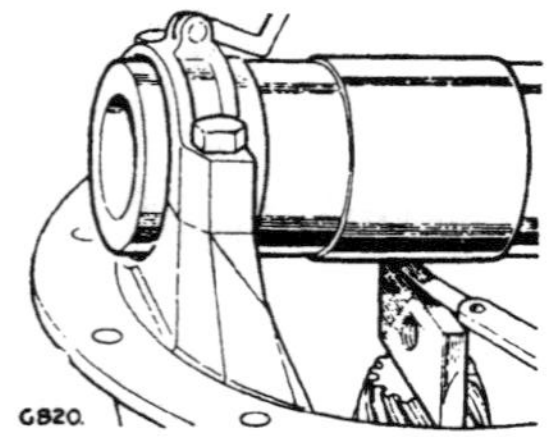

Checking pinion height, using flat slip gauge

8. When gauge, Part No. 600299 is used, that is with a flat slip gauge as illustrated, it is necessary to use a .003 in. (0,07 mm) feeler gauge.
9. Shims, marked B in the illustration, amounting to the thickness measured above must now be placed under the rear bearing outer member, and the same amount must be added to the smaller ones previously fitted, marked A in the illustration. Both large and small shims are available .003 in., .005 in., .010 in. and .020 in. (0,076, 0,127, 0,254 and 0,50 mm) thick.
10. Re-check the torque at the pinion.
11. The oil seal retainer and joint washer can now be fitted with the cutaway in line with the oil feed hole in the casing. Note that the oil seal runs on the driving flange, which should not be worn or damaged.

    Insert the driving bolts in the flange before the flange is finally fitted.
12. Replace the differential wheels, pinions, thrust washers and spindle. The backlash between the wheels should be minimum but definite, and can be reduced by fitting thicker thrust washers which are available .040 in. (1,0 mm), ·045 in. (1,15 mm) and .050 in. (1,3 mm) thick, between the differential wheels and casing.

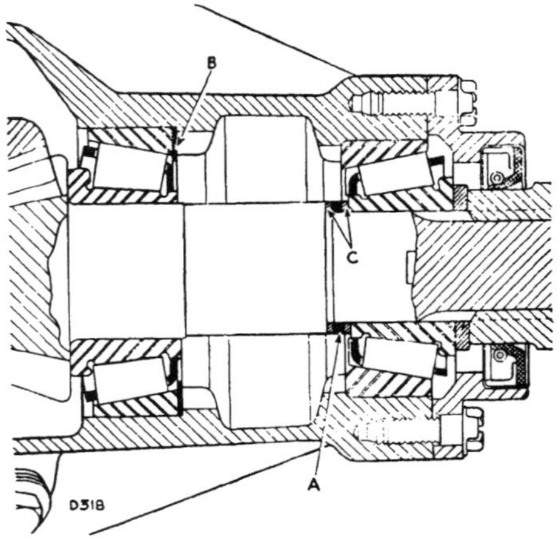

Pinion adjustment shims

A—Shims adjusting bearing pre-load
B—Shims adjusting pinion position
C—Washer for shim

13. Fit the crownwheel, tightening the set bolts evenly and securing with new lockers. Ensure that the two shouldered bolts are fitted diametrically opposite, in the holes from which they were removed.
14. Press on the inner members of the differential bearings.
15. Position the differential in the casing together with the bearing outer members and serrated nuts.
16. Replace the bearing caps in their original position, partially tightening the bolts so that the adjusting nuts can be turned by hand.
17. Ensuring that the crownwheel is not solidly in mesh with the pinion, tighten both adjusting nuts by hand so that the end-float is just eliminated.

Operation M-6—*continued*

Measuring crownwheel backlash

18. With a dial test indicator mounted on the crownwheel, using clamp, Part No. 530106 and the pinion prevented from turning, check the backlash between crownwheel and pinion. This should be .007 in. (0,18 mm) at the tightest point, and should be checked in at least four positions.

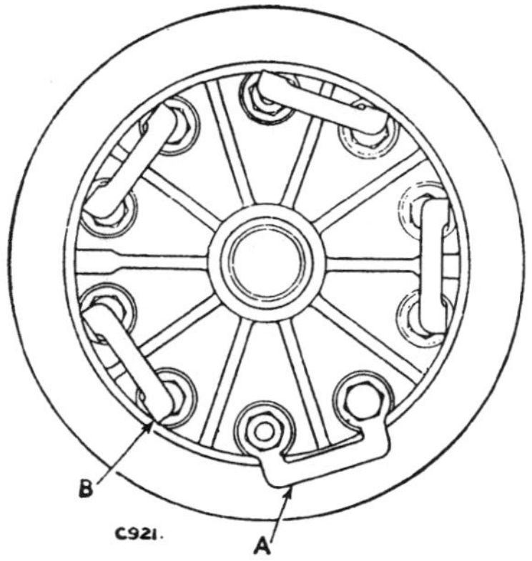

Fitting crownwheel double lockers

A—Lockers before bending
B—Locker bent in position

19. Adjust the backlash by means of the serrated nuts, turning both nuts by the same amount.
20. When the backlash is correct check that the serrated nuts are finger-tight and tighten the bearing cap bolts; turn each serrated nut clockwise one-half of a serration, thus pre-loading the bearings by .005 in. (0,13 mm). A special spanner, Part No. 530105 is available for adjusting the serrated nuts.
21. Drop the locking tabs into slots in the serrated nuts, bending them to one side if necessary; lock the bearing cap bolts and tabs with wire.

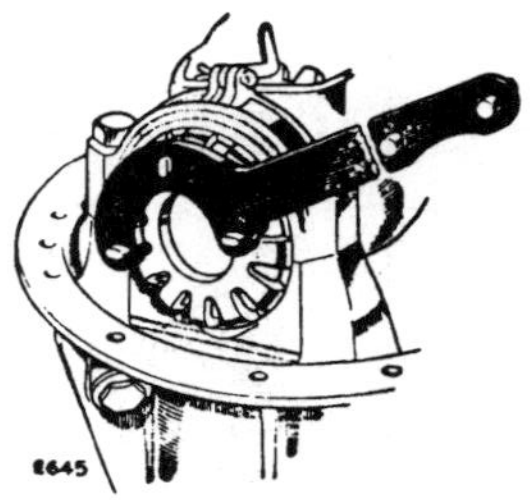

Adjusting serrated nuts

Differential pinion oil seal, remove and replace—Operation M-7

Workshop hand tools: Pliers.

Spanner sizes: $\frac{1}{2}$ in. AF, $\frac{5}{8}$ in. AF, 1 in. AF

Special tools:

Torque wrench

Differential pinion oil seal, remove

It is not necessary to remove the differential unit from the axle in order to renew the pinion oil seal.

1. Disconnect the propeller shaft from the differential end.
2. Remove the split pin, castle nut and pinion driving flange.
3. Remove the oil seal retainer.
4. Remove the oil seal from the retainer and ensure that the retainer is not damaged or distorted. Check that the driving flange, on which the oil seal runs, is not worn or damaged.

Differential pinion oil seal, replace

1. Smear the outside of a new seal with a suitable jointing compound.
2. Fit the seal into the retainer with the lip of the seal face in towards the differential unit.
3. Fit the retainer to the casing, using a new joint washer, with the cutaway in line with the oil feed hole in the casing.
4. Refit the pinion driving flange and castle nut, tightening the nut to 85 lb ft (11,5 mkg) and fit a new split pin.
5. Check that the axle breather is not blocked.
6. Refit the propeller shaft.

DEFECT LOCATION

SYMPTOM	POSSIBLE CAUSE	REMEDY
A—REAR AXLE NOISE	1. Worn gears 2. Worn bearings 3. Incorrect tolerances	1. *Replace* 2. *Replace* 3. *Adjust*
B—OIL LEAKS	1. Flange bolts loose 2. Loose drain filler plug 3. Worn oil seals 4. Damaged gaskets	1. *Tighten* 2. *Tighten* 3. *Renew* 4. *Renew*
C—DRIVE NOT TRANSMITTED	1. Broken axle shaft 2. Damaged gear teeth 3. Differential parts fractured	1. *Replace* 2. *Replace* 3. *Replace*

DATA

Type	Semi-floating with upset axle shaft
Hub bearing lubrication	Pre-packed with grease
Final drive	Spiral bevel
Ratio:	
4-speed gearbox, early models	3.9:1
4-speed gearbox with overdrive	4.3:1
Automatic transmission, Mk I, IA and II	3.9:1
Automatic transmission, Mk III	3.54:1
Backlash, crownwheel to pinion	.007 in. (0,18 mm) at the tightest point
Pinion bearing pre-load	Adjust to give a torque of 9 to 14 in./lb (0,10 to 0,16 mkg) on the pinion shaft
Crownwheel bearing pre-load	.005 in. (0,13 mm)
Pinion height	3.000 to 3.002 in. (76,2 to 76,25 mm), pinion face to crownwheel axis
Axle identity 3.9:1	Differential stamped '3.9' and '3.9' painted on axle casing
4.3:	Stamped '4.3' on axle casing
Tightening torques:	
Pinion flange nut	75 to 95 lb ft (10,0 to 12,8 mkg)
Bearing cap bolts	65 lb ft (9,0 mkg)
Oil seal housing	15 lb ft (2,0 mkg)

Section N — BRAKING SYSTEM

Brief description of the braking system

The brakes are hydraulically operated and servo assisted. The handbrake operates through mechanical linkage to the rear wheels and is applied by a pistol grip lever. A brake fluid level and handbrake warning light is incorporated on later cars.

In the event of a servo failure the brakes remain fully operative although the pedal pressure required to operate the brakes will be higher. Use only Girling Crimson Brake Fluid (Specification SAE 70R3).

INDEX

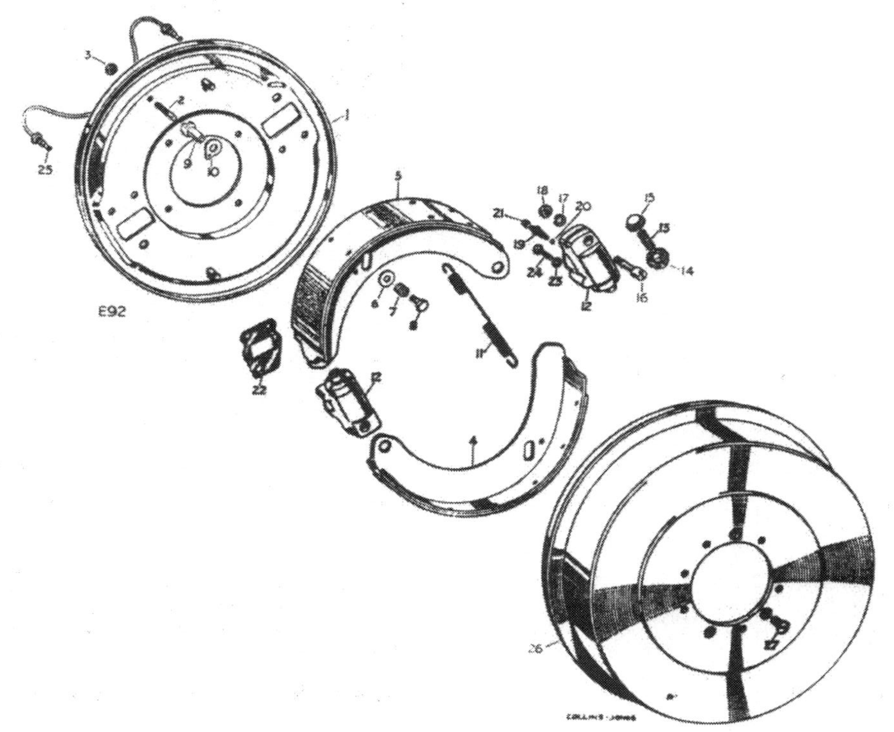

Front brake unit, drum type

1	Brake anchor plate	15	Air excluder, cylinder
2	Steady post	16	Pivot pin } Fixing brake shoe to cylinder
3	Special nut, fixing steady post	17	Spring washer } Fixing brake shoe to cylinder
4	Brake shoe, LH	18	Nut } Fixing brake shoe to cylinder
5	Lining for brake shoe	19	Bleed screw
6	Friction washer } Automatic adjuster	20	Steel ball for bleed screw
7	Spring } Automatic adjuster	21	Dust cap
8	Special screw } Automatic adjuster	22	Gasket for wheel cylinder
9	Link pin } Automatic adjuster	23	Spring washer } Fixing wheel cylinder
10	Link washer } Automatic adjuster	24	Special bolt } Fixing wheel cylinder
11	Pull-off spring	25	Connecting pipe
12	Wheel cylinder, LH	26	Brake drum
13	Spring, wheel cylinder	27	Set screw for brake drum
14	Air excluder, seal		

Front brake shoes, remove and refit—Operation N-1

Workshop hand tools:
Screwdriver, Feeler gauge
Spanner sizes: $\frac{1}{2}$ in. AF, $\frac{3}{4}$ in. AF

Special tools:
Slave drum

Front brake shoes, remove

1. Jack up the car and remove the front road wheels.
2. Remove the brake drums.
3. Slacken the steady post locknut and unscrew the steady post until it is clear of the adjusting device.
4. Loosen the large nut and remove the pivot pin from the wheel cylinder.

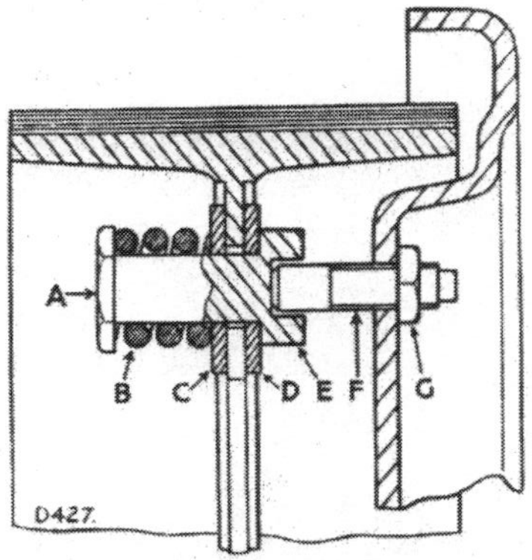

Steady post and automatic adjusting device, drum type brakes
A—Special screw
B—Spring
C—Friction washer
D—Link washer
E—Link pin
F—Steady post
G—Locknut

5. Ease the shoe web from the pivot abutment slot of one wheel cylinder and from the piston slot of the other cylinder.
6. Ensuring that the steady post is clear of the shoe detach the shoe return spring and remove the shoe complete with the automatic adjusting device. Repeat for second shoe.
7. A suitable clip should be fitted to each wheel cylinder to keep the pistons in position and prevent the loss of fluid.
8. Remove the securing bolt of the automatic adjusting device and detach the adjusting device from the shoe.

Front brake shoes, refit

1. When fitting new brake shoes ensure that the ends of the linings are slightly chamfered.
2. Assemble the automatic adjusting device to the brake shoe, ensuring correct alignment of the small dowels on the friction disc in relation to the link pin and brake shoe web. Fit the spring and securing bolt and tighten.
3. Place the long coiled end of the brake shoe return spring on to the spring post on brake anchor plate, and fit other end on to shoe web post. Engage the shoe into the pivot pin abutment slot of wheel cylinder first, then engage other end of shoe into the piston slot of the opposite wheel cylinder.
4. Repeat for the second shoe.
5. Fit the pivot pins and securing nuts to the wheel cylinders.
6. Fit the steady posts to the anchor plate, screwing in until contact is made with the adjusting device, the end of the steady post resting in the slot on the adjusting device body, as illustrated.
7. To adjust the steady posts fit a slave brake drum, which has a section cut away as illustrated, to the hub.
8. Using a feeler gauge, check the clearance between brake shoe linings, at the inner and outer edges, and the slave brake drum. Adjust the steady post until the clearance is equal at inner and outer edges of the lining. Repeat for other end of shoe, then tighten up the locknut on the steady post, and re-check the clearance.
9. Repeat for the opposite brake shoe.

The clearance between the lining and the drum is not laid down, as this will vary from shoe to shoe, but the important factor is that the clearance must be equal at the inner and outer edges of one shoe.

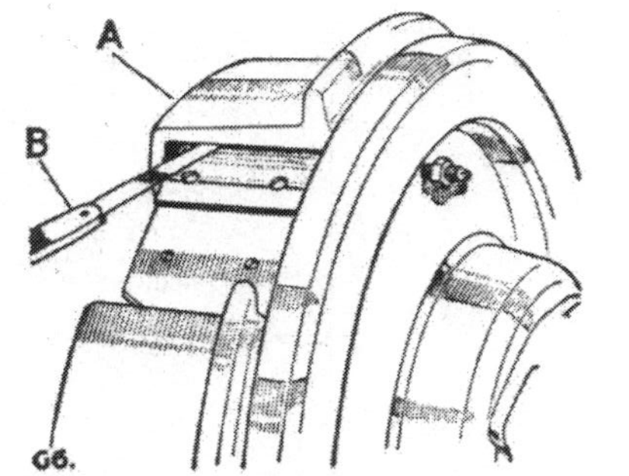

Checking steady post adjustment, drum type brakes
A—Slave brake drum B—Feeler gauge

Front brake drum type, overhaul—Operation N-2

Workshop hand tools:

Screwdriver, Feeler gauge, Bleed tube, Glass container
Spanner sizes: $\frac{7}{16}$ in. AF, $\frac{1}{2}$ in. AF, $\frac{9}{16}$ in. AF, $\frac{5}{8}$ in. AF, $\frac{3}{4}$ in. AF, $1\frac{1}{8}$ in. AF

Special tools:

Slave drum; Front hub adjustment spanner, Part No. 263057; Dial gauge; Dial gauge bracket

Front brake, strip

1. Remove brake shoes as detailed in Operation N-1.
2. To remove the wheel cylinders loosen the bleed nipple on wheel cylinder, and slowly depress the brake pedal. When the pedal is fully depressed, wedge in position to avoid unnecessary loss of brake fluid.
3. Disconnect the brake fluid supply pipe from the flexible pipe at the union and remove the locknut securing flexible pipe to bracket on sub-frame. Unscrew flexible pipe from wheel cylinder.
4. Disconnect the balance pipe and remove the wheel cylinders and gasket.
5. Clean the exterior of each wheel cylinder before removing the piston, seal, air excluders and spring. Remove the bleed nipple, cover and ball, from the cylinders.
6. Remove front hub as detailed in Operation K-1.
7. Remove the brake anchor plate and steady posts.

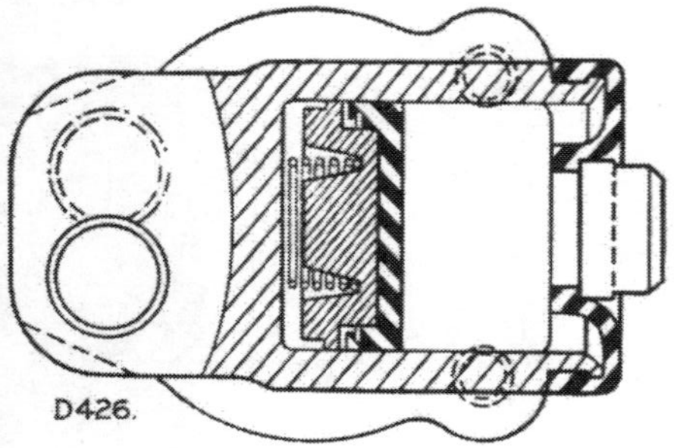

Cross-section of wheel cylinder, front, drum type

Front brake, rebuild

1. Smear the steady post with Girling brake grease before assembling to anchor plate.
2. Absolute cleanliness is essential whenever refitting components. Using a container and a quantity of Girling cleaning fluid, clean the component parts of the wheel cylinder before assembly.
3. Re-assemble the wheel cylinders using only Girling Crimson brake fluid and red rubber grease for lubrication.
4. To rebuild the front brake reverse the removal procedure.
5. Bleed the brakes as detailed in Operation N-23.

Front brake pads, remove and refit—Operation N-3

Workshop hand tools:
Pliers

Front brake pads, remove

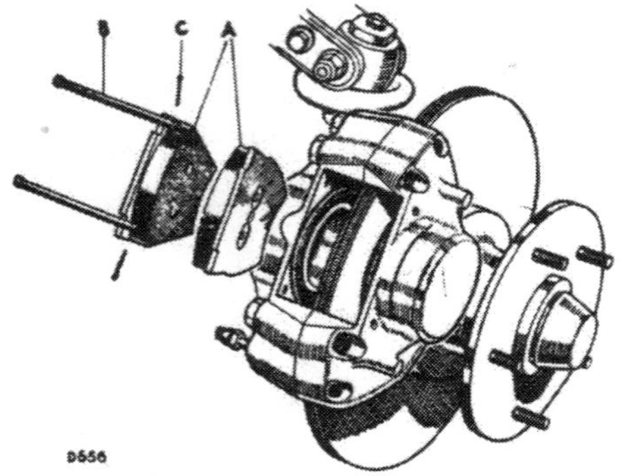

Removing brake pad

A—Pad B—Pad retaining pin
C—Stainless steel split pin

1. Remove road wheel.
2. Remove stainless steel split pins and withdraw the pad retaining pins.
3. Remove the anti-rattle springs if fitted.
4. With a pair of pliers grip the end of the pad and withdraw.
5. If the lining has worn down to $\frac{1}{8}$ in. (3 mm) or less the pad must be renewed. If the pads are not to be replaced, mark each pad in order that it may be refitted to its original position.

Front brake pads, refit

1. Push in the pistons, with an even pressure, to the bottom of the cylinder bores, and slip in the new pads.
2. If anti-rattle springs are fitted, position these over the metal backplate of the pad, with the tangs of the springs downwards and in each case with the cut-out towards the centre of the caliper.

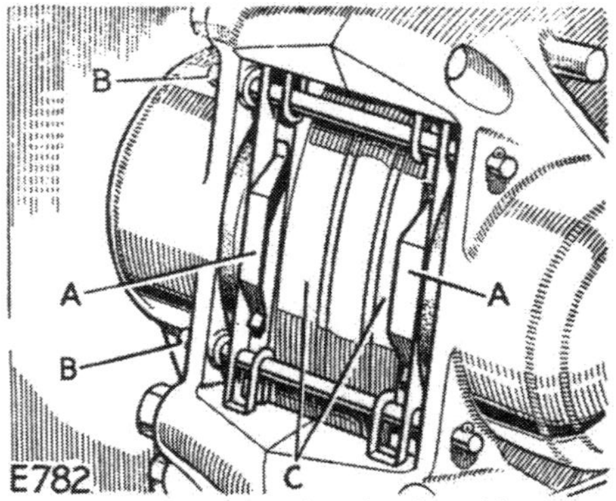

Brake pad anti-rattle springs in position

A—Anti-rattle spring
B—Returning spring
C—Brake pads

3. Replace the pad retaining pins and fit new stainless steel split pins.
4. Pump the foot pedal until a solid resistance is felt. This repositions the piston and puts the pads in slight frictional contact with the disc.

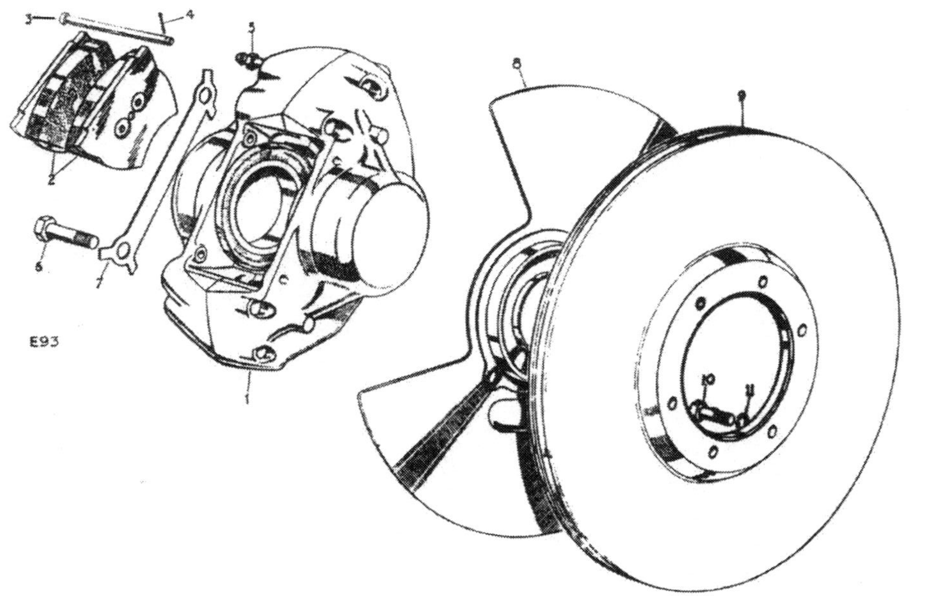

Layout of disc brakes

1 Front brake caliper
2 Pad for disc brake
3 Pad retaining pin
4 Special split pin for retaining pin
5 Bleed screw for caliper
6 Set bolt } Fixing caliper to stub axle
7 Lock plate }
8 Shield for brake disc
9 Disc for brake
10 Set screw } Fixing disc to hub
11 Spring washer }

Front caliper, remove and refit—Operation N-4

Workshop hand tools:
Pliers, Bleed tube, Glass container
Spanner sizes: $\frac{7}{16}$ in. AF, $\frac{5}{8}$ in. AF, $\frac{3}{4}$ in. AF

Special tools:
Torque wrench

Front caliper, remove

1. Remove the road wheel.
2. Remove all external dirt from the caliper.
3. Slacken the bleed nipple and slowly depress the brake pedal, wedge in position to prevent unnecessary loss of brake fluid.
4. Disconnect the brake hose from the caliper, ensure that the two sealing washers are retained with the banjo union.
5. Remove the pads as detailed in Operation N-3.
6. Prise up the tap washers on the bolts securing the caliper to the stub axle.
7. Remove the bolts and withdraw the caliper.

Front caliper, refit

1. To refit the front calipers, reverse the removal procedure, tightening the bolts securing the caliper to the stub axle to a torque of 57 to 63 lb/ft (7,8 to 8,7 mkg).
2. Bleed the brakes as detailed in Operation N-23.

Front caliper, overhaul—Operation N-5

Workshop hand tools:
Pliers, Bleed tube, Glass container
Spanner sizes: $\frac{7}{16}$ in. AF, $\frac{5}{8}$ in. AF, $\frac{3}{4}$ in. AF

Special tools:
Air line, Torque wrench

To overhaul the caliper it is necessary to remove it from the vehicle as detailed in Operation N-4

Front caliper, strip

1. Absolute cleanliness is essential. It is important that the bolts securing the two halves of the brake caliper are not disturbed; pistons and seals must be removed without separating the caliper.
2. Slacken the bleed screw, remove the retaining ring and rubber boot from the piston housing.
3. Pack a piece of clean rag between the pistons and blow the pistons out of their bores with an air line.
4. Remove the sealing rings taking care not to damage the bore or locating groove.

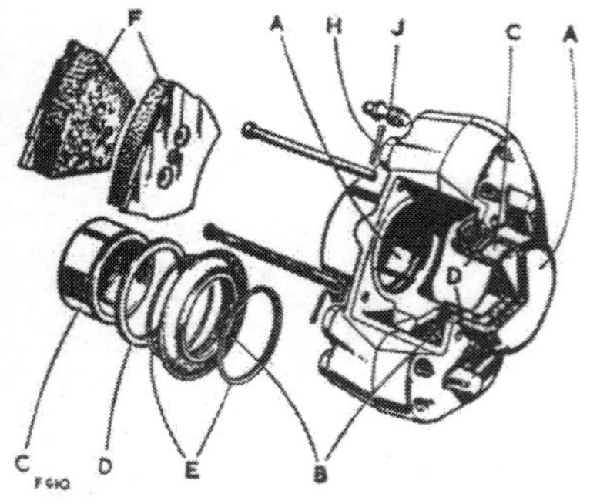

Exploded view of brake caliper

A—Bore
B—Rubber boot
C—Piston
D—Seal
E—Boot retaining rings
F—Pads
G—Pins
H—Split pins
J—Bleed screw

Front caliper, rebuild

1. Wash all components in Girling cleaning fluid.

Absolute cleanliness is essential.

2. Clean out piston sealing ring groove, and fit new sealing ring.
3. Apply Girling crimson brake fluid to the piston bore and piston exterior.
4. Fit rubber boot, retaining ring and piston inserting the piston squarely into the bore Excessive pressure should not be required.

Discs, remove and refit—Operation N-6

Workshop hand tools:
Pliers, Bleed tube, Glass container, Screwdriver
Spanner sizes: $\frac{7}{16}$ in. AF, $\frac{1}{2}$ in. AF, $\frac{5}{8}$ in. AF, $\frac{3}{4}$ in. AF, $1\frac{1}{8}$ in. AF

Special tools:
Torque wrench; Front hub adjustment spanner, Part No. 263057; Dial test indicator; Bracket for dial test

Disc, remove

1. Jack up the car and remove the road wheel.
2. Remove the pads, Operation N-3.
3. Remove the caliper, Operation N-4.
4. Remove the front hub and disc complete, Operation K-1.
5. Remove the disc from the hub, first marking the disc in relation to the hub.

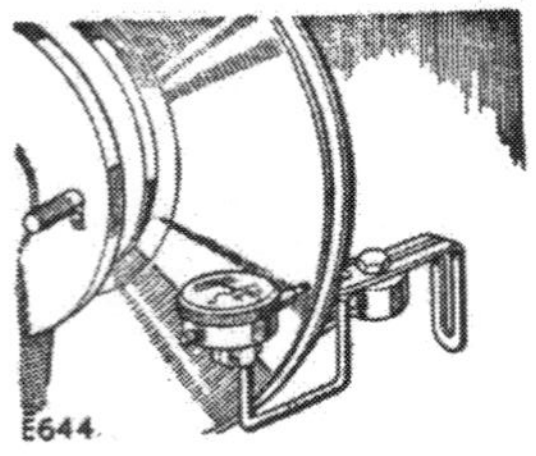

Checking disc radial run-out

Disc, refit

1. Refit disc to hub.
2. Refit front hub and disc complete. Section K.
3. Using a dial test indicator and suitable bracket check the disc for radial run-out, the tolerance permitted is 0.003 in. (0,07 mm). If the run-out exceeds this figure, remove the hub and disc, remove the bolts securing disc to hub and revolve disc on hub, reassemble and check run-out. If the run-out is still not satisfactory, repeat the process with another disc. If satisfaction is still not obtained, fit a new hub and disc, as the mating surface on the hub has possibly been distorted.
4. If there is doubt about the condition of a disc a replacement should always be fitted. If however a replacement is unobtainable reconditioning may be carried out with suitable equipment, see Section X.
5. Refit caliper, Operation N-4.
6. Refit the pads, Operation N-3.
7. Bleed the brakes, Operation N-23.
8. Refit the road wheel, lower jack.

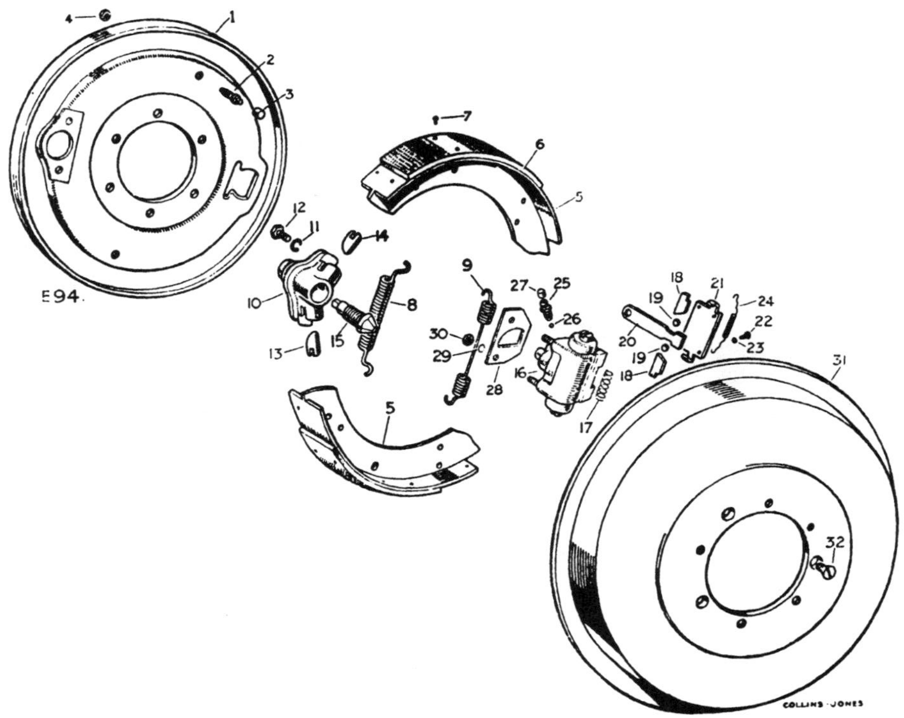

Rear brake unit

1	Brake anchor plate, LH	17	Spring	
2	Steady post	18	Tappet	For hand brake operation
3	Tufnol bush for steady post	19	Roller	For hand brake operation
4	Special nut	20	Draw link	For hand brake operation
5	Brake shoes	21	Cover plate	For hand brake operation
6	Lining, brake shoe	22–23	Fixings	For hand brake operation
7	Rivet	24	Return spring	For hand brake operation
8	Pull-off spring, adjuster end	25	Bleed screw	
9	Pull-off spring, cylinder end	26	Steel ball for screw	
10	Adjuster housing	27	Dust cap	
11–12	Fixings, adjuster housing	28	Dust cover plate	
13	Plunger, LH	29–30	Fixings, wheel cylinder	
14	Plunger, RH	31	Brake drum	
15	Cone for adjuster	32	Set screw for brake drum	
16	Wheel cylinder, LH			

Rear brake shoes, remove and refit—Operation N-7

Workshop hand tools:

Screwdriver. Spanner sizes: $\frac{7}{16}$ in. AF, $\frac{1}{2}$ in. AF

Rear brake shoes, remove

1. Jack up car and remove road wheels.
2. Slacken off the brake shoe adjusters.
3. Slacken off the steady posts.
4. Remove the brake drum.
5. Remove the brake shoes together with the springs. The wheel cylinder pistons should be clipped in position to avoid loss of fluid.

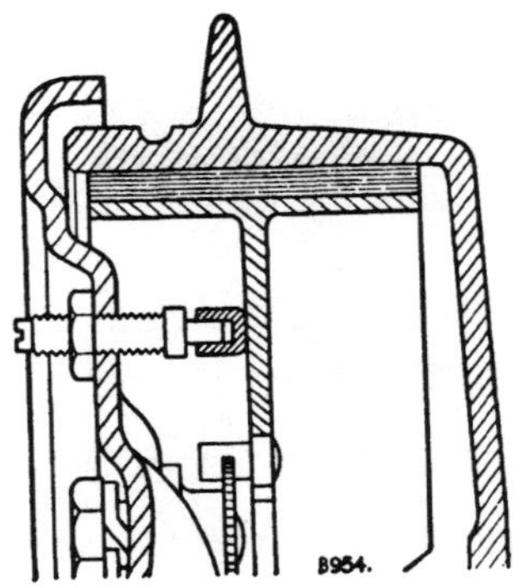

Steady post adjustment, rear

Rear brake shoes, refit

1. If new linings have been fitted the ends must be chamfered slightly. The trailing shoe, having the shorter lining, is the lower of the two. It is strongly recommended that the brake shoe return springs are replaced with the shoes.
2. To refit the brake shoes reverse the removal procedure.
3. Operate brakes to centralise brake shoes; tighten adjusters to hold brake shoes into contact with the drum.
4. Screw in the steady post until contact with the brake shoe webs is felt, then tighten the steady post locknut. Slacken off adjusters.
5. Adjust brakes as detailed in Operation N-9.

Rear brake, overhaul—Operation N-8

Workshop hand tools:

Screwdriver, Pliers, File small, Bleed tube, glass container

Spanner sizes: $\frac{7}{16}$ in. AF, $\frac{1}{2}$ in. AF, $\frac{9}{16}$ in AF

Special tools:

Axle shaft retaining collar tool, Part No. 275870; Adaptor, 514576

Rear brake, strip

1. Remove the brake shoes as detailed in Operation N-7.
2. Disconnect the handbrake linkage at the anchor plate draw link.
3 Depress the brake pedal and wedge in position to prevent brake fluid draining from the reservoir and disconnect the brake pipe at the wheel cylinder.
4. Remove the wheel cylinder complete, together with the dust cover plate.

On Mk III models a rubber boot, as illustrated, is inserted between the dust cover plate and the anchor plate. It should be removed at this stage. This protective boot prevents the ingress of dirt and water through brake anchor plate and into the handbrake mechanism. It cannot be directly

Operation N-8—*continued*

fitted to earlier models as the dust cover plate, draw link and handbrake rods have been modified to suit the rubber boot.

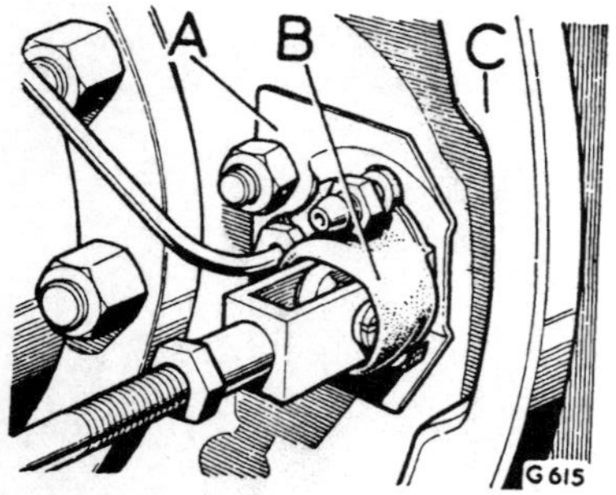

Rubber boot for handbrake linkage. Mk III models

A—Dust cover plate B—Rubber boot C—Brake anchor plate

5. Unscrew the bleed nipple and remove the ball and cover.
6. Remove the pistons, seals, air excluders and spring.
7. Detach the tappet return spring.
8. Remove the tappet cover plate, and lift out the tappets, rollers and draw link.
9. Remove the adjuster housing, withdraw the two plungers and unscrew the adjuster cone.
10. Unscrew the steady posts and remove from anchor plate.
11. If necessary, remove the brake anchor plate. This operation involves the removal and stripping of the half-shaft assembly, as detailed in Section M.

Rear brake, rebuild

1. If removed, refit the brake anchor plate and half-shaft assembly as detailed in Section M.
2. Lightly grease the steady posts with Girling brake grease and refit to the anchor plate.
3. Thoroughly clean all wheel cylinder components in Girling cleaning fluid. **Absolute cleanliness is essential.**
4. Re-assemble the wheel cylinder by reversing the removal procedure, fit new seals and use only the recommended lubricants.

   Clip pistons to prevent them becoming dislodged.

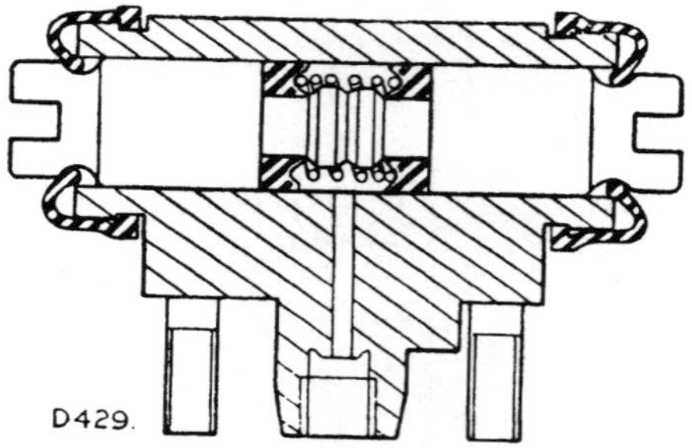

Cross-section of wheel cylinder, rear

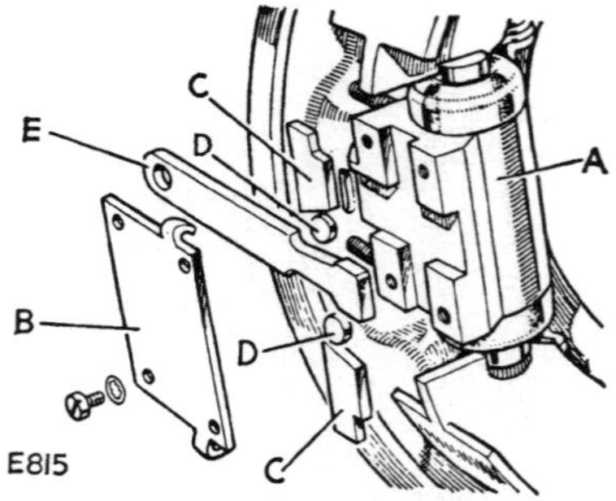

Rear wheel cylinder (handbrake mechanism)

A—Wheel cylinder
B—Cover plate
C—Tappets
D—Rollers
E—Draw link

5. Re-assemble the adjuster unit ensuring that the plungers are a correct pair; this can be checked by placing them end to end, when the slots should be parallel to each other.

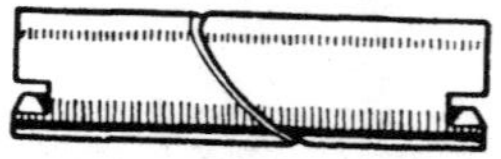

Correct pair of plungers

Operation N-8—*continued*

6. Lubricate the plungers and adjuster cone with Girling brake grease and insert them into the adjuster body.
7. Refit wheel cylinder and adjuster unit to anchor plate, also rubber boot on Mk III models. Leave the wheel cylinder fixing nuts one turn slack so that the cylinders are free to float on the anchor plate.
8. Connect the brake pipe to the wheel cylinders.
9. Re-connect the handbrake linkage at the draw link.
10. Refit the brake shoes as detailed in Operation N-7.
11. Bleed the brakes as detailed in Operation N-23.
12. Check the handbrake adjustment.

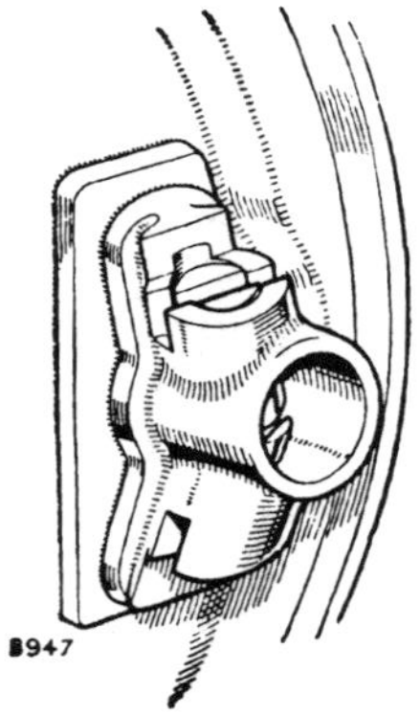

Plungers in bore of housing

Brake adjustment—Operation N-9

Spanner size: $\frac{7}{16}$ in. AF

Front brake adjustment

Drum type. No adjustment of the front brake is necessary; a stabilising arrangement is used in conjunction with the steady post, which keeps the linings close to the brake drum automatically, thereby eliminating need for periodical adjustment.

Disc type. No adjustment is necessary as the brake pads are self-adjusting and run with virtually no clearance.

Rear brake adjustment

1. With the rear of the car jacked up and the handbrake in the off position, ensure the wheels are free to rotate; if necessary, slacken off the adjusters.
2. After giving the brakes a firm application to centralise the shoes, turn the adjuster clockwise until the linings contact the drum, then slacken off two 'clicks' so that the drum rotates freely.

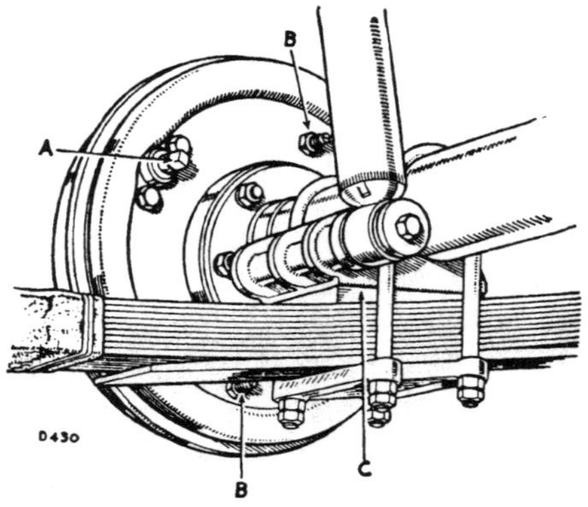

Rear brake adjustment

A—Adjuster B—Steady post C—Wedge, when fitted

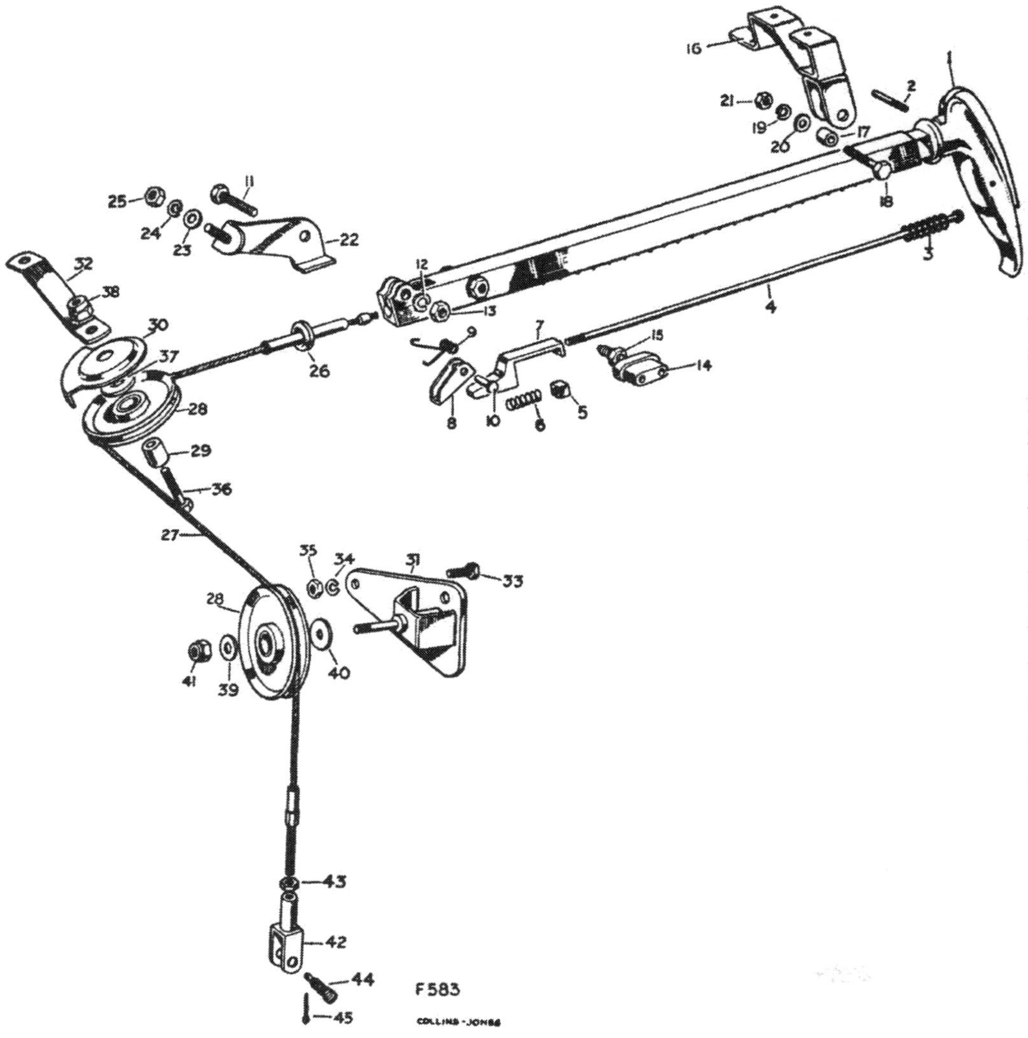

Layout of handbrake mechanism

1	Trigger for handle	
2	Special screw for trigger	
3	Spring for trigger push rod	
4	Push rod	
5	Adjusting nut for push rod	
6	Spring for operating wedge	
7	Operating wedge	
8	Pawl	
9	Spring for pawl	
10	Rivet fixing pawl	
11	Bolt	Fixing hand brake to mounting bracket at front end
12	Spring washer	Fixing hand brake to mounting bracket at front end
13	Nut	Fixing hand brake to mounting bracket at front end
14	Switch for warning light	
15	Nut fixing switch to hand brake	
16	Mounting bracket for hand brake at handle end	
17	Distance tube	
18	Bolt	Fixing mounting bracket to dash rail and hand brake to mounting bracket
19	Spring washer	Fixing mounting bracket to dash rail and hand brake to mounting bracket
20	Plain washer	Fixing mounting bracket to dash rail and hand brake to mounting bracket
21	Nut	Fixing mounting bracket to dash rail and hand brake to mounting bracket
22	Mounting bracket for hand brake at front end	
23	Plain washer	Fixing mounting bracket to dash
24	Spring washer	Fixing mounting bracket to dash
25	Nut	Fixing mounting bracket to dash
26	Grommet for hand brake cable in dash	
27	Hand brake cable, complete	
28	Pulley for hand brake cable	
29	Bush	For pulley
30	Cover plate	For pulley
31	Mounting bracket for pulley	
32	Support bracket for pulley mounting bracket on wing valance	
33	Bolt	Fixing pulley mounting bracket and clutch pedal bracket to dash
34	Spring washer	Fixing pulley mounting bracket and clutch pedal bracket to dash
35	Nut	Fixing pulley mounting bracket and clutch pedal bracket to dash
36	Bolt	Fixing pulley to bracket on valance
37	Plain washer, large	Fixing pulley to bracket on valance
38	Self-locking nut	Fixing pulley to bracket on valance
39	Plain washer, small	Fixing pulley to bracket on dash
40	Plain washer, large	Fixing pulley to bracket on dash
41	Self-locking nut	Fixing pulley to bracket on dash
42	Clevis fork end	
43	Locknut for clevis	
44	Clevis pin complete	
45	Split pin	

Handbrake unit and cable, remove and refit—Operation N-10

Workshop hand tools:

Pliers. Spanner sizes: $\frac{7}{16}$ in. AF, $\frac{1}{2}$ in. AF

Handbrake unit and cable, remove

1. Release the handbrake, and disconnect the handbrake cable from the fulcrum lever beneath the bulkhead. Slacken the pulley spindle locknuts, ease the cover plates aside and remove the cable from the pulleys.
2. Carefully ease away the parcel shelf—back finishing trim from the handbrake.
3. On later models fitted with a warning light switch, disconnect the leads from the switch.
4. Remove the two handbrake fixing bolts and withdraw the assembly complete with cable and cable guide.
5. Slacken the locknut and unscrew the warning light switch.
6. Withdraw the handbrake grip and ratchet assembly from the outer slide, taking care to retain the anti-rattle spring, which may spring out if the grip is withdrawn too quickly.
7. Detach the cable from the grip, remove the clevis fork and locknut from the lower end and remove the cable.

Handbrake unit and cable, refit

1. Fit the handbrake cable to the pulleys and secure the pulley support brackets and cover plates.
2. Pass the nipple end of the cable together with the cable guide through the bulkhead grommet, and then pass the nipple end through the handbrake slide. Fit the nipple into the handbrake grip and ratchet assembly.
3. Fit the grip and ratchet assembly into the outer slide.
4. Push ratchet assembly fully home, screw in warning light switch until it just binds. Turn back three turns, again operate handbrake ratchet and screw out further half turn, lock locknut and test switch operation with a battery-operated light.
5. Mount the unit on to the mounting brackets, ensuring that the cable receives a straight pull. Ensure that the cable guide enters the grommet on the bulkhead.
6. Reconnect the leads to the warning light switch.
7. Refit the locknut and clevis fork to the lower threaded end of the cable, adjust the length of the cable and connect it to the fulcrum lever so that when the handbrake grip is pulled out for approximately six 'clicks' of the ratchet the rear wheels should be fully locked.
8. Ensure that the handbrake warning light illuminates when the handbrake is operated. Tighten the warning light switch locknut.
9. Replace the parcel shelf trim.

Handbrake linkage, reset—Operation N-11

Workshop hand tools:

Pliers. Spanner sizes: $\frac{7}{16}$ in. AF, $\frac{1}{2}$ in. AF, $\frac{11}{16}$ in. AF

Handbrake linkage, reset

In the event of any part of the brake linkage having been removed or disturbed, and the setting thereby lost, it is important that the correct setting be regained as follows:

1. With the handbrake off, adjust the rear brakes until the shoes are hard against the drums.
2. Disconnect one cross-rod and the longitudinal brake rod from the rear balance lever.
3. Loosen the self-locking nut securing the link plate to the axle. Adjust the length of the other cross-rod so that the centre-line of the clevis hole in the balance lever is $1\frac{7}{16}$ in. (36,5 mm) from the rear edge of the cross-rod, as illustrated.
4. Adjust and re-connect the remaining cross-rod without disturbing the balance lever.
5. Adjust and re-connect the rear longitudinal rod to the balance lever and upper clevis hole of the relay lever, so that, without disturbing the setting of the balance lever, the relay lever is approximately vertical.
6. The intermediate brake rod, cross-shaft to relay lever, can now be adjusted so that when it is connected to the lower clevis hole of the relay lever and the longer lever of the two on the cross-shaft, the longer lever is vertical.
7. The foremost operating rod, cross-shaft to fulcrum lever, can be adjusted so that when it is connected to the shorter lever of the cross-shaft and the fulcrum lever, the rear arm of the fulcrum lever should be approximately vertical.

   Adjust the return spring so that its overall length does not exceed 10 in. (254,0 mm) when brake is applied.
8. The self-locking nut securing the link plate can now be tightened.
9. Adjust the rear brakes as detailed in Operation N-9.
10. Adjust the handbrake cable as detailed in Operation N-10.

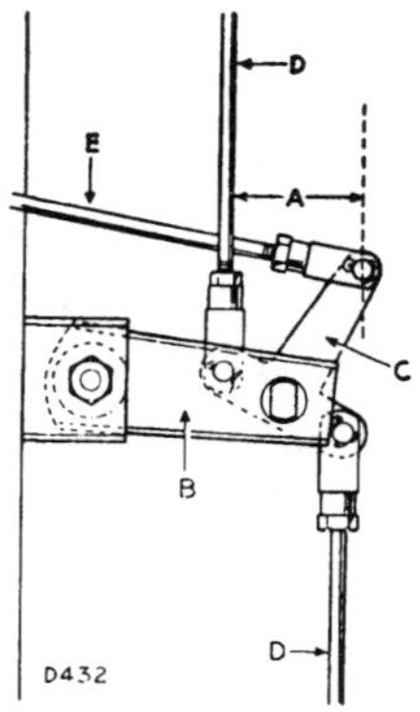

Brake linkage, rear balance lever setting

A—$1\frac{7}{16}$ in. (36,5 mm)
B—Link plate
C—Balance lever
D—Cross-rods
E—Longitudinal rod

Rear balance lever unit, remove, repair and overhaul—Operation N-12

Workshop hand tools:
Pliers. Spanner sizes: $\frac{7}{16}$ in. AF, $\frac{1}{2}$ in. AF, $\frac{11}{16}$ in. AF

Rear balance lever unit, remove and dismantle

1. Disconnect the three brake rods from the balance lever.

2. Remove the bolt, plain washers and self-locking nut securing the unit to the rear axle and remove the unit.

3. Separate the link plate from the balance lever by removing the self-locking nut and plain washer.

4. If necessary, remove the bonded rubber bush and the two oilite bushes from the link plate.

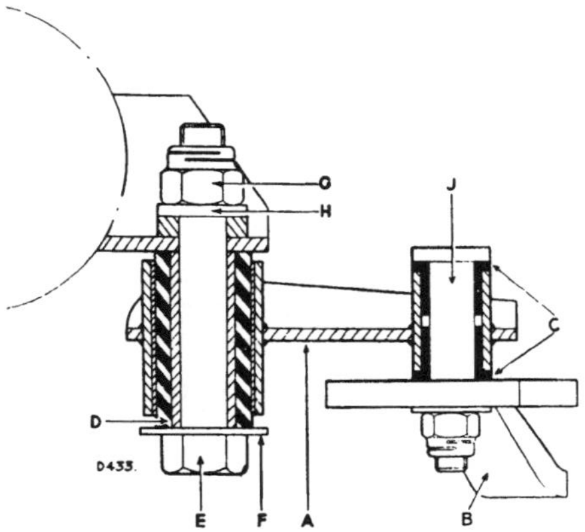

Cross-section of rear balance lever unit

A—Link plate
B—Balance lever
C—Oilite bushes
D—Bonded rubber bush
E—Unit securing bolt
F—Large plain washer
G—Self-locking nut
H—Small plain washer
J—Balance lever pin

Rear balance lever unit, reassemble and refit

1. If removed, refit new oilite and bonded rubber bushes. Both should be a press fit in the link plate, and the balance lever pin should be free to rotate in them when fitted.

2. To rebuild the unit reverse the removal procedure noting the following points:

   (a) The small plain washer is used under the self-locking nut at the top, and the larger one under the bolt head at the bottom of the unit. Do not tighten this bolt until the brake rods are adjusted and connected.

   (b) The balance lever is mounted with the long arm pointing downwards.

   (c) The link plate is fitted with the lipped edges facing uppermost.

3. When the unit is assembled, adjust the linkage, as detailed in Operation N-11.

Cross shaft, relay and fulcrum levers, remove, refit and overhaul—Operation N-13

Workshop hand tools:
Pliers. Spanner sizes: $\frac{7}{16}$ in. AF, $\frac{1}{2}$ in. AF, $\frac{9}{16}$ in. AF, $\frac{11}{16}$ in. AF

Cross-shaft, relay and fulcrum levers, remove and dismantle

1. Disconnect the brake linkage.

2. Remove the cross-shaft, relay and fulcrum lever fixings and remove the shaft and levers from the body; noting specially in the case of the fulcrum lever the position of the spacing collar and plain washers.

3. Refit new bushes and sleeves as necessary ensuring that all bushes are a press fit.

4. The longer bush on the cross-shaft must fit into the outer bracket.

Cross-shaft, relay and fulcrum levers, reassemble and refit

1. Reassemble by reversing the removal procedure.

2. Reset the handbrake linkage as detailed in Operation N-11.

Master cylinder, remove and refit—Operation N-14

Workshop hand tools:
Screwdriver, Pliers, Rule, Feeler gauge, Bleed tube, Glass container
Spanner sizes: $\frac{7}{16}$ in. AF, $\frac{1}{2}$ in. AF, 2 BA

Master cylinder, remove

1. Place a suitable cover over the front wing to protect the paintwork from brake fluid.

2. Remove the carburetter air intake elbow. Section A.

3. Depress the brake pedal, disconnect the hydraulic pipe, servo-to-master cylinder and insert a suitable rubber plug to prevent leakage of fluid. Release the brake pedal.

4. Detach the pedal return spring, and remove the clevis pin from pedal lever and operating rod.

5. Remove the three master cylinder fixing bolts, the two uppermost bolts are fitted to captive nuts. Remove the nut fixing the brake fluid reservoir and remove the master cylinder, distance piece and fluid reservoir as an assembly.

6. Drain off the brake fluid and detach the fluid reservoir from the master cylinder.

Master cylinder, refit

1. Reverse removal procedure.

2. Check and set rod adjustment as detailed in Operation N-17.

3. Bleed the brakes as detailed in Operation N-23.

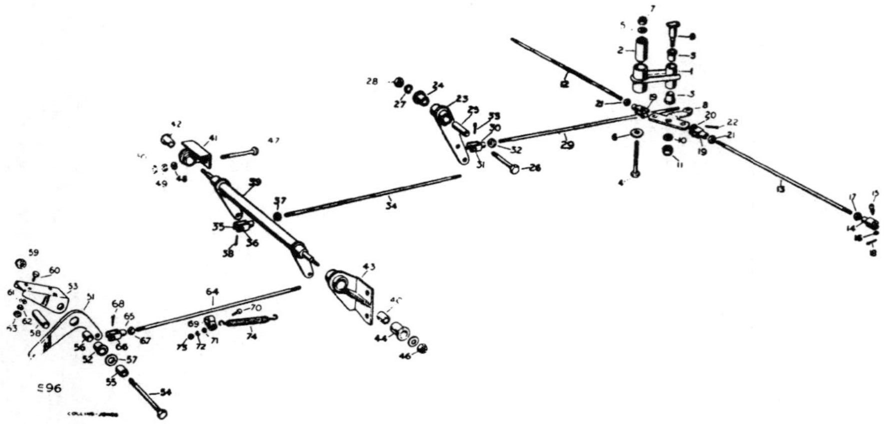

Arrangement of hand brake linkage

1	Link plate	39	Cross-shaft
2	Rubber bush	40	Sleeve for bearing
3	Bush for link plate	41	Bracket for cross-shaft
4–7	Fixings, link plate to axle	42	Bush for bracket
8	Balance lever	43	Bracket for cross-shaft, inner
9	Pin for balance lever	44	Bush for bracket, inner
10–11	Fixings, balance lever to link plate	45–46	Fixings
12	Cross-rod, short	47–48	Fixings
13	Cross-rod, long	51	Fulcrum lever
14–18	Fixings, cross-rods to draw links	52	Bush for fulcrum lever
19–22	Fixings, rods to levers	53	Mounting bracket
23	Relay lever	54–59	Fixings
24	Bush for relay lever	60–63	Fixings
25–28	Fixings for relay lever	64	Rod, cross-shaft to fulcrum lever
29	Rod, relay to balance lever	65–68	Fixings
30–33	Fixings, rod to levers	69	Anchor clip for return spring
34	Rod, relay to cross-shaft	70–73	Fixings
35–38	Fixings, rod to lever and cross-shaft	74	Return spring

Master cylinder, overhaul—Operation N-15

Workshop hand tools:
Screwdriver, Pliers, Rule, Feeler gauge, Bleed tube, Glass container, Circlip Pliers
Spanner sizes: $\frac{7}{16}$ in. AF, $\frac{1}{2}$ in. AF, 2 BA

For removal of master cylinder, see Operation N-14

Master cylinder, strip

1. Remove the end cap and gasket and withdraw the return spring and seal support.
2. Remove the rubber boot, remove the internal circlip and lift out the push rod and retaining washer.
3. Push out the piston and seal through the flanged end of the cylinder, and remove the recuperating seal and shim from the opposite end.
4. Clean all parts in Girling cleaning fluid.
5. Replace all cylinder rubbers and inspect and replace other components as necessary.

Master cylinder, rebuild

1. Reverse the removal procedure, ensuring that the seal support fits snugly into the lip of the recuperating seal, as illustrated.
2. Ensure that a new end gasket is fitted and that the end cap is fully tightened.

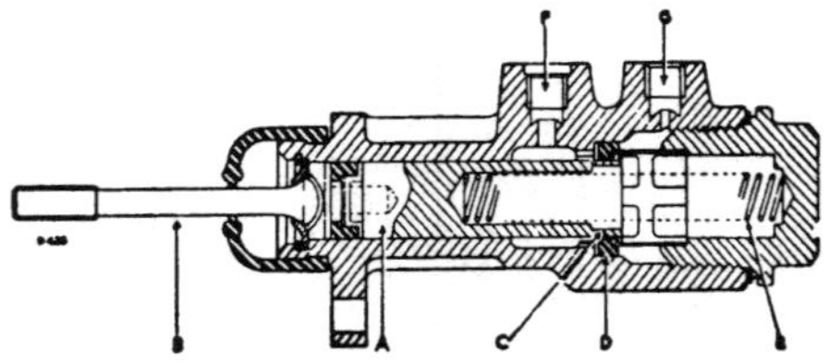

Brake master cylinder

A—Piston
B—Push rod
C—Recuperating holes
D—Recuperating seal
E—Return spring
F—Fluid inlet
G—Fluid outlet

Supply tank, remove and refit—Operation N-16

Workshop hand tools:
Bleed tube, Glass container. Spanner sizes: 2 BA, $\frac{7}{16}$ in. AF

Supply tank, remove

1. Remove the nut and spring washer attaching the supply tank clip to the bracket on the wing.
2. On late models disconnect electrical connectors at cap.
3. Disconnect the hydraulic pipe between the supply tank and the master cylinder and blank off the master cylinder port.
4. Withdraw the supply tank; the clip can be removed by taking out the special bolt and nut; the early cars are fitted with an ordinary screw cap and gasket, late types incorporate a fluid level switch.

Supply tank, refit

1. Reverse the removal procedure.
2. Bleed the brakes as detailed in Operation N-23.

Brake pedal, remove and refit—Operation N-17

Workshop hand tools:
Screwdriver, Pliers, Rule, Feeler gauge, Bleed tube, Glass container.
Spanner sizes: $\frac{7}{16}$ in. AF, $\frac{1}{2}$ in. AF

Brake pedal, remove

1. Disconnect the pedal return spring, and remove the clevis pin connecting the pedal lever to the brake master cylinder operating rod.
2. Place a suitable cover over the front wing to protect the paintwork from spilt brake fluid.
3. Remove the carburetter air intake elbow. Section A.
4. Disconnect the brake pipes from the brake master cylinder to the supply tank and servo unit and insert suitable plugs in the fluid outlets.
5. Detach the master cylinder and distance piece.
6. Remove the pedal support bracket fixings and withdraw the pedal and bracket assembly.

Brake pedal, refit

1. Place the pedal and bracket in position and secure with the fixing bolts, nuts and spring washers.
2. Fit the distance piece and brake master cylinder to the bulkhead, but do not connect the push rod to the pedal.
3. Adjust the pedal against the pedal stop 'B' to give a distance 'A' of 6 in. (152 mm) from the bottom of the pedal pad to the floor.
4. Adjust and connect the push rod of master cylinder so that the pivot pin can be aligned with the hole in the pedal and push rod, with the pedal held against the pedal stop.
5. Fit the pedal return spring with anchor plate to the pivot pin and secure.
6. Finally, adjust the stop 'B' to give a minimum clearance of $\frac{1}{16}$ in. (1,5 mm) free movement of the push rod in the master cylinder.

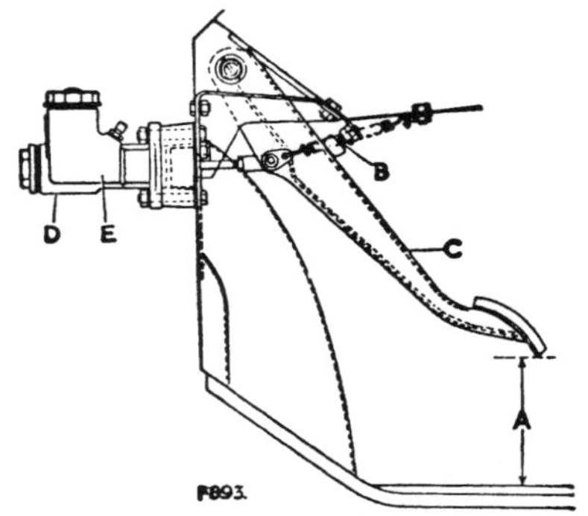

Adjustment of brake pedal

A—6 in. (152 mm)
B—Pedal stop adjustment
C—Pedal
D—Brake master cylinder
E—Clutch master cylinder

7. Bleed the hydraulic system, Operation N-23.
8. Refit the carburetter air intake elbow. Section A.

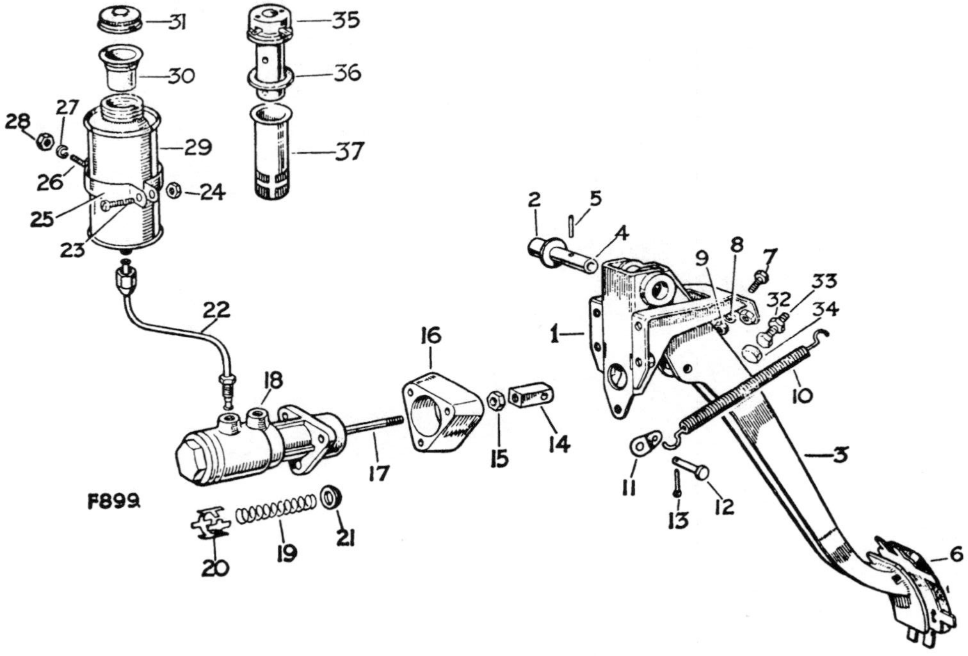

Brake pedal and master cylinder

1	Pedal bracket
2	Bush for bracket
3	Pedal lever
4	Pivot pin
5	Locating pin
6	Rubber pad
7–9	Fixings, bracket to dash
10	Pedal return spring
11	Anchor plate
12–13	Pivot pin and split pin
14	End eye for push rod
15	Locknut
16	Distance piece
17	Push rod
18	Master cylinder
19	Return spring for piston
20	Seal support
21	Retaining washer for push rod
22	Brake pipe
23–24	Fixings, clip to tank
25	Clip for tank
26–28	Fixings, clip to bracket
29	Fluid reservoir tank
30	Filter for tank
31	Cap
32	Locknut } For pedal stop
33	Adjusting screw } For pedal stop
34	Rubber stop } For pedal stop
35	Filler cap complete with fluid level switch
36	Sealing washer for filter
37	Filter for supply tank

Brake pedal, overhaul—Operation N-18

Workshop hand tools:
Screwdriver, Pliers, Rule, Feeler gauge, Bleed tube, Glass container, Small drift
Spanner sizes: $\frac{7}{16}$ in. AF, $\frac{1}{2}$ in. AF

Brake pedal, strip

1. Remove the pedal assembly as detailed in Operation N-17.
2. Remove the small locating pin from the pedal boss and pivot pin and withdraw the pivot pin.
3. Drift out the pivot pin flanged bushes from the bracket.

Brake pedal, rebuild

1. Fit new flanged bushes into the bracket, flanges facing inward.
2. Reverse removal procedure.

Servo unit, remove and refit—Operation N-19

Workshop hand tools:
Screwdriver, Bleed tube, Glass container. Spanner sizes: $\frac{7}{16}$ in. AF, $\frac{1}{2}$ in. AF, $\frac{3}{16}$ in. AF

Servo unit, remove

On all Mk II models it is necessary to remove the carburetter, Section A, and steering box, Section J or J1. It is not necessary to disconnect the pipes from the power steering box. These parts must be removed to enable the servo unit to be withdrawn.

1. Mk II. If necessary, remove the air intake elbow and the air silencer and carburetter. Section A.
2. Depress the brake pedal and secure in position.
3. Mk II. Remove the steering unit. Section J or J1.
4. Mk I and Mk IA. Disconnect the cold start control cable at the carburetter.
5. Mk I and Mk IA. Remove the accelerator countershaft and bracket from the engine. Section A.
6. Disconnect the two hydraulic pipes from the servo unit.
7. Disconnect the vacuum hose-servo-to-manifold, or if vacuum reservoir is fitted, vacuum hose servo-to-reservoir, reservoir-to-manifold.
8. Remove servo unit secured by three bolts and spring washers to the bracket on the sub-frame, then carefully manoeuvre the unit out from between engine and wing valance.

Servo unit, refit

When replacing a Mk I brake unit with a Mk II unit, certain modifications are necessary.

The accelerator lever must be re-positioned further out along the shaft, in order to avoid fouling the new servo unit.

An additional stop clip must be fitted in the original position of the accelerator lever.

1. Before refitting the unit check the operation of the non-return valve in the vacuum line, by ensuring that air will only pass through the valve one way. If this is faulty, renew.
2. Reverse the removal procedure.
3. Bleed the brakes, Operation N-23.
4. If necessary, bleed the power steering unit. Section J1.

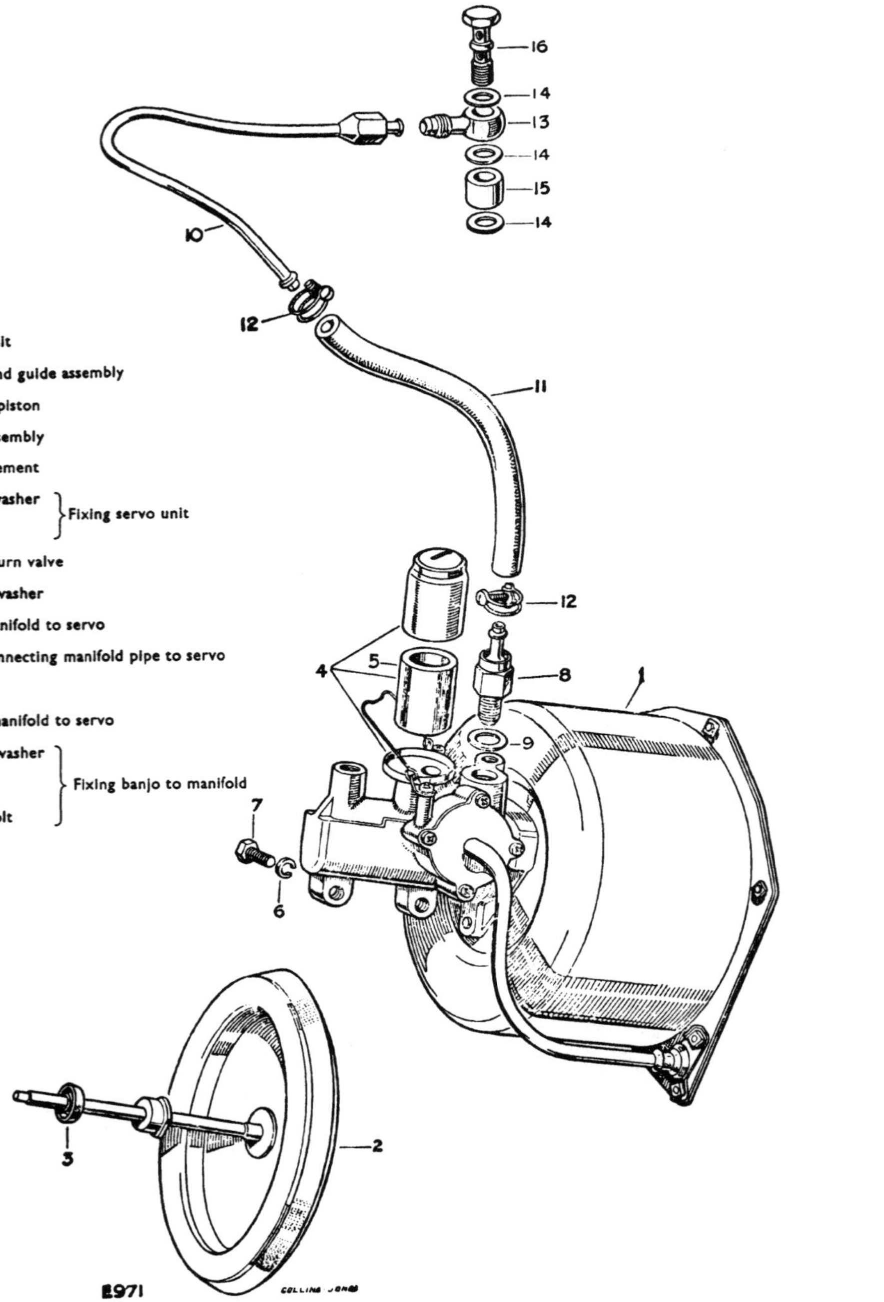

1. Servo unit
2. Piston and guide assembly
3. Seal for piston
4. Filter assembly
5. Filter element
6. Spring washer } Fixing servo unit
7. Bolt } Fixing servo unit
8. Non-return valve
9. Sealing washer
10. Pipe, manifold to servo
11. Hose connecting manifold pipe to servo
12. Clip
13. Banjo, manifold to servo
14. Sealing washer } Fixing banjo to manifold
15. Spacer } Fixing banjo to manifold
16. Banjo bolt } Fixing banjo to manifold

Layout of servo system, late models, Mk II servo

Servo unit, overhaul—Operation N-20

Workshop hand tools:

Screwdriver, Phillips screwdriver, Circlip pliers, Bleed tube, Glass container

Spanner sizes: $\frac{7}{16}$ in. AF, $\frac{1}{2}$ in. AF, $\frac{9}{16}$ in. AF

Servo unit, strip

In the event of failure, this unit should, where possible, be exchanged for a factory reconditioned assembly. When Mk I units are returned for reconditioning, a Mk II unit is automatically supplied as a replacement. These instructions are included for guidance only when reconditioned units are not available.

Absolute cleanliness is essential. All cleaning must be carried out using either Girling cleaning fluid or crimson brake fluid. Nothing else must be used.

1. Remove the unit from the vehicle, Operation N-19.
2. Hold the unit in a vice by the mounting lugs on the body.
3. On Mk I units first mark the end cover plate and cylinder to ensure that the balance pipe will be properly positioned on refitment.
4. Push back the rubber tube covering the vacuum pipe connection and remove the restrictor washer revealed in the open end of the vacuum pipe.
5. On all units remove the screws in the flange, support the cover against the pressure of the spring.
6. Relieve the pressure gradually, allowing the spring to push out the piston.
7. On Mk II units withdraw the small nylon washer or in the case of the Mk IIA unit, bakelite washer from the piston rod.
8. Remove the seal backing ring.
9. Removal of the piston assembly and spring will reveal the set bolts securing the cylinder to the base of the body.
10. Undo the set bolts and remove the cylinder and clamp plate.
11. Remove the rubber grommet which seals the vacuum pipe in the flange of the Mk II unit.
12. If the piston is scored, a replacement unit must be fitted.
13. Remove air filter, Operation N-21.
14. Remove the cover and tube assembly from the valve chest.
15. Remove the two valve retainer screws, lift out the spring and valve retainer.
16. Move the control piston up its cylinder (which is the upper bore) sufficiently to remove the rocking lever and valves by applying pressure to the plug.
17. Jar out the plug by tapping the body on a wooden surface and remove the piston.
18. Compress the spring, push off the circlip and release the retainers and spring.
19. Remove the seals.

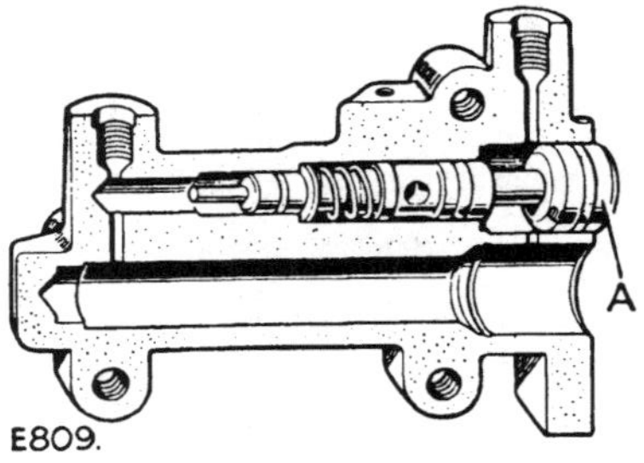

Control cylinder, early type piston
A—End plug

20. If the early type of control piston is fitted as illustrated, replace with latest type.

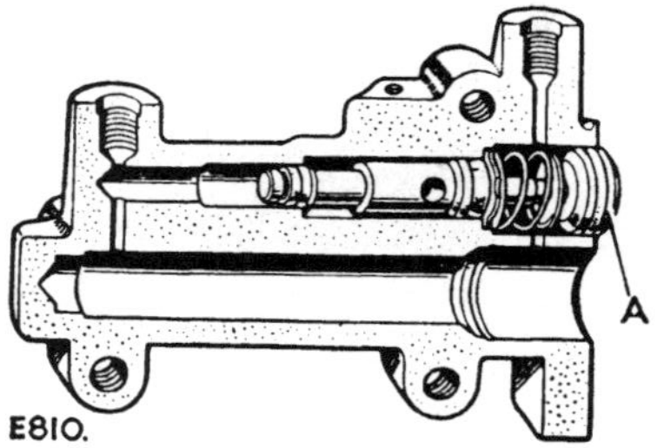

Control Cylinder, new type piston
A—End plug

Operation N-20—*continued*

21. Remove the bush seal and spacer from the output cylinder bore, (or lower bore).
22. A suitable tool must be manufactured for compressing the piston as detailed in illustration.

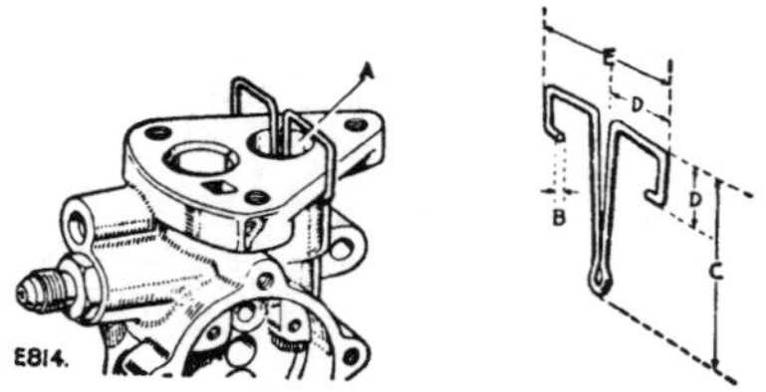

Dimensions of spring compressing tool and tool shown in position

A—Output cylinder
B—$\frac{1}{8}$ in. (3 mm) diameter wire x 12 in. (304 mm) long
C—$2\frac{3}{8}$ in. (60 mm)
D—1 in. (25 mm)
E—$1\frac{3}{4}$ in. (45 mm)

Material: Material used should be a piece of iron wire approx. $\frac{1}{8}$" (3 mm) thick and 12" 304 mm) long.

23. Compress the piston with the tool as illustrated and remove the circlip taking care not to damage the bore.

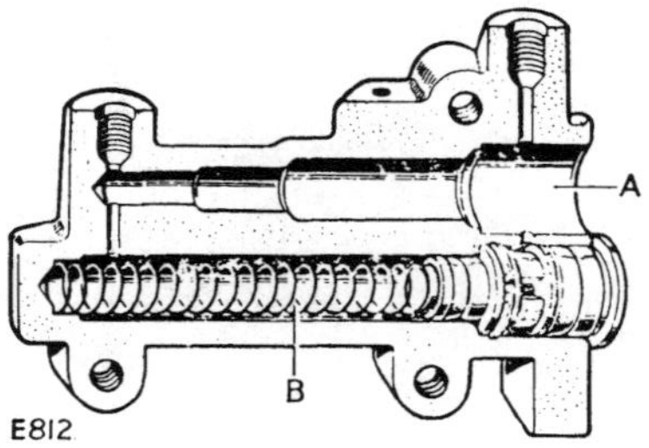

Output cylinder
A—Control piston bore B—Output cylinder

24. Release the compressing tool and remove the washer, piston and spring.

Servo unit, rebuild

Absolute cleanliness is essential. Clean all components in Girling cleaning fluid before assembly.

1. Lubricate components with only crimson brake fluid or red rubber grease.
2. All seals and gaskets must be replaced.
3. Fit a new output cylinder piston as the seal is fitted during manufacture and cannot be replaced separately.
4. Ensure that the seal around the piston has the larger diameter nearer the reduced end of the piston.
5. Refit the output cylinder by reversing the removal procedure.

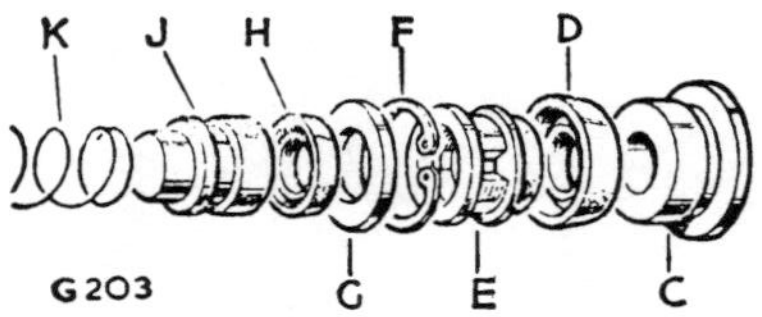

Output cylinder components

C—Bearing bush
D—Gland seal
E—Nylon seal spacer
F—Circlip
G—Abutment washer
H—Piston seal
J—Piston
K—Spring

6. Refit the control cylinder by reversing the removal procedure, ensuring that the hole in the piston lines up with that in the valve chest.
7. Refit the rocking lever with the valves attached into the valve chest so that the spring location above one of the valves is furthest from the retaining screws.
8. Rebuild the valve chest by reversing the removal procedure.
9. Refit air filter, Operation N-21.
10. Insert the assembled body into a vice and locate the vacuum cylinder on to the mounting face.

Operation N-20—*continued*

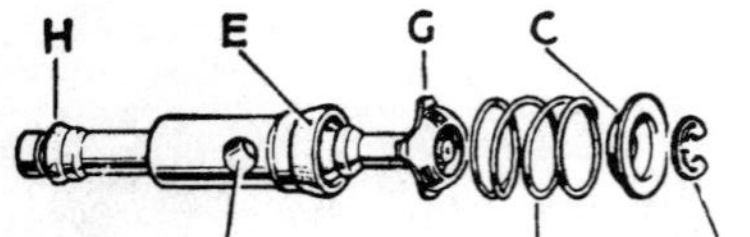

Control cylinder components

B—Circlip
C—Retainer
D—Spring
E—Seal
F—Control piston
G—Abutment
H—Seal

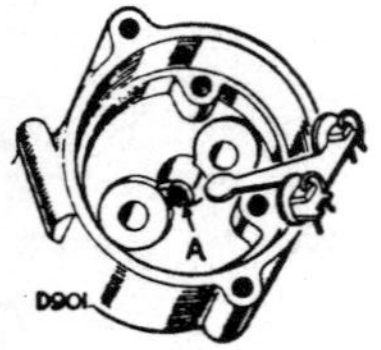

Primary piston in correct position

A—Primary piston orifice

11. On Mk II units fit a new rubber grommet into the flange ensuring that there is space over the grommet for the passage of air when the end cover is fitted.

12. Position the clamp plate inside the cylinder and secure finger tight.

13. Insert the piston and the return spring in position pushing it through its full stroke several times to align the bearing bush.

14. Remove the piston and spring and secure the clamp plate, taking care not to disturb the cylinder. This is important since if the cylinder is misaligned it can cause the brakes to 'hang on'.

15. Secure the valve chest cover and tube assembly.

16. Smear the piston rod with red rubber grease and apply the special lubricant supplied in the kit to the seal on the piston.

17. Fit a new seal backing ring to the piston seal.

18 Fit the small nylon or bakelite washer, whichever is appropriate, to the piston rod.

19. Insert the piston and spring into the cylinder.

20. With the piston held down against the spring, fit a new gasket to the end cover, and secure the end cover in position.

21. Remove the cylinder from the vice and refit to vehicle, Operation N-19.

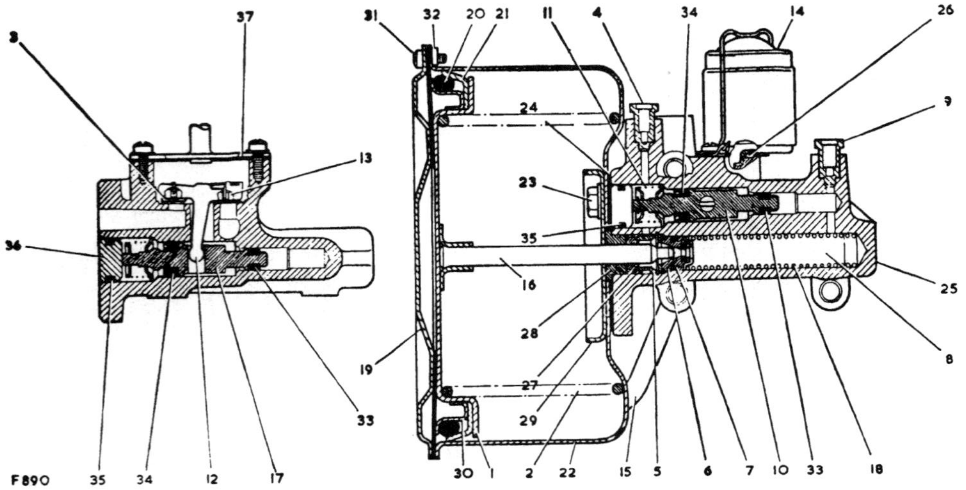

Sectioned view of Girling vacuum servo unit, late models

1	Piston assembly, vacuum
2	Piston return spring
3	Vacuum valve
4	Fluid inlet port
5	Spacer
6	Piston, slave cylinder
7	Seal taper
8	Slave cylinder
9	Fluid outlet port
10	Primary operating valve
11	Return spring, operating valve
12	Valve rocker lever
13	Atmospheric valve
14	Air filter
15	Air pressure pipe
16	Piston rod
17	Secondary valve operating piston
18	Slave cylinder spring
19	End cover plate
20	Sponge rubber seal
21	Seal, piston
22	Vacuum cylinder
23	Self-locking nuts
24	Gasket
25	Valve body
26	Gasket
27	Rubber seal
28	Mild steel bush
29	Clamping plate
30	Seal retainer
31	Screw } Securing end cover
32	Nut } Securing end cover
33	Rubber seal, secondary piston
34	Taper seal
35	Taper seal
36	Mild steel plug
37	Valve cover

Servo air filters, remove and refit—Operation N-21

Workshop hand tools:

Screwdriver, Phillips screwdriver

Servo air filters, remove

The filter element should be replaced every 12,000 miles (20,000 km) or when new pads and shoes are fitted.

1. To remove the filter element on Mk II units, the spring clip under the end plate can be removed by a screwdriver, and the cover and element lifted off.
2. The wire element should be cleaned in Girling cleaning fluid and dipped in brake fluid.
3. To remove the filter on the Mk II unit, the cover can be removed after the spring clip has been pushed aside. The moulded cellular element must be renewed.

Air filter, Mk II brake unit

4. To remove the filter on Mk IIA units the screw and washer must be removed from the centre of the cover.
5. The cover, filter and rubber sealing washer may be lifted off.
6. It is necessary to renew the sealing washer with the filter element.

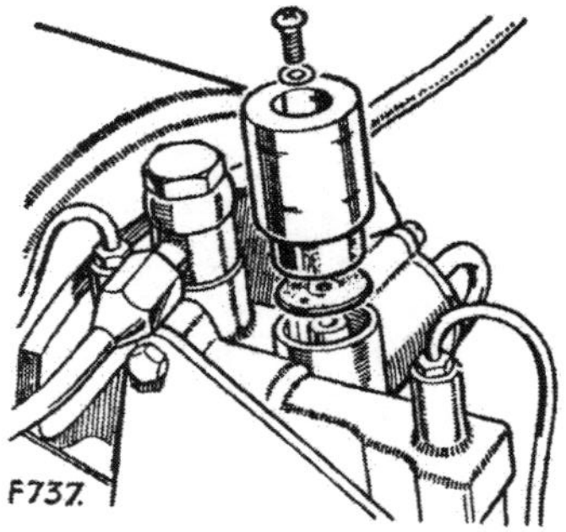

Air filter, Mk IIA and Mk III brake unit

Servo air filters, refit

1. To refit the filter elements on all units, reverse the removal procedure.

Servo reservoir, remove and refit—Operation N-22

Workshop hand tools:

Screwdriver. Spanner size: $\frac{1}{2}$ in. AF

Servo reservoir, remove

The servo reservoir was fitted to Mk I and Mk IA models only. Location under front wing.

1. Remove the air cleaner/silencer. Section A.
2. Remove the banjo bolt retaining the non-return valve (on Mk I models only) and servo pipes to reservoir tank.
3. Remove the three fixing bolts and remove the reservoir tank from beneath the wing.

Servo reservoir, refit

1. Reverse the removal procedure.
2. Start the engine and check for air leaks.

Bleeding the brake system—Operation N-23

Workshop hand tools:

Bleed tube, Glass container. Spanner size: $\frac{7}{16}$ in. AF

Keep brake fluid off paint work.

Brakes, bleed

1. Check fluid in reservoir and if necessary top up with Castrol Girling Crimson Brake Fluid (Specification SAE 70 R3), this level must be maintained during the operation of bleeding.
2. If a vacuum reservoir is fitted the engine must be stopped and the plug removed from the vacuum reservoir to ensure there is no power assistance from the brake servo.
3. Remove the dust cover from the bleed screw of the rear wheel cylinder farthest from the master cylinder.
4. Attach one end of a suitable length of rubber tubing to the bleed screw and place the other end into a clean glass jar, containing some clean brake fluid.
5. Slacken the bleed screw by turning anti-clockwise.
6. With the end of the rubber tube held below the surface of the brake fluid, pump the brake pedal slowly up and down, pausing at the end of each stroke, until the fluid issuing from the tube shows no signs of air bubbles.
7. Depress the brake pedal fully once more and hold down, before tightening the bleed screw and removing the rubber tube. Replace the bleed screw dust cover.
8. Repeat for the other three wheels in turn, continually replenishing the fluid in the supply tank to ensure that the level does not fall too low and so cause a further air lock. Never use fluid that has just been bled from the system for topping up the supply tank—it may be aerated.
9. If applicable, replace the vacuum reservoir plug.

DEFECT LOCATION

SYMPTOM	POSSIBLE CAUSE	REMEDY
A—SPONGY PEDAL ACTION	1. Air in system 2. Swollen rubber components due to incorrect brake fluid 3. Incorrect brake shoe adjustment, early models only	1. *Bleed the hydraulic system* 2. *Drain the system, renew the affected parts and refill with Girling Crimson Brake Fluid* 3. *Adjust*
B—CHATTERING BRAKES	1. Incorrect adjustment of brake shoes, early models 2. Loose front wheel bearings 3. Distorted brake drum or disc	1. *Adjust* 2. *Rectify* 3. *Renew linings as necessary and renew drum or disc*
C—LOSS OF PEDAL PRESSURE	1. Leak at master cylinder 2. Leak at wheel cylinder 3. Leak at servo unit 4. Leak at brake pipes or connections	1. *Renew or rectify* 2. *Renew or rectify* 3. *Renew or rectify* 4. *Renew or rectify*
D—HARD BRAKE PEDAL	1. Incorrect lining 2. Restriction in master cylinder 3. Incorrect shoe adjustment, early models	1. *Renew* 2. *Rectify* 3. *Rectify*
E—HARD BRAKE PEDAL, BRAKES LESS EFFECTIVE	1. Secondary operating piston in servo unit excessively worn or seal defective 2. Vacuum valve-not seating correctly 3. Leaks in pipe-lines between manifold and servo unit 4. Air intake filter choked 5. Vacuum cylinder dented, preventing free movement of piston	1. *Renew or rectify as necessary* 2. *Investigate cause and rectify* 3. *Locate and rectify* 4. *Rectify* 5. *Renew*
F—BINDING BRAKE PEDAL	1. Loose master cylinder mountings 2. Master cylinder operating rod damaged	1. *Rectify* 2. *Renew*
G—POOR BRAKING EFFORT	1. Water soaked linings 2. Incorrect linings 3. Glazed linings 4. Incorrect shoe adjustment, early models only 5. Incorrect pedal setting, giving ineffective master cylinder action 6. Defective servo unit 7. Reservoir servo or connections leaking 8. Fluid level low in reservoir tank	1. *Dry the brake linings by applying the brakes lightly whilst driving* 2. *Renew* 3. *Renew or roughen surface of the linings* 4. *Adjust and check steady post and adjusters on the front brakes* 5. *Reset in accordance with Operation N-17* 6. *Renew or rectify* 7. *Renew or rectify* 8. *Replenish and bleed the system*
H—GRABBING BRAKES OR BRAKING EFFECT EXCESSIVE	1. Servo unit vacuum cylinder end cover plate seal defective 2. Damaged end cover or balance pipe 3. Balance pipe deteriorated 4. Nylon valve cover not seating correctly or seating damaged 5. Restriction washer in balance pipe omitted after overhaul 6. Primary operating piston return sprin defective 7. Atmospheric valve not seating correctly 8. Valve spring broken 9. Scored drum or disc 10. Incorrect shoe adjustment, early models only 11. Incorrect linings 12. Hard spot on drums, early models 13. Loose anchor plate or disc	1. *Renew* 2. *Renew* 3. *Renew* 4. *Renew or rectify* 5. *Refit* 6. *Renew* 7. *Rectify* 8. *Renew* 9. *Renew* 10. *Adjust* 11. *Renew* 12. *Renew* 13. *Rectify or renew*

DEFECT LOCATION—*continued*

SYMPTOM	POSSIBLE CAUSE	REMEDY
J—SIDE PULLING	1. Grease, oil or fluid soaked linings 2. Incorrect shoe adjustment, early models only 3. Loose wheel cylinders 4. Defective brake hose 5. Excessively worn or scored drum or disc 6. Mixed linings 7. Incorrect tyre pressures or worn tyres 8. Water and mud in drums, early models only	1. *Renew and rectify leaks* 2. *Rectify* 3. *Rectify* 4. *Renew* 5. *Renew* 6. *Renew* 7. *Rectify as necessary* 8. *Clean the assembly, examine drums for scoring, linings for wear, renew as necessary*
K—SQUEALING BRAKES	1. Incorrect linings 2. Distorted brake drum or disc 3. Damaged anchor plate, early models only 4. Distorted brake shoes or pads 5. Foreign bodies embedded in brake linings 6. Dust or dirt in the drums, early models only 7. Shoes binding on the steady posts, early models only 8. Loose wheel cylinders 9. Loose linings 10. Badly worn linings	1. *Renew* 2. *Renew* 3. *Renew* 4. *Renew* 5. *Renew* 6. *Clean thoroughly with high pressure air line. If necessary renew the linings and recondition or renew the drums* 7. *Rectify* 8. *Tighten and check the linings. Renew as necessary* 9. *Renew* 10. *Renew*
L—BRAKES OVERHEATING	1. Brake shoes continuously in contact with the drum, early models only 2. High spots on drums, early models only 3. Defective master cylinder or swollen rubber components 4. Incorrect master cylinder adjustment	1. *Adjust* 2. *Recondition or renew* 3. *Renew as necessary* 4. *Rectify. Check brake pedal setting as detailed in Operation N-17*
M—FADING BRAKES	1. Incorrect linings 2. Poor lining contact 3. Excessive heat	1. *Renew* 2. *Adjust* 3. *Check adjustments, renew linings if necessary*
N—BRAKE DRAGS	1. Incorrect adjustment 2. Swollen rubber components in the hydraulic system 3. Seized brake shoe, early models only 4. Weak pull-off springs, early models only 5. Restriction or obstruction in pipe-lines 6. Restriction in master cylinder 7. Distorted brake drum or disc 8. Servo piston sticking 9. Vacuum cylinder end cover seal defective	1. *Rectify* 2. *Renew as necessary* 3. *Free the seized shoe and smear the point of seizure lightly with grease* 4. *Renew* 5. *Renew or rectify* 6. *Remove, clean or renew* 7. *Renew* 8. *Rectify* 9. *Rectify*
P—BRAKES LOCK	1. Grease, oil or fluid soaked linings 2. Damaged or loose lining 3. Loose wheel cylinder 4. Swollen rubber components 5. Servo piston sticks in vacuum cylinder	1. *Renew and rectify any leak* 2. *Renew* 3. *Rectify* 4. *Renew as necessary* 5. *Rectify*
Q—PEDAL GOES TO FLOOR BOARD	1. Linings badly worn 2. Pedal incorrectly set 3. Front brake automatic adjuster not working, early models only 4. Fluid exhausted	1. *Renew or recondition* 2. *Adjust in accordance with Operation N-17* 3. *Reset in accordance with Operation N-1* 4. *Ascertain cause, rectify, refill, bleed and top-up*

DEFECT LOCATION—*continued*

SYMPTOM	POSSIBLE CAUSE	REMEDY
R—GENERAL DETERIORATION OF SERVO ASSISTANCE	1. Vacuum piston leather worn 2. Damaged vacuum cylinder 3. Slave cylinder piston seal worn or deteriorated 4. Primary operating piston or seal worn 5. Piston rod and slave cylinder piston not seating properly 6. Valve springs broken or weak 7. Vacuum valve not seating correctly 8. Vacuum pipe connections loose or pipe damaged or deteriorated 9. Vacuum piston return spring weak or broken 10. Insufficient hydraulic fluid in reservoir	1. *Fit a new assembly* 2. *Renew damaged parts* 3. *Renew seal* 4. *Renew* 5. *Renew* 6. *Renew* 7. *Rectify and renew as necessary* 8. *Rectify or renew* 9. *Renew* 10. *Refill and bleed the system*
S—VACUUM RESERVOIR TANK WILL NOT RETAIN VACUUM AFTER ENGINE STOPS, EARLY MODELS	1. Faulty non-return valve 2. Pipe connections loose 3. Faulty atmospheric valve in servo unit 4. Faulty plug or seal	1. *Investigate cause and rectify* 2. *Rectify* 3. *Investigate cause and rectify* 4. *Renew*

DATA

Master cylinder Girling type $\frac{3}{4}$ CB

Bore	.75 in. (19,1 mm) diameter
Maximum stroke	1$\frac{3}{8}$ in. (34,9 mm)
Brake drum diameter	11 in. (279,4 mm)
Regrind limit	.030 in. (0,75 mm)

Wheel cylinders, front

Bore	1$\frac{1}{4}$ in. (31,7 mm) diameter
Number per wheel	2

Wheel cylinder, rear
drum brake cars

bore	$\frac{5}{8}$ in. (15,8 mm) diameter
Number per wheel	1

Wheel cylinder, rear
disc brake cars

bore	$\frac{3}{4}$ in. (19 mm) diameter
Number per wheel	1

Foot brake—front, drum type

Type	Two trailing shoes, hydraulic—vacuum servo-assisted
Linings:	
length	8.17 in. (207,4 mm)
width	3 in. (76,2 mm)
thickness	.187 in. (4,74 mm)
area (front total)	49 sq in. (316 sq cm)

Foot brake—front, disc type

Thickness of linings when new	$\frac{1}{2}$ in. (12,7 mm)
Minimum thickness of lining	$\frac{1}{8}$ in. (3 mm) to $\frac{1}{16}$ in. (1,5 mm)
Width of segment	2$\frac{3}{8}$ in. (51,1 mm)
Diameter of disc	10$\frac{3}{4}$ in. (273 mm)
Maximum permissible run-out	0.003 in. (0,075 mm)

Foot brake—rear

Type	Leading and trailing, hydraulic—vacuum servo-assisted
Linings:	
length	8.64 in. (208 mm)
width	2.25 in. (57 mm)
thickness	.187 in. (4,74 mm)
area (rear total)	38.88 sq in. (504,95 sq cm)

Pedal setting

All models	The distance from the bottom of the pedal pad to the floor is 6 in. (152 mm)

Pedal stop setting

All models	Adjust to give a minimum clearance of $\frac{1}{16}$ in. (1,5 mm) free movement of the push rod in the master cylinder

Fluid	Castrol Girling Crimson Brake Fluid (Specification SAE 70 R3)

Section P—COOLING SYSTEM

Brief description of cooling system

The engine cooling system operates on the conventional thermo-syphon principle, and is impeller pump assisted.

The pump, which carries a four-bladed fan to assist air flow through the radiator block, is belt driven from the crankshaft pulley.

A thermostat is fitted to ensure rapid engine warm-up. When starting from cold, the thermostat prevents coolant flow through the radiator block, until a predetermined temperature has been attained. Upon reaching the operating temperature the thermostat will automatically re-direct the coolant flow through the radiator.

The cooling system is designed to operate at a pressure of 4 lb/sq in. (0,28 kg/cm^2). In addition to other benefits, this ensures greater engine efficiency.

A pressure relief valve is combined with the radiator cap. If the cap is to be removed when the engine is warm, caution must be exercised to prevent personal injury from scalding. Instructions are stamped on the cap top.

Two points are provided for draining the system, one tap at the side of the cylinder block, and a drain plug at the base of the radiator. However, since it is impossible to completely drain the heater system, a good quality glycol-base anti-freeze solution, should be used during the winter months. In order to avoid an air-lock when draining or refilling the cooling system, the heat control on the heater control panel should be placed in the 'Hot' position.

INDEX

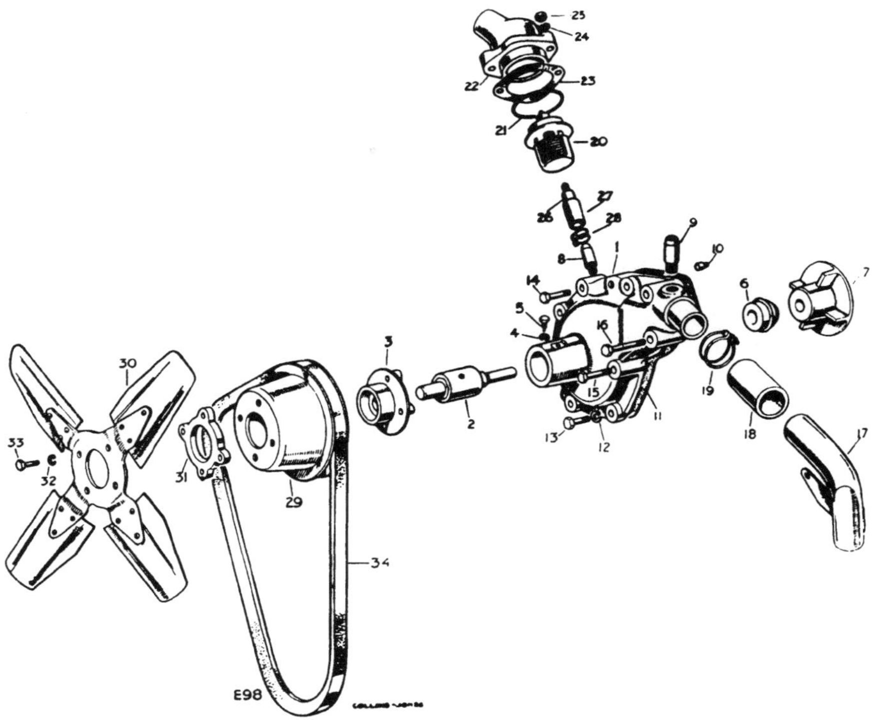

Layout of water pump and thermostat, early models illustrated

1	Casing for water pump
2	Spindle and bearing complete
3	Hub for pulley
4–5	Special set bolt and spring washer
6	Carbon ring and seal unit
7	Impeller for pump
8	Adaptor for thermostat by-pass
9	Adaptor for heater pipe
10	Dowel for water pump casing
11	Joint washer
12–16	Fixings, water pump to block
17	Inlet pipe for water pump
18	Hose
19	Clip for hose
20	Thermostat
21	Joint washer
22	Outlet pipe
23	Joint washer
24–25	Fixings, pipe to cylinder head
26	Adaptor for thermostat by-pass
27	Rubber by-pass pipe
28	Clip for pipe
29	Pulley for fan
30	Fan blade
31	Packing for fan blade
32–33	Fixings, pulley and blade to hub
34	Fan belt

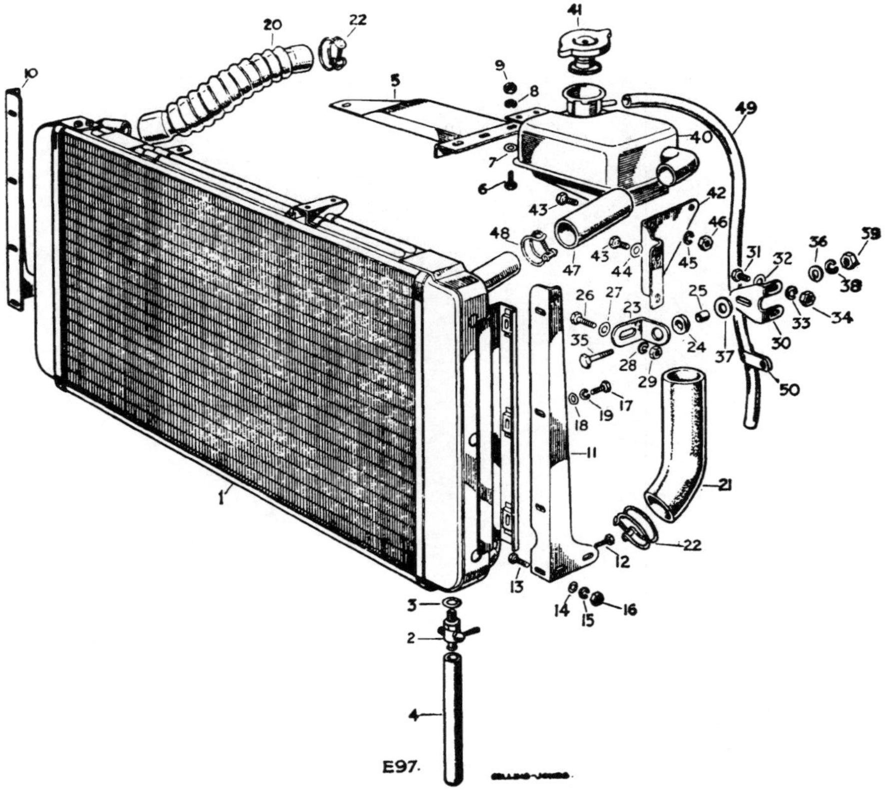

Layout of radiator and fixings

1	Radiator block
2	Drain tap
3	Joint washer
4	Extension tube
5	Fan cowl and header tank support
6–9	Fixings, cowl to radiator and header tank
10	Mounting bracket, RH
11	Mounting bracket, LH
12–16	Fixings, mounting brackets to sub-frame
17–19	Fixings, radiator to brackets
20	Top water hose
21	Bottom water hose
22	Clip for hose
23	Stay for radiator
24–25	Rubber grommet and distance piece
26–29	Fixings, stay to radiator mounting brackets
30	Stay for radiator
31–39	Fixings, stay and valance
40	Header tank
41	Filler cap
42	Bottom support bracket for header tank
43–46	Fixings, support bracket
47	Hose
48	Clip for hose
49	Hose for overflow
50	Clip for hose

Water pump, to overhaul—Operation P-1

Workshop hand tools:
Spanner sizes: $\frac{7}{16}$ in. AF, $\frac{1}{2}$ in. AF, $\frac{5}{8}$ in. AF
Screwdriver, medium
Feeler gauge

Special tools:
Pulley hub extractor

Refer to Section A for removal and refitting of the radiator and water pump

Water pump, overhaul

1. Using a suitable extractor, withdraw the fan pulley hub from the spindle.
2. Remove the bolt and spring washer locating the spindle and bearing assembly.
3. Press out the spindle bearing, seal unit and impeller assembly towards the rear. Inspect and renew components as necessary.
A water pump overhaul kit can be obtained under Part No. 503031 which comprises:
   - Spindle and bearing
   - Water impeller
   - Front washer
   - Fitting instructions.
4. If necessary, support the impeller and drive out the spindle and remove the seal unit. This should only be done where the spindle and bearing are to be used again. Examine the assembly; it need not be renewed if the bearing is satisfactory and the spindle is free from excessive corrosion.
5. Where the original spindle and bearing is being used again, clean any corroded portion of the spindle and paint with chlorinated rubber primer to prevent further corrosion (Part No. 261843 for half-pint tin). As an alternative, good quality aluminium paint or other anti-corrosive paint can be used in place of a rubber primer.
6. Insert a few drops of thick oil into the location hole in the bearing. Press the spindle and bearing assembly and (late models) rubber deflector washer into the pump body, with the longer end of the spindle leading. Take care to align the locating hole in the body and bearing. Locate the bearing with the set bolt and spring washer.
7. Support the spindle and press on the fan pulley hub to a set dimension between the front face of the pulley hub and the mounting face of the water pump casing. This dimension must be 3.80 in. (96,5 mm) for 1959-60 models and 4.456 in. (115,4 mm) for 1961 models onwards.

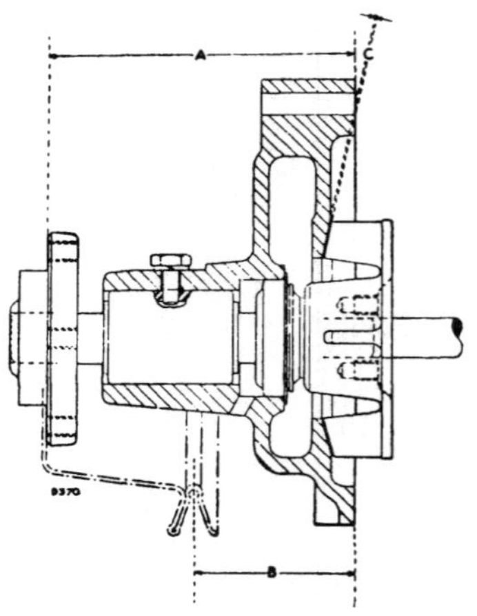

Cross-section of water pump

1959-60 models	1961 onward models
A—3.80 in. (96,5 mm)	A—4.456 in. (115,4 mm)
B—2.0 in. (50,8 mm)	B—2.656 in. (67,5 mm)
C—.020 in. (0,5 mm)	C—.020 in. (0,5 mm)

8. Fit the new carbon ring and seal unit into the bore of the pump body, with the carbon ring towards the mounting face.
9. With the pulley hub end of the spindle supported, press the impeller on to the spindle until there is .020 in. (0,5 mm) clearance between the vanes and pump body face. Check this dimension with a feeler gauge. The impeller must be a **press fit** on the spindle. If the impeller is loose, replace either part as necessary.
10. If removed, refit the heater and thermostat adaptor pipes to the water pump body.

Thermostat, to remove and refit—Operation P-2

Workshop hand tools:
Spanner sizes: $\frac{7}{16}$ in. AF. Screwdriver, medium

Thermostat, remove

1. Partly drain off the coolant and disconnect the water outlet hose from the thermostat cover.
2. Remove the outlet pipe from the water pump casing secured by three nuts and spring washers.

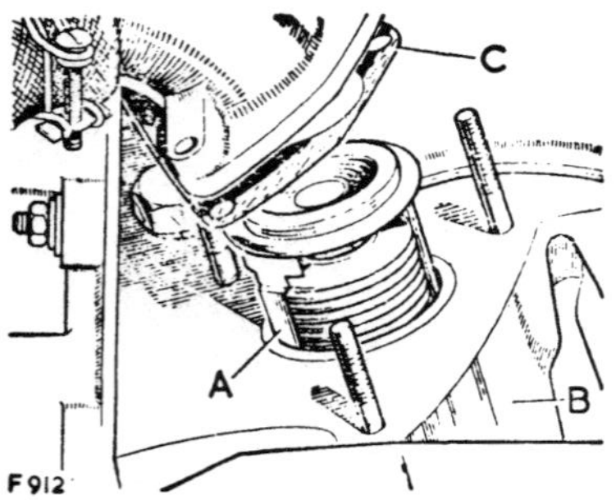

F912

Removing thermostat

A—Thermostat B—Cylinder head C—Joint washer

3. Lift out the thermostat and joint washer.

Thermostat, to check

4. Immerse the thermostat in hot water, expansion of the bellows should commence between 162°F and 171°F (72 - 77°C) and be complete at 191°F (88°C).

Thermostat, refit

1. Reverse removal procedure.
2. Renew the joint washer.
3. Top up the coolant and check for leaks.

Cooling system, to check—Operation P-3

The AC pressure cap and cooling system tester, which is complete with all adaptors, can be used to carry out the following tests in seconds.

Pressure cap

Calibration test

Fit cap to tester, then pump up pressure as far as possible. If pressure release is not within the limits marked on the dial, the cap is fatigued and should be replaced.

Leak test

If the cap will not hold pressure for a minimum of 10 seconds it indicates a leaking seal or valve and the cap should be replaced.

Cooling system

External leak test

Remove pressure cap and fit the tester to the radiator. By pumping up the pressure to the poundage indicated on the cap, near actual running conditions can be assimilated. If the pressure drops, check all seals and joints for leaks—any leaks will be apparent because the pressure forces the coolant to seep out of any leakage points.

Absence of external leaks may indicate that internal leaks are present.

Blown cylinder head gasket test

Care must be exercised in this test to ensure that the cooling system pressure does not exceed that marked on the cap.

Attach tester to radiator and apply pressure. Start engine and set at a slow tick-over—a blown cylinder head gasket will now show itself by fluctuations in pressure on the tester gauge.

DEFECT LOCATION

SYMPTOM	*POSSIBLE CAUSE*	*REMEDY*
A—EXTERNAL LEAKAGE	1. Loose hose clips 2. Defective rubber hose 3. Damaged radiator seams 4. Excessive wear in the water pump 5. Loose core plugs 6. Damaged gaskets 7. Leaks at the heater connections or plugs 8. Leak at the water temperature gauge plug	1. *Tighten* 2. *Renew* 3. *Rectify* 4. *Renew* 5. *Renew* 6. *Renew* 7. *Rectify* 8. *Tighten*
B—INTERNAL LEAKAGE	1. Defective cylinder head gasket 2. Cracked cylinder wall 3. Loose cylinder head bolts	1. *Renew. Check engine oil for contamination and refill as necessary* 2. *Renew cylinder block* 3. *Tighten. Check engine oil for contamination and refill as necessary*
C—WATER LOSS	1. Boiling 2. Internal or external leakage 3. Restricted radiator or inoperative thermostat	1. *Ascertain the cause of engine overheating and correct as necessary* 2. *See Items A and B* 3. *Flush radiator or renew the thermostat as necessary*
D—POOR CIRCULATION	1. Restriction in system 2. Insufficient coolant 3. Inoperative water pump 4. Loose fan belt 5. Inoperative thermostat	1. *Check hoses for crimps, reverse flush the radiator, and clear the system of rust and sludge* 2. *Replenish* 3. *Renew* 4. *Adjust* 5. *Renew*
E—CORROSION	1. Excessive impurity in the water 2. Infrequent flushing and draining of system 3. Incorrect anti-freeze mixtures	1. *Use only soft, clean water (rainwater is satisfactory)* 2. *The cooling system should be drained and flushed thoroughly at least twice a year* 3. *Certain anti-freeze solutions may have a corrosive effect on parts of the cooling system. Only good glycol-base solutions should be used.*
F—OVERHEATING	1. Poor circulation 2. Dirty oil and sludge in engine 3. Radiator fins choked with chaff, mud, etc. 4. Incorrect ignition timing 5. Incorrect valve timing 6. Low oil level 7. Tight engine 8. Choked or damaged exhaust pipe or silencer 9. Dragging brakes 10. Overloading vehicle 11. Driving in heavy sand or mud 12. Engine labouring on grades 13. Low gear work 14. Excessive engine idling 15. Inaccurate temperature gauge 16. Defective thermostat	1. *See Item D* 2. *Refill* 3. *Use air pressure from the engine side of the radiator and clean out passages thoroughly* 4. *See Section—A* 5. *See Section—A* 6. *Replenish* 7. *New engines are very tight during the 'running-in' period and moderate speeds should be maintained for the first 1,000 miles (1.500 km)* 8. *Rectify or renew* 9. *See Section—N* 10. *In the hands of the operator* 11. *In the hands of the operator* 12. *In the hands of the operator* 13. *In the hands of the operator* 14. *In the hands of the operator* 15. *Renew* 16. *Renew*
G—OVERCOOLING	1. Defective thermostat 2. Inaccurate temperature gauge	1. *Renew* 2. *Renew*

TECHNICAL DETAIL DATA

Cooling system	
Water capacity:	
Mk I, Mk IA and Mk II with engines suffix 'A' and 'B'	$22\frac{1}{2}$ Imperial pints; 27 US pints; 13 litres
Mk II with engines suffix 'C' onwards	24 Imperial pints; 29 US pints; 13,7 litres
Mk III	26 Imperial pints; 31 US pints; 14,7 litres
Type	Pump and fan
Temperature control	Thermostat
Thermostat setting (nominal)	Opens at 72° to 77°C (162°F to 171°F)
Pressurised	4 lb/sq in. (0,28 kg/cm²)
Water pump	
Type	Centrifugal impeller
Drive	'V' belt
Fan	
Number of blades	4
Overall diameter	16 in. (406 mm)
Fan belt tension, Single belt	$\frac{5}{16}$ in. to $\frac{7}{16}$ in. (8,0 to 11,0 mm)
Fan belt tension } Twin belts	$\frac{5}{16}$ in. to $\frac{7}{16}$ in. (8,0 to 11,0 mm)
Dynamo belt tension } Twin belts	$\frac{5}{16}$ in. to $\frac{7}{16}$ in. (8,0 to 11,0 mm)
Frost precautions—when the temperature is between 32°F and 0°F (0°C and minus 18°C) a solution of anti-freeze and water is required at the following strength	One part anti-freeze to two parts water. (Only high-quality inhibited glycol-base solutions should be used.)

Section Q – FUEL SYSTEM

Brief description of fuel system

The 14 Imperial gallon ($16\frac{3}{4}$ US gallon, 64 litre) fuel tank is located in the boot of the car, from where fuel is pumped to the carburetter by means of a high pressure electric pump(s) mounted alongside the tank.

A $1\frac{1}{2}$ gallon (7 litre) reserve supply is controlled by a switch on the instrument panel.

The fuel pumped to the carburetter is filtered through a sediment bowl which is located on the wing valance in the engine compartment.

An HD8 type SU carburetter is fitted, which has automatic needle operation controlled by manifold depression acting upon the top of the carburetter piston into which the needle is fixed.

The profile of the needle for a particular engine, identified by the type mark on the shank, is only settled after extensive testing. It is generally inadvisable to change from the standard type.

The fuel level gauge and the tank unit are not precision instruments and only give an approximate indication of the fuel level in the tank.

They are therefore not suitable for taking fuel consumption figures.

INDEX

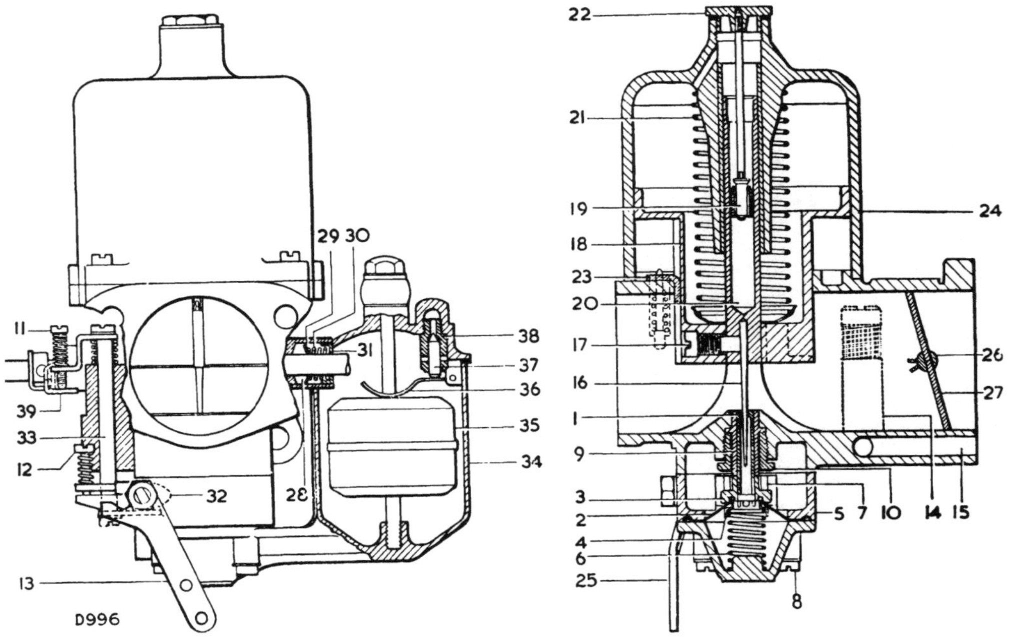

Cross-sectional view of carburetter

1	Jet	14	Slow running adjustment screw	27	Throttle butterfly
2	Diaphragm	15	Slow running orifice	28	Gland for spindle
3	Jet cup	16	Tapered metering needle	29	Dished washer for gland
4	Spring cup	17	Special retaining screw	30	Spring
5	Casing	18	Piston	31	Shroud for spring
6	Return spring	19	Damper	32	Cam
7	Jet actuating lever	20	Oil reservoir	33	Push rod
8	Float chamber securing screw	21	Piston return spring	34	Float chamber
9	Jet bearing	22	Oil cap	35	Float
10	Jet screw	23	Piston guide	36	Float lever
11	Fast idle screw	24	Suction chamber	37	Needle valve
12	Mixture control screw	25	Jet hand control lever	38	Needle valve seat
13	Jet hand control lever	26	Throttle spindle	39	Throttle stop

Carburetter, to remove and refit—Operation Q-1

Workshop hand tools:
Spanner sizes: $\frac{3}{8}$ in. AF, $\frac{7}{16}$ in. AF, $\frac{1}{2}$ in. AF, 2 BA

Carburetter, remove

1. Remove the air cleaner silencer. On early models with oil bath type air cleaners, slacken the hose clip between the top of the air cleaner and silencer and disconnect the hose. All models, remove the air silencer secured to the elbow by a nut and washer, and by a support bracket to a stud on top of the induction manifold.
2. Disconnect the economiser air hose, between the air silencer elbow and carburetter.
3. Remove the air silencer elbow, secured to the carburetter by two nuts and spring washers.
4. Disconnect the fuel supply pipe.
5. Disconnect the vacuum advance pipe.
6. Disconnect the control rod from the throttle lever.
7. Disconnect the throttle return spring.
8. Remove the carburetter, secured by four nuts and spring washers.

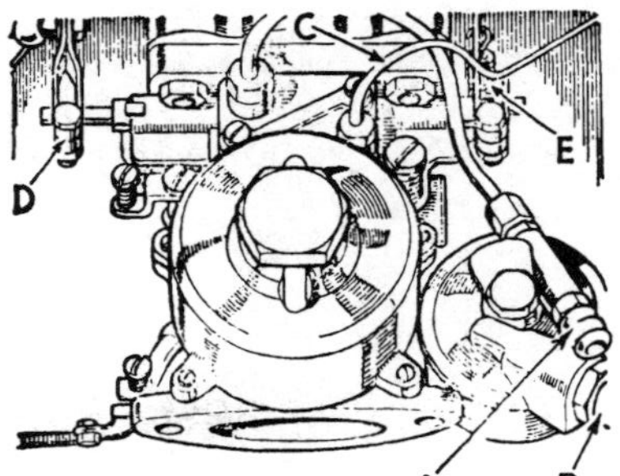

G167

Plan view of carburetter

A—Economiser air hose connection
B—Fuel supply connection
C—Vacuum advance pipe connection
D—Throttle lever
E—Throttle return spring

Carburetter, refit

1. Ensure th · the fitting faces of the carburetter and cylinder head are clean.
2. Reverse removal procedure. Always use a new joint washer.
3. Adjust the cold start control. Operation Q-4.
4. Adjust and tune the carburetter. Operation Q-3.

Carburetter, to overhaul—Operation Q-2

Workshop hand tools:
Spanner sizes: $\frac{11}{32}$ in. AF, $\frac{7}{16}$ in. AF, $\frac{1}{2}$ in. AF, $\frac{1}{4}$ in. Whit, $\frac{5}{16}$ in. Whit, $\frac{3}{8}$ in. Whit., 2 BA
Screwdriver, medium; Pliers

For air cleaner removal see Section A

Carburetter, dismantle

1. Unscrew the oil cap complete with hydraulic damper and washer, and withdraw.
2. Remove the suction chamber, secured by four screws and ensure that the piston spring does not fly out.
3. Remove the piston spring and protection washer from inside the piston.
4. Slacken needle retaining screw in the side of the piston and remove needle.
5. Remove petrol pipe union, fibre washer and gauze filter.
6. Remove banjo bolt and special washer securing top of float chamber and economy device.
7. Remove the adaptor (for economiser and ignition pipes) from the top of the carburetter body, secured by two screws.
8. Remove float chamber top and float.
9. Remove splined pivot from fork, and needle valve from float chamber top.
10. Remove the four screws and shakeproof washers at the base of the carburetter body, together with the bracket and distance piece for choke cable.
11. Carefully remove float chamber and jet return spring.
12. Remove the diaphragm from carburetter body and jet housing; remove jet screw and bearing.
13. Remove the slow running adjustment screw complete with spring, dished brass washer and gland.
14. Remove the cam shoe retaining screw on the bottom end of the sliding rod, remove sliding rod and return spring.
15. Remove throttle return spring lever from throttle spindle.
16. With the butterfly in the fully closed position, mark the butterfly with two lines, one either side of the butterfly spindle and mark to identify the bottom of butterfly. This is to ensure it is refitted in the same position.
17. With a pair of long-nosed pliers, close the split ends of the throttle butterfly retaining screws, and remove; push out butterfly and withdraw spindle.
18. Lever out both gland retainers, and remove spring, dished washer and gland.

Carburetter, rebuild

1. Absolute cleanliness is essential.
2. Check carburetter mounting flange for distortion with a straight edge and face up if necessary.
3. When carburetter spindle has been removed, new glands and retainers must be fitted; renew any other defective parts where necessary.
4. Clean all parts thoroughly in petrol.
5. Place the two smaller spring clips on the inserted end of the spindle and feed the spindle into the opposite bush.

   When the disc slot is central separate the clips and position so that the split is at 90° to the slot, slide clips outwards until they are concealed in the body casting.
6. Rotate the spindle to the 'Full open' position and insert the throttle disc ensuring that the chamfered edges will slope in the correct direction when closed. Close the throttle and insert two securing screws just tight enough to prevent the disc from slipping.
7. Centralise the disc by 'snapping' throttle shut several times, allow .015 to .030 in. (0,3 to 0,7 mm) clearance between stop lever and body then tighten screws and spread ends.

Operation Q-2—*continued*

8. Slide remaining spring clip over throttle spindle. Check that inner spring clip slots are not likely to foul the throttle disc and that the outer spring clips are hard against the throttle bushes.
9. Insert carburetter spindle into carburetter body.
10. Position a new gland dished washer, spring and new retainer, gently ease into carburetter body with a suitable piece of tubing.
11. Remove spindle from carburetter body and insert from the other side; repeat the process. Ensure that the spindle is in its correct position, that is, with the throttle stop to the left-hand side of the carburetter.

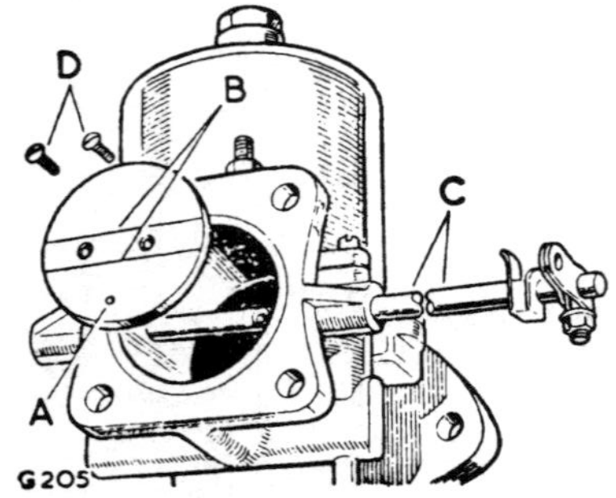

Fitting butterfly

A—Slow running orifice
B—Locating marks
C—Spindle
D—Screws

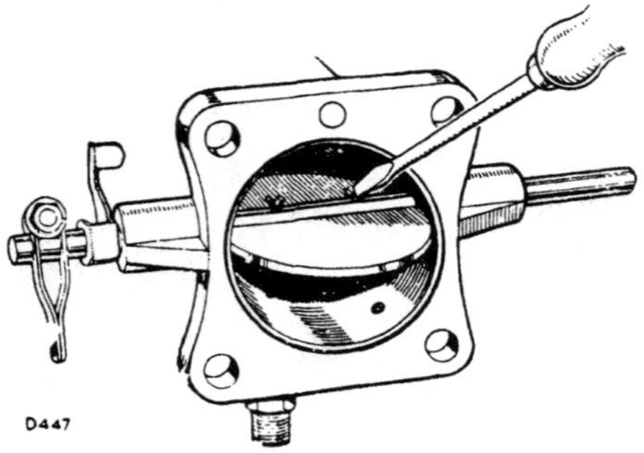

Locking retaining screws

12. Turn the spindle to full throttle position, insert the butterfly using the marks made when dismantling to ensure correct fitting.
13. Refit the throttle return spring lever but do not fully tighten.

Replacing nylon butterfly spindle bushes in latest carburetters. Item 14

14. Slide one of the larger spring clips along the throttle spindle until it is $\frac{1}{4}$ in. from the throttle stop. Insert the nylon bushes from inside the carburetter bore and then feed the throttle spindle through from the throttle stop side, gently rotating and keeping the bush within the casting.

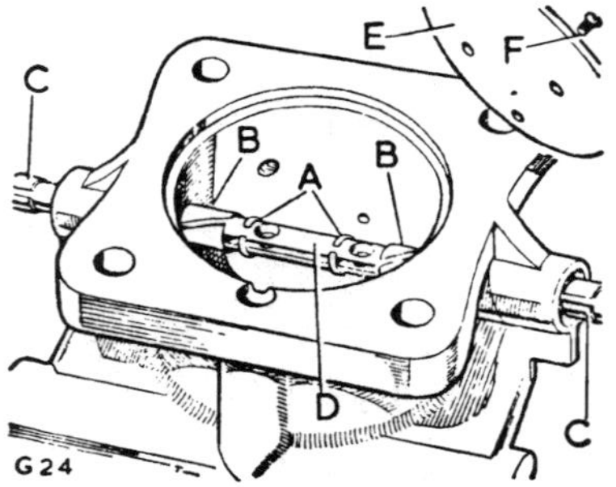

Inserting nylon bushes

A—Small spring clips
B—Nylon bush
C—Large spring clips
D—Throttle spindle
E—Throttle disc
F—Retaining screw

15. Fit needle to piston so that the top of the fitting register is flush with the body of the piston.
16. Insert the piston into the suction chamber and spin the piston to ensure the needle is not bent.
17. Fit jet bearing, short end into the body and retain with the jet screw; do not tighten at this stage.
18. Fit the piston to the carburetter body.
19. Fit protective washer into the body of the piston and fit the spring.
20. Fit suction chamber to carburetter body; revolve suction chamber to align holes for retaining screws.

Operation Q-2—*continued*

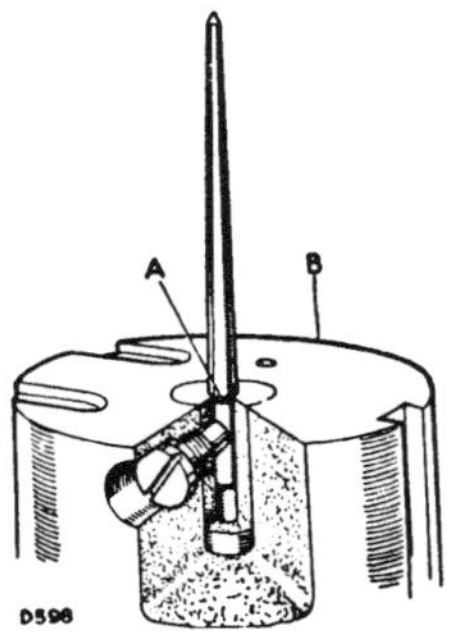

Needle in correct position
A—Needle B—Piston body

21. Fit screws and tighten evenly.
22. Invert the carburetter and insert the jet, gradually tighten the jet screw, ensuring that the needle is not binding on the jet. If the needle is binding: slacken the jet retaining screw, and rotate the bearing to free it, then re-tighten jet retaining screw.
23. Remove jet and fit jet housing to carburetter body.
24. Insert the jet and align the holes in the diaphragm with those corresponding to them in the jet housing.
25. Fit the jet return spring, float chamber and choke cable bracket, secure with four screws and shakeproof washers; do not tighten at this stage.
26. Ensure that the diaphragm can move to the limit of its travel; in this position tighten the retaining screws.
27. Lift and allow the piston to fall sharply several times, to centralise the jet, then tighten jet locking screw. This operation must be repeated until the piston falls freely and hits the jet bridge with a soft metallic click. Take care to keep the jet held firmly upwards during jet centralisation.
28. Refit the slow running gland, washer, spring and slow running screw, which should be screwed right in.
29. Fit the float into the float chamber.
30. Fit the gauze filter, fibre washer and union to the float chamber top.
31. Fit the needle valve, needle valve fork and splined pivot pin to float chamber top.
32. Place a $\frac{7}{16}$ in. (11 mm) round bar between needle valve fork and float chamber top; ensure that with the bar in position the needle valve is held firmly on its seating, that is, air cannot be blown past the needle valve. The fork must be bent at the point illustrated until this condition can be obtained. Where plastic enclosed spring loaded needle valves are fitted it should be noted that when placing a $\frac{7}{16}$ in. (11 mm) bar between the needle valve fork and the float chamber top, the fork should only rest on the top of the needle valve and should not be allowed to compress the spring.
33. Fit float chamber top to float chamber and retain with special washer, economy device and 'banjo bolt.
34. Fit gasket to adaptor housing and fit housing to carburetter body, secure with two screws and shakeproof washers.
35. Fit sliding rod with cam shoe, together with top plate and fast idle screw to the carburetter body. Secure with washers, spring and screw.
36. Insert a few drops of SAE 20 oil into the reservoir and fit oil cap and fibre washers.

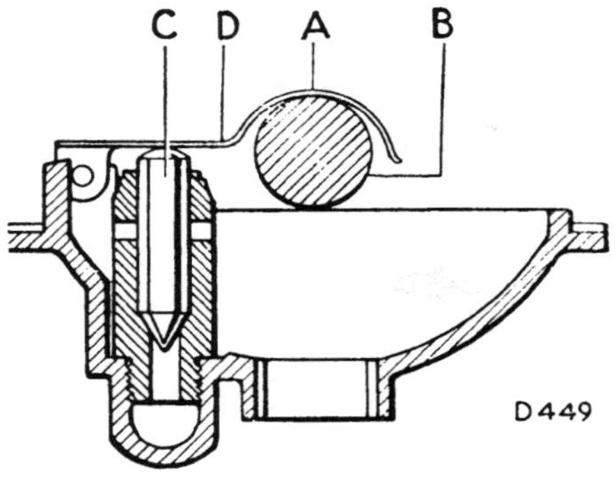

Fitting float level fork
A—Fork
B—$\frac{7}{16}$ in. round bar (11 mm)
C—Needle valve
D—Point at which fork must be bent

Carburetter, to tune—Operation Q-3

Workshop hand tools:
Spanner sizes: 2 BA, $\frac{5}{16}$ in. Whit
Screwdriver, small

Before attempting to tune the carburetter ensure that the engine compression is satisfactory and that there are no air leaks. Check the ignition and sparking plugs for defects and rectify as necessary. See data sheet for idling speeds.

Carburetter, to tune

1. Start the engine and adjust the fast idle screw to give the desired idling speed as indicated by the glowing of the ignition warning light.
2. Turn the slow-run valve until the best idling speed is obtained consistent with even firing.

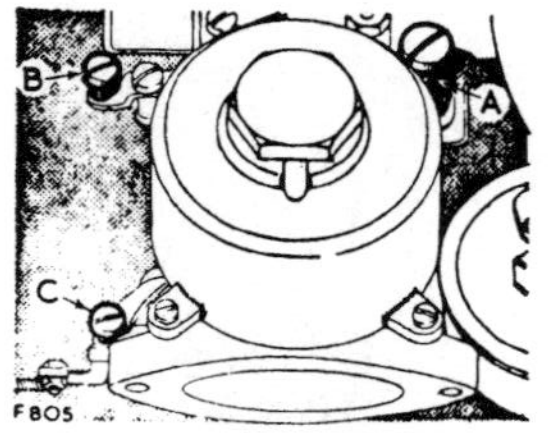

Carburetter adjustment
A—Slow-run valve B—Fast idle adjustment screw
C—Jet adjustment screw

3. As the mixture is adjusted the engine will probably run faster, and it may therefore be necessary to adjust the fast idle screw in order to reduce the speed.
4. By means of the lift pin on the side of the carburetter body lifting the carburetter piston by approximately $\frac{1}{32}$ in. (1 mm) and check the mixture strength, when:
   (a) If the engine speed increases and continues to run faster, this indicates that the mixture is too rich;
   (b) If the engine speed immediately decreases, this indicates that the mixture is too weak;
   (c) If the engine speed momentarily increases very slightly, this indicates that the mixture is correct.
5. When the mixture is correct the exhaust note should be regular and even. If it is irregular, with a splashy type of misfire and a colourless exhaust, the mixture is too weak.
6. If there is a regular or rhythmical type of misfire, together with a blackish exhaust, then the mixture is too rich.
7. With the engine hot, set the cold start control to its maximum travel without moving the carburetter jet and with the warning light just out, adjust the fast idle screw to give an engine speed of about 1,000 rpm.
8. Ensure that the hydraulic damper is replenished with SAE 20 oil to $\frac{1}{2}$ in. (12 mm) above the top of the rod.
9. If the carburetter cannot be satisfactorily tuned as detailed above, the following points should be checked.
10. If the general mixture strength is suspect, or being checked over, first remove the suction chamber and piston unit.
11. Slacken off the needle clamping screw, extract the needle and check that the needle is of the recommended type.
12. Replace the needle and lock it in the standard position, having the shoulder on the shank just flush with the end face of the piston.
13. As the needle size is determined during engine development, tuning of the carburetter is confined to correct idling setting.
14. Screw the slow-run valve until the jet is flush with the bridge of the carburetter. Replace the piston and suction chamber and check that the piston falls freely on to the bridge of the carburetter, do this by means of the piston lifting pin.
15. Lower the jet by turning the slow-run valve two-and-a-half turns.
16. Run the engine until it has attained its normal operating temperature, then close the throttle completely and screw down the fast idle screw on to its seating, then unscrew it three-and-a-half turns. Tune engine by repeating items 1 to 8.

Cold start control, to adjust—Operation Q-4

Workshop hand tools:
Spanner sizes: 2 BA, 4 BA, $\frac{3}{4}$ in. AF
Screwdriver, small

Cold start control, adjust

1. Run the engine until normal operating temperature has been attained.
2. Slacken the nut of clamp securing the inner wire of the cold start control cable to the lever on the carburetter.

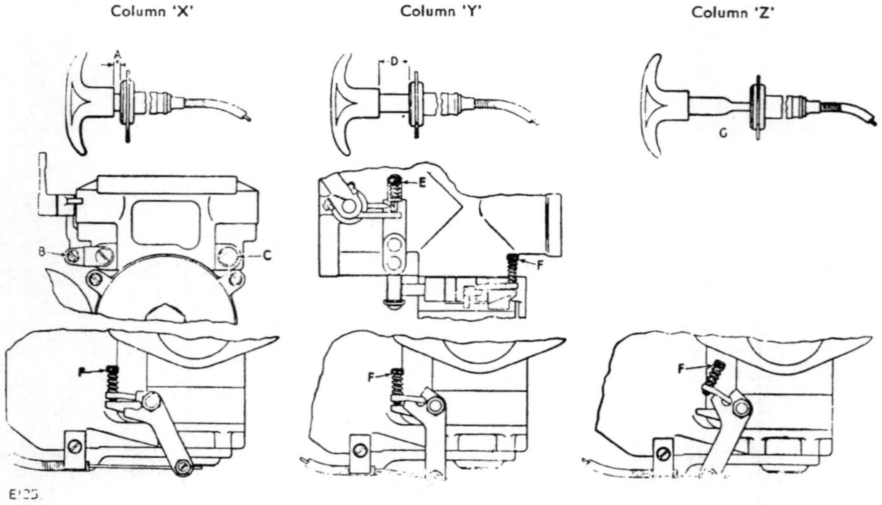

Setting cold start control

	Column 'X'	Column 'Y'	Column 'Z'
Top illustration Cold start control knob setting	A—$\frac{1}{8}$ in. (3 mm) Control off—no fast idle	D—$\frac{5}{8}$ in. (15 mm) Fast idle position	Full operation position
Centre illustration Adjusting screws on carburetter	B—Fast idle C—Mixture volume (Plan view of carburetter)	E—Fast idle F—Jet adjusting screw	
Lower illustration Cold start lever positions	F—Jet adjusting screw Fully forward—off	F—Jet adjusting screw Centre—fast idle	F—Jet adjusting screw Fully rearward—full operation

Operation Q-4—*continued*

3. Secure the cold start lever in the fully forward position. Pull out the control knob $\frac{1}{16}$ in. (1,6 mm) and maintain this position. Re-tighten the cable clamp. (Column X of diagram).

Four-speed and overdrive models

4. Pull out the cold start control $\frac{5}{8}$ in. (15 mm), then fully open the accelerator and allow it to spring back. (This is to allow the throttle linkage to take up its correct position). Adjust the fast idling screw by turning clockwise to increase speed to give 800 to 850 rpm. There must be no enrichment of the mixture at this position and the cold start warning light switch should not have operated. (Column Y of diagram).

Automatic transmission

5. When carrying out the following adjustment **the wheels must be blocked and the hand brake firmly applied.**

   Select 'D' drive position, pull out the cold start control $\frac{5}{8}$ in. (15 mm), then fully open the accelerator and allow it to spring back allowing the throttle linkage to take up its correct position. Adjust the fast idling screw to give 800 to 850 rpm. There must be no enrichment of the mixture and the warning light must not have operated with the control in the above position, but further movement outwards of the control knob must immediately operate the warning light switch and commence progressive enrichment of the mixture. (Column Y of diagram).

Fuel pump, to remove and refit—Operation Q-5

Workshop hand tools:
Spanner sizes: $\frac{7}{16}$ in. AF, $\frac{3}{8}$ in. BSF

Fuel pump(s), remove

1. Disconnect the battery leads.
2. Lift up trim and remove the pump cover from the right-hand rear corner of the boot.
3. Disconnect the wiring at the 'Lucar' connectors.
4. Disconnect both the pipes from the pump.
   Note: Some cars are fitted with twin fuel pumps.
5. Remove the pump from the mounting bracket.

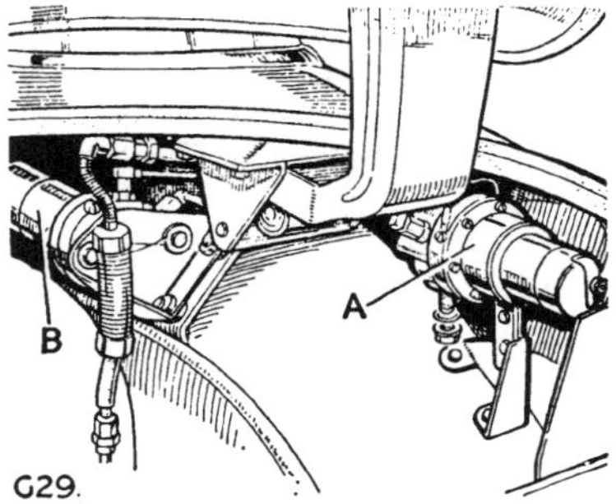

G29.

Twin fuel pumps
A—Main pump B—Reserve pump

Double entry pumps

Late model cars are fitted with double entry fuel pump which have a common outlet.

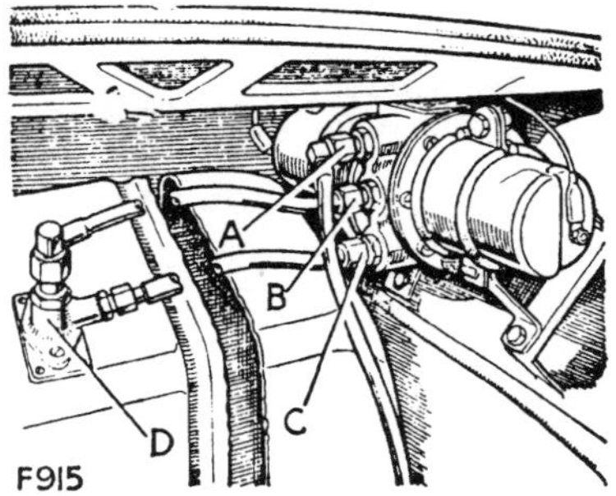

F915

Double entry type fuel pump
A—Supply pipe to carburetter
B—Supply pipe (main) tank to pump
C—Supply pipe (reserve) tank to pump
D—Tank connections

Fuel pump(s), refit

1. Reverse removal procedure.
2. Check pump(s) for correct operation

Operation Q-5—*continued*

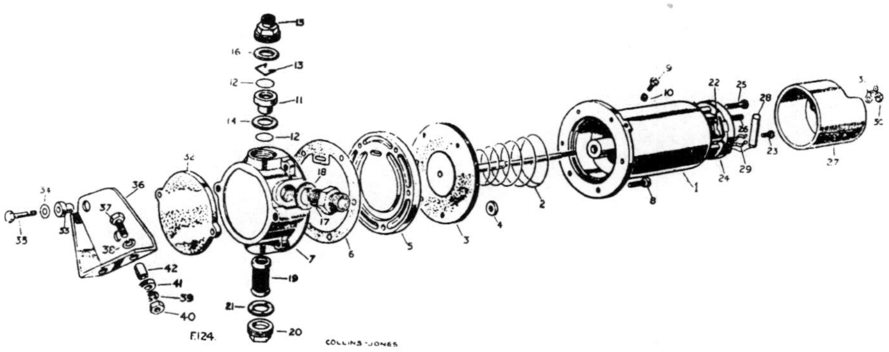

F124.

Layout of electric fuel pump

1	Coil complete
2	Spring for armature
3	Diaphragm
4	Roller for diaphragm
5	Plate body
6	Joint washer for plate body
7	Body
8	Screw fixing coil housing to body
9	Special screw
10	Special spring washer
11	Valve cage
12	Disc for valve
13	Spring clip retaining valve disc
14	Washer for valve cage
15	Outlet union
16	Washer for outlet union
17	Inlet union
18	Washer for inlet union
19	Filter
20	Plug for filter body
21	Washer for filter plug
22	Contact set
23	Special screw for contact blade
24	Moulding for end plate
25	Screw fixing moulding
26	Terminal screw
27	Cover for end plate
28	Condenser for petrol pump
29	Clip for condenser
30	Terminal nut
31	Tag for terminal
32–35	Fixings, pump to mounting bracket
36	Bracket for petrol pump
37	Fixings, bracket to body

Fuel pump, to overhaul—Operation Q-6

Workshop hand tools:

Feeler gauge Screwdriver, medium

Early models, Pump, to strip

1. Dismantle the pump, carefully clean all component parts, renewing the diaphragm, contact breaker assembly and valves as necessary.

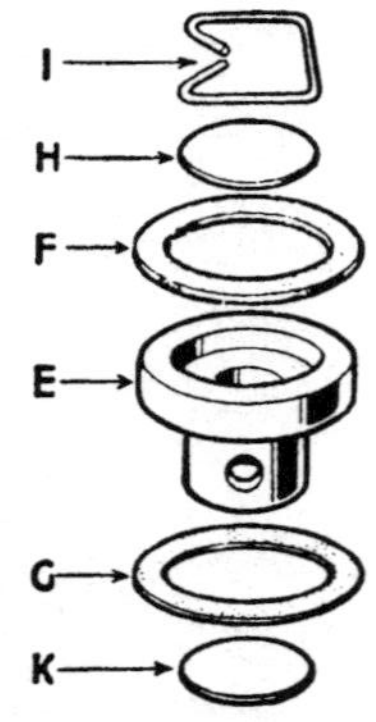

Layout of valve cage

E—Valve cage
F—Thick orange washer
G—Hard red fibre washer
H—The delivery valve
I—Valve retaining clip
K—Suction valve

Valve cage

2. The delivery valve (H) and suction valve (K) should be fitted with smooth side downwards.

3. Care should be taken that the valve retaining clip (I) in the valve cage (E) is located correctly in its groove.

4. The thin fibre washer (G) should be fitted under the valve cage and the thick washer (F) above the cage.

5. Thick fibre washers are also fitted under the inlet union and the gauze filter.

Valve assembly. Models with double entry type pumps

6. Details of one complete valve assembly are given, this arrangement being exactly duplicated in the other section of the pump.

The outlet valve assembly comprises an identical valve which is assembled in the reverse direction, a retaining cap and a fuel filter.

Both assemblies have suitable joint washers and are retained by a single clamping plate which is secured by two self-tapping screws.

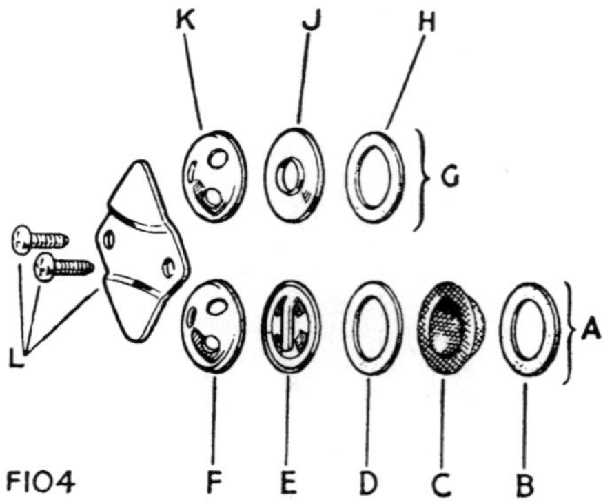

F104

Layout of valve assembly, double entry type pumps

A—Inlet valve assembly
B—Cork washer
C—Filter
D—Cork washer
E—Disc valve
F—Retaining cap
G—Outlet valve assembly
H—Cork washer
J—Disc valve
K—Retaining cap
L—Clamp plate and screw

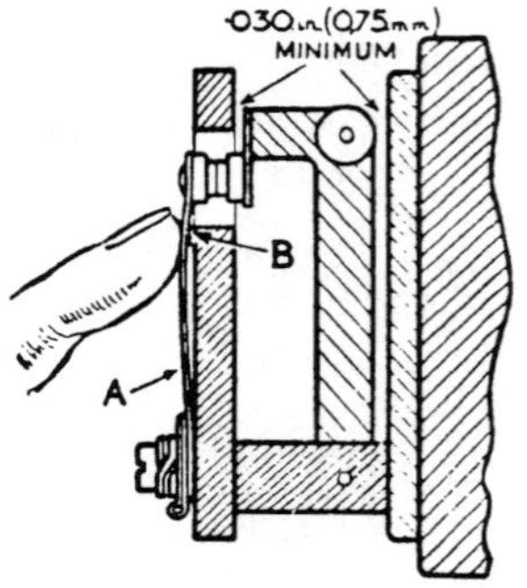

Contact breaker

A—The contact blade B—The ledge

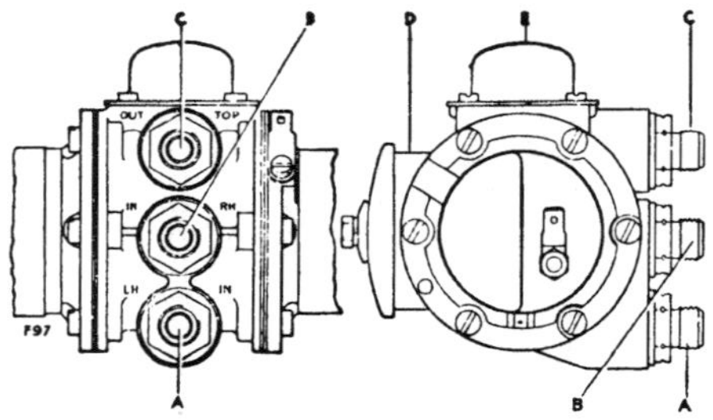

General arrangement of double entry fuel pump

A—Reserve fuel inlet
B—Main fuel inlet
C—Common outlet
D—Inlet air bottle
E—Outlet air bottle

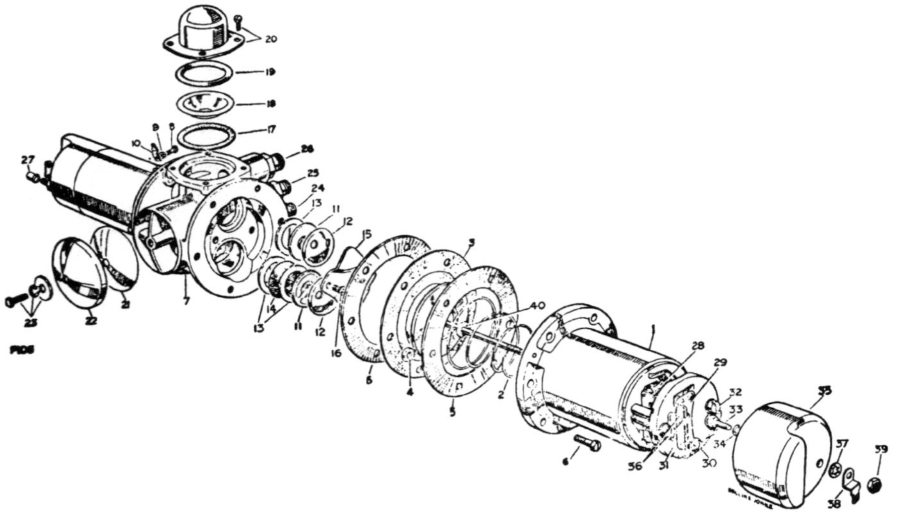

Double entry fuel pump

1 Magnet housing
2 Spring for armature
3 Diaphragm
4 Roller
5 Joint washer
6 Securing screw, body to housing
7 Body
8 Special screw } Earth connection
9 Spring washer } Earth connection
10 Lucar blade } Earth connection
11 Melinex valve assembly
12 Valve cap
13 Sealing washer
14 Fuel filter
15 Clamp plate
16 Clamp plate screws
17 Sealing ring for outlet air bottle
18 Diaphragm for outlet air bottle
19 Rubber sealing ring
20 Outlet air bottle, dome and screw
21 Joint washer for inlet air bottle
22 Cover for inlet air bottle
23 Securing screw and washers
24 Union for reserve fuel supply
25 Union for main fuel supply
26 Union for outlet pipe
27 Nylon protection cap
28 Contacts rocker assembly
29 Spring blade contact
30 Anchor screw
31 Moulded end plate
32 Retaining screw for end plate
33 Terminal screw
34 Composition washer
35 End cover
36 Condenser and clip
37 Shakeproof washer
38 Lucar blade
39 Nut
40 Impact washer for armature.

Operation Q-6—*continued*

7. Check the position by holding the blade in contact with the pedestal, being careful not to press on the overhanging portion, then ensure that .030 in. (0,75 mm) feeler just slides between the white rollers and the cast iron body of the pump. If necessary the tip of the blade may be set in order to obtain the correct clearance.

8. The condenser clip should be fitted under the head of the pedestal bolts, together with the earthing strip and plain washer; the condenser lead is held under the screw holding the contact blade, together with the coil lead.

   The purpose of the condenser is to prevent arcing of the contact breaker points; if the points are badly burnt, the condenser should be tested and renewed if faulty.

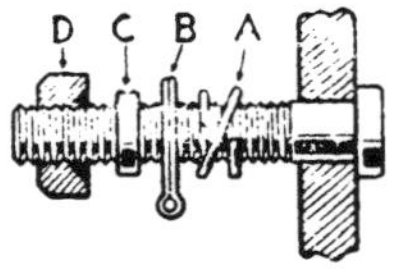

Feed to terminal assembly
A—Spring washer C—Lead washer
B—The tag D—Countersunk nut

9. All connections should be soldered.

10. In the case of the feed terminal screw, which holds the bakelite cover in position, the correct order for assembly is: Spring washer (A), next to bakelite pedestal, then the tag (B), lead washer (C) and countersunk nut (D). Under no circumstances should this assembly be shortened by leaving out the spring washer, or in any other way as this would result in breakage of the pedestal when the nut holding the cover in postion is tightened.

Magnet assembly

11. Fit the armature return spring with its large diameter towards the coil. The spring must not be stretched or the action of the pump will be affected.

12. Swing the contact blade on the pedestal to one side.

13. Fit the impact washer in the recess of the armature.

14. Screw the armature in position.

15. Fit eleven guide rollers in position around the armature.

16. Hold the magnet assembly in the left hand in an approximately horizontal position. Push the armature in firmly but steadily, with the thumb of the right hand.

17. If the contact breaker throws over, the armature should be screwed in further until it ceases to do so. It should then be unscrewed one-sixth of a turn at a time until a position is found at which the contact breaker just throws over, care being taken to avoid jerking the armature. The armature should then be unscrewed for two-thirds of a turn, *i.e.*, four holes, the setting is then correct—do not forget that this setting must be carried out with the points out of contact.

18. When a new diaphragm is fitted, it is possible that considerable pressure will be required to push the armature right home. If there is any doubt about the point at which the contact throws over, come back one-sixth of a turn.

19. Place the cast iron body in a position on the aluminium body, with the drain-hole in the cast iron member in line with the filter plug in the aluminium body. Ensure that all rollers are in their correct position, to prevent the possibility of trapping between the two parts and cutting a hole in the diaphragm.

20. Make sure that the cast iron body seats properly on the aluminium body, insert the six screws and tighten. It is now necessary to check that the top of the contacts inner rocker is in contact with the end face of the magnet housing. If there is a visible gap here the six screws should be slackened off and then re-tightened, until the correct condition is achieved.

    Finally, replace the spring blade contact. The oversize anchor hole in this allows the contacts to be positioned so that a wiping action over the centre line of the contact faces takes place when the pump is operating.

21. Test fuel pump. It is best to use a cut-away cover while testing the pump, as this prevents the hinge pin from falling out, and at the same time makes it possible to observe the action of the contact breaker. The pump should be mounted three feet above the supply tank for testing; either paraffin or petrol may be used. When switched on, the pump should prime itself promptly, and fluid should flow from the outlet union. If the pump outlet is restricted, the pump should slow down gradually, and if completely cut off it should stop for at least 15 seconds.

Fuel tank, to remove and refit—Operation Q-7

Workshop hand tools:
Spanner sizes: $\frac{3}{8}$ in. AF, $\frac{7}{16}$ in. AF, $\frac{1}{2}$ in. AF, $\frac{9}{16}$ in. AF, 2 BA, $\frac{5}{16}$ in. Whit
Screwdriver, medium

Fuel tank, remove

1. Disconnect the battery.
2. Drain the tank. The drain plug is located underneath the car on the nearside immediately in front of the rear axle, and is covered by a small domed plate secured by three set screws and lock washers.
3. Remove the boot trim panel, secured by drive screws.
4. Disconnect the wiring from the petrol tank gauge unit.
5. **Early models.** Disconnect the wiring from the electrically operated reserve tap.
6. Disconnect the petrol filler pipe, main and reserve pipes to the pump(s) and the breather pipework from the tank.
7. Remove the expansion tank, where fitted. This unit is located above the fuel tank and is secured to the body with four bolts and washers.
8. Remove the rear seat squab.
9. Remove the tank mounting bolts.
10. Lift out the tank.

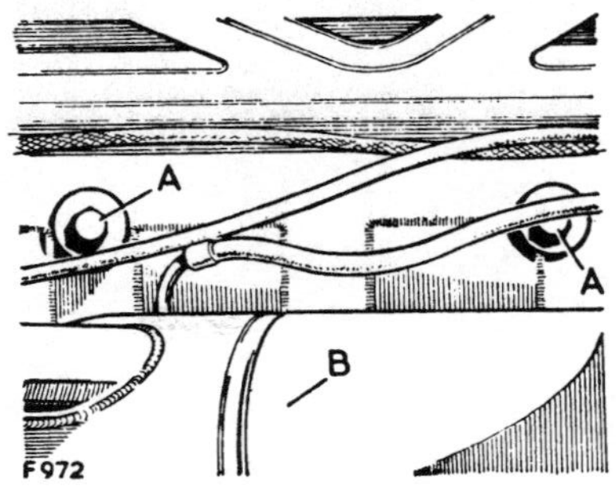

Rear seat squab fixings
A—Squab fixing bolts B—Fuel tank

Fuel tank, refit

1. Reverse removal procedure.

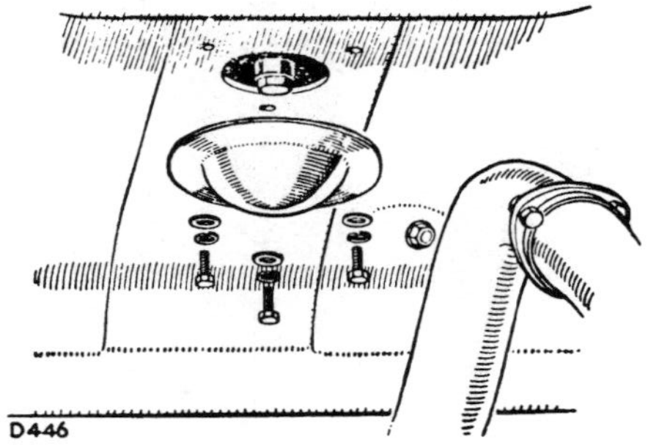

Locating fuel tank drain plug

2. It is important to use a petrol-proof sealing compound, such as Bostik 772, when refitting the filler pipe connections between the filler unit and the tank.

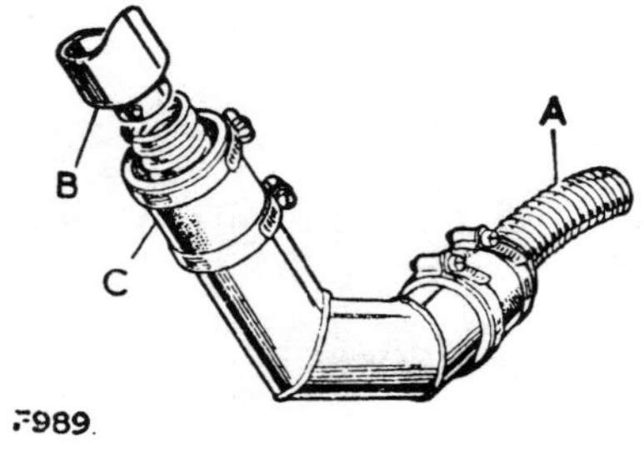

Fuel filler pipe assembly, Mk II and Mk III models
A—Flexible pipe B—Filler neck
C—Hose connection

Fuel gauge tank unit, to remove and refit—Operation Q-8

Workshop hand tools:
Spanner size: 3 BA
Screwdriver, small

Special tools:
Spanner for tank unit, Part No. 600964

Tank unit, remove

1. Disconnect the battery.
2. Remove the trim from the back of the boot secured by three drive screws.
3. **Early models.** Disconnect and remove the expansion tank secured to the body with four bolts; disconnect the breather hose.
4. **Late models.** Disconnect the breather hose and the main and reserve fuel feed pipes between the tank and the pump.
5. Disconnect the wiring from the gauge unit. Note the position and colour code of the wires.
6. **Early models.** Remove the set screws and washers securing the unit to the tank.
7. **Late models.** Remove the locking ring by using the special spanner which can be made as illustrated. Turn the locking ring in an anti-clockwise direction.
8. Withdraw the tank unit and remove the seating ring.

Tank unit, refit

1. Reverse removal procedure.
2. Refill the fuel tank and check for leaks.
3. Check the operation of the fuel level gauge.

G840
Spanner for removal and fitting of tank unit lock ring

Fuel filler cap, to remove and refit—Operation Q-9

Workshop hand tools:
Spanner size: $\frac{5}{16}$ in. AF
Screwdriver, medium; Screwdriver, Phillips; Pliers

Filler cap assembly, Mk I, IA and II, remove

1. **Early models.** Unscrew the fuel filler hose clip; slacken the overflow and breather hose clips and pull off.
2. **Early models.** Remove the filler assembly secured by four nuts and locknuts and mounting pieces.
3. **Late Mk II models.** The fuel filler box is integral with the bodywork. The filler lid can be removed from the filler box; it is secured by two screws. This type of filler has a separate filler cap which is secured to the filler tube by a hinge.

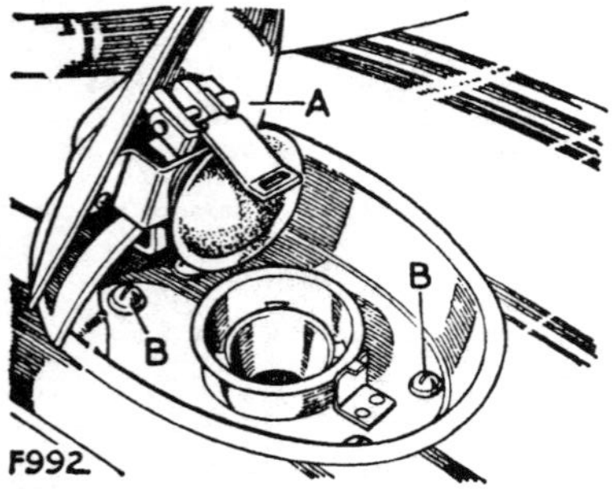

Petrol filler cap assembly, early models
A—Filler lid and cap B—Filler box fixing screw

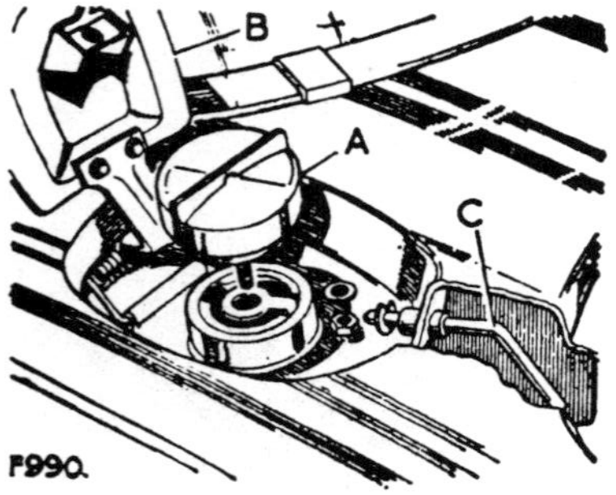

Fuel filler cap assembly, late Mk II models
A—Filler cap B—Filler lid
C—Lid locking device

Filler cap assembly, Mk III, remove

1. Remove the trim-panel inside the boot, secured by drive screws.
2. Disconnect the drain tube from the filler neck inside the boot.
3. Release the worm drive clips from the hose connected to the filler assembly.
4. Remove the filler assembly, secured by four drive screws.

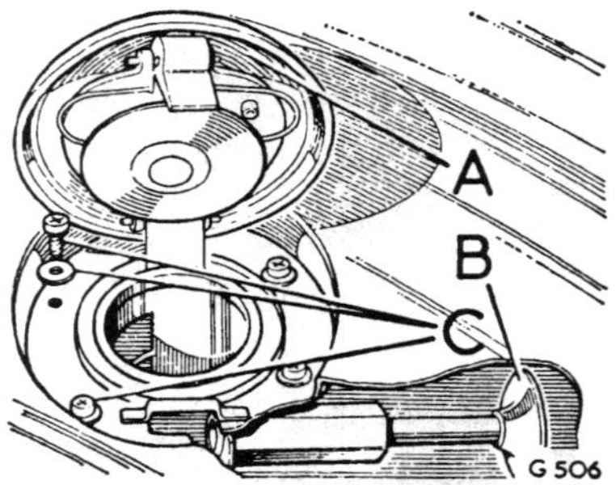

Fuel filler cap assembly, Mk III models
A—Filler cap
B—Locking bolt for filler cap
C—Screws fixing filler cap assembly

Filler cap assembly, refit

1. Reverse removal procedure.
2. It is important to use a petrol-proof sealing compound, such as Bostik 772, when refitting the filler pipe connections between the filler unit and the tank.

Operation Q-9—*continued*

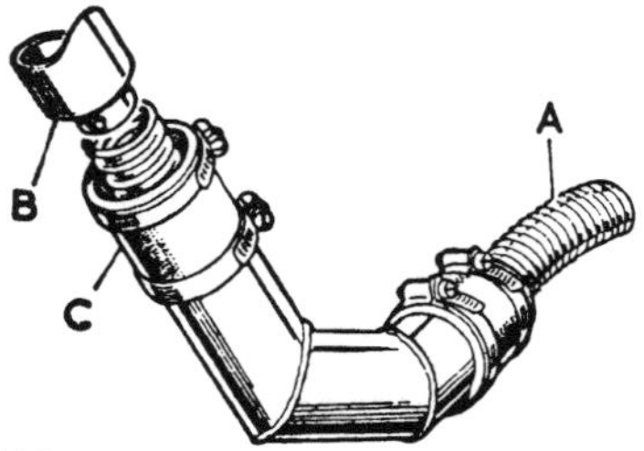

F989

Fuel filler pipe assembly, Mk II and Mk III models

A—Flexible pipe B—Filler neck
C—Hose connection

Fuel filler rectification

A certain amount of trouble has been experienced with petrol loss from the fillers on Mk II suffix letter C' models.

In persistent cases, where fitting a new sealing washer and ensuring the cap pulls down properly on the rim fails to cure the complaint, the following modification can be carried out.

After removing the filler cap it will be seen that the hinge for the filler cap is attached to the inner filler pipe. Cut into-this pipe is a slot for the hinge. At the bottom of the slot on current production vehicles, are two smaller slots to accommodate the arms of the hinge

On early vehicles however either these small slots are non-existent or they are insufficiently deep to accommodate the arms of the hinge. They can be increased in depth quite simply by careful application of a blunt-nosed chisel and a hammer.

By deepening these two small lower slots the hinge is allowed to move lower into the filler pipe, i.e. the arms do not contact the inner pipe and cause the filler cap to tip and therefore not seat correctly.

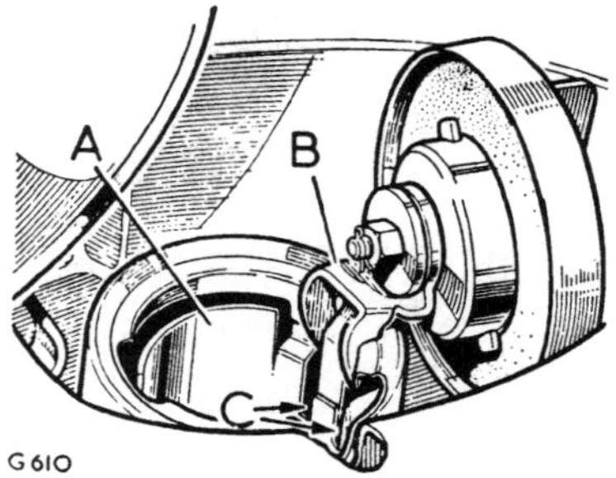

G610

Fuel filler cap and tube

A—Inner filler pipe
B—Filler cap hinge
C—Increase depth of slots at this point

Fuel reserve unit (electrically operated change-over switch) to remove and refit—Operation Q-10

(As fitted to models Mk I and Mk IA)

Workshop hand tools:
Spanner sizes: $\frac{5}{16}$ in. Whit, $\frac{3}{8}$ in. Whit
Screwdriver, medium

Fuel reserve unit, remove

1. Disconnect the battery and the wiring to the feed elbow and reserve tap.
2. Disconnect the petrol pipe between the petrol pump, the feed elbow, and reserve tap.
3. Remove the reserve unit complete with washer, secured by two bolts.

Fuel reserve unit, refit

1. Reverse removal procedure.
2. After connecting the battery leads, check for correct operation of reserve solenoid, which will be indicated by a loud 'click'.

Fuel pipes, to remove and refit—Operation Q-11

Workshop hand tools:
Spanner sizes: $\frac{5}{16}$ in. Whit, $\frac{3}{8}$ in. Whit

Pipes, remove

1. Disconnect the battery.
2. Remove the trim from the back of the boot secured by three drive screws.
3. **Early models.** Disconnect the flexible pipe at the fuel pump; disconnect the fuel pipe at the union immediately above the rear axle.
4. **Models fitted with twin pumps.** Disconnect the pipework from both pumps.
5. Remove the securing clips from the underside of the body and inside the engine compartment.
6. Disconnect the unions at the sediment bowl. and at the carburetter float chamber.

Pipes, refit

1. Reverse removal procedure.

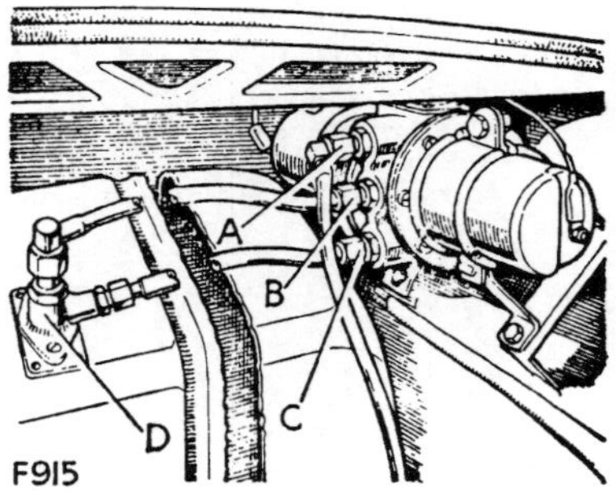

F915

Layout of double entry fuel pump and pipes

A—Supply pipe to carburetter
B—Supply pipe (main) tank to pump
C—Supply pipe (reserve) tank to pump
D—Tank connections

DEFECT LOCATION

SYMPTOM	POSSIBLE CAUSE	REMEDY
A—NO FUEL SUPPLY TO CARBURETTER	1. Blocked pump or bowl filter 2. Stoppage in fuel pipe 3. Sticking float needle 4. Pump inoperative	1. *Clear* 2. *Clear* 3. *Replace needle and seat* 4. *Check and rectify fault*
B—INOPERATIVE FUEL PUMP	1. Foreign matter in pump 2. Faulty pump 3. Faulty diaphragm 4. Sticking valves 5. Choked air vent on fuel tank	1. *Overhaul* 2. *Renew* 3. *Renew* 4. *Clean or renew* 5. *Clean*
C—LACK OF ENGINE POWER	1. Badly adjusted carburetter 2. Sticking carburetter piston 3. Float needle valve sticking 4. Blocked filters or pipes 5. Pump inoperative 6. Engine fault 7. Accelerator linkage stiff 8. Water in fuel	1. *Rectify* 2. *Centre the needle jet* 3. *Replace the needle and seat* 4. *Clean* 5. *Check and rectify fault* 6. *See Section A* 7. *Check and lubricate* 8. *Drain and clean system*
D—HEAVY FUEL CONSUMPTION	1. Badly adjusted carburetter 2. Float chamber flooding 3. Air balance pipe blocked 4. Fuel leaks 5. Damper oil too thick 6. Jet sticking down 7. Engine fault 8. Vacuum advance inoperative 9. Air balance pipe loose on float chamber 10. Float chamber cover gasket broken, cracked or seating improperly 11. Air balance pipe fractured 12. Mixture strength incorrectly adjusted 13. Cold start control incorrectly adjusted 14. Screws securing float chamber to main body loose	1. *Adjust* 2. *Replace the needle and seat* 3. *Clear* 4. *Rectify* 5. *Replace with correct grade* 6. *Lubricate the control cable* 7. *See Section A* 8. *Rectify* 9. *Tighten* 10. *Renew the gasket* 11. *Repair or renew* 12. *Adjust* 13. *Adjust* 14. *Tighten*

DATA

Carburetter:

Type	HD8
Bore	2 in. (50,8 mm)
Needle	UF Alternative to UK on model Mk IA UK Alternative to UF on model Mk IA UR models Mk II and Mk III
Air jet	.116 in.
Piston spring	1003 (283 grms) SU No. AUC 4826
Piston spring identification	Red and green
Jet size	.125 in. dia. (3,17 mm) SU No. AUC 8156
Petrol level, between float chamber spigot and float lever	$\frac{7}{16}$ in. (11,11 mm)
Piston damper oil	SAE 20
Float needle valve TI; Float needle valve seat assembly	SU No. AUC 8170
Normal idling, four-speed and overdrive models ..	Mk I and Mk IA 500 rpm; Mk II and Mk III 520 rpm
Normal idling, automatic transmission models ..	Mk I and Mk IA 520 rpm; Mk II and Mk III 550 rpm
Fast idling, four-speed and overdrive models.. ..	800 to 850 rpm
Fast idling, automatic transmission with 'Drive' selected	700 to 750 rpm
Fuel pump, electric, mounted in boot	Mk I and Mk IA: SU AUB 182 (Mk IA 2 pumps used) Mk II and Mk III: SU AUF 503 double entry type
Delivery pressure	SU AUB 182: 2 to 6 lb/sq in. (0,14 to 0,4 kg/cm²) at carburetter SU AUF 503: 2 to 3.8 lb/sq in. (0,14 to 0,26 kg/cm²) at carburetter

Fuel tank:

Total capacity including reserve	14 Imperial gallons (63,5 litres)
Reserve supply	1½ Imperial gallons (7,0 litres)

Section R – EXHAUST SYSTEM

Brief description of exhaust system

The exhaust system comprises of a front exhaust pipe, intermediate exhaust pipe, front exhaust silencer and rear exhaust silencer and tail pipe.

The components are fitted together with conical couplings.

The exhaust system assembly is secured to the bell housing, and suspended under the body on flexible mountings.

INDEX

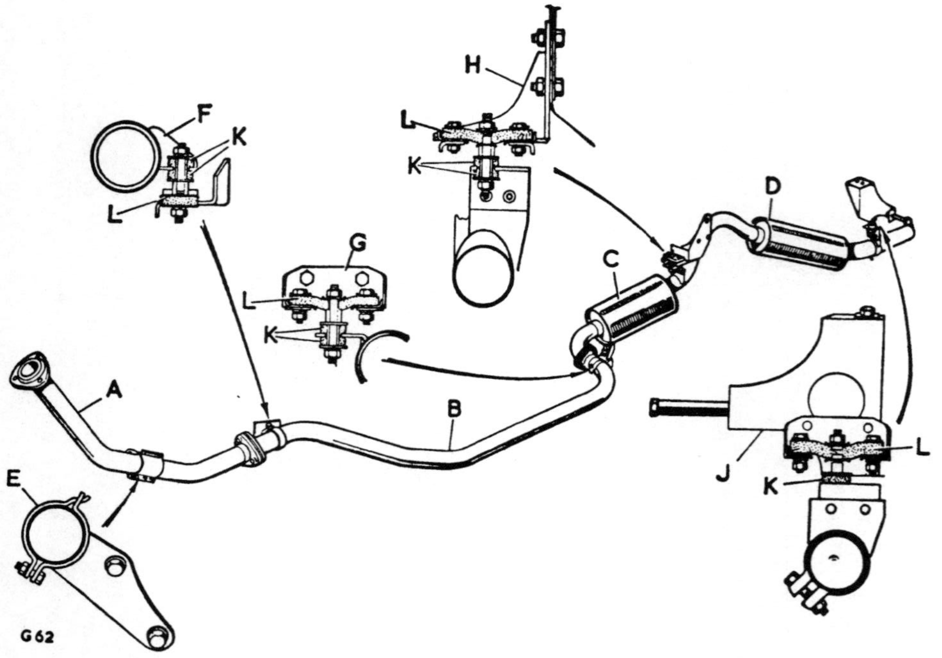

Exhaust system, Mk I and Mk IA models

A—Front exhaust pipe
B—Intermediate exhaust pipe
C—Front silencer
D—Rear silencer and tail pipe
E—Mounting bracket to bell housing (later models)
F—Front mounting bracket (early models)
G—Mounting bracket, rear, intermediate exhaust pipe
H—Mounting bracket, front silencer
J—Mounting bracket, rear silencer and tail pipe
K—Rubber bush
L—Flexible mounting strap

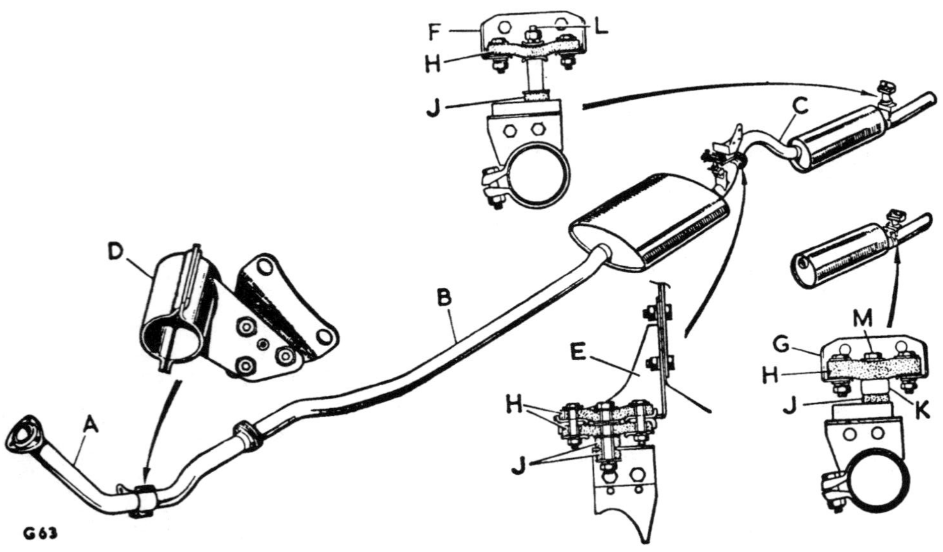

Exhaust system, Mk II models

A—Front exhaust pipe
B—Intermediate exhaust pipe and front silencer
C—Rear exhaust silencer and tail pipe
D—Mounting bracket to bell housing.
E—Mounting bracket, front silencer
F—Mounting bracket, rear silencer and tail pipe. (Mk II models with suffix letters 'A' and 'B')
G—Mounting bracket, rear silencer and tail pipe. (Mk II models with suffix letter 'C' onwards)
H—Flexible mounting strap
J—Rubber bush
K—Distance piece
L—Special stud
M—Special bolt

Front exhaust pipe, to remove and refit—Operation R-1

Workshop hand tools:

Spanner sizes: $\frac{3}{8}$ in. AF, $\frac{7}{16}$ in. AF, $\frac{1}{2}$ in. AF

Pipe, remove

1. Disconnect the pipe from the exhaust manifold, secured by three nuts.
2. On late models remove the nuts securing the front pipe bracket to the gearbox bell-housing.
3. Disconnect the front pipe from the intermediate pipe, secured by three nuts and bolts, and lift the pipe away.

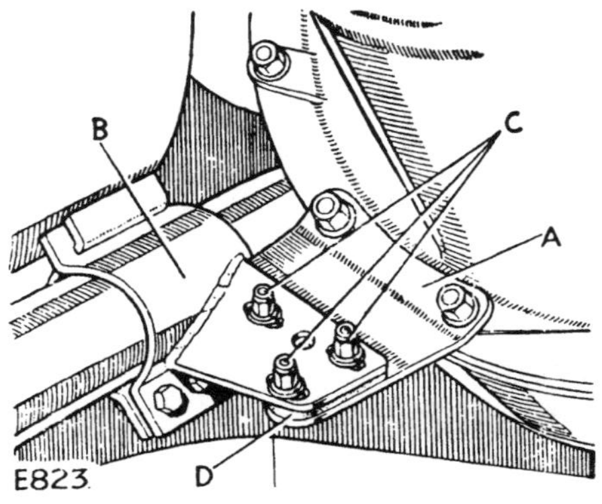

Front exhaust pipe mounting brackets in position late type

A—Mounting bracket
B—Mounting plate
C—Bolts central in slots
D—Special packing

Pipe, refit

1. Reverse removal procedure.
2. It is essential that the rubber mountings supporting the exhaust system are fitted so that they are slightly forwards when the pipes are cold. This will ensure that the exhaust system is not unduly stressed due to expansion when hot.

Any earlier 3 Litre models can be modified to the latest system provided all the latest parts detailed in the Parts Catalogue are supplied and fitted.

When the latest type front exhaust pipe mounting brackets are fitted to early models, the intermediate type front mounting should be removed and discarded.

It is important that the assembly of the mounting is made so that the fixing bolts are as near as possible to the centre of the slots.

After fixing the exhaust down pipe to the manifold, a $\frac{1}{4}$ in. (6 mm) bar or bolt passed through the $\frac{7}{16}$ in. (11 mm) diameter holes in the mounting bracket and plate will enable the fixing bolts to be positioned correctly in the slots.

The bolt heads should be to the front.

Intermediate exhaust pipe, to remove and refit—Operation R-2

Workshop hand tools:

Spanner sizes: $\frac{7}{16}$ in. AF, $\frac{1}{2}$ in. AF

Pipe, remove

1. Disconnect the pipe from the front pipe and the front silencer secured by three nuts and bolts at each end.
2. On early models disconnect the front and rear mounting brackets, then lift the pipe away.
3. On Mk II models the intermediate pipe is integral with the front silencer. Disconnect the pipe at each end, secured by nuts, bolts and washers.
4. Disconnect the mounting bracket to the rear of the front silencer and lift the pipe and silencer away.

Pipe, refit

1. Reverse removal procedure.
2. It is essential that the rubber mountings supporting the exhaust system are fitted so that they are slightly forwards when the pipes are cold. This will ensure that the exhaust system is not unduly stressed due to expansion when hot.

Front silencer, to remove and refit—Operation R-3

Workshop hand tools:

Spanner sizes: $\frac{7}{16}$ in. AF, $\frac{1}{2}$ in. AF

Silencer, remove

Early models, items 1 and 2

1. Disconnect the silencer from the intermediate pipe and rear silencer flange.
2. Disconnect the silencer from the mounting bracket and lift out the silencer.

Late models, items 3 and 4

3. The intermediate pipe is integral with the front silencer. Disconnect the pipe where it joins the front pipe, and where it joins the rear exhaust silencer and tail pipe. The flanges at each end are secured by three bolts, nuts and washers.
4. Disconnect the mounting bracket to the rear of the front silencer and lift the pipe and silencer away.

Silencer, refit

1. Reverse removal procedure.
2. It is essential that the rubber mountings supporting the exhaust system are fitted so that they are slightly forwards when the pipes are cold. This will ensure that the exhaust system is not unduly stressed due to expansion when hot.

Rear silencer and tail pipe, to remove and refit—Operation R-4

Workshop hand tools:

Spanner sizes: $\frac{7}{16}$ in. AF, $\frac{1}{2}$ in. AF

Silencer and pipe, remove

1. Disconnect the rear silencer from the front silencer flange, secured by three nuts, bolts and washers.
2. Disconnect the silencer from the rear mounting bracket and remove the silencer complete with tail pipe.

Silencer and pipe, refit

1. Replace the rear silencer by reversing removal procedure.
2. If necessary renew the rear mounting rubbers as required.
3. Check the position of rubber straps relative to support brackets to ensure that no fouling can take place. Re-check all rubber mountings for adverse strain. It is essential that the rubber mountings supporting the exhaust system are fitted so that they are slightly forwards when the pipes are cold. This will ensure that the exhaust system is not unduly stressed due to expansion when hot.

Section S – ELECTRICAL EQUIPMENT

Brief description of the electrical equipment

Mk I, Mk IA and Mk II models. Positive earth electrical system

Mk III models. Negative earth electrical system

The 12-volt, 57 AH battery is maintained by a high-output charging system which incorporates a compensating control box.

Two headlamps are mounted in the wings; on late models these are of the sealed beam light unit type. A foot operated dipper switch with an organ-type pedal is fitted. All other switches are grouped around the instrument panel and steering column.

Side lamps and flasher lamps are mounted on the front wings, and at the rear, combined rear, stop and flasher lamps are fitted; this unit also incorporates reflectors. On late models there is provision for extinguishing all lamps except the off-side, side and tail lamps for parking purposes. The rear number plate lamp includes the automatically operated reversing lamp. An automatically operated boot lamp is fitted, and coupé models are fitted with inspection lamps under the bonnet.

Interior equipment includes: front and rear courtesy lights, operated either by opening the doors or by independent switches. An electric clock and cigar lighter, are also fitted. The instrument panel has a comprehensive set of warning lights, and on coupé models electrically operated instruments of the bi-metal type are used to indicate fuel contents, water temperature and oil pressure.

The 3 litre Mk III models incorporate a negative earth electrical system, which provides for the eventual use of transistorised units and is in keeping with the latest techniques.

Negative earth polarity affects the coil, dynamo, windscreen washer reservoir connection, harness and revolution counter on coupé models only.

When ordering replacement electrical units ensure that the correct type of parts for use with the negative earth system are obtained and that all units are wired in accordance with the following circuit diagrams.

INDEX

Battery, remove, refit and maintenance—Operation S-1

Workshop hand tools:
Screwdriver, medium

Special tools:
Hydrometer

Battery, remove

1. The battery is located in the right-hand rear corner of the boot.

2. Remove the trim cover from the battery casing, raise the two catches and remove casing.

3. Remove the battery leads from the battery posts secured by drive screws.

4. Remove the two wing nuts, plain washers, clamping plate and lift out battery.

5. Disengage the special bolts from the retaining brackets and remove.

6. Lift out battery tray complete with drain hose and three sealing washers.

7. Remove the base, secured by nuts, bolts and washers.

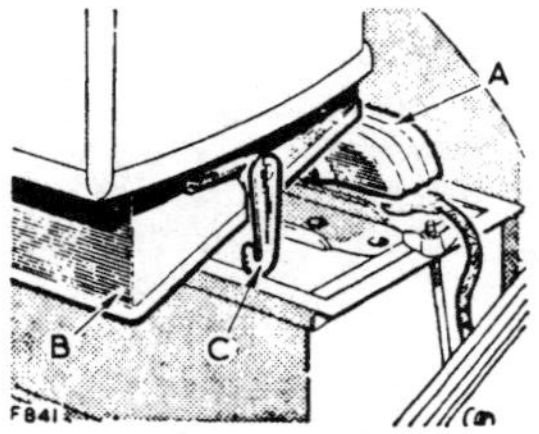

Battery acid level

A—Filler hole cover B—Battery cover C—Securing clip

Battery, refit

1. Ensure sealing rubbers are properly attached to base, if not a suitable sealing compound should be used.

2. Fit base and retaining brackets, secure in position with four nuts, bolts and washers.

3. Fit the three sealing washers on the base floor, the large sealing washer to the centre, fit drain hose and plastic tray.

4. Fit the two special bolts into retaining brackets, and fit battery, passing the special bolt through the aperture in the battery rim.

5. Fit clamping frame, flat washers and wing nuts.

6. Smear battery terminals with petroleum jelly, fit battery leads to their respective posts and retain with drive screws.

   The drive screws securing the battery leads are manufactured from a special non-corrosive metal and must never be replaced with ordinary drive screws which may cause serious corrosion of the battery terminals and must never be used to pull the terminal down into position.

Battery maintenance

7. Check the level of each cell on the battery; using distilled water, top up the cells until the top edges of the separators are just covered.

8. Hydrometer readings indicate the condition and state of charge of the battery and should be checked from time to time. All the cells should give a specific gravity reading of approximately 1.250 when fully charged and in good condition

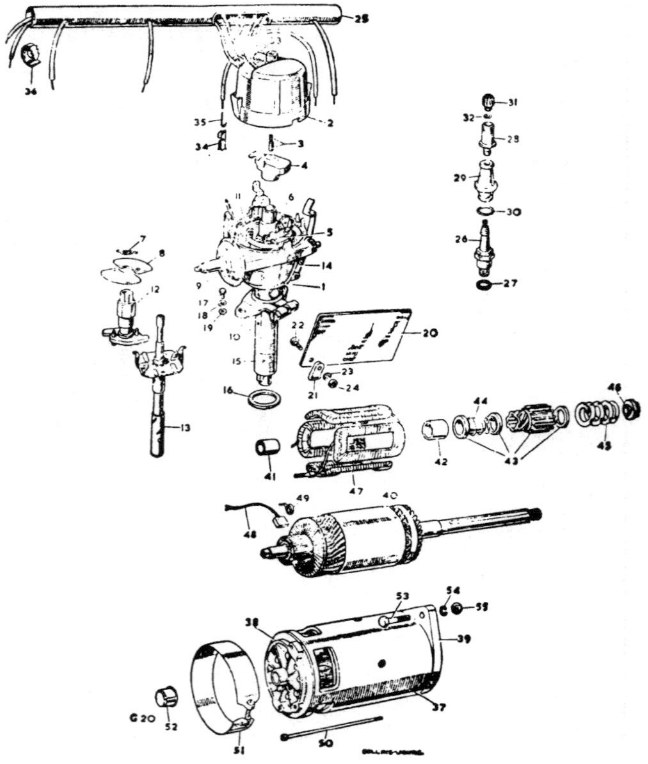

Distributor and starter

1 Distributor complete
2 Distributor cap, latest type shown
3 Brush and spring cap
4 Rotor arm
5 Contact points
6 Condenser
7 Automatic advance spring set
8 Automatic advance weight
9 Vacuum unit
10 Clamping plate
11 Base plate for contact breaker
12 Cam
13 Shaft and action plate
14 Clip for cover
15 Driving dog
16 Cork washer for distributor housing
17 Set bolt
18 Spring washer
19 Plain washer
20 Heat shield for distributor
21 Clip for heat shield
22 Bolt
23 Spring washer
24 Nut
25 Ignition wire carrier
26 Sparking plug
27 Washer for plug
28 Suppressor for sparking plug
29 Cover for sparking plug
30 Rubber sealing ring for plug cover
31 Cable nut
32 Washer for cable nut
33 Sparking plug leads
34 Connector for screw cap nut on leads
35 Staple pin for leads
36 Cleat for plug leads
37 Starter motor complete
38 Bracket for starter commutator end
39 Bracket drive end
40 Armature
41 Bush commutator end
42 Bush pinion end
43 Pinion and sleeve
44 Spring for pinion
45 Main spring for pinion
46 Nut for pinion
47 Field coil for starter
48 Brushes for starter motor
49 Spring set for brushes
50 Bolt for bracket
51 Cover band
52 Grease cap
53–55 Fixings, starter motor to flywheel housing

Distributor, to overhaul—Operation S-2

Workshop hand tools:
Spanner size: 4 BA
Screwdriver, medium
Screwdriver, Phillips
Hide-faced hammer
Pliers
Feeler gauge

For removal of distributor from engine see Section A

Distributor, dismantle

1. Withdraw the rotor arm.
2. Remove the nut, star and plain washer retaining the contact spring and lift off the insulating bush together with the low tension and capacitor leads.
3. Lift off the moving contact point and the insulating washers from the contact pivot and the spring post.
4. Remove the Phillips screw and star washer retaining the capacitor, and lift off the capacitor.
5. Remove the set screw, spring and plain washers retaining the fixed contact plate and lift off the fixed contact.
6. Remove the terminal block from its slot in the distributor body.
7. Remove the circlip from the micrometer adjusting nut.
8. Remove the adjusting nut, ratchet spring and coil spring, taking care that the ratchet spring located at the side of the nut, is not lost.
9. Disconnect the spring connecting the vacuum unit to the base plate and withdraw the vacuum unit.
10. Remove the two Phillips screws and spring washers securing the base plate to the distributor body and lift off the base plate.
11. Rotate the contact breaker moving plate until it is freed from the base plate.

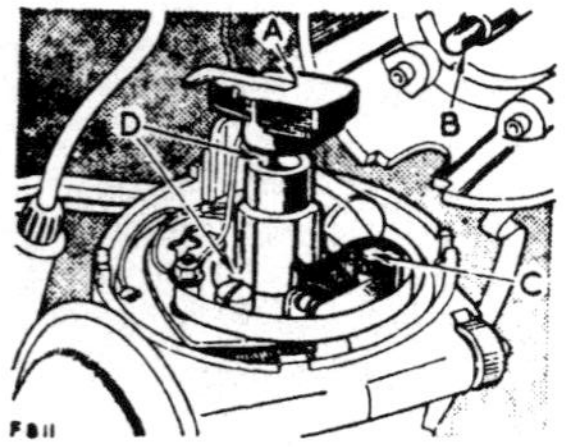

Distributor

A—Rotor arm
B—Carbon brush
C—Contact breaker lever pivot
D—Lubricate at this point

12. Carefully withdraw the two springs from the centrifugal advance unit.
13. Remove the screw from inside the cam and lift off the cam and cam foot, noting the position of the rotor arm slot in relation to the distributor driving dog for assembly purposes.
14. Lift off two weights.
15. Drive out the pin securing the driving dog and remove the dog, brass washer and action plate.
16. Using a shouldered mandrel press out the bush from the body end.
17. Check all parts for wear or damage, and replace as necessary.

The bearing bush is of sintered copper-iron and must be completely immersed in engine oil for at least twenty-four hours prior to fitting.

Distributor, rebuild

1. Reassemble the distributor by reversing the dismantling instructions.
2. Using the hole in the distributor shank as a guide, drill the bush on one side and remove the frazing.
3. Ensure that the drive shaft rotates freely in the bush.
4. When fitting the centrifugal governor springs care must be taken not to stretch them.
5. When fully assembled adjust the contact points to .014–016 in. (0,35 mm–0,40 mm).

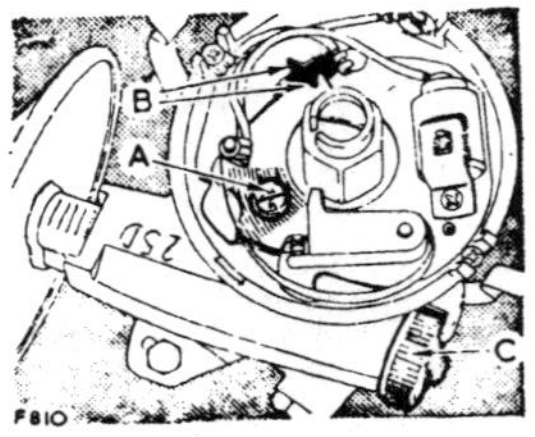

Distributor contact points

A—Securing screw for adjustable contact
B—Adjuster slot for contact points
C—Micrometer adjusting nut

Starter motor, to overhaul—Operation S-3

Workshop hand tools:

Spanner sizes: $\frac{9}{16}$ in. AF, $\frac{1}{4}$ in. Whit
Screwdriver, large
Pliers

Special tools:

Spring balance
"C" spanner

For starter motor removal instruction see Section A

Starter motor, dismantle

1. Remove the cover band, hold back the brush springs and lift out the brushes from their holders.

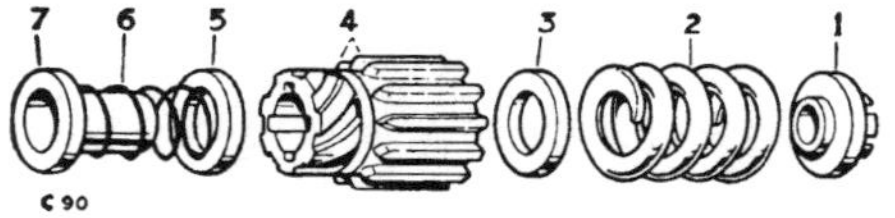

C90

Layout of starter drive

1—Shaft nut
2—Main spring
3—Washer
4—Screwed sleeve and pinion
5—Collar
6—Pinion restraining spring
7—Spring restraining sleeve

2. Remove the starter drive components, secured by a special left-hand threaded nut and a split pin. Use a 'C' spanner to remove this nut. Withdraw the drive components, examine each part for wear and renew as necessary.

3. Remove fibre washer, plain washer and nut from terminal post.

4. Remove the driving end bracket, by unscrewing the two through bolts.

5. Withdraw the armature from the starter yoke and remove end plate

6. Check that the brushes move freely in their holders by holding back the brush spring and pulling gently on the flexible connectors. Any tendency to stick should be corrected by cleaning with a petrol-moistened cloth or in extreme cases by the *light* use of a smooth file. If a brush is damaged or worn so that it does not make good contact on the commutator, all the brushes must be renewed.

7. Check the tension of the brush springs with a spring balance. The correct tension is 30 to 40 oz. (850 to 1134 grammes); new springs must be fitted if the tension is too low.

8 The flexible leads on the brushes are soldered to terminal tags; two are connected to brush boxes and two are connected to the free ends of field coils. When fitting new brushes these flexible leads must be unsoldered and the leads of the new brushes re-soldered in their place. Take care to prevent the solder from travelling along the lead. The new brushes are pre-formed and bedding to the commutator is unnecessary.

9. Clean the commutator with a petrol-moistened cloth. If necessary rotate the armature and, using fine glass cloth, remove pits and burned spots from commutator, remove abrasive dust with a dry air blast. If the commutator is badly worn

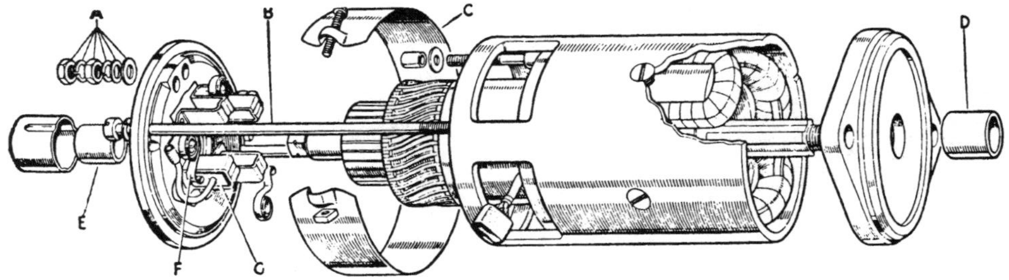

Exploded view of starter motor

A—Terminal nuts and washers
B—Through bolts
C—Cover band
D—Bearing bush
E—Bearing bush
F—Brush spring
G—Brush

Operation S-3—*continued*

mount it in a lathe and, using a very sharp tool, take a light cut, taking care not to remove any more metal than necessary. The insulator between commutator and segments **must not be under-cut.**

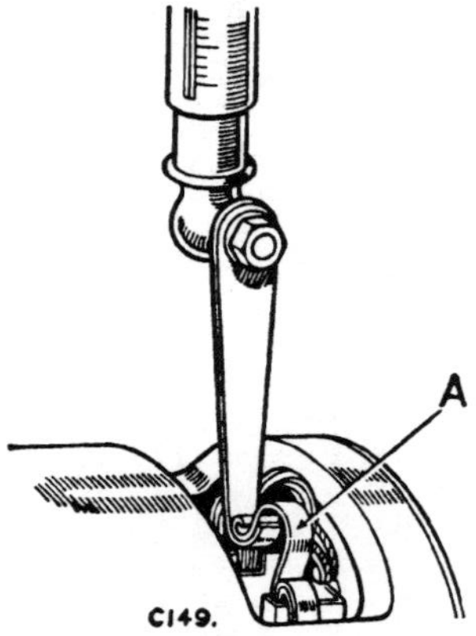

C149.

Checking brush spring tension

A—Brush spring

10. If the armature is damaged, for example 'lifted' conductors or distorted shaft, it must be replaced. Never attempt to machine the armature core, or true a distorted armature shaft.

11. Check field windings for continuity.

Starter motor, rebuild

1. Reverse removal procedure.

2. Ensure that the tufnol washer and nylon insulator are correctly positioned on the terminal post.

3. Ensure that the brushes are quite free to slide in their housings.

4. Fit spring restrainer sleeve, pinion spring collar, screwed sleeve and pinion, distance piece, main spring, shaft nut and split pin. The shaft nut has a left-hand thread.

5. Replace cover band.

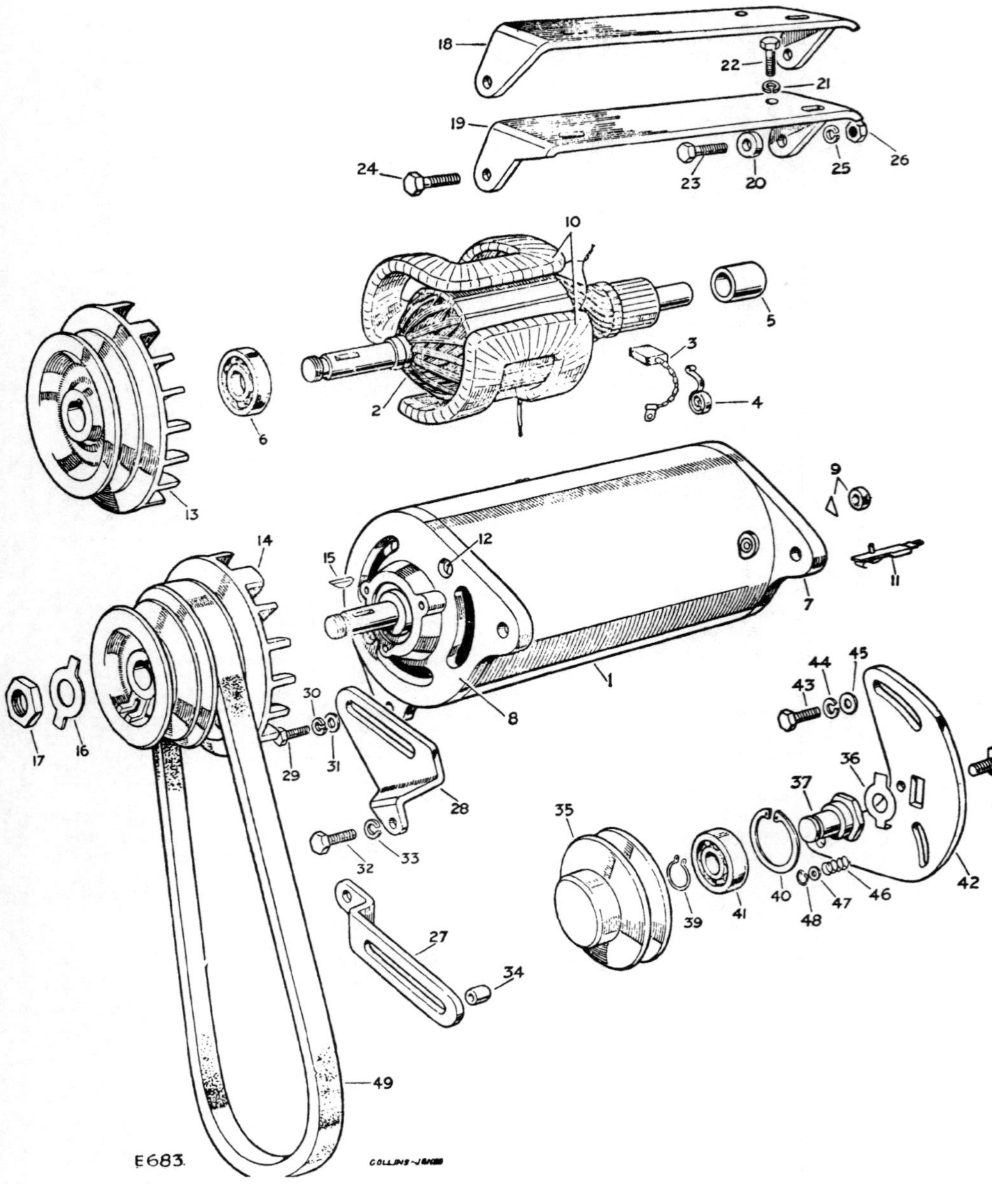

Dynamo layout

Key to dynamo layout

1	Dynamo	26	Nut
2	Armature	27	Adjusting links
3	Brush	28	
4	Brush spring	29	Adjusting link fixings
5	Bush, commutator end	30	
6	Ball bearing, front	31	
7	Support bracket	32	Fixings
8	Support bracket	33	
9	Oiler	34	
10	Field coil	35	Jockey pulley
11	Terminal	36	Lock plate
12	Bolt for bracket	37	Shaft
13	Dynamo pulleys	38	Special bolt
14		39	Retaining ring, small
15	Pulley fixings	40	Retaining ring, large
16		41	Bearing
17		42	Adjusting link
18	Support brackets	43	Adjusting link fixings
19		44	
20	Distance piece	45	
21	Bracket fixings	46	For swivel pin on front cover
22		47	
23	Bolt	48	
24	Bolt	49	Dynamo driving belt
25	Spring washer		

Dynamo, to check—Operation S-4

Workshop hand tools:
Spanner sizes: $\frac{1}{2}$ in. AF

Special tools:
Moving coil voltmeter

Dynamo, to check

1. Check the driving belt tension, which should be $\frac{5}{16}$ in. to $\frac{7}{16}$ in. (8 to 11 mm) by thumb pressure between dynamo and crankshaft pulley; adjust if necessary.

2. Disconnect the cables from the dynamo and connect the dynamo terminals with a short length of wire.

3. Start the engine and run at normal idling speed. Clip the negative lead of a moving coil voltmeter, calibrated 0–20 volts, to one dynamo terminal and the other lead to a good earthing point on the yoke.

4. Gradually increase the engine speed; the voltmeter reading should rise rapidly and without fluctuation. Do not allow the voltmeter reading to reach 20 volts; do not race the engine in an attempt to increase the voltage output. An engine speed of 1,000 rpm should not be exceeded.

5. If there is no reading check the brush gear as described in the dynamo overhaul details. A low reading of approximately $\frac{1}{2}$ to 1 volt indicates a possible faulty field winding. A reading of 4 to 5 volts is probably attributable to faulty armature windings.

   If a radio suppression capacitor is fitted between the output terminal and earth, disconnect this capacitor and re-test dynamo before dismantling. If a reading is now given on the voltmeter, the capacitor is defective and must be replaced.

6. If the dynamo is found serviceable, remove the link from the terminals and connect to their respective cables. Ensure that the larger terminal is connected to the control box terminal marked 'D' and the smaller dynamo terminal to the control box terminal marked 'F'.

Dynamo, to overhaul—Operation S-5

Workshop hand tools:
Spanner sizes: $\frac{11}{16}$ in. AF
Screwdriver, large

Special tools:
Spring balance

For dynamo removal details see Section A

Dynamo, dismantle

1. Remove nut and locking tab, or spring washer and withdraw driving pulley.
2. Unscrew and withdraw the two through bolts.
3. The commutator end bracket can now be withdrawn from the dynamo yoke. Do not lose the fibre thrust washer.
4. The driving end bracket together with the armature can now be lifted out of the yoke.
5. Lift the brushes up into the brush boxes and secure them by positioning the brush spring at the side of the brush.
6. Fit the commutator end-bracket over the commutator and release the brushes.
7. Check that the brushes move freely in their holders by holding back the brush spring and pulling gently on the flexible connectors. Any tendency to stick should be corrected by cleaning with a petrol-moistened cloth, or in extreme cases by the *light* use of a smooth file. If a brush is damaged or worn so that it does not make good contact on the commutator, all brushes must be renewed. Replace the brushes when worn to $\frac{1}{4}$ in. (6 mm).
8. Check the tension of the brush springs with a spring balance. The correct tension is:—

Early models: 22 to 25 oz. (624 to 709 grammes). In service it is permissible for this value to fall to 15 oz. (425 grammes).

Late models: 33 oz. (935,5 grammes) exerted on a new brush and 16 oz. (453,5 grammes) minimum on a well-worn brush.

New springs must be fitted if the tension is low.

New brushes are pre-formed, and bedding to the commutator is unnecessary.

9. Clean the commutator with a petrol-moistened cloth. If necessary rotate the armature and, using fine glass cloth, remove pits and burned spots from the commutator; remove abrasive dust by dry air blast. If the commutator is badly worn mount in a lathe, and, using a very sharp tool take a light cut, taking care not to remove any more metal than necessary.
10. Undercut the insulators between the segments to a depth of $\frac{1}{32}$ in. (0,7 mm) with a hacksaw blade ground to the thickness of the insulator.
11. Check and replace the bearings if necessary. Before fitting a new bearing bush, it should be immersed in good grade SAE 30 engine oil for 24 hours; this will allow the bush to absorb lubricant. The ball race at the fan end should be packed with high melting point grease.

Dynamo, rebuild

1. Reverse removal procedure.
2. When refitting the dynamo driving pulley on late models, which have a spring washer instead of a locking tab, tighten the nut to a torque of 25 lb ft (3,5 mkg).
3. Inject a few drops of engine oil into the hole marked 'oil' at the end of the commutator bearing housing.

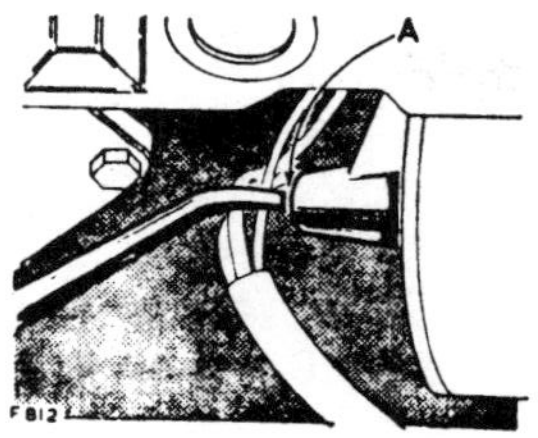

Dynamo lubrication
A—Oil at this point

Wiring, switches and fuses, general information—Operation S-6

Stop light switch

Fitted into the brake pipe connector and located adjacent to the brake master cylinder. A pressure-type switch requiring no adjustment. The warning light cable connectors are the Lucar push-on type on late models.

Flasher unit

Located behind the instrument panel to the right, and is accessible only after the removal of the instrument panel as detailed in Operation T-7.

No adjustment required.

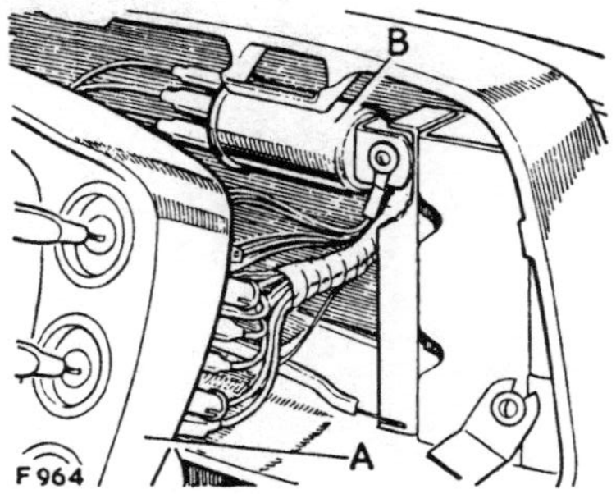

Location of flasher unit
A—Instrument panel B—Flasher unit

Lucar connectors

On late models, liberal use has been made of Lucar connectors on the electrical system: these comprise a terminal blade attached to the component and a push-on spring clip attached to the cable. To detach or connect a cable from any component, all that is necessary is to pull or push on the clip.

Electrical harness

Due to extensive changes between the Mk IA and the Mk II type harness there is no interchangeability.

Engine starter solenoid

The solenoid is a sealed unit, if it should become faulty the unit must be replaced.

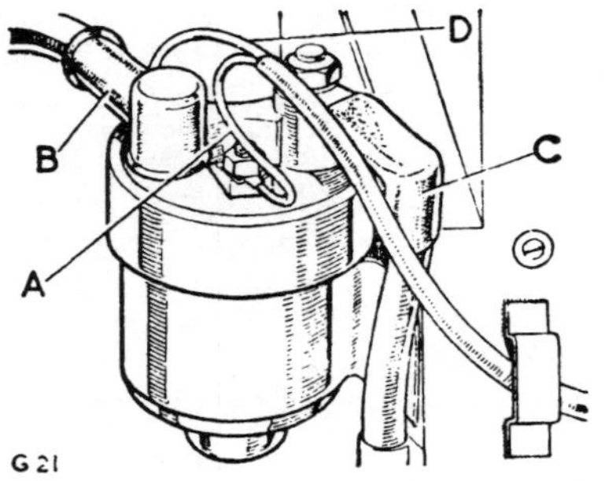

Engine starter solenoid, located on the dash adjacent to the heater

A—Switch cable
B—Battery connection
C—Starter connection
D—Ammeter connection

Fuses, Mk IA and II models

The fuse to terminals numbered 1 and 2 protects the accessories which are connected, so that they operate when the ignition is either on or off; these are clock, map light, cigar lighter and interior lights.

The fuse to terminals numbered 3 and 4 protects the accessories which are connected, so that they operate only when the ignition is on; these are windscreen wipers, heater, direction indicators, stop lights, fuel level gauge, petrol reserve switch and reverse light.

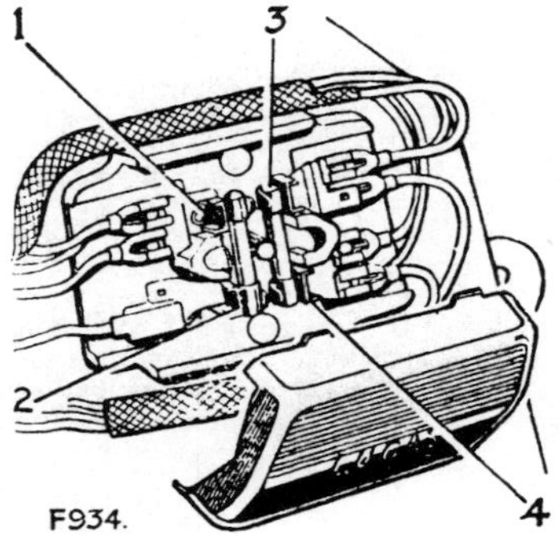

Fuse box, early models

Fuse for terminals 1 and 2 protects: Clock, map light, cigar lighter, interior lights
Fuse to terminals 3 and 4 protects: Windscreen wiper, heater, direction indicators, stop lights, fuel level gauge, petrol reserve switch and reverse light

Operation S–6—*continued*

The instrument panel lights are protected by a 3 amp fuse contained within the plastic fuse unit clipped to the harness above the main fuse box.

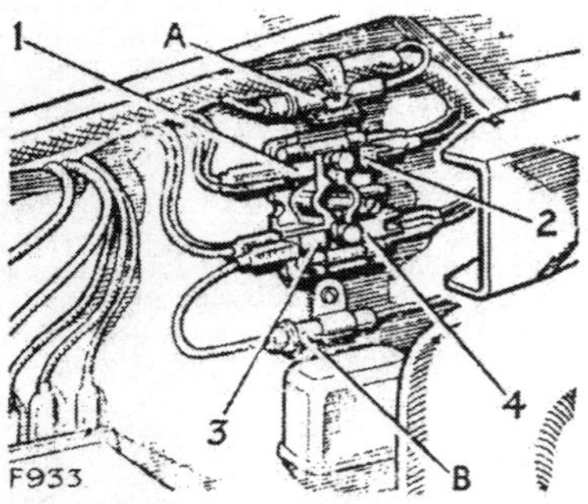

Fuse box, Mk II suffix 'A' and 'B'

Fuse 'A'—Instrument panel lights
Fuse 'B'—Overdrive unit
Fuse to terminals 1 and 2 protects: Clock, map light, cigar lighter, interior lights
Fuse to terminals 3 and 4 protects: Windscreen wiper, heater, direction indicators, stop lights, fuel level gauge, petrol reserve switch and reverse light

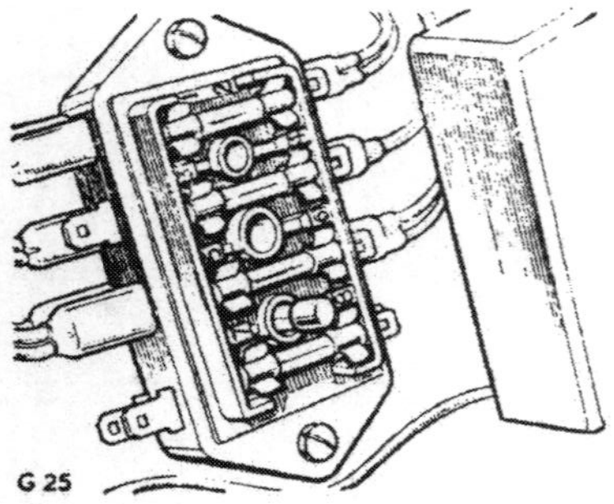

Fuse box, Mk II suffix 'C'

Fuse—Marked 1 and 2 for windscreen wipers, heater, direction indicators, stop lights, fuel level gauge, fuel reserve switch and reverse light
Fuse—Marked 3 and 4 for instrument panel lights
Fuse—Marked 5 and 6 for overdrive unit
Fuse—Marked 7 and 8 for clock, map light, cigar lighter and interior lights

Fuses, Mk III models

The fuses are located on the bulkhead under the bonnet.

To replace a fuse

1. The cover, which indicates the function of each fuse, should be pulled off.
2. Replace fuse as required.

Fuse Number	Fuse Protects	Fuse, Amps
1–2	Battery control, that is, clock, cigar lighters, interior lights, headrest light	25
3–4	Ignition control, that is, stop, reverse and flasher lights, screen washer, water temperature and fuel gauges, tachometer, automatic transmission inhibitor switch, oil pressure transmitter	25
5–6	Parking lights	5
7–8	Side and tail lights	5
9–10	Panel lights	5
11–12	Headlamp RH main beam ..	10
13–14	Headlamp LH main beam ..	10
15–16	Headlamp RH dip beam	10
17–18	Headlamp LH dip beam	10
19–20	Screenwiper motor	15
21–22	Heater motor	15
ˀ3–24	Overdrive	25

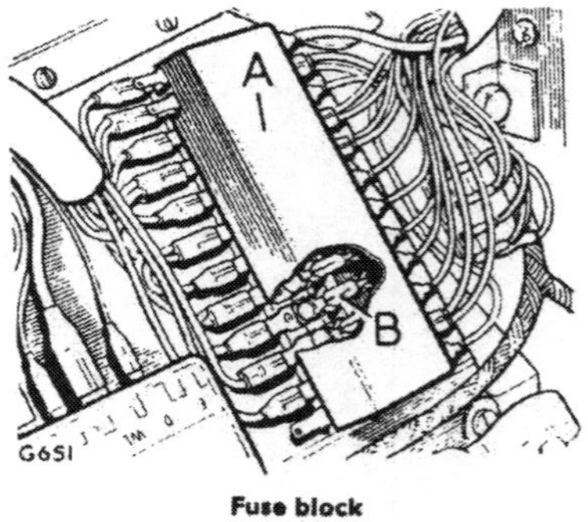

Fuse block

A—Cover B—Fuses

3. Ensure correct replacement is used as detailed above. Replace cover.

A spare 10-amp, 15-amp and 25-amp fuse will be found in the fuse block cover.

Operation S–6—*continued*

Brake fluid level warning light switch and handbrake warning light switch

The main purpose of the warning light which is operated by the above switches is to warn that the level of brake fluid in the reservoir is too low. The same warning light, which is located adjacent to the handbrake, serves to indicate that the handbrake is applied (with the ignition switched "on").

The brake fluid level switch is located in the reservoir cap, situated in the engine compartment above the brake master cylinder. To check the operation of the switch:

(*a*) Release handbrake.

(*b*) Switch ignition "on".

(*c*) Unscrew the reservoir filler cap and lift 1 in. (25 mm) when the warning light should be on.

(*d*) If the warning light does not come on, check the operation of the float and the wiring connections

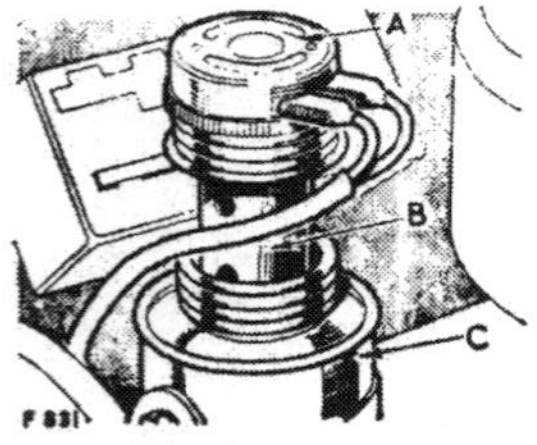

Brake fluid reservoir

A—Cap B—Float unit C—Reservoir

The handbrake warning switch is located on the handbrake assembly. To check the switch:

(*a*) Apply the handbrake.

(*b*) Switch ignition "on". The warning light should now be on.

(*c*) Release the handbrake fully. The light should go out. Details of how to remove, refit and adjust the switch are given in Section N.

Reverse light switch

The reverse light switch fitted to 4-speed and overdrive models is located on the right-hand side of the gearbox and is accessible through the inspection cover on the tunnel.

Adjustment is made by adjusting the set of the striker arm, until, with the reverse gear selected the reverse light is "on" and with neutral selected the reverse light is "off".

On automatic transmission models the switch is situated in the bottom portion of the starter cut-out switch, which is located on the dash, in the engine compartment adjacent to the steering column.

Cold start switches

Two switches are incorporated in the cold start warning light system, a manually operated switch and a thermo or bi-metal switch. No adjustment being required for either switch. The manual switch is located behind the panel on the cold start control fitting. The bi-metal switch is situated in the water jacket of the engine.

Coil

The ignition coil is located at the front of the engine and is secured to the inlet manifold by nuts, bolts and washers.

Cigar lighters

Saloon models have one, and coupe models two, electrically operated lighters. To operate, push in knob; after approximately eight seconds the knob will return to its normal position, the element can then be withdrawn for use. When the panel light is on, the lighter is illuminated to facilitate removal and replacement. Replacement bulb: 12 volt, 2.2 watt.

Auxiliary driving lamps, Mk II and Mk III models

The pick-up points for attaching auxiliary driving lamps to the electrical circuit on the above models is clearly shown on the relevant circuit diagrams.

The following additional information will be found useful when carrying out this work.

The snap connector from which the feed may be taken, will be found behind the instrument panel and adjacent to the lighting and parking switch.

Reference to the circuit diagram will show that the snap connector in question can be identified by the red cable to which it is attached.

For the purpose of fitting auxiliary driving lamps to the above model, spare cables having snap connector end fittings have been included in the wiring harness and are laid between the instrument panel and the appropriate front wing valance.

The function of these cables is to carry the supply from the switch to the lamp.

The cable which runs to the RH side of the vehicle is coloured blue with red.

Operation S-6—*continued*

The colour of the cable to the LH side of the vehicle is yellow with red.

The snap connector ends of these spare cables will be found behind the instrument panel and on the inside of the appropriate front wing valance, adjacent to the common earth terminal.

Two holes are drilled through the underside of the instrument panel (one on each side of the steering column), to accommodate the auxiliary driving lamp switches.

The transparent plastic seal which is fitted over these holes, should be punctured with a suitable instrument when it is desired to fit a switch.

Heated backlight (optional equipment)

The heated backlight is controlled by a push-pull switch fitted to the lower edge of the facia panel, between steering column and hand brake. A white warning light is incorporated in the knob to indicate that the backlight heating element is switched on.

It can also be used with the ignition switch in the auxiliary position.

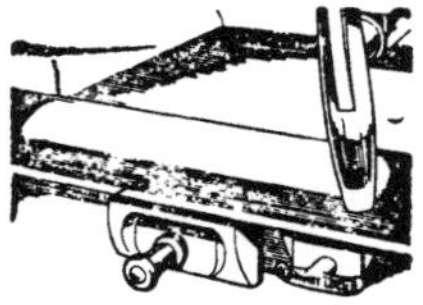

E993

Switch for heated backlight

Boot light

This light is automatically operated when the boot lid is opened and the side lights are switched on. The switch is of the mercury type and is incorporated in the bulb holder; there is no adjustment.

Replacement bulb: Lucas No. 222, 12 volt, 4 watt.

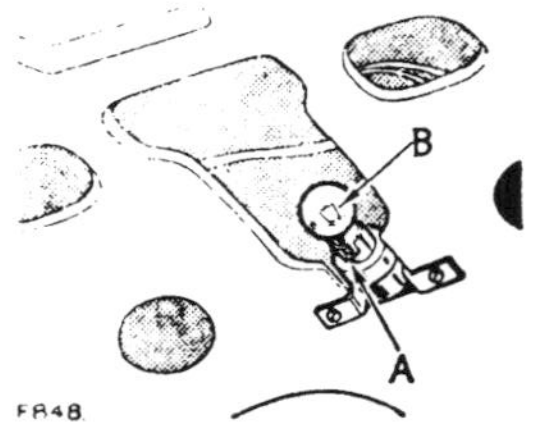

FR48

Boot light

A—Bulb holder B—Bulb

FR47

Bonnet light bulb replacement

A—Plastic cover B—Retaining screws

Under bonnet lights, Coupe models only

There are two lights situated under the bonnet which are operated when the bonnet is opened. To change a bulb, remove the plastic dome secured by two screws.

Replacement bulb: Tex SP No. 209, 12 volt, 6 watt.

Bi-metal instruments

Many bi-metal fuel gauge and water temperature transmitters that include the 10-volt regulator, are being replaced when in actual fact they are perfectly sound, a number of the failures being due to faulty electrical connections.

Below are the circuit diagrams: one showing correct connections and two showing incorrect connections together with details of damage that may result.

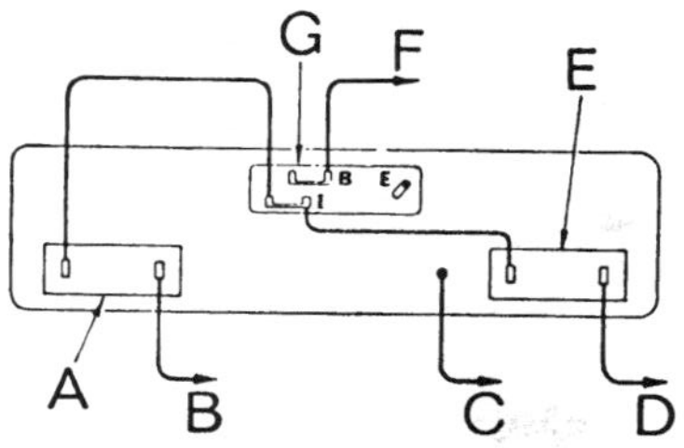

G596

Correct wiring of instruments

A—Fuel gauge
B—Connection to transmitter
C—Connection to battery positive and to chassis
D—Connection to transmitter
E—Temperature gauge
F—Connection to battery negative
G—Bi-metal voltage regulator

Operation S-6—*continued*

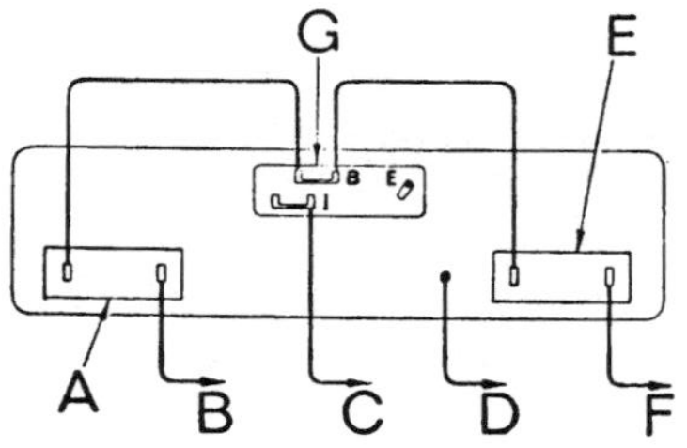

G597

Incorrect wiring of both instruments

A—Fuel gauge
B—Connection to transmitter
C—Connection to battery negative
D—Connection to battery positive and to chassis
E—Temperature gauge
F—Connection to transmitter
G—Bi-metal voltage regulator

With connections made as shown above, 'Incorrect wiring of both instruments', and the ignition switched 'on' the pointer will move rapidly to full or a position above normal as dictated by the amount of petrol in the tank. It will then fall back to zero. No further reading will be obtainable until switched off, when, provided the bi-metal has not been set out too far, the above cycle will be repeated. This will continue until the bi-metal fails or burns out, the amount of sweep decreasing with each 'switch on' as the bi-metal sets out.

The result will be permanent damage to the voltage stabilizer, possible damage to the gauges and tank attachment and probable damage to the temperature transmitter.

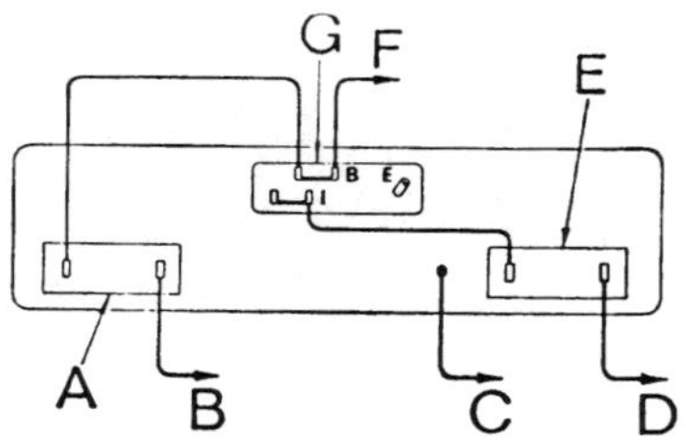

G598

Incorrect wiring of fuel gauge

A—Fuel gauge
B—Connection to transmitter
C—Connection to battery positive and to chassis
D—Connection to transmitter
E Temperature gauge
F—Connection to battery negative
G—Bi-metal voltage regulator

With connections made as shown above, 'Incorrect wiring of fuel gauge' and the ignition switched 'on'. With a small amount of petrol in the tank the indicator will show a reading not very much above normal for correct wiring, but with a larger amount of petrol in the tank the indicator will go towards full condition and gives greater than normal indication. It shows full at about half capacity of the tank depending upon voltage.

The needle remains stationary in the above position even when petrol is exhausted. This may possibly result in damage to the tank attachment and probable damage to the indicator.

If the temperature gauge is incorrectly wired instead of the fuel gauge then a rapid increase in reading will result as coolant temperature increases.

The temperature indicator and transmitter may be damaged. It is essential that everyone concerned should be familiar with the correct wiring of these instruments to avoid premature failure.

Switches on instrument panel, to remove and refit—Operation S–7

These are:

Mk I and Mk IA models

Fuel reserve, Ignition and starter, Main light, Oil level, Panel light, Windscreen wiper.

Mk II and III models

Ignition and starter, Main light, Oil level and main/reserve pump, Panel light, Two-speed heater fan, Windscreen washer, Windscreen wiper, Windscreen wiper speed control.

Switches, remove

1. Disconnect the battery.
2. Remove the instrument panel, secured by two drive screws.

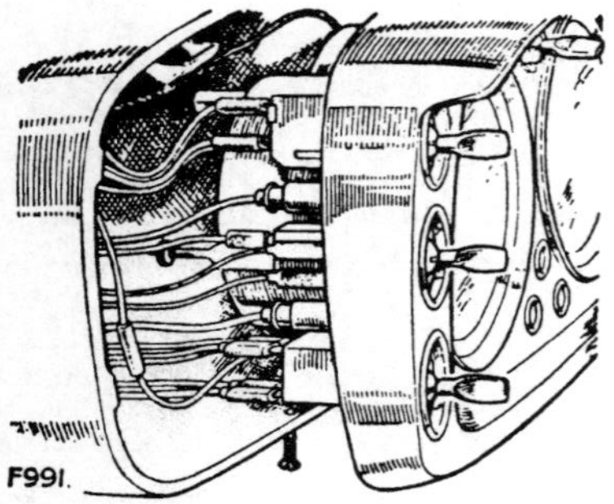

F991.

Removing instrument panel

3. Disconnect the wiring from the switch to be removed, unscrew the bezel in the front of the instrument panel and withdraw the switch and spring washer.

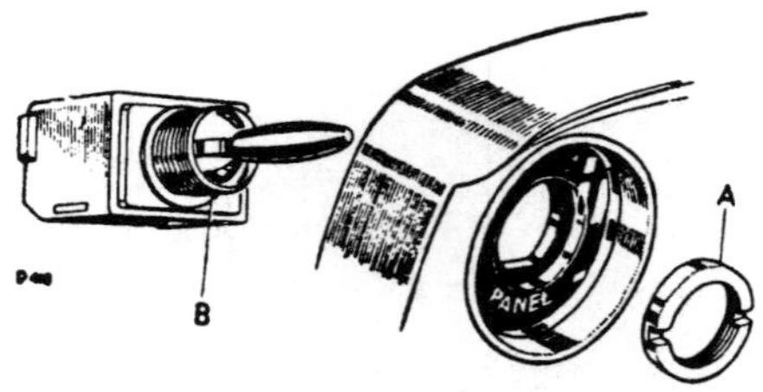

Removing switches

A—Bezel B—Flat on switch

Switches, refit

1. Reverse removal procedure.
2. Connect wiring in accordance with the circuit diagram.

290

Switches on steering column, to remove and refit—Operation S–8

Workshop hand tools:
Screwdriver, medium
Allen key

These are:

Automatic transmission second-speed hold, Direction indicator, Headlamp, Overdrive control.

Switches, remove

1. Disconnect the battery.
2. Withdraw the horn ring, secured by three Allen screws situated on the boss of the steering wheel.

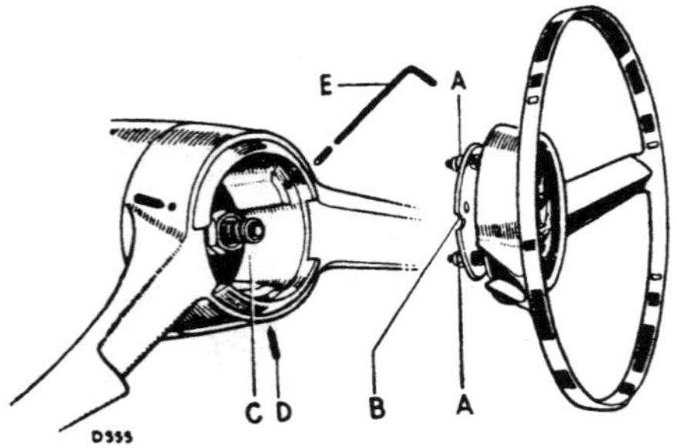

D555

Removing horn ring

A—Adjusting nuts
B—Contact plate
C—Centre contact
D—Allen screw
E—Allen key

3. Remove the steering wheel, secured by a nut and plain washer.
4. Remove the four retaining screws from the steering column shroud, and the four retaining screws from the support plate.
5. Remove the moulding strip between the two shrouds, and pull the shrouds away from the column as far as possible.
6. Remove the appropriate switch.

Switches, replace

1. Refit switch to the shroud.
2. Fit left and right-hand shroud, ensure they are correctly located on their respective dowels, and fit centre moulding strip.
3. Fit the retaining plate and four screws at the top of the shrouds, and the four retaining screws on the sides.
4. With the front wheels in the straight-ahead position, enter the steering wheel on the splined shaft, so that the spokes are as near horizontal as possible. Secure the steering wheel with its nut and flat washer.
5. Fit the horn ring into the steering wheel boss. With slight pressure on the ring, fit Allen screws and fully tighten.
6. Connect battery and test horn and switches.

Switches on body, to remove and refit—Operation S-9

Workshop hand tools:
Screwdriver, medium
Screwdriver, Phillips, small

These are:

Bonnet light, coupé models, Door light (pillar switch) saloon and coupé, Boot light, saloon and coupé—automatically operated.

Switch remove

1. Disconnect the battery.
2. Remove the switch, secured by a small drive screw.
3. Disconnect the wiring.

Switch, refit

1. Reverse removal procedure

Mixture control thermostat switch, to remove and refit—Operation S-10

Workshop hand tools:
Spanner size: 2 BA

With the cold start control pulled out a switch incorporated in the control closes the circuit to the thermobulb switch in the water jacket of the engine. When the engine reaches normal running temperature the thermobulb contacts close and the amber warning light on the instrument panel glows, indicating that the cold start control should be pushed in. Pushing the control in opens the circuit and the warning light goes out.

Switch, remove

1. Disconnect battery.
2. Disconnect wiring from switch.
3. Remove switch from cylinder head secured by three set bolts and spring washers.

Switch, replace

1. Reverse removal procedure.
2. Use a new joint washer.

Stop lamp switch, to remove and refit—Operation S-11

Workshop hand tools:
Spanner sizes: $\frac{9}{16}$ in. Whit

Switch, remove

1. Disconnect the battery.
2. Disconnect the wiring from the stop lamp switch.
3. Depress the brake pedal approximately $1\frac{1}{2}$ in. (4 cm) past free travel and lock in position, to prevent excess loss of fluid and ingress of air.
4. Unscrew the stop lamp switch from union.

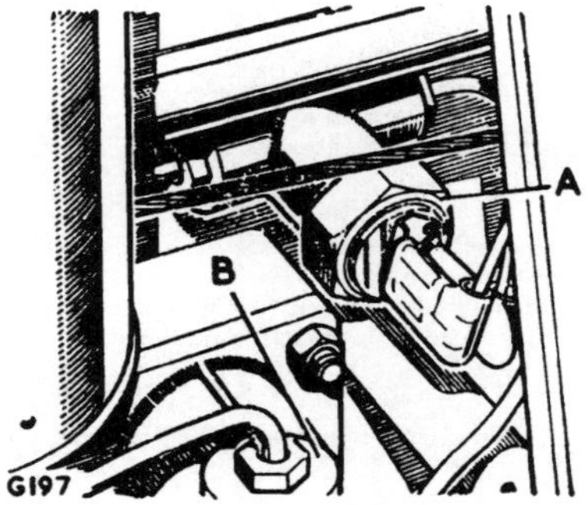

Location of stop lamp switch
A—Stop light switch B—Brake master cylinder

Switch, replace

1. Reverse removal procedure.
2. Top-up reservoir and bleed the brakes. Section N.
3. Check switch for correct operation.

Reverse light switch, to remove and refit (4-speed and overdrive models) Operation S–12

Workshop hand tools:
Spanner sizes: 2 BA

Switch, remove

1. Disconnect the battery.
2. Remove carpet and tunnel cover.
3. Disconnect leads from reverse lamp switch and remove fixings and switch.

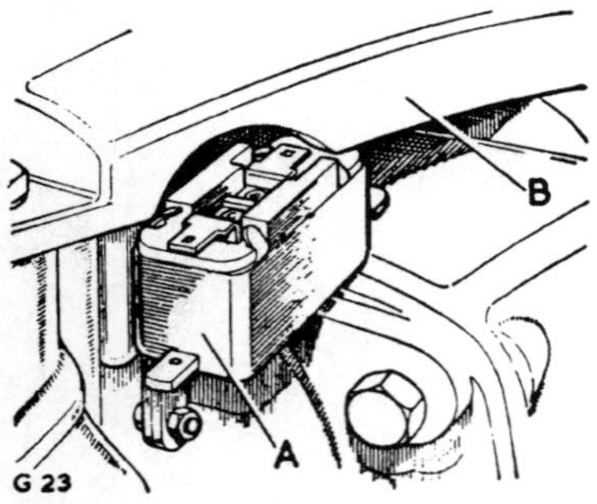

Reverse light switch, 4-speed models

A—Switch
B—Gearbox top support stiffener, on late models

Switch, replace

1. Reverse removal procedure.
2. Connect wiring in accordance with the circuit diagram. Test the switch by selecting reverse gear with the ignition switched on.

Reverse light switch, to remove and refit (automatic transmission models)—Operation S-13

Mk I, IA and II models

The switch is situated in the bottom portion of the starter cut-out switch, which is located on the dash, in the engine compartment adjacent to the steering column.

Switch, remove, Mk I, IA and II

1. Disconnect the battery.
2. Remove the control rod between the splined selector lever and the starter cut-out switch.
3. Disconnect the leads from the starter cut-out switch and remove the switch.

Switch, replace, Mk I, IA and II

1. Reverse removal procedure.
2. With the quadrant selector at park (P), check that the starter cut-out switch on the bulkhead is at the top of its travel. If necessary, adjust the control rod length to obtain this position.
3. Connect the battery.
4. Check that the starter will operate in 'P' and 'N' but not in 'D', 'L' or 'R' positions.

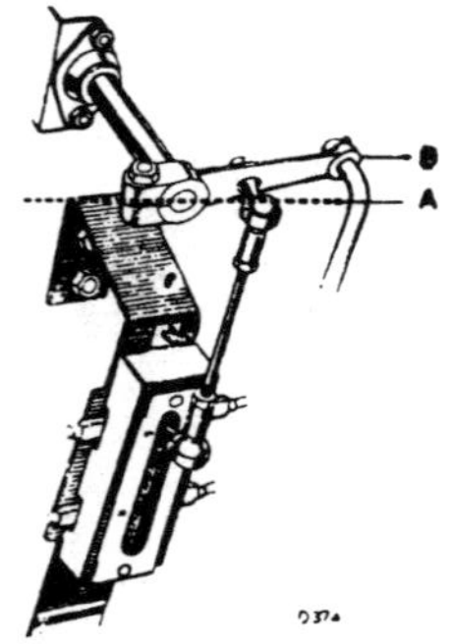

Combined starter cut-out and reverse light switch, Mk I, Mk IA and Mk II models

A—Splined arm in horizontal position
B—Correct position of starter cut-out switch

Switch, remove, Mk III

1. Disconnect the battery, situated in the luggage compartment.
2. Remove gearbox tunnel cover.
3. Disconnect the wiring at the switch connections
4. Slacken the switch locknut.
5. Screw the switch from the transmission case by hand.

Switch, replace, Mk III

1. Reverse removal procedure.
2. Adjust switch as detailed below.

Mk III models

The switch is situated on the gearbox underneath the gearbox tunnel.

Switch, to adjust, Mk III

1. Slide back both front seats as far as possible; lift out the carpet from the tunnel cover and remove the tunnel cover.
2. Ensure that the selector linakge is set correctly. Section EE, Operation EE2-1.

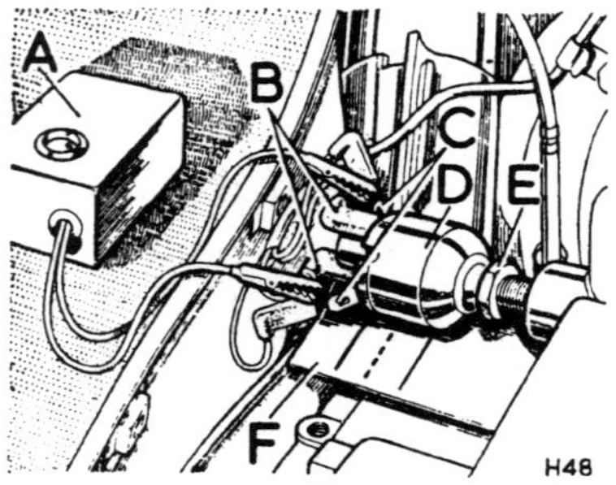

Adjusting inhibitor switch

A—Test lamp
B—Engine isolation terminals
C—Reverse light terminals
D—Starter inhibitor switch
E—Locknut
F—Card

3. Select 'D' (or 'L') position.
4. Disconnect the wiring from the switch at the 'Lucar' connectors.
5. Slacken the locknut and unscrew the switch to its fullest extent.
6. Connect a test lamp (consisting of a small dry battery and bulb) to the pair of terminals which are set at about 45°; these being the reversing light terminals.

Operation S-13—*continued*

7. Screw the switch into the maincase until the test lamp goes out. Note the position of the switch at this point by marking a piece of stiff card held against the transmission case.
8. Now connect the test lamp leads to the other pair of terminals on the switch.
9. Screw the switch in further until the light comes on. Note the position of the switch at this point by marking the card.
10. Turn the switch back until it is midway between the positions marked and tighten the locknut, taking care not to strip the thread of the light alloy switch body.
11. Disconnect the test lamp wiring and reconnect the car wiring.
12. Apply the handbrake firmly and chock the wheels. Apply footbrake during test.
13. Check that the starter operates only when the column selector is at 'P' or 'N'.

Windscreen wiper motor, to remove and refit—Operation S-14

Viper motor, remove

1. Disconnect the battery.
2. Remove the motor drive cover plate secured by four screws on early models, and six screws on late models.
3. Detach the flexible drive from wiper motor by removing the circlip and conical spring from the crankpin. Withdraw the connecting rod. The conical spring is under considerable compression and care should be taken when releasing it.
4. Detach the flexible drive from the connecting rod, and unscrew the outer casing at the wiper motor, detach wiper motor and flexible drive from outer casing.
5. Remove the wiper motor from its mounting bracket, secured by nuts, grommets and distance pieces.

Wiper motor, refit

1. Reverse removal procedure.

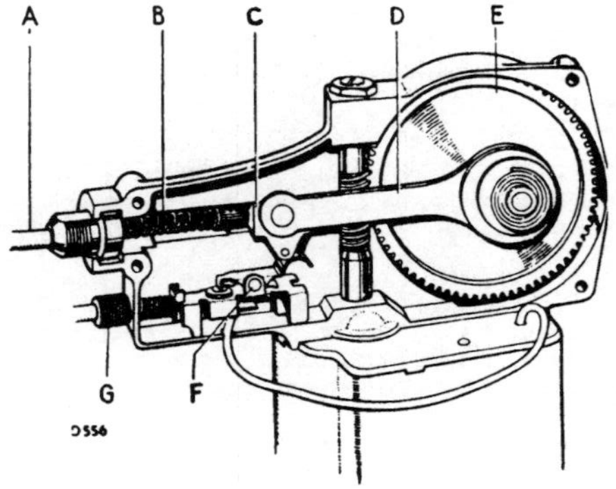

Connecting rod in correct position for fitting

A—Outer casing
B—Flexible drive
C—Crosshead
D—Connecting rod
E—Final gear
F—Self-parking switch
G—Adjusting nut

Windscreen wiper wheel boxes, to remove and refit—Operation S-15

Workshop hand tools:
Spanner size: ⅜ in. AF
Screwdriver, small
Screwdriver, Phillips

Wheel box, remove

1. Disconnect the battery.
2. Remove the motor drive cover plate secured by four screws on early models (or six screws on late models).
3. Detach the flexible drive from wiper motor by removing the circlip and conical spring from the crankpin. Withdraw the connecting rod. The conical spring is under considerable compression and care should be taken when releasing it.
4. Detach the flexible drive from the connecting rod and unscrew the outer casing at the wiper motor; detach wiper motor and flexible drive from outer casing.
5. Remove the windscreen wiper arms and blades complete. The wiper arms are held on the spindle boss by a retaining clip, which should be held back from the boss by means of a suitable tool, until it is clear of the retaining groove.
6. Remove the large nut from the spindle and the small screw retaining the parking ramp. Remove the parking ramp.
7. Remove the fresh air grille secured by drive screws. On early models, disconnect the windscreen washer pipes.
8. Remove the wheel boxes and drive tube complete from the body.
9. Remove the wheel boxes which are secured to the drive tube by two screws.

Wheel box, refit

1. Ensure that the rubber or steel bush is in position on the spindle housing.
2. Lubricate the spindle and spindle gear with Ragosine Listate 225 grease.
3. Place the wheel box over the flexible drive and secure the housing and cover with the two screws. Ensure that the flared ends of the outer casing engage in the slots of the cover in the two outer positions, and the ends of the centre outer casing are on the inside slot to allow for slight transverse adjustment.

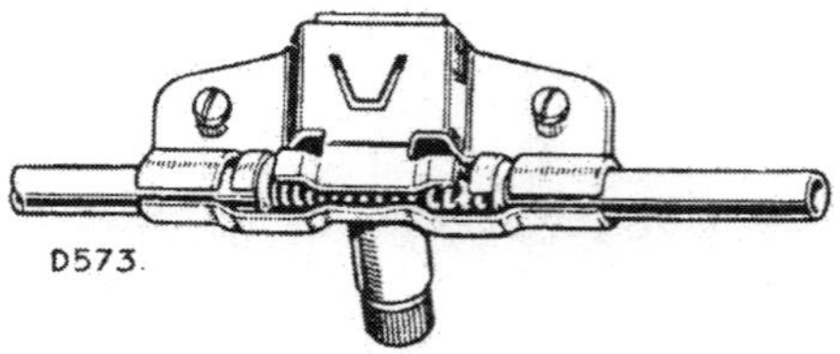

Outer casing in correct position

Early type wheel box illustrated

4. Refit the wheel box and drive assembly to the body.
5. Ensure the cable is not misaligned. Check, if necessary, that the permissible force required to move the cable is not more than 6 lb (2,7 kg).
6. Connect the drive to the motor by reversing removal procedure.
7. Refit the fresh air grille; on early models connect the windscreen washer pipes.
8. Refit the wiper arms and blades and adjust. Operation S-16.

Windscreen wiper and arms, to adjust—Operation S-16

Workshop hand tools:
Screwdriver, medium

General

Many wiper motors are removed as being faulty before the following two points are checked. See windscreen wiper, test and adjust.

(a) Excessive resistance to movement of the cable due to malalignment of the outer tube lengths, lack of grease or tightness in the wheel boxes, etc.

(b) Burning of the limit switch contacts due to incorrect adjustment of the blade parking position.

It should be noted that the wiper motor now being fitted to the Mark II and III models is thermostatically protected against overheating, and faults of this type will result in a temprary shut down of the motor. Upon cooling down, the motor will again commence to operate, this cycle being repeated as long as the switch is left in the 'on' position.

If this thermostat is suspect, supply the motor with a terminal voltage of 12 v., when under motor stall conditions the thermostat should operate within half minute to four minutes. The motor should be initially cold for this test. Replace the motor if the thermostat is faulty. Keep the windscreen damp when testing the wipers, otherwise dust, etc., may cause scratching of the glass.

The windscreen washer may be occasionally operated for this purpose.

Windscreen wiper, test and adjust

1. A quick and simple check for any fault in the transmission system between the wiper motor and wiper blade, can be made by timing the wiping speed of the blade.

Mk I models

The wiper motor is set to run at approximately 60 to 70 wipes per minute.

Mk IA and Mk II suffix letter 'A' and 'B' models

The wiper motor is set to run at approximately 60 to 70 wipes per minute. However, if a customer complains that this is too fast, it is a simple matter to change to a lower speed of approximately 45 wipes per minute as follows:

(a) Remove the green-yellow lead from the wiper motor connector; this will be found just below and adjacent to the wiper motor.

(b) Pull out the green/brown lead which is tucked back inside the PVC tubing at the wiper motor and fit into vacant connector.

(c) Tuck the green/yellow lead inside the PVC tubing.

To change back to the higher speed, reverse the procedure above.

Mk II suffix letter 'C' and Mk III models

With the rheostat switch in the slow position the wiping rate is approximately 45 to 50 wipes per minute. In the fast position the wiping rate is approximately 60 to 70 wipes per minute.

2. Carry out tests with the screen wet.
3. Any fault or undue tightness in the transmission will result in a lesser wiping rate than the above.
4. The maximum permissible force required to move the cable rack in its protective outer tubing, blades away from windscreen and rack disconnected at gearbox on motor, is 6 lb. (2,7 kg). Excessive tightness in wheel boxes should be investigated and rectified.
5. While the end cover is removed from the gearbox for the above test, check the limit switch contacts for signs of burning, as this would result in difficulty being experienced with the self-parking feature of the wiper.
6. If burning is apparent, and no fault has been found in the transmission mechanism, then the limit switch is probably out of adjustment.
7. After carefully cleaning the contacts with a suitable contact file or very fine glass-paper, reassemble the gearbox and reset the limit switch.

Limit switch, to set (Self-parking mechanism)

1. The wiper limit switch is pre-set by the manufacturer before despatch and should require no further adjustment, however, in the event of the wiper not parking the following procedure should be carried out:
2. Wet the screen.
3. Set the limit switch to the condition where it will not park the arms.

To do this, turn the knurled nut located near the **gearbox cable outlet half a turn at a time.**

Operation S-16—*continued*

4. Slowly adjust until the arms just park, then if the motor is cold, add one complete revolution (360°) of the knurled nut in the same direction as to obtain the parked position.

   If the motor is hot (after running or some time) add only half a turn (180°).

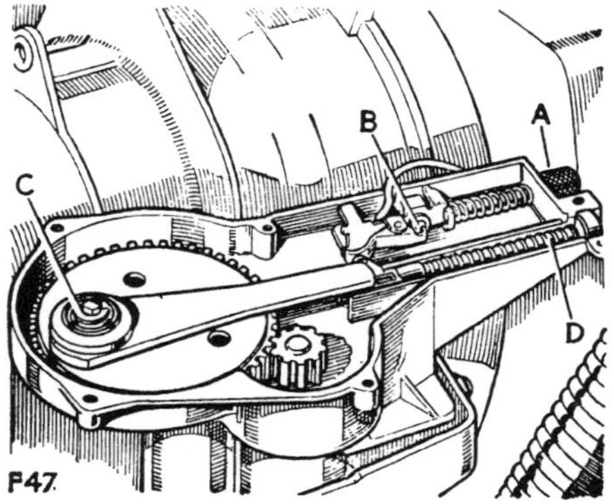

F47

Wiper limit switch adjustment

A—Knurled adjusting nut
B—Limit switch contacts
C—Rack retaining circlip
D—Rack cable

5. Ragosine Listate 225 grease may be applied when required to the wheel boxes and interior of the protective tubing.
6. The wiper blades should be replaced if they have become worn, distorted or frictional.
7. Keep the windscreen clean. Oil and tar, etc., can be removed with methylated spirits.

Wiper arms, adjust

1. The wiper arms are held on the spindle boss by a retaining spring clip. When removing a wiper arm this spring clip should be held back from the boss by means of a suitable tool, until it is clear of the retaining groove.
2. When refitting, ensure that the spring clip is located in the retaining groove on the spindle boss.
3. Ensure that the wiper arms are fitted to the correct spline on the spindle boss, as follows:
4. With the arms removed, allow the motor to move to the "park" position. Push the arm on to the boss, at the same time locating it on the splines so that the RH wiper blade is resting on the park platform, and the LH blade is mid way between the windscreen surround rubber, and the air intake grille surround.

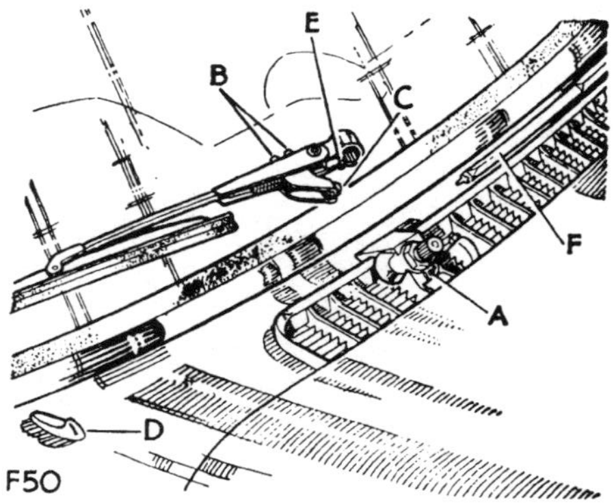

F50

Wiper blade adjustment

A—Ramp adjusting screw
B—Nylon pad adjusting screws
C—Nylon pad
D—Blade parking platform
E—Arm retaining spring clip
F—Park position of L.H. blade

To check the setting of the wiper arm ramps, damp the windscreen and operate the wipers.

The nylon pad attached to the wiper arm should be just making contact with the respective ramp, when at the end of the stroke. This can easily be checked by switching off the ignition switch, and so stopping the wiper motor, when the blade is at the end of its stroke.

If adjustment is required slacken the ramp adjusting screw and the large ramp retaining nut. Move the ramp to the correct position and retighten the screw and nut.

The nylon pad is adjustable by means of two adjusting screws, and this adjustment determines the amount of lift which is imparted to the arm when moving to the park position. This adjustment should be set to give the maximum lift possible while still retaining sufficient pressure to hold the blade firmly against the bodywork, when in the parked position.

Horn ring, to remove, refit and adjust—Operation S-17

Workshop hand tools:
Allen key

Horn ring, remove

1. Disconnect battery leads.
2. Slacken the three Allen screws situated on the boss of the steering wheel and withdraw horn ring.

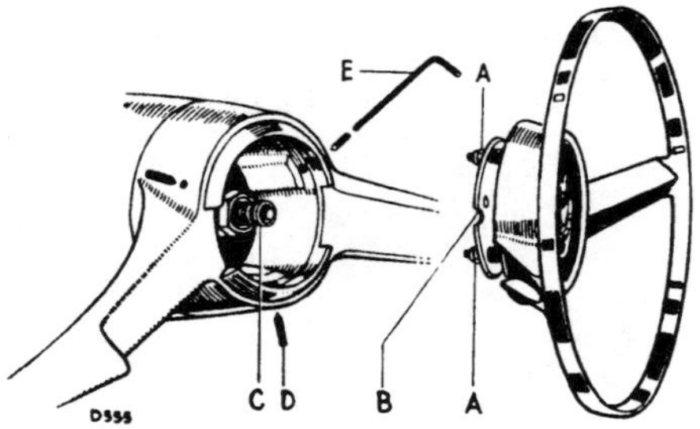

Removing and adjusting horn ring

A—Adjusting nuts
B—Contact plate
C—Centre contact
D—Allen screw
E—Allen key

Horn ring, refit

1. Enter the horn ring into the steering wheel boss and with slight pressure on the ring enter the Allen screws and fully tighten.
2. Connect battery leads and check horns for correct operation.

Horn ring, to adjust

1. On the underside of the horn ring there are three spring-loaded nuts. By either tightening, or slackening, the contact plate is either raised or lowered whichever is required.

Windtone horns, to remove and refit—Operation S-18

Workshop hand tools:
Spanner size: $\frac{7}{16}$ in. AF

Horns, remove

1. Disconnect the battery.
2. Place the car over a pit or on a ramp.
3. From underneath the car, disconnect the wiring.
4. From underneath the car, remove the two bolts, nuts and washers securing each horn to its mounting bracket on the chassis sub-frame.
5. Turn the horn over into a position where the dome can be removed from the horn; this is secured by a single screw with a screwdriver slot. Remove the dome.
6. The horn can now be manoeuvred from the car.

Horns, refit

1. Reverse removal procedure.

Windtone horns, to adjust—Operation S-19

Workshop hand tools:
Spanner size: 2 BA
Screwdriver, medium

1. If a horn fails to work, first check that the cause is not due to faulty wiring or connections; the failure of both horns almost certainly indicates a wiring fault or a discharged battery.
2. To adjust a horn; remove the screw dome, and clip and rotate the fixed contact until the points are just open. Turn the contact back half a turn and check the operation of the horn.
3. If adjusting the contacts does not produce satisfactory results, the horn should be returned to the makers.

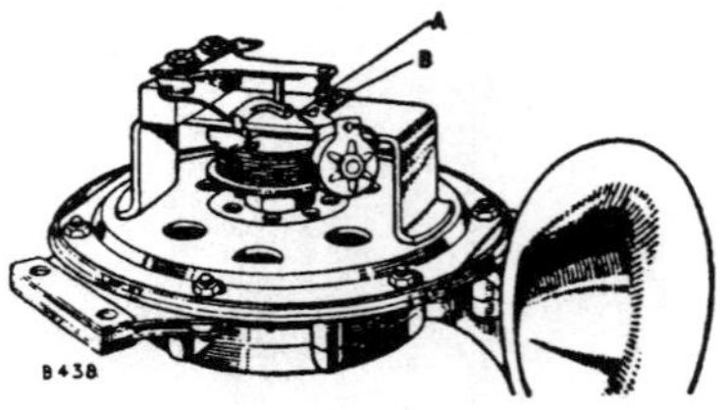

Horn adjustment

A—Adjustable contact B—Locknut

Headlamp bulbs, to remove and replace—Operation S-20

Workshop hand tools:
Screwdriver, medium
Screwdriver, Phillips, small

Bulb, to remove

1. Insert a screwdriver between the headlamp rim and wing, at the bottom centre of the rim and spring off the rim.
2. Remove rubber dust excluder.
3. Press the light unit in against the compression springs of the adjusting screws and turn anti-clockwise to release.

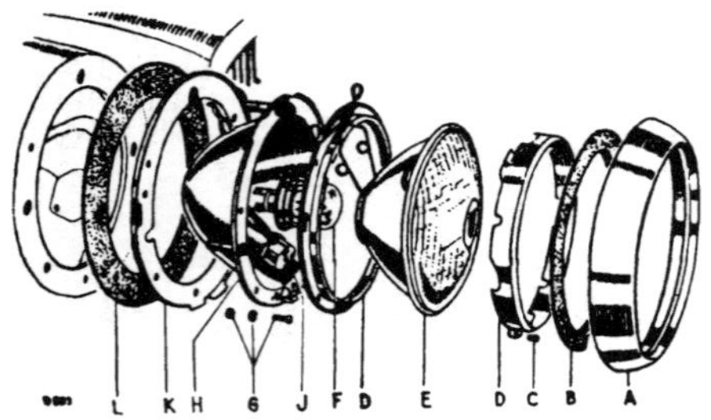

Headlamp

A—Rim for headlamp
B—Rubber gasket for headlamp
C—Screw fixing mounting plate and rim
D—Mounting plate and rim
E—Light unit
F—Bulb
G—Fixings, headlamp to wing
H—Headlamp body
J—Connector
K—Mounting plate
L—Sealing rubber

4. Withdraw Lucar connector from bulb.
5. Squeeze both ends of the bulb retaining clip together and withdraw bulb from light unit.

Bulb, refit

1. Reverse removal procedure.

Sealed-beam headlamps (Home models only)

Unit, replace

1. Insert a screwdriver under the rim at the bottom centre and gently lever off the rim.
2. Remove the rim for light unit retained by three recessed-head screws.

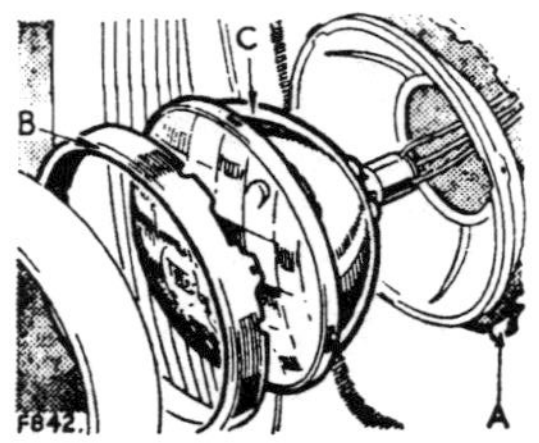

Sealed-beam unit

A—Insert screwdriver at this point
B—Retaining ring
C—Light unit

3. Withdraw the headlamp unit and disconnect the plug at the rear.
4. Replace the unit and reassemble.

Headlamps, to align—Operation S-21

Workshop hand tools:
Phillips screwdriver

Special tools:
Lucas L-Lite

Headlamps with bulbs, adjust

The headlamps should be set so that the main driving beams are parallel with the road surface. If adjustment is required remove the rim as previously described. The vertical setting can be made by turning the screw at the top of the headlamp, and horizontal adjustment by means of the screws at the side of the unit.

In order to adjust headlamps using a beam setting board proceed as follows:—

1. Mark on the board the dimensions shown in the illustration and position the car unladen on level ground.
2. Place board 12 ft (365 cm) in front of the headlamps, ensuring that it is at right-angles to the car centre line on the board, and is in the same plane as the car centre line.
3. Adjust the beam by turning the adjusting screws until the area of concentrated light corresponds with the marks on the beam setting board.

Headlamps with sealed beam unit, adjust

The setting of the headlamps must be made with the Lucas level light beam setter, which is attached to the headlamps.

It is important that this apparatus is set to zero in accordance with the manufacturer's operating instructions, before any adjustments are carried out.

With the beam setter in position the headlamp main beam should be set two divisions from the vertical.

When setting the headlamps the vehicle must be complete with all fittings, and no allowance must be made for the driver or passengers.

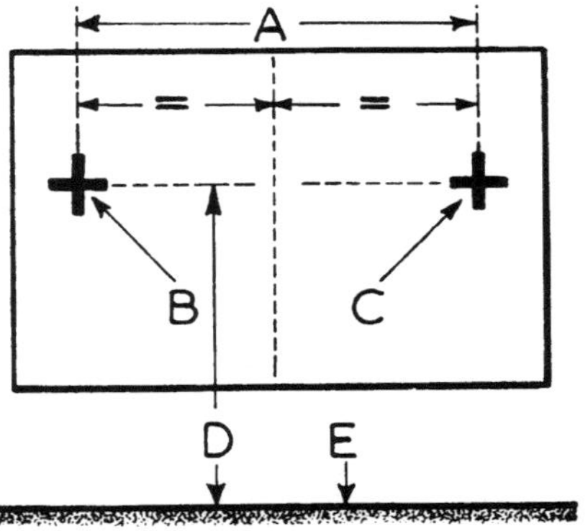

D459

Beam setting board

A—42¼ in. (113 mm)
B—Concentrated area of light LH headlamp
C—Concentrated area of light RH headlamp
D—30$\frac{5}{16}$ in. (84 mm) Mk I, Mk IA and Mk II with high suspension
29$\frac{5}{16}$ in. (744 mm) Mk II with standard suspension
E—Ground level

Side lamp bulb, to replace—Operation S-22

Bulb, remove

1. Press in and turn side lamp glass and rim in an anti-clockwise direction and lift off.
2. Remove plastic sealing ring, rubber sealing ring, and side lamp bulb.

   Replacement bulb: Lucas No. 989, 12 volt, 6 watt.

Bulb, replace

1. Reverse removal procedure.

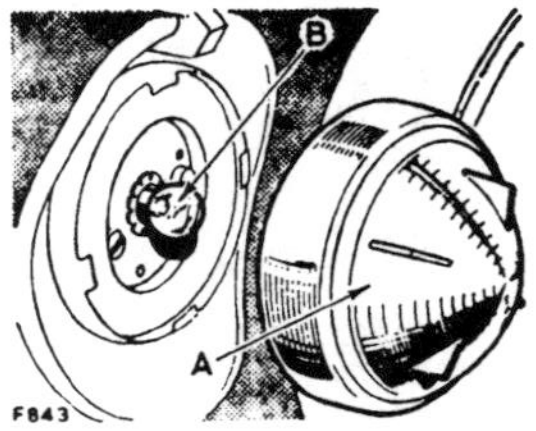

Side lamp bulb replacement
A—White lens B—Bulb replacement

Side lamp, to remove and refit—Operation S-23

Workshop hand tools:
Screwdriver, small

Side lamp, remove

1. Disconnect the battery.
2. Disconnect the lamp wiring at the block connector under the bonnet, withdraw the wiring and grommet from the wing panel.
3. Remove the lamp glass and rim; remove the bulb.
4. Remove the two screws securing side lamp to wing.
5. Lift out bulb holder, lamp body, sealing washer, bezel and rubber washer.

Side lamp, refit

1. Reverse removal procedure.
2. Ensure that the wiring is connected in accordance with the circuit diagram.

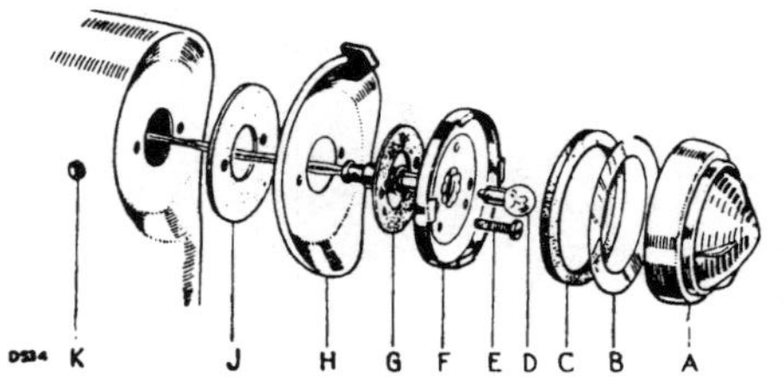

Side lamp

A—Side lamp glass and rim
B—Plastic ring for glass
C—Rubber seal for glass
D—Bulb
E—Screw fixing side lamp
F—Side lamp body
G—Sealing washer for side lamp
H—Bezel for side lamp
J—Sealing rubber for bezel
K—Nut fixing

Flasher lamp bulbs, to replace (front)—Operation S-24

Workshop hand tools:
Screwdriver, small

Bulb, remove

1. Remove the two countersunk screws in the flasher lamp glass and withdraw lamp glass and sealing rubber.
2. Remove flasher lamp bulb.

   Replacement bulb: Lucas No. 382, 12 volt, 21 watt.

Bulb, replace

1. Reverse removal procedure.

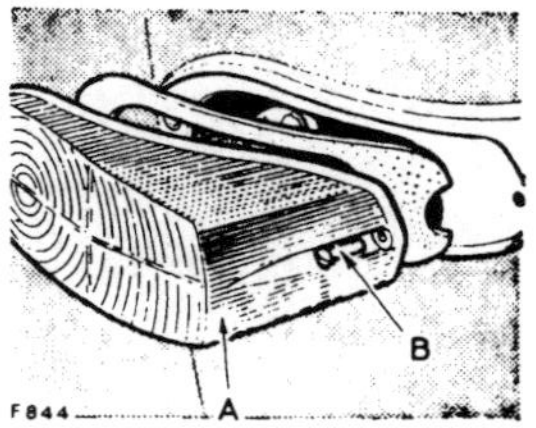

Flasher lamp bulb replacement
A—Amber lens B—Retaining screws

Flasher lamp, to remove and refit—Operation S–25

Workshop hand tools:
Screwdriver, small

Lamp, remove

1. Disconnect battery.
2. Remove the two countersunk screws in the flasher lamp glass and withdraw lamp glass and sealing rubber.
3. Disconnect wiring for lamp at block connector under bonnet.
4. Withdraw wiring and grommet from wing panel.

Flasher lamp, refit

1. Reverse removal procedure.
2. Ensure that the wiring is connected in accordance with the circuit diagram.

Stop/tail and rear flasher bulbs, to replace—Operation S–26

Workshop hand tools:
Screwdriver, small

Bulb, remove

1. Remove the single drive screw at the base of the tail lamp rim, and remove rim.
2. Lift out the flasher and stop/tail lamp glasses.
3. Remove the two sealing rubbers and the bulb.

Stop/tail and rear flasher lamps

A—Amber lens B—Red lens C—Retaining screws

4. The upper lens which is amber, is the direction indicator lamp.

   Replacement bulbs:
   Indicator lamp: Lucas No. 382, 12 volt, 21 watt.
   Stop/tail lamp: Lucas No. 380, 12 volt, 21.6 watt.

Bulb, replace

1. Reverse removal procedure.

Stop/tail and rear flasher lamp, to remove and refit—Operation S–27

Workshop hand tools:
Screwdriver, small

Lamp, remove

1. Disconnect battery.
2. Remove the single drive screw at the base of the tail lamp rim, and remove rim.
3. Lift out the flasher and stop tail lamp glasses.
4. Remove the two sealing rubbers
5. Remove the four drive screws securing the tail lamp assembly mounting plate to wing.
6. Disconnect the wiring at the snap connectors and remove the mounting plate and sealing rubber.

Lamp, refit

1. Reverse removal procedure.
2. Ensure that the wiring is connected in accordance with the circuit diagram.

Reverse and number plate bulbs, to replace—Operation S–28

Workshop hand tools:
Screwdriver, medium

Bulbs, remove

1. Remove the two drive screws securing the reverse lamp cover to the lamp body.
2. Remove the cover and reverse lamp glass.
3. Remove the one reverse and the two plate illumination bulbs.

   Replacement bulbs:
   Number plate: Lucas No. 222, 12 volt, 4 watt.
   Reversing lamp: Lucas No. 382, 12 volt, 21 watt.

Bulbs, replace

1. Reverse removal procedure.

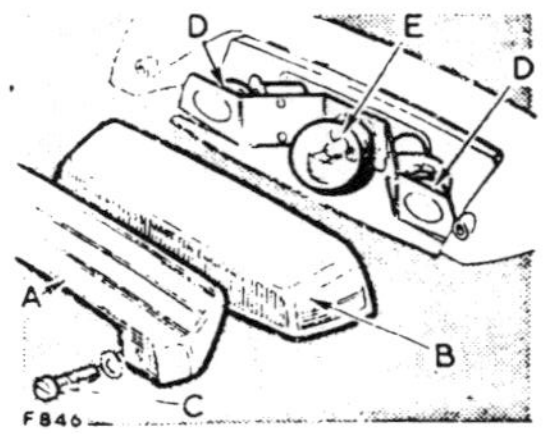

Number plate illumination and reversing lamp

A—Cover
B—Glass
C—Retaining screw
D—Number plate illumination bulbs
E—Reverse light bulb

Reverse and number plate lamp, to remove and refit—Operation S-29

Workshop hand tools:
Screwdriver, medium

Lamp, remove

1. Disconnect battery leads and wiring at snap connector.
2. Remove the two drive screws securing the reverse lamp cover to the lamp body.
3. Remove the cover and reverse lamp glass.
4. Withdraw bulb holders and mounting plate.
5. Remove sealing rubber.
6. Remove the four nuts and washers from the back of the lamp body.
7. Withdraw body and sealing rubber.

Lamp, refit

1. Reverse removal procedure.
2. Ensure that the sealing washers are in sound condition, renew if necessary.
3. Connect the wiring in accordance with the circuit diagram.

Instrument panel and warning light bulbs, to replace—Operation S-30

1. Remove the two retaining screws on the underside of the instrument panel.
2. Carefully ease the facia panel forward and withdraw bulb holder from the instrument. Remove bulb from holder.
3. Carefully ease the instrument panel forward to the nacelle, ensure that the speedometer cable is not kinked, and secure with two drive screws.

   Replacement bulb: Warning and instrument light bulb: Lucas No. 987, 12 volt, 2.4 watt, M.E.S.

   Panel plate light bulbs: Carr Fastener No. 82/036, 12 volt, 1.2 watt.

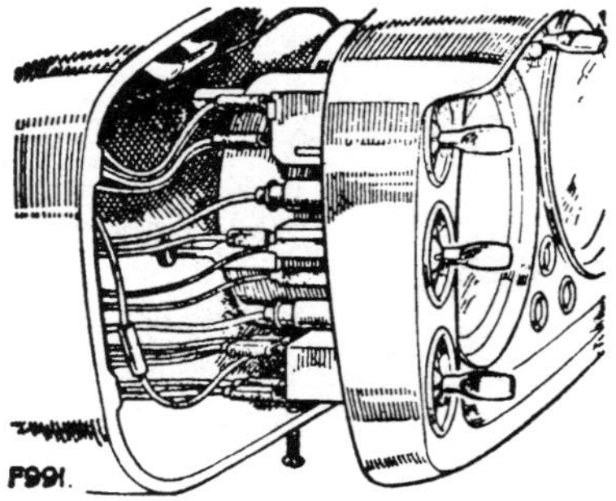

Removing instrument panel

Additional instrument bulbs, Coupé models, to replace—Operation S-31

1. Slacken screw beneath instrument and withdraw unit.
2. Withdraw the rubber sleeve and bulb holder from the rear of the instrument body and renew the bulb.
3. Replace instrument by reversing removal procedure.

   Replacement bulb: Lucas No. 982, 12 volt, 2.2 watt.

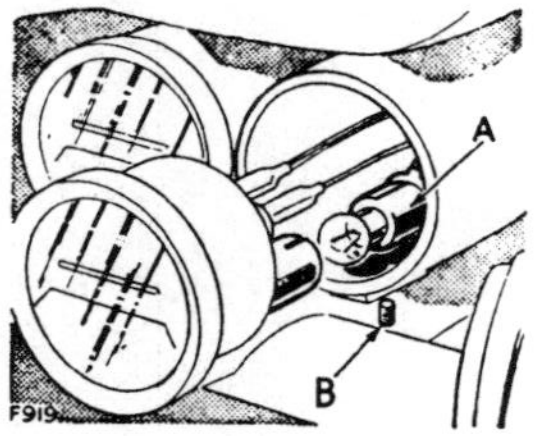

Additional instrument removal and bulb replacement, Coupé models

A—Bulb holder B—Securing screw

Clock illumination bulb, to replace—Operation S-32

1. Slacken screw on the underside of clock nacelle.
2. Withdraw rubber cover and bulb holder from the rear of the clock body, and remove the bulb.
3. Replace bulb, and refit the clock.

   Replacement bulb: Lucas No. 281, 12 volt, 2 watt.

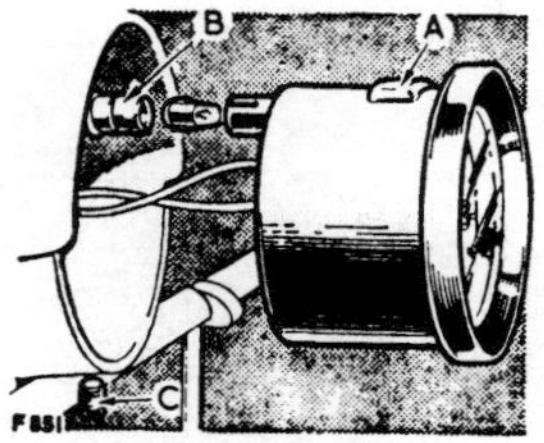

Clock illumination bulb replacement

A—Clock moulding B—Bulb holder C—Fixing screws

Interior light bulb, to replace—Operation S-33

Workshop hand tools:
Screwdriver, small

Bulb, remove

Early models

1. Remove the lamp glass by pressing in and turning in an anti-clockwise direction, lift out complete with spring ring and remove bulb.

Late models

2. Withdraw the cover and glass, secured by two screws and remove bulb.

   Replacement bulbs: Lucas No. 222, 12 volt, 4 watt, Early models.

   Lucas No. 254, 12 volt, 6 watt, Late models.

Bulb, replace

1. Reverse removal procedure.

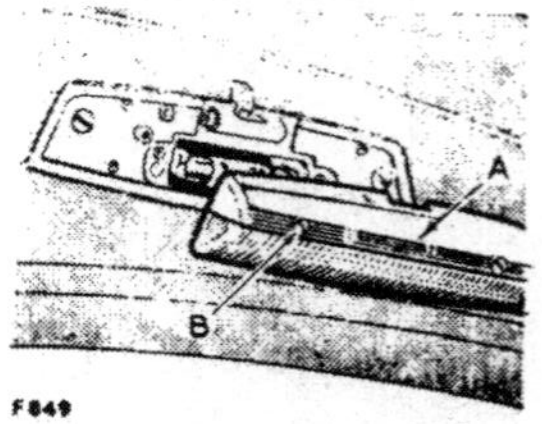

F849

Interior light bulb replacement, late type illustrated

A—Cover B—Retaining screws

Interior lamp, to remove and refit—Operation S-34

Workshop hand tools:
Screwdriver, small

Lamp, remove

Early models

D166

Rear interior lamp, early type illustrated

1. Disconnect battery.
2. Remove lamp glass by pressing in and turning in an anti-clockwise direction, lift out complete with spring ring and remove bulb.
3. Remove the two screws retaining the chromium escutcheon and lift out escutcheon and lamp body, then disconnect wiring at Lucar connectors on lamp body.

Lamp, refit

1. Reverse removal procedure.
2. Connect wiring in accordance with circuit diagram.

Lamp, remove

Late models

1. Disconnect battery.
2. Withdraw the cover and glass, secured by two screws.
3. Remove the drive screw at either end of the lamp body.
4. Lift out lamp body from aperture in lining and disconnect wiring at Lucar connectors. Remove lamp body.

Lamp, refit

1. Connect wiring in accordance with wiring diagram.
2. Fit lamp body into aperture in lining and secure with two drive screws.
3. Ensure switch is in off position, that is, fully forward. otherwise contact may foul and prevent cover from being pushed right on.
4. Connect battery.

Automatic transmission, selector quadrant bulb, to replace—Operation S-35

Remove the small panel in the shroud and remove bulb.

Replacement bulb: Lucas No. 280, 12 volt, 1.5 watt.

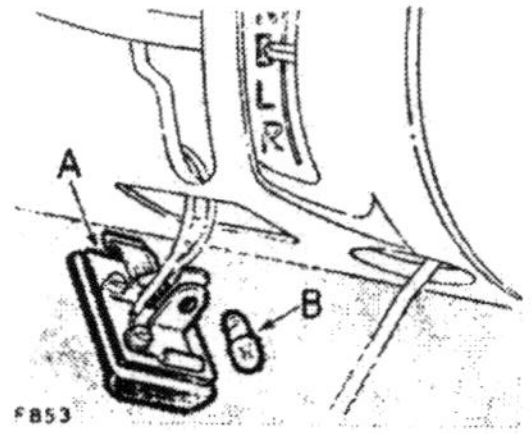

F853

Location of automatic transmission selector quadrant bulb

A—Cover plate B—Bulb

Hand brake warning light bulb, to replace—Operation S-36

Workshop hand tools:
Screwdriver, Phillips type, small

Early models

Unscrew the lens, renew the bulb, refit the lens and test.

Late models

Remove lens secured by two Phillips-headed drive screws, renew the bulb, refit the lens and test.

Replacement bulb:

Early models. Lucas No. 987, 12 volt, 2.2 watt.

Late models. Lucas No. 281, 12 volt, 2 watt.

Current and voltage regulators, to remove and refit—Operation S-37

Workshop hand tools:
Spanner size: $\frac{7}{16}$ in. AF

Regulator, remove

1. Disconnect battery leads.
2. Disconnect all wires from control box.
3. Remove the control box complete from the mounting plate.

Regulator, refit

1. Reverse removal procedure.
2. When replacing a voltage control box, it is essential that the correct control box for the dynamo fitted is used.

   Dynamos type C45, PV5 and PV6, use control box type RB310.

   Dynamo type C42, use control box type RB340.

Current and voltage regulators, to adjust—Operation S-38

Workshop hand tools:

Screwdriver, medium
Feeler gauge

Special tools:

Voltmeter, moving coil type, calibrated 0–20 volts
Ammeter, moving coil type, calibrated 0–40 amps

If the voltage regulator is removed it is essential to fit the replacement in exactly the same position as the original

CONTROL BOX RB340 and RB310

Workshop hand tools:

Spanner size: 4 BA
Screwdriver, medium

Special tools:

Lucas setting tool No. 54381742
Voltmeter, moving coil 0–20 volts
Ammeter 40–0–40 amps

Control box, adjust

1. Before disturbing any electrical adjustments, examine the charging circuit as under to ensure that the fault does not lie outside the control box.
2. Check the battery by substitution or with a hydrometer or heavy discharge tester.
3. Inspect the dynamo driving belt; this should be tensioned to give $\frac{5}{16}$ in.–$\frac{7}{16}$ in. (8–11 mm) deflection by thumb pressure midway between the fan and crankshaft pulleys.
4. Check the dynamo by substitution or in accordance with Operation S-4.
5. Inspect the wiring of the charging circuit and carry out continuity test between the dynamo, control box and when fitted, the ammeter.
6. Check earth connections, particularly that of the control box.
7. In the event of reported undercharging, ascertain that this is not due to low mileage.
8. Should the control box fail to respond correctly to any adjustment given in the following instructions, it should be exchanged for a factory reconditioned unit.

A special tool, Lucas Part No. 54381742 is required for adjustment of the RB340 control box electrical settings. Checking and adjusting should be completed as rapidly as possible to avoid heating errors.

Voltage regulator, adjust

Ambient Temperature	*Voltage Setting* RB310	RB340
10°C (50°F)	15.1–15.7	14.9–15.5
20°C (68°F)	14.9–15.5	14.7–15.3
30°C (86°F)	14.7–15.3	14.5–15.1
40°C (104°F)	14.5–15.1	14.3–14.9

1. Disconnect all cables from control box terminal 'B' and tape ends in such a manner that they are still in contact with each other.
2. Connect a first-grade 0–20 moving coil voltmeter between control box terminal 'D' and a good earthing point.
3. Start the engine and, while observing the voltmeter, gradually speed up to a dynamo speed of 3,000 rpm.
4. The voltmeter pointer should progressively rise to a maximum value, then 'flick' back to a slightly lower reading and remain steady. This is the regulating voltage and should be within the above limits.
5. An unsteady reading of more than ± 0.3 volts may be due to unclean contacts. If the reading occurs outside the appropriate limits, an adjustment must be made. In this event, continue as follows:
6. Stop the engine and remove the control box cover.

Early models with type C45 Dynamo and RB310 Regulator

7. Slacken the adjustment screw locking nut and turn the screw in a clockwise direction to raise the voltage setting, or anti-clockwise to lower the setting. Turn the screw a fraction of a turn only at a time and re-tighten locknut.

Late models with type C42 Dynamo and RB340 Regulator

Insert the special tool in the voltage regulator and turn the cam a very small amount.

Turning clockwise will increase the voltage setting, and vice-versa.

Operation S-38—*continued*

8. Restart the engine and check the setting, as detailed above.

   When the dynamo is run at high speed on open circuit it builds up a high voltage. Do not run the engine up to more than half throttle or a false voltage reading will be given. Complete adjustments within 30 seconds as heating of the regulator winding may cause an inaccurate setting to be made.
9. Repeat this procedure as necessary, until the regulating voltage setting lies within the appropriate limits.
10. Dirty contacts should be cleaned with a fine carborundum stone or silicon carbide paper, followed by methylated spirits. If the contacts setting is disturbed, reset as detailed in Overhaul Instruction (air gap settings), then adjust the electrical settings.
11. When satisfactory, restore the original connections and refit the cover.

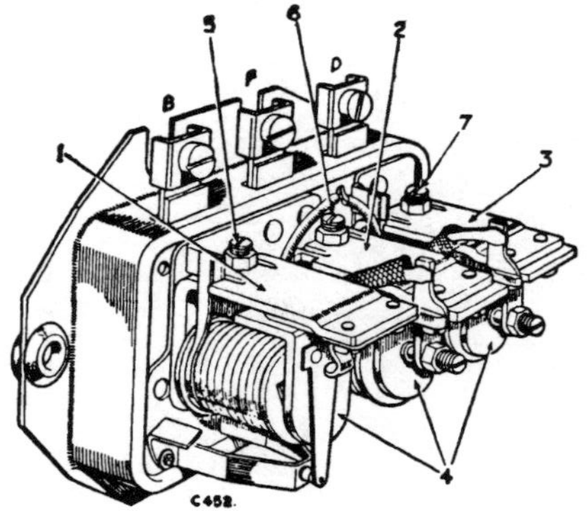

Current voltage regulator, type RB 310

1 Cut-out
2 Current regulator
3 Voltage regulator
4 Armature
5 Cut-out adjusting screw
6 Current adjusting screw
7 Voltage adjusting screw
B—Battery F—Field D—Dynamo

Current regulator, adjust

1. The current regulator on-load setting is equal to the maximum rated output of the dynamo, which is:

Type C45 dynamo PV5	22 amps
Type C45 dynamo PV6	25 amps
Type C42 dynamo	30 amps

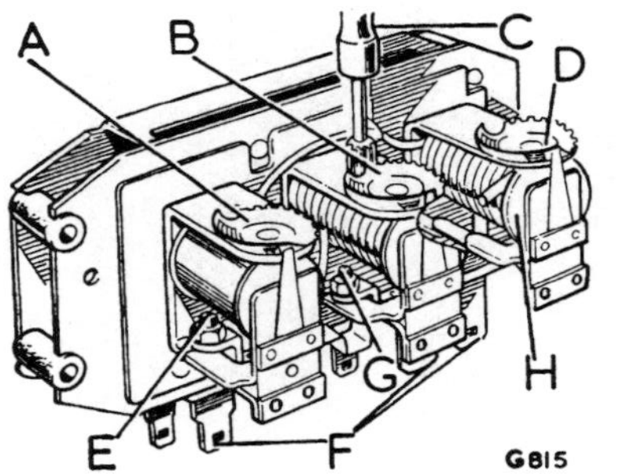

Current voltage regulator, type RB 340

A—Adjustment cam of voltage regulator
B—Adjustment cam of current regulator
C—Special setting tool
D—Adjustment cam of cut-out relay
E—Adjustable contact of voltage regulator
F—'Lucar' connection terminals
G—Adjustable contact of current regulator
H—Core face of cut-out relay

2. The dynamo must be made to develop its maximum rated output, whatever the state of charge of the battery might be at the time of setting. The voltage regulator must therefore be rendered inoperative and this is achieved by shorting-out the voltage regulator contacts.

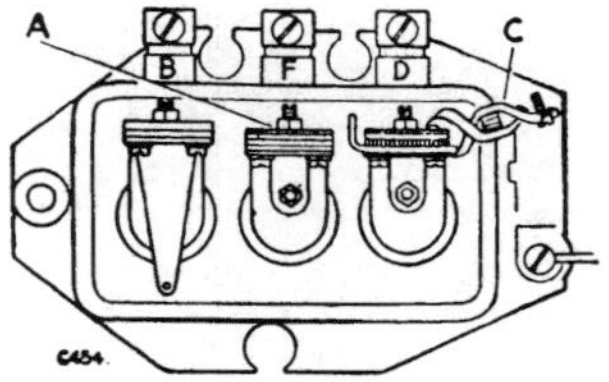

Short-circuiting voltage regulator contacts, type RB 310 regulator illustrated

A—Current regulator adjusting screw
B—Terminal
C—Clip, short-circuiting
D—Terminal
F—Terminal

3. Remove the control box cover with care.
4. Place a crocodile clip across the voltage regulator fixed contact bracket and the voltage regulator frame, to short-out the contacts.

Operation S–38—*continued*

5. Withdraw the leads from the 'B' terminal of the control box and use a 'jumper lead' to connect the two leads together and to the load side of a first grade 0–40 moving coil ammeter.
6. Connect the other side of the ammeter to the 'B' terminal of the control box. It is important that the terminal 'B' carries only the testing ammeter lead.
7. If the battery is well charged switch on an electrical load in excess of the maximum rated output of the dynamo. Start the engine and run the dynamo at 4,500 rpm. Observe ammeter which should be indicating a steady current equal to the maximum rated output of the dynamo.
8. The ammeter pointer should be steady. An unsteady reading (that is one fluctuating more than $\pm$ 1 ampere) may be due to unclean contacts which should be cleaned as described for the voltage regulator. If the reading is too high or too low, an adjustment must be made. In this event, continue as follows:
9. Stop the engine for each adjustment. Insert the special tool in the current regulator and turn the cam a very small amount.

   Clockwise rotation will increase the setting and vice-versa.
10. When the setting is satisfactory (i.e. within $\pm$ 1 ampere of the maximum output figure for the dynamo), switch off the load and restore the original connections.
11. Refit the control box cover with care.

Cut-in voltage, adjust

Checking and adjusting should be completed as rapidly as possible to avoid heating errors.

Cut-in voltage: 12.7–13.3

Drop-off voltage: 9.5–11.0

1. Connect a first-grade 0–20 moving coil voltmeter between control box terminal 'D' and a good earthing point.
2. Switch on an electrical load, such as the head lamps.
3. Start the engine and slowly increase the engine speed.
4. Observe the voltmeter pointer.
5. Closure of the contacts, indicated by a slight drop in the voltmeter reading, should occur between the limits 12.7–13.3 volts. If the cut-in occurs outside these limits, an adjustment must be made. In this event, continue as follows:
6. Reduce the engine speed below the cut-in value, and remove the control box cover.
7. Insert the special tool in the cut-out relay and turn the cam a small amount in the appropriate direction.

   Clockwise rotation will raise the setting and vice-versa.
8. Repeat the checking and setting procedure as necessary, until the correct setting is obtained.
9. Restore the original connections and refit the cover.

Drop-off voltage, adjust

1. Disconnect the cables from control box at terminal 'B' and tape. Connect a first-grade 0–20 moving coil voltmeter between this terminal and a good earth on the chassis.
2. Start the engine and increase engine speed gradually to approximately one-quarter throttle opening.
3. Slowly decelerate and observe the voltmeter pointer.
4. Opening of the contacts, indicated by the voltmeter pointer dropping to zero, should occur between 9.5–11.0 volts. If the drop-off occurs outside these limits, an adjustment must be made. In this event, continue as follows:
5. Stop the engine and remove the control box cover with care.
6. Adjust the drop-off voltage by carefully bending the fixed contact bracket. Reducing the contact gap will raise the drop-off voltage; increasing the gap will lower the drop-off voltage.
7. Repeat items 2 and 3 and, if necessary, readjust until the correct drop-off setting is obtained.
8. Restore the original connections and refit the control box cover with care.
9. To clean the cut-out relay contacts, use a strip of fine glass paper—never carborundum stone or emery cloth.

Control box overhaul (type RB340)

Air gap settings

All air gap settings are accurately adjusted during production and should require no further attention. However, if it has been found necessary to disturb the original setting it must be readjusted as follows, before the electrical settings can be carried out.

Operation S–38—*continued*

Voltage and current regulators

1. To set the air gap between the bobbin and armature on the voltage and current regulators. Disconnect battery. Use the special tool and turn the adjustment cam to the point giving minimum lift to the armature tensioning spring (that is, fully anti-clockwise).
2. Slacken the adjustable contact lock nut and screw back the adjustable contact.
3. Insert a 0.045 in. (1,000 mm) flat feeler gauge between the armature and the core face, taking care not to damage the copper shim. Push the gauge back to the two rivet heads on the under side of the armature.

   The use of non-magnetic material in the top gap has been discontinued, as from December 1963. When servicing late type units use a feeler gauge of 0.052 in.–0.056 in. (1,30 mm–1,40 mm).
4. Screw in the adjustable contact until the gauge is just trapped, that is when it takes a pull of 4 to 5 oz to remove it. Retighten the locknut.
5. Check that narrowest part of back gap, between the armature back face and the frame, on both sides of the armature, is between the limits 0.030 in.–0.040 in. (0,76 mm–1,00 mm) with a maximum of 0.010 in. (0,25 mm) taper for current regulator units.
6. Electrical setting of the voltage regulator can now be carried out; leaving the current regulator unit until the cut-out has been adjusted both mechanically and electrically.

Cut-out

1. With the control box cover removed, turn the adjuster to the point giving minimum lift to the armature tensioning spring, that is by turning the adjuster to its fullest extent anti-clockwise.
2. Press the armature squarely down against the copper separation on the core face. Check that the narrowest part of the back gap, between the armature back face and the frame, on both sides of the armature, is from 0.030 in.–0.040 in. (0,76 mm–1,00 mm).
3. Insert a 0.015 in. (0,38 mm) flat feeler gauge between the head of the core and the armature using the nearest rivet as a datum. Press the armature down and bend the fixed contact bracket until the two contacts just touch, this is the preliminary setting for contact 'follow through'.
4. Insert a 0.015 in. (0,38 mm) feeler gauge between the head of the core and armature as above. Adjust the armature back stop until it just touches the back of the armature.
5. Check that the top gap, controlled by the back stop and using the nearest rivet as a datum, is from 0.035 in.–0.045 in. (0,8 mm–1,1 mm).
6. Proceed with the electrical settings for the cut-out, as detailed.

Control box and switch, rear seat heater (Mk III models), to remove and refit
Operation S-39

Workshop hand tools:
Spanner sizes: ½ in. AF $\frac{9}{16}$ in. AF
Screwdriver small

Control box, remove

1. Where fitted, remove the knob from the rear loudspeaker volume control. The knob is a push-fit, being retained by a spring clip. Remove the control retaining nut from the spindle.
2. Withdraw the control box casing, secured by three small screws.
3. Carefully remove the carpet from around the control box.
4. Disconnect the wiring at the snap connectors.
5. Slacken the two bolts securing the control box to the tunnel and withdraw the control box. The control box bracket is slotted for removal.

Control box, refit

1. Reverse removal procedure.

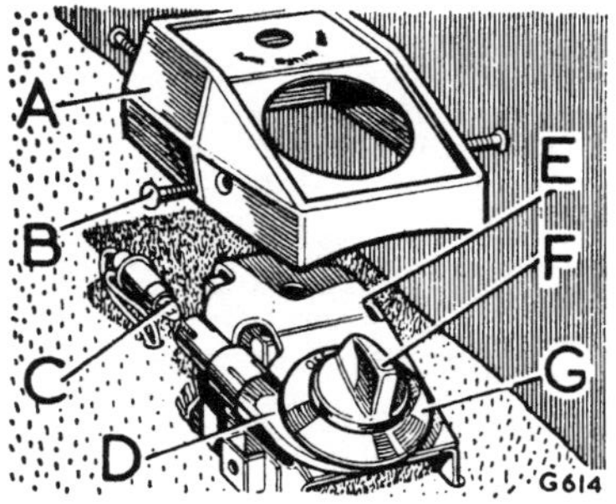

Rear seat heater control box

A—Cover for control box
B—Screw fixing cover
C—Bulb
D—Light diffuser plate
E—Bracket
F—Knob for switch
G—Escutcheon plate for switch

Circuit diagram, positive earth, Mk I and Mk IA Saloon

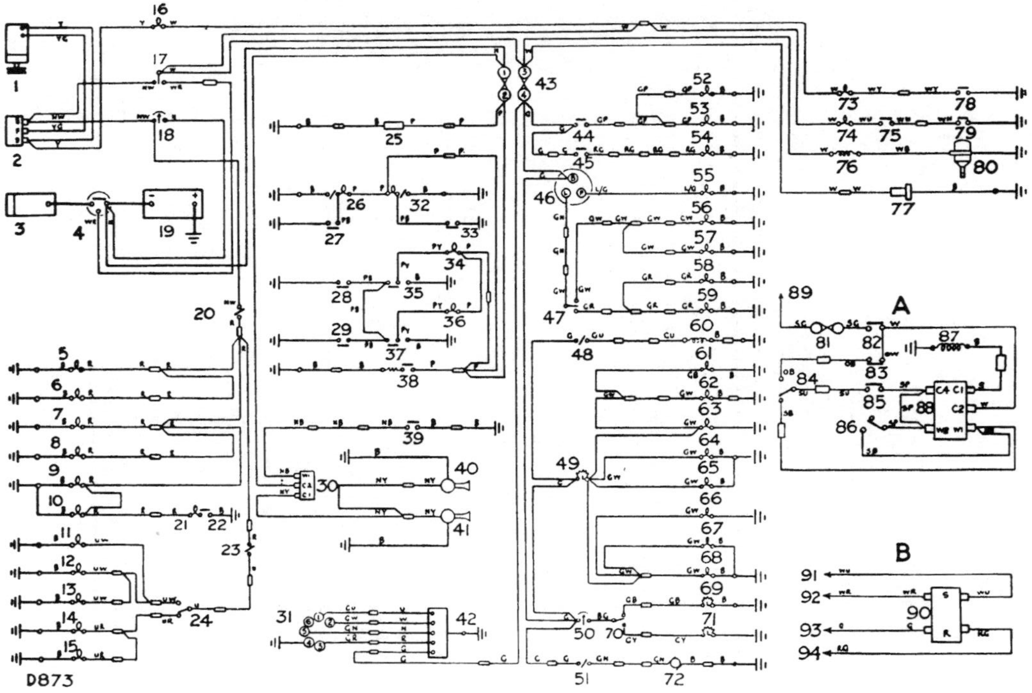

Mk I and Mk IA Saloon. Positive earth electrical system

Key

1 Dynamo
2 Voltage control box RB 310
3 Starter motor
4 Solenoid starter switch
5 Side lamp, RH
6 Side lamp, LH
7 Tail lamp, RH
8 Tail lamp, LH
9 Number plate lamp
10 Number plate lamp
11 Main beam warning light
12 Headlamp main beam, RH
13 Headlamp main beam, LH
14 Headlamp dip beam, RH
15 Headlamp dip beam, LH
16 Ignition warning light
17 Ignition and starter switch
18 Ammeter
19 Battery, 12-volt positive earth
20 Side lamp switch
21 Boot light
22 Boot light switch
23 Headlamp switch
24 Dipper switch
25 Electric clock
26 Front interior light, LH
27 Door switch, LH, front
28 Door switch, RH, rear
29 Door switch, LH, rear
30 Horn relay
31 Windscreen wiper switch
32 Front interior light, RH
33 Door switch, RH, front
34 Rear interior light, RH
35 Pillar switch, RH
36 Rear interior light, LH
37 Pillar switch, LH
38 Cigar lighter
39 Horn push
40 Horn
41 Horn
42 Windscreen wiper motor
43 Fuse unit
44 Stop lamp switch
45 Reverse light switch
46 Flasher unit
47 Flasher switch
48 Fuel reserve switch
49 Panel light rheostat
50 Fuel gauge
51 Heater switch
52 Stop lamp, LH
53 Stop lamp, RH
54 Reverse lamp
55 Flasher warning light
56 Rear flasher lamp, RH
57 Front flasher lamp, RH
58 Front flasher lamp, LH
59 Rear flasher lamp, LH
60 Fuel reserve switch
61 Gear change illumination. Automatic transmission models
62 Clock illumination
63 Grouped instrument panel illumination
64 Panel light, LH
65 Panel light, LH
66 Speedometer illumination
67 Panel light, RH
68 Panel light, RH
69 Fuel tank unit
70 Fuel-oil switch
71 Oil sump unit
72 Heater motor
73 Oil pressure warning light
74 Choke warning light
75 Choke warning switch
76 Ignition coil
77 Fuel pump
78 Oil pressure switch
79 Thermostat
80 Distributor

A—Laycock overdrive kick-down circuit
81 Overdrive fuse box
82 Gearbox switch
83 Throttle switch closed 0–½
84 Column switch
85 Throttle switch open 0–½
86 Kick-down switch
87 Overdrive solenoid
88 Overdrive relay
89 To fuse unit terminal 3

B—Automatic transmission circuit
90 Selector switch. Automatic transmission
91 To starter switch
92 To harness snap connectors adjacent to ignition and starter switch
93, 94 To reverse light switch harness snap connectors, adjacent to selector switch

Snap connectors illustrated this: —▭—

Earth terminals: ——o——||·

CABLE COLOUR CODE

B—Black
U—Blue
N—Brown
R—Red
P—Purple
G—Green
S—Slate
W—White
Y—Yellow
LG—Light Green
O—Orange

NOTE—When a cable has two colour code letters, the first denotes the main colour and the second the tracer colour

Circuit diagram, positive earth, Mk II Saloon Cars with suffix letter 'A' and 'B'

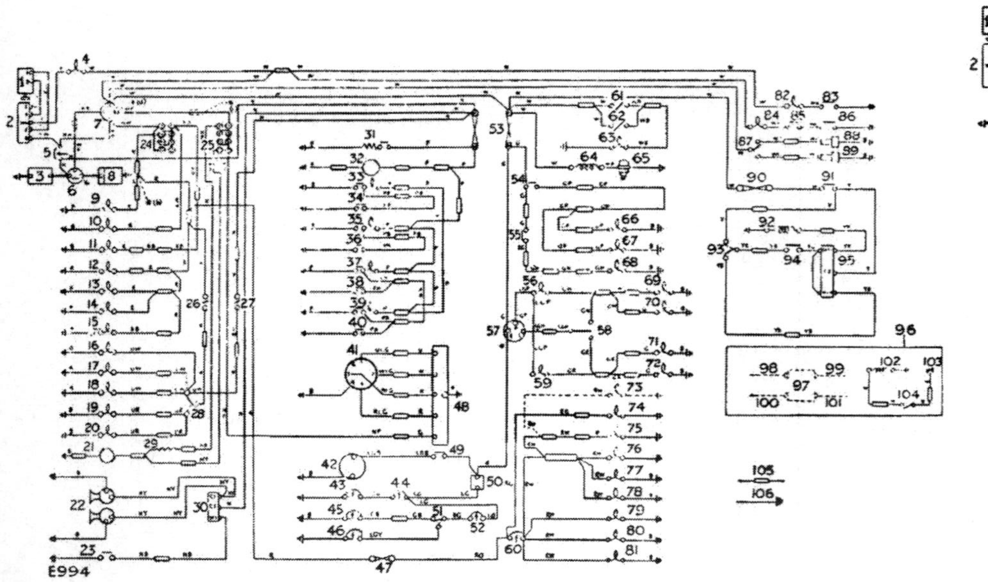

Mk II Saloon Cars with suffix letter 'A' and 'B'. Positive earth electrical system

Key

1 Generator
2 Voltage regulator box
3 Battery
4 Ignition warning light
5 Ammeter
6 Solenoid starter switch
7 Ignition and starter switch
8 Starter motor
9 LH side lamp
10 RH side lamp (Park) } Feed cables reversed
11 RH tail lamp (Park) } for LHD models
12 LH tail lamp
13 Rear number plate lamp
14 Rear number plate lamp
15 Boot lamp and switch
16 Main beam warning light
17 RH headlamp, main beam
18 LH headlamp, main beam
19 LH headlamp, dip beam
20 RH headlamp dip beam
21 Heater motor
22 Horns
23 Horn push switch
24 Main light and parking switch
25 Heater switch
26 Headlamp switch
27 Headlamp flasher switch
28 Dip switch
29 Resistance-heater motor speed
30 Horn relay
31 Cigar lighter
32 Clock
33 Interior lamp and switch, front RH
34 Door switch, front RH
35 Interior lamp and switch, front LH
36 Door switch, front LH
37 Interior lamp and switch, rear LH
38 Door switch, rear LH
39 Interior lamp and switch, rear RH
40 Door switch, rear RH
41 Windscreen wiper switch
42 Windscreen washer pump
43 Water temperature transmitter
44 Water temperature gauge
45 Fuel tank unit
46 Oil sump unit
47 Fuse, panel illumination
48 Windscreen wiper motor
49 Windscreen washer switch
50 10-volt regulator, water temperature and fuel gauge
51 Oil level switch
52 Fuel gauge
53 Fuses, A2 and A4
54 Stop light switch
55 Reverse lamp switch
56 LH flasher warning light
57 Flasher unit
58 Flasher switch
59 RH flasher warning light
60 Panel light rheostat
61 Brake fluid level switch
62 Hand brake switch
63 Hand brake warning light
64 Coil
65 Distributor
66 RH stop lamp
67 LH stop lamp
68 Reversing lamp
69 RH front flasher
70 RH rear flasher
71 LH rear flasher
72 LH front flasher
73 Gear change illumination (automatic transmission models)
74 Cigar lighter illumination
75 Clock illumination
76 Grouped instruments illumination
77 Panel illumination, RH
78 Panel illumination, RH
79 Speedometer illumination
80 Panel illumination, LH
81 Panel illumination, LH
82 Oil pressure warning light
83 Oil pressure switch
84 Mixture control warning light
85 Switch, mixture control warning light
86 Thermostat, mixture control
87 Fuel reserve switch
88 Main fuel pump
89 Reserve fuel pump
90 Fuse, overdrive circuit
91 Gearbox switch }
92 Solenoid }
93 Column switch } 4-speed models
94 Throttle switch }
95 Relay }
96 Automatic transmission circuit
97 Selector switch
98 To harness junction
99 To starter switch
100 To harness junction
101 To reverse light switch
102 Solenoid
103 A3 fuse
104 Switch, intermediate gear hold
105 Snap and Lucar connectors
106 Earth connections

*(a) Radio feed pick-up   *(b) Auxiliary driving lamps pick-up   *(c) Rear window heater pick-up

CABLE COLOUR CODE

B—Black	R—Red	S—Slate	D—Dark
U—Blue	P—Purple	W—White	L—Light
N—Brown	G—Green	Y—Yellow	M—Medium

NOTE—When a cable has two colour code letters, the first denotes the main colour and the second the tracer colour

Circuit diagram, positive earth, Mk II Coupé Cars with suffix letter 'A' (suffix letter 'B' not used on Coupé models)

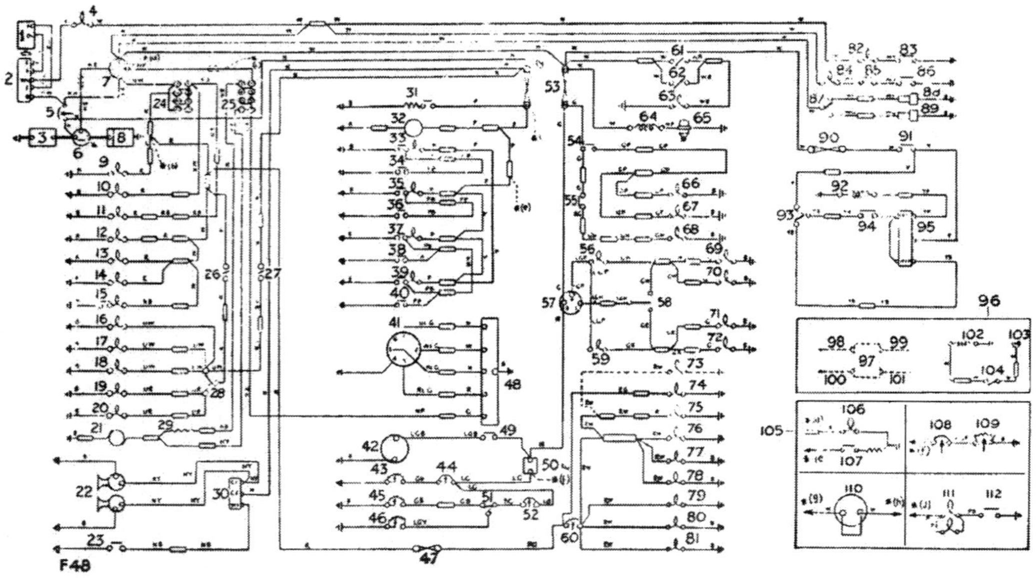

Mk II Coupé Cars with suffix letter 'A' (suffix letter 'B' not used on Coupé). Positive earth electrical system

Key

1 Generator
2 Voltage regulator box
3 Battery
4 Ignition warning light
5 Ammeter
6 Solenoid starter switch
7 Ignition and starter switch
8 Starter motor
9 LH side lamp
10 RH side lamp (Park) } Feed cables reversed
11 RH tail lamp (Park) } on LHD models
12 LH tail lamp
13 Rear number plate lamp
14 Rear number plate lamp
15 Boot lamp and switch
16 Main beam warning light
17 RH headlamp, main beam
18 LH headlamp, main beam
19 LH headlamp, dip beam
20 RH headlamp, dip beam
21 Heater motor
22 Horns
23 Horn push switch
24 Side, tail and parking light switch
25 Heater switch
26 Headlamp switch
27 Headlamp flasher switch
28 Dipper switch
29 Heater motor speed resistance
30 Horn relay
31 Front cigar lighter
32 Clock
33 Interior light and switch, front RH
34 Door switch, front RH
35 Interior light and switch, front LH
36 Door switch, front LH
37 Interior light and switch, rear LH
38 Door switch, rear LH
39 Interior light and switch, rear RH
40 Door switch, rear RH
41 Windscreen wiper switch
42 Windscreen washer pump
43 Water temperature transmitter
44 Water temperature indicator
45 Fuel tank unit
46 Oil sump unit
47 Fuse, panel illumination
48 Windscreen wiper motor
49 Windscreen washer switch
50 10-volt regulator, water temperature and fuel gauge
51 Oil level switch
52 Fuel and oil level indicator
53 Fuses, A2 and A4
54 Stop light switch
55 Reverse lamp switch
56 LH flasher warning light
57 Flasher unit
58 Flasher switch
59 RH flasher warning light
60 Panel lights rheostat
61 Brake fluid level switch
62 Hand brake switch
63 Hand brake warning light
64 Coil
65 Distributor
66 RH stop lamp
67 LH stop lamp
68 Reversing lamp
69 RH front flasher
70 RH rear flasher
71 LH rear flasher
72 LH front flasher
73 Gear change illumination, automatic transmission models
74 Front cigar lighter illumination
75 Clock illumination
76 Grouped instruments illumination
77 Panel illumination, RH
78 Panel illumination, RH
79 Speedometer illumination
80 Panel illumination, LH
81 Panel illumination, LH
82 Oil pressure warning light
83 Oil pressure switch
84 Mixture control warning light
85 Switch, mixture control warning light
86 Thermostat, mixture control
87 Fuel reserve switch
88 Main fuel pump
89 Reserve fuel pump
90 Fuse, overdrive circuit }
91 Gearbox switch }
92 Solenoid } 4-speed models
93 Column switch }
94 Throttle switch }
95 Relay }
96 Automatic transmission circuit
97 Selector switch }
98 To harness junction }
99 To starter switch }
100 To harness junction } Automatic trans-mission models
101 To reverse light switch }
102 Solenoid }
103 A3 fuse connection }
104 Switch, intermediate gear hold }
105 Additional equipment for coupé models
106 Illumination } Rear cigar lighter }
107 Switch and element } }
108 Oil pressure indicator }
109 Oil pressure transmitter } Coupé models
110 Tachometer }
111 Under-bonnet lamps }
112 Bonnet switch }

*(a) Radio feed pick-up
*(b) Auxiliary driving lamps pick-up
*(c) Rear window heater pick-up
*(d) Illumination pick-up } Rear cigar
*(e) Element feed } lighter
*(f) Oil pressure gauge pick-up
*(g) Tachometer feed
*(h) Tachometer connection at coil
*(j) Under-bonnet lamps feed

Snap and Lucar connections: —▭—
Earth connections: —⊪▸

CABLE COLOUR CODE

B—Black	G—Green	L—Light	N—Brown	D—Dark	P—Purple
R—Red	S—Slate	U—Blue	W—White	Y—Yellow	M—Medium

NOTE—When a cable has two colour code letters, the first denotes the main colour and the second the tracer colour

Circuit diagram, positive earth, Mk II Saloon and Coupé Cars with suffix 'C' onwards

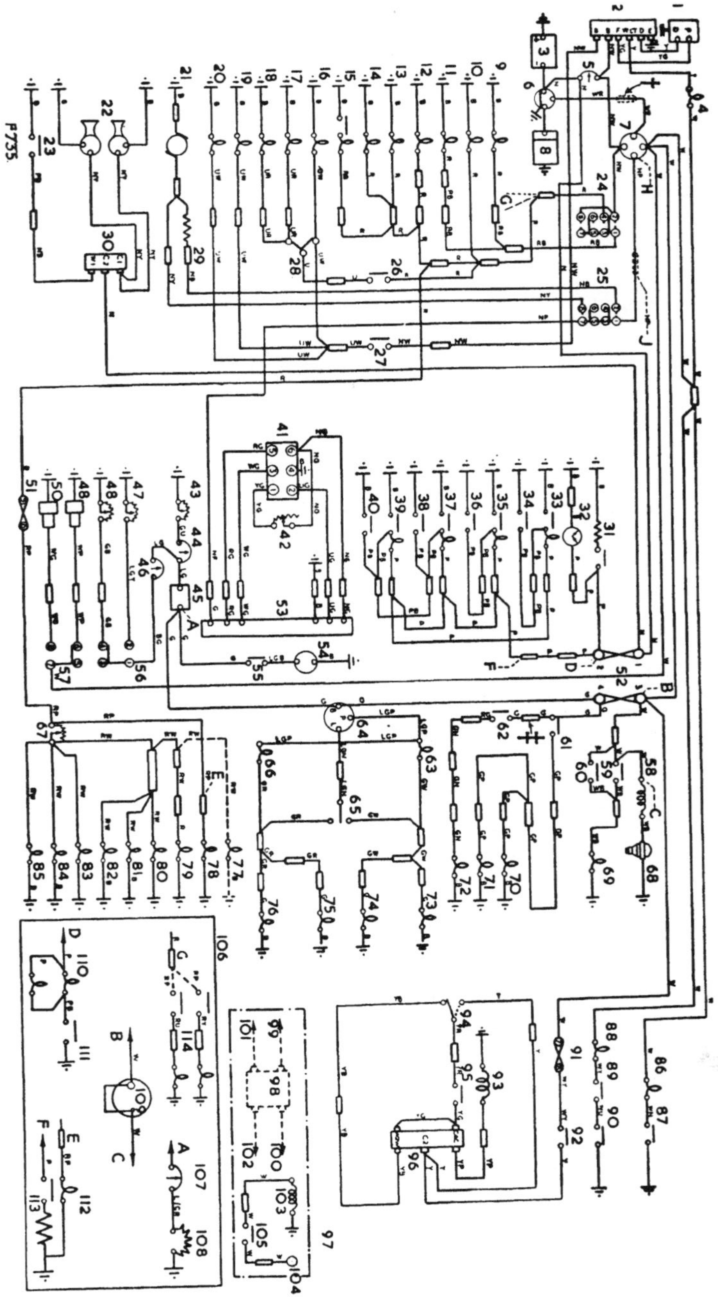

Mk II Saloon and Coupé Cars with suffix letter 'C'. Positive earth electrical system

Key

1 Dynamo
2 Voltage regulator box
3 Battery
4 Ignition warning light
5 Ammeter
6 Solenoid starter switch
7 Ignition and starter switch
8 Starter motor
9 RH side lamp (Park) } Feed cables reversed on LHD models
10 LH side lamp
11 RH tail lamp (Park)
12 LH tail lamp
13, 14 Rear number plate illuminations } Cable movable from connector to connector for LHD side/park requirements
15 Boot lamp and switch
16 Main beam warning light
17 RH headlamp, dip beam
18 LH headlamp, dip beam
19 RH headlamp, main beam
20 LH headlamp, main beam
21 Heater motor, two speed
22 Horns
23 Horn push switch
24 Side, tail and parking light switch
25 Heater switch
26 Headlamp switch
27 Headlamp flasher switch
28 Dipper switch
29 Heater motor speed resistance
30 Horn relay switch
31 Front cigar lighter
32 Clock
33 Interior light and switch, front RH
34 Door switch, front RH
35 Interior light and switch, front LH
36 Door switch, front LH
37 Interior light and switch, rear LH
38 Door switch, rear LH
39 Interior light and switch, rear RH
40 Door switch, rear RH
41 Windscreen wiper "on/off" switch
42 Windscreen wiper speed rheostat switch
43 Water temperature transmitter
44 Water temperature indicator
45 10-volt regulator, water temperature and fuel indicators
46 Fuel indicator
47 Oil sump unit
48 Fuel tank unit
49 Main fuel pump
50 Reserve fuel pump
51 Fuse, panel illumination (3 amp)
52 Fuses, No. 2 and No. 4 (35 amp)
53 Windscreen wiper motor
54 Windscreen washer pump
55 Windscreen washer switch
56 Switch, oil level check
57 Main/reserve fuel changeover switch
58 Coil, ignition
59 Brake fluid level switch
60 Hand brake switch
61 Stop light switch
62 Reverse lamp switch
63 Warning light, direction indicator, LH
64 Direction indicator flasher unit
65 Switch, direction indicators
66 Warning light, direction indicator, RH
67 Panel illumination rheostat
68 Distributor
69 Brake fluid level warning light
70, 71 Stop lamps
72 Reverse lamp
73 Direction indicators, front RH
74 Direction indicators, rear RH
75 Direction indicators, rear LH
76 Direction indicators, front LH
77 Gear change illumination, automatic transmission models
78 Cigar lighter illumination
79 Clock illumination
80 Grouped instruments illumination
81 Panel illumination, LH panel
82 Panel illumination, RH panel
83 Speedometer illumination
84 Panel illumination, LH panel
85 Panel illumination, RH panel
86 Warning light, oil pressure
87 Switch, oil pressure
88 Mixture control warning light
89 Switch, mixture control warning light
90 Thermostat switch, mixture control
91 Fuse (35 amp) } Overdrive circuit 4-speed models
92 Gearbox switch
93 Solenoid
94 Column switch
95 Throttle switch
96 Relay
97 Automatic transmission circuit } Automatic transmission models
98 Selector switch
99 To harness connection } Connected in Series with connector marked thus: †
100 To starter switch
101 To harness connection } Connect in series with connector marked thus: ‡
102 To reverse light switch
103 Solenoid
104 No. 3 fuse connection
105 Switch, intermediatd gear hold
106 Additional equipment for coupé models
107 Oil pressure gauge } Coupé models
108 Oil pressure transmitter
109 Tachometer
110 Under-bonnet lamps
111 Bonnet switch
112 Illumination } Rear cigar lighter
113 Switch and element
114 Auxiliary driving lamps—optional equipment

A—Oil pressure gauge feed } Coupé models
B—Tachometer feed
C—Tachometer connection at coil
D—Under-bonnet lamps feed
E—Illumination feed } Rear cigar lighter
F—Element feed lighter

G—Auxiliary driving lamps feed—optional equipment
H—Radio feed } Optional equipment
J—Rear window heater feed
Snap and lucar connections
Earth connections

CABLE COLOUR CODE

B—Black	R—Red	S—Slate	D—Dark
U—Blue	P—Purple	W—White	L—Light
N—Brown	G—Green	Y—Yellow	M—Medium

Circuit diagram, negative earth, Mk III Saloon and Coupé, RHD

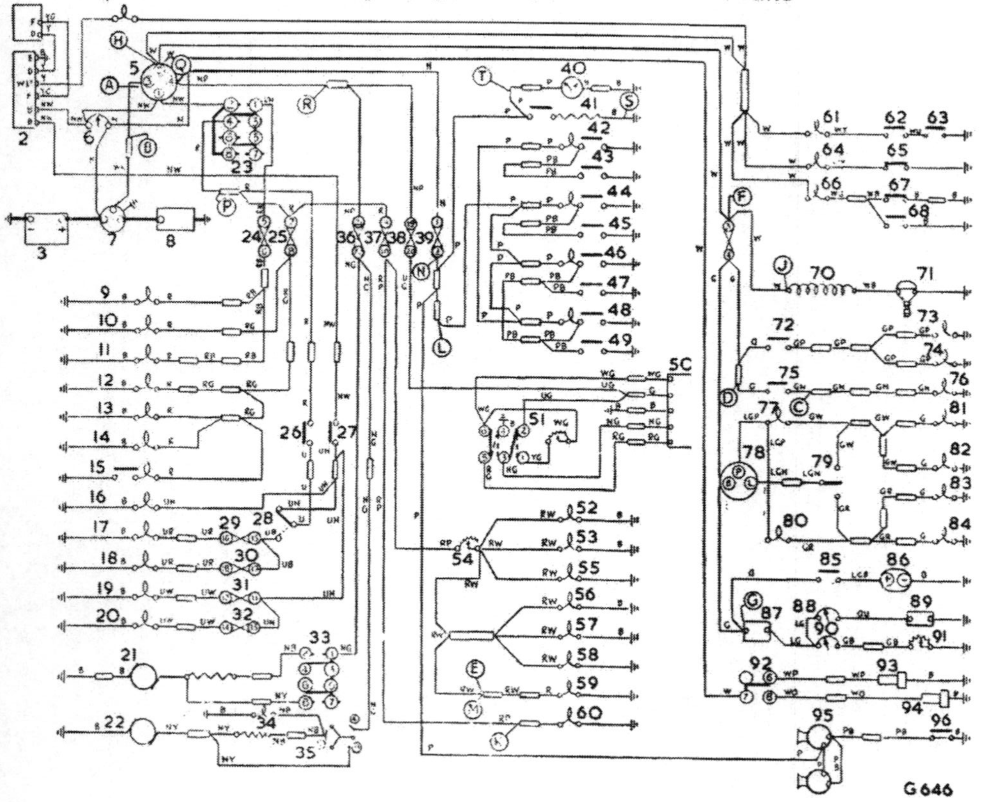

Mk III Saloon and Coupé, RHD. Negative earth electrical system

Key

1 Dynamo
2 Current voltage regulator
3 Battery
4 Warning light, ignition
5 Switch, ignition and starter
6 Ammeter
7 Starter solenoid
8 Starter motor
9 Side lamp, RH (Park)
10 Side lamp, LH
11 Tail lamp, RH (Park)
12 Tail lamp, LH
13 } Rear number plate
14 } illumination
15 Switch and lamp, boot
16 Warning light, main beam
17 Headlamp, RH, dip beam
18 Headlamp, LH, dip beam
19 Headlamp, RH, main beam
20 Headlamp, LH, main beam
21 Heater motor, two-speed, front
22 Heater motor, two-speed, rear
23 Switch, side, tail and park
24 Fuse, 5–6 (5 Amp)
25 Fuse, 7–8 (5 Amp)
26 Switch, headlamp
27 Switch, headlamp flasher
28 Switch, headlamp dip
29 Fuse, 15–16 (10 Amp)
30 Fuse, 17–18 (10 Amp)
31 Fuse, 11–12 (10 Amp)
32 Fuse, 13–14 (10 Amp)
33 Switch, heater, front
34 Heater illumination, rear
35 Switch, heater, rear
36 Fuse, 21–22 (15 Amp)
37 Fuse, 9–10 (5 Amp)
38 Fuse, 19–20 (15 Amp)
39 Fuse, 1–2 (25 Amp)
40 Clock
41 Cigar lighter
42 Interior lamp and switch, front RH
43 Switch, front door, RH
44 Interior lamp and switch, front LH
45 Switch, front door, LH
46 Interior lamp and switch, rear LH
47 Switch, rear door, LH
48 Interior lamp and switch, rear RH
49 Switch, rear door, RH
50 Screen wiper motor
51 Switches, screen wiper
52 } Panel
53 } illumination, LH
54 Switch, panel illumination
55 Speedometer illumination
56 } Panel
57 } illumination, RH
58 Grouped instrument illumination
59 Clock illumination
60 Cigar lighter, front, illumination
61 Warning light, choke
62 Switch, choke
63 Thermostat, choke
64 Warning light, oil pressure
65 Switch, oil pressure
66 Warning light, brake fluid level and handbrake
67 Switch, handbrake
68 Switch, brake fluid level
69 Fuse, 3–4 (25 Amp)
70 Ignition coil
71 Distributor
72 Switch, stop light
73 Stop light, RH
74 Stop light, LH
75 Switch, reverse light
76 Reverse light
77 Warning light, LH direction indicators
78 Direction indicator unit
79 Switch, direction indicators
80 Warning light, RH direction indicators
81 Direction indicator, front RH
82 Direction indicator, rear RH
83 Direction indicator, rear LH
84 Direction indicator, front LH
85 Switch, windscreen washer
86 Windscreen washer
87 Regulator, 10 Volt
88 Gauge, water temperature
89 Transmitter, water temperature
90 Gauge, fuel
91 Tank unit, fuel
92 Switch, fuel pump change-over
93 Fuel pump, main
94 Fuel pump, reserve
95 Horns
96 Switch, horn

Snap and Lucar connections —▭—
Earth connections ——⊪
Encircled letters on circuit diagram show pick-up points for additional and optional equipment

CABLE COLOUR CODE

B—Black	Y—Yellow
P—Purple	U—Blue
W—White	G—Green
R—Red	L—Light
N—Brown	

Circuit diagram, negative earth, Mk III Saloon and Coupé, LHD

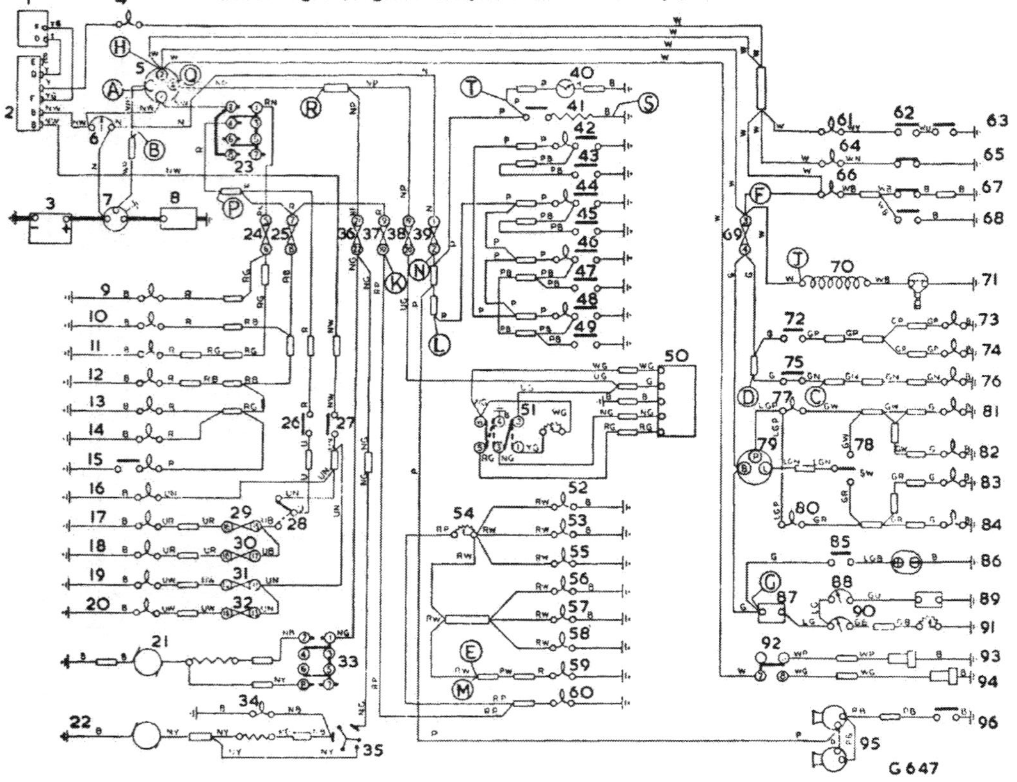

Mk III Saloon and Coupé, LHD. Negative earth electrical system

Key

1 Dynamo
2 Current voltage regulator
3 Battery
4 Warning light, ignition
5 Switch, ignition and starter
6 Ammeter
7 Starter solenoid
8 Starter motor
9 Side lamp, LH (Park)
10 Side lamp, RH
11 Tail lamp, LH (Park)
12 Tail lamp, RH
13 } Rear number plate
14 } illumination
15 Switch and lamp, boot
16 Warning light, main beam
17 Headlamp, RH, dip beam
18 Headlamp, LH, dip beam
19 Headlamp, RH, main beam
20 Headlamp, LH, main beam
21 Heater motor, two-speed, front
22 Heater motor, two-speed, rear
23 Switch, side, tail and park
24 Fuse, 5–6 (5 Amp)
25 Fuse, 7–8 (5 Amp)
26 Switch, headlamp
27 Switch, headlamp flasher
28 Switch, headlamp dip
29 Fuse, 15–16 (10 Amp)
30 Fuse, 17–18 (10 Amp)
31 Fuse, 11–12 (10 Amp)
32 Fuse, 13–14 (10 Amp)
33 Switch, heater, front
34 Heater illumination, rear
35 Switch, heater, rear
36 Fuse, 21–22 (15 Amp)
37 Fuse, 9–10 (5 Amp)
38 Fuse, 19–20 (15 Amp)
39 Fuse, 1–2 (25 Amp)
40 Clock
41 Cigar lighter
42 Interior lamp and switch, front, RH
43 Switch, front door, RH
44 Interior lamp and switch, front, LH
45 Switch, front door, LH
46 Interior lamp and switch, rear, LH
47 Switch, rear door, LH
48 Interior lamp and switch, rear, RH
49 Switch, rear door, RH
50 Screen wiper motor
51 Switches, screen wiper
52 } Panel
53 } illumination, LH
54 Switch, panel illumination
55 Speedometer illumination
56 } Panel
57 } illumination, RH
58 Grouped instrument illumination
59 Clock illumination
60 Cigar lighter, front, illumination
61 Warning light, choke
62 Switch, choke
63 Thermostat, choke
64 Warning light, oil pressure
65 Switch, oil pressure
66 Warning light, brake fluid level and handbrake
67 Switch, handbrake
68 Switch, brake fluid level
69 Fuse, 3–4 (25 Amp)
70 Ignition coil
71 Distributor
72 Switch, stop light
73 Stop light, RH
74 Stop light, LH
75 Switch, reverse light
76 Reverse light
77 Warning light, LH direction indicators
78 Direction indicator unit
79 Switch, direction indicators
80 Warning light, RH direction indicators
81 Direction indicator, front, RH
82 Direction indicator, rear, RH
83 Direction indicator, rear, LH
84 Direction indicator, front, LH
85 Switch, windscreen washer
86 Windscreen washer
87 Regulator, 10 Volt
88 Gauge, water temperature
89 Transmitter, water temperature
90 Gauge, fuel
91 Tank unit, fuel
92 Switch, fuel pump change-over
93 Fuel pump, main
94 Fuel pump, reserve
95 Horns
96 Switch, horn

Snap and Lucar connections —▭—
Earth connections ——⊪
Encircled letters on circuit diagram show pick-up points for additional and optional equipment

CABLE COLOUR CODE

B—Black	Y—Yellow
P—Purple	U—Blue
W—White	G—Green
R—Red	L—Light
N—Brown	

Circuit diagram, negative earth, Mk III Saloon and Coupé, additional and optional equipment

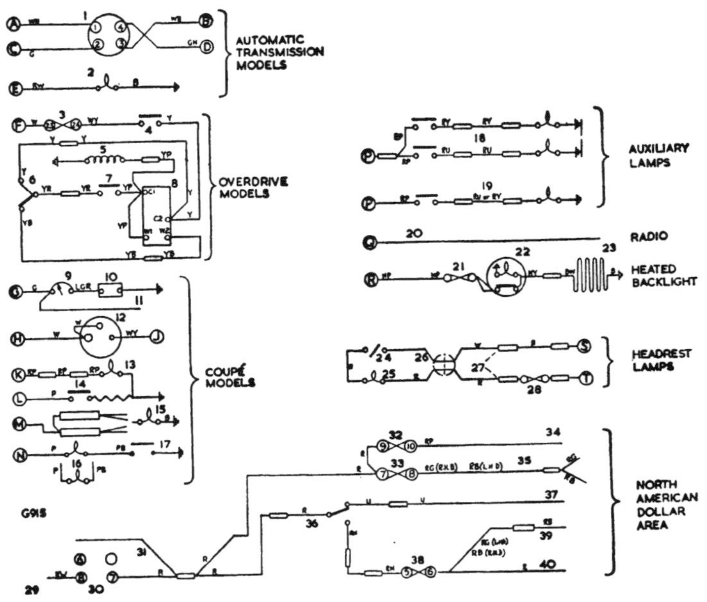

Mk III Saloon and Coupé, additional and optional equipment. Negative earth electrical system

Key

Automatic Transmission models
1 Switch, inhibitor
2 Gear change illumination

Overdrive models
3 Fuse, 23–24 (25 Amp)
4 Switch, gearbox
5 Solenoid
6 Switch, column
7 Switch, throttle
8 Relay

Coupé models
9 Gauge, oil pressure
10 Transmitter, oil pressure
11 To screen washer switch
12 Tachometer
13 Rear cigar lighter illumination
14 Cigar lighter
15 Nacelle illumination, four lamps
16 Bonnet lamp
17 Switch, bonnet lamp

Auxiliary lamps
18 Auxiliary lamps, two, switched separately } Optional equipment
19 Auxiliary lamps, one or two, common switch

Radio
20 Radio pick-up

Heated backlight
21 Fuse (10 Amp), in-line, heated backlight
22 Switch, illuminated, heated backlight
23 Heated backlight

Headrest lamps
24 Switch, headrest lamp
25 Headrest lamp
26 Plug and socket, headrest lamp
27 Pick-up point when two lamps are fitted
28 Fuse (10 Amp) for headrest lamp

(Items 20–28: Optional equipment)

North American Dollar Area Cars
29 Feed from ignition and starter switch
30 Switch, side lamp
31 Connection for fog lamp, etc.
32 Fuse, 9–10 (5 Amp)
33 Fuse, 7–8 (5 Amp)
34 To cigar lighter illumination
35 To tail lamps
36 Switch, headlamp
37 To dip switch
38 Fuse, 5–6 (5 Amp)
39 To RH side lamp
40 To LH side lamp

Replacement headlamp sealed beam units and bulbs

Headlamps

RHD, Lucas No. 416	..12v 60/40w, 3 litre Mk I and Mk IA	
RHD, Lucas Sealed Beam	..12v 60/45w, 3 litre Mk II and Mk III	
LHD, Except North America and Europe, Lucas No. 417	..12v 60/45w	3 litre models, Mk I, Mk IA, Mk II and Mk III
LHD, Europe except France, Lucas No. 410	..12v 45/40w Duplo	3 litre models, Mk I, Mk IA, Mk II and Mk III
LHD, France, Lucas No. 411	..12v 45/40w Duplo (yellow)	3 litre models, Mk I, Mk IA, Mk II and Mk III
North America, Sealed unit	..12v	3 litre models, Mk I, Mk IA, Mk II and Mk III

Side lamps, Lucas No. 222	..12v 4w
Stop/tail lamps, Lucas No. 380	..12v 21/6w
Direction indicator lamps, Lucas No. 382	..12v 21w
Rear number plate lamp, Lucas No. 222	..12v 4w
Instrument panel light, Lucas No. 987	..12v 2.2w
Warning lights, Lucas No. 987	..12v 2.2w
Interior lights, Lucas No. 222	..12v 4w, Early models
Interior lights, Lucas No. 254	..12v 6w, Late models
Automatic transmission selector indicator lamp, Lucas No. 280	..12v 1.5w
Panel plate, Carr Fastener No. 82/036	..12v 1.2w
Clock, Lucas No. 281	..12v 2w
Reverse lamp, Lucas No. 382	..12v 21w
Rear luggage boot lamp, Lucas No. 222	..12v 4w
Brake fluid level warning light, Lucas No. 281	..12v 2w

DEFECT LOCATION

SYMPTOM	POSSIBLE CAUSE	REMEDY
A—BATTERY IN LOW STATE OF CHARGE	1. Broken or loose connection in dynamo circuit 2. Current voltage regulator not functioning correctly 3. Commutator greasy or dirty 4. Brushes worn, not fitted correctly or wrong type	1. *Examine the charging and field circuit wiring. Tighten any loose connections and renew any broken leads. Examine the battery connections* 2. *Adjust or renew* 3. *Clean* 4. *Renew*
B—BATTERY OVERCHARGED, LEADING TO BURNT-OUT BULBS AND FREQUENT NEED FOR TOPPING UP	1. Current voltage regulator not functioning currectly	1. *Adjust or renew*
C—LAMPS GIVING INSUFFICIENT ILLUMINATION	1. Battery discharged 2. Bulbs discoloured through prolonged use	1. *Charge the battery from an independent supply or by a long period of daylight running* 2. *Renew*
D—LAMPS LIGHT WHEN SWITCHED ON BUT GRADUALLY FADE OUT	1. Battery discharged	1. *Charge the battery from an independent supply or by a long period of daylight running*
E—LIGHTS FLICKER	1. Loose connection	1. *Tighten*
F—FAILURE OF LIGHTS	1. Battery discharged 2. Loose or broken connection	1. *Charge the battery from an independent supply or by a long period of daylight running* 2. *Locate and rectify*
G—STARTER MOTOR LACKS POWER OR FAILS TO TURN ENGINE	1. Stiff engine 2. Battery discharged 3. Broken or loose connection in starter circuit 4. Greasy, charred or glazed commutator 5. Brushes worn, not fitted correctly or wrong type 6. Brushes sticking in holders or incorrectly tensioned 7. Starter pinion jammed in mesh with flywheel	1. *Locate cause and remedy* 2. *Charge the battery either by a long period of daytime running or from independent electrical supply* 3. *Check and tighten all battery, starter and starter switch connections and check the cables connecting these units for damage* 4. *Clean* 5. *Renew* 6. *Rectify* 7. *Rotate the squared end of the starter shaft with a spanner to free the pinion*
H—STARTER NOISY	1. Starter pinion of flywheel teeth chipped or damaged 2. Starter motor loose on engine 3. Armature shaft bearing	1. *Renew* 2. *Rectify, checking the pinion and the flywheel for damage* 3. *Renew*
J—STARTER OPERATES BUT DOES NOT CRANK THE ENGINE	1. Pinion of starter does not engage with the flywheel, due to dirt on the screwed sleeve	1. *Clean*
K—STARTER PINION WILL NOT DISENGAGE FROM THE FLYWHEEL WHEN THE ENGINE IS RUNNING	1. Starter pinion jammed in mesh with the flywheel	1. *Rotate squared end of the starter shaft with a spanner until the pinion flies off. On no account run the engine or serious damage to the starter will result*

DEFECT LOCATION—*continued*

SYMPTOM	POSSIBLE CAUSE	REMEDY
L—ENGINE WILL NOT FIRE	1. The starter will not turn the engine due to a discharged battery 2. Sparking plugs faulty, dirty or incorrect plug gaps 3. Defective coil or distributor 4. A fault in the low tension wiring is indicated when no spark occurs between the contacts when separated quickly with an insulated screwdriver with the ignition on 5. Dirty or pitted contacts 6. Contact breaker out of adjustment 7. Controls not set correctly or trouble other than ignition	1. *The battery should be recharged by running the car for a long period during daylight or from an independent electrical supply* 2. *Rectify or renew* 3. *Remove the lead from the centre distributor terminal and hold it approximately $\frac{1}{4}$ in. (6 mm) from some metal part of the engine while the engine is being turned over. If the sparks jump the gap regularly, the coil and distributor are functioning correctly. Renew a defective coil or distributor* 4. *Examine all the ignition cables and check that the bottom terminals are secure and not corroded* 5. *Clean* 6. *Adjust* 7. *See Starting Procedure in the Owner's Instruction Manual*
M—ENGINE MISFIRES	1. Distributor points incorrectly set 2. Faulty coil or condenser 3. Faulty sparking plugs 4. Faulty carburetter	1. *Adjust* 2. *Renew* 3. *Rectify* 4. *Check and rectify*
N—FREQUENT RECHARGING OF THE BATTERY NECESSARY	1. Dynamo inoperative 2. Loose or corroded connections 3. Slipping fan belt 4. Voltage control out of adjustment 5. Excessive use of the starter motor 6. High mica insulation between the commutator segments 7. Vehicle operation confined largely to night driving 8. Abnormal accessory load 9. Internal discharge of the battery	1. *Check the brushes, cables and connections or renew the dynamo* 2. *Examine all connections, especially the battery terminals and earthing straps* 3. *Adjust* 4. *Renew* 5. *In the hands of the operator* 6. *Undercut the mica* 7. *In the hands of the operator* 8. *Superfluous electrical fittings such as extra lamps, etc.* 9. *Renew*
P—DYNAMO NOT CHARGING CORRECTLY	1. Slipping fan belt 2. Voltage control not operating correctly 3. Greasy, charred or glazed commutator 4. Brushes worn, sticking or oily 5. Shorted, open or burnt-out field coils	1. *Adjust* 2. *Rectify or renew* 3. *Clean* 4. *Rectify or renew* 5. *Renew*
Q—DYNAMO NOISY	1. Worn, damaged or defective bearings 2. Cracked or damaged pulley 3. Dynamo out of alignment 4. Dynamo loose in mounting 5. Excessive brush noise	1. *Renew* 2. *Renew* 3. *Rectify at the dynamo mountings* 4. *Rectify* 5. *Check for rough or dirty commutator, badly seating brushes, high mica insulation, incorrect brush tension, loose brushes and loose field magnets. Rectify or renew*
R—DEFECTIVE DISTRIBUTOR	1. Contact breaker gap incorrect or points burned and pitted 2. Distributor cap cracked 3. Weak or broken contact breaker spring 4. Excessive wear in distributor shaft bushes, etc. 5. Rotor arm pitted or burned 6. If the engine lacks power, or misfires, it may be due to a faulty condenser	1. *Clean and adjust* 2. *Renew* 3. *Renew* 4. *Renew* 5. *Clean or renew* 6. *Renew the condenser*

DEFECT LOCATION—*continued*

SYMPTOM	*POSSIBLE CAUSE*	*REMEDY*
S—MIXTURE CONTROL WARNING LIGHT FAILS TO APPEAR WHEN ENGINE REACHES RUNNING TEMPERATURE	1. Mixture control already pushed in 2. Broken connection in warning light circuit 3. Blown bulb 4. Faulty thermostat switch (at cylinder head) 5. Faulty manual switch (at mixture control) 6. Broken operating mechanism at manual switch	1. *In the hands of the operator* 2. *Rectify* 3. *Renew* 4. *Renew* 5. *Renew* 6. *Rectify*
T—MIXTURE CONTROL WARNING LIGHT REMAINS ON WITH ENGINE AT RUNNING TEMPERATURE	1. Mixture control out 2. Faulty manual switch 3. Broken operating mechanism at manual switch	1. *Push control right in* 2. *Renew* 3. *Rectify*
U—POOR PERFORMANCE OF HORNS	1. Low voltage due to discharged battery 2. Bad connections in wiring 3. Loose fixing bolt 4. A faulty horn	1. *Recharge* 2. *Carefully inspect all connections and horn push* 3. *Rectify* 4. *Adjust*

DATA

Electrical system, type:
- Mk I, Mk IA and Mk II .. .. Positive earth
- Mk III .. .. Negative earth

Voltage 12

Battery:
- Capacity .. .. 57 AH
- Location .. .. In the luggage boot, RH side under metal cover

Ignition system:
- Coil .. .. Lucas HA12

Mixture control thermostat switch:
- Makes contact at: 51–55°C (124–131°F)
- Breaks contact at: 47–53°C (117–127°F)

Distributor, type:
- Mk I and Mk IA DMBZ6A
- Mk II and Mk III 25D6

Direction of rotation .. .. Clockwise

Contact breaker gap .. .. .014–.016 in. (0,35–0,40 mm)

Model	Mk I and Mk IA		Mk II suffix 'A' and 'B'		Mk II suffix 'C' and Mk III	
Compression ratio	8.75:1	7.5:1	8.75:1	8.0:1	8.75:1	8.0:1
Maximum centrifugal advance crankshaft degrees	16°	13°	24°	32°	24°	32°
Maximum vacuum advance crankshaft degrees	10°–14°	10°–14°	10°–14°	22°–26°	10°–14°	22°–26°
Advancement begins at (engine rpm)	500	500	520	500	900	900
Advancement finishes at (engine rpm)	2500	2500	4200	4000	4200	4000

Charging circuit:
- Current voltage regulator, Mk I and Mk IA .. Lucas RB310
- Mk II and Mk III .. .. Lucas RB340

Dynamo, type:
- Mk I and Mk IA .. .. Lucas C45, 25 amps
- Mk II and Mk III .. .. Lucas C42, 30 amps

Maximum continuous output:
- C45 dynamo .. .. 25 amps
- C42 dynamo .. .. 30 amps

Starter motor:
- Type .. .. Lucas M418G, 10-tooth pinion

Windscreen wiper, type:
- Mk I and Mk IA .. .. Lucas DR3
- Mk II and Mk III .. .. Lucas 45SA

Screen washer, type:
- Mk I and Mk IA .. .. Lucas 2SJ
- Mk II and Mk III .. .. Lucas 15SA

Section T – FACIA FITTINGS AND CONTROLS

Brief description of facia panel and controls

All instruments and switches are conveniently grouped together. On the saloon model, a multiple gauge comprising a combined fuel/oil level indicator, water temperature gauge and ammeter is mounted adjacent to the speedometer.

Coupé models have oil pressure, ammeter, water temperature and fuel/oil level gauges mounted separately beneath the main instrument unit. These gauges, with the exception of the ammeter are of the bi-metal type. In place of the multiple gauge, there is a tachometer fitted.

Both models have centrally mounted warning lights for oil pressure, ignition, and cold start control. There are also warning lights for main beam headlights, and direction indicators, these being incorporated in the speedometer dial.

An amber warning light is fitted on the lower edge of the facia panel adjacent to the hand brake. The main purpose of this light is to indicate when the level of brake fluid in the reservoir has dropped below the safe limit. With the ignition switched on, the light comes on when the hand brake is applied.

The instrument unit is surmounted by a padded facia crash-rail. The clock is mounted centrally in this rail and on the leading edge at either end there are face-level ventilators.

Mounted below the padded rail of the full-width parcel shelf, are the cold start, bonnet release and ventilator controls.

The heater and demister control levers are situated between the glove box lids on the facia panel.

INDEX

Bonnet lock cable, to remove and refit—Operation T-1

Workshop hand tools:
Spanner sizes: $\frac{1}{4}$ in. AF, $\frac{7}{16}$ in. AF

Cable, remove

1. **Early models, items 1 and 2.** Remove the bolt and ferrule securing the bonnet lock cable to bonnet lock, remove the fixings securing bonnet lock cable to body, and withdraw inner cable.

2. Release the chromium bezel and withdraw outer cable.

3. **Late models, items 3 to 5.** Remove the bonnet lock platform. Section A.

4. Remove the bolt and ferrule securing the bonnet lock cable to lever, removing the fixings securing the bonnet lock cable to body.

5. Withdraw the inner cable, then release the chromium bezel and withdraw outer cable.

Cable, refit

1. Reverse removal procedure.

2. Check the action of locking mechanism, adjust as necessary:

(a) Check that the lock bolt adjustment is correct. The bolt should protrude through the plate approximately $\frac{1}{2}$ in. (12,5 mm), as illustrated.

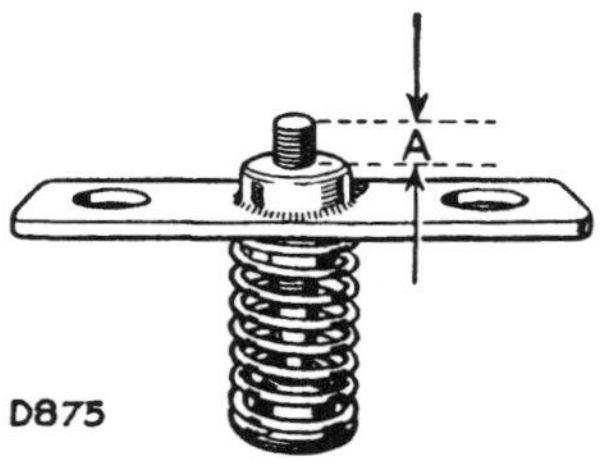

D875

Adjustment of lock bolt

A—$\frac{1}{2}$ in. (12,5 mm)

(b) Ensure that the spring retainer on the bonnet catch locates at the centre of the striker plate.

3. Check operation of slider catch underneath striker plate, as follows:

(a) Ensure that the catch moves freely to the limit of its travel to the right, thereby allowing full engagement in the groove on the bonnet catch.

(b) Ensure that it completely clears the aperture in the striker plate when the operating rod in the car is pulled.

4. Adjust cable operational length as necessary, by repositioning the control rod in the adjustment holes provided.

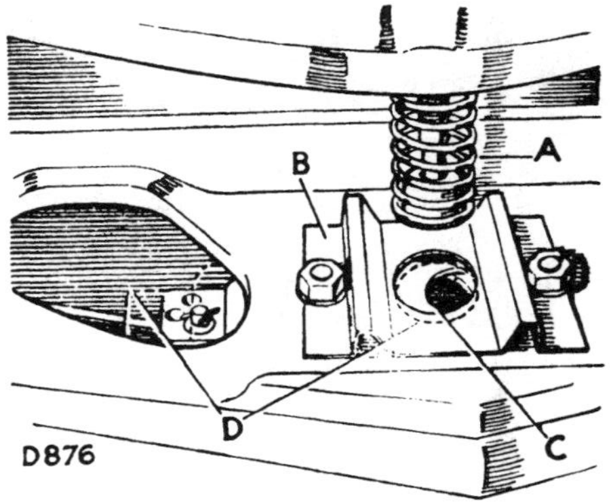

Location of bonnet lock and striker plate

A—Bonnet catch
B—Striker plate
C—Slider catch in locked position
D—Dotted outline shows slider catch in open position

5. Fit two lower brackets to radiator grille, do not tighten, then pull brackets as far back as possible, and fit radiator grille to body, inserting the bottom in first.

6. Tighten the two lower brackets and secure the remainder with nuts, bolts and spring washers; if removed, refit two packing pieces to mounting brackets and secure with nuts, bolts and flat washers.

Clock and nacelle, to remove and refit—Operation T-2

Workshop hand tools:
Spanner sizes: $\frac{5}{16}$ in. AF
Small screwdriver

Clock and nacelle, remove, Mk I, IA and II

1. Disconnect the battery leads.

2. Slacken screw on the underside of clock nacelle, and withdraw clock from nacelle.

3. Withdraw illumination bulb and holder from the rear of clock, and disconnect wiring.

4. Remove clock and the two bolts securing the nacelle to crash rail; remove nacelle and bracket.

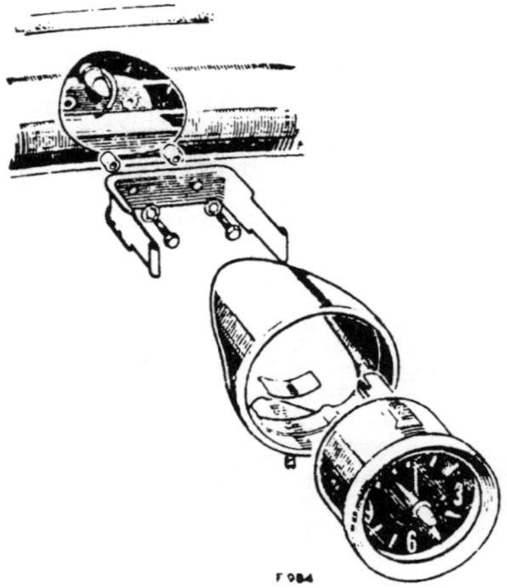

Removal of clock and nacelle

Clock, to remove, Mk III

1. Slacken the small grub screw located beneath the clock (and behind the wooden corner fillet).

2. From behind the corner fillet, carefully push the clock forwards until it is free.

3. Disconnect the wiring from the clock. The bulb holder may be withdrawn from the clock complete with its bulb, it is a push fit into its holder.

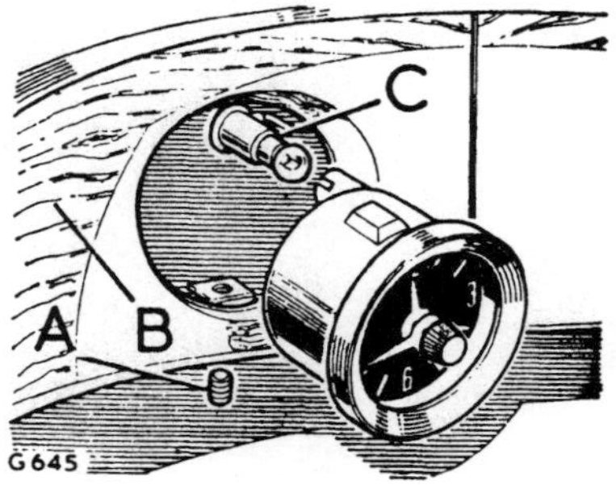

Clock

A—Screw retaining clock
B—Corner fillet
C—Bulb and holder

Clock and nacelle, refit

1. Reverse removal procedure.

Clock, to regulate

2. **Early models.** If necessary, the clock can be regulated by means of the screw in the left-hand front face of the clock.

3. **Late models.** *The clock has a mechanical movement which is electrically wound, automatically, every $2\frac{1}{2}$ minutes. The movement regulator is situated in the rear of the case.* Regulate the clock only if it gains or loses more than two or three minutes per week.

Clock gaining .. turn screw to — mark
Clock losing .. turn screw to + mark

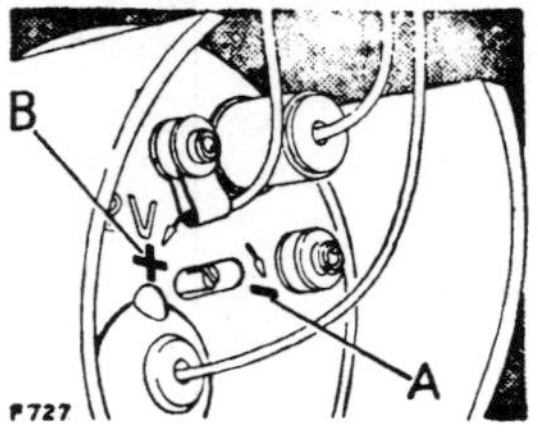

Clock adjustment, late models illustrated

A—Clock gaining, turn to — mark
B—Clock losing, turn to + mark

Facia frame complete, to remove and refit—Operation T-3

Workshop hand tools:
Spanner sizes: $\frac{1}{4}$ in. AF, $\frac{5}{16}$ in. AF, $\frac{7}{16}$ in. AF
Screwdriver, medium

Facia frame, remove

1. Disconnect the battery.
2. Remove the steering wheel. Section J.
3. Remove the steering column shrouds. Section J.
4. Remove the instrument panel and disconnect the wiring from the switches and instruments. Operation T-7.
5. Remove the instrument unit mounting brackets.
6. Remove the parcel shelf trim:
   (a) Remove the parcel shelf back trim first, pulling the trim away at the ends and tilting it forwards to clear the steering column and hand brake.
   (b) Remove the shelf floor trim by pulling it horizontally towards the engine before lifting it out.
   (c) Remove the side trim pieces which are secured by spring clips.

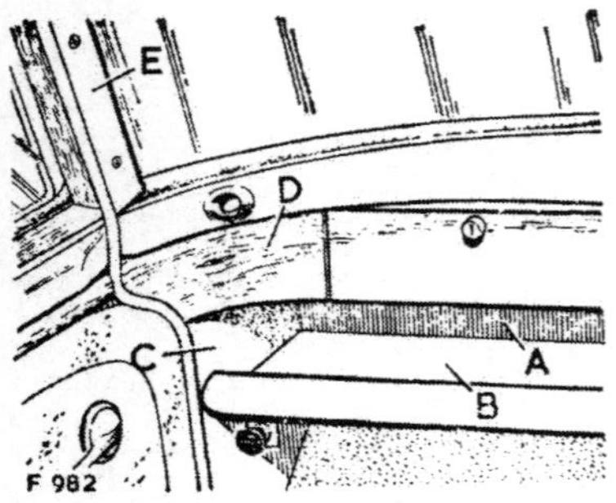

Removing parcel shelf trim

A—Back trim
B—Shelf floor trim
C—Side trim
D—Corner fillet
E—Windscreen side moulding

7. Remove the polished wooden corner fillets, left-hand and right-hand, these are secured by drive screws.
8. On 1959 models remove the chromium cappings from the face-level ventilators, secured by two screws. All models disconnect the rubber boot connecting the ventilator duct to the ventilator.

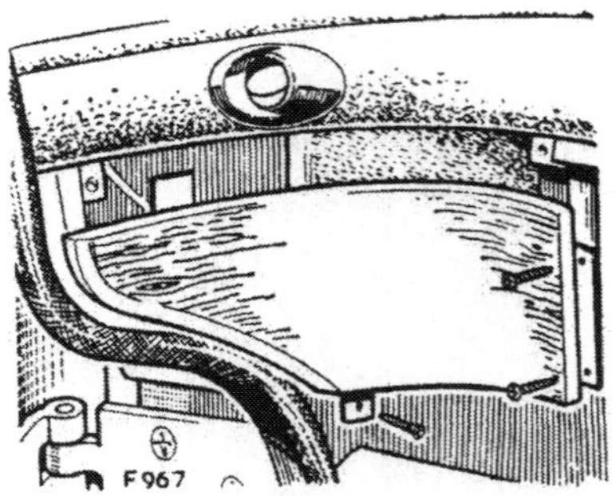

Removing corner fillet

9. Remove the glove box lids, complete with hinges, secured by nuts and spring washers to the facia frame. Remove the glove box trims, which are 'sprung' into position, remove by slightly compressing the sides.
10. Where fitted, remove the radio, secured by two screws under the front lower rail of the facia frame. (On early models a third screw was used to fix the radio to the back rail of the frame). Ease the radio away from frame carefully and disconnect the aerial and battery feed lead.
11. Remove the windscreen side mouldings, each moulding is secured by two drive screws to the 'A' post.
12. Remove the clock and clock nacelle. Slacken the screw on the underside of the nacelle and withdraw the clock from nacelle. Withdraw bulb holder and disconnect clock wiring. Remove clock nacelle secured by two bolts to crash rail.
13. Remove the cover plate above the clock nacelle which joins the windscreen mouldings; this is secured with a spring clip.

Operation T-3—*continued*

14. Remove the windscreen mouldings, L.H. and R H. each moulding is secured by two 10 UNF nuts.
15. Remove the facia crash rail, secured by drive screws to the dash, and by nuts and washers to the facia frame.
16. Disconnect the control cables of the heating and ventilating controls at the heater unit.
17. Remove the facia frame from the body, secured by nuts and bolts.

Facia frame, refit

1. Reverse removal procedure.
2. When fitting the mounting brackets for the instrument unit, make sure that all the fixings are tight.

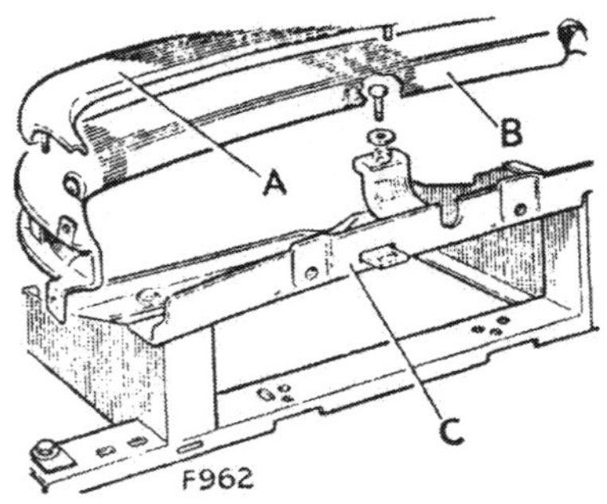

Removing facia frame and crash rail

A—Windscreen moulding B—Crash rail
C—Facia frame

Flasher unit, for direction indicators, to remove and refit—Operation T-4

Workshop hand tools:
Screwdriver, small

Flasher unit, remove

1. Remove the instrument panel, but do not disconnect the wiring. Operation T-7.

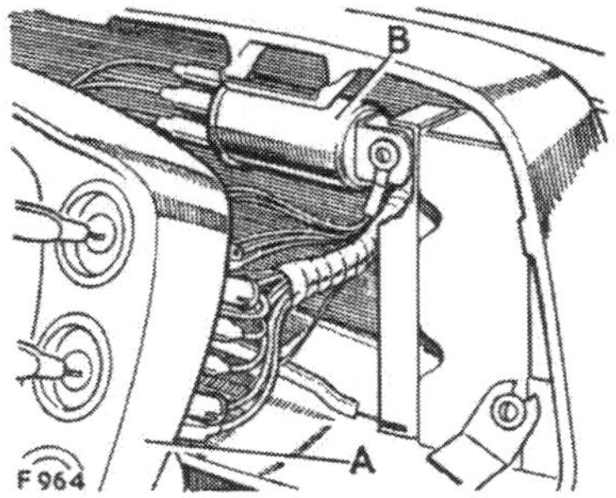

Location of flasher unit
A—Instrument panel B—Flasher unit

2. Disconnect the three wires from the flasher unit, noting the connections.
3. Remove the flasher unit, secured by a drive screw and washers.

Flasher unit, refit

1. Reverse removal procedure.

Fresh air ventilator control cable, to remove and refit—Operation T-5

Workshop hand tools:
Spanner sizes: $\frac{1}{4}$ in. AF, $\frac{3}{8}$ in. AF

Cable, remove

1. Release bolt and ferrule securing control cable to fresh air ventilator, and withdraw inner cable.
2. Remove nut and washer from mounting bracket, and remove outer cable.

Cable, refit

1. Fit outer cable to bracket and secure with a nut and washer.
2. Insert inner cable into outer cable and secure to fresh air ventilator with a bolt and ferrule.

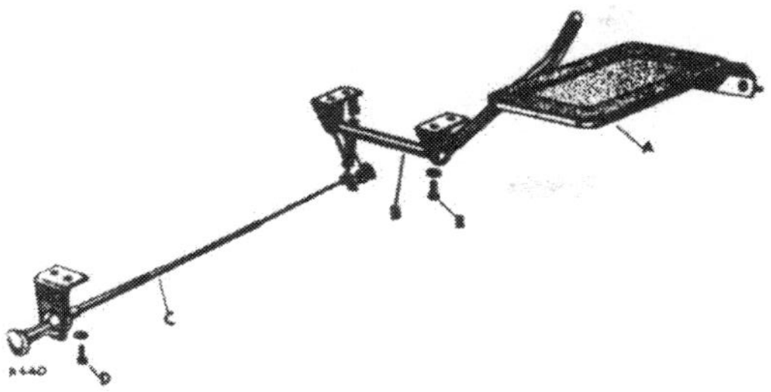

Fresh air ventilator mechanism
A—Ventilator flap
B—Lever mechanism
C—Control cable
D—Fixings, control cable bracket
E—Fixings, lever mechanism

Glove box lids, to remove and refit—Operation T-6

Workshop hand tools:
Spanner size: $\frac{5}{16}$ in. AF

Lids, remove. Early models

1. Remove the three screws securing the lock inside the lid, then remove the covered pad.
2. Remove the screws securing the hinges to the lid; remove the lid; if necessary, remove the set screws securing the striking plate to the lid; remove the chromium beads; remove the wood screws securing the handle to glove box lid.
3. Should it be required to remove the hinges completely, remove the nuts and spring washers securing the hinges to the facia frame, slacken the locknuts and remove the hinges.

Lids, remove. Late models

4. Slightly compress the sides of the glove box and carefully withdraw from the facia frame; remove the lids complete with hinges, secured by nuts, bolts and washers.

Lids, refit

1. Reverse removal procedure.

Instrument panel, to remove and refit—Operation T-7

Workshop hand tools:
Screwdriver, Phillips
Spanner size: $\frac{3}{8}$ in. AF

Instrument panel, remove

1. Disconnect the battery.

Early models, items 2 to 5

2. If the car is fitted with a capillary type water temperature gauge, partially drain the coolant from the radiator and cylinder block.
3. Remove the water temperature thermometer bulb from the cylinder head.
4. Disconnect and remove the capillary tube securing clip and detach the grommet from the bulkhead.

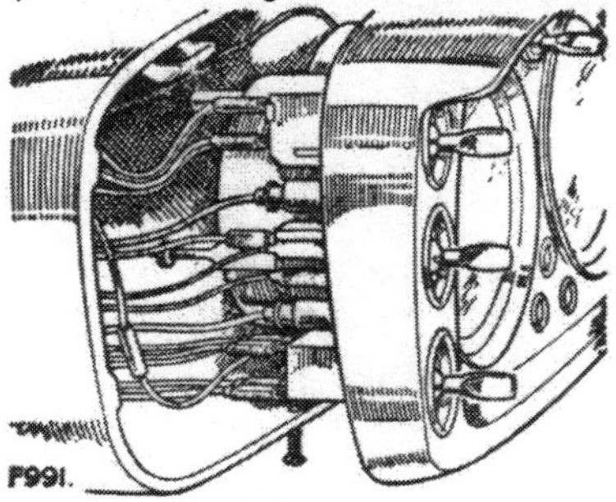

Removing the instrument panel

5. Remove the two screws from the underside of the instrument panel, and carefully ease the instrument panel away from the nacelle pulling the capillary tube through the aperture.

Late models, item 6

6. Remove the two screws from the underside of the instrument panel and carefully ease the panel away.
7. To remove the panel completely, disconnect the wiring and speedometer drive cables. (On Coupé models, disconnect the tachometer.)

Instrument panel, refit

1. Reverse removal procedure.

Instruments, to remove and refit (saloon model)—Operation T-8

Workshop hand tools:
Spanner sizes: 4 BA, ⅜ in. AF

Multiple gauge, individual instruments, to remove

1. Remove the instrument panel. Operation T-7.
2. Disconnect the wiring from the instrument to be replaced.
3. On early models the temperature gauge had a capillary tube connecting the gauge itself to a thermometer bulb in the engine water jacket. Where it is required to remove a gauge of this type, it will be necessary to partially drain off the coolant and remove the thermometer bulb from the engine and withdraw the gauge complete with capillary tube.
4. On early models unscrew the nuts approximately half-way up the thread, turn the clamping plate at right angles to its original position and lift the instruments vertically off the dowels. On late models the instruments are secured with small **screws.**

Instruments, refit

1. Reverse removal procedure.

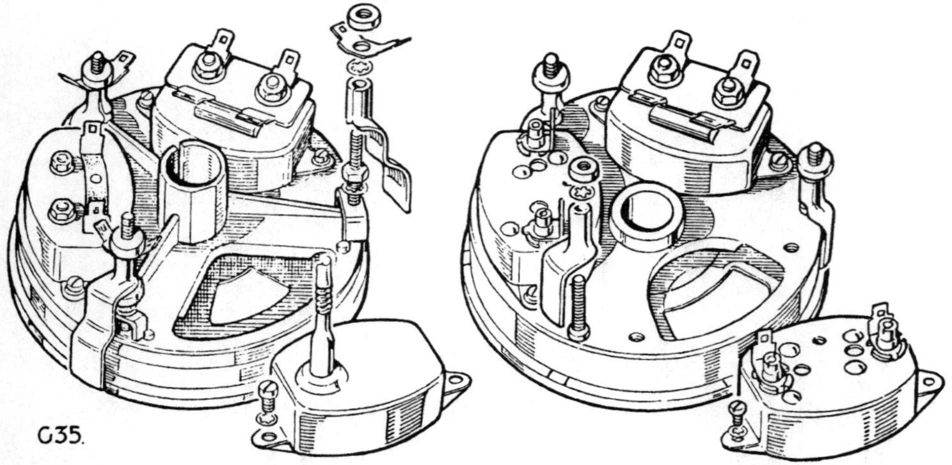

G35.

Exploded view of multiple gauge

Early models **Late models**

Instruments, to remove and refit (Coupé model)—Operation T-9

Workshop hand tools:
Screwdriver, small

Instruments, remove

1. The gauges are housed individually in nacelles mounted below the main instrument unit.
2. Each gauge is secured by a grub screw, beneath the instrument. Slacken this screw and withdraw unit.
3. Withdraw the rubber sleeve and bulb holder from the rear of the instrument body. Disconnect the wiring to the instrument at the connector.

Instruments, refit

1. Reverse removal procedure.

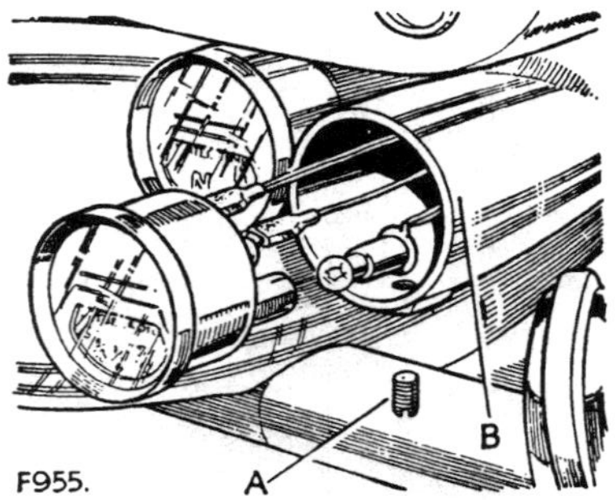

F955.

Instrument removal, Coupé models
A—Fixing screw B—Nacelle

Cold start control, to remove and refit—Operation T-10

Workshop hand tools:
Spanner sizes: $\frac{5}{16}$ in. AF, $1\frac{1}{8}$ in. AF

A plunger switch incorporated in the mixture control is wired in series with a bi-metal thermostat switch at the rear of the cylinder head, and the amber warning light on the instrument panel.

Operation is as follows:

1. With the engine cold and the mixture control pulled out the plunger switch is closed and the thermostat switch open; the light is therefore off.
2. When the engine reaches normal running temperature the thermostat switch closes and the light comes on.
3. When the mixture control is pushed into the normal position, the plunger switch is open and the light goes out.

Mixture control, remove

1. Disconnect the inner wire from carburetter, and withdraw complete with handle from inside the car.
2. Remove the chromium bezel, securing switch body to bracket, and withdraw body and switch from rear of panel.
3. Disconnect the wires and unscrew the switch, washer and shims from the body.

Mixture control, refit

1. Reverse removal procedure, ensuring the washers and shims are correctly positioned.
2. Connect wiring to terminals in accordance with circuit diagram.
3. Ensure that the cold start lever on the carburetter is in the fully closed position, that is, as far forward as it will go, and slide the inner wire into the outer cable and secure to carburetter, allowing the control knob to stand approximately $\frac{1}{16}$ in. (1,5 mm) out from the bezel. For further adjustment see Section Q.

Parcel shelf trim and crash rail, to remove and refit—Operation T-11

Workshop hand tools:
Spanner size: $\frac{5}{16}$ in. AF
Screwdriver, medium

Trim, remove

1. Remove the back trim by pulling the ends away and then tilting slightly forwards to clear the steering column and hand brake. Lift the panel out from the side opposite the steering column.
2. Remove the shelf floor trim by pulling it horizontally towards the engine before lifting it out.
3. Remove the side trim pieces which are secured by spring clips.

Crash rail, remove

4. Remove the ash trays and ash tray slides from beneath the parcel shelf, secured by set screws and drive screws.
5. Remove the crash rail secured by seven nuts and washers to the parcel shelf.

Trim and crash rail, refit

1. Reverse removal procedure.

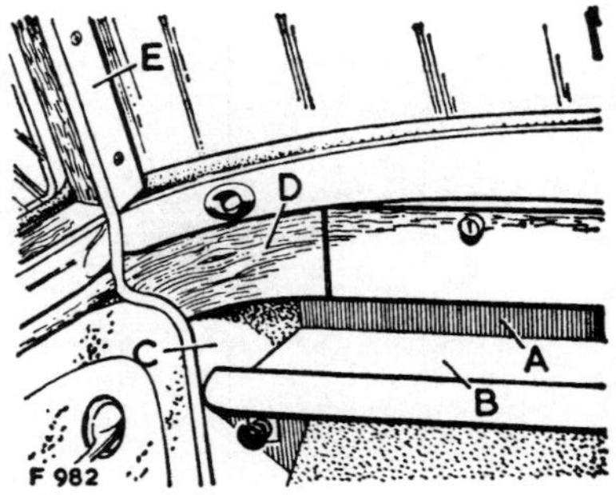

Removing parcel shelf trim

A—Back trim
B—Shelf floor trim
C—Side trim
D—Corner fillet
E—Window mouldings

Radio, to remove and refit—Operation T-12

Workshop hand tools:
Spanner sizes:

Radio, remove

1. Disconnect the battery.
2. **Early models.** Remove the single fixing at the rear of the radio set.
3. **Late models.** Remove the two fixings under the front edge of the set.
4. Ease the set away from the facia just enough to be able to disconnect the aerial and battery feed lead.
5. Carefully lift out the set.

Radio, refit

1. Reverse removal procedure.

Speedometer, to remove and refit—Operation T-13

Workshop hand tools:
Screwdriver, Phillips

Speedometer, remove

1. Remove the instrument panel. Operation T-7.
2. Disconnect the speedometer flexible drive and trip cable, then withdraw the illumination bulb and holder from the speedometer casing.
3. Slacken off the retaining nuts, remove the washers and earth wires, remove the support brackets and push the speedometer through the instrument panel and remove.

Speedometer identification

As axles of two different ratios are in service on 3 litre cars, different speedometer heads are used. These can be identified by the speedometer cable speed printed on the instrument face, immediately beneath the tenths-of-a-mile section on the trip mileage; the Rover part number is also stamped on the face.

3.9 axle ratio, 4-speed:
1,344 cable revolutions per mile
840 cable revolutions per kilometer

3.9 axle ratio, automatic transmission:
1,152 cable revolutions per mile
720 cable revolutions per kilometer

4.3 axle ratio, 4-speed and overdrive:
1,248 cable revolutions per mile
780 cable revolutions per kilometer

Speedometer, refit

1. Reverse removal procedure.

Speedometer cable, to remove and refit—Operation T-14

Workshop hand tools:
Screwdriver, medium

Cable, remove

1. Remove the instrument panel. Operation T-7.
2. Disconnect the speedometer drive from the speedometer head.
3. Remove the grommet from the bulkhead and withdraw cable.
4. Remove the bolt, retaining clip, and grommet from bell housing.
5. **Automatic transmission and overdrive models only**—Unscrew the knurled nut and disconnect cable from gearbox.
6. **Four-speed only**—Remove the three small bolts and securing plate.
7. Withdraw cable from chassis member.

Cable, refit

1. Ensure that the square on the inner cable is fully engaged with the square in the gearbox.
2. **Four-speed only**—Fit the plate and three small bolts to secure the outer cable to gearbox.
3. **Automatic transmission and overdrive models only**—Tighten the knurled nut to secure outer cable to gearbox.
4. Fit grommet and retaining clip to outer cable and secure to bell housing.
5. Pass the cable through the chassis member up to the bulkhead, and fit rubber grommet to cable and pass cable through bulkhead.
6. Fit cable to speedometer head; unless the square on the cable is correctly aligned with the square in the speedometer the cable will not fit properly. Secure with knurled nut.
7. Fit rubber grommet on speedometer cable to bulkhead. Ensure that the speedometer cable is not kinked behind the instrument panel.
8. Re-connect any wiring that might have been disturbed, in accordance with circuit diagram, and fit instrument panel to nacelle and secure with two drive screws.
9. Connect the battery leads and check speedometer and instrument panel lights for correct operation.

Switches for starter and ignition, wiper, panel, oil level, fuel reserve and lights, to remove and refit—Operation T-15

Switches, remove

1. Remove the instrument panel. Operation T-7.
2. Disconnect the wiring, using a suitable tool unscrew the bezel in the front of the instrument panel and withdraw each switch and spring washer.

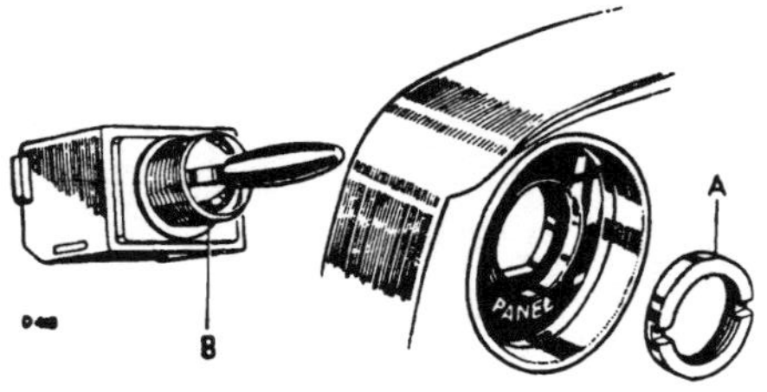

Removing switches
A—Bezel B—Flat on switch

Switches, refit

1. Fit spring washer to switch. Ensure that the flat on the switch is adjacent with the flat in the aperture. The switch should slide in without any undue pressure.
2. Secure the bezel, and connect wiring in accordance with circuit diagram.

Windscreen washer, to remove and refit—Operation T-16

Workshop hand tools:
Spanner sizes: 2 BA, $\frac{7}{16}$ in. AF

Manually operated models

This consists of a pump operated by the foot, and a reservoir mounted on the left-hand wing valance, and two jets situated in the fresh air ventilator, all connected by rubber pipes.

Electrically operated models

This consists of an electrically operated pump, built-in unit with a glass, or plastic, reservoir and mounted in a bracket fixed to the left-hand wing valance. The pump is actuated by a push button, located on the left-hand side of the instrument panel housing.

Nylon tube is used to connect the pump to the jets situated in the fresh air ventilator.

Each nozzle has a ball valve to prevent air being drawn into the system, and a further valve is incorporated in the reservoir pipe.

To prevent freezing in cold weather, fill the reservoir with one-eighth pint of methylated spirits and top up with water.

Washer, remove, manual models

1. Disconnect the hoses from the pump unit which is located under the parcel shelf.
2. Remove the pump unit secured to the parcel shelf by four bolts, nuts and washers.

All models

3. Remove the two windscreen wiper arms and blades by withdrawing the wiper arm and blade from the splined shaft.

Air intake grille, remove

4. Remove the nuts from the outer wiper arm shafts, and remove the grille and intake filter located by drive screws.
5. Disconnect the hoses from the jets.

Jets, remove

6. Unscrew the two jets from the intake grille on early models, or from the bonnet on late models.

Reservoir, remove

7. Disconnect the hoses, and on electrically operated models, the wiring. On early models slacken the clamp retaining the reservoir.
8. Lift out the reservoir.
9. If necessary remove reservoir mounting bracket.

Washer, refit

1. Reverse removal procedure.

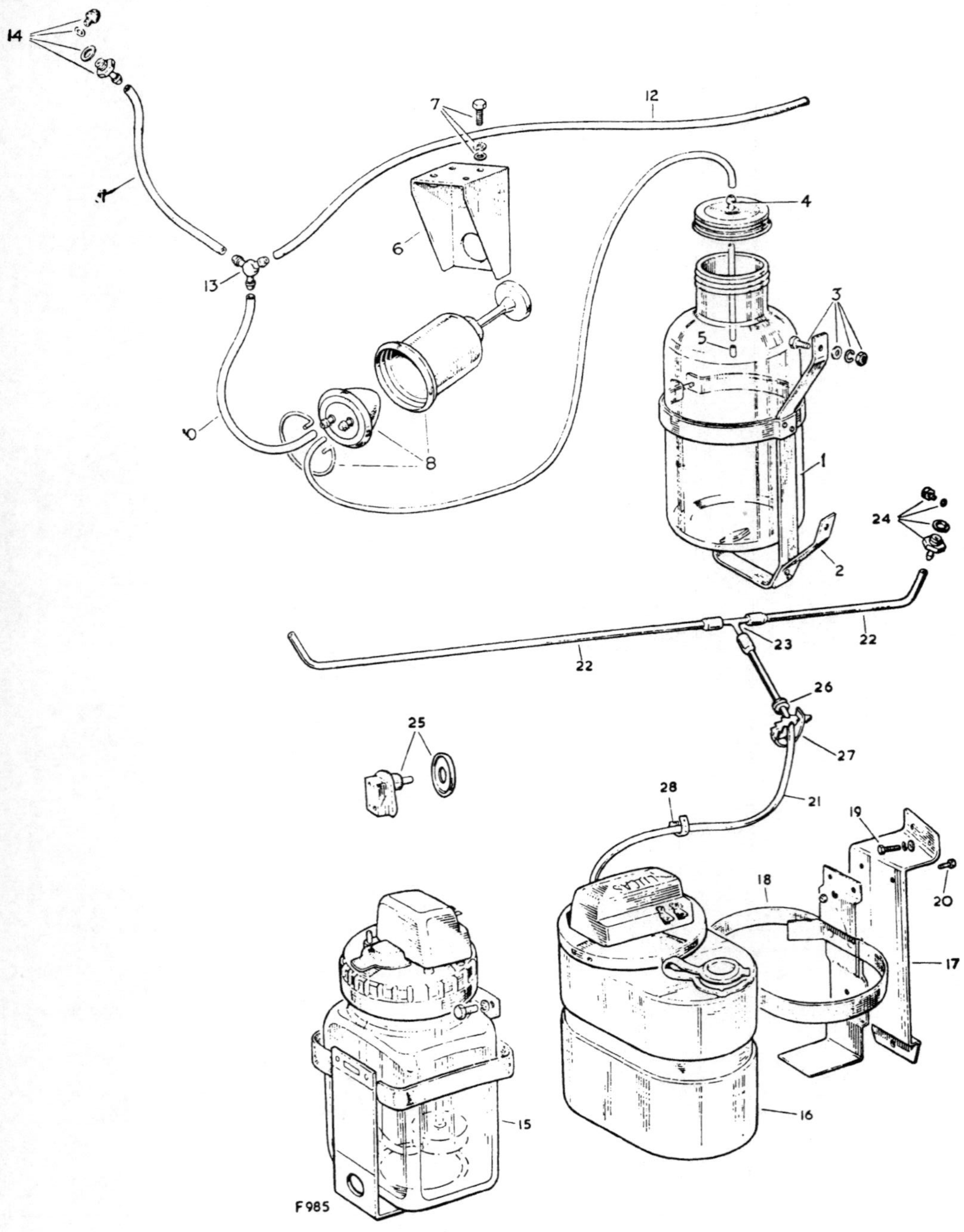

Windscreen washers

1	Reservoir	Manually operated models
2	Reservoir bracket	
3	Bracket fixings	
4	Suction valve top	
5	Suction valve bottom	
6	Pump bracket	
7	Bracket fixings	
8	Pump unit	
9	Pipe, reservoir to pump	
10	Pipe, pump to 'Y' piece	
11	Pipe, 'Y' piece to nozzle, RH	
12	Pipe, 'Y' piece to nozzle, LH	
13	'Y' piece connector	
14	Delivery valve and nozzle	
15	Reservoir and pump, early model	Electrically operated models
16	Reservoir and pump, late model	
17	Reservoir mounting bracket, early model	
18	Reservoir mounting bracket, late model	
19	Bracket fixings	
20	Bracket fixings	
21	Pipe, reservoir to 'T' piece	
22	Pipes, 'T' piece to jets	
23	'T' piece connector	
24	Delivery valve nipple and adjustable jet	
25	Switch and escutcheon	
26	Grommet (for pipe)	
27	Cleat (for pipe)	
28	Clip (for pipe)	

Section U – BODY

Brief description of basic construction

The body is entirely of welded steel construction with a detachable chassis sub-frame which carries the engine and gearbox units. The sub-frame, complete with the engine and gearbox can be removed for servicing purposes.

All four mudwings are bolted to the body shell to facilitate replacement. The doors are all forward hinged and the bonnet and boot lid are counter-balanced by spring-loaded hinges.

Provision has been made for radio and rear extension speaker.

A laminated glass windscreen and rear heated backlight can be supplied as optional equipment. Safety harness fixings are provided, on later models.

INDEX

I N D E X — *continued*

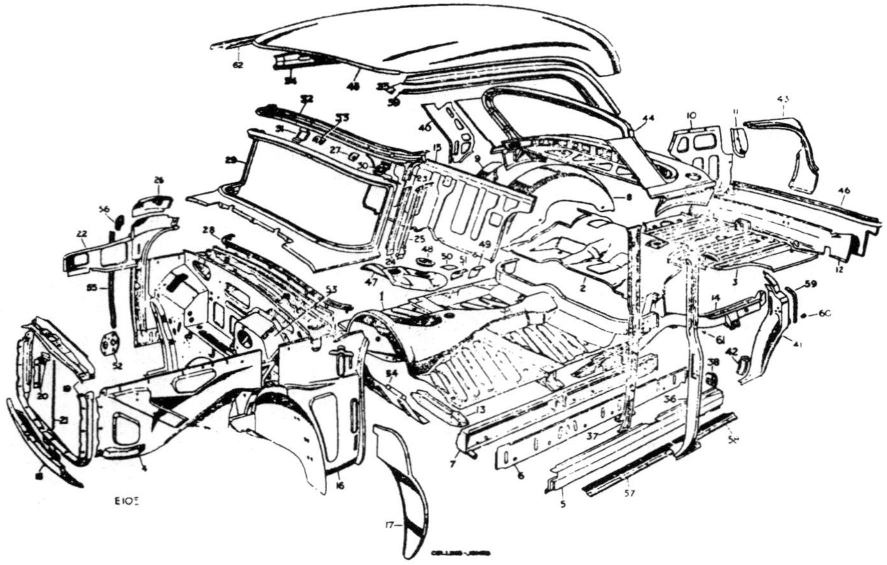

Body panels and fittings, saloon illustrated

1 Floor complete
2 Rear seat panel
3 Boot floor panel
4 Front valance complete
5 Outer sill panel
6 Spacer panel for sill
7 Inner sill panel
8 Wheel arch panel, rear inner
9 Wheel arch panel, rear outer
10 Rear valance panel
11 Rear lamp cover
12 Reinforcement body, rear, lower
13 Intermediate cross-member, centre
14 Longitudinal rear channel complete
15 Rear squab support panel
16 Shroud complete
17 Panel, dash to front wing
18 Lower front body panel
19 Grille surround complete
20 Side gusset for grille surround
21 Stay, bonnet, locking platform to lower front panel
22 'A' post, RH
23 Side header to 'A' post, RH
24 Spacer panel, 'A' post, LH
25 'A' post facing panel
26 Windscreen to dash panel, RH
27 Strap for windscreen glazing attachment
28 Drain channel for windscreen
29 Windscreen panel assembly
30 Visor mounting bracket header, LH
31 Mounting bracket for visor hook
32 Front header panel
33 Plate fixing mirror header
34 Side header panel, RH
35 Cant rail, LH
36 'BC' post complete, LH
37 'BC' post closing plate, LH
38 Striker for door lock, LH
39 Drip moulding, LH
40 Reinforcement, 'D' post to backlight, RH
41 'D' post, LH
42 'D' post to wheel arch panel, lower LH
43 Tonneau panel, RH
44 Backlight aperture complete
45 Roof panel
46 Rear lower outer panel
47 Cover for gearbox
48 Rubber grommet for gearbox cover
49 Cover plate } For gearbox cover
50 Cover plate } For gearbox cover
51 Cover plate } For gearbox cover
52 Cover plate for foot control holes
53 Cover plate for dash, top, LH
54 Passenger's foot rest panel
55 Sealing rubber for 'A' post to front wing
56 Sealing rubber for 'A' post to front wing, upper
57 Sill tread plate, LH front
58 Sill tread plate, LH rear
59 Sealing rubber, rear wing to 'D' post
60 Sealing rubber, rear wing to 'D' post, bottom
61 Rubber buffer for 'BC' post
62 Beading for drip moulding, RH

Car checking points—Operation U-1

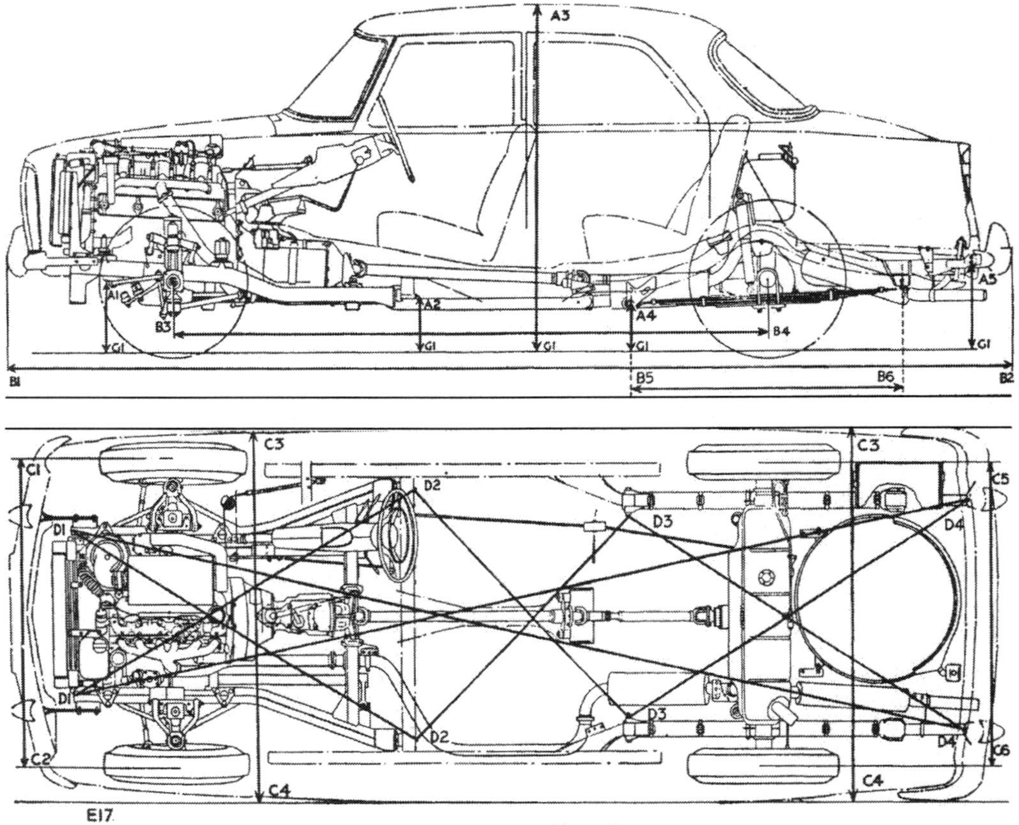

Layout of car checking points

Height dimensions—Mk I, Mk IA, Mk II and Mk III with high suspension

A1—G1	From the front mounting bolt on stabilising anti-roll bar to ground level	13 in. ±.125	330 mm ±3
A2—G1	From torsion bar rear mounting point to ground level ..	10.687 in. ±.125	271,4 mm ±3
A3—G1	Overall height: saloon	60.25 in. ±.125	1,53 m ±3 mm
	coupé	57.25 in. ±.125	1,45 m ±3 mm
A4—G1	From centre of rear spring hanger mounting bolt to ground level	9.3 in. ±.125	236 mm ±3
A5—G1	From lower rear bumper mounting bolt to ground level	16.3 in. ±.125	414 mm ±3

Operation U-1—*continued*

Height dimensions—Mk II with standard suspension

A1—G1	From the front mounting bolt on stabilising anti-roll bar to ground level	12 in. ±.125	305 mm ±3
A2—G1	From torsion bar rear mounting point to ground level ..	9.637 in. ±.125	246 mm ±3
A3—G1	Overall height: saloon	59.25 in. ±.125	1,5 m ±3 mm
	coupé	56.25 in. ±.125	1,4 m ±3 mm
A4—G1	From centre of rear spring hanger mounting bolt to ground level	8.3 in. ±.125	211 mm ±3
A5—G1	From lower rear bumper mounting bolt to ground level	15.3 in. ±.125	381 mm ±3

Height dimensions—Mk III with standard suspension

A1—G1	From the front mounting bolt on stabilising anti-roll bar to ground level	12.5 in. ±.125	317,7 mm ±3
A2—G1	From torsion bar rear mounting point to ground level ..	10.137 in. ±.125	258,7 mm ±3
A3—G1	Overall height: saloon	59.75 in. ±.125	1,5 m ±3
	coupé	56.75 in. ±.125	1,4 m ±3
A4—G1	From centre of rear spring hanger mounting bolt to ground level	8.8 in. ±.125	223,7 mm ±3
A5—G1	From lower rear bumper mounting bolt to ground level	15.8 in. ±.125	393,7 mm ±3

Length dimensions

B1—B2	Overall length	186.5 in.	4,74 m
B3—B4	Wheelbase	110.5 in.	2,81 m
B5—B6	Centre of front eye of rear spring to centre of rear spring mounting	49.187 in. ±.125	1,25 m ±3 mm

Width dimensions

C1—C2	Track: front	55 in.	1,4 m
C3—C4	Overall width	70 in.	1,78 m
C5—C6	Track: rear	56 in.	1,42 m

Diagonals

D1—D2	From the front centre weld on the sub-frame side-member, to the centre of the rear sub-frame mounting bolt	76 in. ±.125	1,93 m ±3 mm
D1—D4	From the centre weld on the sub-frame side-member to centre of rear bumper mounting bolt	171.7 in. ±.125	4,36 m ±3 mm
D2—D3	From the centre of the rear sub-frame mounting bolt, to the centre of nut head on rear spring front hanger bolt	57.4 in. ±.125	1,46 m ±3 mm
D3—D4	From centre of nut head on rear spring to centre of rear bumper mounting bolt	73.9 in. ±.125	1,88 m ±3 mm

Body checking points—Operation U-2

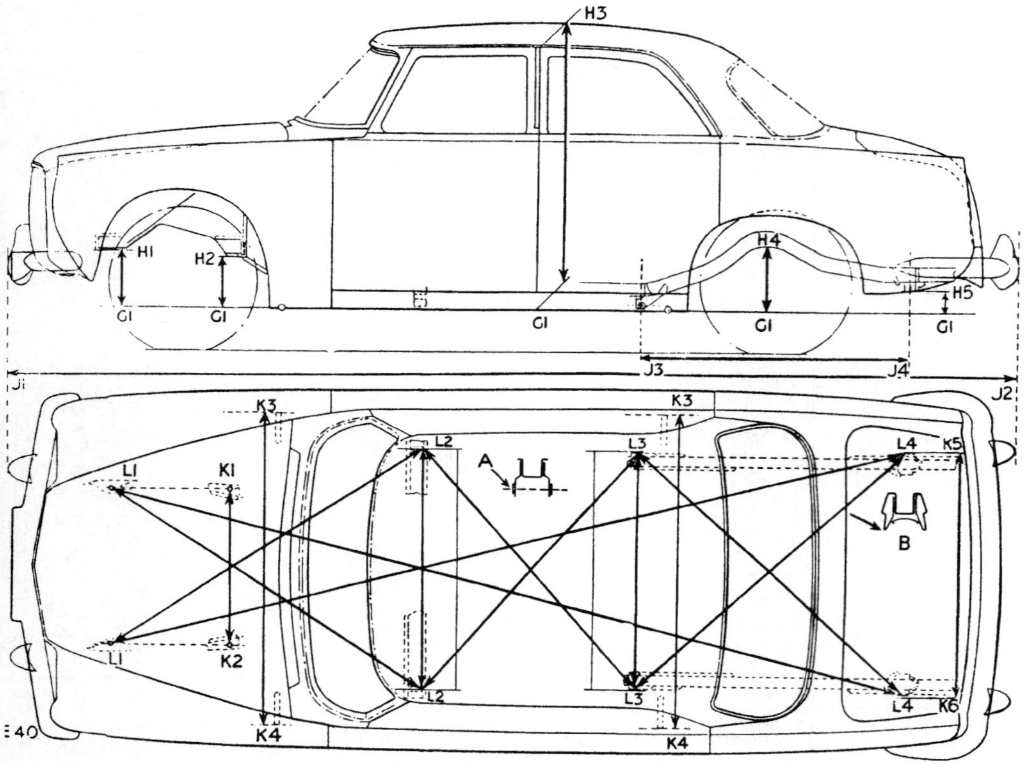

Layout of body checking points

A—Check dimensions at front bracket or rear spring at point arrowed

B—Check dimensions at rear bracket for rear spring at point arrowed

With a surface gauge on a suitable stand ascertain the centre of the jacking point. From this setting the following height dimensions can be checked

Height dimensions

H1—G1	From the underside of the front sub-frame mounting point to the surface gauge, set as described above ..	10.968 in. ±.125	278,5 mm ±3
H2—G1	From the lower edge of the wing panel adjacent to the sub-frame mounting point to the centre of the jacking point	9.468 in. ±.125	240,5 mm ±3
H3—G1	From the top of the door pillar immediately below the gutter to the lower edge of the body panel below the door pillar: saloon	47.234 in. ±.125	1,20 m ±3 mm
	coupé	45.953 in. ±.125	1,16 m ±3 mm
H4—G1	From the centre of chassis wheel arch to the centre of jacking point	11.718 in. ±.125	297,5 mm ±3
H5—G1	From the outside lower edge of rear spring hanger to the centre of jacking point	4 in. ±.125	101,5 mm ±3

Operation U-2—*continued*

Length dimensions

J1—J2	Overall length	186.5 in.	4,74 m
J3—J4	Centre of front eye of rear spring to centre of rear spring mounting	49.187 in. ±.125	1,25 m ±3 mm

Width dimensions

K1—K2	From centre of LH side front sub-frame mounting point to centre of RH side front sub-frame mounting point ..	30 in. ±.125	762 mm ±3
K3—K4	From outer edge of jacking tubes	59.75 in. ±.125	1,50 m ±3 mm
K5—K6	From outer edge of LH side rear spring hanger to the outer edge of RH side rear spring hanger	46.125 in. ±.125	1,17 m ±3 mm
L2—L2	From centre of RH side rear sub-frame mounting point to centre of LH side rear sub-frame mounting point ..	46.375 in. ±.125	1,18 m ±3 mm
L3—L3	From outside edge of LH side front spring hanger to outside edge of RH side hanger	46.25 in. ±.125	1,17 m ±3 mm

Diagonals

L1—L2	From the centre of front sub-frame mounting point, to centre of rear sub-frame mounting point	70.20 in. ±.125	1,79 m ±3 mm
L1—L4	From the centre of front sub-frame mounting point, to centre outside edge of rear spring hanger	153 in. ±.125	3,88 m ±3 mm
L2—L3	From the centre of rear sub-frame mounting point, to centre outside edge of front rear spring hanger ..	61.25 in. ±.125	1,55 m ±3 mm
L3—L4	From the centre outside edge of front rear spring hanger to centre outside edge of rear spring hanger ..	67.46 in. ±.125	1,71 m ±3 mm

Bodywork repairs—Operation U-3

If it is necessary for a complete new body shell to be fitted, the latest type only will be supplied. A kit of parts to enable the original type body fittings to be used, will be supplied. It is essential to quote the chassis number of the vehicle when ordering a new body shell, in order that the correct kit of parts are supplied.

Do not gas weld panels, as they will distort out of alignment.

Checking the alignment of the vehicle after accident damage

The two illustrations show the points at which the complete car and the body only can be checked for correct alignment

All dimensions given are with the car in its static position, that is with the car on level ground complete with normal equipment.

The torsion bars should be adjusted so that the distance between the underside of the jacking tubes and the ground is correct to the dimensions given for high or low suspension.

All dimensions should be obtained with an accurately balanced plumb-bob and a length of fine cord. Using the plumb-line at the points shown, chalk the positions on the floor, then measure between the two relative diagonal points.

New panels, to fit

1. Drill out spot welds; remove old panel and clean and prepare mating panel.
2. Offer new panel to the body. When correct alignment has been achieved locate panel with drive screws.
3. Tack panel to body by either spot welding or brazing. Remove drive screws, then spot weld or braze panel securely into position.

Drilling doors and wings for styling strip clips—Operation U-4

Special tools:

Pop-rivet pliers, Part No. 501264

Marking-out

This operation details the procedure for marking-out, drilling and fitting the styling strips along the sides of a car where a whole side or body shell has been replaced following accident damage.

Replacement wings and door panels are supplied undrilled and the importance of accurate marking and drilling cannot be over-emphasised.

All doors should be properly hung and securely closed before marking-out.

Front wing, Mk I, IA and II

1. Mark a vertical line on the front wing by measuring $34\frac{3}{16}$ in. (868 mm) from the edge of the wing. Offer the finisher to the wing with the fixing stud on the vertical line; mark a horizontal line where the finisher fixing hole is to be drilled.
2. Fit the finisher to the front wing as illustrated, with the top edge of the finisher horizontal.

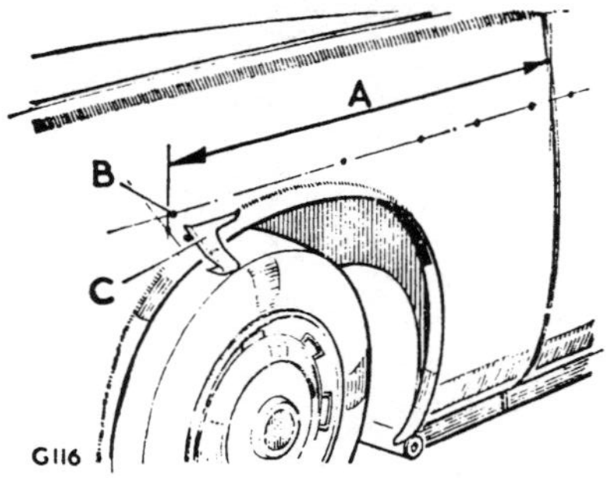

Fitting finisher to front wing, Mk I, Mk IA and Mk II models

A—$34\frac{3}{16}$ in. (868 mm)
B—Position of end clip for styling strip
C—Finisher

3. Mark out the position of the first styling strip securing clip on the wing, $\frac{3}{16}$ in. (4,7 mm) above and $\frac{31}{32}$ in. (24,6 mm) along the top edge of the finisher. This is where the clip will be pop-riveted to the wing.

Rear wing, Mk I, IA and II

4. Use a flexible steel rule and measure $7\frac{1}{2}$ in. (190,5 mm) from the edge of the beading strip on top of the wing. Mark the position.

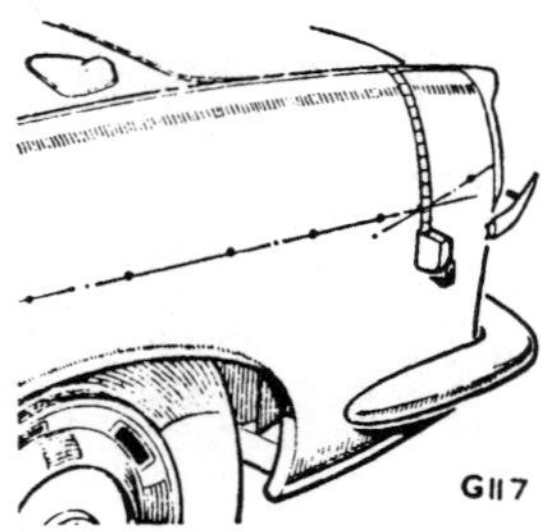

Marking-out rear wing, Mk I, Mk IA and Mk II models

Operation U-4—*continued*

Drilling positions for door and wing styling strip

Use a $\frac{1}{8}$ in. clearance drill No. 30 for pop-rivets, Part No. 78257

Use a $\frac{7}{64}$ in. clearance drill No. 35 for pop-rivets, Part Nos. 78698, 78695

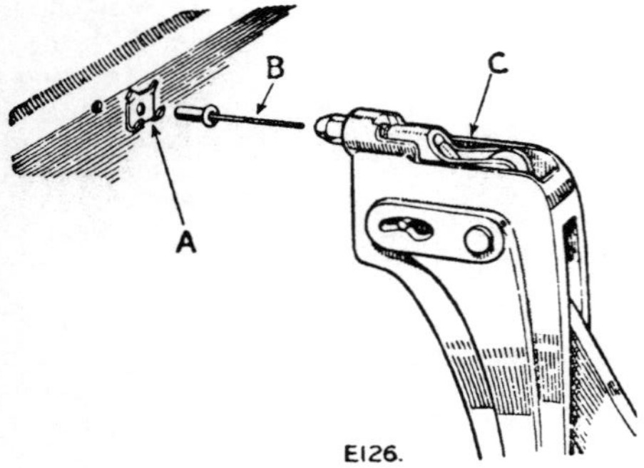

Pop-rivet pliers

A—Clip B—Pop-rivet C—Pliers

5. Mark a line across the door panels from the position of the first clip fixing hole on the front wing, to join the position just marked on the rear wing, as illustrated.
6. Offer the rear wing styling strip, with the finisher pushed on to the end, to the wing. With the end of the styling strip against the edge of the wing adjacent to the door and held in position over the line, mark the position of the finisher fixing hole
7. Drill the finisher fixing hole; remove the finisher from the styling strip and fit the finisher to the wing.
8. Mark the position of the 23 clips along the line as illustrated and drill the fixing holes. Position the clips with the hooks upwards and pop-rivet them to the panels.

Operation U-4—*continued*

Front wing, Mk III

Use a flexible steel rule and mark out the position of the first clip on the wing as shown in the following illustration.

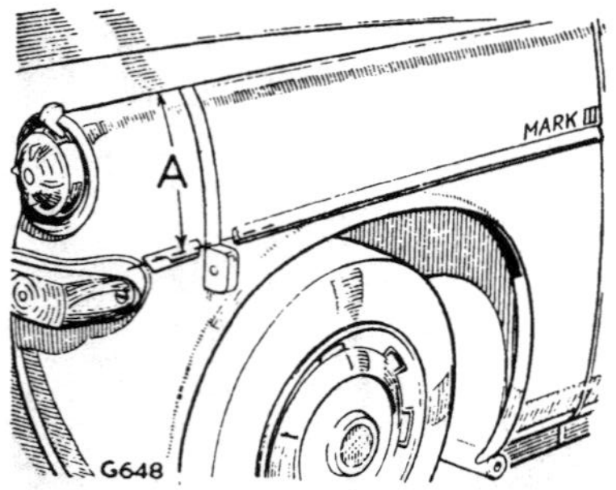

Position of front wing styling strip, Mk III models

A—7½ in. (190,5 mm) following contour of wing
B—1½ in. (38 mm) from rear edge of flasher
All other drillings as in Operation U-4

Rear wing, Mk III

Use a flexible steel rule and mark out the position of rear clip on the wing as shown in the following illustration.

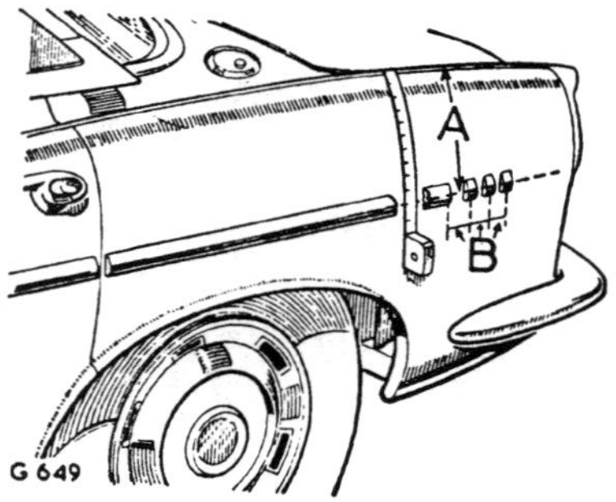

Position of rear wing styling strip, Mk III models

A—8⅜ in. (212.7 mm) following contour of wing and at 8½ in. (216 mm) in from rear edge of wing
B—1 in. (25 mm)
All other drillings as in Operation U-4

Styling strips, to fit

9. Tilt the styling strip to engage on the top of each retaining clip and give a sharp blow with the palm of the hand in a downward direction to engage on the bottom of the clip.

Styling strips, to remove and refit—Operation U-5

Workshop hand tools:
Screwdriver, small
Spanner size: $\frac{1}{4}$ in. AF

Wing and door styling strips, to remove

1. Insert suitable thin-bladed tool under the lower edge of the strip, gently prise up the strip from the bottom of the clips and lift off.

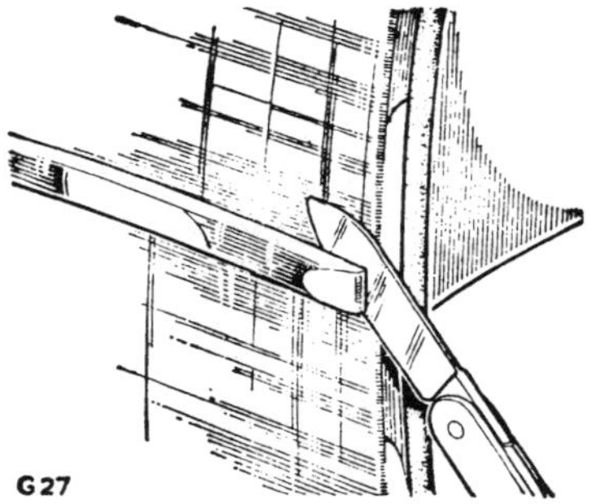

G27

Removing styling strip

2. **Mk I, IA and II.** If necessary remove the front wing finisher, secured by screws, nuts and washers.

3. **Mk I, IA and II.** If necessary remove the rear wing finisher:

(a) Disconnect the battery.

(b) Remove the tail lamp assembly.

(c) Through the tail lamp aperture remove the small nut and washer securing the finisher.

Wing and door styling strips, to refit

1. Reverse removal procedure.

2. Tilt the styling strip very slightly so that it engages on the top of the retaining clip. Give a sharp blow with the palm of the hand in a downward direction to engage on the bottom of the clips.

3. **Mk III.** When fitting styling strips to the doors, the cut-out in the strips must be at front edge of door as illustrated below.

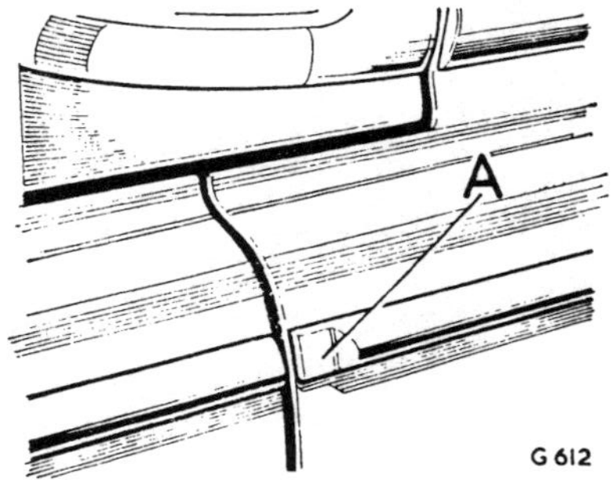

G 612

Position of door styling strip

A—Cut-out in strip must be at front edge of door

Door panel waist rail moulding, to remove and refit—Operation U-6

Workshop hand tools:
Screwdriver, small
Pop-rivet pliers, Part No. 501264

Moulding, remove

1. Close the vent and windows.

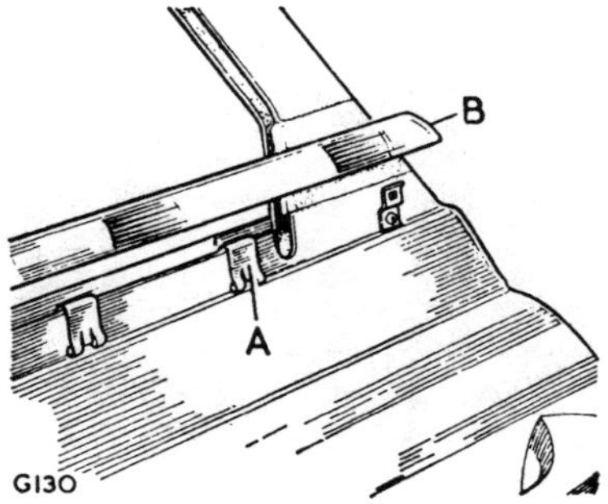

G130

Removing door panel waist moulding
A—Spring clip B—Waist moulding

2. Protect the window pillars above the moulding with masking tape.

3. Tap the waist moulding up gently with a block of hard wood, starting from one end. Lift off moulding taking care not to let the clips fall inside the door panel. Note the position of the clips.

Moulding, refit

1. Place clips in position as noted upon removal.

2. Start the moulding by hand at one end ensuring that the end is flush with the edge of the door. Tap into position with block of wood.

Saloon models

3. If a new door has been fitted, the two end clips must be pop-riveted to the door.

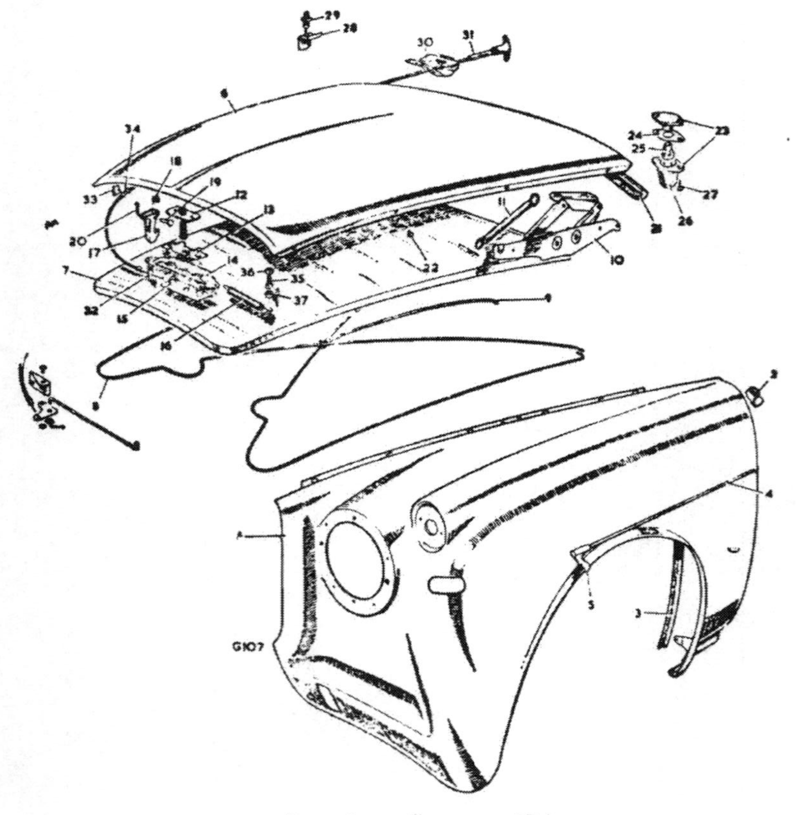

Front wings and bonnet panel fixings

1 Front wing, LH side	13 Striker plate	26 Lens (Coupé only)
2 Support bracket	14 Slider catch	27 Fixing screw (Coupé only)
3 Sealing rubber	15 Support for slider catch	28 Bracket (Coupé only)
4 Styling strip	16 Spring for slider catch	29 Switch (Coupé only)
5 Finisher	17 Bonnet safety catch	30 Bracket for bonnet lock
6 Bonnet panel complete	18–20 Fixings, safety catch	31 Control cable for bonnet complete
7 Insulation pad for bonnet	21 Sealing rubber, for rear of bonnet	32 Nipple
8 Retaining wire for pad	22 Rubber buffer for bonnet side	33 Clip
9 Centre retaining wire for pad	23 Bonnet lamp (Coupé only)	34 Grommet
10 Hinge for bonnet	24 Gasket (For bonnet lamp) (Coupé only)	35 Bolt
11 Spring for bonnet hinge	25 Bulb (For bonnet lamp) (Coupé only)	36 Locknut
12 Bonnet lock		37 Rubber buffer

Front wings, to remove and refit—Operation U-7

Workshop hand tools:
Spanner sizes: $\frac{5}{16}$ in. AF, $\frac{7}{16}$ in. AF, $\frac{9}{16}$ in. AF
Screwdrivers, medium and small

Front wings, to remove

1. Disconnect the battery leads.
2. Remove mounting bolts from front bumper and lift out the bumper.
3. Remove the two top radiator grille mounting bolts and the two lower bolts situated beneath the scuttle.
4. Disconnect the head, side and flasher lamps at the block connector and withdraw lamps, wiring and grommets from the wing.
5. Remove the wing securing bolts situated in the inside of the front and rear of the wing. Leave the three centre mounting bolts slack.
6. It may be necessary to remove the door check strap to open door fully, as two of the front wing bolts are situated between the leading edge of the front door and the wing.
7. Support the wing and remove the three remaining bolts.
8. Remove the rubber baffle strip and sealing rubber.
9. Remove head, side and flasher lamps from wing.

Front wings, to refit

1. Reverse removal procedure.

Bonnet, to remove and refit—Operation U-8

Workshop hand tools:
Spanner sizes: $\frac{7}{16}$ in. AF, $\frac{1}{2}$ in. AF

Bonnet, remove

1. Raise and support the bonnet.
2. On coupé models disconnect the wiring to the bonnet lamps by removing one lead from the switch and the other from the fuse box.
3. On late models, disconnect the windscreen washer pipes from the jets on the bonnet.
4. Remove the springs from the bonnet hinges.
5. Remove the nuts securing the hinge links to the hinge bracket on the bonnet, these face inwards towards the engine.
6. Lift off bonnet.
7. If necessary remove insulation pad from inside bonnet.
8. If necessary remove hinge brackets.

Bonnet, refit

1. Reverse removal procedure.

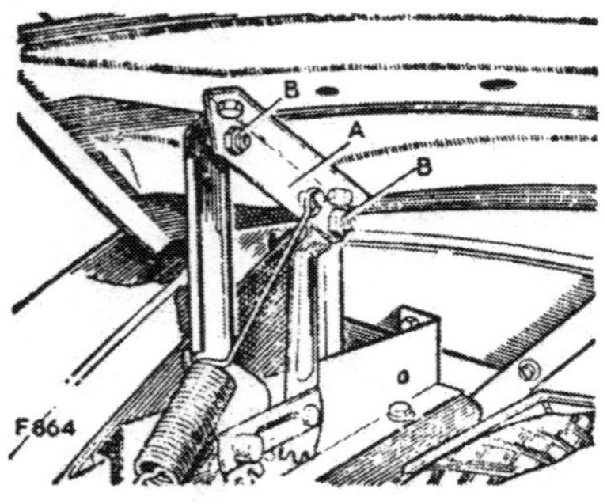

Bonnet hinges
A—Hinge bracket
B—Nuts securing hinge link to hinge bracket

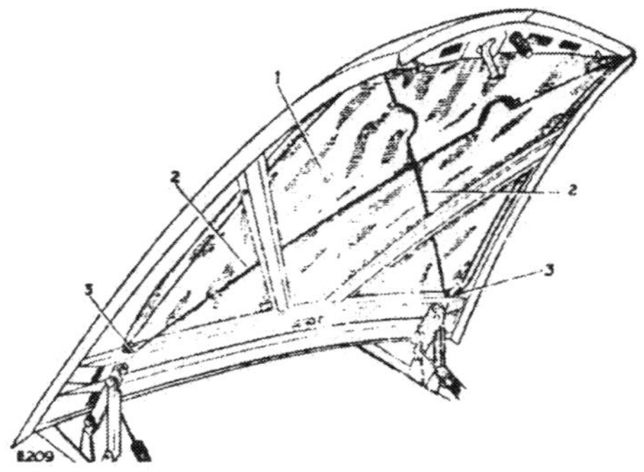

Insulation pad, retaining wires and fixing clips
1—Pad 2—Retaining wires 3—Clips

Bonnet lock, to remove, refit and adjust—Operation U-9

Workshop hand tools:
Spanner size: $\frac{7}{16}$ in. AF
Pliers, long-nosed

Early models

1. Remove the striker plate and catch mechanism from the bonnet lock platform secured by two nuts and plain washers.
2. Disconnect the inner wire of the control cable from the nipple.
3. If necessary remove the control cable completely by removing the cable retaining clips and disconnecting the control from the bracket inside the car. Withdraw the cable from inside the car.

Late models

4. Disconnect the control rod from the bonnet lock, secured by a split pin.

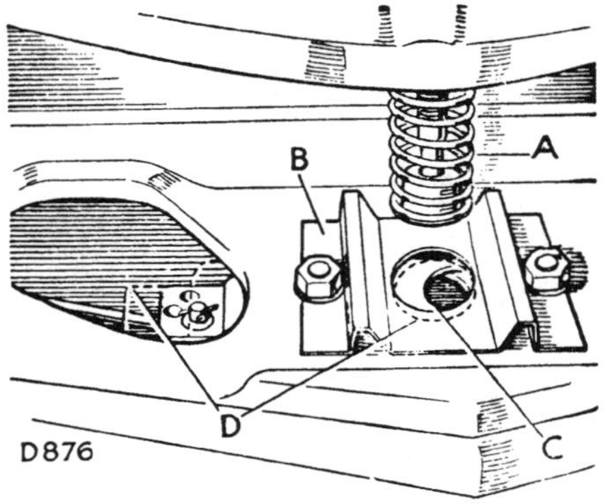

Location of bonnet lock and striker plate
A—Bonnet catch
B—Striker plate
C—Slider catch in locked position
D—Dotted outline shows slider catch in open position

5. Remove the lock, secured by two nuts and washers.
6. If it is necessary to remove the bonnet lock control it will be necessary to remove the radiator grille. Remove the four screws and washers and lift the grille out, removing the top first. Note the position of any shims used.
7. Disconnect the inner wire of the control cable at the nipple.
8. Remove the bell-crank lever bracket and rod, secured by two nuts, bolts and washers.
9. Slacken the two cable clips on the valance.
10. Undo the nut behind the control bracket inside the car and withdraw the cable from inside the car.

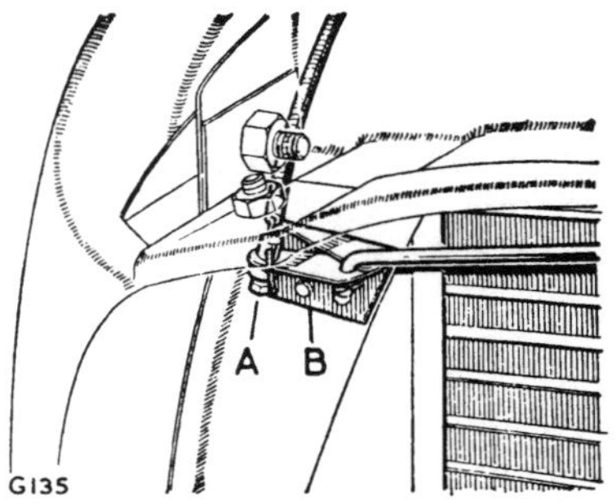

Bonnet lock control mechanism, late type
A—Nipple B—Bracket

Bonnet lock, to refit

1. Reverse removal procedure, but do not fully tighten the nuts securing the lock.
2. Lower the bonnet and align the striker plate with the lock bolt. The bolt should protrude through the plate approximately $\frac{1}{2}$ in. (12,5 mm).
3. The spring retainer on the lock bolt must locate at the centre of the striker plate.

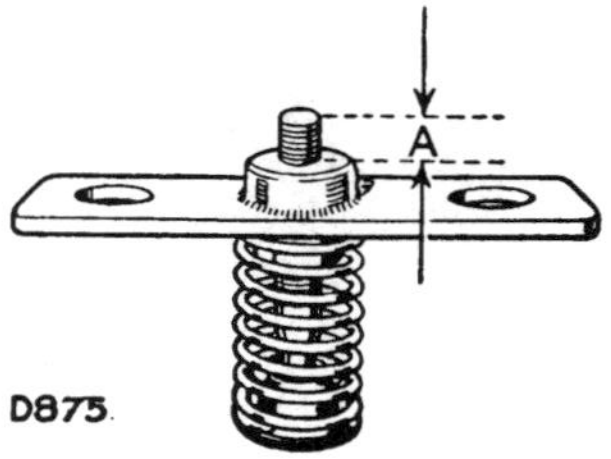

Adjustment of lock bolt
A—$\frac{1}{2}$ in. (12,5 mm)

4. Check operation of slider catch underneath striker plate:
   (a) Slider catch must move freely to limit of its travel to the right; allowing full engagement in groove of bonnet catch.
   (b) Slider catch must completely clear aperture of striker plate when control inside the car is pulled.
5. Adjust the length of the operating cable as necessary.

Radiator grille and bonnet lock platform, to remove and refit—Operation U-10

Workshop hand tools:
Spanner sizes: $\frac{7}{16}$ in. AF, $\frac{1}{2}$ in. AF
Pliers, pointed-nose

Grille, remove

1. Remove two top mounting bolts and the mounting bolts situated beneath the lower front body panel.
2. Lift out radiator grille, removing the top first, remove two lower brackets. Where shims are fitted, note position to ensure correct refitment.
3. Disconnect the bonnet lock mechanism.
4. Remove the two nuts securing the bonnet lock.
5. Remove the bonnet lock platform secured by four bolts, nuts and washers.

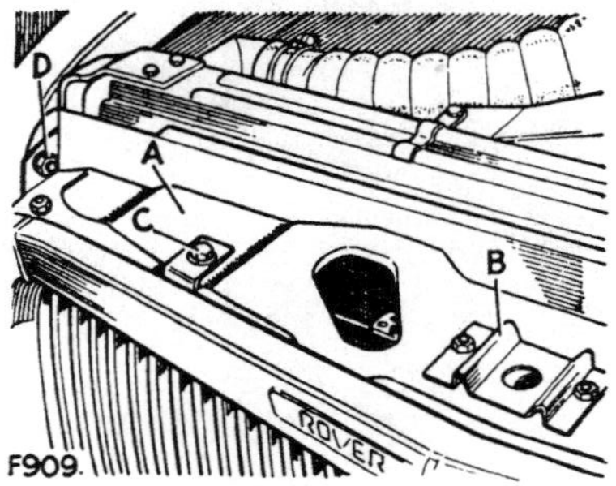

Bonnet lock platform
A—Bonnet lock platform C—Grille fixings
B—Bonnet lock D—Platform fixings

Grille, refit

1. Reverse removal procedure, but do not fully tighten the nuts securing the striker plate.
2. Lower the bonnet and align the striker plate with the lock bolt. The bolt should protrude through the plate approximately $\frac{1}{2}$ in. (12,5 mm).
3. Ensure that the spring retainer on the lock bolt locates at the centre of the striker plate.
4. Check operation of slider catch underneath striker plate, as follows:
   (a) Ensure that the slider catch moves freely to the limit of its travel to the right, thereby allowing full engagement in the groove on the bonnet catch.
   (b) Ensure that it completely clears the aperture in the striker plate when the operating rod in the car is pulled.

   Adjust cable operational length as necessary, by repositioning the control rod in the adjustment holes provided, or on early models by repositioning the nipple on the cable.
5. Fit two lower brackets to radiator grille, do not tighten, then pull brackets as far back as possible and fit radiator grille to body, inserting the bottom first.
6. Tighten the two lower brackets and secure the remainder with nuts, bolts and spring washers; if removed, refit two shims to mounting brackets and secure with nuts, bolts and plain washers.

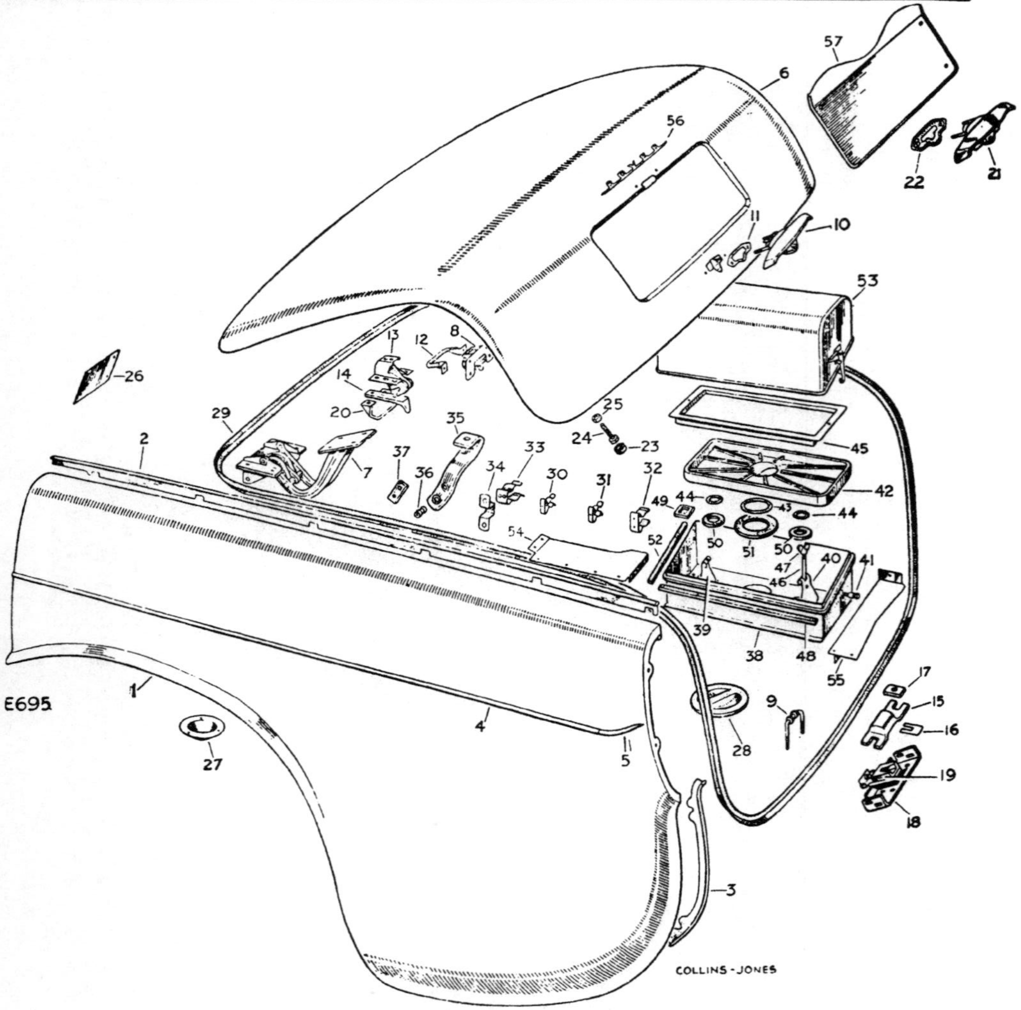

Rear wings and boot lid fittings, Mk II illustrated

1 Rear wing
2 Beading for wing, top
3 Beading for wing, lower
4 Styling strip
5 Finisher for styling strip
6 Boot lid complete
7 Hinge
8 Lock for boot lid
9 Striker, boot lid lock
10 Boot lid handle
11 Packing washer, for handle
12 Securing bracket, for handle
13 Lock for boot lid
14 Dovetail
15 Striker plate
16 Shim
17 Washer plate
18 Mounting bracket for dovetail striker
19 Dovetail striker
20 Securing bracket
21 Boot lid handle less lock
22 Sealing washer
23 Rubber buffer
24 Fixings
25 Fixings
26 Shock-absorber cover
27 Cover, petrol tank drainage
28 Grommet
29 Sealing rubber boot aperture
30 Spring clip for jack
31 Spring clip for starting handle
32 Spring clip for pump
33 Spring clip for jack
34 Support for clip
35 Strap retaining jack
36 Stud for strap
37 Strap retaining wheel cover
38 Base for battery box
39 Retaining bracket, battery front
40 Retaining bracket, battery
41 Pin for battery cover catch
42 Fibre glass tray for battery
45 Clamping frame, for battery
46 Special bolt
47 Wing nut
48 Seal for battery box, long
49 Sealing for earth tag
50 Sealing ring small
51 Sealing ring large
52 Seal for battery box (short)
53 Top cover for battery
54 Filler piece for boot floor
55 Filler piece for boot floor
56 Name plate 'Rover'
57 Mounting plate for rear number plate

Rear wings, to remove and refit—Operation U-11

Workshop hand tools:
Spanner sizes: $\frac{5}{16}$ in. AF, $\frac{7}{16}$ in. AF, $\frac{1}{2}$ in. AF
Screwdriver, small

Rear wing, to remove

1. Disconnect battery leads and remove trim from inside of wing panels. On left-hand wing remove tools and retaining bolts from tool board.
2. Remove the retaining screw from the tail lamp rim, remove tail lamp assembly and sealing rubbers, and disconnect the wiring.
3. Remove the three bolts situated inside the boot.
4. Remove the nut and bolt situated inside tail lamp aperture.
5. Remove the bolts from the front lower corner and rear corner of the wing.
6. Slacken the top bolts from the inside of wheel arch. Do not remove the first three in the top front corner.
7. Remove top and bottom wing moulding, remove all remaining bolts except the first three in the top front corner, lift the wing upwards and off.

Rear wing, refit

1. Reverse removal procedure.
2. Connect battery leads and check operation of tail lamps, stop lamps and flasher lamps.

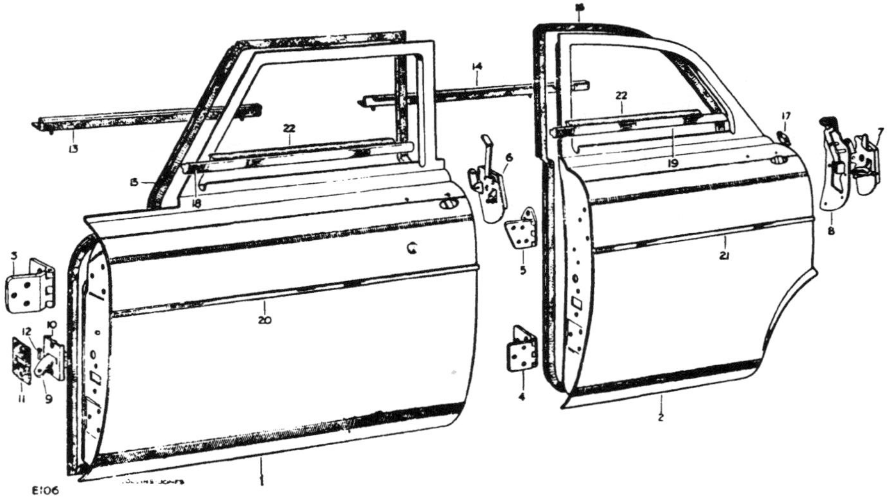

Door panels and hinges, saloon models, LH illustrated

1 Door assembly, front LH
2 Door assembly, rear LH
3 Hinge for front door
4 Hinge, lower, rear door
5 Hinge, upper LH, rear door
6 Lock complete for front door, LH
7 Lock complete for rear door, LH
8 Lever for rear lock, LH
9 Door check arm
10 Retainer for door check arm
11 Packing for door check retainer
12 Special pin fixing door check arm to body
13 Support for outside panel on front door
14 Support for outside panel on rear door, LH
15 Sealing rubber for front door, LH
16 Sealing rubber for rear door, RH
17 Rubber pad for rear door shut pillar, LH
18 Moulding for front door waist, LH
19 Moulding for rear door waist, LH
20 Moulding for front door
21 Moulding for rear door
22 Weather seal for front and rear door waist

Doors, to remove and refit—Operation U-12

Saloon and Coupé

Workshop hand tools:
Spanner size: $\frac{7}{16}$ in. AF
Screwdriver, Phillips type, large

Front and rear doors, remove

1. Withdraw the clevis pin from the check strap, retained by a split pin.
2. Remove the six retaining drive screws from the hinges and lift off door.

Door hinges and check strap

Doors, refit

1. Slacken the screws securing the lower hinge and insert the shim between hinge and body.

   Shim plates are available in one thickness only—18 SWG .048 in. (1,2 mm).

   If they are not to hand, they can be easily made as illustrated below.

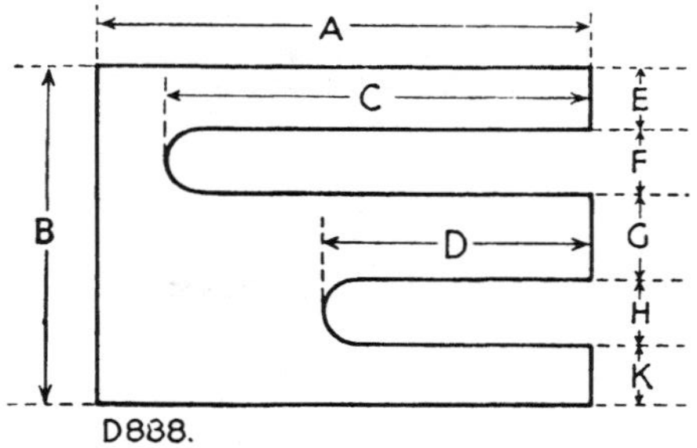

Shim for door hinge

A—2.500 in. (63,5 mm) B—1.750 in. (44,5 mm) C—2.187 in. (55,5 mm) D—1.375 in. (35 mm) E—.281 in. (7 mm) F—.375 in. (9,5 mm) G—.437 in. (11 mm) H—.375 in. (9,5 mm) K—.281 in. (7 mm)

2. Re-tighten with a suitable large screwdriver bent at right-angles to give more leverage.
3. It is advisable to have special screws, (Part No. 350668), available in case of breakage when loosening.
4. On later models shims may already be fitted, in which case the top shim between hinge and body can be removed to carry out door hanging correction.
5. In some cases the shim (Part No. 356227), may be found to give too much correction, and can be replaced with a shim made from 18 SWG .048 in. (1.2 mm) sheet steel.

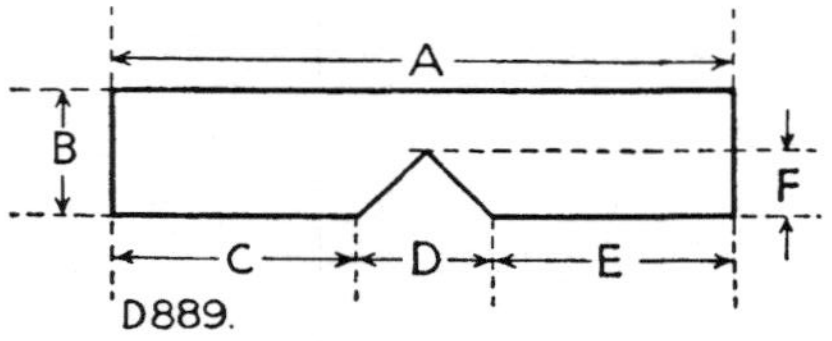

Shim for door hinge, alternative type

A—2.500 in. (63,5 mm) B—.500 in. (12,5 mm) C—1 in. (25 mm) D—.500 in. (12,5 mm) E—1 in. (25 mm) F—.250 in. (6 mm)

6. Insert shim behind single screw on door hinge between hinge and body. This halves the amount of adjustment and can be used on both the upper or lower hinge.
7. The doors, when finally adjusted, should have equal clearance around screen pillar and should be in line with body heading.
8. On no account must door hinges be corrected by using a wrench to twist into position, which may cause fracture of the hinge.

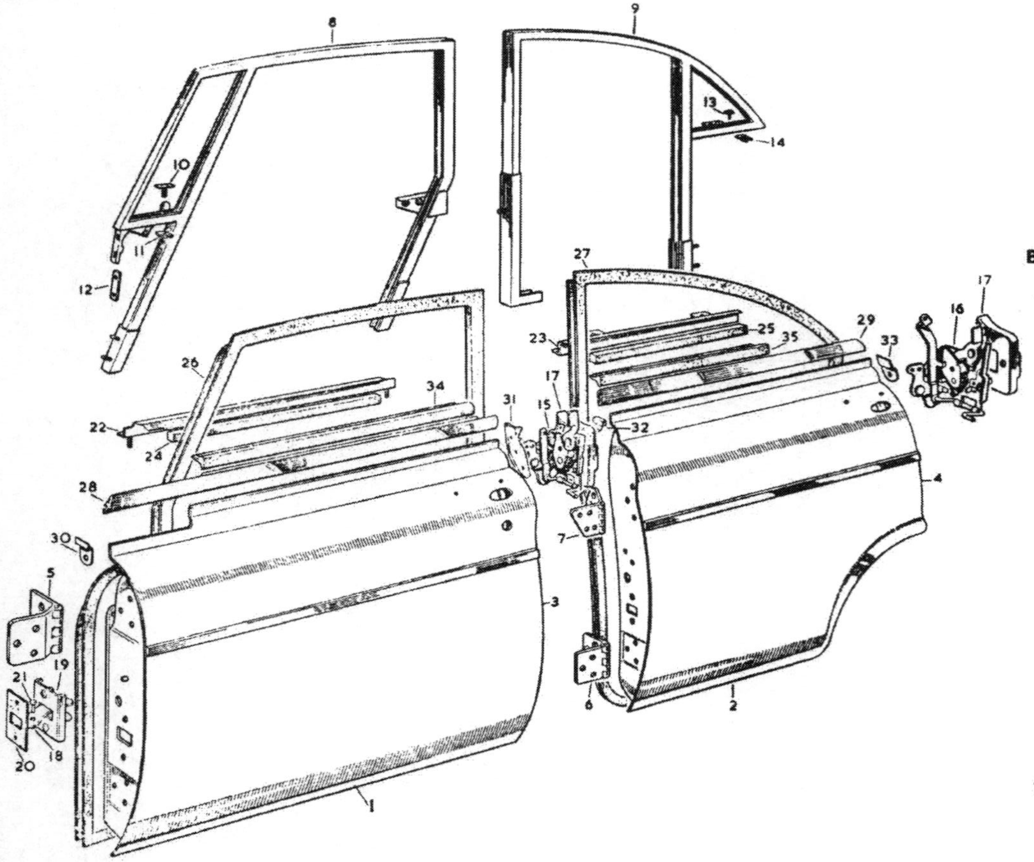

Door panels and hinges, coupé models, LH illustrated

1	Door assembly, front	19	Retainer for check arm
2	Door assembly, rear	20	Packing for retainer
3	Panel, outside, front door	21	Special pin
4	Panel, outside, rear door	22	Angle support, front door
5	Hinge, front door (upper and lower)	23	Angle support, rear door
6	Hinge, rear door (lower)	24	Packing for support, front door
7	Hinge, rear door, (upper)	25	Packing for support, rear door
8	Door frame, front, upper	26	Sealing rubber, front door
9	Door frame, rear, upper	27	Sealing rubber, rear door
10	Stud plate } Front door	28	Moulding for front door waist
11	Shim } Front door	29	Moulding for rear door waist
12	Tapped plate } Front door	30	End finisher, front door, front
13	Stud plate } Rear door	31	End finisher, front door, rear
14	Shim } Rear door	32	End finisher, rear door, front
15	Lock, front door	33	End finisher, rear door, rear
16	Lock, rear door	34	Weather seal, front door waist
17	Lock cover plate	35	Weather seal, rear door waist
18	Door check arm		

Boot lid, to remove and refit—Operation U-13

Workshop hand tools:
Spanner sizes: $\frac{1}{4}$ in. AF, $\frac{5}{16}$ in. AF, $\frac{3}{8}$ in. AF, $\frac{7}{16}$ in. AF, $\frac{1}{2}$ in. AF
Screwdrivers, small and medium

Boot lid, to remove

1. Disconnect battery leads and remove wiring harness and clips from right-hand side of boot lid hinge.

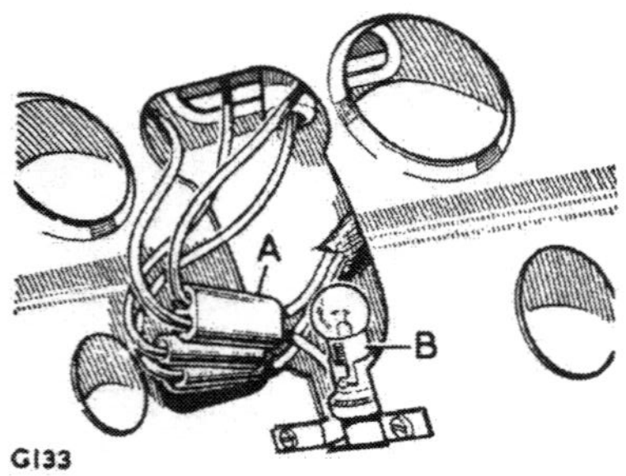

Boot light and wiring

A—Snap connectors B—Boot light

2. Disconnect boot lid light and reverse light at their respective snap connectors and withdraw the harness from the boot lid.
3. With the boot lid suitably supported remove the nuts and bolts securing boot lid to hinges, and lift off.

Boot lid, to refit

1. Reverse removal procedure.
2. Install the wiring harness and connect reverse light and boot light to their respective snap connectors in accordance with circuit diagram.
3. Fit the wiring harness clips to the right-hand side of boot lid hinge. Connect battery. Check reverse and boot lid lights for correct operation.

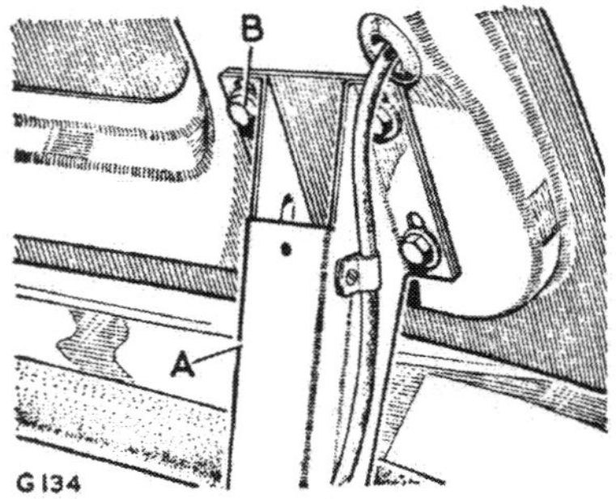

Boot lid hinge, RH illustrated

A—Boot lid hinge B—Fixing bolts

Boot lock, to remove and refit—Operation U-14

Workshop hand tools:
Spanner sizes: $\frac{5}{16}$ in. AF, $\frac{7}{16}$ in. AF, $\frac{1}{2}$ in. AF

Boot lock, remove

1. Remove the dovetail and striker plate from the mounting bracket on the body floor.
2. Remove the lock for boot lid, the dovetail securing bracket and boot lid handle, from the boot lid.

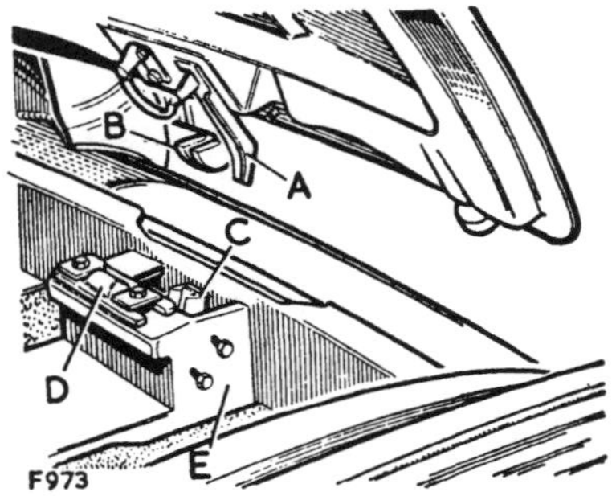

F973
Boot lock
A—Striker B—Catch C—Dovetail striker
D—Striker plate E—Mounting bracket

Boot lock, refit

1. Fit the handle; with sealing washer, lock, dove tail and securing bracket to boot lid.
2. Loosely fit the dovetail striker, and striker plate with shim and packing washer, to the floor mounting bracket.
3. Adjust the dovetail and striker on floor mounting bracket, together with the rubber buffers on the boot lid, so that when the lid is fastened there is no free movement.

Front windscreen, to remove and refit—Operation U-15

Workshop hand tools:
Screwdriver, medium

Front windscreen, to remove

1. When removing the remains of a shattered windscreen, it is advisable to seal off the demister and fresh air vents with masking tape, to prevent fragments of glass entering the ventilation system.

   If this precaution is not carried out, injury to the eyes may be caused when the heater blower is switched on.
2. Open both front doors and remove the drive screws securing the windscreen moulding to 'A' post pillar.
3. Slide the strip down to disengage from corner moulding and lift out; slide out lower corner moulding.
4. Remove the drive screw from moulding securing clip, and slide out clip.

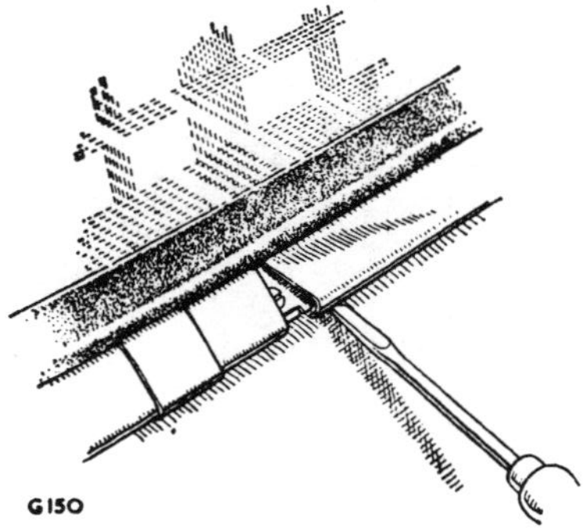
G150
Removing windscreen moulding

D386
Cross-section of windscreen

5. With a screwdriver ease under the bottom windscreen moulding; twist the moulding very slightly in a clockwise direction to disengage it from the bottom clip.
6. Lift the moulding upwards and give a slight twist in an anti-clockwise direction, disengage moulding from top clip. Repeat process at each clip until centre joining clip is reached.
7. Pull moulding outwards to disengage from centre moulding clip. Repeat same process for right-hand lower moulding.
8. Slide top left-hand corner moulding towards the rear of the car to disengage from top moulding. Slide forward and lift off. Repeat same process for top mouldings as for bottom mouldings.
9. Remove all drive screws, washers and clips surrounding windscreen rubber.
10. Insert a screwdriver or pointed instrument between the bottom of the windscreen rubber and the body, slide round the perimeter of windscreen rubber to loosen sealing compound.
11. Tap the windscreen lightly with the palm of the hand and lift out; remove rubber surround from windscreen.

Front windscreen, to refit

1. Ensure the windscreen is firmly seated in the channel of the new windscreen rubber
2. Examine the windscreen frame on the body and remove all traces of sealing compound.
3. Inject a small quantity of sealing compound around the perimeter of the inner channel, with the nozzle of an air pressure gun inserted between the glass and rubber.
4. Offer up the windscreen complete with rubber, to the car body.
5. Insert the top of the windscreen first, then push in the bottom; seat into position by striking the glass with the palm of the hand.
6. Insert six clips, screws and washers at an equal distance around the windscreen rubber.
7. Inject sealing compound along the perimeter of the windscreen rubber with an air pressure gun.

Operation U-15—*continued*

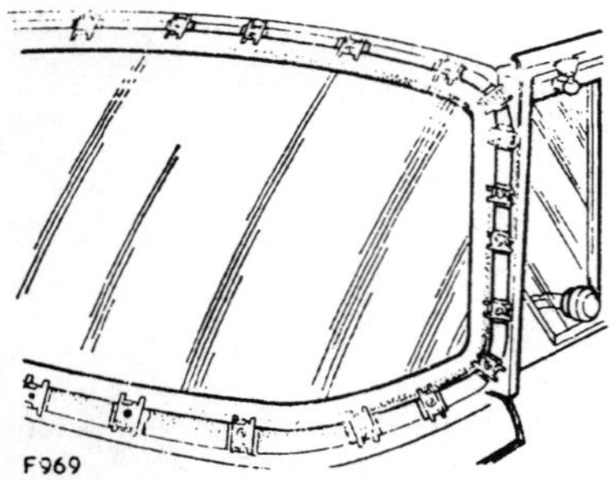
F969

Windscreen support plates and clips in correct position

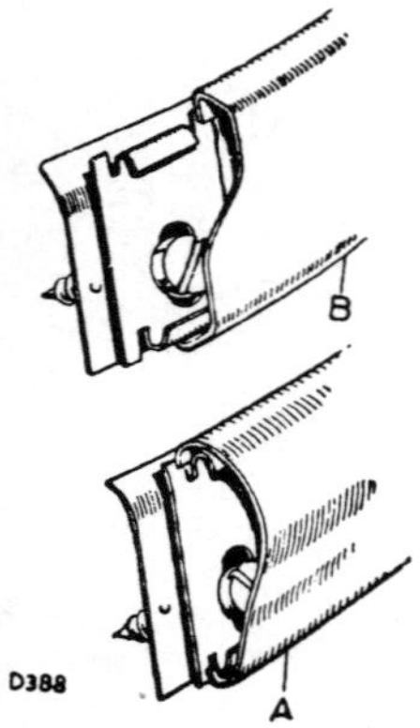

D388

Cross-section of moulding strips, saloon models

A—Top moulding B—Bottom moulding

8. Insert the remaining screws, clips and washers. Ensure that the clips are in line with each other; this is to facilitate the fitting of the moulding strips.
9. Fit the top left-hand strip by engaging on the bottom of the centre clip, give a sharp blow with the palm of the hand to engage over the top of the clip and fit to remainder of clips in a similar manner. Fit the right-hand strip using the same method.
10. Ensure that the mouldings are central on the windscreen, fit joining piece in the centre of the two mouldings and engage on clips.
11. Fit the bottom left- and right-hand mouldings by exactly the same method. Fit end clips on each of the mouldings by sliding into the moulding channel and securing with a drive screw.
12. Fit the left- and right-hand top corner mouldings by engaging the rear end of the moulding in the front of the gutter and sliding rearwards until it is located against the windscreen pillar upright. Ensure that it fits tightly against the top mouldings. Adjust top mouldings if necessary.
13. Slide the left-hand pillar upright moulding into the top corner piece.
14. Engage the left-hand bottom corner piece with the windscreen pillar upright moulding. Ensure that it fits tightly against bottom moulding; adjust bottom moulding if necessary.
15. Repeat same process with right-hand side and insert the drive screws in the side mouldings and tighten fully. Remove all surplus sealing compound.

Rear window, to remove and refit—Operation U-16

Workshop hand tools:
Screwdriver, medium
Spanner size: $\frac{5}{16}$ in. AF

Rear window, to remove, saloon

1. Slide joining strip in the centre of the top moulding towards the left-hand side moulding strip.

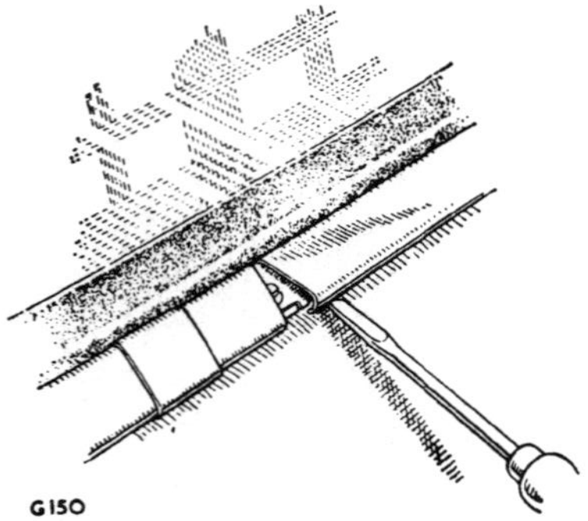
G150

Removing rear window moulding

2. Ease a screwdriver under the left-hand top mould ing at the centre, give a slight twist in a clockwise direction to disengage from moulding clips. Repeat process for each clip.

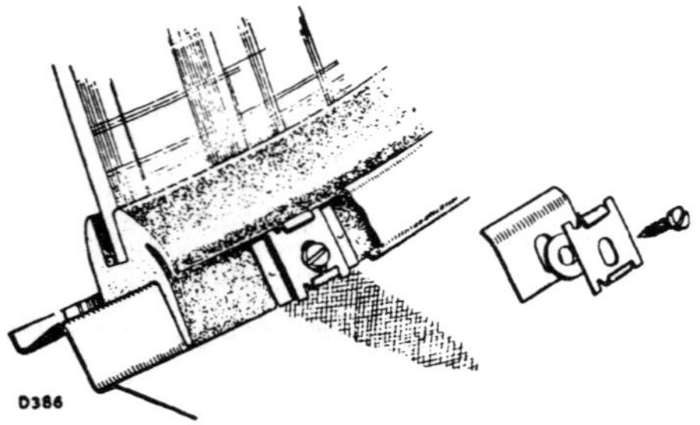
D386

Cross-section of rear window

3. Remove drive screw, washer and plate, securing left-hand bottom corner moulding. Then remove moulding from clips as detailed in the preceding two items.
4. The top right-hand moulding and the right-hand bottom corner moulding are removed by the same method.
5. Starting at the outside, remove the bottom mouldings by the same method as detailed above. Remove all the drive screws, clips, plates and washers securing the rear window rubber.
6. Insert a screwdriver between the edge of the body and rubber surround and slide it around the perimeter of the moulding to break sealing compound.
7. Tap rear window with the palm of the hand and lift out; remove rubber surround from rear window.

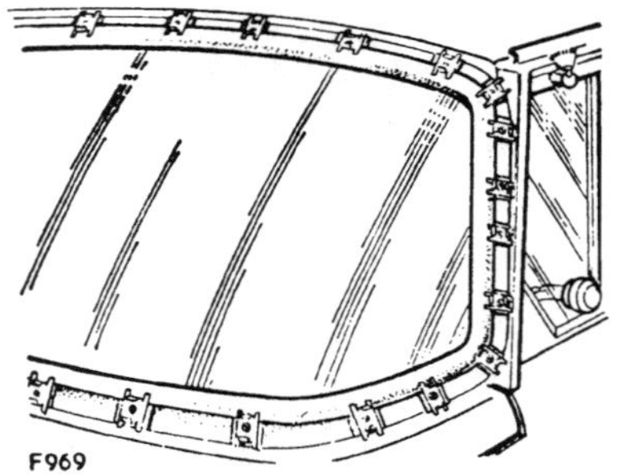
F969

Rear window support plates and clips in correct position

Rear window, to remove, coupé

The following prior operations will have to be carried out; the window removal procedure is then as described for saloon models.

Remove the rear seat squab, secured by bolts accessible from inside the boot, after the trim panel in front of the fuel tank has been removed. This panel is secured by drive screws.

Release the cant rail trim by the screws adjacent to the side header panels.

Prise out the header panels, secured by spring clips.

Remove the exterior mouldings secured inside the body panel by nuts, 'Prestik' and plain washers.

Slide the top and the two joining clips to one side to release the moulding strips.

Operation U-16—*continued*

Rear window, to refit

1. Seat the rear window firmly in the channel of the new sealing rubber and inject a small quantity of sealing compound between rubber and glass
2. Remove all traces of sealing compound from rear window frame, insert the rear window first at the top and then push in the bottom.
3. Insert six clip washers, plates and screws at an equal distance around the perimeter of the rear window rubber.
4. Inject a small quantity of sealing compound between the rubber and body and insert the remaining screws, clips, washers and plates.

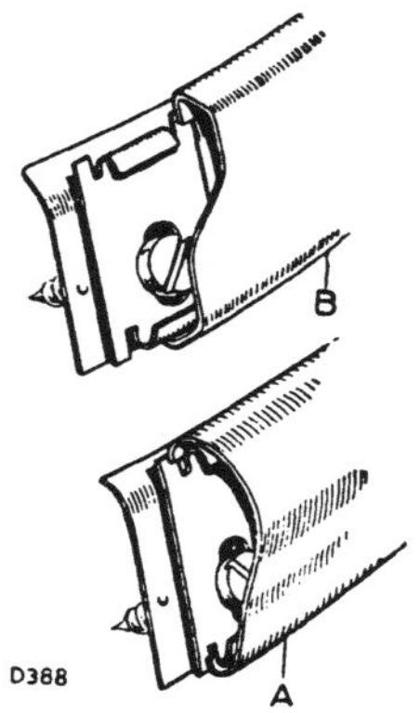

Cross-section of moulding strip, saloon models
A—Top moulding B—Bottom moulding

5. Ensure that the clips are in alignment with each other in order that the moulding will clip on easily.
6. Fit the left-hand lower moulding strip by engaging on the bottom of the clip first; give a sharp blow upwards with the palm of the hand; repeat for remaining clips.
7. Ensure that the mouldings are central on the rear window; fit joining piece in the centre of the two mouldings and engage right-hand lower moulding on the clip as detailed for the left-hand side moulding.
8. Insert the two plates into the channel on each end of the bottom corner mouldings. Secure with two drive screws and washers.
9. Slide the bottom corner mouldings into the lower mouldings. Locate on clips in the manner previously described.
10. Engage top mouldings in the bottom corner mouldings and fit as described for the lower mouldings.
11. Remove all surplus sealing compound. Check that all mouldings fit tightly against each other. Adjust upper or lower mouldings as necessary.

Item 12, coupé models

12. Refit the exterior mouldings, side header panels, cant rail trim, seat squab and boot trim.

Roof trim, to remove and refit—Operation U-17

Saloon models

Workshop hand tools:
Screwdrivers, medium and small Screwdrivers, Phillips type, small and medium

Preliminary procedure

1. Remove the sun visors and driving mirror from the canopy trim above the windscreen. Remove the pillar pulls and coat hooks. These items are secured with drive screws.
2. Disconnect the battery, situated in the luggage compartment.
3. Remove the roof lamps, front and rear, from both sides.

   (a) Withdraw the cover of the the lamp.

   (b) Remove the mounting screws.

   (c) Disconnect the wiring at the snap connectors.
4. If the car is fitted with bench or bucket type seats, the seats will have to be removed.

   (If fully adjustable seats are fitted the cushions should be removed and the seat squabs should be pushed into the fully reclining position. It will not then be necessary to remove the seats from the car.)

Roof trim, remove

5. Carefully prise away the trimmed cant rail and 'D' post casings, secured with spring clips.
6. Remove the canopy trim from above the windscreen and the trim from above the backlight.
7. Prise away the 'BC' post trims, secured by spring clips.
8. The roof trim is assembled on a rigid frame and is secured to the body with drive screws. Withdraw the roof trim complete, through the front passenger door.

Roof trim, refit

1. Reverse removal procedure.

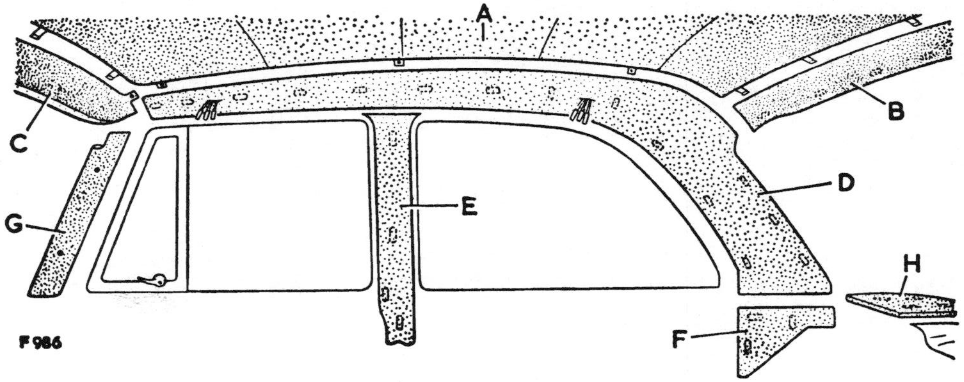

Body trimming, saloon

A—Headlining
B—Backlight trim, top
C—Canopy trim
D—Cant rail
E—'BC' post trim
F—Harness cover
G—'A' post moulding
H—Parcel shelf

Roof trim, to remove and refit—Operation U-18

Coupé models

Workshop hand tools:
Screwdrivers, small and medium   Screwdrivers, Phillips type, small and medium

Preliminary procedure

1. The sun visors and driving mirror must be removed from above the windscreen and the pillar pulls and coat hooks must be removed These items are secured by drive screws.
2. Disconnect the battery, situated in the luggage compartment.
3. Remove the roof lamps, front and rear, from both sides.
   (a) Withdraw the cover of the lamp.
   (b) Remove the mounting screws.
   (c) Disconnect the wiring at the snap connectors.
4. Take out the seat cushions, front and rear and push the front seat squabs into the fully reclining position.

Roof trim, remove

5. Remove the cant rail trimmed fillets from above the doors, secured by drive screws on the underside.
6. Remove the 'A' post trims, secured by drive screws.
7. Take out the rear side header panels, secured with spring clips.
8. Carefully prise away and remove the 'BC' post trims.
9. Remove the front header panel from above the windscreen and the rear centre header panel from above the backlight.
10. Withdraw the roof trim which is assembled on a rigid frame through the front passenger door. The frame is secured to the body with drive screws.

Roof trim, refit

1. Reverse removal procedure.

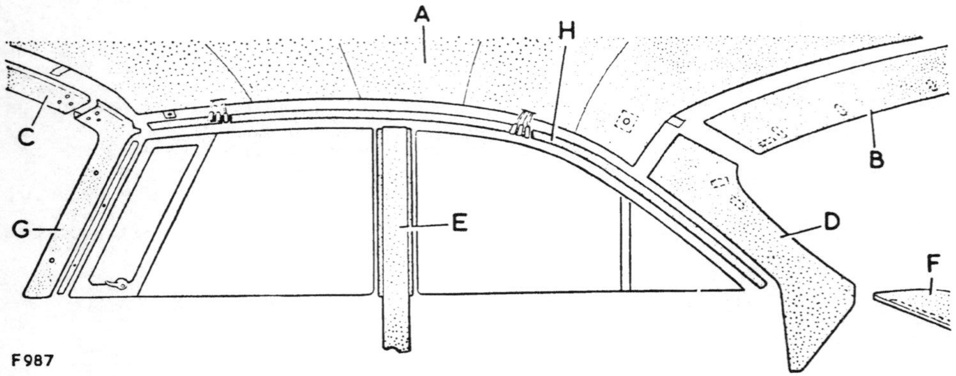

F987

Body trimming, coupé

A—Headlining
B—Centre header pad
C—Front header pad
D—Rear header side panel
E—'BC' post trim
F—Parcel shelf
G—'A' post moulding
H—Cant rail trim

Door locks, to remove and refit—Operation U-19

Saloon models

Workshop hand tools:
Spanner size: $\frac{7}{16}$ in. AF
Screwdrivers, small and medium   Screwdriver, Phillips type, large   Long-nosed pliers

Door lock, remove

1. Take off the interior door handles complete with escutcheon and wearing plates.

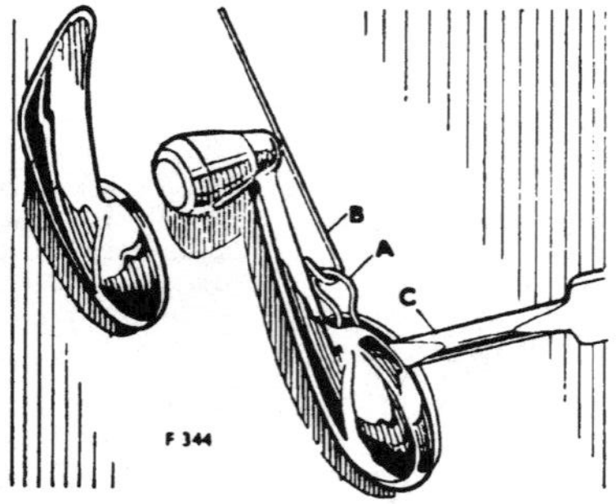

F 344

Removing door handles
A—Retaining spring clip   B—Wire hook
C—Screwdriver

Use a piece of hooked wire to remove the spring clip and a screwdriver to lever the trim panel away from the handle.

Items 2 and 3 Mk I and Mk IA models. Front and rear armrests, to remove

2. Press the button in the centre of the armrest and slide the armrest upwards as high as possible. Remove the two fixing bolts and withdraw the armrest.
3. Prise off the cap in the escutcheon plate of the rear door armrest and remove the fixing screw, spring clip and escutcheon plate. The armrest will now be able to be removed together with the trimmed door casing.

Item 4 Mk II models. Front and rear armrests, to remove

1. Prise out the two plastic retainers from the front door armrest and lift the armrest off its mountings.

Remove the mounting bracket, secured by drive screws, and note the position of the packing washers. Rear door armrests are integral with the trimmed door casing and have no separate fixings.

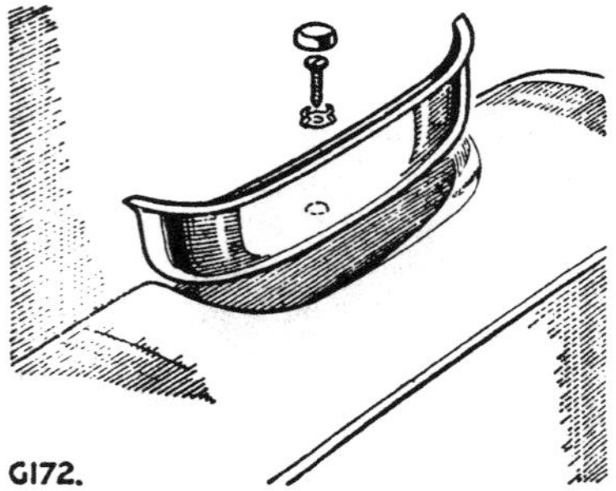
G172.

Removing rear door armrests, Models Mk I and Mk 1A

5. Carefully lever the trimmed door casing, secured by spring clips, away from the door.
6. With a screwdriver as a lever prise out the padded crash-rail, secured by spring clips.
7. Remove the wooden window surround, secured by drive screws.

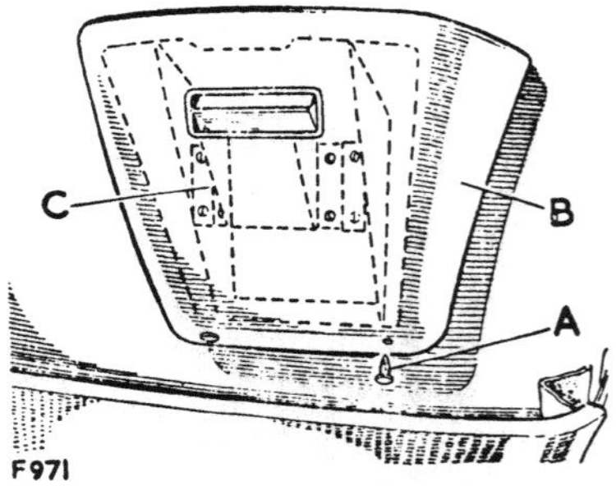

F971

Removing front door armrest, Mk II
A—Retainer   B—Armrest   C—Mounting bracket

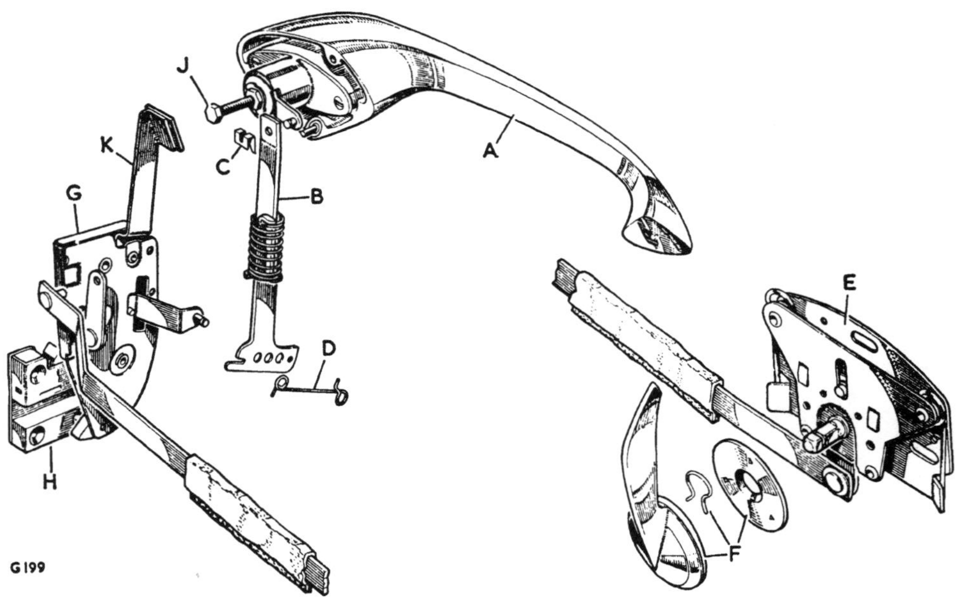

G199

Arrangement of door lock mechanism, saloon models

A—Outside door handle
B—Connecting link, for lock
C—Retaining clip
D—Retaining spring
E—Remote control
F—Inside door handle assembly
G—Door lock
H—Striker
J—Adjusting screw
K—Lock operating arm

Operation U-19—*continued*

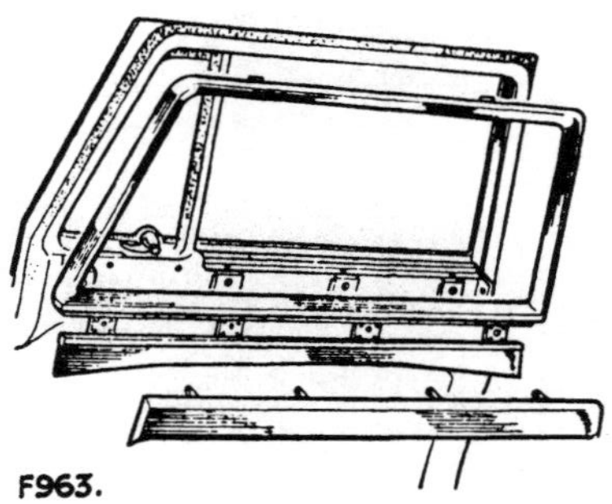
F963.

Removing crash-rail and wooden surround

Items 8 to 11, see illustration on opposite page

8. Through the aperture in the door, remove the retaining spring 'D' and release the connecting link 'B' from the lock 'G'.

9. Disconnect the arm of the remote control 'E' from the lock 'G' and remove the remote control, secured to the door with three set screws and washers.

10. Remove the lock 'G' from the door, taking care that the tapped lock retaining plate does not drop to the bottom of the door.

11. Remove the set screws securing the handle 'A' to door panel and remove the handle complete with link 'B'.

12. If necessary remove the striker from the body.

Locking door handle, to strip

13. Disconnect the link from the handle, secured by a spring clip.

14. Carefully remove the two screws securing the push-button mechanism to the handle and withdraw the push-button and retaining plate.

15. Remove the set screw and locknut and withdraw the operating lever.

16. Take the coil spring and seating washer off the plunger. Remove the self-centring spring by disengaging from the barrel of the push-button.

17. Withdraw the lock barrel from the push-button by driving out the retaining pin.

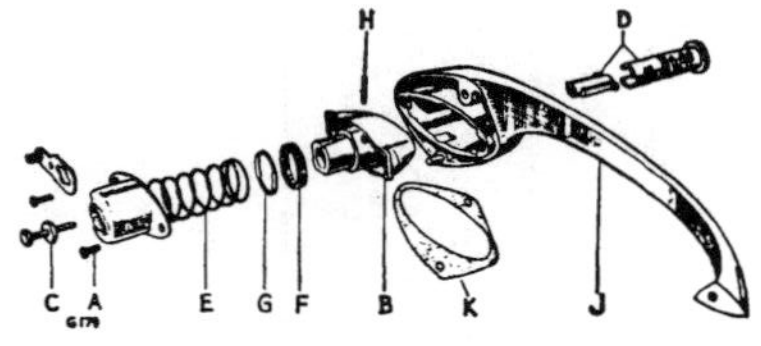

Exploded view of door handle, locking

A—Set screws
B—Push-button
C—Set screw and locknut
D—Barrel lock
E—Spring
F—Self-centring spring
G—Spring retaining plate
H—Pin retaining barrel lock
J—Handle
K—Washer

Handle, rebuild and refit

1. Reverse removal procedure.

Door locks, refit

1. Reverse removal procedure.

Items 2 to 5. Striker plate adjustment

2. If removed, fit the striker plate to the body, tightening the screws sufficiently to allow the striker to be positioned by hand.

3. Push the striker plate fully inwards and close the door fully. If the door fails to latch, the striker plate should be moved slightly outwards.

4. If necessary pull the door outwards, to give correct body panel alignment.

5. Open the door gently and fully tighten the striker securing screws.

Item 6. Push-button plunger adjustment

6. Check the adjustment of the push-button plunger 'J'. The operating arm of the push-button should be in the 'up' position (push-button operative). Adjust the plunger 'J' so that it just touches the operating arm 'K'.

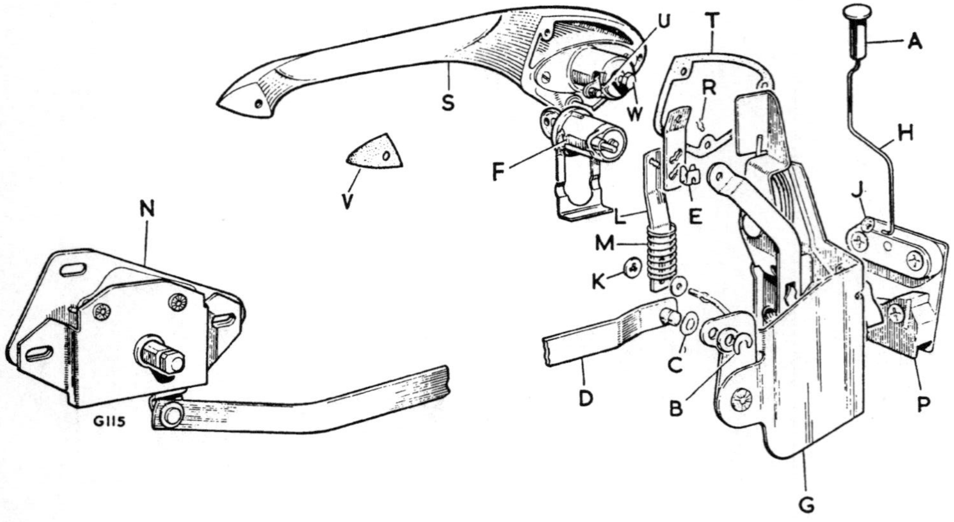

Arrangement of 'zero torque' lock mechanism, coupe models

A—Sill control knob	L—Link
B—Circlip	M—Spring
C—Wave washer	N—Remote control unit
D—Remote control link	P—Striker
E—'U' type clip	R—Spring clip
F—Private lock and retaining clip	S—Door handle
G—Lock unit	T—Seating washer, large
H—Sill control rod	U—Operating arm location hole
J—'Starlock' washer	V—Seating washer, small
K—'Starlock' washer	W—Adjustable plunger

Door locks, to remove and refit—Operation U-20

Coupé models

Workshop hand tools:
Spanner size: $\frac{7}{16}$ in. AF
Screwdrivers, small and medium Screwdriver, Phillips type, large Long-nosed pliers

Brief description of the operation of 'zero torque' locks

The coupé model has 'zero torque' type door locks fitted. A key-operated private lock on both front doors, is interconnected with a knob on the sill inside the car.

When locking the door with the key, it will be found that the key will turn in one direction for part of a turn only and must be turned back to the original position to be withdrawn. The sill knob will go down as the key is turned.

To unlock the door, the key must be turned in the opposite direction for a fraction of a turn.

All the doors may be locked without using the key, by pushing down the sill knob and then closing the door with the push-button of the outside handle depressed. The sill knob, being down, serves as an indicator that the door is locked and the push-button of the outside handle should now be ineffective.

A children's safety device incorporated in the rear door lock is operated by depressing the sill knob. The remote control interior door handle will remain in the locked position when the door is closed and remain so until the sill knob is pulled upwards.

To remove the private locks only, see Operation U-21.

Door lock, remove

1. Take off the interior door handles complete with escutcheon and wearing plates.

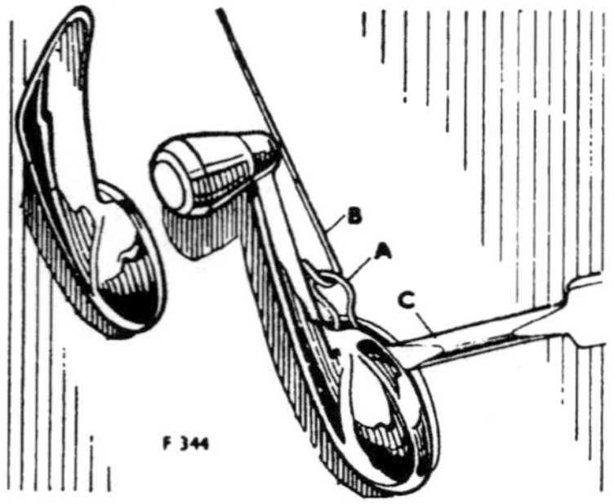

Removing door handles
A—Retaining spring clip B—Wire hook
C—Screwdriver

Use a piece of hooked wire to remove the spring clip and a screwdriver to lever the trim panel away from the handle.

Item 2. Front doors only

2. Remove the armrest from the door casing by prising out the two plastic retainers at the bottom of the armrest cover and removing the cover. Take out the screws securing the armrest mounting bracket to the door. Note the position of any spacing washers.

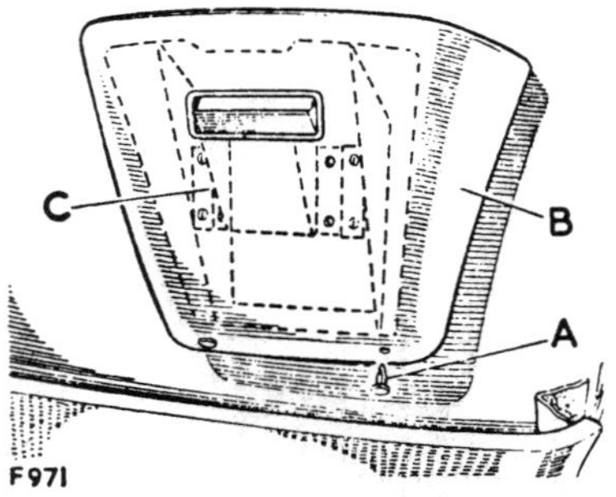

Removing front door armrests
A—Plastic retainer B—Armrest cover
C—Mounting bracket

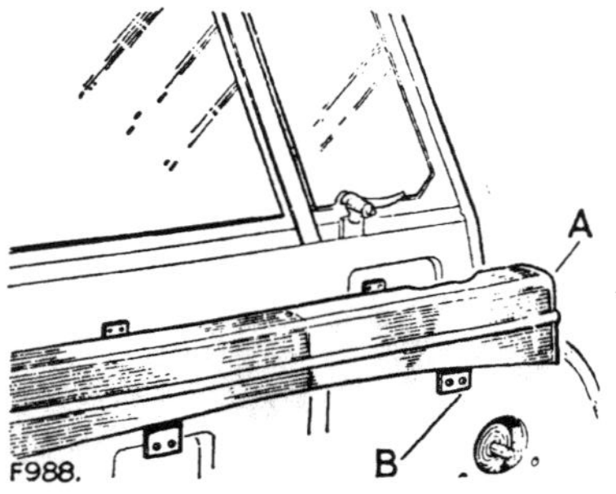

Removing door capping
A—Wooden waist moulding B—Fixing bracket

Operation U-20—*continued*

3. Carefully lever the trimmed door casing secured by spring clips, away from the door.

4. Unscrew the sill knob 'A'; and remove the wooden capping, secured by drive screws. See arrangement of zero torque lock mechanism, page 34.

5. Remove the circlip 'B', securing the remote control link 'D' to the door lock lever.

6. Disconnect the remote control link 'D' and retain the washers for reassembly.

Item 7. Front doors only

7. Disconnect the two links from the private lock 'F', they are retained by a spring clip 'E'.

8. Take out the door lock 'G', secured by three screws. If necessary remove the control rod 'H' and the connecting link 'L' from the lock. The method of securing these items will be obvious from the illustration.

Item 9. Front doors only

9. If necessary remove the private lock 'F', secured to the door panel with a spring clip.

10. If necessary remove the striker 'P', secured to the body with Phillips screws.

Door locks, refit

Item 1. Front doors

1. If removed, refit the private lock device 'F', with the operating arm pointing forwards. Secure in position with the spring clip.

2. Fit the sill control rod 'H' to the long operating lever on the lock 'G'.

Item 3. Front doors

3. Place the spring 'M' over the private lock connecting link 'L'. Fit a plain washer 'C' to the bottom operating rod of the lock unit; compress the spring on the link and connect the link to the rod. Secure with the starlock washer 'K'.

4. Fit the lock 'G' complete with rod 'H' (and link 'L' where fitted) into the aperture of the door. Position the cover plate on to the location plate of the lock and secure with the fixing screws. Ensure that the cover plate engages fully on the location plate of the lock before fully tightening the screws.

5. Fit the wooden capping and sill knob 'A', using a piece of adhesive tape to retain the sill control rod 'H' in position.

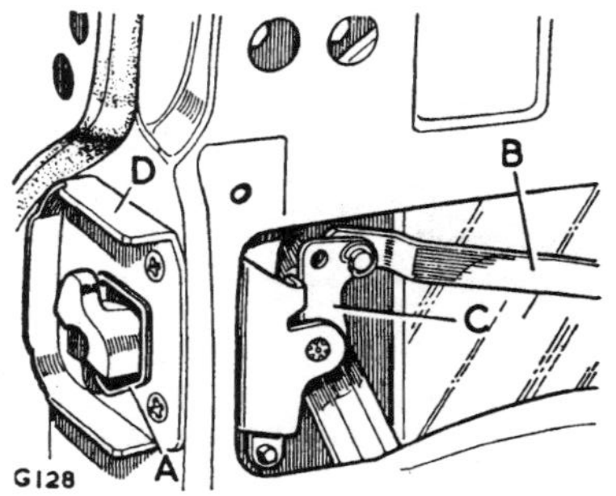

Front door remote control link in position

A—Location plate
B—Remote control link
C—Lock operating lever
D—Cover plate

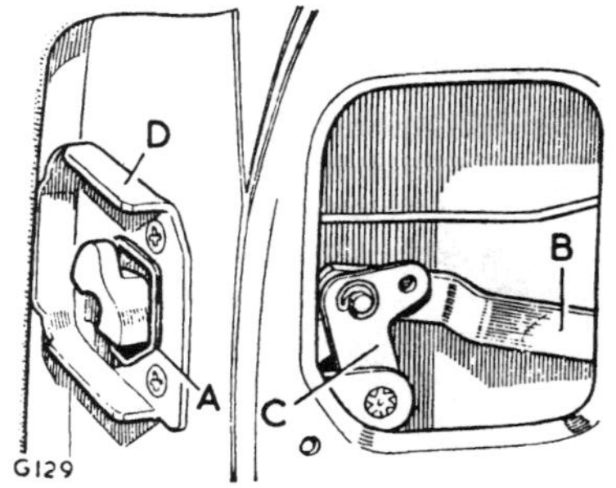

Rear door remote control link in position

A—Location plate
B—Remote control link
C—Lock operating lever
D—Cover plate

Operation U-20—*continued*

6. Place the remote control unit 'N', complete with connecting link into position inside the door and secure loosely.

7. Fit the anti-rattle washer on to the stud at the end of the remote control link 'D' and connect the link to the lock. On front doors the link is connected to the first hole in the lever and on rear doors the second hole is used.

8. Push the remote control mechanism towards the lock, to take up free movement (but do not bulge the link) and tighten the fixing screws. Check that the push-button rotary cam has not rotated during the tightening operation.

9. If removed, fit the striker plate to the body, tightening the screws sufficiently to allow the striker to be positioned by hand.

10. Push the striker plate fully inwards and close the door fully. If the door fails to latch, the striker plate should be moved slightly outwards.

11. Pull the door outwards, without depressing the push-button, to give correct body panel alignment.

12. Open the door gently and fully tighten the striker securing screws.

13. Check the adjustment of the push-button plunger The operating arm of the push-button should be in the 'up' position (push-button operative). The adjustable plunger of the push-button 'W', should be adjusted to rotate the rotary cam of the lock to within 3° of its stop. Free travel of the push-button before it commences to rotate the cam should be $\frac{1}{32}$ to $\frac{1}{16}$ in. (0,79 to 1,5 mm). Check this by holding the cam firmly and operating the push-button.

Items 14 to 16. Front doors

14. Push the sill button down (door locked position). Insert a piece of $\frac{1}{8}$ in. diameter (3 mm) wire into the slot in the push-button retaining plate and through the hole in the push-button operating arm 'U'.

15. Use the key to lock the private lock device 'F', so as to bring its operating arm into the lower position. Fit the link 'L', (lock 'G' to private lock 'F') connecting the link with the nearest of the three holes provided.

16. Fit the short link between the push-button arm 'U' and the private lock 'F', using the nearest of the three holes provided. Should the pin of the link come midway between any two holes, the upper hole should be used. Withdraw the piece of $\frac{1}{8}$ in. wire.

Items 17 to 19. Rear doors

17. Push the sill knob 'A' down.

18. Insert a piece of $\frac{1}{8}$ in. diameter (3 mm) wire into the slot in the push-button retaining plate and through the hole in the operating arm 'U'.

19. Fit the link between the operating arm and the lock 'G' into the nearest of the three holes provided. Secure the link with the spring clip and withdraw the piece of $\frac{1}{8}$ in. wire.

Private lock, to remove and refit—Operation U-21

Coupé models

Workshop hand tools:
Spanner size: $\frac{7}{16}$ in. AF
Pliers, long-nosed, Screwdriver, medium

The key-operated private lock on the front doors can be removed and refitted without removing the 'zero torque' door lock mechanism.

Private lock, remove

1. Remove the interior door handles complete with escutcheon and wearing plates. The spring clip which retains the handle, can be removed with a piece of strong hooked wire.

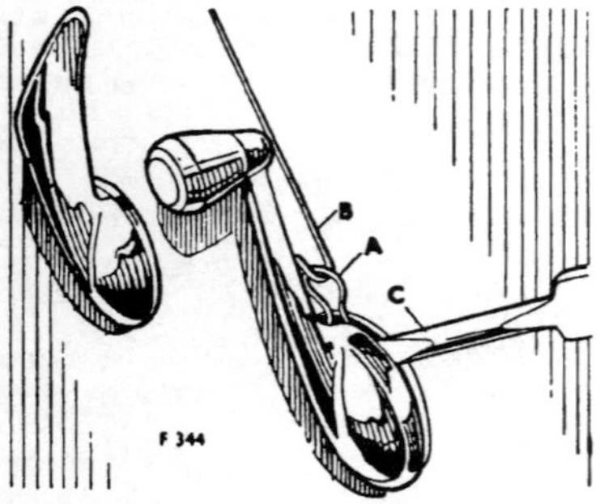

Removing door handles

A—Retaining spring clip B—Wire hook
C—Screwdriver

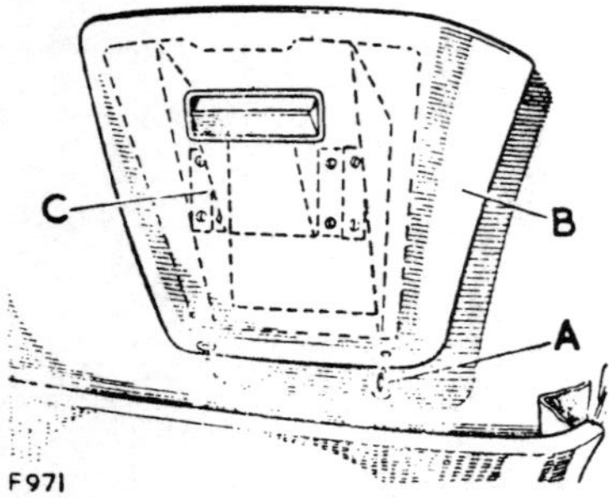

Removing front door armrests

A—Plastic retainer B—Armrest cover
C—Mounting bracket

2. Prise out the two plastic retainers from the armrest and remove the armrest cover.
3. Remove the armrest mounting brackets noting the position of any spacing washers used.
4. Carefully lever the trimmed door casing, secured by spring clips, away from the door.
5. Disconnect the link of the remote control at the door lock by removing the circlip.

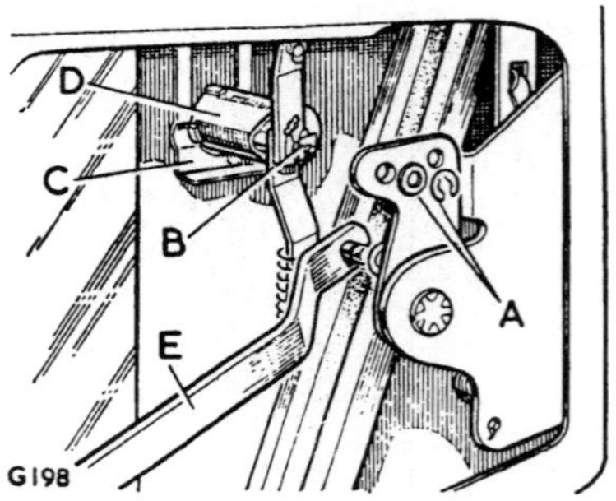

Removing private lock, RH illustrated

A—Fixings, remote control link
B—Spring clip retaining the links to private lock
C—Private lock retaining clip
D—Private lock
E—Remote control link

6. Remove the 'U'-type spring clip retaining the two links to the private lock.
7. Withdraw the retaining clip securing the private lock. Remove the lock from the outside by turning the lock to clear the spigot and pulling outwards.

Private lock, refit

1. Reverse removal procedure.

Interior door handles, to remove and refit—Operation U-22

Saloon and coupé models

Workshop hand tools:
Screwdriver, medium

Handles, remove

1. The handles are retained by spring clips. Use a screwdriver to lever the handle away from the wearing plate and use a piece of hooked wire to remove the spring clip.

Removing door handles

A—Retaining spring clips B—Wire hook
C—Screwdriver

2. Withdraw the handle, escutcheon and wearing plate.

Handles, refit

1. Fit the spring clip into its groove in the handle, place the escutcheon and wearing plates into position on the handle and fit the handle to its spindle.

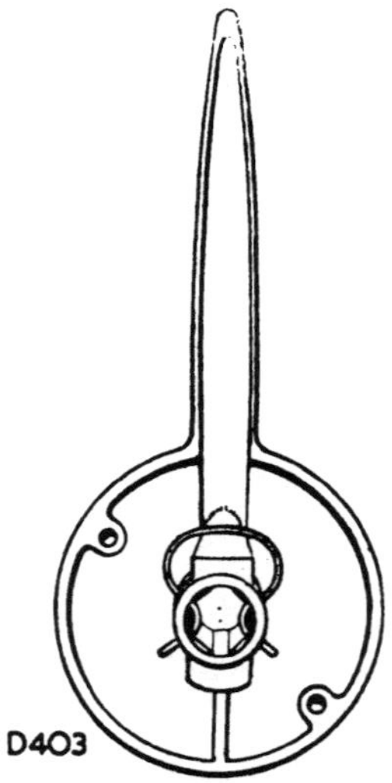

Handle clip in correct position

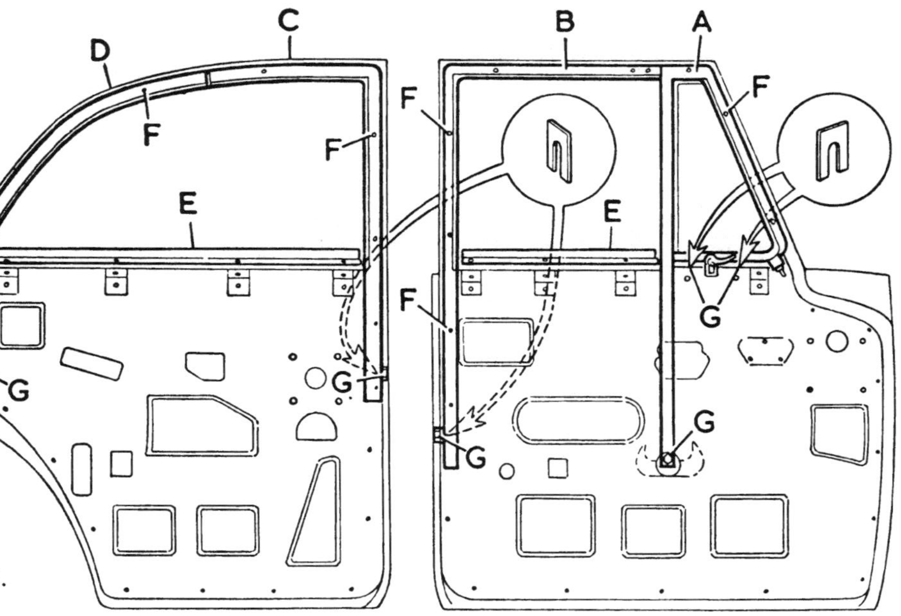

G171.

Front and rear door glass frame fixings, saloon models, LH-side illustrated

A—Window vent, front door
B—Window channel, rear, front door
C—Window channel, front, rear door
D—Window channel, rear, rear door
E—Draught excluders
F—Drive screw fixings, channel to door
G—Windows, channel fixing to door panel

Front door glasses and channels, to remove and refit—Operation U-23

Saloon models

Workshop hand tools:
Spanner sizes: $\frac{5}{16}$ in. AF, $\frac{7}{16}$ in. AF
Screwdrivers, small and medium   Long-nosed pliers

When it is required to replace a vent glass only, it is first necessary to remove the door glass as instructed below.

Glass and channels, remove

1. Insert a screwdriver or suitable lever between the door and crash-rail. Remove the padded crash-rail, secured by spring clips.
2. Withdraw the wooden window surround, secured by drive screws at the bottom and two locating lugs at the top.
3. Remove the draught strip from the inside sill, secured by drive screws.

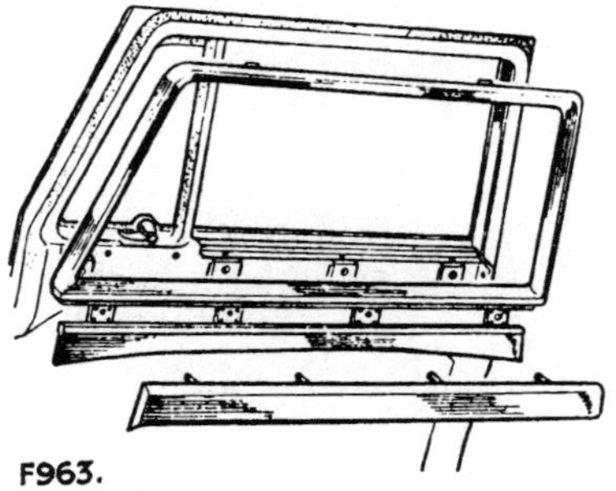

F963.

Removing crash-rail and window surround

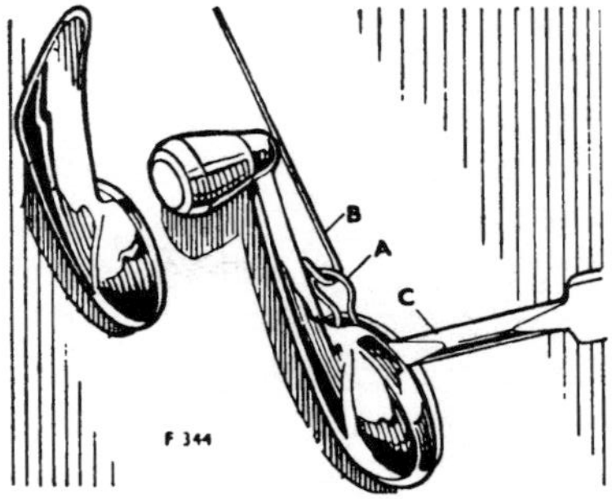

Removing door handles
A—Retaining spring clip   B—Wire hook
C—Screwdriver

4. Remove the door handles, using a piece of hooked wire, as illustrated.

Early models

5. Raise the armrest as far as possible and remove the two mounting bolts. Lift off the armrest and mounting bracket.

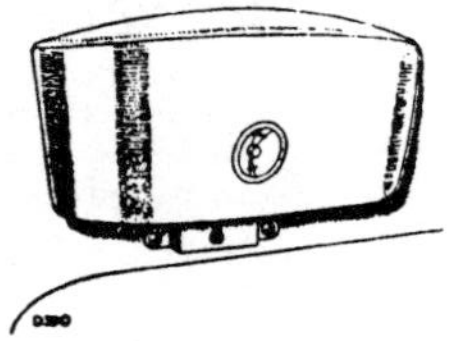

Location of armrest bolts, early models

Late models

Prise out the two plastic retainers from the bottom of the armrest. The armrest can now be removed from its mounting plate and the mounting plate bolts removed. Note the position of the spacing washers.

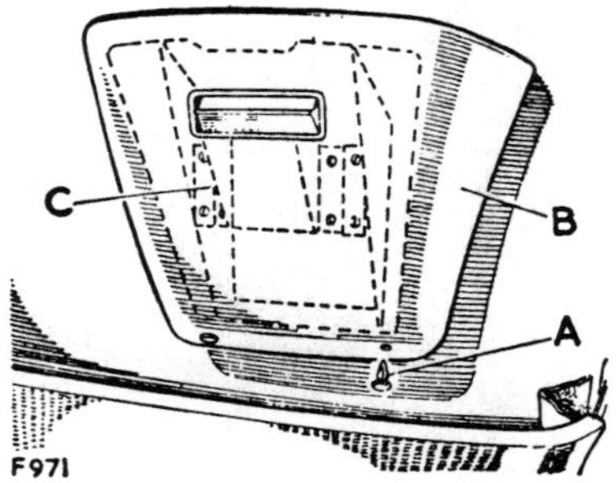

F971

Removing front door armrest, latest type
A—Retainer   B—Armrest   C—Mounting bracket

6. Using a screwdriver as a lever, carefully prise off the trimmed door casing, which is secured by spring clips. Retain the plastic sheet.

Operation U-23—*continued*

7. Replace the window handle loosely and wind down the glass as far as possible.

8. Remove the small drive screws which locate the channel for the glass to the window frame.

9. If the main window glass only is to be replaced, it is not necessary to remove the vent window.

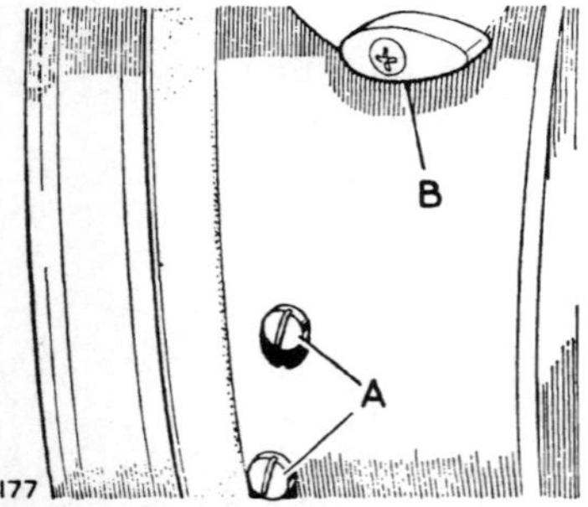

G177

Location of lower window channel fixing screws Mk I and Mk IA models

A—Fixing screws B—Door lock

10. Remove the screws retaining the lower end of the glass channel to the door. (Mk II models have only one screw.) Retain the shims for reassembly.

11. Use a screwdriver to prise the channel downwards from the frame at the top of the door. Twist the channel slightly to clear the frame, and pull the channel upwards and away from the door.

12. Wind the glass upwards and ease the glass away from the frame; tilting the glass as necessary to release the winder mechanism.

13. If necessary remove the vent window assembly completely. This is secured around the window frame with drive screws and by a screw to the door at the lower end of the main glass channel. Tilt the assembly to clear the frame.

14. Remove the vent glass from the frame:

    (a) Remove the split pin, plain washer, spring washer and stop plate from the lower pivot.

    (b) Remove the lower pivot plate secured by two nuts and spring washers.

    (c) Remove the two screws retaining the top pivot bracket to the frame and take out the vent glass.

Vent and door glasses, to refit

1. Reverse removal procedure.

Rear door glass and channels, to remove and refit—Operation U-24

Saloon models

Workshop hand tools:
Spanner sizes: $\frac{5}{16}$ in. AF, $\frac{7}{16}$ in. AF
Screwdrivers, small and medium Long-nosed pliers

Glass and channels, remove

1. Insert a screwdriver or a suitable lever between the door casing and crash-rail. Remove the padded crash-rail, secured by spring clips.
2. Withdraw the wooden window surround, secured by drive screws at the bottom and by two lugs at the top.

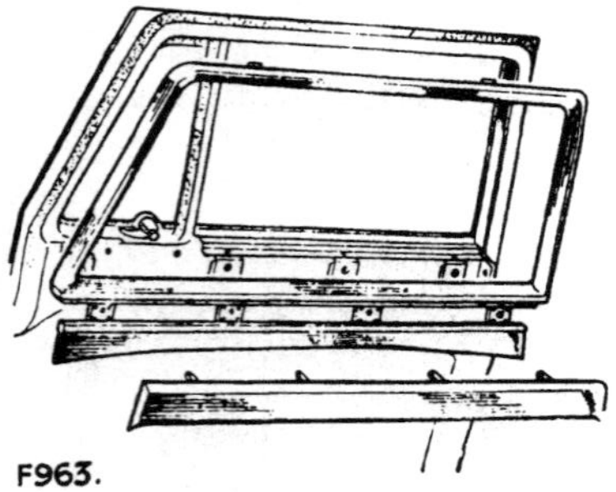

F963.

Removing crash-rail and window surround

3. Remove the draught strip from the inside sill, secured by drive screws.
4. Remove the door handles, using a piece of hooked wire, as illustrated.

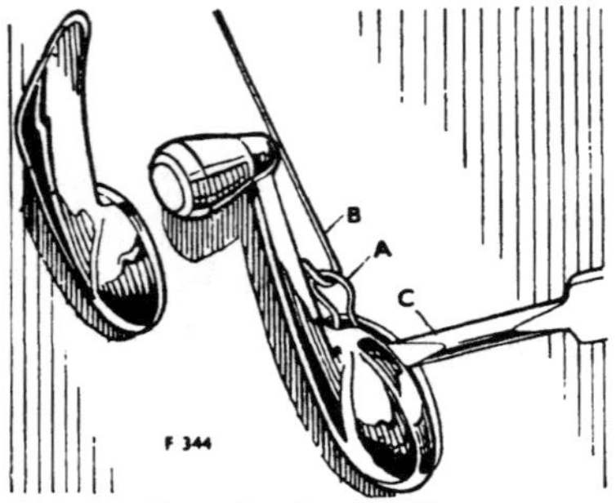

F 344

Removing door handles

A—Retaining spring clip B—Wire hook
C—Screwdriver

Item 5. Models Mk I and Mk IA

5. Remove the small cap, cup washer and drive screw fixing the rear door pull escutcheon.

6. Using a screwdriver as a lever carefully prise off the trimmed door casing which is secured by spring clips.

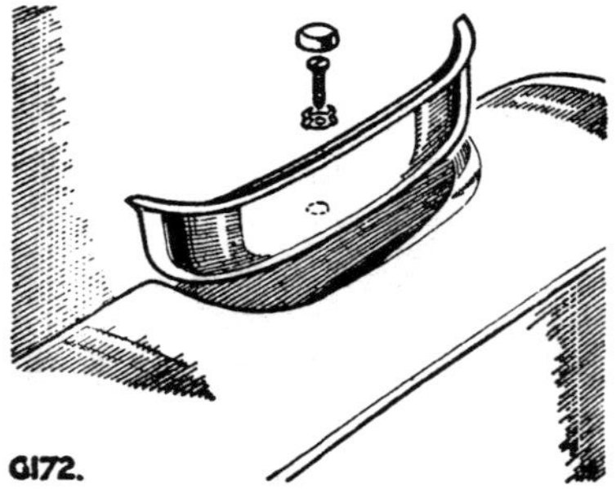

G172.

Removing rear door pull escutcheon

7. Remove the small drive screws securing the glass channel to the window frame and the fixings securing the lower ends of the channel to the door.
8. Open the door as wide as possible. Carefully prise up the end of the waist rail moulding with a suitable lever. Remove the moulding.
9. Wind the window fully down by replacing the winding handle loosely. Use a screwdriver to carefully prise the top edge of the glass channel down from the frame. Note that the channel is in two halves; the half away from the hinges should be removed first.
10. Slightly twist the channel and pull it upwards and away.
11. Remove the channel from the other side.
12. Remove the four screws and washers securing the window winder mechanism to the door.
13. Lift the glass, complete with winder mechanism, as high as possible and tilt to clear the frame. Remove the two spring clips and washers securing the glass to the winder mechanism and lift out the glass.

Glass and channels, to refit

1. Reverse removal procedure.
2. Renew the spring clips and leather washers.

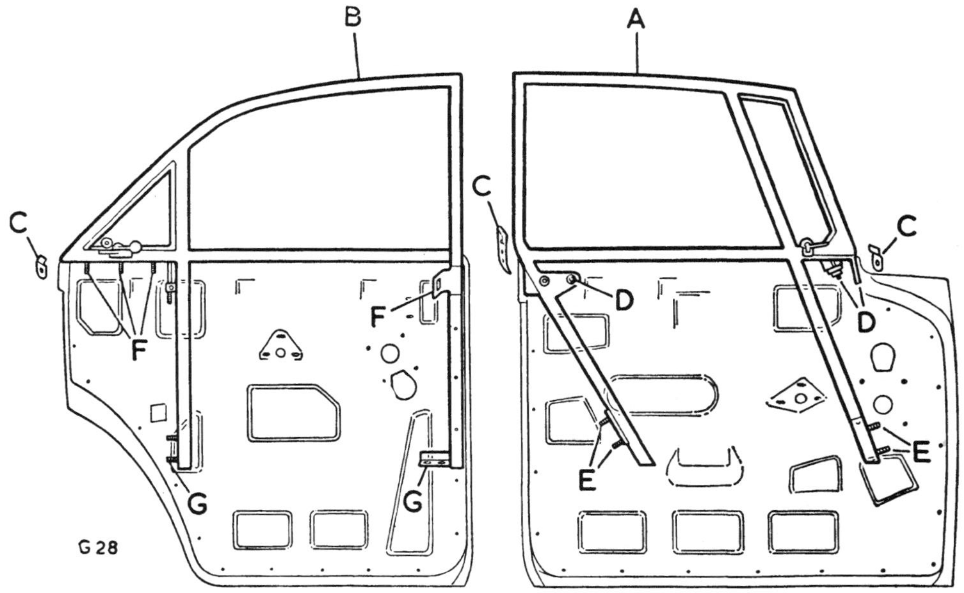

Front and rear door glass frame fixings, coupé models, LH-side illustrated

A—Front door frame
B—Rear door frame
C—End finishers
D—Upper fixings to front door
E—Lower fixings to front door
F—Upper fixings to rear door
G—Lower fixings to rear door

Front door glasses and frames, to remove and refit—Operation U-25

Coupé models

Workshop hand tools:
Spanner sizes: $\frac{5}{16}$ in. AF, $\frac{7}{16}$ in. AF
Screwdriver, medium

When it is required to replace a vent glass **only, it** is first necessary to remove the door glass as instructed below.

Vent and door glasses, to remove

1. Remove the door handles, using a piece of hooked wire, as illustrated.

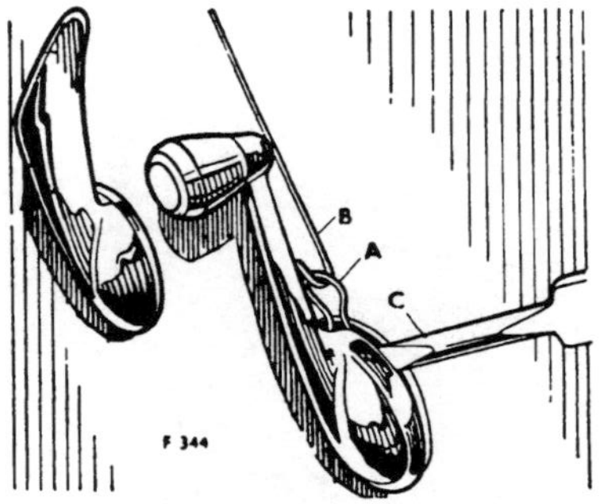

Removing door handles

A—Retaining spring clip B—Wire hook
C—Screwdriver

2. Remove the door lock push-button.
3. Prise out the two plastic retainers from the bottom of the armrest and take off the armrest. Remove the bolts from the armrest mounting bracket, noting the number and position of the spacing washers used.
4. Carefully take off trimmed door casing by using a suitable lever inserted between the door and the trim. The trim is retained by spring clips.
5. Remove the wooden door capping secured by drive screws and the angle support from the window sill, secured by set bolts and washers.

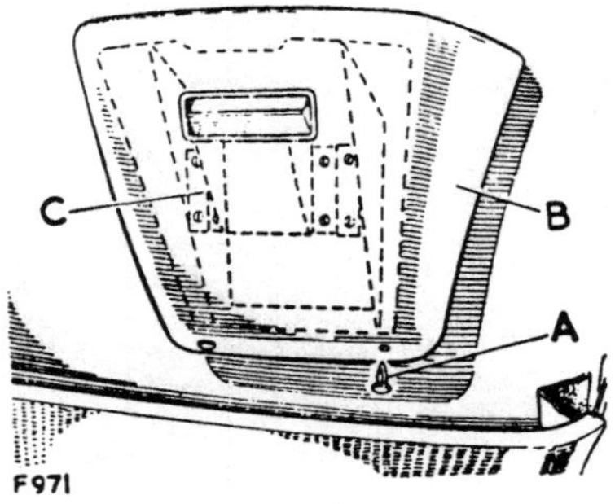

Removing front door armrests

A—Plastic retainer B—Armrest cover
C—Mounting bracket

6. Take off the polished end finisher retained by three drive screws.
7. Disconnect the window regulator mechanism from the glass and remove the mechanism. The regulator and pivot bracket are secured by six set screws, plain and shake-proof washers to the door.
8. Remove the bolts fixing the window frame assembly to the door and remove the frame and glass complete. Note the position and number of shims used and retain for reassembly.
9. If necessary remove the vent window assembly completely. Remove the locknut, plain washer, spring and locating bush from the lower pivot. Drive out the vent window pivot pin.
10. Remove the top pivot secured by two screws and lift out the vent window.

Vent and door glasses, to refit

1. Reverse removal procedure.

Rear door glasses and frames, to remove and refit—Operation U-26

Coupé models

Workshop hand tools:
Spanner sizes: $\frac{5}{16}$ in. AF, $\frac{7}{16}$ in. AF, $\frac{1}{2}$ in. AF
Screwdriver, medium Long-nosed pliers

Vent and door glasses, to remove

1. Remove the door handles, using a piece of hooked wire, as illustrated.

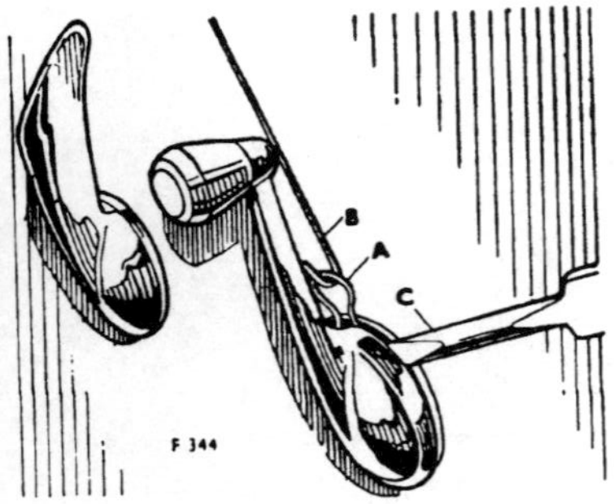

Removing door handles

A—Retaining spring clip B—Wire hook
C—Screwdriver

2. Remove the door sill push-button.

3. Carefully remove the trimmed door casing complete with the armrest, by using a suitable lever inserted between the door and the trim. The trim is retained by spring clips. Retain the plastic sheet for reassembly.

4. Remove the wooden door capping, secured by drive screws and the angle support from the window sill, secured by four set bolts and washers.

5. If it is necessary to replace the vent glass only, this can now be done without removing the whole of the window frame.
   (a) Disconnect the catch from the glass.
   (b) Through the aperture in the door, remove the grub screw from the lower vent pivot and unscrew the pivot.
   (c) Remove the upper pivot bracket secured to the frame by two screws. The glass can now be lifted out.

6. Disconnect the window regulator arm from the glass lifting channel and remove the four set screws securing the regulator to the door.

7. Remove the bolts fixing the window frame assembly to the door and remove the frame and glass complete. Note the position and number of shims used and retain for reassembly. It is helpful to mark the positions of the mounting brackets with a scriber.

Vent and door glasses, to refit

1. Reverse removal procedure.

Window winder mechanism, to remove and refit—Operation U-27

Saloon models

Workshop hand tools:
Screwdrivers, small and medium

Front winder mechanism, remove. Mk I

1. Where stainless steel frames are fitted, pull away rubber draught excluder around the outer edge of the door, remove the drive screws securing finisher and lift out stainless steel finisher.

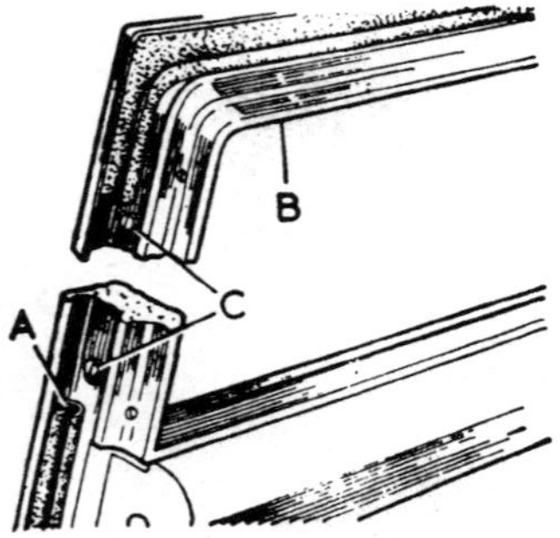

Location of finisher drive screws

A—Draught excluder B—Frame
C—Fixing screws

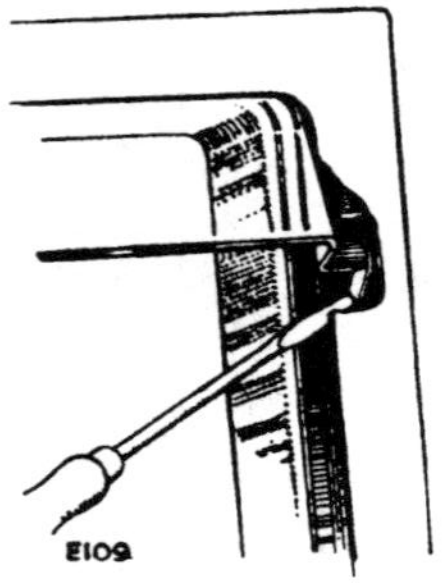

Location of louvre securing tags

2. With a screwdriver ease down both tags securing window louvre and lift out louvre.

3. Remove the drive screws securing the inner window weather strip. Lift off weather strip.

4. Remove front door glasses and channels. Operation U-23.

5. Remove the set screws, securing the winder mechanism to door and lift out through large aperture in panel.

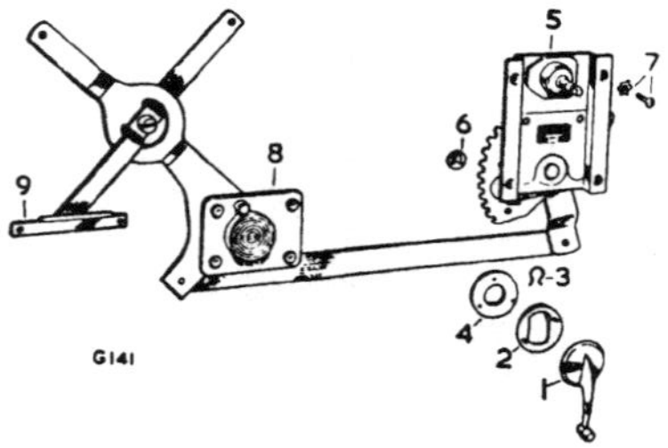

Front window winder mechanism Mk I, LH illustrated

1—Handle	6—Stud retainer
2—Escutcheon	7—Shake-proof washer
3—Spring clip	8—Spring plate
4—Wearing plate	9—Slide
5—Window regulator	

Front winder mechanism, refit

1. Loosely fit the winder mechanism to the door.

2. Turn the winder to the half-way position, and refit the glass to winder slide.

3. Refit the window channels to door.

4. Check the operation of winder mechanism, ensuring free movement of glass in the channels. Fully tighten winder mechanism to door.

5. Refit the trim panel.

Front winder mechanism, remove. Mk IA and Mk II

1. Remove front door glass and channels. Operation U-23.

Operation U-27—*continued*

2. Remove the set screws, securing the winder mechanism to door, and lift out through large aperture in panel.

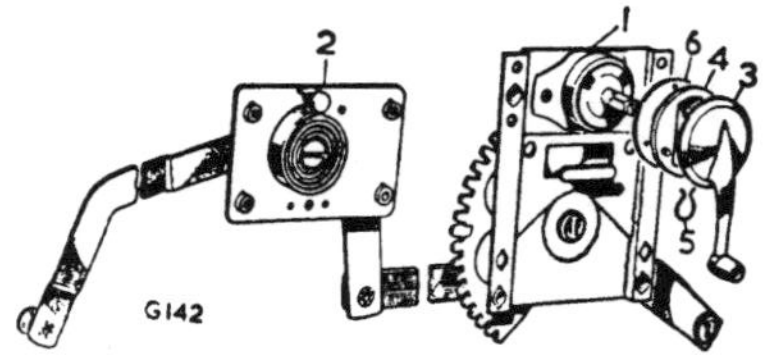

Front window winder mechanism, Mk IA and Mk II, LH illustrated

1—Regulator
2—Spring plate
3—Handle
4—Escutcheon
5—Spring clip
6—Wearing plate

Front winder mechanism, refit

1. Loosely fit the winder mechanism to the door.
2. Turn the winder to the half-way position, and refit the glass to winder slide.
3. Refit the window channels to door.
4. Check operation of winder mechanism, ensuring free movement of glass in channels. Fully tighten winder mechanism to door.
5. Refit the trim panel.

Rear winder mechanism, remove. Mk I, Mk IA and Mk II

1. Remove rear door glass and channels. Operation U-24.
2. Remove the set screws securing the winder mechanism to door and lift out through the large aperture in panel.

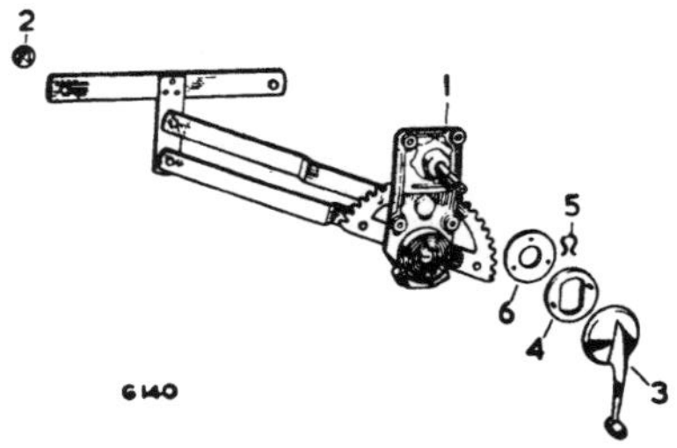

Rear window winder mechanism, Mk I, Mk IA and Mk II, LH illustrated

1—Window regulator
2—Stud retainer
3—Handle
4—Escutcheon
5—Spring clip
6—Wearing plate

Rear winder mechanism, refit

1. Loosely fit the winder mechanism to the door.
2. Turn the winder to the half-way position and refit the glass to winder slide.
3. Refit the window channels to door.
4. Check operation of winder mechanism, ensuring free movement of glass in channels. Fully tighten winder mechanism to door
5. Refit the trim panel.

Window winder mechanism, to remove and refit—Operation U-28

Coupé models

Workshop hand tools:
Screwdrivers, small and medium

Front winder mechanism, remove

1. Remove front door glass and frames. Operation U-25.
2. Remove the set screws, securing the winder mechanism to door, and lift out through large aperture in panel.

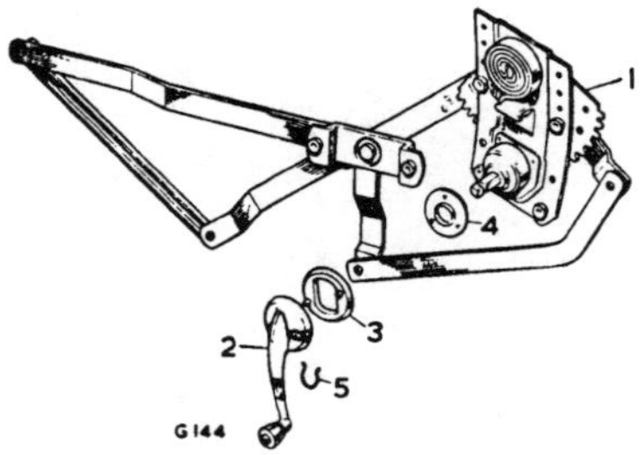

Front window winder mechanism, LH illustrated

1—Window regulator
2—Handle
3—Escutcheon
4—Wearing plate
5—Spring clip

Front winder mechanism, refit

1. Loosely fit the winder mechanism to the door.
2. Turn the winder to the half-way position and refit the glass to winder slide.
3. Refit the window frames to door. Operation U-25.
4. Check operation of winder mechanism, ensuring free movement of glass in the frames. Fully tighten winder mechanism to door.
5. Refit the trim panel.

Rear winder mechanism, remove

1. Remove rear door glass and frame. Operation U-26.
2. Remove the set screws, securing the winder mechanism to door, and lift out through large aperture in panel.

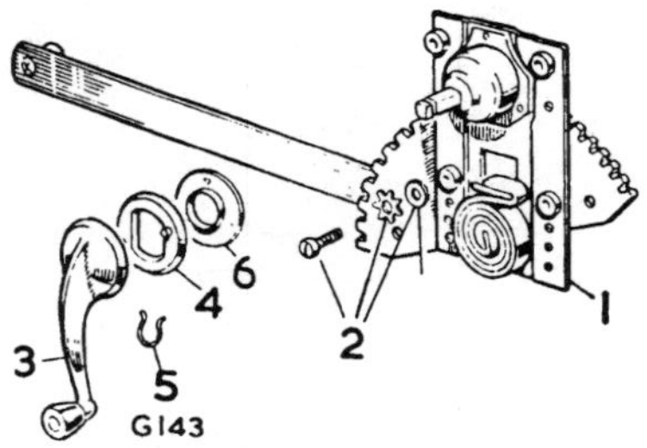

Rear window winder mechanism, LH illustrated

1—Window regulator
2—Fixings
3—Handle
4—Escutcheon
5—Spring clip
6—Wearing plate

Rear winder mechanism, refit

1. Loosely fit the winder mechanism to the door.
2. Turn the winder to the half-way position and refit the glass to winder slide.
3. Refit the window frame to door. Operation U-26.
4. Check operation of winder mechanism, ensuring free movement of glass in the frames. Fully tighten winder mechanism to door.
5. Refit the trim panel

Bench type front seat, to remove and refit (Mk I, Mk IA and Mk II models)—Operation U-29

Workshop hand tools:

Spanner sizes: $\frac{5}{16}$ in. AF, $\frac{7}{16}$ in. AF, $\frac{1}{2}$ in. AF

Seat, remove

1. Remove the front seat cushion.
2. Disconnect the seat adjustment cables at the ferrules on the seat frame.

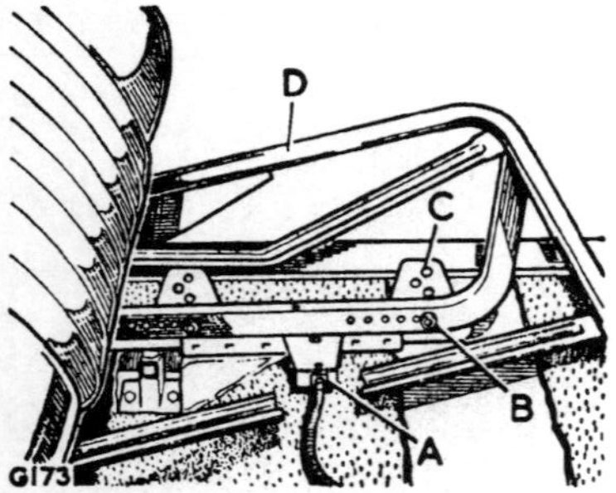

Seat adjustment and fixings, bench type illustrated

A—Seat adjustment cable ferrule
B—Mounting bolts
C—Mounting bracket with adjustment holes
D—Seat frame

3. Remove the four nuts, bolts and washers from the seat runner mounting brackets.
4. Remove seat.
5. Where necessary remove the seat runners and slides from the body floor.

Seat, refit and adjust

1. Align the seat with the mounting in the runner.
2. Insert the four mounting bolts so that the rake and height of the seat is in the desired position.
3. Push the cable through the anchor hole and secure with cable ferrule and adjust as necessary.
4. The seat can be moved forwards or backwards by moving the locking control knob towards right-hand side of the car.
5. To adjust the height or inclination of the seat, remove bolts securing the seat frame supports to the slides; align the bolt holes to suit requirements and refit the bolts.

Bucket type front seat, to remove and refit (Mk I, Mk IA and Mk II models)—Operation U-30

Workshop hand tools:

Spanner sizes: $\frac{5}{16}$ in. AF, $\frac{7}{16}$ in. AF, $\frac{1}{2}$ in. AF

Models Mk I and Mk IA. Seat, remove

1. Remove the seat cushion.
2. Disconnect the seat adjustment cable from the seat slide mechanism.
3. Remove the seat mounting bolts from the seat runners and remove the seat.

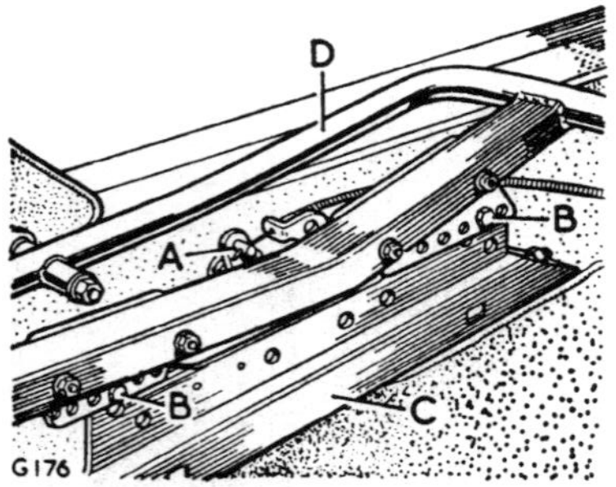

Seat adjustment and fixings

A—Seat adjustment cable
B—Mounting bolts
C—Mounting bracket with adjustment holes
D—Seat frame

Models Mk II. Seat, remove

4. Remove the front seat cushion.
5. Disconnect the seat adjustment cable at the ferrule on the seat frame.
6. Release the ferrule from the seat adjuster cable controls.
7. Remove the four nuts, bolts and washers from the seat adjuster mounting brackets.
8. Remove seat.
9. Where necessary remove the seat runners and slides from the body floor.

Seat, refit and adjust

1. Align the seat with the mounting in the runner.
2. Insert the four mounting bolts so that the rake and height of the seat is in the desired position.

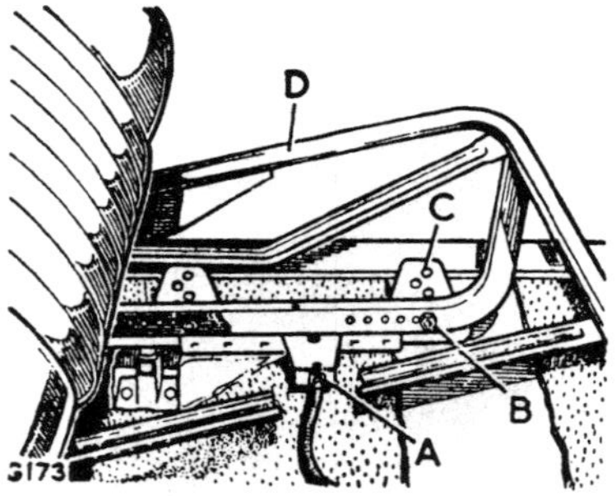

Seat adjustment and fixings, bucket type illustrated

A—Seat adjustment cable ferrule
B—Mounting bolts
C—Mounting bracket with adjustment holes
D—Seat frame

3. Push the cable through anchor hole and secure with cable ferrule and adjust as necessary.
4. Fit front seat cushion.
5. The seat can be moved forwards or backwards by moving the locking control knob towards right-hand side of the car.
6. To adjust the height or inclination of the seat, remove bolts securing the seat frame supports to the slides; align the bolt holes to suit requirements and refit the bolts.
7. The angle of the backrest squab in relation to the seat cushion can also be altered by adjustment of the four knurled nuts in the rearmost lower corner of the seat frames.

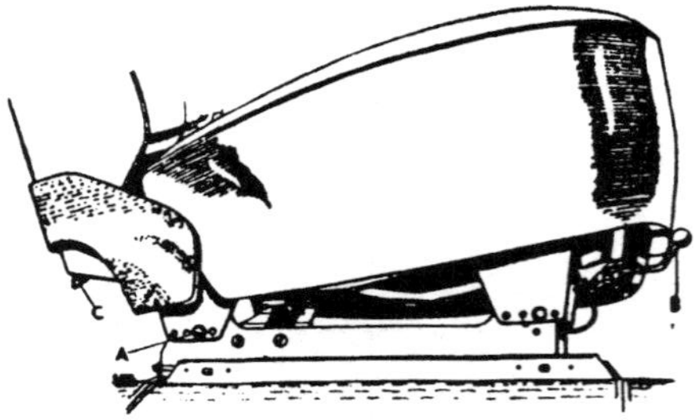

Bucket seat squab adjustment

A—Adjusting bolts B—Operating handle
C—Squab inclination adjuster

Fully adjustable type bucket seats, to remove and refit (Mk IA and Mk II models)—Operation U-31

Workshop hand tools:

Spanner sizes: $\frac{5}{16}$ in. AF, $\frac{7}{16}$ in. AF, $\frac{1}{2}$ in. AF

Seat, to remove

1. Remove the front seat cushion.

2. Disconnect the seat adjustment cables at the ferrule on the seat frame.

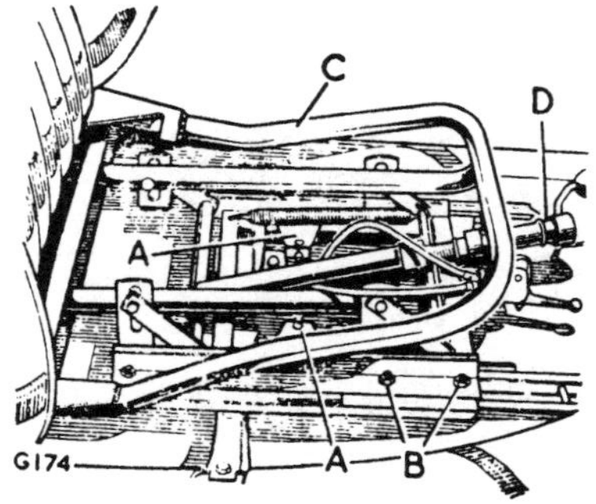

G174

Seat adjustment and fixings, fully adjustable type

A—Seat adjustment cable
B—Nuts, securing seat to slide
C—Seat frame assembly
D—Seat adjuster

3. Remove the seat from the seat slides, secured by six nuts. Lift out the seat.

4. Where necessary remove the seat runners and slides from the body floor.

Seat, to refit

1. Reverse removal procedure.

Seat, to adjust

2. The seat can be moved forwards or backwards by pulling the adjustment handle (on inboard side of seat) upwards.

3. To adjust the seat height, a winding handle is provided; adjust to suit requirements.

4. To alter the angle of the backrest squab in relation to the seat cushion; sit in the seat and operate the lever on the outboard side of the seat, pull lever upwards and release when desired angle is obtained.

5. If the backlash in the seat back mechanism becomes excessive, the squab may, as a result of this, drop back under the weight of the body. To restore the normal action of the mechanism proceed as follows:

(a) Sit sideways on seat cushion to steady seat frame, thus avoiding a false impression of backlash the seat movement would give.

To facilitate checking and subsequent adjustment, the centre armrest should be folded down.

Check amount of backlash first at inner hinge by moving squab backwards and forwards. The backlash can be felt with the finger at point A on the mounted part of the hinge.

(b) Slacken locknut B and turn bolt C clockwise until the backlash has been almost taken up.

(c) Lock the adjusting bolt by means of the locknut.

(d) Repeat the above operations for the outer hinge.

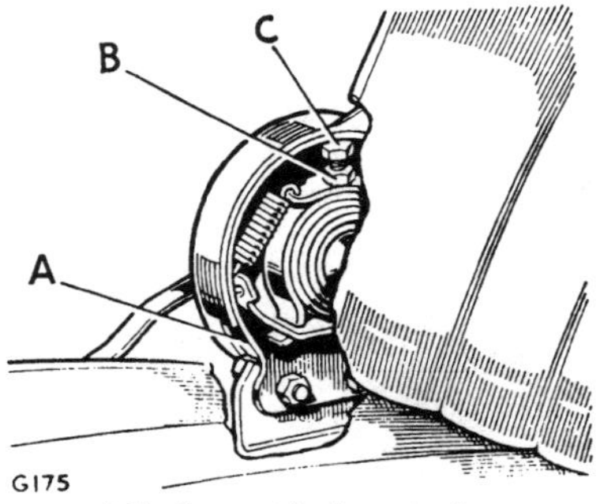

G175

Adjusting seat back mechanism

A—Check backlash at this point
B—Locknut for adjusting bolt
C—Adjusting bolt

Front seats, to remove and refit (Mk III models)—Operation U-32

Workshop hand tools:

Spanner size: $\frac{1}{2}$ in. AF

Seats and runners, remove

1. Slide the seat fully forward to gain access to the rear mountings, and fully rearward to gain access to the front mountings. Remove the four mounting bolts from each seat and withdraw the seat complete with its runners.

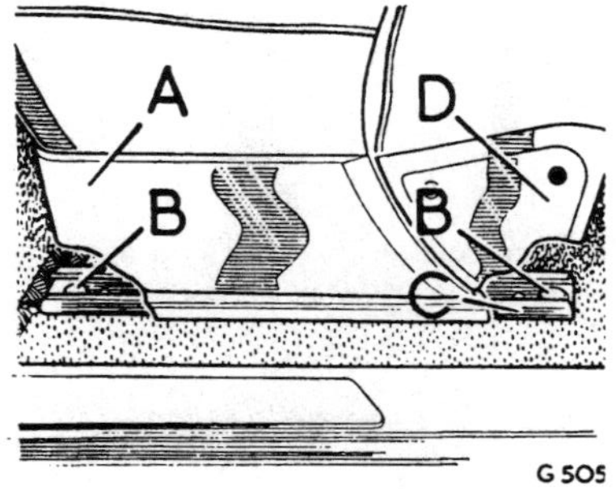

G 505

Front seat mountings

A—Front seat
B—Mounting bolts
C—Seat runner
D—Finisher for seat

Seats and runners, refit

1. Reverse removal procedure.

Front seat back finisher, to remove and refit (Mk III models)—Operation U-33

Workshop hand tools:
Screwdriver, Phillips

Back finisher, remove

1. Slide the front seats into a position from where the screws retaining the polished cover plates can be removed. Remove both plates.

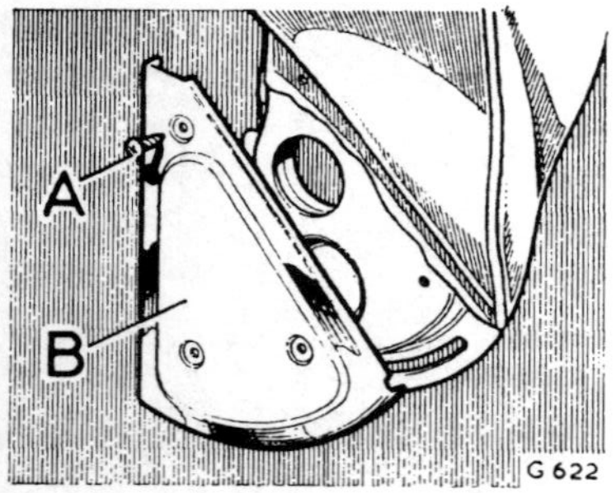

Front seat cover plates

A—Cover plate fixing screws B—Cover plates

2. Pull the bottom of the seat back finisher outwards to release the spring clips. Slide the finisher upwards to disengage the upper fixings.

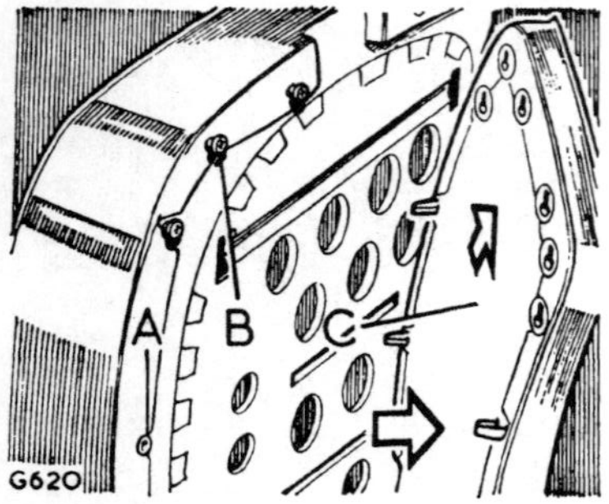

Front seat back finisher removal

A—Lower fixing clips B—Upper fixings
C—Back finisher

Back finisher, refit

1. Reverse removal procedure.

Front seat (Mk III models), to dismantle and rebuild—Operation U-34

Workshop hand tools:
Spanner size: $\frac{9}{16}$ in. AF Hammer, light Plastic-faced mallet Screwdriver, small Screwdriver, Phillips

Front seat, dismantle

1. Remove the Phillips drive screws securing the left-hand and right-hand polished metal covers.
2. Remove the screw securing the torsion bar retainer and drift the torsion bar out about 1 in. (25 mm) towards the lever to release spring tension. Then withdraw the bar.

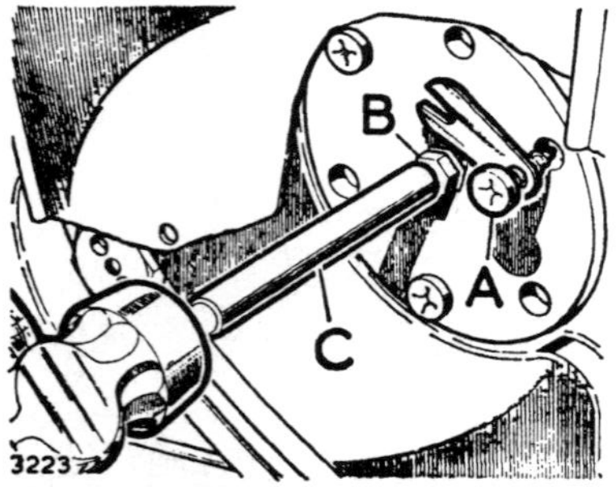

Removing the seat torsion bar

A—Torsion bar retainer and securing screw
B—Torsion bar
C—Drift

3. Remove the two remaining screws securing the adjuster plate and remove, then lever the plate out.
4. Remove the spring ring from the loose bearing on squab frame; remove bearing. This operation must be carried out to prevent spreading of squab frame when dismantling.
5. Remove the long locking screw from the locking pad opposite lever side, and the short locking screw from lever side.
6. Using a spanner, unscrew the outer locking pad, lever side, from the brake rod, then withdraw the rod complete with the other locking pad from opposite lever side.
7. The seat squab may now be eased off the seat frame.
8. Withdraw the compression tube complete with locking lever. If necessary unscrew lever. Unscrew the coarse adjustment locking pad, lever side, and the fine adjustment locking pad from the compression tube.
9. Examine all parts for wear and renew as necessary.

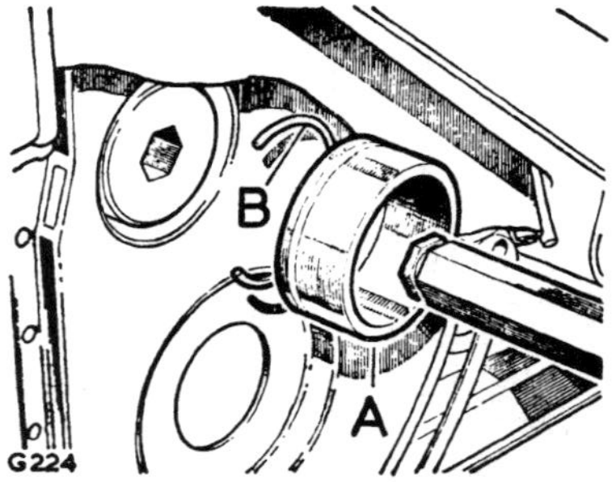

Removing the torsion bar spigot bush

A—Spigot bush B—Retaining clip

10. If necessary remove the bearing, secured by one drive screw, from opposite side of the lever.

Front seat, rebuild

1. Smear the locking lever with grease, then screw on to the compression tube as far as possible, mark tube and lever boss, then unscrew lever approximately one complete turn to arrive at a dimension of $18\frac{11}{16}$ in. (475 mm) as illustrated.
2. Smear with grease, screw the coarse adjustment locking pad into the lever, leaving the pad $\frac{3}{32}$ in. (2,5 mm) proud of lever boss.

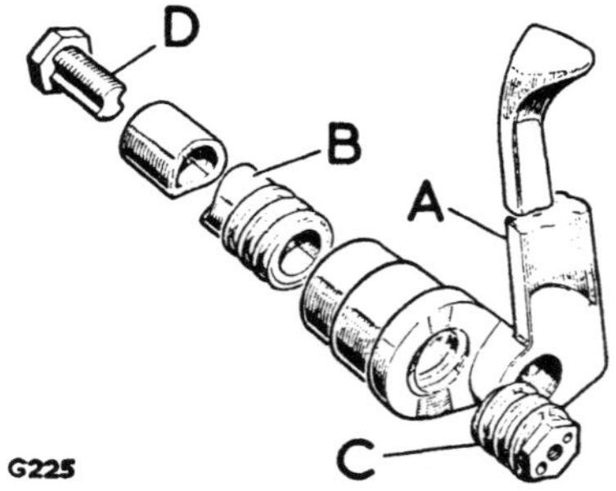

Compression tube details

A—Seat locking lever C—Coarse adjustment brake pad
B—Compression tube D—Fine adjustment brake pad

Operation U-34—*continued*

3. Smear the thread of the fine adjustment locking pad with grease, then screw it into the compression tube, ensuring that previous adjustments are not disturbed. Adjust as necessary to inside width of squab frame, at the same time ensuring that the locking pad screw holes align in the compression tube.

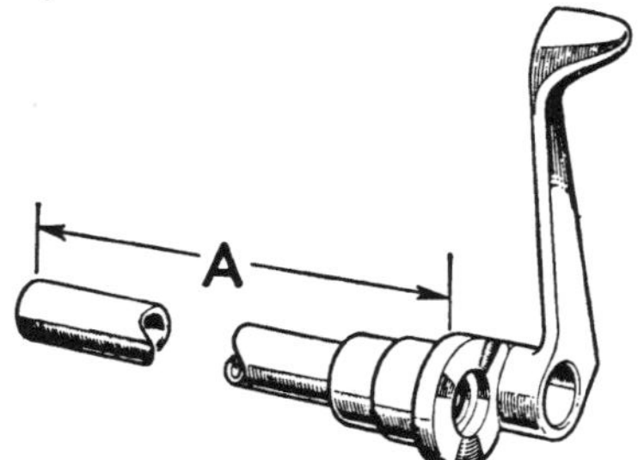

Seat compression tube dimensions

A—Adjust tube to obtain a dimension of 18$\frac{11}{16}$ in. (475 mm)

4. If previously removed the bearing for compression tube should be smeared with grease on the inner diameter and refitted to the seat cushion frame.

5. Lightly smear boss of lever and bearing end of tubes with grease. Insert the lever and compression tube complete through the seat frame in such a way that the lever is at right-angles to seat, that is, vertical, also ensure that the lever is not turned on the compression tube.

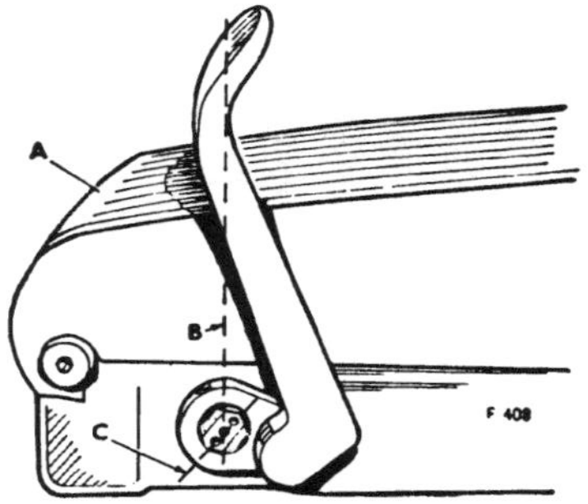

Fitting seat to squab

A—Seat cushion
B—Position of lever to be as shown
C—Position of seat squab fixing bolts

6. Offer the seat squab to the seat frame and locate torsion bar spigot in squab frame. While the squab is being located ensure that fine adjuster is not disturbed.

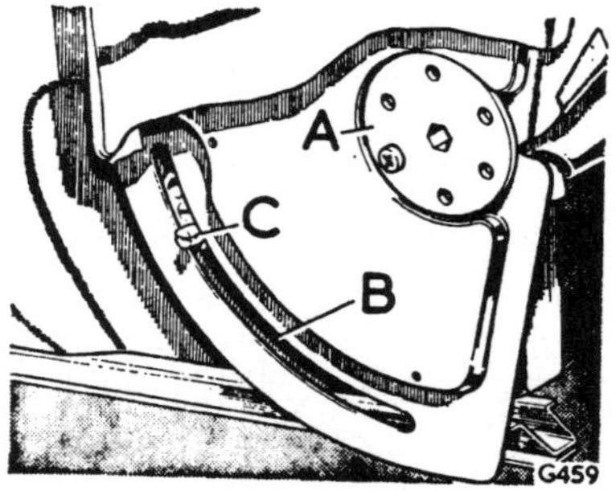

Squab frame location

A—Torsion bar adjuster B—Slot in squab frame
C—Locking screw

7. Smear adjuster for torsion bar with grease, then insert it into the squab and secure with one screw, this will locate the frames whilst the remainder of the parts are assembled.

8. Align the coarse and fine adjustment locking pads with the slot in squab frame and insert the locking screws in the lower holes. The short locking screw is always fitted in the lever side.

9. Smear the long locking rod with grease, screw it into an outer locking pad, so that it is flush with pad outer face.

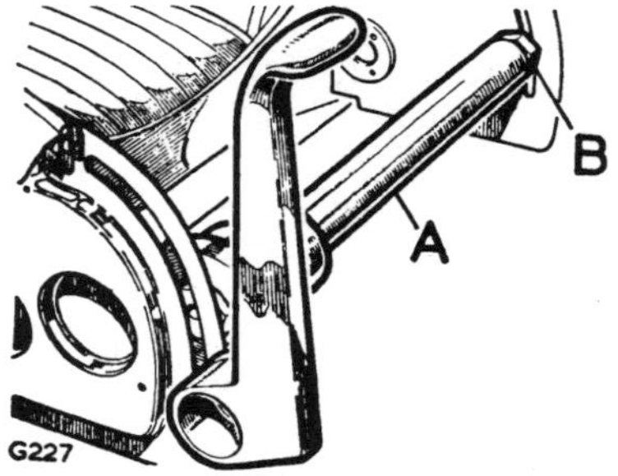

Adjusting the compression tube to the squab

A—Compression tube offered to squab frame
B—Adjust pad as necessary to squab

Operation U-34—*continued*

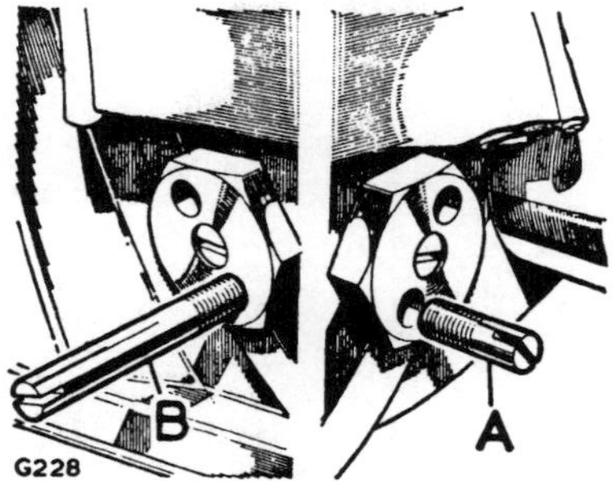

Fitting locking screws

A—Short locking screw B—Long locking screw

10. Insert locking rod and pad through squab and seat from the opposite side to the lever.

11. Insert rod and locking pad, then locate the outer locking pad over the locating screw previously fitted.

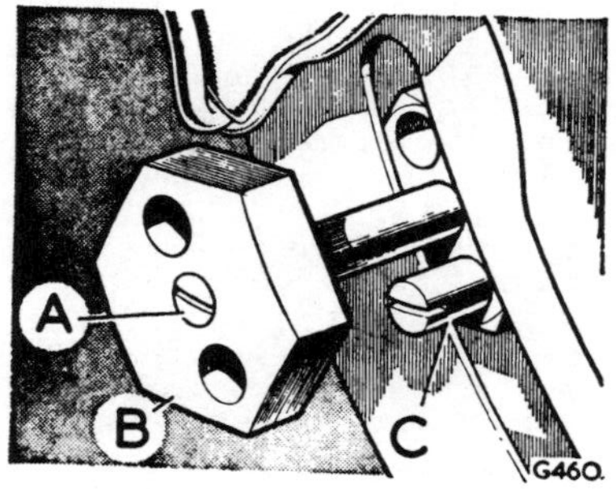

Fitting locking rod and outer pad

A—Locking rod B—Locking pad
C—Locking screw

12. Remove the short locking screw from lever side.

13. Screw the outer locking pad, lever side, right on to the locking rod. Tighten until the holes align, ensure that lever remains upright. Then retain pad in position with short locking screw.

14. Smear with grease the torsion bar spigot bush. Then insert with the clip groove innermost and fit the clip.

Fitting squab pivot bearing

A—Squab pivot bearing C—Locking screw
B—Spring clip D—Locking pad

Check operation of seat lock as follows:

15. Move lever fully rearwards and recline seat, the action should be fairly smooth. Move lever to the locked position where it should be just above the seat trim, ensure that the seat squab can not be moved. Repeat the above check in the fully upright position. If necessary remove short locking screw and adjust outer locking pad to obtain free movement with lever to rear and fully locked with lever forwards.

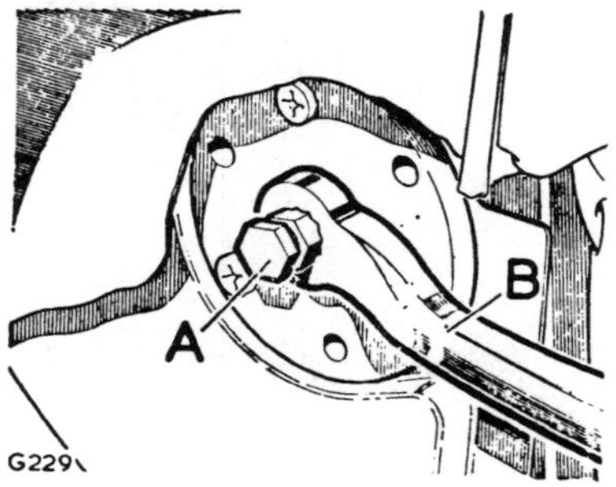

Loading the torsion bar

A—Torsion bar B—Loading spanner

Operation U-34—*continued*

Torsion bar, refit—squab in upright position

16 Remove screw previously fitted to secure torsion bar adjuster with the seat squab in the upright position, smear the torsion bar with grease and insert it, retainer groove first, from the lever side until the bar is projecting through the adjuster $\frac{3}{8}$ in. (9,5 mm).

17. Wind the torsion bar up in a clockwise direction to align the three screw holes, insert and tighten two of the screws.

18. Tap the torsion bar back far enough for the retainer plate and remaining screw to be fitted

19. Re-check operation of seat, ensuring that the seat will come upright from the reclining position without assistance.

20. Refit polished covers and drive screws.

Front seat slide mechanism (Mk III models), to adjust—Operation U-35

Workshop hand tools:
Spanner size: $\frac{5}{16}$ in. AF

Slides, adjust

1. If the seat cannot be moved forward or backwards when the lever is operated, check the adjustment of the mechanism as follows:

2. Look beneath the seat whilst the lever is being operated. Observe whether the latch is clearing the slots in each slide.

3. Slacken the two bolts in the adjustment block and shorten the rods until the lever, when operated, lifts both latches from the slots in the slides.

4. Finally tighten the bolts when the adjustment has been completed.

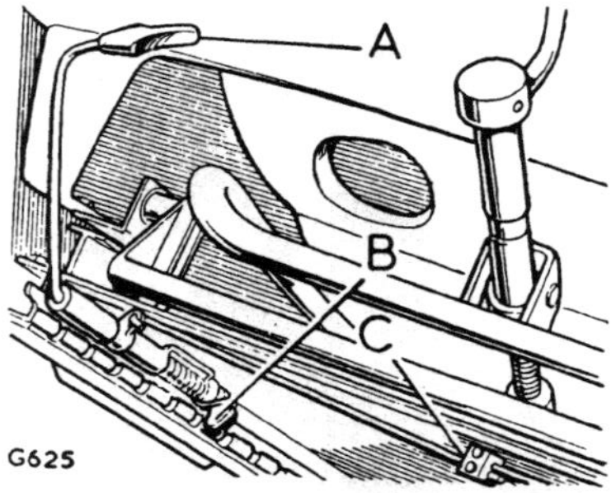

Front seat slide mechanism

A—Operating lever B—Catch for slide
C—Adjuster and rods

Front seat armrest (Mk III models), to remove and refit—Operation U-36

Workshop hand tools:
Spanner size: $\frac{7}{16}$ in. AF Screwdriver

Armrest, remove

1. Prise out the button from the escutcheon plate.
2. Carefully lever off the escutcheon plate and retaining washer.
3. Withdraw armrest from spindle.
4. Remove adjusting lever from between cam retaining plate and armrest stop.
5. Remove three bolts and withdraw cam retaining plate, armrest stop and cover plate.
6. Lift off the adjusting mechanism cover plate from the base plate spindles.
7. Remove the two countersunk screws securing the base plate to the seat squab and withdraw base plate.

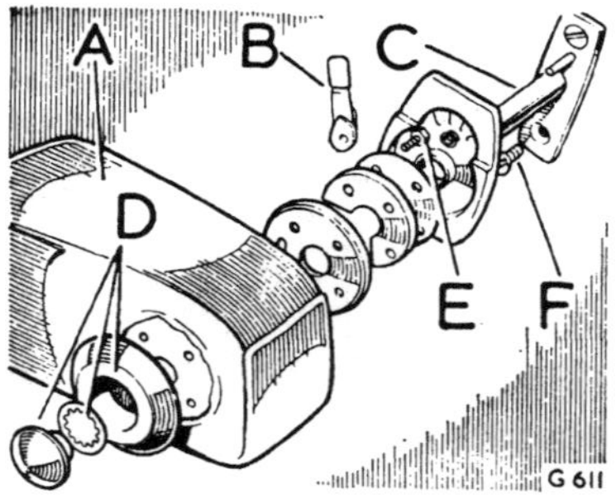

Armrest components

A—Armrest D—Cover, spring and plug
B—Lever for armrest rake E—Bolt fixing armrest
C—Base plate F—Screw fixing base plate

Operation U-36—*continued*

Armrest, refit

1. Secure base plate to squab frame with two countersunk screws. The short peg is uppermost as illustrated.
2. Locate the adjusting mechanism cover on to the spindle and peg of the base plate.
3. Assemble cover plate, armrest stop and cam retaining plate to the appropriate side of the armrest and secure with three bolts.
4. Locate cam lever assembly between the cam retaining plate and the armrest stop, with the ratchet spring facing outwards.
5. Manoeuvre the front seats to allow the armrest to be mounted.
6. Fit the armrest over the spindle and peg, taking care to ensure that the cam lever assembly is located on the peg.
7. Fit the escutcheon plate and secure the assembly with the serrated washer.
8. Press finisher plug into the end of the spindle.

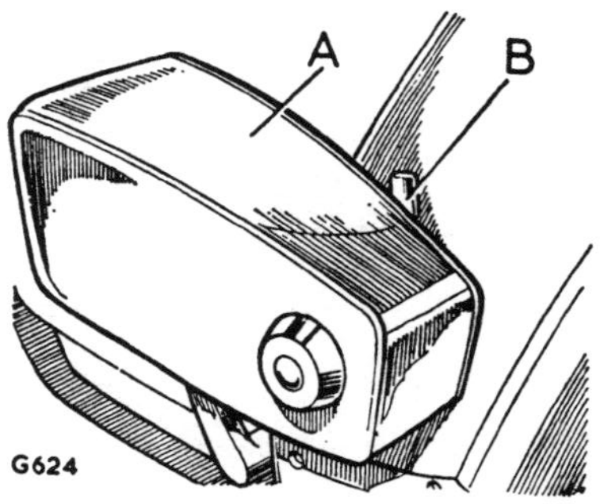

G624

Armrest in position

A—Armrest B—Adjustment lever for armrest rake

Front head rest (Mk III models), to fit—Operation U-37

Workshop hand tools:

The front head rest, which is fitted with a rear passengers' light, is adjustable up or down, pull or push into position as required, head rest held by friction on support tongue.

To adjust forward movement, pull into position; head rest will remain locked as selected. Rearward movement, which is spring-loaded, is controlled by pushing in the button at the right-hand side of the head rest.

Reading lamp on rear of head rest is controlled by push button at left-hand underside of head rest.

Front head rest, to fit

1. Remove plastic plug from top of seat back rest.
2. Insert electrical plug into socket of aperture for head rest tongue.
3. Push support tongue into position and adjust as necessary.

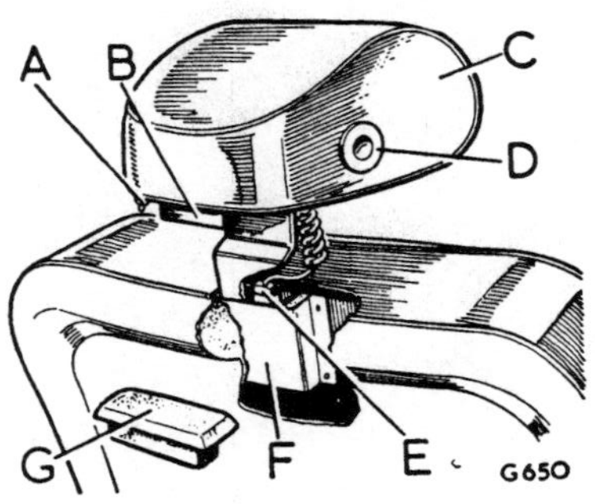

G650

Front head rest

A—Switch for rear light
B—Rear passengers' light
C—Head rest
D—Push button for fore and aft adjustment
E—Electrical plug and wire
F—Bracket for tongue
G—Plastic plug for head rest aperture

Rear seat and squab, to remove and refit—Operation U-38

Workshop hand tools:
Spanner size: $\frac{7}{16}$ in. AF
Screwdriver, medium

Seat squab and cushion, remove

1. From inside the luggage compartment remove the trim panel in front of the fuel tank, secured by drive screws. Remove the fixings securing the rear seat squab to the body panel. Lift out the squab.
2. Lift out the rear seat cushion.

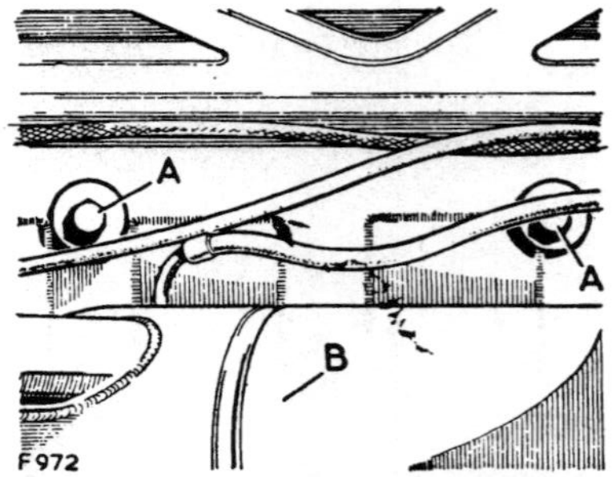

Rear seat squab fixings, as seen from inside the boot
A—Squab fixings B—Fuel tank

Seat squab and cushion, refit

1. Reverse removal procedure.

Rear head rest (Mk III models), to fit—Operation U-39

Rear head rest

1. The rear head rest is located between the back of the rear squab and parcel shelf trim, there are no fixings.

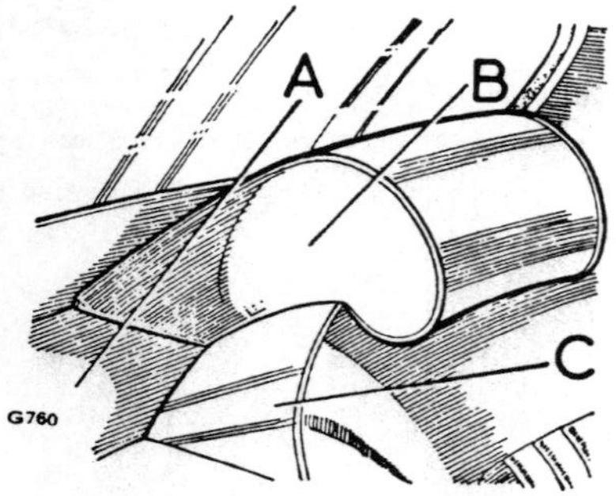

Rear head rest
A—Rear parcel shelf B—Head rest, rear C—Rear squab

Pillar pulls, to remove and refit—Operation U-40

Saloon models only

Workshop hand tools:
Screwdrivers, small and medium Screwdriver, Phillips type, small

Pillar pulls, to refit. Early models, with circular rear interior lamps, items 1 and 2

Measurement 'B' to be made first. Measurement 'A' to be drawn at right-angles to measurement 'B'.

1. Mark the roof trim with a pencil as illustrated.
2. Using a $\frac{3}{32}$ in. (2,38 mm) drill, drill lower hole first.

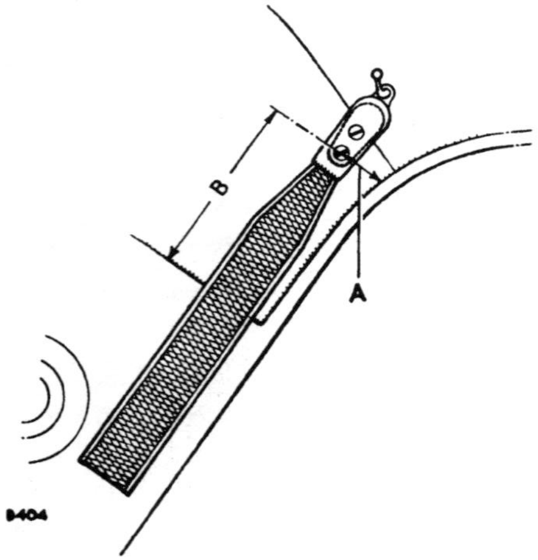

Marking out pillar pull securing points, early models
A—1¼ in (31,3 mm) B—4½ in. (113,7mm)

Late models

3. Using the illustration as a guide, the pre-drilled holes in the cant rail can be located through the trim by running the fingers over the area.
4. Secure pillar pull with a drive screw, but do not tighten fully.
5. Align the handle of the pillar pull so that it runs parallel with the door frame.
6. When this condition has been achieved, drill the second hole and secure with a drive screw. Fully tighten both fixings.

The drive screws are not screwed into the roof lining frame, but into the cant rail running along the top of the door frames.

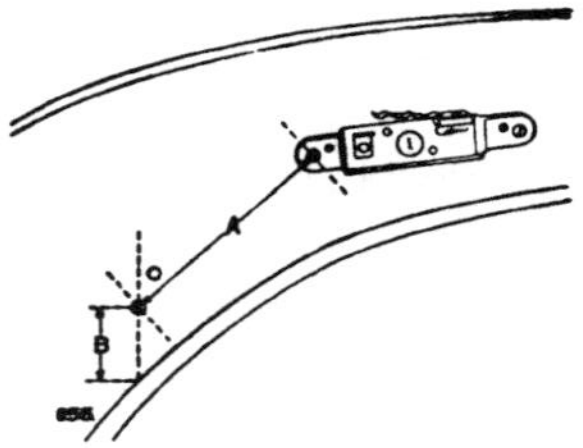

Locating pillar pull securing points, late models
A—4½ in. (114 mm) B—1¼ in. (31 mm)

Pillar pull, remove. Mk II models

1. Remove the two screws, securing the pillar pull to cant rail.

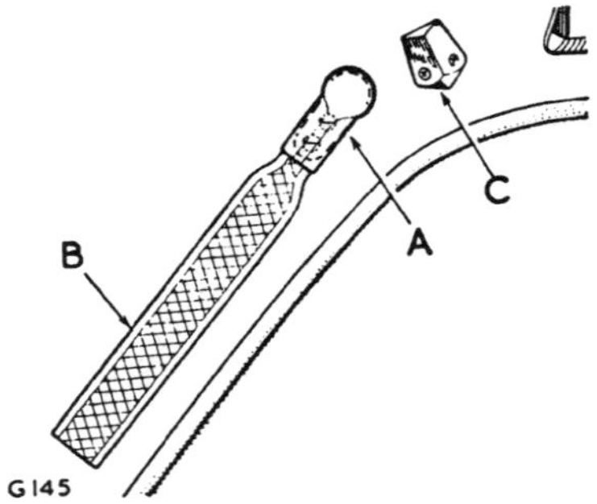

Pillar pull fixings, Mk II
A—Fixing screws B—Pillar pull C—Coat hook

Pillar pull, refit

1 Reverse removal procedure.

Gutter beading, to remove and refit—Operation U-41

Workshop hand tools:
Screwdriver, medium

Beading, remove

1. To remove the gutter beading, withdraw the drive screws on the inside rim of gutter and lift off.

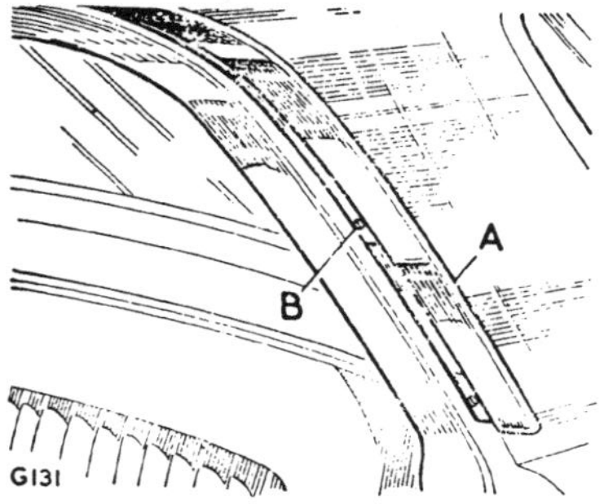

G131

Removing gutter beading

A—Gutter beading B—Fixing screws

Coupé models

2. If necessary remove the motif and texture plate, secured by drive screws.

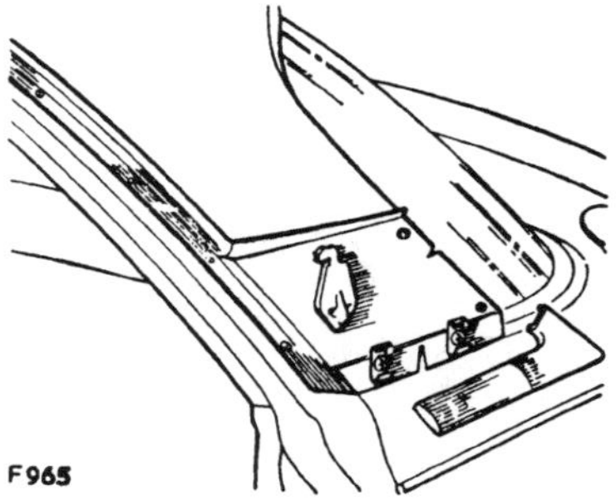

F965

Removing motif and texture plate, Coupé models

Door sill tread plates, to remove and refit—Operation U-42

Workshop hand tools:
Screwdriver, Phillips type, small

Door sill tread plates, remove

1. To remove the door sill tread plates, remove the drive screws and lift off.

Door sill tread plates, refit

1. Reverse removal procedure.

Spare wheel housing, to remove and refit—Operation U-43

Workshop hand tools:
Spanner sizes: $\frac{7}{16}$ in. AF, $\frac{1}{2}$ in. AF

Spare wheel housing, to remove

1. Lower spare wheel housing and remove spare wheel, unhook the tray from the bolt.
2. Remove two nuts, bolts and washers from each hinge, and remove spare wheel housing.
3. If necessary, remove the housing operating screw secured to the boot floor by nuts and bolts.

Spare wheel housing, to refit

1. Reverse removal procedure.

Rear cigar lighter and ashtray, to remove and refit (Mk II and Mk III coupé models) Operation U-44

Workshop hand tools:
Spanner size: $\frac{5}{16}$ in. AF

Ashtray, remove

1. Disconnect the battery.
2. Remove the cigar lighter and lift out the ashtray from the ashtray and cigar lighter holder, situated between the rear seats.

F 993

Removing rear cigar lighter and ashtray

3. Withdraw the holder, secured to its plinth by two screws and washers. Disconnect the wiring at the snap connectors.

Ashtray, refit

1. Reverse removal procedure.

Rear ashtray and pull escutcheon on door, to remove and refit (Mk III saloon models)—Operation U-45

Workshop hand tools:
Screwdriver, Phillips

Rear ashtray

1. Lever out ashtray.
2. Remove screws retaining holder.

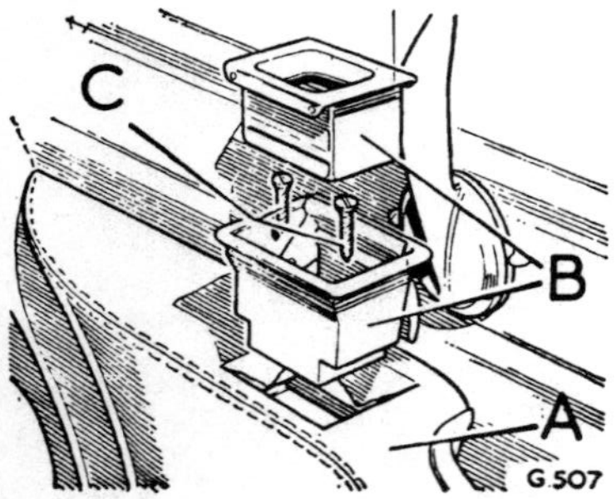

G 507

Rear ashtray on doors

A—Armrest
B—Ashtray and holder
C—Screw fixing ashtray holder

Rear door pull escutcheon

1. Remove retaining screws and lift out escutcheon.

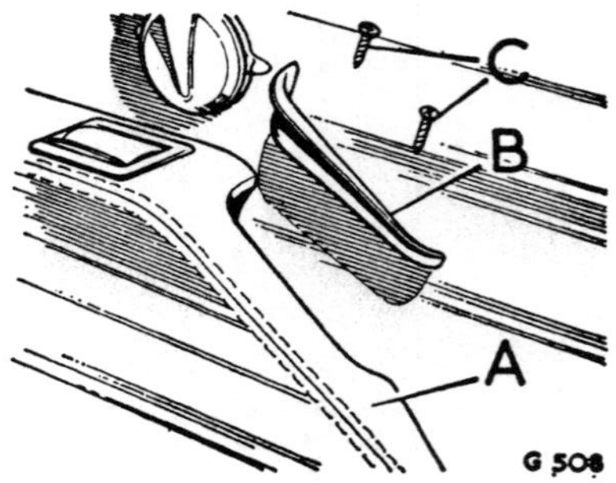

G 508

Rear door pull escutcheon

A—Armrest B—Escutcheon C—Screw fixing escutcheon

Fresh-air grille, to remove and refit—Operation U-46

Workshop hand tools:
Spanner size: $\frac{3}{8}$ in. AF, thin type
Screwdriver, small Screwdriver, Phillips type, small

Grille, remove

1. Remove the two windscreen wiper arms and blades by withdrawing wiper arm and blade from splined shaft. Do this by carefully levering the arms off the shafts.

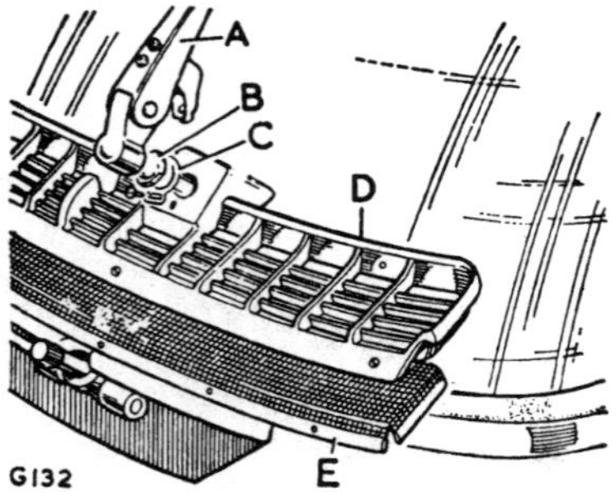

G132

Removing grille

A—Wiper arm D—Air intake grille
B—Special nut E—Filter for air intake
C—Parking ramp

2. Remove the large nuts securing the wiper wheel boxes to the air intake grille.
3. Remove the special screw securing the parking ramp to air intake grille.
4. Raise the bonnet and remove the six large drive screws from the front of the fresh-air grille, and four smaller drive screws from the back of the grille.
5. Lift out grille and filter for air intake and on early models, disconnect the windscreen washer pipes. (Early models had a two-piece grille.)
6. Remove the drive screws securing filter for air intake to air intake grille.

Grille, refit

1. On early models, pass the windscreen washer unions through the apertures in the filter for air intake and connect the hoses to the air intake grille.
2. Secure filter for air intake to grille with drive screws.
3. Enter the windscreen wiper spindles through the filter and fresh-air grille, ensure that the wiper wheelboxes are properly located in their housings.
4. Fit the parking ramps and loosely secure ramps and wheelboxes with large nuts: align the grille with the fixing holes in the body and secure with drive screws.
5. Fit drive screws and washers locating parking ramps; turn the ramps clockwise as far as possible and tighten drive screws.
6. Fully tighten large nuts securing wheelboxes.
7. Refit wiper blade and arm, if necessary slacken two screws at base of each arm and adjust nylon follower so that it is below the crown of the parking ramp; retighten screws.
8. Check for correct operation of wiper and windscreen washer. Instructions for the adjustment of the wiper arms and limit switch are given in Section S.

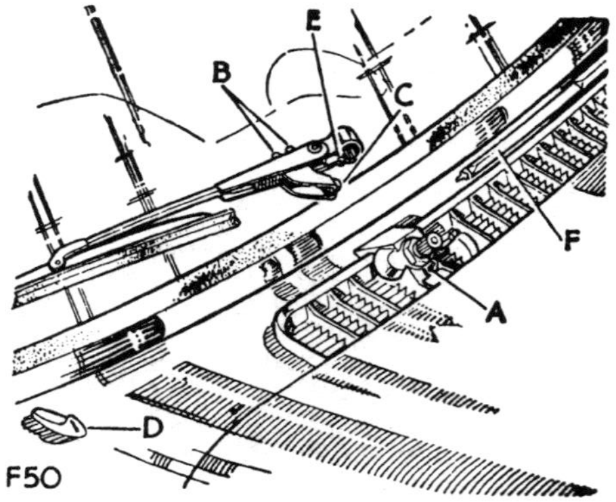

F50

Wiper blade adjustment

A—Ramp adjusting screw D—Blade parking platform
B—Nylon pad adjusting screws E—Arm retaining spring clip
C—Nylon pad F—Park position of LH blade

Bumpers, to remove and refit—Operation U-47

Workshop hand tools:

Spanner sizes: $\frac{7}{16}$ in. AF, $\frac{1}{2}$ in. AF, $\frac{9}{16}$ in. AF

Front bumper, remove

1. Remove the front bumper as an assembly by removing the bolts and washers securing the brackets to the chassis sub-frame.
2. Dismantle the bumper assembly on the bench.

Front bumper, to reassemble and fit

3. Assemble the bumper on the bench but do not fully tighten the bolts until all the parts have been put together. Tighten the bolts alternately and evenly. Bolt the assembly securely to the frame.

Rear bumper, to remove and refit

1. Remove the assembly complete with the support brackets from the body mountings. Further dismantling should be done on the bench.
2. Reassemble the bumper on the bench and tighten the bolts evenly.
3. Fit the bumper to the body mountings.

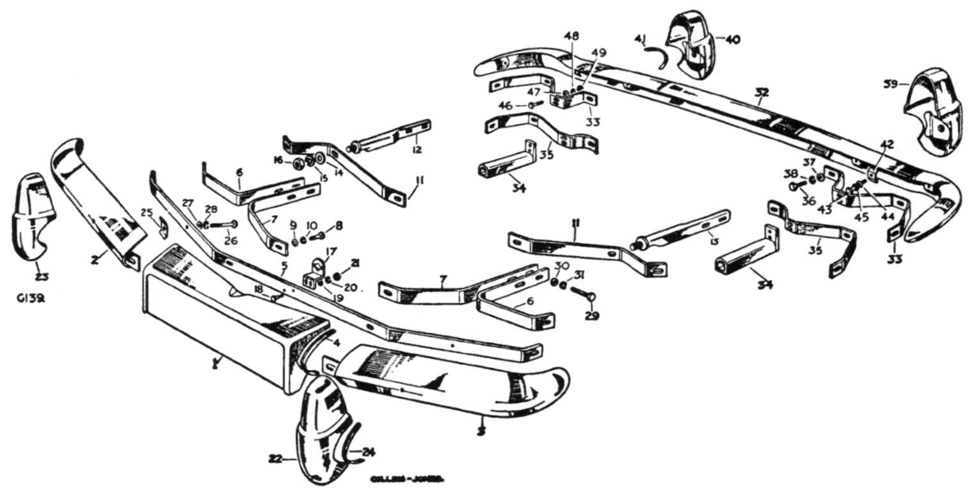

G132

Front and rear bumpers and fittings

1	Centre bar } For front bumper
2	Outer bar, RH } For front bumper
3	Outer bar, LH } For front bumper
4	Protective moulding
5	Support bracket, centre
6	Support bracket, outer
7	Support bracket, inner
8–10	Fixings
11	Support bracket, front bumper
12	Mounting bracket, RH } For front bumper
13	Mounting bracket, LH } For front bumper
14–16	Fixings
17	Bracket for starting handle
18–21	Fixings
22	Overrider, LH
23	Overrider, RH
24	Protective moulding
25	Clamp
26–31	Fixings, bumper to chassis sub-frame
32	Rear bar
33	Support bracket, Mk I models
34	Mounting bracket } Mk IA and Mk II models
35	Support bracket } Mk IA and Mk II models
36–38	Fixings
39	Overrider, LH
40	Overrider, RH
41	Protective moulding
42–49	Fixings

Section V—WHEELS AND TYRES

Brief description of the wheels and tyres

Pressed steel, easy-clean wheels with polished stainless steel trim and hub cover plate embodying the Rover symbol.

The wheels are secured to the hubs with five studs and ball-faced nuts.

In the interests of safety and comfort all wheel assemblies are balanced during car production.

INDEX

Tyre, to remove and refit—Operation V-1

Workshop hand tools:

Wheel brace — Valve core key
Tyre levers — Valve fitting tool, Part No. 268723 (tubeless tyres only)
Pressure gauge

This operation covers removal and fitting instructions for both tubed and tubeless tyres.
Whenever a tyre is replaced always check the wheel for any possible damage.

Tyre, remove

As inextensible wires are incorporated in the beads of the outer cover, the beads must not be stretched over the wheel rim.

The correct method of tyre removal is as follows:

1. Remove the valve cap and core and deflate the tyre.
2. Free each bead from its taper seating in the usual way. Note that the bead on the wide flat seat side fitted to late 3 litre models will have to be pushed away from the flange further than usual before it is free.

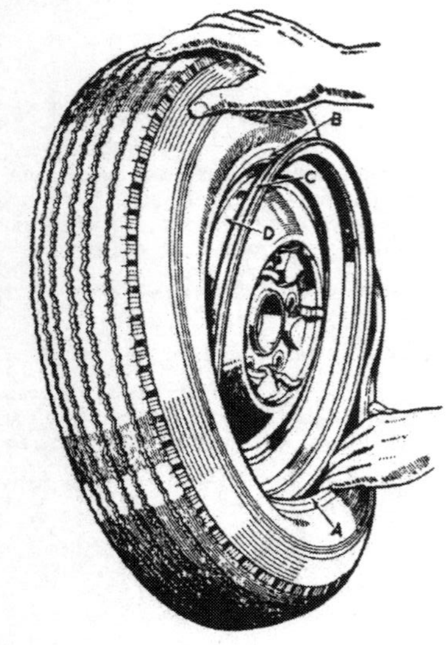

Tyre removal

A and B—Cover bead
C—Rim shoulders
D—Rim well

3. Before lifting the beads over the rim flange lubricate the tyre beads and levers with tyre bead lubricant or with a thin vegetable oil soap solution.
4. Remove both beads, one at a time, over the flange side of the rim which has the narrower bead seat. If the tyre is removed with the wheel lying flat, the narrower bead seat should be uppermost.
5. Where fitted, remove the inner tube and pull the second bead over the rim.

Tyre, refit (tubed)

1. Place the cover over the wheel and press the lower bead over the rim edge into the well.
2. Inflate the inner tube until it is just rounded out and insert it in the cover.
3. Press the upper bead into the well diametrically opposite the valve and lever the bead over the rim edge.
4. Push the valve inwards to ensure that the tube is not trapped under the bead, pull it back and inflate the tyre.
5. Check the concentricity of the fitting line on the cover and the top of the wheel flange. Deflate the tube completely to relieve any strains in the tube, then re-inflate to the correct pressure.

Tyre, refit (tubeless)

1. Rim preparation. Remove mud and dirt from wheel, taking care not to damage the paint.
2. Hammer out any dents in the rim flanges.
3. Clean the rim bead seats thoroughly. Use emery cloth, steel wool, a wire brush or file, depending on the amount of dirt, rust, rubber and surface irregularities to be removed. Smooth paint need not be removed.
4. File or buff away any high spots at the welded joint.
5. Wipe rim clean with a moist rag.

Operation V-1—*continued*

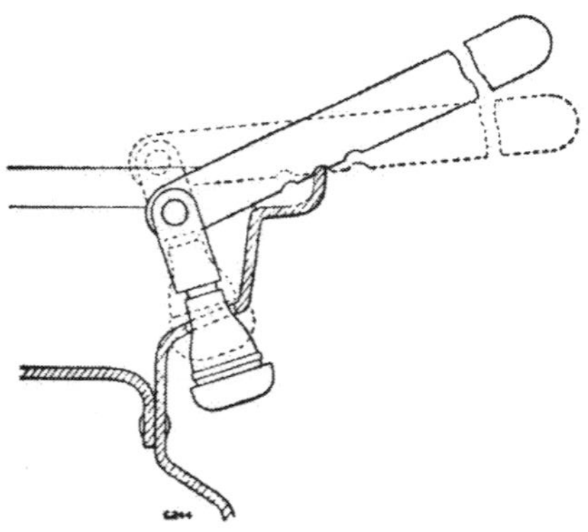

Valve fitting and removal

6. Valve fitting. The valve can be pulled into position or extracted with the aid of special tool (Part No. 268723) as illustrated.
   If fitting a new tubeless valve, make sure that it is of the correct diameter and length.
7. Extraction of the valve is brought about by continuing the downward pressure on the tool handle, thus drawing the broad rubber base through the valve hole in rim.
8. Tyre fitting. The tyre beads and their rubber surfaces must not be damaged during fitting. Do not use a hammer or mallet.
9. Remove spacers from between the beads.
10. Wipe beads clean with a damp cloth.
11. Lubricate tyre beads, rim flanges, rim bead seats and levers with a liberal amount of lubricant or a thin vegetable oil soap solution.
12. Fit tyre in normal manner; both beads (one at a time) must be fitted over the flange on the narrow seat side of the rim. If fitting is carried out with the wheel flat, the narrower bead seat should be uppermost. Use narrow levers in good condition and free from sharp edges. Take small bites so as not to strain or damage the beads. Exercise particular care to ensure that the rubber bead toes are not torn when lifted over the rim flanges.
13. The second bead should be fitted so that the part nearest the valve goes over the rim last.
14. **Inflating.** During fitting, check pressure frequently to make sure that 40 lb/sq in. (2,8 kg/cm²) air pressure is not exceeded as there can be a risk of severe bead damage. If this pressure will not seat the beads properly, deflate, lubricate, centralise the tyre and reinflate. If the tyre beads do not seat properly at the second attempt the wheel rim seat circumferences are suspect and should be checked; if necessary, fit a new wheel.
15. After beads have seated properly, adjust pressure to the recommended operating pressure.

IMPORTANT

16. Lock wheels down when using a fitting machine.
17. Stand clear of the tyre when inflating and do not lean over it until the beads are properly seated.
18. In stubborn cases a tyre tourniquet (Part No. 268722) can be used to assist the sealing of tyre against rim seats.

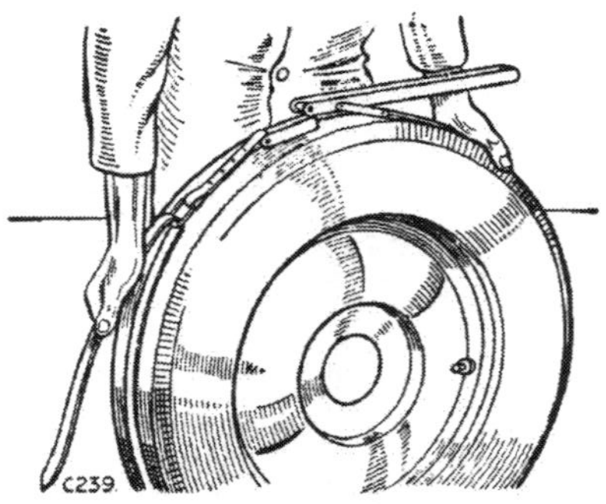

Fitting tourniquet on tyre

Operation V-1—*continued*

19. With the tool in open position, buckle the strap centrally around the tread of the deflated tyre and wheel assembly. Pull strap through buckle as tightly as possible.
20. Thread the loose end of strap through gap between rivet and roller on link mechanism and compress tread by pulling handle through 180°.
21. With valve core removed, attach the air line and inflate until the beads are sealed against the flanges. If they fail to seal at the first attempt, move the handle back and re-tighten the strap. When the beads are home, disconnect the air supply and fit the valve core, then remove the tourniquet before final inflation.
22. To remove the tourniquet, move the handle back and press the thumb on the end of buckle—pushing the slider bar on the buckle inwards and upwards.
23. Testing for leaks. A few minutes after inflating, immerse the tyre and wheel in a water tank and check for air leaks.
24. Place assembly in tank with valve uppermost. Submerge valve and check.
25. Release and allow the assembly to float, with channel between the rim flange and tyre filled with water. Check carefully for air bubbles above the rim flange.
26. Turn wheel assembly over and submerge wheel rivets if they are not already under water. Check for leaks at rivets.
27. Submerge the assembly to fill between flange and tyre, then allow to float. Check for air bubbles at rim flange.

Checking wheel and tyre for air leaks

28. To seal leaks—Leak at top of rim flange:
    Mark on tyre and rim, the position of leak and deflate tyre. The leak may be caused by dirt, rust, a high weld or chipped paint. By holding the bead away from rim seat, the cause of the leak can often be located and cleared without removing the tyre.
29. Make sure that the rim is clean after cause of leak has been removed.
30. Leak at wheel rivets: Mark position of leak on rim then deflate and remove tyre. Peen the head of the defectively sealed rivet with a ball peen hammer whilst it is supported by another hammer or suitable tool.
31. Leak at valve base: The valve should be replaced if after ensuring that it is properly seated, the leak continues.

Repair of tubeless tyres—Operation V-2

Equipment required:

Dunlop Reddiplug repair kit
or
Standard puncture repair kit

Tubeless tyre repair

Normally a tubeless tyre will not leak when penetrated by a nail or other normal puncturing object, provided that it is left in the tyre.

These objects should be withdrawn every 2,000 or 3,000 miles, at a time when loss of air will cause least inconvenience. If they are left in the tyre indefinitely, the original injuries may extend and cause more serious damage and possibly a road delay.

The tyre can be repaired without complete deflation or removal from rim by using a Dunlop 'Reddiplug' repair kit as follows:

1. Mark the point of penetration and extract the puncturing object, noting the angle of entry. If the tyre is leaking and the cause of puncture cannot be located by visual inspection, the inflated tyre should be immersed in water to facilitate location.

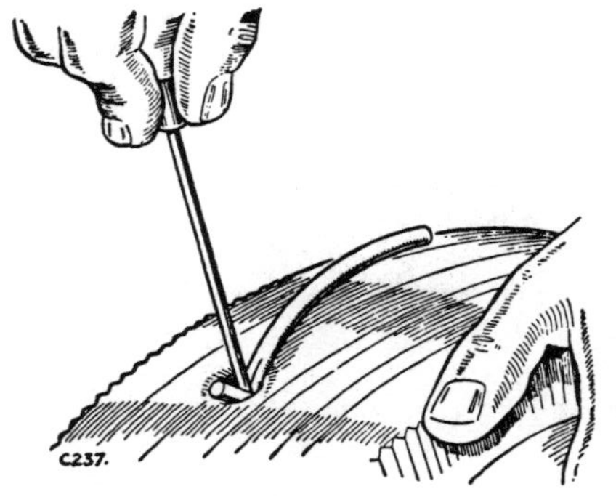

Inserting plug

2. Dip the needle into flask of solution and insert through the hole in tyre, following same direction as puncturing object. Repeat until the hole is well moistened with solution.
3. Select a plug about twice the diameter of the puncturing object, then stretch and roll into the eye of needle.
4. Dip plug into solution, then press the plug and needle through hole in tyre, again following direction of original penetration.

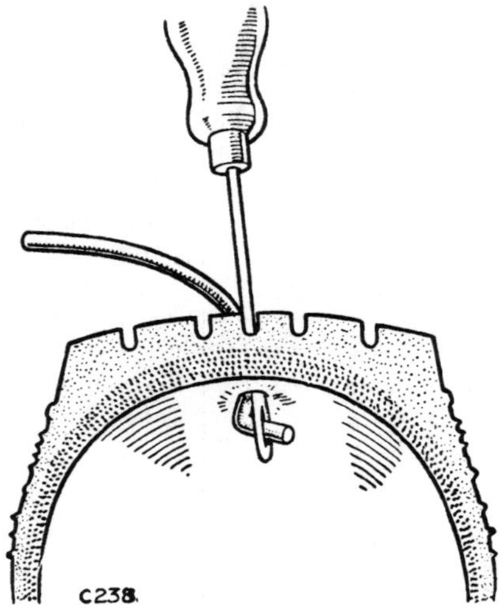

Needle ready for withdrawal

5. Withdraw needle and cut off surplus plug about $\frac{1}{8}$ in. (3 mm) from surface of tread.

Method of repair when 'Reddiplug' kit is not available

1. Remove the tyre from rim, taking care not to damage the beads and clean the area around hole on the inside of the tyre with naphtha.
2. Lightly buff or scratch brush an area slightly larger than the patch to be used.
3. Apply one coat of solution to the prepared area and allow to dry thoroughly.
4. Take a suitable size of tube repair patch, remove the protective backing, place in position and roll down firmly.

More severe injuries which are outside the scope of simple puncture repair methods are dealt with in a manner similar to that used on conventional type covers.

Operation V-2—*continued*

Changing tyre positions

To ensure the best tyre mileage and even wear, it is desirable that the position of the tyres on the car be changed as detailed in the appropriate Owner's Maintenance Manual.

Wheel maintenance and balance

1. The lateral variation measured on the vertical inside face of flanges must not exceed $\frac{3}{32}$ in. (3 mm).
2. On a truly mounted and revolving wheel the difference between high and low points, measured at any location on either tyre bead seat, must not exceed $\frac{3}{32}$ in. (3mm).
3. There is no effective method of truing eccentric pressed steel wheels economically, and they should be replaced.
4. Wheel nuts should be free on their studs. When fitting a wheel all the nuts should be screwed up very lightly, making sure that their seatings register with the seatings in the wheel.
5. Final tightening should be done progressively and alternately by short turns of opposite nuts to ensure correct seating and to avoid distortion.
6. Wheels with damaged or elongated stud holes, should be changed.
7. Rim seatings and flanges in contact with the tyre beads should be free from rust and dirt.
8. Wheel balance. Apart from fitting the outer cover correctly as previously detailed, the wheel and tyre complete should be balanced dynamically, using standard garage equipment. If suitable equipment is not available, the wheel and tyre may be balanced statically on a slave hub which is itself in balance.

DEFECT LOCATION

SYMPTOM	*POSSIBLE CAUSE*	*REMEDY*
A—EXCESSIVE WEAR ON FRONT TYRES	1. Tyres under-inflated 2. Incorrect toe-in 3. Excessive use of brakes or high-speed driving 4. Front wheels out of balance	1. *Inflate to the pressures recommended.* 2. *See Section J* 3. *In the hands of the operator* 4. *Re-balance*
B—RATTLES FROM FRONT WHEELS	1. Loose or damaged wheel bearings	1. *See Section K*
C—SQUEAKS FROM FRONT WHEELS	1. Wheel nuts loose 2. Lack of lubrication to front wheel bearings 3. Front wheel bearings adjusted too tightly or damaged	1. *Examine studs for damage and tighten nuts* 2. *Lubricate* 3. *See Section K*
D—OTHER NOISES FROM THE FRONT WHEELS	1. Variation in tread surface 2. Type or condition of tyre tread 3. Under-inflated tyres 4. Foreign body embedded in tyre	1. *Renew outer cover* 2. *Renew tyres* 3. *Inflate to the pressures recommended* 4. *Extract the embedded matter and repair the tyre as necessary*
E—OVERHEATING OF FRONT WHEEL BEARINGS	1. Insufficient lubricant 2. Use of a poor quality or incorrect grade of lubricant 3. Front wheel bearings adjusted too tightly or damaged 4. Excessive use of the brakes	1. *Lubricate* 2. *Replenish with the correct grade* 3. *See Section K* 4. *In the hands of the operator*
F—EXCESSIVE WEAR ON REAR TYRES	1. Under-inflated tyres 2. Rear wheel run-out or wobble 3. Excessive use of brakes or high-speed driving 4. Wheels or tyres out of balance	1. *Inflate to the pressures recommended* 2. *Check for loose wheel nuts. Check for a damaged wheel or incorrectly fitted tyres* 3. *In the hands of the driver* 4. *Rectify*
G—REAR WHEEL NOISE	1. Wheel hub nuts or studs loose 2. Type or condition of tyre tread 3. Wear in the differential	1. *Rectify* 2. *Renew the tyres* 3. *See Section L*

DATA

Tyre size .. .. 6.70 x 15 in.

Wheels .. .. 500 K rims, 15 in.

Wheel nuts .. .. $\frac{7}{16}$ in. UNF, ball faced (Right-hand threads all round)

Tyre pressures, check with tyres cold

6.70 x 15 in. Dunlop C41 Gold Seal or Avon HM — Speed	Front normal load	Front fully laden	Rear normal load	Rear fully laden
Speeds up to 80 mph (120 kph)				
lb/sq in.	24	26	22	30
Kg/cm²	1,7	1,8	1,5	2,1
Speeds over 80 mph (120 kph)				
lb/sq in.	30	32	28	36
Kg/cm²	2,1	2,2	1,9	2,5
7.10 x 15 in. Dunlop or Avon				
Speeds up to 80 mph (120 kph)				
lb/sq in.	22	24	20	28
kg/cm²	1,5	1,7	1,4	1,9
Speeds over 80 mph (120 kph)				
lb/sq in.	28	30	26	34
kg/cm²	1,9	2,1	1,8	2,4

6.70 x 15 in. Dunlop Roadspeed or Avon Turbospeed	Front normal load	Front fully laden	Rear normal load	Rear fully laden
Speeds up to 105 mph (168 kph)				
lb/sq in.	26	30	26	30
kg/cm²	1,8	2,1	1,8	2,1
Speeds over 105 mph (168 kph)				
lb/sq in.	30	34	30	34
kg/cm²	2,1	2,4	2,1	2,4

Section W — HEATING AND VENTILATING SYSTEM

Brief description of heating and ventilating system

A fresh-air type heater is used. This has a powerful two-speed blower unit, which is mounted separately and which draws air from a grille below the windscreen.

The heater controls are placed one on either side of the centre glove box and the control switch is mounted on the instrument panel, two-speed motor on Mk II models. The controls provide for demisting and defrosting of the windscreen as well as for regulating the heat inside the car.

Cool air inlets at two levels are provided, these being at face-level and at the toe board on either side of the car. This system operates only with the forward movement of the car and is progressive as the speed increases.

It is impossible to drain the heater unit when draining the remainder of the cooling system. During winter conditions recommended anti-freeze must be used.

For operating instructions of the ventilating, heating and cooling system, see Owner's Instruction Manual.

INDEX

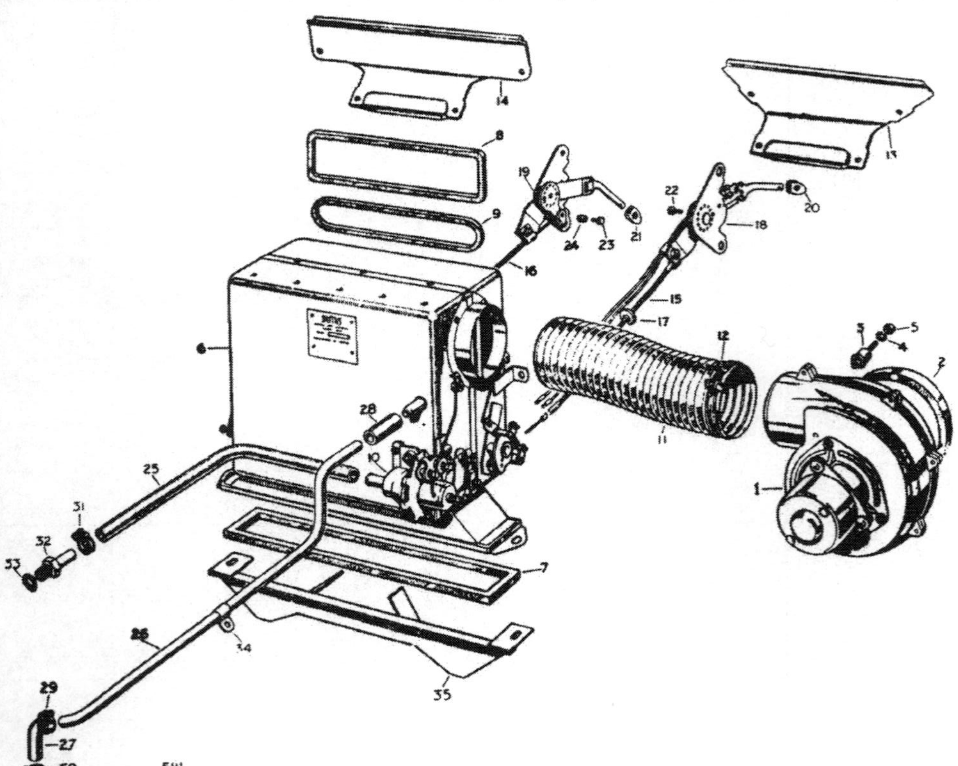

E111

Car heater and blower

1	Blower	19	Lever control complete, demister
2	Rubber seal for blower to dash	20	Control knob
3	Rubber mounting bush	21	Control knob
4	Spring washer } Fixing blower	22	Special screw, long, for cable
5	Nut } to dash	23	Special screw, short, for cable
6	Heater	24	Nipple for cable
7	Rubber seal at heater base	25	Inlet hose for water heater
8	Rubber seal, large } Heater	26	Outlet pipe for water heater
9	Rubber seal, small } to dash	27	Hose, outlet pipe to engine
10	Tap for heater	28	Hose, outlet pipe to heater
11	Hose, blower to heater	29	Clip } For hose, outlet
12	Clip for hose	30	Clip } pipe to engine
13	Demister nozzle, LH	31	Clip for hose except outlet pipe to engine
14	Demister nozzle, centre	32	Adaptor for car heater inlet pipe
15	Control cable, heat	33	Joint washer for adaptor
16	Control cable, demister	34	Clip for outlet pipe
17	Grommet for control cable	35	Distribution plate
18	Lever control complete, heat		

Heater control levers, to adjust—Operation W-1

Workshop hand tools:
Spanner size: ¼ in. AF

In the event of accidental damage to the cables or valve linkages, or if the heater should fail to function correctly, the adjustments should be made in the following sequence:

There is no part of the mechanism of the heater inside the heater radiator case, all adjustments can be made outside.

Controls, adjust

1. Move interior heat control lever to 'Off' position; the heater tap lever should now be in its extreme clockwise position.

2. If this is not so, slacken screw 'E', set the lever in its correct position and re-tighten screw.

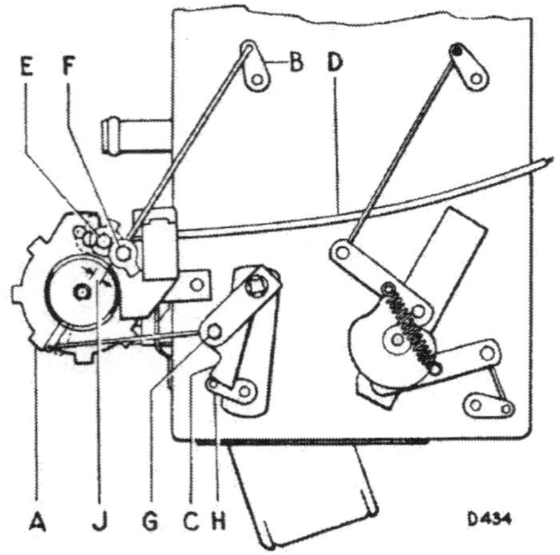

D434

Heater tap and levers

A—Heater tap
B—Air mixing lever
C—Air outlet lever
D—Control cable
E—Screw fixing control cable
F—Screw fixing air mixing control rod
G—Screw fixing air outlet rod
H—Air outlet remote control lever
J—Adjust air outlet valve with heater tap lever ⅛ in. (3 mm) from end of slot

3. The lever on the heater tap is linked to the air mixing and air outlet valves. When it is in the fully clockwise position, the air mixing valve should be at rest in the horizontal position, inside the heater box; to check this, slacken screw 'F', and turn the upper lever fully clockwise, then re-tighten screw 'F'.

4. To check that the air outlet valve is fully closed, move the interior heat control lever away from the off position until the heater tap lever is ⅛ in. (3 mm) from the end of its slot, as shown in the illustration.

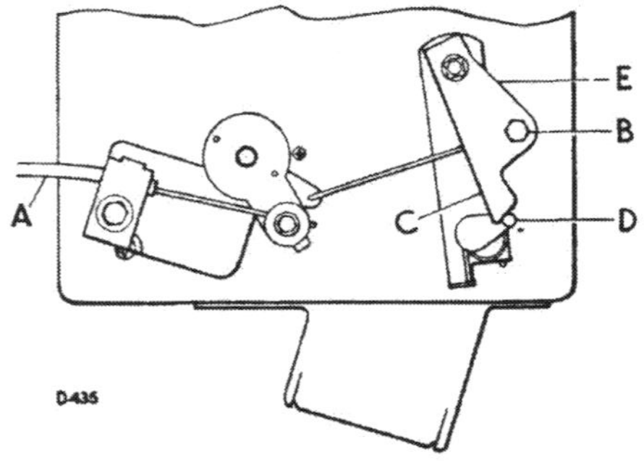

D435

Screen control levers

A—Control cable
B—Fixing screw for air control rod
C—Push at this point
D—Air outlet valve lever
E—Cam lever

5. Slacken screw 'G', rotate air outlet lever fully clockwise by applying finger pressure on cam lever, and re-tighten screw 'G'.

Ensure that the air outlet valve on the right-hand side of the heater box is in its correct position when the screen lever is fully open:

Slacken screw 'B', rotate air outlet valve lever fully anti-clockwise by applying finger pressure at the point 'C', and re-tighten screw 'B'.

Blower unit, to remove and refit—Operation W-2

Workshop hand tools:
Spanner sizes: $\frac{5}{16}$ in. AF, $\frac{7}{16}$ in. AF
Screwdriver, medium

Blower unit, remove

1. Disconnect battery leads.
2. Remove air hose between heater radiator and blower motor.
3. Disconnect wiring for heater motor at snap connections.
4. Remove the three nuts securing motor to blower body, and withdraw motor and fan.
5. Through the blower motor aperture locate and remove the fixings securing the blower body to the bulkhead panel, and remove blower body.

Blower unit, refit

1. Fit blower body to bulkhead panel, and blower fan to blower body.
2. Connect wiring in accordance with the circuit diagram.
3. Fit air hose between blower and heater radiator.
4. Connect battery leads and check blower motor for correct operation.

Front heater, to remove and refit—Operation W-3

Workshop hand tools:
Spanner sizes: $\frac{7}{16}$ in. AF
Screwdriver, medium

Heater, remove

1. Drain cooling system (drain taps under radiator and on cylinder block) and also the heater by disconnecting water hose at heater tap and moving interior heat control lever to fully open position.
2. Remove the air hose between heater radiator and blower.
3. Slacken hose clips and slide the water hose on inlet pipe clear of heater radiator.
4. Disconnect heater control cables, do not disturb the linkage fixings unless necessary.
5. Remove the fixings, which also secure the distribution plate on 1960 models, from heater radiator mountings situated on the bulkhead panel.
6. Pull heater radiator slightly forward, then lift out; if necessary remove rubber seals from rear and base of heater radiator.

Heater, refit

1. If removed, fit the rubber seals to the rear and base of heater radiator with suitable adhesive.
2. Place the heater radiator unit in position and fit the lower fixing bolts first. (On 1960 models these also secure the distribution plate.)
3. Re-connect the water hoses.
4. Move both control levers inside the car fully down, and the levers on the heater radiator fully forward; connect both cables.
5. Fit air hose between blower and heater radiator.
6. Refill cooling system, anti-freeze in winter, and run engine until normal operating temperature has been obtained, then check for water leaks and correct operation of heater.

   Capacity of cooling system:
   Mk I and Mk IA—
   22½ Imperial pints, 27 US pints, 13 litres.
   Mk II—
   24 Imperial pints, 29 US pints, 13,7 litres.
   Mk III—
   26 Imperial pints, 31 US pints, 14,7 litres.

Heater tap, front heater, to remove and refit—Operation W-4

Workshop hand tools:
Spanner sizes: 2 BA, $\frac{1}{4}$ in. AF

Tap, remove

1. Drain cooling system (drain tap under radiator and on cylinder block) and also the heater by disconnecting water hose at heater tap and moving interior heat control to fully open position.
2. Disconnect control cable from heater tap, and remove the control rods between the heater tap and air mixing and air outlet levers.
3. Remove and withdraw heater tap.

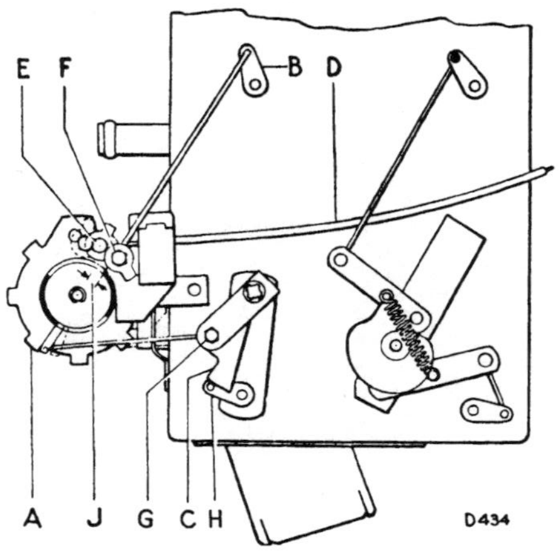

Heater tap and levers

A—Heater tap
B—Air mixing lever
C—Air outlet lever
D—Control cable
E—Screw fixing control cable
F—Screw fixing air mixing control rod
G—Screw fixing air outlet control rod
H—Air outlet remote control lever
J—Adjust air outlet valve with heater tap lever $\frac{1}{8}$ in. (3 mm) from end of slot

Tap, refit

1. Fit heater tap to heater radiator, secured by nuts, spring washers and drive screws.
2. Move the interior heat control lever to the 'off' position and turn the heater tap lever fully clockwise; fit control cable.
3. Turn air mixing valve lever fully clockwise and connect control rod to heater tap.
4. Move the interior heat control lever away from the 'off' position until the heater tap lever is $\frac{1}{8}$ in. (3 mm) from the end of its slot, as shown in the illustration.
5. Fit the control rod and rotate air outlet lever fully clockwise, then tighten clamping screw.
6. Re-connect water hose to heater tap and refill cooling system, anti-freeze in winter.
7. Run engine until normal operating temperature has been obtained, then check correct operation of heater.

   Capacity of cooling system:
   Mk I and Mk IA—
   22½ Imperial pints, 27 Us pints, 13 litres.
   Mk II—
   24 Imperial pints, 29 US pints, 13,7 litres.
   Mk III—
   26 Imperial pints, 31 US pints, 14,7 litres.

Lever controls and cables, front heater, to remove and refit—Operation W-5

Workshop hand tools:

Spanner sizes: 2 BA, 6 BA, $\frac{1}{4}$ in. AF, $\frac{5}{16}$ in. AF

Control levers, remove

1. Disconnect battery leads.
2. Open centre glove box locker lid and remove trim panel by depressing both side panels inwards, then twist and withdraw. When a radio set is fitted disconnect aerial and feed leads and withdraw radio.
3. Disconnect cables from heater radiator.
4. Disconnect wiring from heater control switch at snap connectors under glove box, and remove the control lever knobs; these are secured by small Allen screws on the underside of the knobs.
5. Remove bolts securing controls to facia frame, lift out and withdraw cables through bulkhead.
6. If necessary, disconnect cables from controls.

Control levers, refit

1. If removed, fit cables to controls.
2. Insert cables through bulkhead, ensuring that the rubber grommets are securely in position.
3. Secure controls to facia frame and refit control knobs, 'heat' on left-hand control and 'screen' on right-hand control.
4. Connect wiring for heater control at snap connections in accordance with circuit diagram.
5. Refit glove box trim panel, ensuring the sides are pushed fully home; where radio is fitted, refit and connect aerial and battery feed leads.
6. Move both control levers inside the car fully down and the levers on the heater radiator fully forward; connect both cables.
7. Connect battery leads, run engine until normal operating temperature has been obtained and then check for correct operation of heater.

Rear heater and air outlets, to remove and refit (Mk III models)—Operation W-6

Workshop hand tools:

Spanner size: $\frac{7}{16}$ in. AF Screwdriver, small Pliers, long-nosed

Heater, remove

1. Drain the cooling system. Drain taps are located under radiator and on the side of the cylinder block.
2. Lift out the rear seat cushions.

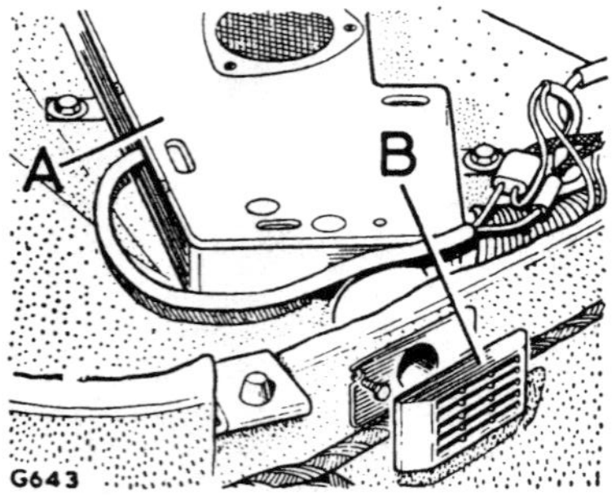

Rear seat heater unit

A—Heater B—Air grille

3. Release spring clips securing flexible hoses to heater unit and disconnect the hoses.
4. Disconnect the electrical wiring from the heater at the snap connectors. Pull the wiring through the grommet in the floor panel from below the car.
5. Disconnect the water hoses from the rear heater unit, from below the rear seat pan.
6. Remove the two bolts and plain washers securing the heater unit to the floor. Lift the unit out.
7. Pull the short flexible air hose off the RH air outlet flange.
8. Withdraw the long flexible air hose from LH air outlet flange.
9. If necessary remove the retaining clips, air outlet grilles to flanges, and withdraw grilles and flanges.

Heater, refit

1. Reverse removal procedure.
2. Connect wiring in accordance with the circuit diagram.
3. Refill system with coolant, anti-freeze in winter and check for leaks.
4. Make good the seal between the heater and body with a suitable sealing compound.
5. When testing heater ensure tap adjacent to front heater is turned on.

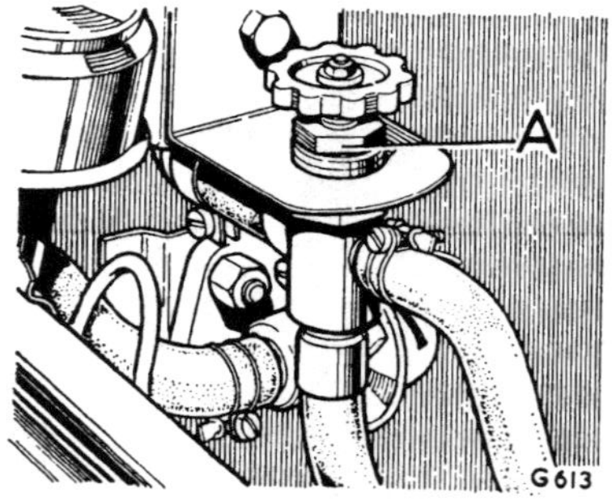

Tap for rear heater

A—Tap

Capacity:
26 Imperial pints, 31 US pints, 14,7 litres.

Rear heater, water hoses (Mk III models), to remove and refit—Operation W-7

Workshop hand tools:
Screwdrivers, small and medium

Hoses, remove

1. Drain the coolant from the system. Drain taps are located under radiator and on the side of the cylinder block.
2. Disconnect the water hoses from the rear heater unit, from below the rear seat pan.
3. Disconnect the water hoses from the copper supply pipes beneath the RH toe-board at the front of the car.
4. Bend back the hose retaining clips below the car floor and withdraw the hoses.

Hoses, refit

1. Reverse removal procedure.
2. Refill the system with coolant, anti-freeze in winter, and check for leaks.

Capacity:
24 Imperial pints, 31 US pints, 14,7 litres.

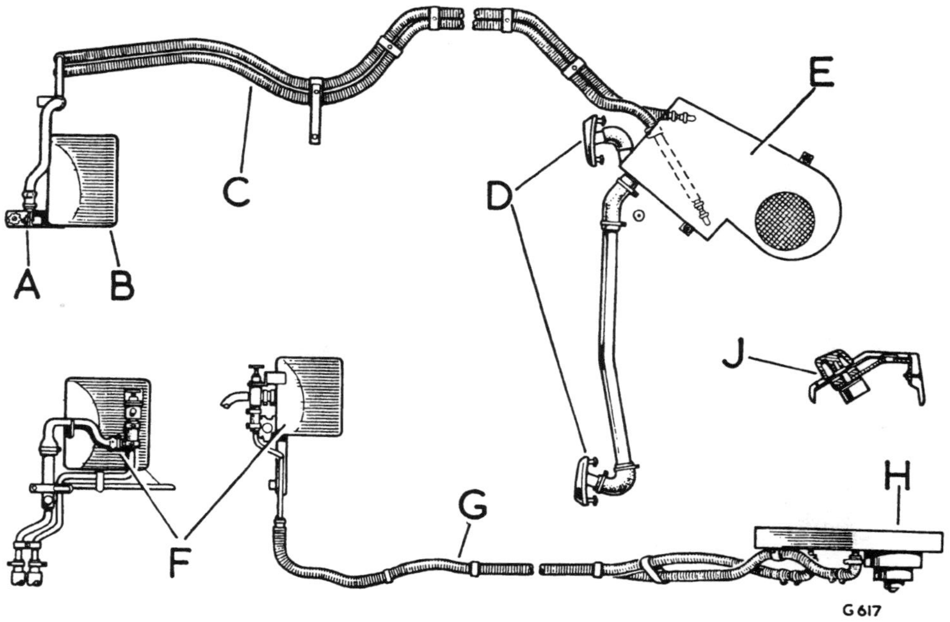

Water pipe layout for rear seat heater

A—Tap for heater
B—Heater, front
C—Hoses to rear heater
D—Air outlet grilles at rear seat
E—Heater, rear
} Plan view

F—Heater, front, showing hose connections
G—Hoses to rear heater
H—Heater, rear
} Side elevation
J—Switch for rear heater

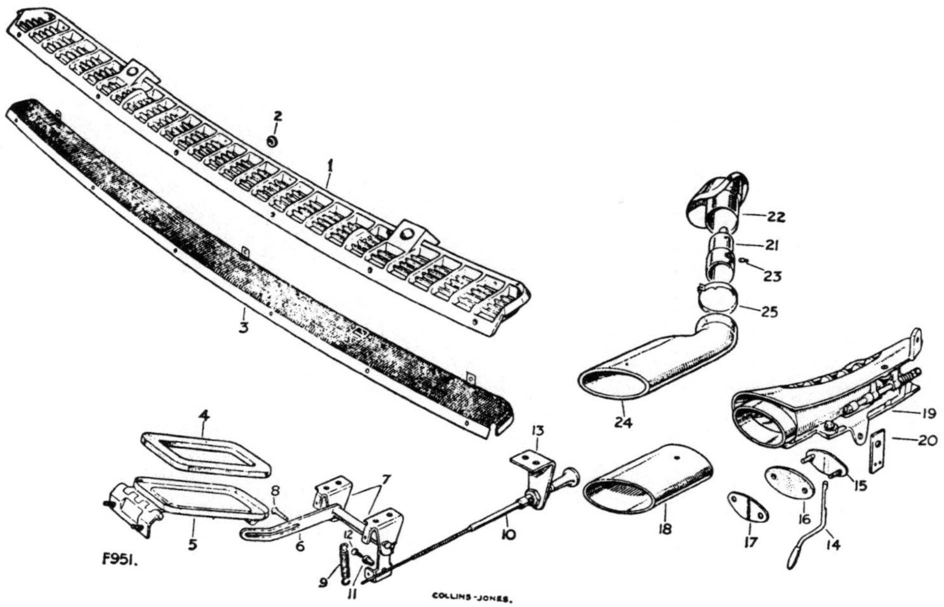

Fresh air grille and ventilators

1 Fresh air intake grille
2 Rubber grommet
3 Filter for intake grille
4 Sealing rubber for ventilator
5 Ventilator flap
6 Ventilator control mechanism
7 Mounting brackets for mechanism
8 Joint pin
9 Control return spring
10 Control cable
11 } Bolt and ferrule fixing
12 } control cable
13 Mounting bracket for control
14 Spindle for ventilator butterfly
15 }
16 } Ventilator butterfly and sealing rubber
17 }
18 Ventilator tube
19 Face-level ventilator
20 Ventilator fixing bracket
21 Butterfly and housing
22 Escutcheon
23 Special rivet fixing escutcheon
24 Rubber boot } For
25 Spring clip } ventilator

Face-level ventilators, to remove and refit—Operation W-8

Workshop hand tools:
Spanner size: $\frac{5}{16}$ in. AF
Screwdriver, medium

Ventilators, remove. Early models

1. Remove drive screws securing chromium cappings at the end of the face-level ventilator.

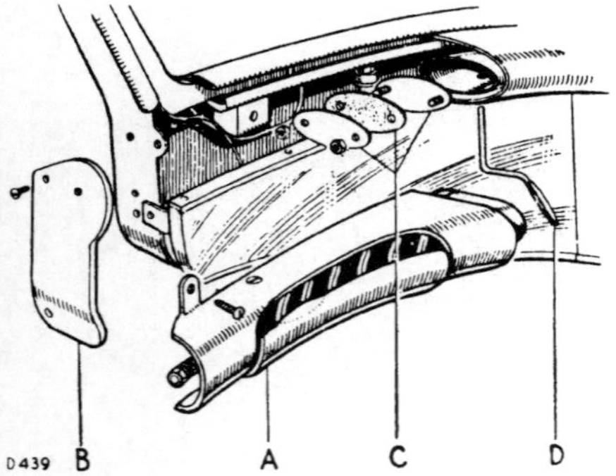

Removing face-level ventilator and butterfly, early models

A—Face-level ventilator
B—Chromium capping
C—Butterfly valve
D—Spindle

2. Remove the windscreen side trim panel.

3. If necessary, lift up windscreen bottom trim panel, remove the drive screw securing each face-level ventilator, and withdraw ventilator.

4. Remove the two nuts and washers securing each butterfly valve to spindle, and withdraw butterfly valves and spindles.

Ventilators, remove. Late models

5. Remove the parcel tray trim panels.

6. Remove the wooden corner fillet from the driver's side, this is secured by a nut and washers to the facia frame adjacent to the hand brake mounting bracket, and by a drive screw to the door hinge pillar.

7. Remove the wooden corner fillet from the passenger side, secured by drive screws.

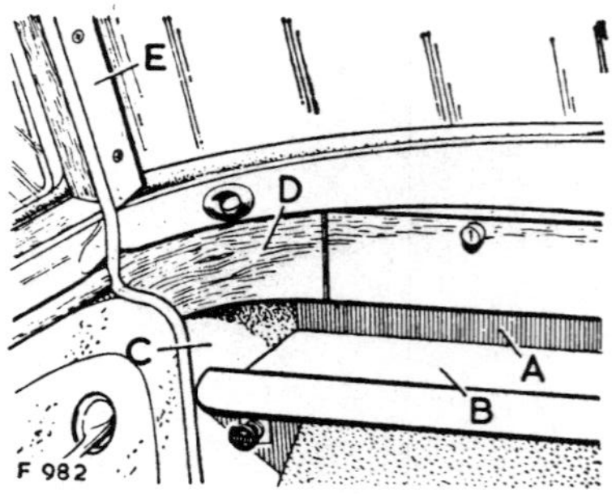

Removing parcel tray trim

A—Back trim
B—Shelf floor trim
C—Side trim
D—Corner fillet
E—Windscreen side moulding

8. Detach the rubber boot from each ventilator, remove the circlips and withdraw the ventilators.

Removing corner fillet

Operation W-8—*continued*

Ventilators, refit. Early models

1. Enter each butterfly valve and spindle into the fresh air passage.

2. Ensure that the rubber seal on each butterfly valve is correctly positioned, secure to spindle with nuts and flat washers.

3. Offer face-level ventilators to fresh air passages and secure with one drive screw.

4. If removed, refit windscreen bottom trim panel and windscreen side trim panel, refit chromium cappings.

Ventilators, refit. Late models

5. Press the ventilator assemblies firmly into the crash rail and secure with the circlips. Press the circlips well home. Connect the rubber hoses.

6. Refit the wooden corner fillets and refit the parcel tray trim panels.

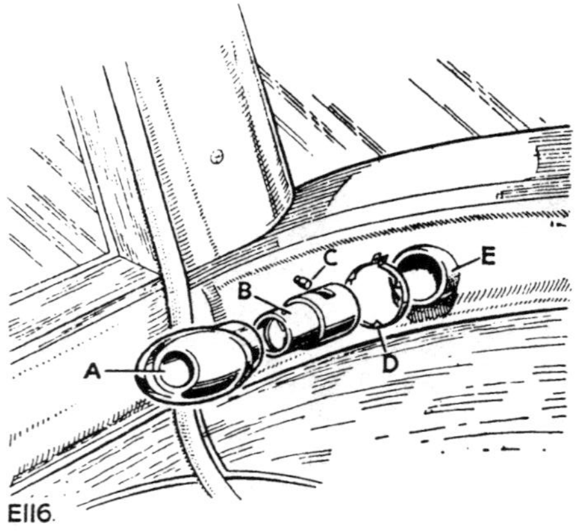

Face-level ventilators, late models

A—Nozzle
B—Butterfly
C—Dowel
D—Spring clip
E—Hose

Fresh air intake grille, to remove and refit—Operation W-9

Workshop hand tools:
Spanner size: $\frac{3}{4}$ in. AF
Screwdriver, medium

Grille, remove

1. Remove the two windscreen wiper arms and blades by withdrawing wiper arm and blade from splined shaft.
2. Remove the large nuts securing the wiper wheel boxes to the air intake grille.
3. Remove the special screw securing the parking ramp to air intake grille.
4. Remove the six large drive screws from the front of the fresh air grille, and four smaller drive screws from the back of the grille.

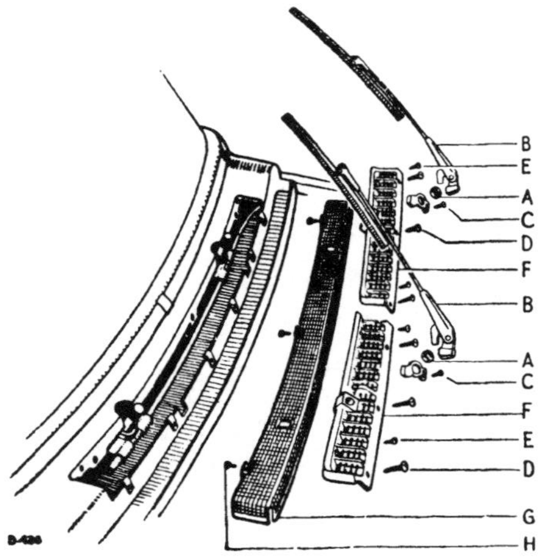

Removing air intake grille

A—Large nuts
B—Wiper arm and blade
C—Special screw
D—Large drive screw
E—Small drive screw
F—Air intake grille
G—Filter for air intake
H—Drive screws

5. Lift out grille and filter for air intake, and on early models, disconnect the windscreen washer hoses.
   Mk III models. The air intake grille has been redesigned to accommodate rubber bushes which are fitted on the windscreen wiper wheel boxes and insulate the wheel boxes from the grille.
6. Remove the drive screws securing filter for air intake to air intake grille.

Grille, refit

1. Pass the windscreen washer unions through the apertures in the filter for air intake and connect the hoses to the air intake grille.
2. Secure filter for air intake to intake grille with drive screws.
3. Enter the windscreen wiper spindles through the filter and fresh air grille, ensure that the wiper wheel boxes are properly located in their housings.
4. Fit the parking ramps, and loosely secure ramps and wheel boxes with large nuts; align the air intake grille with the holes drilled in the body, and secure with the drive screws.
5. Fit drive screws and washers locating parking ramps; turn the ramps clockwise as far as possible and tighten drive screws.
6. Fully tighten large nuts securing wheel boxes.
7. Refit wiper blade and arm, if necessary slacken two screws at the base of each arm and adjust nylon follower so that it is below the crown of the parking ramp; re-tighten screws.
8. Check for correct operation of wiper and windscreen washer.

Fresh air ventilator control cable, to remove and refit—Operation W-10

Workshop hand tools:
Spanner sizes: $\frac{1}{4}$ in. AF, $\frac{5}{16}$ in. AF, $\frac{3}{4}$ in. AF

Control cable, remove

1. Release control inner cable secured by a bolt and ferrule.
2. Remove control outer cable secured by a large nut to the support bracket.

Control cable, refit

1. Reverse removal procedure.

Fresh air ventilator flap, to remove and refit—Operation W-11

Workshop hand tools:
Spanner sizes: $\frac{1}{4}$ in. AF, $\frac{5}{16}$ in. AF
Long nosed pliers
Screwdriver, medium

Ventilator flap, remove

1. Release bolt and ferrule securing inner wire of control cable.
2. Remove joint pin fixing operating lever to flap, secured by a split pin.
3. Lift out parcel tray trim and remove the operating mechanism complete, secured to the underside of the parcel tray by set bolts.
4. Remove flaps, secured by nuts and washers situated below the heater blower unit on one side, and below the voltage and current control regulator on the other side of the engine compartment.

Ventilator flap, refit

1. Reverse removal procedure.

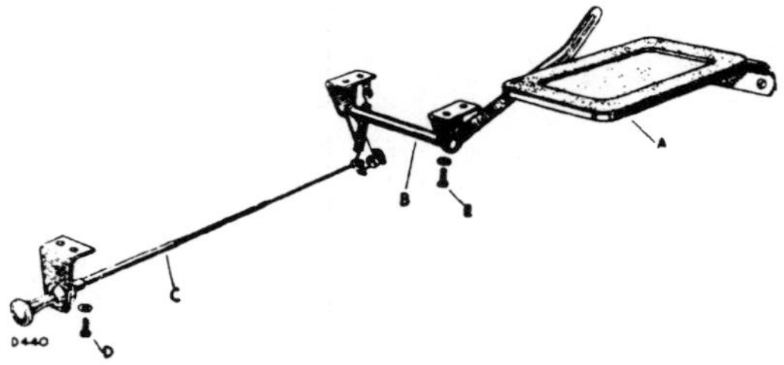

Removing fresh air ventilator flap

A—Fresh air ventilator flap
B—Lever mechanism
C—Control cable
D—Fixings, control cable bracket
E—Fixings, lever mechanism to bracket

Section X – RECLAMATION SCHEMES

Flywheel—Operation X-1

Instructions for the removal of the flywheel are given in Section A

Flywheel pressure, face to machine

If the flywheel pressure face is scored and worn; proceed as follows:

1. Remove the ring gear from the flywheel, secured by bolts, and remove the clutch bolts and dowels.
2. Machine the whole pressure face until the score marks are removed.
3. The maximum amount of metal which may be removed from a flywheel face is .030 in. (0,76 mm), if the face is not satisfactory after removing this amount, the flywheel must be scrapped. The minimum thickness at the outer edge of the flywheel after refacing is .742 in. (18 mm).
4. Replace the bolts and dowels and renew the primary pinion spigot bush as necessary.
5. Refit flywheel ring gear, and secure with bolts.

Clutch pressure plate—Operation X-2

Instructions for the removal of the clutch pressure plate are given in Section C

Clutch pressure plate, to machine

If the clutch pressure plate is scored and worn, the face should be machined.

1. The main body thickness of the pressure plate is .640 to .660 in. (16,25 to 16,76 mm) and regrinding is permissible to .010 in. (.254 mm) of bottom limit quoted.

Section Y – RECOMMENDED LUBRICANTS

Recommended lubricants

These recommendations apply to temperate climates where operational temperatures may vary between approximately 10°F (—12°C) and 90°F (32°C).

Information on recommended lubricants for use under extreme winter or tropical conditions can be obtained from The Rover Co. Ltd., Technical Service Department.

Mk I and Mk IA models

COMPONENTS	SAE	BP	CASTROL	DUCKHAM'S	ESSO	MOBIL	REGENT TEXACO/ CALTEX	SHELL
ENGINE AND AIR CLEANER	20W	Energol SAE 20W	Castrolite	Duckham's NOL Twenty	Esso Extra 20W/30 Motor Oil	Mobiloil Arctic	Advanced Havoline 20/20W	Shell X100 SAE 20/20W
GEARBOX 4-SPEED REAR AXLE STEERING BOX, MANUAL BALL SWIVEL PINS	90EP	Energol EP SAE 90	Castrol Hypoy	Duckham's Hypoid 90	Esso Gear Oil GP 90/140	Mobilube GX 90	Universal Thuban 90	Spirax 90 EP
AUTOMATIC TRANSMISSION AND POWER STEERING RESERVOIR	—	Energol ATF Type A	Castrol TQ Fluid Grade A	Duckham's Nolmatic ATF Type A	Esso Automatic Transmission Fluid	Mobil Fluid 200	Texamatic Fluid 3528	Shell Donax T6
FRONT HUBS AND PROPELLER SHAFT REAR SPRING AND FRONT TORSION BAR GREASE SLEEVES	—	Energrease L2	Castrolease LM	Duckham's LB 10 Grease	Esso Multi-purpose Grease H	Mobilgrease MP	Marfak Multi-purpose 2	Retinax A
BRAKE FLUID RESERVOIR		Castrol Girling Brake and Clutch Fluid Crimson						
CLUTCH FLUID RESERVOIR, 4-SPEED GEARBOX		Castrol Girling Brake and Clutch Fluid Crimson						

Mk II and Mk III models

COMPONENTS	SAE	BP	CASTROL	DUCKHAM'S	ESSO	MOBIL	REGENT TEXACO/ CALTEX	SHELL
ENGINE AND AIR CLEANER	20W	Energol SAE 20W	Castrolite	Duckham's NOL Twenty	Esso Extra Motor Oil 20W/30	Mobiloil Arctic	Advanced Havoline 20/20W	Shell X100 20W
GEARBOX ONLY	90EP	Energol SAE 90EP	Castrol Hypoy	Duckham's Hypoid 90	Esso Gear Oil GP90/140	Mobilube GX 90	Universal Thuban 90	Spirax 90 EP
OVERDRIVE ONLY	20W	Energol SAE 20W	Castrolite	Duckham's NOL Twenty	Esso Extra Motor Oil 20W/30	Mobiloil Arctic	Advanced Havoline 20/20W	Shell X100 20W
AUTOMATIC TRANSMISSION AND POWER STEERING	—	Energol ATF Type A	Castrol TQ Automatic Transmission Fluid	Duckham's Nolmatic ATF Type A	Esso Automatic Transmission Fluid	Mobil Fluid 200	Texamatic Fluid 3528	Shell Donax T6
REAR AXLE, STEERING BOX (MANUAL) Ball swivel pins on Mk II, suffix letter 'A' and 'B' only.	90EP	Energol SAE 90EP	Castrol Hypoy	Duckham's Hypoid 90	Esso Gear Oil GP90/140	Mobilube GX 90	Universal Thuban 90	Spirax 90 EP
FRONT HUBS, PROPELLER SHAFT, REAR SPRING AND FRONT TORSION BAR SLEEVES	—	Energrease L2	Castrolease LM	Duckham's LB 10 grease	Esso Multi-purpose grease H	Mobilgrease MP or Mobilgrease Special	Marfak Multi-purpose 2	Retinax A
BRAKE FLUID RESERVOIR		Castrol Girling Brake and Clutch Fluid Crimson						
CLUTCH FLUID RESERVOIR, 4-SPEED GEARBOX		Castrol Girling Brake and Clutch Fluid Crimson						

CAPACITIES

Mk I and Mk IA models

Component	Imperial Unit	US Unit	Litres
Engine sump oil	10 pints	12 pints	5,5
Extra when refilling after fitting new filter	1 pint	1.2 pints	0,5
Gearbox oil, 4-speed models	3½ pints	4 pints	2
Gearbox oil, 4-speed and overdrive	5 pints	6 pints	2,75
Automatic transmission	15 pints	18 pints	8,5
Rear axle	3 pints	3.5 pints	1,75
Power steering	3 to 3½ pints	3.5 to 4 pints	1,75 to 1,8

Mk II and Mk III models

Component	Imperial Unit	US Unit	Litres
Engine sump oil	10 pints	12 pints	5,5
Extra when refilling after fitting new filter	1 pint	1.2 pints	0,5
Gearbox oil, 4-speed models	3 pints	3.5 pints	1,75
Overdrive unit	1½ pints	2 pints	0,85
Automatic transmission, Mk II models	15 pints	18 pints	8,5
Automatic transmission, Mk III models	14 pints	17 pints	8,0
Rear axle	3 pints	3.6 pints	1,75
Power steering	3 to 3½ pints	3.5 to 4 pints	1,75 to 1,8

Overdrive unit lubrication system

3 litre Mk I and Mk IA models have gearbox and overdrive units with a common lubrication system. Filling of the overdrive unit is effected through the gearbox filler. The level of lubricant in both units being indicated by the gearbox dipstick.

Mk II and Mk III models have a separate gearbox and overdrive lubrication system. The overdrive unit has its own dipstick located in the filler orifice which is accessible through the inspection hole on top of the gearbox cover.

Oil additives

Must not be used in the overdrive or automatic transmission units. The oils selected for the engine, gearbox and axle, etc., are complete in themselves and afford every protection.

Section Z – SPECIAL TOOLS

In this section will be found details of special tools which are recommended to facilitate service work on the Rover 3 litre.

All tools are also illustrated in the appropriate sections, together with an explanation of their use.

INDEX

Description	*Function*	*Section*	*Illustration No.*	*Part No.*	*Symbol*
Accumulator housing 'O' ring replacer	Assembly overdrive unit	D	27	268714	‡
Accumulator piston housing remover	Dismantling overdrive unit	D	20	268715	*
Adaptor for power steering unit	Checking hydraulic pressure on the power steering unit	J1	44	601304	*
Axle shaft retaining collar removal and replacement tools	Removing and fitting axle shafts	M	50	275870 514576	*
Ball swivel rubber boot tool	Fitting rubber boot to ball swivel	K	45	511041	†
Bracket for dial gauge	Dial gauge support	A, M and N	5	530106	‡
Clutch spring compressor	Automatic transmission, Model 35, overhauling rear clutch	EE	39	601283	*
Collar retaining power steering components	Overhauling power steering unit	J1	43	601303	*
'C' spanner for power steering unit	Dismantling and assembling power steering unit	J1	42	525375	*
Differential pinion pre-load tool	Assembling differential	M	49	600968	*
Drive shaft oil seal remover	Dismantling overdrive unit	D	18	268709	‡
Drive shaft oil seal replacer, cone clutch and spring thrust housing dismantling tool	Dismantling and assembling overdrive unit	D	22	268710	*
Drift, valve guide removal	Removing valve guides	A	2	274400 274401	*
Dummy drive shaft	Assembling overdrive unit	D	23	268718	†
Endplay checking tool	Automatic transmission, Model 35, measuring gear train endplay	EE	37	601281	†
Engine sling	Removing and fitting engine	A	15	600963	†
Extractor	Removing camshaft gudgeon pin and pulling in connecting rod bolts	A	8	530101	‡
Extractor, chain wheel	Removing chain wheel	A	10	507231	†
Extractor, differential pinion bearing	Removing pinion bearing	M	51	262757	*
Extractor, rocker shafts	Removing rocker shafts	A	9	262749	*
Extractor, steering drop arm	Removing steering drop arm	J and J1	41	600446	*
Fitting tool, exhaust valve seat	Replacing exhaust valve seats	A	1	530625	*
Fitting tool, gudgeon pin	Replacing gudgeon pin	A	7	272103	‡
Fitting tool, valve guides	Replacing valve guides	A	3	600959 601508	*
Forked wedge, petrol pump	Assembling petrol pump	Q	53	263058	‡

*—Essential †—Advantageous ‡—Required when volume of work justifies use

INDEX—*continued*

Description	Function	Section	Illustration No.	Part No.	Symbol
Free-wheel assembly ring	Assembling overdrive unit	D	28	268711	†
Front servo gauge and adaptor	Automatic transmission, Model 35, adjusting front brake band	EE	36	601287	*
Gauge, differential pinion	Assembling differential	M	52	600299	*
Gauge plate, clutch release levers	Assembling clutch unit	C	16	530103	†
Gearbox cradle	Automatic transmission, Model 35, supporting unit during overhaul	EE	32	601280	†
Guides for rear main bearing cap seals	Fitting main bearing cap seals	A	11	270304	†
Hydraulic test equipment	Testing overdrive unit	D	29	268721	*
Insertion and extraction tool	Removing and fitting tyre valve	V	56	268723	*
Jig block, cylinder boring	Reboring cylinder block	A	12	261288	*
Operating piston fitting tool	Fitting operating piston into housing	D	30	268713	†
Piston fitting tool	Assembling overdrive unit	D	26	268712	†
Pop rivet pliers	Fitting chrome trim strips	U	55	501264	*
Press block, cylinder liner	Fitting liners to cylinder block	A	13	246650	*
Press block, differential bearings	Assembling differential	M	47	262758	*
Pressure gauge and tachometer	Automatic transmission, Model 35, checking downshift cable adjustment	EE	31	601284	*
Protection plate	Removing exhaust valve seats	A	4	263050	†
Pump barrel replacer	Assembling overdrive unit	D	25	268717	*
Pump barrel remover	Dismantling overdrive unit	D	19	268716	*
Rear clutch and seal inserter	Automatic transmission, Model 35, overhauling rear clutch	EE	40	601290	*
Retainer clip for torque converter	Automatic transmission, Model 35, removing gearbox and torque converter	EE	33	601467	*
Setting bar	Fitting solenoid to overdrive unit	D	17	278328	*
Snap ring pliers	Automatic transmission, Model 35, removing circlip retaining governor	EE	38	601282	*
Spanner	Dismantling and assembling differential	M	48	530105	†
Spanner, front hub adjustment	Assembling front hubs	K	46	263057	‡
Spanner, starter dog	Removing and fitting starter dog	A	14	530102	‡
Spanner, fuel tank unit	Removing tank gauge unit	Q	54	600964	*
'Spintorq' screwdriver set	Automatic transmission, Model 35, adjusting front brake band, replacing components	EE	35	601286	*
Tailshaft bearing remover	Dismantling overdrive unit	D	21	268720	†
Tailshaft bearing replacer	Assembling overdrive unit	D	24	268719	‡
Torque wrench set	Automatic transmission, Model 35, adjusting rear brake band, replacing components	EE	34	601285	*
Tyre fitting tourniquet	Fitting tubeless tyres	V	57	268722	‡
Valve spring compressor	Valve removal and replacement	A	6	276102	‡

*—Essential †—Advantageous ‡—Required when volume of work justifies use

Valve seat fitting tool * →

The seat must be pulled in carefully to avoid shattering.

Part No. 530625

Section A

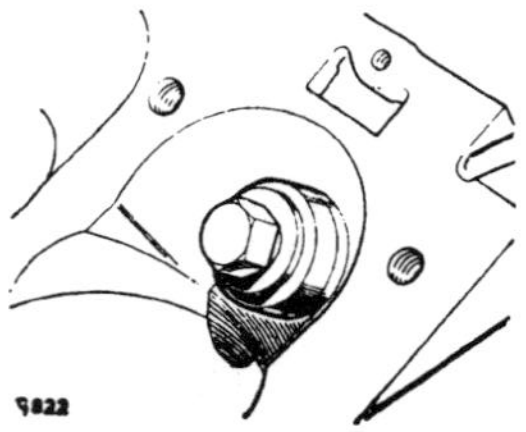

Illustration No. 1

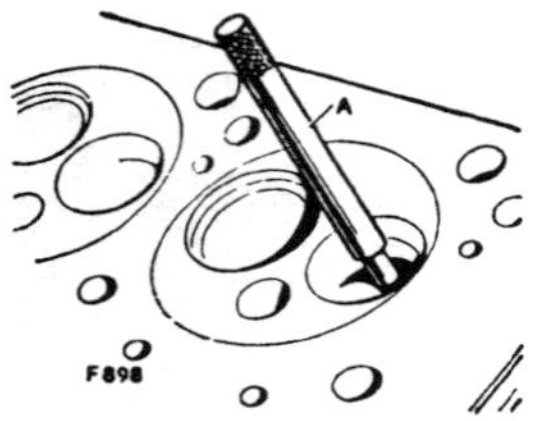

Illustration No. 2

← **Drifts, valve guide removal †**

Facilitates removal of the valve guides.

Mk I and IA Inlet and exhaust .. Part No. 274401
Mk II and III Inlet .. .. .. Part No. 274400
Exhaust .. .. Part No. 274401

Section A

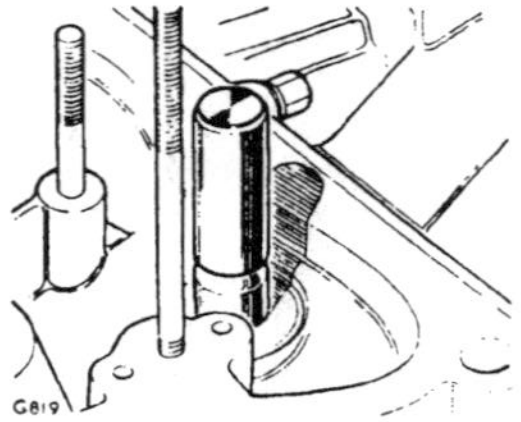

Illustration No. 3

Fitting tool valve guides * →

These tools are necessary to overcome the possibility of damage to the seal groove.

Mk I and IA Inlet and exhaust .. Part No. 600959
Mk II and III Inlet .. .. .. Part No. 601508
Exhaust .. .. Part No. 600959

Section A

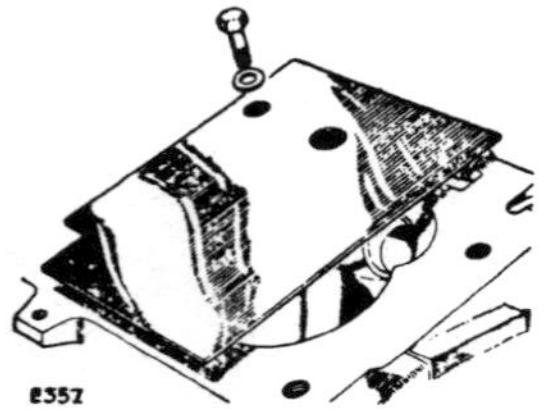

Illustration No. 4

← **Protection plate for exhaust valve seat removal †**

The seat insert is removed by breaking, following grinding, and the use of the plate will prevent injury to the operator.

Part No. 263050

Section A

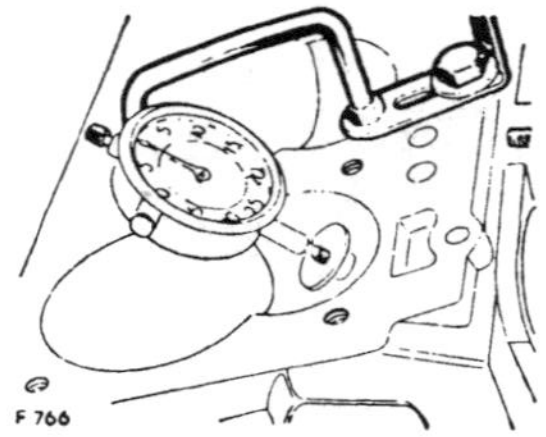

Illustration No. 5

Bracket for indicator, valve timing ‡ →

Its use enables the employment of a standard indicator. Also used for checking camshaft and crankshaft end-float, flywheel run-out.

Part No. 530106

Sections A, M and N

*—Essential †—Advantageous ‡—Required when volume of work justifies use

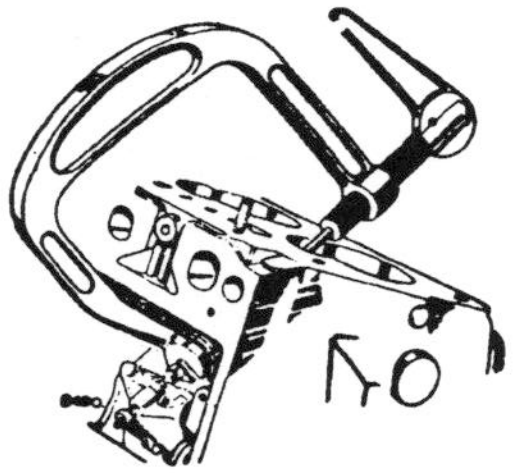

Illustration No. 6

Valve spring compressor ‡

Suitable for extracting the cotters on both inlet and exhaust valves.

Part No. 276102

Section A

Fitting tool, gudgeon pin ‡

Facilitates refitting of gudgeon pin.

Part No. 272103

Section A

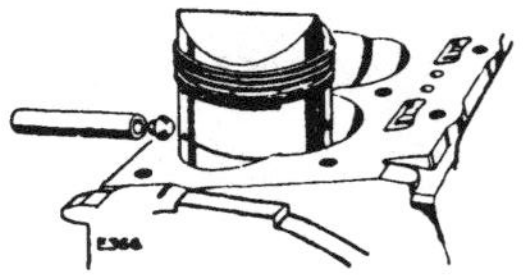

Illustration No. 7

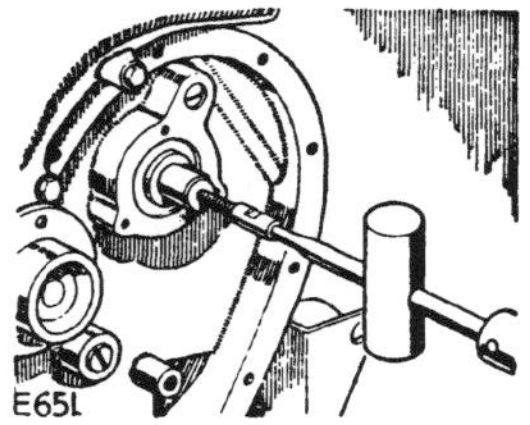

Illustration No. 8

Extractor, camshaft and gudgeon pin ‡

Part No. 530101

Section A

May also be used for pulling in connecting rod bolts.

Extractor, rocker shafts *

Essential when removing and refitting rockers with engine in position.

Part No. 262749

Section A

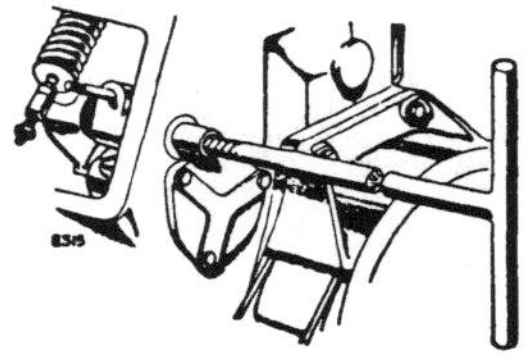

Illustration No. 9

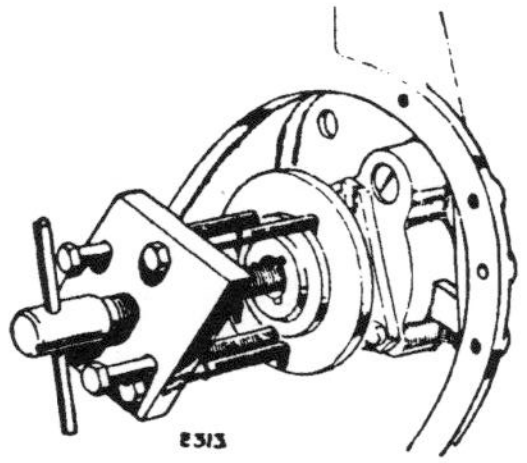

Illustration No. 10

Extractor, chain wheel †

Facilitates chain wheel removal.

Part No. 507231

Section A

*—Essential †—Advantageous ‡—Required when volume of work justifies use

Guides for rear main bearing cap seals †

Provides a leading edge for the rear main seals.

Part No. 270304

Section A

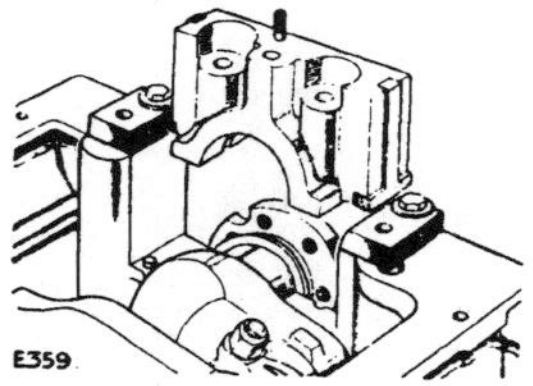

Illustration No. 11

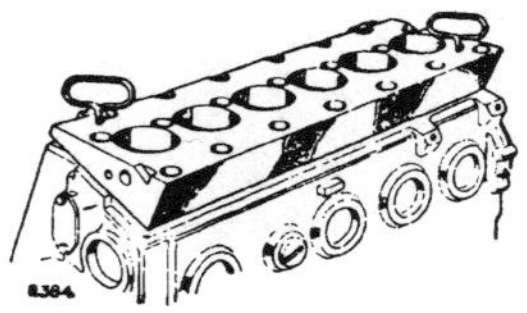

Illustration No. 12

Jig block, cylinder boring *

Enables standard boring equipment to be used on sloping head engines.

Part No. 261288

Section A

Press block, cylinder liner *

Essential for fitting liners on sloping head engines.

Part No. 246650

Section A

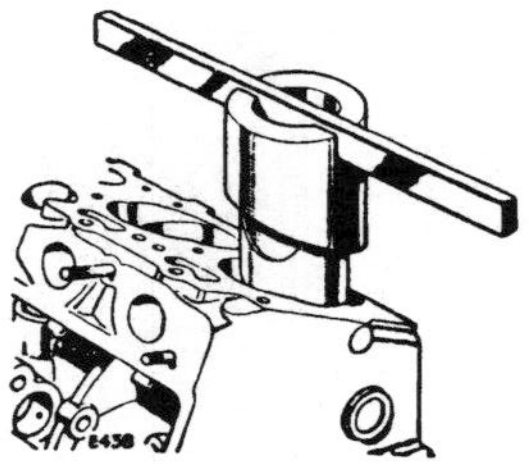

Illustration No. 13

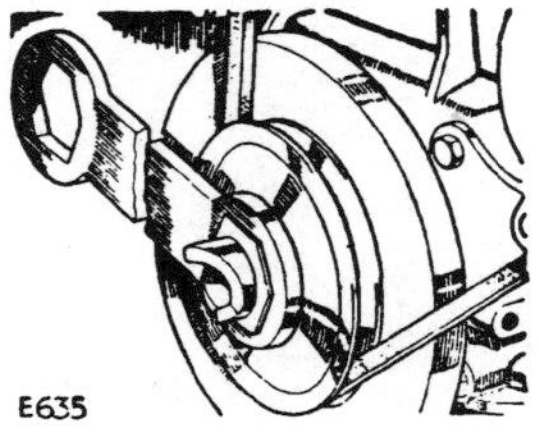

Illustration No. 14

Spanner for starter dog ‡

Facilitates removal and refitting of the starter dog.

Part No. 530102

Section A

Engine sling †

Facilitates removal and refitting of the engine.

Part No. 600963

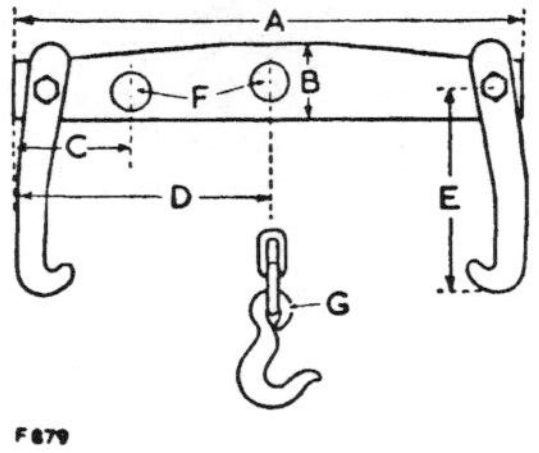

Illustration No. 15

*—Essential †—Advantageous ‡—Required when volume of work justifies use

Illustration No. 16

Setting bar for solenoid operating lever * →

Must be used when adjusting the solenoid lever.

Part No. 278328

Section D

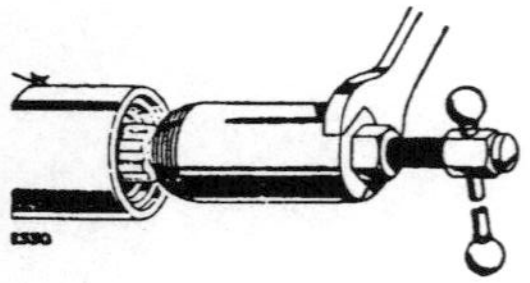

Illustration No. 18

Pump barrel remover * →

Essential when removing the pump barrel.

Part No. 268716

Section D

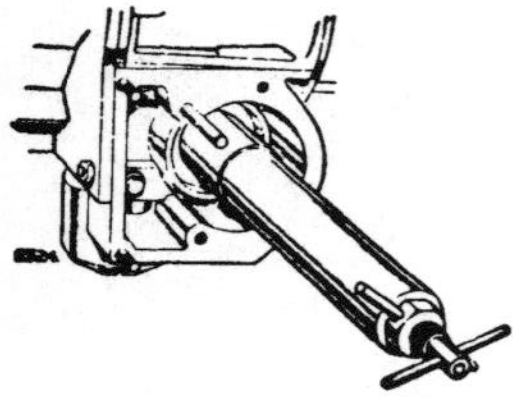

Illustration No. 20

← **Gauge plate, clutch release levers †**

Clutch lever thrust faces must be set, using these gauges, from the flywheel face.

Part No. 530103

Section C

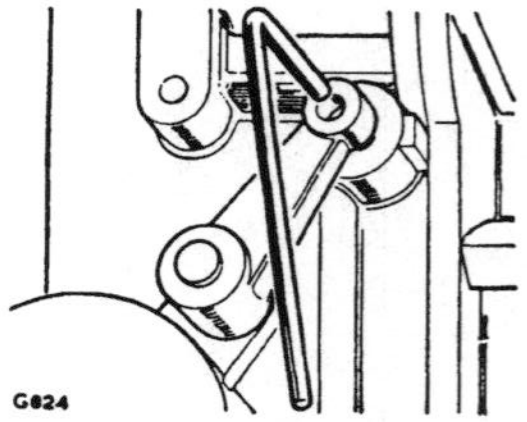

Illustration No. 17

← **Drive shaft oil seal remover ‡**

Facilitates removal of the drive shaft oil seal with overdrive unit in position.

Part No. 268709

Section D

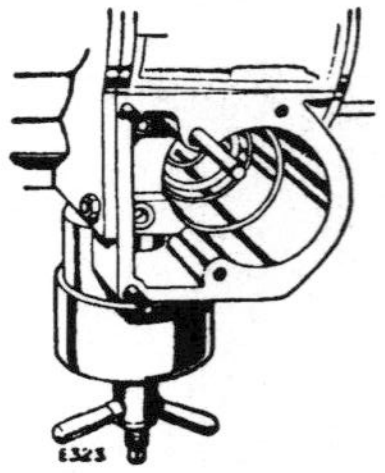

Illustration No. 19

← **Accumulator piston housing remover ***

Essential when removing the accumulator piston housing.

Part No. 268715

Section D

*—Essential †—Advantageous ‡—Required when volume of work justifies use

Tailshaft bearing remover and replacer † →

Facilitates removal of tailshaft bearing. Use in conjunction with Churchill Hand Press, S4221, RG4221 or similar.

Part No. 268720

Section D

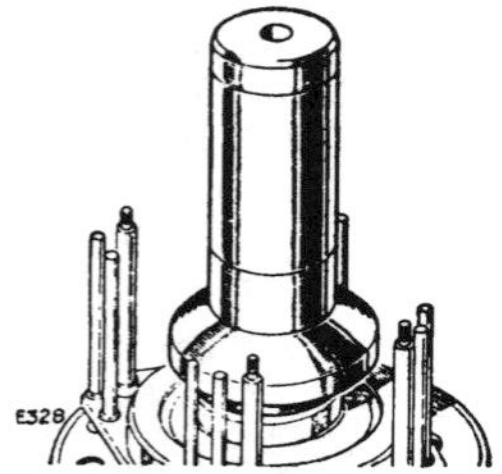

Illustration No. 22

Dummy drive shaft † →

Facilitates refitting the drive shaft.

Part No. 268718

Section D

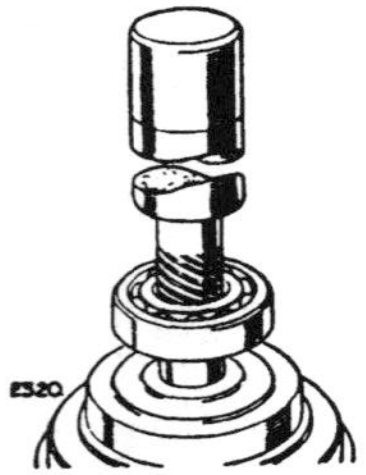

Illustration No. 24

Pump barrel replacer * →

Essential when replacing the pump barrel.

Part No. 268717

Section D

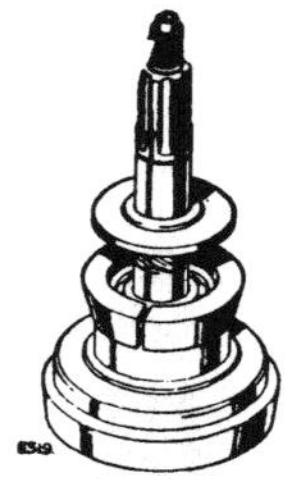

Illustration No. 21

← **Drive shaft oil seal replacer, cone clutch and spring thrust housing dismantling tool ***

Essential when dismantling the cone clutch.

Part No. 268710

Section D

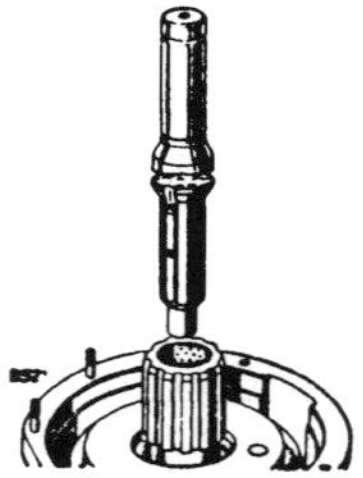

Illustration No. 23

← **Tailshaft bearing replacer ‡**

Facilitates refitting the tailshaft bearing.

Part No. 268719

Section D

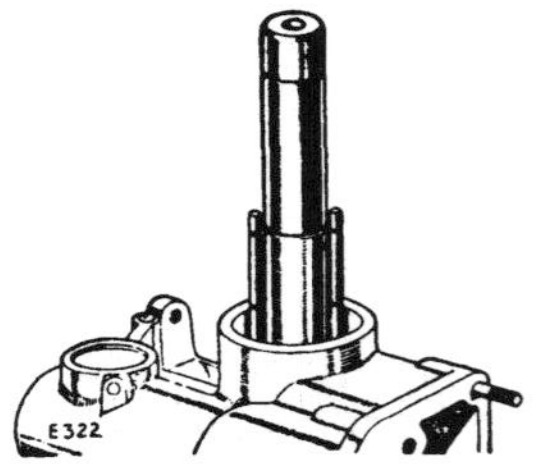

Illustration No. 25

*—Essential †—Advantageous ‡—Required when volume of work justifies use

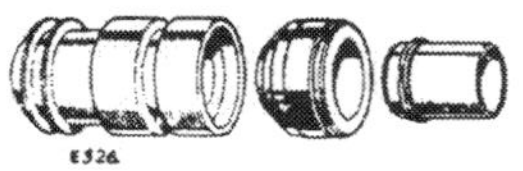

Illustration No. 26

Accumulator housing 'O' ring replacer ‡ ⟶

Used when fitting accumulator housing 'O' rings.

Part No. 268714

Section D

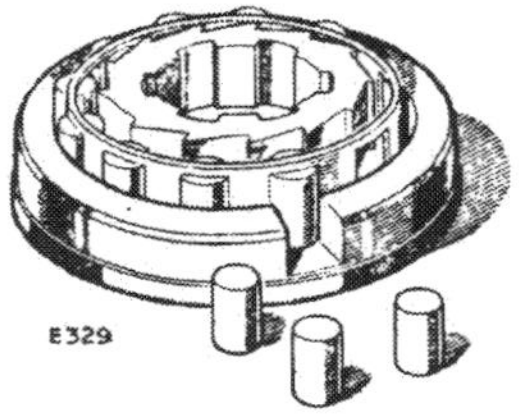

Illustration No. 28

Hydraulic test equipment * ⟶

Essential for checking the working oil pressure on the overdrive unit, also used to test the hydraulic pressure in the power steering system.

Part No. 268721

Section D and J1

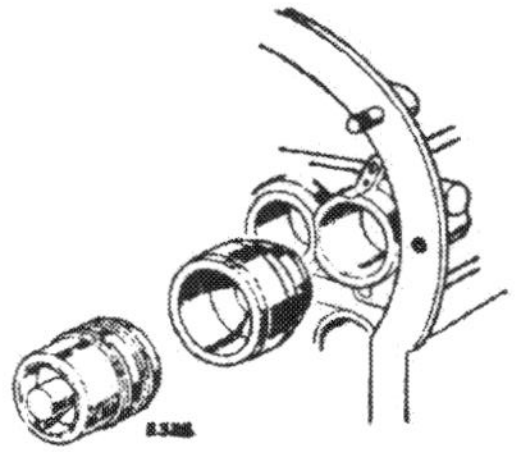

Illustration No. 30

⟵ **Piston fitting tool $1\frac{1}{8}$ in., for accumulator piston †**

Facilitates refitting piston to accumulator housing.

Part No. 268712

Section D

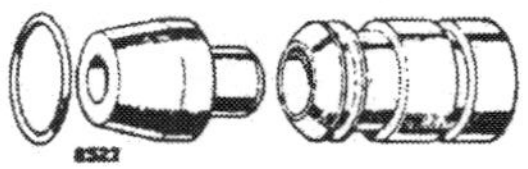

Illustration No. 27

⟵ **Free-wheel assembly ring †**

The use of this tool is advisable when replacing the free-wheel rollers.

Part No. 268711

Section D

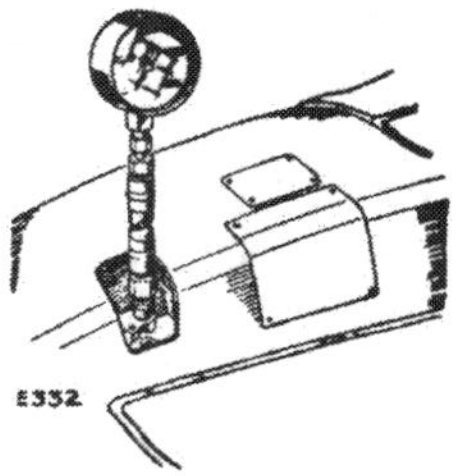

Illustration No. 29

⟵ **Operating piston fitting tool, $1\frac{3}{8}$ in., for operating piston †**

Facilitates fitting the operating piston into the housing.

Part No. 268713

Section D

*—Essential †—Advantageous ‡—Required when volume of work justifies use

Pressure gauge and tachometer* ⟶

Essential when checking downshift cable adjustment.

Part No. 601284

Section EE

Illustration No. 32

Retainer clip for torque converter* ⟶

Essential when removing gearbox and torque converter as one unit.

Part No. 601467

Section EE

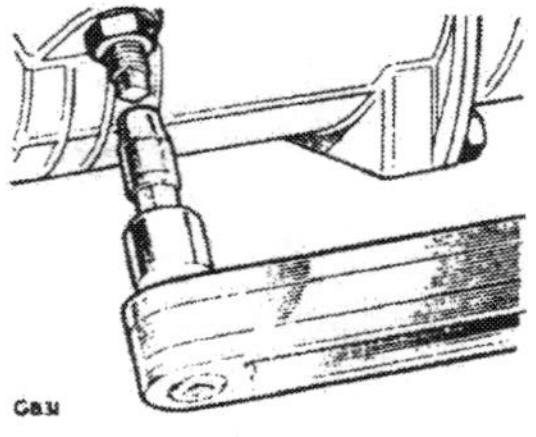

Illustration No. 34

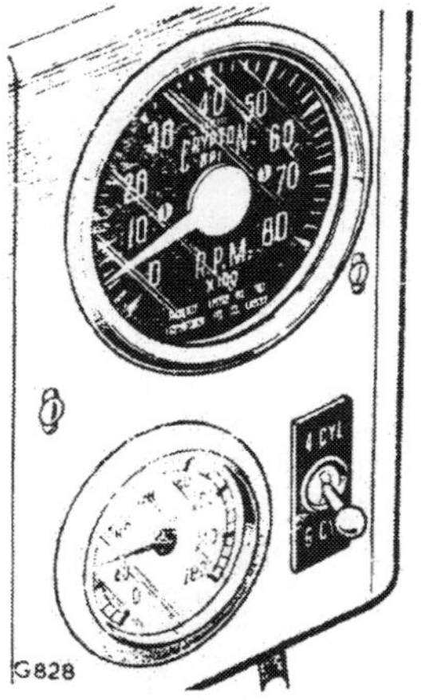

Illustration No. 31

⟵ **Gearbox cradle†**

Used to support the unit during overhaul.

Part No. 601280

Section EE

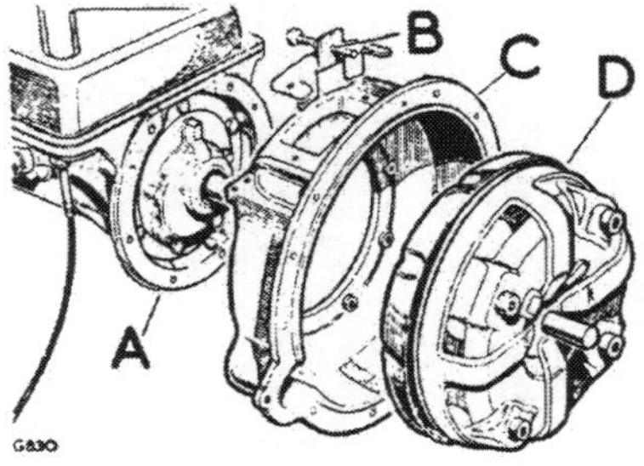

Illustration No. 33

⟵ **Torque wrench set***

Essential for adjusting rear brake band and to obtain correct tightening torques when replacing components

Part No. 601285

Section EE

*—Essential †—Advantageous ‡—Required when volume of work justifies use

'Spintorq' screwdriver set* ⟶

Essential for adjusting front brake band and to obtain correct tightening torques when replacing components.

Part No. 601286

Section EE

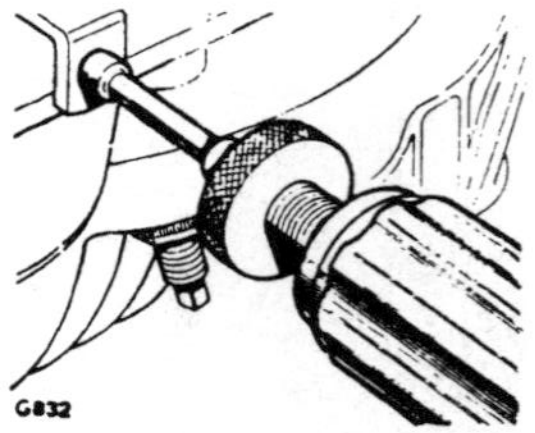

Illustration No. 35

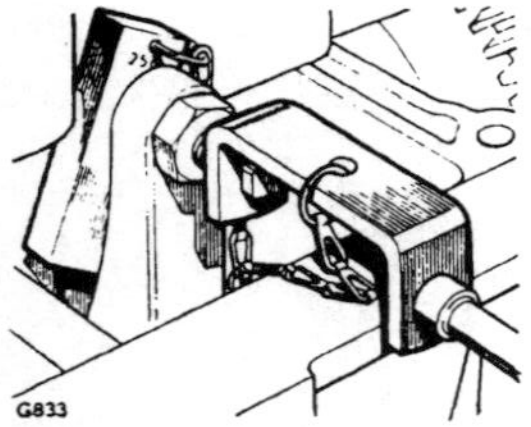

Illustration No. 36

⟵ **Front servo gauge and adaptor***

Essential when adjusting front brake band, use in conjunction with 'Spintorq' screwdriver.

Part No. 601287

Section EE

End-play checking tool† ⟶

Facilitates checking gear train end-play.

Part No. 601281

Section EE

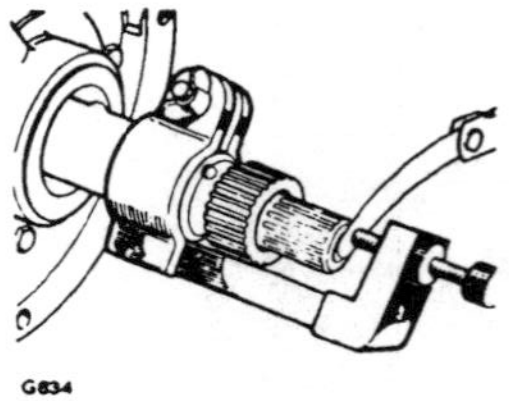

Illustration No. 37

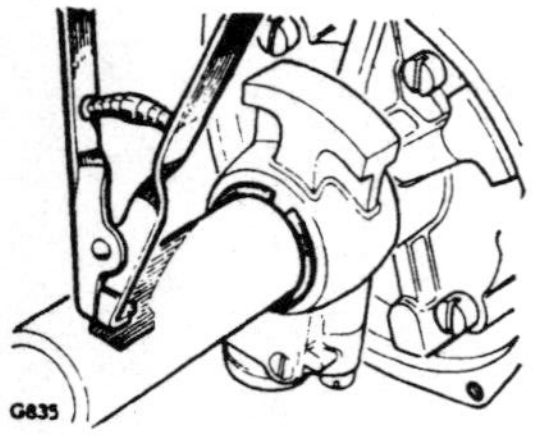

Illustration No. 38

⟵ **Snap ring pliers***

Used to remove circlip retaining governor.

Part No. 601282

Section EE

*—Essential †—Advantageous ‡—Required when volume of work justifies use

Clutch spring compressor* ⟶

Essential when overhauling the rear clutch.

Part No. 601283

Section EE

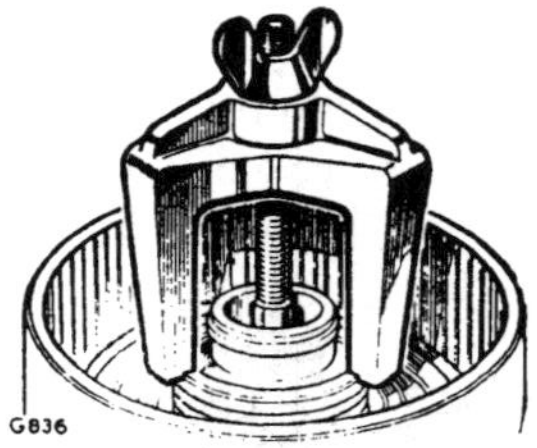

Illustration No. 39

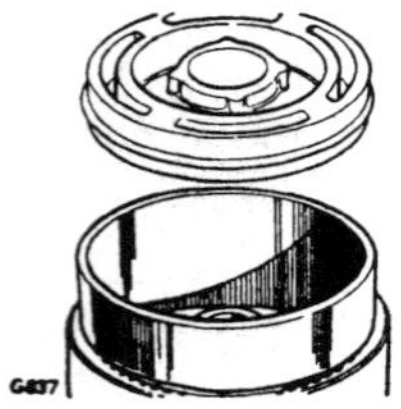

Illustration No. 40

⟵ **Rear clutch and seal inserter***

Essential when overhauling the rear clutch.

Part No. 601290

Section EE

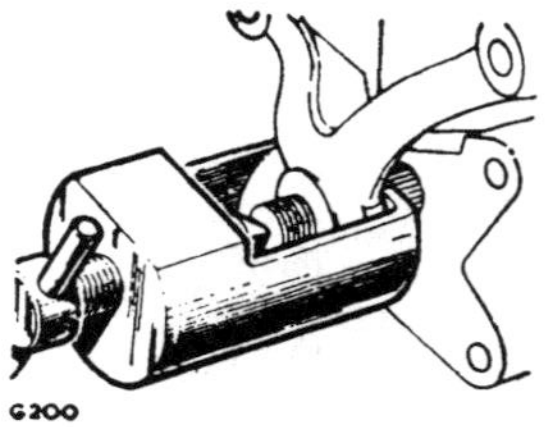

Illustration No. 41

Extractor for steering drop arm* ⟶

Essential when withdrawing drop arms when the steering box is removed. Recommended for power steering.

Part No. 600446

Sections J and J1

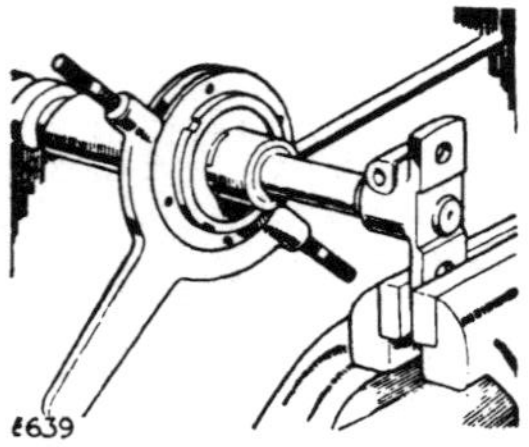

Illustration No. 42

⟵ **'C' spanner for power steering***

Essential to unlock and lock up the valve spool halves.

Part No. 525375

Section J1

*—Essential †—Advantageous ‡—Required when volume of work justifies use

Collar, retaining power steering components*

Essential when overhauling the power steering unit.

Part No. 601303

Section J1

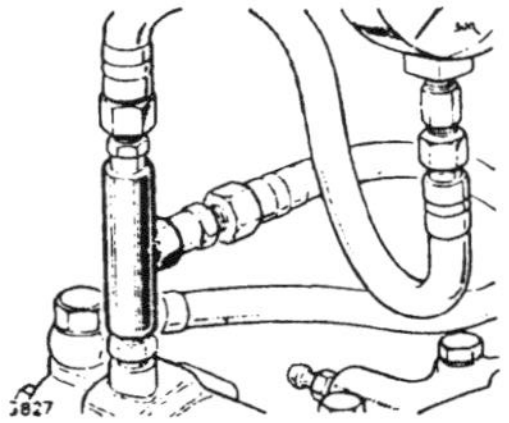

Illustration No. 44

Ball swivel rubber boot replacing tool †

It is important that the rubber boot is correctly refitted, and this tool facilitates the operation.

Part No. 511041

Section K

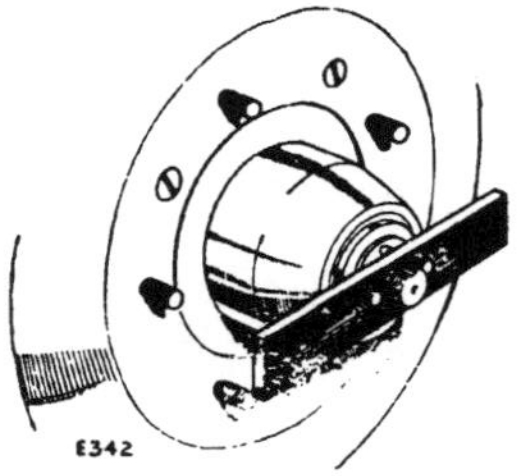

Illustration No. 46

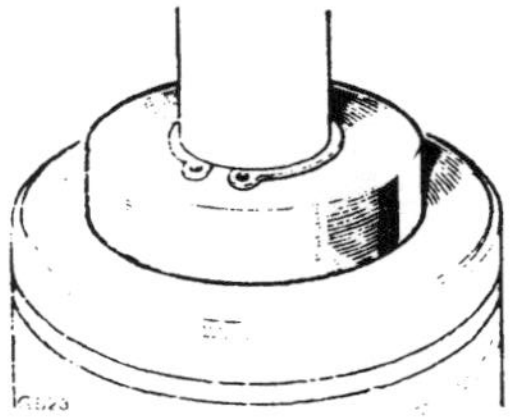

Illustration No. 43

Adaptor for power steering unit*

Essential when checking hydraulic pressure on the power steering unit.

Part No. 601304

Section J1

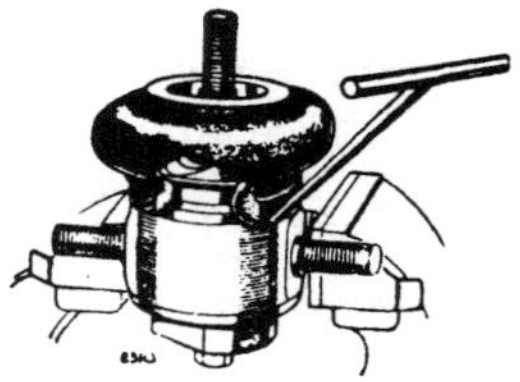

Illustration No. 45

Spanner, front hub adjustment ‡

Facilitates front hub adjustment.

Part No. 263057

Section K

Press block differential bearings *

This tool must be purchased with Tool No. 262757 as the cross-piece is common to both.

Part No. 262758

Section M

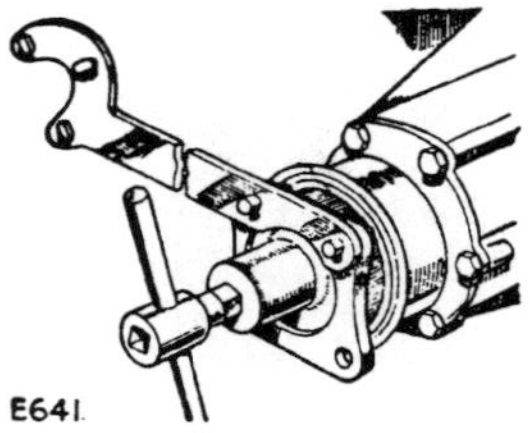

Illustration No. 48

Differential pinion pre-load tool *

Essential when overhauling the differential unit.

Part No. 600968

Section M

Illustration No. 50

Extractor, differential pinion rear bearing *

Essential when removing roller bearing outer race.

Part No. 262757

Section M

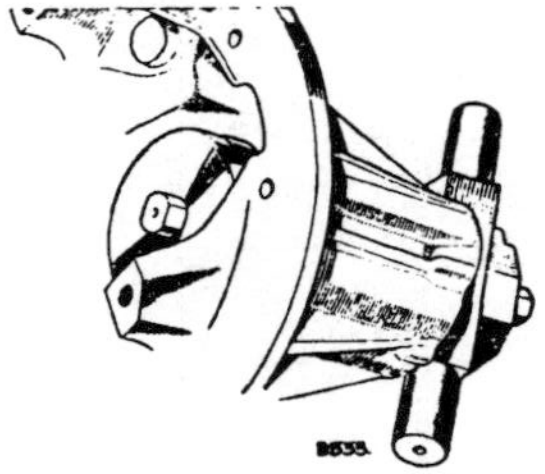

Illustration No. 47

Spanner for differential flange and crownwheel locking nuts †

Facilitates holding the differential flange when tightening nut retaining flange, can also be used to tighten the crown wheel locking nuts.

Part No. 530105

Section M

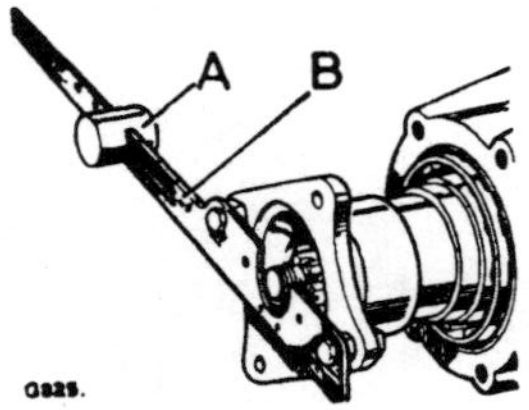

Illustration No. 49

Axle shaft retaining collar removal and replacement tools *

Essential when removing and replacing axle shaft retaining collar.

Part No. 275870

Adaptor 514576

Section M

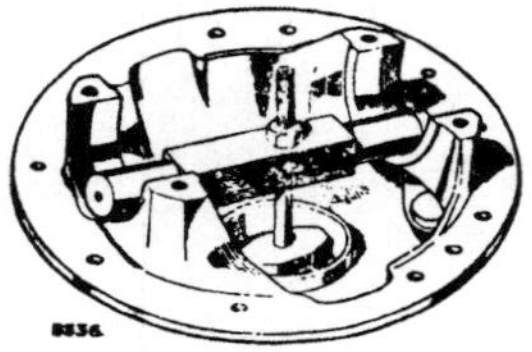

Illustration No. 51

G820
Illustration No. 52

Forked wedge, petrol pump ‡ ⟶

The pump body must be assembled with the diaphragm fully stretched, using this tool.

Part No. 263058

Section Q

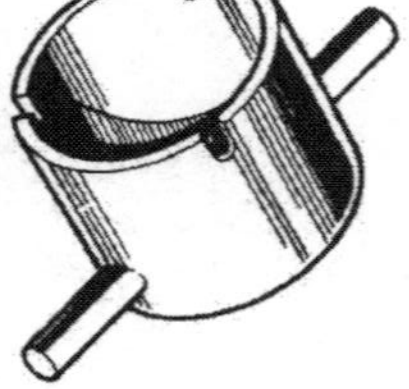
G840
Illustration No. 54

Pop rivet pliers * ⟶

Essential when fitting chrome trim strips to doors and wings on cars. These pliers are suitable only for the size of rivet used on the trim strips.

Part No. 501264

Section U

⟵ **Gauge, differential pinion setting ***

In use the tool provides the correct dimension from pinion to crownwheel when using a .003 in. feeler gauge.

Part No. 600299

Section M

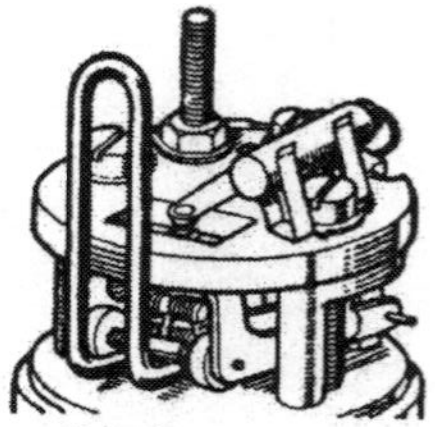
E439
Illustration No. 53

⟵ **Spanner for fuel tank gauge***

Essential when removing the fuel tank gauge unit

Part No. 600964

Section Q

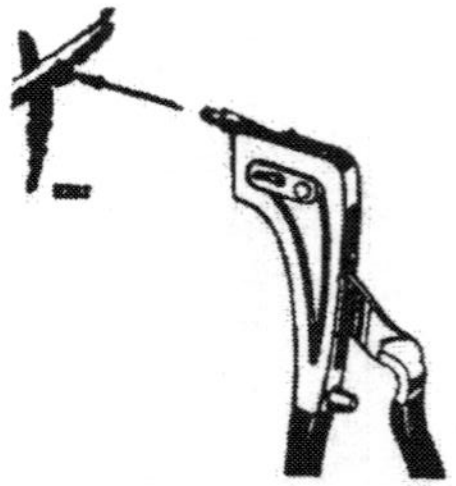
Illustration No. 55

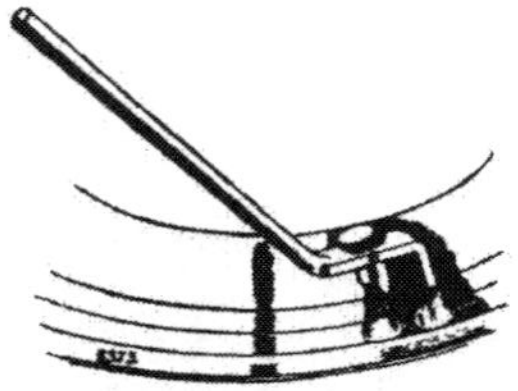
Illustration No. 56

Tourniquet tubeless tyres ‡ ⟶

Facilitates sealing the tubeless tyre if difficulty is experienced.

Part No. 268722

Section V

⟵ **Insertion and extraction tool for rubber valve, tubeless tyres ***

Essential for fitting and removing the rubber moulded valves used on tubeless tyres.

Part No. 268723

Section V

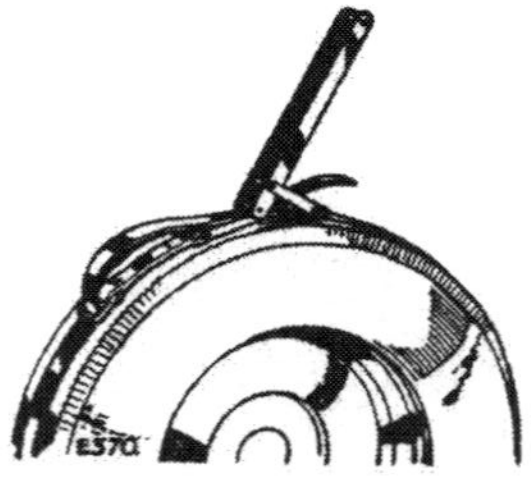
E570
Illustration No. 57

The following numbers refer to the special tools necessary for servicing the automatic transmission fitted to 3 litre cars as optional equipment.

The tools are not supplied by Rover-British Leyland UK Limited, but are available from the manufacturers:

Messrs. V. L. Churchill and Company Limited
P.O. Box No. 3
London Road
Daventry
Northants

	Churchill No.		Churchill No.
Hydraulic test gauge and adaptors (8)	B-W 1A	Mainshaft end-float gauge	B-W 13
Brake band adjuster	B-W 2B	Bench cradle	B-W 15A
Converter aligning gauge	B-W 3	Drive flange oil seal replacer	B-W 16
Spline aligning fixture	B-W 5	Oil seal driver	550 (handle)
Spring retainer remover	B-W 8A	Pulling tools	6312A
Piston installing pins	B-W 10	Pulling tools	B-W 6312A/1
Clutch assembling and dismantling tool	B-W 11A	Mainshaft bearing replacer	B-W 7
Lubrication valve test rod	B-W 12A	Circlip pliers	7065

Rover 3.5 Litre Workshop Manual Supplement Saloon & Coupe (P5)

Rover-British Leyland UK Limited
Solihull, Warwickshire, England

First issue - September 1967

BRITISH LEYLAND ROVER

Service Department
Solihull, Warwickshire,
Telephone : 021-743 4242
Telgrams : Rovrepair Solihull
Telex : 33-156

This Supplement, which should be used in conjunction with the Rover 3 Litre Workshop Manual, Part No. 4661, gives workshop procedure details for all the new items introduced on the Rover 3.5-Litre model, which is fitted only with automatic transmission.

Parts Department
P.O. Box 79
Cardiff
Great Britain
Telephone : Cardiff 33681
Telgrams : Rovparts, Cardiff
Telex : 49-359

Please note that all prices and specifications are subject to alteration without note

Always quote type and number of vehicle when ording

By Appointment to Her Majesty Queen Elizabeth II — *Manufacturers of Motor Cars and Land-Rovers*

By Appointment to Her Majesty Queen Elizabeth the Queen Mother — *Suppliers of Motor Cars and Land-Rovers*

Part No. 606358

Rover 3.5 Litre Workshop Manual Supplement Saloon & Coupe (P5)

Location of car and unit numbers

Chassis number

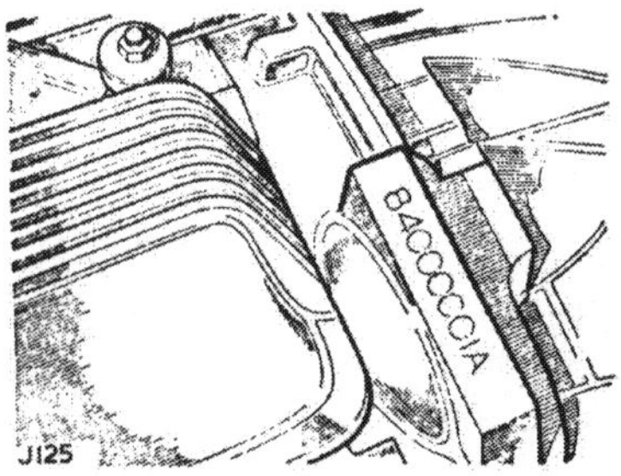

Engine number

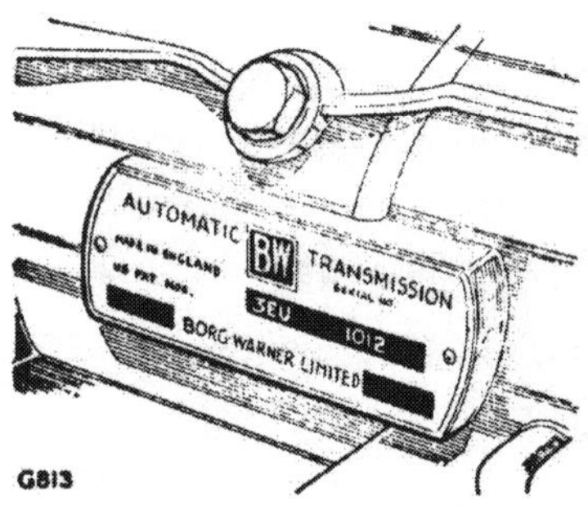

Automatic transmission number

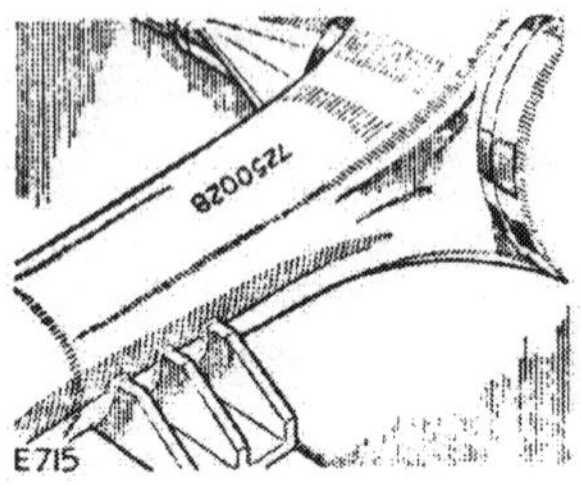

Rear axle number

Commencing chassis and unit numbers

Rover 3.5-Litre Saloon

Model	Chassis Numbers	Engine Numbers	Automatic Transmission Numbers	Rear axle Numbers
Automatic transmission, Home, RHD	84000001A			
Automatic transmission, Export, RHD	84100001A			
Automatic transmission, CKD, RHD	84200001A	84000001A	FU 1001	84000001A
Automatic transmission, Export, LHD	84300001A			
Automatic transmission, CKD, LHD	84400001A			

Rover 3.5-Litre Coupé

Model	Chassis Numbers	Engine Numbers	Automatic Transmission Numbers	Rear axle Numbers
Automatic transmission, Home, RHD	84500001A			
Automatic transmission, Export, RHD	84600001A			
Automatic transmission, CKD, RHD	84700001A	84000001A	FU 1001	84000001A
Automatic transmission, Export, LHD	84800001A			
Automatic transmission, CKD, LHD	84900001A			

CONTENTS

H893

ROVER 3.5 LITRE, SALOON ILLUSTRATED

GENERAL EXPLANATION

This Supplement, which should be used in conjunction with the Rover 3-Litre Workshop Manual, Part No. 4661, gives workshop procedure details for all the new items introduced on the Rover 3.5-Litre model, which is fitted only with automatic transmission.

The main features of the Rover 3.5-Litre model are summarised below.

(1) Identification

A. External

i **Wheels:** 5J x 15 magnum type wheels, finished in chrome and silver, featuring a centre TC type badge, are fitted. The wheel nuts are also chromium plated.

Rover 3.5 litre, three-quarter front view

ii **Motifs:** The '3.5-LITRE' motif is fitted as follows: boot lid and rear edge of front wings, below repeater flashers.

iii **Radiator:** The redesigned radiator grille no longer comprises an aperture for the starting handle. New centre spine with badge cast in gilding metal. Both spine and grille bars are finished in silver grey.

iv **Fog lamp:** The twin Lucas 6 WFT 50 watt foglamps are accommodated in depressions in the front wings, below the headlamps.

v **Exhaust system:** Twin tail pipes are fitted.

vi **Bumpers:** The over-riders are redesigned and have rubber inserts fitted.

vii **Body side mouldings with repeater flashers:** The body side mouldings have been modified to take the flasher repeaters. These are fitted into a recess as follows: Rear edge of front wing and rear edge of rear wing.

viii **Coach lines:** Coach lines are painted below the body side mouldings. On Coupé models a second coach line is painted on the roof, above the gutter, following the roof line.

ix **Sills:** The one-piece sills are finished in matt black.

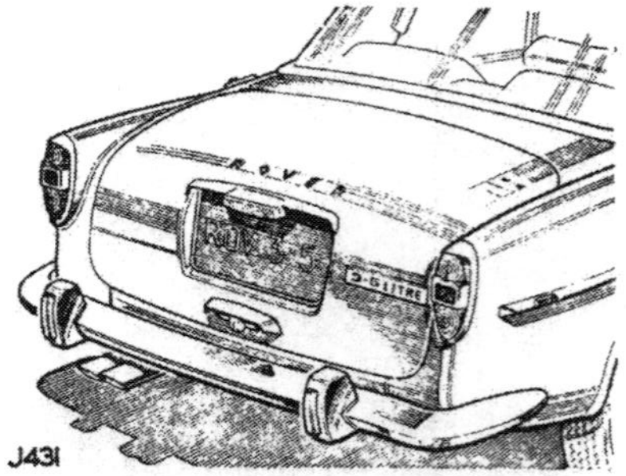

J431

Rover 3.5 litre, three-quarter rear view

B. Internal

i **Console:** The console unit on the tunnel comprises the selector lever finisher surround, trinket tray and a Rover '2000' type ashtray.

ii **Instruments:** The instruments are basically as on the 3-Litre Mk III, with the exception of the following:

(a) Speedometer. Red zone from 115 mph onwards.

(b) Tachometer. Red zone from 5,200 to 6,000 rpm.

(c) Ammeter. 60-0-60 calibration.

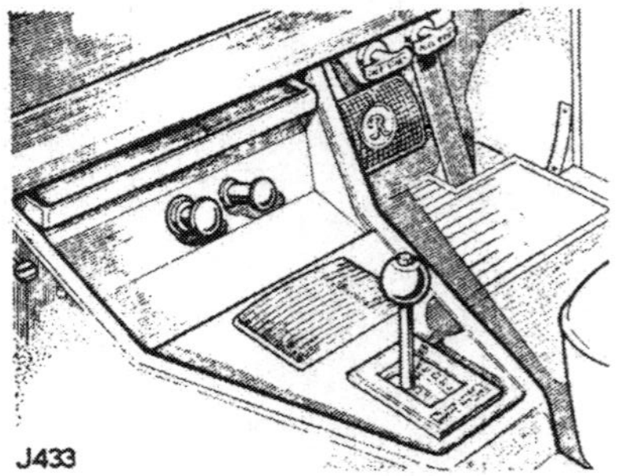

J433

Console unit

iii **Switch panel:** The leather cloth covered switch panel below the picnic tray carries the cigar lighter, one fog lamp switch controlling both lamps, and where fitted, the switch for the heated backlight.

iv **Parcel shelf crash roll:** The ashtrays are deleted from the underside of the parcel shelf crash roll. A large Rover '2000' type ashtray is built into the console unit.

(2) Engine: The cylinder block is cast aluminium fitted with cylinder liners, maximum permissible rebore .020 in. It has two banks of four cylinders each, which form a 90° angle.

The crankshaft is supported by five bearings. The thrust is taken by the centre bearing. The connecting rods are forged steel, and aluminium alloy pistons are used. These are fitted with two compression and one oil control ring above the gudgeon pin.

The cylinder heads are also an aluminium casting. Iron valve seat inserts and valve guides are used. The valves are arranged in line and operate at an angle of 10° above the cylinder bore centre line. The camshaft is located between the two banks of cylinders, above the crankshaft and runs in five bearings. It is driven at half the crankshaft speed by a single chain. No chain tensioner is provided.

The valves are operated by means of hydraulic tappets which ensure quiet engine running and maintain tappet adjustment at the correct clearance.

Lubrication of the engine is by means of a pressure fed oil system, which incorporates an oil pump located in the timing chain cover, and an external full-flow oil filter.

Main engine data

Type	V8
Bore	3.500 in. (88,90 mm)
Stroke	2.800 in. (71,12 mm)
Number of cylinders	8
Cylinder capacity	215 cu in. (3.531 ccm)
Compression ratio	10.5:1
BHP	183 at 5,000 rpm
Maximum torque	226 lb ft (31 mkg) at 3,000 rpm
Firing order	1, 8, 4, 3, 6, 5, 7, 2
Sparking plugs	Champion L87Y

(3) Transmission

The transmission consists of an up-rated converter and model 35 automatic transmission to suit the higher power output of the engine. The transmission has no rear pump which means that the car cannot be towed or push started. Furthermore, for anything exceeding local recovery the propeller shaft must be disconnected.

The gear ratios are as on the Rover 3-Litre Mk III.

An oil cooler is incorporated in the radiator.

(4) Fuel system

The fuel system comprises an AC mechanical fuel pump, mounted on the front left-hand side of the engine. Two SU type HS6 carburetters are used, fitted with twin paper element air cleaners. A spill return fuel system is used.

The petrol reserve is similar to the Rover 2000 type, and the petrol tank has been suitably altered to accommodate the spill return pipe. The petrol tank breather system, too, is similar to that used on the Rover 2000.

(5) Cooling system

The cooling is by pump, 5 blade fan and thermostat. The system is pressurised to 15 lb/sq in. (1,0 kg/cm²). A radiator of the cross-flow type is used incorporating an oil cooler for the automatic transmission.

(6) Suspension

Both front and rear suspension follow the pattern used on the 3-Litre models, but the damper setting at the front has been altered to compensate the reduced weight at the front end of the car.

(7) Brakes

The braking system is similar to that used on the 3-Litre Mk III cars with the following exceptions:

(a) New Ferodo 2424F type front pads.
(b) New $\frac{7}{8}$ in. brake master cylinder.
(c) Lockheed type 7 brake servo unit.
(d) $\frac{3}{4}$ in. wheel cylinders for rear brakes.
(e) Fine turned brake drums.
(f) New simpler handbrake linkage.
(g) AC mechanical stop lamp switch.

(8) Steering

The steering is identical to that used on the 3-Litre Mk III with the exception of the power steering pump, which is now pulley driven, instead of dynamo driven.

(9) Tyres

6.70 in. x 15 in. Avon Turbospeed or Dunlop RS5 tyres are fitted.

(10) Electrical

The main innovation of the electrical installation, which is of the negative earth type as on the 3-Litre Mk III, is the fitting of a Lucas 11 AC alternator with an output of 43 amps minimum.

The starter motor fitted is of the pre-engaged type.

Section A1 – Rover 3.5 Litre – ENGINE UNIT – Part One

The operations in this Section are peculiar to the Rover 3.5-Litre model. They replace all the operations in Section A1 and Section B in the Rover 3-Litre Workshop Manual.

Section A is divided into two parts:

Part I .. .. .. Dismantling, overhaul and assembling
Part II .. .. .. Defect location and data

When carrying out a complete engine overhaul, the section can be worked straight through in the order presented.

Alternatively, the individual operations which form the greater percentage of maintenance work undertaken by Distributors and Dealers, are detailed under appropriate headings, and will be found to be complete in themselves.

Some operations are marked with an asterisk * to indicate that they can be carried out with the engine installed. In all other cases it is necessary to remove the engine unit in order to carry out the work detailed.

Brief description of engine

The cylinder block is cast aluminium fitted with cylinder liners, maximum permissible rebore 0.020 in. It has two banks of four cylinders each, which form a 90° angle.

The crankshaft is supported by five bearings. The thrust is taken by the centre bearing. The connecting rods are forged steel, and aluminium alloy pistons are used. These are fitted with two compression and one oil control ring above the gudgeon pin.

The cylinder heads are also an aluminium casting. Iron valve seat inserts and valve guides are used. The valves are arranged in line and operate at an angle of 10° above the cylinder bore centre line.

The camshaft is located between the two banks of cylinders, above the crankshaft and runs in five bearings. It is driven at half the crankshaft speed by a single chain. No chain tensioner is provided.

The valves are operated by means of hydraulic tappets which ensure quiet engine running and maintain tappet adjustment at the correct clearance.

Lubrication of the engine is by means of a pressure fed oil system, which incorporates an oil pump located in the timing chain cover, and an external full-flow oil filter.

Bolt tightening torques

IMPORTANT: As the V8 engine is fitted with a cast aluminium cylinder block it is of critical importance to adhere to the specified tightening torque for all bolts. It is equally important to maintain the designed thread engagement lengths, otherwise irreparable damage may be done to the cylinder block.

Always use bolts of the correct length and where specified use the thread lubricant and sealer.

INDEX—ENGINE UNIT—PARTS ONE AND TWO

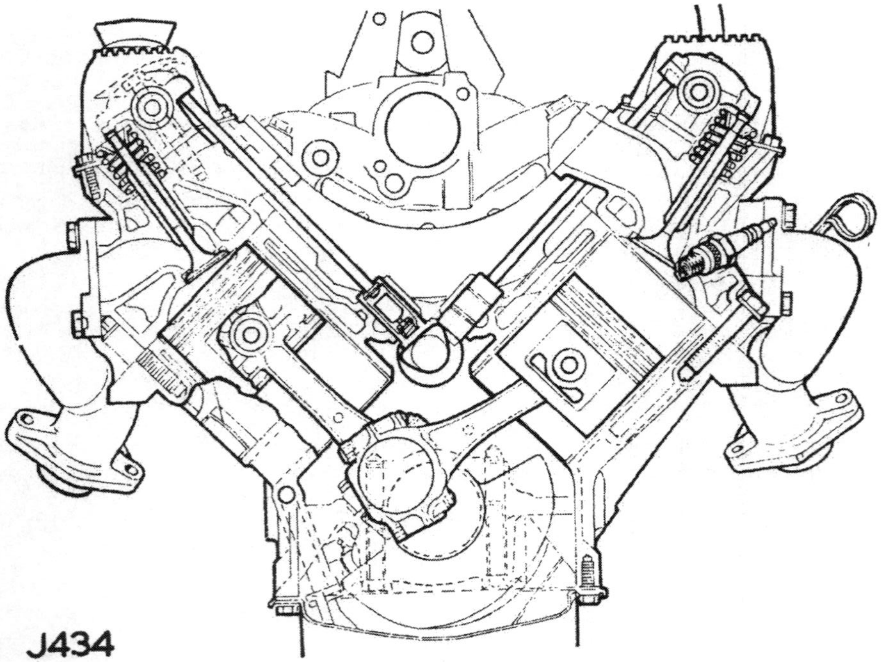

Cross-section of engine, end view

*Bonnet, to remove and refit—Operation A1-1

Time allowed: hours

Workshop hand tools:
Spanner size: ½ in. AF

Bonnet, remove

1. Raise and support the bonnet.
2. **Coupé models only.** Disconnect the wiring to the bonnet lamp by removing one lead from the switch and the other from the fuse box.
3. Disconnect pipe, windscreen washer reservoir to jets.
4. Remove the springs from the bonnet hinges.
5. Mark position of plain washers relative to bracket on bonnet to obviate the need for bonnet catch mechanism adjustment when replacing the bonnet.
6. Remove the nuts securing the hinge links to the hinge bracket on the bonnet, these face inwards towards the engine. Do not remove the bracket from the bonnet.
7. Lift off bonnet and store in a convenient place.

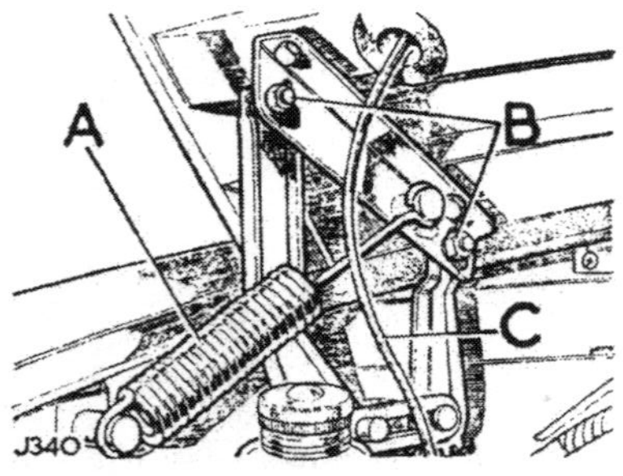

Bonnet hinge and spring

A—Spring for bonnet hinge
B—Nuts fixing hinge links to bracket
C—Pipe, windscreen washer

Bonnet, refit

1. Reverse removal procedure.
2. Check and ensure correct fit also correct operation of bonnet lock mechanism.

   Adjust as necessary. See Operation A1-3.

Operations which are identified by an asterisk (*) can be carried out with the engine installed in the car

*Radiator, to remove and refit, including frost precautions and engine protection—Operation A1-2

Time allowed: hours

Workshop hand tools:
Spanner size: $\frac{1}{2}$ in. AF Screwdriver, medium

Radiator, remove

1. Remove radiator cap and drain off coolant. As the system is filled with anti-freeze and/or inhibitor, use of a clean container is essential.

   Note: The cooling system is pressurised and great care must be taken when removing the radiator filler cap, especially when the engine is hot. When removing the filler cap first turn it anti-clockwise to the stop and allow all pressure to escape, before pressing it down and turning it further in the same direction to lift it off.

2. Disconnect top and bottom hoses from radiator.

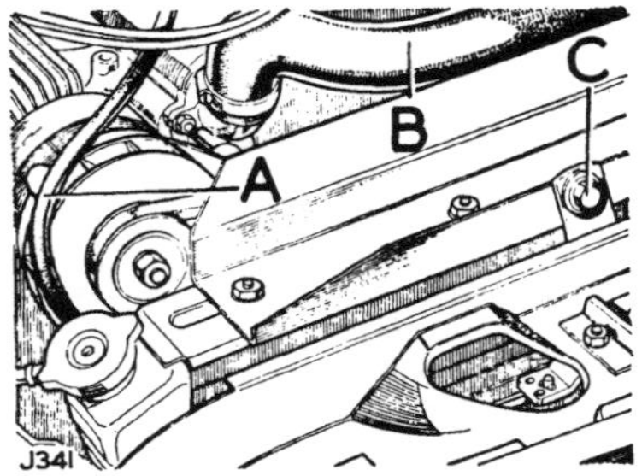

Radiator mounting bracket, at top

A—Hose, radiator to inlet manifold
B—Top hose for radiator
C—Bolt fixing radiator at top

3. Disconnect the hose from the radiator header tank to the inlet manifold.
4. Disconnect the two oil cooler pipes.
5. Remove the radiator fixing, one at each side comprising nut, bolt, plain and spring washers and one at the top fixing radiator to bracket on top panel of grille surround.
6. Incline radiator to the left to drain coolant remaining in the radiator.
7. Lift out radiator.

Radiator, refit

1. Reverse removal procedure.

   Note: Because of the possibility of air-locking in the cooling system it is essential that the following procedure is adopted when filling.

   To prevent corrosion of the aluminium alloy engine parts it is imperative that the cooling system is filled with a solution of water and anti-freeze, winter or summer, or water and inhibitor Part No. 605765 during the summer only. Never fill or top-up with plain water.

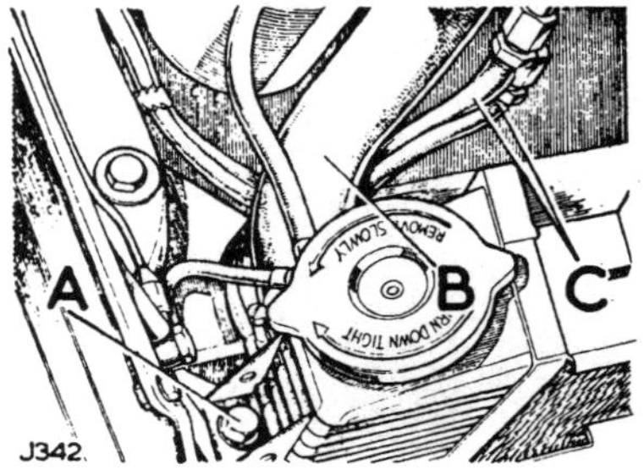

Radiator mounting bracket at side

A—Bolt fixing radiator at side
B—Bottom hose for radiator
C—Oil cooler pipes

2. Open the front and rear heater taps, fill the system with the engine stationary, until the coolant is level with the bottom of the radiator filler neck.
3. Close the rear heater tap.
4. Allow the engine to idle or fast idle and top-up the cooling system to the bottom of the radiator filler neck.
5. Open the rear heater tap and close the front heater tap by operating the 'Heat' control in the car. Run the engine at 1,500 rpm for one minute to purge the air from the rear heater. Reopen the front heater tap.

Operations which are identified by an asterisk (*) can be carried out with the engine installed in the car

Operation A1-2—*continued*

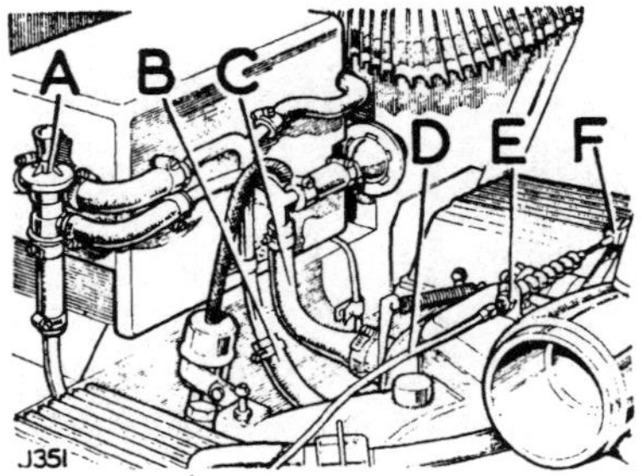

Heater taps

A—Rear heater tap
B—Hose, heater inlet
C—Hose, heater outlet
D—Accelerator cable
E—Locknut for accelerator cable
F—Clevis for accelerator cable

6. With the engine idling top-up radiator to the bottom of the radiator filler neck.
7. Run the engine until it attains normal running temperature, i.e. thermostat open. Check the level of the coolant and top-up if necessary. With the engine cold, the final level of the coolant will be one inch below the lowest point of the filler neck.

   Important: During the warm-up period of the filling schedule, the radiator filler cap should be removed **only** when the engine is idling.

8. Use soft water wherever possible; if the local water supply is hard, rain water should be used.

Frost precautions and engine protection

During the winter months a special anti-freeze mixture and in the summer months a special inhibitor is used in Rover 3.5-Litre cars to prevent corrosion of the aluminium alloy engine parts. It is most important therefore if the cooling system is drained at any time to refill with a solution of water and anti-freeze during winter or summer, or water and inhibitor during the summer only.

Recommended solutions are:

Anti-freeze—Bluecol AA, coloured green.

Inhibitor—Marston Lubricants, SQ 36 coolant inhibitor concentrate. Part No. 605765.

Use one part of anti-freeze to two parts of water.

Use 3 fluid ounces of inhibitor per gallon of water.

To ensure that the solution is fully effective at all times the cooling system should be drained and refilled every twelve months.

Proceed as follows:

1. Ensure that the cooling system is leakproof; anti-freeze solutions are far more searching at joints than water.
2. Drain and flush the system.
3. Pour in approximately 1 gallon (4,5 litres) of water, add solution, $5\frac{1}{4}$ pints (3 litres) of anti-freeze summer or winter, or 6 fluid ounces of inhibitor if frost protection is not required. Then top up as detailed previously.

   During the winter months Rover 3.5-Litre cars leaving the Rover Factory have the cooling system filled with $33\frac{1}{3}\%$ of anti-freeze mixture.

   This gives protection against frost down to minus 25° Fahrenheit (minus 32° Centigrade). Cars so filled can be identified by the green label affixed to the right-hand side of the windscreen and a green label tied to the engine.

   In the summer cars have 6 fluid ounces of SQ 36 inhibitor added, that is 3 fluid ounces per gallon of water.

*Radiator grille and bonnet lock platform, to remove and refit—Operation A1-3

Time allowed: hours

Workshop hand tools:
Spanner sizes: $\frac{7}{16}$ in. AF, $\frac{1}{2}$ in. AF, $\frac{5}{16}$ in. Whit Pliers, long nose

Grille, remove

1. Remove two top mounting bolts and the mounting bolts situated beneath the lower front body panels.
2. Lift out radiator grille, removing the top first. Where packing pieces are fitted note position to ensure correct refitment.
3. Remove radiator. Operation A1-2

Bonnet lock platform, remove

4. Disconnect the bonnet lock mechanism, including the return spring.

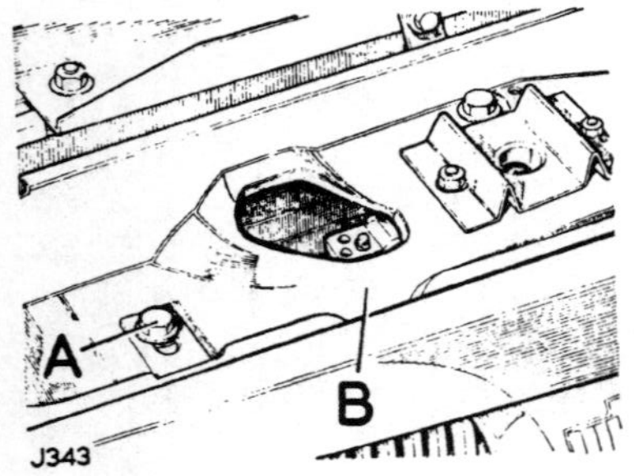

Radiator grille

A—Bolt fixing grille B—Bonnet lock platform

5. Remove the two nuts securing the bonnet lock.
6. Remove the two bottom nuts of the radiator grille bars and screw up the upper of the bottom fixing nuts until it is possible to remove the grille bars. A flexible drive shaft or universal joint will facilitate the removal of the lower nuts.
7. Disconnect the radiator mounting brackets from the bonnet lock platform. Loosen off the brackets and move to one side.
8. Remove the eight bolts securing the bonnet lock platform and remove it by tilting the top towards the engine.

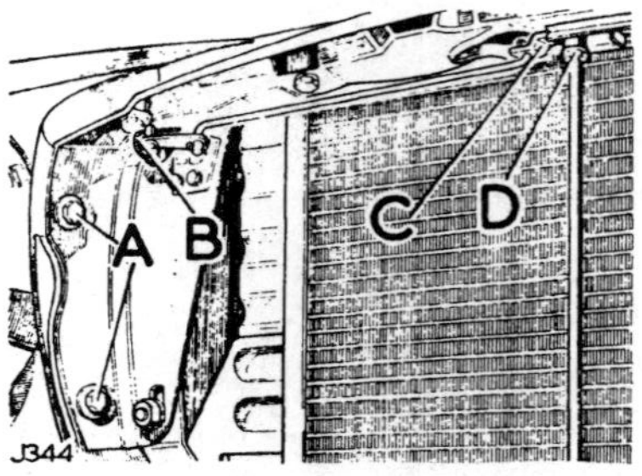

Bonnet lock and platform

A—Bolts fixing platform to wing valance
B—Cable for bonnet lock
C—Bonnet lock
D—Nut fixing bonnet lock

Grille and bonnet lock platform, refit

1. Reverse removal procedure, but do not fully tighten the nuts securing the striker plate.

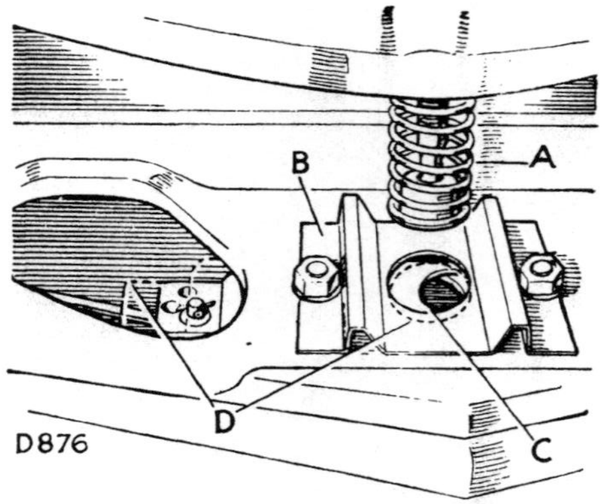

Location of bonnet lock and striker plate

A—Bonnet lock bolt
B—Striker plate
C—Slider catch in locked position
D—Dotted outline shows slider catch in open position

Operations which are identified by an asterisk (*) can be carried out with the engine installed in the car

Operation A1-3—*continued*

2. Lower the bonnet and align the striker plate with the lock bolt.
3. Ensure that the spring retainer on the lock bolt locates at the centre of the striker plate.
4. Check operation of slider catch underneath striker plate, as follows:
   (a) Ensure that the catch moves freely to the limit of its travel to the right, thereby allowing full engagement in the groove on the bonnet catch.
   (b) Ensure that it completely clears the aperture in the striker plate when the operating rod in the car is pulled.

   Adjust cable operational length as necessary, by repositioning the control rod in the adjustment holes provided.

   If necessary, adjust the lock bolt which should protrude through the plate approximately $\frac{1}{2}$ in. (12,5 mm).
5. Fit radiator grille to body, inserting the bottom in first.
6. Tighten the two lower brackets and secure the remainder with nuts, bolts and spring washers; if removed, refit the packing pieces to mounting brackets and secure with nuts, bolts and flat washers.

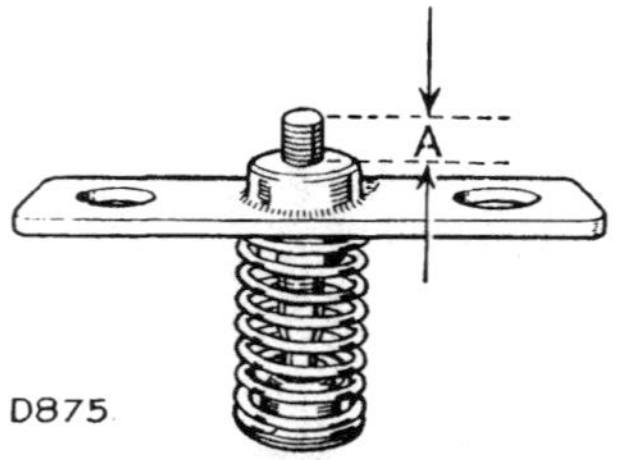

Adjustment of lock bolt

A—$\frac{1}{2}$ in. (12,5 mm)

*Air cleaner-silencer and elbows, to remove and refit—Operation A1-4

Time allowed: hours

Workshop hand tools:
Screwdriver, medium

Air cleaner, remove

1. Release the hose clips on either side of the air cleaner and withdraw the two elbows.
2. Disconnect hose, engine breather filter to air cleaner, disconnect the return petrol pipe clipped to the front of the air cleaner, unclip the choke cable from the air intake and remove the air cleaner body by easing from over the domed retaining studs.
3. To replace the elements, release the three clips on either side of the air cleaner, withdraw the end plates, and remove the old elements, secured by retainers, wing nuts and plain washers.

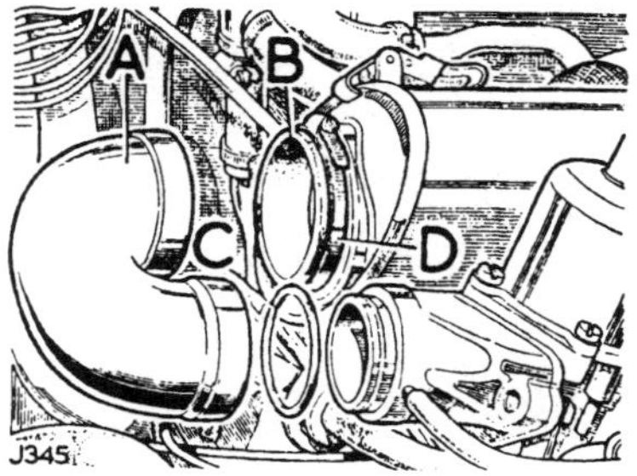

Air cleaner and elbow

A—Elbow for air cleaner
B—Hose, elbow to air cleaner
C—Seal, air intake elbow
D—Clip, elbow to air cleaner

Air cleaner, refit

1. Reverse removal procedure.
2. Fit new paper elements and renew sealing washers on air cleaner body and carburetter elbow adaptors as necessary.

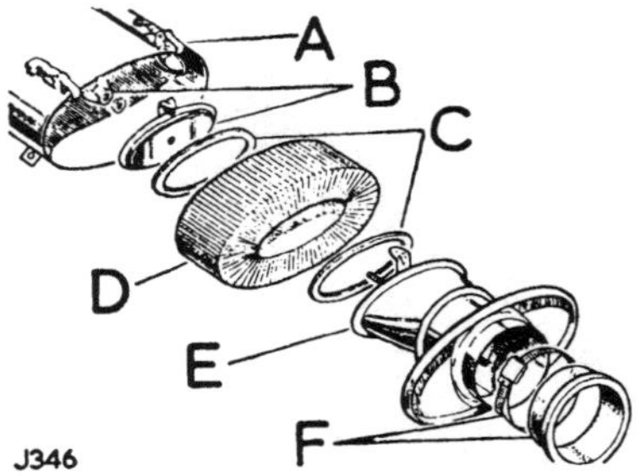

J346

Air cleaner element

A—Body for air cleaner
B—Retainer and fixings for element
C—Sealing washer for element
D—Element
E—End plate for element
F—Hose clip and hose

Operations which are identified by an asterisk (*) can be carried out with the engine installed in the car

Engine and transmission, remove and refit—Operation A1-5

Time allowed: hours

Workshop hand tools:
Spanner sizes: $\frac{7}{16}$ in. AF, $\frac{1}{2}$ in. AF, $\frac{9}{16}$ in. AF, $\frac{5}{8}$ in. AF, 1 in. AF, 2 BA, 4 BA
Screwdriver, medium Pliers

Special tool:
Engine sling, Part No. 600963

If a service replacement engine is to be fitted, the following parts must be removed from the original engine and fitted to the replacement unit. Remove and refit: Fuel pump, fuel filter, oil filter, oil level rod, fan, fan belt, alternator, carburetters, distributor, fuel pipes on engine, ignition harness, exhaust manifolds, air cleaner, starter motor, steering pump, belt for pump and oil pump cover. If the engine is to be completely overhauled after removal, the work should be carried out in the order presented in this Section, Part One. Any components which have been removed to enable the engine to be lifted from the car, should not be refitted until the engine has been re-installed.

Overhaul of the Automatic transmission see Section EEE.

Engine and transmission, remove

It is considered more practicable to remove the engine and transmission assemblies in one operation, rather than to remove the engine unit only.

1. Disconnect the battery.
2. Remove trim panel at front of boot. With fuel reserve control pushed in, disconnect main feed pipe from the tank. This will prevent fuel being siphoned out when pipes are disconnected at the rear of the engine.

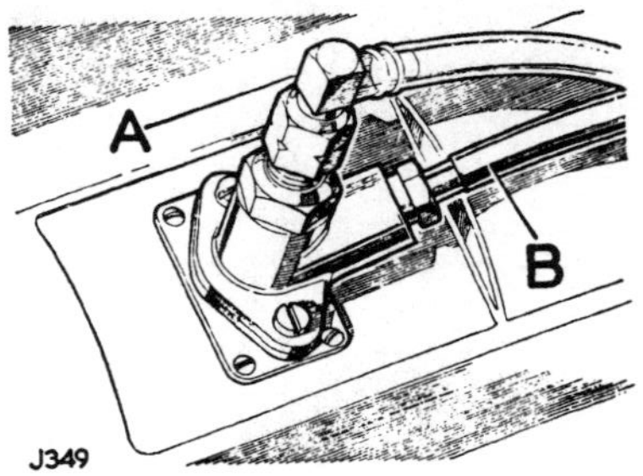

J349

Fuel pipe connections at tank

A—Fuel pipe, main
B—Fuel pipe, reserve

3. Remove the bonnet. Operation A1-1.
4. Remove the radiator. Operation A1-2.
5. Remove the grille. Operation A1-3.
6. Place the car on a suitable ramp.
7. Drain the cylinder block. **Note:** there is a drain tap on either side of the engine cylinder block, and both must be opened.
8. Remove the front exhaust pipe.

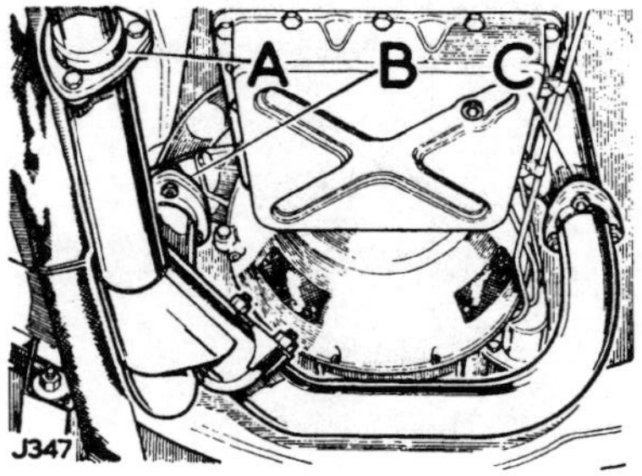

Front exhaust pipe

A—Coupling, front to intermediate pipe
B—Coupling at manifold, left-hand
C—Coupling at manifold, right-hand

9. Disconnect the following items:
   (a) Propeller shaft
   (b) Speedometer cable.
   (c) Rods at the gear selector lever.
   (d) Main fuel pipe at union adjacent to reserve tap.
   (e) Wires from the starter solenoid.
   (f) Starter cable.
   (g) Wires from the inhibitor switch on the automatic transmission.
   (h) Earth lead from the engine to the body.

Operation A1-5—*continued*

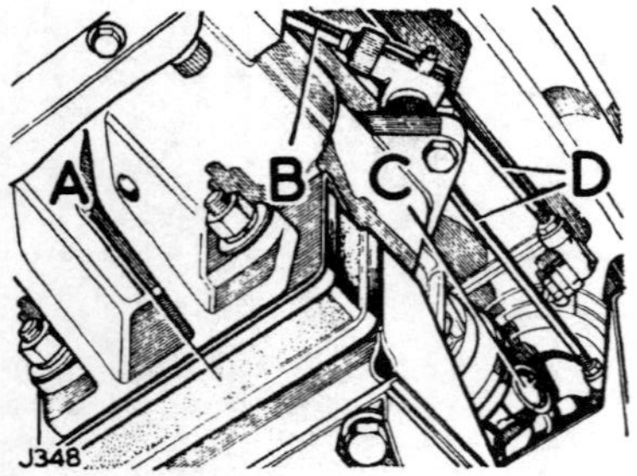

Rear mounting, engine and transmission

A—Rear mounting
B—Speedometer cable
C—Propeller shaft
D—Rods for gear selector lever

10. Remove the power steering hose clip from the sump.

11. Remove both the hoses from the power steering pump and drain into a suitable container.

12. Remove and drain the oil filter.

13. Remove the nuts and bolts holding the gearbox mounting bracket to the frame crossmember.

14. Remove the nuts and special washers from the lower end of the engine mountings.

15. Remove the two bolts, spring and plain washers, together with the plate, from the lower end of the engine tie rod.

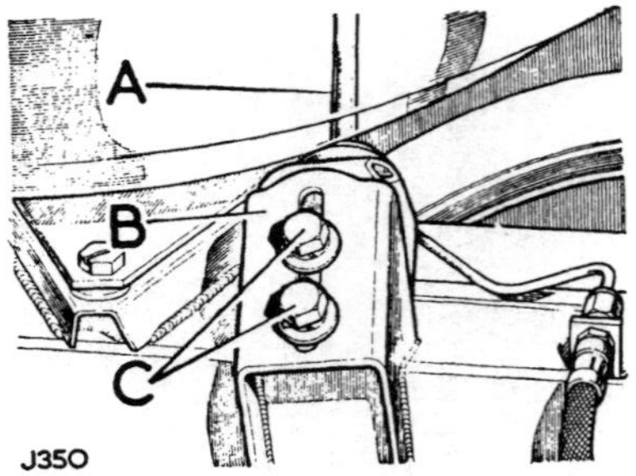

Engine tie-rod

A—Engine tie-rod
B—Bracket for tie-rod on chassis frame
C—Bolts fixing tie-rod

16. Disconnect the inhibitor switch cable from the clip on the bell housing.

17. Disconnect the speedometer cable from the clip on the bell housing.

18. Lower the ramp and move the car to a suitable position.

19. Remove the air cleaner/silencer and elbows. Operation A1-4.

20. Remove the heater inlet and outlet hoses from the rear of the inlet manifold.

21. Disconnect the throttle cable.

22. Disconnect the overflow pipe to the right-hand carburetter.

Operation A1-5—*continued*

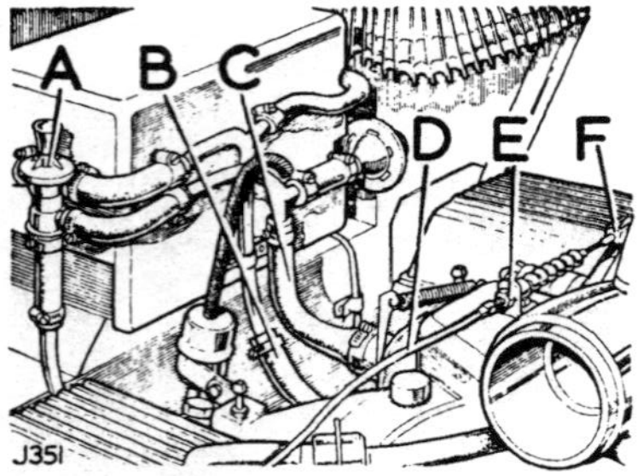

Heater water hoses

A—Rear heater tap
B—Hose, heater inlet
C—Hose, heater outlet
D—Accelerator cable
E—Locknut for accelerator cable
F—Clevis for accelerator cable

23. Disconnect the choke cable junction box, and remove the cable, junction box to cold-start control. Unclip the cold-start control cable from the two clips on the right-hand rocker cover and move to one side.

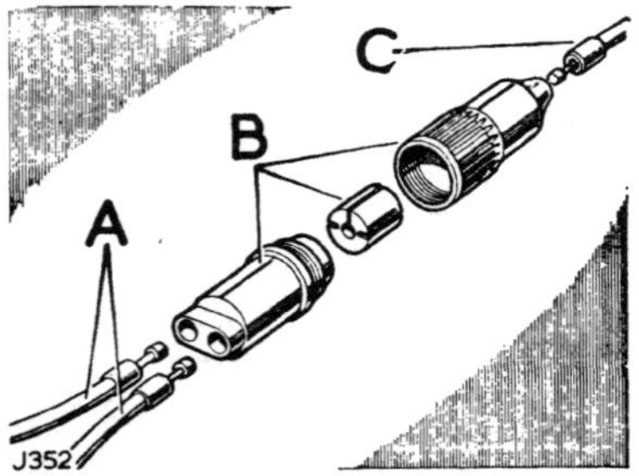

Cold-start cable junction box

A—Cables to carburetter
B—Junction box
C—Cable to cold-start control

24. Disconnect the brake servo pipe from the inlet manifold.

25. Remove the high and low tension leads, coil to distributor.

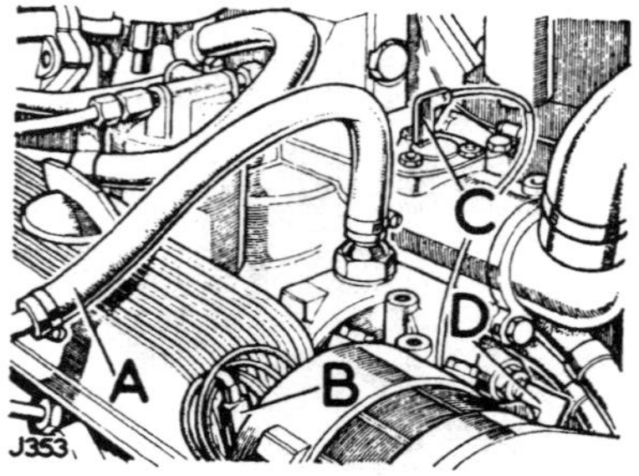

Servo hose and alternator connections

A—Servo hose
B—Alternator connections
C—Lead for cold-start control thermostat switch
D—Lead for water temperature indicator

26. Remove the leads to the alternator and disconnect the clip on the bottom alternator fixing bolt.

27. Disconnect the lead to the thermostat switch for cold-start control warning light.

28. Disconnect the lead to the oil pressure switch.

29. Disconnect the lead to the water temperature unit.

30. Attach suitable engine lifting tackle to the lifting brackets, ensuring that the balance of the engine is central.

Operation A1-5—*continued*

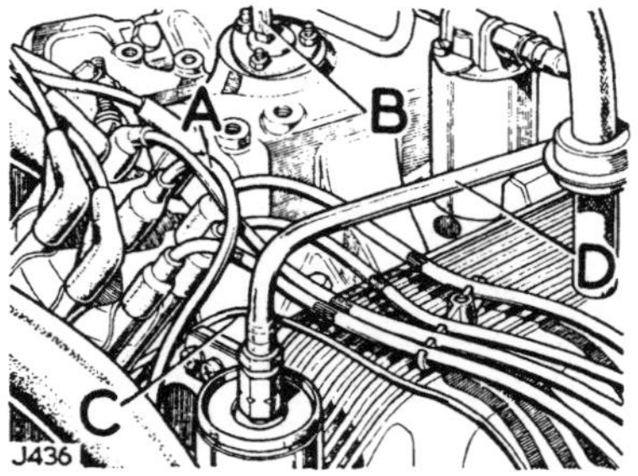

Distributor connections

A—H.T. lead
B—Connector for cold-start control switch
C—L.T. lead
D—Fuel pipe at filter

31. Lift engine until just clear of the mounting brackets and draw forward slightly. Lift again and draw forward. Proceed in this manner until the engine and transmission are clear of the frame.

Transmission and torque converter, removal from engine

1. Disconnect the downshift cable at carburetter.
2. Remove transmission oil filler pipe and dipstick.
3. Disconnect fuel pipe at fuel pump, then remove clips at transmission sump and at rear of engine.
4. Remove bell housing cover plate.
5. Remove the four torque converter fixing bolts through the aperture left by the removal of the cover plate.
6. Remove the eight bell housing fixing bolts and draw off the transmission unit and torque converter.

   Note: It is advised that precautions are taken against the spillage of oil from the torque converter should it become separated from the transmission.

Transmission and torque converter, refit to engine

1. Reverse the removal procedure.

Torque figures

Torque converter housing to flexible drive housing 30 lbs/ft (4,0 mkg).

Torque converter to drive plate 25 to 30 lbs/ft (3,5 to 4,0 mkg).

Engine and transmission, refit

1. Attach a suitable engine sling to the front and rear lifting brackets so that the engine and transmission assembly can be suspended from a hoist in a level position.
2. Now lower the assembly into the engine compartment ensuring that the transmission enters the tunnel without fouling, continue to lower and push rearwards until the rear mounting is in position on the crossmember and the front mountings are located on the chassis brackets. At all times during this operation care must be taken to ensure complete freedom from fouling pipes, cables, etc.
3. Reconnect the lead to the water temperature unit at the front of the inlet manifold.
4. Connect the lead to the oil pressure switch located on the oil pump housing.

Operation A1-5—*continued*

5. Connect the lead to the cold-start control warning light thermostat switch situated on top of the inlet manifold.
6. Connect all alternator leads to their respective terminals and attach the harness to the clip on the bottom fixing bolt securing the alternator bracket to the cylinder head.
7. Connect the low tension lead to the distributor and the high tension lead to the coil.
8. Couple the brake servo pipe to the adaptor on the inlet manifold.
9. Connect the cold-start control cable at the junction box. Clip the cable into the brackets on the right-hand rocker cover.
10. Connect the return fuel pipe to the union on the right-hand carburetter.
11. Connect the throttle cable to the carburetter linkage.
12. Fit the heater inlet and outlet hoses to ‘he rear of the inlet manifold and secure the hose clips.
13. Fit the two hoses to the power steering pump and refit the clip to its position on the front of the engine.
14. Fit the tie rod to the engine and to the sub-frame bracket, but do not tighten the lower fixings fully at this stage.
15. Refit the grille. Operation A1-3
16. Refit the radiator. Operation A1-2.
17. Raise the car on a suitable hoist and connect the following items:

    Speedometer cable, inhibitor switch wiring, rear mounting bracket to chassis crossmember, earth lead from engine to body, starter cables, gear selector linkage rods, propeller shaft.

Reconnect fuel pipe at union adjacent to reserve tap.

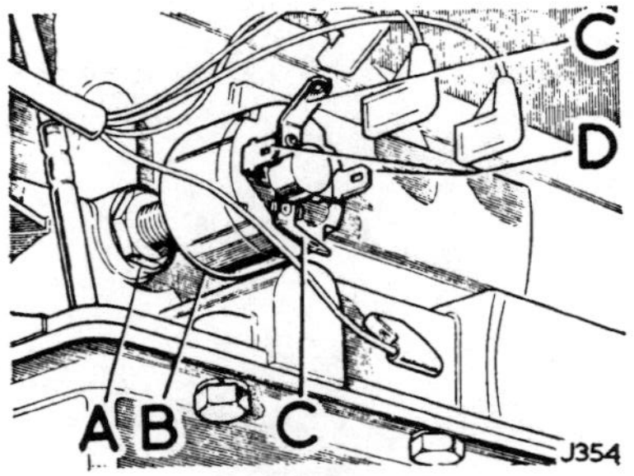

Inhibitor switch

A—Locknut for switch
B—Starter inhibitor switch
C—Reverse light terminals
D—Starter isolator terminals

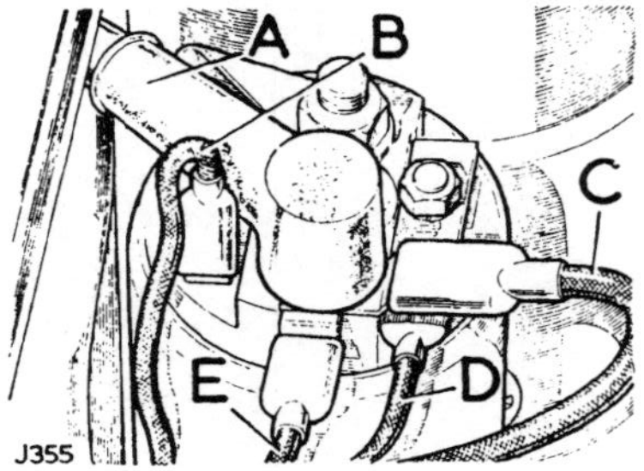

Starter motor

A—Feed lead for starter motor
B—Lead, thick, white with brown
C—Lead, thick, brown
D—Lead, thin, white with brown
E—Lead, thin, brown

Operation A1-5—*continued*

18. Fit the front exhaust pipe.
19. Lower the car and connect the battery. Refit main fuel pipe and replace trim panel.
20. Refill the cooling system with suitable coolant plus anti-freeze or inhibitor in accordance with the instructions given in Operation A1-2.

    Check engine and transmission oil levels and top-up if necessary using recommended grades of oil. See Section Y.

    Refill the power steering pump reservoir with the correct grade of oil (see Section Y). Bleed and test the system as laid down in Section J.
21. Set the carburetter linkage and tune the carburetters. Operation A1-8.
22. Fit the air cleaner/silencer and elbows. Operation A1-4.
23. Using a Tach-Dwell meter or Oscilloscope set the dwell angle of the distributor. Operation A1-20.
24. Using an approved timing lamp, set the ignition timing. Operation A1-20.
25. Fit the bonnet. Operation A1-1.
26. Road test the car and finally check adjustments and also check for oil or water leaks.

*Engine breather filter, to remove and refit—Operation A1-6

Time allowed: hours

Workshop hand tools:
Spanner size: $\frac{9}{16}$ in. AF

Engine breather filter, remove

1. Remove the air cleaner and silencer. Operation A1-4.
2. Unscrew the domed stud to release the engine breather filter.
3. Lift off the engine breather filter.

Engine breather filter, replace

1. Reverse removal procedure, ensuring that the word 'IN' is on the bottom of the filter and that the flange is above the mounting bracket.

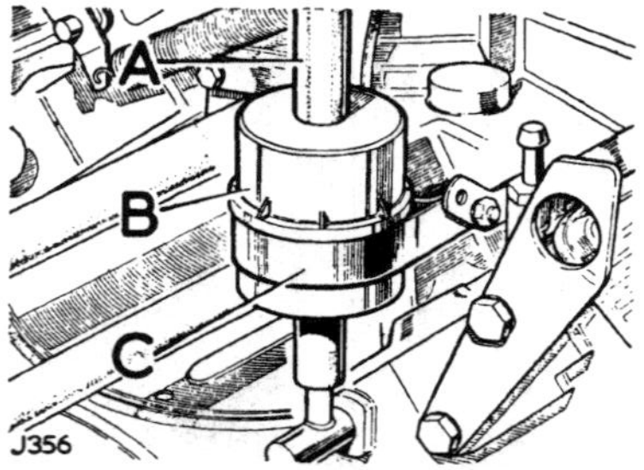

Engine breather filter

A—Hose
B—Breather filter
C—Retaining clip

*Alternator, remove and refit—Operation A1-7

Time allowed: hours

Workshop hand tools:
Spanner sizes: $\frac{1}{2}$ in. AF, $\frac{9}{16}$ in. AF

To overhaul the alternator, see Section S

Alternator, remove

1. Disconnect the wiring from the terminals at the rear of the alternator noting their positions.
2. Remove bolt, plain and spring washer securing adjusting link to alternator.
3. Slacken the nuts and bolts securing the alternator to the mounting bracket and remove the fan belt.
4. Remove bolts securing alternator to mounting bracket and lift off the alternator, noting the position of the clip for wiring harness.

Alternator, refit

1. Reverse removal procedure, connecting the wiring prior to fitting the alternator.
2. Adjust the fan belt to give $\frac{7}{16}$ in. to $\frac{9}{16}$ in. (11 mm to 14 mm) free movement when checked midway between the alternator pulley and the crankshaft pulley, by hand.

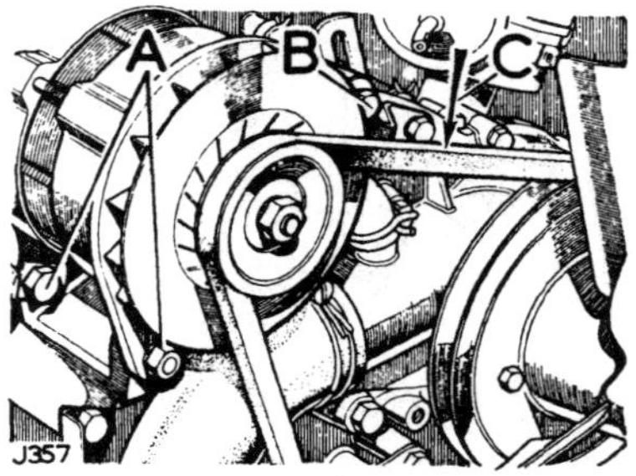

Alternator

A—Bolts fixing alternator to mounting bracket
B—Bolt fixing adjusting link to alternator
C—Check for free movement at this point—$\frac{7}{16}$ in. to $\frac{9}{16}$ in. (11mm to 14 mm)

Operations which are identified by an asterisk (*), can be carried out with the engine installed in the car

*Carburetters, to remove, refit and adjust—Operation A1-8

Time allowed: Remove and refit hours
Adjust hours

Workshop hand tools:
Spanner sizes: $\frac{5}{16}$ in. AF, $\frac{7}{16}$ in. AF, $\frac{1}{2}$ in. AF, $\frac{11}{16}$ in. AF, 4 BA
Pair of pliers Screwdriver, medium

Special tools:
Carburetter balancing device, Part No. 605330

See Section Q for carburetter overhaul procedure

Carburetter, remove

1. Remove air cleaner. Operation A1-4.
2. Disconnect cold-start control cable and move to one side.
3. Remove the breather pipes at the rocker covers.

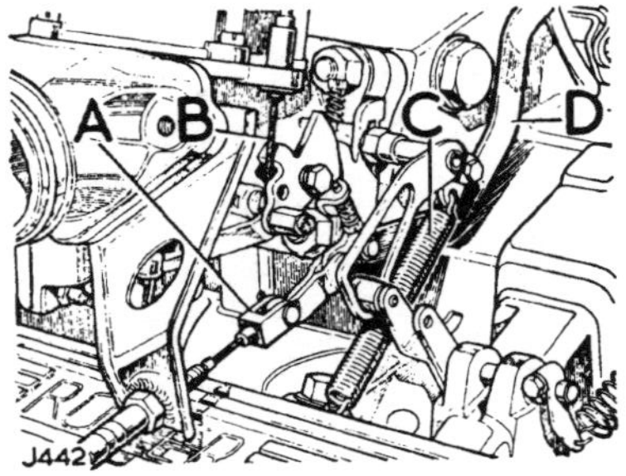

Carburetter linkage, left-hand

A—Downshift cable
B—Cold-start control cable
C—Return spring for throttle
D—Throttle link

4. If the left-hand carburetter is being removed the downshift cable should be disconnected and also the vacuum pipe to the distributor.
5. Remove throttle linkage return springs.
6. Disconnect the throttle link.
7. When removing the left-hand carburetter, disconnect the fuel inlet pipe from the float chamber and also the connecting fuel pipe between the carburetters.

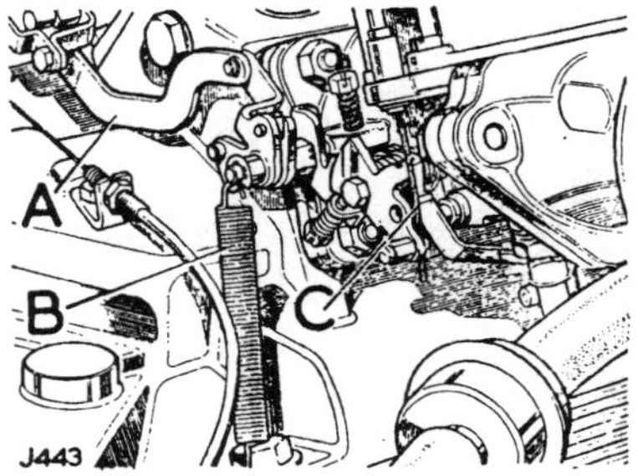

Carburetter linkage, right-hand

A—Throttle link
B—Return spring for throttle
C—Cold-start control cable

8. When removing the right-hand carburetter disconnect the fuel spill return pipe from the float chamber to the tank and also disconnect the fuel connecting pipe.

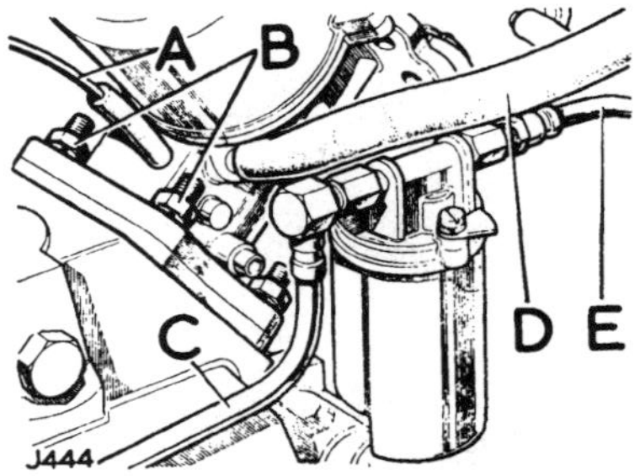

Fuel connections for carburetter, left-hand illustrated

A—Vacuum pipe
B—Nuts fixing carburetter
C—Fuel connecting pipe
D—Breather hose
E—Fuel inlet pipe

Operations which are identified by an asterisk (*), can be carried out with the engine installed in the car

Operation A1-8—*continued*

9. Remove the four nuts securing the carburetter to the inlet manifold and withdraw the carburetter.
 Note: On the left-hand carburetter it is not necessary to disconnect the throttle lever as, with care, it can be withdrawn together with the carburetter.
10. If necessary, the insulator and the liner for carburetter may be withdrawn together with the joint washers.

Carburetter, refit

1. Replace the insulator and liner. The arrow on the top edge of the insulator should match up with that on the inlet manifold. The liner should also be fitted fully into the insulator.

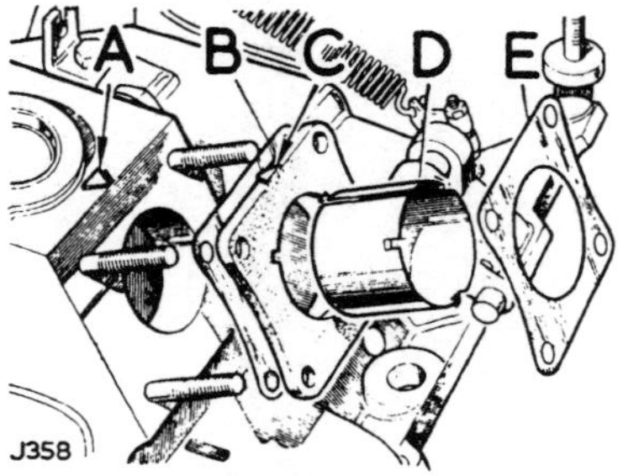

Carburetter insulator and liner

A—Location marks on inlet manifold
B—Joint washer, insulator to inlet manifold
C—Location marks on insulator
D—Liner, carburetter to inlet manifold
E—Joint washer, insulator to carburetter

2. Complete the refitting of the carburetters by reversing the removal procedure, and then adjust and tune as follows.

Carburetter adjustment

1. Move the gear selector to the 'P' (park) position.
2. Run the engine until it is warm.
3. Remove the air cleaner. Operation A1-4.
4. Slacken screws securing throttle lever to carburetter lever on each carburetter.
5. Using the approved carburetter throttle balancing device, Part No. 605330, turn the two slow-running screws until an identical reading is obtained on both carburetters at a speed of 600 to 650 rpm.
 Tachometer must be used to obtain accurate engine speed.

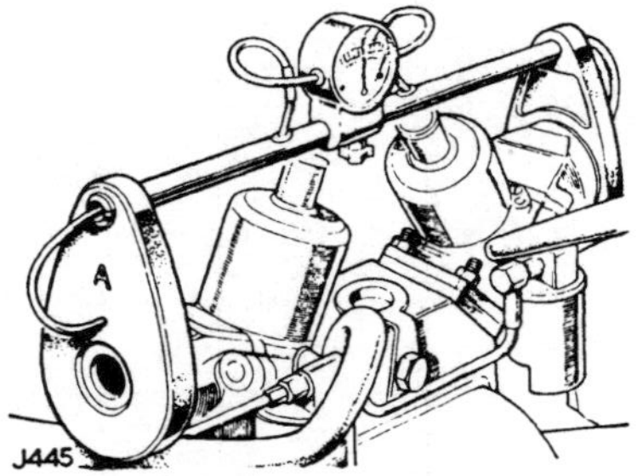

Carburetter balancing device

6. On the right-hand carburetter, place a .006 in. (0,15 mm) feeler between the right leg of the fork on the adjusting lever and the pin on the throttle lever. Apply light pressure to the linkage to hold the feeler, then tighten throttle lever securing screw.

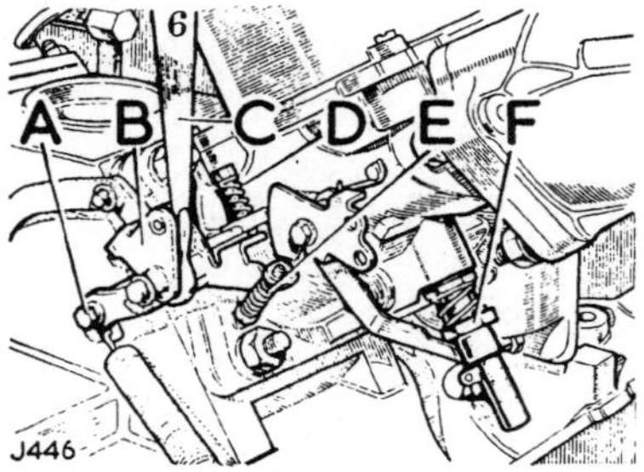

Throttle lever setting, right-hand

A—Screw fixing throttle lever and carburetter lever, right-hand
B—Lever with pin for throttle link
C—Feeler gauge
D—Slow-running adjustment screw
E—Fast-idle adjustment screw
F—Mixture adjustment nut

Operation A1-8—*continued*

7. On the left-hand carburetter place a .006 in. (0,15 mm) feeler between the roller on the counter shaft lever and the throttle lever. Apply pressure to the throttle lever to hold the feeler, then tighten the throttle lever securing screw.

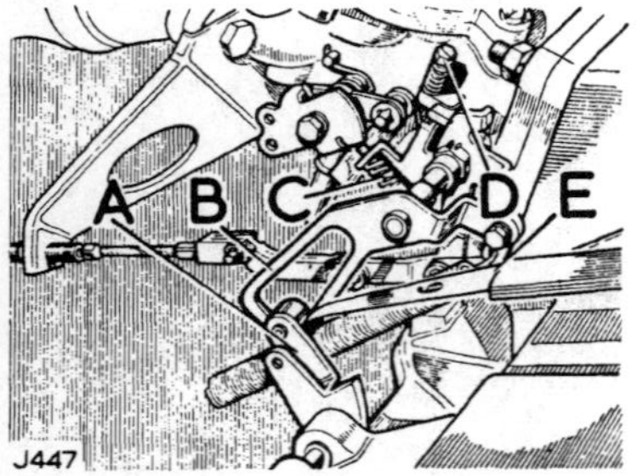

Throttle lever setting, left-hand

A—Countershaft lever with nylon roller
B—Throttle lever, left-hand
C—Fast-idle adjustment screw
D—Slow-running adjustment screw
E—Feeler gauge

8. If necessary, adjust the fast idle by pulling the cold start control out until the warning light just comes on. At 1,400 rpm adjust the fast idle screw until an identical reading is obtained from both carburetters, with the balancing device. Return cold start control to its original position.

9. Refit the air cleaner. Operation A1-4.

10. Check the mixture on each carburetter separately, by lifting the carburetter piston approximately $\frac{1}{32}$ in. (1 mm) by means of the lift pin on the front of the carburetter body. There is approximately $\frac{3}{16}$ in. (4,5 mm) free movement on the lift pin before it contacts the piston.

11. If the engine speeds up immediately, the mixture is too rich and the mixture adjustment nut must be turned anti-clockwise. If the engine speed decreases immediately, the mixture is too weak and the adjusting screw must be turned clockwise. In either case turn one flat at a time and check after each adjustment. If the engine speed momentarily increases very slightly, the adjustment is correct.

12. Adjust downshift cable so there is a .010 in. (0,25 mm) gap between end of the adjuster and the crimped stop on the cable, with throttle fully closed.

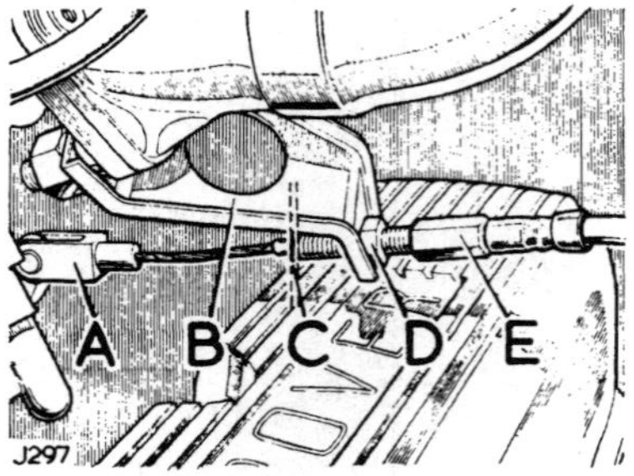

Downshift cable adjustment

A—Clevis for cable
B—Bracket for cable
C—.010 in. (0,25 mm) clearance between crimped stop and end of adjuster
D—Locknut for adjuster
E—Adjuster

13. The vehicle should be run for a few miles to stabilise the carburetter temperature and Items 10 and 11 should be repeated. The idling speed should also be re-checked, and if found to be incorrect should be adjusted by turning the slow running screws equal amounts.

*Inlet manifold, remove and refit—Operation A1-9

Time allowed: hours

Workshop hand tools:
Screwdriver, medium Pliers
Spanner sizes: $\frac{5}{16}$ in. AF, $\frac{1}{2}$ in. AF, $\frac{9}{16}$ in. AF

Special tools:
Torque wrench

Inlet manifold, remove

1. Drain radiator and engine block. Operation A1-2.
2. Remove the air cleaner/silencer. Operation A1-4.
3. Remove carburetters. Operation A1-8.
   Important—This operation is necessary to enable the inlet manifold bolts to be tightened to the correct torque figure.
4. Disconnect the following items as detailed below:
   (a) Throttle linkage and cable.
   (b) Brake vacuum pipe connection at manifold.

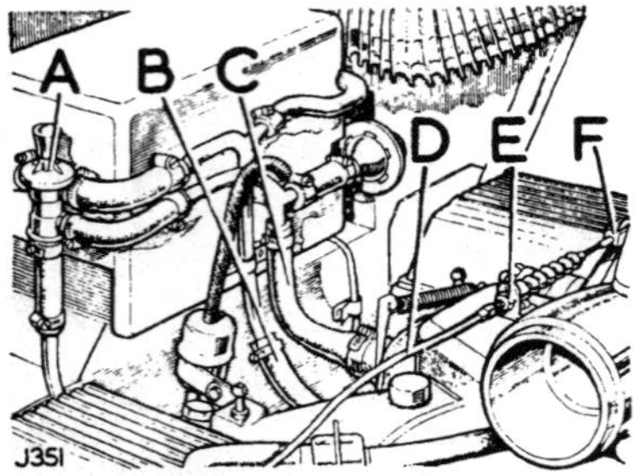

Water hoses and throttle cable

A—Rear heater tap
B—Hose, heater inlet
C—Hose, heater outlet
D—Accelerator cable
E—Locknut for accelerator cable
F—Clevis for accelerator cable

   (c) Plug leads and plastic retainers on rocker covers together with distributor cap.
   (d) The six water hoses as follows:
   Radiator top hose.
   Water pump to inlet manifold.
   Water pump to heater return pipe front end.
   Heater to heater inlet pipe and heater to heater return pipe.
   Pressure relief pipe, radiator to inlet manifold.
   (e) Water temperature indicator lead.
   (f) Cold-start control warning light thermostat switch lead.

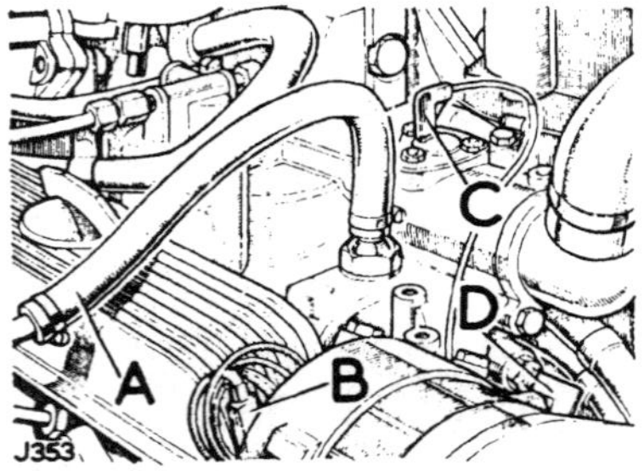

Servo hose and leads

A—Servo hose
B—Connections for alternator
C—Lead for cold-start control thermostat switch
D—Lead for water temperature indicator

   (g) Engine breather filter from clamp at rear of engine.

5. Remove the twelve bolts securing the inlet manifold to the cylinder heads. It should be noted that the throttle butterfly return springs are located on brackets held on the third bolt from the rear on each side of the engine. Push the rear heater hoses clear and lift the inlet manifold rearwards to clear the hose from the water pump, and remove. Lift off the fibre glass insulation pad.

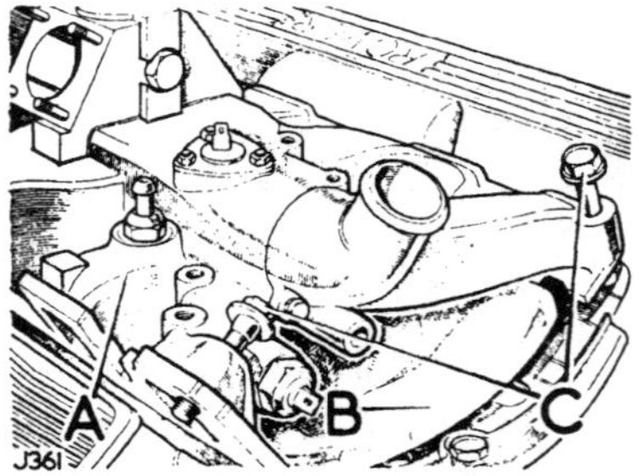

Inlet manifold removal

A—Inlet manifold
B—Fibreglass insulation pad
C—Bolts, inlet manifold to cylinder head

Operations which are identified by an asterisk (*), can be carried out with the engine installed in the car

Operation A1-9—*continued*

6. Make sure that there is no coolant lying on the top of the inlet manifold gasket, then remove the gasket clamps and lift off the gasket, now remove the rubber gasket seals.

Inlet manifold, refit

1. Fit new inlet manifold gasket seals and make sure that the ends of the seals are fitted correctly in the notches formed between the cylinder head and cylinder block.

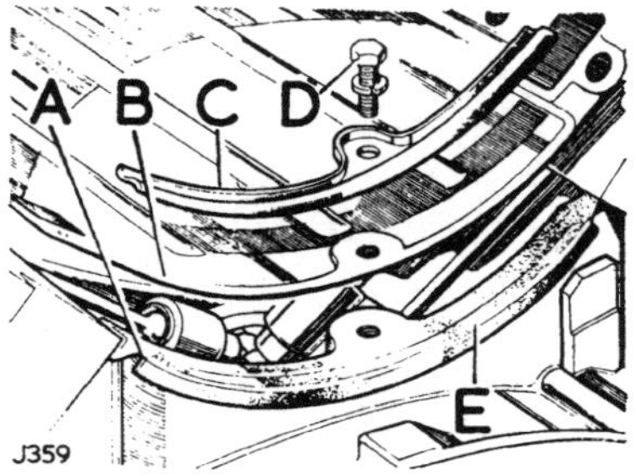

Inlet manifold gasket

A—Notch for ends of rubber gasket seals
B—Gasket, inlet manifold
C—Clamp for gasket
D—Bolt fixing gasket clamp
E—Rubber gasket seals

2. Place the inlet manifold gasket in position with the word 'FRONT' to the front, the open bolt hole will be positioned to the front, right-hand side.

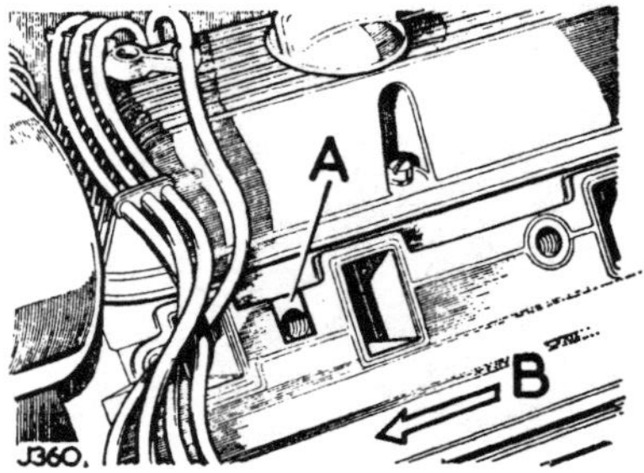

Position of inlet manifold gasket

A—Open hole in gasket to be at front right-hand of engine
B—To front of engine

3. Fit the gasket clamps and bolts but do not fully tighten at this stage.

4. Fit the fibre-glass insulation pad to the inlet gasket, ensuring that it does not become trapped between the faces of the inlet manifold and the cylinder head. This pad is held in position by the compression pressure of the inlet manifold.

5. Position the inlet manifold on the cylinder heads and connect up the water hoses.

6. Check to ensure that the manifold and gasket clamps are properly positioned and fit all the bolts into the cylinder head, the two longer bolts are installed at the front, and the brackets for the throttle return springs are located on the third bolt from the rear of the engine.

   As the bolt holes are not at right angles to the inlet manifold cylinder head faces there may be an illusion of malalignment.

7. Tighten all the manifold to cylinder head bolts a little at a time. Tighten evenly alternate sides working from centre of engine to each end. Finally tighten to a torque figure of 25/30 lbs/ft (3,5/4,0 mkg) following the sequence detailed above.

   The clamp bolts at the front and rear of the gasket can now be tightened to a torque figure of 10/15 lbs/ft (1,4/2,0 mkg).

Operation A1-9—*continued*

8. Ensure that all water hoses are located correctly and fully tighten all hose clips, this is of the utmost importance, as the cooling system of this engine is pressurised to 15 lbs per square inch. (1,06 kg/cm²)

   Reverse the removal procedure for the remaining items and adjust the downshift cable as follows:

   The adjuster on the outer cable should be screwed into the bracket until there is a clearance of .010 in. (0,25 mm) between the adjuster and the crimped stop on the inner cable with the throttle in the fully-closed position.

9. **Note:** See instruction in Operation A1-2 for refilling the radiator.

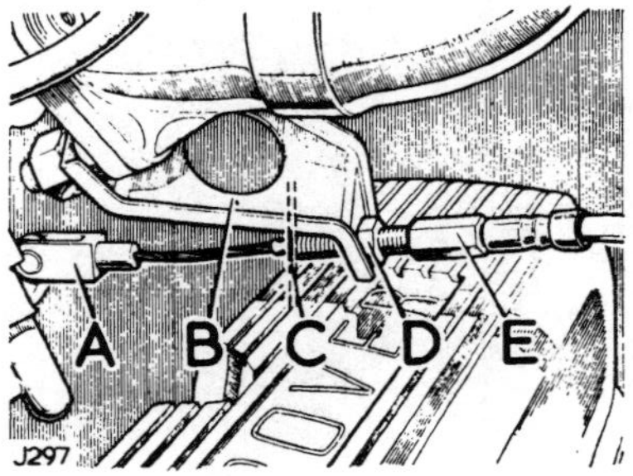

Downshift cable adjustment

A—Clevis for cable
B—Bracket for cable
C—.010 in. (0,25 mm) clearance between crimped stop and end of adjuster
D—Locknut for adjuster
E—Adjuster

*Valve rocker shafts, push-rods and hydraulic tappets, to remove and refit
Operation A1-10

Time allowed: Valve rocker shafts, remove and refit hours
Valve rocker shafts, overhaul hours
Hydraulic tappets, remove and refit hours

Workshop hand tools:
Spanner sizes: $\frac{1}{2}$ in. AF, $\frac{9}{16}$ in. AF
Screwdriver, medium
Phillips screwdriver, medium Pliers

Special tools:
Torque wrench
Bostik 1775, Part No. 601736

Valve rocker shaft, push rods and hydraulic tappets, remove

1. If engine is installed remove air cleaner. Operation A1-4.
2. Remove inlet manifold. Operation A1-9.
3. Release plug leads from plastic retainer on rocker cover and disconnect engine breather pipe.
4. Remove the four screws securing the rocker cover to the cylinder head.

   Right-hand side only: Move the two clips retaining the cold-start control cable to the rocker cover to one side.

   Lift off cover and gasket.
5. Release the four bolts securing the rocker shaft assembly to the cylinder head, and lift off this assembly complete with shield and bolts.

   IMPORTANT
   When removing rocker shaft only take care to ensure that the push rods are not lifted as hydraulic tappets may be dislodged.

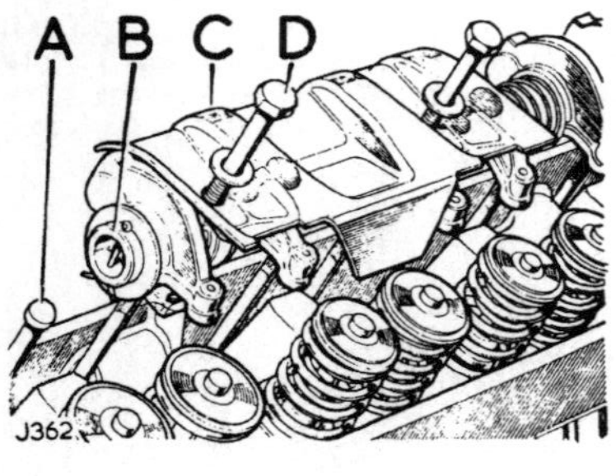

Rocker shaft

A—Push-rod
B—Rocker shaft assembly
C—Shield
D—Bolt fixing rocker shaft to cylinder head

6. If rocker shaft assembly is to be overhauled remove the split pin from one end and withdraw the plain washer and wave washer followed by the component parts, these should be retained in the correct sequence for re-assembly.
7. To assemble the rocker shaft insert split pin and fit a plain washer and wave washer and then assemble the rocker arms, springs and brackets to the shaft. Note that two different rocker arms are used and that the valve ends of the arm slope away from the brackets. Compress springs, brackets and rockers to fit wave washer, plain washer and split pin to the other end of the shaft.

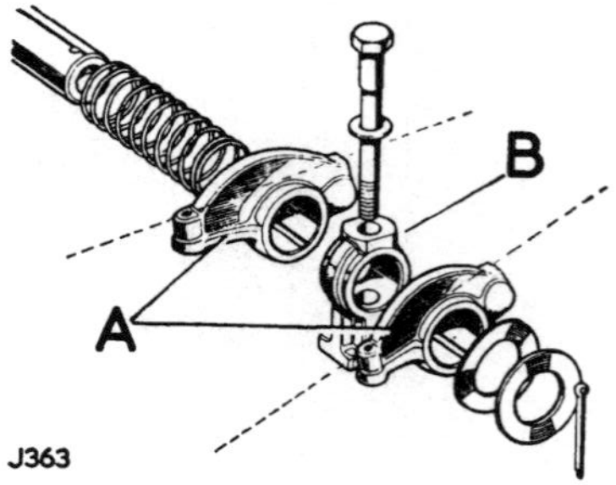

Location of valve rocker arms

A—Rocker arms sloping away from bracket
B—Bracket

8. Fit the bolts through the brackets and shaft so that the notch on the one end of the shaft is uppermost towards the front on the right-hand side and towards the rear on the left-hand side.

   With the notch up, the oil holes in the shaft are correctly positioned in relation to the valve rocker arms. Note that the oil baffle is fitted to the rear of the engine on the right-hand side and to the front on the left-hand side.

Operations which are identified by an asterisk (*), can be carried out with the engine installed in the car

Operation A1-10—*continued*

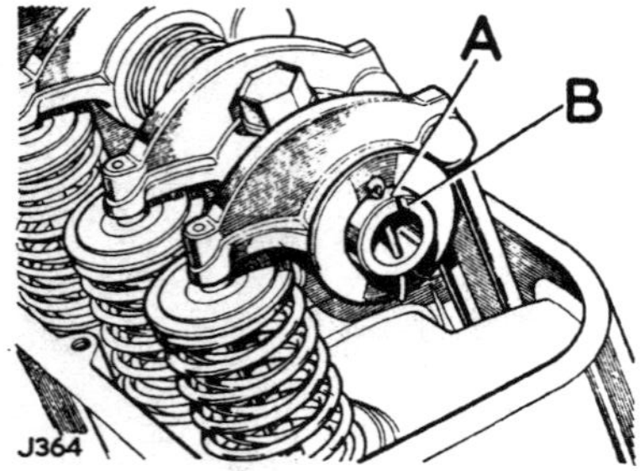

End view of valve rocker shaft

A—Valve rocker shaft
B—Notch

9. If the rocker shaft assemblies only are to be removed and refitted continue with Item 1. 'Valve rocker shafts, push rods and hydraulic tappets, refit.'
10. Lift out the push rods and hydraulic tappets.

    These should be retained in the sequence in which they are removed from the engine.

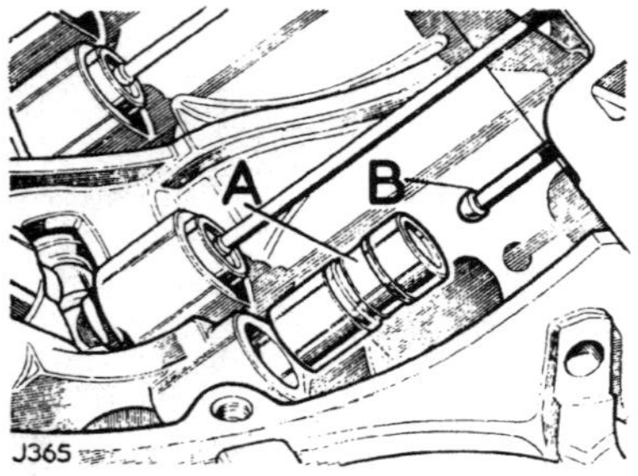

Push-rods and hydraulic tappets

A—Hydraulic tappet
B—Push-rod

Inspection of hydraulic tappets and push-rods

1. Hydraulic tappet: Inspect inner and outer surfaces of body for blow holes and scoring. Replace hydraulic tappet if body is roughly scored or grooved, or has a blow hole extending through the wall in a position to permit oil leakage from lower chamber.

   The prominent wear pattern just above lower end of body should not be considered a defect unless it is definitely grooved or scored; it is caused by side thrust of cam against body while the lifter is moving vertically in its guide.

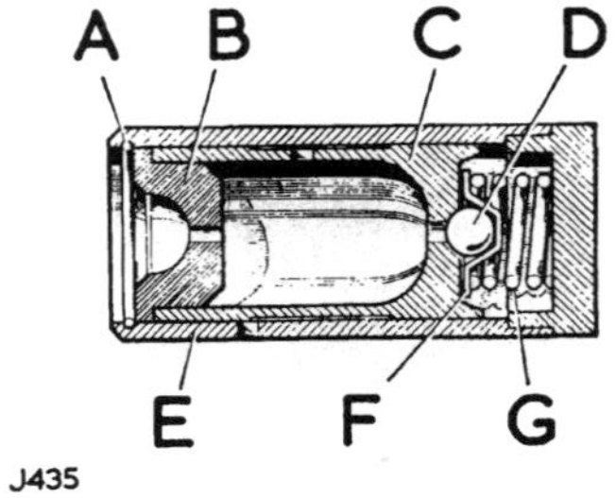

Cross section of hydraulic tappet

A—Retainer for plunger
B—Push-rod seat
C—Plunger
D—Check ball
E—Body
F—Retainer for ball
G—Spring for plunger

Inspect the cam contact surface on lower end of hydraulic tappet. Replace the hydraulic tappet if this surface is excessively worn, or otherwise damaged. A hydraulic tappet body that has been rotating will have a round wear pattern and a non-rotating lifter body will have a square wear pattern with a very slight depression near the centre.

Operation A1-10—*continued*

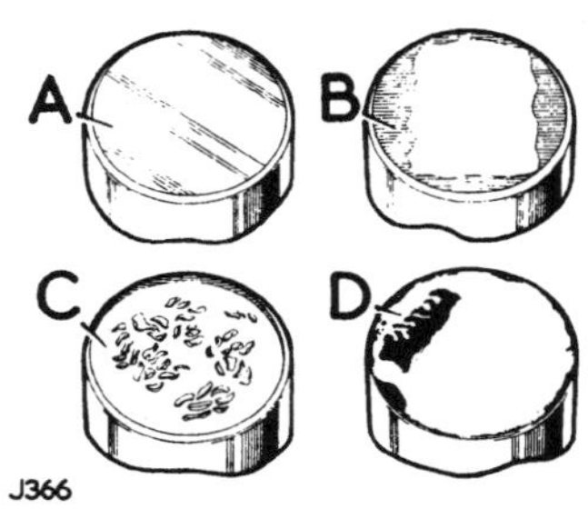

Hydraulic tappet wear pattern

A—Normal rotating pattern
B—Normal non-rotating pattern
C—Excessively worn
D—Soft worn

Either condition is normal and such bodies may be continued in use if the surface is free of defects. See illustration.

Replace the hydraulic tappet if the area where the push-rod contacts is rough or otherwise damaged.

2. Push-rod. Replace any push-rod having a rough or damaged ball end or seat.

Valve rocker shafts, push rods and hydraulic tappets, refit

1. Fit the hydraulic tappets into the cylinder block and locate each push rod into its seat in the tappet. Unless they have been renewed ensure that tappets and push rods are refitted to their original positions.

   Note: The oil feed to the rockers and push rod ball ends is by way of the rocker shaft bore. Because of this the rocker shaft assembly is handed.

   Each rocker shaft is notched at one end and on one side only.

   The notch should be uppermost and towards the front on the right-hand side and towards the rear on the left-hand side.

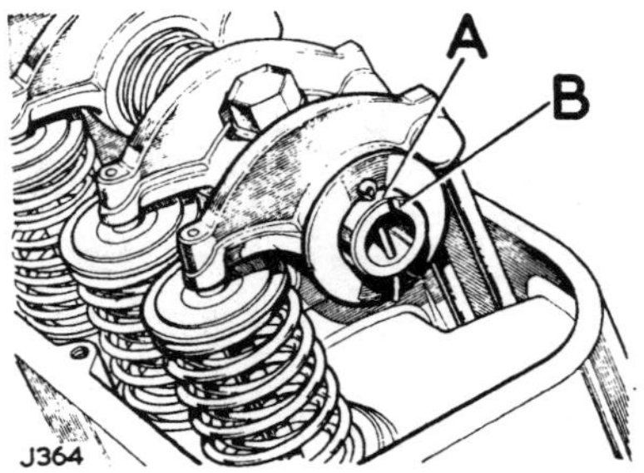

Correct location of valve rocker shaft

A—Valve rocker shaft
B—Notch

2. Fit the rocker shaft assemblies, ensuring that the push rods locate correctly in the cups of the rocker arms, and that the baffle plates are fitted at the front on the left-hand side and at the rear on the right-hand side. Pull the bolts down evenly and finally tighten to a torque figure of 25 to 30 lbs/ft (3,5 to 4.0 mkg). Do not overtighten.
3. Position the rocker covers and their gaskets on the cylinder heads, place the two choke cable clips in position on the right-hand side and retain with the four special screws.

   If it is necessary to renew the rocker cover gasket, proceed as follows:

   (a) Clean and dry the seal mounting surface using either Trichloroethylene, Bostik cleaner No. 6001 or a suitable spirit cleaner.

   (b) Apply an even film of Bostik 1775, Part No. 601736, which is an impact adhesive, to both the cover seal face and gasket by dispensing direct from the tube and following with a brushing operation. The brushing operation is most important to ensure an even film of adhesive over both surfaces. On no account must the two parts be rubbed together in an attempt to spread the adhesive.

   (c) Allow the two films to dry for approximately 15 minutes or until they are touch dry.

Operation A1-10—*continued*

   (d) Place the one end of the gasket into the recess of the cover taking care to place it accurately first time with the edge firmly against the recess wall. (N.B. The gasket will only fit one way since the cover holding screw holes are not symmetrical. It is important that the placing be accurate first time since any subsequent movement may adversely affect the bond.) At the same time, hold the remainder of the gasket clear of the cover; then work round the cover, pressing the gasket into place a little at a time making sure that the outer edge of the gasket is firmly up to the recess wall.

   Do not attempt to place the whole gasket into position at one time.

   (e) Allow the assembled cover to stand for at least half an hour before fitment to the engine.

4. Refit the inlet manifold. Operation A1-9.
5. If previously removed refit air cleaner. Operation A1-4.

Note: Tappet noise

It should be noted that tappet noise can be expected on initial starting up after an overhaul due to oil drainage from the tappet assemblies or indeed if the vehicle has been standing over a very long period. If excessive noise should be apparent after an overhaul, the engine should be ruin at approximately 2,500 rpm until the noise is eliminated.

*Cylinder head, to remove, overhaul and refit—Operation A1-11

Time allowed: Cylinder head, to remove and refit hours
Cylinder head, overhaul hours

Workshop hand tools:
Spanner sizes: ½ in. AF, $\frac{9}{16}$ in. AF, ⅝ in. AF
Screwdriver, medium Pliers

Special tools:
Torque wrench
Thread lubricant/sealant 3M EC 776, Part No. 605764
Valve spring compressor, Part No. 276102
Valve guide remover, Part No. 274401
Valve guide drift, Part No. 600959
Distance piece for valve guide drift, Part No. 605774

CAUTION: Aluminium parts can easily be damaged by careless handling. Be particularly careful of gasket surfaces

Cylinder head, remove

1. Completely drain off coolant through both radiator and cylinder block drain taps.
2. If engine is installed remove air cleaner. Operation A1-4.
3. Remove inlet manifold. Operation A1-9.
4. Remove rockers and shafts. Operation A1-10.
5. If engine is installed disconnect front exhaust pipe from manifold. This is most easily done from beneath the car.

Left-hand cylinder head. Items 6, 7, 8, 9, 10 and 11

6. Remove the exhaust manifold from the cylinder head by knocking back the lock tabs and removing the bolts.

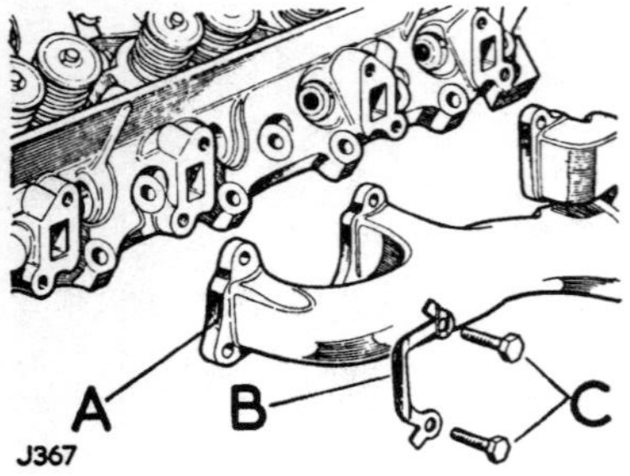

Exhaust manifold

A—Manifold
B—Lock plate
C—Bolts fixing exhaust manifold

7. Remove the trim panel at the front of the boot. With the fuel reserve control pushed in, disconnect the main feed pipe from the tank. This will prevent fuel being siphoned out when the outlet pipe is disconnected from the fuel pump.
8. Disconnect the fuel outlet pipe from the fuel pump.
9. Disconnect the fuel filter bracket from the mounting bracket, and lift off the filter bracket, filter and fuel pipes complete.
10. Disconnect the tie rod bracket from the front of the cylinder head, and remove the clip for the downshift cable at the rear of the left-hand cylinder head.

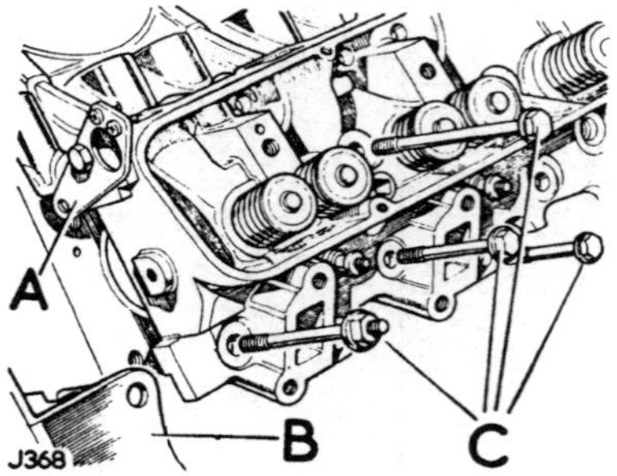

Cylinder head and tie-rod bracket

A—Fuel filter bracket
B—Tie-rod bracket
C—Bolts fixing cylinder head

11. Note also that there is a special cylinder head bolt which carries the retaining clip for the dipstick tube, this is on the left-hand side of the engine. Do not forget to lift out the dipstick when removing the left-hand cylinder head.

Right-hand cylinder head. Items 12, 13 and 14

12. When removing the right-hand cylinder head only it will be necessary to remove the gearbox dipstick and oil filler tube attached to the rear of the cylinder head by a bolt, spring washer and spacing washers.

Operations which are identified by an asterisk (*), can be carried out with the engine installed in the car

Operation A1-11—*continued*

13. Remove alternator. Operation A1-7.
14. Disconnect the two oil cooler pipes from the clip on the alternator mounting bracket.
15. Slacken off the cylinder head bolts evenly and remove them, together with the plain washers, then lift off the cylinder head and discard the gasket. Place the bolts in white spirit to remove the sealing compound used on them.
16. If necessary repeat for opposite side. If both cylinder heads have been removed, mark them appropriately so that they may be refitted in their original position.

Cylinder head, overhaul

Reconditioning valves and guides

CAUTION: Aluminium can be dented or nicked if carelessly handled. Use particular care to protect gasket surfaces against damage.

1. Place cylinder head on clean, smooth surface.
2. Using suitable spring compressor, Part No. 276102, compress valve spring and remove valve collets. Release tool and remove spring and cap.

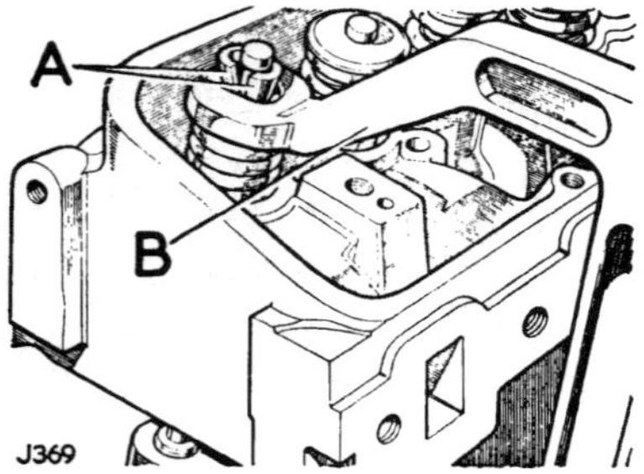

Removing valves

A—Valve collets
B—Spring compressor, Part No. 276102

3. Remove valve. Valves should be set aside so they may be refitted in their original location. A small board with numbered holes is handy for this purpose.
4. Remove carbon from combustion chamber of heads taking care to avoid scratching the aluminium head or the valve seats. A **soft** wire brush is suitable for this purpose.
5. Clean carbon and gum deposits from valve guide bores.
6. Clean valves. Inspect valve faces and seats for pits, burned spots or other evidence of poor seating.
7. Grind or replace valves as necessary. If a valve head must be ground to a knife edge to obtain a true face, the valve should be replaced, as a sharp edge will run too hot. 45° is the correct angle for valve faces.
8. Check fit of valve in valve guide. If clearance is excessive, replace guides as follows:
   (a) Drive old guide out from combustion chamber side using special tool, Part No. 274401.
   (b) Lubricate and install new guide from top of head using special tool, Part No. 600959 and distance piece Part No. 605774.
   The tool is designed to bottom when the guide is correctly positioned.

Note: Service guides are .001 in. (0,025 mm) larger on the outside diameter than original equipment in order to obtain a good press fit in the aluminium cylinder head.

9. If it is necessary to replace valve seat inserts, proceed as follows:
   (a) Remove the valve seat insert by carefully grinding the seat insert away; when thin enough, the insert can be prised out.

Operation A1-11—*continued*

(b) To fit new valve seat inserts to a cylinder head, heat the head evenly for a few minutes to approximately 150°F (65°C), the temperature of a normal degreaser, enter the seat squarely into the cylinder head recess, which must be thoroughly clean, and press insert into position.

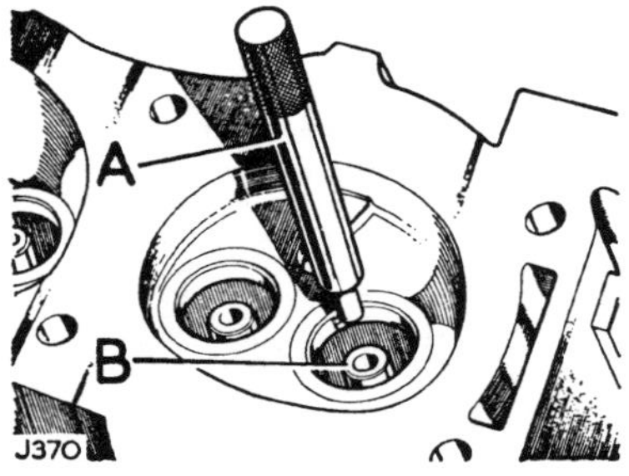

Removing valve guide

A—Special tool, Part No. 274401
B—Valve guide

10. True up valve seats to 45°. Cutting a valve seat results in lowering the valve spring pressure and increases the width of the seat. The nominal width of the valve seat is $\frac{1}{16}$ in. (1,5 mm). If a valve seat is over $\frac{5}{64}$ in. (1,98 mm) wide after truing up it should be narrowed to specified width by the use of 20° and 70° stones.

Improper hydraulic valve lifter operation may result if valve and seat are refinished to the extent that the valve stem is raised more than .050 in. (1,27 mm) above normal height. In this case it will be necessary to grind off the end of the valve stem or replace parts.

The normal height of the valve stem above the valve spring seat surface of the head is 1.825 in. (46,36 mm).

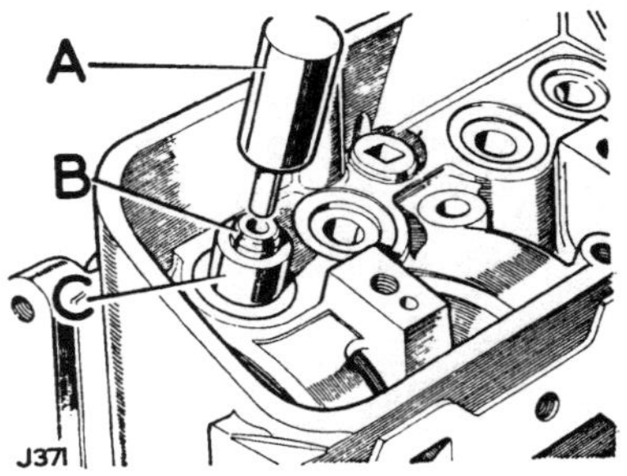

Fitting valve guide

A—Special tool, Part No. 600959
B—Valve guide
C—Distance piece, Part No. 605774

11. Lightly lap the valves into seats with fine grinding compound. The refacing and reseating operations should leave the refinished surfaces smooth and true so that a minimum of lapping is required. Excessive lapping will groove the valve face preventing a good seat when hot.

12. Test valves for concentricity with seats and for tight seating. The usual test is to coat the valve face lightly with Prussian blue and turn the valve against seat. If the valve seat is concentric with the valve guide a mark will be made all around the seat, while if the seat is not concentric with the guide, a mark will be made on only one side of the seat. Next, coat the valve **seat** lightly with Prussian blue. Rotate the valve against the seat to determine if the valve face is concentric with the valve stem, and if the valve is seating all the way round. Both of these tests are necessary to prove that a proper seat is being obtained.

13. Lubricate with engine oil and fit valves, valve springs, caps and valve collets, using same equipment used for removal.

Operation A1-11—*continued*

Cylinder head, refit

CAUTION: Aluminium parts can be damaged by careless handling. Be particularly careful of gasket surfaces.

1. Wipe off engine block gasket surface and be certain no foreign material has fallen in the cylinder bores, bolt holes, or in the area of the hydraulic tappets. It is a good practice to clean out bolt holes with an air hose.
2. Fit a **new** head gasket on cylinder block, ensuring that the word 'TOP' printed on the gasket is uppermost. Dowels in the block will hold the gasket in position. Always handle gaskets carefully to avoid kinking or damage to the surface treatment of the gasket. Do not use any type of sealing material on head gaskets. The gaskets are coated with a special lacquer to provide a good seal once the parts have warmed up.
3. Clean gasket surface of cylinder head and carefully set in place on the engine block dowel pins. If any difficulty is experienced in locating the cylinder head gasket on the dowels, two $\frac{3}{8}$ in. (9,5 mm) UNC slave studs may be used.
4. Clean the cylinder head bolts and lubricate the threads with Minnesota Mining and Manufacturing Co. Ltd. Thread Lubricant/Sealant EC 776, Part No. 605764.

   Bolt lengths:
   Bolts 1, 2 and 4 are $3\frac{13}{16}$ in. (96 mm) long.
   Bolts 3, 5, 6, 7, 8, 9, and 10 are $2\frac{5}{8}$ in. (66 mm) long.
   Bolts 11, 12, 13 and 14 are $2\frac{5}{32}$ in. (54 mm) long.
5. Tighten the head bolts a little at a time about three times around in the sequence shown, then tighten the bolts in the same sequence to 65 to 70 lbs/ft (9,0 to 9,6 mkg) torque.

   Note: Damage to the aluminium cylinder block threads can result if bolts are not lubricated with 'EC 776' prior to installation. A false torque reading may also be obtained.

   Use an accurate torque wrench when tightening head bolts and do not over-tighten. Uneven tightening of the cylinder head bolts can distort the cylinder bores, causing compression loss and excessive oil consumption.

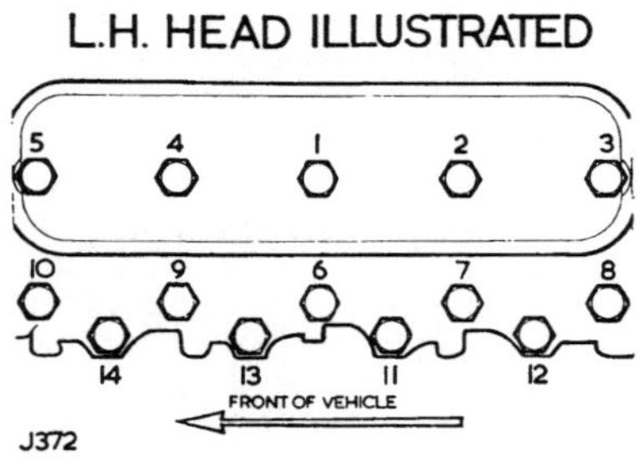

Sequence for tightening cylinder head bolts

Right-hand cylinder head. Items 6 and 7

6. Fit the gearbox dipstick and oil filler tube and secure to the rear of the right-hand cylinder head. Connect the two oil cooler pipes to the clip on the alternator bracket.
7. Refit alternator. Operation A1-7.

Left-hand cylinder head. Items 8 and 9

8. Refit the exhaust manifold, by reversing removal procedure and tightening the fixing bolts to 10 to 15 lbs/ft (1,4 to 2,0 mkg). **Note:** Do not overtighten. Bend the tab of the locking plates over the bolt.
9. Refit the fuel filter bracket, fuel filter and pipes, and connect the outlet pipe to the fuel pump. Refit the main feed pipe to the fuel tank and replace the boot trim panel.
10. Refit rockers and shafts. Operation A1-10.
11. Refit inlet manifold. Operation A1-9.
12. Refit air cleaner. Operation A1-4.
13. Tightening torques:
    Cylinder head bolts: 65 to 70 lbs/ft (9,0 to 9,6 mkg).
    Rocker shaft bolts: 25 to 30 lbs/ft (3,5 to 4,0 mkg).
    Exhaust manifold bolts: 10 to 15 lbs/ft (1,4 to 2,0 mkg).
14. Refill radiator. **Important:** See Operation A1-2 for full details.

*Timing chain and chain wheels, to remove and refit—Operation A1-12

Time allowed: hours

Workshop hand tools:
Screwdriver, medium Pliers
Spanner sizes: $\frac{7}{16}$ in. AF, $\frac{1}{2}$ in. AF, $\frac{9}{16}$ in. AF
$\frac{5}{8}$ in. AF, $\frac{15}{16}$ in. AF

Special tools:
Torque wrench

Timing chain and chain wheels, remove

1. Remove radiator. Operation A1-2.
   Note: When draining coolant, the cylinder block should also be drained at the two taps, one on either side.
2. Remove fan blades and pulley.
3. Slacken off alternator fixings, and remove fan belt. Then remove bolt fixing alternator adjusting bracket to front cover and move alternator to one side.
4. Slacken the timing pointer bolts and move the pointer to one side. Slacken off power steering pump fixings and remove the drive belt. Remove the two bolts holding the adjusting bracket to the front cover, and the bolt holding the rear mounting plate to the bracket. Move power steering pump to one side.

Fan belt removal
A—Bolts fixing alternator to mounting bracket
B—Bolt fixing adjustment link to alternator
C—Check for free movement at this point $\frac{7}{16}$ to $\frac{9}{16}$ in. (11 to 14 mm)

5. Disconnect the water hoses, water pump to inlet manifold, water pump to heater return pipe.
6. Disconnect distributor vacuum pipe also remove distributor cap, unclip leads from clip on left-hand rocker cover and push cap to one side, disconnect the distributor low tension lead. Also disconnect the oil pressure warning light switch lead.

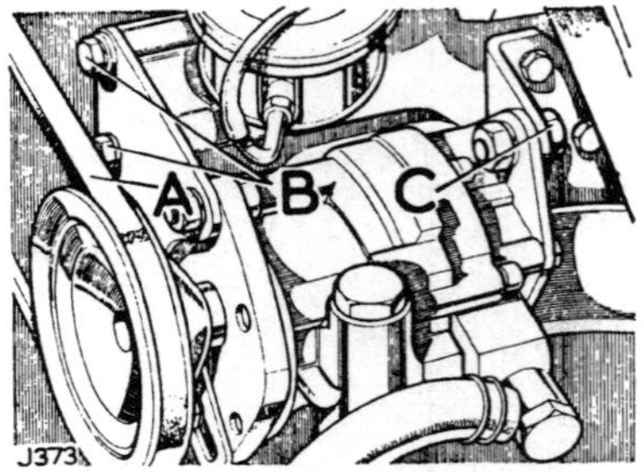

Power steering pump fixings
A—Drive belt
B—Bolt fixing adjusting bracket to front cover
C—Bolt fixing rear mounting bracket

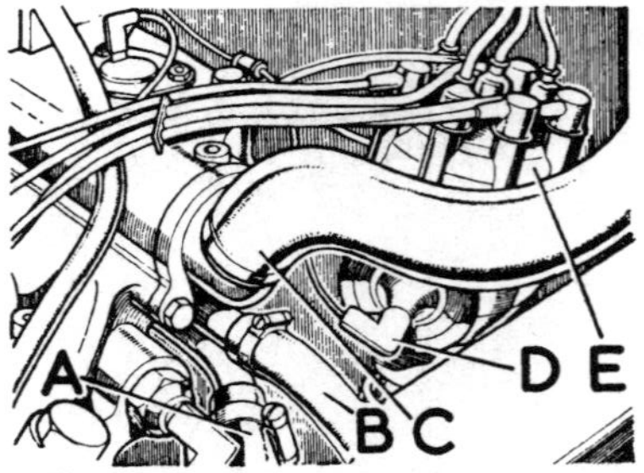

Front water hoses and distributor
A—Water hose, pump to heater return pipe
B—Hose, water pump to inlet manifold
C—Water hose, pump to radiator
D—Vacuum pipe
E—Distributor cap

7. If the engine is installed disconnect the fuel filter retaining clip from the lifting bracket, remove the two bolts fixing the fuel pump to the front cover, withdraw the pump together with the gasket, and move to one side. Do not disconnect the fuel pipes at the pump or fuel will drain from the tank.

Operations which are identified by an asterisk (*), can be carried out with the engine installed in the car

Operation A1-12—*continued*

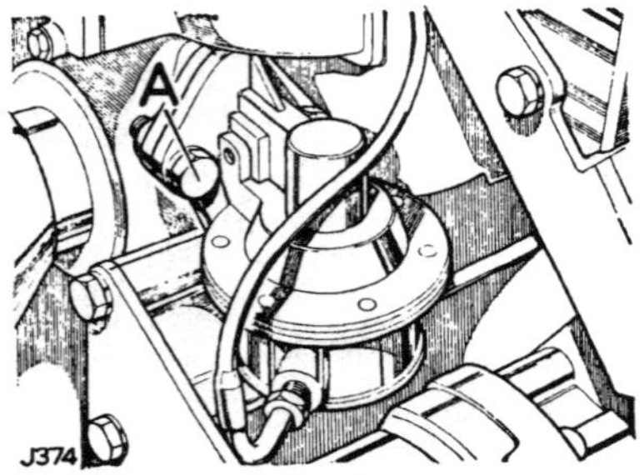

Fuel pump
A—Bolt fixing fuel pump

8. Lock the engine and slacken the bolt securing the crankshaft vibration damper. Before removing the damper, turn the engine so that No. 1 piston is at TDC on the firing stroke, then mark the distributor body in relation to the centre line of the rotor arm, to enable correct replacement of the distributor to be made. If the distributor is to be removed, make a mark on the body of the distributor and a corresponding mark on the timing cover.
   Note: It is suggested that to lock the engine, the flywheel housing cover plate is removed, and a suitable bar is positioned between the lower engine face and a convenient bolt head. It is *not* recommended that the ring gear teeth are used.
9. Remove the bolt and special washer fixing the vibration damper assembly to the crankshaft and withdraw the damper assembly.

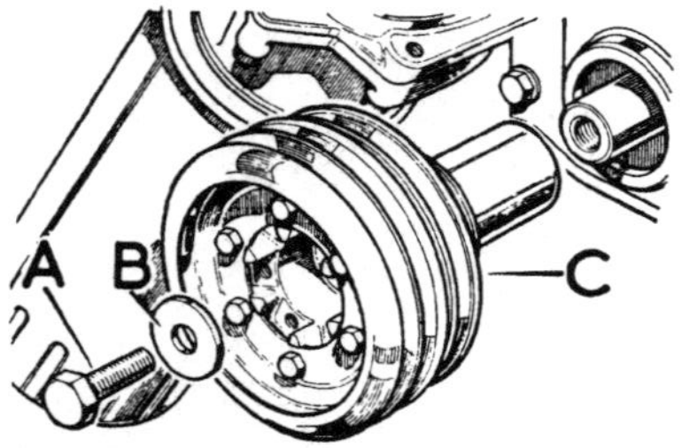

J375
Crankshaft vibration damper
A—Bolt B—Special washer C—Vibration damper

10. Remove all the $\frac{1}{2}$ in. (12,5 mm) AF bolts fixing the front cover to the cylinder block including the two fixing the sump to the front cover. Note the clip securing the power steering hose fitted to the right-hand bolt.
11. Withdraw front cover complete with distributor, water pump, oil pump and oil filter. Remove gasket and withdraw oil thrower from crankshaft.
12. Remove bolt and special washer fixing distributor drive gear, fuel pump cam and camshaft chainwheel to camshaft and withdraw distributor drive shaft gear and fuel pump cam.

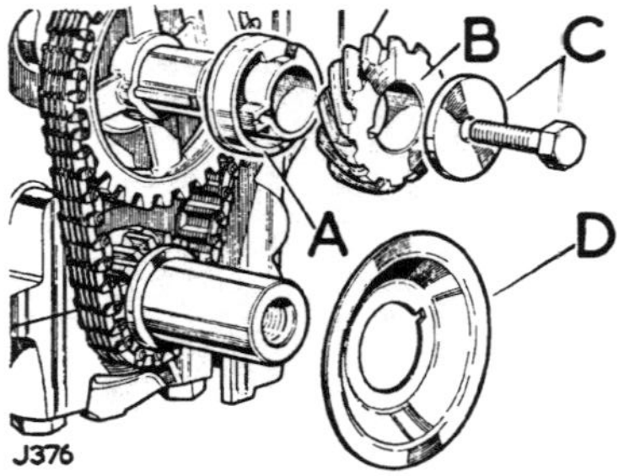

Driving members on camshaft
A—Fuel pump cam
B—Distributor drive gear
C—Bolt and washer fixing driving members to camshaft
D—Oil thrower on crankshaft

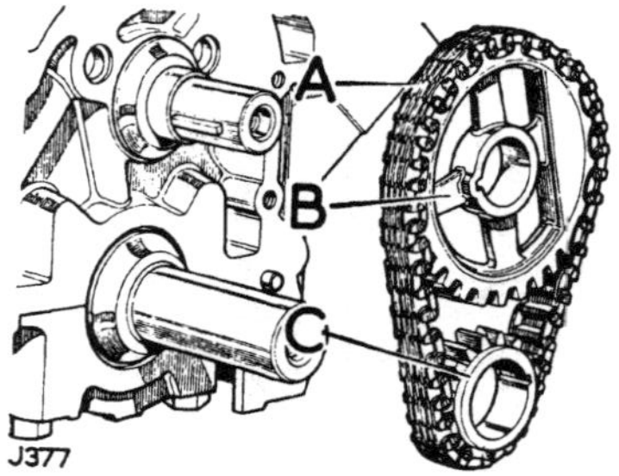

Timing chain and chainwheel
A—Chain B—Camshaft chainwheel
C—Crankshaft chainwheel

Operation A1-12—*continued*

13. Withdraw camshaft chainwheel and crankshaft chainwheel complete with chain.

Front cover oil seal replacement

1. Use a punch to drive out the old seal and oil thrower. Drive from the front towards the rear of the cover.

2. Coil new packing into a new oil thrower. Carefully drive the assembly into the front cover, ensuring that the ends of the packing are at the top. Stake in place, using a small chisel, at three equidistant points.

3. Size the packing by rotating a hammer handle or similar round tool around the packing until the vibration damper can be inserted.

Timing chain and chainwheels, refit

Note: If the crankshaft and/or camshaft have **NOT** been rotated, commence assembly at Item 3, otherwise commence at Item 1.

1. Turn the crankshaft so that number one piston is at top dead centre.

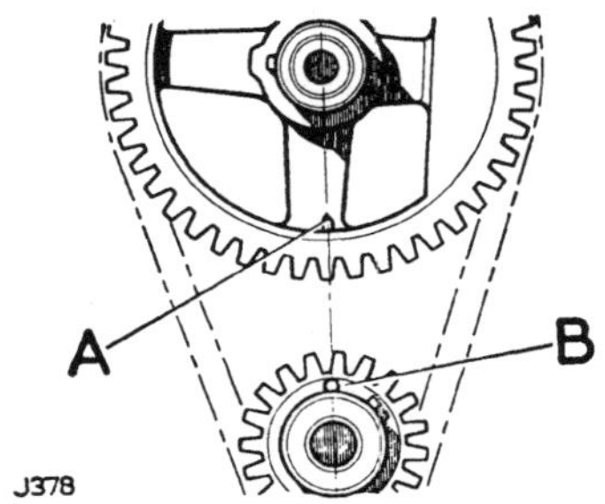

Chainwheel markings

A—Marking on camshaft chainwheel
B—Marking on cranshaft chainwheel

2. Temporarily fit the camshaft chainwheel and turn the camshaft so that the mark on the chainwheel is at the six o'clock position; now remove the chainwheel, being careful not to turn the camshaft.

   The camshaft chainwheel timing mark is a raised boss on the alloy centre of the chainwheel.

   The chainwheel should be fitted with the marking 'FRONT' to the outside. On some early models, however, this marking may not be present, and it is most important to ensure that the chamfer on the camshaft chainwheel is fitted **towards** the engine.

3. Locate the chainwheels to the chain so that the two marks are in line as illustrated.

   Fit the assembly to the camshaft and crankshaft locating the two chainwheels on their respective keys.

   Make a further check to ensure that the two markings are in their closest together position and in line with the chainwheel centre line.

4. Continue assembly by reversing the removal procedure, tightening the bolt fixing distributor drive gear and cam to the camshaft to a torque figure of 40 to 45 lbs/ft (5,5 to 6,2 mkg). Fit the fuel pump cam with the marking 'F' to the front.

   Do not forget to refit the oil thrower with the concave section to the front. When refitting the front cover, the distributor rotor arm should be positioned approximately 30° before the final positioning mark on the distributor body to compensate for 'skew' gear engagement.

   Check the final position carefully against the marks made previously to ensure correct ignition timing.

   Tighten the torsional vibration damper bolt to a torque of 140 to 160 lbs/ft (19,3 to 22,3 mkg).

5. Adjust belt tension to give a deflection of $\frac{7}{16}$ to $\frac{9}{16}$ in. (11 to 14 mm) when checked midway between pulleys as illustrated.

6. Check and if necessary adjust ignition timing. Operation A1-20.

7. For details of refilling the radiator see Operation A1-2.

Operation A1-12—*continued*

Alternator belt adjustment

A—Pivot bolts
B—Adjusting bolt
C—Check at this point $\frac{7}{16}$ to $\frac{9}{16}$ in. (11 to 14 mm)

Power steering pump, refit

It is essential that the procedure be strictly adhered to in order to avoid noise transmission into vehicle and vibration of steering column.

1. Assemble front and rear mounting brackets **loosely** to timing cover and cylinder block respectively. All bolts are to be left completely slack.

2. Assemble steering pump to front and rear support brackets and nip up (finger tight) the two pivot bolts and the adjusting bolt at bottom of front bracket with the pump held at about half travel in the adjusting slot.

3. Nip up (finger tight) the two bolts securing front bracket to timing cover pedestals.

4. Tighten the two bolts securing rear bracket to cylinder block to a torque of 20 to 25 lbs/ft (2,8 to 3,5 mkg).

5. Tighten the two bolts securing front bracket through the timing cover to the cylinder block to a torque of 20 to 25 lbs/ft (2,8 to 3,5 mkg).

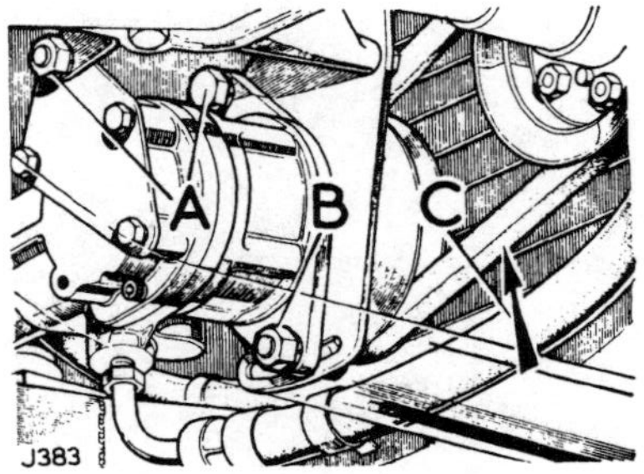

Power steering pump belt adjustment

A—Pivot bolts
B—Adjusting bolt
C—Check at this point—$\frac{1}{4}$ to $\frac{3}{8}$ in. (6 to 9 mm)

6. Adjust belt tension to give a deflection of $\frac{1}{4}$ to $\frac{3}{8}$ in. (6 to 9 mm) when checked midway between the crankshaft vibration damper and the power steering pump pulley. Then tighten pivot bolts and pump adjusting bolt.

Torque-tightening figures

1. Vibration damper pulley bolt: 140 to 160 lbs/ft (19,3 to 22,3 mkg).
2. Bolt—distributor drive gear and fuel pump cam to camshaft: 40 to 45 lbs/ft (5,5 to 6,2 mkg).
3. Front cover bolts: 20 to 25 lbs/ft (2,8 to 3,5 mkg)
4. Power steering pump bolts: 20 to 25 lbs/ft (2,8 to 3,5 mkg).

*Camshaft, to remove and refit—Operation A1-13

Time allowed: hours

Workshop hand tools:
Spanner sizes: $\frac{1}{2}$ in. AF, $\frac{9}{16}$ in. AF, $\frac{5}{8}$ in. AF, $\frac{15}{16}$ in. AF
Screwdriver, medium. Pliers

Special tools:
Torque wrench

Camshaft, remove

1. Remove radiator. Operation A1-2.
2. Remove radiator grille. Operation A1-3.
3. Remove air cleaner if engine is installed in car. Operation A1-4.
4. Remove alternator. Operation A1-7.
5. Remove inlet manifold. Operation A1-9.
6. Remove valve rocker shafts, push rods and hydraulic tappets. Operation A1-10.
7. Remove timing chain and chainwheels. Operation A1-12.
8. Withdraw camshaft taking great care not to damage the white metal bearings as these are not replaceable.

Inspection

Check all bearing surfaces for excessive wear and score marks, also check cam lobes for excessive wear, check key and keyway.

Camshaft, refit

1. Reverse removal procedure.

Torque-tightening figures

1. Bolt fixing distributor drive gear and cam to camshaft: 40 to 45 lbs/ft.
2. Vibration damper bolt: 140 to 160 lbs/ft (19,3 to 22,3 mkg).
3. Timing cover retaining bolts: 20 to 25 lbs/ft (2,8 to 3,5 mkg).
4. Power steering pump bolts: 20 to 25 lbs/ft (2,8 to 3,5 mkg).

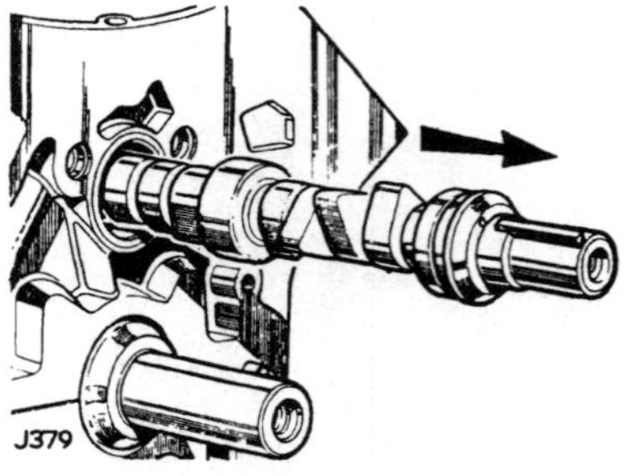

Camshaft removal

Note: Refer to Operation A1-2 for full details concerning refitting the radiator

Operations which are identified by an asterisk (*), can be carried out with the engine installed in the car

*Pistons and connecting rods, to remove, overhaul and refit—Operation A1-14

Time allowed: Pistons and connecting rods, remove and refit hours
Pistons and connecting rods, to overhaul hours

Workshop hand tools:
Spanner sizes: $\frac{7}{16}$ in. AF, $\frac{1}{2}$ in. AF, $\frac{9}{16}$ in. AF, $\frac{5}{8}$ in. AF, $\frac{11}{16}$ in. AF, $\frac{7}{8}$ in. AF
Screwdriver, medium. Pliers

Special tools:
Torque wrench; Piston ring clamp; Connecting rod guide bolts, Part No. 605351; Plastigauge, Part No. 605238; Tool for fitting and removing gudgeon pin Part No. 605350; Hydraulic press; Feeler gauge; Piston ring expander

Pistons and connecting rods, remove

1. Drain radiator. Operation A1-2. The engine cylinder block should also be drained at both drain taps.
2. Remove air cleaner. Operation A1-4.
3. Remove alternator. Operation A1-7.
4. Remove inlet manifold. Operation A1-9.
5. Remove valve rocker shafts, push rods and hydraulic tappets. Operation A1-10.
6. Remove cylinder heads. Operation A1-11.
7. Remove torque converter cover plate to gain access to the sump bolts. This also allows the engine to be rotated by the flywheel.

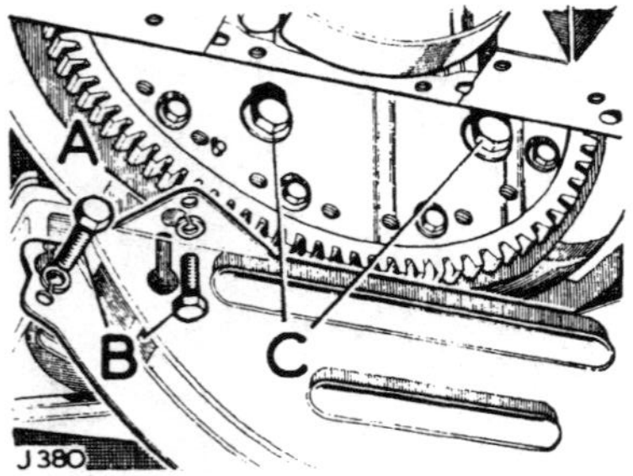

Torque converter cover plate

A—Cover plate
B—Bolts fixing cover plate
C—Bolt fixing torque converter

8. Disconnect one end of track rod and move to one side.
9. Drain oil and remove sump. Note the two clips and spacing washers holding the oil cooler pipes to the right-hand side of the sump. Discard sump washer.
10. Remove baffle plate, secured by six $\frac{7}{16}$ in. AF bolts. Note carefully that the baffle plate will be holding a certain quantity of oil.
11. Remove sump oil strainer.
12. Carefully rotate the crankshaft to gain access to the connecting rod cap securing nuts and disconnect the connecting rods two at a time from each crankshaft journal. Then push the piston and connecting rod assemblies one at a time up the cylinder bore, using special tool, Part No. 605351.

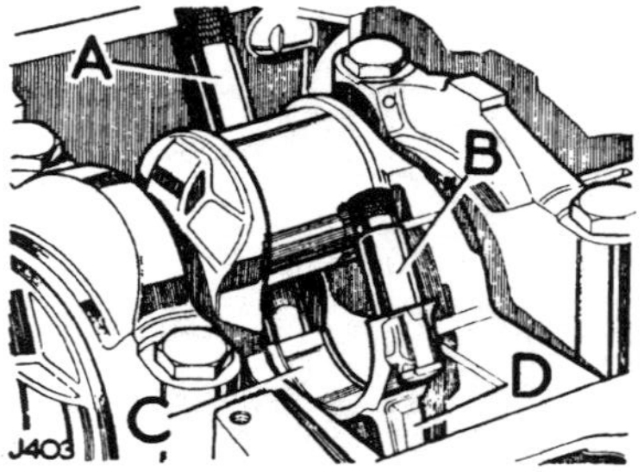

Connecting rod bolt guide tool

A—Guide tool, long } Special tool,
B—Guide tool, short } Part No. 605351
C—Bearing shell located by guide tool
D—Connecting rod

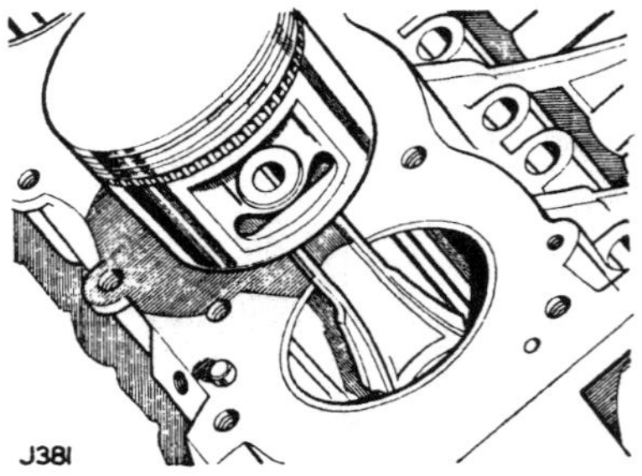

Piston and connecting rod removal

Operations which are identified by an asterisk (*), can be carried out with the engine installed in the car

Operation A1-14—*continued*

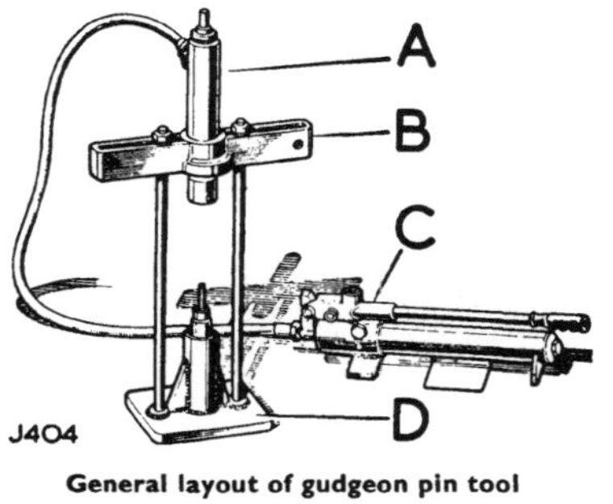

General layout of gudgeon pin tool
A—Hydraulic ram
B—Beam for hydraulic ram
C—Hydraulic pump
D—Gudgeon pin tool, Part No. 605350

Pistons, piston rings and connecting rods, overhaul

1. Separate the piston and connecting rod by pressing out the gudgeon pin using special tool, Part No. 605350 and a hydraulic press with a capacity of at least 8 tons (8128 kg). Should a workshop press of this type not be available a hydraulic ram of 8 tons (8128 kg) capacity of the type manufactured by J. W. Picavant & Co. Ltd., can be used with the special tool, Part No. 605350

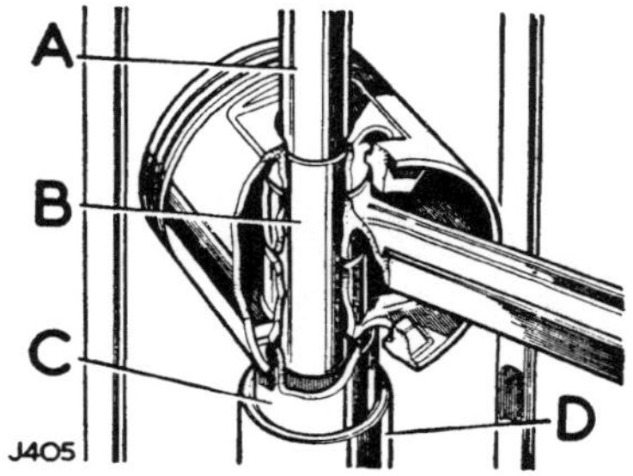

Gudgeon pin removal
A—Drift for gudgeon pin. Part of 605350
B—Gudgeon pin
C—Support for piston. Part of 605350
D—Base plate. Part of 605350

2. If the same piston assembly is to be refitted to the engine it should be marked to ensure that piston and connecting rod are reassembled in the same relative position.

Pistons and piston rings, overhaul

1. If the same pistons are to be fitted to the engine, any carbon should be cleaned from the piston surfaces and particularly from the piston ring grooves and any gum or varnish deposits should be removed using a suitable solvent. Carefully examine pistons for rough or scored bearing surfaces, cracks in the skirt or in the head of the piston, broken ring lands or chipping and uneven wear which would cause the rings to seat improperly or to have excessive clearance in the ring grooves. Damaged or faulty pistons must be replaced.
2. New piston assemblies are available for replacement purposes in graded standard sizes and oversizes of .010 in. (0,25 mm) and .020 in. (0,50 mm).
3. Standard pistons are graded in diameter and the grade letter is stamped on the crown of the piston, and also on the cylinder block; this grading does not apply to oversize pistons.

   Standard pistons are graded as follows:

   Grade letter 'Z' cylinder bore diameter nominal to + .0003 in. (0,0075 mm).
   'A' .0003 in. (0,0075 mm) to .0006 in. (0,015 mm) above nominal.
   'B' .0006 in. (0,015 mm) to .0009 in. (0,0225 mm) above nominal.
   'C' .0009 in. (0,0225 mm) to .0012 in. (0,03 mm) above nominal.
   'D' .0012 in. (0,03 mm) to .0015 in. (0,0375 mm) above nominal.
4. If for any reason standard pistons are to be fitted into a comparatively low mileage engine a graded piston corresponding to the piston removed should be fitted; however, a check should still be made to ensure that the clearance falls within the limits laid down—for example if the car has done little mileage and there is no appreciable bore wear a graded piston of the same size as that taken out can be used. However, if a certain amount of bore wear is apparent, not in excess of .003 in. (0,08 mm) it may be necessary to fit a piston two or even three grades larger than the one removed.

   When reboring cylinders, all crankshaft bearing caps must be in place and tightened to the proper torque figures to avoid distortion of bores in final assembly. Always be sure the crankshaft is out of the way of the boring cutter when boring each cylinder. When taking the final cut with boring bar leave .001 in. on the diameter for finish honing to give the clearance specified.

   In the case of a top limit piston fitted as original equipment it may be necessary to rebore to the first over-size to obtain a correct piston fit.
5. When fitting pistons standard or over-size into a new or rebored cylinder the clearance should be checked and must be within the limits .0005 in. to .0011 in. (0,0127 mm to 0,026 mm). **Note:** Both block and piston must be at very nearly the same temperature when measurements are made or errors due to expansion will occur. A difference of 10°F between parts is sufficient to produce a variation of .0005 in. (0,012 mm). It should be noted that service pistons will be supplied complete with a selectively fitted gudgeon pin.

   Check piston clearance as follows:

   (a) Measure the inside of cylinder bore at right angles to the gudgeon pin and between 1½ to 2 in. (38 to 50 mm) from the top.

   (b) Measure the piston to be installed at right angles to the gudgeon pin and ¼ in. (6,0 mm) below the compression ring groove.

   (c) The piston dimension must be between .0005 to .0011 in. (0,0127 to 0,026 mm) smaller than the dimension of the cylinder bore.
6. If new piston rings are to be fitted into a bore without reboring it will be advantageous to deglaze the cylinder walls using a suitable hone without actually increasing the bore diameter.
7. New piston rings must be checked for clearance in the piston grooves and for gap in the cylinder bores, gapping applies to the two compression rings and not to the special oil control ring.

Operation A1-14—*continued*

8. To gap the compression rings place each ring one at a time in the cylinder in which it will be fitted, square it to the bore using the piston, measure the gap with feeler gauges, this should be .017 in. to .022 in. (0,46 mm to 0,60 mm). If necessary, a fine cut flat file can be used to increase the gap as required. Should the gap exceed the maximum figure given, another compression ring should be selected.

Note: Compression rings are marked 'top' on one face and must be fitted to the piston accordingly. Note also that the chrome compression ring is fitted to the top groove.

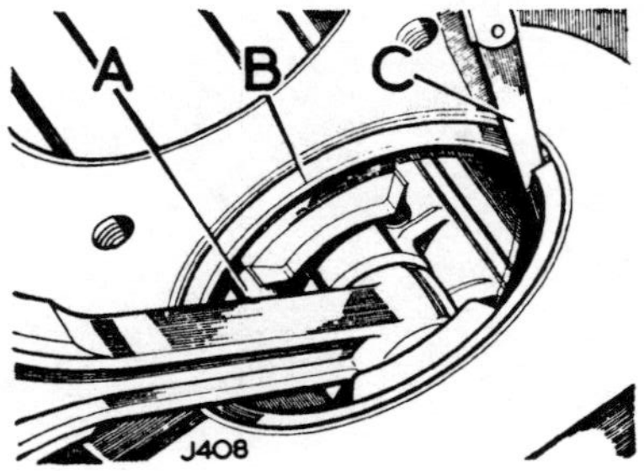

Checking piston ring gap
A—Piston assembly used to square up ring in cylinder bore
B—Piston ring
C—Feeler gauge

9. Check the side clearance of the compression rings in the piston groove, this side clearance should be .003 in. to .005 in. (0,08 mm to 0,13 mm).

Operation A1-14—*continued*

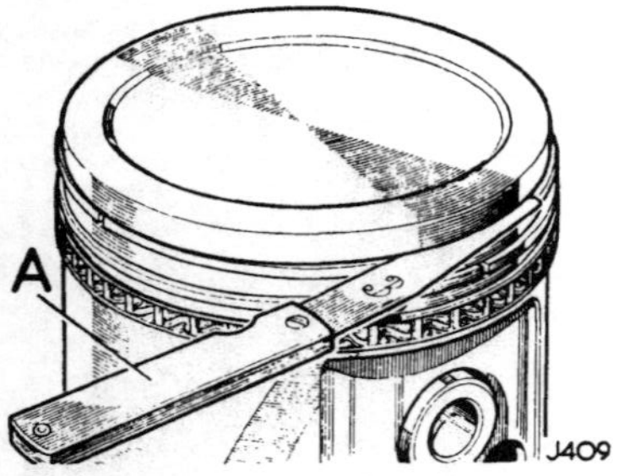

Checking piston ring clearance in groove

A—Feeler gauge

Pistons and connecting rods, assemble

1. Using special tool Part No. 605350 in conjunction with either a hydraulic press or with the hydraulic ram equipment previously described, assemble the piston to the connecting rod.

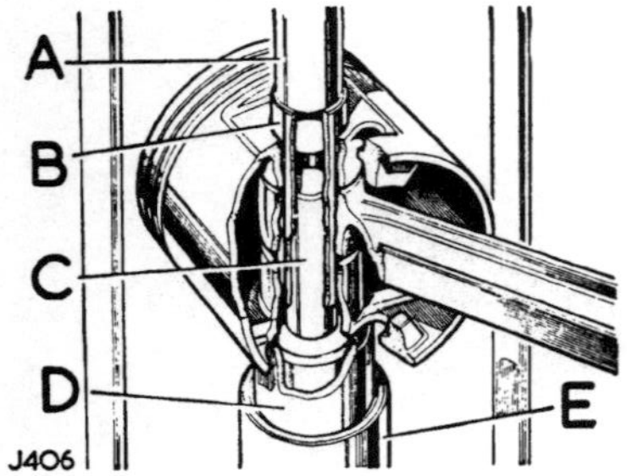

Gudgeon pin refitting

A—Drift for gudgeon pin. Part of 605350
B—Gudgeon pin
C—Guide for gudgeon. Part of 605350
D—Support for piston. Part of 605350
E—Base plate. Part of 605350

2. The piston and connecting rod should be positioned on to the guide and support tube, the gudgeon pin should then be pushed into the piston bore until the inner diameter is located over the guide pin, the gudgeon pin can now be pressed into the connecting rod and piston assembly until it abuts on the shoulder of the special guide tool, this will ensure that the gudgeon pin is accurately located to the piston and connecting rod assembly.

   It will be of some advantage if the gudgeon pin is lubricated during this operation as this will assist in the assembly. Check to ensure that the piston moves freely on the gudgeon pin and that no damage has been incurred during the pressing operation.

Piston rings, refit

1. To fit the special oil control ring, first fit the expander into the groove making absolutely certain that the ends of the expander ring abut and do not overlap. Fit the oil ring rails one at a time and ensure correct location within the piston groove.

   The two compression rings can now be installed in the normal manner ensuring that the 'T' or 'Top' marking is towards the piston crown, and that the chrome compression ring is in the top groove.

Pistons and connecting rods, refit

1. Make sure all cylinder bores, pistons, connecting rod bearings and crankshaft journals are absolutely clean.

2. Before fitting the piston and connecting rod assembly into its bore, position the crankshaft journal straight down, that is, in the bottom dead centre position.

3. Place the bearing upper shell in position in the connecting rod and retain using the connecting rod bolt guides, special tool, Part No. 605351.

Operation A1-14—*continued*

4. Insert the piston and connecting rod assembly into its respective bore. Note carefully that on each connecting rod there is a small dome-shaped boss. When fitting the piston and connecting rod assembly the small boss should face the front of the engine on the right-hand bank of cylinders and the rear of the engine on the left-hand bank of cylinders. This will mean that with the connecting rods fitted to each crankshaft journal the bosses will face inwards towards each other.

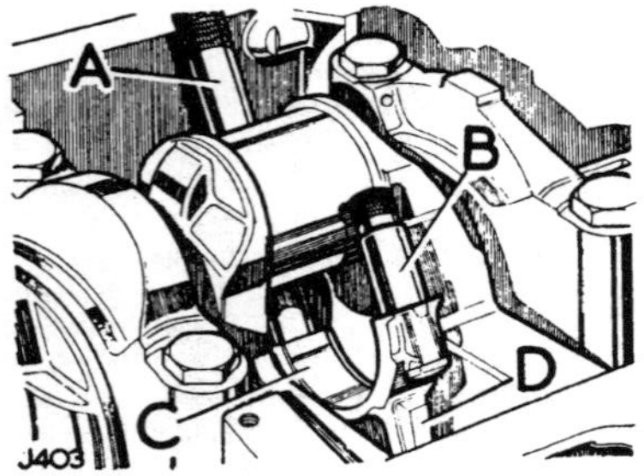

Connecting rod bolt guide tool

A—Guide tool, long } Special tool,
B—Guide tool, short } Part No. 605351
C—Bearing shell located by guide tool
D—Connecting rod

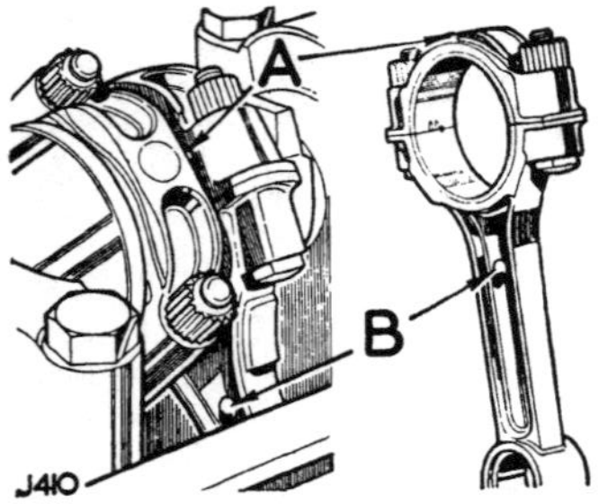

Connecting rod showing identifying boss

A—Boss on connecting rod cap
B—Boss on connecting rod

5. Using a suitable ring compressor, fit the piston into the cylinder bore ensuring that the bearing locates correctly on the crankshaft journal.

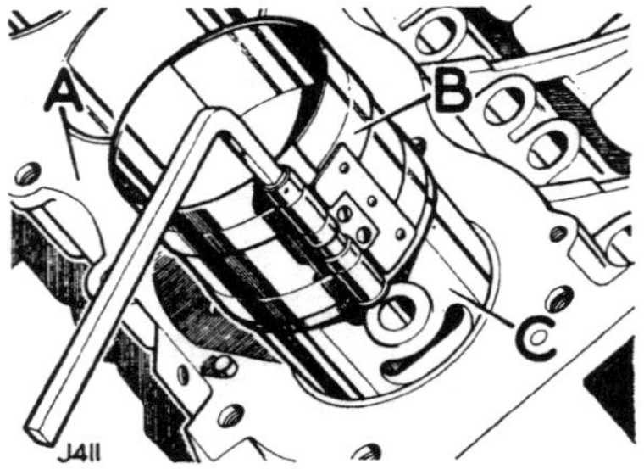

Fitting piston using ring compressor

A—Cylinder block B—Piston ring compressor
C—Piston

6. Place a piece of Plastigauge, Part No. 605238, lengthwise across the bottom centre of the lower bearing shell (if the engine is removed from the car and is in the inverted position it will be easier if the Plastigauge is placed on to the crankshaft journal).

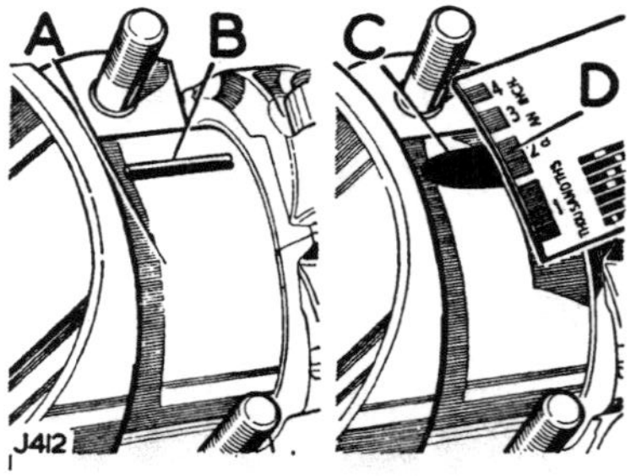

Position of Plastigauge, Part No. 605238, for checking bearing clearance

A—Connecting bearing journal
B—Initial position of Plastigauge
C—Plastigauge, flattened
D—Graduated scale on Plastigauge packet

Operation A1-14—*continued*

7. Fit the bearing cap with the shell and tighten the securing nuts to a torque figure of 30 to 35 lbs/ft (4,0 to 4,9 mkg).
   Note: The rib on the edge of the cap and the dome-shaped boss on the web of the connecting rod must be towards the rear of the engine on all connecting rods in the left-hand cylinder bank and towards the front of the engine in the right-hand cylinder bank.
   Important: Under no circumstances must the crankshaft be turned with Plastigauge in the bearing.
8. Remove the bearing cap complete with bearing shell, the flattened Plastigauge will be found adhering to either the bearing shell or the crankshaft journal. DO NOT REMOVE IT.
9. Using the scale printed on the Plastigauge packet measure the flattened Plastigauge at its widest point. The number within the graduations which most closely corresponds to the width of the Plastigauge indicates the bearing clearance in thousands of an inch.
10. The desired clearance with a new bearing is .0006 in. to .0022 in. (0,013 mm to 0,06 mm).
   Note: If a bearing has been in service it is advisable to fit a new bearing if the clearance exceeds .003 in. (0,08 mm). However, if the bearing is in good condition and is not being checked because of bearing noise it is not necessary to replace the bearing.
11. If a new bearing is being selected it will be necessary to use selective assembly until the correct clearance between bearing and crankpin journal is obtained.
   NEVER under any circumstances file the connecting rods or caps to adjust bearing clearance.
12. Having selected the correct size bearing clean off the Plastigauge, oil the bearing thoroughly and refit the cap with bearing shell and tighten the securing nuts to 30 to 35 lbs/ft (4,0 to 4,9 mkg).
13. With the selected bearing fitted and the bolts tightened it should be possible to move the connecting rod freely back and forth on the crankpin as allowed by end clearance, if the rod cannot be moved either the bearing is too much undersized or a misaligned rod is indicated.
14. Fit all other piston and connecting rod assemblies in exactly the same manner. When all assemblies are fitted, a check should be made to ensure that they are fitted correctly, the oil holes in the connecting rods will be up towards the camshaft, the small boss on the edge of the bearing cap will be on the same side as the boss on the connecting rod web and these bosses will be towards each other on the same crank journal.
15. Check the end-float between the connecting rods on each crank journal using feeler gauges, this clearance should be between .005 in. and .015 in. (0,13 mm to 0,38 mm).

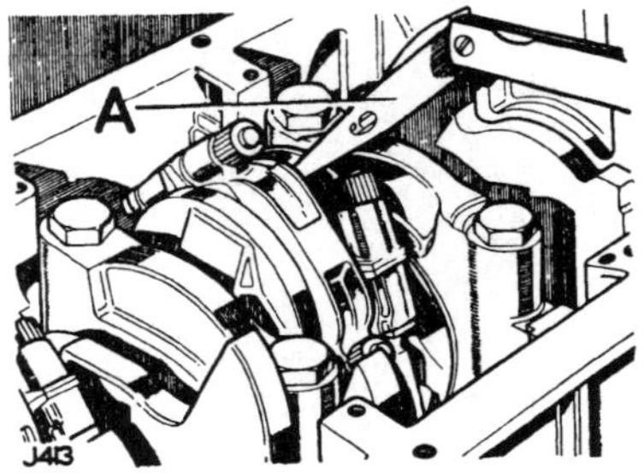

Checking connecting rod end-float

A—Feeler gauge inserted between connecting rods

16. Reverse the removal procedure for the remaining items.
17. Fill the engine to the correct level and with the correct grade of lubricant. Capacity: 10 Imperial pints, 12 US pints, 5,5 litres, plus 1 Imperial pint 1.2 US pints, 0,5 litres, if oil filter element has been replaced. For recommended grades of oil, see chart in Section Y.
18. Refill radiator as per instructions in Operation A1-2.
19. Finally, run the engine and check for oil or water leaks and carry out any adjustments that may be necessary.

*Flexible drive plate and ring gear, remove and refit—Operation A1-15

Time allowed: hours

Spanner size: $\frac{5}{8}$ in. AF

Flexible drive plate and ring gear, remove

1. Remove automatic transmission complete. Operation EEE2-5.
2. Remove the six bolts securing the flexible drive plate to the crankshaft flange and lift off the reinforcing plate, flexible drive plate and spacer ring.
3. Inspect flexible drive plate for cracks at bolt holes, check ring gear for wear.

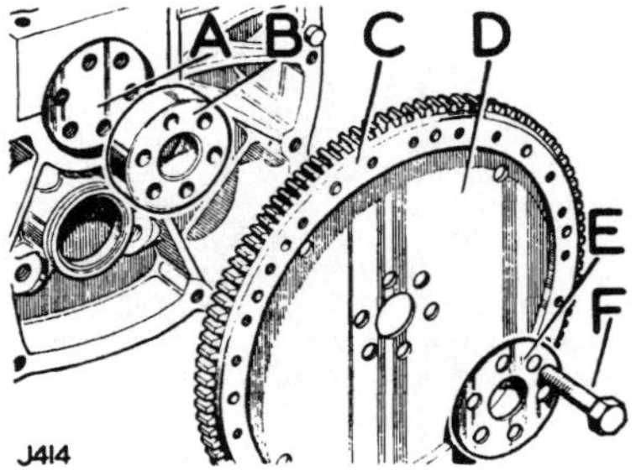

Flexible drive plate and ring gear

A—Crankshaft
B—Spacer ring
C—Ring gear
D—Flexible drive plate
E—Reinforcement plate
F—Bolt fixing flexible drive plate

Flexible drive plate and ring gear, refit

1. Reverse removal procedure.
   Note: The reinforcing plate and the spacer ring each have a chamfer on one outer edge and this chamfer should be fitted towards the flexible drive plate.
2. The bolt holes are unevenly spaced so that the flexible drive plate can only be fitted in one position, with the starter ring bolt heads towards the engine.
3. Before tightening the bolts, take up any clearance in the flexible drive plate by rotating it in direction of engine rotation. Tighten the bolts to a torque of 50 to 60 lbs/ft (7,0 to 8,5 mkg).
4. Refit automatic transmission. Operation EEE2-5

Operations which are identified by an asterisk (*), can be carried out with the engine installed in the car

Crankshaft, bearings and rear main bearing oil seal, to remove and refit
Operation A1-16

Time allowed: Crankshaft, remove and refit, complete overhaul hours
Main bearings and rear main oil seal, remove and refit hours
Rear main oil seal, to renew hours

Workshop hand tools:
Spanner sizes: 7/16 in. AF, 1/2 in. AF, 9/16 in. AF, 5/8 in. AF, 3/4 in. AF, 7/8 in. AF, 15/16 in. AF
Screwdriver, medium. Pliers
Sparking plug spanner

Special tools:
Torque wrench
Plastigauge, Part No. 605238

This operation to be carried out with the engine removed from the car.

When carrying out a complete engine overhaul proceed through this operation as detailed for complete overhaul. However if main bearings and/or rear main bearing oil seals only are being replaced, carry out the items listed under the headings 'Crankshaft, remove and refit, main bearings and/or rear main oil seal only'.

Crankshaft, remove, complete overhaul

1. Remove engine and transmission. Operation A1-5.
2. Remove alternator. Operation A1-7.
3. Remove inlet manifold. Operation A1-9.
4. Remove rockers and shafts. Operation A1-10.
5. Remove cylinder heads. Operation A1-11
6. Remove front cover assembly. Operation A1-12.
7. Remove pistons and connecting rods. Operation A1-14
8. Remove flexible drive plate. Operation A1-15.
9. Remove the main bearing cap bolts, lift off the caps and then lift out the crankshaft and place to one side.
10. If they are to be used again retain the bearing shells in pairs and suitably mark them with the number of each respective journal.

Crankshaft, remove—main bearings and/or rear main oil seal only

1. Remove engine and transmission. Operation A1-5.
2. Remove front cover assembly. Operation A1-12.
3. Remove flexible drive plate. Operation A1-15.
4. Drain oil and remove sump and sump baffle plate.
5. Remove sump oil strainer.
6. Remove all connecting rod cap nuts and lift off bearing caps together with the lower bearing shells.
7. Remove the main bearing cap bolts, lift off the caps and cover bearing shells, then lift out the crankshaft.
8. If the bearing shells are to be used again, retain them in pairs and mark them to facilitate their replacement in the same position from which they were removed.
9. If necessary carry out the inspection procedure as detailed for crankshaft bearings and crankshaft.

Inspection of crankshaft bearings and crankshaft

The following procedure is suggested to check crankshaft for straightness.

1. Rest crankshaft on the blocks at number one and number five main bearing journals.
2. Check with a dial test indicator the run-out at numbers two, three and four main bearing journals.
3. The total indicator readings at each journal should not exceed .003 in. (0,08 mm).
4. While checking run-out at each journal, note the relation of maximum eccentricity on each journal to the others. The maximum on all journals should come at the same angular location—if they do not come at nearly the same location, the crankshaft may well have a 'dog leg' in it and is therefore unsatisfactory for service.
5. Check each crankshaft journal for ovality—if the ovality is more than .0015 in. (0,04 mm) the crankshaft should be re-ground as applicable since the full mileage cannot be expected from bearings used with an excessively out-of-round crankshaft.

Operation A1-16—*continued*

Crankshaft, refit

1. Make sure that the crankshaft journals, the bearing seats in the crankcase and bearing caps are thoroughly clean, also ensure that initially crankshaft journals and bearings are free from oil. This is essential when checking bearing clearances using Plastigauge as it is soluble in oil.

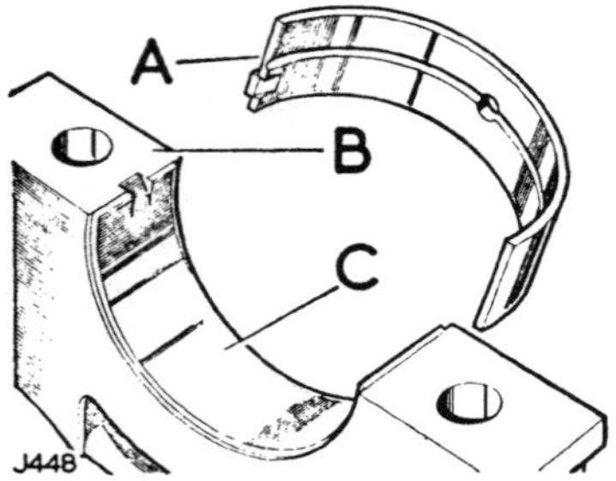

Main bearing shells

A—Upper bearing shell
B—Main bearing cap
C—Lower bearing shell

2. Fit the upper bearing shells to the cylinder block. **These must be the shells with the oil drilling and oil grooves.**
3. Braided fabric seals are pressed into grooves formed in the crankcase and rear main bearing cap to the rear of the oil collecting groove.

   Cork/neoprene composition seals are fitted in the grooves in the sides of the bearing cap to seal against leakage in the joints between cap and crankcase. The cork/neoprene composition swells in presence of oil and heat, forming a tight seal.

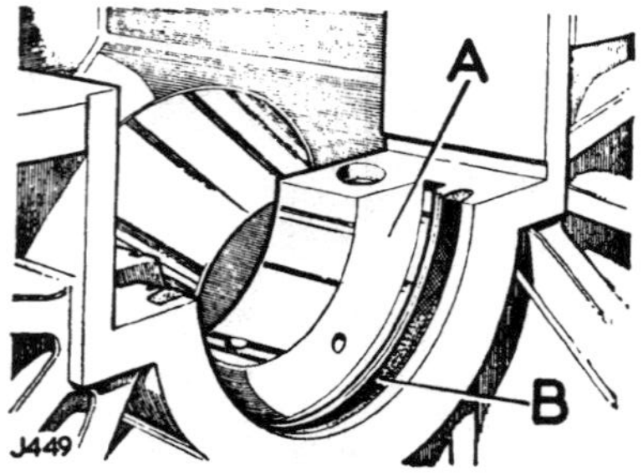

Rear main bearing seal in cylinder block

A—Cylinder block B—Fabric seal

The braided fabric seal can only be installed in the crankcase when the crankshaft is removed. However, the seal can be replaced in the cap whenever the cap is removed.

Remove old seal and place new seal in groove with both ends projecting above the parting surface of the cylinder block. Force the seal into the groove by rubbing down with a hammer handle or smooth stick until seal projects above the groove not more than 1/16 in. (1,5 mm). Cut ends off flush with surface of cylinder block, using a sharp knife or razor blade. Lubricate the seal with heavy engine oil just before installation of crankshaft.

Crankshaft, refit—main bearings and/or rear main oil seal only. Items 4 to 9 inclusive

4. Place suitable blocks, approximately 1/2 in. (12,5 mm thick, on to each end of the cylinder block so that they cover the front and rear upper bearing shells.

Operation A1-16—*continued*

5. Lift the crankshaft into position with the ends supported on the blocks.
6. Holding the connecting rods in position, remove one of the blocks, and carefully lower the crankshaft on to the connecting rod bearings. Repeat for the opposite end.
7. Where necessary, draw the connecting rods up on to the crankshaft journals using connecting rod guide tool, Part No. 605351. It is suggested that the end of the guide is drilled, and a suitable bar is used to form the guide bolt into a 'T' bar.

   If necessary, check connecting bearing clearance. See Operation A1-14.
8. Refit the connecting rod bearing caps ensuring that the boss on each bearing cap is facing its partner on the journal.
9. Tighten the connecting rod bearing caps to a torque of 30 to 35 lbs/ft (4,0 to 4,9 mkg).

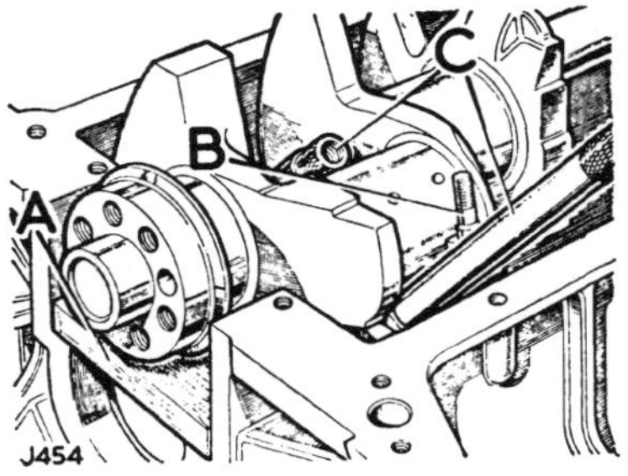

Crankshaft supported on cylinder block

A—Support block, ½ in. (12,5 mm) thick
B—Connecting rod
C—Connecting rod guide tool, Part No. 605351

Crankshaft, refit—complete overhaul, item 10

10. Gently place the crankshaft in position in the bearings.

Checking main bearing clearance

11. Place a piece of Plastigauge on each of the main bearing journals. Fit the plain bearing shells to the caps and fit the caps to the cylinder block. **Note:** The rear main bearing seals should not be fitted to the cap until after the bearing clearances have been checked and are correct. Tighten the fixing bolts to the correct torque figure; rear main bearing bolts 65 to 70 lbs/ft (9,0 to 9,6 mkg); other main bearing bolts 50 to 55 lbs/ft (7,0 to 7,6 mkg).
12. Remove the main bearing caps complete with bearing shells, the flattened Plastigauge will be found adhering to either the bearing shells or the crank journals. **DO NOT REMOVE IT.**

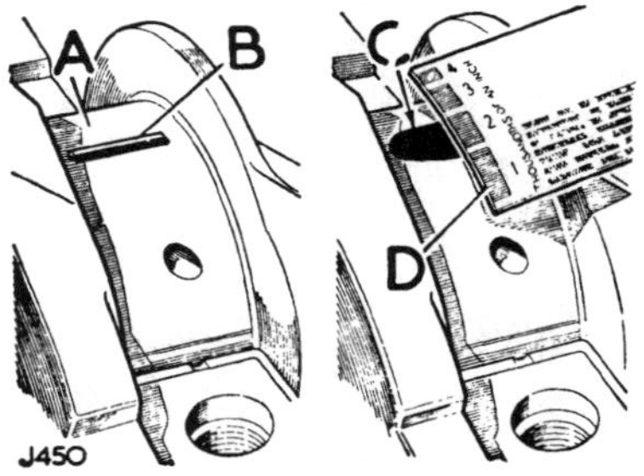

Position of Plastigauge, Part No. 605238, for checking bearing clearance

A—Main bearing journal
B—Initial position of Plastigauge
C—Flattened Plastigauge
D—Graduated scale on Plastigauge packet

13. Using the scale printed on the Plastigauge packet, measure the flattened Plastigauge on each bearing at its widest point. The figure within the graduation which most closely corresponds to the width of the Plastigauge indicates the bearing clearance in thousandths of an inch.

Operation A1-16—*continued*

14. The desired clearance with a new bearing is 0.0009 in. to 0.0025 in. (0,0254 mm to 0,065 mm). If this clearance is not obtained initially then selective assembly of bearing shells will be necessary.
15. When bearings of the correct clearance have been selected, clean off all the Plastigauge and oil the crankshaft journals, turn the crankshaft to ensure lubrication of upper bearing shells.
16. Lubricate the lower bearing shells and fit numbers one to four (1 to 4) bearing caps leaving the bolts just finger tight at this stage.
17. Fit the fabric seal to the rear main bearing cap following exactly the procedure in paragraph 3 then fit the cork/neoprene seals.

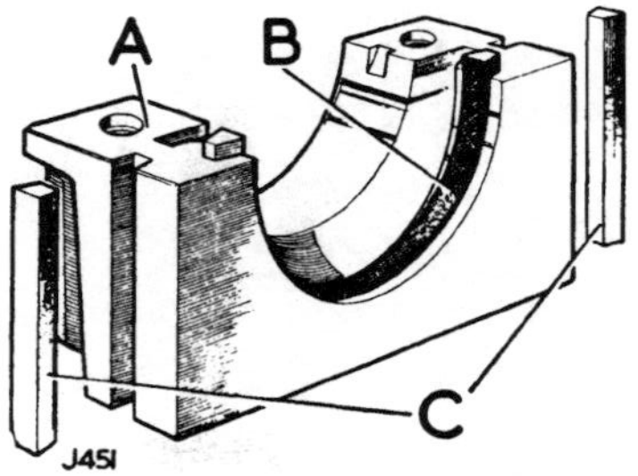

Rear main bearing cap seals

A—Rear main bearing cap
B—Fabric seal
C—Cork/neoprene seal

The cork/neoprene composition seals are $\frac{1}{16}$ in. (1,6 mm) longer than the grooves in the bearing cap. The seals MUST NOT be cut to length. Just before installation of bearing cap in crankcase fit the seals into the bearing cap with the upper end (i.e. cap parting face) protruding very slightly. Lightly lubricate outer faces only of cap seals and fit the bearing cap to the crankcase.

After the cap is installed, push seals up into the cap with a blunt instrument to be sure of a seal at the upper parting line between cap and crankcase.

18. **Note:** When replacement main bearings are being fitted or the original main bearings are being refitted, it is necessary to line up the thrust surfaces of the centre main bearing shell before the cap bolts are finally torqued.

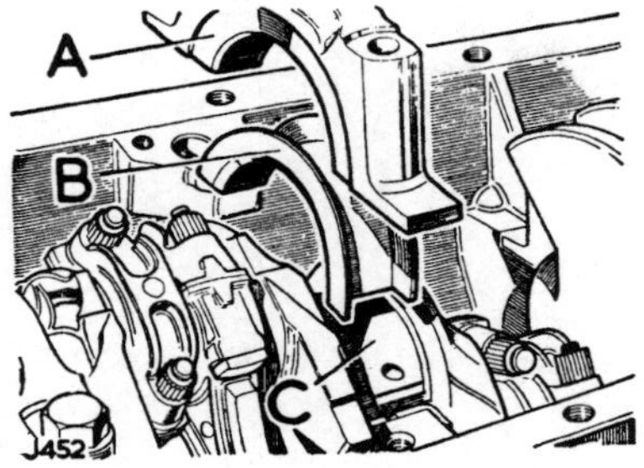

Centre main bearing thrust surfaces

A—Centre main bearing cap
B—Centre main bearing thrust surfaces
C—Centre main journal

Using a hide hammer, tap the crankshaft rearwards to the limit of its travel and then tap the crankshaft forward again, to the limit of its travel.

Operation A1-16—*continued*

Finally, tighten the main bearing bolts to the following torque figures:

Rear main bearing bolts 65 to 70 lbs/ft (9,0 to 9,6 mkg).

Other main bearing bolts 50 to 55 lbs/ft (7,0 to 7,6 mkg.)

If the crankshaft has been removed, but the main bearings not disturbed, it is still recommended that the above procedure be followed.

19. The end-float of the crankshaft should be between the limits .004 in. to .008 in. (0,10 mm to 0,20 mm) and is achieved by selective assembly.

Crankshaft regrinding

An important point to note is that bearings are available in undersizes of .010 in. (0,25 mm), .020 in. (0,50 mm), .030 in. (0,76 mm) and .040 in. (1,02 mm). In the case of the centre bearing, which controls crankshaft thrust, the thrust faces are increased in thickness, as shown on the chart.

When a crankshaft is to be re-ground the thrust faces on either side of the centre main journal must be machined in accordance with the dimensions on the following charts.

For example, if a .020 in. (0,508 mm) undersize bearing is to be fitted, .005 in. (0,127 mm) must be machined off the thrust face of the centre journal, maintaining the radius as illustrated.

20. Reverse the removal procedure for the remaining items.

CAUTION: The engine must be operated at low speed when first started after fitting a new braided seal. (1,000 rpm maximum).

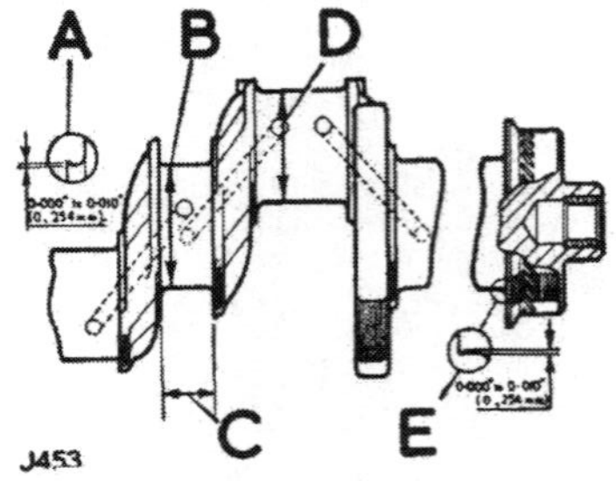

Crankshaft dimensions

A—Radius for all journals except rear main bearing .075 to .090 in. (1,905 to 2,286 mm)
B—Main bearing journal diameter
C—Thrust face width
D—Connecting rod journal diameter
E—Radius for rear main bearing journal 120 in. (3.048 mm)

Operation A1-16—*continued*

Main bearing journal size	Thrust face width
Standard	Standard
.010 in. (0,254 mm) undersize	Standard
.020 in. (0,508 mm) undersize	.010 in. (0,254 mm) oversize
.030 in. (0,762 mm) undersize	.010 in. (0,254 mm) oversize
.040 in. (1,06 mm) undersize	.020 in. (0,508 mm) oversize

Crankshaft dimensions, metric sizes

Crankshaft grade	Diameter 'B'	Width 'C'	Diameter 'D'
Standard	58,399–58,412 mm	26,975–27,026 mm	50,800–50,812 mm
0,254 mm U/S	58,146–58,158 mm	26,975–27,026 mm	50,546–50,559 mm
0,508 mm U/S	57,892–57,904 mm	27,229–27,280 mm	50,292–50,305 mm
0,762 mm U/S	57,638–57,650 mm	27,229–27,280 mm	50,038–50,051 mm
1,016 mm U/S	57,384–57,396 mm	27,483–27,534 mm	49,784–49,797 mm

Crankshaft dimensions, British sizes

Crankshaft grade	Diameter 'B'	Width 'C'	Diameter D'
Standard	2.2992–2.2997 in.	1.062–1.064 in.	2.0000–2.0005 in.
.010 in. U/S	2.2892–2.2897 in.	1.062–1.064 in.	1.9900–1.9905 in.
.020 in. U/S	2.2792–2.2797 in.	1.072–1.074 in.	1.9800–1.9805 in.
.030 in. U/S	2.2692–2.2697 in.	1.072–1.074 in.	1.9700–1.9705 in.
.040 in. U/S	2.2592–2.2597 in.	1.082–1.084 in.	1.9600–1.9605 in.

*External oil filter, to remove and refit—Operation A1-17

Time allowed: hours

Workshop hand tools:

Spanner size: $\frac{5}{8}$ in. AF

External oil filter, remove

The oil filter must be renewed every 5,000 miles (8.000 km); this should be carried out at a routine oil change. To remove the filter proceed as follows:

1. Place a suitable oil tray under the engine.
2. Unscrew the oil filter from the oil pump cover assembly on the engine and discard together with rubber washer.

Oil filter

A—Rubber washer B—Oil filter

External oil filter, refit

1. Make sure that mating surfaces on oil pump cover assembly are perfectly clean.
2. Place a new rubber washer in position on the sealing face of the new oil filter and fit the filter to the oil pump cover on the engine.

   On fitting the oil filter it is essential that it is tightened by hand. The filter should be spun on until the rubber sealing ring touches the oil pump cover face and then a further half-turn should be given by **hand.**

   Note: The hexagon on the AC Delco filter casing is for **removal** purposes only. Alternatively a removal strap may be used.
3. Refill the engine with 11 Imperial pints, 13 US pints, 6 Litres, of the correct grade of engine oil. Run the engine for 5 minutes, and check around oil filter for any sign of leakage.
4. Check the oil level after the engine has been switched off and sufficient time has elapsed for the oil around the engine to drain back into the sump. Replenish if necessary.

*Oil pressure warning light switch, to replace—Operation A1-18

Time allowed: hours

Workshop hand tools:

Spanner size: $\frac{3}{8}$ in. Whit

Oil pressure switch, replace

1. The oil pressure switch is screwed into the oil filter adaptor on the right-hand side of the front cover. Its function is to cause the oil warning light to operate if the oil pressure drops below 8 to 10 lbs per square inch (0,6 to 0,7 kg/cm sq.)
2. The switch can be removed from the adaptor by disconnecting the electrical connection and using a $\frac{3}{8}$ in. Whit spanner to unscrew the complete unit.
3. If a faulty switch is suspected it can be checked by substitution or by temporarily fitting a pressure gauge in its place.
4. When replacing the switch fit a new sealing washer.

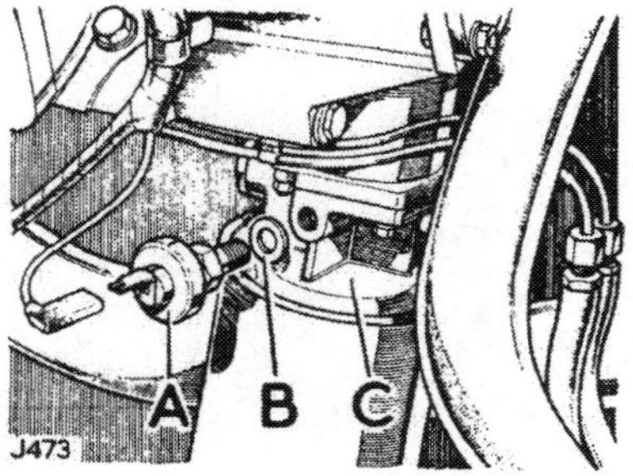

Oil pressure warning light switch

A—Warning light switch B—Sealing washer C—Oil filter adaptor

*Oil pump, to remove and refit—Operation A1-19

Time allowed: hours

Workshop hand tools:

Spanner sizes: $\frac{5}{16}$ in. AF, $\frac{5}{8}$ in. AF, 1 in. AF

Oil pump, remove

1. Remove oil filter. Operation A1-17.
2. Disconnect wire from oil pressure indicator switch in the oil pump cover assembly.
3. Remove special bolts securing oil pump cover assembly to front cover; remove cover and slide out oil pump gears.

Inspection

1. Clean off gears and inspect for wear, scoring, etc., replace gears not found to be serviceable.
2. Remove the oil pressure relief valve cap spring and valve also remove the oil filter by-pass valve cap spring and valve.
3. Wash the parts thoroughly and inspect the relief valve for wear or scoring. Check the relief valve spring to see that it is not worn on its sides or collapsed. Replace the relief valve spring if it is not serviceable. Thoroughly clean the gauze filter in the relief valve bore of the cover.
4. Check the valve in its bore in the cover, the valve should have no more clearance than an easy slide fit. If any perceptible side movement can be felt the valve and/or the cover should be replaced.
5. Check filter by-pass valve for cracks, nicks, or warping. The valve should be flat and free of nicks or scratches.

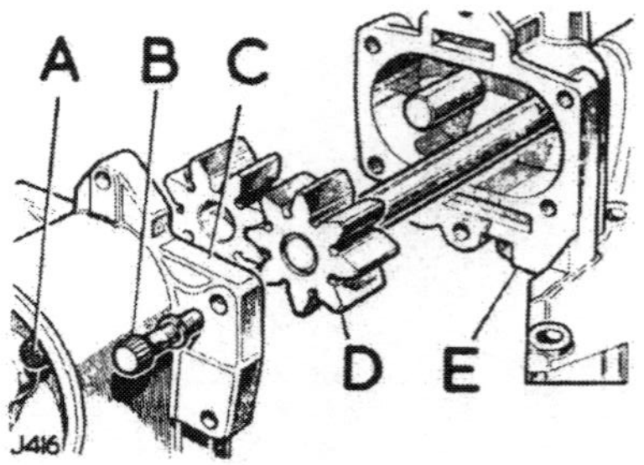

Oil pump

A—Gauze filter for adaptor body
B—Screw fixing adaptor body
C—Oil pump cover
D—Oil pump gears
E—Front cover

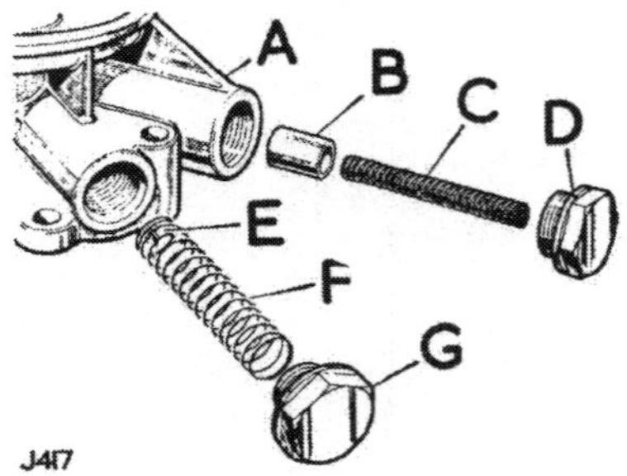

Oil pump valves, exploded view

A—Oil filter adaptor body
B—Pressure relief valve
C—Spring for pressure relief valve
D—Pressure relief valve cap
E—Filter by-pass valve
F—Spring for by-pass valve
G—Filter by-pass valve cap

Operations which are identified by an asterisk (*), can be carried out with the engine installed in the car

Operation A1-19—*continued*

Oil pump, refit

1. Lubricate and fit the pressure relief valve and spring into the bore of the oil pump cover. Fit the cap and sealing washer and tighten to a torque figure of 30 to 35 lbs/ft (4,0 to 4,9 mkg). Do not over-tighten.
2. Fit the filter by-pass valve into the end of the spring, then fit the spring, cap and gasket and tighten to a torque figure of 30 to 35 lbs/ft (4,0 to 4,9 mkg).
3. Fit the oil pump gears and shaft into the front cover.
4. Place a straight-edge across the gears and measure the clearance between the straight-edge and the surface of the front cover; the clearance should be between .0018 in. and .0058 in. (0,05 mm to 0,15 mm). If the clearance is less than .0018 in. (0,05 mm) check the timing front cover gear pocket for evidence of wear.
5. If the gear end clearance is satisfactory remove the gears and **fully pack the housing with petroleum jelly. Note:** Use only petroleum jelly, no other grease is suitable.
6. Fit the gears so that the petroleum jelly is forced into every cavity and between the teeth of the gears. **Note: This is very important, unless the pump is fully packed with petroleum jelly it may not prime itself when the engine is started.**
7. Fit a new gasket and place the oil pump cover assembly in position. Fit the special fixing bolts and tighten alternatively and evenly to a torque of 10 to 15 lbs/ft (1,4 to 2,0 mkg).
8. Fit filter to oil pump body.
9. Reconnect wire to oil pressure switch.
10. The oil pressure settings for the 3.5-Litre engine are as follows:

    Oil pressure at 2,400 rpm 30 to 40 lbs/sq in. (2,109 to 2,812 kg/cm²).

    Oil pressure at 4,000 rpm 55 lbs/sq in. (3,867 kg/cm²).

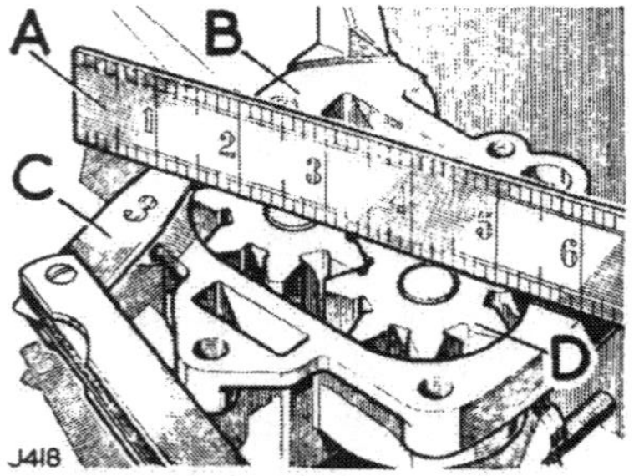

Checking oil pump gear end-float

A—Straight edge
B—Front cover
C—Feeler gauge
D—Oil pump gears

*Distributor, to remove and refit, ignition timing and dwell angle setting
Operation A1-20

Time allowed: Distributor, remove and refit hours
Distributor, timing hours

Workshop hand tools:
Spanner size: $\frac{9}{16}$ in. AF
Screwdriver, medium Screwdriver, Phillips
Set of feeler gauges

Special tools:
Stroboscopic timing lamp
Tach-Dwell Meter

See Section S for distributor overhaul

Distributor and HT leads, remove

1. Disconnect battery.
2. Disconnect the vacuum advance pipe from the distributor.
3. Disconnect the low tension lead, coil to distributor.
4. Unclip the distributor cap also the leads from the retainer on the left-hand rocker cover and move cap to one side.

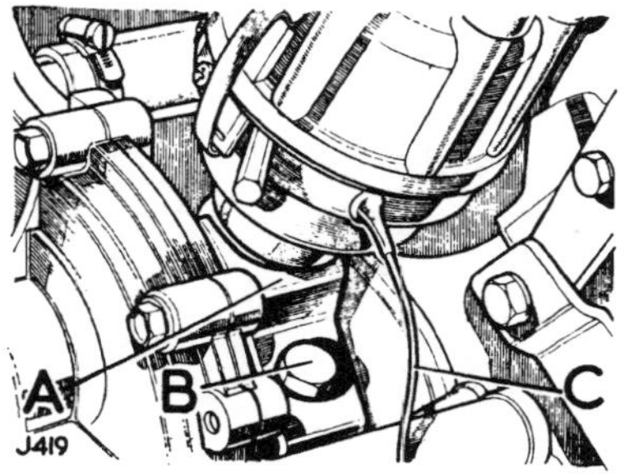

Distributor

A—Clamp for distributor
B—Bolt fixing clip
C—Low-tension lead

5. Mark the distributor body and make a corresponding mark on the front cover to identify position of distributor in relation to the engine.
6. This will enable the distributor to be replaced in exactly the same position when refitting. Note: If the engine is turned while the distributor is removed, complete ignition timing procedure must be followed.
7. Remove the distributor clamp and fixing bolt and lift out the distributor. Mark the top edge of the body in line with the centre line of the rotor arm.

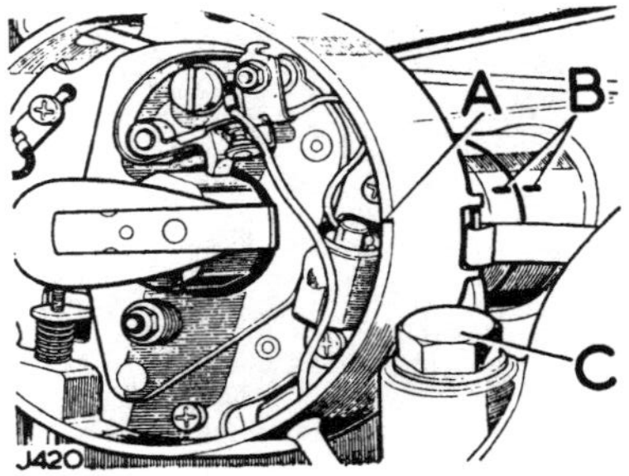

Correct location of distributor marks

A—Mark on distributor body in relation to centre of rotor arm
B—Marks on distributor body and front cover
C—Front left-hand bolt of inlet manifold

Distributor, refit

Note: If a new distributor is being fitted, mark body in same relative position as distributor removed.

Leads for distributor caps should be connected as shown in the illustration.

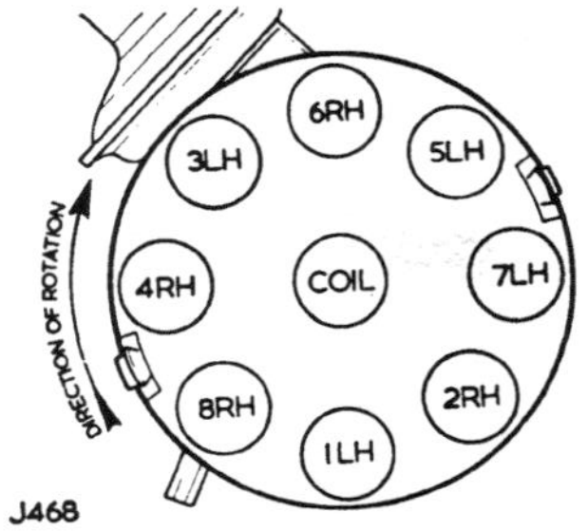

Distributor leads sequence

Operations which are identified by an asterisk (*), can be carried out with the engine installed in the car

Operation A1-20—*continued*

1. If the engine has not been disturbed while the distributor has been removed from the engine proceed as follows:
2. Fit a new 'O' ring seal to the distributor housing.
3. Turn the distributor drive so that the centre line of the rotor arm is 30° anti-clockwise with the mark previously made on the top edge of the distributor body.
4. Refit the distributor to its position in the front timing cover, making sure that the mark on the distributor body lines up with the mark on the timing cover.

   It may be necessary to align the oil pump drive shaft to enable the distributor drive shaft to engage in the slot.
5. Fit the distributor clamp and fixing bolt and tighten to secure distributor in the exact original position.
6. Connect the low tension lead, distributor to coil.
7. Refit distributor cap.
8. Reconnect the battery.
9. Using suitable electronic equipment, set the dwell angle and the ignition timing as detailed under 'ignition timing' and 'dwell angle settings' in this section.
10. If, with the distributor removed, the engine has been turned it will be necessary to carry out the following procedure.
11. Fit the distributor to the engine with the rotor aligned with the number one sparking plug lead position on the cap, line up the vacuum control in position to connect the vacuum pipe.
12. Fit the distributor clamp and fixing bolt leaving both loose at this stage.
13. If the distributor does not seat correctly in the timing cover press down lightly on the distributor while turning the engine, the drive on the end of the distributor shaft should then engage with the slot in the oil pump drive shaft.

    Use a socket spanner on the vibration damper securing nut to rotate engine.

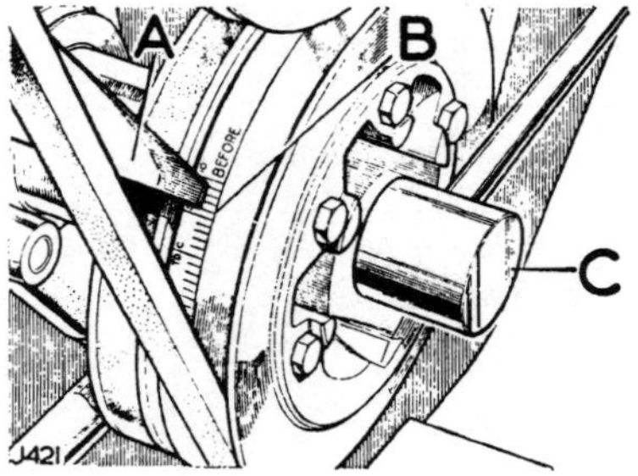

Ignition timing mark

A—Timing pointer
B—6° mark
C—Socket spanner

14. Turn the engine back until the 6° timing mark on the crankshaft vibration damper passes the indicator on the front cover, then rotate the engine, slowly this time, in a forward direction until the 6° mark is in line with the indicator.

    Now check the position of the distributor to ensure that the rotor is in the correct firing position for number one cylinder and that the vacuum advance unit is correctly positioned for connecting the vacuum advance pipe.
15. Rotate the distributor in an anti-clockwise direction until the contact points just start to open.
16. Secure the distributor in this position by tightening the clamp bolt.

Operation A1-20—*continued*

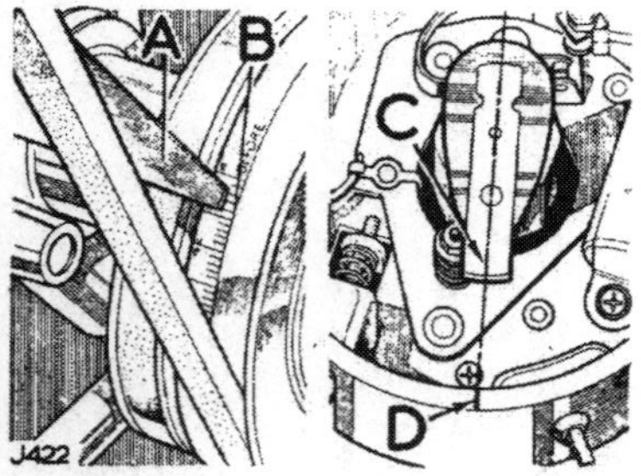

Fitting distributor to engine

A—Timing pointer
B—6° mark on vibration damper
C—Centre of rotor arm
D—Mark on body to indicate No. 1 plug lead position

17. Connect the low tension lead, coil to distributor, also connect the vacuum advance pipe.
18. Refit distributor cap.
19. Reconnect battery.
20. Using suitable electronic equipment, set the dwell angle and ignition timing as detailed below.

Ignition timing and dwell angle settings

Static and dynamic ignition timing: 6° BTDC.

Dwell angle: 26° to 28°.

Note: It is essential that the following procedure is adhered to. Inaccurate timing can lead to serious engine damage.

1. Set ignition timing statically, prior to the engine being run, by the basic lamp timing method. (This sequence is to give only an approximation in order that the engine may be run. On no account should the engine be started before this check is carried out.)
2. Start engine and set to an idling speed of 600 rpm.
3. Set dwell angle as follows:
   (a) Couple up Tach-dwell meter to engine following manufacturers' instructions.
   (b) Set selector knob to 'calibrate' position. Adjust calibration knob to give a zero reading on the meter.
   (c) Set selector knob to 8 cylinder position and Tach-dwell selector knob to 'dwell'. Adjust distributor dwell angle by turning the hexagon headed adjustment screw adjacent to the forward distributor cap clip until the meter reads 26° to 28°. If meter used does not have an 8-cylinder position, set selector knob to 4-cylinder position and adjust at distributor until meter reads 52° to 56°.

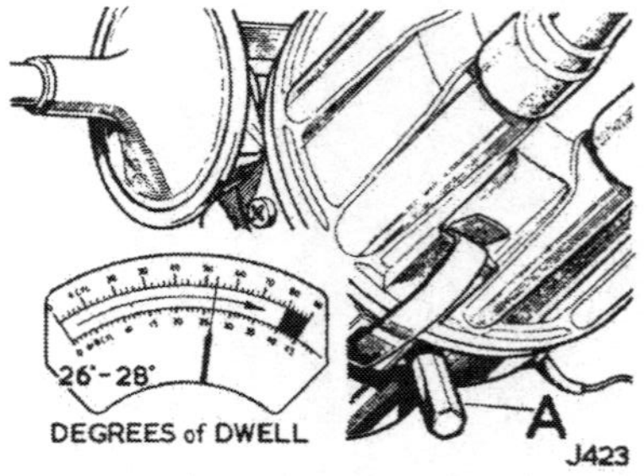

Adjusting dwell angle

A—Adjustment screw for dwell angle

   (d) Uncouple Tach-dwell meter.

Note: Care should be taken to switch the Tach-dwell meter selector switch to the 'off' position after use otherwise battery life will be impaired.

4. Set ignition timing as follows:
   (a) Couple Stroboscopic timing lamp to engine following manufacturers' instructions, with the high tension lead attached into No. 1 cylinder plug lead. (See Data Section for cylinder numbering sequence.)

Operation A1-20—*continued*

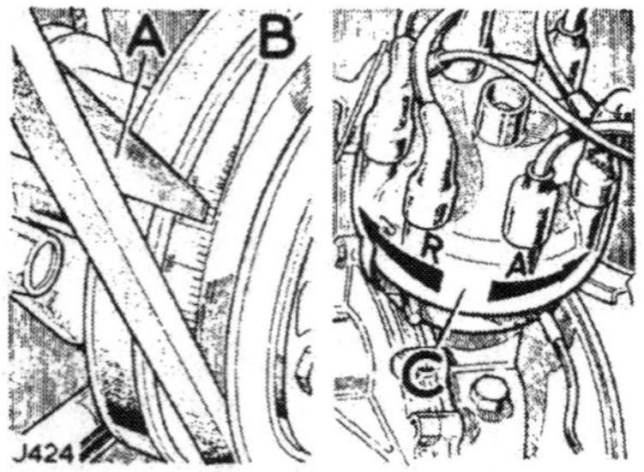

Setting ignition timing

A—Timing pointer
B—6° mark
C—Distributor, adjust as indicated to advance or retard

   (b) Disconnect vacuum advance pipe from distributor and block vacuum advance pipe by suitable means.
   (c) With distributor clamping bolt slackened and engine idling at a speed of 600 rpm, turn distributor until the Stroboscopic lamp synchronises the timing pointer and the timing mark at 6° BTDC on the vibration damper rim.
   (d) Retighten the distributor clamping bolt securely.
   (e) Disconnect Stroboscopic timing lamp.
   (f) Refit vacuum advance pipe.

Note: Engine speed accuracy during ignition timing is of paramount importance. Any variation from the required 600 rpm particularly in an upwards direction will lead to wrongly set ignition timing.

*Fan blades and water pump, to remove and refit—Operation A1-21

Time allowed: Fan blades and water pump, remove and refit hours

Workshop hand tools:
Spanner sizes: $\frac{3}{8}$ in. AF, $\frac{1}{2}$ in. AF, $\frac{7}{16}$ in. AF, $\frac{9}{16}$ in. AF
Screwdriver, medium

Special tool:
3M EC 776 sealant/lubricant, Part No. 605764

See Section P for water pump overhaul procedure

Water pump and fan blades, remove

1. Drain the cooling system, using a clean container as system is filled with either anti-freeze or inhibitor.
2. Remove the fan blades and slacken off the three fan pulley bolts.

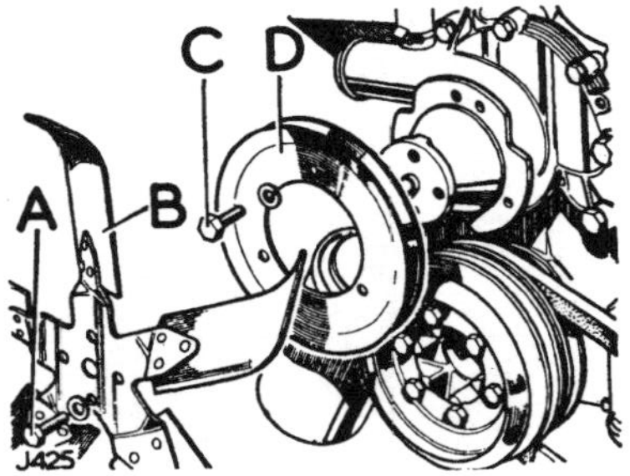

Fan blades and pulley

A—Bolt fixing fan blades
B—Fan blades
C—Bolt fixing fan pulley
D—Fan pulley

3. Slacken the alternator fixings, remove fan belt and lift off the fan pulley.
4. Remove the bolt securing the alternator to the alternator adjusting bracket and move the alternator to one side.
5. Disconnect the heater return pipe, thermostat by-pass pipe and the bottom hose at the water pump.
6. Remove the bolts securing the water pump assembly to the front cover and lift off water pump complete with gasket.

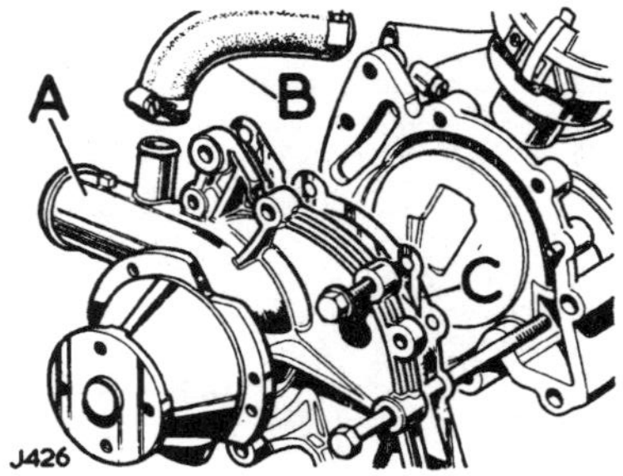

Water pump

A—Water pump
B—By-pass hose
C—Joint washer for pump

Water pump and fan blades, refit

1. Ensure that the fitting faces of the water pump and the front timing cover are clean.
2. Lightly grease a new joint washer and position it on the face of the timing cover.
3. Reverse the removal procedure making sure that in the case of the four $\frac{1}{2}$ in. AF bolts the threads are cleaned and then lubricated with 3M thread lubricant sealant EC 776, Part No. 605764, prior to refitting.
4. Tighten the water pump bolts to the following torques:

   Water pump and timing chain cover to block

   20 to 25 lbs/ft (2,8 to 3,5 mkg).

   Water pump to timing chain cover: 6 to 8 lbs/ft (0,8 to 1,0 mkg).

Operations which are identified by an asterisk (*), can be carried out with the engine installed in the car

Operation A1-21—*continued*

5. Adjust the fan belt to the correct tension. Fan belt tension $\frac{7}{16}$ in. to $\frac{9}{16}$ in. (8 mm to 11 mm) when checked midway between the alternator pulley and crankshaft pulley, by hand.
6. To refill radiator, refer to Operation A1-2.

Fan belt adjustment

A—Pivot bolts
B—Adjusting bolt
C—Adjust at this point—$\frac{7}{16}$ to $\frac{9}{16}$ in. (8 to 11 mm) free movement

*Fuel pump, to remove and refit—Operation A1-22

Time allowed: Fuel pump, remove and refit hours
Fuel pump, overhaul hours

Workshop hand tools:
Spanner sizes: $\frac{7}{16}$ in. AF, $\frac{1}{2}$ in. AF

See Section Q for fuel pump overhaul

Fuel pump, remove

1. Remove trim panel at front of boot. With fuel reserve control pushed in, disconnect main feed pipe from tank. This will prevent fuel being syphoned out when pipes are disconnected from fuel pump.
2. Disconnect the fuel inlet and outlet pipes from the fuel pump.
3. Remove the two bolts securing the fuel pump to the front timing cover and withdraw fuel pump together with gasket.

Fuel pump, refit

1. Reverse removal procedure.
2. Check for leakage after tightening fuel inlet and outlet unions.

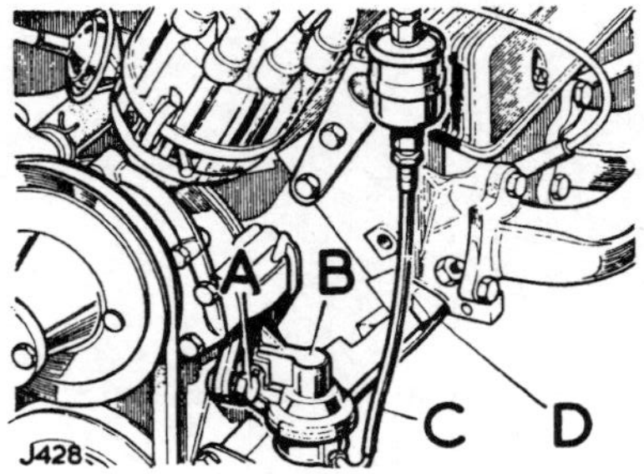

Fuel pump

A—Bolts fixing fuel pump
B—Fuel pump
C—Fuel outlet
D—Fuel inlet

Operations which are identified by an asterisk (*), can be carried out with the engine installed in the car

*Starter motor, to remove and refit—Operation A1-23

Time allowed: Starter motor, remove and refit hours
Starter motor, overhaul hours

Workshop hand tools:

Spanner sizes: $\frac{7}{16}$ in. AF, $\frac{1}{2}$ in. AF, $\frac{9}{16}$ in. AF, $\frac{7}{16}$ in. BSF Screwdriver, large

Starter motor, to overhaul, see Section S

Starter motor, remove

1. Place the car on a suitable hoist.
2. Disconnect the leads from the solenoid and starter motor.
3. Remove the two bolts securing the starter motor to the flywheel housing and draw the starter motor forward and remove from under the car by raising the front end (terminal end) and turning the unit over to allow it to be withdrawn rear end (starter dog end) first.

Starter motor, refit

1. Reverse the removal procedure.
2. Tighten the bolts securing starter motor to cylinder block to a torque figure of 30 to 35 lbs ft (4,0 to 4,9 mkg).

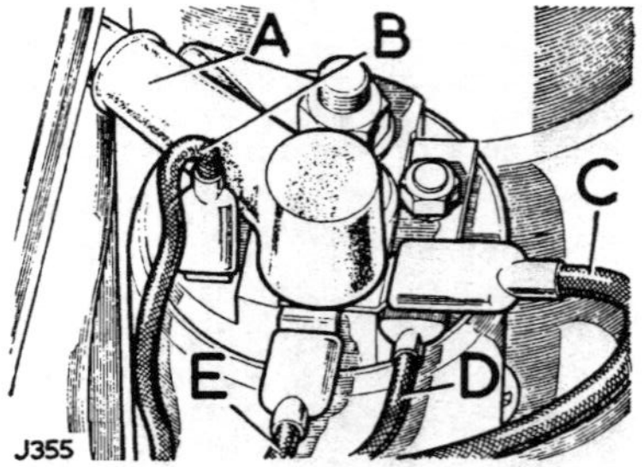

Starter motor

A—Feed lead for starter motor
B—Lead, thick, white with brown
C—Lead, thick, brown
D—Lead, thin, white with brown
E—Lead, thin, brown
(B–E) Connections for solenoid

*Thermostat, to renew—Operation A1-24

Time allowed: hours

Workshop hand tools:

Spanner size: $\frac{7}{16}$ in. AF Screwdriver, medium

If the thermostat becomes faulty either overheating or over-cooling of the engine may result. To check the operation of the thermostat remove it from its housing as detailed below. When immersed in hot water the thermostat should commence expansion between 78°C to 83°C (173°F to 182°F).

Thermostat, remove

1. Partly drain off the coolant and disconnect the water outlet hose from the outlet pipe.
2. Remove outlet pipe secured to the front of the inlet manifold casting by three $\frac{1}{4}$ in. UNF nuts and spring washers.
3. Lift out the thermostat together with the joint washer.
4. Carry out the test as detailed above.

Thermostat, refit

1. Reverse removal procedure.
2. If necessary a new thermostat complete with new joint washer should be fitted.
3. It is essential that the thermostat is fitted with its jiggle pin uppermost in the 12 o'clock position. This is to assist in filling and to prevent air locks.
4. Top up the coolant and check for leaks.

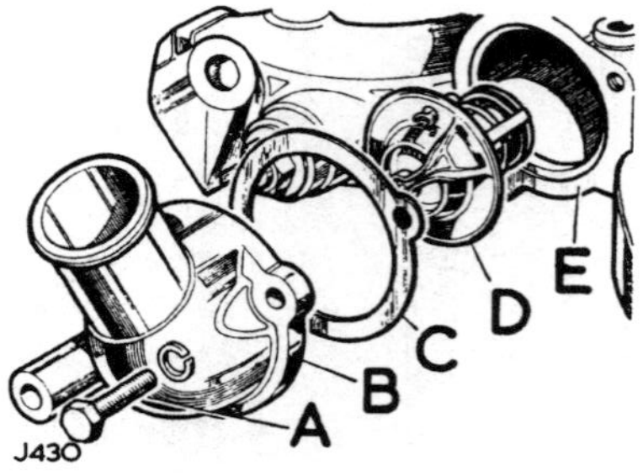

Thermostat

A—Bolt fixing outlet elbow
B—Outlet elbow
C—Joint washer
D—Thermostat
E—Inlet manifold

Operations which are identified by an asterisk (*), can be carried out with the engine installed in the car

*Water temperature transmitter and mixture control switch for mixture control, to remove and refit—Operation A1-25

Time allowed: hours

Workshop hand tools:

Spanner size: $\frac{5}{8}$ in. AF

Water temperature transmitter or mixture control switch, remove

1. Disconnect the battery.
2. Disconnect the wiring at the Lucar connector on the unit being removed. Both are situated in the inlet manifold at the front of the engine.
3. Remove unit from the inlet manifold.

Water temperature transmitter or mixture control switch, refit

1. Reverse the removal procedure being sure to renew joint washer.

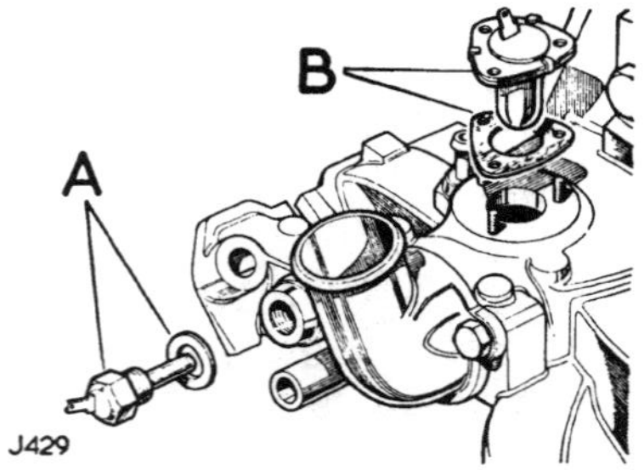

Water temperature transmitter and mixture control switch

A—Water temperature transmitter and washer
B—Mixture control switch and washer

*Compression pressure, to check—Operation A1-26

Workshop hand tools:
Plug spanner
Screwdriver, medium

Special tools:
Compression gauge

1. Remove sparking plugs.
2. Secure the throttle in the fully open position.
3. Insert a suitable compression gauge into the sparking plug hole of each cylinder in turn and crank the engine with the starter motor, for as short a period as possible.
4. Check pressure reading.
5. If the compression is appreciably less than the correct figure, the piston rings or valves are faulty.

   Low pressure in adjoining cylinders indicates a faulty cylinder head gasket.

Starter motor cranking speed 185 rpm

Compression ratio	10.5:1
Compression pressures	180 to 190 lb/in.² (12,6 to 13,4 kg/cm²)

Operations which are identified by an asterisk (*), can be carried out with the engine installed in the car

Section A1 – Rover 3.5 Litre – ENGINE UNIT – Part Two

DEFECT LOCATION

SYMPTOM	POSSIBLE CAUSE	REMEDY
A—ENGINE FAILS TO START	1. Incorrect starting procedure 2. Starter motor speed too slow 3. Faulty ignition system 4. Water or dirt in fuel system 5. Carburetter(s) flooding 6. Defective fuel pump system 7. Defective starter motor 8. Starter pinion jammed in flywheel 9. Starter pinion not engaging	1. *See Instruction Manual* 2. *Check battery and connections* 3. *See Section S* 4. *See Section Q* 5. *See Section Q* 6. *See Section Q* 7. *See Section S* 8. *Rotate armature shaft with spanner to free pinion* 9. *Clean drive pinion and sleeve with paraffin*
B—ENGINE STALLS	1. Low idling speed 2. Faulty sparking plugs 3. Faulty coil or condenser 4. Faulty distributor points 5. Incorrect mixture 6. Foreign matter in fuel system	1. *Adjust carburetter. See Section Q* 2. *Clean and test, renew if necessary* 3. *Renew* 4. *Rectify or renew. See Section Q* 5. *Adjust carburetter. See Section Q* 6. *See Section Q*
C—LACK OF POWER	1. Poor compression 2. Badly seating valves 3. Faulty exhaust silencer 4. Incorrect ignition timing 5. Leaks or restrictions in fuel system 6. Faulty sparking plugs 7. Excessive carbon deposit 8. Brakes binding 9. Faulty coil, condenser or battery	1. *If the compression is appreciably less than the correct figure, the piston rings or valves are faulty. Low pressure in adjoining cylinders indicates a faulty cylinder head gasket* 2. *Rectify or renew* 3. *Renew* 4. *Rectify* 5. *See Section Q* 6. *Rectify* 7. *Decarbonise* 8. *See Section N* 9. *See Section S*
D—ENGINE RUNS ERRATICALLY	1. Faulty electrical connections 2. Defective sparking plugs 3. Low battery charge 4. Defective distributor 5. Foreign matter in fuel system 6. Faulty fuel pump 7. Sticking valves 8. Defective valve springs 9. Incorrect ignition timing 10. Worn valve guides or valves 11. Faulty cylinder head gaskets 12. Damaged exhaust system	1. *Rectify* 2. *Renew or rectify* 3. *Recharge battery* 4. *Rectify* 5. *See Section Q* 6. *See Section Q* 7. *Rectify or renew* 8. *Renew* 9. *Rectify* 10. *Renew* 11. *Renew* 12' *Rectify or renew*
E—ENGINE STARTS, BUT STOPS IMMEDIATELY	1. Faulty electrical connections 2. Foreign matter in fuel system 3. Faulty fuel pump 4. Low fuel level in tank	1. *Check HT leads for cracked insulation; check low tension circuit* 2. *See Section Q* 3. *See Section Q* 4. *Replenish*
F—ENGINE FAILS TO IDLE	1. Incorrect carburetter setting 2. Faulty fuel pump 3. Sticking valves 4. Faulty cylinder head gasket(s)	1. *See Section Q* 2. *See Section Q* 3. *Rectify or renew* 4. *Renew*
G—ENGINE MISFIRES ON ACCELERATION	1. Distributor points incorrectly set 2. Faulty coil or condenser 3. Faulty sparking plug 4. Faulty carburetter	1. *Rectify. See Section A* 2. *Renew* 3. *Rectify* 4. *See Section Q*

DEFECT LOCATION—*continued*

SYMPTOM	POSSIBLE CAUSE	REMEDY
H—ENGINE KNOCKS	1. Ignition timing advanced 2. Excessive carbon deposit 3. Incorrect carburetter setting 4. Unsuitable fuel 5. Worn pistons or bearings 6. Distributor advance mechanism faulty 7. Defective sparking plugs	1. *Adjust* 2. *Decarbonise* 3. *See Section Q* 4. *Adjust ignition timing. See Section A1* 5. *Renew* 6. *Rectify. See Section S* 7. *Rectify or renew*
J—ENGINE BACKFIRES	1. Ignition defect 2. Carburetter defect 3. Sticking valve 4. Weak valve springs 5. Badly seating valves 6. Excessively worn valve stems and guides 7. Excessive carbon deposit 8. Incorrect sparking plug gap 9. Air leak in induction or exhaust systems	1. *See Section S* 2. *See Section Q* 3. *Rectify* 4. *Renew* 5. *Rectify or renew* 6. *Renew* 7. *Decarbonise* 8. *Reset* 9. *Renew faulty gaskets or components*
K—BURNED VALVES	1. Sticking valves 2. Weak valve springs 3. Excessive deposit on valve seats 4. Distorted valves 5. Excessive mileage between overhauls	1. *Rectify* 2. *Renew* 3. *Re-cut* 4. *Renew* 5. *Decarbonise*
L—NOISY VALVE MECHANISM	1. Excessive oil in sump, causing air bubbles in hydraulic tappets 2. Worn or scored parts in valve operating mechanism 3. Valves and seats cut down excessively, raising end of valve stem .050 in. (1,27 mm) above normal position 4. Sticking valves 5. Weak valve springs 6. Worn timing chain or chainwheels	1. *Drain and refill to correct level* 2. *Replace faulty parts* 3. *Grind off end of valve stem or replace parts* 4. *Rectify* 5. *Renew* 6. *Renew worn parts*
M—NOISE FROM HYDRAULIC TAPPETS 1. Rapping noise only when engine is started 2. Intermittent rapping noise 3. Noise on idle and low speed 4. General noise at all speeds 5. Loud noise at normal operating temperature only	1. Oil too heavy for prevailing temperature. Excessive varnish in tappet 2. Leakage at check ball 3. Excessive leakdown 4. High oil level in sump Leakage at check ball Worn tappet body Worn camshaft 5. Excessive leakdown rate or scored lifter plunger	1. *Drain and refill with correct grade* *Replace tappet* 2. *Replace tappet* 3. *Replace tappet* 4. *Drain and refill to correct level* *Replace tappet* *Replace tappet* *Replace camshaft* 5. *Replace tappet*
N—MAIN BEARING RATTLE	1. Low oil level 2. Low oil pressure 3. Excessive bearing clearance 4. Burnt-out bearings 5. Loose bearing caps	1. *Replenish as necessary* 2. *See Item O* 3. *Renew bearings; grind crankshaft* 4. *Renew* 5. *Tighten*

DEFECT LOCATION—*continued*

SYMPTOM	*POSSIBLE CAUSE*	*REMEDY*
O—LOW OIL PRESSURE WARNING LIGHT REMAINS ON, ENGINE RUNNING	1. Thin or diluted oil 2. Low oil level 3. Choked pump strainer 4. Faulty release valve 5. Excessive bearing clearance 6. Oil pressure switch unserviceable 7. Electrical fault 8. Relief valve plunger sticking 9. Weak relief valve spring 10. Pump rotors excessively worn 11. Excessively worn bearings; main, connecting rod, big end, camshaft, etc.	1. *Drain and refill with correct oil* 2. *Replenish* 3. *Clean* 4. *Rectify* 5. *Rectify* 6. *Renew* 7. *Check circuit* 8. *Remove and ascertain cause* 9. *Renew* 10. *Renew* 11. *Ascertain which bearings and rectify*
P—RATTLE IN LUBRICATION SYSTEM	1. Oil pressure relief valve plunger sticking	1. *Remove and clean*
Q—ENGINE OVERHEATING	1. Low coolant level 2. Faulty cooling system 3. Faulty thermostat 4. Incorrect timing 5. Defective lubrication system	1. *Check for leaks* 2. *See Section P* 3. *Renew* 4. *Rectify* 5. *See Section A1*

GENERAL DATA

Engine type	'V8' OHV
Number of cylinders	Eight, two banks of four
Capacity	3,525 cc (215.5 cu in.)
Bore diameter	3.5 in. (88,9 mm)
Stroke	2.8 in. (71,3 mm)
Compression ratio	10.5:1
BHP	160.5 at 5,200 rpm
Max. torque	210 lb/ft (29 mkg) at 2,750 rpm
Ignition timing	6° BTDC

Contact/breaker settings only to be used if specialist equipment for setting the dwell angle is not available

Dwell angle	26° to 28°
Firing order	1–8–4–3–6–5–7–2
Number system front to rear:	
Left bank	1–3–5–7
Right bank	2–4–6–8
Sparking plug type	Champion L87Y
Sparking plug gap	.025 in. (0,70 mm)
Compression pressure	180 to 190 lbs/in.^{2} (12,6 to 13,4 kg/cm^2)
Starter motor cranking speed	185 rpm

TECHNICAL DETAIL DATA

Camshaft

Position	Central
Material	Cast iron
Drive	Chain
Bearings: Type	Steel backed babbit lined
Number	5

Carburetter

Make	SU HS 6
Number	Two, one LH and one RH
Standard needle	KK
Jet	0.100 in. (2,54 mm)
Barrel size	1.75 in. dia (44,45 mm)

Connecting rod

Length	Centres 5.662 to 5.658 in. (143,8 to 143,7 mm)
Bearings:	
Material and type	Vandervell VP lead indium
Clearance	.0007 in. to .0027 in. (0,0178 to 0,068 mm)
End play	.005 in. to .015 in. (0,13 to 0,40 mm)
Overall length	.732 in. to .742 in. (18,6 to 18,85 mm)

Cooling system

Type	Pressure vented
Pressurised to	15 lbs/sq in. (1,06 kg/cm^2)
Thermostat opening	173°F to 182°F (78°C to 83°C)
Radiator core	Tube and fin
Capacity	16 Imperial pints, 9.1 litres, 19 US pints

Crankshaft

Material	Iron, spheroidal graphite
No. of main journals	5
End thrust	Taken on Number 3
End play	.004 in. to .008 in. (0,10 to 0,20 mm)
Crankpin journal diameter	2.0000 in. to .20005 in. (50,8 to 50,813 mm)
Main bearing:	
Material and type	Vandervell lead indium
Clearance	.0009 to .0024 in. (,023 to ,061 mm)
Journal diameter	2.2992 in. to 2.2997 in. (58,4 to 58,413 mm)
Bearing overall length	.797 in. to .807 in. (20,244 to 20,498 mm). Nos. 1, 2, 4 and 5 1.056 in. to 1.058 in. (26,82 to 26,87 mm) Number 3
Crankshaft vibration damper type	Torsional

Cylinder block

Material	Aluminium alloy
Cylinder liner type	Dry
Liner reboring limit	.020 in. (0,50 mm)

Cylinder heads

Material	Aluminium alloy
Type	Two heads with separate alloy inlet manifold
Inlet and exhaust valve seat material	Piston ring iron
Inlet and exhaust valve seat angle	45°

Electrical

Battery	Lucas C9, negative earth, 57 amp/hr
Alternator	Lucas 11 AC, 45 amp
Alternator control box	Lucas 4T–R
Starter motor	Lucas M45G, pre-engaged
Distributor	Lucas 35D8
Coil	Lucas BA7

Flexible drive plate and ring gear

Number of teeth on starter ring	156

Lubrication system

Oil pump type	Gear
Normal pressure	30 to 40 lbs/in.^{2} (2,11 to 2,81 kg/cm^2) at 2,400 rpm
Capacity of crankcase	8.5 Imperial pints, 10.2 US pints, 4,688 litres

Pistons and gudgeon pins

Pistons

Type	Aluminium alloy, flat topped
Clearance: Top land	.0255 in. to .0310 in. (0,65 to 0,8 mm)
Skirt Top	.0005 in. to .0011 in. (0,0127 to 0,28 mm)
,, Bottom	.0003 in. to .0017 in. (0,008 to 0,043 mm)
Ring groove depth	.194 in. to .2015 in. (4,93 to 5,118 mm)

Gudgeon pins

Length	2.861 in. to 2.866 in. (72,67 to 72,8 mm)
Diameter	.8746 in. to .8749 in. (22,215 to 22,22 mm)
Fit in rod	Press fit
Clearance in piston	.0001 in. to .0003 in. (0,0025 to 0,0076 mm)
Clearance in rod	.00075 in. to .00125 in. (0,019 to 0,0318 mm)

Piston rings

Number of compression	2
Number of oil	1
No. 1 compression ring	Chrome faced
No. 2 compression ring	Stepped to 'L' shape and marked 'TOP'
Width of compression rings	.078 in. to .079 in. (1,98 to 2,01 mm)
Compression ring gap	.017 in. to .022 in. (0,44 to 0,57 mm)
Oil ring type	Perfect circle, type 98
Oil ring width	.1894 in. max. (4,811 mm)

Tappets

Hydraulic tappets are fitted and are not serviceable

Timing chain and wheels

Timing chain type	Inverted tooth
Number of links	54
Width	.875 in. (22,225 mm)
Pitch	.375 in. (9,525 mm)
Crankshaft chainwheel	Sintered iron
Camshaft chainwheel	Aluminium alloy, teeth covered with nylon

Torque figures

Inlet manifold bolts	25 to 30 lbs ft (3,5 to 4,0 mkg)
Inlet manifold clamp bolts	10 to 15 lbs ft (1,4 to 2,0 mkg)
Rocker shaft bolts	25 to 30 lbs ft (3,5 to 4,0 mkg)
Cylinder head bolts	65 to 70 lbs ft (9,0 to 9,6 mkg)
Exhaust manifold bolts	10 to 15 lbs ft (1,4 to 2,0 mkg)
Bolt fixing distributor drive gear and fuel pump cam to camshaft	40 to 45 lbs ft (5,5 to 6,2 mkg)
Crankshaft bearing bolts	30 to 35 lbs ft (4,0 to 4,9 mkg)
Flexible drive plate to crankshaft bolts	50 to 60 lbs ft (7,0 to 8,5 mkg)
Rear main bearing bolts	65 to 70 lbs ft (9,0 to 9,6 mkg)
Other main bearing bolts	50 to 55 lbs ft (7,0 to 7,6 mkg)
Oil pump fixing bolts	10 to 15 lbs ft (1,4 to 2,0 mkg)
Pressure relief valve to oil pump cover	30 to 35 lbs ft (4,0 to 4,9 mkg)
Bypass valve to oil pump cover	30 to 35 lbs ft (4,0 to 4,9 mkg)
Starter motor to cylinder block	30 to 35 lbs ft (4,0 to 4,9 mkg)
Torsional vibration damper bolt	140 to 160 lbs ft (19,3 to 27,9 mkg)
Timing cover bolt to cylinder block	20 to 25 lbs ft (2,8 to 3,5 mkg)
Power steering pump bolts	20 to 25 lbs ft (2,8 to 3,5 mkg)
Water pump and timing chain cover to block	20 to 25 lbs ft (2,8 to 3,5 mkg)
Water pump to timing chain cover	6 to 8 lbs ft (0,8 to 1,0 mkg)
Torque converter housing to flexible drive housing	30 lbs ft (4,0 mkg)
Torque converter to flexible drive plate	25 to 30 lbs ft (3,5 to 4,0 mkg)

Valves

	Inlet	Exhaust
Opens	30° BTDC	68° BBDC
Closes	75° ABDC	37° ATDC
Duration	285°	285°
Valve peak	112.5° ATDC	105.5 BTDC

Valves, inlet

Overall length	4.590 in. to 4.620 in. (116,586 to 117,348 mm)
Actual overall head diameter	1.495 in. to 1.505 in. (37,973 to 38,227 mm)
Angle of face	45°
Stem diameter	.3402 in. to .3412 in. (8,64 to 8,666 mm) at the head and increasing to .3407 in. to .3417 in. (8,653 to 8,679 mm)
Stem clearance in guide	Top .001 in. to .003 in. (0,0254 to 0,0762 mm) Bottom.0015 in. to .0035 in. (0,038 to 0,0889 mm)

Valves, exhaust

Overall length	4.590 in. to 4.620 in. (116,586 to 117,348 mm)
Actual overall head diameter	1.3075 in. to 1.3175 in. (33,215 to 33,466 mm)
Angle of face	45°
Stem diameter	.3397 in. to .3407 in. (8,628 to 8,654 mm) at the head and increasing to 3.402 in. to 3.412 in. (8,64 to 8,666 mm)
Stem clearance in guide	Top .0015 in. to .0035 in. (0,038 to 0,0889 mm) Bottom .002 in. to .004 in. (0,0508 to 0,1016 mm)
Valve lift	.39 in. (9,906 mm) both valves
Valve spring length:	
Outer	1.6 in. (40,64 mm) at pressure of 39 to 45 lbs (17,69 to 20,41 kg)
Inner	1.63 in. (41,402 mm) at pressure of 21.5 to 26.5 lbs (9.75 to 12.02 kg)

Section C, Section D, Section E and Section EE

The above Sections are not applicable to the Rover 3.5-Litre. See Section EEE for full details of the Automatic Transmission fitted to the Rover 3.5-Litre model.

SECTION EEE ROVER 3.5 LITRE AUTOMATIC TRANSMISSION, MODEL 35

PART ONE

Section EEE is divided into four parts, namely:

Part I .. .. General description and working principles
Test procedure

Part II .. .. Adjustments
Automatic transmission unit, removal and refit
Sub-assemblies, removal and refit

Part III .. .. Unit dismantling and overhaul procedure

Part IV .. .. Defect location
Data
Recommended lubricants

Model 35 automatic transmission units applicable to Rover 3.5-Litre models can be identified by the serial number commencing FU1001 on a blue plate.

The model 35 transmission unit can be separated from the engine and removed from the car, leaving the engine and torque converter in position.

When carrying out a complete unit overhaul, the section can be worked straight through in the order presented.

Alternatively, the individual operations which form the greater percentage of maintenance work undertaken by Distributors and Dealers are detailed under appropriate headings and will be found to be complete in themselves.

Certain units and operations can be carried out without removing the transmission from the car; these operations are marked with an asterisk (*).

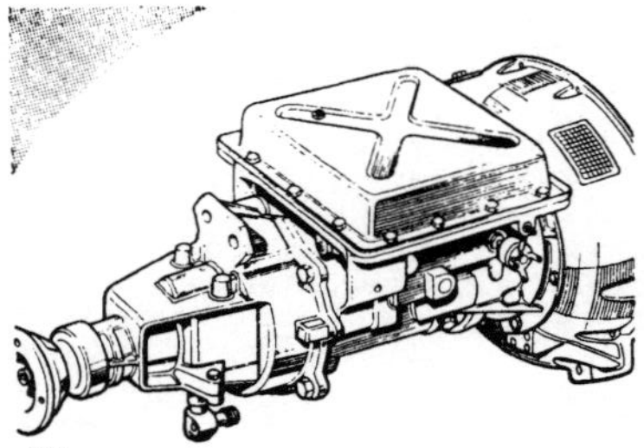

J271

INDEX—ROVER 3.5 LITRE AUTOMATIC TRANSMISSION MODEL 35 PARTS ONE, TWO, THREE AND FOUR

Rover 3.5 Litre Automatic transmission, model 35

Description and operation

The model 35 three-speed automatic transmission is coupled to the engine by a three-element torque converter. Engine power is converted into hydro-kinetic energy and this provides smooth application or driving torque.

Torque multiplication in all gears ratios is provided by the converter, which is infinitely variable between the ratio of 2:1 and 1:1. Extreme low-speed flexibility in third gear is the result. The speed range during which torque multiplication can be achieved is also variable, depending upon the position of the accelerator.

The torque converter

The torque converter consists of an impeller, connected to the engine crankshaft; a turbine connected to the transmission input shaft and a stator incorporating a sprag-type one-way clutch. This assembly is supported by a tube attached to the gearbox; it is co-axial with the input shaft.

The impeller, driven by the engine, causes fluid to flow from its vanes to the turbine vanes and to return to the impeller through the stator vanes.

The vanes of the components are designed and curved to affect the angle of fluid flow when a speed differential exists between impeller and turbine. The angle of the fluid flow from the turbine is changed by the stator vanes in such a way that the fluid from the stator assists in driving the impeller; torque multiplication taking place.

This varies from 2:1 when the turbine is stalled* to 1:1 when the turbine speed reaches approximately 90 per cent of the impeller.

With the speed differential between impeller and turbine achieved the angle of fluid flow from the turbine drives the stator in the same direction as the turbine and impeller. In this state the converter acts as a fluid coupling and no torque multiplication takes place.

The mechanical system

A planetary gear set, having helical involute tooth form throughout, provides three forward speeds and reverse. The planetary gear set comprises of two sun gears (forward and rear); two sets of pinions located in a pinion carrier; and ring gear which is attached to the output shaft.

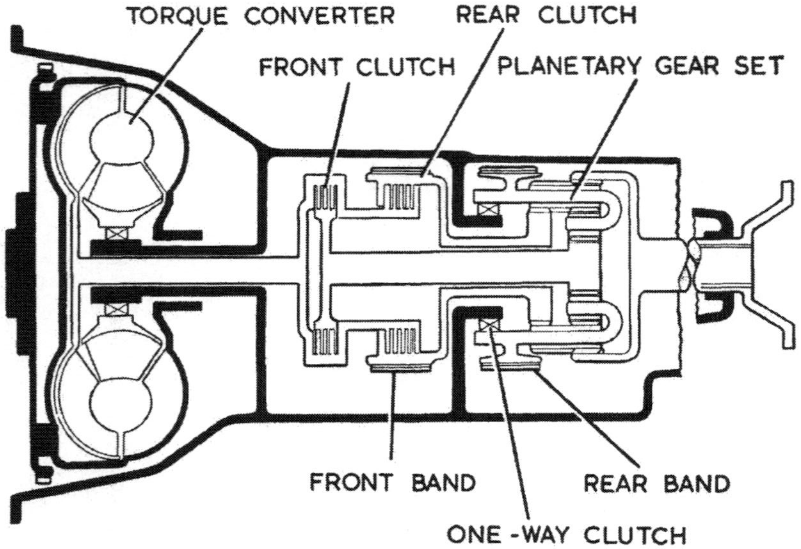

H6

Mechanical layout

*When the car is held stationary with the engine operating at maximum throttle opening and any one of the driving ranges selected.

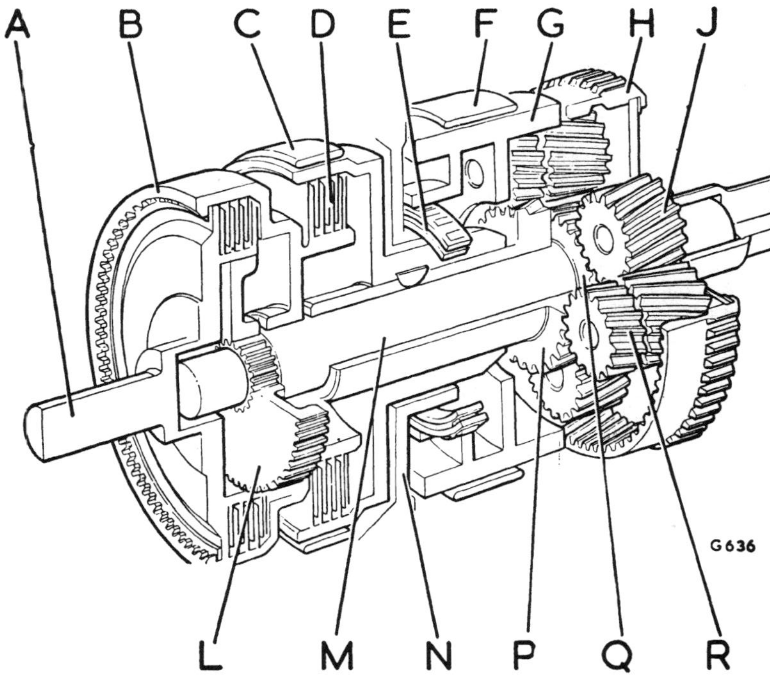

Identification of mechanical parts

A—Input shaft
B—Front clutch
C—Front brake band
D—Rear clutch
E—One-way clutch
F—Rear brake band
G—Planetary gear carrier
H—Ring gear
J—Pinion, short
K—Output shaft
L—Hub for front clutch
M—Shaft for forward sun gear
N—Centre support
P—Reverse sun gear
Q—Forward sun gear
R—Pinion, long

Power enters through one of the sun gears and leaves the gear set through the ring gear. In all forward gears, power enters through the forward sun gear and in reverse through the rear sun gear.

A single set of pinions is engaged when reverse is selected, causing the ring gear to rotate in the opposite direction to the sun gear. A double set of pinions, engaged when forward gears are selected, cause the ring gear to rotate in the same direction as the sun gear.

The pinions are housed in a carrier which locates them in their respective position relative to the two sun gears and the ring gear. The carrier is in the form of a drum which may rotate or be held stationary by a brake band or the one-way clutch.

Gear ratios are engaged by hydraulically-operated clutches and brake bands, of which there are two of each.

The clutches

These are operated by hydraulic pistons and connect the torque converter to the gear set.

In forward gears the front clutch connects the converter to the forward sun gear and in reverse the rear clutch connects the torque converter to the reverse sun gear.

Both clutches are of the multi-disc type.

The one-way clutch

This functions in place of the rear brake band when the selector is at the 'D'–Drive position. It prevents anti-clockwise rotation of the planetary gear carrier.

In first gear the gear set therefore freewheels, providing smooth changes first to second and vice versa.

The brake bands

There are two bands which hold elements of the gearing stationary to effect lower ratio output and increased torque. Both bands are hydraulically operated by servos.

The front band holds the reverse sun gear stationary; the rear band holds the planetary gear carrier stationary.

In lock-up the pinion or planetary gear carrier is held stationary by the rear band and provides the first gear ratio of 2.39:1.

A double set of pinions are engaged so that the output shaft rotates in the same direction as the input shaft.

In reverse gear the planetary gear carrier is again held stationary, but a single set of pinions causes the driven shaft to rotate in the opposite direction.

For second gear ratio the front band holds the reverse sun gear stationary and the gearing produces a ratio of 1.45:1.

Mechanical power flow—first gear; selector at the 'L' position

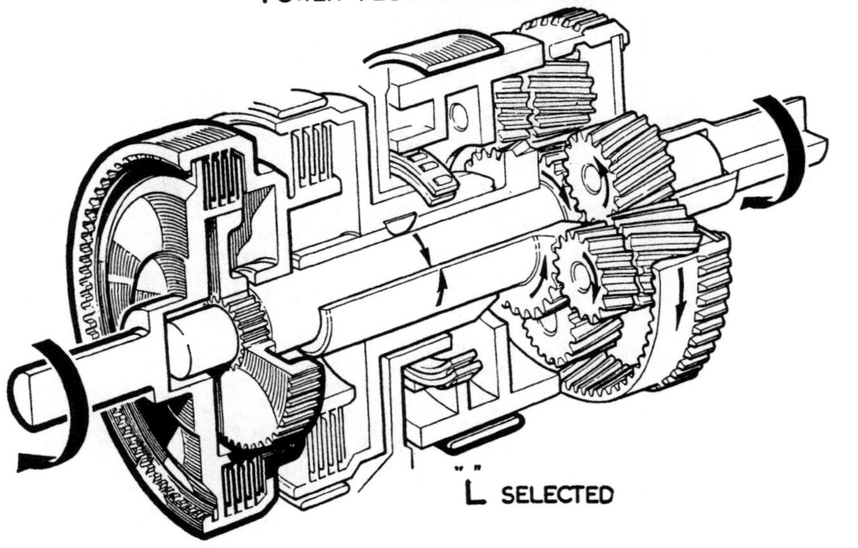

Application of bands and clutches—front clutch and rear band

Power from the turbine of the torque converter is transmitted through the front clutch to the forward sun gear, which is in mesh with a double set of pinions in the planetary gear carrier.

Power leaves the planetary gear set by the ring gear, which is attached to the driven shaft. The carrier itself is held stationary by the rear brake band.

The reverse sun gear, which is also in mesh with a single set of pinions in the planetary set, rotates freely in the opposite direction to the forward sun gear.

Mechanical power flow—first gear; selector at the 'D1' position

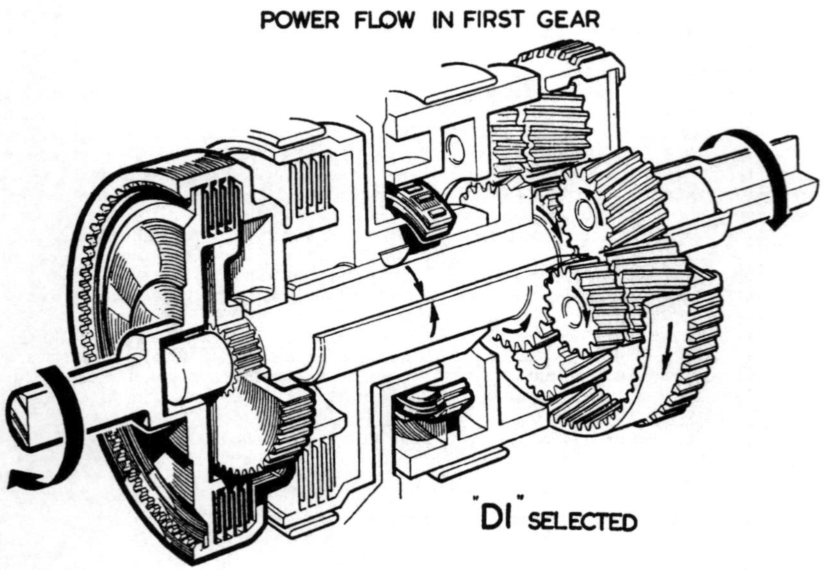

H531

Application of bands and clutches—front clutch and one-way clutch

Power is again transmitted from the turbine of the torque converter to the forward sun gear, through the front clutch. The forward sun gear is in mesh with a double set of pinions in the planetary gear set.

A one-way clutch, incorporated in the carrier of the planetary gears, prevents anti-clockwise rotation of the carrier and allows the gearbox to freewheel when on the overrun.

Power leaves the planet gear set by the ring gear and driven shaft.

Mechanical power flow—second gear; selector at the 'L', 'D1' or 'D2' position

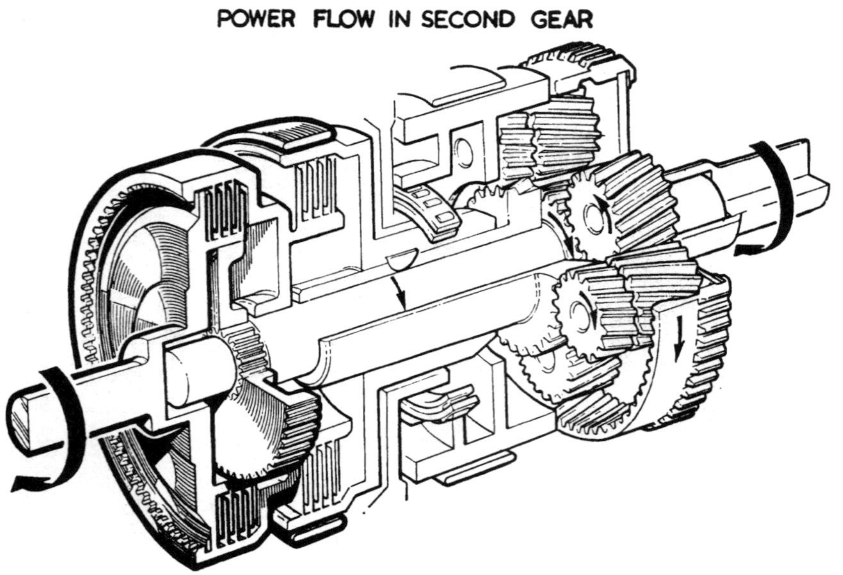

H532

Application of bands and clutches—front clutch and front brake band

The front clutch is applied, connecting the power from the converter to the forward sun gear and the planetary gear set. The front band is applied holding the reverse sun gear stationary; this allows the planetary gear carrier to be driven around the stationary reverse sun gear and provides the reduction of 1.45:1.

Power again leaves the gearbox by the ring gear and driven shaft.

Mechanical power flow—top gear; selector at the 'D1' or 'D2' position

POWER FLOW IN TOP GEAR

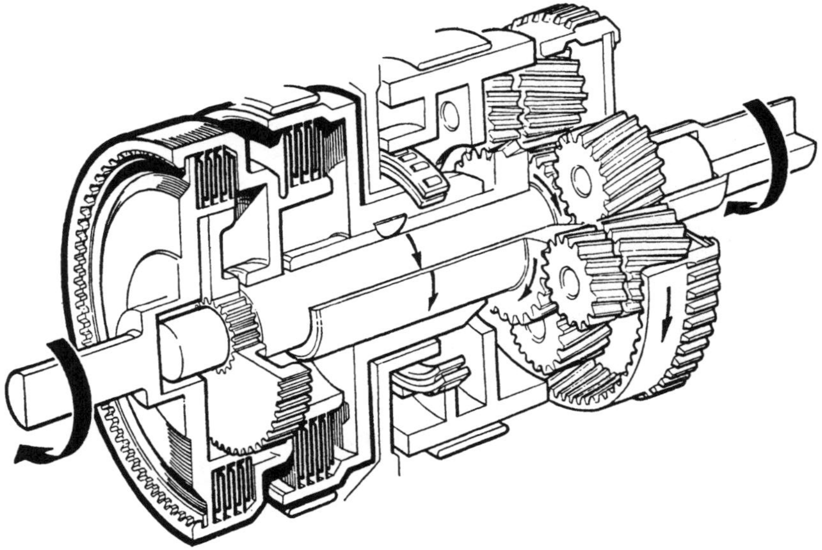

H533

Application of bands and clutches—front clutch and rear clutch

Power enters the gearbox from the torque converter through the front clutch, to the forward sun gear.

The rear clutch is applied which connects the power from the converter to the reverse sun gear; both sun gears being locked together, the gear set rotates as a unit providing a 1:1 ratio.

Mechanical power flow—selector at the 'R' position

POWER FLOW IN REVERSE

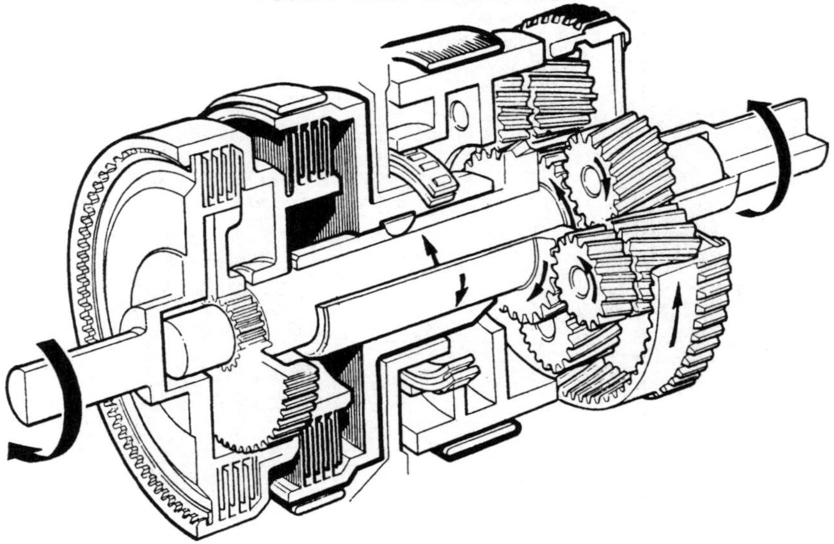

H534

Application of bands and clutches—rear clutch and rear band

Power enters the gearbox from the converter and through the rear clutch to the reverse sun gear.

The rear band is applied which holds the planetary gear carrier stationary. A single set of pinions in the planetary set between the reverse sun gear and the ring gear of the driven shaft provides a reduction of 2.09:1 in the reverse direction to the input shaft.

Neutral and Park

The front and rear clutches are off and no power is transmitted from the converter to the gear set. The front and rear bands are also released, except in 'P', where for constructional reasons the rear band is applied as long as the engine is running.

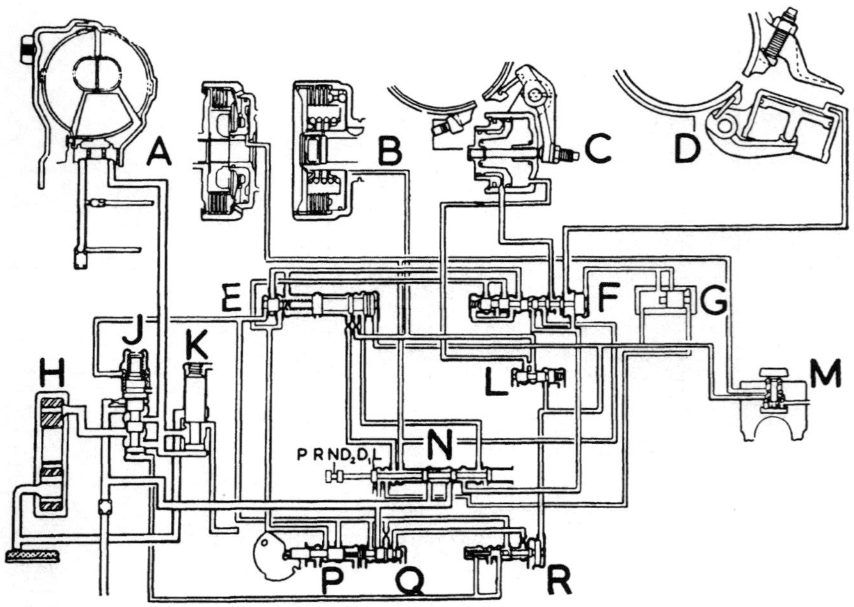

J272

Identification of hydraulic parts

A—Front clutch
B—Rear clutch
C—Front servo
D—Rear servo
E—2 to 3 shift valve
F—1 to 2 shift valve
G—D1–D2 control valve
H—Front pump
J—Primary regulator valve
K—Secondary regulator valve
L—Servo orifice control valve
M—Governor valve
N—Manual control valve
P—Downshift valve
Q—Throttle valve
R—Modulator valve

The hydraulic system consists of a front pump and a centrifugally-operated hydraulic governor. Pressure and direction of flow of fluid to the various mechanical components is regulated by a series of valves.

Front pump (H)

The front pump is driven by the converter impeller and is in operation whenever the engine is running. This pump supplies fluid to the hydraulic control system and to the torque converter, and also controls lubrication.

H14

Front pump

Primary regulator valve (J)

The primary regulator valve controls line pressure in the transmission.

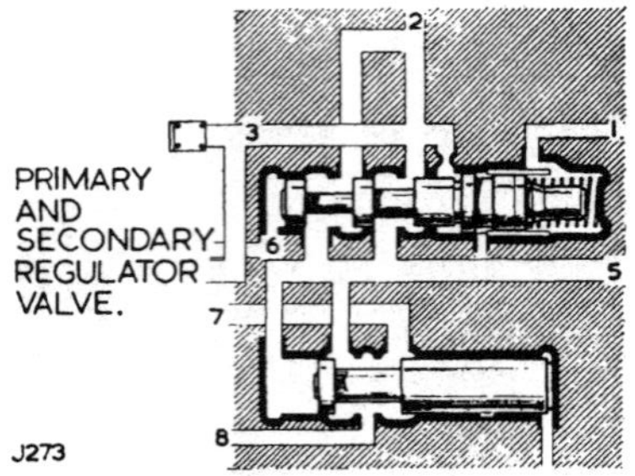

J273

Primary and secondary valve at regulating position

1—Throttle pressure
2—Front pump pressure
3—Line pressure
4—Converter pressure
5—Modulator pressure
6—Return to front pump
7—Lubrication

Secondary regulator valve (K)

The secondary regulator valve controls pressure in the torque converter and also provides lubrication.

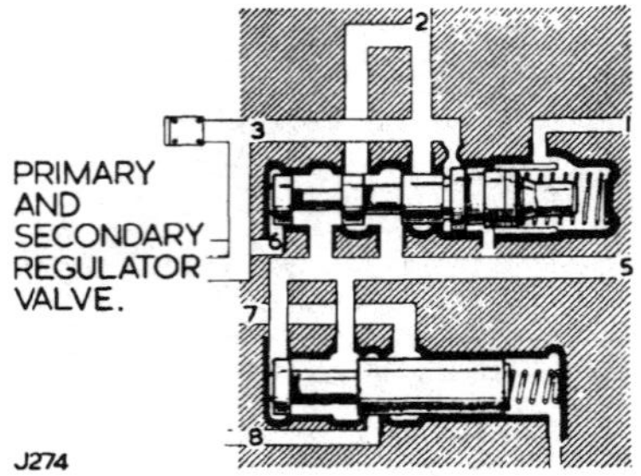

J274

Primary and secondary valve at closed position

1—Throttle pressure
2—Front pump pressure
3—Line pressure
4—Converter pressure
5—Modulator pressure
6—Return to front pump
7—Lubrication

Manual control valve (N)

The manual valve is operated by the selector and directs fluid to the shift valves, clutches, servos and governor.

Governor valve (M)

The governor, driven by the output shaft, regulates the fluid pressure applied to the ends of the shift valves, according to the vehicle road speed.

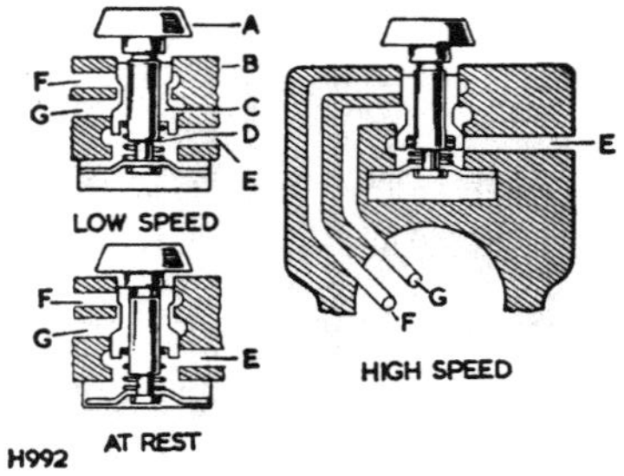

H992

Governor valve

A—Weight for governor
B—Body for governor
C—Valve for governor
D—Spring for governor
E—Exhaust port
F—Main line pressure
G—Governor pressure

Throttle valve (Q)

The throttle valve is operated by the downshift valve via a compression spring and directs fluid to the shift valves to delay upshifts and effect downshifts.

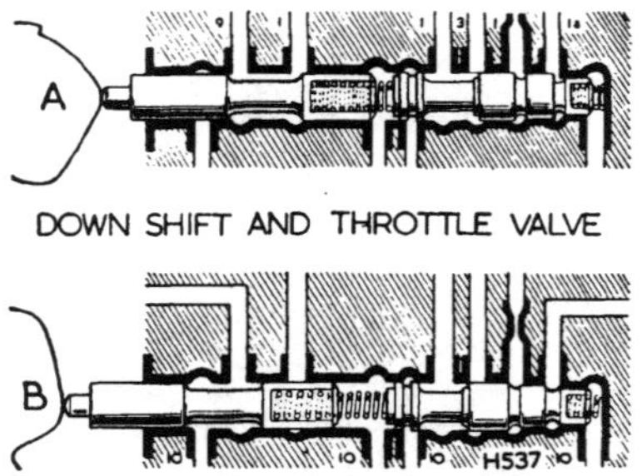

Downshift and throttle valve

A—Kickdown position
B—Part throttle position
1—Throttle pressure
1a—Throttle pressure, modulated
3—Line pressure
9—Kickdown throttle pressure
10—Exhaust ports

Downshift valve (P)

The downshift valve is operated by the downshift cable and cam and directs fluid to the shift valves, further delaying upshifts and effecting downshifts.

Modulator valve (R)

The modulator valve provides high line pressure during stall or part throttle conditions. This valve varies the line pressure relative to throttle and governor pressure.

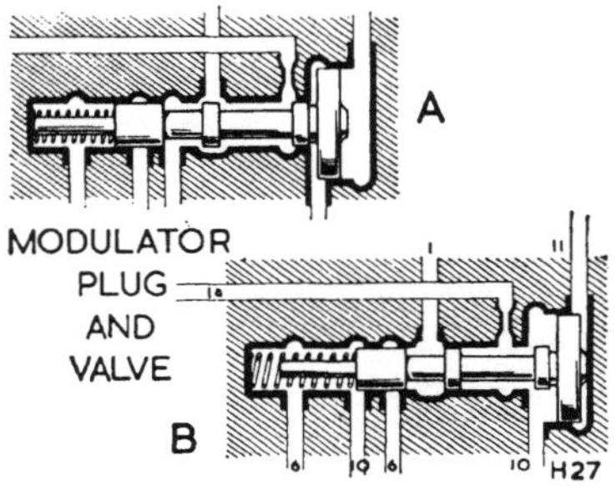

Modulator valve

A—Governor pressure applied
B—Closed position
1—Throttle pressure
1a—Throttle pressure, modulated
6—Modulator pressure
10—Exhaust ports
11—Governor pressure

Servo orifice control valve (L)

The servo orifice control valve is operated by governor pressure, and opposed by spring pressure. This valve controls the quality of 2 to 3 and 3 to 2 shifts.

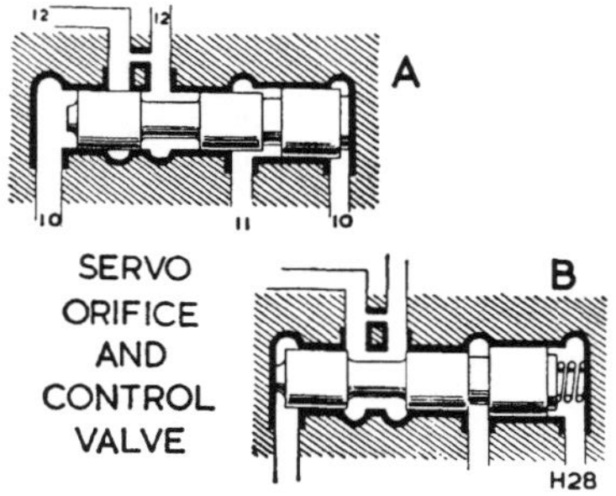

Servo orifice control valve

A—Operation at high speed, orifice in circuit
B—Operation at low speed, orifice by-passed
10—Exhaust ports
11—Governor pressure
12—Line pressure to front servo release

1 to 2 shift valve (F)

The 1 to 2 shift valve is operated by governor pressure and opposed by spring and throttle pressure. This valve effects upshifts or downshifts between first and second gears.

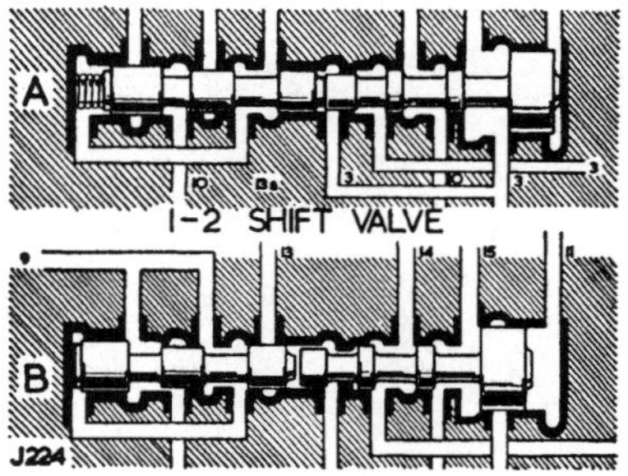

1 to 2 shift valve

A—First gear position
B—Second gear position
3—Line pressure
9—Kickdown throttle pressure
10—Exhaust ports
11—Governor pressure
13—Reduced throttle pressure
13a—Reduced throttle pressure
14—Line pressure to front servo apply
15—Line pressure to rear servo

2 to 3 shift valve (E)

The 2 to 3 shift valve is operated by governor pressure and opposed by spring and throttle pressure. This valve effects upshifts or downshifts between second and third gears.

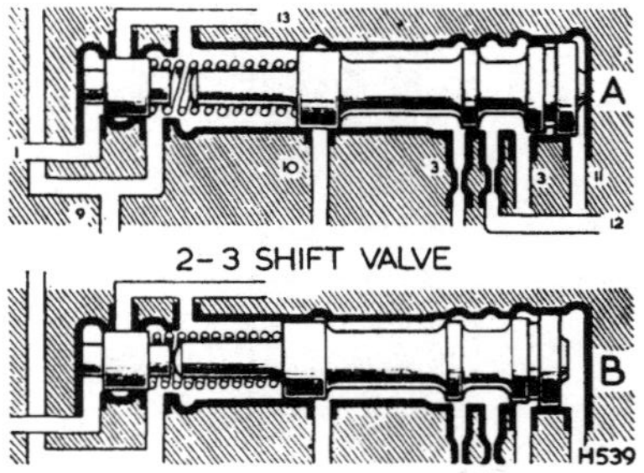

2 to 3 shift valve

A—Second gear position
B—Third gear position
1—Throttle pressure
3—Line pressure
9—Kickdown throttle pressure
10—Exhaust port
11—Governor pressure
12—Line pressure to front servo release
13—Reduced throttle pressure

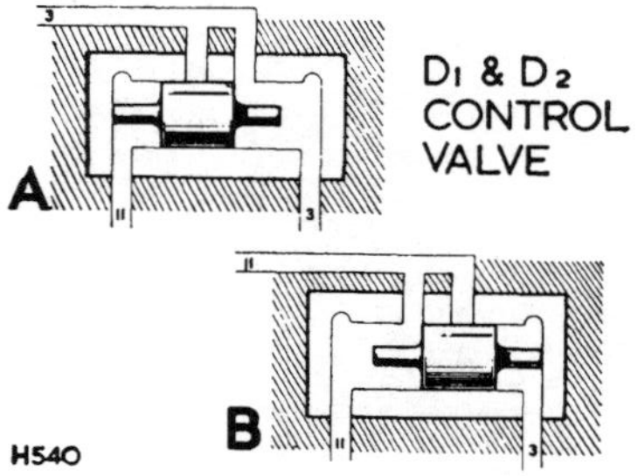

Control valve, 'D1–D2'

A—'D2' selected
B—'D1' selected
3—Line pressure
11—Governor pressure

Control valve, 'D1–D2' (G)

The 'D1–D2' control valve is operated by either line or governor pressure. With 'D1' selected governor pressure is applied to the 1–2 shift valve, allowing the three speed ranges to be used.

With 'D2' selected line pressure is applied to the 1–2 shift valve, which prevents first gear engagement.

Front servo (C)

The front servo is a double-acting unit, hydraulically operated by line pressure to engage or release the front band (second gear).

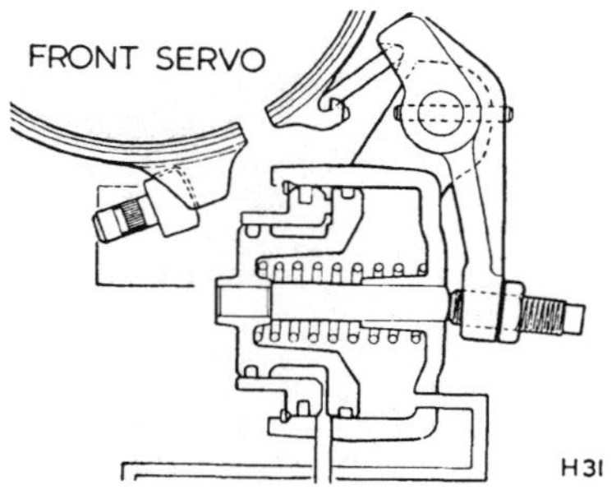

Front servo

Rear servo (D)

The rear servo is a single-acting unit, hydraulically operated by line pressure to apply the rear band (lock-up and reverse gear).

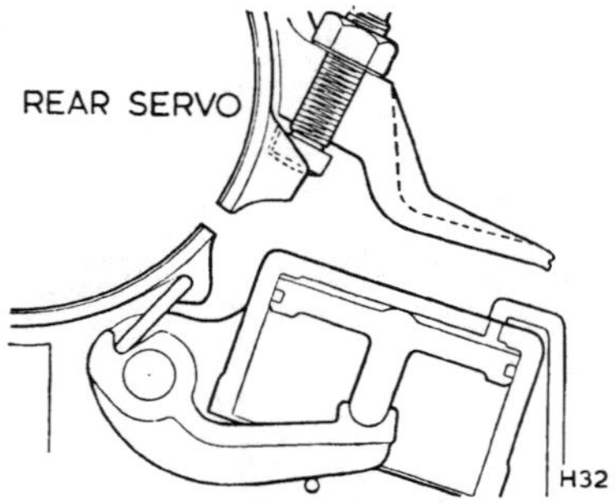

Rear servo

Front and rear clutches (A and B)

Both front and rear clutches are of the wet multi-plate type operated by line pressure.

Hydraulic circuit—neutral selected, light throttle

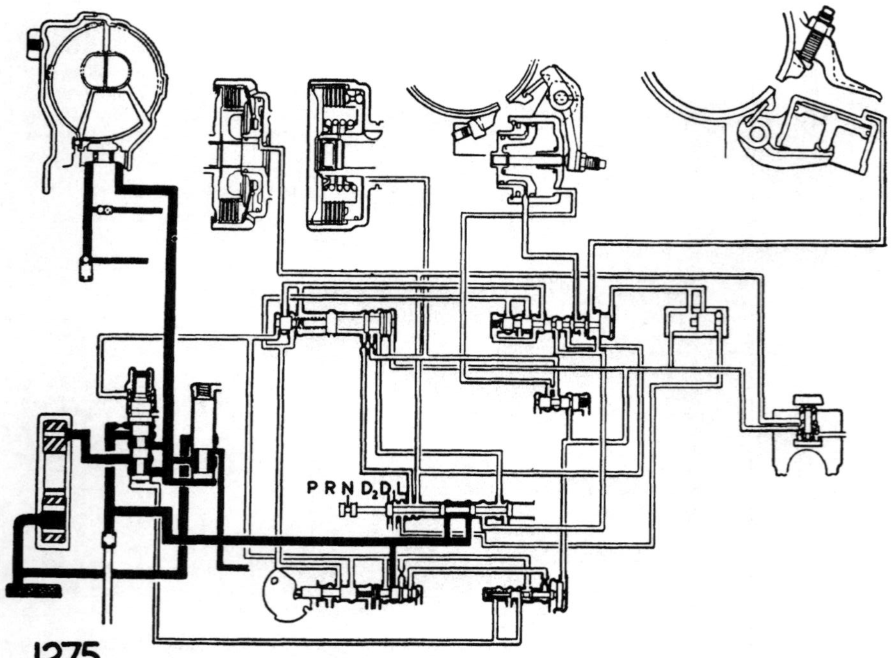

J275

Hydraulic circuit—neutral selected, light throttle

With the engine running the pump check valve closes and pressure is supplied by the front pump.

The primary regulator valve regulates line pressure which is directed to the manual valve and throttle valve. It also permits fluid to reach the secondary regulator valve.

The secondary regulator valve regulates pressure to the converter and lubrication of the front and rear of the gear train.

Excess pressure is exhausted from the primary regulator valve through the secondary regulator valve to the input side of the front pump and also to the oil pan.

Hydraulic circuit—park selected, light throttle

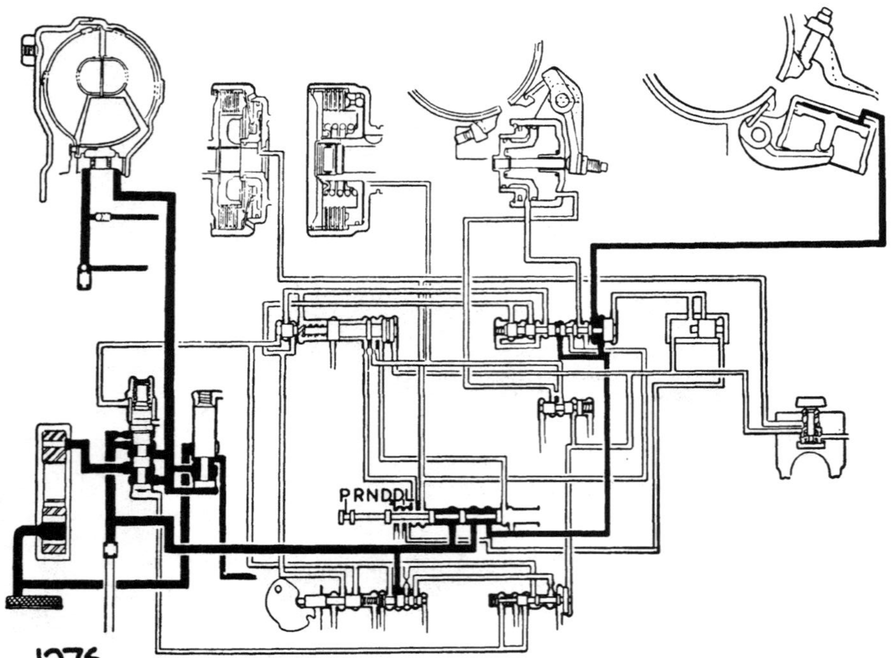

J276

Hydraulic circuit—park selected, light throttle

An internal linkage from the manual valve detent lever engages the parking pawl with teeth formed on the driven shaft ring gear.

With the engine running, the operation of the hydraulic system is identical to the neutral circuit, except that the manual valve directs line pressure through the 1–2 shift valve to the rear servo.

This arrangement is based upon the design of the hydraulic system without the rear servo or band performing any function in this selector position.

Hydraulic circuit—reverse selected, medium throttle

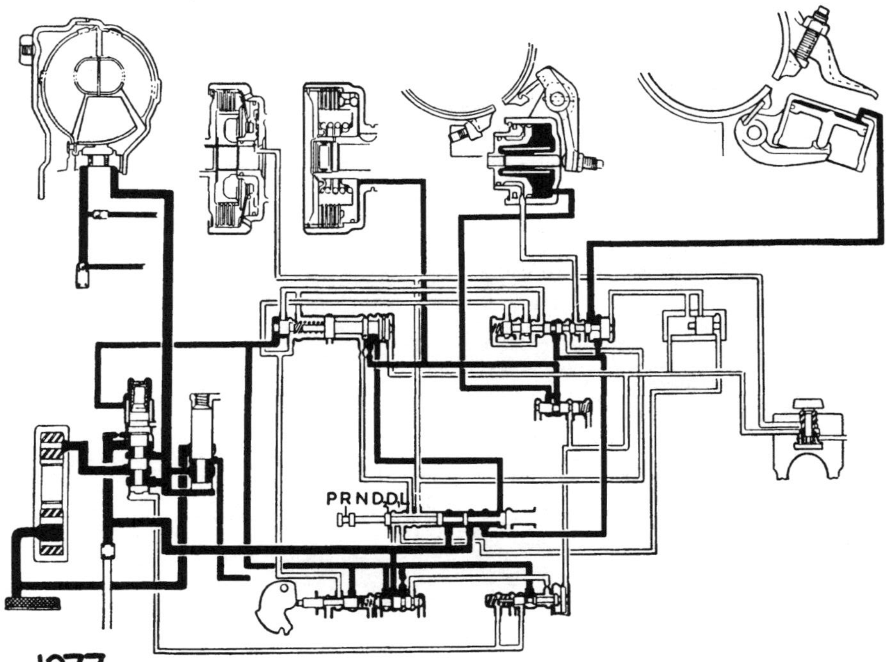

J277

Hydraulic circuit—reverse selected, medium throttle

Front pump operates as detailed for neutral selected, but depending upon accelerator pedal depression; throttle pressure is directed to the spring end of the primary regulator valve, thus increasing line pressure in accordance with torque capacity requirements.

The manual valve directs line pressure through the 1–2 shift valve to the rear servo and line pressure through the 2–3 shift valve to the rear clutch and front servo release. Due to absence of governor pressure, the shift valves and servo orifice control valve perform no function in this selector position.

Hydraulic circuit—first gear, 'D1' selected, full throttle

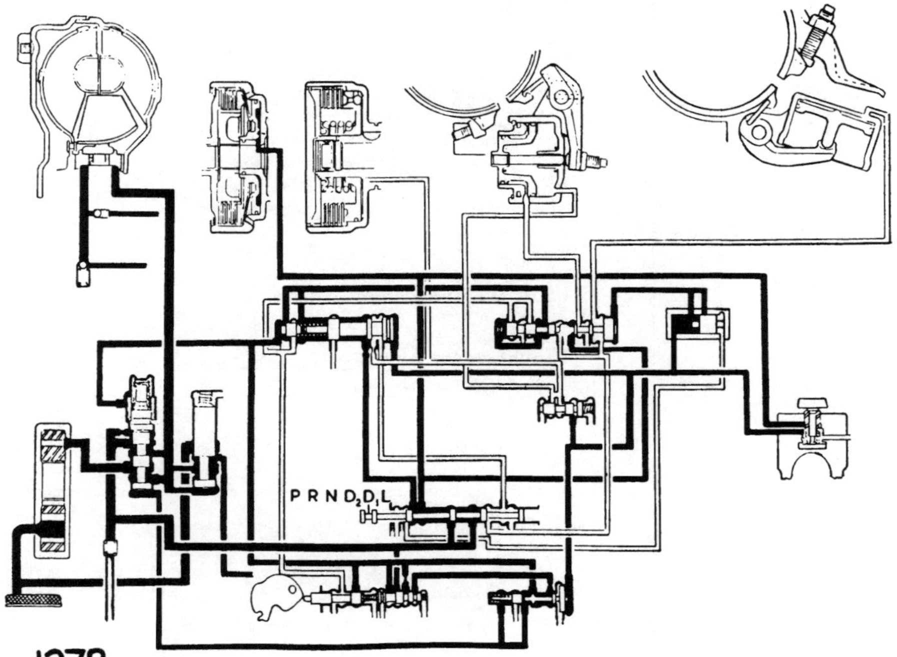

J278

Hydraulic circuit—first gear, 'D1' selected, full throttle

Pressure control of the front pump will be as for neutral selected but with the throttle valve in the full throttle position as illustrated, throttle pressure regulated by the modulator valve plunger acts upon the primary regulator valve opposing throttle pressure and spring force, thus modulating line pressure in the interest of shift quality.

The manual valve directs line pressure to the front clutch, governor feed and 1–2 shift valve for the subsequent 1–2 shift. Line pressure also reaches the 2–3 shift valve for the subsequent 2–3 shift.

The front clutch, applied in conjunction with the one-way clutch, permits the car to move off from rest in first gear.

Hydraulic circuit—second gear, 'D1' selected, kickdown

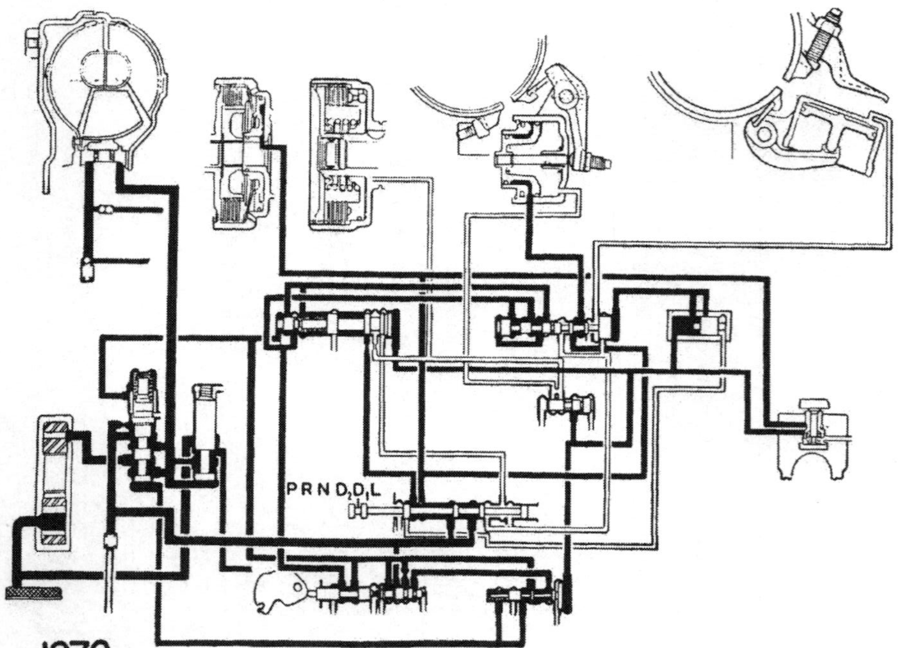

J279

Hydraulic circuit—second gear, 'D1' selected, kickdown

Pressure control by the primary regulator valve will be of the front pump output; this also provides torque converter and lubrication requirements. Throttle pressure acts upon the primary regulator valve.

Shift control is provided by the 1–2 shift valve moving under influence of governor pressure opposed by spring force and throttle pressure.

With the downshift valve in the forced throttle position, as illustrated, forced throttle pressure acts only upon the 2–3 shift valve, thus further delaying the upshift (or providing a 3–2 downshift at speeds when there is little governor pressure).

This permits line pressure to reach the apply side of the front servo. The front band thus applied, in conjunction with the front clutch, provides second gear.

Hydraulic circuit—second gear, 'D2' selected, kickdown

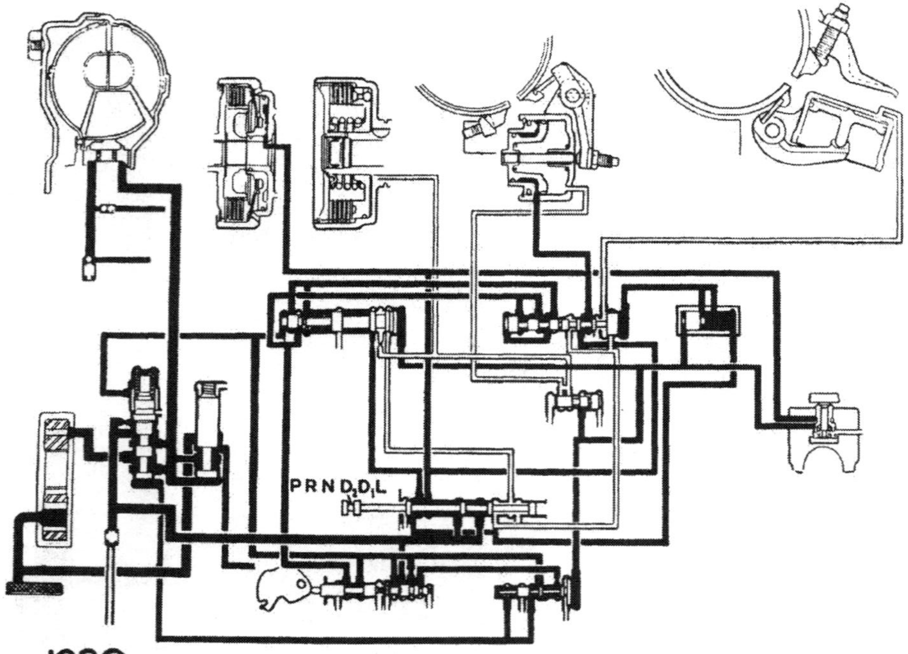

J280

Hydraulic circuit—second gear, 'D2' selected, kickdown

Pressure control by the primary regulator valve will be of the front pump output; this also provides torque converter and lubrication requirements. Throttle pressure acts upon the primary regulator valve.

Selector position 'D2' directs line pressure via the 'D1–D2' control valve to the 1–2 shift, which prevents engagement of first gear.

Shift control is provided by the 2–3 shift valve moving under influence of governor pressure opposed by spring force and throttle pressure.

With the downshift valve in the forced throttle position, as illustrated, forced throttle pressure acts only upon the 2–3 shift valve, thus further delaying the upshift (or providing a 3–2 downshift at speeds when there is little governor pressure).

This permits line pressure to reach the apply side of the front servo. The front band thus applied, in conjunction with the front clutch, provides the second gear.

Hydraulic circuit—third gear, 'D1' selected, light throttle

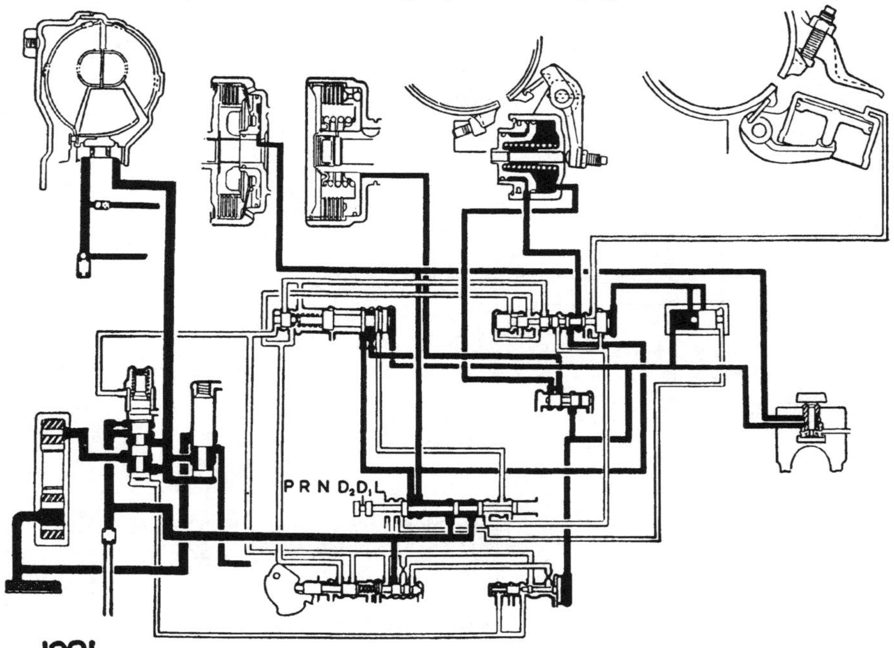

J281

Hydraulic circuit—third gear, 'D1' selected, light throttle

Pressure control will be as second gear, 'D1' selected, except that in the throttle valve position shown (light throttle) no throttle pressure or modulated throttle pressure acts upon the two ends of the primary regulator valve.

Shift control is provided by the 2–3 shift valve moving against spring force under influence of governor pressure. This permits line pressure to reach the rear clutch and the release side of the front servo through the servo orifice control valve. When governor pressure is apparent, the servo orifice control valve closes, forcing line pressure through a .052 in. (1,32 mm) orifice which thus affects the relationship between rear clutch apply and front servo release in accordance with road speed.

Because the release side of the front servo has a larger area than the apply side, the front servo will disengage the band. The rear clutch now engaged in conjunction with the front clutch provides third gear.

The absence of throttle pressure, as mentioned above, will cause the 2–3 shift valve to move early, under influence of governor pressure, thus providing a low-speed 2–3 shift.

With 'D2' selected the circuit and operation is the same as detailed above, except line pressure, via the 'D1–D2' control valve, replaces governor pressure on the 1–2 shift valve.

Hydraulic circuit—first gear, lock-up selected, medium throttle

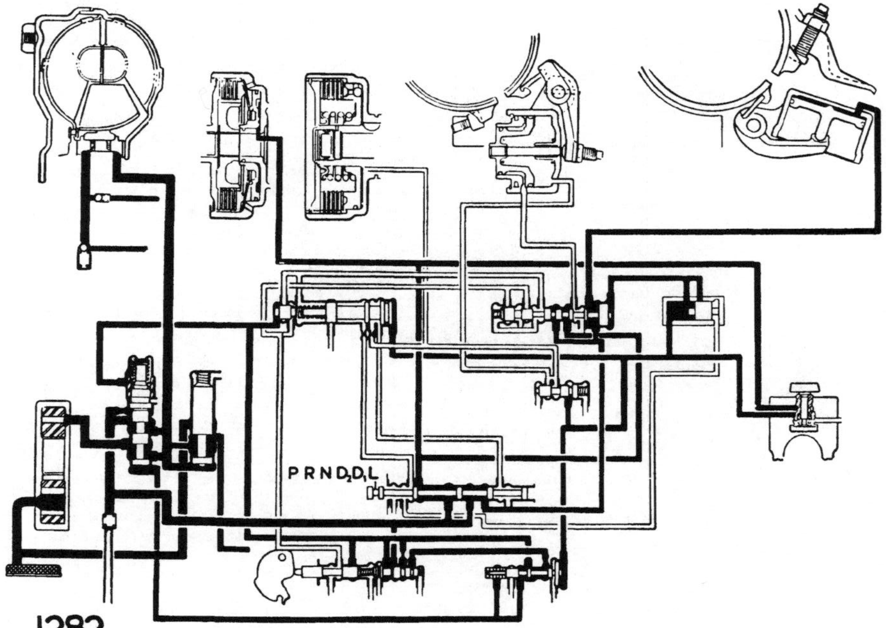

J282

Hydraulic circuit—first gear, lock-up selected, medium throttle

Pressure control of the front pump will be as second gear, 'D1' selected.

The manual valve directs line pressure to the front clutch, governor feed and 1–2 shift valve. In the position illustrated, the 1–2 shift valve is subjected to insufficient governor pressure to overcome spring and line pressure, thereby locking the system in first gear.

At the same time, the manual valve opens to exhaust the rear clutch and front servo release circuit from the 2–3 shift valve. This causes a downshift from third gear whenever 'L' is selected at speed. Reduction of road speed to 18 mph (28 kph) then allows line and spring pressure to overcome governor pressure; this directs line pressure to operate the rear servo, giving first gear.

Driving procedure

The notes which follow have been divided into two sections:

(i) A brief general description of the transmission and its method of handling.

(ii) The manual control aspects of the transmission.

General description of controls

In addition to the accelerator pedal, there are two controls:

(i) The selector lever.

(ii) A kickdown mechanism on the accelerator pedal.

Selector lever

The selector lever moves through a quadrant and by means of a pointer indicates the various positions, which are marked 'P', 'R', 'N', 'D2', 'D1' and 'L'.

Depress button in centre of selector lever, then move to the position required. Button must be depressed to engage all positions, except between 'D2' and 'D1'; the lever can also be moved from 'L' into 'D1' or 'D2' and from 'R' into 'N' without depressing the button.

'P' – Park: use this position whenever the car is parked
'R' – Reverse
'N' – Neutral.
} Never select these positions when car is moving

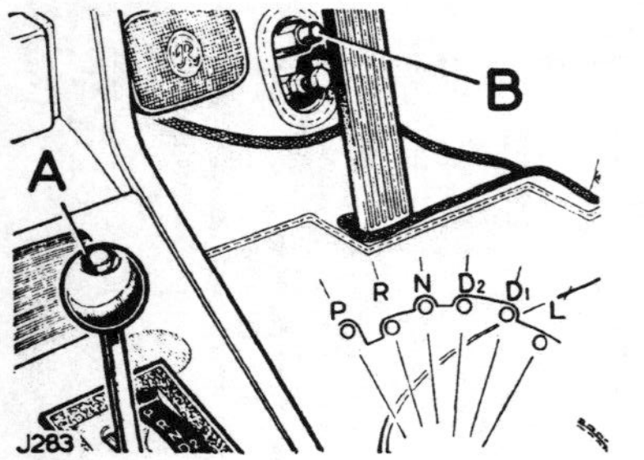

Selector lever and accelerator kickdown mechanism
A—Gear selector lever B—Kickdown mechanism

'D2' – Drive: this position dispenses with first gear. Select and leave in 'D2' for normal leisurely driving and in town conditions where changes into first gear are not required. This position should also be used when driving on slippery surfaces.

'D1' – Drive: this position gives a first gear start and provides facilities for using the full performance of the car. See following detailed description for the use of this selector position.

'L' – Lock-up: not normally required. See following detailed description for the use of this selector position. Never select 'L' when road speed is above 77 mph (124 kph) as there is a risk of over-speeding the engine.

Accelerator kickdown mechanism

The accelerator pedal should be depressed beyond its full throttle travel to operate the kickdown mechanism when:

(i) A lower gear is required for rapid overtaking or hill climbing.

(ii) Maximum acceleration is required, and can safely be used, on starting from rest.

The maximum kickdown speeds are pre-set to give optimum performance without overspeeding the engine.

If the accelerator pedal is eased back from the kick-down position during acceleration, up-changes will be made at lower road speeds.

Driving the car

Ensure that the handbrake is firmly applied and that the selector is in either the 'P' or 'N' position. As a safety measure an isolation switch prevents the starter being operated in any other position. Operate the starter switch. With the engine started and idling easily, depress the button and move the selector lever to either the 'D2', 'D1' or 'R' position as required, release handbrake and gently depress the accelerator pedal. Use footbrake to control car when manoeuvring in confined spaces. With the selector at 'D2' or 'D1', the car will move forward controlled by the accelerator and gear changes will be made automatically, depending on road speed and accelerator position; minimum accelerator pedal pressure will result in low up-change speeds. The further the accelerator pedal is depressed the faster the car will go before changing into a higher gear. The kickdown position referred to previously can be used for changing down into a lower gear or to obtain maximum acceleration as required.

It is not possible to tow-start the car with the type of automatic transmission used on the Rover 3.5-Litre. In the unlikely event of the car having to be towed any distance, disconnect the propeller shaft.

Manual control aspects of the transmission

The following paragraphs provide a more detailed description of the use of manual control aspects of the transmission.

'D2'–Drive

The drive position 'D2' covers an automatic range of two ratios with second gear start, operating in conjunction with a torque converter, the ratios being engaged progressively according to car speed and accelerator position.

Top gear will be retained, unless using the kickdown, until the car speed has fallen to about 10 mph (16 kph), when second gear will be automatically engaged.

Provided road speed is below 55 mph (88 kph), second gear can be obtained by use of the kickdown mechanism and can be held up to a maximum speed of 70 mph (112 kph), at which it will automatically change into top gear.

With the engine running and the selector at the 'D2' position the car will not roll back on an incline. This feature can be used when car is stopped on an upward slope; slip selector into 'D1' as car accelerates away.

First gear cannot be engaged with the selector at the 'D2' position.

'D1'–Drive

The drive position 'D1' covers a fully-automatic range of three ratios, with first gear start, operating in conjunction with a torque converter, the ratios being engaged progressively according to car speed and accelerator position.

When the road speed has fallen to about 5 mph (8 kph), first gear will be engaged.

Provided road speed is below 55 mph (88 kph), second gear can be obtained by use of the kickdown mechanism and can be held up to a maximum speed of 70 mph (112 kph), at which it will automatically change into top gear. Similarly, first gear can be engaged below 35 mph (56 kph) and can be held up to 40 mph (64 kph), at which speed it will automatically change into second.

'L'–Lock-up

The 'L' position (lock-up) provides the ability to hold the car in either first gear or second gear and therefore, in effect, to drive the car in manual control, the torque converter, however, replacing the conventional clutch.

At any time, when first or second gear is in operation in lock-up, full overrun braking is obtained from the gear in question. The lock-up should never be engaged at speeds above 77 mph (124 kph).

If the selector lever is placed in 'L' when starting from rest, the transmission starts and will remain locked in first gear regardless of road speed or throttle position. This gear gives maximum engine braking, but a speed of 46 mph (74 kph) must not be exceeded in first gear. To move from first gear lock-up to second gear lock-up, the lever must be moved to 'D1' or 'D2' and then returned to 'L', which will put the transmission into second gear, where it will remain locked.

Maximum speed in this gear should not exceed 77 mph (124 kph).

The change to top gear is made simply by moving the lever to 'D1' or 'D2' and leaving it there.

On saloon models the maximum recommended speeds in first and second gear, referred to previously, are indicated by yellow figures on the speedometer dial.

When the transmission is in top gear, selector position 'D2' and 'D1', movement of the lever to 'L' will immediately give second gear, but first gear will be automatically selected if the road speed drops below 12 mph (20 kph).

With second gear in operation, first gear can be engaged at speeds below 35 mph (56 kph) by operating the kickdown mechanism, but to change up into second the lever must be moved to 'D1' or 'D2' and returned to 'L', as referred to above.

The 'L' position is particularly useful in the following conditions:

(i) For unusually long and steep up-gradients or descents where a low gear is required, either for pulling or overrun braking.

(ii) Where hard pulling may be encountered, as in deep snow or heavy mud.

(iii) Driving slowly but where it is desirable to maintain reasonable engine speed so that the alternator can balance the heavy electrical load placed upon it by lights, windscreen wiper, heater, etc; that is, in foggy conditions at night.

(iv) To select and hold a lower gear when overtaking, within the permissible maximum speed limits stated previously.

Driving in mountainous areas

If the car is heavily laden, or towing a trailer, then 'D1' selector position should always be used when climbing any long hill of Alpine type. This will make available first gear, by use of the kickdown, when negotiating hairpin corners and also allow a restart in first gear should this become necessary.

When descending a hill of this type, under similar load conditions, use the 'L' selector position. This will provide engine braking in second and first gears, so reducing the load on the wheel brakes.

When approaching a corner, if the speed drops below 12 mph (20 kph), first gear will be obtained.

Should this not be required during acceleration between corners, second gear may be obtained by moving the selector lever to 'D1' or 'D2', and then back into 'L' after the transmission has changed gear.

It will then be locked in second gear until the next occasion on which the car speed falls below 12 mph (20 kph).

Static test procedure

1. Check and, if necessary, correct the fluid level:
   (a) Apply handbrake firmly and chock the wheels.
   (b) Select 'P'–Park, start engine and allow engine to idle for two minutes.
   (c) Take several dipstick readings.
   (d) Top up as necessary with recommended grade of transmission fluid.
2. When testing or making a diagnosis, it is important that the transmission fluid is at operating temperature but the fluid temperature must **not** exceed 110°C at any time.
3. Check that starter will operate only with the selector in 'P' and 'N' positions—but **not** in 'D1', 'D2', 'L' or 'R'.

4. Check that reverse light comes on when 'R' is selected.
5. Check the freedom of the transmission with the selector lever at 'N'. There should be no tendency for the engine to drive the car, nor should there be any engine braking effect.
6. Apply the hand and foot brakes firmly and chock the wheels.

   With the engine at normal idling speed, select 'N–D1', 'N–D2', 'N–L' and 'N–R'.

   Transmission engagement should be felt in each position selected.

   Check for slip or clutch squawk.

Stall speeds

'Stall speed' is the maximum speed at which the engine can drive the torque converter impeller whilst the turbine is held stationary. It is dependent on both engine and torque converter characteristics and will vary according to the condition of the engine.

An engine in poor condition will give a lower stall speed.

1. Connect a revolution counter, Rover Part No. 601284, to the engine. See Operation EEE2-3.
2. Apply the handbrake firmly and chock the wheels; whilst testing apply the footbrake.
3. Start engine and move selector lever to 'L' and allow to idle for approximately one minute to ensure circulation of fluid.
4. Depress accelerator to full throttle position and note the revolution counter reading.

   DO NOT STALL FOR LONGER THAN TEN SECONDS OR TRANSMISSION WILL OVERHEAT.
5. The stall speed of an engine in good condition should be 1,950 to 2,150 rpm.
6. If the stall speed is below 1,950 rpm, change the torque converter.

Road test procedure

1. Check and, if necessary, correct the fluid level:
   (a) Apply handbrake firmly.
   (b) Select 'P'–Park, start engine and allow engine to idle for two minutes.
   (c) Take several dipstick readings.
   (d) Top up as necessary with recommended grade of transmission fluid.
2. (a) All normal forward running is done in 'D2' or 'D1' selector position. The following table of change speeds apply with the selector linkage correctly adjusted and selector at the 'D1' position.

   The speeds in the above table are 'indicated'.

   Maximum permissible tolerances in both speedometer and transmission have been taken into account, together with tyre make and expansion due to speed.

   (b) Selector at 'D2' position, check that car starts in second gear; first gear should not be available in this selector position.

Light throttle	mph	kph
1 to 2 2 to 3	6 to 12 13 to 20	10 to 19 20 to 32
Full throttle		
1 to 2 2 to 3	23 to 31 48 to 58	37 to 50 77 to 93
Kickdown		
1 to 2 2 to 3	33 to 43 63 to 75	53 to 69 101 to 120

   (c) At 25 mph (40 kph)

   'D1' selected in top gear, depress accelerator to full throttle position. Transmission should not change down.

   (d) At 40 mph (64 kph)

   'D1' selected, depress accelerator to kick-down position. Transmission should change down into intermediate.

   Release the accelerator pedal immediately, when transmission should revert to direct gear.

   (e) At 20 mph (32 kph)

   'D1' selected, depress accelerator to kick-down position. Transmission should change down into first gear.

   Release the accelerator pedal immediately, when transmission should revert to top gear.

   (f) 'D2' or 'D1' selected. Driving at 30 mph (48 kph) in top gear, select 'L'.

   The transmission should change into intermediate, giving engine braking. Slow vehicle to rest. At under 12 mph (20 kph) the transmission should engage first, thus increasing the engine braking and ensuring a first speed start from rest.

   Accelerate to 30 mph (48 kph) and close throttle. Transmission must not change up.

   (g) Stop on a hill and select 'P'–Park.

   Note: THIS TRANSMISSION DOES **NOT** INCORPORATE ANY SAFETY INTERLOCKS ON 'PARK' OR 'REVERSE'. 'P' or 'R' must never be selected unless the vehicle is stationary.

   Release the brakes when facing up or down hill, the car should remain stationary. On steep slopes some force may be needed to disengage the 'Park' position.
3. Stop and select 'R'. Release brakes and reverse, using full throttle if possible. Check for slip or clutch squawk.

PART TWO

This section provides the instructions necessary for the adjustment and for the removal and refitting of various units of the automatic transmission.

It is rarely necessary to completely dismantle the unit, which has basic assemblies, each of which may be renewed and dismantled without affecting the others.

With the unit removed from the vehicle, it should be supported on gearbox cradle, Rover Part No. 601280, when carrying out any of the operations in this section. It will be necessary to remove the torque converter and bell housing, Operation EEE2-6, to enable this to be done.

High standards of cleanliness are required when working on the automatic transmission. Petrol, paraffin or an industrial cleaning solvent may be used to clean components. Use nylon rag—never material that is fluffy or that leaves lint—when drying any components.

IMPORTANT

Before any dismantling of the transmission unit is commenced it is essential that the following checks are made in accordance with the procedure as detailed:

1. Fluid level in transmission unit. Operation EEE2-4.
2. Gear selector linkage adjustment. Operation EEE2-1.
3. Downshift cable adjustment. Operation EEE2-3.

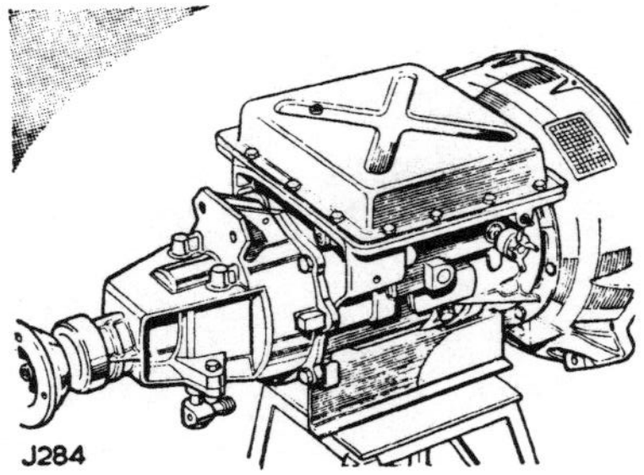

J284

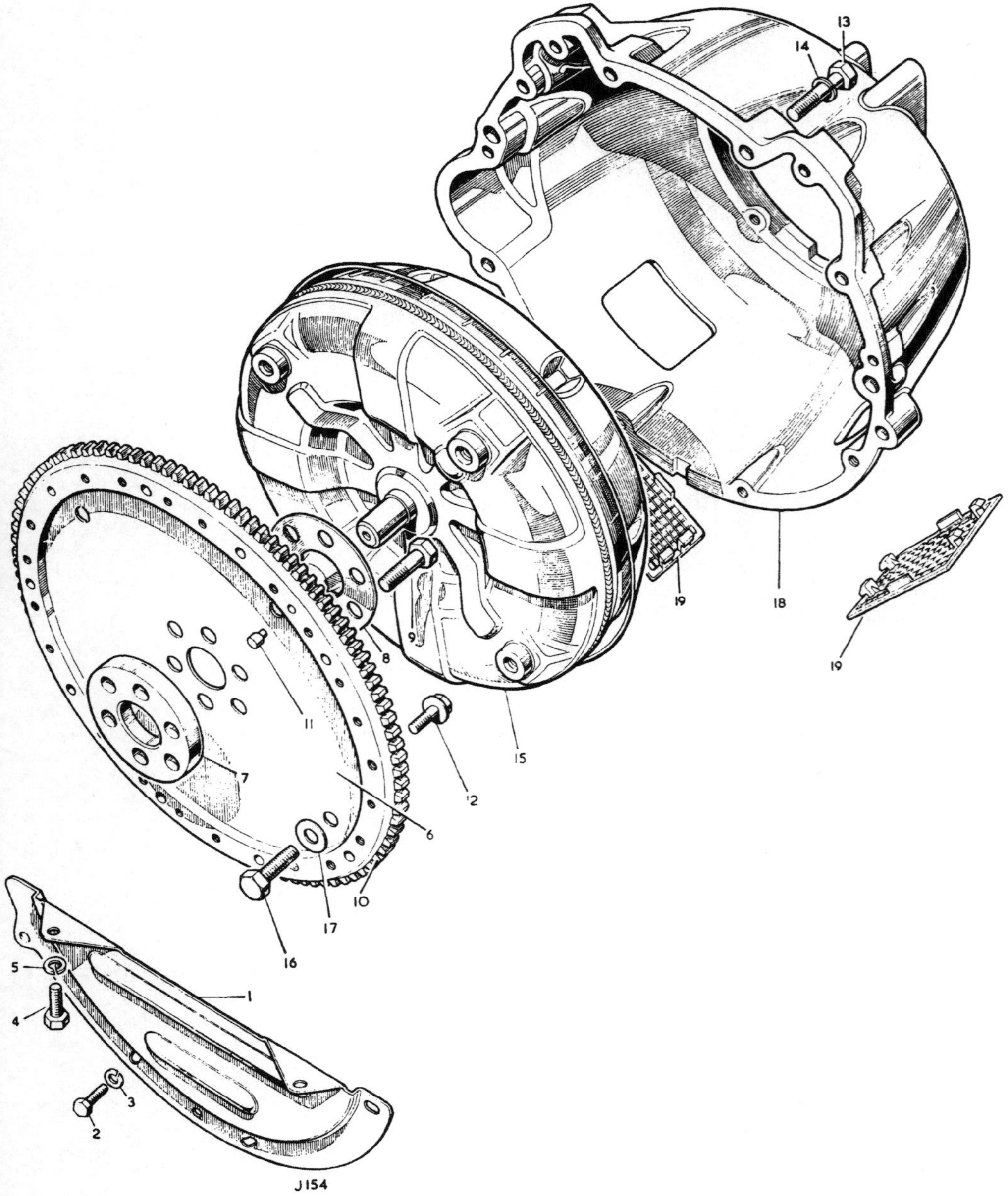

Torque converter and bell housing

Torque converter and housing

1	Front cover plate	
2	Bolt ($\frac{1}{4}$ in. UNC x $\frac{1}{2}$ in. long)	Fixing cover plate and transmission to engine
3	Spring washer	
4	Bolt ($\frac{5}{16}$ in. UNC x $\frac{5}{8}$ in. long)	
5	Spring washer	
6	Flexible drive plate	
7	Spacer for drive plate	
8	Reinforcing plate	
9	Bolt fixing flexible drive plate	
10	Starter ring	
11	Dowel for flexible drive plate	
12	Special bolt and washer fixing starter ring	
13	Bolt ($\frac{3}{8}$ in. UNC x 2 in. long)	Fixing torque converter housing
14	Spring washer	
15	Torque converter	
16	Bolt ($\frac{3}{8}$ in. UNF x $\frac{5}{8}$ in. long)	Fixing flexible drive plate to torque converter
17	Plain washer	
18	Housing for torque converter	
19	Stone guard for housing	

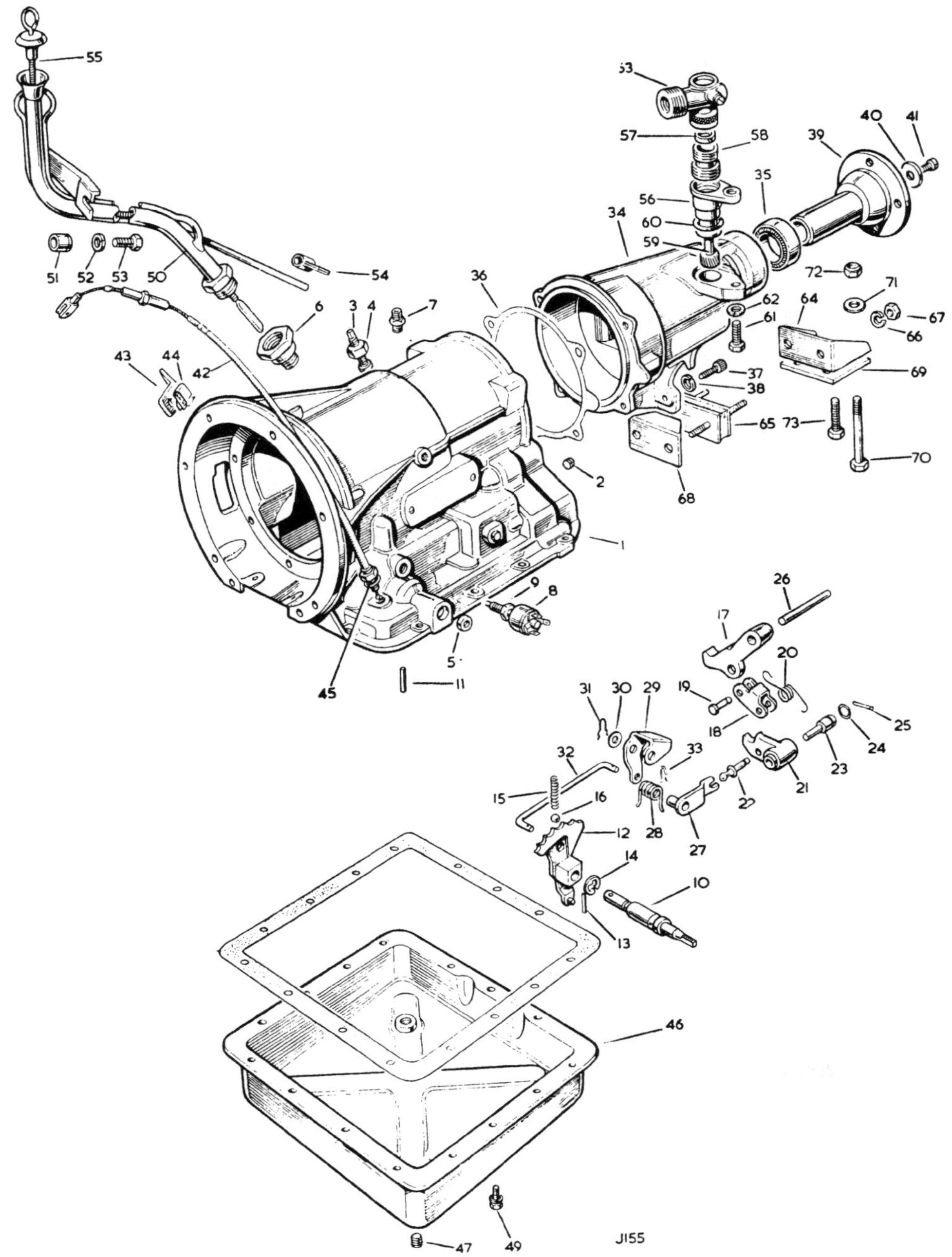

Transmission case

1 Main case assembly
2 Pipe plug
3 Screw, rear servo adjusting
4 Nut, locking adjusting screw
5 Oil seal, manual control shaft
6 Adaptor for tube connector
7 Connector tube outlet, oil cooler
8 Inhibitor switch
9 Locknut for inhibitor switch
10 Shaft, manual valve lever
11 Pin retaining shaft
12 Lever, manual valve detent
13 Retaining pin for lever
14 Circlip
15 Spring, manual valve detent
16 Ball ($\frac{3}{8}$ in. diameter), manual valve detent
17 Pawl, parking brake
18 Link for parking brake
19 Pin for toggle link, pawl end
20 Spring, parking brake release
21 Toggle lever
22 Pin for toggle lever, ball-ended
23 Pin for toggle lever, shouldered
24 'O' ring for toggle lever
25 Roll pin fixing toggle lever pin
26 Anchor pin for pawl
27 Toggle lift lever, forked
28 Spring for lift lever
29 Torsion lever for parking brake
30 Plain washer for torsion lever
31 Retaining spring for torsion lever
32 Link for parking brake
33 Clip for linkage rod
34 Extension housing assembly
35 Oil seal for housing
36 Gasket for extension housing
37 Special bolt and washer fixing extension housing
38 Lock washer
39 Coupling flange
40 Plain washer for flange
41 Special screw fixing flange
42 Downshift cable complete
43 Bracket for downshift cable
44 Clip fixing downshift cable to bracket
45 Sealing washer for downshift cable
46 Oil pan
47 Drain plug
48 Gasket for oil pan
49 Special bolt and washer fixing oil pan
50 Oil filler tube
51 Distance piece
52 Spring washer
53 Set bolt ($\frac{1}{4}$ in. UNC x $1\frac{5}{8}$ in. long)
54 Clip for breather tube
55 Dipstick
56 Housing for speedometer drive
57 Oil seal, small, for housing
58 Adaptor for housing
59 Speedometer driven gear and spindle
60 'O' ring for speedometer housing
61 Bolt ($\frac{1}{4}$ in. UNC x 1 in. long) } Fixing speedometer housing to extension case
62 Spring washer } Fixing speedometer housing to extension case
63 Right-angled drive for speedometer
64 Mounting bracket for transmission
65 Rubber mounting
66 Spring washer
67 Nut ($\frac{3}{8}$ in. UNF)
68 Backplate for transmission mounting
69 Shim plate
70 Bolt ($\frac{3}{8}$ in. UNF x $4\frac{3}{4}$ in. long)
71 Plain washer
72 Self-locking nut ($\frac{3}{8}$ in. UNF)
73 Bolt ($\frac{3}{8}$ in. UNF x 1 in. long)

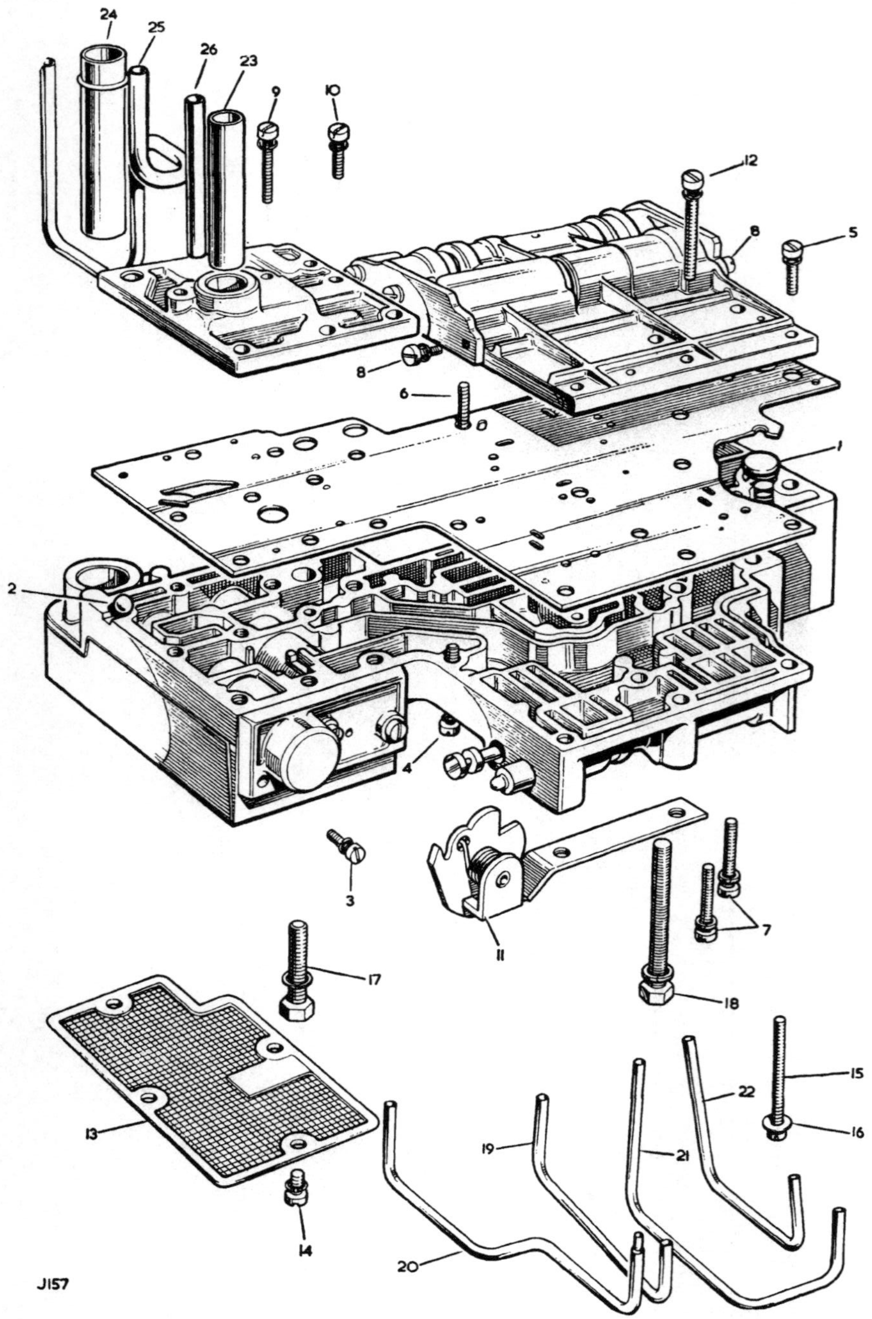

Valve bodies

Valve bodies

Valve bodies assembly
1 Check valve
2 Ball ($\frac{1}{4}$ in. diameter) converter check valve
3 Screw and washer fixing end plate
4 Screw and washer fixing valve body, upper
5 Screw and washer fixing valve body, upper
6 Screw and washer fixing valve body, upper
7 Screw and washer fixing 'D1–D2' control valve
8 Screw and washer fixing end plates to upper valve body
9 Screw and washer fixing oil tube plate
10 Screw and washer fixing oil tube plate
11 Cam for downshift valve
12 Screw and washer fixing cam
13 Oil strainer, front pump
14 Screw and washer fixing strainer, front
15 Screw and washer fixing valve body, lower
16 Plain washer
17 Bolt and washer fixing valve body to transmission case
18 Bolt and washer fixing valve body to transmission case
19 Tube, front servo apply
20 Tube, front servo release
21 Tube, rear clutch
22 Tube, rear servo
23 Tube, from pump outlet
24 Tube, front pump inlet
25 Tube, converter out and oil cooler inlet
26 Tube, oil cooler inlet

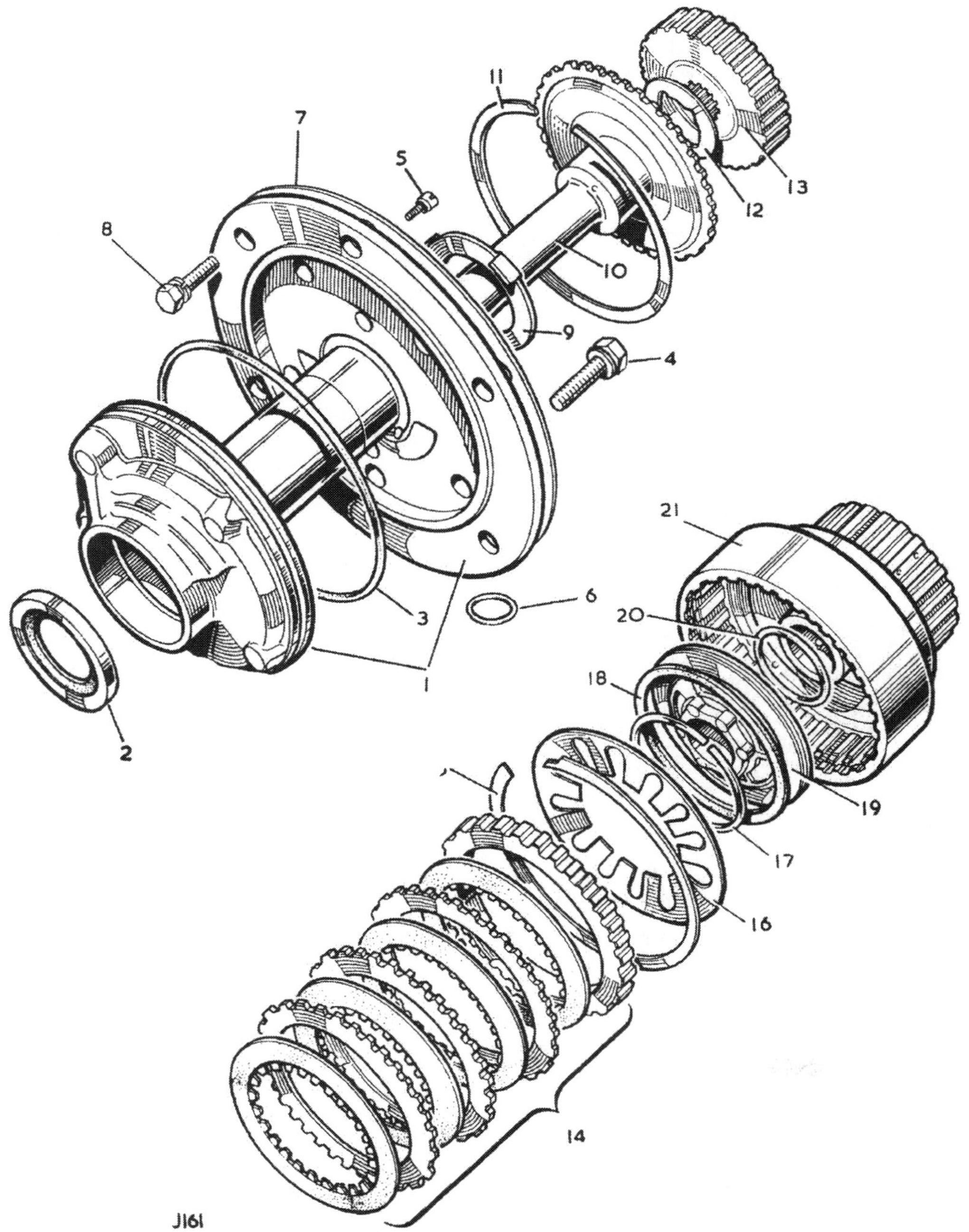

Front pump and front clutch

Front pump and front clutch

1 Front pump assembly
2 Seal for pump
3 'O' ring for pump
4 Bolt and washer ($\frac{7}{8}$ in. long)
5 Screw and washer ($\frac{5}{8}$ in. long)
6 'O' ring for pump inlet tube
7 Gasket, pump to main case
8 Bolt and washer fixing pump
9 Thrust washer
10 Input shaft
11 Snap ring for input shaft
12 Thrust washer
13 Hub for front clutch
14 Clutch plates
15 Snap ring for front clutch spring
16 Diaphragm spring for front clutch
17 Bearing ring for front clutch spring
18 Sealing ring, large, for piston
19 Piston and reed assembly, front clutch
20 'O' ring, small, for piston
21 Cylinder, front clutch

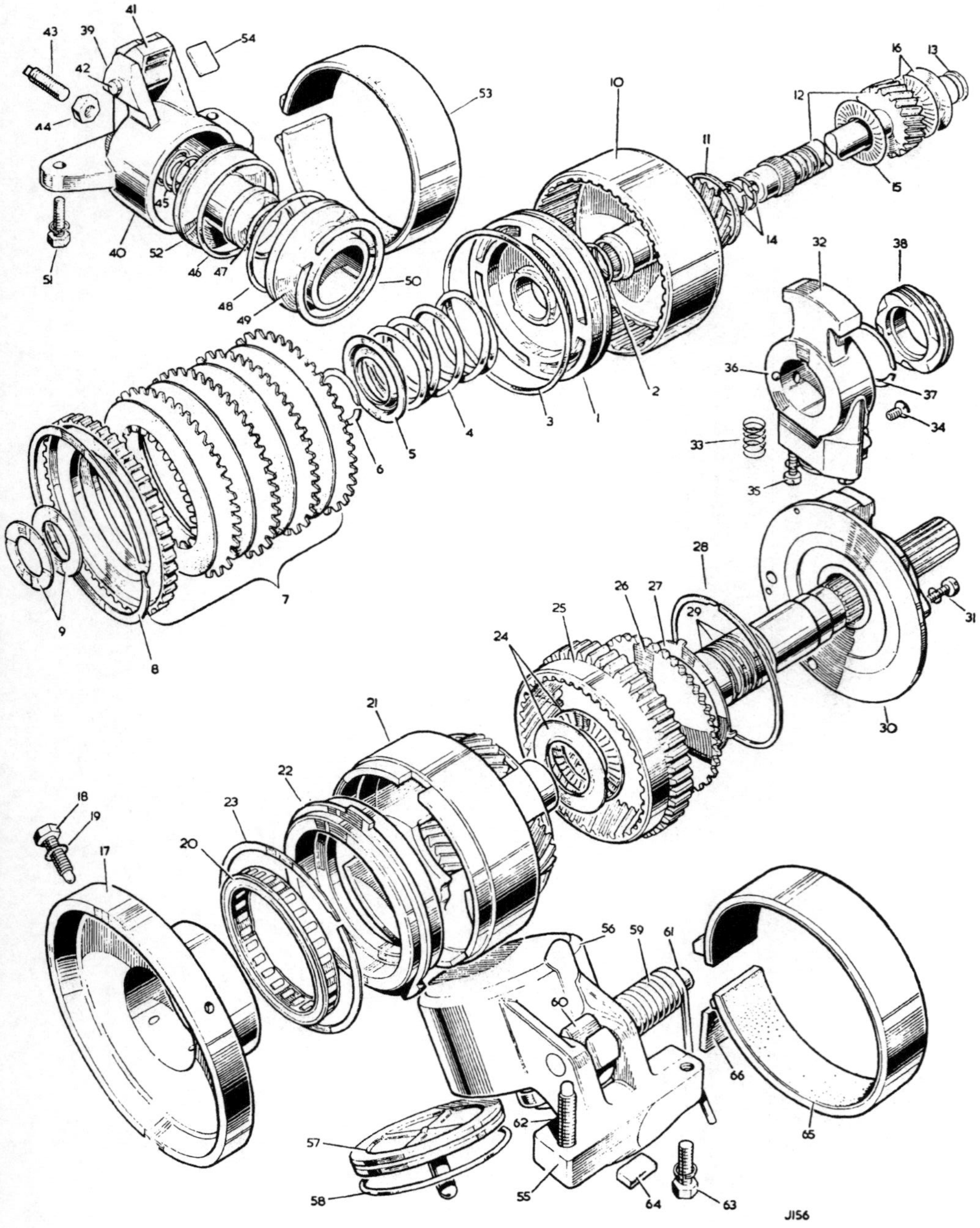

Rear clutch, servo and governor

Rear clutch, servo and governor

1 Piston and reed assembly, rear clutch
2 'O' ring, small, rear clutch piston
3 Sealing ring, large, rear clutch piston
4 Spring, rear clutch
5 Seat, rear clutch spring
6 Snap ring for spring
7 Clutch plates and spacer
8 Snap ring, large
9 Thrust washer
10 Front drum assembly
11 Oil seal ring
12 Forward sun gear assembly
13 Oil seal ring, nylon
14 Oil seal ring for forward sun gear
15 Thrust needle bearing
16 Thrust needle bearing and plate
17 Centre support assembly
18 Bolt, centre support
19 Lockwasher, centre support
20 One-way clutch assembly
21 Planet gears and rear drum assembly
22 Outer race, one-way clutch
23 Snap ring, one-way clutch race
24 Thrust needle bearing and plate
25 Ring gear
26 Driven shaft assembly
27 Thrust washer
28 Snap ring for ring gear
29 Oil sealing ring, driven shaft
30 Adaptor plate
31 Screw and washer fixing adaptor plate
32 Governor assembly
33 Spring, governor
34 Lockscrew, governor cover plate
35 Screw and washer, governor
36 Steel ball ($\frac{1}{4}$ in. diameter)
37 Snap ring, governor
38 Gear, speedometer drive
39 Servo assembly, front
40 Body, front servo
41 Lever, front servo
42 Pivot pin, front servo
43 Adjusting screw, front servo
44 Locknut, adjusting screw
45 Spring, front servo
46 'O' ring, large, front servo piston
47 'O' ring, small, front servo piston
48 Oil sealing ring
49 Sleeve, front servo piston
50 Snap ring, front servo piston
51 Bolt ($1\frac{3}{8}$ in. long) fixing front servo
52 Piston, front servo
53 Brake band, front servo
54 Strut for brake band
55 Servo assembly, rear
56 Body, rear servo
57 Piston, rear servo
58 'O' ring, piston
59 Spring, rear servo
60 Lever, rear servo
61 Pivot pin, rear servo
62 Bolt, rear servo
63 Bolt fixing rear servo
64 Magnet
65 Brake band, rear servo
66 Strut, brake band

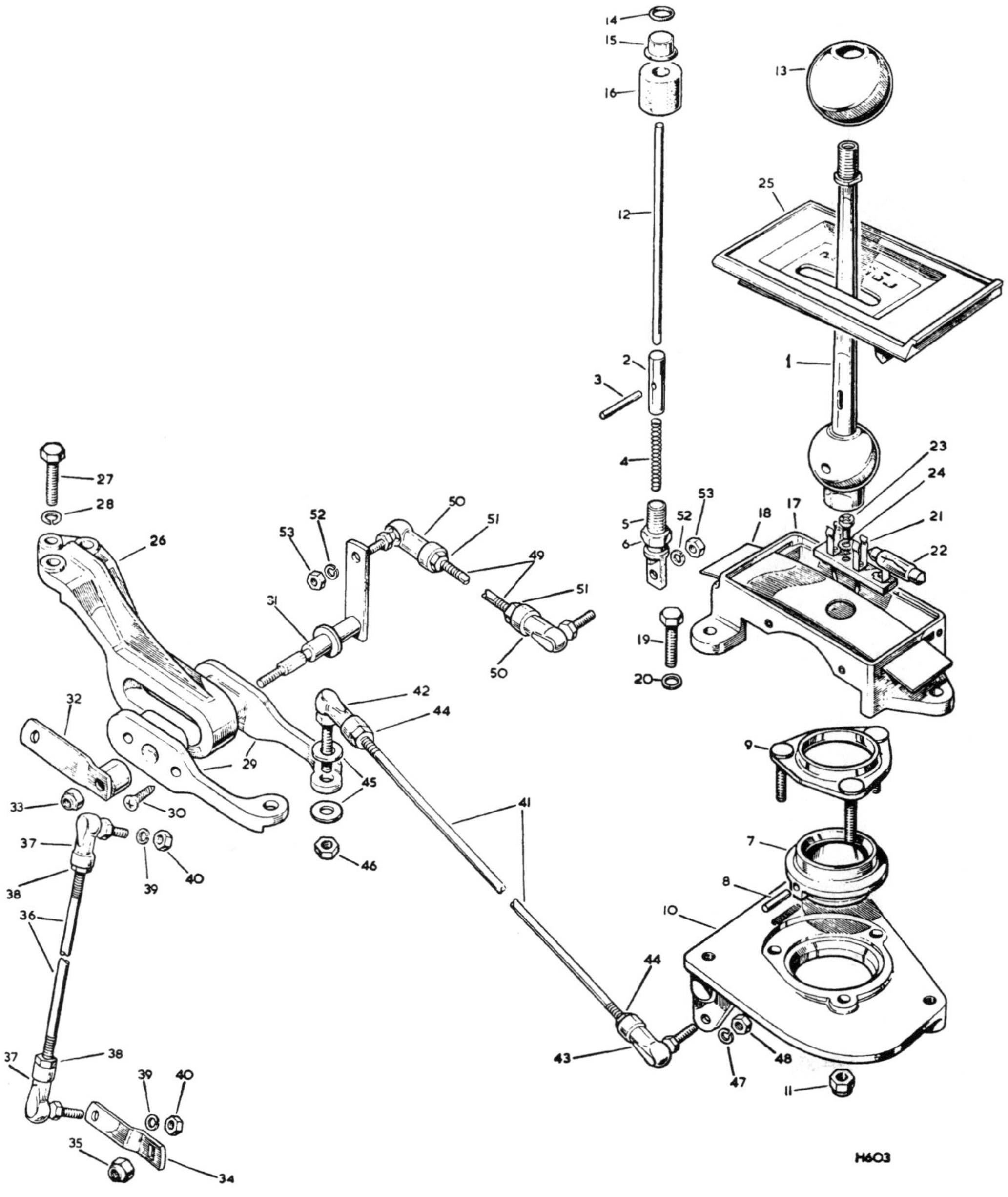

Gear selector lever and linkage

Gear selector lever and linkage

1 Gear selector lever
2 Plug for lever
3 Pin for selector gate
4 Spring for plug
5 Eye bolt } For gear selector lever
6 Nut ($\frac{3}{8}$ in. UNF) for eye bolt } For gear selector lever
7 Spherical seat for lever
8 Locating pin for spherical seat
9 Retaining cap for spherical seat
10 Pivot housing
11 Special nut ($\frac{1}{4}$ in. UNF) fixing retaining cap to pivot housing
12 Control rod for gear selector lever
13 Knob for gear selector lever
14 'O' ring for knob
15 Button for knob
16 Rubber insert for knob
17 Housing for gear selector lever
18 Shield for gear selector lever
19 Set bolt ($\frac{5}{16}$ in. UNC x $\frac{7}{8}$ in. long) } Fixing gear selector lever housing to pivot housing
20 Plain washer } Fixing gear selector lever housing to pivot housing
21 Illumination lamp for gear selector
22 Bulb, 12-volt 3-watt, festoon
23 Screw (10 UNF x $\frac{3}{8}$ in. long) } Fixing lamp to housing
24 Shakeproof washer } Fixing lamp to housing
25 Indicator plate for gear selector lever
26 Compensator bracket for gear linkage
27 Set bolt ($\frac{5}{16}$ in. UNC x $\frac{3}{4}$ in. long) } Fixing bracket to torque converter housing
28 Spring washer } Fixing bracket to torque converter housing
29 Compensator block
30 Drive screw fixing compensator blocks
31 Shaft and lever for compensator
32 Selector lever, upper
33 Self-locking nut ($\frac{1}{4}$ in. UNF) fixing upper lever to shaft
34 Selector lever, lower
35 Self-locking nut ($\frac{5}{16}$ in. UNF) fixing lower lever to transmission unit
36 Lower control rod
37 Ball joint for rod
38 Locknut ($\frac{1}{4}$ in. UNF) for ball joint
39 Spring washer } Fixing lower rod to levers
40 Locknut ($\frac{1}{4}$ in. UNF) } Fixing lower rod to levers
41 Tie rod, compensator block to pivot housing
42 Ball joint for tie rod, compensator end
43 Ball joint for tie rod, pivot housing end
44 Locknut ($\frac{1}{4}$ in. UNF) for ball joints
45 Plain washer } Fixing tie rod to compensator
46 Locknut ($\frac{1}{4}$ in. UNF) } Fixing tie rod to compensator
47 Spring washer } Fixing tie rod to pivot housing
48 Locknut ($\frac{1}{4}$ in. UNF) } Fixing tie rod to pivot housing
49 Control rod, gear selector lever to compensator
50 Ball joint for control rod
51 Locknut ($\frac{1}{4}$ in. UNF) for ball joint
52 Spring washer } Fixing control rod to levers
53 Locknut ($\frac{1}{4}$ in. UNF) } Fixing control rod to levers

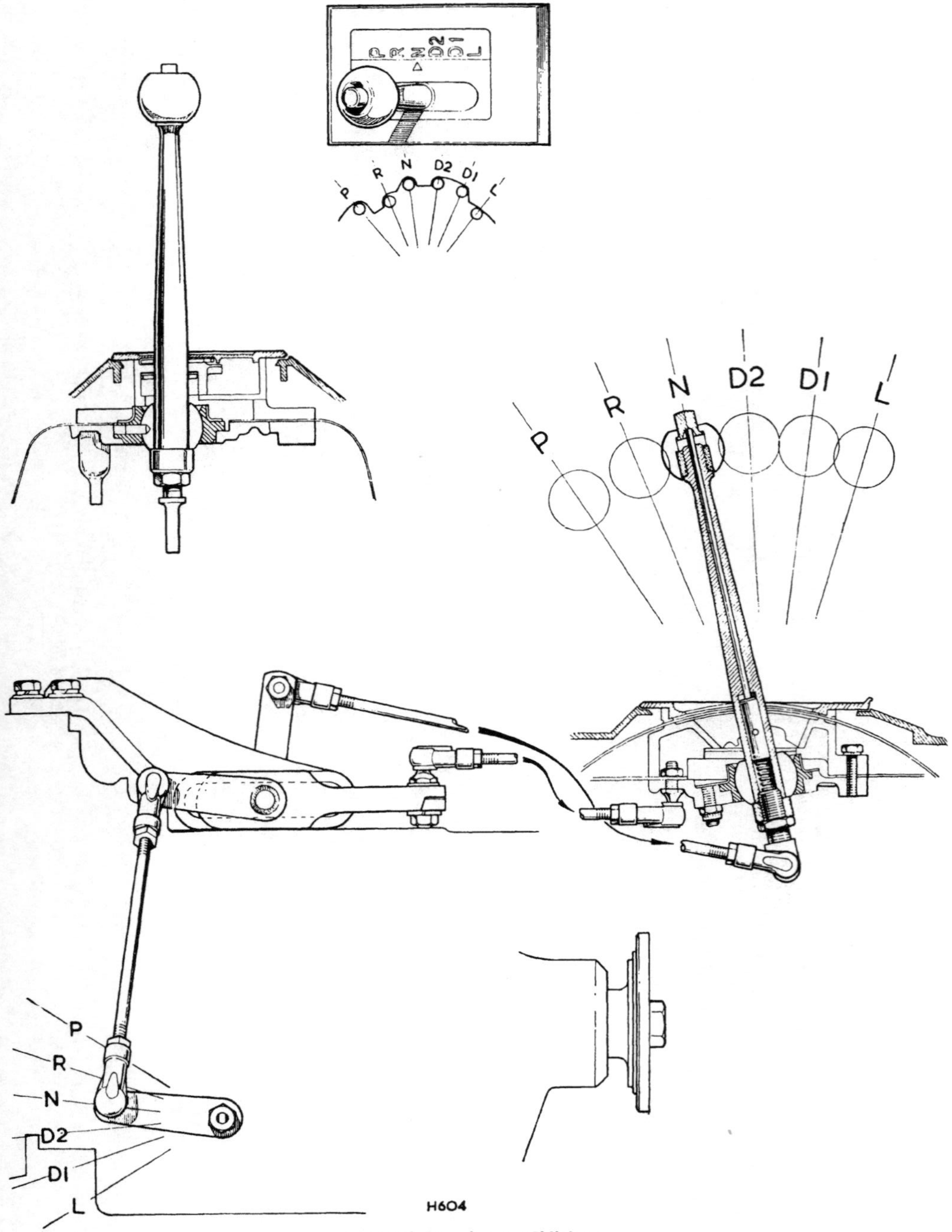

H6O4

Layout of gear selector and linkage

Gear selector linkage, remove, refit and adjust—Operation EEE2-1

Workshop hand tools:

Spanner sizes: Open-ended $\frac{7}{16}$ in. AF, $\frac{1}{2}$ in. AF

Linkage, remove

1. Unscrew the knob from the top of the gear lever.
2. Lift off the plastic indicator cover for gear selector.
3. Remove the Phillips' screw securing the trim panel to the top of the transmission tunnel and lift off the trim panel.

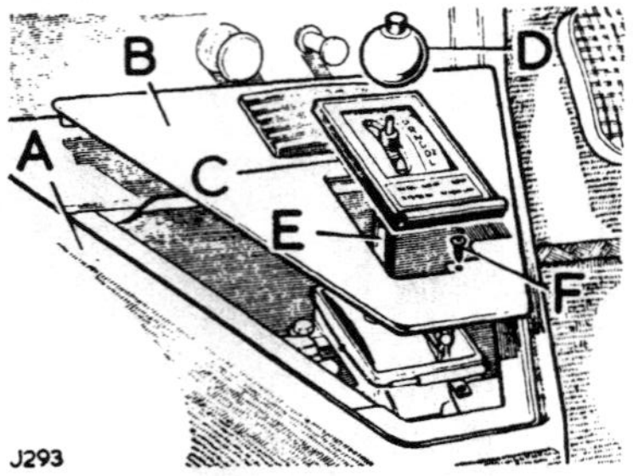

J293

Trim panel

A—Transmission tunnel
B—Trim panel
C—Indicator plate
D—Knob for gear selector lever
E—Gear selector lever
F—Screw fixing trim panel

4. Push the two front seats back as far as they will go.
5. Remove the two nuts, spring washers and plain washers securing the gearbox console to the tunnel cover, lift the rear of console and draw out; at this stage the wiring harness can be disconnected from the cigar lighter and fog lamp switch. Withdraw the console unit complete from the car.

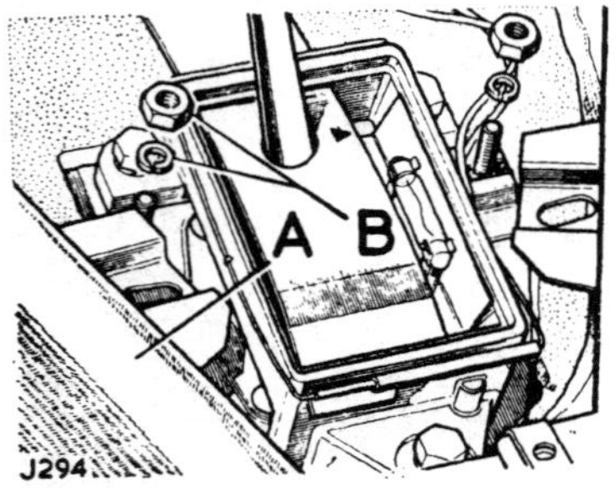

J294

Console unit

A—Console unit
B—Nut and spring washer fixing console unit

6. Remove cover plate to gain access to the compensator bracket fixing bolts.
7. Remove the three bolts securing compensator bracket to top of bell housing; the complete assembly of compensator and rods can now be withdrawn.
8. Disconnect operating rod at selector lever and tie rod at pivot housing.

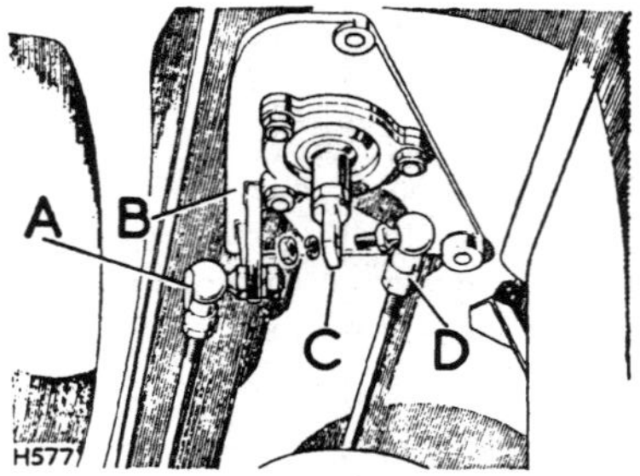

H577

Selector linkage rods

A—Tie rod
B—Pivot housing
C—Selector lever
D—Operating rod

9. Disconnect lower control rod at automatic transmission unit.
10. If necessary, remove upper selector lever from shaft and tie rod from compensator blocks.

The compensator blocks can be withdrawn from the bracket after removing the two drive screws.

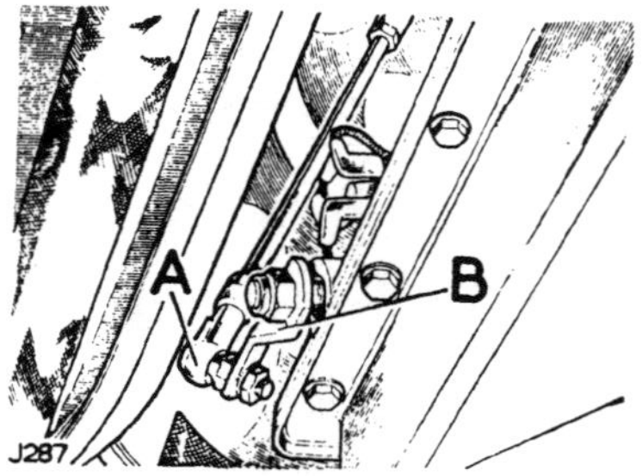

J287

Lower control rod

A—Lower control rod B—Selector lever, lower

Operation EEE2-1—*continued*

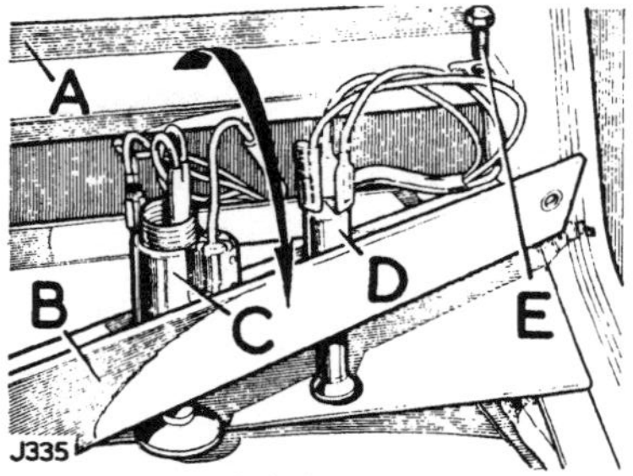

Switch panel

A—Console unit
B—Switch panel
C—Cigar lighter
D—Fog lamp switch
E—Bolt fixing console unit

Remove panel in direction of arrow

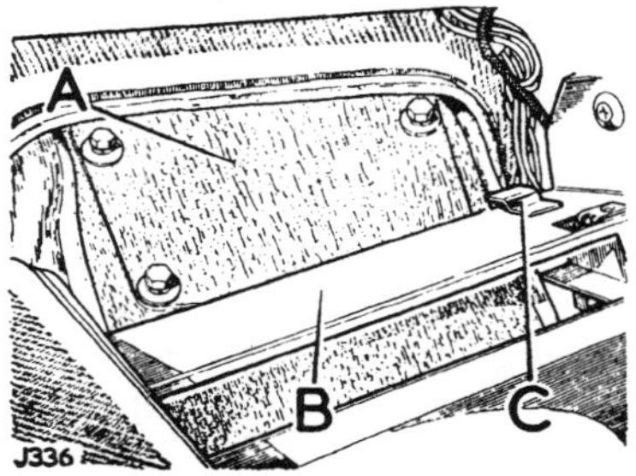

Console unit, front end fixing

A—Panel on transmission tunnel
B—Console unit
C—Clip fixing console unit

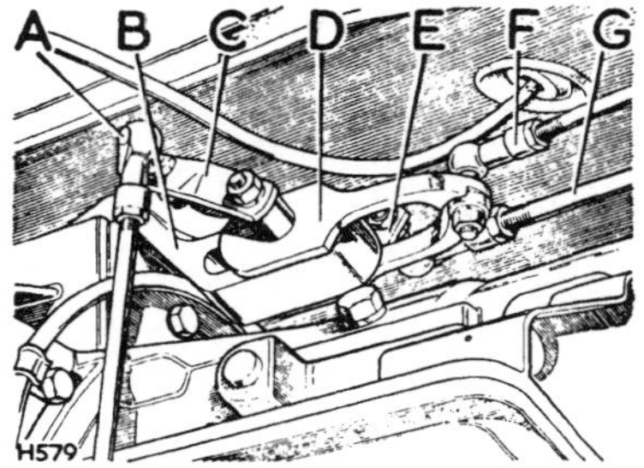

Compensator bracket for gear linkage

A—Lower control rod
B—Compensator bracket
C—Selector lever, upper
D—Compensator block
E—Selector lever and shaft
F—Tie rod
G—Operating rod

Linkage, refit

1. Reverse removal procedure.
2. Ensure that upper selector lever is fitted facing forwards and at right-angles to the other lever.
3. Adjust linkage in accordance with the details given below. Connect operating rod and tie rod at both ends. Connect vertical rod at top position only.

IMPORTANT

The gear selector linkage must be correctly adjusted to give satisfactory operation of the transmission unit.

Ensure that the linkage is never allowed to override the transmission detent; a definite 'click' must be felt in each selector position.

Linkage, adjust

1. Check and, if necessary, adjust length of rods to the dimensions detailed, which represents the length between the centres of the ball joints:

(a) Operating rod .. .. $18\frac{3}{16}$ in. (462 mm)
(b) Tie rod .. .. .. $13\frac{1}{8}$ in. (333 mm)
(c) Vertical rod .. .. $7\frac{3}{4}$ in. (197 mm)

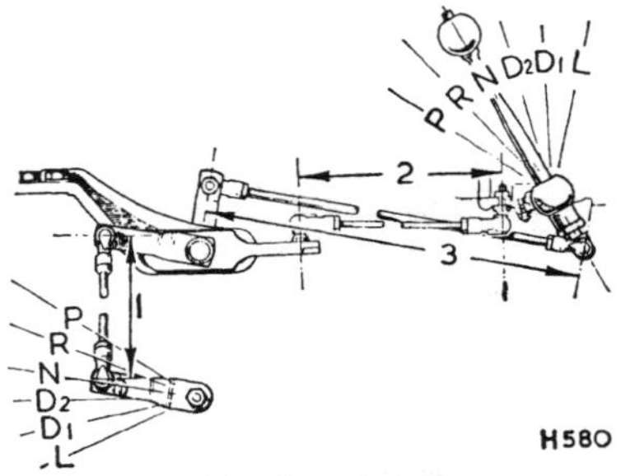

Rod dimensions

1—Vertical rod $7\frac{3}{4}$ in. (197 mm
2—Tie rod $13\frac{1}{8}$ in. (333 mm)
3—Operating rod $18\frac{3}{16}$ in. (462 mm)

2. Select 'N' at the selector lever on the transmission unit.
3. Place the gear selector lever at the neutral ('N') position.

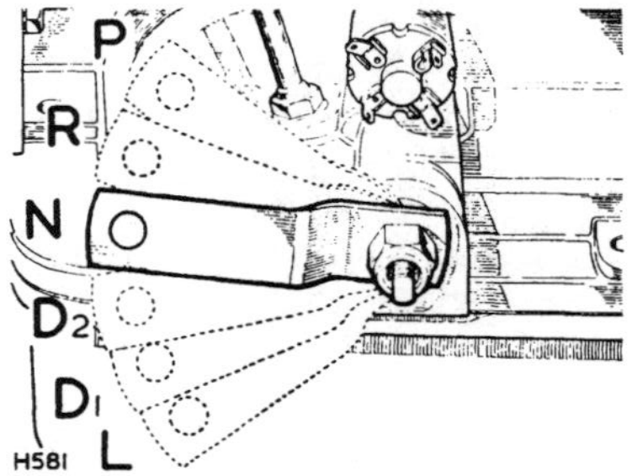

Selector lever, lower, on the transmission unit at the 'N'—neutral position

4. Adjust as necessary at lower control rod, ensuring that the ball joint can be connected to the lower selector lever without strain. Check quadrant gating in all selector positions, ensuring that linkage is not overriding the transmission detent.

Gear selector lever at 'N' position

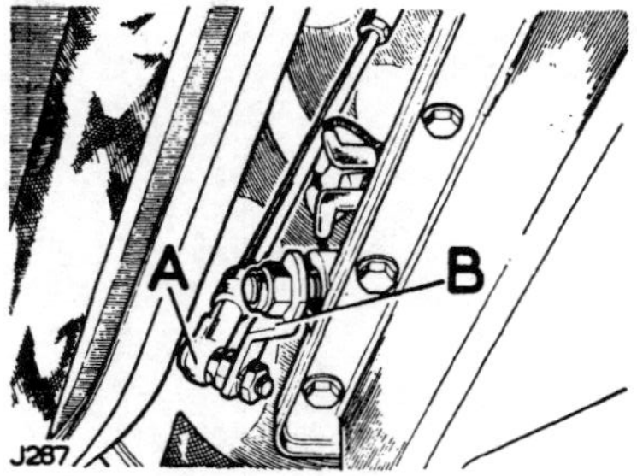

Control rod, lower

A—Control rod, lower B—Selector lever, lower

Starter inhibitor switch, adjust—Operation EEE2-2

Workshop hand tools:

Spanner size: Open-ended $\frac{11}{16}$ in. AF

Special tools:

Test lamp

Starter inhibitor switch, adjust

1. Remove front exhaust pipe; this will facilitate adjustment of the switch.
2. Ensure that the selector linkage is set correctly. Operation EEE2-1.
3. Select 'D2', 'D1' or 'L' position.
4. Disconnect the wiring from the switch at the 'Lucar' connectors.

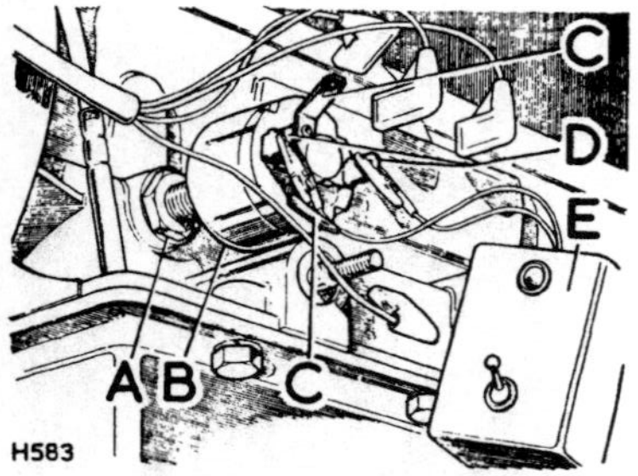

Adjusting inhibitor switch

A—Locknut for switch
B—Starter inhibitor switch
C—Reverse light terminals
D—Engine isolation terminals
E—Test lamp

5. Slacken the locknut and unscrew the switch to its fullest extent.
6. Connect a test lamp (consisting of a small dry battery and bulb) to the pair of terminals which are set at about 45°; these being the reversing light terminals.
7. Screw the switch into the maincase until the test lamp goes out.
8. Now connect the test lamp leads to the other pair of terminals on the switch.
9. Screw the switch in approximately one turn until the light comes on.
10. Turn the switch back approximately half a turn; that is, midway between the two points previously noted. Then tighten the locknut, taking care not to strip the thread of the light alloy switch body.
11. Disconnect the test lamp wiring and reconnect the car wiring and front exhaust pipe.
12. Apply the handbrake firmly and chock the wheels. Apply footbrake during test.
13. Check that the starter operates only when the selector lever is at 'P' or 'N'.

*Downshift valve cable, adjust—Operation EEE2-3

Workshop hand tools:

Spanner sizes: $\frac{1}{2}$ in. AF, $1\frac{5}{16}$ in. AF
Allen key $\frac{3}{16}$ in. AF

Special tools:

Pressure gauge and tachometer, Rover Part No. 601284
Torque wrench set, Rover Part No. 601285
Carburetter balancing device, Rover Part No. 605330

IMPORTANT

The downshift valve cable must be correctly adjusted to give satisfactory operation of the transmission unit. For production purposes the adjustment is pre-set at the factory where a stop is crimped on to the inner cable at the engine end.

If, however, the stop has not been crimped, or if it is necessary to check the adjustment of the cable, carry out one of the following two procedures. **Always adjust carburetters first.**

Method A
Adjusting downshift valve cable, using service test gauges

1. Chock front wheels of the car and apply handbrake firmly. Apply footbrake during test.
2. Remove the line pressure take-off plug from the rear of the transmission case, using an Allen key.
3. Connect the line pressure gauge to the pressure take-off point.

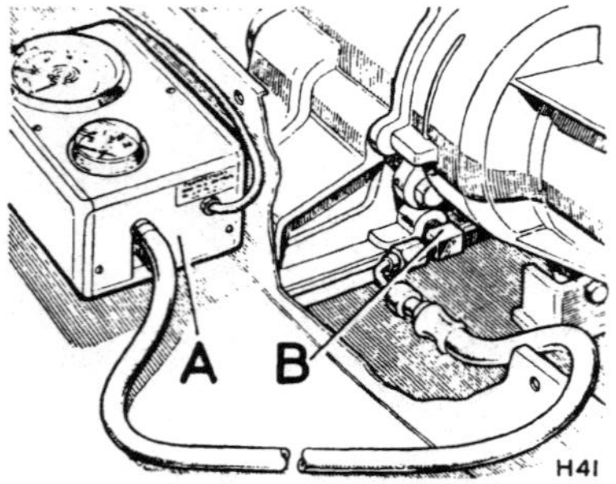

Pressure gauge connected to transmission

A—Pressure take-off connection
B—Pressure gauge

4. Connect a suitable tachometer.
5. Start the engine and allow to warm up.

   Take the line pressure reading when engine is running at 600 rpm in 'D2' or 'D1'.

   Increase the rpm to 1,000 when the line pressure should increase by 15 to 20 lb sq in. (1,05 to 1,40 kg/cm²).

   If the pressure rise is less than 15 lb sq in. (1,05 kg/cm²), the effective length of the outer cable should be increased by screwing out the cable adjuster.

   If the pressure rise is more than 20 lb sq in. (1,40 kg/cm²), then the effective length of the cable should be decreased by screwing in the cable adjuster.

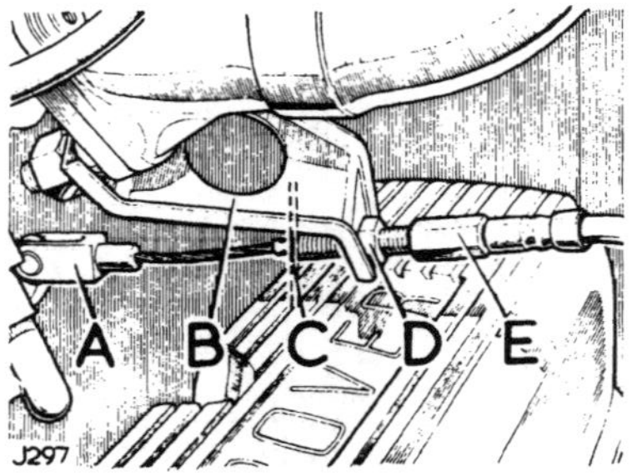

Downshift cable

A—Clevis for cable
B—Bracket for cable
C—.010 in. (0,25 mm) clearance between crimped stop and adjuster
D—Locknut for adjuster
E—Adjuster for cable

Operations which are identified by an asterisk (*) can be carried out with the automatic transmission installed in the car

Operation EEE2-3—*continued*

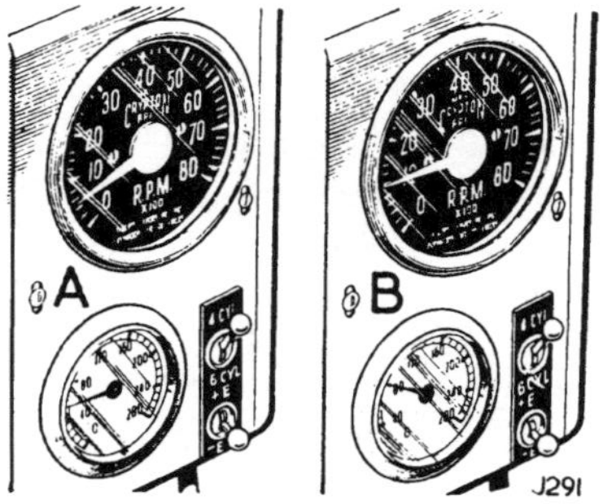

Pressure reading using test gauge

A— 600 rpm—approximate pressure: 60 lb/sq in. (4,2 kg/cm²)
B—1000 rpm—approximate pressure: 80 lb/sq in. (5,6 kg/cm²)

Method B

Adjusting downshift valve cable, visual method

1. Drain the fluid from the transmission oil pan and remove the oil pan. Operation EEE2-7.
2. Ensure that the accelerator pedal is fully released and that the carburetter butterfly is fully closed.

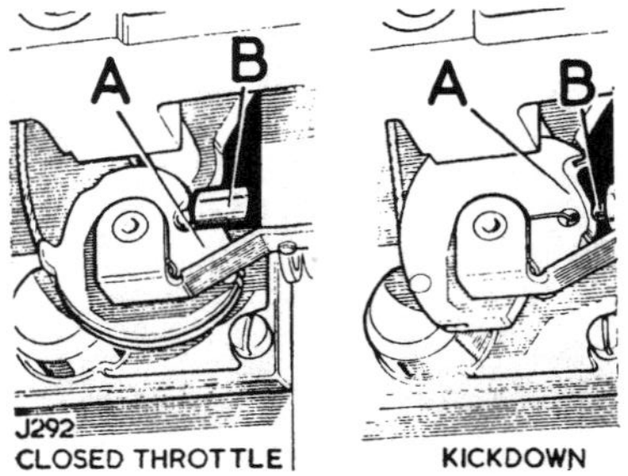

Downshift valve cable adjustment, visual method

Closed throttle { A—Heel of the cam; B—Downshift valve }
Kickdown { A—Constant radius of cam; B—Downshift valve }

3. Check the position of the downshift valve cam; the heel of the cam should contact the full diameter of the downshift valve, with all the slack of the inner cable taken up.
4. With accelerator pedal fully depressed to kick-down position and the carburetter butterfly fully open, the constant radius area of the valve cam should be the point of contact with the downshift valve.

Fluid level, automatic transmission—every 5,000 miles (8.000 km)—Operation EEE2-4

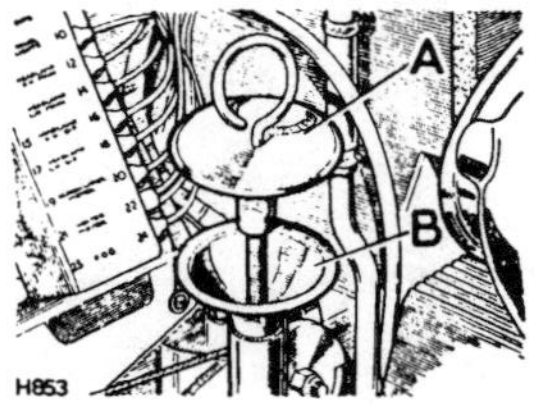

Fluid level dipstick plug in engine compartment

A—Dipstick B—Tube for dipstick

The torque converter and automatic gearbox are lubricated as one unit. As the fluid for operating the torque converter is fed from the transmission casing it is essential when checking the level or topping-up the automatic gearbox that the engine is run at idling speed for about two minutes to transfer fluid from transmission casing to torque converter, otherwise a false level reading will be obtained. Do not add anti-friction additives to the automatic transmission fluid. Check as follows:

1. Absolute cleanliness is essential. Use only nylon rag for cleaning.
2. Stand car on level ground, engine idling and selector at the 'P' position.
3. Lift bonnet to expose dipstick, which is adjacent to the windscreen washer bottle.
4. Clean area around dipstick and oil filler hole. Remove dipstick, wipe dry and check fluid level. Take the dipstick reading immediately after the dipstick has been fully inserted to avoid mis-readings by splashing. The difference between full and low marks on dipstick represents approximately one pint (0,5 litre). See paragraph 6.
5. With the engine idling and the selector at 'P', add the recommended grade of fluid to bring the level up to the 'full' mark. Do not overfill.
6. When the transmission is hot, top up to the upper mark on the side of the dipstick marked 'HOT'. With transmission cold, top up to the upper mark on the side of the dipstick marked 'COLD'. It is most important to ascertain if the transmission is hot or cold when topping up and to use the appropriate mark, otherwise overfilling or under-filling will result.
7. If significant topping-up is required, check for leakage at oil seals and sump joint; rectify immediately.

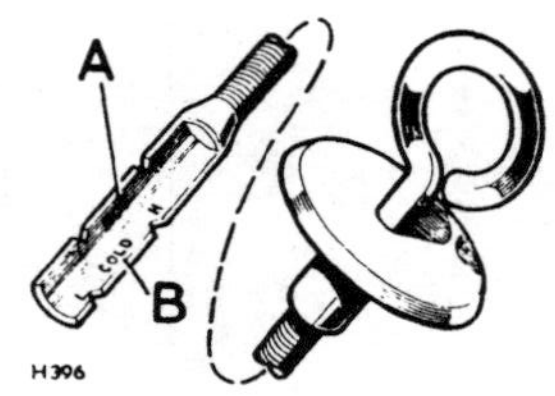

Fluid level dipstick

A—Transmission cold, top up to upper mark on 'COLD' side of dipstick
B—Transmission hot, top up to upper mark on 'HOT' side of dipstick

Automatic transmission, remove and refit—Operation EEE2-5

This operation does NOT involve removal of the engine from the car

Workshop hand tools:

Spanner sizes:

Open-ended $\frac{7}{16}$ in. AF, $\frac{1}{2}$ in. AF, $\frac{9}{16}$ in. AF, $1\frac{5}{16}$ in. AF

Sockets $\frac{1}{2}$ in. AF, $\frac{9}{16}$ in. AF

Pliers, long-nosed   Allen key $\frac{3}{16}$ in. AF

High standards of cleanliness are required when working on the automatic transmission. Before attempting to remove or dismantle the unit, clean the outside of the transmission case thoroughly with petrol/paraffin or an industrial cleaning solvent.

Place the car on a suitable floor lifting hoist, but carry out the prior operations before raising the car

Automatic transmission, remove

1. Unscrew the knob from the top of the gear selector lever.
2. Lift off the plastic indicator cover for gear selector lever.
3. Remove the Phillips' screw securing the trim panel to the top of the transmission tunnel and lift off trim panel.

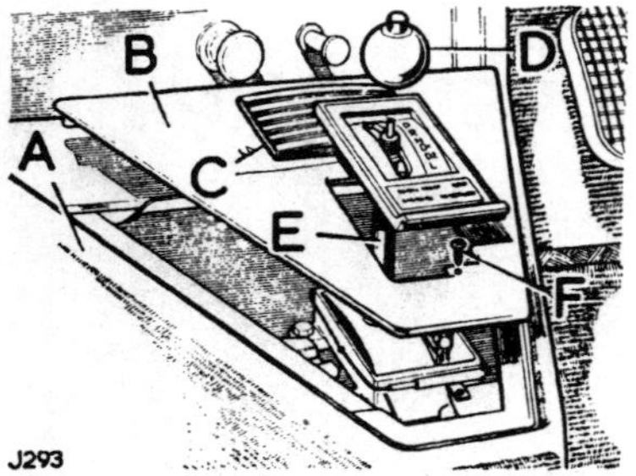

Trim panel

A—Transmission tunnel
B—Trim panel
C—Indicator plate
D—Knob for gear selector lever
E—Gear selector lever
F—Screw fixing trim panel

4. Push the two front seats back as far as they will go.
5. Remove the two nuts, spring washers and plain washers securing the gearbox console to the tunnel cover. Lift the rear of the console and draw out; at this stage the wiring harness can be disconnected from the cigar lighter and fog lamp switch. Withdraw the console unit complete from the car.
6. Disconnect wiring from gear selector indicator lamp.
7. Move the gear selector lever to the fully forward position and remove the three bolts, spring and plain washers securing the gear selector lever housing to the gearbox tunnel cover. Lift off the housing, and allow the gear selector lever to rest on top of the gearbox.

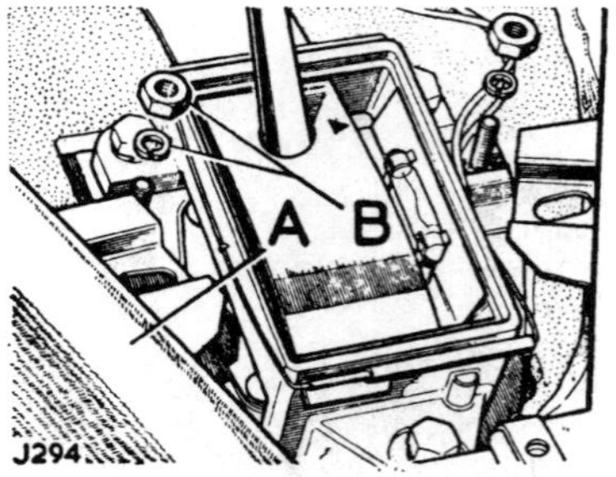

Console unit

A—Console unit
B—Nut and spring washer fixing console unit

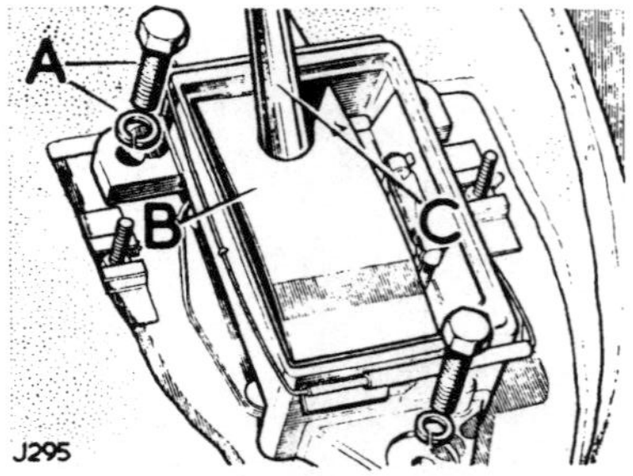

Gear selector lever

A—Bolt and spring washer fixing housing
B—Housing for gear selector lever
C—Gear selector lever

8. Remove remainder of floor carpet from the front end of tunnel cover.

Operation EEE2-5—*continued*

9. Remove 18 bolts and washers securing tunnel cover to body and lift off tunnel cover.
10. The gear linkage vertical rod should be disconnected at the ball joint on the selector lever on the gearbox. The three bolts securing the compensator bracket assembly to the bell housing should be removed; the complete gear selector linkage can then be lifted clear.

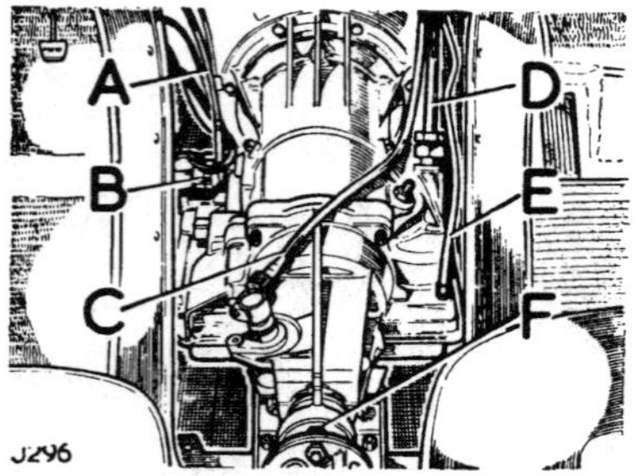

Gear selector mechanism

A—Downshift cable
B—Inhibitor switch
C—Speedometer cable
D—Oil filler tube
E—Oil cooler pipes
F—Propeller shaft fixing bolts

11. Disconnect the speedometer cable from the drive unit at the rear of the gearbox.
12. Remove the four bolts securing the propshaft to the drive flange.
13. Disconnect the union nuts securing the dipstick filler tube to the gearbox.
14. Disconnect the wiring from the inhibitor switch and release it from the clip on the bell housing.
15. Disconnect the oil cooler pipe unions at the gearbox.

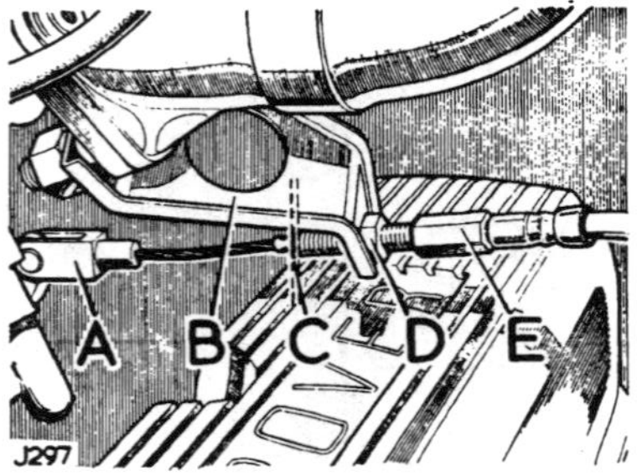

Downshift cable

A—Clevis for cable
B—Bracket for cable
C—.010 in. (0,25 mm) clearance between crimped stop and adjuster
D—Locknut for adjuster
E—Adjuster for cable

16. Disconnect the downshift cable from the bracket on the inlet manifold.
17. Raise the car on a suitable hoist.

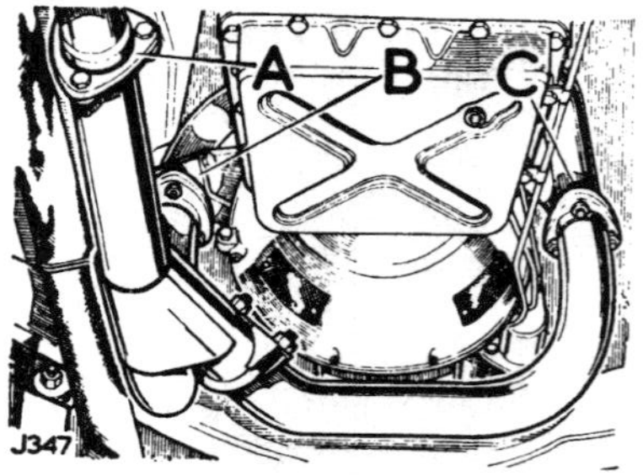

Exhaust pipe

A—Coupling, front pipe to intermediate pipe
B—Coupling at manifold, left-hand
C—Coupling at manifold, right-hand

Operation EEE2-5—*continued*

18. Remove the front exhaust pipe complete by disconnecting at the two flanges on the right-hand and left-hand exhaust manifolds, and also at the flange coupling the front exhaust pipe to the intermediate exhaust pipe.
19. Remove the two bolts and spring washers securing the fuel line clips to the gearbox sump.
20. Support the rear end of the engine, using a suitable block, and remove the bolts securing the rear mounting to the chassis and the nuts and washers securing the rear mounting bracket to the gearbox, and withdraw the rear mounting complete.
21. Release the two oil cooler pipes from the clips alongside the engine sump.

Rear mounting transmission

A—Rear mounting C—Propellor shaft
B—Speedometer cable D—Rods for gear selector

22. Remove the six bolts securing the transmission to the bell housing. Support the transmission and draw it rearwards; care should be taken at this stage because of oil which will be released from the torque converter as the transmission is drawn rearwards. To remove the transmission, the rear end should be raised into the car until the shaft at the front is clear of the torque converter; the complete transmission assembly can then be lowered from under the car.

Automatic transmission, refit

1. It will be found advantageous when refitting the unit to provide some means of lifting the transmission unit into position in order to avoid any undue strain on the front pump drive flanges or the front oil seal.

   One method is to make an extension tube of suitable length to fit a hydraulic trolley jack with a platform on which the transmission unit can be safely supported.
2. Make sure that the driving flanges on the torque converter and the corresponding drive slots on the transmission front pump are positioned in the same relative alignment; this will ensure correct and easy engagement of the transmission unit to the torque converter.
3. Raise gearbox into position by lifting the tail end up into the car and then gently easing the unit forward until the splines and the front pump drive engage. Fit the six retaining bolts.
4. Refit rear mounting. The slots are provided in this for alignment.
5. Reverse removal procedure for the remaining items.
6. Tightening torque—transmission case to bell housing: 8 to 10 lb ft (1,0 to 1,4 mkg).

Operation EEE2-5—*continued*

7. Refill the torque converter and automatic transmission with a suitable oil in the following manner:
   (a) Quantity—10 Imperial pints (12 US pints, 5,5 litres) transmission fluid of the recommended grade.
   (b) The car should be on a level surface.
   (c) Select 'P' and allow engine to idle for two minutes.
   (d) Add fluid in small quantities. With engine still idling in 'P', wipe dipstick with a non-fluffy rag or clean paper and take frequent readings by inserting the dipstick and withdrawing it immediately.

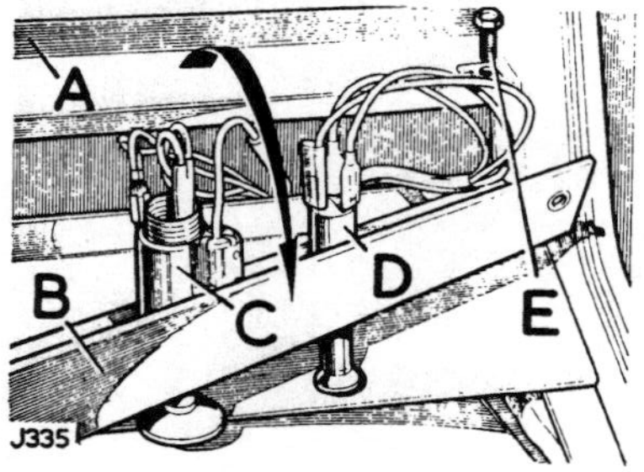

Switch panel

A—Console unit D—Fog lamp switch
B—Switch panel E—Bolt-fixing console unit
C—Cigar lighter
Remove panel in direction of arrow

   (e) With the transmission 'cold', fill to the 'high' mark on the side of the dipstick marked 'cold'.

   Capacity of transmission unit from dry: 14 Imperial pints (17 US pints, 8 litres).
8. If necessary, check and adjust the following:
   (a) Gear selector linkage. Operation EEE2-1.
   (b) Starter inhibitor switch. Operation EEE2-2.
   (c) Downshift valve cable. Operation EEE2-3.

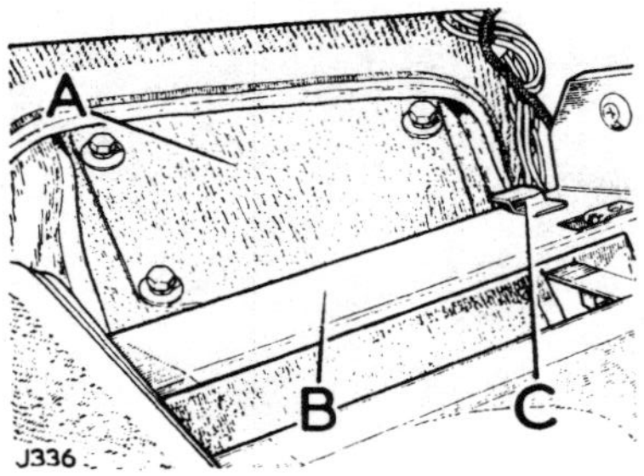

Console unit, front end fixing

A—Panel on transmission tunnel
B—Console unit
C—Clip fixing console unit

Torque converter and bell housing, remove and refit—Operation EEE2-6

Workshop hand tools:
Spanner sizes:
Open-ended $\frac{1}{2}$ in. AF, $\frac{7}{16}$ in. AF, $\frac{9}{16}$ in. AF, $1\frac{5}{16}$ in. AF
Sockets $\frac{1}{2}$ in. AF, $\frac{9}{16}$ in. AF
Allen key $\frac{3}{16}$ in. AF   Pliers, long-nosed

Torque converter and bell housing, remove

1. Disconnect battery terminal.
2. Remove automatic transmission. Operation EEE2-5.
3. Remove bell housing.

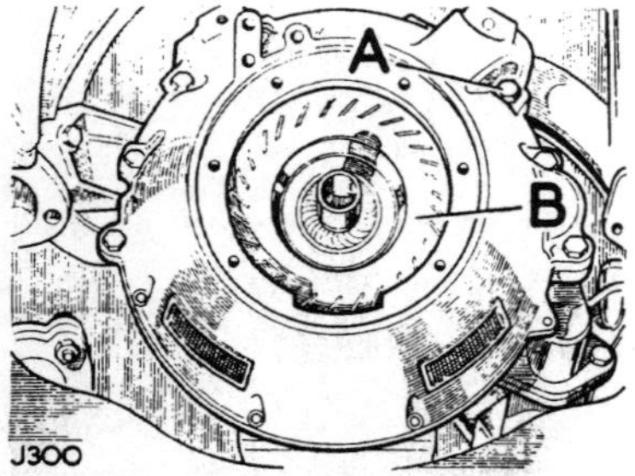

Bell housing and torque converter
A—Bolt fixing bell housing
B—Torque converter

4. Remove front cover plate.
5. Turn engine and remove the four bolts retaining the torque converter.

   Ensure that the torque converter is supported while the four fixing bolts are removed. Withdraw unit, taking care as a certain amount of oil will be retained in the torque converter.

Torque converter and bell housing, refit

1. The removal procedure should be reversed, ensuring that the bolts fixing the bell housing to the flywheel housing are tightened **before** the bolts fixing the torque converter to the flexible drive plate.
2. Tightening torques:
   (a) Bell housing to flexible drive plate housing: 30 lb ft (4,0 mkg).
   (b) Torque converter to engine drive plate: 32 lb ft (4,4 mkg).
3. Refill with fluid of the recommended grade. Capacity: 14 Imperial pints (17 US pints, 8 litres).

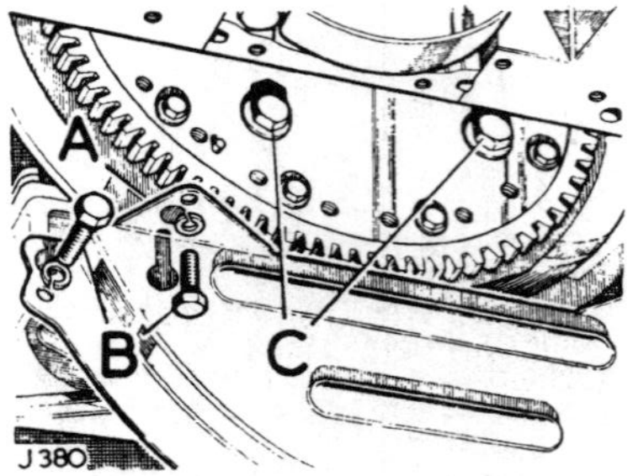

Torque converter fixing bolts
A—Front cover plate
B—Bolt for torque converter
C—Bolt fixing torque converter

*Oil pan and valve bodies, remove and refit—Operation EEE2-7

Workshop hand tools:
Spanner sizes:
Open-ended $\frac{7}{16}$ in. AF, $\frac{1}{2}$ in. AF
Sockets $\frac{7}{16}$ in. AF, $\frac{1}{2}$ in. AF
Screwdriver, large   Pliers, long-nosed
Allen key $\frac{1}{4}$ in. AF

Special tools:
Gearbox cradle, Rover Part No. 601280
Torque wrench set, Rover Part No. 601285

Instructions for overhauling the valve bodies are given in Part Three of this Section

Oil pan and valve bodies, remove

Operations 1 and 2 apply only if the unit is fitted to the car

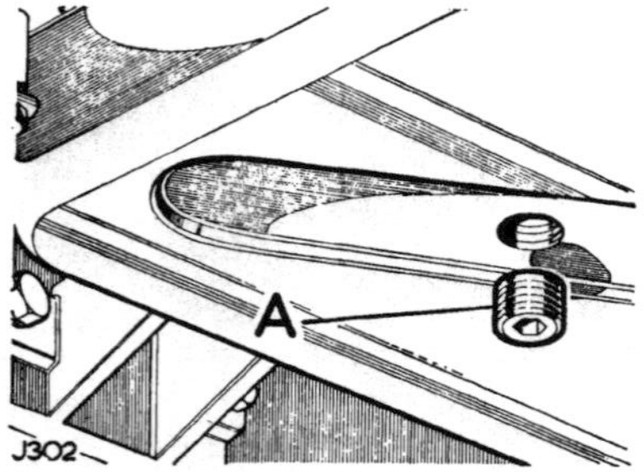

Oil drain plug
A—Oil drain plug

1. Remove the oil drain plug and allow fluid to drain away. Take great care if the car has just returned from a run as the fluid will be hot enough to cause scalding.

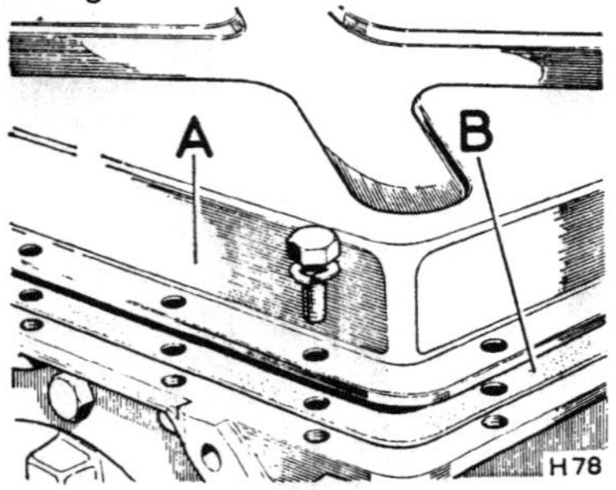

Removing the oil pan
A—Oil pan   B—Gasket for oil pan

2. When the oil has been drained, replace the oil drain plug. It is not possible to completely drain the oil pan.
3. Remove the oil pan and gasket, secured by 15 bolts and spring washers. Drain off remainder of the oil.

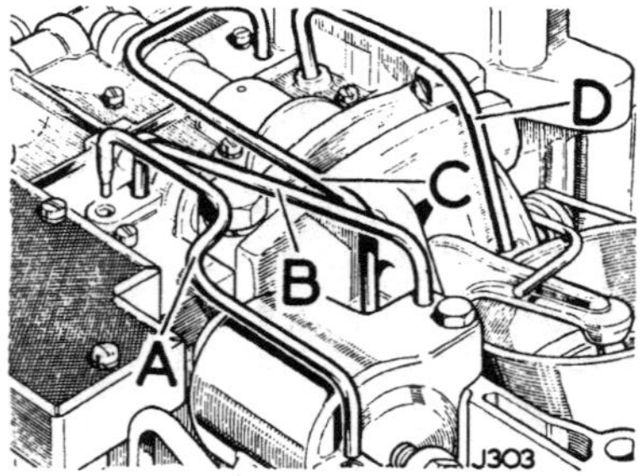

Location of oil tubes in valve body
A—Tube, front servo release   C—Tube, rear clutch
B—Tube, front servo apply   D—Tube, rear servo

4. Withdraw the four oil tubes from the valve bodies assembly. These tubes are a push fit into their respective locations and should be removed by carefully levering out of position with a screwdriver. Take care that no distortion or damage is caused to the tubes.
5. If unit is still fitted to the car, disconnect the downshift cable at the throttle end. Pull the downshift valve cam forwards, as indicated by the arrow, and release the cable at the valve bodies end.

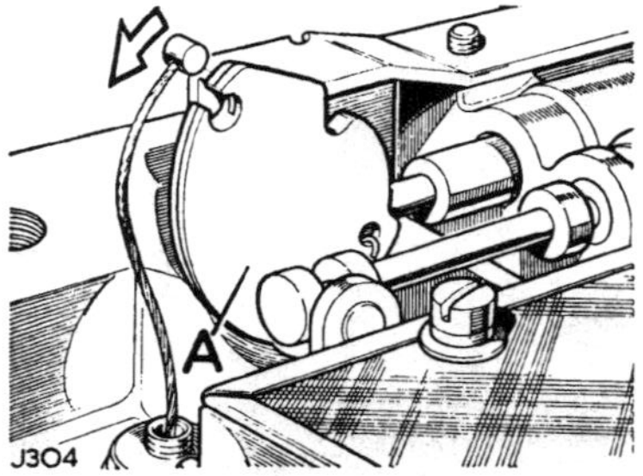

Downshift valve cam and cable
A—Cable for downshift valve

Operations which are identified by an asterisk (*) can be carried out with the automatic transmission installed in the car

Operation EEE2-7—*continued*

6. Lift off the valve bodies assembly, which is secured by three bolts and spring washers. Take care not to disturb the oil tubes located between the valve body and front pump casing.

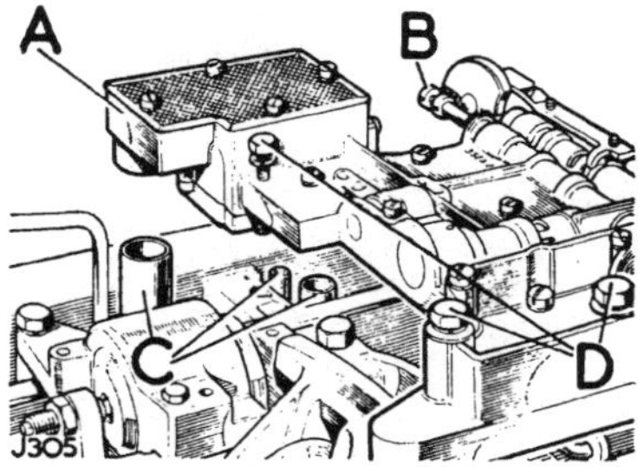

Valve bodies assembly

A—Valve bodies
B—Manual control valve
C—Oil tubes
D—Bolts fixing valve bodies

Oil pan and valve bodies, refit

1. When placing the valve bodies into position, ensure that the oil tubes between valve body and front pump casing are correctly located, flange on front pump inlet tube must be towards front pump, and that the peg on the manual valve detent lever engages in the groove of the manual control valve.

   If the oil tubes have been inadvertently disturbed, it is important that the 'O' ring, which is located at the pump end of the front pump inlet tube, is not omitted or dropped into the transmission casing.

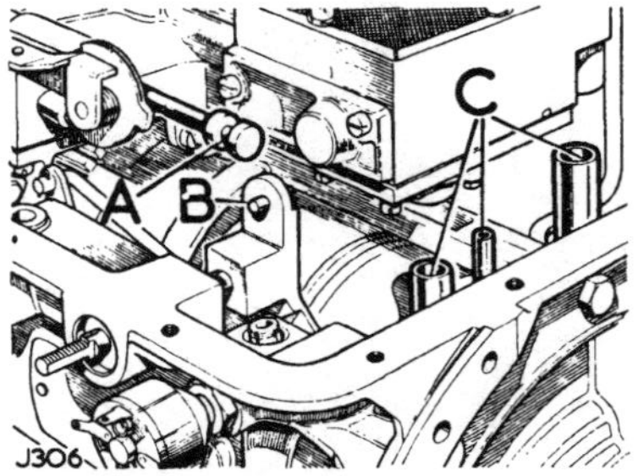

Engaging groove of manual control valve with peg on detent lever

A—Groove in manual control valve
B—Peg on detent lever
C—Oil tubes

2. Tighten the valve bodies, securing bolts to a torque of 4 to 5 lb ft (0,55 to 0,7 mkg).
3. Pull downshift valve cam forward, as indicated by the arrow, and connect the cable. Reconnect cable at accelerator end if unit is still fitted to vehicle.
4. Replace the four oil tubes. Ensure that they are pushed firmly into position, and that the restricted end of tube, front servo release, is inserted into the valve bodies assembly.
5. Check adjustment of downshift cable in accordance with method 'B'. Operation EEE2-3.
6. Use a new oil pan gasket and locate it on transmission casing with petroleum jelly. Fit oil pan and tighten the bolts to a torque figure of 8 to 10 lb ft (1,0 to 1,4 mkg).
7. If the above operation has been carried out with the unit in the vehicle, refill with fluid of the recommended grade. Capacity: 14 Imperial pints (17 US pints, 8 litres).

*Front servo, remove, refit and adjust—Operation EEE2-8

Workshop hand tools:
Spanner sizes:
Open-ended $\frac{7}{16}$ in. AF, $\frac{1}{2}$ in. AF, $\frac{9}{16}$ in. AF
Sockets $\frac{1}{2}$ in. AF, $\frac{9}{16}$ in. AF
Screwdriver, large Allen key $\frac{1}{4}$ in. AF

Special tools:
Gearbox cradle, Rover Part No. 601280
Torque wrench set, Rover Part No. 601285
Spintorq screwdriver set, Rover Part No. 601286
Front servo gauge, Rover Part No. 601287

Instructions for overhauling the front servo are given in Part Three of this Section

Front servo, remove

Operations 1 and 2 apply only if the unit is fitted to the car

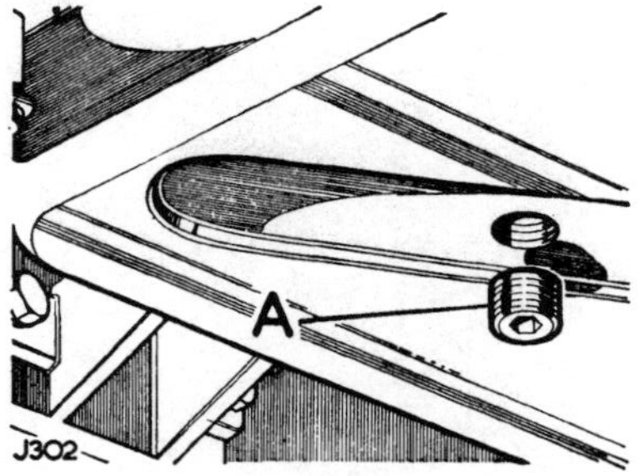

Oil drain plug

A—Oil drain plug

1. Remove the oil drain plug and allow fluid to drain away. Take great care if the car has just returned from a run as the fluid will be hot enough to cause scalding.
2. When the fluid has drained, refit the plug. It is not possible to completely drain the oil pan.
3. Remove the oil pan and gasket, secured by 15 bolts and spring washers. Drain off remainder of oil.
4. Withdraw the two oil tubes fitted between front servo and valve bodies. These tubes are a push fit into their locations. If necessary, very carefully lever them out, using a screwdriver. Take care not to cause distortion or damage.

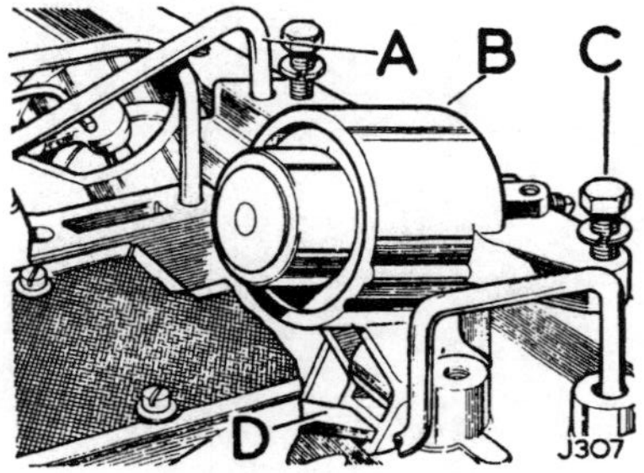

Front servo, removing oil tubes

A—Oil tube, front servo apply
B—Front servo
C—Bolt fixing servo
D—Strut for servo

5. Slacken locknut and adjusting screw to relieve tension and remove the front servo, retained by two bolts and spring washers.

   Take care not to lose the servo strut, which is a loose item.

Front servo, refit

1. Install the servo into the main casing. To facilitate location of the servo strut, attach it to the servo lever with petroleum jelly and ensure that it engages with the slot in the brake band. Tighten the two servo fixing bolts to a torque figure of 8 to 10 lb ft (1,0 to 1,4 mkg).
2. Replace the oil tubes. Ensure that they are pushed firmly into position, and that the restricted end of tube, front servo release, is inserted into the valve bodies assembly.

Operations which are identified by an asterisk (*) can be carried out with the automatic transmission installed in the car

Operation EEE2-8—*continued*

Front servo, adjusting the brake band

The oil pan must be removed to enable the front servo to be adjusted.

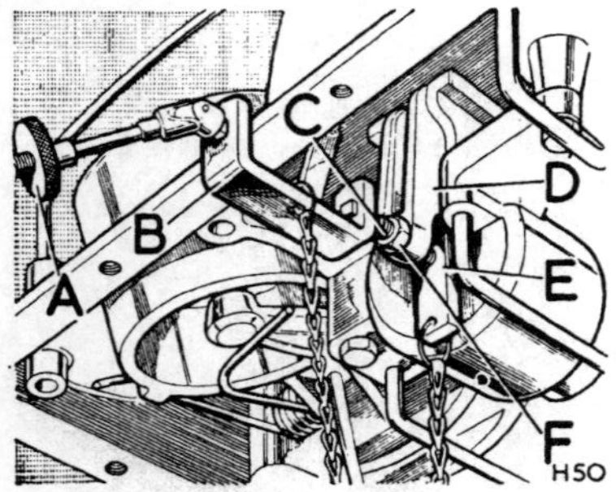

Front brake band, adjust

A—Spintorq screwdriver
B—Adaptor
C—Adjusting screw for front servo
D—Servo lever
E—Gauge block
F—Locknut for servo adjusting screw

1. Slacken the locknut and unscrew the adjuster. Pull the servo lever outwards and place the front servo gauge between the adjusting screw and the servo piston pin.
2. Tighten the servo lever adjusting screw to a torque figure of 10 lb in. (0,11 mkg), using the Spintorq screwdriver and the adaptor attached tc the gauge block, together with the universal joint.
3. Using a screwdriver between servo body and adjuster lever, release pressure from gauge block and withdraw it.
4. Tighten adjuster lever locknut to a torque figure of 15 to 20 lb ft (2,0 to 2,8 mkg).
5. Use a new oil pan gasket and locate it on transmission casing with petroleum jelly. Fit oil pan and tighten the bolts to a torque figure of 8 to 10 lb ft (1,0 to 1,4 mkg).
6. If the operation has been carried out with the unit in the vehicle, refill with the recommended grade of fluid. Capacity: 14 Imperial pints (17 US pints, 8 litres).

*Rear servo, remove, refit and adjust—Operation EEE2-9

Workshop hand tools:
Spanner sizes:
Open-ended $\frac{7}{16}$ in. AF, $\frac{1}{2}$ in. AF, $\frac{3}{4}$ in. AF
Sockets $\frac{1}{2}$ in. AF, $\frac{9}{16}$ in. AF, $\frac{3}{4}$ in. AF
Screwdriver, large Allen key $\frac{1}{4}$ in. AF

Special tools:
Gearbox cradle, Rover Part No. 601280
Torque wrench set, Rover Part No. 601285

Instructions for overhauling the rear servo are given in Part Three of this Section

Rear servo, remove

Operations 1 and 2 apply only if the unit is fitted to the car

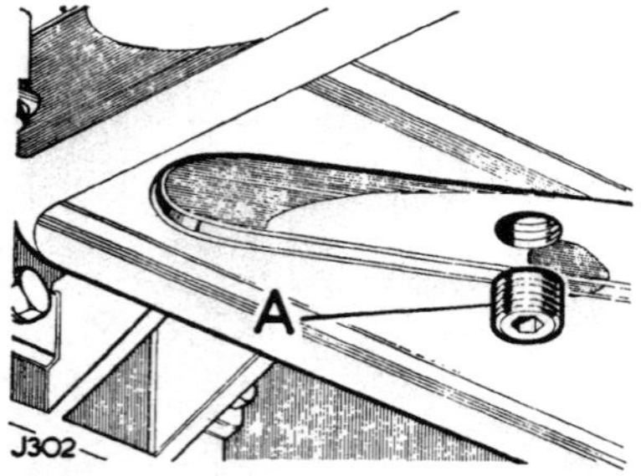

Oil drain plug

A—Oil drain plug

1. Remove the oil drain plug and allow fluid to drain away. Take great care if the car has just returned from a run as the fluid will be hot enough to cause scalding.
2. When the oil has drained, replace the drain plug. It is not possible to completely drain the oil pan.
3. Remove the oil pan, secured by 15 bolts and spring washers. Drain off remainder of oil.
4. Withdraw the oil tubes between the rear servo and valve body, rear clutch to valve body and front servo to valve body. They are a push fit into their respective locations. If necessary, very carefully lever out, using a screwdriver. Take care not to cause distortion or damage.
5. Lift off the magnet from the rear bolt, then remove the servo retained by two bolts and spring washers. Note that the longer bolt is special as it has a dowel end to locate the centre support. Take care not to lose the servo strut, which is a loose item.

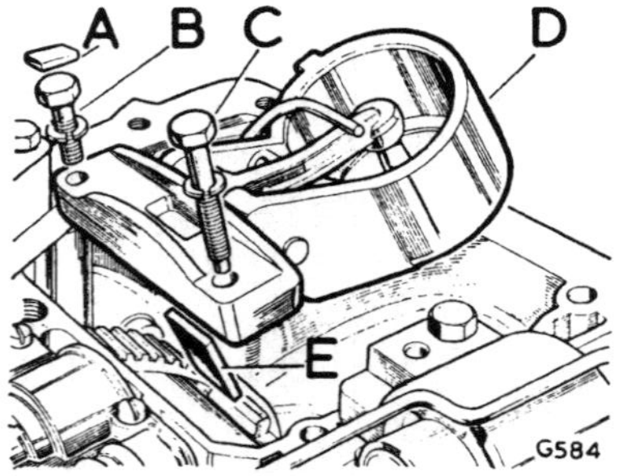

Rear servo, remove

A—Magnet
B—Bolt fixing servo, short
C—Special bolt fixing servo
D—Rear servo
E—Strut for rear servo

Rear servo, refit

1. Install the rear servo into the transmission case. Ensure that the brake band is located on the head of the adjustment bolt. To facilitate location of the servo strut, attach it to the servo lever with petroleum jelly; make sure that the strut engages with the slot in the brake band. The special bolt must be fitted into the hole adjacent to the centre cross-support of the transmission case. The magnet should be located on the head of the rear bolt. Tighten the two fixing bolts to a torque figure of 10 to 13 lb ft (1,4 to 1,7 mkg).
2. Replace the oil tubes. Ensure that they are pushed firmly into position.
3. Use a new oil pan gasket and locate it on the transmission casing with petroleum jelly. Fit oil pan and tighten the bolts to a torque figure of 8 to 10 lb ft (1,0 to 1,4 mkg).

Operations which are identified by an asterisk (*) can be carried out with the automatic transmission installed in the car

Operation EEE2-9—*continued*

Rear servo, adjusting the brake band

1. The adjuster for the rear band servo is located on the outside of the transmission case. When the unit is fitted in the car, the adjuster is accessible from inside the car by removing the tunnel cover.

2. Slacken the locknut of the adjusting screw.

3. Using the torque wrench adaptor, tighten the adjusting screw to a torque figure of 10 lb ft (1,4 mkg), then turn it back one complete turn and tighten the locknut to 25 to 30 lb ft (3,5 to 4,0 mkg).

4. If the operation has been carried out with the unit in vehicle, replace the rubber grommet and carpet, then refill unit with recommended grade of fluid. Capacity: 14 Imperial pints (17 US pints, 8 litres).

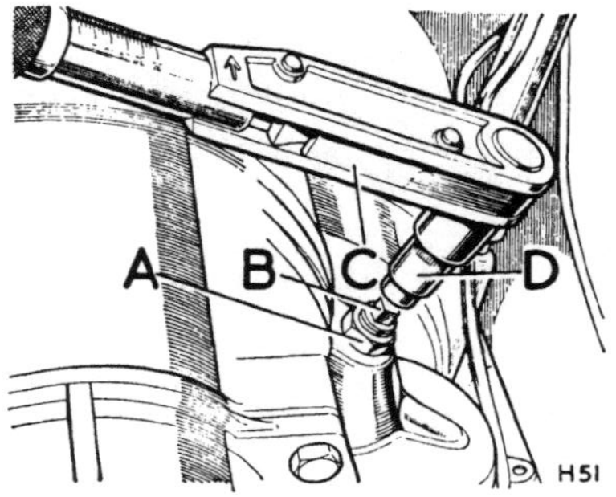

Rear brake band, adjust

A—Locknut for adjuster
B—External adjusting screw
C—Adaptor for torque wrench
D—Torque wrench

Front pump, remove and refit—Operation EEE2-10

Workshop hand tools:
Spanner sizes:
Open-ended $\frac{7}{16}$ in. AF, $\frac{1}{2}$ in. AF
Sockets $\frac{7}{16}$ in. AF, $\frac{1}{2}$ in. AF
Screwdriver, large Feeler gauges
Allen key $\frac{1}{4}$ in. AF

Special tools:
Gearbox cradle, Rover Part No. 601280
Torque wrench set, Rover Part No. 601285
End-play checking tool, Rover Part No. 601281, or dial test indicator

Instructions for overhauling the front pump are given in Part Three of this Section

Instructions for the removal of the unit from the car are given in Operation EEE2-5

Front pump, remove

1. Remove the oil pan and valve bodies. Operation EEE2-7.

2. Withdraw the oil tubes from the front pump assembly. These tubes are a push fit into their locations.

   Note that the front pump inlet tube has an 'O' ring seal on the end that locates into the front pump assembly; this 'O' ring must be renewed.

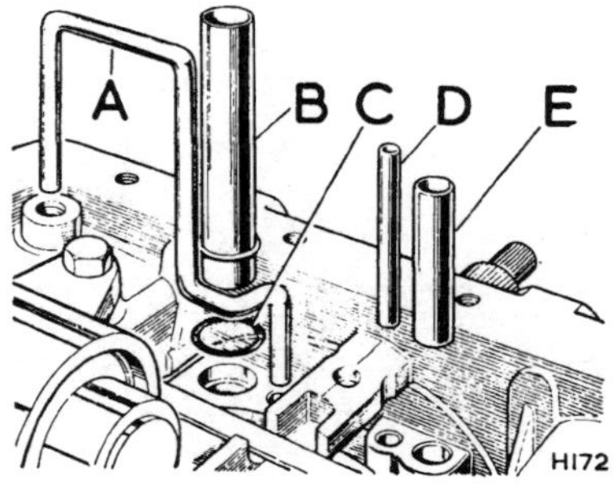

Front pump and converter fluid tubes

A—Tube, converter outlet
B—Tube, front pump inlet
C—'O' ring seal for front pump inlet tube
D—Tube, converter inlet
E—Tube, front pump outlet

3. At this stage measure the gear train end-float. This measurement must be made before the removal of the front pump so that compensation for thrust washer wear may be made on re-assembly. Thrust washers are available in two thicknesses: .061 to .063 in. (1,54 to 1,6 mm) and .078 to .080 in. (1,97 to 2,03 mm).

   Two methods of measuring the end-float are illustrated, depending upon the tools used.

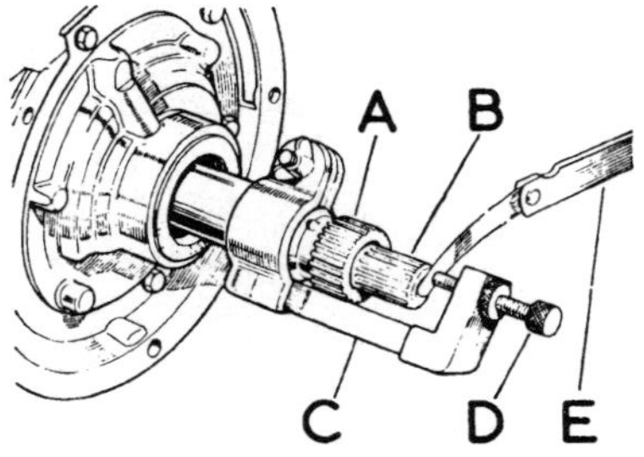

Measuring gear train end-play, using feeler gauges

A—Converter support tube
B—Input shaft
C—End-play checking tool
D—Adjusting screw
E—Feeler gauge

Feeler gauge method, using end-play checking tool, Rover Part No. 601281

(a) Clamp the tool on to the converter support tube.
(b) Pull the input shaft outwards and adjust the abutment screw to just contact the end of the shaft. Tighten knurled locknut.
(c) Push the input shaft inwards and measure the gap between screw and shaft, using feeler gauges.
(d) The permissible end-float is .010 to .030 in. (0,25 to 0,75 mm). If the reading is outside the permissible limit, a new thrust washer must be fitted on reassembly.
(e) Remove end-play checking tool.

Dial test indicator method

(a) Clamp the dial test indicator bracket to one of the holes in the main casing flange.
(b) With the knob of the dial indicator touching the end of the shaft, push the shaft inwards.
(c) Zero the indicator, then pull the shaft outwards and note the reading; the permissible end-float is .010 to .030 in. (0,25 to 0,75 mm). If the reading is outside the permissible limit, a new thrust washer must be fitted on reassembly.

Operation EEE2-10—*continued*

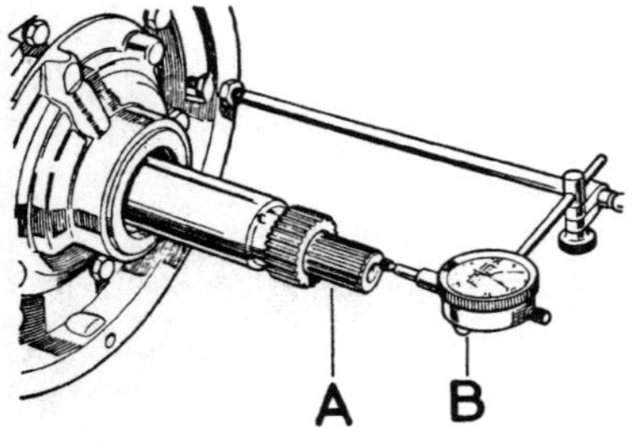

Measuring gear train end-play, using dial test indicator

A—Input shaft B—Dial test indicator

5. Now remove front pump, secured by six bolts and spring washers. Hold the input shaft inwards whilst withdrawing the front pump assembly from the main casing, to ensure that the front clutch is not disengaged from the rear clutch assembly.
6. Discard the paper gasket.
7. Retain the tabbed thrust washer, located behind the front pump assembly if the end-float of the gears was within the limits .010 to .030 in. (0,25 to 0,75 mm).

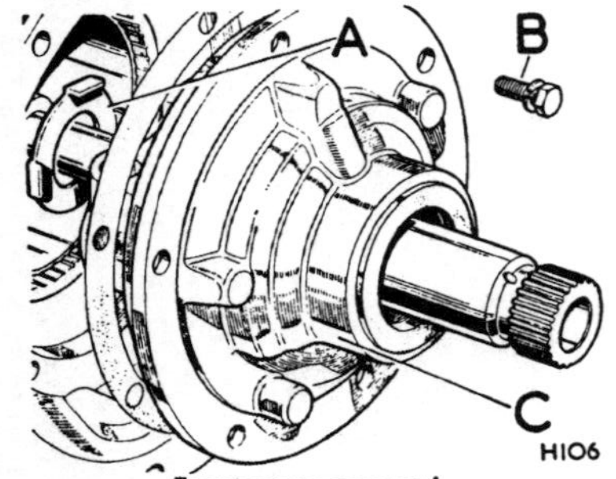

Front pump removal

A—Tabbed thrust washer B—Bolts for front pump C—Front pump

Front pump, refit

1. Fit a new paper gasket between the front pump and the transmission case. Locate the gasket on transmission case with petroleum jelly.
2. If necessary, correct the gear train end-float. Thrust washers are selective and available in two sizes: .061 to .063 in. (1,54 to 1,6 mm) and .078 to .080 in. (1,97 to 2,3 mm). Locate the thrust washer on to the pump with petroleum jelly.
3. Check the gear train end-float.
4. Fit the front pump to the transmission case with the oil tube locations facing the valve body. Tighten the six mounting bolts to a torque figure of 8 to 10 lb ft (1,0 to 1,4 mkg).
5. Fit new 'O' ring to the large tube and insert the tube with 'O' ring in the pump. Refit the remaining three tubes.
6. Refit oil pan and valve bodies. Operation EEE2-7.

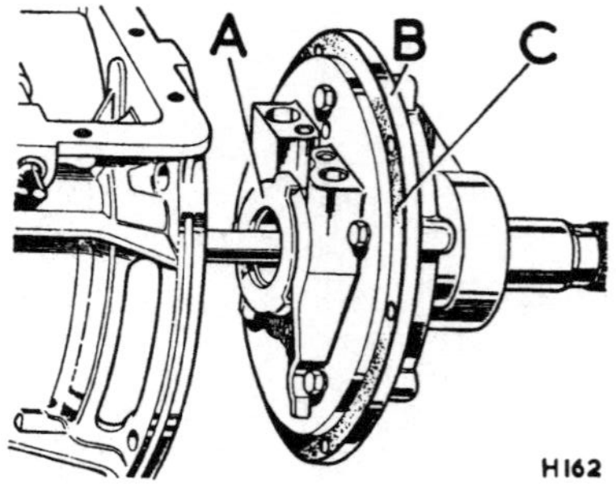

Front pump, refit

A—Thrust washer for front pump
B—Front pump C—Gasket for front pump

Front brake band, remove and refit—Operation EEE2-11

Workshop hand tools:
Spanner sizes:
Open-ended $\frac{7}{16}$ in. AF, $\frac{1}{2}$ in. AF
Sockets $\frac{7}{16}$ in. AF, $\frac{1}{2}$ in. AF, $\frac{9}{16}$ in. AF
Screwdriver, small Screwdriver, large
Feeler gauges Allen key $\frac{1}{4}$ in. AF

Special tools:
Gearbox cradle, Rover Part No. 601280
Torque wrench set, Rover Part No. 601285
End-play checking tool, Rover Part No. 601281, or dial test indicator

Front brake band, remove

1. Take off the oil pan and valve bodies assembly. Operation EEE2-7.
2. Remove the front servo. Operation EEE2-8.
3. Remove the front pump. Operation EEE2-10.
4. Withdraw the brake band through the front of the main casing; take care not to disturb the front clutch and input shaft.

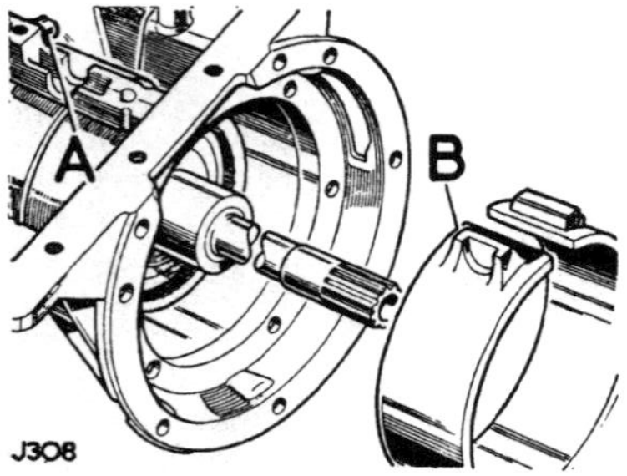

Withdrawing front brake band

A—Support pin in transmission casing
B—Front brake band

Front brake band, refit

1. Reverse removal procedure, ensuring that the brake band is fitted into the transmission case with the larger external lug located on the support pin in the casing.
2. Tightening torques:
   Bolts, front pump to transmission casing, 8 to 10 lb ft (1,0 to 1,4 mkg).
   Bolts, front servo to transmission casing, 8 to 10 lb ft (1,0 to 1,4 mkg).
   Adjusting screw, front servo, 10 lb in. (0,11 mkg).
   Locknut, front servo adjuster screw, 15 to 20 lb ft (2,0 to 2,8 mkg).
   Bolts, valve bodies, 4 to 5 lb ft (0,55 to 0,7 mkg).
   Bolts, oil pan, 8 to 10 lb ft (1,0 to 1,4 mkg).

Front clutch, rear clutch and forward sun gear, remove and refit Operation EEE2-12

Workshop hand tools:
- Spanner sizes:
  - Open-ended $\frac{7}{16}$ in. AF, $\frac{1}{2}$ in. AF
  - Sockets $\frac{7}{16}$ in. AF, $\frac{1}{2}$ in. AF, $\frac{9}{16}$ in. AF
- Screwdriver, small Screwdriver, large
- Feeler gauges Allen key $\frac{1}{4}$ in. AF

Special tools:
- Gearbox cradle, Rover Part No. 601280
- Torque wrench set, Rover Part No. 601285
- End-play checking tool, Rover Part No. 601281, or dial test indicator

Instructions for overhauling the front clutch, rear clutch and forward sun gear are given in Part Three of this Section

Clutch assembly, remove

1. Remove oil pan and valve bodies. Operation EEE2-7.
2. Remove front servo. Operation EEE2-8.
3. Remove front pump. Operation EEE2-10.
4. Withdraw the front brake band.
5. Ease the rear clutch forward with a screwdriver, as illustrated, and withdraw the assembly of front and rear clutch out through the transmission case. Ensure that the needle thrust bearing and bearing plate, located on the forward sun gear shaft, have not dropped into the planetary gear set.

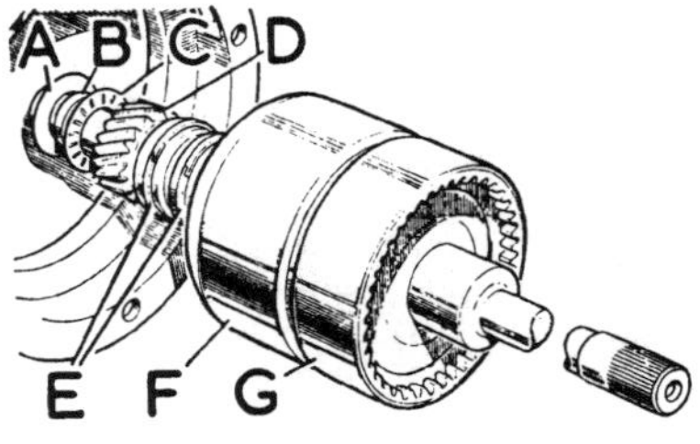

Installing front and rear clutch

A—Bearing plate
B—Nylon seal
C—Needle thrust bearing
D—Forward sun gear
E—Oil sealing rings, rear clutch to centre support
F—Rear clutch
G—Front clutch

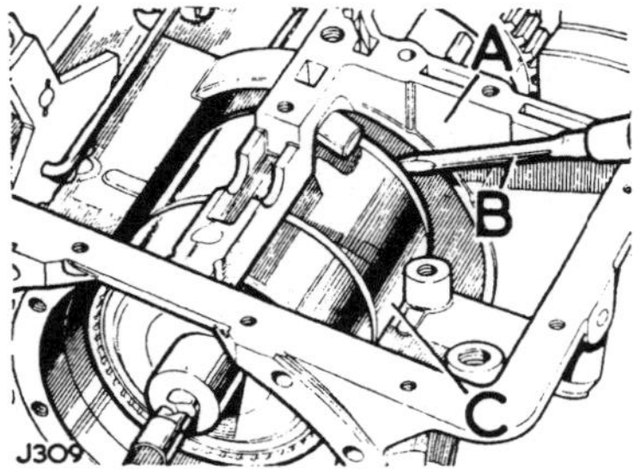

Front and rear clutch withdrawal

A—Centre support
B—Screwdriver, insert in position shown
C—Front and rear clutch assembly

6. Take care not to withdraw front clutch from rear clutch at this stage, unless some repair work is to be carried out on these units. If the units are inadvertently disengaged, see Part Three of this Section for assembly procedure.

Clutch assembly, refit

1. Fit a new nylon seal on the forward sun gear shaft, then locate the needle thrust bearing followed by the bearing plate, lip towards nylon seal. Ensure that oil sealing rings are correctly interlocked.
2. Then install the assembly of front and rear clutch. Turn output shaft to engage the gears of the planetary set.
3. Fit the brake band into the transmission case, with the larger external lug towards the support pin in the casing.
4. Then reverse removal procedure.
5. Tightening torques:
   - Bolts, front pump to transmission casing, 8 to 10 lb ft (1,0 to 1,4 mkg).
   - Adjusting screw, front servo, 10 lb in. (0,11 mkg).
   - Locknut, front servo adjuster screw, 15 to 20 lb ft (2,0 to 2,8 mkg).
   - Bolts, valve bodies, 4 to 5 lb ft (0,55 to 0,7 mkg).
   - Bolts, oil pan, 8 to 10 lb ft (1,0 to 1,4 mkg).
   - Bolts, front servo to transmission casing, 8 to 10 lb ft (1,0 to 1,4 mkg).

Centre support and planetary gears, remove and refit—Operation EEE2-13

Workshop hand tools:
- Spanner sizes:
  - Open-ended $\frac{7}{16}$ in. AF, $\frac{1}{2}$ in. AF
  - Sockets $\frac{7}{16}$ in. AF, $\frac{1}{2}$ in. AF, $\frac{9}{16}$ in. AF
- Screwdriver, small Screwdriver, large
- Feeler gauges Allen key $\frac{1}{4}$ in. AF

Special tools:
- Gearbox cradle, Rover Part No. 601280
- Torque wrench set, Rover Part No. 601285
- End-play checking tool, Rover Part No. 601281, or dial test indicator
- Spintorq screwdriver set, Rover Part No. 601286

Instructions for overhaul of centre support and planetary gears are given in Part Three of this Section

Centre support and planetary gears, remove

1. Take off the oil pan and valve bodies assembly. Operation EEE2-7.
2. Remove the front servo. Operation EEE2-8.
3. Remove the rear servo. Operation EEE2-9.
4. Remove the front pump. Operation EEE2-10.
5. Withdraw the front brake band. Operation EEE2-11.
6. Lift out the front and rear clutch, together with the forward sun gear assembly. Operation EEE2-12.
7. Remove the two special bolts and lock washers retaining the centre support. These fixings are located on the outside of the transmission case.
8. Withdraw the centre support and planetary gear through the front of the transmission case.
9. Note the needle thrust bearing and plate, located on the rear end of the planetary gear assembly.

Centre support and planetary gears, refit

1. Locate the lipped bearing plate on to the rear of the planet carrier with the lip facing rearward, followed by the needle thrust bearing. Locate in position with petroleum jelly.
2. Position centre support and planetary gears into transmission case.
3. It is most important that the centre support is correctly located. The fluid passages in the support must correspond with those in the main casing, that is, with three drillings towards the valve bodies.
4. The lock washers of the centre support bolts also act as oil retainers and must be fitted with the 'flat rim' facing the bolt head.

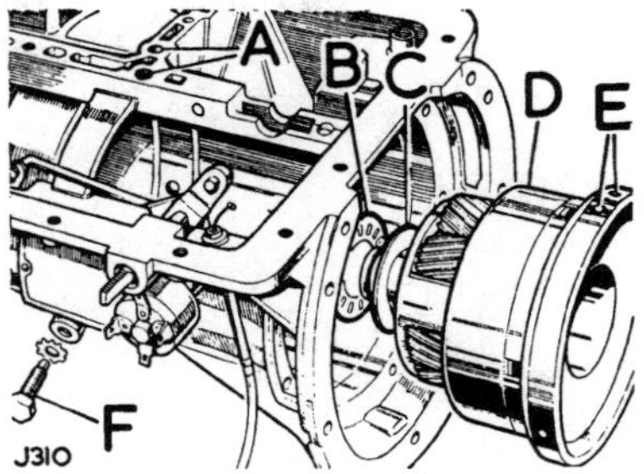

Locating centre support

A—Drillings in transmission casing
B—Needle thrust bearing
C—Thrust plate for needle bearing
D—Planet gear carrier
E—Drillings in centre support
F—Special fixing bolt for centre support

5. Tighten the centre support locating bolts to a torque figure of 10 to 13 lb ft (1,4 to 1,7 mkg).
6. Then reverse removal procedure.
7. Other tightening torques:
   - Bolts, front pump to transmission casing, 8 to 10 lb ft (1,0 to 1,4 mkg).
   - Bolts, front servo to transmission casing, 8 to 10 lb ft (1,0 to 1,4 mkg).
   - Bolts, rear servo to transmission casing, 10 to 13 lb ft (1,4 to 1,7 mkg).
   - Adjusting screw, front servo, 10 lb in. (0,11 mkg).
   - Adjusting screw, rear servo, 10 lb ft (1,4 mkg).
   - Locknut, front servo adjusting screw, 15 to 20 lb ft (2,0 to 2,8 mkg).
   - Locknut, rear servo adjusting screw, 25 to 30 lb ft (3,5 to 4,0 mkg).
   - Bolts, valve bodies, 4 to 5 lb ft (0,55 to 0,7 mkg).
   - Bolts, oil pan, 8 to 10 lb ft (1,0 to 1,4 mkg).

Rear brake band, remove and refit—Operation EEE2-14

Workshop hand tools:

Spanner sizes:
Open-ended $\frac{7}{16}$ in. AF, $\frac{1}{2}$ in. AF
Sockets $\frac{7}{16}$ in. AF, $\frac{1}{2}$ in. AF, $\frac{9}{16}$ in. AF, $\frac{3}{4}$ in. AF
Screwdriver, small Screwdriver, large
Feeler gauges Allen key $\frac{1}{4}$ in. AF

Rear band, remove

1. Take off the oil pan and valve bodies assembly. Operation EEE2-7.
2. Remove front servo. Operation EEE2-8.
3. Remove rear servo. Operation EEE2-9.
4. Remove front pump. Operation EEE2-10.
5. Withdraw front brake band. Operation EEE2-11.
6. Remove front and rear clutch. Operation EEE2-12.
7. Remove centre support and planetary gears. Operation EEE2-13.
8. Withdraw the brake band by tilting the band through 45° to clear the main casing.

Removing rear brake band

A—Rear brake band

Special tools:

Gearbox cradle, Rover Part No. 601280
Torque wrench set, Rover Part No. 601285
End-play checking tool, Rover Part No. 601281, or dial test indicator
Spintorq screwdriver set, Rover Part No. 601286

Rear brake band, refit

1. Reverse removal procedure, ensuring that the band is put in the correct way round, that is, with the slotted lug for the servo strut towards the valve bodies and the larger lug located on the head of the adjuster bolt.
2. Tightening torques:
   Bolts, centre support, 10 to 13 lb ft (1,4 to 1,7 mkg).
   Bolts, front pump to main casing, 8 to 10 lb ft (1,0 to 1,4 mkg).
   Bolts, front servo to main casing, 8 to 10 lb ft (1,0 to 1,4 mkg).
   Bolts, rear servo to main casing, 10 to 13 lb ft (1,4 to 1,7 mkg).
   Adjusting screw, rear servo, 10 lb ft (1,4 mkg).
   Adjusting screw, front servo, 10 lb in. (0,11 mkg).
   Locknut, front servo adjuster screw, 15 to 20 lb ft (2,0 to 2,8 mkg).
   Bolts, valve bodies, 4 to 5 lb ft (0,55 to 0,7 mkg).
   Bolts, oil pan, 8 to 10 lb ft (1,0 to 1,4 mkg).

*Speedometer drive housing, remove and refit—Operation EEE2-15

Workshop hand tools:
Spanner size: $\frac{7}{16}$ in. AF

Speedometer drive housing, remove

1. Withdraw the end of the speedometer cable from the housing, retained by a knurled nut.
2. Remove the speedometer drive housing from its location in the transmission extension case, retained by one set bolt.
3. Withdraw the 'O' ring oil seal from the housing.
4. If necessary, renew the driven gear and spindle which may be pulled out of the housing. If the spindle and gear is being withdrawn, it will be necessary to unscrew the adaptor from the housing and remove and discard the oil seal.

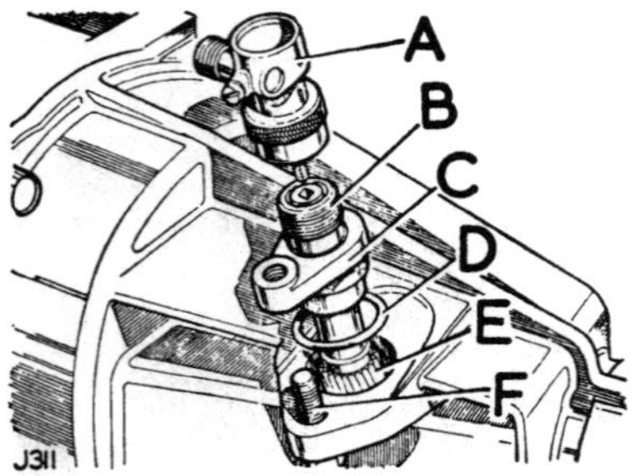

Speedometer cable and housing for driven gear

A—Right-angled drive
B—Adaptor for spindle
C—Housing for driven gear
D—Oil seal for housing
E—Driven gear
F—Bolt fixing housing

Speedometer drive housing, refit

1. Reverse removal procedure.
2. Renew the 'O' ring oil seal on the outside of the housing.
3. If the driven gear and spindle has been withdrawn, renew the oil seal located beneath the adaptor. When replacing the adaptor the threads should be smeared with a little 'Loctite' sealant grade 'AVV', Rover Part No. 600303.

Operations which are identified by an asterisk (*) can be carried out with the automatic transmission installed in the car

*Coupling flange and extension housing, remove and refit—Operation EEE2-16

Workshop hand tools:
Spanner sizes:
Open-ended $\frac{7}{16}$ in. AF, $\frac{1}{2}$ in. AF
Sockets $\frac{7}{16}$ in. AF, $\frac{1}{2}$ in. AF, $\frac{3}{4}$ in. AF
Screwdriver, large   Allen key $\frac{1}{4}$ in. AF

Special tools:
Gearbox cradle, Rover Part No. 601280
Torque wrench set, Rover Part No. 601285

Coupling flange and extension housing, remove Items 1, 2, 3 and 4 only apply if unit is fitted to the car

1. Drain the fluid from the oil pan by removing the oil drain plug. Take great care if the care has just returned from a run as the fluid will be hot enough to cause scalding.
2. Disconnect the front propeller shaft at front end and push to one side.
3. Disconnect rear mounting at gearbox and remove.
4. Disconnect speedometer cable.
5. Lock the box in the park position. If unit is out of vehicle, turn lever clockwise.
6. Withdraw the driving flange, secured by bolt and plain washer.

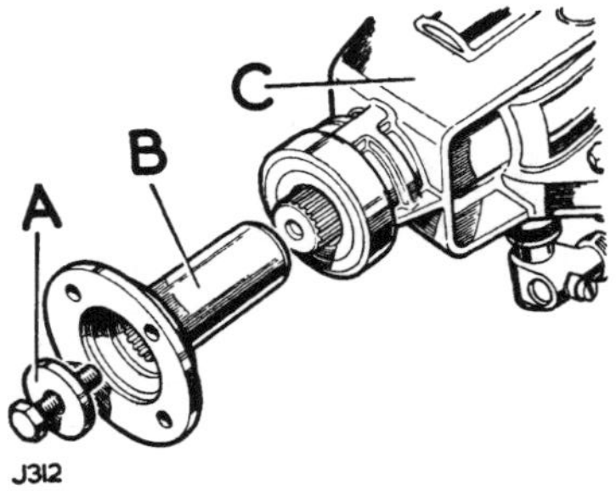

Coupling flange

A—Bolt and special plain washer
B—Coupling flange
C—Extension casing

7. Remove the extension case, secured by four bolts and spring washers. Discard the paper gasket.
8. The speedometer drive pinion can be withdrawn from the shaft if necessary.
9. The oil seal in the extension housing should be levered out with a screwdriver. Press or drift a new seal into position.
10. If necessary, remove speedometer driven gear from extension housing.

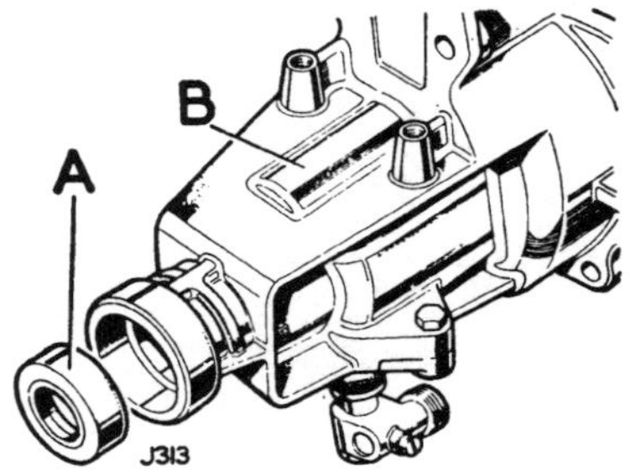

Extension housing oil seal

A—Oil seal   B—Extension housing

Operations which are identified by an asterisk (*) can be carried out with the automatic transmission installed in the car

Operation EEE2-16—*continued*

Coupling flange and extension housing, refit

1. Reverse removal procedure, using a new paper gasket for the extension housing.
2. Tighten the bolts securing the extension housing to the transmission case to a torque figure of 8 to 10 lb ft (1,0 to 1,4 mkg).

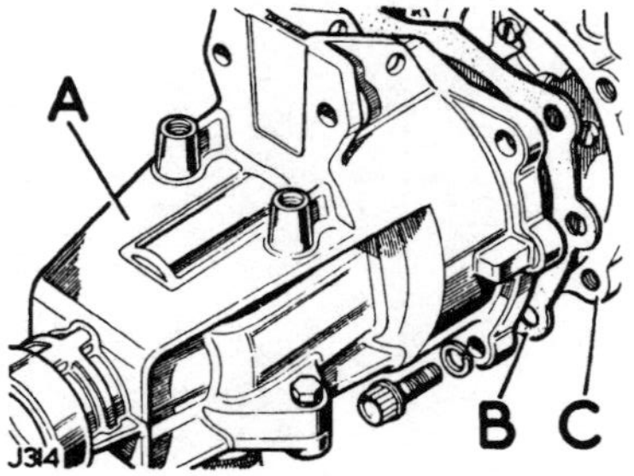

Extension housing, refit

A—Extension housing
B—Gasket
C—Transmission case

3. Smear the threads of the bolt retaining the coupling flange to the driven shaft with 'Loctite' sealant grade 'CV', Rover Part No. 601168. Tighten the bolt fully to ensure that flange nips speedometer pinion. Looseness at this point can cause speedometer fluctuation.
4. Release the parking pawl engagement.
5. If the gearbox is completely dismantled, hold the ring gear and driven shaft firmly whilst fitting the extension housing and the coupling flange.
6. If the above operation has been carried out with the unit in the vehicle, refill with fluid of the recommended grade. Capacity: 14 Imperial pints (17 US pints, 8 litres).

*Governor, remove and refit—Operation EEE2-17

Workshop hand tools;
Spanner sizes:
Open-ended $\frac{7}{16}$ in. AF, $\frac{1}{2}$ in. AF,
Sockets $\frac{7}{16}$ in. AF, $\frac{1}{2}$ in. AF, $\frac{3}{4}$ in. AF
Screwdriver, large

Special tools:
Gearbox cradle, Rover Part No. 601280
Torque wrench set, Rover Part No. 601285
Snap ring pliers, Rover Part No. 601282

Instructions for dismantling the governor valve are given in Part Three of this Section

Governor, remove

1. Remove the coupling flange and extension housing. Operation EEE2-16.

2. Release park position, then rotate the driven shaft so that the governor centrifugal weight is at the 6 o'clock position, that is, downwards as illustrated. This is a precaution to prevent the steel retaining ball from being lost when the governor is withdrawn from the shaft.

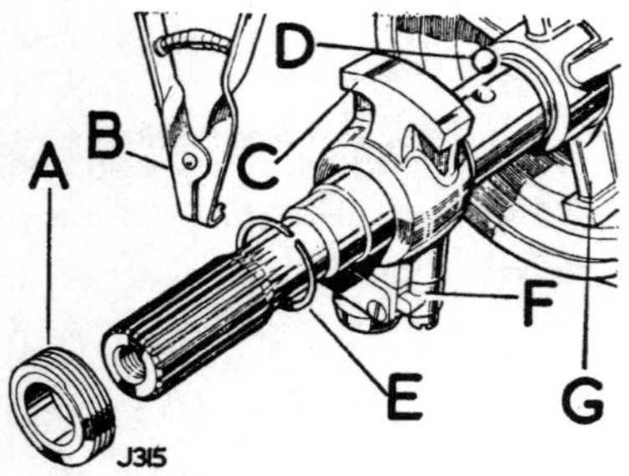

Governor, remove

A—Speedometer drive gear
B—Snap ring pliers
C—Governor sleeve
D—Governor retaining ball
E—Snap ring
F—Governor body
G—Adaptor plate

3. Remove the snap ring locating the governor on to the driven shaft, using the special snap ring pliers.
4. Slide the governor off the shaft, taking care not to lose the steel ball which keys the governor to the shaft.

Governor, refit

1. Reverse removal procedure.
2. Ensure that the governor is the correct way round, that is, with the governor valve cover plate facing rearwards.

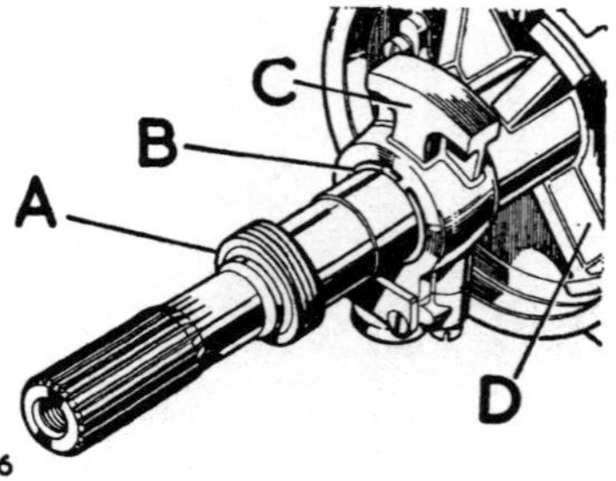

Governor in position on shaft

A—Speedometer drive gear
B—Snap ring for governor
C—Governor assembly
D—Adaptor plate

3. If the transmission case has been completely dismantled, hold the ring gear and drive shaft firmly in position whilst fitting the governor and the snap ring.
4. Tightening torques:
Bolts, securing extension housing, 8 to 10 lb ft (1,0 to 1,4 mkg).

Operations which are identified by an asterisk (*) can be carried out with the automatic transmission installed in the car

Driven shaft and ring gear assembly, remove and refit—Operation EEE2-18

Workshop hand tools:
Spanner sizes:
Open-ended $\frac{7}{16}$ in. AF, $\frac{1}{2}$ in. AF, $\frac{9}{16}$ in. AF, $\frac{3}{4}$ in. AF
Sockets $\frac{7}{16}$ in. AF, $\frac{1}{2}$ in. AF, $\frac{9}{16}$ in. AF, $\frac{3}{4}$ in. AF
Screwdriver, small   Screwdriver, large
Allen key $\frac{3}{16}$ in.   Feeler gauges
Allen key $\frac{1}{4}$ in. AF

Special tools:
Gearbox cradle, Rover Part No. 601280
Torque wrench set, Rover Part No. 601285
Spintorq screwdriver set, Rover Part No. 601286
Front servo gauge, Rover Part No. 601287
End-play checking tool, Rover Part No. 601281, or dial test indicator
Snap ring pliers, Rover Part No. 601282

The driven shaft is a service exchange item

Driven shaft and ring gear, remove

1. Remove all items detailed under previous operations in this section.
2. Remove adaptor plate.
3. Withdraw the shaft and ring gear forwards from the transmission case, taking care that the white metal bush in the rear of the transmission case is not damaged. This bush is not serviced separately.

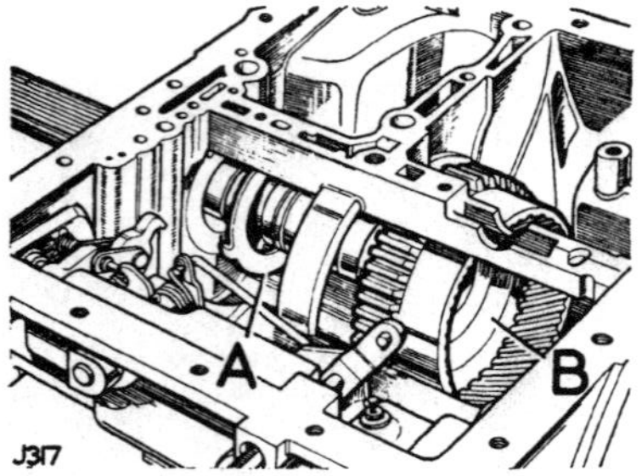

Driven shaft and ring gear assembly, remove

A—Tabbed thrust washer
B—Driven shaft and ring gear assembly

4. Lift off the tabbed thrust washer, located between the driven shaft and the rear bearing of the transmission case.
5. If necessary, remove the snap ring and separate the driven shaft from the ring gear. Examine and pressure test the plug in the front of the driven shaft to ensure that it is not loose. A loose plug necessitates a replacement shaft.
6. If necessary, remove the three oil sealing rings from the driven shaft.
7. Check components for wear and ensure all oilways are clear.
8. At this stage check the transmission case for signs of damage or stripped threads. Clear all oil passages with an air line.

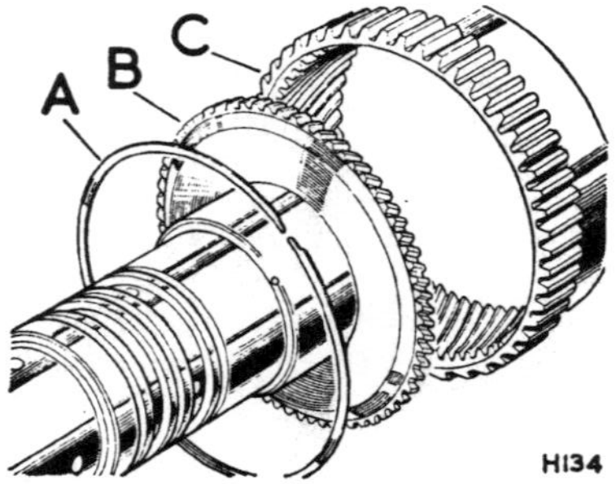

Separating ring gear from driven shaft

A—Snap ring B—Driven shaft C—Ring gear

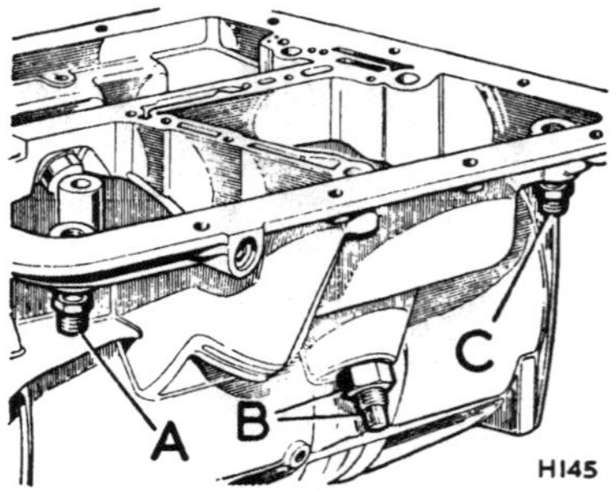

Transmission case details

A—Oil cooler pipe union, inlet
B—Rear brake band adjuster and locknut
C—Oil cooler pipe union, return

Operation EEE2-18—*continued*

9. If necessary, check or remove the following:
   (a) Rear brake band adjusting screw and locknut.
   (b) Oil cooler pipe unions. If replaced, use 'Loctite' sealant grade 'AVV', Rover Part No. 600303, on the threads.
   (c) Do not remove the driven shaft bush. This is not a service item.
   (d) Pressure take-off plug at rear face of transmission case.
   (e) Oil dipstick tube adaptor.
   (f) Check that parking brake torsion lever pin is a tight fit.
   (g) Ensure that the front brake band anchor pin is tight.

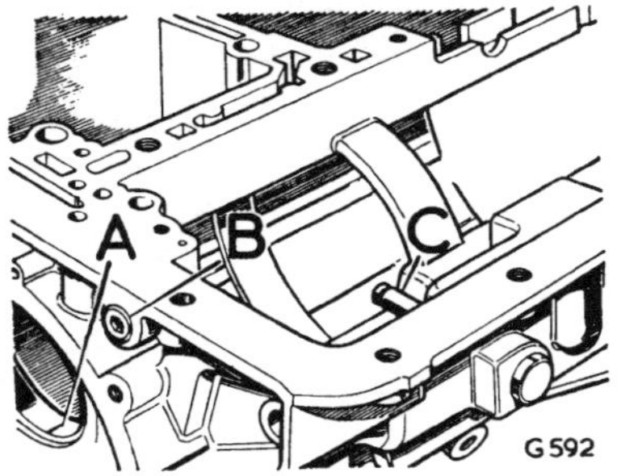

Transmission case details

A—Bush for driven shaft
B—Pressure take-off plug
C—Pin for parking brake torsion lever

Driven shaft and ring gear assembly, refit

1. Fit the driven shaft to the ring gear and secure with snap ring. Check and ensure that there is no end-float between driven shaft and ring gear.
2. The snap ring retaining the driven shaft to the ring gear is available in the following thicknesses to enable end-float to be eliminated: .055, .057 and .059 in. (1,39, 1,44 and 1,49 mm).
3. Fit the three oil sealing rings and line up with gaps uppermost as viewed with the box inverted, centralise the rings in their grooves, retaining them in position with a little petroleum jelly.
4. Locate the tabbed thrust washer on to the boss of the transmission case with petroleum jelly. The tabs of the washer locate on the boss in such a manner that one tab will be pointing upwards, as seen with the box on the gearbox cradle.

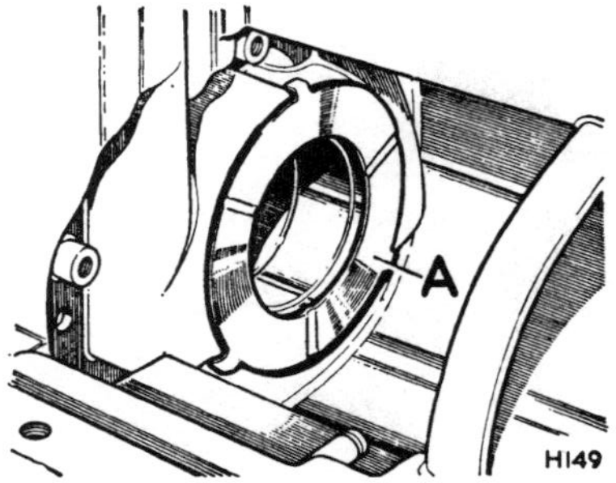

Driven shaft thrust washer

A—Thrust washer

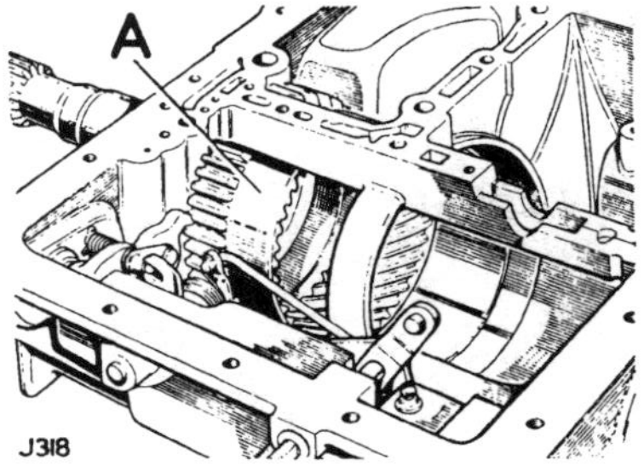

Driven shaft and ring gear, refit

A—Driven shaft and ring gear assembly

Operation EEE2-18—*continued*

5. Insert the driven shaft and ring gear assembly. Great care must be taken when installing it into the transmission case to prevent damage to the bush in the rear of the case.
6. Rotate the driven shaft to bring location hole for governor, retaining ball uppermost with the gearbox inverted.
7. Refit the adaptor plate.

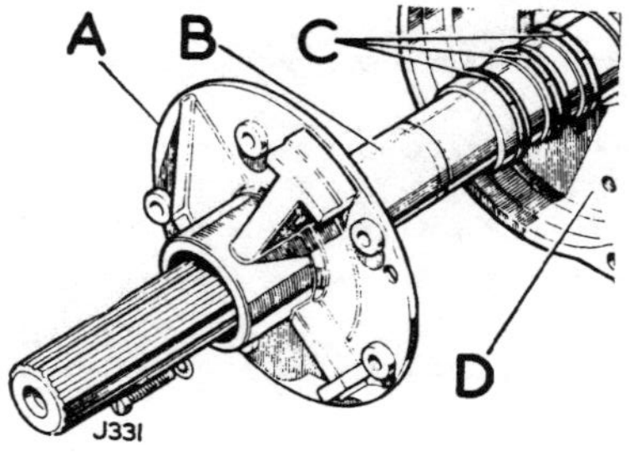

Adaptor plate

A—Adaptor plate
B—Driven shaft
C—Oil sealing rings
D—Main casing

8. Refit governor. Operation EEE2-17.
9. Refit extension housing and coupling flange. Operation EEE2-16.
10. Refit rear brake band. Operation EEE2-14.
11. Refit centre support and planetary gears. Operation EEE2-13.
12. Refit front and rear clutch. Operation EEE2-12.
13. Refit front brake band. Operation EEE2-11.
14. Fit a new paper gasket for front pump to the transmission case. Locate with petroleum jelly.
15. If necessary, check and correct gear train end-float. See Operation EEE2-10.
16. Fit the front pump to the transmission case with the oil tube locations facing the valve bodies. Fit oil tubes to front pump.
17. Install the rear servo into the transmission case. To facilitate the location of the servo strut, attach it to the servo lever with petroleum jelly and ensure that the strut engages with the slot in the brake band. The long special bolt must be fitted into the hole adjacent to centre cross-support of the transmission case. The short bolt also locates the magnet.
18. The adjuster for the rear band servo is located on the outside of the transmission case.
19. Slacken the locknut of the adjusting screw.
20. Tighten the adjusting screw to a torque of 10 lb ft (1,4 mkg), then turn the adjusting screw back one complete turn and tighten the locknut to a torque figure of 25 to 30 lb ft (3,5 to 4,0 mkg).
21. Install the front servo into the transmission case. To facilitate location of the servo strut, attach it to the servo lever with petroleum jelly and ensure that the strut engages with the slot in the brake band.

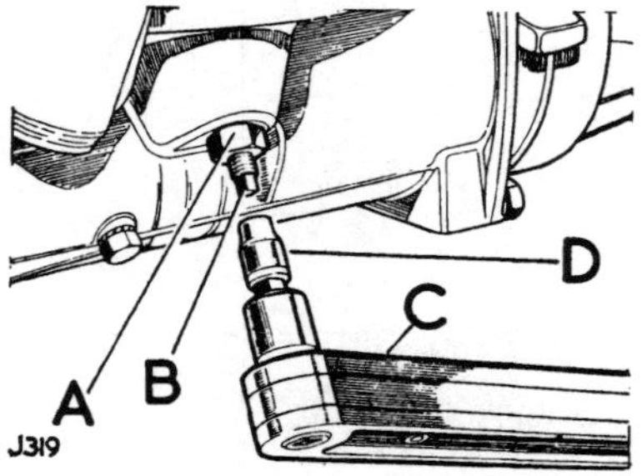

Rear brake band adjustment

A—Locknut for adjuster
B—Adjusting screw for brake band
C—Torque wrench
D—Adaptor

Operation EEE2-18—*continued*

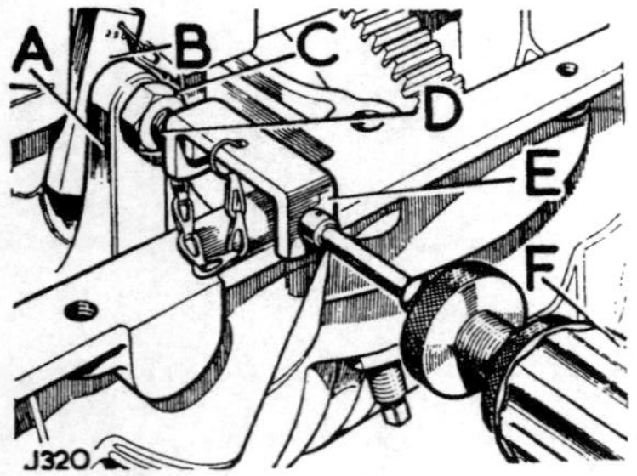

Front brake band, adjustment

A—Servo lever
B—Gauge block
C—Locknut for adjuster
D—Adjuster screw for servo
E—Adaptor
F—Spintorq screwdriver

22. To adjust the front servo, slacken locknut and unscrew the adjuster. Pull the servo lever outwards and place the gauge block between the adjusting screw and the servo piston pin.
23. Tighten the servo lever adjusting screw to a torque figure of 10 lb in. (0,11 mkg), using a torque screwdriver and the adaptor attached to the gauge block.
24. Use a screwdriver between servo body and adjuster lever to release pressure from gauge block and withdraw.
25. Tighten the adjuster lever locknut to a torque figure of 15 to 20 lb ft (2,0 to 2,8 mkg).
26. Refit valve bodies and oil pan. Operation EEE2-7.
27. Tightening torques for all the previous operations as applicable are:

Bolts, extension housing, 8 to 10 lb ft (1,0 to 1,4 mkg).

Bolts, centre support, 10 to 13 lb ft (1,4 to 1,7 mkg).

Bolts, front pump to transmission casing, 8 to 10 lb ft (1,0 to 1,4 mkg).

Bolts, front servo to transmission casing, 8 to 10 lb ft (1,0 to 1,4 mkg).

Bolts, rear servo to transmission casing, 10 to 13 lb ft (1,4 to 1,7 mkg).

Adjusting screw, rear servo, 10 lb ft (1,4 mkg).

Adjusting screw, front servo, 10 lb in. (0,11 mkg).

Locknut, front servo adjusting screw, 15 to 20 lb ft (2,0 to 2,8 mkg).

Locknut, rear servo adjusting screw, 25 to 30 lb ft (3,5 to 4,0 mkg).

Bolts, valve bodies, 4 to 5 lb ft (0,55 to 0,7 mkg).

Bolts, oil pan, 8 to 10 lb ft (1,0 to 1,4 mkg)

Manual valve lever control shaft, remove and refit—Operation EEE2-19

Workshop hand tools:

Spanner sizes:

Open-ended $\frac{7}{16}$ in. AF, $\frac{1}{2}$ in. AF

Sockets $\frac{7}{16}$ in. AF, $\frac{1}{2}$ in. AF

Screwdriver, large — Pin punch $\frac{1}{8}$ in. diameter (3 mm)

Pliers, pointed-nose — Brass drift — Hammer, light

Allen key $\frac{1}{4}$ in. AF

Special tools:

Torque wrench set, Rover Part No. 601285

Manual valve lever control shaft, remove

1. Remove oil pan and valve bodies. Operation EEE2-7.
2. Remove the clip retaining the parking brake link at the torsion lever end.
3. Remove the spring clip retaining the detent lever.
4. Push lever towards casing, then drive out the $\frac{11}{16}$ in. (17 mm) roll pin from the manual valve detent lever shaft with a suitable drift. Take care not to drop the pin.
5. Withdraw the detent lever—take great care as the detent ball is under strong spring pressure—then remove the spring.
6. Remove the operating lever from the end of the shaft outside the box.
7. Remove the taper pin retaining the shaft.
8. Withdraw the shaft, taking out the oil seal.
9. Clean and examine all the components. Renew defective parts.

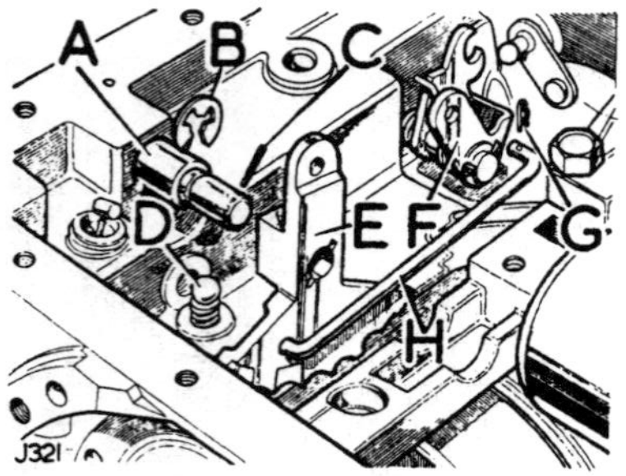

Detent lever

A—Shaft
B—Spring clip
C—Roll pin
D—Ball and spring
E—Detent lever
F—Torsion lever
G—Clip for parking brake link
H—Braking brake link

Manual valve lever shaft, refit

1. Renew the oil seal in the transmission case.
2. Reverse removal procedure.

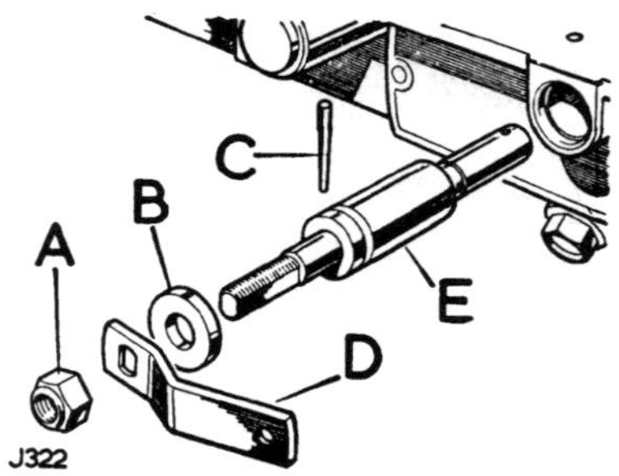

Shaft for detent lever

A—Self-locking nut for lever
B—Oil seal
C—Taper pin retaining shaft
D—Lever
E—Shafr

Operation EEE2-19—*continued*

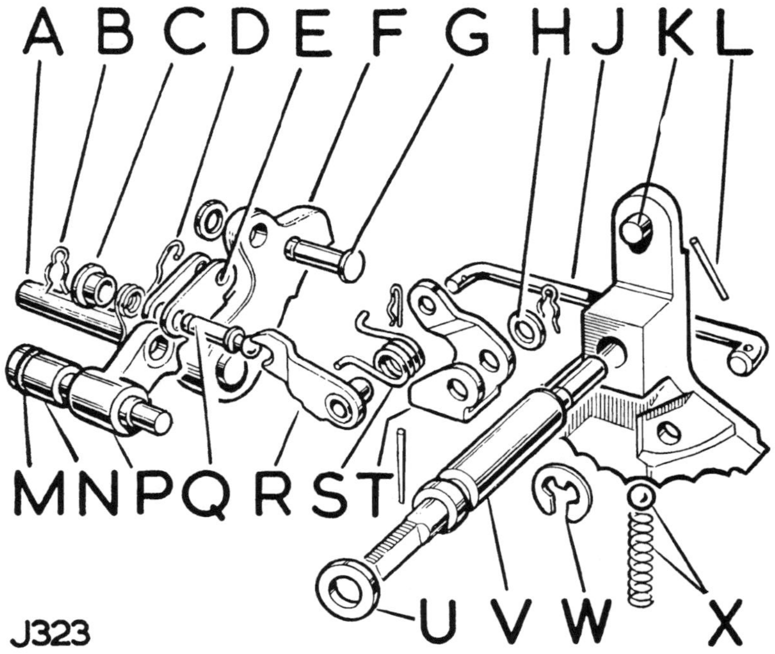

J323

Manual valve shaft, link and parking pawl and torsion lever assembly

A—Anchor pin
B—Circlip for toggle lever pin
C—Retainer for spring
D—Parking brake release spring
E—Toggle link
F—Parking brake pawl
G—Pin for toggle link
H—Plain washer for torsion lever
J—Linkage rod, detent lever to torsion lever
K—Detent lever
L—Roll pin
M—'O' ring for toggle pin
N—Toggle pin
P—Toggle lever
Q—Pin for toggle lever
R—Toggle lift lever
S—Toggle lever spring
T—Torsion lever
U—Oil seal for manual lever shaft
V—Shaft
W—Spring clip
X—Detent ball and spring

*Parking pawl and torsion lever assembly, remove and refit—Operation EEE2-20

Workshop hand tools:
Spanner sizes:
Open-ended $\frac{7}{16}$ in. AF, $\frac{1}{2}$ in. AF
Sockets $\frac{7}{16}$ in. AF, $\frac{1}{2}$ in. AF, $\frac{3}{4}$ in. AF
Screwdriver, large Hammer
Pin punch $\frac{1}{8}$ in. diameter (3 mm) Pliers, pointed-nose
Magnet Allen key $\frac{1}{4}$ in. AF

Special tools:
Torque wrench set, Rover Part No. 601285

Parking pawl and torsion lever assembly, remove

1. Remove oil pan and valve bodies. Operation EEE2-7.
2. Remove extension housing and coupling flange. Operation EEE2-16.
3. Tap out the roll pin locating the parking pawl toggle pin in the transmission case.

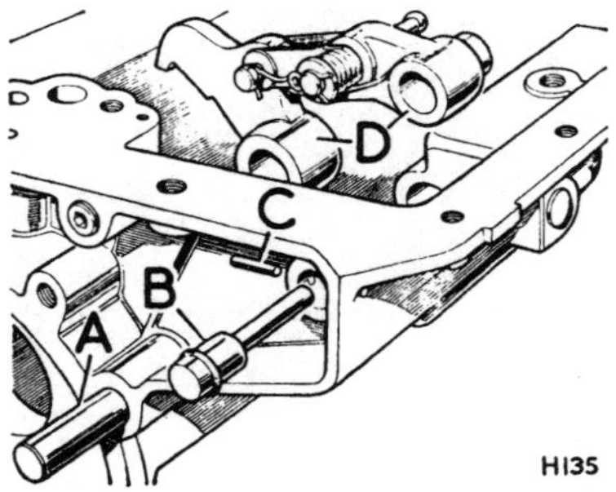

Parking pawl and torsion lever assembly

A—Parking pawl anchor pin
B—Parking brake toggle pin
C—Retaining roll pin
D—Parking pawl assembly

4. Use a suitable magnet to withdraw the toggle pin complete with 'O' ring, also the anchor pin.
5. Lift out the parking pawl assembly. If necessary, the parking pawl assembly can be dismantled as follows:
6. Remove spring clip from the toggle lever pin, withdraw spring retainer and disconnect release spring.
7. Separate the components by withdrawing the toggle lever pin and toggle link pin; note plain washer on link pin.
Item 8 can only be carried out after the removal of the rear servo and sliding the brake band fully to the rear.
8. Remove the spring clip retaining the link rod, also the spring clip retaining the torsion lever assembly to the pin in the casing and withdraw the assembly.

Torsion lever assembly

A—Spring clip for torsion lever
B—Plain washer for torsion lever
C—Parking brake lever and toggle assembly
D—Spring clip for link

Parking pawl and torsion lever, refit

1. Examine components for wear, renew as necessary and assemble by reversing dismantling procedure.
2. Use a new 'O' ring on the toggle pin.

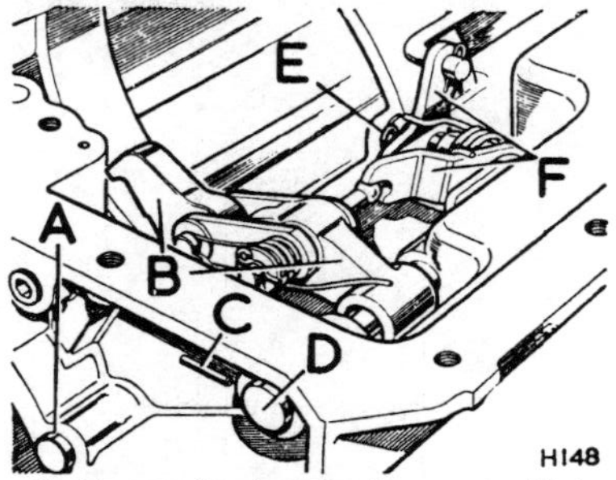

Parking pawl and torsion lever assembled

A—Anchor pin for parking pawl
B—Parking pawl assembly
C—Roll pin for toggle pin
D—Toggle pin
E—Spring clip for torsion lever
F—Torsion lever assembly

Operations which are identified by an asterisk (*) can be carried out with the automatic transmission installed in the car

*Starter inhibitor switch, remove and refit—Operation EEE2-21

Workshop hand tools:
Spanner size: Open-ended $\frac{11}{16}$ in. AF

Inhibitor switch, remove

1. Remove the front exhaust pipe.
2. Disconnect the wiring at the switch connections. The illustration shows the switch being removed after the gearbox has been dismantled, but this operation can be carried out without dismantling the gearbox.
3. Slacken the switch locknut.
4. Screw the switch from the transmission case by hand.

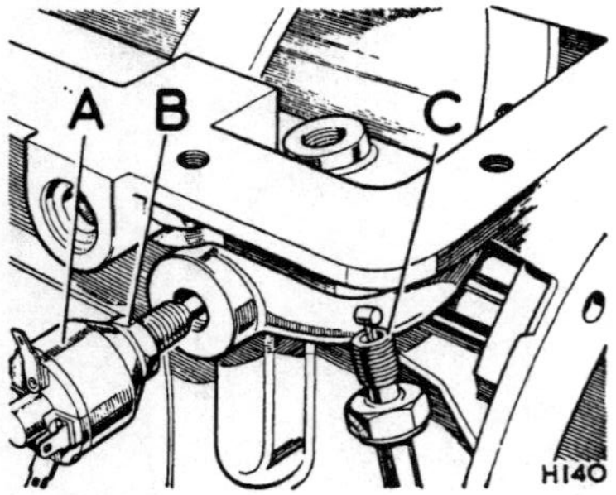

Starter inhibitor switch, remove

A—Inhibitor switch
B—Switch locknut
C—Downshift valve cable

Inhibitor switch, refit

1. Reverse removal procedure.
2. For adjustment, see Operation EEE2-2.

*Downshift valve cable, remove and refit—Operation EEE2-22

Workshop hand tools:
Spanner sizes:
Open-ended $\frac{7}{16}$ in. AF, $\frac{1}{2}$ in. AF, $\frac{3}{4}$ in. AF Sockets $\frac{7}{16}$ in. AF, $\frac{1}{2}$ in. AF
Allen key $\frac{1}{4}$ in. AF

Cable, remove

1. Drain the fluid from the oil pan by removing the drain plug. Take great care if the car has just returned from a run as the fluid will be hot enough to cause scalding.
   It is not possible to completely drain the oil pan. Replace drain plug.
2. Remove the oil pan and pull the downshift valve cam forward in direction of arrow and disconnect the cable from the valve bodies end.
3. Disconnect the cable at the engine end.
4. Unscrew the ferrule of the cable from the transmission case.

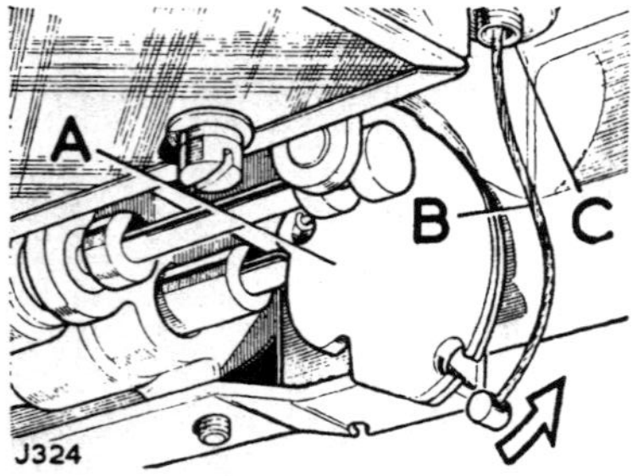

Downshift valve cable, remove at transmission unit

A—Downshift valve cam B—Cable C—Ferrule for cable

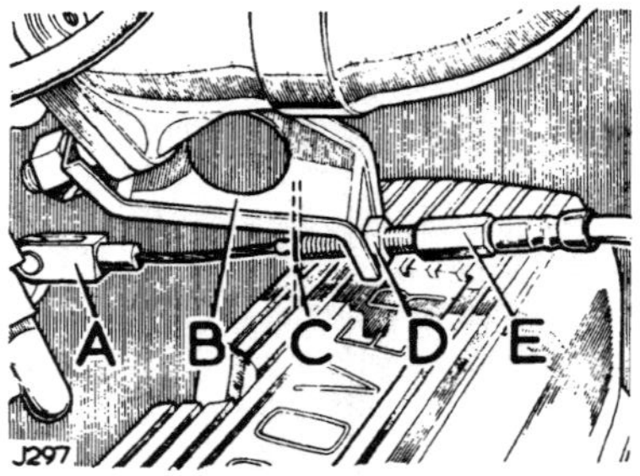

Downshift valve cable, remove at engine

A—Clevis for cable
B—Bracket for cable
C—.010 in. (0,25 mm) clearance between crimped stop and adjuster
D—Locknut for adjuster
E—Adjuster for cable

Cable, refit

1. Reverse removal procedure.
2. Tightening torque:
   Bolts, oil pan, 8 to 10 lb ft (1,0 to 1,4 mkg).
3. If the above operation has been carried out with the unit in the vehicle, refill with fluid of the recommended grade. Capacity: 14 Imperial pints (17 US pints, 8 litres).
4. To adjust cable, see Operation EEE2-3.

*Air pressure checks—Operation EEE2-23

Workshop hand tools:

Spanner sizes:

Open-ended $\frac{7}{16}$ in. AF, $\frac{1}{2}$ in. AF

Sockets $\frac{7}{16}$ in. AF, $\frac{1}{2}$ in. AF, $\frac{3}{4}$ in. AF

Allen key $\frac{1}{4}$ in. AF

Special tools:

Torque wrench set, Rover Part No. 601285

Air pressure checks to determine whether the clutch and brake bands are operating can be made with the transmission unit in the car, or on the bench.

If the clutch and bands operate satisfactorily with air pressure, faulty operation of the transmission must be due to malfunction of the hydraulic control system.

The valve bodies assembly must then be dismantled, cleaned, inspected and reassembled.

Instructions for dismantling the valve bodies assembly is given in Part Three of this Section.

Prior operations necessary if the unit being tested is fitted in the car

1. Remove the oil pan and valve bodies assembly. Operation EEE2-7.
2. Remove the extension housing and coupling flange. Operation EEE2-16.

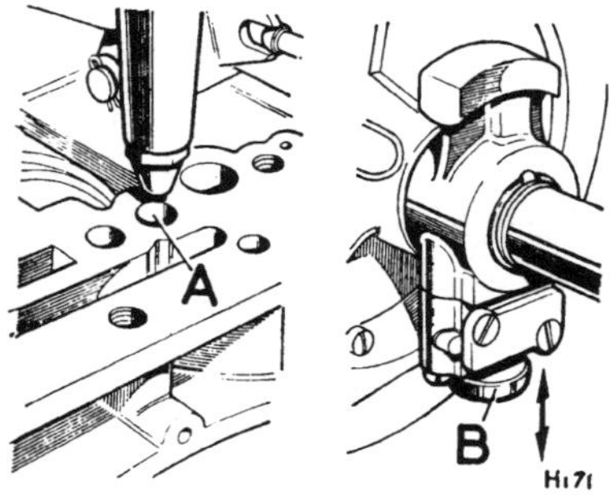

Front clutch and governor feed pressure check

A—Drilling in transmission case
B—Governor weight

Front clutch and governor feed

3. Apply air pressure to the drilling 'A' in the transmission case.
   (a) Listen for thump indicating that the clutch is functioning.
   (b) Rotate driven shaft so that the governor weight is in the 6 o'clock position. Apply and release air pressure and observe whether governor weight rises and falls. If the unit is on the bench, apply air pressure and rotate the driven shaft by hand and observe that the input shaft rotates.

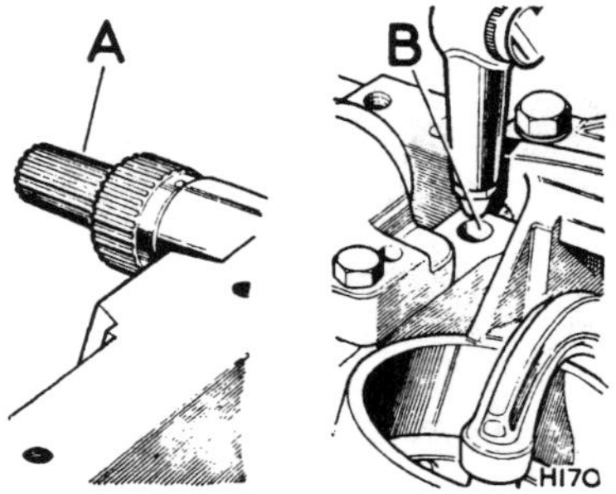

Rear clutch pressure check

A—Input shaft B—Drilling in transmission case

Rear clutch

4. Apply air pressure to the drilling 'B' in the transmission case.
   (a) If the unit is on the bench, apply air pressure and try to turn the input shaft by hand; note resistance as long as air pressure is applied. Keep air pressure applied for several seconds to check for leaks.
   (b) Listen for thump as air pressure is released indicating that clutch is releasing and not sticking.

Front servo

5. Apply air pressure to the servo apply tube location 'B' on servo body, adjacent to the rear retaining bolt. Observe the movement of the piston pin indicating that the servo is working.

Operations which are identified by an asterisk (*) can be carried out with the automatic transmission installed in the car

Operation EEE2-23—*continued*

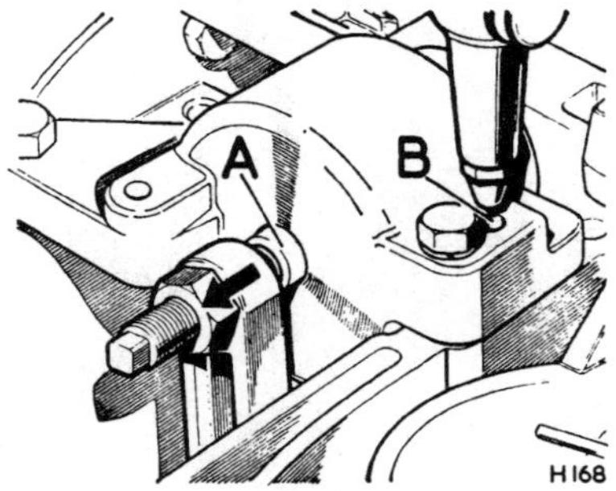

Front servo pressure check

A—Piston pin B—Servo apply tube location

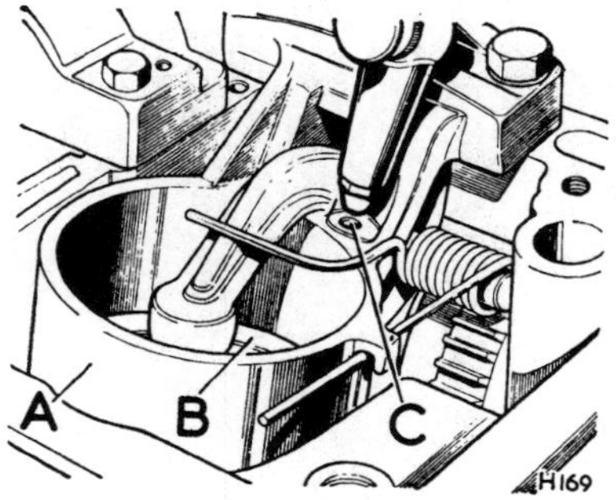

Rear servo pressure check

A—Cylinder B—Piston C—Oil tube location

Rear servo

6. Apply air pressure to tube location 'B' on the servo body. Observe the movement of the servo lever indicating that the servo is working.

On completion of tests continue assembly of the unit or, if the unit tested is fitted in the car, fit the following:

Extension casing and coupling flange. Operation EEE2-16.

Oil pan and valve bodies assembly. Operation EEE2-7.

Tightening torques

Bolts, securing valve bodies assembly to transmission casing, 4 to 5 lb ft (0,55 to 0,7 mkg).

Bolts, securing extension housing to transmission casing, 8 to 10 lb ft (1,0 to 1,4 mkg).

Bolts, securing oil pan to transmission casing, 8 to 10 lb ft (1,0 to 1,4 mkg).

Gear selector lever, remove and refit—Operation EEE2-24

Workshop hand tools:

Spanner sizes: Open-ended $\frac{7}{16}$ in. AF, $\frac{1}{2}$ in. AF
Screwdriver, Phillips'

Instructions for overhauling the gear selector lever are given in Part Three of this Section

Gear selector lever, remove

1. Unscrew the knob from the top of the gear selector lever.
2. Lift off the plastic indicator cover for gear selector lever.

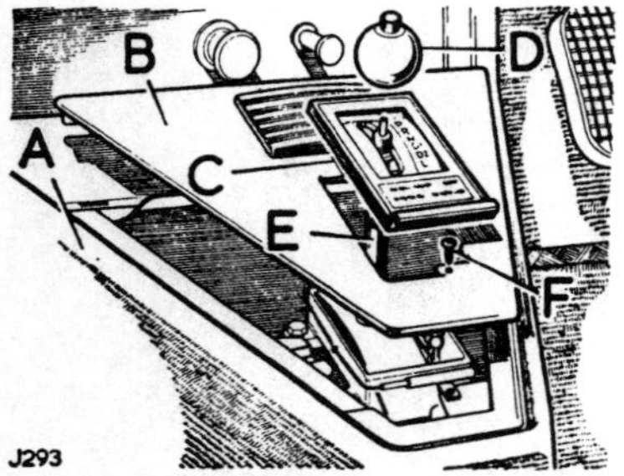

Trim panel

A—Transmission tunnel
B—Trim panel
C—Indicator plate
D—Knob for gear selector lever
E—Gear selector lever
F—Screw fixing trim panel

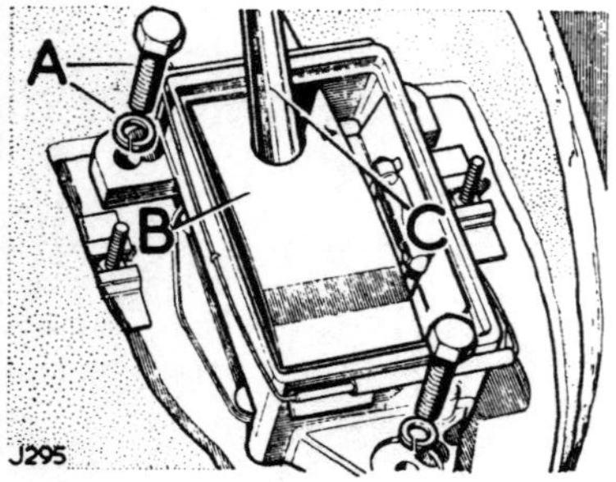

Gear selector lever

A—Housing for gear selector lever
B—Gear selector lever
C—Set bolt and spring washer fixing housing

3. Remove the Phillips' screw securing the trim panel to the top of the transmission tunnel and lift off the trim panel.
4. Remove the three bolts securing the gear selector housing.
5. Disconnect wiring from illumination lamp.
6. From under the car, disconnect the operating rod at selector lever and tie rod at pivot housing.
7. Remove the three nuts securing the spherical seat cover to the housing.
8. The pivot housing can now be removed from under the car and the gear selector mechanism withdrawn from inside the car.

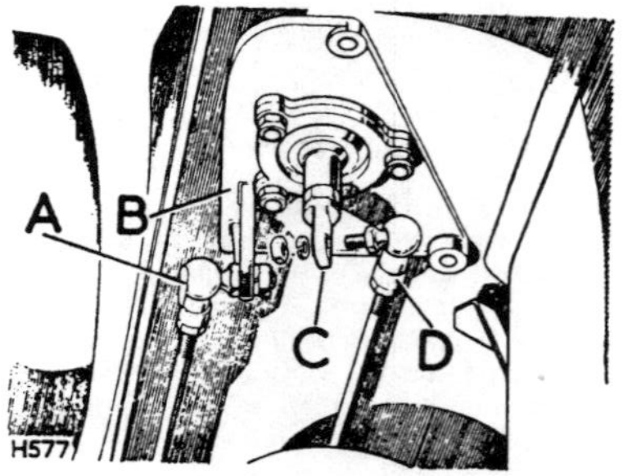

Selector linkage rods

A—Tie rod
B—Pivot housing
C—Selector lever
D—Operating rod

Gear selector lever, refit

1. Reverse removal procedure.
2. Adjust linkage, if necessary. Operation EEE2-1.

PART THREE

This section provides the instructions necessary for overhauling the various units of the automatic transmission.

High standards of cleanliness are required when working on the automatic transmission. Petrol, paraffin or an industrial cleaning solvent may be used to clean components. Use nylon rag—never material that is fluffy or that leaves lint—when drying any components.

Valve bodies, overhaul—Operation EEE3-1

Workshop hand tools:

Screwdriver, medium

Special tools:

Spintorq screwdriver set, Rover Part No. 601286

Instruction for the removal of the valve bodies assembly is given in Part Two of this Section

Valve bodies, dismantle

1. Withdraw the manual control valve.
2. Remove the front pump oil strainer, secured by screws, plain and spring washers.

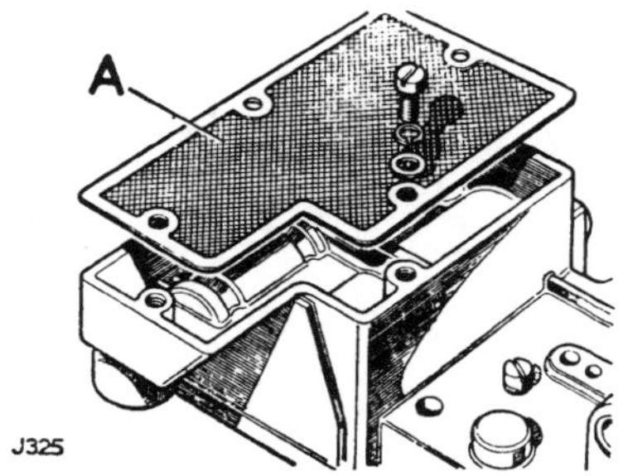

Oil strainers, front pump

A—Oil strainer, front pump

3. Remove eight screws and spring washers securing the lower valve body to the upper valve body; two screws and washers are located in the oil strainer housing, these retain the D1–D2 valve body. If necessary, remove stop and withdraw D1–D2 control valve and spacer.

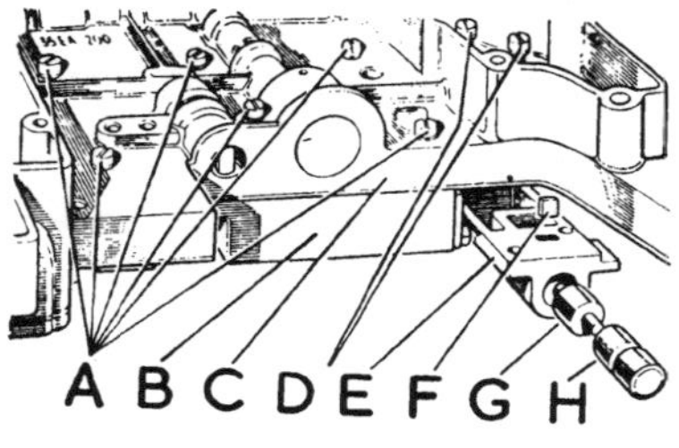

Valve bodies

A—Screws for valve bodies
B—Upper valve body
C—Lower valve body
D—Screws for D1–D2 control
E—Valve body, D1–D2 control
F—Stop for spacer
G—Valve, D1–D2 control
H—Spacer, D1–D2 control

4. Turn the unit over and remove the oil tube collector plate, secured by six short and two long screws and spring washers to the lower valve body.

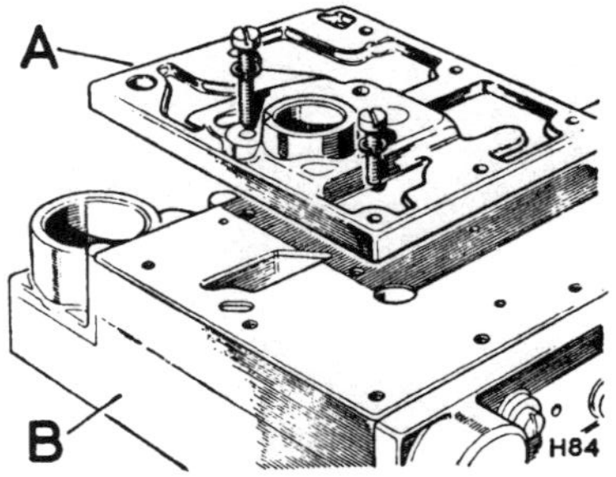

Oil tube collector plate

A—Oil tube collector plate
B—Lower valve body

5. Remove the downshift valve cam, which is secured by two screws and spring washers.
6. Remove the two remaining screws securing the upper valve body to the lower valve body and separate the two bodies.

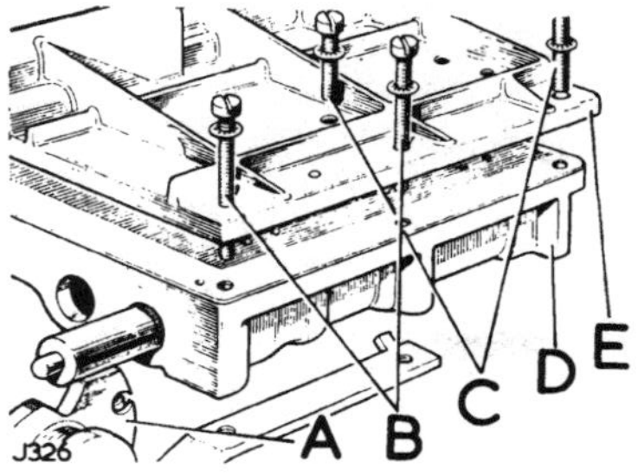

Downshift valve cam

A—Downshift valve cam
B—Screws fixing valve cam
C—Screws fixing upper to lower valve body
D—Lower valve body
E—Upper valve body

Operation EEE3-1—*continued*

7. Lift off the separating plate.
8. Take all the loose valves and components from the lower valve body, these are:

   Rear pump check valve and spring, disc and coil spring.

   Converter check valve and spring, ball and coil spring.

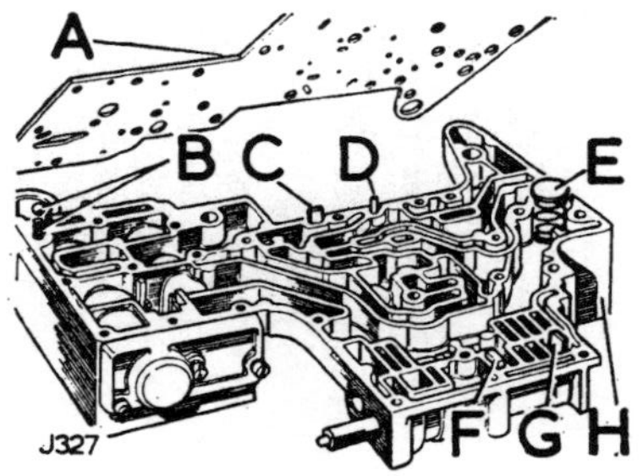

Separating plate, remove

A—Separating plate
B—Converter 'out' check valve
C—Servo orifice valve stop
D—Dowel pin for modulator valve
E—Rear pump check valve
F—Retainer for throttle valve
G—Stop for throttle valve spring
H—Lower valve body

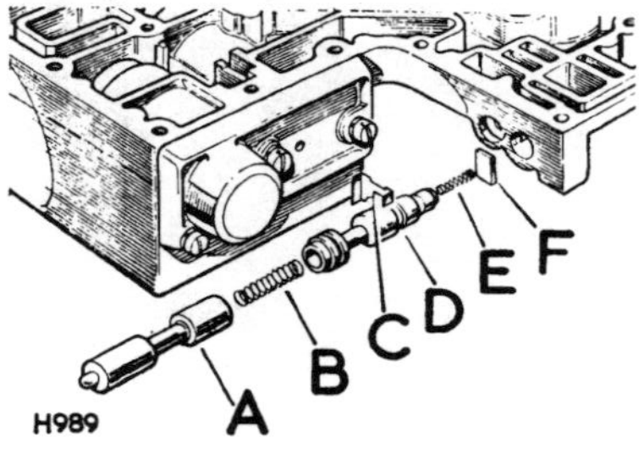

Downshift and throttle valve

A—Downshift valve
B—Spring for downshift valve
C—Valve retainer
D—Throttle valve
E—Spring for throttle valve
F—Stop for throttle valve spring

9. Withdraw the downshift valve and retainer for throttle valve, then tilt valve body to allow throttle valve and spring to slide out, finally remove stop for throttle valve spring.

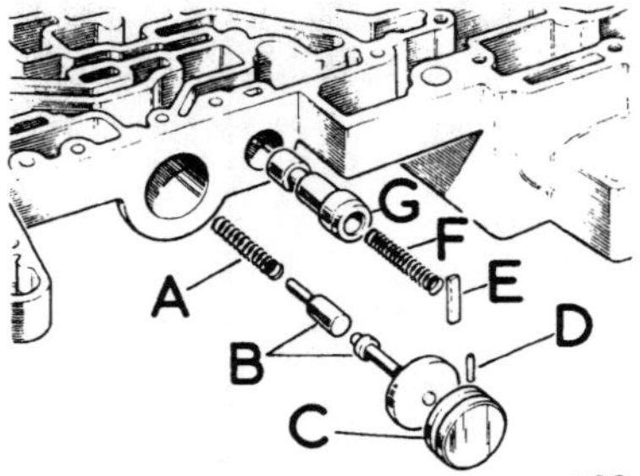

Modulator and servo orifice valve components

A—Spring, modulator valve, 1 in. (25 mm) long, $\frac{3}{16}$ in. (4,5 mm) diameter
B—Modulator valve
C—Plug, modulator valve
D—Dowel pin for modulator valve
E—Stop for servo orifice valve
F—Spring, servo orifice control valve, $1\frac{1}{8}$ in. (28 mm) long, $\frac{3}{16}$ in. (4,5 mm) diameter
G—Servo orifice control valve

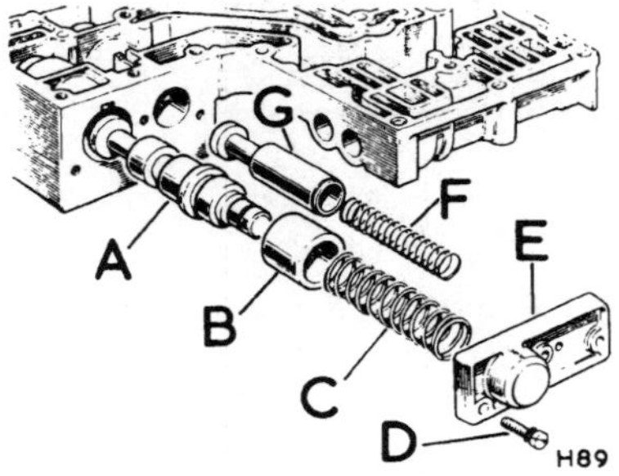

Primary and secondary regulator valves

A—Primary regulator valve
B—Sleeve, primary regulator valve
C—Spring, primary regulator valve
D—Screw fixing cover plate
E—Cover plate
F—Spring, secondary regulator valve
G—Secondary regulator valve

Operation EEE3-1—*continued*

10. Turn the valve body over to remove:

    Orifice control valve stop.

    Modulator valve dowel.

    It may be necessary to depress the valve plug to release the dowel pin. Withdraw the plug, valve, spacer and spring of the modulator valve and the servo orifice control valve spring and valve.

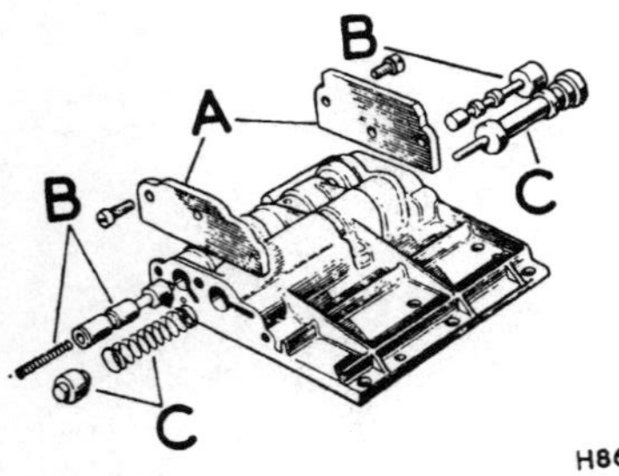

H86

Upper valve body components

A—End cover plates
B—1st, 2nd shift valve, plunger and spring
C—2nd, 3rd shift valve, plunger and spring

11. Remove the lower body end-plate, secured by three screws and spring washers. Withdraw the primary and secondary regulator valve components. Note there is considerable spring pressure behind the cover plate.

12. Dismantle the upper valve body, which has already been removed from the lower valve body. The upper body end-plates are each retained by three screws and spring washers. Remove the plates and withdraw the valve components.

Preparation before rebuild

1. Carefully clean all the components, using petrol as the cleaning medium. Use only nylon or non-fluffy rag. Clear fluid passages with the aid of an air line. Assemble parts dry to check fit in bores.

2. Examine all components for wear and verify the free movement of all the valves in their bores.

Valve bodies, rebuild

1. Note that no gaskets are used throughout the valve bodies assembly. It is essential that a torque screwdriver is used exclusively on reassembly.

2. Assembly the upper valve body in the order as illustrated. Tighten the six end-plate fixing screws to 20 to 30 lb in. (0,23 to 0,35 mkg).

3. Place on one side until required for final assembly.

4. Assemble in accordance with the illustration the servo orifice control valve and secure with the stop.

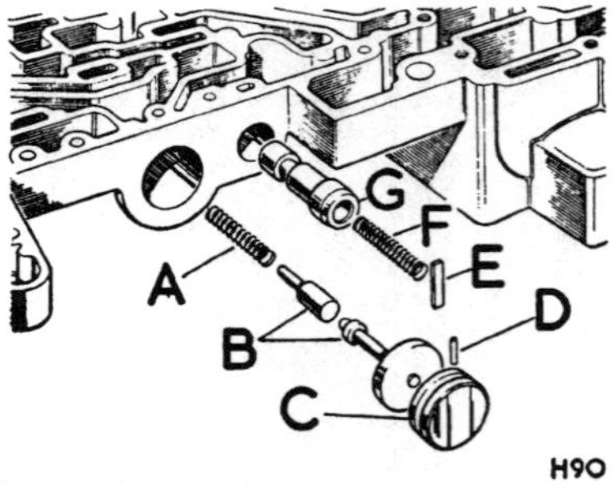

H90

Modulator and servo orifice valve components, assemble

A—Spring, modulator valve, 1 in. (25 mm) long, $\frac{3}{16}$ in. (4,5 mm) diameter
B—Modulator valve and plug
C—Retaining plug
D—Dowel pin, modulator valve
E—Stop, servo orifice valve
F—Spring, servo orifice control valve, $1\frac{1}{8}$ in. (28 mm) long, $\frac{3}{16}$ in. (4,5 mm) diameter
G—Servo orifice control valve

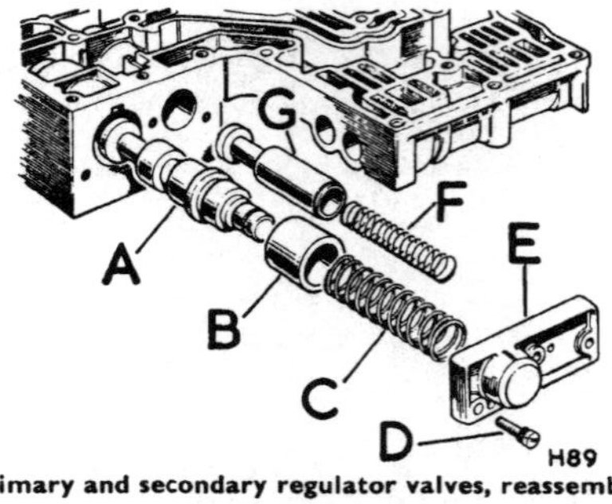

H89

Primary and secondary regulator valves, reassemble

A—Primary regulator valve
B—Sleeve, primary regulator valve
C—Spring, primary regulator valve
D—Screw fixing cover plate
E—Cover plate
F—Spring, secondary regulator valve
G—Secondary regulator valve

Operation EEE3-1—*continued*

5. Fit the modulator valve to the lower valve body, and secure the assembly with the dowel pin.

6. Insert the primary and secondary regulator valves into the lower valve body and fit the cover plate. Tighten the three screws securing the cover plate to the body to a torque figure of 20 to 30 lb in. (0,23 to 0,35 mkg).

7. Place the two check valves, rear pump and converter 'out', into position on the lower valve body. Place the stop for throttle valve spring into position.

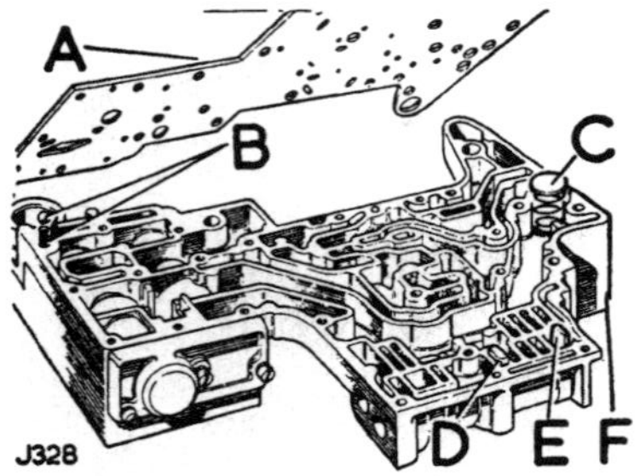

J328

Lower valve body components, assemble

A—Separating plate
B—Converter 'out' check valve
C—Rear pump check valve
D—Retainer for throttle valve
E—Stop for throttle valve spring
F—Lower valve body

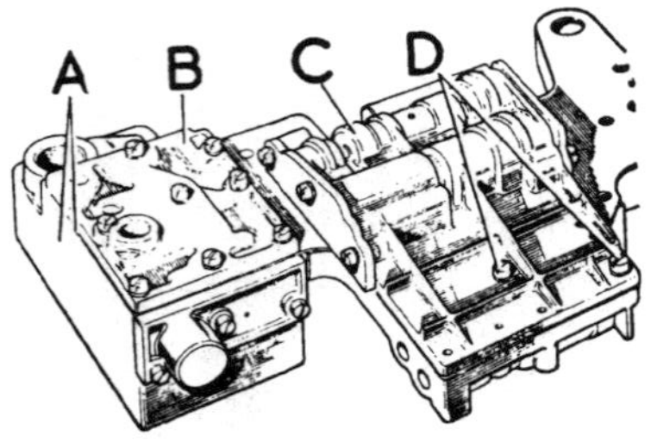

H 92

Valve bodies, reassemble

A—Separating plate and lower valve body
B—Oil tube collector plate
C—Upper valve body
D—Screws fixing valve bodies

8. Fit the throttle valve and spring and locate valve retainer, as illustrated.

9. Carefully place the separating plate into position, ensuring that the valves beneath it are locating correctly.

10. Position the upper valve body assembly on to the separating plate and locate with the two screws as shown, but do not fully tighten the screws at this stage.

11. Fit the oil tube collector plate to the valve body. Tighten the eight fixing screws (six short and two long) to 20 to 30 lb in. (0,23 to 0,35 mkg).

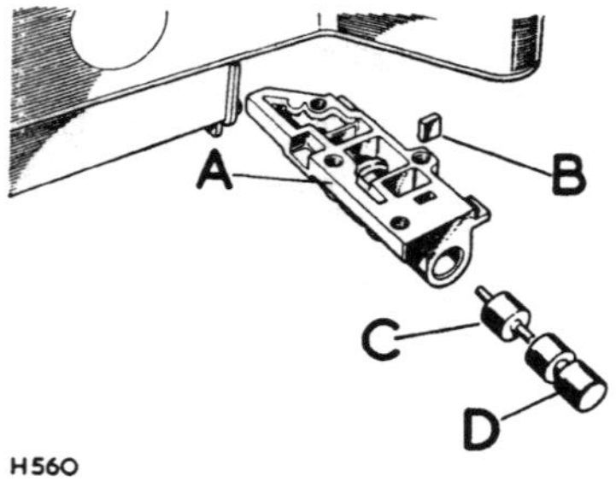

H560

Control valve, D1–D2

A—Valve body, D1–D2 control
B—Stop for spacer
C—Valve, D1–D2 control
D—Spacer, D1–D2 control

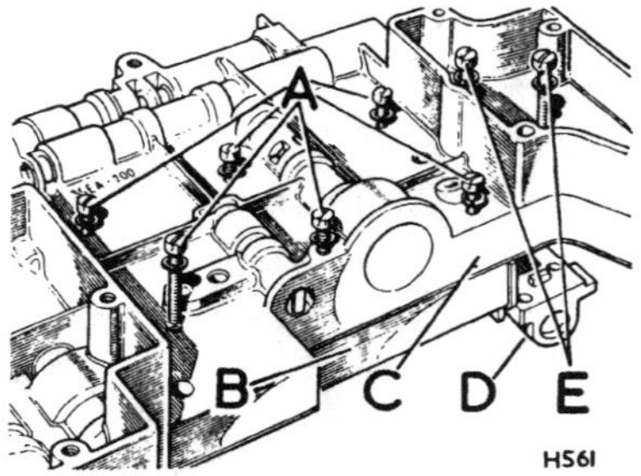

H561

Valve bodies and line plate, reassemble

A—Screws fixing valve bodies
B—Upper valve body
C—Lower valve body
D—Control valve, D1–D2
E—Screws fixing D1–D2 valve

Operation EEE3-1—*continued*

12. Assemble the D1–D2 control valve in the order illustrated.
13. Place the D1–D2 control valve into position on the valve bodies. Turn the unit over and secure the plate loosely with the two screws located inside the oil intake chamber of the valve body. Before finally tightening these two screws to 20 to 30 lb in. (0,23 to 0,35 mkg) insert the other two long screws loosely (these also locate the oil strainer) to ensure correct alignment. After tightening, remove the long screws.
14. Fit the six remaining screws securing the upper valve body to the lower valve body. Tighten to a torque figure of 20 to 30 lb in. (0,23 to 0,35 mkg).

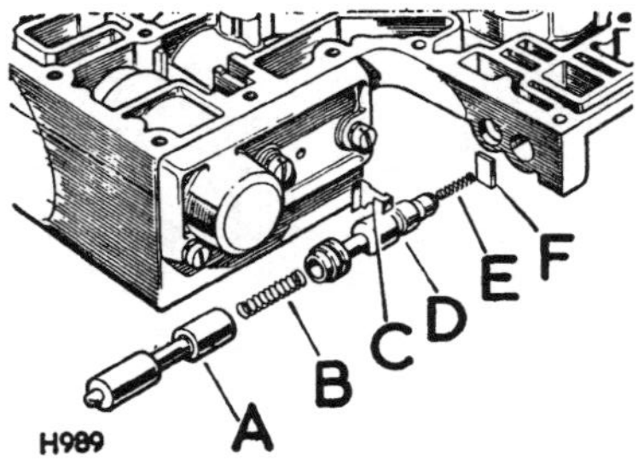

H989

Downshift and throttle valve, reassemble

A—Downshift valve
B—Spring for downshift valve
C—Valve retainer
D—Throttle valve
E—Spring for throttle valve
F—Stop for throttle valve spring

15. Fit the downshift valve and throttle valve in the order illustrated.
16. Fit the downshift valve cam. To ensure that the return spring is correctly tensioned, the cam should be turned in the direction of the arrow and held in this position whilst the assembly is secured to the valve body with two screws and spring washers.
17. Replace the front pump strainer, tightening the screw to 20 to 30 lb in. (0,23 to 0,35 mkg).
18. Insert the manual control valve. The valve body assembly is now completely assembled.

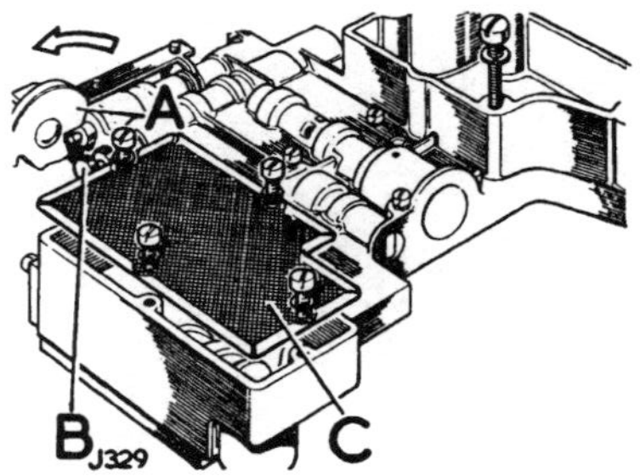

J329

Downshift valve cam and oil strainers, reassemble

A—Downshift valve cam assembly
B—Manual control valve
C—Oil strainer, front pump

Front servo, overhaul—Operation EEE3-2

Workshop hand tools:

Spanner sizes: Open-ended ½ in. AF, 9/16 in. AF
Screwdriver, small Drift Light hammer

Instruction for the removal and refitting of the front servo is given in Part Two of this Section

Front servo, dismantle

1. Use a screwdriver to prise out the snap ring.
2. Withdraw the sleeve and piston from the body of the servo and separate the components.

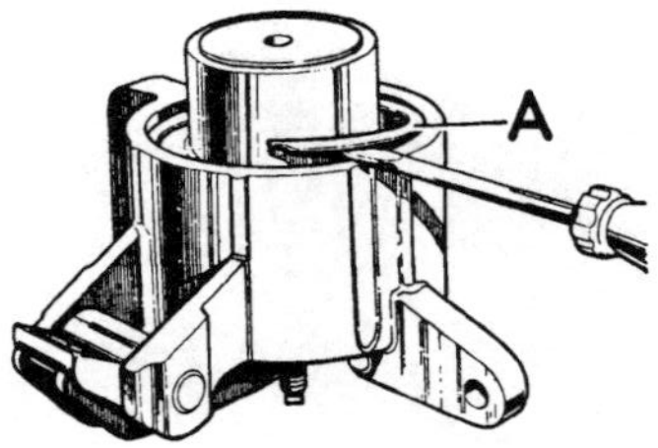

H96

Front servo, dismantle

A—Snap ring

3. Remove the large and small 'O' ring from the piston and the seal from the piston sleeve.
4. Remove the adjusting screw, operating lever and pivot pin.

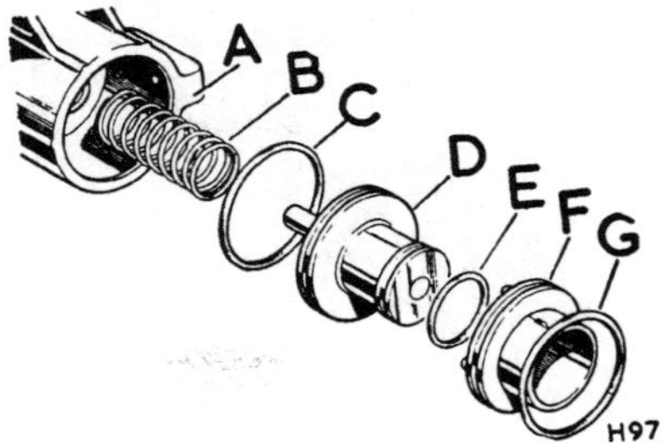

H97

Front servo components

A—Servo body
B—Piston retracting spring
C—'O' ring for piston, large
D—Piston assembly
E—'O' ring for piston, small
F—Piston sleeve
G—Sealing ring for piston sleeve

Preparation before rebuild

1. Clean all components, using petrol and nylon rag. Examine all components for defects.

   The nominal free length of the spring is 31/32 in. (24,5 mm).

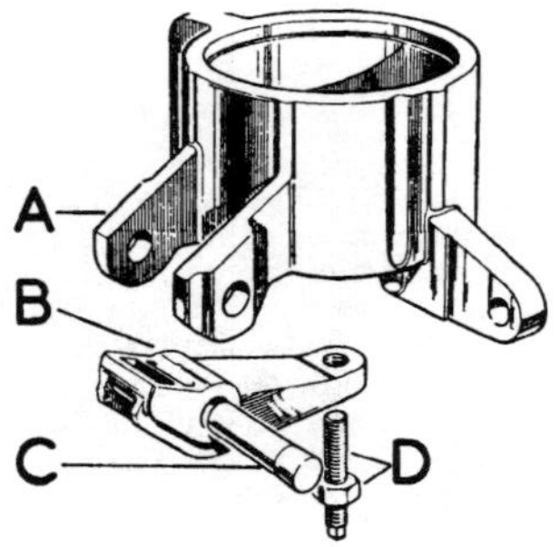

H98

Front servo body

A—Servo body
B—Operating lever
C—Pivot pin
D—Adjusting screw and locknut

Front servo, rebuild

1. Renew the 'O' ring and the square section oil sealing ring.
2. Prior to assembly, lubricate the components with clean transmission fluid.
3. Assemble the components and secure with the snap ring. Note that the collar of the sleeve fits inwards.

Rear servo, overhaul—Operation EEE3-3

Workshop hand tools:

Drift Light hammer

Instruction for the removal and refitting of the rear servo is given in Part Two of this Section

Rear servo, dismantle

1. Release return spring from lug on servo body.

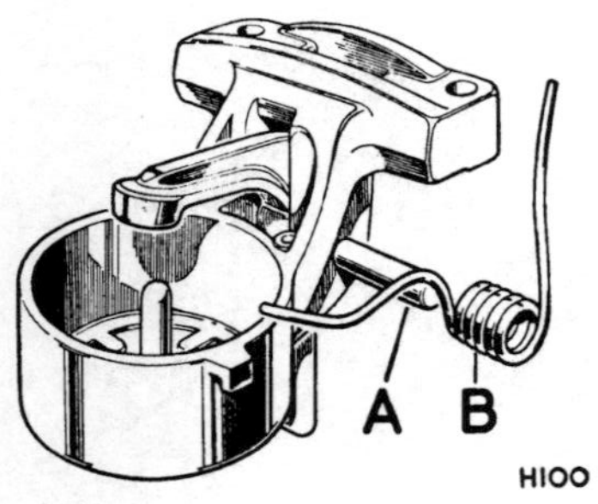

Rear servo, dismantle

A—Pivot pin for spring and lever
B—Return spring for servo

2. Drift out the pivot pin, then withdraw the operating arm.

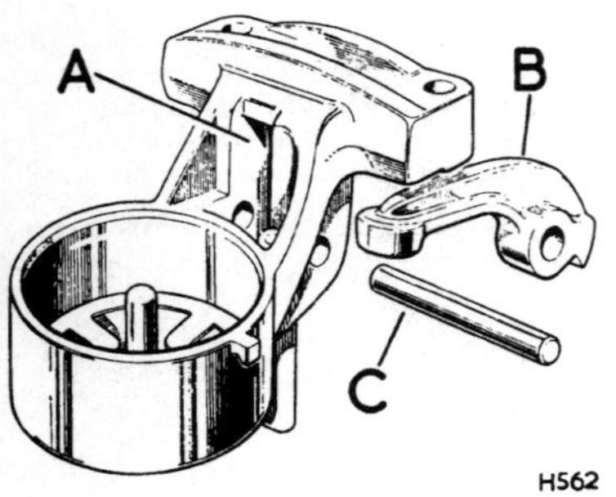

Servo operating lever, removal

A—Servo body
B—Operating lever for servo
C—Pivot pin for spring and lever

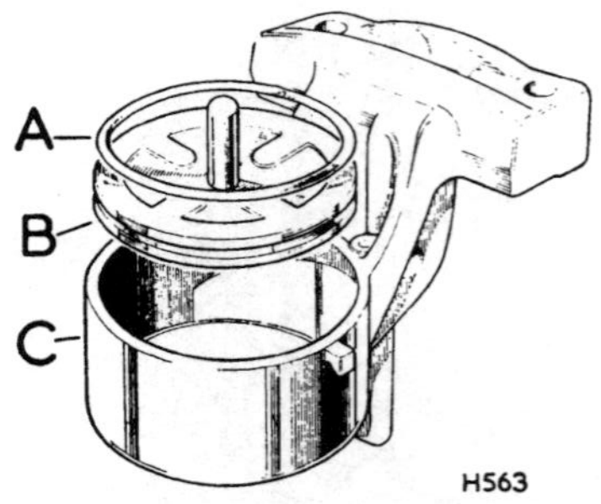

Rear servo piston

A—Sealing ring for piston
B—Servo piston
C—Rear servo body

3. Withdraw piston.
4. Remove the 'O' ring from the piston.

Preparation before rebuild

1. Clean and examine all the components for defects. Use petrol and nylon rag for cleaning purposes.

Rear servo, rebuild

1. Renew the piston 'O' ring.
2. Prior to assembly of the piston into the body, lubricate all components with transmission fluid.
3. Reverse dismantling procedure.

Front pump assembly, overhaul—Operation EEE3-4

Workshop hand tools:

Spanner size: Socket $\frac{1}{2}$ in. AF
Screwdriver, medium Hammer, plastic-faced

Special tools:

Spintorq screwdriver set, Rover Part No. 601286
Torque wrench set, Rover Part No. 601285

Instruction for the removal and refitting of the front pump is given in Part Two of this Section

Front pump, dismantle

1. Separate the pump housing from the adaptor and converter support by removing the five bolts and spring washers and the small locating screw and spring washer.

   If necessary, tap the assembly lightly with a plastic-faced hammer to separate the housing and adaptor.

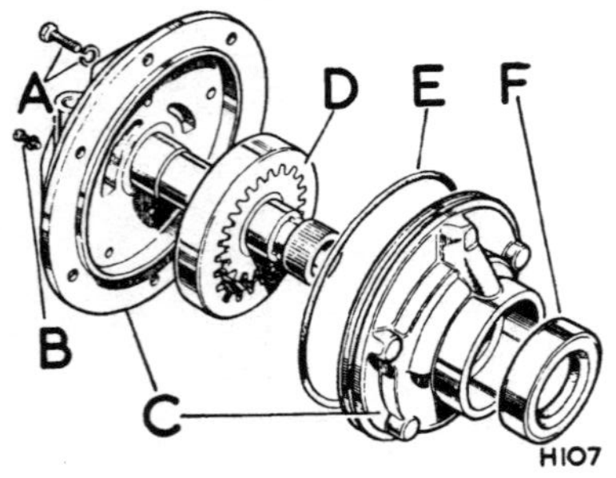

Front pump assembly

A—Bolts for front pump
B—Locating screw and washer
C—Two halves of pump assembly
D—Pump gears
E—'O' ring, large
F—Outer oil seal

2. Mark the outside face of each pump gear to ensure that they are fitted the same way round on assembly. Lift out the gears.
3. Remove the large 'O' ring from the outside diameter of the pump housing and discard.
4. Prise out the lipped oil seal from the pump housing and discard.

Preparation before rebuild

1. Clean all parts thoroughly and examine for wear and defects. Renew the seal and 'O' ring and, if necessary, the fixing bolts and washers.
2. The bushes in the converter support tube are not service items.

Front pump assembly, rebuild

1. Position the new large 'O' ring on to the pump housing and fit a new lipped oil seal.
2. Assemble the pump gears; locate in position with petroleum jelly the correct way round, as marked, position the pump housing to the adaptor and converter support. Loosely locate with the five bolts and spring washers and small screw and washer. Push the pump housing into the adaptor. Tighten the five bolts to a torque figure of 17 to 22 lb ft (2,3 to 3,0 mkg) and the screw to a torque figure of 25 to 35 lb in. (0,3 to 0,4 mkg).

Front clutch assembly, overhaul—Operation EEE3-5

Workshop hand tools:

Screwdriver, small

Instruction for the removal and refitting of the front clutch is given in Part Two of this Section

Front clutch, dismantle

1. Separate front clutch from rear clutch.
2. Use a screwdriver to remove the snap ring retaining the input shaft. Lift off the input shaft.

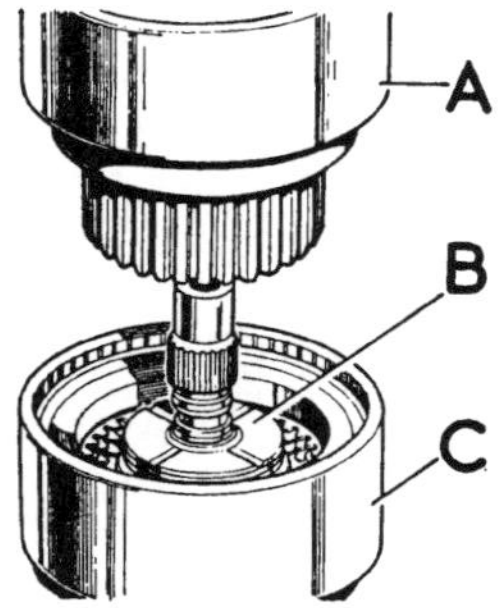

Front and rear clutch

A—Front clutch B—Thrust washers
C—Rear clutch

3. Remove the bronze thrust washer, located in the recess of the clutch hub, and lift out the clutch hub.

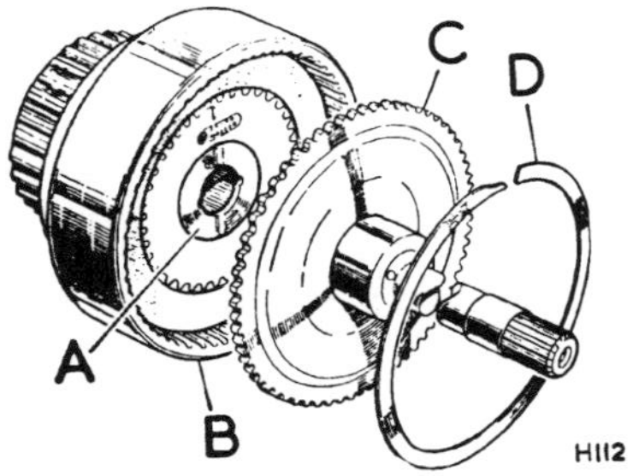

Input shaft and front clutch assembly

A—Bronze thrust washer C—Input shaft
B—Front clutch cylinder D—Snap ring

4. Withdraw the clutch plates, four inner and three outer. The outer 'drive' plates are steel and the inner friction plates are paper-faced.
5. Lift out the pressure plate.

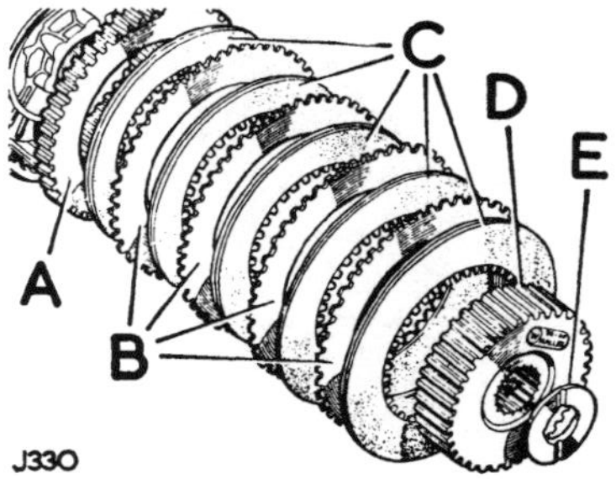

Hub and clutch plates, remove

A—Pressure plate D—Clutch hub
B—Outer clutch plates E—Bronze thrust washer
C—Inner clutch plates

6. Prise out the inner snap ring with a screwdriver and remove the diaphragm-type spring. Note that the inner edge of the diaphragm spring is dished inwards.

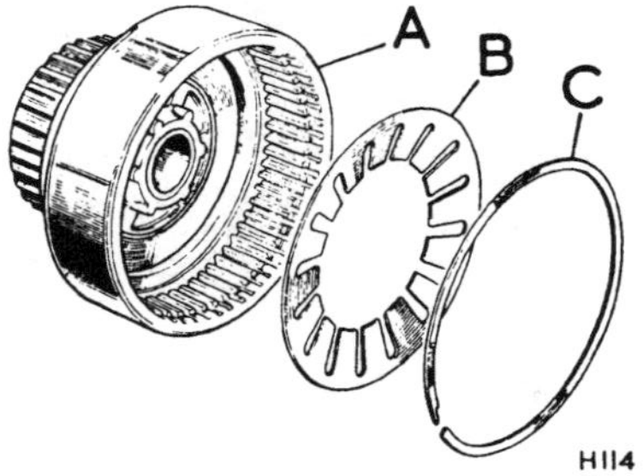

Clutch spring, remove

A—Clutch cylinder B—Diaphragm spring
C—Snap ring

7. Remove the clutch piston. This may be facilitated by applying an air line through the hole in the internal bore whilst the second hole is blanked off.
8. Withdraw the bearing ring from the top of the piston.
9. Remove the large sealing ring from the piston.
10. Remove the small 'O' ring from the cylinder spigot.

Operation EEE3-5—*continued*

11. Check that the reed valve on the piston is not bent and that it can be closed with light finger pressure.

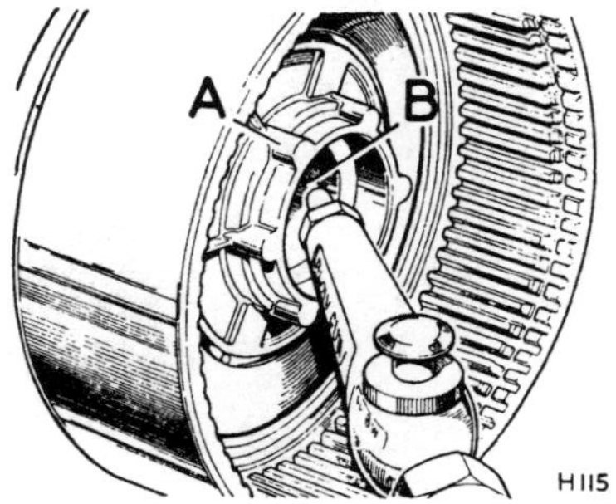

Clutch piston, remove

A—Piston B—Drilling to which air pressure is applied

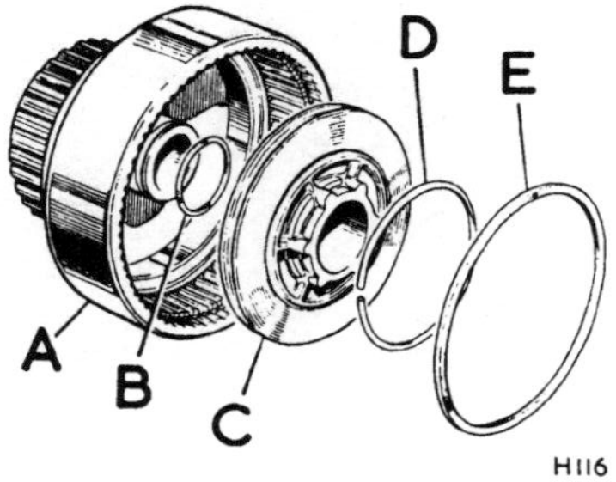

Front clutch piston components

A—Clutch cylinder D—Spring bearing ring
B—Inner 'O' ring seal E—Seal for piston
C—Piston

Preparation before rebuild

1. Clean the component parts thoroughly and inspect for defects. Use nylon rag and petrol for cleaning purposes.

Front clutch, rebuild

1. Lubricate the cylinder with clean transmission fluid. Smear a new small 'O' ring with clean fluid and fit the ring into the cylinder.
2. Fit new sealing ring on to the clutch piston, after lubricating both parts with clean transmission fluid. Place the bearing ring into position in its groove on top of the piston.
3. Replace the diaphragm spring, dished edge inwards, and secure in position with the snap ring.
4. Install the clutch pressure plate with the plain side uppermost.
5. Replace the clutch plates; an inner splined plate first, followed by an outer splined plate, alternately.
6. Line up the internal teeth of the inner plates, then fit the clutch hub, with the flat face uppermost. If necessary, turn the hub slightly to pick up the splines of the clutch plates.
7. Place the bronze thrust washer into the recess of the hub.
8. Fit the input shaft to the cylinder and secure with the large snap ring.

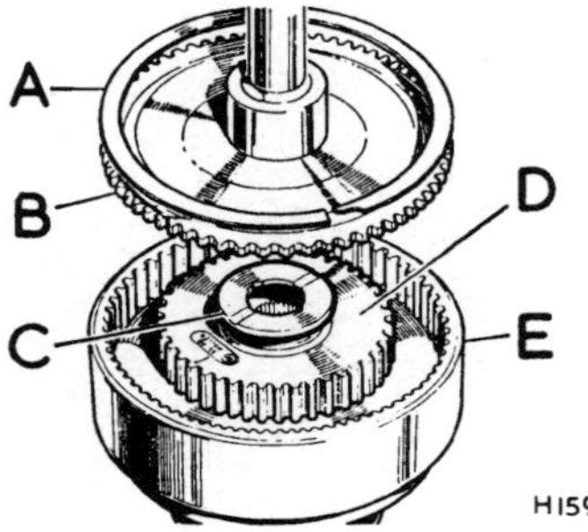

Clutch plates and hub

A—Snap ring for input shaft D—Clutch hub
B—Input shaft flange E—Clutch cylinder
C—Bronze thrust washer

9. Support the rear clutch and forward sun gear assembly in a vertical position, centralise the two sealing rings on the shaft of the forward sun gear assembly. Lubricate freely with petroleum jelly and gently lower the front clutch cylinder into position.
10. Take care not to disengage the front clutch from rear clutch during handling.

Rear clutch, overhaul—Operation EEE3-6

Workshop hand tools:

Screwdriver, small

Special tools:

Clutch spring compressor, Rover Part No. 601283
Snap ring pliers, Rover Part No. 601282
Rear clutch piston and seal inserter, Rover Part No. 601290

Instruction for the removal and refitting of the rear clutch is given in Part Two of this Section

Rear clutch, dismantle

1. With the front and rear clutch assembly in a vertical position, carefully lift off the front clutch and place on one side.
2. Remove needle thrust bearing and lipped thrust plate from rear end of shaft, also the steel and bronze thrust washers from the rear clutch housing.

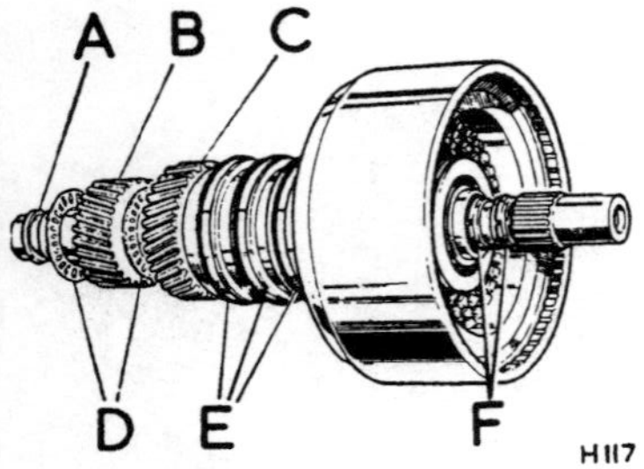

Rear clutch, dismantle

A—Rear end sealing ring, nylon
B—Forward sun gear and shaft
C—Rear clutch assembly
D—Needle thrust bearing
E—Large sealing rings
F—Front end oil sealing rings

3. Remove the oil sealing rings from the front end of the forward sun gear shaft before attempting to remove the forward sun gear assembly.
4. Withdraw the forward sun gear assembly from the clutch, noting the position of the needle thrust bearing between the two gears. The sun gear cannot be removed from its shaft.
5. Use a screwdriver to remove the outer snap ring retaining the clutch components.
6. Invert drum and remove plates. Mark plate serrations to ensure correct assembly if original plates are being replaced.
7. Lift out the pressure plate, spacer and clutch plates. Note that the outer plates are dished and the inner plates are paper-faced.

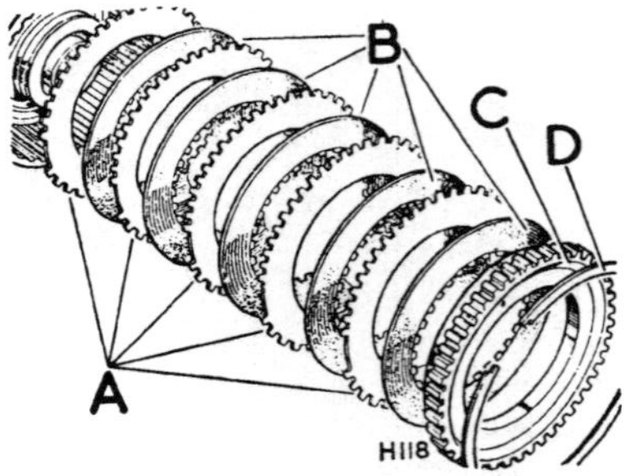

Rear clutch components

A—Outer clutch plates
B—Inner clutch plates
C—Pressure plate
D—Snap ring for pressure plate

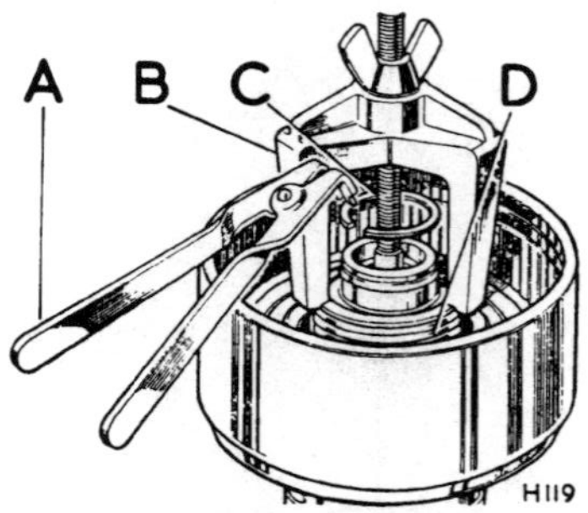

Clutch piston spring, remove

A—Snap ring pliers
B—Clutch spring compressor
C—Snap ring for piston spring
D—Piston spring

8. Insert threaded rod of service tool, Rover Part No. 601283, through clutch and use legs of tool, together with the wing nut, to compress the clutch spring. Use snap ring pliers, Rover Part No 601282, to remove the circlip. Rotate the snap ring gap to the milled flat on the boss of the drum to facilitate removal.

   Remove spring compression tool.

Operation EEE3-6—*continued*

9. Withdraw spring seat and spring.
10. To facilitate removal of the piston, use an air line through the hole adjacent to the drum, as illustrated.

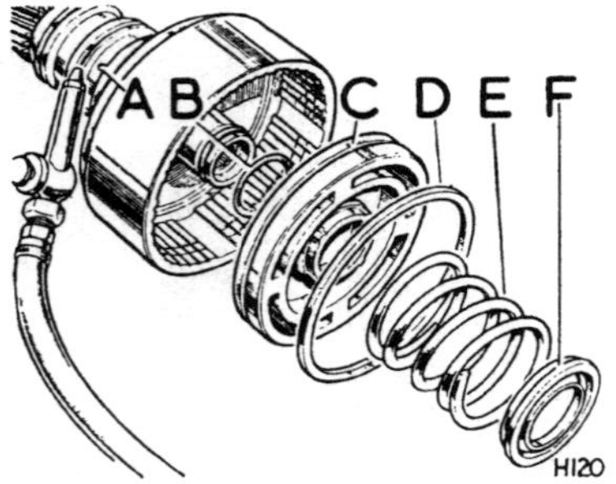

Clutch piston removal

A—Orifice for air line
B—Inner 'O' ring, small
C—Piston
D—Seal for piston
E—Clutch spring
F—Clutch spring seat

11. Remove the 'O' ring from the inner boss of the drum and the oil seal from the piston.

Preparation before rebuild

1. Use petrol and nylon rag to clean all the components.
2. Examine all the parts for wear or defects.
3. Check that the reed valve on the piston is not bent or stuck open and that it can be closed with light finger pressure.

Rear clutch, rebuild

1. Fit new 'O' ring to boss in clutch cylinder.
2. Fit new sealing ring to piston.
3. Locate the rear clutch piston and seal inserter in clutch cylinder, then install piston, flat side downwards, ensure that it is correctly aligned with the bore during fitting. Remove the rear clutch piston and seal inserter.

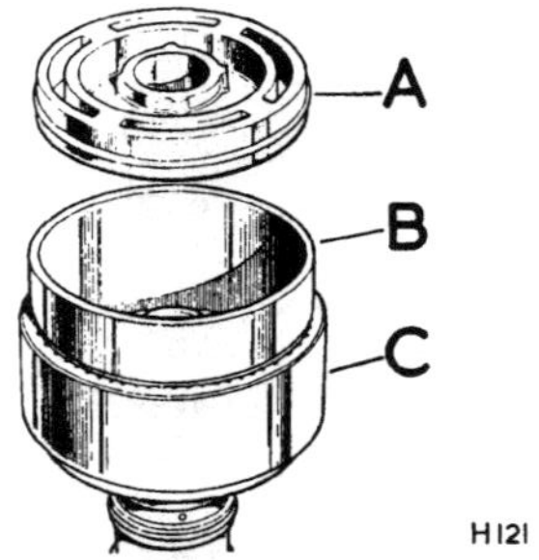

Clutch piston, refit

A—Piston
B—Rear clutch piston and seal inserter
C—Clutch cylinder

4. Locate the piston spring and spring seat on to the piston. Position circlip on spring seat, then use the special tool to compress the spring. Fit the circlip, using circlip pliers.
5. Fit the clutch plates, noting that an outer plate is fitted first. The dishing of the outer plates must all face in one direction, but it does not matter which way the dishing of the plates face in the drum. If necessary, check for dishing on a flat surface.

   Replace the spacer and pressure plate with the flat face inwards and secure with the snap ring.

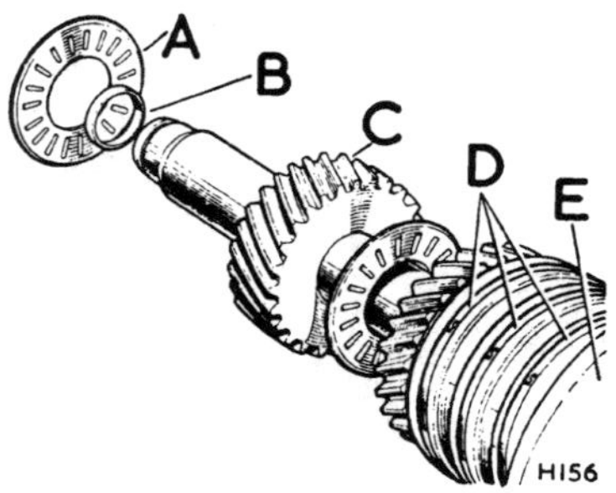

Forward sun gear and rear clutch

A—Needle thrust bearing
B—Nylon ring
C—Forward sun gear
D—Oil sealing ring, clutch to centre support
E—Rear clutch

Operation EEE3-6—*continued*

6. Fit new oil sealing rings to the rear outer boss of the drum.
7. Place a needle thrust washer over the shaft against the front face of the forward sun gear, then insert shaft into the clutch.
8. Fit two new oil sealing rings to the front end of the forward sun gear shaft.

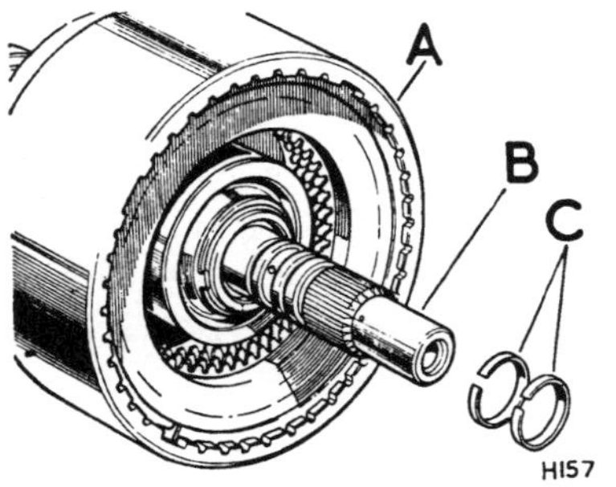

Oil sealing rings, fit

A—Rear clutch
B—Forward sun gear shaft
C—Oil sealing rings

9. Locate the steel and bronze thrust washer over the centre hub of the drum and retain with petroleum jelly.
10. With the assembly in a vertical position, first line up the internal teeth of the clutch plates, then centralise the small oil sealing rings on the shaft, lubricating with petroleum jelly and gently lower the front clutch over the shaft.

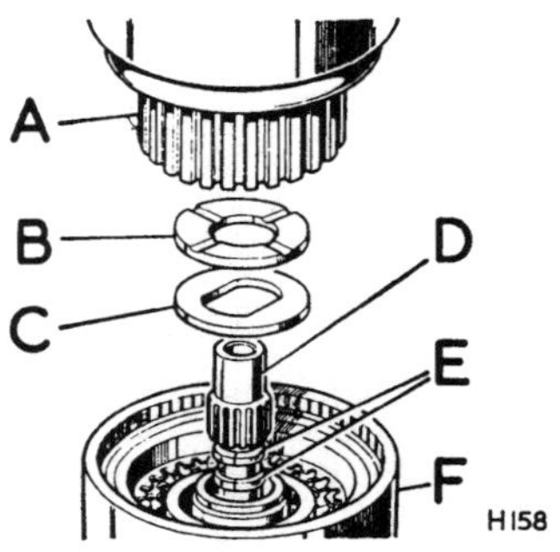

Front and rear clutch

A—Front clutch	D—Forward sun gear shaft
B—Bronze thrust washer	E—Oil sealing rings
C—Steel thrust washer	F—Rear clutch

11. If difficulty is experienced when carrying out this operation, the front clutch should be checked to ensure that the internal thrust washer has not been displaced.
12. Fit new nylon sealing ring to rear end of forward sun gear shaft and place needle thrust washer in position and retain with petroleum jelly.

Planet gears and rear drum, overhaul—Operation EEE3-7

Workshop hand tools:

Screwdriver, small Screwdriver, large Mallet, plastic-faced

Instruction for the removal and refitting of the planet gear and rear drum assembly is given in Part Two of this Section

Rear drum, dismantle

1. Remove needle thrust bearing and plate from the rear end of the drum.
2. Separate the centre support from the planet gear assembly.
3. Withdraw the one-way clutch from its outer race.
4. Support the drum in a soft-jawed vice. Prise out the snap ring with a screwdriver. Remove the one-way clutch outer race by levering with a large screwdriver alternately in the three slots. This race is a tight fit. Take care not to damage outer surface of drum.

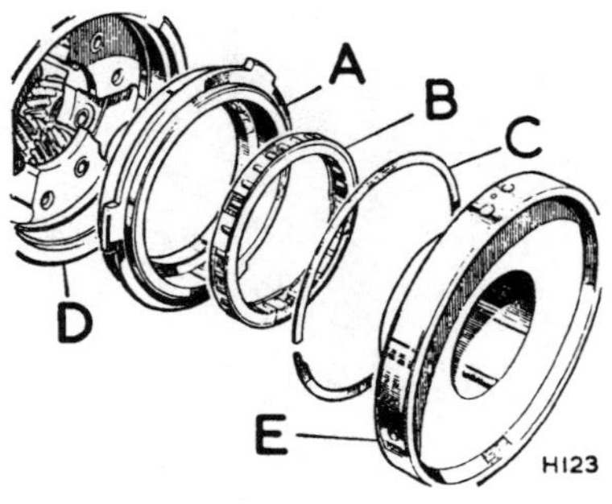

Planet gears and rear drum assembly

A—Outer race for one-way clutch
B—One-way clutch
C—Snap ring for outer race
D—Planet carrier
E—Centre support

Preparation before rebuild

1. Clean all the components, using transmission fluid and nylon rag. Examine all components for defects.

Rear drum, rebuild

1. Lubricate all the components with clean transmission fluid.
2. Lightly tap the one-way clutch outer race into position, using a soft-faced mallet, and ensure correct alignment. Secure with the snap ring.
3. Position the one-way clutch in the outer race with the lip of the one-way clutch outwards.
4. Place the centre support into position on the drum.
5. First place the bearing plate lip outwards, followed by the needle thrust washer in position at the rear of the assembly and retain, using petroleum jelly.

Governor, overhaul—Operation EEE3-8

Workshop hand tools:

Screwdrivers, medium and large

Special tools:

Spintorq screwdriver, Rover Part No. 601286

Instruction for the removal and refitting of the governor is given in Part Two of this Section

Governor, dismantle

1. Remove the two screws and spring washers retaining the body to the governor sleeve.
2. Compress and withdraw the retainer and remove the governor weight, valve and spring.
3. If necessary, remove the governor cover plate, retained by two countersunk-head lock screws.

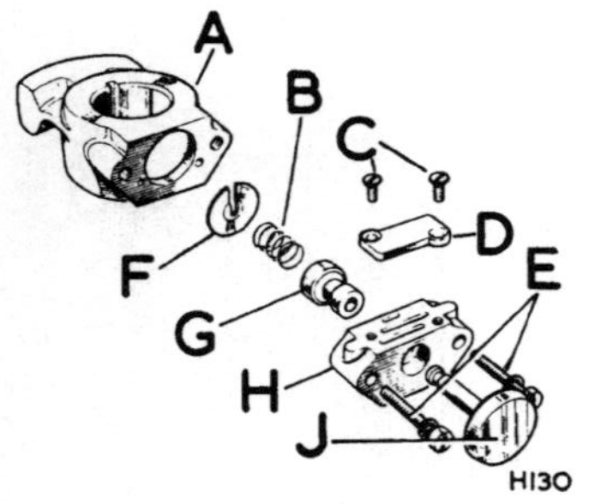

Governor assembly

A—Sleeve for governor
B—Spring for governor
C—Countersunk head lock screws
D—Cover plate
E—Screws fixing governor body
F—Retainer for spring
G—Valve for governor
H—Body for governor
J—Weight for governor

Preparation before rebuild

1. Clean and examine all components. Use nylon rag and transmission fluid for cleaning.

Governor, rebuild

1. Reverse removal procedure.
2. Align oil holes between body and sleeve.
3. Tighten the screws retaining the cover plate to the valve body to a torque figure of 20 to 30 lb in. (0,23 to 0,35 mkg).

   The screws retaining the valve body to the sleeve should be fully tightened, using a large screw-driver.

Gear selector lever, overhaul—Operation EEE3-9

Workshop hand tools:

Spanner size: Open-ended $\frac{9}{16}$ in. AF

Pliers, pointed-nose Screwdriver, Phillips'

Instructions for removal and refitting of the gear selector lever are given in Part Two of this Section

Gear selector lever, dismantle

1. Unscrew gear selector lever knob. If necessary, remove rubber insert, 'O' ring and button.

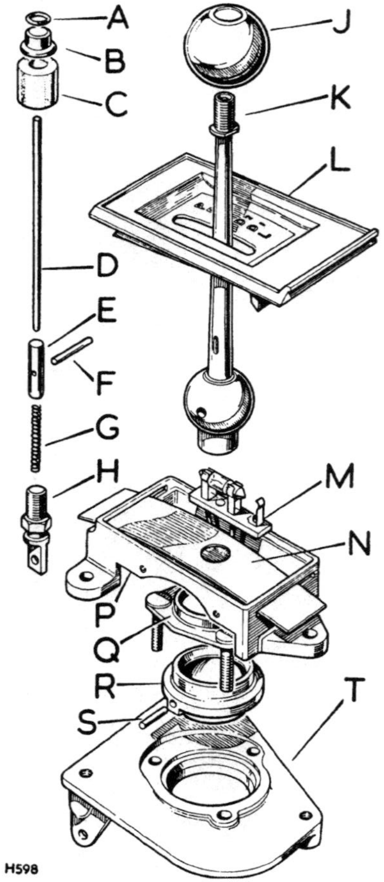

Layout of gear selector lever

A—'O' ring for button
B—Button for knob
C—Rubber insert
D—Control rod
E—Plug for control rod
F—Detent pin
G—Spring for control rod
H—Eyebolt and locknut
J—Knob for gear selector lever
K—Gear selector lever
L—Indicator for gear selector lever
M—Illumination lamp
N—Shield for gear selector lever
P—Housing for gear selector lever
Q—Anti-rattle spring for shield
R—Cover for spherical seat
S—Spherical seat for gear selector lever
T—Locating pin for spherical seat
U—Pivot housing

2. Withdraw gear selector lever through stainless steel shield and gear-change housing. Shield can now be withdrawn from the housing and the illumination lamp removed.
3. Withdraw control rod and remove cover for spherical seat.
4. Use pointed-nose pliers to withdraw the locating pin from the spherical seat. The seat can then be forced off the lever by hand.
5. Remove eyebolt and locknut, the spring, plug for control rod and detent pin can then be withdrawn from the lever.

Gear selector lever, rebuild

1. Reverse removal procedure.
2. If new control rod is being fitted, it should be cut to length on assembly so that $\frac{1}{2}$ in. (12,7 mm) protrudes from the top of the gear selector lever. This dimension is important to ensure correct engagement of the detent pin in the selector gate.

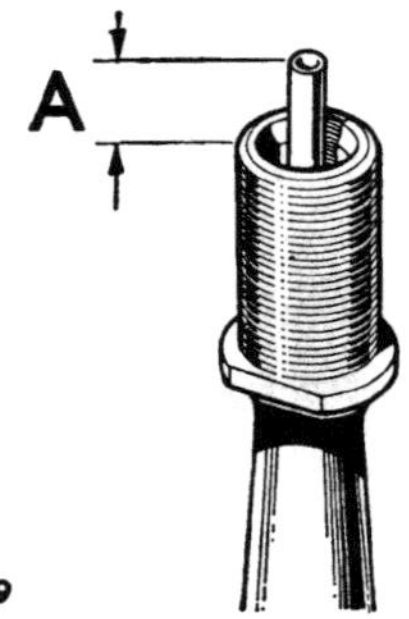

Control rod for gear selector lever

A—$\frac{1}{2}$ in. (12,5 mm)

PART FOUR

This section covers a quick reference defect location chart, general data, recommended lubricants, a list of tightening torques and special tools.

MODEL 35—QUICK REFERENCE DEFECT LOCATION CHART

Note: The numbers indicate the recommended sequence of fault investigation
See opposite page for Action Key

	1	2	3	4	5	6	7	8	9	10	11	12	13
ENGAGEMENT OF 'R', 'D1', 'D2' or 'L'													
Bumpy	D	B	d	f	c	O	Q	—	—	—	—	—	—
Delayed	A	C	D	a	d	c	b	s	N	P	S	X	q
None	A	C	a	b	c	d	V	W	X	Y	—	—	—
TAKE-OFF													
None forward	C	c	b	N	T	—	—	—	—	—	—	—	—
None reverse	C	F	m	n	c	b	a	S	P	—	—	—	—
Seizure reverse	E	O	—	—	—	—	—	—	—	—	—	—	—
No neutral	C	O	c	—	—	—	—	—	—	—	—	—	—
UPSHIFTS													
No 1 to 2	C	E	h	m	R	f	g	a	b	c	t	—	—
No 2 to 3	C	h	n	p	P	f	g	a	b	c	—	—	—
Above normal speeds	B	f	h	m	n	p	g	b	c	d	—	—	—
Below normal speeds	B	f	h	p	b	c	—	—	—	—	—	—	—
UPSHIFT QUALITY													
Slip 1 to 2	A	B	C	E	R	d	f	a	b	c	—	—	—
Slip 2 to 3	A	B	C	E	P	R	d	f	a	b	c	—	—
Rough 1 to 2	B	E	d	f	g	h	T	U	N	c	—	—	—
Rough 2 to 3	B	E	d	f	Q	c	—	—	—	—	—	—	—
Seizure 1 to 2	F	Q	T	U	b	c	—	—	—	—	—	—	—
Seizure 2 to 3	E	a	b	c	—	—	—	—	—	—	—	—	—
DOWNSHIFTS													
No 2 to 1	B	m	h	S	t	—	—	—	—	—	—	—	—
No 3 to 2	B	m	h	Q	R	—	—	—	—	—	—	—	—
Involuntary high speed 3 to 2	A	a	P	—	—	—	—	—	—	—	—	—	—
Above normal shift speeds	B	h	p	f	b	c	—	—	—	—	—	—	—
Below normal shift speeds	B	h	p	f	b	c	m	n	—	—	—	—	—
DOWNSHIFT QUALITY													
Slip 2 to 1	T	—	—	—	—	—	—	—	—	—	—	—	—
Slip 3 to 2	E	R	l	d	f	a	b	c	P	—	—	—	—
Rough 2 to 1	T	N	b	—	—	—	—	—	—	—	—	—	—
Rough 3 to 2	E	l	d	f	c	P	Q	R	—	—	—	—	—
LINE PRESSURE													
Low, idling	A	C	D	d	c	a	s	b	W	—	—	—	—
High, idling	B	D	d	f	e	—	—	—	—	—	—	—	—
Low at stall	A	B	d	g	f	a	c	b	h	X	—	—	—
High at stall	d	f	g	c	—	—	—	—	—	—	—	—	—
STALL SPEED													
Below 1,000	Y	—	—	—	—	—	—	—	—	—	—	—	—
Over 2,000	A	C	F	a	b	c	d	N	P	S	T	V	Y
OVERHEATING	A	E	F	Y	—	—	—	—	—	—	—	—	—

PRELIMINARY ADJUSTMENT FAULTS

A Fluid level incorrect
B Downshift valve cable incorrectly assembled or adjusted
C Manual linkage incorrectly assembled or adjusted
D Incorrect engine idling speed
E Incorrect front band adjustment
F Incorrect rear band adjustment

MECHANICAL FAULTS

N Front clutch slipping due to worn plates or faulty parts
O Front clutch seized or plates distorted
P Rear clutch slipping due to worn plates or faulty check valve in piston
Q Rear clutch seized or plates distorted
R Front band slipping due to faulty servo, broken or worn band
S Rear band slipping due to faulty servo, broken or worn band
T One-way clutch slipping or incorrectly installed
U One-way clutch seized
V Input shaft broken
W Front pump drive tangs on converter hub broken
X Front pump worn
Y Converter blading and/or one-way clutch failed

HYDRAULIC CONTROL FAULTS

a Oil tubes missing or not installed correctly
b Sealing rings missing or broken
c Valve body assembly screws missing or not correctly tightened
d Primary regulator valve sticking
e Secondary regulator valve sticking
f Throttle valve sticking
g Modulator valve sticking
h Governor valve sticking, leaking or incorrectly assembled
l Orifice control valve sticking
m 1 to 2 shift valve sticking
n 2 to 3 shift valve sticking
p 2 to 3 shift valve plunger sticking
q Converter 'out' check valve missing or sticking
s Pump check valve missing or sticking
t 'D1–D2' control valve sticking

DATA

Type	Hydraulic torque converter, providing torque multiplication between the ratios 2:1 and 1:1. Planetary gear set, comprising two sun gears, two sets of pinions, a pinion carrier and a ring gear. The various mechanical ratios are obtained by the engagement of hydraulically operated multi-disc clutches and brake bands.

Gear ratios		Torque converter ratio	Torque converter stall ratio
Direct (top)	1:1		2.16
Intermediate (second)	1.45:1		2.16
Low (first)	2.39:1		2.16
Reverse	2.09:1		

Rear axle gear ratio	3.54:1	
Engine stall speed	1,950 to 2,150 rpm	
Transmission fluid capacity from dry	Torque converter	9 pints
	Gearbox	4¼ pints
	Cooler and pipes	¾ pints
	TOTAL	14 pints
Fluid temperature	Normal operating range 80° to 100°C approximately.	
Identification	The Rover 3.5-Litre automatic transmission model 35 has a blue nameplate attached to the side of the transmission maincasing with the commencing serial number FU1001.	

Recommended lubricants

BP	Castrol	Duckham's	Esso	Mobil	Regent Texaco/ Caltex	Shell
BP Automatic Transmission Fluid Type A	Castrol TQ	Nolmatic ATF	Esso Automatic Transmission Fluid	Mobil ATF 200	Texamatic Fluid	Shell Donax T6

Tightening torques

Component	Torque lb ft	Torque mkg
Torque converter to drive plate	25 to 30	3,5 to 4,0
Drive plate to crankshaft	50	7,0
Transmission case to bell housing	8 to 10	1,0 to 1,4
Extension housing to transmission case	8 to 10	1,0 to 1,4
Oil pan to transmission case	8 to 10	1,0 to 1,4
Front servo to transmission case	8 to 10	1,0 to 1,4
Rear servo to transmission case	10 to 13	1,4 to 1,7
Pump adaptor to front pump body (locating screw)	2 to 3 (25 to 35 lb in.)	0,3 to 0,4
Pump adaptor to front pump body	17 to 22	2,3 to 3,0
Pump adaptor to transmission case	8 to 10	1,0 to 1,4
Rear adaptor to transmission case	4 to 5	0,55 to 0,7
Centre support to transmission case	10 to 13	1,4 to 1,7
Outer lever to manual valve shaft	10 to 15	1,4 to 2,0
Pressure take-off plug	4 to 5 (50 to 60 lb in.)	0,55 to 0,7
Oil pan drain plug	10 to 14	1,4 to 1,9
Oil tube collector to lower valve body	1.7 to 2.5 (20 to 30 lb in.)	0,23 to 0,35
'D1–D2' control valve to lower valve body	1.7 to 2.5 (20 to 30 lb in.)	0,23 to 0,35
Lower body end plate to lower valve body	1.7 to 2.5 (20 to 30 lb in.)	0,23 to 0,35
Upper body end plate, front or rear, to upper valve body	1.7 to 2.5 (20 to 30 lb in.)	0,23 to 0,35
Upper valve body to lower valve body	1.7 to 2.5 (20 to 30 lb in.)	0,23 to 0,35
Valve bodies assembly to transmission case	4 to 5 (50 to 66 lb in.)	0,55 to 0,7
Pump strainers to lower valve body	1.7 to 2.5 (20 to 30 lb in.)	0,23 to 0,35

Tightening torques *(continued)*

Component	Torque lb ft	Torque mkg
Downshift valve cam bracket to valve body	1.7 to 2.5 (20 to 30 lb in.)	0,22 to 0,35
Body to governor sleeve	Tighten fully with large screwdriver	
Cover plate to governor body	1.7 to 2.5 (20 to 30 lb in.)	0,23 to 0,35
Adjusting screw, front servo	10 lb in.	0,11
Locknut, front servo lever	15 to 20	2,0 to 2,8
Adjusting screw, rear servo	10	1,4
Locknut, rear servo to case	25 to 30	3,5 to 4,0
Starter inhibitor switch locknut	4 to 6 (48 to 72 lb in.)	0,55 to 0,8
Downshift valve cable adaptor to transmission case	8 to 9 (96 to 108 lb in.)	1,0 to 1,2
Filler tube connector adaptor to transmission case	20 to 30	2,8 to 4,0
Filler tube to connector sleeve nut	17 to 18	2,3 to 2,4
Stone guards to converter housing	1.4 to 1.6 (17 to 19 lb in.)	0,19 to 0,22
Coupling flange to driven shaft	20 to 25	2,8 to 3,5
Oil cooler to transmission case connector	6 to 10 (72 to 120 lb in.)	0,8 to 1,4
Extension housing to mounting bracket on sub-frame	25	3,5
Torque converter housing to flexible drive plate housing	30	4,0

Special tools

Below will be found details of special tools which are recommended to facilitate service work on the model 35 automatic transmission.

All tools are illustrated in the appropriate sections, together with an explanation of their use.

Special service tools for the model 35 automatic transmission

	Rover Part No.
Service tool kit assembly	601279
Comprising the following 11 items	
Gearbox cradle	601280
End-play checking tool	601281
Snap ring pliers	601282
Clutch spring compressor	601283
Pressure gauge and tachometer	601284
Torque wrench set	601285
Spintorq screwdriver set	601286
Front servo gauge	601287
Locknut wrench	601288
Service tool box	601289
Rear clutch and seal inserter	601290

All the tools listed may be ordered from the Rover Parts Department or through any Rover Distributor or Dealer.

Section F - ACCELERATOR LINKAGE

Operations F-1 to F-6 are not applicable, see following Operation F-7 for Rover 3.5-Litre models.

Accelerator linkage, remove, refit and adjust—Operation F-7

Time allowed: hours

Workshop hand tools:

Spanner sizes: $\frac{5}{16}$ in. AF, $\frac{7}{16}$ in. AF, $\frac{9}{16}$ in. AF
Screwdriver, medium Pliers, long-nosed

Accelerator linkage, remove

1. Disconnect cable from throttle pivot arm.
2. Remove nut, bolt and spring washer securing the pivot arm to the bracket.
3. Remove accelerator pedal and pivot arm, secured to the floor by two screws and plain washers.
4. If necessary, remove the pivot arm from the pedal, secured by a split pin and washer.

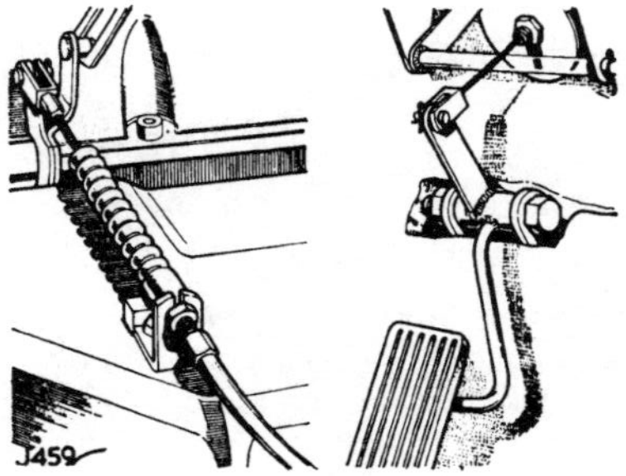

Accelerator pedal and cable

5. Disconnect the cable from the countershaft lever and remove the adjusting nut from the bracket on the inlet manifold. It is now possible to remove the cable by lifting it through the bracket.

Accelerator linkage, refit

1. Reverse removal procedure.
2. Before the engine is tested, ensure that the linkage is correctly adjusted.

Downshift cable adjustment

1. With the downshift cable attached to the extension arm of the throttle lever on the left-hand carburetter, and with the butterfly in the idling position, adjust the downshift cable abutment screw until there is a gap of .010 in. (0,25 mm) between the end of the abutment screw and the crimped stop on the inner cable.

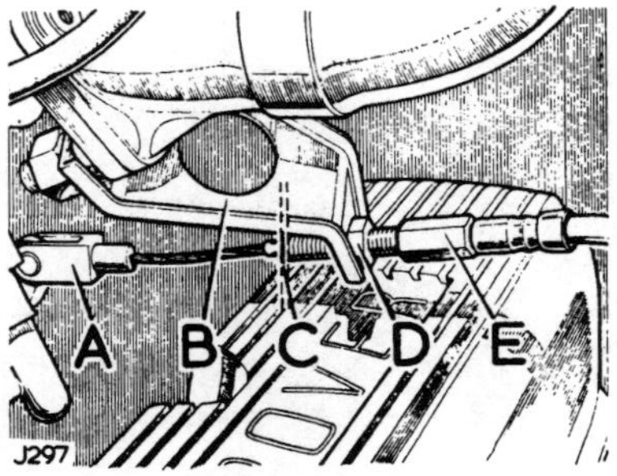

Downshift cable adjustment

A—Clevis for cable
B—Bracket for cable
C—Clearance .010 in. (0,25 mm) between crimped stop and adjuster
D—Locknut for adjuster
E—Adjuster

2. With the abutment screw in this position, tighten the locknut to the bracket stop.

   Note: Should the crimp be missing, or if it is suspected that the crimp is in the incorrect position, a full check should be carried out as outlined under Operation EE2-3.

Operation F-7—*continued*

3. With the butterfly in the idling position, check that on the left-hand carburetter there is a .006 in. (0,15 mm) gap between the roller on the countershaft lever and the throttle lever, and on the right-hand carburetter a .006 in. (0,15 mm) gap between the right leg of the fork on the adjusting lever and the pin on the throttle lever. Should these not be correct, carry out adjustments as detailed under Operation A1-8.

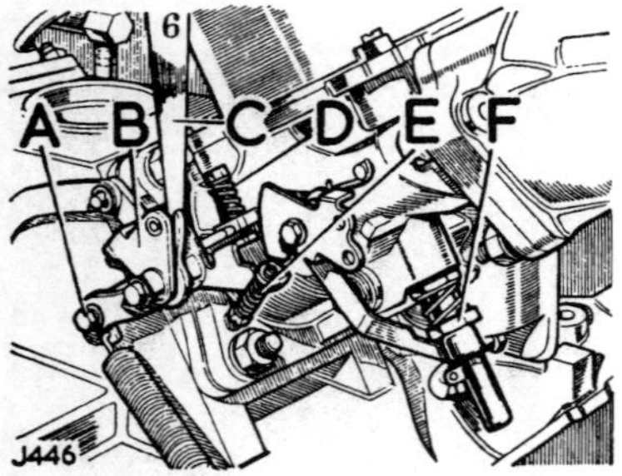

Throttle lever setting, right-hand

A—Screw fixing throttle lever and carburetter lever, right-hand
B—Lever with pin for throttle link
C—Feeler gauge
D—Slow running adjustment screw
E—Fast idle adjustment screw
F—Mixture adjustment screw

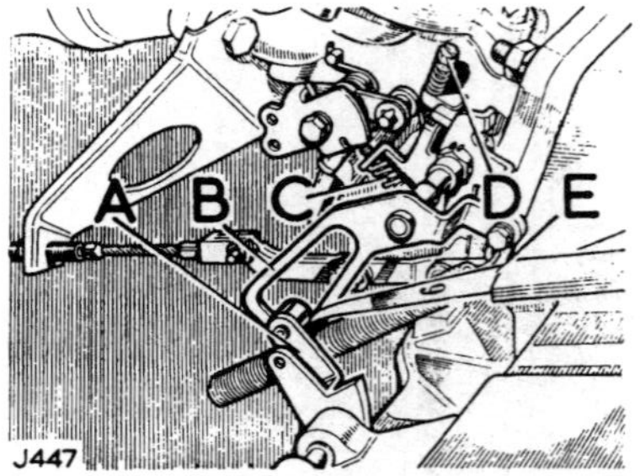

Throttle lever setting, left-hand

A—Countershaft lever with nylon roller
B—Throttle lever, left-hand
C—Fast idle adjustment screw, left-hand
D—Slow running adjustment screw
E—Feeler gauge

Section G - PROPELLER SHAFTS

Information contained in the Rover 3-Litre Workshop Manual is applicable, except that the front propeller shaft has a splined end for centre flange in place of the tapered end and Woodruff key type of fixing used on Rover 3-Litre models.

Section H – SUB-FRAME

The sub-frame has been modified to accept the new V-8 engine. However basically the workshop procedures as detailed for Rover 3-Litre models fitted with Automatic transmission are applicable. See Section A-1, Engine and transmission, remove and refit for items to be disconnected when removing and refitting sub-frame with engine and transmission.

Section J

This Section is not applicable to Rover 3.5-Litre models.

Section – J1 POWER STEERING

The steering is identical to that used on the 3-Litre Mk III with the exception of the power steering pump, which is now pulley driven, instead of dynamo driven.

Therefore, most of the information in this Section is applicable except that:

Operation J1-6 is replaced by Operation J1-6A.

Operation J1-7 is replaced by Operation J1-7A.

Operations J1-10, J1-11 and J1-12 are not applicable.

Power steering hydraulic pump, remove and refit—Operation J1-6A

Time allowed: hours

Workshop hand tools:

Spanner sizes: $\frac{7}{16}$ in. AF, $\frac{1}{2}$ in. AF, $\frac{9}{16}$ in. AF, $\frac{5}{8}$ in. AF, 1 in. AF
Screwdriver, medium

To overhaul power steering hydraulic pump, see Operation J1-7A

Hydraulic pump, remove

1. Remove the reservoir filler cap and disconnect the hydraulic pipe, reservoir to pump, by releasing the clip at the adaptor. Allow the oil to drain into a suitable container. This oil must not be used again.
2. Remove the high pressure pipe, hydraulic pump to steering box, at the pump.

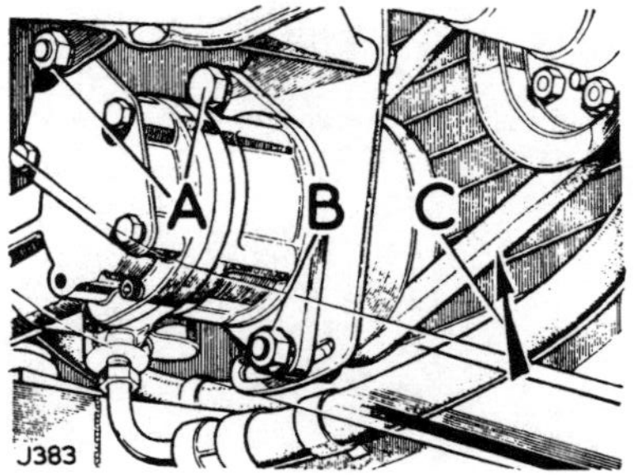

Power steering hydraulic pump belt adjustment

A—Pivot bolts
B—Adjusting bolt
C—Check at this point $\frac{1}{4}$ in. to $\frac{3}{8}$ in. (6 to 9 mm) free movement

3. Slacken the hydraulic pump pulley bolt.
4. Slacken the adjustment bolt and release the belt. To remove the belt, the fan, fan pulley and fan belt must be removed, and the timing pointer moved to one side.
5. Remove the two bolts, pump bracket to timing cover, and the nut, spring and plain washers from the rear mounting bracket. Lift out the hydraulic pump.

Hydraulic pump, refit

It is essential that this procedure is strictly adhered to in order to avoid noise transmission into the vehicle and vibration of the steering column.

1. Assemble front and rear mounting brackets **loosely** to timing cover and cylinder block respectively. All bolts are to be completely slack.
2. Assemble steering pump to front and rear support brackets and nip up (finger tight) the two pivot bolts and the adjusting bolt at bottom of front bracket with the pump held at about half-travel in the adjusting slot.
3. Nip up (finger tight) the two bolts securing front bracket to timing cover pedestals.
4. Tighten the two bolts securing rear bracket to cylinder block.
5. Tighten the two bolts securing front bracket to timing cover pedestals.
6. Refit the belt and adjust the tension to give a deflection of $\frac{1}{4}$ in. to $\frac{3}{8}$ in. (6 to 9 mm) when checked midway between the crankshaft pulley and the power steering pump pulley when depressed by hand, and tighten pivot bolts and pump adjusting bolt.
7. Refit the fan belt, pulley and fan. Adjust the fan belt to give a deflection of $\frac{7}{16}$ in. to $\frac{9}{16}$ in. (11 to 14 mm).
8. Reposition the timing pointer.
9. Refit the hydraulic pipes, reservoir to pump, and pump to steering box.
10. Refill the system with the correct grade of oil. (See Section Y). Bleed the system as laid down in Operation J1-9.
11. Test the steering, with the engine running, by holding the steering hard on full lock in both directions. Do not maintain this pressure for more than 30 seconds in any one minute to avoid causing the oil to overheat and possible damage to the seals.
12. Road test the car.

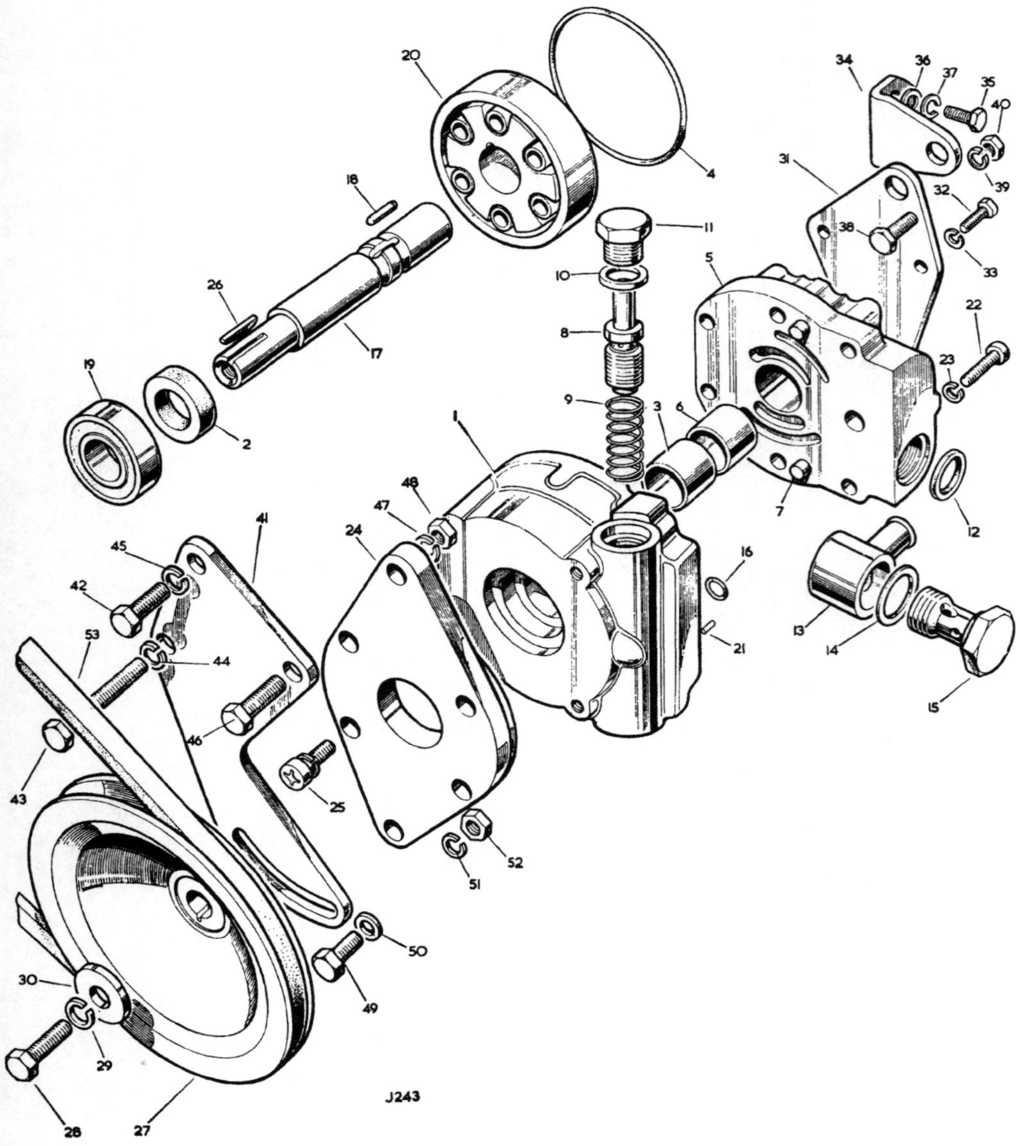

Power steering hydraulic pump layout

1	Body assembly	
2	Oil seal	For body
3	Bush	
4	'O' ring, body to cover	
5	End cover assembly	
6	Bush	For end cover
7	Dowel	
8	Valve assembly	
9	Spring, flow control	
10	'O' ring for valve cap	
11	Valve cap	
12	Seal for adaptor	
13	Adaptor banjo	
14	Fibre washer for adaptor	
15	Banjo bolt	
16	'O' ring for by-pass	
17	Shaft	
18	Drive pin	
19	Bearing	
20	Vane carrier and roller vane	
21	Cam lock peg	
22	Special screw	Fixing end cover to body
23	Lock washer	
24	End plate	
25	Special screw and washer fixing end plate	
26	Key for pump shaft	
27	Pulley	

28	Bolt ($\frac{5}{16}$ in. UNC x $\frac{7}{8}$ in. long)	Fixing pulley to steering pump
29	Spring washer	
30	Plain washer	
31	Mounting arm for pump, rear	
32	Bolt ($\frac{1}{4}$ in. UNF x $\frac{5}{8}$ in. long)	Fixing mounting arm to pump
33	Spring washer	
34	Mounting bracket, rear	
35	Bolt ($\frac{5}{16}$ in. UNC x $\frac{7}{8}$ in. long)	Fixing mounting bracket, rear, to cylinder block
36	Plain washer	
37	Spring washer	
38	Bolt ($\frac{3}{8}$ in. UNF x $\frac{3}{4}$ in. long)	Fixing pump to rear bracket
39	Spring washer	
40	Nut ($\frac{3}{8}$ in. UNF)	
41	Mounting bracket, front	
42	Bolt ($\frac{3}{8}$ in. UNC x $\frac{7}{8}$ in. long)	Fixing mounting bracket, front, to cylinder block
43	Bolt ($\frac{5}{16}$ in. UNC x 3.82 in. long)	
44	Spring washer	
45	Spring washer	
46	Bolt ($\frac{3}{8}$ in. UNF x 1 in. long)	Fixing steering pump to brackets
47	Spring washer	
48	Nut ($\frac{3}{8}$ in. UNF)	
49	Bolt ($\frac{3}{8}$ in. UNF x $1\frac{1}{8}$ in. long)	For steering pump driving belt adjustment
50	Plain washer	
51	Spring washer	
52	Nut ($\frac{3}{8}$ in. UNF)	
53	Belt, driving steering pump	

Power steering hydraulic pump, overhaul—Operation J1-7A

Time allowed: hours

Workshop hand tools:

Spanner sizes: $\frac{7}{16}$ in. AF, $\frac{1}{2}$ in. AF, $\frac{9}{16}$ in. AF, 1 in. AF
Screwdriver Allen key $\frac{3}{16}$ in. Feeler gauge Straight edge

To remove and refit power steering hydraulic pump, see Operation J1-6A

Hydraulic pump, dismantle

Thoroughly clean the exterior of the pump assembly using care so that the dirt does not enter the inlet or outlet holes. During assembly operations extreme caution should be used to prevent any dirt from entering the pump. All parts should be lightly oiled before assembly.

1. Remove the hydraulic pump pulley, bolt and special washer.
2. Remove the front mounting bracket.
3. Remove the body end-plate, secured by four Phillips' screws.
4. Remove the rear bracket.
5. Clamp the body of the pump in a vice. Remove the adaptor screw, and withdraw the adaptor, fibre washer and rubber seal. The venturi flow director is pressed into the cover and should not be removed.
6. Remove the six Allen screws securing the cover to the pump body, and remove the pump from vice. Separate the cover from the body vertically to prevent parts from falling out.
7. Remove the 'O' ring seals from the groove in the pump body.
8. Carefully tilt the pump body, and remove the six rollers.
9. Draw the carrier off the shaft, and remove the drive pin.
10. Remove the shaft from the body.
11. Remove the cam and the cam lock peg from the pump body.
12. If necessary, remove the key from the shaft, and withdraw the sealed bearings.
13. Remove the shaft seal from the body, ensuring that no damage is caused to the shaft bushing.
14. Remove the valve cap, valve and valve spring from the body. Place all parts where they will not be damaged, or subject to contamination.
15. Wash all parts in a suitable solvent, air dry, or wipe clean with a lint-free cloth if air is not available.
16. Check pump body and cover for wear. Replace either part if faces or bushes are worn.

Hydraulic pump, rebuild

1. Install a new shaft seal in the pump body with the lip towards the carrier pocket. Care should be taken to ensure that damage is not caused to the lip of the seal.
2. Replace the cam lock peg in the hole in the pocket. Inspect the cam for wear and replace if worn or damaged. Refit the cam in the pocket with the slot over the retaining pin, and ensure that the cam is seated on to the pocket face.
3. If the sealed bearing has been removed, replace it and move it to the limit of its travel on the shaft. Replace the pulley key.
4. Insert the shaft from the seal side of the body, ensuring that there are no sharp edges on the shaft to cut the seal lip.
5. Replace the carrier drive pin in the shaft.
6. Inspect the carrier and replace in position, ensuring that the greater angle on the vein is in the leading position, as illustrated.
7. Inspect rollers, paying particular attention to the finish on the end. Replace if scored, damaged or oval. Refit rollers to carrier.
8. Using a straight edge across the cam surface, and a feeler gauge, check the end clearance of the carrier and rollers in the pump body. If the end clearance is more than .002 in. (0,05 mm), replace the carrier and rollers.
9. Replace the flow control valve spring in the bore. The spring tension should be 8 to 9 lb (3,6 to 4,8 mkg) at .820 in. (21 mm). If not, replace with a new spring.
10. Replace the valve in the bore, inserting the valve so that the exposed ball end enters last. Ensure that the valve is not sticking.
11. Replace the 'O' ring on the valve cap and assemble in the pump. Tighten the cap to a torque figure of 30 to 35 lb ft (4,0 to 4,9 mkg).

Operation J1-7A—*continued*

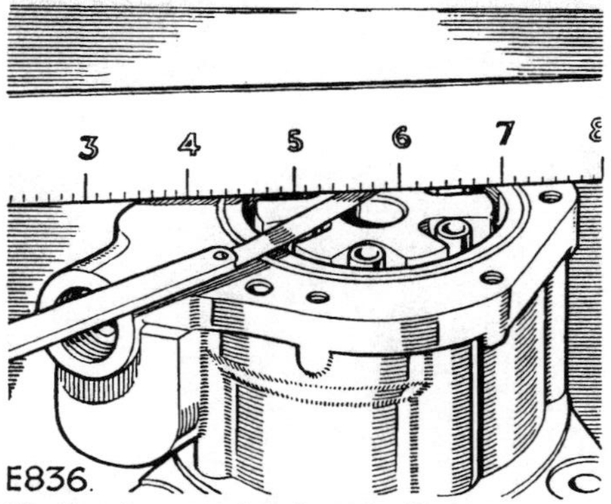

Checking clearance of carrier and roller in pump body

12. Install new 'O' rings to the body of the pump.
13. Replace the cover on the pump body and tightly secure with the six Allen screws.
14. Having tightened the Allen screws, check that the shaft rotates freely, and is not binding.
15. Refit the square sectioned oil seal to the groove around the inlet port, and replace the adaptor, fibre washer and adaptor screw.
16. Refit the end plate to the body, ensuring that the larger radius is in line with the valve.
17. Refit the rear bracket.
18. Refit the front bracket, ensuring that the adjustment slot is at the bottom, and that the retaining bolt holes are on the opposite side to the valve.
19. Refit the pulley to the shaft, and secure with the special washer, spring washer and bolt. This should be tightened to a torque figure of 10 to 12 lb ft (1,4 to 1,6 mkg).

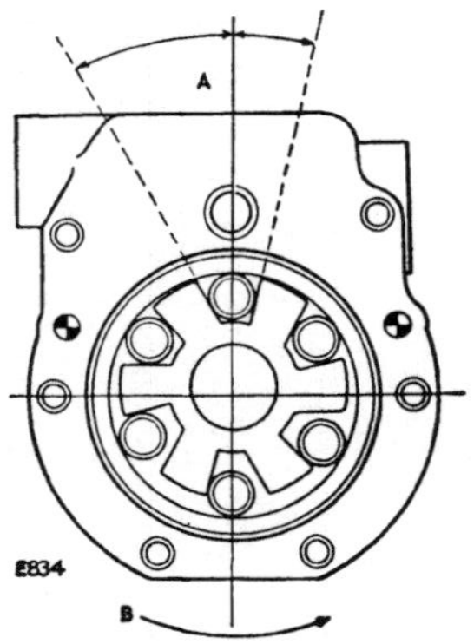

Installation of vein carrier

A—Greater angle in leading position
B—Direction of rotation

Section K — FRONT SUSPENSION

Section L — REAR SUSPENSION

Section M — REAR AXLE

All the information in the above Sections as detailed for Rover 3-Litre Mk III models is applicable to the Rover 3.5-Litre, but the damper setting at the front has been altered to compensate for the reduced weight at the front end of the car.

Section N – BRAKING SYSTEM

The braking system is similar to that used on the 3-Litre Mk III cars with the following exceptions:

(a) New Ferodo 2424F type front pads.
(b) New $\frac{7}{8}$ in. brake master cylinder.
(c) Lockheed type 7 servo.
(d) $\frac{3}{4}$ in. wheel cylinders for rear brakes.
(e) Fine turned brake drums.
(f) New, simpler handbrake linkage.
(g) Mechanical stop lamp switch.

This affects the following Operations which replace similar items in the Rover 3-Litre Workshop Manual.

Operation N-11A.
Operation N-15A.
Operation N-17A.
Operation N-19A.
Operation N-20A.
Operation N-22A.

Handbrake linkage, re-set—Operation N-11A

Time allowed: hours

Workshop hand tools:
Spanner sizes: $\frac{7}{16}$ in. AF, $\frac{1}{2}$ in. AF
Pliers

Handbrake linkage, reset

In the event of any part of the brake linkage having been removed or disturbed, and the setting thereby lost, it is important that the correct setting be regained as follows:

1. With the handbrake off, disconnect the two brake rods from the rear brakes.
2. Adjust the rear brakes at the screw adjusters on the back plates until the shoes are hard against the drums.
3. Adjust the handbrake lever so that the distance between the centre line of the lever pivot and the centre line of the clevis hole is 1 in. (25 mm), as illustrated. Also that the distance between the centre line of the clevis hole and the centre line of the return spring clip hole is 7¼ in. (184 mm).
4. Holding the lever in this position, adjust the relay so that the distance between the centre line of the pivot and the lower clevis hole on the relay is 1 in. (25 mm), as illustrated.
5. With these settings correctly made, make a mark on the compensating lever, and a corresponding mark on the link plate.
6. Maintaining these two marks in line, adjust the brake rods and couple up with the rear brakes.
7. Slacken the adjusters on the back plate two clicks so that the wheels rotate freely.
8. Adjust the locknut and clevis fork on the lower threaded end of the cable so that when the hand-brake grip is pulled out for approximately six 'clicks' of the ratchet the rear wheels are fully locked.

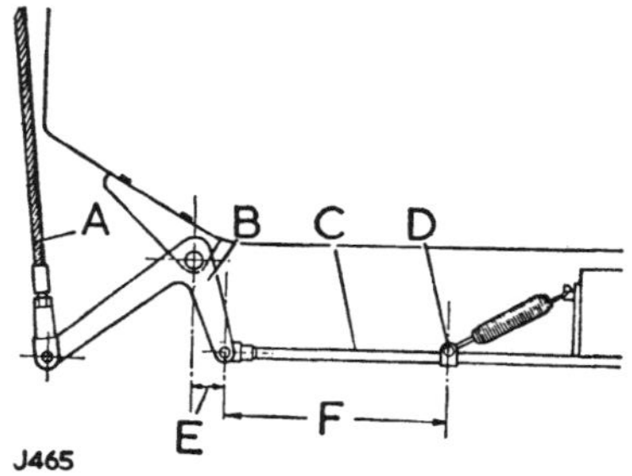

J465

Handbrake lever setting dimensions

A—Handbrake cable
B—Lever pivot
C—Handbrake rod, lever to relay
D—Clip for return spring
E—1 in. (25 mm)
F—7¼ in. (184 mm)

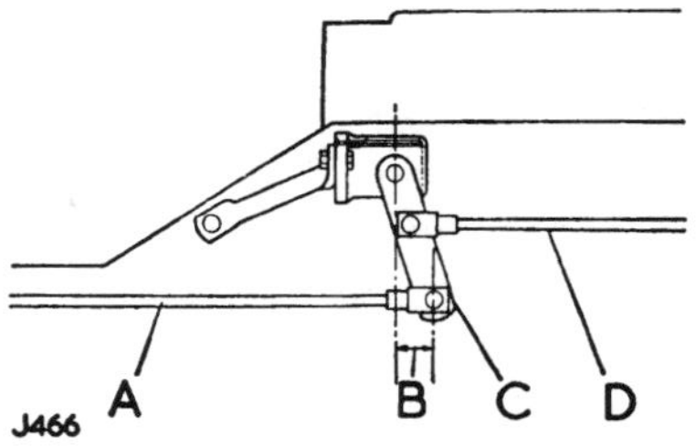

Relay setting dimensions

A—Handbrake rod, lever to relay
B—1 in. (25 mm)
C—Relay
D—Handbrake rod, relay to compensator

Master cylinder, overhaul—Operation N-15A

Time allowed: hours

Workshop hand tools:
Circlip pliers Screwdriver, medium

Extreme cleanliness must be observed when carrying out this operation

Master cylinder, dismantle

1. Remove the dust cover.
2. Remove the circlip, and withdraw the push rod complete with the dished washer.
3. Remove the piston and valve stem by applying low air pressure to the inlet port.
4. Lever the locking prong of the spring retainer clear of the piston shoulder and withdraw the piston.
5. Compress the return spring and position the valve stem to align with the larger hole in the spring retainer. Withdraw the spring and retainer.
6. Slide the valve spacer over the valve stem. Remove the spring washer and valve seal from the stem.
7. Remove the piston seal from the piston.

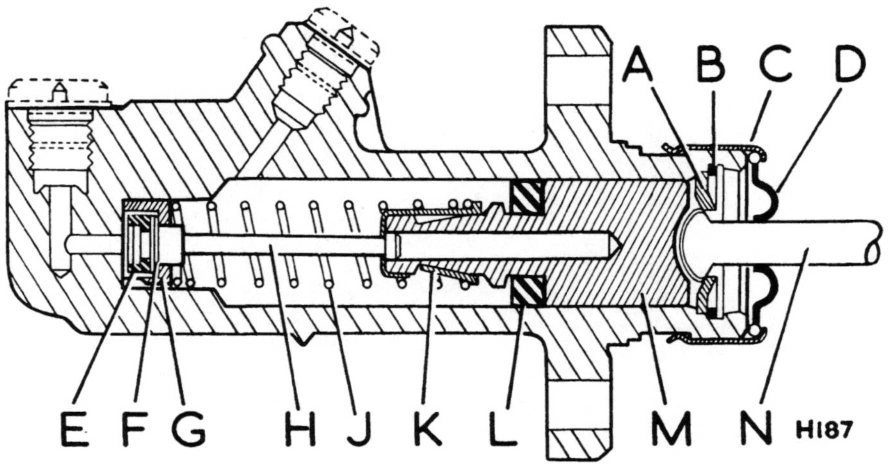

Brake master cylinder components

A—Dished washer
B—Circlip
C—Retainer for dust cover
D—Dust cover
E—Valve seal
F—Spring washer
G—Valve spacer
H—Valve stem
J—Return spring
K—Spring retainer
L—Piston seal
M—Piston
N—Push rod

Operation N-15A—*continued*

Master cylinder, assemble

1. Examine all components and renew as necessary. Clean the parts thoroughly in brake fluid.

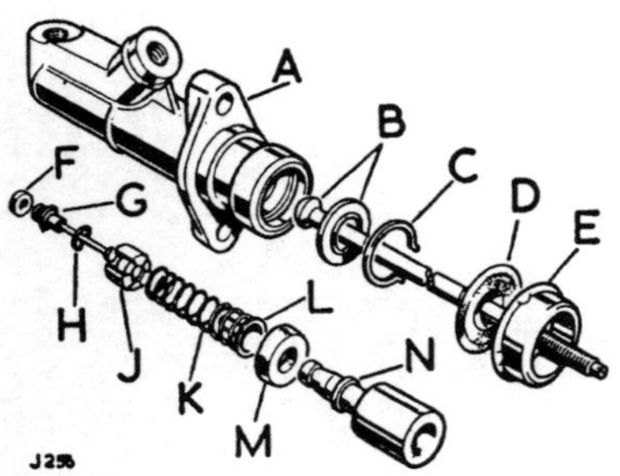

Master cylinder components

A—Master cylinder body
B—Push rod and retaining washer
C—Circlip
D—Dust seal
E—Retainer for dust seal
F—Valve seal
G—Valve stem
H—Spring washer
J—Valve spacer
K—Return spring
L—Spring retainer
M—Piston seal
N—Piston

2. Reverse the dismantling procedure, ensuring that the seals are assembled in correct direction.
3. The spring washer must be assembled as illustrated.
4. Fit a new spring retainer, ensuring that the prong is in the locked position, as illustrated.
5. Fill the dust excluder with rubber grease.

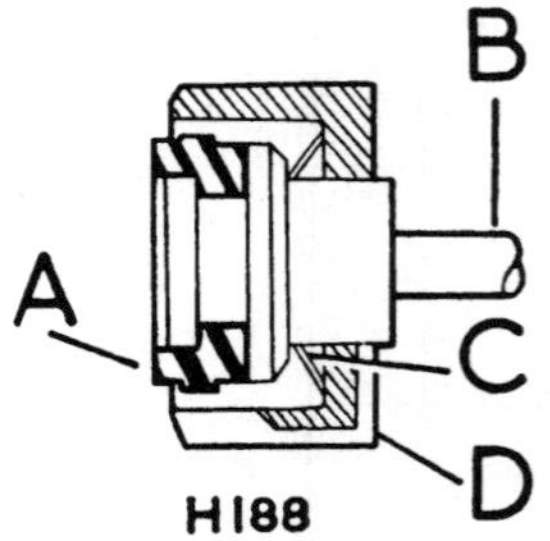

Valve assembly

A—Valve seal
B—Valve stem
C—Spring washer correctly fitted
D—Valve spacer

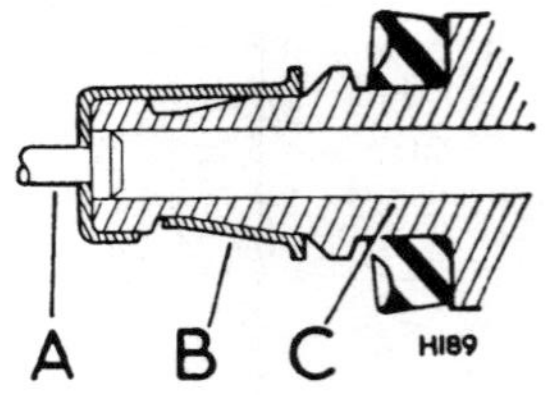

Piston and spring retainer

A—Valve stem
B—Prong in locked position
C—Piston

Brake pedal, remove and refit—Operation N-17A

Time allowed: hours

Workshop hand tools:
Spanner sizes: $\frac{7}{16}$ in. AF, $\frac{1}{2}$ in. AF
Screwdriver Pliers Rule Bleed tube Glass container

Brake pedal, remove

1. Remove master cylinder. Operation N-14.
2. Disconnect the wiring from the stop light switch.
3. Remove the pedal support bracket fixings and withdraw the pedal and bracket assembly.

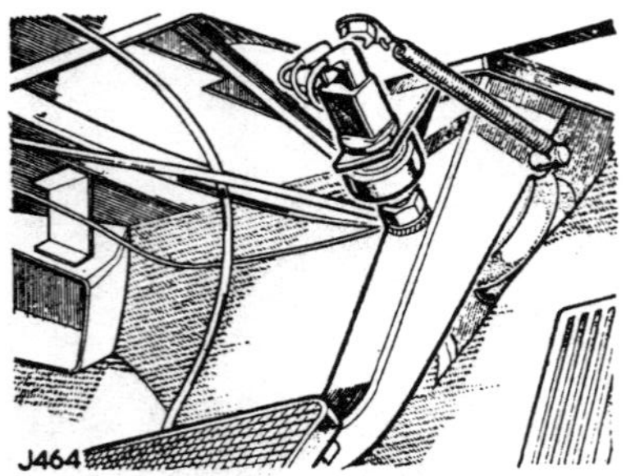

Brake pedal and stop light switch

Brake pedal, refit

1. Place the pedal and bracket in position and secure with the fixing bolt, nut and spring washers.
2. Fit the distance piece and brake master cylinder to the bulkhead, but do not connect the push rod to the pedal.
3. Adjust the pedal against the stop light switch to give a distance 'A' of 6 in. (152 mm) from the bottom of the pedal pad to the floor.
4. With the pedal held against the stop light switch, adjust and connect the push rod of the master cylinder so that the pivot pin can be aligned with the hole in the pedal and the push rod.
5. Fit the pedal return spring with anchor plate to the pivot pin and secure.
6. Connect up the wiring to the stop light switch.
7. Bleed the hydraulic system. Operation N-23.

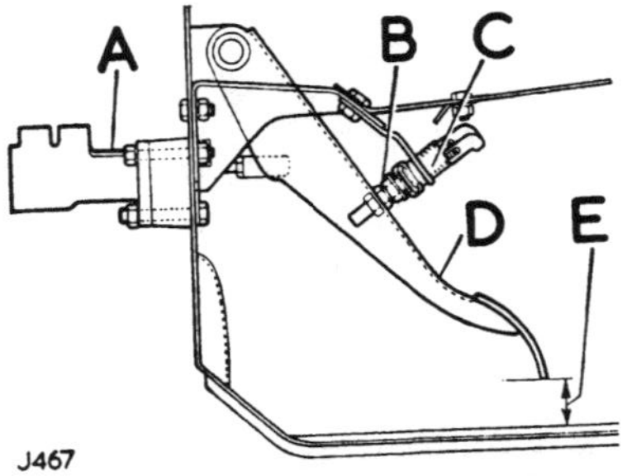

Adjustment of brake pedal

A—Brake master cylinder
B—Pedal adjustment
C—Stop light switch
D—Pedal
E—6 in. (152 mm)

Servo unit, remove and refit—Operation N-19A

Time allowed: hours

Workshop hand tools:
Spanner sizes: $\frac{7}{16}$ in. AF, $\frac{1}{2}$ in. AF
Bleed tube Glass container

Special tools:
Bar for brake pedal

To overhaul servo unit, see Operation N-20A

Servo unit, remove

1. Depress the brake pedal and secure in position.
2. Disconnect hydraulic pipe, master cylinder to servo unit.
3. Remove clip on rear servo unit mounting bracket.
4. Disconnect hydraulic pipe, servo unit to brakes.
5. Disconnect vacuum hose, reservoir to manifold. Remove nut, spring and plain washer securing the vacuum hose clip to the servo front mounting bracket.
6. Remove the two nuts, bolts, spring and plain washers securing the servo unit mounting bracket to the wing valance.
7. Draw off the servo unit, at the same time removing the vacuum hose, servo unit to reservoir; if necessary, remove the bracket from the servo unit by removing the remaining $\frac{1}{2}$ in. AF nut.

Servo unit, refit

1. Before refitting the unit, check the operation of the non-return valve in the vacuum line by ensuring that air will only pass through the valve one way. Renew if this is faulty.
2. Reverse removal procedure.
3. Bleed brakes. Operation N-23.

Servo unit, 7 in., overhaul—Operation N-20A

Time allowed: hours

Workshop hand tools:
Spanner sizes:
$\frac{7}{16}$ in. AF, $\frac{1}{2}$ in. AF, $\frac{1}{2}$ in. socket
Screwdriver, small Screwdriver, large
Hammer, small Drift

Special tools:
Cover removal tool, Part No. 601315
Torque screwdriver
Torque spanner

To remove and refit servo unit, see Operation N-19A

Servo unit, to dismantle

1. Hold the unit in a soft-jawed vice at the slave cylinder. Carefully insert a screwdriver in one of the cover holes of the air filter and prise the cover away. Remove the sorbo washer, filter and spring, as illustrated.
2. Remove the five screws securing the valve cover to the housing and withdraw the cover from the rubber hose, lift off the reaction valve diaphragm and support, and separate.

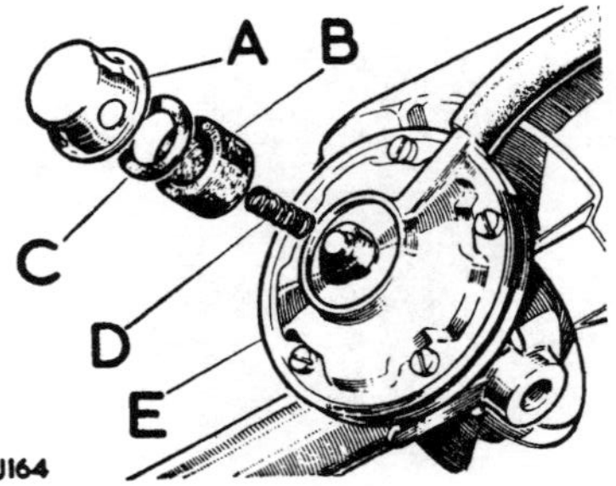

J164

Withdrawing filter and cover

A—Air filter cover
B—Filter
C—Sorbo washer
D—Spring for valve
E—Valve cover

3. Remove the three countersunk-headed screws and separate the valve housing, together with gasket from the slave cylinder body.
4. Remove the air valve piston by applying low air pressure to the fluid inlet connection whilst blanking off the hydraulic outlet.
5. Remove the cup from the valve piston.
6. Prise out the vacuum non-return valve from the vacuum chamber.
7. Reposition the unit in the vice so that the vacuum chamber is uppermost. Fit the special tool, Part No. 601315, to the end cover fixing with two $\frac{5}{16}$ in. UNF nuts, and remove the cover by turning the tool in an anti-clockwise direction; considerable pressure is required and an extension bar may be necessary.

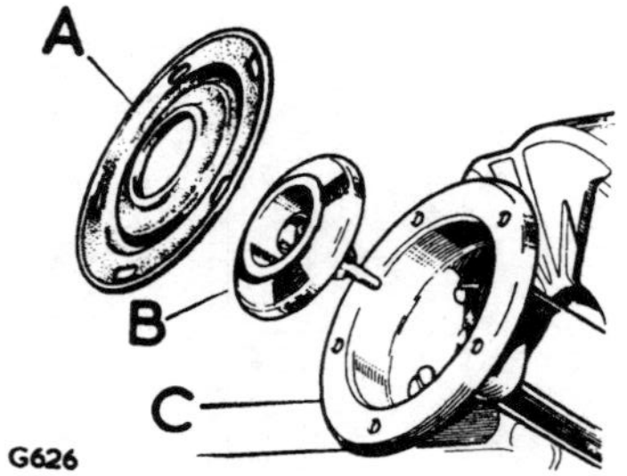

G626

Reaction valve diaphragm separated from support

A—Reaction valve diaphragm
B—Diaphragm support
C—Valve housing

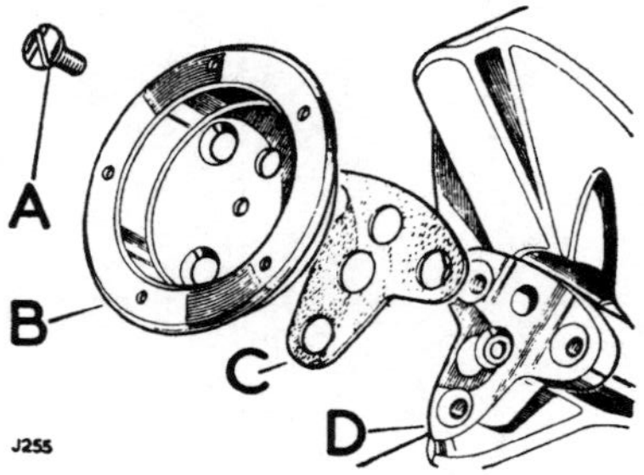

J255

Removing air valve body

A—Screw fixing body
B—Body for air valve
C—Gasket
D—Slave cylinder body

Operation N-20A—*continued*

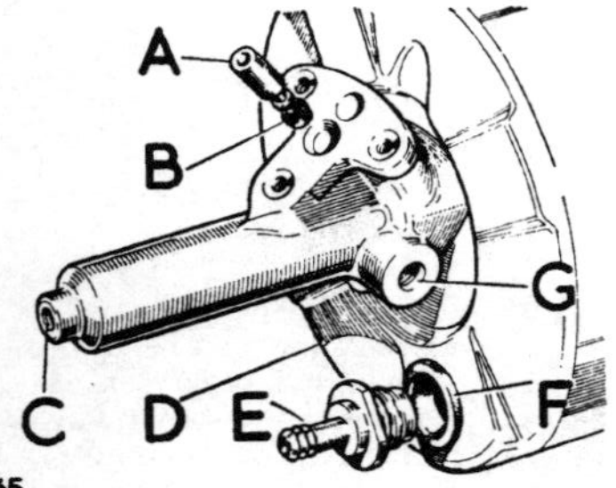

J165

Removing air valve piston and non-return valve

A—Air valve piston
B—Seal for air valve piston
C—Outlet connection
D—Vacuum chamber
E—Non-return valve
F—Seal for non-return valve
G—Inlet connection

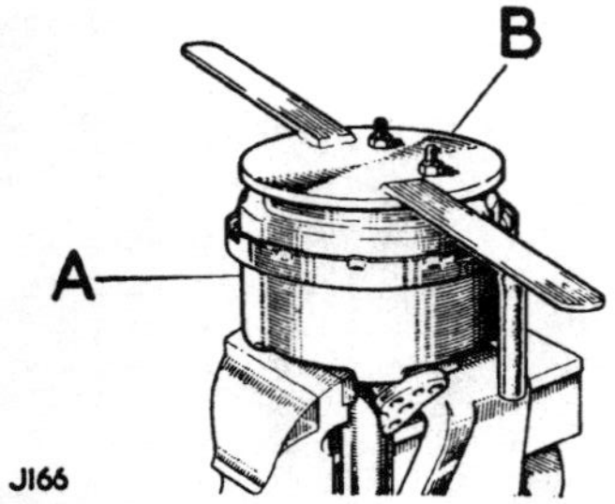

J166

Removing end cover with special tool

A—End cover
B—Special tool, Part No. 601315

8. Disengage the diaphragm from the diaphragm support by peeling it out of the rim of the vacuum chamber and off the lip of the support.
9. Lightly press the diaphragm support inwards and shake the key from the diaphragm support. Remove the support and the return spring.

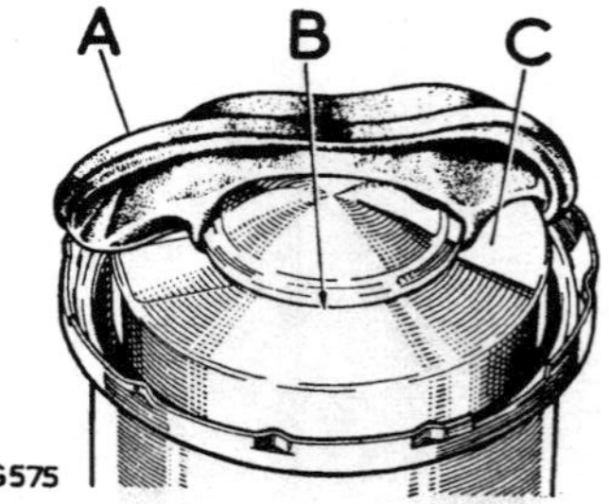

G575

Removing diaphragm

A—Diaphragm
B—Groove
C—Diaphragm support

10. Bend back the tabs on the locking plate, remove the set bolts, and withdraw locking tab and abutment plate. Separate the vacuum chamber, together with gasket from the slave cylinder body.

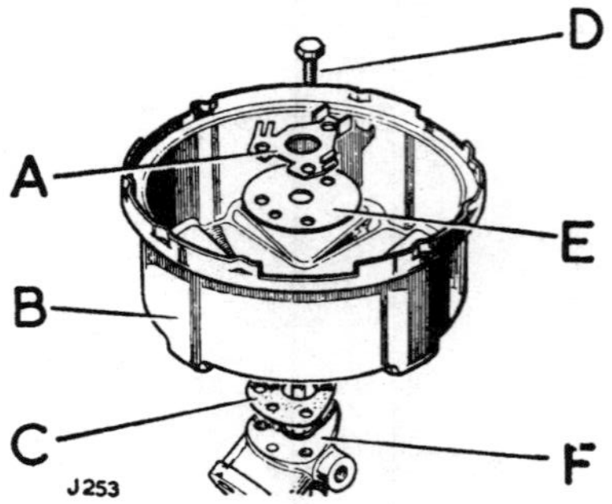

J253

Vacuum chamber removal

A—Lock plate
B—Vacuum chamber
C—Gasket
D—Bolt fixing vacuum chamber
E—Abutment plate
F—Slave cylinder

Operation N-20A—*continued*

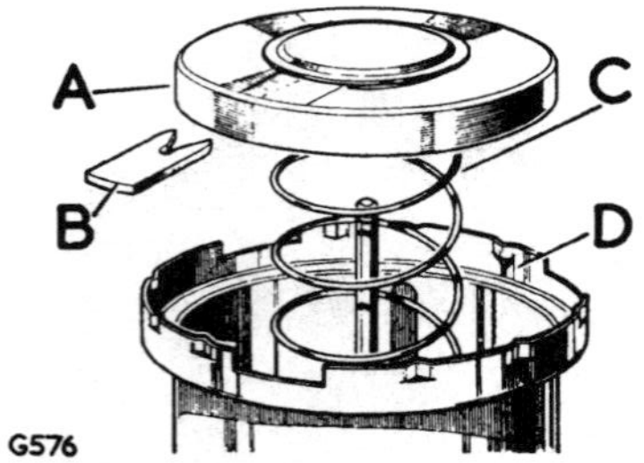

G576

Removing the diaphragm, support and spring

A—Diaphragm support
B—Key securing diaphragm support
C—Return spring
D—Vacuum chamber

11. Withdraw the push rod and internal parts from the slave cylinder.
12. Remove the guide, large gland seal and spacer from the push rod, as illustrated. Remove the small piston seal from the piston.

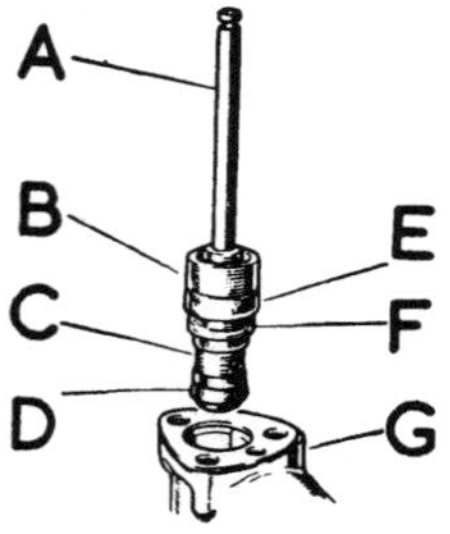

J167

Removing push rod and internal parts

A—Push rod	E—Gland seal
B—Push rod guide	F—Spacer
C—Piston	G—Slave cylinder body
D—Piston seal	

13. If it is considered necessary to remove the piston from the rod, proceed as follows:

    Hold the push rod in a soft-jawed vice, then use a small screwdriver to expand the spring clip on the piston and gently ease the clip off along the piston. Take care not to damage the piston surface.

    Separate the piston from the push rod by pressing out the small pin, as illustrated.

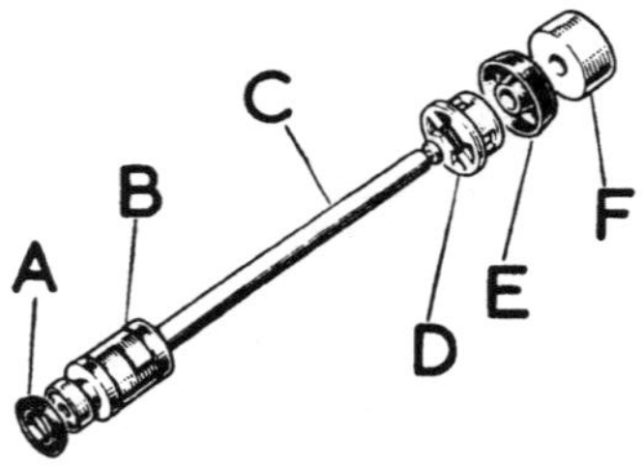

J168

Push rod and components

A—Piston seal	D—Spacer
B—Piston	E—Gland seal
C—Push rod	F—Push rod guide

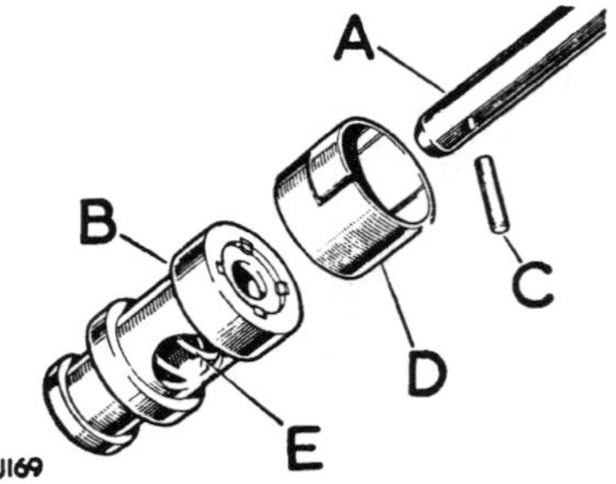

J169

Removing piston from push rod

A—Push rod	D—Spring clip
B—Piston	E—Piston spring
C—Pin	

Operation N-20A—*continued*

Servo unit, rebuild

1. Examine all components for wear or damage and replace any parts necessary. If the bore of the slave cylinder is scored or rusty, this must also be replaced.
2. The piston and all rubber parts should be renewed and are available in a repair kit.
3. If the piston has been removed from the rod, refit as follows:

   Hold the push rod in a soft-jawed vice, then slide the slave cylinder piston over the tapered end of the push rod.
4. Hold the small spring within the piston back towards the diaphragm end of the push rod, and insert the small pin into the hole in the push rod, ensuring that the end of the spring rests against the pin and that it does not pass through the coil of the spring.

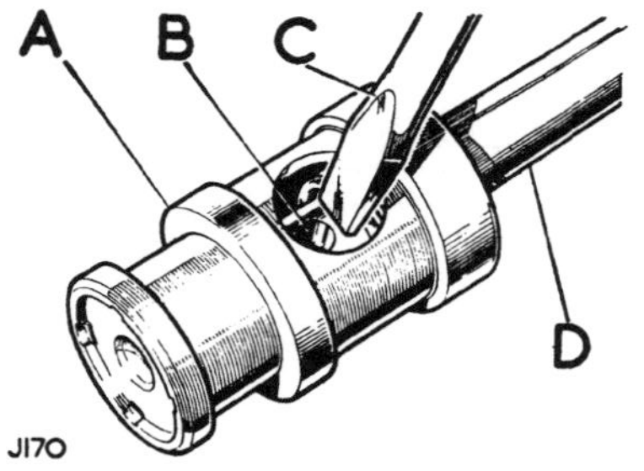

Fitting piston to push rod

A—Piston C—Screwdriver
B—Hole for pin D—Push rod

5. With the pin correctly positioned, expand the spring clip and pass it over the piston to secure the pin. It is most important that the outside diameter of the piston is not damaged in any way, however slight, during this operation. Remove push rod from vice.

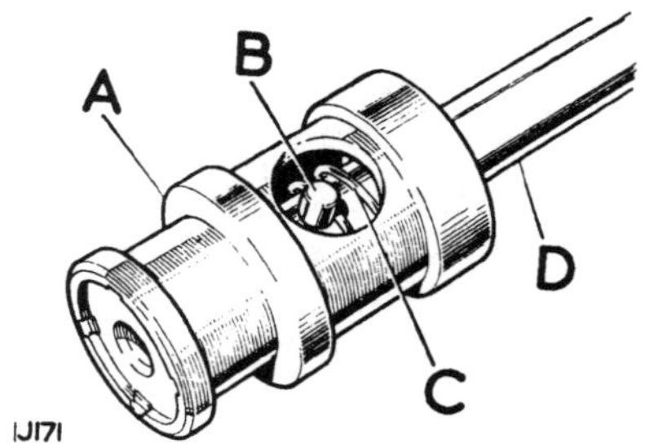

Fitting pin

A—Piston C—Spring
B—Pin D—Push rod

6. Fit a new small 'U' section seal to the slave cylinder piston so that the groove in the seal is towards the head of the piston. Assemble the spacer with the large diameter against the head of the piston and follow up with the large gland seal, grooved face leading, on to the push rod.

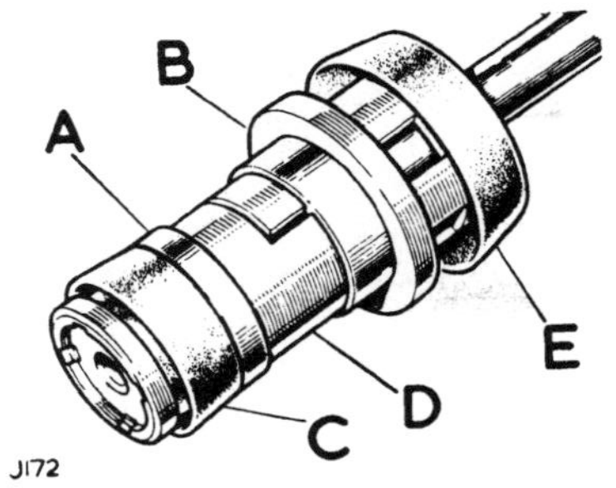

Piston assembled

A—Piston D—Spring clip
B—Spacer E—Gland seal
C—Piston seal

Operation N-20A—*continued*

7. Hold the slave cylinder body in a soft-jawed vice, then fit the push rod assembly into the bore of the slave cylinder, ensuring that the seals are not damaged or distorted.
8. Refit the push rod guide into the end of the slave cylinder so that its flat face is innermost in the bore.
9. Locate a new gasket over the push rod guide following up with the vacuum chamber, abutment plate and locking plate, line up the holes with the tapped holes in the slave cylinder, and insert the three set bolts, tightening to a torque figure of 12 to 14 lb ft (1,6 to 1,9 mkg). Bend over the locking tabs.
10. Ensure that the push rod is withdrawn fully and place the return spring over the push rod and locate the diaphragm support on the end of the push rod. Compress support and secure by fitting the key into the slot in the side of the diaphragm support. Ensure that the key engages the groove in the push rod and that it is pushed right in.

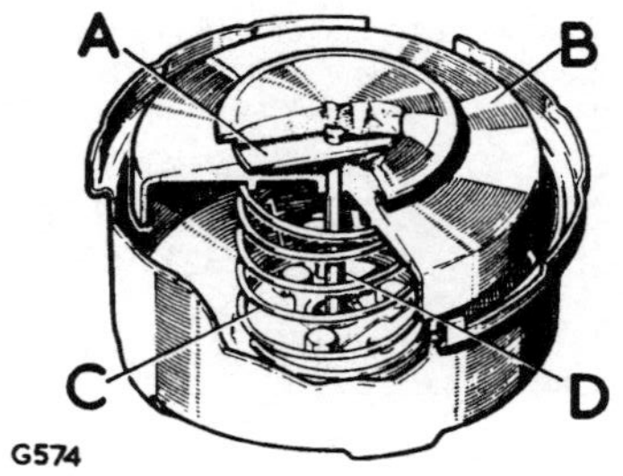

Fitting key to diaphragm support

A—Key C—Return spring
B—Diaphragm support D—Push rod

11. Stretch the smaller diameter of the diaphragm into position on the diaphragm support, ensuring that it is correctly bedded into its groove. Locate outer edge of diaphragm in the vacuum chamber.
12. If the flat face of the diaphragm appears buckled, this indicates that the diaphragm has not been assembled correctly. Ensure correct location in groove of diaphragm support and rim of vacuum chamber.
13. With the special tool attached to the end cover, refit the cover by pressing downwards and turning in a clockwise direction. Ensure that the end cover air pipe is positioned in correct relationship with the face of the air valve. Remove special tool.
14. Reposition slave cylinder in vice so that the air valve face is uppermost. Ease the cup into the groove in the air valve piston so that the lip of the cup faces the shouldered end of the piston. Insert the piston into the valve bore of the slave cylinder.
15. Position a new gasket on the slave cylinder following up with the valve housing, line up the holes, and secure by fitting the three countersunk-headed screws. The screws should be tightened to a torque figure of 5 to 7 lb ft (0,6 to 0,9 mkg).
16. Stretch the reaction valve diaphragm on to the diaphragm support and insert the push rod portion of the diaphragm support through the hole in the valve housing.
17. Stretch the valve rubber, and, with the groove around its inside diameter, force it on to the valve stem flange with the fingers. Insert the valve stem through the hole in the valve cover, fit the other valve rubber over the valve stem, and secure by fitting the snap-on cap. If necessary, warm cap in hot water for ease of assembly.

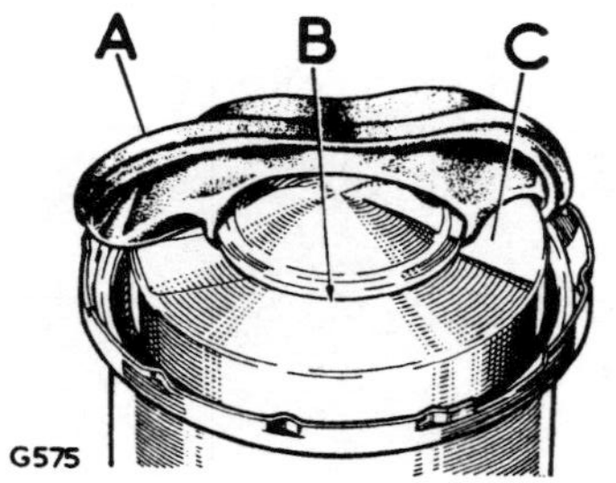

Fitting diaphragm and support

A—Diaphragm B—Groove C—Diaphragm support

Operation N-20A—*continued*

18. If necessary, fit new rubber hose, insert valve cover end into hose, then position cover on the valve housing. Secure the cover with the five self-tapping screws. Take care to ensure that the reaction valve diaphragm is not trapped between the valve cover bosses and the valve housing. If, on removal of the air filter cover, the valve and valve seals were found to be unserviceable, a new filter cover assembly complete with seals and valve must be fitted; this is essential as valve stem and seals are a selective assembly.
19. Examine air filter and, if necessary, renew; any light dust may be cleared by washing the filter in methylated spirits and drying with an air line. Do not use any other cleaning fluid.

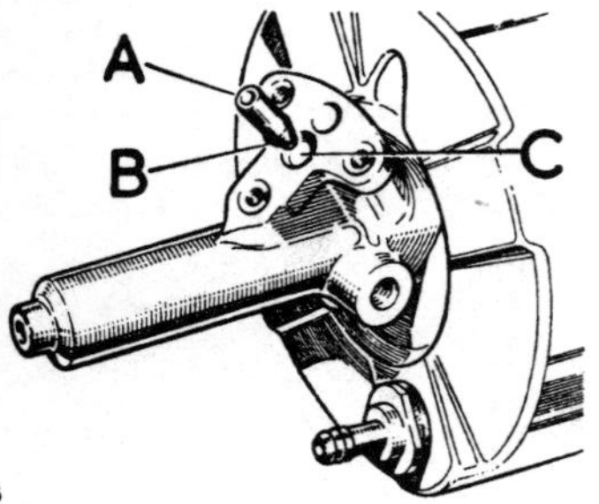

J173

Fitting air valve piston to bore

A—Air valve piston B—Piston seal C—Valve bore

20. Position the air filter over the air valve, then position the small spring over the snap-on cap.
21. Fit the sorbo washer in the air filter cover, then snap the assembly on to the air valve cover.
22. If necessary, replace sealing rubber for non-return valve, then push non-return valve into position.

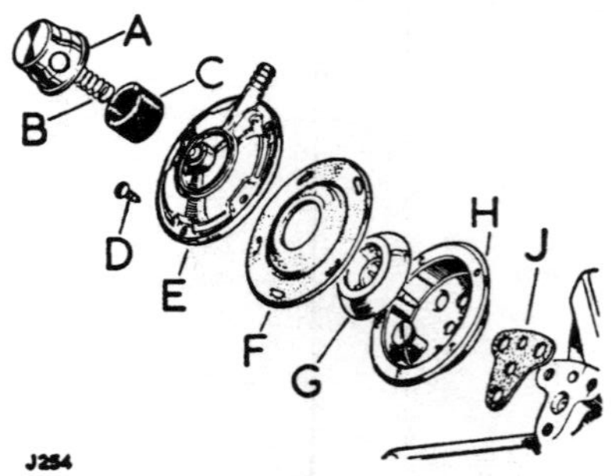

J254

Air valve components

A—Cap for filter
B—Spring for filter
C—Filter
D—Screw fixing cover
E—Cover for air valve
F—Diaphragm
G—Support
H—Body for air valve
J—Gasket

Servo reservoir, remove and refit—Operation N-22A

Time allowed: hours

Workshop hand tools:
Spanner sizes: $\frac{1}{2}$ in. AF, $\frac{7}{8}$ in. AF

The servo reservoir is fitted under the right-hand front wing.

Servo reservoir, remove

1. Remove the banjo bolt connecting the servo pipes to the reservoir.
2. Remove the three fixing nuts and bolts, and draw out the reservoir from beneath the wing. Note the position of the engine earth lead, which is attached to the lower rear of he set bolts.

Servo reservoir, refit

1. Reverse removal procedure.
2. Start the engine and check for air leaks.

Section P – COOLING SYSTEM

The cooling is by pump, 5-blade fan and thermostat in conjunction with a cross-flow radiator which also incorporates an oil cooler for the Automatic transmission. The system is pressurised to 15 lb/sq in.

Operation P-1 is replaced by Operation P-1A. Thermostat removal will be found in Section A.

Water pump, overhaul—Operation P-1A

Time allowed: hours

Workshop hand tools:
Rule, 12 in.

Special tools:
Extractor for pulley hub
Press for impeller

See Section A for water pump removal.

Water pump overhaul

Replacing the water pump seals

1. Pull off fan blade pulley hub, taking care to avoid damage.

2. Place the water pump assembly into very hot water, and leave for a short period.

3. Using a suitable press, push out the water pump impeller assembly. This item which includes the seals should not be dismantled and the water pump must be reassembled using all the parts contained in the overhaul kit.

4. Reassemble by reheating the water pump housing and pressing in a new spindle assembly into position until the bearing outer race is flush with the nose of the water pump housing, as illustrated. This operation should be carried out using a suitable press and **applying load only to the outer race.**

5. Smear the outside diameter of the seal with sealer Stag 'A' or Pettman's cement. The seal face must be coated with Shell Donax 'C'. Then fit the seal over the spindle and into the housing. Ensure that flange on seal is firmly seated on water pump housing.

6. Fit seal mating face over spindle.

7. Support spindle, then press impeller into position to the dimension as illustrated.

8. Support spindle at other end, ensure position of impeller is not disturbed, then refit the fan blade pulley hub, again using a suitable press, ensuring that it is fitted in accordance with the dimensions in the illustration.

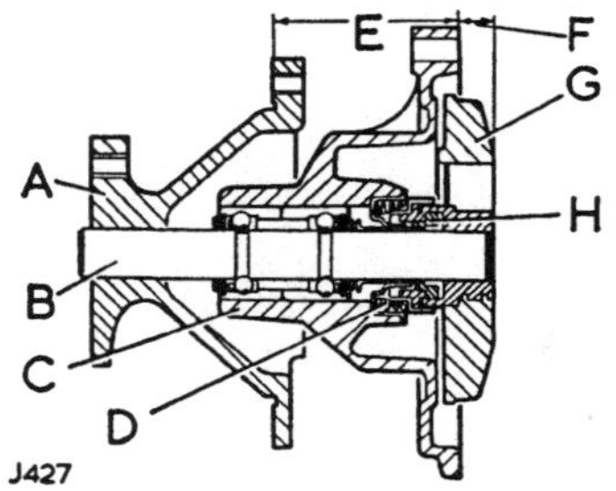

J427

Cross-section of water pump

A—Hub for fan blade pulley
B—Spindle and bearing
C—Water pump housing
D—Seal for water pump
E—2.262 in. (57,5 mm)
F—.320 in. (8,0 mm)
G—Impeller
H—Seal mating face

TECHNICAL DETAIL DATA

Cooling system

Capacity	16 Imperial pints, 19 US pints, 9 Litres
Type	Pump, fan and thermostat
Temperature control	Thermostat
Pressurised to	15 lb/sq in.
Thermostat opens at	78°C to 83°C (173°F to 182°F)

Fan

Number of blades	5

Water pump

Type	Centrifugal impeller, driven by a 'V' belt
Belt adjustment	$\frac{7}{16}$ in. to $\frac{9}{16}$ in. (11 to 14 mm) free movement

Frost precautions and engine protection

During the winter months special anti-freeze mixture and in the summer a special inhibitor is used in Rover 3.5-Litre cars to prevent corrosion of the aluminium alloy engine parts. **It is most important therefore if the cooling system is drained at any time, to refill with a solution of water and anti-freeze during winter or summer, or water and inhibitor during the summer only.**

Recommended solutions are:

Anti-freeze—Bluecol AA, coloured green.

Inhibitor—Marston Lubricants SQ36. Coolant inhibitor concentrate.

Use one part of anti-freeze to two parts of water or 3 fluid ounces of inhibitor per gallon of water if frost precautions are not being taken.

To ensure that the solution is fully effective at all times the cooling system should be drained and refilled every twelve months.

Proceed as follows:

1. Ensure that the cooling system is leak-proof; anti-freeze solutions are far more 'searching' at joints than water.
2. Drain and flush the system.

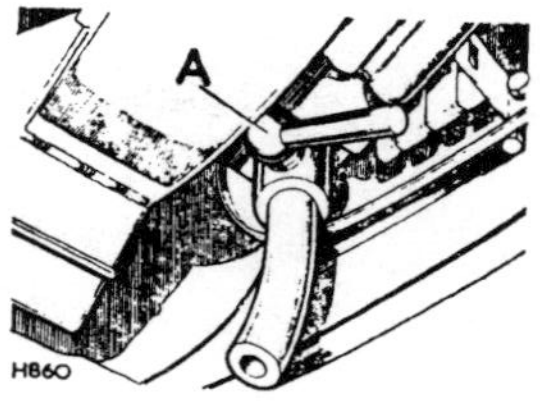

Radiator drain plug

A—Drain plug, under valance at right-hand side

3. Pour in approximately one gallon (4,5 litres) of water, add solution, 5$\frac{1}{4}$ pints (3 litres) of anti-freeze, summer or winter, or 6 fluid ounces of inhibitor if frost protection is not required. Then top up as detailed under Section A1, Operation A1-2.

During the winter months Rover 3.5-Litre cars leaving the Rover factory have the cooling system filled with 33% of anti-freeze mixture. This gives protection against frost down to minus 25°F (minus 32°C). Cars so filled can be identified by the blue label affixed to the right-hand side of the windscreen and a blue label tied to the engine.

In the summer cars have 6 fluid ozs of SQ36 inhibitor added, that is 3 fluid ozs per gallon of water.

Cylinder block drain tap

A—Drain tap, two fitted, one each side of engine

Section Q—FUEL SYSTEM

The fuel system comprises a mechanical fuel pump, mounted on the front left-hand side of the engine. Two SU type HS6 carburetters are used, fitted with twin paper element air cleaners. A spill return fuel system is used, with the fuel tank suitably altered to accommodate the spill return pipe. An anti-spill breather system is also fitted to the fuel tank. The petrol reserve is manually operated from inside the car.

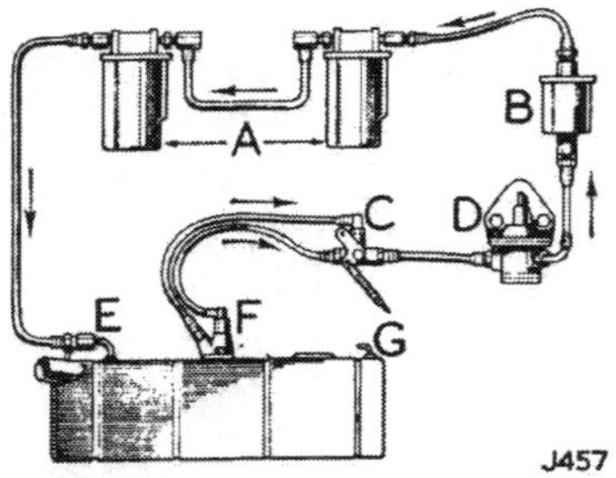

J457

Diagrammatic view of fuel system

A—Carburetter, left-hand and right-hand
B—Fuel filter
C—Fuel reserve tap
D—Fuel pump
E—Spill return
F—Dual outlet from fuel tank
G—Breather for fuel tank

Only Operations Q-7, Q-8 and Q-9 apply to the Rover 3.5-Litre model.

For carburetter and fuel pump removal see Section A. Carburetter overhaul and fuel pump overhaul are detailed on the following pages.

*Carburetter, overhaul—Operation Q-2A

Time allowed: hours

Workshop hand tools:

Spanner sizes: $\frac{5}{16}$ in. AF, $\frac{7}{16}$ in. AF, $\frac{1}{2}$ in. AF, $\frac{11}{16}$ in. AF, 4 BA
Pair of pliers Screwdriver, medium Phillips screwdriver, small

See Section A for carburetter removal

Carburetter, dismantle

1. Unscrew the oil cap with hydraulic damper and withdraw together with the washer.
2. Remove the three screws retaining the carburetter suction chamber, lift off the suction chamber together with the piston spring.
3. Remove the piston and needle, if necessary slacken the needle retaining screw at the side of the piston and remove the needle.
4. Remove balance pipe, float chamber to intake.
5. Remove the three screws and spring washers retaining the float chamber lid and lift off the lid complete with the float and gasket.
6. If necessary the mills pin securing the float can be withdrawn and the float removed, the needle valve can then be lifted from its seating and the seating can be removed from the float chamber lid.

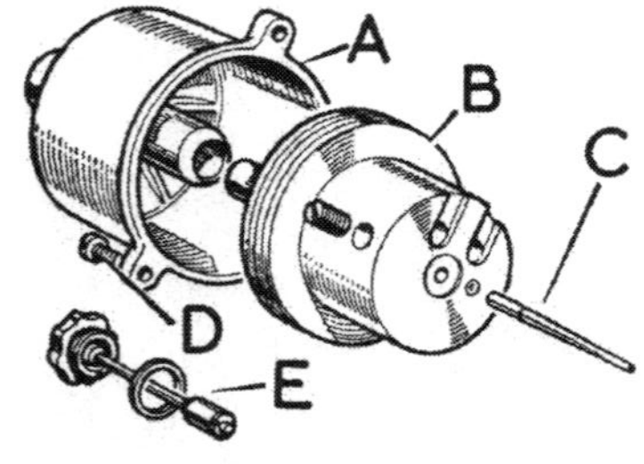

J182

Suction chamber and piston complete

A—Suction chamber
B—Piston
C—Needle KK
D—Screws retaining suction chamber
E—Oil cap and hydraulic damper complete

7. Relieve the load on the pick-up lever return spring by applying pressure to the cam lever and remove the Phillips drive screw from the base of the jet head assembly and release the pick-up link.

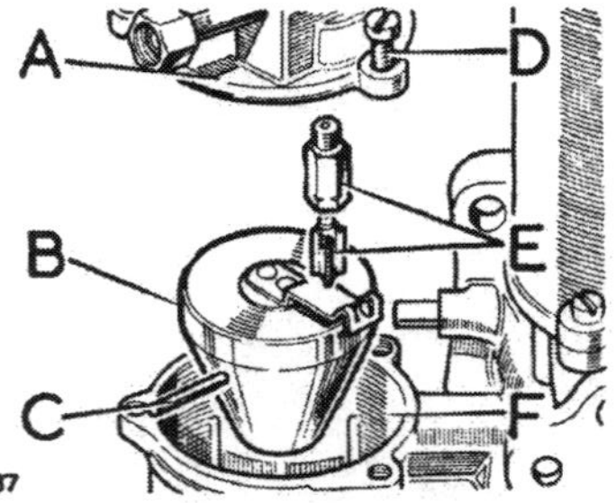

J437

Float Chamber

A—Float chamber lid
B—Float and lever complete
C—Mills pin
D—Screws retaining float chamber lid
E—Needle valve and seat
F—Float chamber

8. Remove the bolt and double spring brass washer securing the pick-up link assembly, at the same time releasing the return spring.

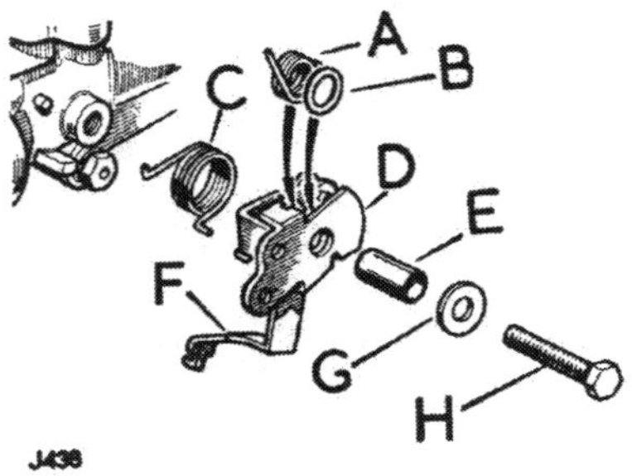

J438

Detail of carburetter pick-up link assembly

A—Spring for pick-up lever
B—Shim washer for pick-up lever
C—Return spring for cam lever
D—Cam lever
E—Distance tube
F—Pick-up link
G—Plain washer for securing bolt
H—Bolt securing assembly to carburetter body

Operations which are identified by an asterisk (*), can be carried out with the engine installed in the car

Operation Q-2A—*continued*

9. Withdraw the pick-up link assembly comprising, pick-up lever, spring, distance tube, cam lever, spring and shim washer. Note carefully the assembly arrangement.

10. To remove the jet and flexible pipe from the float chamber release the gland nut and remove the jet and flexible pipe complete with gland washer and brass washer.

11. Remove the bolt, spring washer and plain washer retaining the float chamber to the carburetter body and lift off the float chamber and adaptor.

12. Remove the jet adjusting nut together with the spring and then remove the jet bearing nut together with the jet bearing and brass washer.

13. Disconnect the throttle link from the right-hand throttle lever.

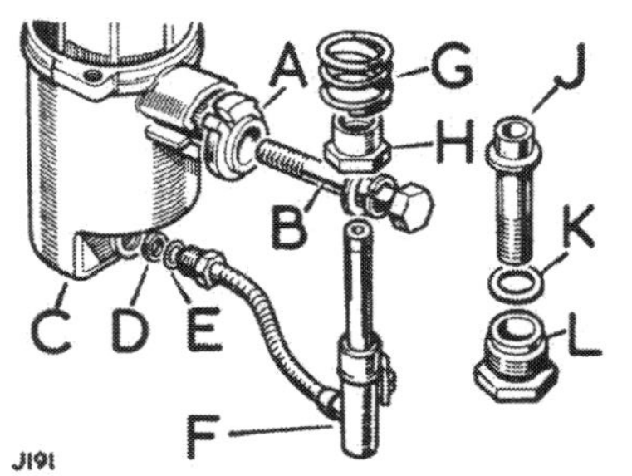

J191

Float chamber and jet assembly

A—Adaptor for float
B—Bolt fixing float chamber
C—Float chamber
D—Gland washer
E—Brass washer
F—Jet and pipe complete
G—Lock spring
H—Adjusting nut
J—Jet bearing
K—Brass washer
L—Special nut fixing jet bearing

14. **On left-hand carburetter.** Remove the throttle lever secured by a bolt, spring and brass washer to the carburetter lever.

15. Release the tab washer from the spindle extension nut and remove the nut and tab washer, then remove the carburetter lever, brass washer and throttle link.

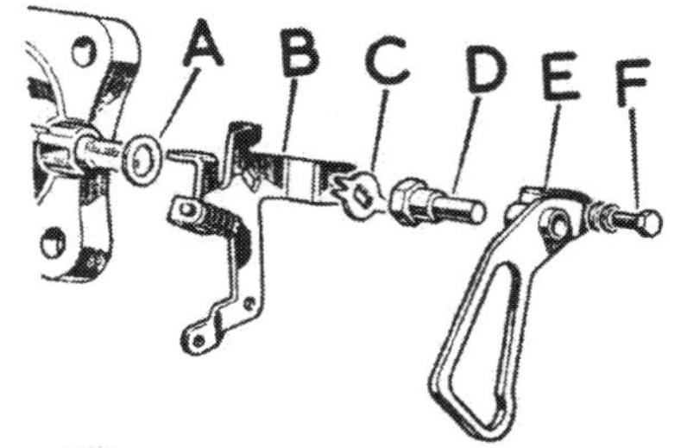

J439

Throttle lever assembly, left-hand carburetter

A—Brass washer
B—Carburetter lever
C—Tab washer
D—Special nut
E—Throttle lever
F—Bolt, spring and brass washer securing throttle lever

16. **On right-hand carburetter:**
    (a) Remove the circlip from the spindle and draw off the right-hand throttle lever.

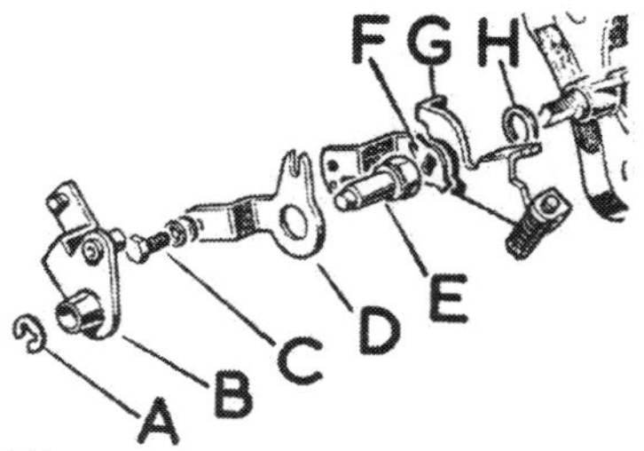

J440

Throttle lever assembly, right-hand carburetter

A—Circlip securing throttle lever
B—Throttle lever
C—Bolt, spring and plain washer for lever
D—Adjusting lever
E—Extension nut
F—Tab washer
G—Carburetter lever
H—Brass washer

Operation Q-2A—*continued*

(b) Remove the adjusting bolt, spring and plain washer from the adjusting lever and draw off.
(c) Release the tab washer from the spindle extension nut and remove the nut and tab washer.
(d) Remove the carburetter lever and brass washer.

17. Close the ends of the two special screws retaining the throttle butterfly, remove the screws and withdraw the butterfly from the spindle. The throttle spindle can now be withdrawn from the carburetter body. If necessary the piston lift pin can be removed by removing the circlip, the brass washer, the neoprene washer and the lift pin together with the spring.

Inspection

Check the throttle spindle and carburetter body for wear, also check all levers and linkage for excessive free movement indicating wear and replace these as necessary. Clean the inside bore of the suction chamber and the outside diameters of the piston with a clean cloth moistened with petrol. Inspect the jet and the jet bearing for signs of wear and replace as necessary. Make sure that all the components are thoroughly clean in preparation for assembly.

Carburetter, assemble

1. If previously removed position the spring over the lift pin and locate into the carburetter body, fit the neoprene washer, brass washer and secure with the circlip.

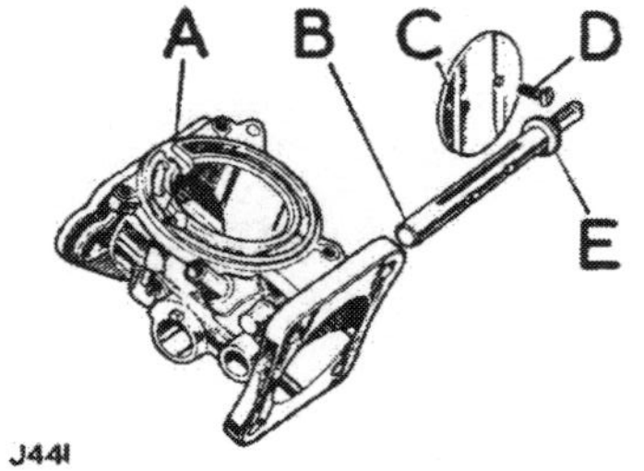

J441

Fitting throttle butterfly and spindle to carburetter body

A—Carburetter body
B—Spindle
C—Butterfly
D—Screws fixing butterfly
E—Brass washer

2. Insert the spindle into the carburetter body with the plain end on the float chamber side.

3. Slide the butterfly through the spindle so that the top of the butterfly will move away from the engine when opening the throttle and the chamfered edge locates with the bore when closed.

4. Fit two new screws but do not fully tighten at this stage.

5. Place the brass washer for throttle spindle on to the threaded end of the spindle ensuring that it is located on the larger diameter of the spindle which will just be protruding from the carburetter body.

6. Fit the carburetter lever and, on the left-hand carburetter, the throttle link, locating it correctly on the threaded portion of the spindle, then fit the tab washer and extension nut.

7. Tighten the extension nut to secure the lever to the spindle and lock with the tab washer.

8. With the throttle butterfly held in the fully closed position apply light pressure to the spindle at the end with the extension nut to bring the lever into contact with the brass washer, hold this position and fully tighten the two screws fixing the throttle butterfly to the spindle and lock them by opening the slots.

9. **On left-hand carburetter.** Refit the throttle lever to carburetter lever with bolt, spring and plain brass washer, do not tighten at this stage.

10. **On right-hand carburetter:**
    (a) Refit adjusting lever, and secure with adjusting bolt, spring and plain washer. Do not tighten at this stage.
    (b) Refit the right-hand throttle lever to extension, and secure to spindle with circlip.
    (c) Refit throttle link to throttle lever, and secure with the circlip.

11. Locate the jet bearing, short end first, into the carburetter body followed by the brass washer and bearing nut, do not tighten at this stage. Insert the jet into the jet bearing.

Operation Q-2A—*continued*

12. Fit the jet needle into the piston so that the shoulder on the shank is flush with the face of the piston and secure with the clamping screw.

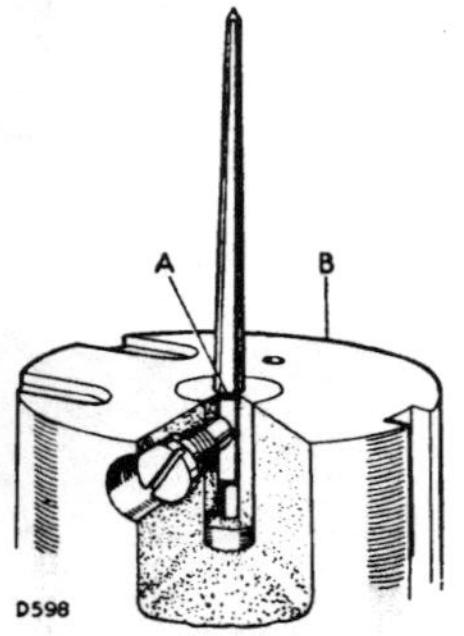

D598

Needle in correct position

A—Needle B—Piston body

13. Insert the piston into the carburetter body locating the needle into the jet bearing.

14. With a few drops of thin oil on the piston rod only, position the piston spring and suction chamber on to the carburetter body and secure with the three screws.

15. With the damper or oil cap removed and using a pencil or something similar on top of the piston rod, gently press the piston and needle down on to the jet bridge.

16. Tighten the jet locking nut observing that the jet head is still in correct angular position.

17. Lift the piston and check that it falls freely and evenly hitting the jet bridge with a soft metallic click. Fully lower the jet and re-check to see if there is any difference in the sound of the impact, if there is, and the second test produces a sharper impact sound, the centring operation will have to be repeated until successful.

18. Remove the jet and locate the spring and adjusting nut on to the jet bearing.

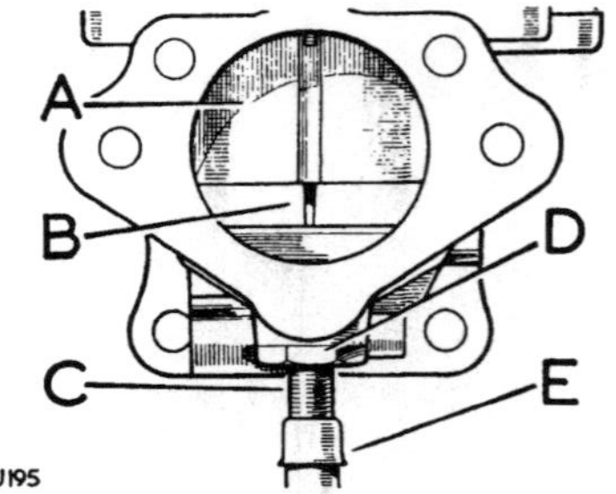

J195

Centring the carburetter jet

A—Piston
B—Needle
C—Jet bearing
D—Nut for bearing
E—Jet assembly

19. Fit the gland nut, brass washer and a new gland to the jet tube and position in the base of the float chamber, but do not tighten at this stage.

20. Offer the float chamber with the adaptor on to the carburetter body at the same time locating the jet into the jet bearing.

21. Secure the float chamber to the carburetter body with a special bolt, plain washer and spring washer.

22. Tighten the gland nut on the jet pipe at the base of the float chamber.

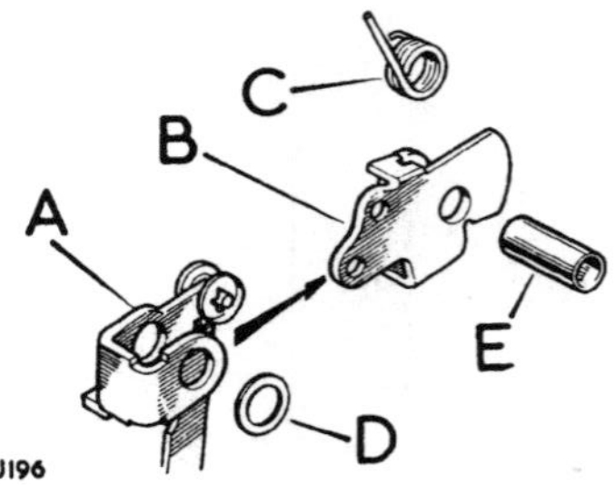

J196

Cam lever, pick-up lever and link assembly

A—Pick-up lever and link
B—Cam lever
C—Cam lever spring
D—Shim washer
E—Distance tube

Operation Q-2A—*continued*

23. Assemble the cam lever, pick-up lever and link, cam lever spring, distance tube and shim washer, ensuring correct sequence.

24. Place the spring for pick-up lever over the bolt ensuring that the outer end of the spring locates in the slot in the pick-up lever.

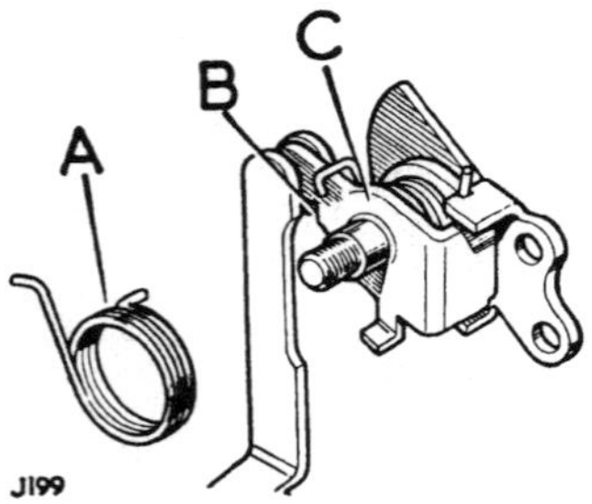

J199

Pick-up lever spring

A—Return spring B—Slot in lever
C—Pick-up lever

25. Now secure this assembly to the carburetter body and using a suitable piece of hooked wire locate the inner end of the pick-up lever spring over the projection on the carburetter body.

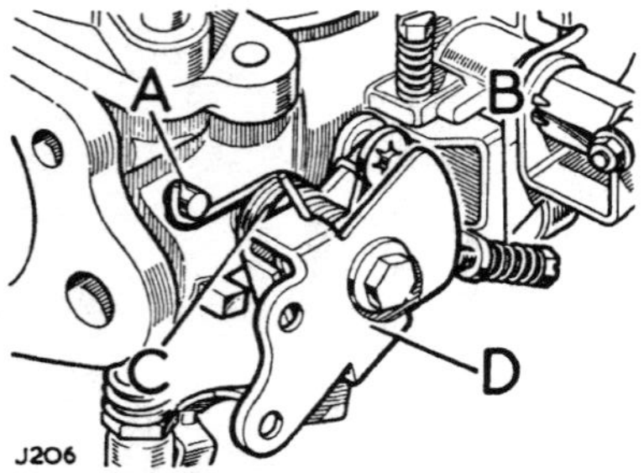

J206

Cam lever and pick-up lever assembly on carburetter body

A—Location for inner end of spring on carburetter body
B—Fast idling adjusting screw
C—Return spring
D—Lever assembly

26. Turn the cam lever in a clockwise direction and hold against spring pressure while securing the pick-up link bracket to the jet head, with the self-tapping screw.

27. Fit the needle valve seat into the float chamber lid and replace the valve.

28. Fit the float to the float chamber lid and secure with the mills pin.

29. A check should be made to ensure that the float level will be correct. With the float chamber lid inverted and the needle valve in the shut off position there should be a $\frac{1}{8}$ in. to $\frac{3}{16}$ in. (3 to 4,5 mm) gap between the float lever and the rim of the float chamber lid.

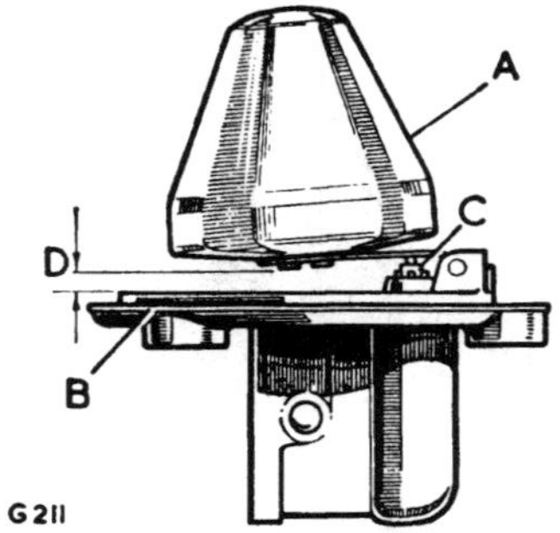

G211

Setting the float chamber fuel level

A—Nylon float
B—Gasket
C—Needle valve
D—Correct clearance $\frac{1}{8}$ in. to $\frac{3}{16}$ in. (3 to 4,5 mm)

30. Fit the lid complete with a new gasket to the float chamber and secure with the three screws and spring washers.

31. Fill the damper reservoir in the suction piston with SAE 20 engine oil to within $\frac{1}{2}$ in. (12 mm) from the top of the hollow piston rod, replace the damper and washer.

32. Refit the balance pipe, float chamber to intake.

*Fuel pump, overhaul—Operation Q-6A

Time allowed: hours

Workshop hand tools:
Screwdriver, medium Small chisel

See Section A for fuel pump remove and refit

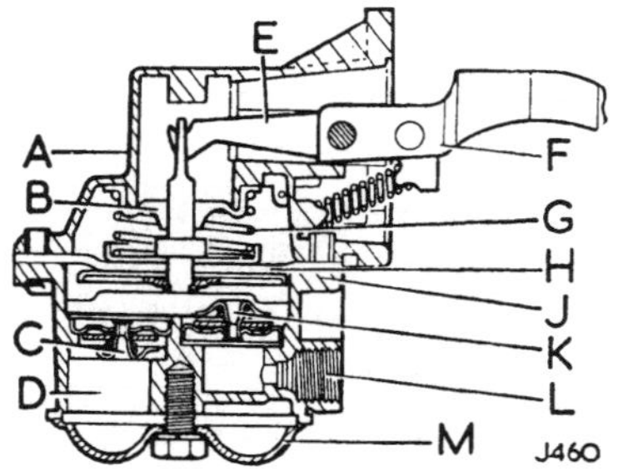

Cross-section of fuel pump

A—Pump body
B—Oil seal and retainer
C—Outlet valve
D—Outlet port
E—Link
F—Rocker arm
G—Diaphragm spring
H—Diaphragm
J—Fuel cover
K—Inlet valve
L—Inlet port
M—Pulsator cover

Fuel pump, overhaul

(a) Dismantling fuel pump

1. Mark edges of fuel cover and pump body so that cover may be refitted in its original position on body.
2. Remove all fuel cover screws and separate cover from pump body. If cover sticks to body, rap with soft mallet—**do not pry between the faces with a screwdriver.**
3. Remove pulsator cover and diaphragm from fuel cover. Scrape out burrs produced by staking valves and drive both valves and gaskets from cover.
4. Block pull rod link in position farthest toward diaphragm by jamming a thin tool between link and pump body. Depress diaphragm very lightly until blocked link just touches end of slot in pull rod. Then tilt diaphragm away from body mounting flange, apply a heavy side pressure on pull rod away from mounting flange, and while still applying this pressure, tilt diaphragm toward mounting flange to unhook pull rod from link. Remove diaphragm and spring from pump body.

Operations which are identified by an asterisk (*), can be carried out with the engine installed in the car

Operation Q-6A—*continued*

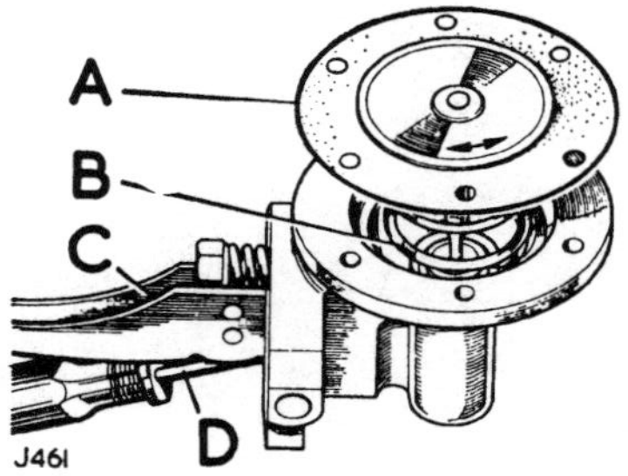

Diaphragm assembly

A—Diaphragm
B—Diaphragm spring
C—Rocker arm
D—Screwdriver blocking link

5. Scrape out burrs produced by staking and pry out oil seal and retainer.

(b) Removal of rocker arm and link

To install a **diaphragm kit,** it is not necessary to remove the rocker arm pin. However, when overhauling a high mileage pump, it is advisable to use the **repair kit** which contains a rocker arm pin and a link. Remove as follows:

1. File or grind riveted end of rocker arm pin flush with steel washer, or cut off end with a $\frac{3}{8}$ in. drill. Then drive pin out with a drift punch and hammer.
2. Remove rocker arm, rocker arm spring, and link from pump body.

(c) Inspection of pump parts

1. Clean and rinse all parts to be re-used in solvent. Blow out all passages with air hose.
2. Inspect pump body and fuel cover for cracks, breakage, or distorted flanges. Examine screw holes for stripped or crossed threads.
3. Inspect rocker arm for wear at pad and at point of contact with link. Check for excessive rocker arm side-play due to wear on rocker arm pin.
4. If a damaged casting or a badly worn rocker arm is found, it is advisable to discard old parts and install a new fuel pump.

(d) Assembly of fuel pump

When overhauling pump, always use all new parts in kit as amount of wear of these parts cannot be determined visually.

1. If rocker arm and link were removed (see above), place new rocker arm spring and link in position in pump body with rocker arm and use a slightly undersize rod through pin hole to line them up. Drive new rocker arm pin through body, forcing line-up rod ahead of it. Install new steel washer over small end of rocker arm pin, support head of pin on a suitable steel block, and peen small end of pin to retain washer and pin in place.
2. Install new oil seal in retainer and drive retainer into body with flat end of a rod $\frac{7}{8}$ in. in diameter. Stake body in four places around retainer.
3. Block link in position farthest towards diaphragm by jamming a thin tool between link and pump body. Place diaphragm spring in body, place cup shaped spring retainer on ends of spring, then push diaphragm pull rod through these parts with flat of rod at 90° to link in body. Hook pull rod over end link.
4. Place a new gasket in each valve seat in fuel cover. Place valve in seat nearest 'IN' connector with spring cage facing up. Place other valve in outlet valve seat with spring cage down.

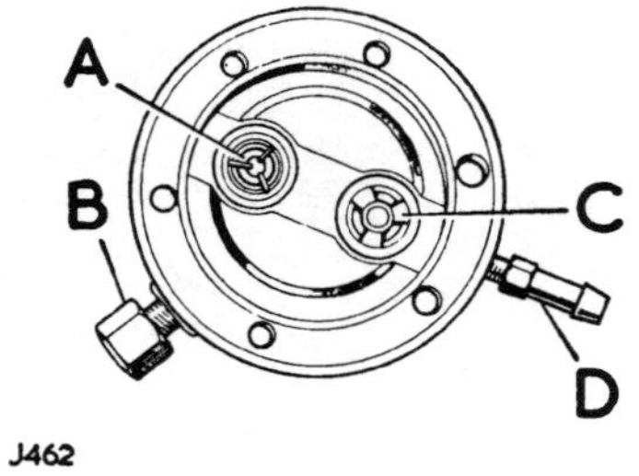

Valves in position in fuel cover

A—Outlet valve
B—Outlet port
C—Inlet valve
D—Inlet port

5. Seat valves firmly against gaskets and stake cover in four places around edge of each valve.

Operation Q-6A—*continued*

6. Install new pulsator diaphragm and cover on fuel cover and tighten screws securely.
7. Place fuel cover in position so that file marks on cover and pump body are in line and install all cover screws and lockwashers until screws just engage lockwashers. **Be sure that screws pass through holes in diaphragm without damaging fabric.**
8. Tighten screws alternately and evenly until all screws are tight.

(e) Testing repaired fuel pump

Bench tests of the fuel pump require equipment which is not available in most service organisations; therefore, tests must be made after installation of the pump on an engine.

Fuel reserve tap, remove and refit—Operation Q-10A

Time allowed: hours

Workshop hand tools:

Spanner sizes: $\frac{1}{2}$ in. AF, $\frac{11}{16}$ in. AF, $\frac{5}{16}$ in. Whit

Pliers, long-nosed Screwdriver, small

Fuel reserve tap, remove

1. Remove trim panel at rear of boot.
2. Slacken off both main and reserve fuel pipes. This **will cause an air lock and prevent the fuel being syphoned out.**

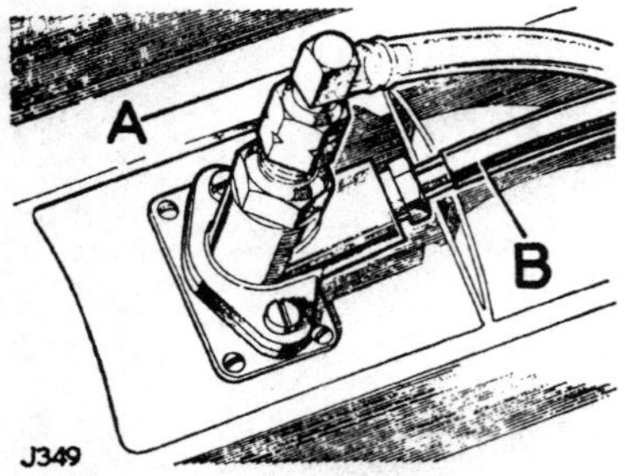

Fuel pipe connections at tank

A—Main feed pipe B—Reserve pipe

3. Disconnect the pipes from the reserve tap.
4. Disconnect operating cable and return spring.
5. Remove large locking nut and withdraw tap from bracket.

Fuel reserve tap, refit

1. Reverse removal procedure.

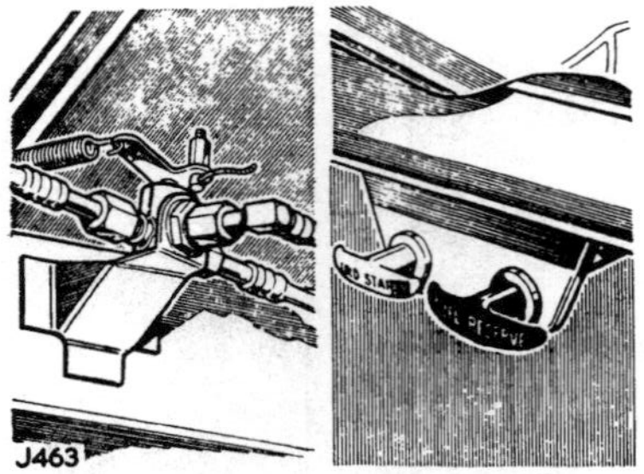

Fuel reserve tap and control

DATA

Carburetter

Type	SU HS6
Number	2
Bore	1.75 in. (44,45 mm)
Needle	KK
Jet size	0.100 in. (2,54 mm)
Float level	$\frac{1}{8}$ in. to $\frac{3}{16}$ in. (3,0 to 4,5 mm)
Damper oil	SAE 20

Fuel pump

Type	AC mechanical
Delivery pressure	3.5 to 5 lbs/sq in. (0,246 to 0,351 kgs/cm²)

Fuel tank

Total capacity including reserve	14 Imperial gallons (63,5 litres)
Reserve capacity	$1\frac{1}{2}$ Imperial gallons (7,0 litres)

Section R – EXHAUST SYSTEM

All the Operations in this Section are replaced by the items that follow

Front exhaust pipe, remove and refit—Operation R-1A

Time allowed: hours

Workshop hand tools:
Spanner size: ½ in. AF

Pipe, remove

1. Disconnect the pipe at the two exhaust manifolds, each secured by three nuts and washers.
2. Disconnect the front pipe from the intermediate pipe, secured by three nuts, bolts and washers, and lift the pipe away.

Pipe, refit

1. Reverse removal procedure.

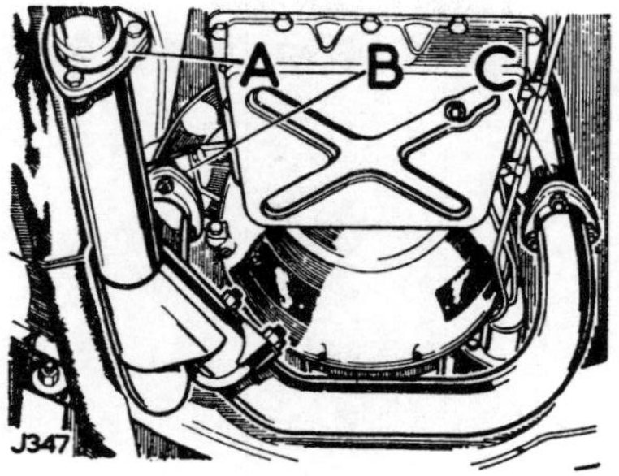

Front exhaust pipe

A—Coupling, front to intermediate pipe
B—Coupling at manifold, left-hand
C—Coupling at manifold, right-hand

Intermediate exhaust pipe and front silencer, remove and refit—Operation R-2A

Time allowed: hours

Workshop hand tools:
Spanner sizes: $\frac{7}{16}$ in. AF, $\frac{1}{2}$ in. AF
Hammer, hide

Pipe and silencer, remove

1. The front silencer and intermediate pipe form an integral unit. Disconnect the pipe from the front pipe and the rear exhaust silencer. The flanges each end are secured by three bolts, nuts and washers.
2. Carefully knock the front flange to the rear and remove the two split ring halves. Remove the flange.
3. Disconnect the pipe from the front mounting bracket, which is situated just behind the front crossmember.
4. Disconnect the mounting bracket at the rear of the front silencer.
5. Draw the whole unit to the rear until it is clear of the crossmember and remove.

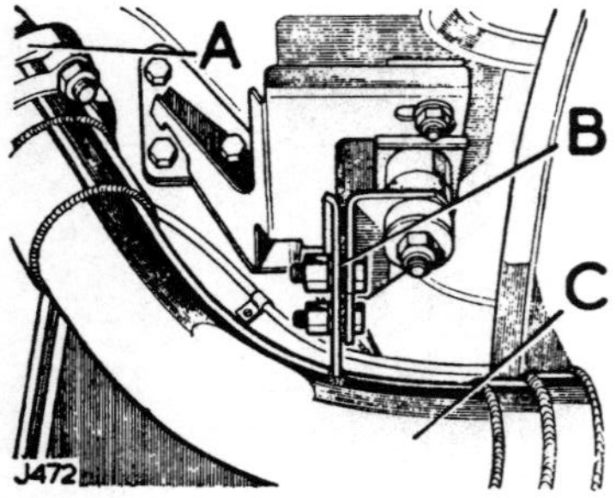

Mounting for intermediate exhaust pipe

A—Flange B—Intermediate mounting
C—Intermediate exhaust pipe

Pipe and silencer, refit

1. Reverse removal procedure.
2. It is essential that the rubber mountings supporting the exhaust system are fitted so that they are slightly forwards when the pipes are cold. This will ensure that the exhaust system is not unduly stressed due to expansion when hot.

Rear silencer and tail pipe, remove and refit—Operation R-4A

Time allowed: | hours

Workshop hand tools:
Spanner size: $\frac{1}{2}$ in. AF

Rear silencer and tail pipe, remove

1. Disconnect the rear silencer from the front silencer flange, secured by three nuts, bolts and spring washers.
2. Disconnect the silencer from the rear mounting bracket and remove the silencer complete with tail pipes.

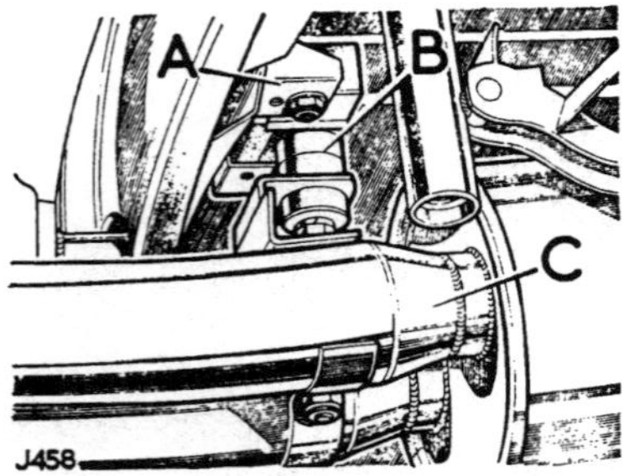

Mounting for rear pipe and silencer

A—Mounting bracket B—Rubber mounting
C—Silencer and tail pipes

Rear silencer and tail pipe, refit

1. Reverse removal procedure.
2. Renew mounting rubbers as necessary.
3. Ensure that all mountings are fitted slightly forward when cold. Expansion when hot will then not put the exhaust system under undue stress.

Section S — ELECTRICAL SYSTEM

The main differences between the 3-Litre and 3.5-Litre electrical system is the introduction of an alternator replacing the dynamo, a pre-engaged starter replacing the inertia type, and two fog lamps fitted as standard equipment.

All the changes are shown on the following pages.

INDEX

Distributor, overhaul—Operation S-2A

Workshop hand tools:
Spanner size: 4 BA
Screwdriver, medium Screwdriver, Phillips Hammer, hide faced Pliers Feeler gauge

For removal of distributor from engine see Section A-1

Distributor, dismantle

1. Unclip and remove distributor cap.
2. Withdraw rotor arm.
3. Remove nut retaining the contact spring, and lift off the insulating bush together with the low tension and capacitor leads.
4. Lift off the moving contact point and the insulating washer from the contact pivot and spring post.
5. Remove the Phillips screw and spring washer retaining the capacitor, and lift off the capacitor.
6. Remove the set screw, spring and plain washers retaining the fixed contact plate and lift off the fixed contact.

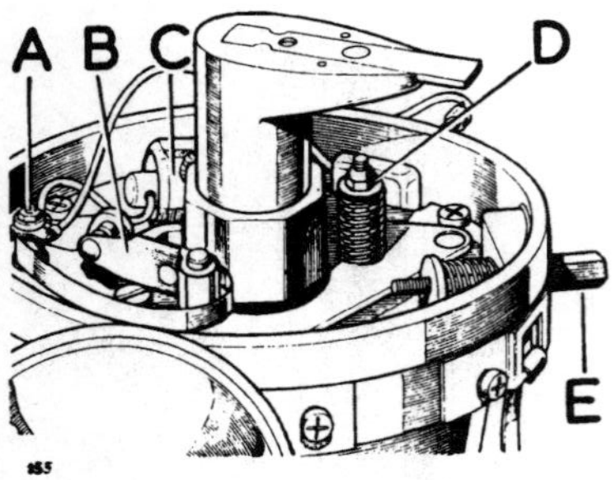

Distributor contact points

A—Nut and insulating washer for contact points
B—Contact points
C—Capacitor
D—Nut for base plate pivot pin
E—Dwell angle adjuster

7. Remove the nut, plain washer and spring from the contact breaker base plate pivot pin.
8. Remove the dwell angle adjuster screw and spring.
9. Remove the Phillips screw and spring washer retaining the earth lead to the centrifugal advance cover plate.
10. Remove the contact breaker base plate.
11. Remove the two Phillips screws, spring and plain washers retaining the vacuum unit and remove the vacuum unit and grommet.
12. Remove the remaining two Phillips screws and spring washers securing the centrifugal advance cover plate to the distributor body, and lift off the cover plate.
13. Carefully withdraw the two springs from the centrifugal advance unit.
14. Remove the screw from inside the cam and lift off the cam and cam foot, noting the position of the rotor arm slot in relation to the distributor driving gear for assembly purposes.
15. Lift off the two weights.
16. Drive out the pin securing the driving gear, and remove the gear and tab washer.
17. Check all parts for wear or damage and replace as necessary.

Operation S-2A—*continued*

Distributor, rebuild

1. Reassemble the distributor by reversing the dismantling instructions.
2. When fitting the centrifugal governor springs care must be taken not to stretch them.
3. When fully assembled the points can be set to a clearance of .014 to .016 in. (0,35 to 0,40 mm) as an initial guide before refitting to the engine.

Note: It is most important that the dwell angle is adjusted to 26° to 28° using specialised equipment when the distributor has been refitted.

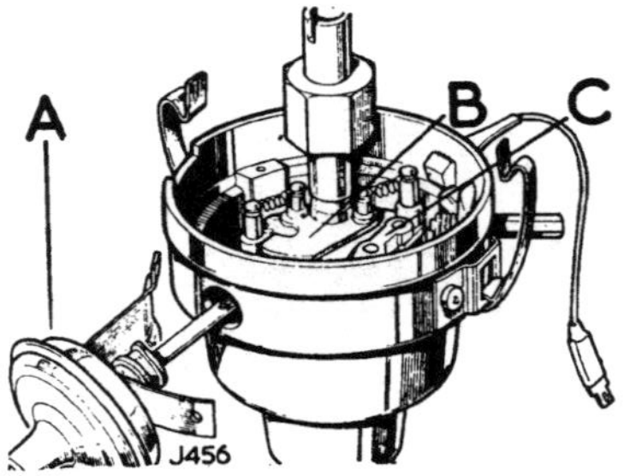

Distributor centrifugal advance unit

A—Vacuum unit B—Centrifugal advance unit
C—Centrifugal weights

Starter motor, overhaul—Operation S-3A

Workshop hand tools:
Spanner sizes: $\frac{7}{16}$ in. AF, $\frac{1}{2}$ in. AF, $\frac{7}{16}$ in. BSF
Screwdriver, large Hammer

Special tools:
Spring balance

For starter motor removal see Section A

Starter motor, overhaul
To strip

1. Disconnect the copper link between the lower solenoid terminal and the starter motor casing.
2. Remove the solenoid securing nuts and spring washers and withdraw the solenoid from the drive end bracket.
3. Move the starter pinion away from the armature to the end of its travel then disengage the solenoid plunger from the engagement lever, withdraw plunger and spring.
4. Slacken the screw retaining the cover band and remove the band.
5. Hold back the brush springs and remove brushes as illustrated.

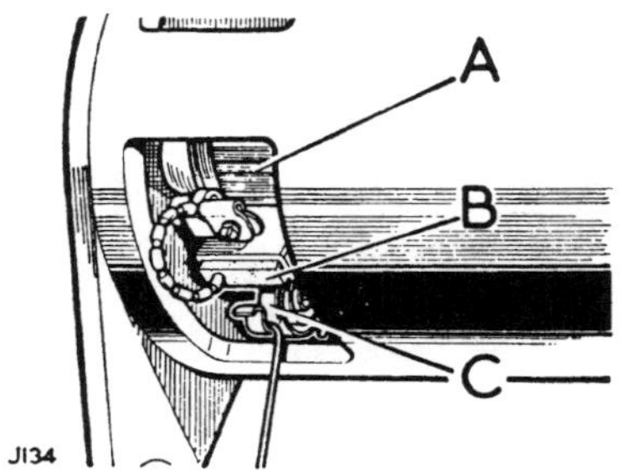

Removal of brushes
A—Commutator B—Brush C—Spring

6. Unscrew and withdraw the two through bolts from the commutator end bracket and remove the bracket from the starter yoke.
7. Separate the yoke from the intermediate and drive end bracket.
8. Disengage the armature from the engagement lever and withdraw the armature, drive gear and intermediate bracket.
9. From the armature shaft extension, remove the collar and jump ring by first driving the collar back along the shaft with a suitable tube. Remove the jump ring, and lift off the collar, drive assembly, intermediate bracket and rubber seal.
10. From the commutator end bracket withdraw the brake ring complete, steel washer and tufnol washer.
11. From the drive end bracket remove the nut securing the eccentric pin on which the drive engagement lever pivots and withdraw the pin and engagement lever.

To overhaul

1. Examine the brushes in the drive end bracket, intermediate and commutator end brackets, renew as necessary.

Clutch

2. The roller clutch drive is sealed in a rolled steel outer cover and cannot be dismantled.

   Check that the clutch will:

   (a) Give instantaneous take up of the drive in one direction.

   (b) Rotate easily and smoothly in the other direction.

   (c) Be free to move round and along the shaft splines without roughness or any tendency to bind. All moving parts should be smeared liberally with Shell Retinax 'A' grease or an equivalent.

Brushes

3. Check that brushes move freely in their holders while holding back the brush springs. If a brush is damaged or worn so that it does not make good contact with the commutator, all the brushes must be renewed.

   The new brushes are pre-formed, 'bedding' to the commutator is therefore unnecessary.
4. The flexible connectors are soldered to the terminal tabs, two to the field coils and two to the brush boxes, the flexible connectors must be unsoldered and the new brushes secured in position by re-soldering.
5. Using a spring balance as illustrated check that the tension of the brush springs is between 30 ozs to 40 ozs (0,85 kg to 1,13 kg). If the tension is low, fit new springs.

Operation S-3A—*continued*

6. Check the commutator, having first cleaned with a petrol moistened cloth, if necessary rotate the armature and, using fine glass paper remove pits and burns. If commutator is badly worn, mount in a lathe and with a very sharp tool take a light cut, removing no more metal than is necessary. Commutator segments MUST NOT BE UNDERCUT.

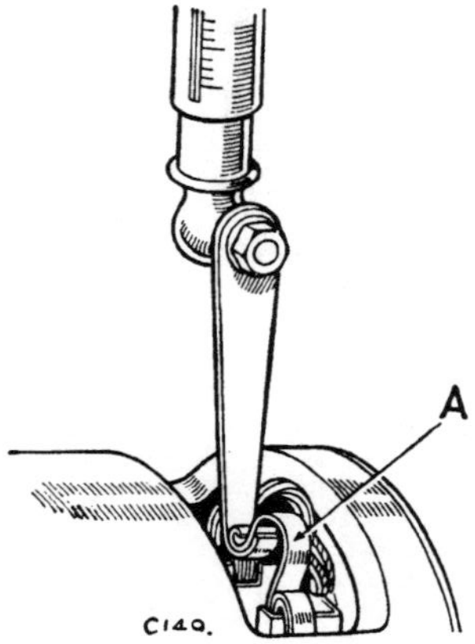

Testing brush springs
A—Brush spring

Solenoid, to check

7. Normally an earth return starter solenoid has three terminals, two large and one small, but model 10S starter solenoid carries an additional small terminal marked 'IGN' and is used in conjunction with the ignition coil ballast resistor. These solenoid units have an auxiliary phosphor bronze contact which serves to cut out the ballast resistor during starting, thus ensuring that the terminal voltage (therefore the performance) of the coil at this time remains almost unaffected by the drop in battery voltage.

Auxiliary contacts, to check

1. Disconnect all the cables from the solenoid terminals and connectors.
2. Connect a test lamp between the connector marked 'IGN' (B) and a good earth.
3. Connect the battery to the small unmarked connector (D).
4. Momentarily connect the large battery terminal (A) to earth. The solenoid contacts should close fully and remain closed, the test lamp should emit a steady light.
5. Disconnect the battery from the small unmarked connector (D). The contacts should open, the solenoid released, and the test lamp extinguished.

   The period of energising should be as brief as possible to avoid overheating the windings.

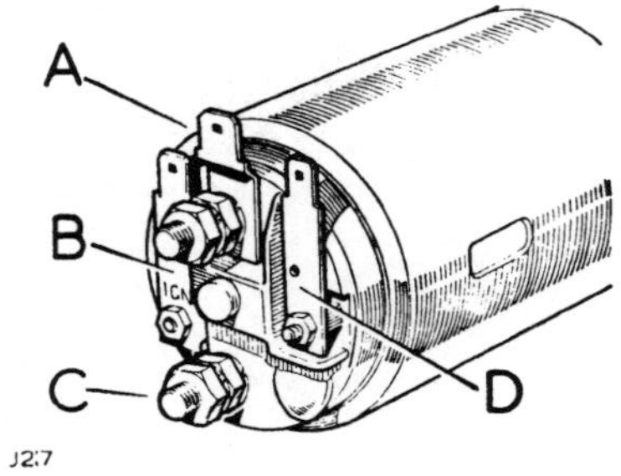

Pre-engaged starter solenoid terminals
A—Battery C—Starter
B—Ignition D—Starter switch

To assemble

1. Position the pre-engagement lever into the drive end bracket so that the flat face at the solenoid engagement end of the lever will face away from the solenoid.
2. Fit the eccentric pivot pin into the drive end bracket, at the same time locating engagement lever on to the pivot pin, replace the securing nut but do not tighten at this stage.
3. Fit the intermediate bracket on to the armature together with the drive assembly, stop collar, new jump ring and thrust washer.
4. Fit the armature in to the drive end bracket, at the same time locating the engagement fork into the drive assembly, position the intermediate bracket on to the dowel in the drive end bracket and locate rubber seal in the solenoid aperture.

Operation S-3A—*continued*

5. Fit the yoke over the armature and locate on to end bracket dowel.
6. Fit the tufnol washer, thrust washer and brake ring into the commutator end bracket.
7. With the brushes positioned clear of the commutator fit the bracket on to the yoke, locating the dowel and the brake drive pin into the brake ring.
8. Fit the two through bolts, replace brushes and cover band.
9. Position the solenoid plunger so that the fork end with the spring loaded plunger is located under the small hole in the end bracket. Pass a ⅛ in. (3,175 mm) rod through the hole and depress the plunger.
10. With the drive assembly held in the forward position locate the solenoid plunger over the engagement lever and withdraw the rod.
11. Fit the return spring over the plunger, fit the solenoid on to the plunger and locate it in the drive end bracket, secure with two nuts and spring washers.
12. Refit the copper link between the lower solenoid terminal and the starter motor casing.
13. Before tightening the lock nut on the eccentric bolt it is necessary to check the pinion movement by connecting the small terminal on the solenoid to one side of a six volt battery, using a switch, connect the other side of the battery to a solenoid fixing stud.
14. Close the switch, thus throwing the drive assembly forward into the engaged position. Measure the distance between the pinion and the collar on the armature shaft as illustrated.
15. This measurement should be taken with the pinion pressed lightly towards the armature to take up any free play in the engagement linkage. The setting should be 0.005 in. to 0.015 in. (0,12 mm to 0,40 mm).

    Adjustment is made by rotating the eccentric bolt until the correct clearance is obtained, then secure with the lock nut.

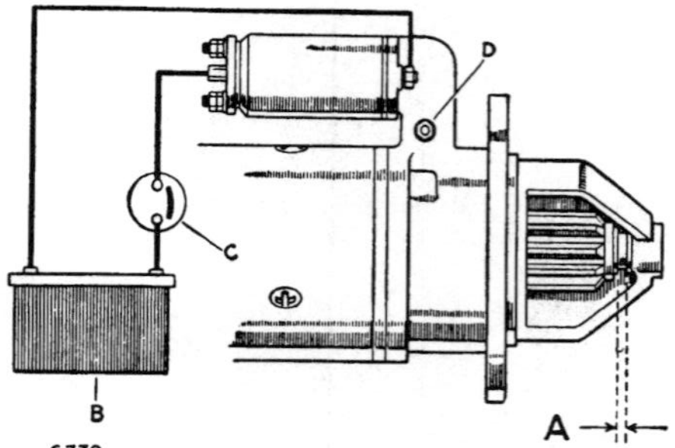

C739.

Adjusting pinion clearance with solenoid energised

A—Clearance 0.005 in. to 0.015 in. (0,12 mm to 0,40 mm)
B—Battery
C—Switch
D—Eccentric pivot pin

Battery charging system—alternator—Operation S-5A-1

For alternator, remove and refit, see Section A1

Description

Battery charging is maintained by a 43-ampere. three-phase alternator. The eight-pole rotor carries the field winding, which is connected to two face-type slip rings. The rotor is supported by a ball bearing in the drive end bracket, and a needle roller bearing in the slip-ring end cover.

The slip-ring end cover also carries six silicon diodes connected in a three-phase bridge circuit to give rectification of the generated AC output.

Output control

The alternator terminal voltage is controlled by an electronic voltage regulator that utilises transistors as switching devices in place of moving contacts.

At zero or very low rotor speeds the alternator diodes prevent battery current flowing through the output windings, so that a cut-out unit is unnecessary,

IMPORTANT

Precaution when using a fast charger

Before using a fast charger, either to boost the battery or to start the engine, first withdraw the three-way connector from the 4TR control unit terminals. Do not reconnect the terminals until the charger has been disconnected, and in the case of assisted starting the engine speed is reduced to idling.

Failure to observe this precaution may result in irreparable damage to the semi-conductors in the control unit.

Field isolation

The voltage regulator and alternator field windings are isolated from the battery when the ignition is switched off by the normally open contacts of a model 6RA relay. The operating coil of the relay is supplied by the ignition switch.

Alternator warning light

This is similar in operation to the ignition warning light or 'no charge' warning light used with generator charging systems. It is operated by a thermal relay, model 3AW, connected to one pair of the alternator diodes.

Warning

The diodes and transistors in the alternator and voltage regulator, and any other transistorised equipment that may be fitted, will be irreparably damaged if the battery connections are reversed. Care must be taken to check the polarity of all connections in the electrical system.

Damage to the diodes can also be caused by a short circuit to earth of a live lead of the charging system. Battery voltage is applied to the alternator output cable even when the ignition is switched off, so it is recommended that the battery be disconnected when any work is being done in the vicinity of the alternator or voltage regulator.

The battery should also be disconnected when repairs to the body structure are being done by arc-welding.

Alternator driving belt tension, adjust—Operation S-5A-2

Workshop hand tools:
Spanner size: $\frac{1}{2}$ in. AF

Alternator driving belt tension, adjust

1. When correctly adjusted, it is possible to deflect the driving belt by thumb pressure $\frac{7}{16}$ in. to $\frac{9}{16}$ in. (11 mm to 14 mm) mid-way between the crankshaft and fan pulleys.
2. Loosen the bolts securing the alternator to the support bracket.
3. Loosen the bolts securing the alternator adjusting link to the alternator and top compressor bracket.
4. Position the alternator so that the driving belt can be deflected by thumb pressure $\frac{7}{16}$ in. to $\frac{9}{16}$ in. (11 mm to 14 mm) mid-way between the crankshaft and fan pulleys. Apply leverage only to the drive end bracket of the alternator to avoid damage to the bearings.
5. Tighten the alternator and adjusting link securing bolts.
6. Recheck the driving belt tension.

Adjustment of alternator driving belt

A—Securing bolt, link to top bracket
B—Securing bolt, link to alternator
C—Check belt tension at this point, $\frac{7}{16}$ in. to $\frac{9}{16}$ in. (11 mm to 14 mm)

Alternator output control unit. Model 4TR

Maintenance

The output control unit does not require any regular maintenance, but the moulded cover should be kept clean, and the terminals checked for tightness.

Control unit, test—Operation S-5A-3

Workshop hand tools:
Screwdriver

Special tools:
Voltmeter, Ammeter

Control unit, test

1. Before checking and adjusting the control unit it must be established that the alternator and charging circuit wiring are in good order. See Operation S-5A-8. The battery to control unit wiring, including the 6RA field isolating relay, must also be in good order. See Operation S-5A-8, item 9. The resistance of this circuit, including the relay, must not exceed 1 ohm. Higher resistance must be traced and remedied.
2. Disconnect the alternator main output lead from the alternator or starter solenoid, and connect an ammeter of 50-amp range in series with the lead and its connection.
3. Connect a voltmeter of 1 per cent accuracy or better between the battery terminals and note the reading with all electrical equipment switched off. If available, use a voltmeter of the suppressed—zero type, reading 12–15 volts.

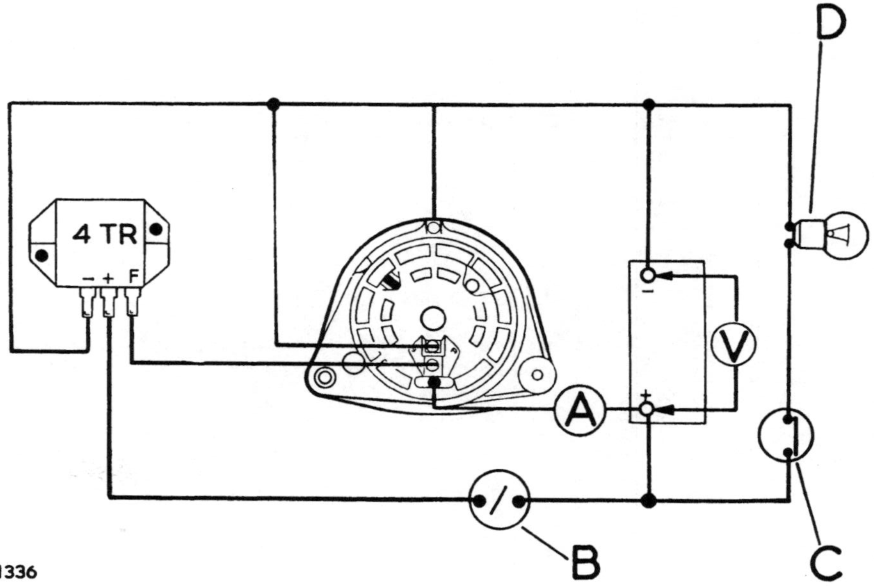

H336

4TR control unit test circuit

A—Ammeter
B—Field isolating relay
C—Side and tail lamp switch
D—Side and tail lamps
V—Voltmeter

Operation S-5A-3—*continued*

4. Switch on the side and tail lights to give an electrical load of approximately 2 amperes.
5. Start the engine and run the alternator at approximately 3,000 rpm for at least 8 minutes to ensure the system voltage has stabilised. If the charging current is greater than 10 amperes, continue to run the engine until this figure is reached. The voltmeter should then read 13.9 to 14.3 volts.
6. If the reading obtained is stable, but outside these limits, the unit can be adjusted to obtain the correct voltage. See Operation S-5A-4.
7. If the voltmeter reading remains unchanged at open circuit battery voltage, or increases in an uncontrolled manner, the control unit is faulty and must be replaced.

Control unit, adjust—Operation S-5A-4

Workshop hand tools:

Screwdriver

Control unit, adjust

1. Test control unit. Operation S-5A-3.
2. Stop the engine and remove the control unit securing screws, insert the unit and carefully scrape away the sealing compound that conceals the potentiometer adjuster.
3. Start the engine and run the alternator at approximately 3,000 rpm with the voltmeter firmly connected to the battery terminals. Turn the potentiometer adjuster slot clockwise to increase the voltage setting, or counter-clockwise to decrease it. A small movement of the adjuster causes an appreciable difference in the voltage reading.
4. Recheck the setting by stopping the engine, then restarting and running the alternator at 3,000 rpm.
5. Disconnect the voltmeter and ammeter. Reconnect the alternator output lead.
6. Refit the control unit.

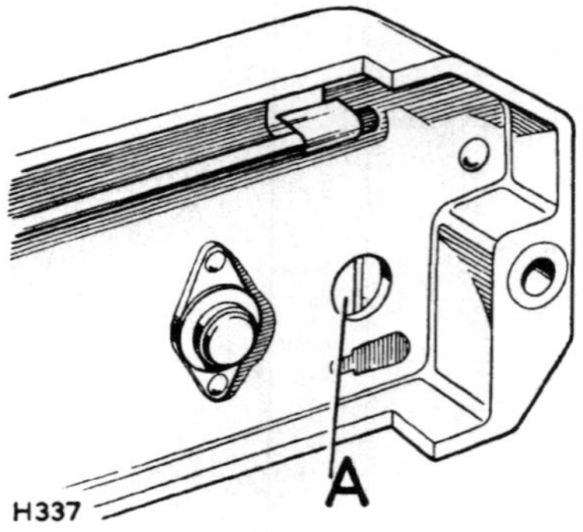

4TR alternator control, rear view

A—Potentiometer adjuster

Alternator field isolating relay. Model 6RA

The relay has a pair of normally open contacts, is actuated by a continuous rated winding, and has four blade-type terminals, marked C1, C2, W1 and W2.

Terminal C1 is associated with the fixed contact post, C2 with the moving contact; W1 and W2 are the ends of the operating winding. The relay is protected by a metal case secured to the base by gimping.

The relay should be replaced as a unit in the event of failure. Where facilities are available, the case can be removed for checking the contacts, mechanical settings and soldered connections.

Maintenance

Check the tightness of the terminals.

Field isolating relay, test—Operation S-5A-5

Workshop hand tools:

Screwdriver, medium
Screwdriver, electrician's
Pliers, long-nosed

Special tools:

Variable DC supply 0–15 volts
Voltmeter, 0–20 volts
Bulb, 12 volts 1.5 watt

Field isolating relay, test

1. Connect terminals C1 and C2 in series with a 1.5-watt bulb and terminals of a 12-volt battery.
2. Connect terminals W1 and W2 of the relay to the terminals of the battery.
3. The bulb should light when the relay winding between W1 and W2 is energised. If the bulb does not light, the relay winding or contacts are faulty and the relay should be replaced.

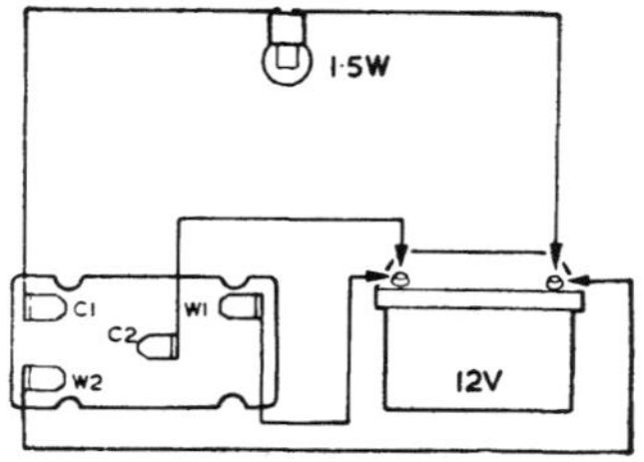

6 RA relay winding and contact test

Field isolating relay, adjust—Operation S-5A-6

Workshop hand tools:

Screwdriver Pliers Pliers, long-nosed

Special tools:

Voltmeter, variable DC supply, 0–15 volts

Field isolating relay, adjust

1. Prise open the gimping securing the cover to the base.
2. Connect a first grade moving coil voltmeter across the relay operating winding, terminals W1 and W2.
3. Connect a variable direct current supply 0–15 volts to the winding terminals, W1 and W2.
4. Check the cut-in setting by raising the supply voltage from zero. The contacts should close when the voltage is 6.0 to 7.5 volts. The setting is raised by increasing the air gap between the underside of the armature and the bobbin core, and lowered by decreasing the air gap.
5. Check the drop-off setting by raising the voltage to 15 volts then slowly reducing it. The contacts should open at 4.0 volts minimum. The drop-off setting is raised by raising the height of the fixed contact post to increase the contact pressure. The drop-off setting is lowered by lowering the fixed contact post and contact pressure.
6. Disconnect the voltmeter and voltmeter supply.
7. Place the sealing gasket in the case flange and insert the relay assembly. Press the components firmly together and secure at four points by gimping the case lip.
8. Recheck the cut-in and drop-off settings.

Alternator warning light control. Model 3AW

The warning light control is a thermally operated relay for controlling the switching on and off of an instrument panel warning light. It is connected to the centre point of one pair of the alternator diodes through terminal 'AL' on the alternator, and to earth. The indication given by the warning light is similar to that provided by the ignition ('no charge') warning light used with dynamo charging systems.

Warning. Due to the external similarity of the alternator warning light control model 3AW to flasher unit model FL5, a distinctive green label is applied to the aluminium case of model 3AW.

Care must be taken to avoid connecting either of these units into a circuit designed for the other.

Maintenance

Check the tightness of the terminals. Model 3AW is a sealed unit.

Alternator warning light control, bench test—Operation S-5A-7

Special tools:

12-volt battery with accessible intercell connections
2.2-watt 12-volt bulb in holder
Three battery connector clips
Three Lucar connections
Watch with second hand

Warning light control, test

1. Connect terminal 'E' of the warning light control to the battery negative terminal.
2. Connect the 2.2-watt bulb in series with the terminal 'WL' of the warning light control and the positive battery terminal. The bulb should light up immediately. If the bulb does not light up, the warning light control is faulty and must be replaced.
3. With the terminals connected as in 1 and 2 above, connect terminal 'AL' of the warning light control to the 6-volt tapping of the battery. The bulb should go out within five seconds.
4. Transfer the battery connection of terminal 'AL' to the positive battery terminal for ten seconds only. Then quickly transfer it to the battery 2-volt tapping. The bulb should light up within five seconds.
5. If the performance in items 3 and 4 differs appreciably from the test requirements, the unit is faulty and must be replaced.

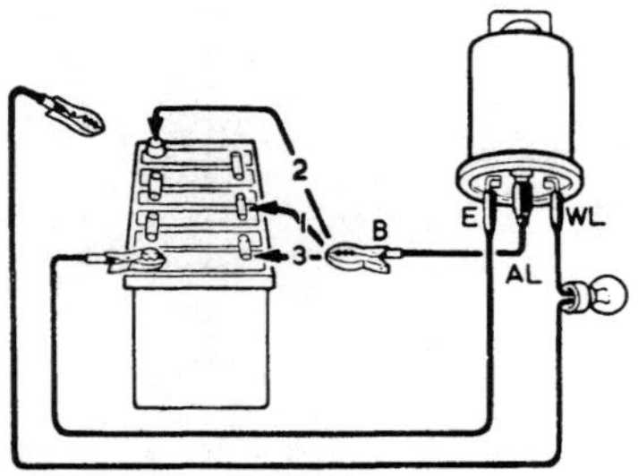

H339

Bench test for warning light control, model 3AW

Connect battery clip 'B' in sequence 1, 2 and 3

Battery charging system, test—Operation S-5A-8

Special tools:

Ammeter, 0–50 amperes
Extension leads with clips
Voltmeter, 0–15 volts

Charging system, test

1. Check the alternator driving belt for wear and tension. Adjust if necessary. Operation S-5A-2.
2. Disconnect the battery negative terminal.
3. Disconnect the 35-amp alternator output lead from the alternator and connect a good quality moving coil ammeter between the output terminal and alternator output lead.
4. Disconnect the leads from the alternator field terminals, and connect them to the battery terminals with the extension leads. Polarity is unimportant.

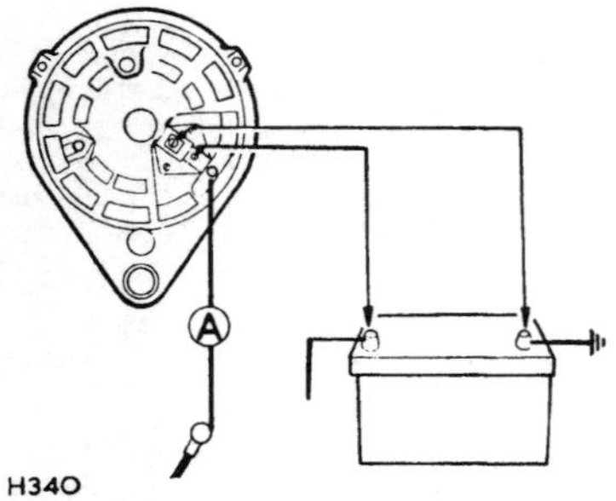

H340

Alternator output test

A—Ammeter

5. Reconnect the battery negative terminal. Start the engine and increase the speed until the alternator is running at approximately 4,000 rpm. The ammeter reading should be approximately 40 amps and if this figure is obtained the alternator and output cable are in order.
6. If a zero or low reading is obtained, check the output circuit and wiring by connecting a voltmeter between the alternator output terminal and the battery positive terminal and noting the reading; then transfer the voltmeter to the alternator frame and the battery negative terminal and noting the reading. If either reading exceeds 0.5 volt there is high resistance in the circuit that must be traced and remedied.

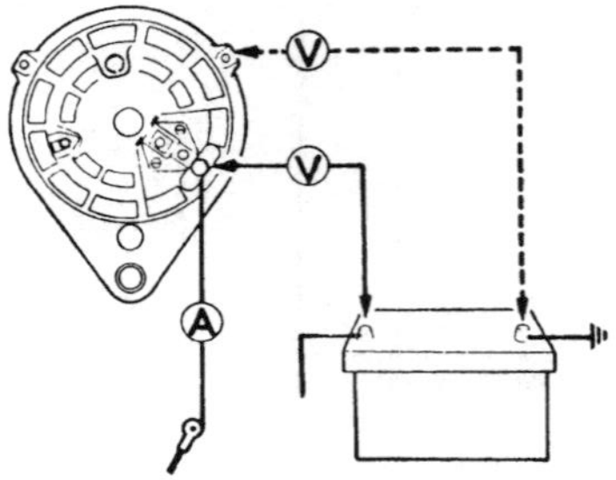

H341

Charging circuit voltage drop test

A—Ammeter V—Voltmeter

7. If the test in item 6 does not reveal high resistance, and alternator output is low, remove and examine the alternator brush gear. Retest and, if low output persists, replace or overhaul the alternator.
8. If the alternator output is in order, disconnect the battery negative terminal, remove the ammeter and connect the alternator output cable to its terminal. Remove the extension leads from the alternator field cables.
9. Connect the battery negative terminal. Switch on the ignition, and check that battery voltage is applied to the cable ends normally attached to the alternator field terminals by connecting a voltmeter across them. A reading of battery voltage proves that the field isolating relay circuit and wiring is in order. Conversely, a low or zero reading indicates a fault in the field isolating relay associated wiring, or the alternator output control unit. See Operation S-5A-5 for testing of field isolating relay. Refer to circuit diagram for continuity testing of wiring in the charging system.

Alternator, overhaul—Operation S-5A-9

Workshop hand tools:
Spanner sizes:
$\frac{5}{16}$ in. AF, $\frac{3}{8}$ in. AF, $\frac{11}{16}$ in. AF
Screwdriver, electrician's
Screwdriver, large
Pliers, long-nosed

Special tools:
Hand press
Soldering iron
Ohmmeter, Ammeter
Mains AC supply
15-watt 110-volt bulb
1.5-watt 12-volt bulb

For alternator removal, see Section A1

Cleaning

Maintain the alternator free from dirt and oil that may collect, particularly around the slip-ring end cover vents.

Lubrication

The bearings are packed with grease during assembly and do not require periodic attention.

Terminal connections

Ensure that all terminal connections are clean and tight.

Alternator, strip

1. Remove the nut and spring washer from the rotor shaft. Withdraw the pulley and fan.
2. Scribe the drive end bracket, lamination pack and slip ring end bracket so that they can be re-assembled in correct angular relation to each other.
3. Remove the three through bolts and washers. Withdraw the drive end bracket and rotor as an assembly from the stator.
4. Remove the Woodruff key and bearing collar. Press out the rotor shaft from the drive end bracket.

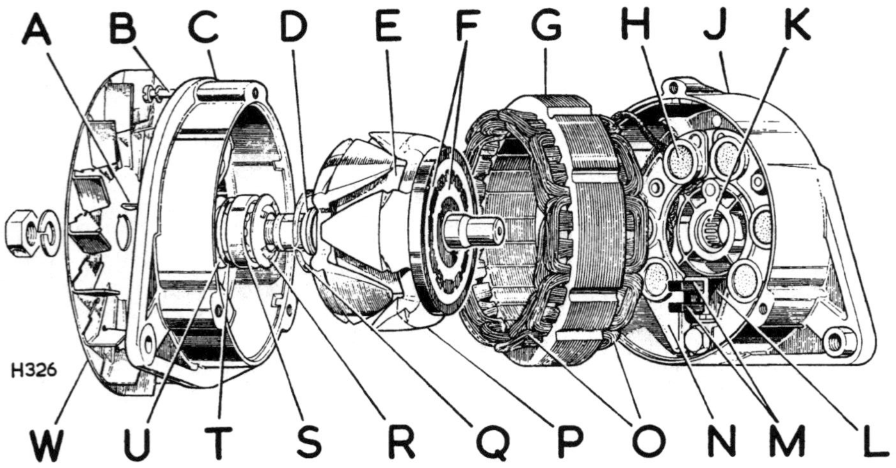

H326

Alternator model 11AC dismantled

A—Woodruff key
B—Through bolt (3)
C—Drive end bracket
D—Jump ring shroud
E—Rotor (field) winding
F—Slip rings
G—Stator laminations
H—Silicon diodes (6)
J—Slip ring end bracket
K—Needle roller bearing
L—Brush box
M—Brushes (2)
N—Diode heat sink (2)
O—Stator winding
P—Rotor
Q—Circlip
R—Bearing retaining plate
S—Ball bearing, drive end
T—'O' ring
U—'O' ring retaining washer
W—Fan

Operation S-5A-9—*continued*

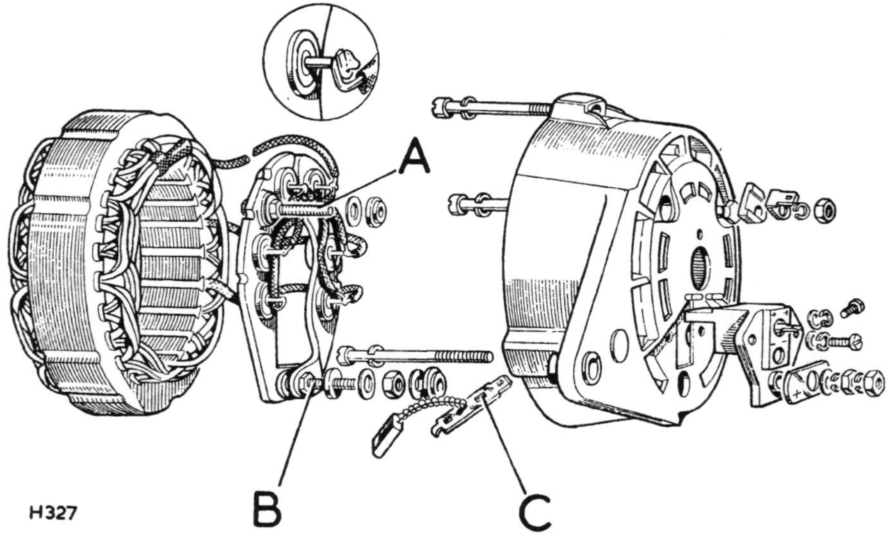

H327

Slip ring end, showing heat sinks withdrawn

A—Warning light terminal 'AL' B—Output terminal C—Terminal block retaining tongue

5. Remove the circlip from the drive end bracket and remove the retaining plate. Press out the ball bearing and remove the 'O' ring and retaining washer.

6. Remove the nut, spring washer, 35-amp Lucar blade and plastic strip from the output terminal. Remove the locknut and washer. Remove the two securing screws and washers and withdraw the brush box, noting the two small insulating washers between the brush box and end bracket.

7. Close up the retaining tongue at the root of each field terminal blade. Withdraw the brush spring and terminal assemblies from the brush box.

8. Remove the nut and washer from the warning light 'AL' terminal. Lift off the $17\frac{1}{2}$-amp Lucar blade and the insulation bush.

9. Remove the bolt and washer securing the slip ring end bracket to the heat sinks. Withdraw the stator and heat sinks from the end bracket, noting the insulating and plain washers on the 'AL' and output terminal posts.

10. Note the connections of the wires to the diodes and unsolder the wires, using a pair of long-nosed pliers as a thermal shunt, as in the illustration. Great care must be taken to avoid overheating the diodes, or bending the diode pins and the operation should be done as quickly as possible. Remove the nut securing the heat sinks together, and separate the heat sinks, noting the insulation washers.

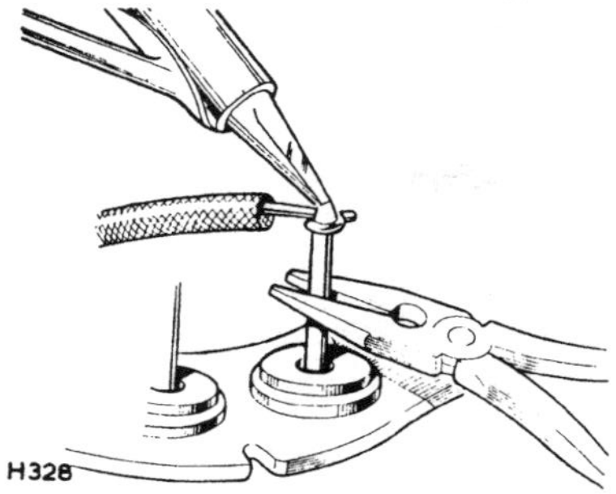

H328

Use of thermal shunt when soldering diode connections

Operation S-5A-9—*continued*

Inspection and testing of alternator parts
Brushgear

1. Measure the brush length. A new brush is $\frac{5}{8}$ in. (15,9 mm) long; a fully worn brush is $\frac{5}{32}$ in. (4 mm) long, and must be replaced at, or approaching, this length. Brush spring pressures can be checked against the specifications in the technical data.

   Check that the brushes move freely in their holders. Clean the brushes with a petrol-moistened cloth, and lightly polish the brush sides with a smooth file if necessary.

   Note. The brush which bears on the inner slip ring is the positive brush, as the lower linear speed results in reduced mechanical wear and helps to offset the higher rate of electrical wear peculiar to the positive connected brush.

2. **Slip-rings.** The surfaces of the slip rings should be smooth and free from oil. Clean the surfaces with a petrol-moistened cloth, or very fine glass paper if there is evidence of burning. No attempt should be made to machine the slip-rings, as any eccentricity will adversely affect the high speed performance of the alternator.

3. **Rotor.** Test the rotor winding by connecting an ohmmeter between the slip rings. The resistance reading should be 3.8 ohms at 68°F.

   An alternative test can be made using a 12-volt battery and large-scale ammeter in series with the winding. The ammeter reading should be approximately 3.2 amperes.

   Test the slip-ring/rotor winding insulation by using an AC mains supply and a test lamp in series with a slip-ring and rotor pole. If the lamp lights, the insulation is faulty and the rotor must be replaced.

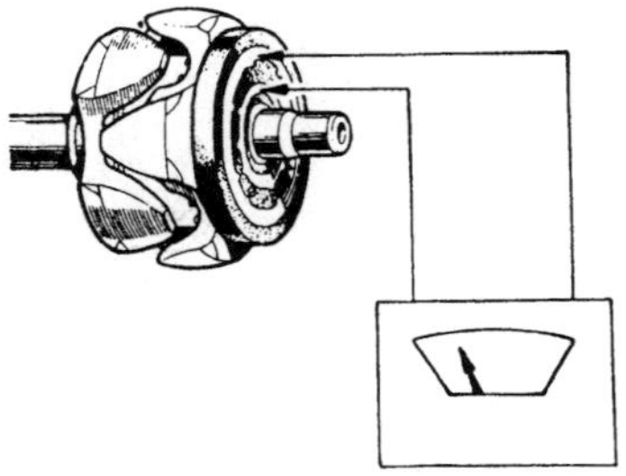

H329

Measuring rotor winding resistance with ohmmeter (alternator dismantled)

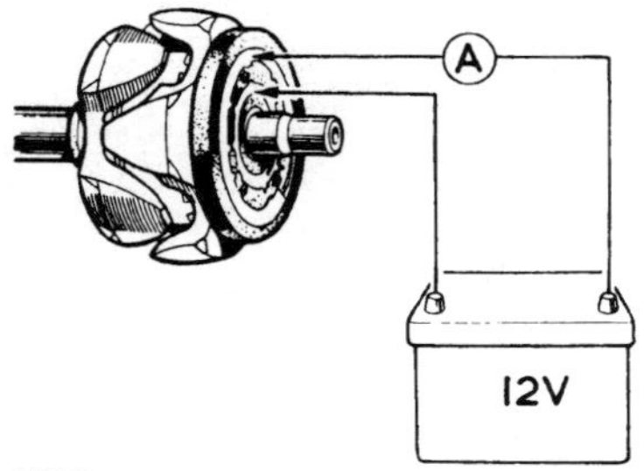

H330

Measuring rotor winding resistance with battery and ammeter (alternator dismantled)

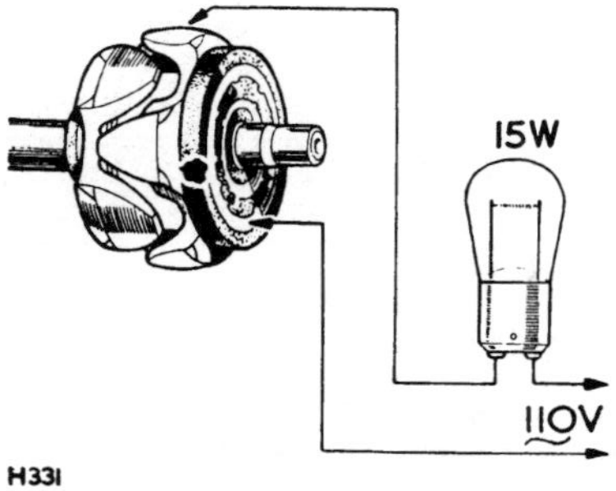

H331

Insulation test of rotor winding

No attempt should be made to machine the rotor poles or true a distorted shaft.

4. **Stator.** Check the continuity of the stator windings with the stator cables separated from the heat sinks. Connect any two of the three stator cables in series with a 1.5-watt test lamp and a 12-volt battery. Repeat the test, replacing one of the two cables by the third cable. Failure of the test lamp to light on either occasion means that part of the stator winding is open-circuit, and the stator must be replaced.

   Test the insulation between the stator coils and lamination pack with an AC mains supply and a bulb in series with any one of the three cable ends and the lamination pack. If the bulb lights, the stator coils are earthing and the stator must be replaced.

Operation S-5A-9—*continued*

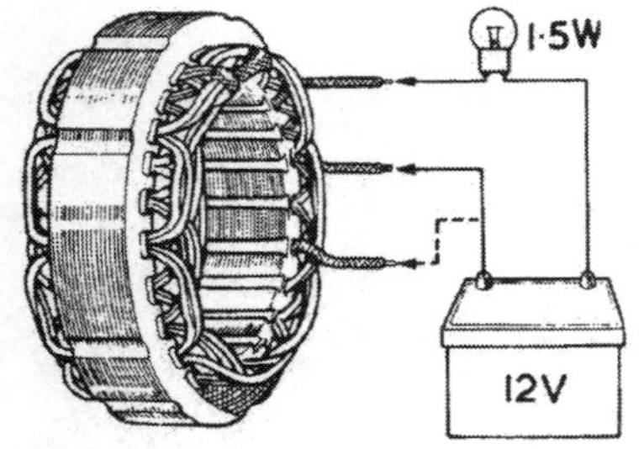

H332

Stator winding continuity test

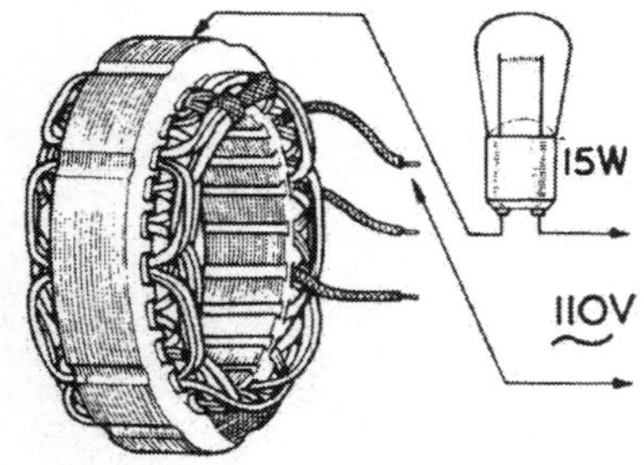

H333

Stator winding insulation test

Heat sinks and diodes

There are two heat sink assemblies, one of positive polarity and the other negative. Each carries three diodes that are pressed into position. The diodes are not individually replaceable, and if a diode is found defective the heat sink must be replaced.

The diodes can be tested for service purposes with the stator wires separated from the heat sinks. Connect a 12-volt battery and 1.5-watt bulb in series with each diode, and reverse the connections. Current should flow, and the bulb light up, in one direction only. If the bulb lights up in both directions, or does not light up in either, the diode is defective and the heat sink assembly must be replaced.

Accurate measurement of diode resistance requires factory equipment. Since the forward resistance of a diode varies with the voltage applied, no realistic readings can be obtained with battery-powered ohmmeters. If a battery ohmmeter is used, a good diode will yield infinity in one direction, and some indefinite but much lower reading in the other.

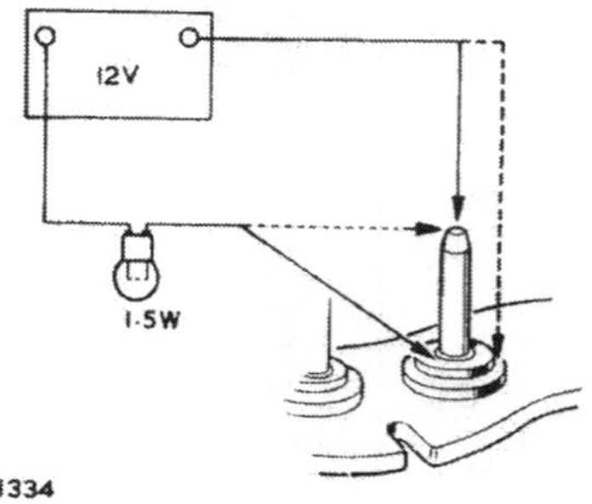

H334

Service test of diodes

WARNING. Ohmmeters of the type incorporating a hand-driven generator must never be used for checking diodes.

Bearings. Bearings that are worn to the extent that they allow excessive side movement of the rotor shaft must be renewed. The needle roller bearing in the slip-ring end bracket is not serviced separately, and in the unlikely event that it becomes unserviceable the end bracket must be replaced.

Alternator, assemble

1. Resolder the stator wires to the diodes using M grade 45–55 tin/lead solder. A pair of long-nosed pliers should be used as a thermal shunt, and care must be taken to avoid overheating the diodes or bending the diode pins. Soldering must be carried out as quickly as possible.

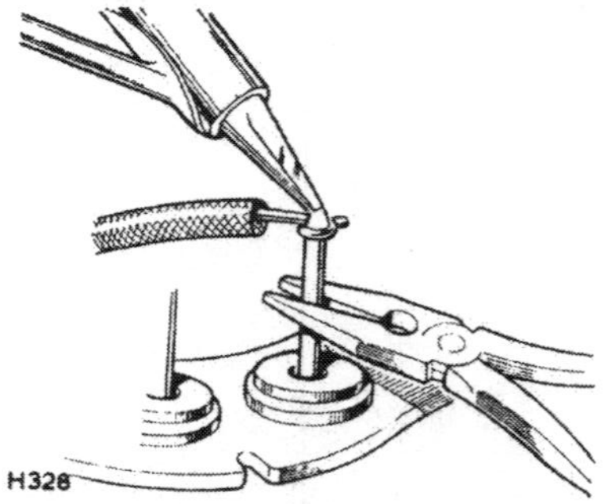

H326

Use of thermal shunt when soldering diode connections

Operation S-5A-9—*continued*

2. After soldering, the connections must be neatly arranged around the heat sinks to ensure adequate clearance for the rotor, and tacked down with 3 M EC 1022 adhesive where indicated in the illustration. The stator connections must pass through the appropriate notches at the edge of the heat sink.

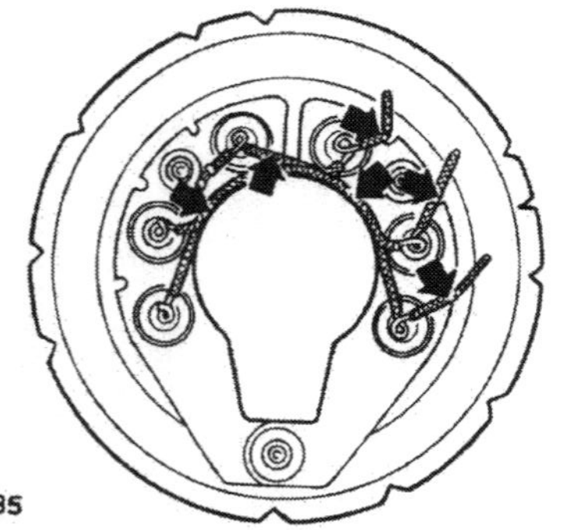

H335

Heat sink cable securing points

3. Assembly is the reverse of the stripping procedure, observing the torque values given in the Data section. Note the order of the insulation washers between the heat sinks—thick plain washer, thin plain washer and small plain washer.
4. Refit the plain and insulating washers to the 'AL' and output terminal posts before fitting the stator to the slip-ring end bracket.
5. Fit the two small insulating washers under the brush box.
6. To ensure the Lucar terminals of the brushes are properly retained the tongue should be levered up with a fine screwdriver to make an angle of 30° with the terminal blade.
7. Support the inner journal of the drive end bearing when pressing in the rotor shaft. Do not use the bracket as a support for the bearing while fitting the rotor shaft.
8. Align the drive end bracket, lamination pack and slip-ring bracket, and tighten the three bolts evenly. Check that the rotor is quite free in its bearing.

Cold start control, remove and refit—Operation S-10A

Time allowed: hours
Workshop hand tools:
Spanner sizes: $\frac{1}{4}$ in. AF, $\frac{3}{4}$ in. AF
Screwdriver, small

Cold start cables, remove

1. Disconnect the inner wires at the carburetters.
2. Disconnect the junction box and remove the main choke inner wire coming from the cold start handle. Place the cables, junction box to carburetters, to one side.
3. Disconnect the wires to the plunger switch.
4. Release the bolt on the chrome retaining arm on the plunger switch. Slide off the retaining arm and remove the plunger switch.
5. Release the nut and spring washer retaining the chrome guide to the bracket.
6. Draw out the inner and outer cables together into the car.

Cold start cables, refit

1. Reverse removal procedure, ensuring that the plunger switch fits into the third hole in the cable guide.
2. Connect wiring to terminals in accordance with the circuit diagram.
3. Any slack in the cable between the control lever and the junction box can be taken up by screwing in the adjustment bolt, thus shortening the effective length of the cable. With the cables attached to the carburetters there should be a movement at the control lever of approximately $\frac{1}{16}$ in. (1,5 mm) before any movement takes place at the carburetters. For further adjustment see Section A1.

Stop lamp switch, remove and refit—Operation S-11A

Time allowed: hours
Workshop hand tools:
Spanner size: $\frac{3}{4}$ in. AF
Pliers, long-nosed

Stop lamp switch, remove

1. Remove pedal return spring from beneath the parcel shelf.
2. Disconnect wiring from the stop lamp switch.
3. Hold down the brake pedal and remove rubber boot covering the lower part of the switch.
4. Remove nut from switch and lift switch out of the bracket.

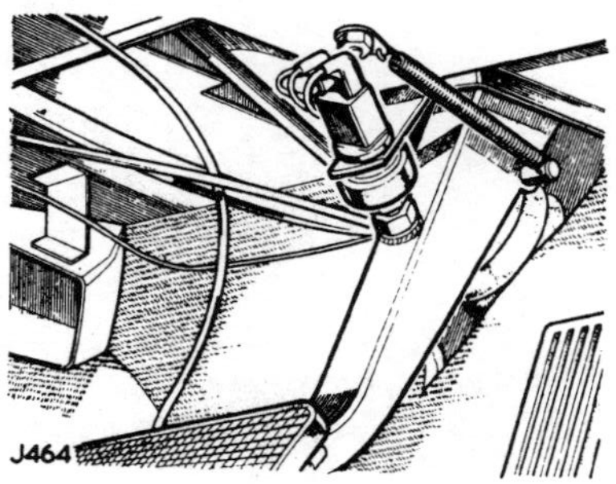

Location of stop lamp switch and pedal return spring

Stop lamp switch, refit

1. Reverse removal procedure.
   Note. The switch has a flat on the thread and will only fit into the bracket in one position.
2. Check switch for correct operation.

Flasher repeater bulbs, replace—Operation S-26A

Time allowed: hours

Workshop hand tools:
Screwdriver, Phillips', small

To remove and refit flasher repeater unit, see Operation S-27A

Bulb, remove

1. Remove the two Phillips' screws and withdraw the cover.
2. Remove flasher bulb.

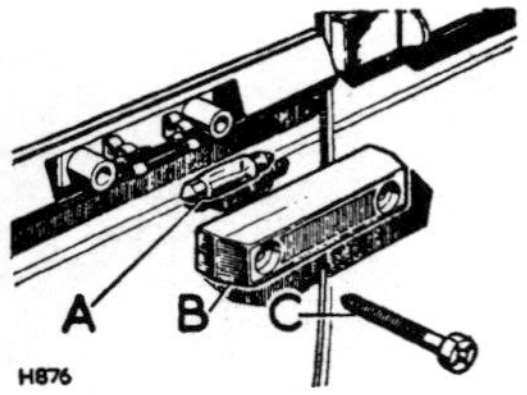

Repeater flasher

A—Festoon bulb B—Amber lens C—Retaining screw

Bulb, replace

1. Reverse removal procedure.

Flasher repeaters, remove and refit—Operation S-27A

Time allowed: hours

Workshop hand tools:
Screwdriver, Phillips', small Screwdriver, medium

Flasher repeater, remove

1. Disconnect the battery.
2. Disconnect the wiring connectors. The two front flasher connectors can be reached by removing the kick plate and the scuttle trim panel. The connectors for the two rear flasher repeaters may be reached by removing the boot side trim. On the left-hand side it will be necessary also to remove the tool tray.
3. Unscrew the two Phillips' screws, but do not remove.
4. By pulling the two screws the whole unit, including the two leads, will come away.

Flasher repeater, refit

1. Reverse removal procedure.

Cigar lighter bulb, replace—Operation S-40

Time allowed: hours

Workshop hand tools:
Spanner size: $\frac{7}{16}$ in. AF

Bulb, remove

1. Remove picnic tray.
2. Remove the two bolts holding the console switch panel to console and draw forward. If necessary, unclip wiring, noting its position.
3. The bulb is held in a retainer clipped to the side of the cigar lighter. Unclip by pressing at the base of either side and withdraw.
4. Replace bulb by withdrawing the bulb and holder which is clipped into the retainer.

Bulb, replace

1. Reverse removal procedure.

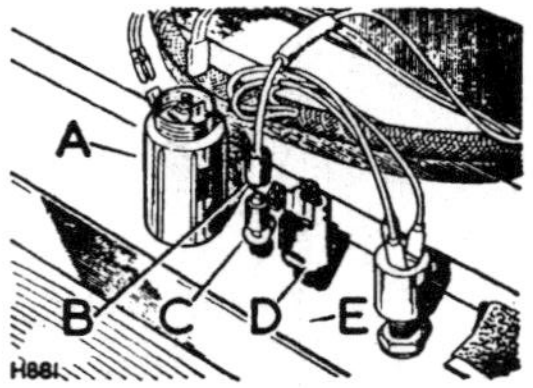

Cigar lighter

A—Cigar lighter
B—Bulb holder
C—Bulb
D—Retainer for bulb holder
E—Console unit

Fog lamp unit, remove, refit and adjust—Operation S-41

Time allowed: hours

Workshop hand tools:
Spanner size: $\frac{5}{8}$ in. AF
Screwdriver, medium

Fog lamp, remove

1. Remove screw at base of lamp, draw forwards, disconnect the wiring, noting its position, and withdraw sealed beam unit and rim.
2. Withdraw rubber boot from bolt thread from beneath the wing.
3. Withdraw the wiring by drawing it back through the unit.
4. Remove locknut, nut and spring washer, holding and lamp, and draw it forward away from the car.

Fog lamp, replace

1. Reverse removal procedure.

Fog lamp, adjust

1. Remove the rubber boot from thread beneath the wing.
2. Slacken off the locknut and nut, and adjust the lamp as required.
3. Tighten up locknut and nut, and replace rubber boot.

Fog lamp sealed beam units, replace—Operation S-42

Time allowed: hours

Workshop hand tools:
Screwdriver, medium

Sealed beam unit, remove

1. Remove screw at the base of the unit.
2. Draw lamp forward and remove wiring, noting its position.
3. Remove the five wire clips securing the unit to the rim and withdraw. Replace if necessary.

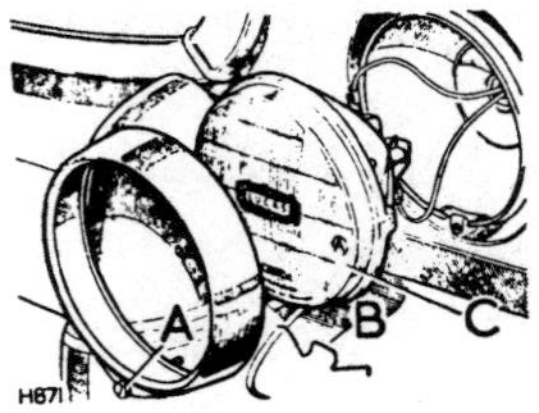

Fog lamps

A—Retaining screw for rim
B—Clip retaining light unit
C—Light unit

Sealed beam unit, refit

1. Reverse removal procedure.

Circuit diagram, negative earth, all models

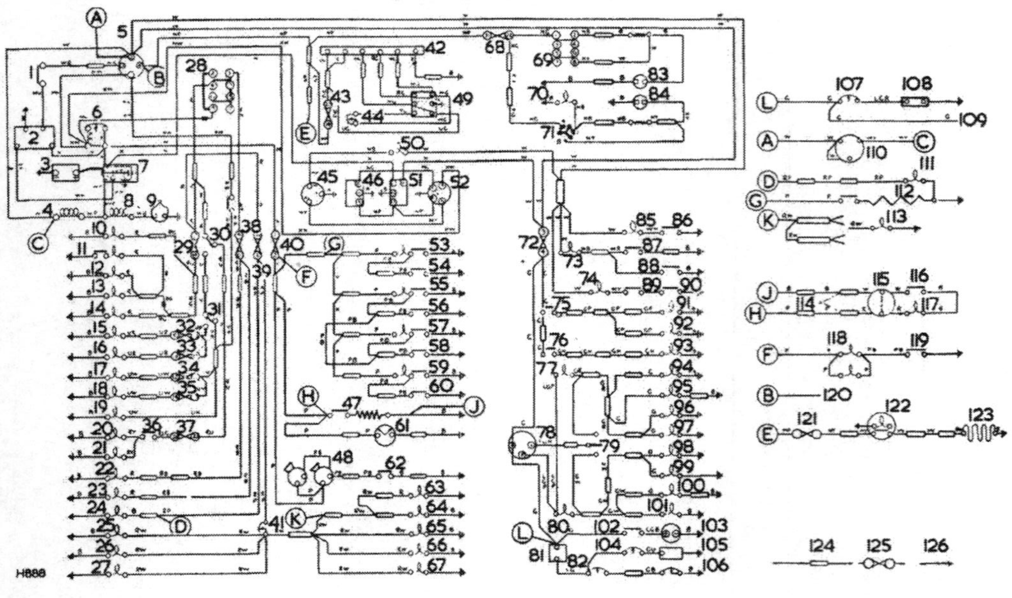

H888

Key to circuit diagram, negative earth, all models

1 Inhibitor switch
2 Relay for ignition
3 Battery
4 Ballast resistance
5 Switch, ignition and starter
6 Ammeter
7 Starter motor
8 Ignition coil
9 Distributor
10 Side lamp, left-hand RHD, right-hand LHD
11 Switch and lamp, boot
12} Rear number plate
13} illumination
14 Tail lamp, left-hand RHD, right-hand LHD
15 Headlamp, RH, dip beam
16 Headlamp, LH, dip beam
17 Headlamp, RH, main beam
18 Headlamp, LH, main beam
19 Warning light, main beam
20 Fog lamp, RH
21 Fog lamp, LH
22 Tail lamp, (park) right-hand RHD, left-hand LHD
23 Side lamp, (park) right-hand RHD, left-hand LHD
24 Cigar lighter, front, illumination
25} Panel
26} illumination, LH
27 Speedometer illumination
28 Switch, side, tail and park lamps
29 Fuse, 7–8 (5 amp)
30 Switch, headlamp, on steering column
31 Switch, headlamp dip
32 Fuse, 15–16 (10 amp)
33 Fuse, 17–18 (10 amp)
34 Fuse, 11–12 (10 amp)
35 Fuse, 13–14 (10 amp)
36 Switch, fog lamp
37 Fuse, 23–24
38 Fuse, 5–6 (5 amp)
39 Fuse, 9–10 (5 amp)
40 Fuse, 1–2 (15 amp)
41 Switch, panel illumination
42 Screen wiper motor
43 Fuse, 19–20 (15 amp)
44 Switch, rheostat, screen wiper
45 Relay 3AW, warning lights
46 Control 4TR, alternator
47 Cigar lighter and switch
48 Horns
49 Switch, screen wiper
50 Warning light, ignition
51 Relay 6RA, starter motor
52 Alternator, 11AC
53 Interior lamp and switch, front, LH
54 Switch, front door, LH
55 Interior lamp and switch, rear, LH
56 Switch, rear door, LH
57 Interior lamp and switch, rear, RH
58 Switch, rear door, RH
59 Interior lamp and switch, front, RH
60 Switch, front door, RH
61 Clock
62 Switch, horns
63 Clock illumination
64 Gear selector illumination
65} Panel
66} illumination, RH
67 Grouped instrument illumination
68 Fuse, 21–22 (15 amp)
69 Switch, heater, front
70 Heater illumination, rear
71 Switch, heater, rear
72 Fuse, 3–4 (15 amp)
73 Warning light, brake fluid level and hand brake
74 Warning light, cold start
75 Switch, stop light
76 Switch, reverse light
77 Warning light, RH, direction indicators
78 Direction indicator unit
79 Switch, headlamp flasher
79 Switch, direction indicators
80 Warning light, LH, direction indicators -
81 Regulator, 10 volt
82 Gauge, fuel
83 Heater motor, two-speed, front
84 Heater motor, two-speed, rear
85 Warning light, oil pressure
86 Switch, oil pressure
87 Switch, handbrake
88 Switch, brake fluid level
89 Switch, cold start
90 Thermostat, cold start
91 Stop light, RH
92 Stop light, LH
93 Reverse light
94 Direction indicator, front, LH
95 Repeater direction indicator, LH front
96 Repeater direction indicator, LH rear
97 Direction indicator, rear, LH
98 Direction indicator, rear, RH
99 Repeater direction indicator, RH rear
100 Repeater direction indicator, RH front
101 Direction indicator, front RH
102 Switch, windscreen washer
103 Windscreen washer
104 Gauge, water temperature
105 Transmitter, water temperature
106 Tank unit, fuel
107 Gauge, oil pressure } Coupé
108 Transmitter, oil pressure } Coupé
109 To screen washer switch } Coupé
110 Tachometer } Coupé
111 Rear cigar lighter illumination } Coupé
112 Cigar lighter } Coupé
113 Nacelle illumination, four lamps } Coupé
114 Pick-up point when two lamps are fitted } Optional equipment
115 Plug and socket, headrest lamp } Optional equipment
116 Switch, headrest lamp } Optional equipment
117 Headrest lamp } Optional equipment
118 Bonnet lamp* } Optional equipment
119 Switch, bonnet lamp* } Optional equipment
120 Radio pick-up } Optional equipment
121 Fuse (10 amp) in line, heated backlight } Optional equipment
122 Switch, illuminated, heated backlight } Optional equipment
123 Heated backlight } Optional equipment
124 Snap and Lucar connections
125 Fuses
126 Earth connections

*Standard on coupé

Encircled letters on circuit diagram show pick-up points for additional and optional equipment

CABLE COLOUR CODE: B—Black P—Purple W—White R—Red N—Brown Y—Yellow U—Blue G—Green L—Light

Replacement headlamp sealed beam units and bulbs

Headlamps	
RHD, Lucas No. 59679, sealed beam..	12v 75/45w
LHD except France, Lucas No. 410	12v 45/40w Duplo
LHD France, Lucas No. 411	12v 45/40w Duplo (yellow)
Automatic transmission selector indicator lamp, Lucas No. 256	12v 3w
Bonnet light, coupé models, Tex SP No. 209	12v 6w
Brake fluid level warning light, Lucas No. 281 ..	12v 2w
Cigar lighter illuminator, Tex No. GBP-V-2.2 ..	12v 2.2w
Clock, Lucas No. 281	12v 2w
Direction indicator lamps, Lucas No. 382	12v 21w
Fog lamp, Lucas No. 54522163, sealed beam	12v 50w
Instrument panel switches, Lucas No. 981	12v 2w
Interior lights, Lucas No. 254, festoon bulb	12v 6w
Panel plate, Carr Fastener No. 82/036	12v 1.2w
Rear luggage boot lamp, Lucas No. 222	12v 4w
Rear number plate lamp, Lucas No. 989	12v 6w
Repeater flasher lights, Lucas No. 256	12v 3w
Reverse lamp, Lucas No. 382	12v 2w
Side lamps, Lucas No. 989	12v 6w
Speedometer and grouped instruments, tachometer on coupé, Lucas No. 984	12v 3.6w
Stop/tail lamps, Lucas No. 380	12v 21/6w
Warning lights, Lucas No. 987	12v 2.2w

GENERAL DATA

Electrical system, type	Negative earth
Voltage	12 volts
Alternator:	
Type	Lucas 11 AC
Rating	45 amps
Alternator control box	Lucas 4T-R
Battery:	
Capacity	57 ampere hour
Location	Right-hand side of boot, under metal cover
Coil	Lucas BA 7
Distributor:	
Type	Lucas 35 D8
Dwell angle	26° to 28°
Contact breaker gap	.014 in. to .016 in. (0,36 to 0,40 mm) approx. To be used only when specialist equipment is not available
Centrifugal advance begins at	560 to 840 rpm
Maximum centrifugal advance	28° at 4,800 rpm
Starter motor:	
Type	Lucas M45G pre-engaged
Engine cranking speed	185 rpm
Number of teeth	9
Windscreen wiper type	Lucas variable speed electric
Windscreen washer type	Lucas electric

TECHNICAL DETAIL DATA

Alternator

Type	Lucas 11AC
Nominal voltage	12 volts
Nominal direct current output	43 amperes
Resistance of field coil at 68°F (20°C)	3.8 ohms
Maximum rotor speed	12,500 rpm
Stator phases	3
Stator connection	Star
Number of rotor poles	8
Number of field coils	1
Slip-ring brushes length	
New	$\frac{5}{8}$ in. (15,9 mm)
Replace at	$\frac{5}{32}$ in. (4 mm)
Brush spring tension	
Load at $\frac{25}{32}$ in. (19,9 mm)	4 to 5 oz (113 to 142 grms)
Load at $\frac{13}{32}$ in. (10,3 mm)	7.5 to 8.5 oz (212 to 241 grms)
Assembly torques, maximum	
Brushbox fixing screws	10 lb in. (0,115 mkg)
Diode heat sink fixings	25 lb in. (0,288 mkg)
Through bolts	45 to 50 lb in. (0,518 to 0,576 mkg)

Alternator field isolating relay

Nominal voltage	12 volts
Cut-in voltage	6.0 to 7.5 volts
Drop-off voltage	4.0 volts minimum
Resistance of operating winding	76 ohms

Alternator warning light control

Resistance of actuator wire and internal ballast resistor (terminals AL and E)	14 to 16 ohms
Warning light bulb	2.2 watts 12 volts, MES cap

Section T – FACIA FITTINGS AND CONTROLS

The instruments are basically as on the 3-Litre Mk III, with the exception of the following:

(a) Speedometer. Red zone from 115 mph onwards.
(b) Tachometer. Red zone from 5,200 to 6,000 rpm.
(c) Ammeter. 60–0–60 calibration.

All operations as specified for the Rover 3-Litre Mk III models apply except T-10 which is replaced by T-10A detailed on the following pages.

Cold start control, remove and refit—Operation T-10A

Time allowed: hours

Workshop hand tools:

Spanner sizes: $\frac{1}{4}$ in. AF, $\frac{3}{4}$ in. AF Screwdriver, small

A plunger switch incorporated in the mixture control is wired in series with a bi-metal thermostat switch at the rear of the cylinder head, and the amber warning light on the instrument panel.

Operation is as follows:

1. With the engine cold and the mixture control pulled out the plunger switch is closed and the thermostat switch open; the light is therefore off.
2. When the engine reaches normal running temperature the thermostat switch closes and the light comes on.
3. When the mixture control is pushed into the normal position, the plunger switch is open and the light goes out.

Cold start cables, remove

1. Disconnect the inner wires at the carburetters.
2. Disconnect the junction box and remove the main choke inner wire coming from the cold start handle. Place the cables, junction box to carburetter to one side.
3. Disconnect the wires to the plunger switch.
4. Release the bolt on the chrome retaining arm on the plunger switch.
   Slide off the retaining arm and remove the plunger switch.
5. Release the nut and spring washer retaining the chrome guide to the bracket.
6. Draw out the inner and outer cables together into the car.

Cold start cables, refit

1. Reverse removal procedure, ensuring that the plunger switch fits into the third hole in the cable guide.
2. Connect wiring to terminals in accordance with the circuit diagram.
3. Any slack in the cable between the control lever and the junction box can be taken up by screwing in the adjustment bolt, thus shortening the effective length of the cable. With the cables attached to the carburetters, there should be a movement at the control lever of approximately $\frac{1}{16}$ in. before any movement takes place at the carburetters. For further adjustment see Section A1.

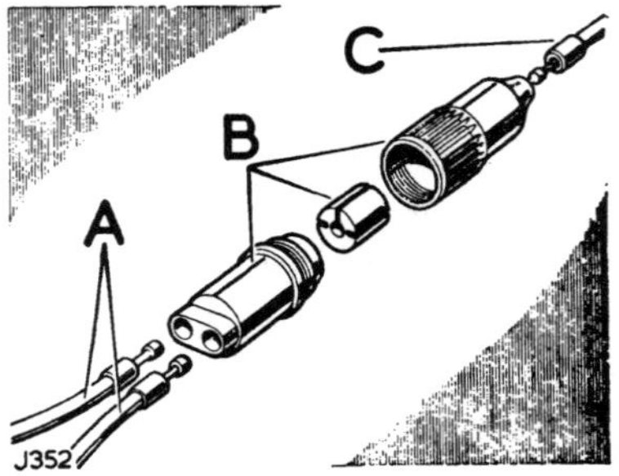

Cold start cable junction box

A—Cables to carburetter B—Junction box
C—Cable to control

Section U — BODY

All items as specified for the Rover 3-Litre Mk III also apply to the Rover 3.5-Litre models.

Section V — WHEELS AND TYRES

Magnum type wheels are fitted, however all the information in this Section applies to the Rover 3.5-Litre models.

Section W — HEATING AND VENTILATING SYSTEM

All items specified for Rover 3-Litre Mk III models apply to the 3.5-Litre models except that the tap for the rear heater is operated by a push-pull action in place of the rotating type.

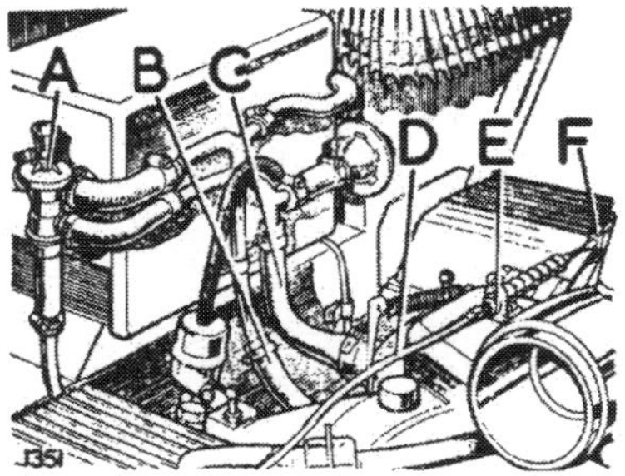

Heater hoses and tap

A—Rear heater tap
B—Hose, heater inlet
C—Hose, heater outlet
D—Accelerator cable
E—Locknut for cable
F—Clevis for cable

Section X — RECLAMATION SCHEMES

This Section does not apply to the Rover 3.5-Litre models.

Section Y

Recommended lubricants and fluids

These recommendations apply to temperate climates where operational temperatures may vary between approximately 10°F (—12°C) and 90°F (32°C).

Lubricants marked with an asterisk (*) are multi-grade oils suitable for all temperature ranges.

Information on recommended lubricants for use under extreme winter or tropical conditions can be obtained from the Rover Co. Ltd., Technical Service Department.

Components	BP	Castrol	Duckham's	Esso	Mobil	Regent Texaco/ Caltex	Shell
Engine	*BP Super Visco-Static 10W-40	Castrolite	Duckham's Q20-50 Motor Oil	Esso-Extra 10W-30	Mobiloil Special 10W-30 or Mobiloil Super	Havoline 10W-30	*Shell Super Oil
Automatic Transmission and power steering	BP Automatic Transmission Fluid Type 'A'	Castrol TQ	Duckham's Nolmatic ATF	Esso Automatic Transmission Fluid	Mobil ATF 200	Texamatic Fluid	Shell Donax T6
Rear axle	BP Gear Oil SAE 90 EP	Castrol Hypoy	Duckham's Hypoid 90	Esso Gear Oil GP 90/140	Mobilube GX 90	Multigear Lubricant 90	Spirax 90 EP
Propeller shaft sliding spline, front hubs, rear spring and front torsion bar sleeves	BP Energrease L2	Castrolease LM	Duckham's LB 10 Grease	Esso Multi-purpose Grease H	Mobilgrease MP or Mobilgrease Special	Marfak Multi-purpose 2	Retinax A
Brakes	Castrol Girling Brake and Clutch Fluid Crimson, Specification SAE 70 R3						
Anti-freeze solution for cooling system	Bluecol AA, coloured green, or any other anti-freeze solution conforming to British Standard No. 3150						
Inhibitor solution for cooling system	Marston Lubricant SQ 36—Coolant inhibitor concentrate. For summer use only						

CAPACITIES

Component	Imperial Unit	US Unit	Litres
Engine sump oil	9 pints	10½ pints	5,0
Extra when refilling after fitting new filter	1 pint	1.2 pints	0,5
Automatic transmission, with oil cooler	14 pints	17 pints	8,0
Rear axle oil	3 pints	3½ pints	1,75
Power steering unit	3 to 3½ pints	3½ to 4 pints	1,75 to 1,8

OIL ADDITIVES

Oil additives must not be used in the automatic transmission unit. The oils selected for the engine, automatic transmission and axle, etc., are complete in themselves and afford every protection.

Section Z — SPECIAL TOOLS

The following special tools apply to the Rover 3.5-Litre models, illustration numbers 2, 3, 6, 15, 31, 32, 34, 35, 36, 37, 38, 39, 40, 41, 42, 43, 44, 45, 46, 47, 48, 49, 50, 51, 52, 54, 55, 56 and 57.

Four additional tools, illustrated in Section A-1, are required to service the V-8 engine, as follows:

Gudgeon pin removal and refitting tool, Part No. 605350.
Connecting rod bolt guides, Part No. 605351.
Distance piece for valve guide drift.
Carburetter balancing device, Part No. 605330.

Brooklands Rover Titles

Brooklands Books supplies owners, restorers and professional repairers with official factory literature and other reading material.
Available from Amazon and all good motoring bookshops.

Workshop Manuals

Rover Workshop Manual 1950-1964 (P4)	4503	9780907073970
Rover 3 & 3.5 Litre Saloon & Coupe Workshop Manual (P5)	AKM 4661 & 605358	9781855201446
Rover 3 Litre Saloon & Coupe (P5) without supp.	AKM 4661	9781783180608
Rover 2000-2200 Repair Operation Manual (P6)	AKM3625	9781855208254
Rover 3500, 3500S Repair Operation Manual (P6)	AKM3621	9781855201156
Rover SD1 2300 . 2600 . 3500 Repair Operation Manual	AKM3616A & AKM4331	9781783180639
Rover 25 & MG ZR Workshop Manual	RCL0534ENGBB	9781855208834
Rover 75 & MG ZT Workshop Manual	RCL0536ENGBB	9781855208841

Parts Catalogues

Rover 80, 100 and Mk. 1, 95 and 110 (P4)	4505	9781783181667
Rover 3 & 3.5 Litre Saloon & Coupe Parts Catalogue (P5)	608264	9781855202375
Rover 2000 (P6) Parts Catalogue	RTC 9021A	9781783181193
Rover 2200 (P6) Parts Catalogue	RTC9011	9781855201514
Rover 3500 & 3500S (P6) Parts Catalogue	RTC9022B	9781870642408

Instruction Manuals

Rover 3.5 Litre Owners Instruction Manual (P5)	605214	9781855204270

Maintenance Manual

Rover 3.5 Maintenance Manual (P5)	605215	9781855202948

Owners Manuals and Handbooks

Rover 3500 & 3500S Owners Manual (P6)	607875	9781855201149
Rover Vitesse, Vanden Plas & VP EFI (SD1)	AKM5106	9781855202894

Autobooks

Rover 60, 75, 80, 90, 95, 100, 105, 110 1953-1964 OWM857	9781783181438
Rover P5 3 Litre 1958-1967 OWM812	9781783181421
Rover P6 2000, 2200 1963-1977 OWM890	9781783181414
Rover SD1 3500 1976-1984 (SD1) OWM921	9781783181384
Rover SD1 2000 . 2300 . 2600 (SD1) 1977-1984 OWM951	9781783181391

Other Rover Titles

Rover 2000 & 2200 1963-1977 (Brooklands Road Test Book)	9780907073864
Rover P6 1963-1977 by James Taylor	9781855209442
SU Carburetters Tuning Tips & Techniques	9781855202559

Brooklands Books Ltd., PO Box 406, Amersham,
Bucks, HP6 9JA, England
E-mail: sales@brooklands-books.com www.brooklandsbooks.com

ISBN: 9781855201446 Part No. 4461 and 605358 Ref: RV48WH 4W4/2969

Printed in Great Britain
by Amazon

49959972R00275